Q-R Volume 16

The World Book Encyclopedia

World Book, Inc.

a Scott Fetzer company

Chicago

The World Book Encyclopedia

World Book, Inc.
233 North Michigan
Chicago, IL 60601

www.worldbook.com

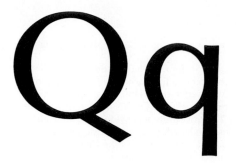

Qq

Q is the 17th letter of our alphabet. It was also a letter in the alphabet used by the Semites, who once lived in Syria and Palestine. They named it *qoph* which may have been their word for *ape* or *monkey,* and they wrote it with a picture symbol that may represent a monkey. The Greeks later took the letter into their alphabet for a time, calling it *koppa.* The Romans adopted it from the Greeks, and gave it its present capital Q form. They also originated the usage of following *q* with *u.* See **Alphabet.**

Uses. *Q* or *q* is about the 25th most frequently used letter in books, newspapers, and other printed material in English. *Q* is used as an abbreviation for Quebec. In titles, *Q* may indicate *queen,* as in *Q.C.* for *Queen's Counsel,* and it can mean Quarter as in *QMC* for *Quartermas-*

ter Corps, a military unit. The lower case *q* is used to abbreviate *quart, quarter, quarterly,* and *question.* A Latin phrase, *quod vide,* or *which see,* is represented by *q.v.* This abbreviation is used in footnotes and other citations.

Pronunciation. *Q* followed by *u* in English has the sound of *kw* as a rule. People make this sound by narrowing and rounding their lips. The back of the tongue touches or is near the velum, or soft palate. The vocal cords do not vibrate. Final *que* as in *unique* has the sound of *k.* The combination *qu* also has the sound of *k* in such words as *liquor* and *croquet.* This combination has the sound of *k* or *kw* in French, of *kv* in German, and of *k* in Spanish. The Romans pronounced it like *kw.* See **Pronunciation.**   Marianne Cooley

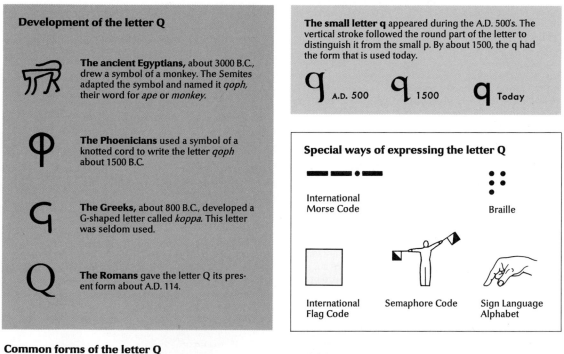

Development of the letter Q

The ancient Egyptians, about 3000 B.C., drew a symbol of a monkey. The Semites adapted the symbol and named it *qoph,* their word for *ape* or *monkey.*

The Phoenicians used a symbol of a knotted cord to write the letter *qoph* about 1500 B.C.

The Greeks, about 800 B.C., developed a G-shaped letter called *koppa.* This letter was seldom used.

The Romans gave the letter Q its present form about A.D. 114.

The small letter q appeared during the A.D. 500's. The vertical stroke followed the round part of the letter to distinguish it from the small p. By about 1500, the q had the form that is used today.

q A.D. 500   **q** 1500   **q** Today

Special ways of expressing the letter Q

International Morse Code

Braille

International Flag Code

Semaphore Code

Sign Language Alphabet

Common forms of the letter Q

Handwritten letters vary from person to person. *Manuscript* (printed) letters, *left,* have simple curves and straight lines. Cursive letters, *right,* have flowing lines.

Roman letters have small finishing strokes called *serifs* that extend from the main strokes. The type face shown above is Baskerville. The italic form appears at the right.

Qq Qq

Sans-serif letters are also called *gothic letters.* They have no serifs. The type face shown above is called Futura. The italic form of Futura appears at the right.

Computer letters have special shapes. Computers can "read" these letters either optically or by means of the magnetic ink with which the letters may be printed.

Q fever. See Rickettsia.

Qadhafi, *guhd DAH fee,* **Muammar Muhammad al-,** *moo ahm MAHR moo HAM uhd ahl* (1942-   ), took over the leadership of Libya's government in 1969. He came to power after he led a military overthrow of Libya's monarchy. He is a colonel and commander in chief of the Libyan armed forces. Other spellings of his name include Gadhafi, Kaddafi, and Qaddafi.

© Rosy Rouleau, SYGMA

Muammar al-Qadhafi

Qadhafi is an outspoken radical leader with a strong belief in Arab unity under Islam, the religion whose followers are called Muslims. He has sought to spread his influence. For example, he has given military and financial aid to revolutionaries and terrorists in many parts of the world. Leaders of many countries denounced him for interfering in other nations' affairs. In 1992 and 1993, the United Nations (UN) imposed sanctions on Libya for refusing to turn over Libyans suspected of placing bombs on two international civilian flights. In 1999, Libya handed over to UN officials two men suspected of planting the bomb on one of the flights. As a result, the United Nations suspended its sanctions on Libya. For details, see **Libya** (History).

As Libya's leader, Qadhafi encourages strict obedience to the laws of Islam. Oil income enabled Qadhafi to build many schools, houses, and hospitals, and his government provides free social services for all citizens. However, a downturn in oil prices in the 1980's and 1990's and the UN sanctions significantly reduced Libya's prosperity.

Qadhafi was born in a desert tent near the town of Surt (also spelled Sirte). He attended the Libyan Military Academy in Benghazi and the Royal Military Academy at Sandhurst, England.   Malcolm C. Peck

Qandahar, *KAN duh hahr,* also spelled *Kandahar* (pop. 191,345), is the second largest city of Afghanistan. Only Kabul, the capital, is larger. Qandahar lies in southern Afghanistan. For the location of Qandahar, see **Afghanistan** (map).

The old section of Qandahar includes many ancient buildings and bazaars. The city also has modern sections. Qandahar serves as the center of an important trade route between India, Iran, Pakistan, and Kabul. It also processes and exports fruits grown in the area.

Qandahar existed as early as 1000 B.C. It became the capital of an Afghan empire in A.D. 1747. Ahmad Shah Durrani, the founder of the empire, built the modern city of Qandahar in 1761. Kabul replaced Qandahar as the capital in 1776.   Riffat Sardar

Qatar, *KAH tahr* or *GAH tahr,* is a small Arab country in southwestern Asia. It occupies a peninsula that juts from eastern Arabia into the Persian Gulf. Doha is Qatar's capital and largest city.

More than two-thirds of Qatar's people were born in other countries. The native-born are called Qataris. Until the 1940's, most Qataris tended camel herds, fished, or dived for pearls for a living. Today, most work in cities or oil fields.

Qatar's economy depends largely on oil. Since the 1950's, the government has earned much income from oil exports and used it to develop Qatar. Qatar ranks among the richest nations in terms of average income per person. The government provides free education. It also provides free health care and housing for the poor.

Qatar became a protectorate of the United Kingdom in 1916. It gained full independence in 1971.

Government. Qatar is an *emirate*. An *emir* (prince) rules the country. The emir is a member of the al-Thani family, which has ruled Qatar since the mid-1800's. He

Facts in brief

Capital: Doha.
Official language: Arabic.
Official name: State of Qatar.
Area: 4,247 sq. mi. (11,000 km²). *Greatest distances*—north-south, 115 mi. (185 km); east-west, 55 mi. (89 km). *Coastline*—235 mi. (378 km).
Population: *Estimated 2000 population*—605,000; density, 142 persons per square mile (55 per km²); distribution, 91 percent urban, 9 percent rural. *1997 census*—520,500.
Chief products: Petroleum and petroleum products.
Flag: The left third is white with a vertical series of points on the right side. The right two-thirds is maroon. See **Flag** (picture: Flags of Asia and the Pacific).
Money: *Basic unit*—Qatar riyal. One hundred dirhams equal one riyal.

Qatar

▬▬▬	International boundary
———	Road
———	Oil pipeline
⬭	Salt flat
⊛	National capital
•	Other city or town
+	Elevation above sea level

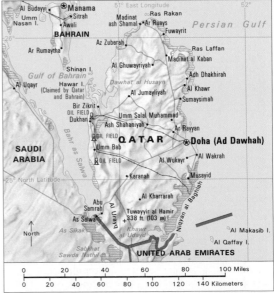

WORLD BOOK maps

© Robert Azzi, Woodfin Camp, Inc.

Doha is the capital and largest city of Qatar. Examples of the city's traditional Islamic architecture are shown here. But much of Doha has a modern appearance.

appoints an 18-member Council of Ministers. An advisory council, made up of 30 elected deputies and 3 appointed by the Council of Ministers, also aids the emir. The government allows no political parties.

People. Oil was discovered in Qatar in 1939. By the 1950's, the oil industry was providing more jobs than had ever been available in Qatar before. As a result, thousands of people moved to Qatar from other Arab countries.

Arabs make up most of the population of Qatar. Arabic is the official language, but many business executives and government officials use English when they deal with people from other countries. Islam is the state religion.

Most of Qatar's people live in or near Doha in modern houses or apartments. Some Qataris wear Western clothing, but most prefer traditional Arab garments.

The government requires children from the ages of 6 to 16 to go to school. The number of schools in Qatar rose from 1 in 1952 to about 160 today. Most of Qatar's adults can read and write.

Land and climate. Most of Qatar's land is stony desert. Barren salt flats cover the southern part of the country.

Summer temperatures sometimes rise above 120 °F (49 °C), but the winter is cooler. Qatar seldom gets more than 4 inches (10 centimeters) of rain a year.

Qatar has little natural water. It must distill most of its drinking water, which comes from the sea. The people grew few crops until the late 1950's, when the government dug wells and made crop growth possible.

Economy. Oil is Qatar's most important product and chief export. The exportation of petroleum and petroleum products provides 95 percent of the nation's income. The government encourages the development of manufacturing, farming, and fishing so Qatar will not have to depend entirely on its oil for income. The government owns and operates the oil wells and refineries; flour mills; a fishing fleet; and plants that produce fertilizers, cement, steel, petrochemicals, and plastics. Fertilizers are Qatar's second most important export.

Qatar produces enough vegetables for its people but

must import much meat and other food, and most manufactured goods. The government aids grain and fruit cultivation by distributing free seeds and insecticides.

Doha has a port and a modern airport. Roads link Doha to the rest of Qatar and to neighboring Saudi Arabia and the United Arab Emirates. The government owns and operates a radio and television station.

History. People have lived in what is now Qatar for thousands of years. Before oil was discovered, they made a living by raising camels, fishing, or pearl diving.

The people of Qatar had no strong government until the late 1700's, when the Wahhabis, an Islamic sect from Saudi Arabia, took control of the country. During the mid-1800's, *sheiks* (Arab chiefs) of the al-Thani family became the leaders of Qatar's tribes. The Ottomans extended their territory to Qatar during the late 1800's. In 1916, Qatar became a British protectorate.

Exploration for oil in Qatar began in 1930. The government granted a 75-year drilling right to the foreign-owned Qatar Petroleum Company in 1935. The company first found oil in 1939 in western Qatar. But World War II began that year and delayed oil exportation until 1949.

Qatar became an independent nation in 1971. In 1972, Khalifa bin Hamad al-Thani, the deputy ruler, became emir after peacefully overthrowing his cousin, Emir Ahmad bin Ali al-Thani. In the mid-1970's, the government took ownership of Qatar's petroleum industry. In 1981, Qatar and other states of eastern Arabia formed the Gulf Cooperation Council (GCC) to work together in such matters as defense and economic projects.

In August 1990, Iraq invaded Kuwait. After the invasion, Qatar allowed the United States and other allied forces to use a Qatari air force base to attack the Iraqi forces. As part of the GCC, Qatar took part in the bombing of Iraqi military targets and in the ground offensive to liberate Kuwait in early 1991.

In 1995, Hamad bin Khalifa al-Thani, the crown prince, peacefully overthrew his father, Khalifa bin Hamad al-Thani, to become emir. The new ruler had long served as Qatar's defense minister.   Robert Geran Landen

See also **Doha; Gulf Cooperation Council; Persian Gulf War; Organization of Petroleum Exporting Countries.**

Qin dynasty, *chihn,* also spelled *Ch'in,* was a Chinese *dynasty* (family of rulers) that governed from 221 B.C. to 206 B.C. The dynasty began after Shi Huangdi, ruler of the state of Qin in northwestern China, conquered rival northern and central states. He later extended his rule to southeastern China. The dynasty had complete control over the areas it ruled. Earlier, local Chinese chiefs had much control over their regions.

Shi Huangdi ruled his empire with an iron hand. He made former local rulers move to his new capital at Xianyang and appointed local administrators who were responsible to him. He banned most books in an attempt to silence critics, to promote obedience, and to blot out knowledge about the past. He ordered large numbers of laborers to build new walls that connected with older Chinese border walls to keep invaders out. This marked the start of the Great Wall of China. But Shi Huangdi gave his country a lasting ideal—national unity. The name *China* came from the name of his dynasty.

Shi Huangdi died in 210 B.C., and his son proved to be a weak ruler. Rebellions began in 209 B.C., and the

Qin dynasty soon collapsed. The Han dynasty then gained control of China.　　Eugene Boardman

See also **Great Wall of China; Shi Huangdi.**

Quadrilateral, *KWAHD ruh LAT uhr uhl,* is the name given to a plane figure with four straight sides—that is, a four-sided *polygon.* A quadrilateral whose opposite sides are parallel is a *parallelogram.* The opposite sides and opposite angles of any parallelogram are equal. If the angles of a parallelogram are right angles, the figure is a *rectangle.* If all four sides are equal, the figure is a *rhombus.* A parallelogram that has four equal sides and four right angles is a *square.* The area, *A,* of any parallelogram with base *b* and altitude *h* is given in the formula $A=bh.$ The altitude is the perpendicular distance between the base and the side opposite it.

A *trapezoid* is a quadrilateral with one set of parallel sides of unequal length. The trapezoid is *isosceles* if the nonparallel sides are equal.　　Arthur F. Coxford, Jr.

See also **Rhombus; Square.**

Quadruplets. See Multiple birth.

Quail is a type of small bird that belongs to the same family as pheasants and partridges, grouse, turkeys, and guineafowl. They live on every continent except Antarctica. There are about 45 species of quail, about 20 of which are found in North America. Quail are often hunted for sport or food.

Most adult quail are 8 to 12 inches (20 to 30 centimeters) long. Males are shades of brown or gray and may have striking patterns of reddish-brown, blue, white, or black feathers. Most females are patterned in shades of brown, tan, or gray. These colors help protect quail from enemies by making the birds hard to see when they sit quietly in a pasture or woodland.

During the fall and winter, quail live together in groups called *coveys.* Depending on the kind of quail, a covey may have 10 or fewer birds or as many as 100 or more. The covey helps protect its members from foxes, owls, and hawks. When such an enemy or a hunter approaches a covey, the quail squawk loudly and fly away in all directions. The covey breaks up in spring, and

Leonard Lee Rue, NAS

The mountain quail lives in the mountains of the Pacific Coast States, southwestern Canada, and northwestern New Mexico.

males and females form pairs for the nesting season.

The best-known type of quail in North America is the *northern bobwhite.* These birds are found chiefly in the middle and eastern parts of the continent and in Mexico. During spring, they build their nests on the ground and conceal them with grass. Females lay 8 to 16 eggs. The chicks hatch in about three weeks. Chicks grow quickly and can fly short distances about a week after birth. Like their parents, chicks eat insects and seeds.

Another kind of quail common to the United States is the *California quail.* California quail are grayish with a teardrop-shaped feather rising from the forehead. Many live in the foothills and valleys of the Western mountains. Others nest and raise their young in residential areas of even the largest Western cities.

Other kinds of quail found in the United States are *scaled quail, Gambel's quail, mountain quail,* and *montezuma quail.* The mountain quail is the largest quail, measuring $10\frac{1}{2}$ to $11\frac{1}{2}$ inches (26.7 to 29.2 centimeters) long and weighing about 8 ounces (230 grams); the montezuma quail is the smallest, measuring 8 to $9\frac{1}{2}$ inches (20 to 24 centimeters) long. All these birds live in the Western and Southwestern states. The *European quail* is found in much of Europe and Africa. The European populations migrate chiefly to northern Africa and the Middle East.　　Richard F. Johnston

Scientific classification. Quail make up the quail subfamily, Odontophorinae, in the family Phasianidae. The scientific name for the northern bobwhite is *Colinus virginianus.* The California quail is *Callipepla californica.*

See also **Partridge; Grouse; Bird** (pictures).

Quaker-ladies. See Bluet.

Quakers is the popular name for members of the Religious Society of Friends. Quakerism developed in England in the 1600's. Today, a majority of its followers live in the United States. England and Kenya also have large Quaker populations. Smaller Quaker groups exist in most other parts of the world.

Quakers have been known throughout their history for their humanitarian activities. They reject war and stress peace education. They have been pioneers in removing barriers to racial equality and have been among the leaders in prison reform and in the humane treatment of mental patients. Quakers have always been concerned with education, and the high quality of their many schools and colleges has been widely recognized.

History. George Fox of England founded Quakerism. His spiritual experience led him to witness what he called the *Inner Light* of Christ that dwells in the hearts of ordinary people. Those who followed that Inner Light were truly spiritual and following God's will. Fox began preaching in 1647 and attracted a variety of religious seekers. The word *Quaker* was originally meant as an insult to Fox, who told an English judge to "tremble at the Word of the Lord." The judge called Fox a "quaker."

From the beginning, the Quakers emphasized inward spiritual experiences rather than specific creeds. The early Quakers, or Friends, developed radically fresh forms of worship and business proceedings. These forms were based on a trust in the Holy Spirit and faith that ordinary lay people were able to receive the Spirit.

In 1681, a Quaker, William Penn, received a charter from the king of England to establish the colony of Pennsylvania. Penn hoped to make the colony a haven for the continually persecuted English Quakers who wished to emigrate to the New World. Penn gave the colony a constitution that was a model for safeguarding the religious liberties of its citizens. While the Quakers governed the colony from 1682 to 1756, Pennsylvania maintained no militia and only a modest police force.

Worship. Quakers regard all life as sacramental and observe no special sacraments. Business and worship are conducted in monthly, quarterly, and yearly meetings. Originally, Quakers worshiped by gathering for periods of group silence. During the silence, the faithful attentively waited for the Lord to exercise His power upon their lives; to lay on them "the burden of the world's suffering" and their responsibility to respond to it. Anyone who felt he or she had been given a message during the silence could speak at the meeting.

Quaker business meetings are guided by a *clerk.* After a period of silent waiting, the clerk states a particular problem and listens to the members' suggestions. Then, without being bound to anyone's specific suggestion, the clerk presents for group consideration a *minute* that seeks to resolve the problem. No votes are taken, but the process continues until even opposing minorities are at least satisfied that their position has had a hearing and that it has been considered.

The loose organizational structure of the Religious Society of Friends has always given a great deal of liberty to its regional yearly meetings. This liberty has resulted in a variety of worship and spiritual patterns throughout the world. The Friends World Committee for Consultation in Birmingham, England, is a communications center for many regional yearly meetings in the world.   Henry Warner Bowden

Related articles in *World Book* include:

American Friends Service Committee	New Jersey (English control)
Dyer, Mary	Penn, William
Fox, George	Pennsylvania (picture: A Quaker meeting house)
Marriage (Wedding ceremonies and customs)	Prison (Early prison reform)
Mott, Lucretia Coffin	Whittier, John Greenleaf
	Woolman, John

Additional resources

Barbour, Hugh, and Frost, J. W. *The Quakers.* Rev. ed. Friends United, 1994.
Williams, Jean K. *The Quakers.* Watts, 1998.

Quanah, *KWAH nuh* (1845-1911), was a chief of the Comanche Indians. He led his people against white settlers in an attempt to stop the slaughter of buffalo in the tribe's homeland in Texas.
Quanah surrendered to the United States Army in 1875. In June 1875, Quanah's band moved to a reservation near Fort Sill, in what is now southwestern Oklahoma. Quanah encouraged his people to get an education and to farm the land. He also persuaded the Comanche to increase their income by leasing pastureland to white ranchers. Quanah obtained full U.S. citizen-

Smithsonian Institution National Archives, Washington, D.C.

Quanah

ship for every member of his band long before other Indian chiefs did so for their people.

Quanah was born near what is now Lubbock, Texas. He was the son of a Comanche chief named Nokoni and of Cynthia Ann Parker, a white captive. He was also called Quanah Parker. The name Quanah comes from the Comanche *kwaina,* meaning *fragrant.* Quanah, Texas, was named for him.   W. Jean Hurtado

Quanta. See Photon; Quantum mechanics.

Quantico Marine Corps Combat Development Command, *KWAHNT uh кон,* in Quantico, Virginia, is the main center for training United States Marine Corps officers. Enlisted personnel are also trained there. The Marine Corps develops and tests new weapons and equipment and develops techniques of amphibious warfare at Quantico. The command lies about 35 miles (56 kilometers) south of Washington, D.C. Schools at Quantico include the Amphibious Warfare School, the Basic School for commissioned officers, the Command and Staff College, the Communications Officer School, the Officer Candidate School, and the Staff Noncommissioned Officer Academy. It also has a U.S. Navy hospital and schools for computer science, instructor training, and ordnance. The Quantico Marine Corps Air Facility and part of the Federal Bureau of Investigation Academy are also there. Quantico was founded in 1917.

Critically reviewed by the United States Marine Corps

Quantrill, *KWAHN trihl,* **William Clarke** (1837-1865), led a Confederate guerrilla band during the American Civil War (1861-1865). Born in Ohio, he went to Kansas in 1857 and started farming. The next year, he rode west with a wagon train and became a gambler. He returned to Kansas in 1859 and taught school. Quantrill was accused of stealing cattle and horses and of killing several people, but he escaped arrest.

At the start of the Civil War, Quantrill formed a band of guerrilla troops. He led his men on raids against Kansas and Missouri farmers and townspeople who favored the Union. Quantrill's band was mustered into Confederate service in 1862, but continued to operate independently. On Aug. 21, 1863, he and his men burned most of the town of Lawrence, Kansas, and killed about 150 people. Frank James, Jesse James's brother, rode with the band that day. Quantrill was killed during a raid in Kentucky.   Thomas L. Connelly

Quantum mechanics, *KWAHN tuhm,* is a field of physics that describes the structure of the atom and the motion of atomic particles. It also explains how atoms absorb and give off energy as light, and it clarifies the nature of light.

Quantum mechanics goes beyond the limits of classical physics, which is based on the laws formulated by the English scientist Sir Isaac Newton. It ranks as one of the major scientific achievements of the 1900's. Quantum mechanics has contributed greatly to the development of such important devices as lasers and transistors. It also has enabled scientists to gain a better understanding of chemical bonds and chemical reactions.

Understanding quantum mechanics. In an atom, tiny particles of negative electric charge called *electrons* move in orbits around a nucleus of positive charge. Quantum mechanics shows that the electrons can move only in certain orbits. Each orbit, called a *quantized* orbit, has a particular value of energy. When an electron is in a given orbit, it exists at a specific energy level and does not release or absorb energy. An electron remains in this normal state as long as its atom is not disturbed. But if outside forces act on the atom, the electron can change to another quantized orbit.

When an electron jumps from an orbit of higher energy to one of lower energy, it gives off energy as light. This light is released in the form of a tiny bundle of energy called a *quantum* or *photon*. The energy of a photon corresponds to the difference in energy of the two orbits between which the jump occurs. An electron also can absorb a photon and jump from an orbit of lower energy to one of higher energy.

Scientists once believed light was a wave emitted as a continuous flow. But quantum mechanics explains that light is a stream of separate photons, which have characteristics of both particles and waves. A photon behaves like a particle because it occupies a fixed amount of space. A photon also behaves like a wave because it has a definite *frequency* (number of vibrations per second), which is proportional to its energy.

A photon's frequency forms a single spectrum line that represents a particular wavelength or color. The atoms of a chemical element give off photons of a wide range of frequencies to produce many different lines. This series of lines makes up the chemical element's spectrum, which differs from that of any other element.

Quantum mechanics shows that electrons and other atomic particles of matter are also associated with waves. These waves, called *matter waves,* have a specific wavelength. The wavelength is inversely proportional to the particle's *momentum.* The particle's momentum is calculated by multiplying the mass of the particle by its velocity.

Matter waves provide an explanation for the arrangement of electrons in separate orbits. When an electron is undisturbed, its wave fits around the atom's nucleus at a distance such that the wave can join smoothly onto itself. The electrons of a single atom have waves of different wavelengths. These electrons form orbits at varying distances from the nucleus.

Another fundamental idea of quantum mechanics is the *uncertainty principle.* According to this principle, the position and velocity of a particle cannot simultaneously be measured with exactness. The principle is valid because a particle has certain wave properties.

History. In 1900, the German physicist Max Planck introduced the idea of quanta to explain the spectrum of light emitted by certain heated objects. In 1905, the German-born physicist Albert Einstein broadened Planck's idea to explain a phenomenon called the *photoelectric effect.* In doing so, Einstein firmly established that light consists of particles of energy that have wave properties. Niels Bohr, a Danish physicist, proposed the theory of the atom's electron structure in 1913. He also showed how atoms radiate light. Scientists call Bohr's work *quantum theory* to distinguish it from the broader system of quantum mechanics.

Louis de Broglie, a French physicist, introduced the idea of matter waves in 1924. The physicists Erwin Schrödinger of Austria and Werner Heisenberg of Germany independently developed forms of quantum mechanics in the mid-1920's. Since that year, these forms have been unified into a system and applied to several scientific fields, including chemistry, molecular biology, and solid-state physics.   Francis T. Cole

Related articles in *World Book* include:

Atom	Einstein, Albert	Physics (Quantum
Bohr, Niels	Heisenberg, Werner	theory)
Born, Max	Jordan, Ernst P.	Planck, Max K. E. L.
De Broglie, Louis	Light (Quantum me-	Schrödinger,
Victor	chanics)	Erwin
Dirac, Paul A. M.	Photon	Solid-state physics

Quantum theory. See Quantum mechanics.

Quarantine occurs when people, animals, or plants are isolated or their movements restricted to prevent the spread of infection. The period of quarantine depends on the amount of time necessary for protection against the spread of a particular disease. The word *quarantine* comes from the Latin *quadraginta,* meaning 40. In early times, officials held a ship outside of port for 40 days if they suspected it carried infection among its passengers or freight.

International quarantine. All people entering a country from foreign areas are subject to quarantine. The officer in command of a ship or airplane is required to report illnesses or deaths on board to officials at the port of entry. People infected with certain diseases may be detained, placed in isolation, or denied entry.

In the United States, the Public Health Service (PHS) develops and enforces quarantine regulations. The United States maintains a quarantine over Asiatic cholera, plague, and yellow fever. In addition, the PHS may apply quarantine restrictions in cases of diphtheria, tuberculosis, and suspected cases of smallpox or certain fevers. Quarantine regulations in Canada are administered by Health and Welfare Canada. The World Health Organization, an agency of the United Nations, helps national health agencies develop quarantine laws.

Plant and animal quarantine. Harmful insect pests and disease organisms have been brought into the United States and Canada by diseased plants and animals. The governments of both nations have laws that provide for the inspection of all plants and animals entering the country. Some states have quarantines to keep out diseased plants and animals or insect pests. Local areas may be quarantined to prevent the spread of such animal diseases as foot-and-mouth disease, which affects livestock.   Alan R. Hinman

Related articles in *World Book* include:

Bill of health	Insect (Insect control)
Epidemic	Plant quarantine
Fumigation	Sanitation

Quark, *kwawrk,* is one of the three families of particles that serve as "building blocks" of matter. The other two families are the leptons and the fundamental, or gauge, bosons. Quarks are *elementary particles*—that is, they have no known smaller parts.

There are six types of quarks, each of which carries a fraction of an electric charge. Three of the quarks, called *down* (or *d*), *strange* (or *s*), and *bottom* (or *b*), have $\frac{1}{3}$ unit of negative charge. The other three—the *up* (or *u*), *charm* (or *c*), and *top* (or *t*)—have $\frac{2}{3}$ unit of positive charge.

A quark is always combined with one or two other quarks. *Composite particles* made up of quarks are known as *hadrons*. These include protons and neutrons, which form the nuclei of atoms.

There are two kinds of hadrons—(1) baryons and (2) mesons. A baryon is a three-quark combination. A proton is a baryon consisting of two *u* quarks and one *d*, while a neutron is a baryon made up of two *d*'s and one *u*. A meson is made up of a quark and an *antiquark*. Antiquarks are the antimatter equivalents of quarks, opposite in electric charge and certain other properties.

Quarks have no measurable size. Physicists describe them as "pointlike." The *t* quark is the heaviest known elementary particle. Its mass is about 190 atomic mass units. This is almost as heavy as an entire atom of gold. The lightest quark, the *u*, has about 35,000 times less mass than the *t*.

The *s, c, b,* and *t* quarks are much heavier than the *u* and *d*. All the heavy quarks are unstable, and they do not exist in ordinary matter. They usually break down into *u*'s, *d*'s, and other lighter particles in less than a billionth of a second. Physicists must create *s, c, b,* and *t* quarks with devices called *particle accelerators*. An accelerator causes subatomic particles to collide violently with one another to produce these quarks.

Two California Institute of Technology physicists, the American Murray Gell-Mann and Russian-born George Zweig, independently proposed the first theory of quarks in 1964. The original theory required only *u, d,* and *s* quarks to build all known hadrons. In the late 1960's and early 1970's, experiments showed that protons and neutrons contain parts much smaller than they are, and that these parts carry fractional charges. Discoveries in 1974, 1977, and 1995 proved the existence of the *c, b,* and *t,* in that order. Robert H. March

See also **Boson; Gluon; Hadron; Lepton; Psi particle.**

Quarles, *kwawrlz,* **Benjamin Arthur** (1904-1996), was an American historian. He wrote many books about African Americans and their role in United States history. His books include *Frederick Douglass* (1948), *The Negro in the Civil War* (1953), *The Negro in the American Revolution* (1961), and *The Negro in the Making of America* (1964). Quarles was born in Boston. He became professor of history at Dillard University in 1939 and was dean of Dillard from 1946 to 1953. He served as head of the department of history at Morgan State College from 1953 to 1974. Edgar Allan Toppin

Quarrying, *KWAWR ee ihng,* is a method of mining a deposit that lies at the surface of the earth. This method is commonly used to dig out large slabs or blocks of stone called *dimension stone.* The stone is removed from a large pit called a *quarry.* Quarries have nearly vertical walls that in some cases can be 1,000 feet (300 meters) high. Dimension stone cut from quarries includes flagstone, granite, limestone, marble, sandstone, and slate. It is used mainly as a building material and for flooring and decorative wall coverings.

The value of dimension stone depends on its color, strength, and freedom from cracks and flaws. To preserve these qualities, workers must remove the stone from a quarry with great care. Workers begin the quarrying of a deposit by removing a large section of stone called a *key block.* They separate individual blocks from the surrounding rock by channeling, cutting, or sawing. When the stone has been taken from the entire length and width of the quarry, workers remove another key block to establish a new working level.

Quarrying is not a common method of mining because only limited amounts of dimension stone are used each year. In the United States, the leading producers of dimension stone are Georgia, Indiana, and Vermont.

The word *quarrying* is sometimes used to refer to the removal of such materials as crushed rock and gravel from an open pit. These materials are mined in enormous amounts each year. William Hustrulid

See also **Mining** (Quarrying).

Quart is a unit of volume and capacity for both dry and liquid substances in the inch-pound system of measurement. This system is used in the United States. The liquid quart equals $\frac{1}{4}$ of a gallon and contains 57.750 cubic inches. It equals 0.946 liter in the metric system. The dry quart equals $\frac{1}{32}$ of a bushel and contains 67.200 cubic inches. It equals 1.101 liters. Quarts are divided into two pints. The *imperial quart* was once used in Britain and such countries as Canada and New Zealand. But it has been replaced with metric units of measurement. The imperial quart contains 69.355 cubic inches, or 1.137 liters. See also **Weights and measures.** Richard S. Davis

Quarter is a United States coin worth 25 cents, or a quarter of a dollar. The government issued the first quarters in 1796. The Washington quarter was first minted in 1932, the 200th anniversary of George Washington's birth. Washington's head appears on one side, and an eagle is on the other side. Quarters of several other designs were used before the Washington quarter. In 1975 and 1976, the government issued special bicenten-

WORLD BOOK photo by James Simek

The traditional Washington quarter pictures George Washington on one side. An eagle appears on the coin's reverse side.

nial quarters. The coins featured a colonial drummer, instead of an eagle, on one side. In 1999, the government began issuing quarters that replaced the eagle with one of 50 designs that each commemorates a U.S. state.

Until 1965, quarters contained 90 percent silver and 10 percent copper. Because of a shortage of silver, the Coinage Act of 1965 eliminated silver from the coin. Since then, it has consisted of a layer of copper between layers of a copper-nickel mixture. Burton H. Hobson

Quartz, *kwawrts,* is a common mineral that occurs in many types of rocks. Pure quartz is transparent. It is made of silicon dioxide and has the chemical formula SiO_2. Quartz has many uses in science and industry.

Quartz can be found in several forms and in all three major kinds of rocks—*igneous, metamorphic,* and *sedimentary* (see **Rock**). Except for feldspar, it is the most common rock-forming material in the earth's continental crust. Quartz is also one of the hardest minerals. Beryl, spinel, topaz, corundum, and diamond are among the few harder minerals. Erosion does not wear away quartz as rapidly as it wears away most other rock materials.

Types. There are many varieties of quartz. Geologists often divide them into two general groups, *coarse crystalline* and *cryptocrystalline.*

Coarse crystalline forms of quartz include six-sided prismlike crystals and massive, granular clumps in which the individual grains of quartz can be seen. *Rock crystal* is a coarse crystalline quartz that occurs as colorless, transparent crystals. Some colored varieties of coarse crystalline quartz crystals, such as *amethyst* and *citrine,* also called *false topaz,* are cut into gemstones. Granular forms of coarse crystalline quartz include *quartz sandstone* and *quartz sand. Rose quartz* and *milky quartz* are colored granular forms.

The color of a type of coarse crystalline quartz results from small amounts of aluminum, calcium, iron, lithium, magnesium, sodium, or other elements in its crystal structure. For example, the bluish-violet color of amethyst is caused by the presence of iron and manganese. Coloring may also result from changes or defects in the crystal structure of quartz. The smoky appearance of *cairngorm,* also called *smoky quartz,* is produced by such alterations. The decay of a radioactive element, such as uranium or thorium, in quartz releases high-energy radiation that alters the crystal structure of quartz. Because of this change, light rays cannot penetrate the quartz crystal, and a smoky color results.

Cryptocrystalline forms of quartz have individual grains of quartz that can be seen only with a microscope. These forms include *chalcedony, chert, flint,* and *jasper.* Petrified wood consists of chalcedony that has replaced the original wood fiber. *Carnelian* and *agate* are varieties of chalcedony used as gems.

Properties and uses. Quartz has an important property called the *piezoelectric effect* (see **Piezoelectricity**). When a *plate* (slice) from a quartz crystal is mechanically compressed, it develops a positive charge on one side and a negative charge on the other. This phenomenon is piezoelectric generation of voltage across the crystal. It enables an electric current or signal to pass through the crystal.

Quartz crystals are used in the wave transmitters of radios, TV sets, and most radars. In such transmitters, the electric signal generated is amplified and changed into a radio wave of a certain frequency. The piezoelectric property of quartz also provides the basis for the operation of quartz watches and clocks. Voltage applied to a quartz crystal plate causes the plate to expand and contract, producing vibrations at a uniform rate. The size of the plate determines the number of vibrations per second. The vibrations are translated into seconds, minutes, and hours. See **Watch** (Electronic watches).

Quartz does not expand much when heated, or crack when cooled rapidly. These properties make quartz an important material in making glass containers that can withstand extremely high temperatures.

Rock crystal is used in making lenses for some microscopes and telescopes. Large crystals of quartz are also used in the manufacture of certain other optical devices. Most quartz crystals used for industrial purposes are produced synthetically because of the limited supply of suitable natural crystals. Quartz sandstone is a common building material. Quartz sand is used in making sandpaper and grindstones.   Robert W. Charles

Related articles in *World Book* include:

Agate	Chalcedony	Jasper
Amethyst	Flint	Mineral (pictures)
Carnelian	Hardness	Onyx

Quartzite, *KWAWRT syt,* is a rock composed chiefly of the mineral quartz. The quartz occurs both as individual grains and as the cementing material that holds the grains together. Quartzite, one of the hardest rocks, is a common type of metamorphic rock (see **Metamorphic rock**). It forms when heat and pressure change the grains in quartz sandstone. In this process, called *recrystallization,* quartz grains become so firmly bonded that any breaks that occur in quartzite go through the grains rather than pass around them.   John C. Butler

Quasar, *KWAY sahr* or *KWAY zahr,* is an extremely luminous object at the center of some distant galaxies. The word *quasar* is a shortened form of the term *quasi-stellar* (starlike) *radio source,* which was applied to the first type of quasar identified. Because quasars look much like stars in photographs, they are sometimes called *quasi-stellar objects.* Most quasars are about the size of the solar system. But they can be a trillion times brighter than the sun. Quasars are among the most distant objects yet detected in the universe. Some are estimated to be as far as 12 billion to 16 billion light-years from the earth (see **Light-year**).

Astronomers determine how distant a quasar is by measuring its *red shift.* Red shift is a shift in the wavelength of light given off by an astronomical object toward the longer, or red, wavelengths of the object's spectrum. It indicates an object is moving away from the earth. The more distant the object is, the larger is its red shift. All quasars have large red shifts. See **Red shift**.

Quasars give off enormous amounts of energy in the form of visible light, ultraviolet light, infrared rays, X rays, gamma rays, and in some cases, radio waves. Energy from quasars takes billions of years to reach the earth. For this reason, the study of quasars can provide information about early stages of the universe.

Quasars were first identified in 1963 by a group of astronomers at the Palomar Observatory, near San Diego. Since then, over a thousand have been discovered. Astronomers are not yet sure how quasars generate their vast quantities of radiation. Some believe quasars

Robert Weldon, © Gemological Institute of America, 1990, Stone Collection

Smoky quartz gets its smoky color from changes in the crystal structure of colorless quartz. The mineral appears as a six-sided crystal on the right and as a cut gem on the left.

are powered by a giant black hole that produces energy by swallowing clouds of gas from the surrounding galaxy (see **Black hole**). Timothy M. Heckman

See also **Telescope** (Radio telescopes).

Quasicrystal is a solid composed of atoms arranged in an orderly pattern that differs from the pattern in a crystal. In a crystal, the atomic structure is composed of a single type of atom cluster called a *unit cell.* The unit cell repeats throughout the structure so that the distance between the centers of the unit cells is the same throughout. A quasicrystal is composed of two, or sometimes more, kinds of unit cells. The unit cells repeat with different spacings between the different types of unit cells. The ratio of the spacings is an irrational number—that is, a number that cannot be expressed as a fraction (see **Rational number**).

Bell Laboratories
Quasicrystals have shapes that are impossible in crystals. For example, these quasicrystals have five-sided faces.

Both crystals and quasicrystals display *symmetry*—that is, it is possible to rotate their atomic structure by certain angles and have the structure appear identical to the first view. However, because quasicrystals have more than one shape of unit cell, they have types of symmetry that are impossible in crystals. For example, many quasicrystals have fivefold symmetry, meaning that they look the same after every one-fifth rotation around a circle. Crystals cannot have this type of symmetry because it is not possible to pack together a single shape of unit cell so that there is both five-fold symmetry and equal distance between the unit cells. Physicists discovered quasicrystals in 1984. Paul Joseph Steinhardt

See also **Symmetry**.

Quasimodo, *KWAH ZEE MOH doh,* **Salvatore,** *SAHL vah TAW reh* (1901-1968), an Italian poet, won the 1959 Nobel Prize for literature. Until about 1942, Quasimodo belonged to the *hermetic* school, a group of poets who wrote in a difficult, personal style that seemed sealed off from everyday life. Largely because of World War II, Quasimodo turned to a style that dealt with the events of his time. Beginning with *Day after Day* (1947), his poetry became an accurate reflection of the grief and destruction that the war had brought to humanity.

Quasimodo was born in Modica, near Syracuse, Sicily. In 1918, he moved to Italy. His first poems were published in literary magazines in Florence and later as a collection called *Waters and Lands* (1930). He also wrote many essays on literature and translated the work of William Shakespeare and other writers. Richard H. Lansing

Quayle, Dan (1947-   ), served as vice president of the United States from 1989 to 1993, during the term of President George Bush. Before becoming vice president, Quayle represented Indiana in the U.S. Senate

from 1981 to 1989. He previously had served two terms in the U.S. House of Representatives.

© R. Maiman, Sygma
Dan Quayle

Early life. Quayle, whose full name is James Danforth Quayle, was born on Feb. 4, 1947, in Indianapolis. Quayle's maternal grandfather, Eugene Pulliam, was an influential and wealthy publisher of several newspapers in Indiana and Arizona. Quayle graduated from DePauw University in Greencastle, Indiana, in 1969 with a degree in political science. In 1974, he received a law degree from Indiana University in Indianapolis. While attending law school at night, Quayle worked in the offices of the governor and attorney general of Indiana and directed the state's Inheritance Tax Division. From 1974 to 1976, he was associate publisher of *The Huntington Herald-Press,* a paper owned by his family.

In 1972, Quayle married Marilyn Tucker of Indianapolis. They had three children: Tucker Danforth, the oldest; Benjamin Eugene; and Mary Corinne, the youngest.

Political career. Quayle was elected to the United States House of Representatives in 1976 and in 1978 from a district in northeastern Indiana. In the House, he had a consistently conservative voting record. In 1980, Quayle won election to the U.S. Senate, defeating Democratic Senator Birch E. Bayh, Jr. Quayle was reelected in 1986. He served on the Senate's Budget, Armed Services, and Labor and Human Resources committees.

In 1988, the Republican National Convention nominated Quayle for vice president at Bush's request. The selection sparked controversy. Much of it centered on charges that Quayle used family influence to get into the Indiana National Guard in 1969, thereby avoiding the draft and possible combat in the Vietnam War (1957-1975). Quayle's experience and accomplishments were also questioned, but Bush stood by his choice. In the 1988 election, Bush and Quayle defeated their Democratic opponents, Governor Michael S. Dukakis of Massachusetts and Senator Lloyd Bentsen of Texas. Questions concerning Quayle's capabilities persisted throughout his term, but Bush loyally defended his vice president. Quayle also received support from the conservative branch of the Republican Party.

As vice president, Quayle traveled throughout the United States and to other countries to promote the Bush administration's policies. He also headed the National Space Council and the Council on Competitiveness. As head of the competitiveness council, Quayle sought to end government regulations he considered harmful to U.S. economic efficiency. But critics claimed many of the regulations were needed for environmental protection and other purposes.

In 1992, Bush and Quayle again became Republican nominees. But they were defeated by the Democratic candidates, Governor Bill Clinton of Arkansas and Senator Al Gore of Tennessee. Quayle briefly sought the Republican presidential nomination for the 2000 election but withdrew after attracting little support. Lee Thornton

Huge Percé Rock off the coast of the Gaspé Peninsula

Quebec

Quebec, *kwih BEHK,* or Québec, *kay BEHK,* is the largest province of Canada. It also has more people than any other province except Ontario. About 80 percent of Quebec's people have French ancestors, and some of the people in this group speak only French. These French Canadians write the name of the province as *Québec.* Montreal is the largest city in Quebec. The capital of the province is also named Quebec, but it is often called Quebec City.

The strong French influence makes Quebec quite different from the rest of Canada. For example, almost 90 percent of the people belong to the Roman Catholic Church. Many Quebec schools teach the Roman Catholic religion, and most schools use French as the language of instruction. The province's older buildings are French in architecture. Beautiful French-style homes can still be seen in the countryside. Almost every village has a Catholic church, and crosses and shrines stand by the roadsides. Nevertheless, Quebec has churches of a

The contributors of this article are Robin B. Burns, Professor of History at Bishop's University; and Roger Nadeau, Head of the Department of Geography at the University of Sherbrooke.

number of other denominations. The province also has hospitals, schools, and universities that serve English-speaking people. Government services use both French and English.

The early French settlers in the Quebec region were interested chiefly in the fur trade. Rapid economic growth during the 1900's placed Quebec among the great industrial regions of North America. Factories and mills use the power provided by hydroelectric plants on Quebec's many rivers. Quebec is a leading producer of hydroelectric power in North America.

Quebec produces about a fourth of all the goods manufactured in Canada. The Montreal area ranks second to the Toronto area among Canada's leading manufacturing centers. Important products manufactured in Quebec include processed foods, aircraft, and chemicals. Quebec leads all North American regions in the manufacture of paper. Also, Quebec ranks first among the Canadian provinces in the production of aluminum.

The province's vast natural resources provide its industries with huge supplies of valuable raw materials. The far northern wilderness of Quebec has vast deposits of iron ore, the province's leading mineral product. Quebec mines produce nearly all of Canada's asbestos. The

Montreal, Quebec's largest city

© Yves Marcoux, Stone

Interesting facts about Quebec

WORLD BOOK illustrations by Kevin Chadwick

The Cathedral-Basilica of Mary, Queen of the World, in downtown Montreal, is a reproduction of St. Peter's Basilica in Vatican City. The cathedral covers about one-fourth the area of St. Peter's. It was dedicated in 1870.

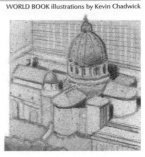

Cathedral

The Haskell Opera House in Rock Island, Quebec, has performances on a stage in Canada while the audience watches from seats in the United States. North of the U.S.-Canadian boundary line is Rock Island. To the south is Derby Line, Vermont. Many other buildings in the area were built before the international boundary was firmly established. In some houses, meals are prepared in Canada and served in the United States.

Joseph-Armand Bombardier of Valcourt helped to launch the sport of snowmobiling when his company began mass-producing sled-sized snowmobiles in 1959. Bombardier began building his first snowmobile in 1922, when he was only 15 years old.

Snowmobiles

province also is a leading producer of gold, copper, and titanium. Forests cover about half of the province. They provide balsam firs, spruces, and other trees for Quebec's great paper industry.

The St. Lawrence River Valley and the rolling Eastern Townships, south of the river, have rich soils. Quebec ranks among North America's leading producers of dairy cattle, hogs, and milk, and leads in the production of maple syrup.

Quebec's great St. Lawrence River is one of the most important waterways in North America. The word *Quebec* came from the Algonquian Indian word *kebec (the place where the river narrows).* The French explorer Samuel de Champlain heard the Indians use this word for a place on the St. Lawrence River. He founded Quebec City there in 1608. It was the first permanent European settlement in Canada. The battlefield at the Plains of Abraham, where France lost Canada to Britain in 1759, lies within the city. Because of the province's rich historical background, Quebec is sometimes called the *Storied Province.*

For the relationship of Quebec to the other provinces of Canada, see **Canada; Canada, Government of; Canada, History of.**

Bob Anderson, Masterfile

Towing logs on the Gatineau River

Quebec in brief

Symbols of Quebec

The provincial flag was adopted in 1948. The provincial coat of arms, adopted in 1939, combines the emblems of France, Britain, and Canada. The three *fleurs-de-lis* represent the coat of arms of the French kings. The British lion stands across the center. The three maple leaves symbolize Canada.

Provincial flag

Quebec (brown) is Canada's largest province.

General information

Entered the Dominion: July 1, 1867, as one of the original four provinces.
Provincial abbreviation: PQ (postal).
Provincial motto: *Je Me Souviens* (I Remember).

The National Assembly Building is in Quebec City, the capital since 1867 and from 1608 to 1841. The Quebec region had several capitals as part of the Province of Canada.

Land and climate

Area: 594,860 sq. mi. (1,540,680 km²), including 71,000 sq. mi. (184,000 km²) of inland water.
Elevation: *Highest*—Mont d'Iberville, 5,322 ft. (1,622 m) above sea level. *Lowest*—sea level.
Record high temperature: 104° F. (40° C) at Ville Marie on July 6, 1921.
Record low temperature: −66° F. (−54° C) at Doucet on Feb. 5, 1923.
Average July temperature: 63° F. (17° C).
Average January temperature: 7° F. (−14° C).
Average yearly precipitation: 40 in. (101 cm).

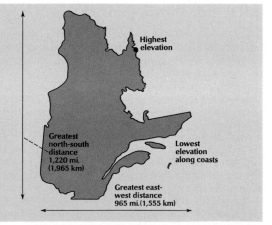

Highest elevation

Greatest north-south distance 1,220 mi. (1,965 km)

Lowest elevation along coasts

Greatest east-west distance 965 mi. (1,555 km)

Important dates

Samuel de Champlain established Quebec City, the first permanent European settlement in Canada.

Quebec became one of the original four provinces on July 1.

1534   **1608**   **1763**   **1867**

Jacques Cartier reached the Gulf of St. Lawrence and claimed the Quebec region for France.

Britain acquired the Quebec region by the Treaty of Paris.

**Provincial
coat of arms**

Provincial seal

**Floral
emblem**
White
garden lily

People

Population: 7,138,795 (1996 census)
Rank among the provinces: 2nd
Density: 12 persons per sq. mi. (4 per
km²), provinces average 12 per sq. mi.
(4 per km²)
Distribution: 78 percent urban, 22 per-
cent rural
Largest cities and towns*

Montreal	1,016,376
Laval	330,393
Quebec	167,264
Longueuil	127,977
Gatineau	100,702
Montréal-Nord	81,581

*1996 census.
Source: Statistics Canada.

Population trend

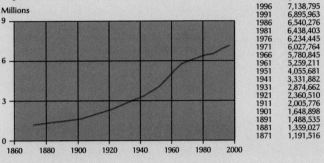

Millions

Source: Statistics Canada.

Year	Population
1996	7,138,795
1991	6,895,963
1986	6,540,276
1981	6,438,403
1976	6,234,445
1971	6,027,764
1966	5,780,845
1961	5,259,211
1951	4,055,681
1941	3,331,882
1931	2,874,662
1921	2,360,510
1911	2,005,776
1901	1,648,898
1891	1,488,535
1881	1,359,027
1871	1,191,516

Economy

Chief products

Agriculture: milk, hogs, chickens,
beef cattle, corn, potatoes.
Manufacturing: paper products,
transportation equipment, food
and beverage products, chemicals,
printed materials.
Mining: gold, iron ore, titanium.

Gross domestic product

Value of goods and services produced in 1998: $193,243,000,000.*
Services include community, business, and personal services; finance; government; trade; transportation and communication;
and utilities. *Industry* includes
construction, manufacturing, and
mining. *Agriculture* includes agriculture, fishing, and forestry.

*Canadian dollars.
Source: Statistics Canada.

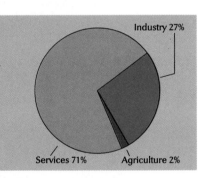

Industry 27%

Services 71%   Agriculture 2%

Government

Provincial government

Premier: term of up to 5 years
Members of the National Assembly: 125;
terms of up to 5 years

Federal government

Members of the House of Commons: 75
Members of the House of Senate: 24

Sources of information

For information on tourism in Quebec, write to: Tourisme
Québec, P.O. Box 979, Montreal, PQ H3C 2W3. Tourisme
Québec's Web site at www.tourisme.gouv.qc.ca also pro-
vides tourist information. Communication-Québec handles
requests for information about the province's economy,
government, and history. Write to: Communication-
Québec, Les Façades de la Gare, 400 Boulevard Jean-
Lesage, Bureau 105, Quebec, PQ G1K 8W1.

The provincial government bought all privately owned electric power companies.

The Quebec legislature made French
the province's official language.

1912   **1963**   **1967**   **1974**

Quebec nearly doubled in size by acquiring
territory east of Hudson Bay.

Expo 67, a world's fair, was held in Montreal
as part of Canada's centennial celebration.

Population. The 1996 Canadian census reported that Quebec had 7,138,795 people. The population of the province had risen about 4 percent over the 1991 figure of 6,895,963.

About four-fifths of the people of Quebec live in cities and towns. A little less than half live in the metropolitan area of Montreal. Quebec has four other Census Metropolitan Areas as defined by Statistics Canada. They are Chicoutimi-Jonquière, Ottawa-Hull, Quebec, and Trois-Rivières. For the population of these areas, see the *Index* to the political map of Quebec.

Montreal is the largest city in Quebec. It ranks as Canada's largest city based on city limits population. However, Toronto, Ontario, has a larger metropolitan area population. Montreal ranks second in population only to Paris among French-speaking cities in the world. Other large cities of Quebec include Laval, Quebec City, and Longueuil. For more information, see the articles on Quebec cities listed in the *Related articles* at the end of this article.

Most of the people of Quebec are French Canadians. Nearly all are descendants of the French settlers who came to the Quebec region during the 1600's and 1700's. The French colony came under British rule in 1763, but not many British settlers arrived until the early 1800's. They soon controlled the colony economically as well as politically. But the French Canadians lived apart and continued to follow their own ways of life.

French Canadians make up 80 percent of Quebec's population. People of British descent form 10 percent. There are about 50,000 North American Indians and about 7,000 Inuit (formerly called Eskimos). Another 63,000 people have some American Indian ancestry. French is the only tongue spoken by three-fifths of the people of Quebec. About a third of the population speaks French and English. Most of the rest speak only English.

Ninety-two percent of Quebec's population was born in Canada. The others came from Britain, France, Italy, the United States, and other countries.

Roman Catholics make up 88 percent of the province's population. Other large religious groups include members of the Anglican Church of Canada, the United Church of Canada, and the Jewish faith.

Schools. During the 1600's, Roman Catholic missionaries from France established the first schools in the Quebec region. The missionaries taught Indian and white children. Priests and nuns provided the only formal schooling in Quebec for many years. During that

Population density

Most of Quebec's people live in the southern part of the province. Montreal, Quebec's largest city, is located there. The vast northern areas have few settlements.

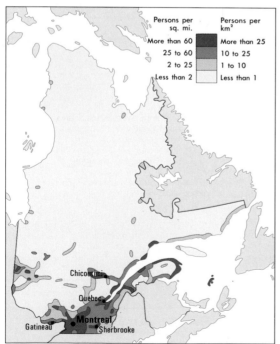

Persons per sq. mi.	Persons per km²
More than 60	More than 25
25 to 60	10 to 25
2 to 25	1 to 10
Less than 2	Less than 1

WORLD BOOK map; based on the *National Atlas of Canada*

Derek Caron, Masterfile

Montreal's St. Denis Street has a number of charming open-air restaurants. Montreal ranks second in population only to Paris among the French-speaking cities of the world.

Quebec Department of Tourism

The International Jazz Festival in Montreal is one of Quebec's most popular annual events. Each summer, about 1 million jazz fans attend this 10-day festival.

period, nearly all of the settlers were French Roman Catholics.

British colonists began arriving during the late 1700's. They were Protestants and wanted their own schools. In 1801, the provincial legislature set up a system of free public education under Protestant control. But the French Canadians were opposed to these schools. In 1846, the colony established two separate school systems under church control, one for Roman Catholics and the other for Protestants.

Until 1964, the two school systems were headed by a superintendent of education. In 1964, the provincial government assumed greater control of the two systems. The province created the Cabinet post of minister of education. The minister, who administers the school program, is advised on educational policies by the superior council of education. Roman Catholic and Protestant committees supervise religious teaching.

In mid-1998, the school systems in Quebec were reorganized based on language. French and English school boards replaced Catholic and Protestant ones. However, individual schools may decide whether they will be Roman Catholic or Protestant by submitting a request to the Roman Catholic or Protestant committee. Children begin school at age 5 or 6 and must complete 11 years of schooling. For the number of students and teachers in Quebec, see **Education** (table).

Libraries. Canada's first public library was established in Quebec City in 1779. The province now has about 950 public libraries. Laval University, McGill University, the University of Quebec at Montreal, and the University of Montreal have outstanding libraries. The provincial government operates the National Library in Montreal and the Library of the National Assembly in Quebec City.

Museums. The Montreal Museum of Fine Arts houses collections of Canadian paintings and decorative arts. The Château de Ramezay, built in 1705 by Governor Claude de Ramezay in Montreal, is a fine historical museum. The Montreal Museum of Contemporary Art exhibits works completed since 1940. The McCord Museum of Canadian History, operated by McGill University in Montreal, displays arts and costumes of native-born Canadians. The Musée du Québec in Quebec City features Canadian art dating from the 1600's to the present. The Quebec Seminary Museum in Quebec City has a fine collection of old and rare coins.

Exhibits at the Musée de la Civilisation in Quebec City concentrate on aspects of human civilization and culture. La Maison Chevalier, which is part of the museum, houses a collection of furniture dating back to the time of French rule. The Canadian Museum of Civilization in Hull reflects the country's cultural heritage. The Canadian Center for Architecture in Montreal has a collection of public records, blueprints, books, and photographs.

Universities and colleges

This table lists the universities and colleges in Quebec that grant bachelor's or advanced degrees and are members of the Association of Universities and Colleges of Canada.

Name	Mailing address
Advanced Commercial Studies, School for	Montreal
Bishop's University	Sherbrooke
Concordia University	Montreal
Laval University	Quebec
McGill University	Montreal
Montreal, University of	Montreal
Polytechnic School of Montreal	Montreal
Quebec, University of	*
Sherbrooke, University of	Sherbrooke

*For campuses, see **Quebec, University of.**

Laval University

Laval University, in Ste.-Foy, became a degree-granting institution in 1852. It was established as a Roman Catholic seminary in 1663 by Bishop François Xavier de Laval.

Ray Chen, Masterfile

McGill University, in Montreal, conducts courses in English. Bishop's and Concordia are also English-language universities. Quebec's other universities teach courses in French.

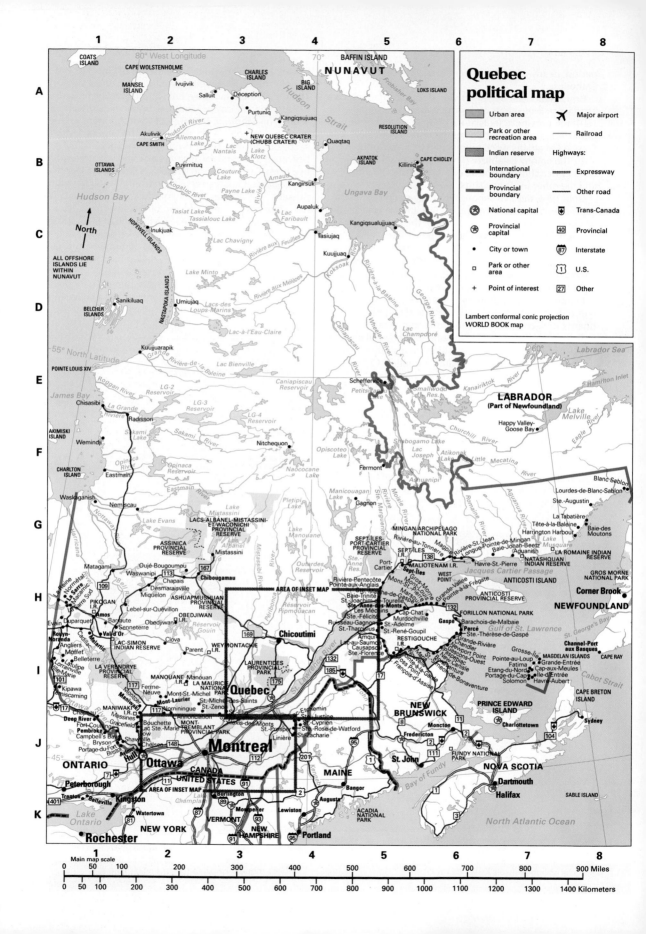

Quebec political map

Legend:

- Urban area
- Park or other recreation area
- Indian reserve
- ----- International boundary
- ——— Provincial boundary
- ✈ Major airport
- ——— Railroad

Highways:
- ═══ Expressway
- ----- Other road

- National capital
- Provincial capital
- City or town
- Park or other area
- + Point of interest
- Trans-Canada
- 40 Provincial
- 87 Interstate
- 1 U.S.
- 27 Other

Lambert conformal conic projection
WORLD BOOK map

Main map scale
0 50 100 200 300 400 500 600 700 800 900 Miles
0 50 100 200 300 400 500 600 700 800 900 1000 1100 1200 1300 1400 Kilometers

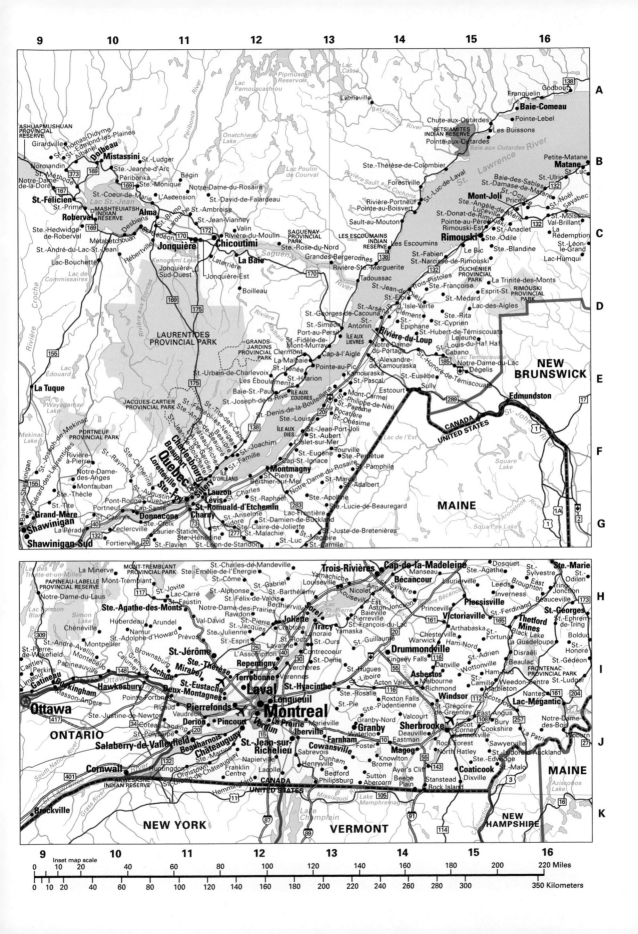

Quebec map index

Neuville* ....1,013 .G 1
New Carlisle ...1,538 .I 6
New Richmond† ...3,941 .I 6
Newport* ....729 .H 6
Nicolet ....4,352 .H 14
Noranda, see Rouyn-Noranda
Normandin ......3,873 .B 9
Normétal ....1,129 .H 1
North Hatley ....758 .J 14
Notre-Dame-de-l'Île-Perrot* ......7,059 .J 11
Notre-Dame-de-Lourdes* ...2,087 .H 16
Notre-Dame-des-Pins* ....1,025 .H 16
Notre-Dame-des-Prairies* ..6,837 .H 12
Notre-Dame-du-Bon-Conseil* ....1,343 .J 13
Notre-Dame-du-Lac ....2,193 .E 15
Notre-Dame-du-Laus† .....412 .H 9
Notre-Dame-du-Mont-Carmel* ....4,835 .C 9
Notre-Dame-du-Rosaire ...394 .B 11
Nouvelle ....2,009 .I 5
Obedjiwan Indian Reserve ...1,464 .H 2
Omerville* ....2,068 .J 14
Ormstown ....1,604 .J 11
Otterburn Park* ....7,320 .I 12
Outremont .....22,571 .I 11
Papineauville ...1,628 .I 10
Parc Mailloux*† ...518 .D 14
Parc Rémillard*† ...651 .J 13
Parent ....387 .I 2
Paspébiac ....2,945 .I 6
Percé ....3,993 .H 6
Petit-Saguenay* ...918 .J 4
Philipsburg .....245 .K 13
Pierrefonds ...52,986 .I 12
Pierreville ......976 .H 13
Pincourt ....10,023 .I 11
Plaisance* ......992 .I 10
Plessisville ....6,810 .H 15
Pohénégamook* ...3,259 .E 14
Pointe-au-Pic ...952 .E 13
Pointe-aux-Outardes ..1,339 .B 15
Pointe-au-Père ...4,145 .C 15
Pointe-Calumet* ..5,443 .I 12
Pointe-Claire* ..28,435 .I 12
Pointe-des-Cascades* ...910 .J 12
Pointe-Lebel ...2,011 .A 16
Pont-Rouge ....4,676 .G 10
Pontbriand* ....858 .H 16
Port-Cartier ...7,070 .H 5
Portage-du-Fort ...289 .J 1
Portneuf* ....1,470 .G 10
Port-St-François*† ...981 .H 13
Povungnituk ...1,091 .B 2
Price ....1,916 .C 16
Princeville ....3,997 .H 15
Quebec ......167,264 .I 3
Quyon*† ....789 .J 2
Radisson† ....813 .F 1
Rawdon ....3,855 .H 12
Repentigny ...53,824 .I 12
Restigouche Indian Reserve ...920 .I 5
Richelieu* ......3,195 .I 13
Richmond ....3,053 .I 14
Rigaud ....6,057 .I 11
Rimouski ......31,773 .C 15
Rimouski-Est ...2,119 .C 15
Ripon* ....601 .I 10
Rivière-à-Pierre ...694 .F 10
Rivière-au-Tonnerre ...476 .G 6
Rivière-du-Loup ...14,721 .D 14
Robertsonville* ...1,829 .J 4
Roberval ......11,640 .C 10
Rock Forest ..16,604 .J 14
Rock Island ...1,067 .K 14
Rosemère* ....12,025 .I 12
Rougemont* ...1,237 .J 13
Rouyn-Noranda ..28,819 .H 1
Roxboro* ......5,950 .J 12

Roxton Falls ....1,371 .I 14
St-Adelme* ......543 .H 5
St-Adelphe* ....1,014 .J 3
St-Adrien ....337 .I 13
St-Alban* ....621 .G 10
St-Alexis-de-Matapédia* ...747 .J 5
St-Alexis-des-Monts ...2,741 .J 3
St-Alphonse* ...2,889 .J 13
St-Alphonse-de-Rodriguez* ....2,461 .J 3
St-Amable* .....7,105 .J 12
St-Ambroise ...3,605 .C 11
St-Ambroise-de-Kildare* ...3,406 .H 12
St-Anaclet-de-Lessard* ...2,546 .C 15
St-André-Avellin ...1,710 .J 10
St-André-d'Acton* ...2,487 .I 14
St-André-du-Lac-St-Jean ...580 .C 10
St-André-Est* ....1471 .I 11
St-Anicet* ......2,549 .J 11
St-Anselme .....1,912 .G 12
St-Antoine* ...10,806 .I 11
St-Antoine-de-Lavaltrie* ...4,385 .H 12
St-Antonin* .....3,368 .D 14
St-Arsène ......1,198 .D 14
St-Athanase* ...6,546 .J 13
St-Augustin* .....741 .G 8
St-Augustin-de-Desmaures* ...14,771 .F 10
St-Barnabé* ...1,284 .H 13
St-Barthélémy* ...2,075 .H 13
St-Basile-le-Grand* ...11,771 .J 12
St-Basile-Sud* ...1,7684 .J 3
St-Benjamin* ....917 .H 16
St-Benoît-Joseph-Labre* ...2,179 .C 16
St-Boniface-de-Shawinigan* ...3,998 .G 9
St-Bruno-de-Montarville* ...23,714 .I 12
St-Camille ....459 .G 13
St-Camille-de-Lellis* ...963 .J 4
St-Césaire* .....2,990 .I 13
St-Charles ....979 .G 12
St-Christophe-d'Arthabaska* ...2,264 .H 15
St-Chrysostome* ...850 .J 12
St-Columban* ...3,645 .I 11
St-Côme ....1,921 .H 12
St-Constant* ...21,933 .J 12
St-Cuthbert* ...1,722 .H 13
St-Cyrille-de-Wendover* ...3,849 .I 14
St-Damase ....1,362 .J 13
St-Damien-de-Buckland ...2,216 .G 12
St-David-de-l'Auberivière*† ...5,769 .J 4
St-Denis ....994 .I 13
St-Denis-de-Brompton* ...2,289 .J 12
St-Dominique* ...2,236 .J 13
St-Donat ....812 .C 15
St-Donat-de-Montcalm* ...1,419 .H 11
St-Édouard-de-Frampton* ...1,278 .J 4
St-Élie ....1,455 .J 3
St-Élie-d'Orford* ...6,148 .J 15
St-Elzéar* ......952 .J 1
St-Émile* ......9,889 .F 11
St-Ephrem-de-Tring ...1,248 .H 16
St-Épiphane ....895 .D 14
St-Esprit ....1,908 .J 12
St-Étienne-de-Beaumont* ...2,067 .G 11
St-Étienne-des-Grès* ...3,823 .G 9
St-Eugène ....1,158 .F 13
St-Eustache ..39,848 .I 12
St-Fabien .....1,838 .C 15
St-Fabien-de-Panet* ...1,061 .F 12
St-Félicien .....9,599 .C 10
St-Félix-de-Valois ...1,530 .H 12

St-Fidèle-de-Mont-Murray ...946 .E 13
St-Flavien ....796 .G 11
St-François-d'Assise* ...897 .J 5
St-François-du-Lac ...907 .H 13
St-François-Xavier-de-Brompton* ...1,834 .I 14
St-Gabriel ....2,862 .H 12
St-Gabriel-de-Brandon ...2,608 .H 12
St-Gédéon ....1,770 .I 16
St-Georges ...3,929 .C 9
St-Georges ...20,057 .H 16
St-Georges-de-Cacouna ...1,130 .D 14
St-Georges-Est* ...2,990 .I 16
St-Gérard* ......514 .I 13
St-Gérard-des-Laurentides ...2,133 .C 9
St-Gérard-Majella* ...4,207 .J 12
St-Germain-de-Grantham* ...1,594 .I 14
St-Gilles* .....1,806 .G 11
St-Grégoire-de-Greenlay ...611 .I 15
St-Grégoire-le-Grand* ...2,138 .J 13
St-Guillaume ...741 .I 13
St-Hilarion ...1,215 .E 12
St-Hippolyte* ...5,672 .I 11
St-Hubert* ...77,042 .I 12
St-Hugues .....1,340 .I 13
St-Hyacinthe ..38,981 .I 13
St-Isidore ....833 .G 11
St-Isidore .....2,401 .J 12
St-Jacques ...2,261 .H 12
St-Janvier* .....373 .I 11
St-Jean-Baptiste* ...2,913 .J 13
St-Jean-Baptiste-de-Nicolet* ...3,076 .H 14
St-Jean-Chrysostome* ...16,161 .G 12
St-Jean-de-Boischatel ...3,878 .F 11
St-Jean-de-Matha* ...3,260 .I 11
St-Jean-sur-Richelieu ...36,435 .J 12
St-Jérôme ...23,916 .J 11
St-Jérôme-de-Matane* ...1,165 .C 10
St-Joachim* ...1,493 .F 12
St-Joseph-de-Beauce* ...3,240 .H 16
St-Joseph-de-Maskinongé* ...1,151 .H 13
St-Joseph-de-Sorel* ...1,875 .H 13
St-Joseph-du-Lac* ...4,930 .I 11
St-Jovite ....4,609 .H 11
St-Lambert* ...20,971 .I 12
St-Lambert-de-Lauzon* ...4,590 .G 11
St-Laurent* ...74,240 .I 12
St-Lazare* ...11,193 .J 11
St-Léon-de-Standon ...1,237 .G 12
St-Léon-le-Grand ...1,145 .C 16
St-Léonard* ...71,327 .I 12
St-Léonard-d'Aston* ...1,006 .H 14
St-Léonard-de-Portneuf* ...988 .G 10
St-Liboire ......904 .I 13
St-Liguori* ....1,730 .H 12
St-Lin* ....6,734 .I 6
St-Louis-de-France* ...7,327 .I 3
St-Louis-de-Gonzague* ...1,413 .J 4
St-Louis-du-Ha! Ha! ...1,471 .E 14
St-Luc* ....18,371 .J 12
St-Ludger ....173 .B 10
St-Malachie-d'Ormstown* ...2,096 .J 11
St-Marc-des-Carrières* ...2,955 .G 10
St-Martin* ....2,546 .I 16
St-Mathias-sur-Richelieu* ...4,014 .J 13
St-Maurice* ...2,295 .H 14
St-Michel* .....2,451 .J 12

St-Moïse* ....625 .C 16
St-Narcisse* ...1,995 .C 9
St-Narcisse-de-Rimouski ...996 .C 15
St-Nicolas* ....7,600 .J 4
St-Noël ....509 .C 16
St-Octave-de-Dosquet* ...908 .G 15
St-Odilon-de-Cranbourne* ...1,448 .H 16
St-Omer* ......1,381 .I 5
St-Ours ....1,619 .I 13
St-Pamphile ...2,990 .F 13
St-Pascal .....2,504 .E 13
St-Patrice-de-Beaurivage* ...1,125 .J 4
St-Patrice-de-la-Rivière-du-Loup* ...3,080 .D 14
St-Paul-de-Abbotsford* ...2,789 .J 13
St-Philippe .....3,656 .J 13
St-Philippe-de-Néri* ...967 .E 13
St-Pie ....2,249 .J 13
St-Pierre* .....4,739 .J 12
St-Pierre* ......357 .J 13
St-Pierre-de-Sorel* ...5,467 .H 13
St-Prime ......2,685 .C 10
St-Raphaël ...1,285 .G 12
St-Raphaël-de-l'Île-Bizard* ...11,352 .J 12
St-Raymond ...8,733 .F 10
St-Rédempteur* ...6,358 .J 12
St-Rémi* ......5,707 .J 12
St-René-de-Matane* ...1,065 .B 16
St-Roch-de-l'Achigan* ...4,305 .J 12
St-Romuald ..10,604 .G 11
St-Sauveur ....3,970 .H 11
St-Sauveur-des-Monts* ...2,904 .I 12
St-Séverin* .....976 .J 3
St-Siméon .....1,012 .D 13
St-Sulpice* ...3,307 .J 12
St-Sylvestre ...363 .H 16
St-Thomas* ...2,987 .H 12
St-Thomas-d'Aquin* ...4,196 .I 13
St-Tite ....2,555 .G 9
St-Ulric ....754 .B 16
St-Urbain .....1,528 .E 12
St-Victor* .....1,253 .H 16
St-Zénon .....1,067 .I 3
St-Zotique* ...3,683 .J 11
Ste-Adèle ....5,837 .H 11
Ste-Agathe .....675 .H 15
Ste-Agathe-des-Monts ...5,669 .H 11
Ste-Agathe-Sud* ...2,209 .J 2
Ste-Angèle-de-Monnoir* ...1,481 .J 13
Ste-Anne-de-Beaupré ...3,023 .F 12
Ste-Anne-de-Bellevue* ...4,700 .I 12
Ste-Anne-des-Monts ...5,617 .H 5
Ste-Anne-des-Plaines* ...12,908 .I 12
Ste-Blandine .2,114 .C 16
Ste-Catherine .13,724 .J 12
Ste-Croix ......1,618 .G 10
Ste-Élisabeth* ...1,559 .H 12
Ste-Émélie-de-l'Énergie ...1,437 .I 12
Ste-Famille ......913 .F 12
Ste-Félicité .....718 .A 15
Ste-Foy ......72,330 .G 11
Ste-Geneviève* ...3,339 .I 12
Ste-Geneviève-de-Batiscan ...1,044 .G 9
Ste-Geneviève-de-Berthier* ...2,402 .H 12
Ste-Hedwidge-de-Roberval† ...847 .C 10
Ste-Helene-de-Breakeyville* ...3,423 .G 11
Ste-Hélène-de-Kamouraska* ...941 .E 13
Ste-Hénédine ..1,175 .G 12
Ste-Jeanne-d'Arc ...1,158 .B 10
Ste-Julie* ....24,030 .I 12

Ste-Julienne ...6,092 .H 12
Ste-Justine ...1,939 .J 4
Ste-Louise† .....78 .F 13
Ste-Madeleine* ...1,993 .J 13
Ste-Madeleine-de-Rigaud* ...3,267 .J 12
Ste-Marguerite* ...985 .H 11
Ste-Marie ...10,966 .H 16
Ste-Marie-de-Monnoir* ...2,126 .J 13
Ste-Marthe-sur-le-Lac* ...7,410 .J 11
Ste-Martine ...2,316 .J 12
Ste-Mélanie* ...2,474 .J 12
Ste-Monique ...192 .B 10
Ste-Perpétue* ...1,013 .J 13
Ste-Pétronille .1,090 .F 11
Ste-Rosalie ...4,153 .J 13
Ste-Thérèse ..23,477 .J 12
Ste-Victoire-d'Arthabaska* ...7,313 .J 15
Ste-Victoire-de-Sorel* ...2,318 .H 13
Salaberry-de-Valleyfield ..26,600 .J 11
Salluit ....929 .A 3
Sault-au-Mouton ...643 .C 14
Sawyerville ....832 .J 15
Schefferville ...578 .E 5
Scotstown .....680 .I 16
Scott* ....542 .J 4
Senneterre ...3,488 .H 1
Senneville* ....906 .J 12
Sept-Îles ....25,224 .G 5
Sept-Îles Indian Reserve ...735 .G 5
Shawinigan ..18,678 .G 9
Shawinigan-Sud ...11,804 .G 9
Shawville ....1,632 .J 2
Shefford* ....4,496 .J 13
Sherbrooke ..76,786 .J 15
Shipton* ......2,753 .I 15
Sillery ....12,003 .G 11
Sorel ....23,248 .H 13
Squatec* .....1,390 .J 4
Stanstead .....3,112 .K 14
Stanstead Plain* ...1,059 .J 14
Stoke* ....2,409 .J 14
Stoneham-et-Tewkesbury* ...4,842 .F 11
Stukely-Sud* ....882 .J 14
Sutton ....1,617 .J 13
Tache*† ....939 .C 10
Tadoussac .....913 .D 13
Taschereau* ...641 .H 1
Témiscaming ..3,112 .J 1
Terrebonne ..42,214 .I 12
Thetford Mines ...17,635 .H 16
Thurso ....2,498 .J 10
Tingwick* ....1,278 .I 15
Tourelle* .....1,566 .H 5
Tracy ....12,7731 .H 13
Tremblay* ....3,665 .C 11
Tring-Jonction ...1,387 .H 16
Trois-Pistoles .3,807 .D 14
Trois-Rivières .48,419 .H 14
Trois-Rivières-Ouest* ...22,886 .H 14
Upton* ....1,070 .J 13
Val-Barrette* ...611 .J 2
Val-Bélair* ...20,176 .E 10
Val-David .....3,473 .H 11
Val-d'Or .....24,285 .H 1
Valcourt ......2,442 .J 14
Vanier* ......11,174 .J 7
Varennes .....18,842 .I 12
Vaudreuil ....11,187 .J 11
Vaudreuil-sur-le-Lac* ...928 .J 11
Verchères ....4,854 .J 12
Verdun ....59,714 .J 12
Victoriaville .38,174 .H 15
Ville-Marie ...2,850 .J 1
Wakefield*† ....611 .J 9
Warwick ......2,904 .J 14
Waterloo .....4,040 .J 14
Waterville* ....1,332 .J 14
Weedon-Centre ...1,213 .J 15
Wemindji .....1,013 .F 1
Westmount* ..20,420 .I 12
Weymontachie Indian Reserve ...856 .J 3
Windsor ......4,904 .J 14
Wottonville ....627 .J 15
Yamachiche ...2,776 .H 13
Yamaska ....466 .H 13

*Not on map. Key shows general location.
†Unincorporated place.
Source: 1996 census for most places; 1991 census for places not individually counted in 1996 census.

Quebec attracts about 30 million tourists yearly, including many from the United States. Probably no other Canadian province is so rich in places of historical interest. Vacationers find the charm of Old France as they wander through the winding cobblestone streets of historic Quebec City. Every year, pilgrims visit the many religious shrines.

The rugged Gaspé Peninsula attracts artists, hikers, and mountain climbers. The Eastern Townships have lovely lakes, mountains, and rolling farmland. Many tourists take canoe trips down the rushing rivers of the Laurentian Mountains. Sports fans visit Montreal to see the Canadiens of the National Hockey League, the Expos baseball team of the National League, and the Alouettes of the Canadian Football League. In winter, thousands of skiers from all parts of Canada and the United States speed down Quebec's fine ski trails. Hockey, ice skating, snowmobiling, and snowshoeing are also popular.

On June 24, French Canadians honor their patron saint, Saint-Jean-Baptiste (John the Baptist). The province observes this legal holiday, called Fête nationale des Québécois (Quebec National Day), with solemn ceremonies followed by lively festivities and art and sports events.

George Hunter

Saint-Jean on Île d'Orléans in the St. Lawrence River

Places to visit

Following are brief descriptions of some of Quebec's many interesting places to visit:

Bonaventure Island, off the Gaspé Peninsula near Percé, is one of the largest water-bird refuges that people can visit. More than 250,000 birds nest on the island during the summer months.

Île d'Orléans is an island that is located in the middle of the St. Lawrence River near Quebec City. About 7,100 French Canadians live on the island. Old Norman-style houses, numerous churches, and a number of religious shrines attract visitors to the island.

Mount Royal Park, in Montreal, is a lovely wooded area. The top of Mount Royal, which is 763 feet (233 meters) high, offers a magnificent view of Montreal and the St. Lawrence. For more information on Mount Royal Park, see **Montreal** (Cultural life).

Percé Rock, about 200 feet (60 meters) off the Gaspé coast, rises straight out of the water to a height of 154 to 290 feet (47 to 88 meters). The rock is 1,565 feet (477 meters) long and 300 feet (90 meters) wide.

Quebec City, founded in 1608, is known as the cradle of French civilization in North America. The Citadel, a walled fortress, overlooks the city. Another major landmark of Quebec City is a district called Place Royale. The area includes a number of houses dating from the 1600's and 1700's and the Notre-Dame-des-Victoires Church, completed in 1688. The church stands on the former site of the first settlement of the French explorer Samuel de Champlain. See **Quebec** (City).

Sainte-Anne-de-Beaupré, in Montmorency County, is a Roman Catholic shrine where miracles are said to have occurred. See **Sainte-Anne-de-Beaupré.**

National parks and sites. Quebec has three national parks—Forillon, La Mauricie, and Mingan Archipelago—and one national marine park—Saguenay-St. Lawrence. It has 27 national historic parks and sites, including Fort Chambly and Fort Lennox. See **Canada** (National parks).

Provincial parks. Quebec has 38 provincial parks and reserves. They include large areas of the Canadian Shield and Gaspé Peninsula. For information on these parks, write to Environment and Wildlife Ministry, 675 Boulevard René-Lévesque Est, Quebec, PQ, G1R 5V7.

Quebec Winter Carnival in Quebec City

Roland Weber, Masterfile

Annual events

January-June

Quebec International Bonspiel in Quebec City (late January); Quebec Winter Carnival in Quebec City (early February); Chicoutimi Carnival Souvenir (mid-February); International Fireworks Festival in Montreal (early June-mid-July); Canadian Grand Prix in Montreal (early June); Shrimp Festival in Matane (late June).

July-December

Montreal International Jazz Festival (early July); Quebec Summer Festival in Quebec City (early July); World Folklore Festival in Drummondville (early July); Valleyfield International Regattas (early July); Just for Laughs Festival in Montreal (mid-July); Haut-Richelieu Hot-Air Balloon Festival in St-Jean-sur-Richelieu (August); World Film Festival in Montreal (late August-early September); Montreal International Marathon (September); International Festival of New Cinema and New Media in Montreal (October).

Derek Caron, Masterfile

The Basilica of Sainte-Anne-de-Beaupré

W. Griebeling, Miller Services

An old, narrow street in Quebec City

Land regions. Quebec has four main land regions: (1) the Canadian Shield, (2) the St. Lawrence Lowland, (3) the Appalachian Region, and (4) the Hudson Bay Lowland.

The Canadian Shield is a vast, horseshoe-shaped region. It covers almost half of Canada and dips into the Northern United States. In Quebec, this rough, rocky plateau lies north of the St. Lawrence Lowland and Appalachian regions, and covers about nine-tenths of the province. It includes the North Shore, which extends along the St. Lawrence River from the Saguenay River to Labrador.

Through the ages, the Canadian Shield was scraped by glaciers, and much of its soil was worn away by wind and water. In many sections, the ancient rocks have no soil at all. Most of the region has remained a wilderness of forests, lakes, rivers, and streams. Treeless tundras with mosses and lichens cover the northern part of the Canadian Shield (see **Tundra**). The region has little land that can be farmed, but it has a variety of great mineral deposits.

Mont d'Iberville (called Mount Caubvick in Newfoundland), the highest point in Quebec, rises 5,322 feet (1,622 meters) in the northeastern part of the Canadian Shield. The Laurentian Mountains, or Laurentides, form the southeastern edge of the Canadian Shield in Quebec. Some of the province's highest ranges rise in the Laurentides Provincial Park and Mont Tremblant Provincial Park areas. See **Canadian Shield**.

The St. Lawrence Lowland consists chiefly of the St. Lawrence River Valley and the Montreal Plain. It includes Anticosti Island and islands in the river's mouth. The lowland is about 10 miles (16 kilometers) wide near Quebec City, and broadens to about 100 miles (160 kilometers) at Montreal. The plain lies less than 500 feet (150 meters) above sea-level, but is broken by some rocky hills. Eight hills called the Monteregians rise in the southwestern part of the lowland. The best known is Mount Royal, which is 763 feet (233 meters) high. It overlooks Montreal.

The St. Lawrence River Valley has always been the most important part of the province. Its fertile soil supports most of Quebec's farming. The many cities and towns in the valley make it one of the most heavily populated regions of Canada.

The Appalachian Region is the northeastern extension of the Appalachian Mountains of the Eastern United States. It extends from Vermont along the province's southeastern boundary. This region consists of three main sections: (1) the Eastern Townships, between the St. Lawrence River Valley and the Canadian-United States border; (2) the South Shore, which extends along the mouth of the St. Lawrence from the Eastern Townships to the Gaspé Peninsula; and (3) the Gaspé Peninsula, north of New Brunswick. The land is broken by lakes, mountains, and streams.

In the gently rolling Eastern Townships, the Notre-Dame Mountains form an extension of the Green Mountains of Vermont. The South Shore has two separate areas. The Piedmont Region along the St. Lawrence estuary is a rich farming area, and the inland plateau has thick forests. The Gaspé Peninsula is also heavily forested. Mountain ranges in the interior of the peninsula make transportation between the northern and southern coasts difficult. See **Gaspé Peninsula**.

The Hudson Bay Lowland extends into Quebec from Ontario. It covers a small strip of land south of James Bay.

Coastline. Water forms most of Quebec's boundaries. The province has a coastline of 8,558 miles (13,773 kilometers), including bays, inlets, and offshore islands. The main bodies of water that surround Quebec are James and Hudson bays on the west, Hudson Strait and Ungava Bay on the north, and the Gulf of St. Lawrence on the southeast and south.

North of the Gulf of St. Lawrence, the coastline is uneven. Many bays cut into the land, and rocks rise along the water's edge. To the south, along the Gaspé Peninsula, the coastline is more regular. The waters along the

Map index

Land regions of Quebec

CANADIAN SHIELD

HUDSON BAY LOWLAND

St. Maurice R.

Ottawa R.

APPALACHIAN REGION

ST. LAWRENCE LOWLAND

St. Lawrence R.

WORLD BOOK map

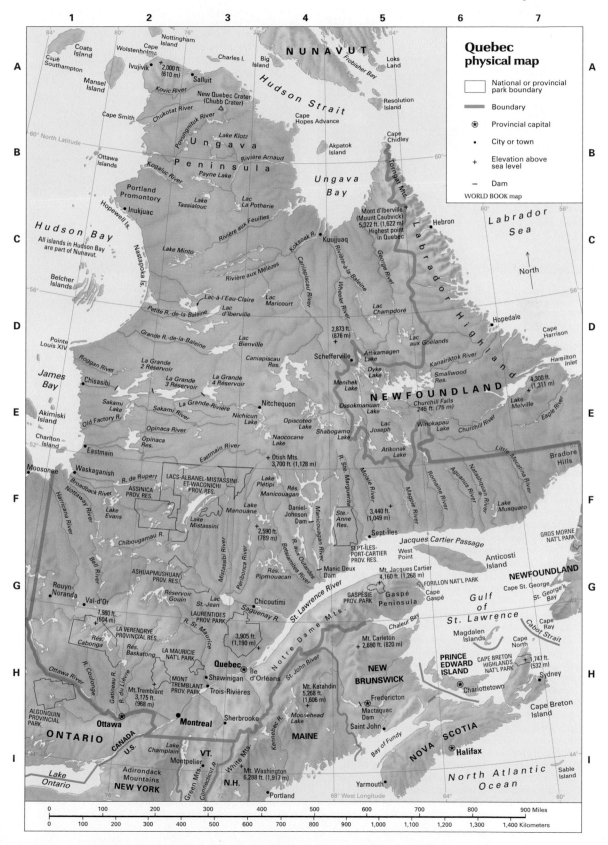

Quebec
physical map

National or provincial park boundary

Boundary

Provincial capital

City or town

Elevation above sea level

Dam

WORLD BOOK map

NUNAVUT

Coats Island
Cape Southampton
Mansel Island
Nottingham Island
Wolstenholms
Cape Wolstenholms
Ivujivik
+2,000 ft. (610 m)
Salluit
Charles I.
Big Island
Hudson Strait
Frobisher Bay
Loks Land
Resolution Island

Kovic River
New Quebec Crater (Chubb Crater) △
Chukotat River
Cape Smith
Cape Hopes Advance
Cape Chidley

Ungava Peninsula

Ottawa Islands
Kogaluc River
Portland Promontory
Inukjuac
Hopewell Is.
Lake Klotz
Payne Lake
Rivière Arnaud
Lake Tassialouc
Lac La Potherie
Akpatok Island

Ungava Bay

Mont d'Iberville (Mount Caubvick) 5,322 ft. (1,622 m) Highest point in Quebec
Hebron

Labrador Sea

Hudson Bay
All islands in Hudson Bay are part of Nunavut.
Belcher Islands
Nastapoka Is.
Lake Minto
Rivière aux Feuilles
Koksoak R.
Kuujjuaq
Rivière-à-la-Baleine
George River
Caniapiscau River
Rivière aux Mélèzes
Lac Champdoré

North

Labrador Highland

Pointe Louis XIV
Petite R.-de-la-Baleine
Grande R.-de-la-Baleine
Lac-à-l'Eau-Claire
Lac d'Iberville
Lac Maricourt
Lac Bienville
2,873 ft. (876 m)
Scefferville
Attikamagen Lake
Lac aux Goelands
Hopedale
Cape Harrison
Hamilton Inlet

James Bay
Roggan River
Chisasibi
La Grande 2 Reservoir
La Grande 3 Réservoir
La Grande 4 Réservoir
Caniapiscau Res.
Dyke Lake
Menihek Lake
Smallwood Res.
Kaniariktok River
4,300 ft. (1,311 m)

Sakami Lake
Sakami River
La Grande-Rivière
Nichicun Lake
Nitchequon
Opiscoteo Lake
Ossokmanuan Lake
Churchill Falls 245 ft. (75 m)
Lac Joseph
Winokapau Lake
Lake Melville
Churchill River
Eagle River

NEWFOUNDLAND

Akimiski Island
Old Factory R.
Opinaca River
Opinaca Res.
Shabogamo Lake
Lac Joseph
Atikonak Lake
Little Mecatina River
Bradore Hills

Charlton Island
Eastmain
Eastmain River
Naococane Lake
Otish Mts. 3,700 ft. (1,128 m)
R. Ste. Marguerite
Moisie River
Magpie River
Romaine River
Aguanus River
Natashquan River
Lake Musquaro

Moosonee
Waskaganish
R. de Rupert
LACS-ALBANEL-MISTASSINI-ET-WACONICHI PROV. RES.
Lake Plétipi
Rés. Manicouagan
ASSINICA PROV. RES.
Ste. Anne Res.
3,440 ft. (1,049 m)

Broadback River
Nottaway River
Lake Evans
Harricana River
Chibougamau R.
Lake Mistassini
Lake Manouane
Daniel-Johnson Dam
2,590 ft. (789 m)
Peribonca River
Bersimites River
Rés. Pipmuacan
Manic Deux Dam
Sept-Îles
West Point
Jacques Cartier Passage
Anticosti Island
GROS MORNE NAT'L PARK

Rouyn-Noranda
Val-d'Or
Bell River
ASHUAPMUSHUAN PROV. RES.
Réservoir Gouin
Lac St.-Jean
Mistassibi River
Chicoutimi
Saguenay R.
St. Lawrence River
SEPT-ÎLES-PORT-CARTIER PROV. RES.
Mt. Jacques Cartier 4,160 ft. (1,268 m)
Cape Gaspé
Gaspé
FORILLON NAT'L PARK
Cape St. George
St. George's Bay
NEWFOUNDLAND

1,980 ft. (604 m)
LA VERENDRYE PROVINCIAL RES.
Rés. Cabonga
LAURENTIDES PROV. PARK
R. St. Maurice
3,905 ft. (1,190 m)
GASPÉSIE PROV. PARK
Gaspé Peninsula
Chaleur Bay
Mt. Carleton 2,690 ft. (820 m)
Gulf of St. Lawrence
Magdalen Islands
Cape North
Cape Ray
Cabot Strait

Ottawa River
R. Coulonge
Gatineau R.
R. du Lièvre
Rés. Baskatong
LA MAURICIE NAT'L PARK
MONT TREMBLANT PROV. PARK
Mt. Tremblant 3,175 ft. (968 m)
Quebec ⊛
Shawinigan
Trois-Rivières
Île d'Orléans
Notre Dame Mts.
St. John River
Mt. Katahdin 5,268 ft. (1,606 m)
NEW BRUNSWICK
Fredericton
Mactaquac Dam
1,747 ft. (532 m)
Sydney
Charlottetown
Cape Breton Island
PRINCE EDWARD ISLAND
CAPE BRETON HIGHLANDS NAT'L PARK

ALGONQUIN PROVINCIAL PARK
ONTARIO
Ottawa
Montreal
Sherbrooke
Kennebec R.
Moosehead Lake
MAINE
Saint John
Bay of Fundy
NOVA SCOTIA
Halifax

CANADA
U.S.
Lake Champlain
VT.
Montpelier
White Mts.
Mt. Washington 6,288 ft. (1,917 m)
Saguenay R.
N.H.
Cape Breton Island
Cape Breton Island

Lake Ontario
Adirondack Mountains
NEW YORK
Green Mts.
Connecticut R.
Portland
68° West Longitude
Yarmouth
Sable Island
North Atlantic Ocean

0   100   200   300   400   500   600   700   800   900 Miles
0   100 200 300 400 500 600 700 800 900 1,000 1,100 1,200 1,300 1,400 Kilometers

Sherman Hines, Masterfile

Rugged, rocky land with scattered forests forms part of the Canadian Shield region of Quebec. This region has large mineral deposits, but little of the area can be farmed.

John C. Whyte, Hot Shots

The St. Lawrence River Valley lies in the St. Lawrence Lowland region of southern Quebec. The fertile valley supports most of the province's agriculture.

northern and western coasts usually remain frozen from the end of December to May.

Rivers, waterfalls, and lakes. Inland waters in Quebec cover 71,000 square miles (184,000 square kilometers). Quebec has a greater total area of fresh water than any other province. Its many rivers help make it a leading producer of hydroelectric power in Canada and the United States.

Quebec's principal river is the St. Lawrence. The river enters Quebec at the point where the province, New York, and Ontario meet. The St. Lawrence then flows northeast into the Gulf of St. Lawrence. Ever since the French explorer Jacques Cartier sailed up the St. Lawrence in 1535, this important trade route has influenced the life and development of Quebec and Canada. The St. Lawrence River has been called the *Mother of Canada.* Its importance increased greatly in 1959, when the St. Lawrence Seaway was completed. The seaway allows large oceangoing ships to travel up the river and to the Great Lakes. See **Saint Lawrence River; Saint Lawrence Seaway.**

All the other important rivers in Quebec flow into the St. Lawrence. Most of them, including the Saguenay, St. Maurice, and Ottawa, rise in the Canadian Shield and join the St. Lawrence from the north or northwest. The principal rivers south of the St. Lawrence include the Chaudière, Richelieu, and St. Francis.

Rivers flowing east, north, or west into James Bay, Hudson Bay, Hudson Strait, and Ungava Bay drain more than half the province. They are used to produce hydroelectricity, and many of them are more than 200 miles (320 kilometers) long.

Most of Quebec's rivers have waterfalls and rapids. Many of the rapids, such as Rapide Blanc on the St. Maurice River and Rapide des Quinze on the Ottawa River, are used to produce hydroelectric power. The best-known falls include Shawinigan Falls, which drops 146 feet (45 meters) on the St. Maurice River; 114-foot

(35-meter) Joffre Falls on the Chaudière River; and 251-foot (77-meter) Montmorency Falls on the Montmorency River.

Beautiful lakes lie throughout Quebec. More than 20 of them cover over 100 square miles (260 square kilometers) each. The Canadian Shield has the largest lakes, of which 840-square-mile (2,180-square-kilometer) Lake Mistassini is the biggest. Other lakes in this region include Lac-à-l'Eau-Claire, Lac St.-Jean, and Lakes Bienville, Caniapiscau, and Minto. Lakes Megantic and Memphremagog, just north of Maine, are famous among fishing enthusiasts.

Plant and animal life. Forests cover about 319,000 square miles (825,000 square kilometers), about 55 per cent of Quebec's land. The southern part of the Canadian Shield has important stands of balsam fir and spruce, Quebec's most valuable trees. Maples, pines, and white and yellow birches also grow there. Small stands of balsam, birch, black and white spruce, dwarf aspen, and willow trees grow in northern Quebec. Mosses and lichens grow west of Ungava Bay and Hudson Strait. The Appalachian Region has thick stands of timber. Most of Quebec's maple trees grow in the Eastern Townships. Forest wild flowers include bellworts, bloodroots, dogtooth violets, spring beauties, squirrel corn, and trilliums. Buttercups, daisies, and prairie strawberries and raspberries grow on Quebec's prairies.

Beavers, foxes, martens, minks, muskrats, and seals are the most numerous fur-bearing animals in Quebec. Bears are found throughout the province. Large numbers of deer, moose, and raccoons live in the southern regions. Game birds include black ducks and geese. Fish in the waters off Quebec include cod, herring, and redfish. Crabs, lobsters, and scallops also live in these waters. Fish in Quebec's inland rivers and lakes include bass, pike, muskellunge, salmon, and trout.

Climate. Quebec's climate varies greatly. The average annual temperature ranges from 44 °F (7 °C) in the far south to 17 °F (−8 °C) in the far north. The highest recorded temperature, 104 °F (40 °C), was in Ville Marie on July 6, 1921. The lowest temperature, −66 °F (−54 °C), occurred in Doucet on Feb. 5, 1923.

Quebec's winters are long and cold. The average January temperature in the north ranges from −5 to −11 °F (−21 to −24 °C). In July, the average temperature there ranges from 50 to 54 °F (10 to 12 °C). In southern Quebec, the average January temperature ranges from 1 to 14 °F (−17 to −10 °C). Summers are warm, but short. The average July temperature ranges from 64 to 70 °F (18 to 21 °C).

In southern Quebec, *precipitation* (rain, melted snow, and other forms of moisture) ranges from 37 to 41 inches (94 to 104 centimeters) a year. The north receives from 15 to 31 inches (38 to 79 centimeters) annually. Southern Quebec gets from 85 to 163 inches (215 to 415 centimeters) of snow yearly, most of it between late November and mid-March. Northern Quebec has from 69 to 163 inches (175 to 415 centimeters) of snow a year.

Average monthly weather

	Montreal					Quebec City				
	Temperatures °F		Temperatures °C		Days of rain or snow		Temperatures °F		Temperatures °C		Days of rain or snow
	High	Low	High	Low			High	Low	High	Low	
Jan.	21	5	−6	−15	16	Jan.	18	1	−8	−17	18
Feb.	25	7	−4	−14	13	Feb.	21	3	−6	−16	15
Mar.	36	19	2	−7	13	Mar.	32	16	0	−9	14
Apr.	52	34	11	1	13	Apr.	46	28	8	−2	13
May	66	45	19	7	13	May	63	41	17	5	14
June	73	55	23	13	13	June	72	50	22	10	14
July	79	59	26	15	12	July	77	55	25	13	14
Aug.	77	57	25	14	13	Aug.	73	54	23	12	14
Sept.	68	48	20	9	11	Sept.	64	45	18	7	14
Oct.	55	39	13	4	13	Oct.	52	36	11	2	14
Nov.	41	28	5	−2	15	Nov.	37	25	3	−4	17
Dec.	27	12	−3	−11	17	Dec.	23	9	−5	−13	19

Average January temperatures
There is a wide range of temperatures in Quebec during winter. The area along the southern border is the mildest.

Average July temperatures
The southwestern area has the warmest summers. The temperature decreases sharply toward the far north.

Average yearly precipitation
Quebec's precipitation is heaviest in the southeastern section. The province becomes steadily drier northward.

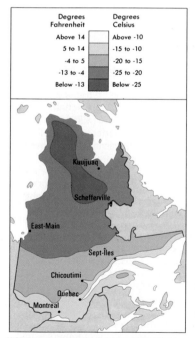

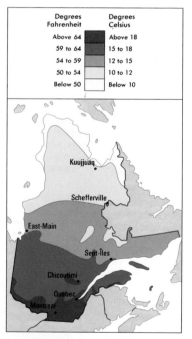

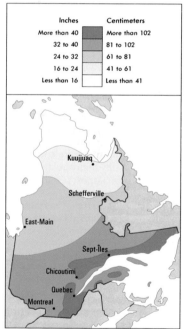

WORLD BOOK maps; based on the *National Atlas of Canada.*

Economy

Many early settlers of Quebec earned their living by fishing or by fur trading. Logging and farming became important in the early 1800's, and manufacturing and mining began to develop during the early 1900's. Service industries have grown rapidly in importance since the mid-1900's. The development of Quebec's economy has been boosted by the province's natural resources, which include rivers well-suited to shipping and hydroelectric power.

Today, service industries combine to account for the largest portion of Quebec's *gross domestic product* (GDP)—the total value of goods and services that are produced in the province in a year. Quebec has a higher GDP than any province except Ontario.

Natural resources of Quebec include rich soils and vast mineral deposits. The province also has great forests, much wildlife, and plentiful supplies of water.

Soil. The St. Lawrence Lowland has the province's richest soils. They are composed chiefly of *sediments* (material that settles to the bottom of liquid). The sediments were deposited by the sea and various lakes and streams that covered the region after the most recent ice age, which ended about 11,500 years ago. The soils include clays, loams, sands, and silts.

Material deposited by the ice age glaciers, and some lake sediments, cover most of the Appalachian Region. These soils include clays, limestone and slate loams, sands, and sandy loams. Stony soils occur in much of the Eastern Townships. The Gaspé Peninsula has sandy soils broken by boulders. Heavy loams occur on the southern shores of the peninsula.

Granites, schists, and other stone are found in most of the Canadian Shield. Most of the soil covering is thin and not suitable for agriculture. A rock and clay soil covers the Hudson Bay Lowland.

Minerals. The Canadian Shield has some of the world's largest deposits of metallic minerals. Vast iron ore deposits lie along the central part of the Labrador border and near Ungava Bay. Most copper deposits are in the Chibougamau and Noranda areas and on the Gaspé Peninsula. Lead and zinc are also found on the Gaspé Peninsula. The largest known beds of asbestos in the Western Hemisphere lie in the Eastern Townships. Northern Quebec also has asbestos deposits, as well as nickel deposits.

The most important gold-bearing ore deposits are located near Rouyn-Noranda and Val-d'Or. This area also has deposits of uranium and zinc. Another rich mining territory lies west and northwest of Montreal. This area has deposits of a great variety of minerals, including feldspar, granite, graphite, kaolin, magnesite, mica, molybdenum, and silica.

Service industries are concentrated in the Montreal and Quebec City metropolitan areas. These industries account for the largest portion of Quebec's gross domestic product.

Community, business, and personal services form the most important service industry group in Quebec. This industry employs more than a third of the province's workers. Community, business, and personal services include such activities as education and health care, engineering and legal services, and the operation of hotels and sports franchises. Many people are employed by five of Canada's largest universities: the University of Quebec, Laval University, the University of Montreal, McGill University, and Concordia University. Several of the world's largest engineering research companies are based in Montreal. Quebec's large tourist trade benefits hotels and restaurants in Montreal and Quebec City.

Finance, insurance, and real estate form the second most important service industry group in Quebec in terms of the gross domestic product. Real estate is the major part of this industry because of the large amounts of money involved in the selling and leasing of homes, office buildings, and other property. Montreal ranks second only to Toronto among Canada's leading financial centers. Such major banks as the Bank of Montreal, the National Bank of Canada, and the Royal Bank have large

Production and workers by economic activities

Economic activities	Percent of GDP* produced	Employed workers	
		Number of people	Percent of total
Community, business, & personal services	25	1,023,400	35
Manufacturing	21	612,800	21
Finance, insurance, & real estate	14	154,300	5
Wholesale & retail trade	12	507,300	17
Transportation & communication	8	201,700	7
Government	7	167,100	6
Construction	5	131,500	5
Utilities	4	†	†
Agriculture	2	75,700	3
Mining	1	15,100	1
Forestry	1	6,000	‡
Total	100	2,894,800	100

*GDP = gross domestic product, the total value of goods and services produced in a year.
†Included in Transportation & communication.
‡Less than one-half of one percent.
Figures are for 1998.
Source: Statistics Canada.

operations in the city, which also has a stock exchange. The Confederation of Caisses Populaires (credit unions) has its headquarters in Lévis.

Wholesale and retail trade form the third-ranking service industry in Quebec. Much of the activity in this industry involves distributing and selling food products and motor vehicles. The transportation and communication industry ranks next. Information on transportation and communication appears later in this section. Other service industries are government and utilities. Several federal agencies have their headquarters in the Hull area. Most provincial and local government employees work in the Montreal and Quebec City areas.

Manufacturing. Products manufactured in Quebec have an annual *value added by manufacture* of more than 45 billion Canadian dollars. This figure represents the value created in products by Quebec's industries, not counting such costs as materials, supplies, and fuel.

The province's vast raw materials and hydroelectric power have helped the industries develop. Quebec's approximately 10,000 factories, mills, and refineries account for about a fourth of the value of Canada's total industrial production. Most of Quebec's production occurs in the Montreal area. Around 5,000 plants operate in the Montreal area, which ranks second only to the Toronto area among Canada's manufacturing centers.

The production of paper products is Quebec's leading manufacturing activity in terms of value added by manufacture. The province has approximately 65 pulp and paper mills, most of which are located in Trois-Rivières, Quebec City, North Shore, and the Eastern Townships. Quebec leads the provinces and the states in the production of paper. Newsprint (paper used for newspapers) is its most valuable paper product. Quebec produces approximately $4\frac{1}{2}$ million tons (4 million metric tons) of newsprint a year and provides almost half of Canada's print exports. Quebec's paper mills also produce book and writing paper, paperboard, wallboard,

Denis Trudel, Quebec Government

The production of maple syrup begins with the collection of sap from maple trees. Quebec leads the provinces and states in maple syrup production.

Farm, mineral, and forest products

This map shows where the province's leading farm, mineral, and forest products are produced. The major urban areas (shown in red) are the province's most important manufacturing centers.

WORLD BOOK map

wrapping paper, and other paper products.

Transportation equipment is Quebec's second most valuable manufacturing industry in terms of value added by manufacture. Montreal is a major center of the aerospace industry in Canada. Such leading aerospace companies as Bell Helicopter Textron, Bombardier/Aerospace, Pratt and Whitney Canada, and Rolls-Royce Canada employ many people in the Montreal area. General Motors manufactures automobiles in Quebec. Companies in the province also make trains and buses.

Food and beverage processing is Quebec's third most valuable manufacturing activity. Food-processing plants are concentrated in the area between Montreal and Quebec City. Dairy products account for about a quarter of food and beverage processing income. Quebec makes more butter and cheese than any other province. Large commercial bakeries and meat-packing plants in the Montreal area are also major parts of Quebec's food-processing industry. The industry also turns out large amounts of beer, bottled water, candy, canned fruits and vegetables, coffee and tea, and livestock feed.

Other leading manufactured products in Quebec include chemicals, electrical equipment, printed materials, and primary metals. Pharmaceuticals, industrial chemicals, and toiletries are the leading types of chemicals made in the province. Montreal has large plants that make telecommunications equipment and electronic components. Commercial printing companies are the leading producers of printed materials. Aluminum plants along the St. Lawrence and Saguenay rivers and a

steel plant in Contrecoeur account for most of Quebec's primary metals production. Other top manufactured products include clothing, fabricated metal products, machinery, and wood products.

Agriculture. Quebec has about 33,000 farms. Farmland covers about $2\frac{1}{2}$ percent of the province's land area. About 3 percent of the people live on farms. Most farmland lies along the St. Lawrence River.

Milk production accounts for about a third of Quebec's farm income. Quebec ranks among the leading provinces and states in milk production and in the number of dairy cattle. Most of Quebec's dairy farms are in the southernmost part of the province. More than 70 percent of the milk goes into the manufacture of butter, cheese, ice cream, powdered milk, and yogurt. The farmers sell most of the rest of the milk for drinking.

Hogs are the most valuable meat animals raised in Quebec. Farmers in the rural areas surrounding Montreal and Quebec City raise the largest number of hogs. They also raise the most beef cattle and poultry. Only Ontario raises more chickens and eggs than Quebec. Quebec farmers also raise sheep and turkeys.

Nearly all farmers in the province raise some vegetables. Potatoes are grown on more land than any other vegetable. Other important vegetables include carrots, sweet corn, lettuce, onions, and tomatoes. Growing ornamental plants also has become an important activity.

Apples, Quebec's most important fruit crop, are grown chiefly in the Montreal area. Farmers also raise blueberries, cranberries, raspberries, and strawberries.

Corn is Quebec's leading field crop. Most of the corn is grown in the far southern part of the province. Quebec's farmers also grow barley, oats, soybeans, and wheat. Much of the grain grown in the province is used as livestock feed.

Quebec leads the provinces and states in the production of maple products. About 70 percent of the world's maple syrup, sugar, and taffy comes from Quebec. The annual maple harvest provides about 5 million gallons (20 million liters) of maple products, including syrup, sugar, taffy, and maple butter.

Mining. Gold and iron ore are the leading mineral products of Quebec. Together, they account for about a third of the total mining income. Gold mines operate around Rouyn-Noranda and Val-d'Or. Some of the gold ore also contains silver. The Fermont area near the Labrador border supplies most of Quebec's iron ore. Quebec produces about a fourth of Canada's gold and two-fifths of its iron ore.

Titanium is Quebec's third most important mineral product. It is obtained from ilmenite ore in the Lake Allard area. Titanium is a metal that is highly resistant to corrosion and heat. It is used in the production of aircraft engines, paint, and many other items.

Limestone, copper, asbestos, and zinc are also important mineral products in Quebec. The main limestone deposits are in the Eastern Townships and in the St. Lawrence and Ottawa river valleys. Limestone is used mainly to make cement and roadbeds. Quebec's other mined products include clays, dimension stone, peat, salt, and sand and gravel.

Forestry. Quebec is one of the leading timber-producing areas of North America. Balsam firs, jack pines, and spruce provide much of the province's tim-ber. The most productive forests in Quebec lie in a broad belt that extends west from Sept-Îles to the Ontario border. More than half the timber in Quebec is used by the paper industry.

Electric power. Quebec is a leading producer of hydroelectric power in North America. The province produces hydroelectric power more cheaply than most other regions in North America because it has great water resources.

Hydroelectric plants supply about 95 percent of Quebec's electric power. Most of the rest comes from a nuclear plant near Bécancour. Quebec's hydroelectric plants are managed primarily by Hydro-Quebec, a government corporation. The major hydroelectric plants lie on the La Grande and Manicouagan rivers. Some of Quebec's power is sold to the United States.

Transportation. Montreal is Canada's chief transportation center. All early highways in French Canada were called *les Chemins du Roi* (the King's Highways). The first one linked Montreal and Quebec City in the 1700's. Canada's first major canal, the Lachine Canal, bypassed Lachine Rapids on the St. Lawrence River near Montreal. This canal was opened in 1825. It was closed in 1970 after ships began using the new South Shore Canal. A 15-mile (24-kilometer) railroad, the first one in Canada, began operating between Laprairie and Saint-Jean in 1836.

Quebec has three international airports. They are the Montreal International Airport at Dorval, the Montreal International Airport at Mirabel, and the Jean Lesage International Airport at Ste.-Foy. The province also has several domestic airports and many landing facilities for helicopters and seaplanes.

Quebec has about 4,000 miles (6,500 kilometers) of railroad tracks, mainly in the St. Lawrence Lowland and the Appalachian Region. Branch lines reach the mining areas to the north. Provincial highways and roads total about 18,000 miles (29,000 kilometers). About 90 percent of them are paved.

About 65 ports handle water transportation in Quebec. Most of the chief ports, such as Baie-Comeau, Montreal, Port-Cartier, Quebec City, Sept-Îles, and Sorel, lie along the St. Lawrence River. The ports of Baie-Comeau, Montreal, Quebec City, Sept-Îles, and Trois-Rivières are kept ice-free all year. Montreal is at the gateway to the St. Lawrence Seaway. Ocean ships moving up the St. Lawrence River use the seaway to reach the Great Lakes. Sorel is at the head of a waterway leading south to New York City. From its harbor, boats and small barges can travel to the Hudson River by way of the Richelieu River and Lake Champlain. The Richelieu and Ottawa rivers, like the St. Lawrence Seaway, have systems of canals.

Communication. Quebec has over 400 magazines and more than 240 newspapers, including 13 dailies. Ten of the dailies are printed in French. Publishing in the province began in 1764 with the founding of the Quebec City *Gazette.* This newspaper was published in both French and English until 1842, when it began being published in English only. In 1884, the newspaper became the *Quebec Chronicle-Telegraph*, and it is still published by that name today.

In 1776, a French printer, Fleury Mesplet, came to Montreal with Benjamin Franklin. The two men pub-

Cameramann International, Ltd.

The St.-Lambert Lock, in Montreal, is part of the St. Lawrence Seaway. The seaway links the chief port cities in Quebec with cities located along the Great Lakes.

lished propaganda material for the 13 American Colonies during the Revolutionary War in America (1775-1783). In 1778, Mesplet began publishing *La Gazette du Commerce et Littéraire, pour la Ville et District de Montréal,* which is now *The Gazette* of Montreal.

Le Journal de Montréal is the newspaper with the largest daily circulation in Quebec. Other large Montreal newspapers include *La Presse, Le Devoir,* and *The Gazette.* Quebec City's two daily newspapers are *Le Journal de Québec* and *Le Soleil.*

In 1919, the Canadian Marconi Company made the first radio broadcast in Canada, from Montreal. Its station, CFCF, began regular broadcasts in 1920. The government-owned Canadian Broadcasting Corporation introduced television broadcasting in the province in 1952. Station CBFT of Montreal began broadcasting that year, chiefly in French. Today, Quebec has over 130 radio stations and 50 television stations. Most of the stations broadcast in French. A number of smaller television stations rebroadcast programs from the major stations to distant areas of Quebec. Cable television systems service most Quebec communities.

Government

Lieutenant governor of Quebec represents Queen Elizabeth II of the United Kingdom in her role as the queen of Canada. The lieutenant governor is appointed by the governor general in council of Canada. The position of lieutenant governor is largely honorary.

Premier of Quebec is the actual head of the provincial government. Quebec, like Canada itself, has a parliamentary form of government. The premier is an elected member of the National Assembly. The person who serves as premier is usually the leader of the majority party in the Assembly.

The premier presides over the Executive Council (cabinet). The council includes other ministers chosen by the premier from among the majority party's members in the legislature. The ministers direct about 20 departments of the government. The council resigns if it loses the support of a majority of the legislature.

Legislature. Quebec has a one-house legislature called the National Assembly. Each of its 125 members is elected from an electoral district and serves a term of up to five years. If the lieutenant governor, on the advice of the premier, calls for an election before five years have passed, all Assembly members must run again for office. The legislature meets at least once a year.

Quebec formerly had a two-house legislature. The lower house was called the Legislative Assembly and the upper house the Legislative Council. But in 1968, the Legislative Council was abolished, and the Legislative Assembly became the National Assembly.

Courts. The highest court in Quebec is the Court of Appeal. It consists of a chief justice and 19 *puisne* (associate) judges. The Superior Court has 143 judges, including a chief justice, a senior associate chief justice, and an associate chief justice. It meets in the major cities of 36 judicial districts. The governor general in council appoints all judges of the Court of Appeal and the Supe-

The premiers of Quebec

	Party	Term
Pierre-J.-O. Chauveau	Conservative	1867-1873
Gédéon Ouimet	Conservative	1873-1874
C.-B. de Boucherville	Conservative	1874-1878
Henri-G. Joly	Liberal	1878-1879
J.-Adolphe Chapleau	Conservative	1879-1882
J.-Alfred Mousseau	Conservative	1882-1884
John Jones Ross	Conservative	1884-1887
L.-Olivier Taillon	Conservative	1887
Honoré Mercier	Parti National	1887-1891
C.-B. de Boucherville	Conservative	1891-1892
L.-Olivier Taillon	Conservative	1892-1896
Edmund J. Flynn	Conservative	1896-1897
F.-Gabriel Marchand	Liberal	1897-1900
S.-Napoléon Parent	Liberal	1900-1905
Lomer Gouin	Liberal	1905-1920
L.-Alexandre Taschereau	Liberal	1920-1936
Adélard Godbout	Liberal	1936
Maurice Duplessis	Union Nationale	1936-1939
Adélard Godbout	Liberal	1939-1944
Maurice Duplessis	Union Nationale	1944-1959
J.-Paul Sauvé	Union Nationale	1959-1960
Antonio Barrette	Union Nationale	1960
Jean Lesage	Liberal	1960-1966
Daniel Johnson	Union Nationale	1966-1968
Jean-Jacques Bertrand	Union Nationale	1968-1970
Robert Bourassa	Liberal	1970-1976
René Lévesque	Québécois	1976-1985
Pierre Marc Johnson	Québécois	1985
Robert Bourassa	Liberal	1985-1994
Daniel Johnson	Liberal	1994
Jacques Parizeau	Québécois	1994-1996
Lucien Bouchard	Québécois	1996-

Quebec National Assembly

Quebec's National Assembly meets in the National Assembly Chamber in Quebec City. Each of the 125 members of the assembly serves a term of up to five years.

rior Court. The judges hold office until the age of 75. The lower courts of Quebec include the Court of Quebec, which has approximately 290 judges, and the municipal courts. Provincial authorities appoint the judges of these courts.

Quebec is the only province in which judges do not decide civil cases chiefly on the basis of *common law.* Under the common-law system, developed in England, rulings are determined by previous court decisions and by the customs of the people. In Quebec, judges decide civil cases mainly on rules in the Civil Code, which has its origins in the Napoleonic Code. The judges can disregard the decisions of other judges in similar cases. In criminal matters, the courts follow a federal criminal code.

Local government is based on Quebec's 96 regional county municipalities and 3 urban communities. The regional county municipalities include the areas of *cantons* (townships), parishes, towns, cities, and villages. They are governed by a council made up of the mayors of the communities within their borders. Quebec's three urban communities are the metropolitan areas of Hull, Montreal, and Quebec City. They are also governed by a council of mayors. All of Quebec's cities, towns, and villages have the mayor-council form of government.

Revenue. Taxes account for about two-thirds of the province's *general revenue* (income). Quebec is the only province that collects provincial personal income taxes, instead of having the federal government collect them.

Corporation income and sales are also taxed.

The provincial government receives about a fifth of its revenue from federal-provincial tax-sharing arrangements. Most of Quebec's other revenue comes from license and permit fees and from the sale of liquor. The sale of liquor in Quebec is under government control.

Politics. Since 1867, the provincial government has been controlled by one of five parties. These groups are the Conservative Party, the Liberal Party, Parti National, the Union Nationale, and Parti Québécois.

The Conservatives held power during the first 30 years, except for two brief administrations, one under the Liberals and the other under Parti National. In 1896, Wilfrid Laurier, a Liberal from Quebec, became the first French-Canadian prime minister of Canada. His victory helped bring the Liberals to power in Quebec in 1897. They controlled Quebec until 1936.

The Union Nationale party, led by Maurice Duplessis, came to power in 1936. Duplessis opposed federal control over Quebec and fought to protect French-Canadian rights—economic, political, and social. He led the government for a combined total of 18 years, longer than any other premier. The Liberal Party returned to power in 1960. From 1960 to 1976, power shifted between the Liberal and Union Nationale parties.

In 1976, the Parti Québécois won control of Quebec's government. In 1985, the Liberal Party returned to power. But the Parti Québécois regained control of the government in 1994.

History

Indian days. Inuit (formerly called Eskimos) and several Indian tribes were living in what is now Quebec when the first white settlers came. The Inuit lived in the far north, chiefly west of Ungava Bay and along Hudson Bay. The Naskapi Indians hunted in the eastern part of the Quebec region. Naskapi Indians who lived toward the south, between the St. Maurice River and present-day Sept-Îles, were called *Montagnais* (mountaineers) by the French. The Cree Indians roamed between the Naskapi and Inuit lands and south of James Bay. Other tribes were the Algonquin, Maliseet, and Micmac.

In 1534, the French explorer Jacques Cartier sailed into what is now the Gulf of St. Lawrence and claimed the Quebec region for France. This region became the base of France's colonial empire in North America, called New France. For information on the early history of Quebec, see **New France; Canada, History of.**

Early years as a province. Britain won control of Quebec in 1763 in the Treaty of Paris. The British North America Act of 1867 created the Dominion of Canada (see **British North America Act**). Quebec was one of the original provinces in the Dominion. French, in addition to English, was recognized as one of Quebec's two official languages. The act gave the province direct control over education and civil law. In 1867, Pierre-J.-O. Chauveau, a Conservative, became the first premier of Quebec.

Many French Canadians resented British rule. The federal system established in 1867 and the rights it granted the French Canadians satisfied them temporarily. The British North America Act had guaranteed the

school rights of Canada's two major religious groups. In Quebec, the Protestant, English-speaking minority received provincial funds for its schools. But the French Canadians of Quebec soon discovered that French Canadians in some of the other provinces were prevented from using public funds to establish Roman Catholic, French-language schools.

Relations between French and English Canadians grew worse after the *métis* (people of mixed white and Indian ancestry) of Saskatchewan rebelled in 1885. Louis Riel, their leader, surrendered and was hanged later that year. Many French Canadians considered Riel a hero who had been unjustly killed. Many English Canadians regarded him as a traitor. See **North West Rebellion.**

Tension between the French- and English-speaking Canadians rose again in 1899. That year, Britain went to war against the Boers in South Africa. Many French Canadians opposed fighting in the Boer War. Some English-speaking Canadians considered it Canada's duty to send troops to support the British Empire.

Sir Wilfrid Laurier of Quebec, the Dominion's first French-Canadian prime minister, spent government funds to equip volunteers and send them to South Africa. This policy created much anger in Quebec. Many French Canadians, led by Laurier's former ally Henri Bourassa, objected to providing support for Britain and held that Canadians should be loyal first to Canada. See **Laurier, Sir Wilfrid.**

About 1900, a period of rapid industrialization began in Quebec. In 1912, Quebec nearly doubled in size. Its

Historic Quebec

The British captured the city of Quebec in 1759. The victory enabled Britain to obtain almost all France's Canadian lands in the 1763 Treaty of Paris.

Separatists were French-Canadians in Quebec who wanted it to secede from Canada. They demonstrated in the 1960's and 1970's.

Sir Wilfrid Laurier of Quebec was the first French-Canadian prime minister. He sent troops to aid Britain in the Boer War in 1899.

French was adopted as the province's official language by the Quebec National Assembly in 1974.

The Expo 67 world's fair was held in Montreal as part of Canada's centennial celebration.

WORLD BOOK illustrations by Kevin Chadwick

Important dates in Quebec

1534 Jacques Cartier reached the Gulf of St. Lawrence and claimed the Quebec region for France.

1608 Samuel de Champlain established Quebec City, the first permanent European settlement in Canada.

1663 King Louis XIV of France made the Quebec region a royal province.

1759 The British captured Quebec City during the French and Indian War.

1763 Britain acquired Quebec by the Treaty of Paris.

1774 The British Parliament approved the Quebec Act, extending Quebec's borders and establishing French-Canadian political and religious rights.

1791 The Constitutional Act divided Quebec into the colonies of Upper Canada and Lower Canada.

1841 The Act of Union joined Upper Canada and Lower Canada under one government.

1867 The British North America Act created the Dominion of Canada, forming the province of Quebec.

1912 Quebec nearly doubled in size by acquiring territory east of Hudson Bay.

1927 The British Privy Council set the present Quebec-Labrador boundary.

1963 The provincial government bought all privately owned electric power companies.

1967 Expo 67, a world's fair, was held in Montreal as part of Canada's centennial celebration.

1974 The Quebec legislature made French the official language of the province.

1976-1985 The Parti Québécois, a separatist political party, controlled the provincial legislature.

1990 The Meech Lake accord, a constitutional amendment that would have recognized Quebec as a distinct society, failed to pass all 10 provincial legislatures.

1994 The Parti Québécois regained control of the government.

1995 Quebec voters narrowly rejected a referendum proposal that called for independence for Quebec.

northwestern boundaries were extended to Hudson Bay and Hudson Strait. Interest in the region's natural resources grew, and Quebec and Newfoundland disputed the Quebec-Labrador boundary. The British Privy Council settled the dispute in 1927 in favor of Newfoundland.

World War I. Tensions again developed between English and French Canadians during World War I (1914-1918). At first the country was united behind the war effort, but soon some English Canadians accused French Canadians of not enlisting. French Canadians pointed out that most English Canadian volunteers had been born in Britain. Matters worsened when courts upheld a decision by Ontario to abolish the use of French in its schools. French Canadians asked why they should fight for Britain when Britain's supporters were denying them equal rights in their own country.

In 1917, Canada began drafting men into the army. In 1918, the army was used to put down antidraft riots in Quebec City, and there was some talk of Quebec separating from Canada. Nevertheless, French-Canadian troops served heroically in the war.

Between the wars. After World War I, industry continued to expand rapidly. More people from rural areas found work in the cities. Until this time, they had been moving to Ontario or the United States.

Many French-Canadian leaders resented the industrial expansion, which was controlled by the English Canadians and Americans. The French Canadians feared that their language and culture would not survive in the cities, where English was the main language used in business. But the people accepted this threat because the new industry offered an improved living standard.

World War II. During World War II (1939-1945), Quebec was of great value to the Allies. The province had a large labor force, plentiful electric power, and huge deposits of asbestos, copper, and zinc. Quebec's industrial production nearly tripled.

Tension between French and English Canadians developed again during the war. In 1944, the federal government, under the Liberal Party, set up a military draft for service overseas, despite promises to Quebecers that it would not do so. As a result, Quebec voters elected the Union Nationale party to power in 1944. The new government, under Premier Maurice Duplessis, emphasized French-Canadian political rights in Quebec and opposed control by the federal government.

The mid-1900's. The economic growth in Quebec that followed World War II extended into the 1950's and 1960's. In 1950, mines near Havre-Saint-Pierre began to produce ilmenite, a titanium ore. In 1954, an asbestos fiber mill that was then the largest in the world opened in Asbestos. In 1960, huge asbestos deposits were discovered in the Ungava Peninsula.

In 1960, the Liberal Party won control of Quebec's government, and Jean Lesage became premier. He served in this position from 1960 to 1966, a period often called Quebec's *Quiet Revolution,* because of its many reforms. A new labor code made it easier to form trade unions. A new Ministry of Education was established, and it increased the number of high schools, colleges, and universities. During the 1960's, Quebec and other provinces became dissatisfied with joint federal and provincial social programs and division of taxes. Quebec exercised the provinces' right to withdraw from these programs and to administer its share of taxes without federal supervision. Quebec then gained control of its pension plans, social security programs, and student loans. In 1963, the province bought all privately owned electric companies in Quebec.

The 1960's also saw an upsurge of strong French-Canadian nationalist feelings among some of Quebec's people. A number of French Canadians wanted Quebec to *secede* (withdraw) from the Canadian confederation and form a separate nation. Some Quebecers used demonstrations to promote secession, and a few extremists used bombings. In 1968, many separatist groups joined forces and formed the Parti Québécois. René Lévesque, a Quebec legislator, led the party.

Recent developments. In October 1970, members of the *Front de Libération du Québec* (FLQ), a revolutionary separatist group, kidnapped British Trade Commissioner James R. Cross and Quebec Labor Minister Pierre Laporte. Canadian Prime Minister Pierre Trudeau sent thousands of federal troops to major cities in Quebec to protect government officials and public buildings. Provincial police made about 3,000 raids and arrested about 450 people. Laporte was later murdered, and four FLQ members were charged with the crime. All of them were convicted and sent to prison. Trudeau and Quebec authorities allowed Cross's kidnappers to go to Cuba in return for their release of Cross.

The largest strike in Canadian history broke out in Quebec in 1972. More than 200,000 public employees left their jobs in a dispute over wages and related matters. The 11-day strike closed most schools and limited hospital service and government operations.

In 1974, the National Assembly adopted French as Quebec's official language. This act promoted French-language instruction in schools and made French Quebec's chief language of business and government.

In 1976, the Parti Québécois won 71 of the 110 seats in Quebec's legislature and took control of the government. Lévesque became premier. In 1977, the legislature adopted the Charter of the French Language. The charter established deadlines and fines to help enforce the program to make French the chief language in all areas of Quebec life. But the Supreme Court of Canada ruled that parts of the charter were unconstitutional.

In a referendum held in 1980, the Lévesque government asked voters for the authority to negotiate a *sovereignty association* with the rest of Canada. Such an association would give Quebec political independence but maintain its economic ties to Canada. However, voters rejected the proposal.

In 1981, proposed changes in Canada's Constitution upset many French-speaking Quebecers. They felt the proposals would not help preserve and promote Quebec's French-Canadian character. In 1982, the proposals became part of a revised Constitution that was accepted by all provincial legislatures except Quebec.

Lévesque resigned as party leader on Sept. 29, 1985, and as premier on Oct. 3, 1985. He was succeeded in both posts by Pierre Marc Johnson, who had been Lévesque's minister of justice and intergovernmental relations. In December 1985, the Liberal Party won a majority of seats in the legislature. Robert Bourassa, the premier from 1970 to 1976, again became premier and held the position until he retired in 1994.

In 1987, a proposed constitutional amendment recognizing Quebec as a distinct society in Canada offered promise of winning the province's acceptance of the Canadian constitution. The amendment was developed by Canadian Prime Minister Brian Mulroney and the provincial first ministers at Meech Lake, Quebec, in April. Mulroney and the provincial leaders approved the proposed amendment, known as the Meech Lake accord, in June 1987.

To go into effect, the accord had to be ratified by the assemblies of all 10 provinces by June 23, 1990. However, Manitoba and Newfoundland refused to ratify the amendment. After the failure of the accord, many Quebecers began to demand increased independence for Quebec from the rest of Canada. In 1992, fundamental changes to the national government were again under consideration, primarily to keep Quebec part of Canada. Among the possible changes was the transfer of certain federal powers to the provinces. In a referendum held in October 1992, a majority of Canadians in Quebec and each of five other provinces voted against the proposed changes.

Legislative elections were held in 1994. The separatist Parti Québécois won a majority of seats and its leader, Jacques Parizeau, became premier. In October 1995, the Quebec government held a referendum on independence for Quebec. The proposal was narrowly defeated, and Quebec remained a part of Canada. Following the defeat of the proposal he had supported, Parizeau decided to resign as premier and as head of the Parti Québécois. In January 1996, Lucien Bouchard succeeded him as leader of the party and as premier of Quebec. Bouchard led the PQ to victory in elections held in 1998 and remained premier.

In late 1995 and early 1996, the Canadian Parliament passed resolutions aimed at promoting national unity. One resolution recognized Quebec's unique language, culture, and civil law. Another gave Quebec and four other parts of Canada a veto over changes in the Canadian constitution.   Robin B. Burns and Roger Nadeau

Related articles in *World Book* include:

Biographies

Abbott, Sir John J. C.
Bourassa, Henri
Brock, Sir Isaac
Carleton, Sir Guy
Cartier, Sir George É.
Cartier, Jacques
Champlain, Samuel de
Charest, Jean
Chrétien, Jean
Drummond, William H.
Garneau, Marc
Gregoire, Paul Cardinal
Laurier, Sir Wilfrid
Laval de Montmorency, François
Léger, Jules
Lemelin, Roger
Lévesque, René
McGill, James
Montcalm, Marquis de
Mulroney, Brian
Papineau, Louis J.
Saint Laurent, Louis S.
Scott, F. R.
Taché, Sir Étienne-P.
Trudeau, Pierre E.
Turner, John N.
Vanier, Georges-Philias
Verchères, Marie M. J. de
Wolfe, James

Cities

Laval
Montreal
Quebec (city)
Sherbrooke

History

Acadia
Bloc Québécois
British North America Act
Canada, History of
French and Indian wars
Mohawk Indians

Montagnais Indians
Parti Québécois
Quebec, Battle of
Quebec Act
United Empire Loyalists
War of 1812

Physical features

Anticosti
Canadian Shield
Gaspé Peninsula
Gulf of Saint Lawrence
Hudson Bay
James Bay
Lake Champlain
Ottawa River
Saguenay River
Saint Lawrence River

Outline

I. **People**
  A. Population
  B. Schools
  C. Libraries
  D. Museums
II. **Visitor's guide**
  A. Places to visit
  B. Annual events
III. **Land and climate**
  A. Land regions
  B. Coastline
  C. Rivers, waterfalls, and lakes
  D. Plant and animal life
  E. Climate
IV. **Economy**
  A. Natural resources
  B. Service industries
  C. Manufacturing
  D. Agriculture
  E. Mining
  F. Forestry
  G. Electric power
  H. Transportation
  I. Communication
V. **Government**
  A. Lieutenant governor
  B. Premier
  C. Legislature
  D. Courts
  E. Local government
  F. Revenue
  G. Politics
VI. **History**

Questions

Why is Quebec called the *Storied Province*?
What percentage of Quebec's people are French Canadians?
What is Canada's chief transportation center?
What were some developments in the *Quiet Revolution*?
What part of Quebec produces the most iron ore?
Who was the first French Canadian prime minister of Canada?
How did Quebec receive its name?
What is Quebec's chief manufacturing activity?
How was Quebec's school system changed in 1964?

Additional resources

Level I
Hamilton, Janice. *Quebec*. Lerner, 1996.
LeVert, Suzanne. *Quebec*. Chelsea Hse., 1991.
McLean, Eric. *The Living Past of Montreal*. 3rd ed. McGill-Queens Univ. Pr., 1993.
Provencher, Jean. *Quebec*. Childrens Pr., 1992.
Wartik, Nancy. *The French Canadians*. Chelsea Hse., 1989.
Wright, J. V. *Quebec Prehistory*. National Museums of Canada, 1979.

Level II
Bothwell, Robert. *Canada and Quebec*. Univ. of Br. Columbia Pr., 1995.
Guindon, Hubert. *Quebec Society*. Univ. of Toronto Pr., 1988.
Kevan, Martin. *The Best of Montreal & Quebec City*. Crown, 1992. A guidebook.
Linteau, Paul-André, and others. *Quebec: A History, 1867-1929*. James Lorimer, 1983. *Quebec Since 1930: A History*. 1991.
Little, J. I. *Nationalism, Capitalism, and Colonization in Nineteenth-Century Quebec*. McGill-Queens Univ. Pr., 1989.
Ouellet, Fernand. *Economic and Social History of Quebec, 1760-1850*. Carleton Univ. Pr., 1980. *Lower Canada, 1791-1840: Social Change and Nationalism*. McClelland, 1980.
Trofimenkoff, Susan M. *The Dream of Nation: A Social and Intellectual History of Quebec*. Gage, 1983.

Eberhard E. Otto, Miller Services

Quebec, the capital of the province of Quebec, lies on the St. Lawrence River. The Château Frontenac, *left,* a hotel, helps give Quebec the charm of an old European city.

Quebec, *kwih BEHK,* is the capital of the province of Quebec and the oldest city in Canada. In French, the city's name is spelled with an accent—Québec (pronounced *kay BEHK).* The French explorer Samuel de Champlain founded Quebec in 1608. Quebec ranks as an important Canadian port and tourist center. Among the cities in the province, only Montreal and Laval have more people. Quebec lies at the point where the St. Charles River flows into the St. Lawrence River. Nearby, the St. Lawrence narrows to about $\frac{1}{2}$ mile (0.8 kilometer). The city's name comes from an Algonquian Indian word meaning *the river narrows here.*

Quebec is the only walled city in North America. But most of the present-day city lies outside the walls. Quebec's many churches, old stone houses, and crooked cobblestone streets give it the charm of an old European city. The Château Frontenac, a castlelike hotel with towers, red brick walls, and a steep copper roof, rises dramatically from the Quebec skyline.

The city has been called the *Cradle of New France* because it served as the main base of early French explorers and missionaries in North America. Quebec also has the nickname *Gibraltar of America* because of the Citadel, a huge fort on the cliffs above the St. Lawrence River. In 1759, British troops defeated the French on the Plains of Abraham, west of the Citadel. In 1763, the Treaty of Paris gave Canada to Britain.

Most people who live in Quebec have French ancestors. Sir Wilfrid Laurier, the nation's first French-Canadian prime minister, said that "Quebec is to French Canadians what Mecca is to Arabs—the most sacred city."

The city

Quebec covers 34 square miles (89 square kilometers). The city has an old section that makes up about 4 square miles (10 square kilometers). The old section, in turn, has two parts, Upper Town and Lower Town. The

Quebec metropolitan area spreads over 1,216 square miles (3,150 square kilometers). The metropolitan area includes 45 suburbs, among them Beauport, Charlesbourg, Lévis-Lauzon, Sainte-Foy, and Val-Bélair.

The Citadel, Quebec's most famous landmark, overlooks the city from a height of 347 feet (106 meters). It stands on the highest point of *Cap Diamant* (Cape Diamond). The cape drops sharply toward the St. Lawrence River but slopes more gradually to the St. Charles. Massive walls and cannons surround the fort and its 140 acres (57 hectares) of parade ground. The British completed the Citadel in 1832.

Upper Town lies north of the Citadel atop Cap Diamant. A stone wall, rebuilt at the time the Citadel was built, encircles part of Upper Town. The wall averages 35 feet (11 meters) in height and has four entrance gates.

Most of Quebec's best hotels, luxury shops, monuments, parks, and fine restaurants are in Upper Town. This section of Quebec also has the Parliament buildings, fashionable residential areas, and most of the city's private schools.

The Dufferin Terrace, a planked walkway 60 feet (18 meters) wide, extends along the cliffs from the Citadel to the Château Frontenac. The terrace offers excellent

Facts in brief

Population: 167,264. *Metropolitan area population*—671,889.
Area: 34 sq. mi. (89 km²). *Metropolitan area*—1,216 sq. mi. (3,150 km²).
Altitude: 162 ft. (49 m) above sea level at City Hall.
Climate: *Average temperature*—January, 12 °F (–11 °C); July, 68 °F (20 °C). *Average annual precipitation* (rainfall, melted snow, and other forms of moisture)—42 inches (107 centimeters).
Government: Mayor-council. *Terms*—4 years each for the mayor and the 21 council members.
Founded: 1608. Incorporated as a city in 1832.

views of Lévis-Lauzon on the opposite bank of the St. Lawrence and of the Beaupré Coast and the Isle of Orleans downstream.

Lower Town, northeast of Upper Town, includes the business and industrial districts of Quebec. It lies 19 feet (6 meters) above sea level on a strip of land between the rivers and the cliffs of Cap Diamant. Lower Town has many large stores and some factories. A number of its homes date back to the 1700's and 1800's. Some of the area's oldest streets are very narrow. Sous-le-Cap measures only 8 feet 10 inches (2.69 meters) at its narrowest point and may be the narrowest street in North America.

A square called Place Royale is Lower Town's best-known landmark. The Notre-Dame-des-Victoires Church there has an altar built to look like a fort. This church, completed in 1688, stands on the site once occupied by Samuel de Champlain's first settlement.

The people

About 98 per cent of Quebec's people were born in Canada. About 95 per cent have French ancestors, and the rest have English, Irish, or Scottish ancestry. More than 95 per cent of the people are Roman Catholic. About 80 per cent of the Quebecers speak French, so signs and other public notices appear in that language.

Major problems in Quebec include unemployment and deterioration of old neighborhoods in Lower Town.

Lack of adequate housing is also a problem. The city has built a number of low-rent projects to provide needed housing. The provincial government paid 95 per cent of the cost of the projects, and the city paid 5 per cent.

The economy

Industry and commerce. Quebec lies about 180 miles (290 kilometers) from Montreal, a major center of Canadian industry. The city's nearness to Montreal has limited its industrial development, but more than 500 manufacturing companies operate in the Quebec area. They employ almost 20,000 workers and produce about $1\frac{1}{4}$ billion worth of goods annually. Most of the industrial sites are along the St. Charles River and in industrial parks along the Autoroute de la Capitale. Shipbuilding, papermaking, and the manufacture of cement are the leading industries. Tourism also is important to the city's economy. The port of Quebec handles more than 16 million short tons (14.5 million metric tons) of goods yearly. Its chief exports are grain, ore, and pulp and paper.

Transportation. Quebec's harbor stays open the year around and can handle oceangoing ships. The waterfront extends 6 miles (10 kilometers) along both the east and west sides of the cape and into the mouth of the St. Charles River. A ferry crossing and two bridges link Quebec to the south shore of the St. Lawrence River. Railroad passenger trains and three rail freight

City of Quebec

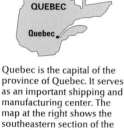

Quebec is the capital of the province of Quebec. It serves as an important shipping and manufacturing center. The map at the right shows the southeastern section of the city, which includes Quebec's major points of interest.

City boundary
Old city wall
Expressway
Main road
Other road
Railroad
■ Point of interest
Park

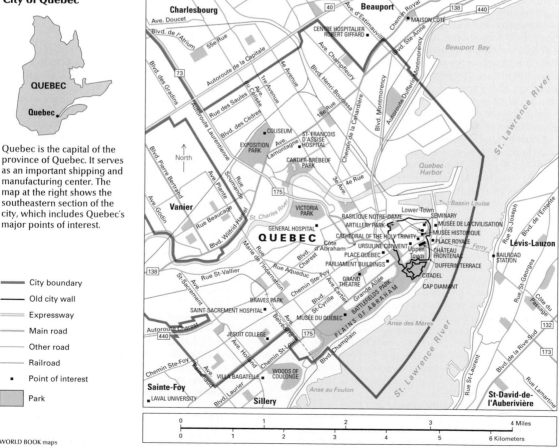

lines serve the city. Commercial airlines use the Quebec International Airport, which lies 10 miles (16 kilometers) from Quebec. A public transit system provides local bus transportation.

Communication. Two daily French-language newspapers, *Le Journal de Québec* and *Le Soleil,* serve Quebec. The city has four French-language TV stations and one that broadcasts in English. One English-language and 10 French-language radio stations serve the Quebec area.

Education

Schools. Quebec's public school system consists of about 45 French-language schools and 5 English-language schools, with a total of about 18,500 students. A campus of the University of Quebec and Laval University are in nearby Ste.-Foy. Laval University was founded in 1852.

Libraries. Quebec has six public libraries, including the library of the Canadian Institute and of the Bibliothèque Municipale, which has five branches. The libraries of the provincial legislature and Laval University also have large collections of books.

Cultural life

The arts. Cultural activity in Quebec centers around the Grand Theatre. This building includes an 1,800-seat concert hall and an 800-seat theater. Choral groups, the Quebec Symphonic Orchestra, and a local drama company perform there.

Museums. The Musée du Québec, the largest museum in Quebec province, has both traditional and modern paintings and sculpture. The Musée Historique features life-sized wax figures that illustrate scenes from Canadian history. The Seminary Museum displays old paintings, coins, and stamps. The Musée de la Civilisation, which opened in 1988, features exhibits on human culture and civilization. Many of the exhibits encourage participation of museum visitors.

Churches. Quebec has over 100 basilicas, chapels, and churches. Important Roman Catholic structures include the Basilique Notre-Dame, with walls built in 1647, and the Ursuline Convent, founded in 1639. The Anglican Cathedral of the Holy Trinity, the first cathedral of the Church of England built outside Britain, opened in 1804.

Recreation

Many visitors enjoy touring Quebec in horse-drawn buggies called *calèches.* During the summer, sightseeing boats operate on the St. Lawrence River.

Parks. Quebec's park system covers a total of about 350 acres (142 hectares). The system includes about 45 parks and playgrounds. Also in the city is National Battlefields Park. This park includes the historic Plains of Abraham. The Quebec Zoo in nearby Charlesbourg specializes in Canadian animals. About 6½ miles (10.5 kilometers) northeast of Quebec, the waters of Montmorency Falls plunge 251 feet (77 meters) into the St. Lawrence River.

Annual events and places to visit. About half a million tourists attend the Quebec Winter Carnival, held every February. This event lasts almost two weeks and includes costume balls, dog-sled and ice-canoe races,

parades, and street dancing. The Festival D'Eté in July features top performers from many parts of the world. A 10-day provincial fair at Exposition Park, ending on Labor Day in September, features agricultural and industrial exhibits.

Many visitors attend the changing-the-guard ceremony that is held in the Citadel each summer day. During this colorful ceremony, Canadian soldiers wear elaborate British uniforms and march to military music and commands.

Government

Quebec has a mayor-council form of government. The voters of Quebec elect the mayor and the 21 council members to four-year terms.

Taxes on property, sales, and business companies provide most of the city's revenue. However, Quebec collects little or no taxes on about a third of its property, including churches, government buildings, hospitals, and various other institutions. As a result, the city depends on grants from the federal government and the provincial government to meet many of its financial needs.

History

Early days. Algonquian and Iroquoian Indians once farmed and hunted in the area that is now Quebec. The French explorer Jacques Cartier spent the winter of 1535 near the Iroquoian village of Stadacona. Samuel de Champlain established a permanent settlement there on July 3, 1608, and named it Quebec (see **Champlain, Samuel de** [The founding of Quebec]).

Louis Hébert, the first Canadian farmer, established his household at Quebec in 1617. In 1620, Champlain built Fort St. Louis on the site where the Château Frontenac now stands.

In 1628, Quebec underwent the first of several attacks by English forces. A fleet under Admiral David Kirke captured the settlement in 1629. Fewer than 60 people lived in Quebec at that time. France regained Quebec in 1632 through the Treaty of Saint-Germain-en-Laye. In 1659, Monsignor François Xavier de Laval de Montmorency arrived in Quebec. He helped make Quebec the center of New France. In 1674, he became the first bishop of Quebec. The population of the village reached 547 in 1666. See **Laval de Montmorency, François Xavier de.**

In 1690, the English general Sir William Phips tried to capture Quebec. Louis de Buade, Comte de Frontenac, the governor general of New France, headed the successful defense of the city. At that time, Quebec had 1,500 residents.

The 1700's. In 1711, a British fleet under Admiral Hovenden Walker turned back from a planned attack on Quebec after a storm wrecked many of the ships on the Isle-aux-Oeufs reef. However, in September 1759, General James Wolfe's British troops defeated French forces under the Marquis de Montcalm on the Plains of Abraham. The British captured Quebec five days later (see **Quebec, Battle of**). By 1760, the city's population had grown to 7,900. The Treaty of Paris, which ended the French and Indian War in 1763, gave Canada to the British.

In 1775, during the Revolutionary War in America,

American troops led by General Richard Montgomery and Colonel Benedict Arnold attacked Quebec. They suffered a disastrous defeat on New Year's Eve. General Montgomery was killed.

Upper and Lower Canada (now the southern parts of Ontario and Quebec) were formed in 1791. Quebec City became the capital of Lower Canada at that time.

The 1800's. Through the years, Quebec became increasingly important as an industrial port and a center of government. Business people took advantage of Quebec's nearby forests and the city's river location, and developed lumber and shipbuilding industries.

Quebec received a city charter in 1832. In 1841, Upper and Lower Canada united. Quebec twice served as capital of the Province of Canada, from 1851 to 1855 and from 1859 to 1865. When the Dominion of Canada was established in 1867, the area that had been Lower Canada became the province of Quebec. Quebec City was named the capital of the province. The city's population stood at almost 60,000 that year.

During the mid-1800's, the Montreal Harbour Commission deepened the St. Lawrence River from Quebec to Montreal. As a result, Quebec's importance as a port declined sharply. Montreal, which is closer to the heart of the continent and is connected by canal to the Great Lakes, took much of Quebec's trade. At about the same time, iron ships began to replace wooden vessels, which hurt Quebec's lumber and shipbuilding industries.

The early 1900's brought further industrialization. By 1911, Quebec had 80,000 people. During World War II (1939-1945), its factories expanded to manufacture war materials. The increased labor demand helped raise the population to 164,016 by 1951.

Twice during the war, in 1943 and 1944, Prime Minister Winston Churchill of Britain and President Franklin D. Roosevelt of the United States met in Quebec. They conferred at the Château Frontenac and the Citadel about important war matters.

Recent developments. In 1970, the Quebec Urban Community was formed to deal with area problems and to promote tourism and industrial development. It consists of Quebec and 12 suburbs and has a council made up of mayors and other representatives of the communities. In the early 1970's, Quebec annexed four suburbs and its area increased from 8 square miles (21 square kilometers) to 34 square miles (89 square kilometers).

In 1974, a $50-million hotel-convention center was completed at Place Québec, which is located opposite the Parliament buildings. This project included a 600-room hotel and convention facilities. Since 1974, other hotels have been built at Place Québec. In addition, a larger convention center was completed at the site in 1996. The city has become a popular convention destination.   Denis Angers

See also **Quebec** (province); **Champlain, Samuel de; French and Indian wars** (The French and Indian War).
Quebec, *kwih BEHK,* **Battle of,** settled the fate of the French empire in America. France's defeat at Quebec in 1759 led to the Treaty of Paris of 1763 that gave Canada and all French territory east of the Mississippi River to Britain.

About 2 million British colonists were living along the eastern seaboard when the Seven Years' War began in 1756 (see **Seven Years' War**). About 60,000 French lived in America, mostly in Canada. Skirmishes between the British and French had taken place for about two years before war broke out. The British wanted to expand westward, but a chain of French posts blocked their move. Without a formal declaration of war, the British attacked French settlements in Ohio. The Marquis de Montcalm took command of French troops in 1756. He captured Forts Oswego (1756) and William Henry (1757) and successfully defended Fort Ticonderoga (1758). But British victories forced him to fall back on Quebec, where he gathered about 14,000 troops to defend the city. Quebec stood on heights dominating the Saint Lawrence River, and seemed impregnable to attack. French cannon covered all ship movements.

In 1758, the British seized Louisbourg, a fortress on Cape Breton Island that was the center of French power in the area. They assembled a huge fleet of ships and set sail for Quebec in May 1759. The 250 ships carried 8,000 soldiers under the command of General James Wolfe. For three months, the British urged the French in the fortified city to surrender. Wolfe could not decide whether to attack the French positions at Beauport, east of Quebec, or to climb the steep cliffs leading to the wide plateau called the *Plains of Abraham,* west of the city. He feared his ships would be unable to pass before Quebec under the fire of French batteries.

Bombardment of Quebec. British troops landed on the Île d'Orléans, 5 miles (8 kilometers) east of Quebec, in June. Other forces occupied Pointe Lévis on the south bank. Protected by cannon fire, a few British ships sailed past the city to Anse des Mères on July 18. Wolfe then decided to attack Beauport. Under Montcalm and General François de Lévis, French, Canadian, and Indian soldiers repelled the attack.

Wolfe, depressed by the loss, vowed to make a last attempt by assaulting Quebec from the west. Montcalm believed that the British could not land at Anse au Foulon, at the foot of the cliffs leading to the Plains of Abraham. But he wanted French troops at Cap Rouge farther west to occupy the Plains of Abraham. The Marquis de Vaudreuil-Cavagnal, governor of Canada, ordered these troops to stay at Cap Rouge.

The attack on Quebec began during the cloudy, calm night of Sept. 12-13, 1759. The tide bore British flatboats to the Anse au Foulon. The men climbed silently to the Plains and surprised a larger enemy post. By dawn, 5,000 British regulars had scaled the cliffs and were ranged for battle. Montcalm had expected an attack at Beauport. He quickly moved up 4,000 troops to meet the enemy. They arrived about 10 that morning.

The French fired too quickly at the British, who advanced in closed ranks and held their fire. When the French were near at hand, the British fired, reloaded, fired again, and then charged with bayonet and sword. The French retreated in disorder. Wolfe was wounded mortally in the first shots. Montcalm, who had been trying to rally his men, was wounded about the same time. His men brought him back to Quebec, where he died a few hours later. In 15 minutes, the fate of the French empire in America had been settled. General Jean-Baptiste Ramezay carried out the request of the townspeople by surrendering Quebec to General George Townshend on September 18.

The French tried to recapture Quebec in April 1760. They defeated the British at Sainte Foy. This victory proved to be a useless one. The British fleet arrived in the river below Quebec soon after the battle, and the British army coming up from Lake Champlain forced the surrender of Montreal in September. The Treaty of Paris of 1763 reduced all French possessions in North America to two small islands off the coast of Newfoundland, St.-Pierre and Miquelon. In 1908, the site of the battles of Quebec and Sainte Foy became the National Battlefields Park.   P. B. Waite

Related articles in *World Book* include:

Acadia	Montcalm, Marquis de
Canada, History of (picture)	Murray, James
French and Indian wars (The	Wolfe, James
French and Indian War)	

Quebec, University of, or Université du Québec, is Canada's largest university. It is a coeducational university with campuses in Chicoutimi, Hull, Montreal, Rimouski, Rouyn and Noranda, and Trois-Rivières. It also includes the National Institute for Scientific Research, the National School of Public Administration, and the Tele-University in Ste.-Foy, a suburb of Quebec City; the Armand-Frappier Institute in Laval; and the School of Higher Technology in Montreal. All courses are in French. The university offers programs in business and public administration, fine arts, health services, humanities, paralegal studies, sciences, and social sciences. It grants bachelor's, master's, and doctor's degrees. The University of Quebec opened in 1969. Its administrative offices are in Ste.-Foy.   Critically reviewed by the University of Quebec

Quebec Act, *kwih BEHK,* was a group of laws passed by the United Kingdom in 1774. It guaranteed the use of French civil law in Quebec, then a British colony with a largely French population. It also guaranteed the French Canadians the right to practice Roman Catholicism and allowed the Catholic Church in Quebec to collect a tax from its members. The act enlarged Quebec to include much of what is now Quebec, Ontario, and the Midwestern United States.

The United Kingdom passed the act to settle questions about law and government in Quebec. The United Kingdom also had a more selfish reason. It faced a possible revolution in its 13 American Colonies to the south. The United Kingdom hoped to have some French support if the revolution began, or, at least, to keep the French in Quebec from joining it.

In the same year the United Kingdom passed the Quebec Act, it passed four acts designed to punish Massachusetts. The Americans bitterly resented all five acts and called them the *Intolerable Acts* (see **Intolerable Acts**). The Americans invaded Quebec shortly after their revolution began in April 1775 but were turned back. Most French Canadians remained neutral during the invasion, because they considered the invasion mainly a quarrel between the United Kingdom and its colonies.   P. B. Waite

Quebec Conference, *kwih BEHK,* was a meeting at which Canadian leaders completed plans for forming a united Canada. It was held in the city of Quebec from Oct. 10 to Oct. 27, 1864. At that time, eastern Canada consisted of five self-governing colonies of the United Kingdom—the Province of Canada, New Brunswick, Newfoundland, Nova Scotia, and Prince Edward Island. The

Hudson's Bay Company, a fur-trading firm, controlled most of western Canada. British Columbia and Vancouver Island were two British colonies in the far west.

Three chief factors made union desirable: (1) The United Kingdom felt Canadians could better defend themselves if they united. (2) Union could aid economic growth. (3) Union might help end friction between the French- and English-speaking groups of the Province of Canada.

The delegates to the Quebec Conference, now called the Fathers of Confederation, proposed a union of all the eastern provinces under a central government. They also made provision for future admission of the western territories. Within two years, the Province of Canada, New Brunswick, and Nova Scotia agreed to the plan. The Province of Canada was divided into the provinces of Quebec and Ontario. Quebec, Ontario, New Brunswick, and Nova Scotia were the provinces when the British North America Act formed the Dominion of Canada in July 1867.   P. B. Waite

See also **Confederation of Canada.**

Quebec separatist movement. See Canada, History of (The Quebec separatist movement; The separatist threat); **Lévesque, René; Montreal** (The separatist movement); **Quebec** (The mid-1900's).

Quebracho, *kay BRAH choh,* is a type of South American tree that grows mainly in Argentina and Paraguay. The wood of quebracho trees contains 20 to 30 percent tannin. Workers extract the tannin and export it to the United States for use in tanning leather. The name *quebracho* means *ax-breaker* in Spanish. Quebracho trees have hard, tough wood called *quebracho colorado wood.* The name *quebracho* is also used for other South American trees that have hard wood.   Alwyn H. Gentry

Scientific classification. Quebracho trees belong to the cashew family, Anacardiaceae. They make up the genus *Schinopsis.*

Quechan Indians, *kweh CHAHN,* also called the Yuma Indians, live along the Colorado River in southeastern California and southwestern Arizona. Traditionally, the Quechan lived in villages, in airy houses made from branches or reeds plastered with mud. They cultivated corn, beans, squash, and melons in the fertile soils created by the flooding each spring of the Colorado River. They also fished; gathered wild beans, seeds, and nuts; and made pottery and baskets. Dreams played an important role in their religion.

About 1540, Spanish explorers probably became the first white people to encounter the Quechan. In 1780, the Spanish built two settlements in Quechan territory, near what is now Winterhaven, California. To protect their homeland, the Quechan attacked and destroyed the settlements in 1781. For years, the Quechan remained independent of government control. But in 1852, the United States Army established Fort Yuma, also near what is now Winterhaven. In 1884, the U.S. government set up the Fort Yuma Reservation, and the Indians agreed to live there. The reservation lies in California and Arizona and includes the sites of the destroyed settlements and of the fort. Today, Quechan living on the reservation grow large amounts of vegetables for sale. According to the 1990 U.S. census, there are about 2,000 Quechan.   Victoria D. Patterson

See also **Indian, American** (Table of tribes).

Quechua. See **Inca** (Communication and learning); **Peru** (Languages).

Queen, the insect. See **Ant** (Life in an ant colony); **Bee; Insect** (Family life); **Termite.**

Queen is the title of a woman who rules a kingdom in her own right, or who is the wife of a king. If she rules in her own right, she is called a *queen regnant.* She has the same powers that a king would have, depending on the constitution of the country she rules.

If the queen is the wife of the king, she is called a *queen consort.* The mother of the ruling monarch is the *queen mother,* and the widow of a king is a *queen dowager.* Each of the queens has her own household. But none are able to exercise any official power in the government.

Kings or queens of the United Kingdom and other constitutional monarchies have few powers of government. But they can refuse the advice of the prime minister, and they can influence public opinion.

Robert E. Dowse

For names of queens, see names of individuals; for example, **Elizabeth II.** See also **Coronation; King; Prince consort; Royal Household of the United Kingdom.**

Queen, Ellery, was the pen name of two cousins, Frederic Dannay (1905-1982) and Manfred B. Lee (1905-1971), who became successful detective-story writers. Ellery Queen is also the name of their chief fictional character. They also published under the name of Barnaby Ross.

Dannay and Lee were both born in New York City. They became full-time writers soon after they won a detective-story contest in 1928. The story became their first Ellery Queen novel, *The Roman Hat Mystery* (1929). The early Ellery Queen novels especially are excellent examples of the cleverly plotted mystery puzzle. In 1941, Dannay and Lee founded *Ellery Queen's Mystery Magazine,* which publishes original detective fiction and reprints detective fiction classics. As editor and anthologist, Ellery Queen made a major contribution to the popularity of mystery fiction in America.   David Geherin

Queen Anne's lace. See **Wild carrot.**

Queen Charlotte Islands is a group of about 150 islands in the North Pacific Ocean. The islands are part of the Canadian province of British Columbia. Hecate Strait separates the islands from the mainland of the province. About 5,500 people live on the islands, which cover about 4,100 square miles (11,000 square kilometers). George Dixon, a British navigator, explored the islands in 1787 and named them for his ship, the *Queen Charlotte.* Queen Charlotte was the wife of King George III of the United Kingdom.

The largest islands of the group are Graham and Moresby. Lumbering, fishing, and tourism are the islands' chief economic activities. Part of Gwaii Haanas National Park lies on Moresby Island. The old Haida Indian village of Ninstints, on Skungwai Island, has spectacular totem poles.   Graeme Wynn

Queen Mary, a ship. See **Ship** (Ocean liners).

Queens is the largest of New York City's five *boroughs* (districts) in area. It covers 126 square miles (326 square kilometers), all of Queens County. It has a population of 1,951,598.

Mainly a residential area, Queens Borough has several well-known sections. These include Flushing, Forest Hills, and Kew Gardens. La Guardia Airport and John F. Kennedy International Airport are located in Queens. The site of present-day Queens was settled by the Dutch in 1635. It became part of the British province of New York in 1683 and was named for England's Catherine of Braganza, Queen of Charles II. Queens became part of New York City in 1898.   Owen Moritz

See also **New York City** (Queens; map).

Queen's University at Kingston is a coeducational university in Kingston, Canada. It grants bachelor's, master's, and doctor's degrees. Queen's has faculties of applied science, arts and science, education, law, and medicine. It also includes schools of business, graduate studies and research, industrial relations, nursing, physical and health education, public administration, rehabilitation therapy, and urban and regional planning.

Queen's was founded in 1841. Queen's Theological College is affiliated with the university.

Critically reviewed by Queen's University at Kingston

Queensberry, Marquess of (1844-1900), a British sportsman, sponsored the boxing code that bears his name (see **Queensberry Rules**). His given name was John Sholto Douglas. The Queensberry Rules were actually written by John Graham Chambers of the Amateur Athletic Club. Douglas became the eighth marquess when only 14. He served in the British Parliament from 1872 to 1880.   Bert Randolph Sugar

Queensberry Rules are a set of rules for boxing matches. Their official name is the Marquess of Queensberry Rules. They were drawn up under the supervision of the Marquess of Queensberry in the mid-1860's. At that time, matches were fought with bare fists. John Graham Chambers, an English athlete, composed the Queensberry Rules to replace the Revised London Prize Ring Rules of 1853.

The new rules were first used in a professional tournament in London in 1872. They called for three-minute rounds, a one-minute rest between rounds, and the wearing of gloves. The Queensberry Rules were first used in the United States in the early 1880's. The Amateur Athletic Union (AAU) adopted them in 1888. In 1892, James J. Corbett defeated John L. Sullivan and became the first boxer to win the heavyweight title fighting under the Queensberry Rules.   Bert Randolph Sugar

See also **Boxing** (From bare knuckles to gloves); **Queensberry, Marquess of.**

Queensland is the second largest state in Australia. It occupies the entire northeastern part of the continent and has 3,236 miles (5,208 kilometers) of seacoast. The Great Barrier Reef is one of the wonders of Queensland. It is a coral ridge that rises out of the sea some distance from the shore. The Great Barrier Reef follows the coastline for about 1,250 miles (2,010 kilometers). See **Great Barrier Reef.**

Location, size, and surface features. Queensland covers 666,900 square miles (1,727,200 square kilometers). For detailed maps, see **Australia.**

The eastern section of the state is rugged and mountainous. The Great Dividing Range runs in a north-south direction through this section. The state's highest peak is 5,287-foot (1,611-meter) Mount Bartle Frere.

Most of Queensland's rivers flow south and west from the Great Dividing Range. Cooper Creek and the Diamantina River flow southwest to Lake Eyre in central

Australia. Rivers flowing east from the mountains have fertile lowlands. Dense forests cover the state's coastal ranges, and mangrove thickets occur along the coast.

Location of Queensland

WORLD BOOK map

Farther south, the War- rego and Condamine rivers flow southward and join the Darling River in New South Wales. Central and western Queensland have vast grazing areas. Artesian wells provide this region with water for livestock (see **Artesian well**).

Natural resources. Forests, including subtropical rain forests, grow on the mountain slopes of southern Queensland. The state is rich in bauxite, coal, copper, natural gas, petroleum, silver, and tin.

Climate. Temperatures in Queensland rarely rise above 95 °F (35 °C). Temperatures average 65 °F (18 °C) in July and 90 °F (32 °C) in January. The rainfall on the east- ern coast is heavy, especially in the north where it aver- ages 160 inches (406 centimeters) a year. In the extreme west, as little as 6 inches (15 centimeters) of rain may fall in a year.

The people. Queensland has a population of 2,978,617, including 48,000 Aborigines. Most of the peo- ple were born in Australia or in the British Isles. About 45 percent of the people live in the capital, Brisbane (see **Brisbane**). Gold Coast is Queensland's second largest city.

Agriculture. Queensland depends on crops and herds for much of its wealth. Sugar cane is the chief crop. Other important crops include barley, oats, wheat, and several kinds of hay. Many kinds of tropical fruits thrive on the coast. Cotton, peanuts, and tobacco are also grown in Queensland. The state raises about a third of Australia's cattle. Sheep raising is also important.

Manufacturing. Queensland's chief industries are brewing, meat packing, sugar refining, and tanning. Ex- ports include wool, fruit, meat, sugar, and minerals.

Education. Primary education is free and compul- sory. Queensland University was set up in Brisbane in 1911. A university was founded at Townsville in 1961. A second university opened in Brisbane in 1972. Various technical and secondary schools receive government support.

Government. A governor appointed by the British Crown on the advice of the Queensland government serves as the chief executive in Queensland. An execu- tive council of 11 ministers assists the governor. The state parliament has most of the governing power in Queensland. The parliament consists of 82 members in a single assembly who serve three-year terms. Queens- land is represented in the federal parliament by 24 rep- resentatives and 10 senators. All adults can vote.

History. The English navigator James Cook explored the coast of Queensland in 1770 and took possession of the region. Cook called it New South Wales. See **Cook, James; New South Wales**.

The first settlement in Queensland was a *penal* (prison) colony, established on Moreton Bay in 1824.

After 1840, free settlers entered the region.

Queensland was a part of New South Wales until 1859, when it became a separate colony. In 1867, the dis- covery of gold brought a rush of immigration. In January 1901, Queensland and the other Australian colonies be- came states when they united to form the Common- wealth of Australia. Robin Peter Simson

Quemoy, *kih MOY,* is the name of a group of islands about 5 miles (8 kilometers) off the coast of China, in the Taiwan Strait. *Quemoy* is also the name of the largest is- land in the group. The Chinese call this island *Jinmen.* For location, see **Taiwan** (map).

The Quemoy islands have a population of about 48,000 and an area of 58 square miles (150 square kilo- meters). The Chinese Nationalist government continued to control the islands after the Chinese Communists conquered mainland China in 1949. The Chinese Com- munists bombarded the islands with artillery fire heavily in 1958 and occasionally during the 1960's. They officially announced a cease-fire in 1979. Parris H. Chang

Querétaro, *kay RAY tah roh,* is a mountainous state in central Mexico (see **Mexico** [political map]). It has a pop- ulation of 1,051,235, and covers 4,420 square miles (11,449 square kilometers). Farm products include wheat, corn, beans, and lentils. Mines there produce opals, silver, gold, lead, and copper. The city of Queré- taro is the capital. The Mexican Constitution was drafted in the city in 1916 and 1917. Querétaro is one of the orig- inal Mexican states. James D. Riley

Quesnay, *keh NAY,* **François,** *frahn SWAH* (1694- 1774), was a French economist who made some of the earliest contributions to the development of economics. He headed a group of economic writers called the *phys- iocrats.* The physiocrats believed that natural laws direct economic activity, and they tried to discover these laws. They devised early forms of economic *models,* charts or sets of formulas showing the relationships between vari- ous parts of a nation's economy.

Quesnay developed the idea that wealth flows contin- uously between producers and consumers. He and his followers considered land the only source of wealth. Only agriculture, they believed, could yield products of greater value than the resources used for production. In a chart called the *Tableau Économique* (1758), Quesnay traced the relationships between different economic classes, such as farmers and merchants. He showed how the wealth created by agricultural production cir- culates throughout the economy.

Quesnay was born in Méré, France, near Paris. Before taking up economics, he studied medicine and served as the personal physician of King Louis XV of France.
Barry W. Poulson

See also **Physiocrats**.

Question mark. See Punctuation.

Quetzal, *keht SAHL,* is a brilliantly colored bird of the trogon family. There are four species of quetzals. They are found in Central and South America. The head, back, and chest of the *resplendent quetzal* of Central America are glittering emerald-green, and the underparts are crimson. The head has a wide crest of golden-green, hairlike feathers. The upper tail feathers are enormously developed and form a train about 3 feet (90 centimeters) long. The brown and buff-colored female has no long tail feathers. As in trogons, the quetzal's feet are small and weak. The bird sits quietly for long periods on a perch in dense forest. The quetzal builds its nest in a hole in a tree.

Ancient Maya chiefs used the long tail feathers of the quetzal as a symbol of authority. One of the legends about this bird says that it loves freedom too much to survive captivity. The quetzal is the national bird of Guatemala.   John W. Fitzpatrick

Scientific classification. The resplendent quetzal belongs to the trogon family, Trogonidae. It is *Pharomacrus mocinno.*

See also **Bird** (picture: Birds of Central and South America).

Quetzalcóatl. See Aztec (Religion); **Mythology** (American Indian mythology; picture); **Orozco, José Clemente** (picture).

Quevedo, *kay VAY doh,* **Francisco de** (1580-1645), was the leading Spanish humanist of the 1600's. He wrote extensively on social, political, religious, and aesthetic problems of Spanish Renaissance life. His works include *Life of the Swindler* (written about 1605 and published in 1626), a cruelly ironic picaresque novel; *Visions* (1627), a satirical prose portrait of Spanish society; and hundreds of poems on moral and sentimental themes.

Quevedo's political ideology, which is expressed in the *Politics of God* (1626) and other works, was modeled on the life and teachings of Christ and contrasted with the harsh realities of Spanish court intrigue. Quevedo's theological and philosophical essays generally reflect an ascetic and stoic point of view.

Quevedo was born in Madrid. His bitter satires caused him much personal trouble. He was jailed from 1639 to 1643 as the supposed author of verses ridiculing corruption in the court of King Philip IV.   Harry Sieber

Quezon City, *KAY sawn* (pop. 1,587,140), is a beautiful city in the Philippines. It lies 10 miles (16 kilometers) northeast of Manila. For the location of Quezon City, see **Philippines** (map). The city is named for Manuel Luis Quezon, first president of the Commonwealth of the Philippines. Stately buildings stand along Quezon City's palm-lined boulevards. Ateneo de Manila University and the campus of the University of the Philippines are in the city.

The Philippine government purchased the land where Quezon City now stands in 1939. The land was part of a private estate and was bought chiefly to serve as a residential area. Many Filipinos moved to the city from Manila after World War II ended in 1945. In 1948, the government officially transferred the capital from Manila to Quezon City. But Manila again became the official capital in 1976. However, Quezon City is part of *Metro Manila,* the Philippine National Capital Region. Several federal government agencies are located in Quezon City.

David J. Steinberg

Quicksand is a deep mass of extremely fine sand. It usually forms on the bottoms of streams and on sand flats along seacoasts. The sand body behaves like a fluid because water flowing through the sand forces individual grains apart and prevents them from settling. In the *quick* condition, the sand loses its firmness and cannot support heavy weight. Thick layers of quicksand are dangerous and may cause the death of trapped people.

People caught in deep quicksand must remain calm. They should fall flat on their back with arms stretched out at right angles to the body. In this position, the body will float on the sand. The person should roll slowly off the sand to firm ground. Building on quicksand requires special foundations.   Ray E. Ferrell, Jr.

Quicksilver. See Mercury [element].

Quill. See Feather; Pen; Porcupine.

Quillwort. See Plant (Lycopsids).

Quilt is a cloth bedcover. A quilt consists of two layers of cloth filled with an *interlining* of a soft, insulating material, such as cotton, down, or wool. The layers are fastened by tiny stitches that run in plain rows or in decorative designs. Many beautifully decorated quilts are considered outstanding examples of folk art.

The top layer of a quilt is often decorated with colorful geometric forms or pictures of animals, buildings, people, and plants. Designs may commemorate historic events or important family occasions. A quilt design can be created in several ways. In a *pieced quilt,* the top layer consists of many different pieces of cloth sewed together in a design. An *appliquéd quilt* has cutout designs sewed onto one large piece of cloth (see **Appliqué**). *Cord quilts* and *trapunto-stuffed quilts* feature a raised design that is made by cotton cording or padding inserted between the top and bottom layers of cloth.

The technique of quilting originated in prehistoric times. Quilting in the United States began during colonial days, when immigrants began practicing the quilting skills they learned in Europe. Quilters frequently made quilts together at social gatherings that were called *bees.*

Colonial quilters mainly made pieced quilts from scraps of linen and wool they saved because cloth was scarce. During the 1800's, a variety of cotton materials became readily available and quilting developed into an art form. During the mid-1800's, *album quilts* became popular. Many album quilts bear verses, quotations, and the quilters' signatures in needlework or ink. These

Baltimore Album Quilt (about 1847-1850); the Baltimore Museum of Art, gift of Dr. William Rush Dunton, Jr., Baltimore

An appliquéd quilt has cutout designs sewed onto a large piece of cloth. This one, made in Maryland, has an embroidered picture of Baltimore's Washington Monument in the third row.

quilts were often presented as gifts to a guest of honor at a quilting bee. *Crazy quilts* were popular in the late 1800's. Most often, they consisted of randomly placed pieces of silk of various sizes, colors, and shapes. Traditional patterns were also used.

Today, quilting styles have been revived by needlework artists who often gather to exchange ideas and practice their craft. Quilters still use traditional patterns and techniques, but with a fresh approach that produces unusual designs.   Dena S. Katzenberg

Quince, *kwihns,* is a type of attractive shrub or small tree that is closely related to apple and pear trees. The *common quince* has many large, pinkish-white flowers and twisted branches. Its fragrant, fuzzy fruit is round to pear-shaped and is golden-yellow. The fruit grows up to 3 inches (7.6 centimeters) in diameter and bears many seeds in its core. Botanists call this type of fruit a *pome.* The fruit of the common quince is hard and has an acid

Eric Crichton, Bruce Coleman Ltd.

The hard, golden-yellow quince puckers the mouth when tasted raw, but it has a delightful flavor when it is cooked.

taste and is almost never eaten fresh. It is used in marmalades and jellies, often in combination with other fruits.

The common quince can be grown from cuttings or by *grafting* (joining) a quince seedling to another plant. Buds from pear trees sometimes are grafted to quince rootstocks to produce dwarf pear trees (see **Pear** [How pears are grown]). The common quince has been cultivated since ancient times and was originally grown in central Asia. It is rarely grown commercially in the United States.

Another type of quince, the Japanese *flowering quince,* is a thorny shrub with showy red blossoms. It bears a very sour fruit that grows up to $1\frac{1}{2}$ inches (3.8 centimeters) in diameter.   John A. Barden

Scientific classification. Quinces belong to the rose family, Rosaceae. The common quince is *Cydonia oblonga.* The flowering quince is *Chaenomeles japonica.*

Quinine, *KWY nyn* or *kwih NEEN,* is a drug made from the bark of the cinchona tree. Quinine was once the only known treatment for malaria. It reduces the fever of malaria, and, especially when used with other drugs, can cure some types of the disease.

Beginning in the mid-1940's, when supplies of quinine became scarce because of World War II, synthetic drugs, such as chloroquine, mefloquine, and primaquine, were developed to treat malaria. These drugs are generally less dangerous to use than quinine. However,

in Southeast Asia and many other regions, types of malaria have developed that are resistant to synthetic drugs. As a result, physicians in those areas are again using quinine. They have found that quinine can help save the lives of people infected with multidrug-resistant forms of the disease.

Quinine is also used to relieve nighttime leg cramps. Many physicians prescribe the drug *quinidine* to treat and correct certain disorders of heart rhythm. Quinidine has the same chemical formula as quinine and differs from quinine only in the way its atoms are arranged. Physicians believe that both drugs, particularly quinine, may cause abnormalities in unborn children. For this reason, pregnant women should not take quinine and quinidine without first consulting a physician.

Cinchona trees first grew along the eastern slopes of the Andes Mountains in South America. In the early 1600's, Spanish explorers and missionaries found that the Indians of the region used the bark of the trees as medicine. The trees began to die out during the mid-1800's, but other cinchona trees were planted in India and Indonesia, especially Java. Most of the quinine used today comes from Indonesia.   Frank Welsch

See also **Alkaloid; Cinchona; Malaria** (Treatment and prevention).

Quinoa, *KEE noh ah* or *KEEN wah,* is a grain plant native to the Andes Mountains of South America. For centuries, quinoa has been one of the chief foods of Andean Indians. It has been called the "mother grain" of the Inca because of its importance to the ancient Inca civilization. Quinoa was introduced into the United States during the 1980's. It is cultivated at high elevations in parts of Colorado, Oregon, and Washington.

The quinoa plant is related to lamb's-quarters, a common weed. The quinoa grows from 3 to 6 feet (0.9 to 1.8 meters) tall. It bears large clusters of seeds at the tips of its stalks. The leaves of the quinoa are shaped like a goose's foot.

Quinoa seeds are cooked and eaten whole like rice. They may be ground into flour and made into breads, tortillas, and pastas. The seeds also may be popped like corn or added raw to soups and hot breakfast cereals. The leaves of the quinoa are cooked and eaten like spinach. They also may be used as feed for livestock. Both the seeds and the leaves of the quinoa are rich in protein and other nutrients. Most quinoa grown and sold in the United States is marketed through health food stores.   Stephen G. Diver

Scientific classification. The quinoa plant belongs to the goosefoot family, Chenopodiaceae. Its scientific name is *Chenopodium quinoa.*

Quinolone, *KWIHN uh lohn,* is any of a group of synthetic drugs used to treat a variety of bacterial infections. Doctors prescribe quinolones to treat urinary tract infections; diarrhea; chronic bronchitis; pneumonia; gonorrhea and certain other sexually transmitted diseases; and bone, joint, and skin infections.

The first quinolone, nalidixic acid, was produced in 1962. It was used to treat urinary tract infections. Since then, researchers have developed quinolones that are effective against a broad range of bacterial infections. These drugs include ciprofloxacin, enoxacin, lomefloxacin, norfloxacin, and olfloxacin. Each has a fluorine atom as part of its chemical structure. As a result, these newer

drugs are sometimes called *fluoroquinolones.* All quinolones can be taken by mouth. Physicians sometimes administer ciprofloxacin and olfloxacin by injecting it di
rectly into a vein.

Quinolones rarely cause severe side effects. Some
people who take the drugs develop minor discomforts,
such as headaches, nausea, or dizziness. Laboratory
tests have not ruled out the possibility that quinolones
may have harmful effects on developing bones and cartilage of young animals. For this reason, physicians usually do not give quinolones to pregnant or nursing
women, or to children.

Quinolones fight bacteria by interfering with production of the bacteria's *DNA (deoxyribonucleic acid).*
Quinolones disrupt the activity of *DNA gyrase,* an enzyme that helps duplicate DNA. If DNA gyrase fails to
function properly, DNA cannot be duplicated, and the
bacteria therefore cannot multiply.   N. E. Sladek

Quintilian, *kwihn TIHL ee uhn* (A.D. 35?-95?), was a
Roman teacher of oratory. He is best known for his 12-
volume *Institutio Oratoria* (often called *The Training of
an Orator),* a manual for the training of public speakers
from infancy to adulthood.

In the manual, Quintilian outlined a program that
combined broad, general education with specialized
training in *rhetoric* (the art of persuasion). He stressed
that an orator must have both technical ability and moral
worth. Quintilian also provided brief judgments regarding the value of many Greek and Latin writers in the
training of young orators. Quintilian's manual influenced
many later literary figures, especially during the Renaissance.

Marcus Fabius Quintilianus was born in Calagurris
(now Calahorra), Spain. He was educated in Rome and
became a great teacher of the art of rhetoric there in the
A.D. 70's and 80's.   Joseph R. Tebben

Quintuplets, *KWIHN too plihts* or *kwihn TUHP lihts,*
are five babies born to the same mother at one time. The
first set of quintuplets known to have lived more than a
few hours after birth were five girls born to Elzire and
Oliva Dionne on May 28, 1934. The Dionne quintuplets
were born in Canada, near Callander, Ontario. The Fischer quintuplets were the first set of quintuplets born in
the United States to survive early infancy. The four girls
and a boy were born to Andrew James and Mary Ann
Fischer on Sept. 14, 1963, in Aberdeen, South Dakota.
      Lois Kazmier Halstead

See also **Multiple birth.**

Quipu. See **Inca** (Communication and learning).

Quirinal Hill, *KWIHR uh nuhl,* is the northernmost of
the famous seven hills of Rome. It was named for the
god Quirinus. Evidence of the ancient settlement of the
Sabines has been found on this hill. There were many famous temples on the hill, including the oldest shrine of
the god Jupiter. Julius Caesar had large gardens on the
edge of the hill, and the emperor Constantine built a famous public bath there. In the A.D. 1500's, a large palace
and garden were built on the hill for the Roman Catholic
popes. These were later used by the kings of Italy. The
palace now serves as the official residence and offices
of the president of the Italian Republic. See also
Sabines.   David I. Kertzer

Quirinus. See **Mythology** (Roman divinities).

Quisling, *KWIHZ lihng,* **Vidkun Abraham Lauritz**

(1887-1945), was a Norwegian traitor of World War II
(1939-1945). The word *quisling* came to stand for *traitor*
because of his aid to German occupation forces. At the
end of the war, he was convicted on charges of treason
and executed.

Quisling was born in Telemark. He joined the army
and rose to the rank of captain. In 1931, Quisling formed
his own political party, the National Union. He contacted
German Nazi leaders and conferred with Adolf Hitler in
1940. Shortly afterward, the Germans attacked Norway.
Quisling served briefly as head of the puppet Norwegian government.   Raymond E. Lindgren

Quito, *KEE toh* (pop. 1,281,849), is the capital and second largest city of the Republic of Ecuador. Only Guaya-
quil has more people. Quito is Ecuador's principal textile
center. The city lies almost on the equator, 9,350 feet
(2,850 meters) above sea level in the Andes Mountains.
For location, see **Ecuador** (map).

The name *Quito* comes from the word *Quitus,* the
name of an ancient people who lived in Ecuador long
before the Spanish conquerors arrived in 1534. The

Shostal

Quito lies high in the Andes Mountains. The city's skyline is a
blend of old tile-roofed buildings and modern skyscrapers.

Spaniards ruled Quito until 1822, when General Antonio
José de Sucre defeated them in the Battle of Pichincha
on a mountain slope overlooking the city. The victory
helped Ecuador become an independent republic.

Under Spanish rule, Quito was a great center of religious art. Today, many of the city's old churches and
monasteries have paintings and sculptures from the period.   Murdo J. MacLeod

See also **Ecuador** (picture).

Quixote, Don. See **Don Quixote.**

Quoits, *kwoyts,* is a game in which players toss a metal
ring, called a *quoit,* at a peg, called a *mott.* The mott is
level with the ground. A white target about 4 inches (10
centimeters) in diameter surrounds the mott so players
can see where it is located. Rules vary, but in championship competition players toss quoits at two motts 54 feet
(16 meters) apart. Each player stands behind one mott
and alternately throws two quoits at the other mott. A
quoit closer to the mott than an opponent's quoit counts
one point. Most games end when a side has 21 points. If

the score is tied at 20-20, play continues until one side leads by 2 points.

Quoits vary in size and weight. Those used in championship tournaments weigh $3\frac{1}{2}$ pounds (1.6 kilograms) and measure 6 inches (15 centimeters) in diameter with a hole $2\frac{3}{4}$ inches (7 centimeters) in diameter. Informal games of quoits often follow the rules of horseshoe pitching.   W. Scott Johns III

Quoll is a small, spotted mammal that lives in the forests of New Guinea and Australia, including Tasmania. Quolls are *marsupials*—that is, the females give birth to extremely immature young that complete their development attached to the mother's nipples. There are six species of quolls.

Quolls have brown or black fur with white spots. The *tiger quoll,* the largest meat-eating marsupial on the

WORLD BOOK illustration by Colin Newman, Bernard Thornton Artists

The eastern quoll lives in forests in the southeastern part of mainland Australia and on the island of Tasmania.

Australian continent, grows up to 4 feet (1.2 meters) long, including the tail. The animal may weigh more than 13 pounds (6 kilograms). Quolls eat chiefly insects but also feed on birds, mice, and small lizards.

The female quoll normally has five to eight young, which attach themselves firmly to nipples within a pouch on her belly. The young leave the mother's pouch after about three or four months. However, they may cling to the mother's fur for a few more weeks.

Michael L. Augee

Scientific classification. Quolls make up the genus *Dasyurus* in the family Dasyuridae.

Quonset hut, *KWAHN siht,* is a corrugated steel building made in the shape of a half cylinder. The flat side forms the floor. The building usually measures about 50 to 100 feet (15 to 30 meters) long and from 20 to 40 feet (6 to 12 meters) high. The first Quonset hut was constructed for the United States Navy in 1941 at Quonset Point, Rhode Island.   Jack M. Landers

Quorum. See **Parliamentary procedure** (Holding meetings).

Quota International is a service organization of executives and professionals who work to help people with hearing and speech disabilities. Its motto, "We Share," is from the Latin word *quota,* meaning *a share.* The organization was founded in Buffalo, New York, in 1919. It has about 12,000 members in about 460 clubs in the United States, Canada, Australia, New Zealand, the Philippines, Singapore, India, Sri Lanka, Aruba, Curaçao, and China. Headquarters are in Washington, D.C.

Critically reviewed by Quota International

Quota system. See **Immigration** (Immigration to the United States).

Quran, *ku RAHN* or *ku RAN,* is the sacred book of the Muslims. It is also spelled Koran. The name *Quran* means *a recitation* or *something to be recited,* presumably in worship.

Muslims believe the angel Gabriel revealed the Quran to the Prophet Muhammad a little at a time. The revelations began about A.D. 610 and continued until Muhammad's death in 632. Muhammad's followers, who wrote down the revelations, collected them into the book that is now known as the Quran. The standard text of the Quran was formed during the reign of Caliph Uthman, who ruled from 644 to 656. Muslims consider the Quran to be the words of God Himself, and in no sense the composition of Muhammad. They believe that the earthly book, bound between covers, is a copy of an eternal book that is kept in heaven.

The Quran consists of verses grouped into 114 chapters. The chapters vary in length from a few lines to over 200 verses. Much of the Quran is written in rhymed Arabic prose. Muslims believe that the rich, forceful language of the text is humanly unmatchable, and a miracle that confirms Muhammad's prophethood.

Teachings. The central teaching of the Quran is that there is only one God. The word for God in Arabic is *Allah.* Allah is the creator of the universe and requires *Islam* (submission) to Himself. Allah, in His mercy, sent the Quran as a guide for humanity. Another important teaching concerns the prophets who have been God's messengers to different peoples. The Quran mentions the prophets Abraham, Moses, Jesus, and many others. It describes Muhammad as the last of the prophets.

The Quran speaks of a day of judgment when people shall stand before God to account for their lives. It contains many teachings to regulate Muslim daily life. It requires daily prayers, and stresses charity and brotherly love among Muslims. The Quran teaches that one should be humble, temperate, brave, and just.

Influence. The Quran is one of the most widely read books in the world. Its teachings formed the basis of the great Islamic civilization of the past, and it guides and inspires millions of Muslims. The Quran is the final authority in matters of faith and practice for all Muslims. It is the highest authority for Islamic law.

The Quran has been taught orally and is memorized, at least in part, by virtually all Muslims. Thus, even illiterate Muslims possess and prize the text. The reverence for the holy book is so great that many Muslims learn the entire work by heart. The art of properly reciting the Quran has been preserved and passed on through the centuries, and has been enhanced by the modern technology of audio cassette recording.

For hundreds of years, Muslims refused to translate the Quran into other languages. They thought they should preserve the words of God in their original form. But in the early 1900's, Muslims began to translate the Quran into Eastern and Western languages.

Richard C. Martin

See also **Islam; Muhammad.**

Additional resources

Cleary, Thomas. *The Essential Koran.* Harper, 1993.
Irving, Thomas B., and others. *The Qur'an: Basic Teachings.* New Era Pubns., 1979.
Rahman, Fazlur. *Major Themes of the Qur'an.* Bibliotheca Islamica, 1980.

Rr

R is the 18th letter of our alphabet. It was also a letter in the alphabet used by the Semites who once lived in Syria and Palestine. They named it *resh,* their word for *head,* and adapted an Egyptian *hieroglyphic* (picture symbol) for a human head to represent it. The Greeks later called the letter *rho.* When the Romans adopted it, they gave it its present capital R form. See **Alphabet.**

Uses. *R* or *r* is about the sixth most frequently used letter in books, newspapers, and other printed material in English. *R* is used to stand for *Respond* or *Response* in prayer books and liturgies. *R* indicates *radius* or *ratio* in mathematics; *radical* in chemistry; and *resistance* in electricity. In titles, *R* may mean *royal* as in *RN,* for *Royal Navy,* or *registered* as in *R.N.* for *Registered Nurse. R*

may mean *regular* as in *R.A.* for *Regular Army,* or *reserve* as in *USNR* for *U.S. Naval Reserve.* In some countries, *r* is the abbreviation for a unit of money, for *ruble* in Russia and for *rupee* in India. It is an abbreviation for *rook* in chess.

Pronunciation. When speaking English, a person pronounces *r* by placing the sides of the tongue against the molars, with the point of the tongue toward the hard palate. The person contracts the tongue to form the *r* and the vowel that follows it. The velum, or soft palate, is closed, and the vocal cords vibrate. In some dialects, the *r* is trilled. In some English dialects, *r* is not pronounced in such words as *farm* or *here.* See **Pronunciation.**   Marianne Cooley

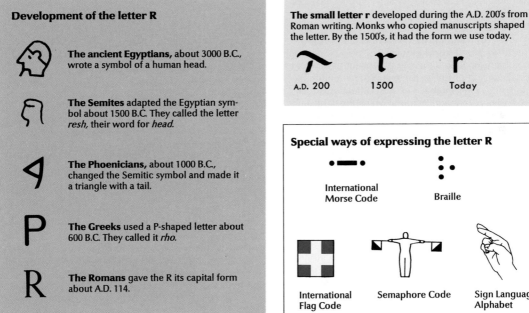

Development of the letter R

The ancient Egyptians, about 3000 B.C., wrote a symbol of a human head.

The Semites adapted the Egyptian symbol about 1500 B.C. They called the letter *resh,* their word for *head.*

The Phoenicians, about 1000 B.C., changed the Semitic symbol and made it a triangle with a tail.

The Greeks used a P-shaped letter about 600 B.C. They called it *rho.*

The Romans gave the R its capital form about A.D. 114.

The small letter r developed during the A.D. 200's from Roman writing. Monks who copied manuscripts shaped the letter. By the 1500's, it had the form we use today.

A.D. 200   1500   Today

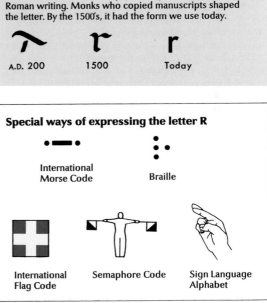

Special ways of expressing the letter R

International Morse Code

Braille

International Flag Code

Semaphore Code

Sign Language Alphabet

Common forms of the letter R

Handwritten letters vary from person to person. *Manuscript* (printed) letters, *left,* have simple curves and straight lines. Cursive letters, *right,* have flowing lines.

Roman letters have small finishing strokes called *serifs* that extend from the main strokes. The type face shown above is Baskerville. The italic form appears at the right.

Sans-serif letters are also called *gothic letters.* They have no serifs. The type face shown above is called Futura. The italic form of Futura appears at the right.

Computer letters have special shapes. Computers can "read" these letters either optically or by means of the magnetic ink with which the letters may be printed.

℞ is a symbol used on prescriptions written by doctors. It is generally accepted as representing the Latin word *recipe,* which means *take.* ℞ is traceable to ♃, the sign of Jupiter, which was placed on ancient prescriptions to appeal to that god for favorable action of the medicine. A more recent explanation of the cross at the end of the letter *R* is that it represents a period.   Edward J. Shahady

Ra. See Re.

Rabat, *rah BAHT* (pop. 623,457), is the capital of Morocco. Rabat is in the northern part of the country. It is located on the Atlantic coast at the mouth of the Bou Regreg, a shallow river (see **Morocco** [map]). The Bou Regreg separates Rabat from the city of Salé.

Rabat is divided into old and new sections. The old section, called the *medina,* is in the northern part of the city. It has small, white, flat-roofed houses and several *mosques* (Muslim houses of worship). The new section spreads out around the medina. It has broad streets and modern European-style buildings. The royal palace is located in this part of Rabat. The two sections of the city are connected by Avenue Muhammad V, the main business street. Hassan Tower, the *minaret* (prayer tower) of an incomplete mosque, stands on a bluff overlooking the Bou Regreg. Nearby is the tomb of Muhammad V, the first ruler of independent Morocco.

Rabat is chiefly a government and administrative center. It has textile and cork-processing industries. It also produces asbestos products, bricks, cement, and flour. Craftworkers in the city make baskets, carpets, leather goods, tapestries, and other handicrafts.

Muhammad V University was founded in Rabat in 1957. Rabat's Archaeological Museum exhibits objects from prehistoric and Roman times.

The Romans occupied the site of present-day Rabat in the first century after Christ. Ruins of Roman buildings stand in southeastern Rabat. The Berber leader Abd-al-Mumin and his grandson Yakub-al-Mansur established the present city in the 1100's. In 1912, France established a protectorate over most of Morocco. The French made Rabat their headquarters. When the protectorate ended in 1956, Rabat became the capital of the independent nation of Morocco.   Kenneth J. Perkins

See also **Morocco** (picture).

Rabbi, *RAB eye,* is the title given to an ordained Jewish minister. The word is Hebrew and means *my master* or *my teacher.* The title of rabbi was popularized in the Mishnah, an important book of Jewish law compiled about A.D. 200.

Many influential leaders of medieval Jewish communities were rabbis. They wrote books and helped people with their religious and worldly concerns, and they frequently represented Jewish communities to non-Jewish groups. They often judged civil and religious legal cases. Some of the most famous rabbis were also doctors.

Today, the role of the rabbi has changed. The main responsibilities of rabbis are to preach, counsel, officiate at religious services, teach, and conduct important personal and community celebrations. Some also serve as authorities on Jewish law.

Despite the importance of ordination to become a rabbi, no uniform course of study is required for all rabbis. Students may attend seminaries or special schools called *yeshivas.* Seminaries teach a variety of subjects, including the Bible and Talmud, and Jewish philosophy,

history, and literature. Yeshivas concentrate mainly on teaching the Talmud. The major American schools also train future rabbis in teaching, preaching, and caring for the needs of their congregations. Individual rabbis may train and certify their students as rabbis.   B. Barry Levy

See also **Judaism** (The rabbi).

Rabbit is a furry animal with long ears and a short, fluffy tail. Wild rabbits live throughout the world in all climates. Tame varieties of rabbits make excellent pets.

Rabbits are closely related to hares. Rabbits and hares look similar and are often mistaken for one another. Some rabbits and hares are misnamed. For example, the *Belgian hare* is a rabbit, and the *jack rabbit* is a hare. Rabbits and hares can be told apart most easily at birth. Newborn rabbits have no fur and are blind and helpless. Newborn hares have fur and their eyes are open. Also, mother rabbits shelter their young in a soft, fur-lined nest. Mother hares do not make nests for their young.

Kinds of rabbits

Biologists classify rabbits into 10 groups called *genera* and into many *species* within the genera. Numerous species, such as the *volcano rabbit* of Mexico, have become rare. The most widespread rabbits are *cottontails* and *European rabbits.* Domestic rabbits are tame varieties of European rabbits.

Cottontails are wild rabbits of North America and parts of Central and South America. Most species have fluffy white fur on the underside of the tail. Perhaps the most common species is the eastern cottontail. Cottontails inhabit fields, prairies, marshes, and swamps— wherever they can find bushes or clumps of tall grass in which to hide. They may also live in wooded areas bordering open country.

European rabbits originally lived in southern Europe and northern Africa, and on some western Mediterranean islands. From these places they spread throughout Europe. People brought European rabbits to many other parts of the world, including Australia, New Zealand, and South America. Rabbits have often become pests in these regions. The animals reproduce quickly in areas where they have few natural enemies, and they can present a threat to plant life.

Domestic rabbits are raised for their meat and fur, for use in scientific research, and as pets. People around the world eat rabbit meat, which is tasty and nutritious. Rabbit breeds raised commercially for meat include the Californian and New Zealand. Many people raise other breeds for meat in small backyard "rabbitries."

Artificial furs have largely replaced rabbit fur in clothing. However, people still raise the Angora rabbit for its long fur, which is spun into a soft, warm yarn. Rabbit fur is also used in making stuffed toys.

The use of rabbits in research laboratories requires great numbers of highly similar animals, which only large commercial breeders can provide. The Californian, Florida White, and New Zealand White are breeds frequently used in laboratories.

Many of the more than 40 rabbit breeds are raised for show or as pets. Popular show breeds include the Californian, Dutch, Holland lop, Mini Rex, Netherland Dwarf, and Satin. Judges rate rabbits on such features as size and shape, and the quality and color of the fur. Favorite pet breeds include the Netherland Dwarf, Dutch,

A young cottontail sits motionless to escape hunters, but hops away quickly if they come near.

A Lop rabbit has floppy ears that may be more than 2 feet (0.6 meter) long. The Lop is a favorite pet breed.

Holland Lop, and Mini Lop. The ears of the English Lop may grow more than 2 feet (60 centimeters) long.

The body of a rabbit

Wild rabbits have brownish fur that mixes white, light brown, gray, dark reddish-brown, and black hairs. Domestic rabbits may be black, brown, gray, white, or even spotted in various combinations of these colors.

An adult cottontail rabbit grows about $21\frac{1}{2}$ inches (55 centimeters) long and can weigh up to 6 pounds (2.7 kilograms). European rabbits may be somewhat smaller. Domestic rabbits can grow larger than wild rabbits. The White Flemish Giant, the largest breed of rabbit, weighs up to 17 pounds (8 kilograms). The smallest species of rabbit, the volcano rabbit, measures only about 12 inches (30 centimeters). Female rabbits, called *does,* tend to grow larger than males, called *bucks.* In most species, the tail of a rabbit measures about $\frac{3}{5}$ to $2\frac{3}{4}$ inches (1.5 to 7 centimeters) long and is covered with soft, fluffy fur.

Rabbits generally move in a hopping motion using their long, powerful hind legs. This motion enables them to travel quickly. A rabbit's hind legs have long toes hidden beneath a thick cushion of fur. The toes are webbed to keep them from spreading when the rabbit jumps.

A rabbit's eyes are on the side of its head, toward the back. As a result, the animal can see better to the side than forward. A rabbit's keen sense of smell helps alert it to danger. But rabbits rely mostly on their hearing. They may move their long, sensitive ears together or one at a time to catch sounds from any direction. The ears also keep the rabbit cool in hot weather by giving off heat.

Rabbits' teeth grow continually throughout their lives. Their chisellike front teeth, the *upper incisors* and *lower incisors,* resemble those of rodents. Unlike rodents, rabbits have two pairs of upper incisors. One pair is directly behind the other. Rabbits use the incisors to gnaw and clip off plants. They then chew their food with sideways movements of the lower jaw, which grinds the food and helps wear down the ever-growing teeth.

The life of a rabbit

Rabbits have many natural enemies and can protect themselves mainly by hiding or running from danger.

An angora rabbit is raised for its fur. The long white hairs are plucked from the animal's coat and spun into soft yarn.

Belgian hares are raised for show. The Belgian hare is not really a hare but is a breed of European rabbit.

The skeleton of a rabbit

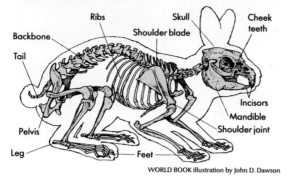

WORLD BOOK illustration by John D. Dawson

Although pet rabbits may live as long as 10 to 15 years, wild rabbits rarely survive beyond 6 years of age.

Homes. Cottontail rabbits spend most of the daylight hours resting in shallow depressions in the ground called *forms.* In cold weather underneath deep snow, a cottontail may take over another wild animal's abandoned burrow and make a network of connected paths called *runs.* Cottontails live mostly solitary lives, but they share territory with others and come together for mating. The *pygmy rabbit* constructs its own burrow.

European rabbits live in large colonies and will warn one another about danger by making loud thumps with their hind feet before running off. They share vast underground burrows called *warrens.* Warrens may be dug up to 10 feet (3 meters) underground and have several entrances and exits. They consist of interconnecting tunnels, living chambers, and nesting chambers where females give birth to and nurse their babies.

Food. Most rabbits eat and play from dusk to dawn, and spend the day resting and sleeping. In spring and summer, rabbits eat green leafy plants, including clover, grass, and herbs. In winter, they eat the twigs, bark, and fruit of bushes and trees. Rabbits sometimes damage crops because they nibble the tender sprouts of beans, lettuce, and other vegetables.

The plant foods that rabbits eat are hard to digest. To get the most nutrients from these foods, rabbits pass the plant matter through their digestive system more than once. Rabbits produce two kinds of solid wastes: moist pellets, which they swallow again and redigest, and solid pellets, which are true wastes.

Young. Because wild rabbits often die before reaching maturity, they must produce many young to survive. A female rabbit usually has four to five young at a time, and she may give birth several times a year. Female cottontails may bear about four litters of young per year.

A female cottontail rabbit carries her young, called *kits,* inside her body for 26 to 30 days before giving birth The mother keeps the newborns in a nest she has dug in the ground. She lines the nest with fur pulled from her chest with her teeth. The mother stays near the nest and covers the kits with grass and fur to keep them warm. Kits develop a coat of soft fur around 10 days after birth.

About two weeks after birth, the kits leave the nest and hide in long grass and leaves. The mother nurses her young for only a few weeks. Some females start their own families when less than 6 months old.

Enemies. People rank as the greatest enemies of rabbits. Every year, hunters kill millions of rabbits for sport and for food. Farmers kill rabbits to protect crops. Human beings also kill rabbits by destroying the animals' natural habitats. Other rabbit enemies include coyotes, foxes, weasels, snakes, hawks, and owls.

Rabbits usually try to hide from enemies. If a rabbit is in the open, it may sit still, unnoticed, and wait for the foe to go away. If the enemy comes too close, the rabbit flees. A frightened rabbit can leap 10 feet (3 meters) or more and can travel as fast as 25 miles (40 kilometers) an hour. But it tires quickly. It tries to confuse its enemy by zigzagging. It sometimes circles back and follows its own trail for a while, and then leaps off in another direction. It may dive into a burrow or into brush to escape.

Wild rabbits often die from the disease *tularemia,* also known as *rabbit fever.* Tularemia can spread to people who handle sick rabbits (see **Tularemia**).

Pet rabbits

Many people keep domesticated rabbits as pets. All rabbits initially avoid human contact. Rabbit owners must use frequent, gentle handling to teach their pets not to fear people. Owners also need to provide proper cages, food, and medical care for these animals.

Handling. Never pick up a rabbit by the ears. Lifting it that way can cause pain and injury to the rabbit. Instead, grasp the animal by the scruff of the neck with one hand and support its rear quarters with the other hand. You can also hold a rabbit against your body by using the crook of the supporting arm's elbow to cover the animal's head. Use both hands to restrain its rump and rear legs. Rabbits scratch or sometimes bite people who have not restrained them properly. They can also break their own backs or legs if allowed to struggle too much.

Cage. You can buy a *hutch* (rabbit cage) at a pet store, or you can build one. Rabbits may be housed outdoors or indoors as long as they have good ventilation. Elevate outdoor hutches to prevent predators from reaching the rabbits and to help keep the rabbits healthy. Outdoor hutches must also protect rabbits from rain, wind, direct sunlight, extreme cold and heat, and wild animals.

When constructing a hutch, use cleanable materials that are strong enough to withstand a rabbit's chewing. Such materials include wire mesh, sheet metal for roofing, and hardwood framing. Make the hutch large enough for the rabbit to move freely. Provide food and water bowls that the animal cannot tip over and cannot chew. Rabbits can also learn to drink water from *siphons* (sucking tubes). Rabbits should have safe, indestructible toys and chew sticks to prevent boredom. Remove uneaten food and waste from the hutch each day and clean the hutch thoroughly at least three times a week. Rabbits kept indoors can learn to use a litter box.

Male rabbits may fight with one another and even kill baby rabbits. Owners should house them individually.

Food. Rabbits have sensitive digestive systems. They do best when their diets consist mainly of high-quality commercial rabbit pellets. Supplement the main diet with hay or straw to provide fiber. Fiber helps prevent hairballs and other serious intestinal problems. Owners can also feed rabbits small amounts of bread, tender tree growths, and such fruits and vegetables as apples, cabbage, cauliflower, leaf lettuce, spinach, and turnips.

Do not give your rabbit all the day's food at once. Two meals each day help prevent boredom. Provide water and a *mineral block* at all times. Mineral blocks, also called *salt licks,* are blocks of salt injected with other minerals that the animal needs.

Health. Owners must brush pet rabbits at least once a week, especially when the animals *molt* (shed their hair). Molting occurs about once a year. Long-haired breeds, such as the Angora, must be brushed every day. Excess hair licked off by the rabbit can cause a hairball to form in the stomach. During brushing, examine the rabbit for ear mites, fur mites, and fleas. Consult a veterinarian if you find such parasites.

Trim your rabbit's toenails if they do not wear down naturally. The animal also may need its teeth trimmed by a veterinarian if the teeth have grown irregularly. Signs of bad teeth include drooling and lack of appetite.

Rabbits not used for breeding should undergo *neutering* (removal of some of the sex organs) between 4 and 6 months of age. Female neutering, called *spaying,* removes the ovaries and uterus and prevents uterine cancer, a common cause of death among does. Male neutering, called *castration,* can make bucks less aggressive.

Owners should not ignore any signs of illness in rabbits because the animals often die quickly from disease. Signs of disease include diarrhea, runny eyes, sneezing, and loss of appetite. 　　Terri McGinnis

Scientific classification. Rabbits are in the rabbit and hare family, Leporidae. Cottontails make up the genus *Sylvilagus.* The eastern cottontail is *S. floridanus.* European and domestic rabbits are genus *Oryctolagus.* The volcano rabbit makes up the genus *Romerolagus.* The pygmy rabbit is *Brachylagus idahoensis.*

See also **Hare; Jack rabbit.**

Rabbit fever. See **Tularemia.**

Rabelais, *RAB uh* LAY or *ra BLEH,* **François,** *frahn SWA* (1494?-1553?), a French humanist, wrote the comic narrative *Gargantua and Pantagruel.* Gargantua and his son Pantagruel are giants with enormous appetites. In the work, Rabelais used laughter to question and examine the most important institutions of his time. For example, the comic descriptions of Gargantua's education really satirize the educational methods of the time and express Rabelais's own ideas on the subject. Although famous for the earthy quality of his humor, Rabelais wrote earnestly about many subjects.

Rabelais was born near Chinon in the province of Touraine. He became a Franciscan friar in 1520. He practiced and lectured on medicine from 1532 to 1546.

In 1532, Rabelais published *Pantagruel,* a continuation of an anonymous popular work, *Chronicles of the Giant Gargantua* (1532). While preserving its popular tone, Rabelais added much learned material and showed extraordinary gifts as a satirist and storyteller. *Pantagruel* was condemned for obscenity by the Sorbonne, the theological college of the University of Paris. In 1534, Rabelais published *Gargantua,* his own version of the episodes preceding *Pantagruel.* This book, which introduces the mischievous monk Frère Jean, was also condemned by the Sorbonne.

In 1546, Rabelais published Book Three, which the Sorbonne condemned for heresy. He published Book Four in two parts, in 1548 and 1552. He may have written only parts of Book Five, which appeared in 1562 and 1564, after his death.

With his linguistic creativity, Rabelais invented many words, some of which remain in the French language. His verve, his optimism, his delightful storytelling, and his ability to become involved in both fun and ideas have made him one of the greatest and most loved French writers. 　　Mary B. McKinley

See also **French literature** (The Renaissance); **Humanism.**

Rabies, *RAY beez,* is an infectious disease that destroys the nerve cells of part of the brain and almost always causes death. Human beings and most other mammals can get the disease. The word *rabies* is Latin for *rage* or *fury.* The disease probably received its name because infected animals often become excited and attack any object or animal in their way. Because one of the symptoms of rabies is an inability by the infected animal to swallow water, the disease is sometimes called *hydrophobia,* which means *fear of water.*

Cause. Rabies is caused by a virus known as a *rhabdovirus.* Most mammals can carry this virus, which usually lives in the nerve cells and glands of the *host* (carrier). The rabies virus can be carried in the salivary glands for long periods of time. If the host bites another animal or a human being, or if some of its infected saliva enters an open wound, the victim may get rabies. Dogs, cats, and wild animals are common sources of infection for people. Research indicates that rabies virus can also enter mucous membranes, such as those lining the nose and eyes. People and other mammals can develop rabies after breathing the air in caves that house large numbers of bats, which may carry the virus.

When rabies virus enters the body, it travels along nerves to the spinal cord and up to the brain, producing inflammation. Symptoms of the disease generally develop about 10 days to 7 months after exposure.

Symptoms in human beings. Among the first symptoms are pain, burning, or numbness at the site of the infection. The victim complains of headaches and is extremely restless. Muscle spasms make the throat feel full, and swallowing becomes difficult. Later, the patient may have convulsions. After a day or two, a quiet period can occur, which can progress to unconsciousness and, finally, death. Symptoms generally last from 2 to 12 days.

Symptoms in animals. The development of rabies in animals follows the same pattern as in people. During the period of excitation, the animal may wander great distances. It vocalizes almost constantly, often becomes aggressive, and will attack without reason. The disease then usually progresses to paralysis of the jaw and throat muscles, followed by general paralysis and death. Some animals with rabies never show signs of excitation but only of paralysis. This form of the disease is sometimes called *dumb rabies.* Some animals that recover from rabies continue to carry and spread the virus.

Treatment. The first step in treating a person bitten by any animal should be to wash the wound with soap and water. The animal should either be caged and watched for signs of rabies, or killed and its brain tissue tested for rabies virus. If either procedure indicates the presence of rabies, a doctor should begin preventive treatment at once. If the animal cannot be found, the doctor may follow such treatment as a safety measure.

Standard preventive treatment in the United States consists of one injection of antirabies globulin followed by five injections of rabies vaccine. Vaccinating all dogs and cats against rabies is an important means of controlling the disease.   Lawrence D. McGill

See also **Pasteur, Louis.**

Rabin, *rah BEEN,* **Yitzhak,** *YIHTS hahk* (1922-1995), was prime minister of Israel from 1974 to 1977 and from 1992 until his death. On Nov. 4, 1995, he was assassinated in Tel Aviv, Israel. A right-wing Israeli university student who opposed Rabin's policies confessed to the murder.

Yitzhak Rabin
© Johnson, Gamma/Liaison

Rabin was born in Jerusalem and was the nation's first prime minister born in Israel. Israel's previous prime ministers were born in Europe. In 1941, during World War II, Rabin joined the *Palmach,* a unit of the Jewish underground army in Palestine. He was deputy commander of the Palmach in 1948 during the first Arab-Israeli war. Rabin headed Israel's defense forces from 1964 to 1967. He planned the strategy in a 1967 war in which the Israelis defeated the Arabs and occupied the Arab lands of the Gaza Strip and West Bank.

From 1968 to 1973, Rabin was ambassador to the United States. A Labor Party member, he was elected to Israel's parliament in 1973. He became Labor Party head and prime minister in 1974, and held those posts until 1977. He was minister of defense from 1984 to 1990.

Rabin again became Labor Party head in February 1992. Elections in June brought the party to power, and Rabin became prime minister again. He appointed himself minister of defense. In 1993, Rabin's government and the Palestine Liberation Organization (PLO) signed an agreement that included the start of a plan for self-government for, and Israel's withdrawal from, the Gaza Strip and West Bank. Israel and the PLO also agreed to try to work out their conflicts. Rabin, Israeli foreign minister Shimon Peres, and PLO leader Yasir Arafat shared the 1994 Nobel Peace Prize for their peace efforts. Also in 1994, talks between Rabin and King Hussein I of Jordan led to a peace treaty ending a state of war that had technically existed between their countries since 1948.
    Bernard Reich

See also **Israel** (Recent developments).

Rabinowitz, Solomon. See Sholom Aleichem.

Raccoon is a furry animal that has a bushy, ringed tail and a band of black hair around its eyes. This black hair looks like a mask. Raccoons, which are often called *coons,* belong to the same family as coatis, kinkajous, and ringtails. Raccoons live in North America and South America. There are two main species, the northern raccoon and the crab-eating raccoon. The northern raccoon lives in Canada, the United States, and Central America. The crab-eating raccoon lives in Costa Rica, Panama, and South America. Several kinds of raccoons live on tropical islands.

The body of a raccoon. The northern raccoon measures from 24 to 42 inches (61 to 107 centimeters) long, including its tail. Most raccoons weigh from 8 to 20 pounds (3.6 to 9 kilograms), though some males may weigh more than 40 pounds (18 kilograms). Male raccoons are usually larger than females.

A raccoon has coarse, long hair that is generally gray in color, but sometimes tinged with yellow or brown. Northern raccoons and crab-eating raccoons both have pale brown or gray underfur. But a crab-eating raccoon has shorter hair and thinner underfur.

The tail of both the northern and the crab-eating raccoon may grow as long as 15 inches (38 centimeters). Most raccoon tails have from five to seven rings. Both main species have a pointed snout and long, flexible fingers. Raccoons have strong, sharp claws, which help them climb. They can handle objects almost as skillfully as monkeys can.

The life of a raccoon. Raccoons live both on the ground and in trees. They live alone or in small family groups. Each raccoon has a *home range.* Most raccoons in good *habitats* (living areas) have home ranges of about 100 to 250 acres (40 to 100 hectares). Adult males may roam up to 10 miles (16 kilometers). Within its home range, the raccoon mates, locates its home, and

A raccoon has a "mask" of black hair around its eyes. This furry mammal eats fish and frogs that it catches in rivers and streams.

The feet of a raccoon

Hind foot   Front foot

Raccoon tracks

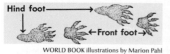

Hind foot ——→
↓   ←Front foot→

WORLD BOOK illustrations by Marion Pahl

Hans Reinhard, Bruce Coleman Ltd.

searches for food. Raccoons usually hunt for food at night and stay in their dens during the day. They walk like bears, with all four feet flat on the ground, and are good swimmers.

Raccoons in captivity may live 15 years or more because they have a constant food supply and are not attacked by enemies. But most raccoons in their natural habitats probably live fewer than 5 years.

Raccoons that live in wooded areas have their den in a hollow log, stump, or tree. They also make their home in an abandoned barn or farmhouse. In marshy, treeless areas, raccoons make their nest in high grass, or they may take over an abandoned muskrat house.

Both northern and crab-eating raccoons eat crabs. Their other food includes crayfish, frogs, fish, and other freshwater animals. Raccoons also eat acorns, birds' eggs, corn, fruit, nuts, seeds, and small land animals, such as grasshoppers and mice.

Many people think raccoons "wash" their food because they frequently dunk food in water before eating it. But experiments show that the animals dunk food that is already clean or wet as often as they dunk dirty or dry food. This habit of dunking food in water seems much more common among raccoons in captivity than in their natural environment. Some scientists say captive raccoons are simply imitating the way they would pull fish or other animals from rivers and streams. For these reasons, scientists do not believe that the animals actually wash their food.

Raccoons in the southern United States and South America remain active the year around. In colder areas of the northern United States and Canada, raccoons sleep for long periods during the winter, but they do not hibernate. During true hibernation, an animal's heart rate and temperature decrease greatly. On mild winter days, a raccoon may wake up and leave its den to search for food. Raccoons in such colder areas prepare for winter by eating extra food during the fall. They store up a layer of fat under their skin, and this fat keeps them alive during the long winter sleep.

Northern raccoons mate once a year between January and June. About nine weeks after mating, the female has from one to eight babies. Most females have three or four young a year. Newborn raccoons have no mask around their eyes or rings on their tail. Their eyes do not open until about 20 days after birth. The mother raccoon protects her young and does not even let the father near them. The babies stay in the den from 8 to 10 weeks. Then they follow their mother when she searches for food. The mother teaches her young to feed and protect themselves. They may stay with her until the beginning of winter, when they find their own dens.

People and raccoons. The American Indians hunted raccoons for their furs. After the arrival of Dutch, English, and French fur traders, the Indians exchanged pelts for guns and other items. The American colonists made the pelts into caps, overcoats, and sleigh robes. They also used the furs as money before paper currency was established. The settlers traded pelts for such items as flour and sugar. During the 1830's and 1840's, the Whig Party in the United States used the raccoon as its emblem.

In the 1920's, long-haired raccoon furs—especially overcoats—again became popular in the United States.

Today, fashion designers sometimes make coats out of raccoon furs that have had the long hairs plucked out. The pale-brown underfur remaining is called *sheared raccoon.*

Raccoon hunts are a favorite sport in some rural areas of North America. People use dogs to chase the animals until the raccoons jump up into trees to escape. Hunters sometimes roast and eat the raccoons that are caught in a hunt.

Some people keep raccoons as pets. Raccoons are more intelligent than cats and can be easily trained. But after they reach the age of about 1 year, they may be easily angered and, as a result, often bite and scratch.

Raccoons can be a serious nuisance if they break into chicken houses and kill poultry. They also damage corn crops by breaking the stalks of the plant and eating the growing corn.

Scientific classification. Raccoons belong to the raccoon family, Procyonidae. The scientific name for the northern raccoon is *Procyon lotor.* The crab-eating raccoon is *P. cancrivorous.*   John H. Kaufmann and Arleen B. Kaufmann

See also **Coati; Fur; Kinkajou; Panda; Ringtail.**

Raccoon dog. See **Fox** (Raccoon dogs; picture).

Raceme, *ray SEEM* or *ruh SEEM,* is a type of flower cluster. A raceme has a single central stem that bears several flowers, each on a stalk, in a spiral arrangement. The central stem is called the *peduncle.* The stalk bearing each flower is called a *pedicel.* Each flower bud of a raceme forms above a small modified leaf called a *bract.* The flowers of a raceme develop in a spiral pattern, with the lowest flowers on the peduncle developing first. Flowers continue to develop at the tip of the peduncle as it grows. This type of flowering is called an *indeterminate inflorescence.* Such plants as the hyacinth and the lily-of-the-valley produce flowers in racemes.

Joseph E. Armstrong

See also **Inflorescence.**

Racer is the name of a group of harmless, fast-moving snakes of the United States. Racers usually measure about $3\frac{1}{2}$ feet (107 centimeters) long, but they sometimes grow nearly 6 feet (1.8 meters) long.

There are several varieties of racers. The *northern black racer* is found from southern Maine to central Alabama. The skin of its back is glossy and slaty-black. The belly of the northern black racer is bluish-gray, and the chin and throat are white. A bluish variety of racer, called the *blue racer,* is found between the Great Lakes and the Ohio River. A mottled variety of racer found in Louisiana is known as the *buttermilk snake.* Racers live chiefly in the eastern United States. Varieties found west of the Mississippi Valley have tan to olive coloration on their backs.

Racers often climb trees to reach birds' nests, and eat the eggs and young birds. They also eat insects, frogs, small mammals such as mice, and other snakes. Some people believe racers kill large rattlesnakes, but racers never attack other snakes of their own size. When cornered, they defend themselves by biting. But they prefer to run away.

Scientific classification. Racers are members of the common snake family, Colubridae. The scientific name for the northern black racer is *Coluber constrictor constrictor.*

D. Bruce Means

See also **Snake** (picture: Eastern yellow-bellied racer).

© Michal Heron, Woodfin Camp, Inc.

Human beings resemble one another in many essential ways. However, people also differ from one another. The youngsters in this photo exhibit variations in skin color and hair color. Today, most experts avoid classifying people into races based on such variable physical characteristics.

Human races

Races, Human. All human beings are descended from people who lived hundreds of thousands of years ago. Thus, we all share a common ancestry. This means that all people living today are related to one another. But even though we are all related, we do not all look alike. Our bodies have different sizes and shapes, our skins have varying shades, our eyes differ in color and shape, our lips and noses have different shapes, and our hair has different colors and textures.

Most anthropologists believe that human beings originated in Africa and gradually spread throughout the world (see **Prehistoric people** [The first human beings]). They have observed that groups of people who have lived in certain parts of the world for many thousands of years tend to differ from groups living in other parts of the world. Living in regions with differing environments is one reason human beings have developed different appearances. For example, people whose ancestors lived for many generations in northern parts of the world—such as northern Europe or northern Japan—tend to have light-colored skin. People who come from places near the equator, such as central Africa or south-

ern India, tend to have dark-colored skin. People who come from places between those two environmental extremes tend to have medium-colored skin. For information on how skin colors result from adaptations to the environment, see the *Climatic adaptations* section of this article.

In some instances, we observe that certain physical traits tend to cluster in a group. For example, we might associate blond hair, blue eyes, and fair skin with people from Denmark, Norway, and Sweden. We also might associate red hair, green eyes, and a freckled complexion with people from Ireland. However, many people in these four countries actually have brown hair, brown eyes, and light brown skin. This example shows some of the problems facing human biologists who attempt to classify human beings into races.

Biologists define a race as a subdivision of a plant or animal *species*. The members of the same species resemble one another in many essential ways. Most importantly, they can breed with one another and produce fertile offspring. Members of different species usually cannot interbreed and produce fertile offspring. Grizzly bears and black bears, for example, are closely related North American bears. Despite their similarities, grizzly bears and black bears do not interbreed. Therefore, they belong to different species.

Many plant and animal species can be subdivided

Alan Swedlund, the contributor of this article, is Chairman of the Department of Anthropology at the University of Massachusetts at Amherst.

into groups that differ from one another. These groups have been called *races, subspecies, natural populations, breeds,* or *varieties.* Among grizzly bears, for instance, biologists observe distinct physical differences from region to region. They group grizzly bears into subspecies based on these differences.

All living human beings belong to the subspecies *Homo sapiens sapiens.* But like those of the grizzly bear, human populations differ from one region to another. Scholars have used these differences to classify people into various races. They have devised racial categories for human beings according to such physical characteristics as the color of the skin, the color and texture of the hair, and the shape of the eyes.

But some people assigned to the same race—and even some members of the same family—have widely differing features. Over the years, scientists have disagreed over how many races of human beings can be devised, and over which individuals belong to what race. For this reason, many anthropologists and biologists have come to believe that the assignment of a racial label to any group of people is arbitrary and thus open to argument.

For many years, most scholars believed that "pure" races of human beings existed some time in the prehistoric past. According to these scholars, the "pure" human races developed in complete isolation from one another, and the members of each race exhibited physical characteristics that the members of other races did not possess.

Today, however, most *physical anthropologists* (scientists who study the physical differences and prehistoric development of human beings) doubt that "pure" races ever existed. They point out that people have probably always taken mates from outside their own population as well as from within. They also note that as transportation and communication have become easier, populations have blended more and more. For these reasons, the biological definition of race does not describe human populations well. Most anthropologists now avoid classifying people into races. Instead, they try to learn more about human diversity by studying how human traits vary throughout the world.

Despite the lack of a scientifically valid racial classification system, people generally consider those who "look different" from themselves to be members of a different race. As a result, the concept of race remains important in a sociological sense. Societies continue to divide their members into "races"—though the criteria and labels used may vary from society to society.

The idea of race has often been misunderstood, and the term has sometimes been misused on purpose. The biological concept of race has often been confused with culture, language, nationality, or religion. Differences in physical appearance have led some people to mistakenly conclude that members of different groups are born with differences in intelligence, talents, and moral standards. Race has also been a major basis of *discrimination*—that is, the treatment of other groups as inferior to one's own group. For more information, see the *World Book* articles on **Minority group, Racism,** and **Segregation.**

This article describes some racial classification systems that have been used over the years and discusses alternative approaches to the study of human variation. It also describes how the physical characteristics of human beings change, and it discusses the social significance of race.

Systems of racial classification

Physical differences among human beings have long been recognized, and many of these differences have been used throughout history as bases of racial classification. Obvious physical characteristics, such as size, build, skin color, eye form, hair form, and nose shape, were the main criteria of early classifications of race, with skin color considered most important.

Since the beginning of recorded history, scholars have classified human beings in different ways, and the number of categories recognized by each system varied. The development of racial classification systems was influenced by three important theories: (1) the three-race theory, (2) evolutionary theory, and (3) the geographical-race theory.

The three-race theory. Ancient Egyptians, Greeks, and Romans knew about dark-skinned, curly-haired peoples that lived in Africa. They also knew about the so-called "yellowish-skinned" peoples of Asia, most of whom had folds of skin that extended from their eyelids over the inner corners of their eyes. Limited knowledge of the peoples of the world at this time suggested the existence of three races—European, or "white"; African, or "black"; and Asian, or "yellow." These groups eventually became known as Caucasoid, Negroid, and Mongoloid, respectively. For many years, scholars attempted to classify all human populations in terms of these three races, or some variation of the three. They believed that all people belonged to one of a limited number of racial types. They also believed that the traits of each race were fixed and unchanging.

The major period of European overseas exploration, which began in the late 1400's, provided increased contacts with peoples of different cultures. By the 1800's, it became evident that much of the world's population did not easily fit into the three-race system. For example, as Europeans came into contact with more and more Asian peoples, they realized that the skin of the people they had classified as Mongoloids was not really yellow, but that it varied from very dark to very light brown. They also discovered that the *epicanthic fold*—the inner eyefold thought to characterize Mongoloids—was rare in some Asian populations but present in some of the native peoples of southern Africa and North America. Lip form and hair form were also found to vary across the traditional racial groupings.

Evolutionary theory. The view that human beings could be classified into races based on fixed physical characteristics began to change dramatically as biologists came to accept the theory of evolution. During the early 1800's, most biologists believed that all plant and animal species remained the same from generation to generation. However, geologists found fossils of animals and plants that were not the same as living species, thus providing evidence that species were not fixed.

Even though scientists could now see that species could change, they did not know how evolution worked. It was the idea of *natural selection* as the mechanism for evolution that helped scientists understand how organ-

The three-race theory

For many years, scholars classified all human populations into one of three races—Caucasoid, Negroid, or Mongoloid. The three illustrations below show the physical characteristics that were believed to typify the members of each race.

WORLD BOOK illustrations by Nathan Greene

Typical Caucasoid traits were believed to include fair skin and fine, light-colored hair that was either straight or wavy. Blue eyes, a narrow nose, and fairly thin lips were also considered Caucasoid traits.

Typical Negroid traits were believed to include dark brown or black skin and coarse, kinky black hair. Brown eyes, a broad nose, and thick lips were also thought to characterize Negroids.

Typical Mongoloid traits were believed to include yellowish skin and coarse, straight black hair. A fold of skin across the inner corner of the eye was thought to characterize Mongoloids.

isms could change over many generations. This idea, set forth by the British naturalist Charles R. Darwin in his book *The Origin of Species* (1859), states that populations of organisms can change over generations as they adapt to their physical environment. This new understanding of the processes of evolution through natural selection, when applied to human populations, showed that many of the supposedly "fixed" traits that had been used to identify races were actually adaptations that had evolved over time in response to environmental conditions. See **Evolution; Darwin, Charles R.**

Scientists saw that widely separated groups could develop similar characteristics as a result of adapting to similar environments, even if they shared no recent ancestral relationship. For example, the Quechua, a people who live in the Andes Mountains of South America, and the Sherpas, a people of the Himalaya in Asia, are only remotely related. However, they have many similar physical characteristics as a result of prolonged adaptation to living in their high mountain environments.

As they came to understand evolutionary theory, experts began to see the difficulty of trying to use adaptable traits to fit people into just a few major races. Physical anthropologists began to search for *nonadaptive,* or *neutral,* traits—that is, physical characteristics that would persist even if a population moved to a different environment. They viewed race as something fixed and unchanging and wanted to discover traits that were also unchanging. Anthropologists compared many traits and physiological processes of people living in different environments, including blood groups and rates of respiration, circulation, and metabolism. These comparisons

are discussed later in this article, in the section on *How human populations develop and change.*

The geographical-race theory. In an effort to reconcile the theory of evolution with the observed variations among the world's populations, some anthropologists developed a new system of racial classification during the 1950's. They divided human beings into large categories called *geographical races.* These races were collections of populations that exhibited similar characteristics. One popular classification system recognized nine geographical races: (1) African, (2) American Indian, (3) Asian, (4) Australian, (5) European, (6) Indian, (7) Melanesian, (8) Micronesian, and (9) Polynesian.

In general, the geographical races extended throughout major continental areas and large island chains. But they did not correspond exactly to the continents. For example, the European geographical race included populations throughout Europe, in the Middle East, and north of the Sahara in Africa. It also included descendants of these populations in other parts of the world, such as the "whites" of North America and Australia.

Geographical races were believed to exist because of the isolation caused by such natural barriers as oceans, mountains, and deserts. The idea was that these barriers separated groups of people for many thousands of years, allowing the populations to evolve in different directions. India, for example, is partly isolated from the rest of Asia by the Himalaya. According to the geographical-race theory, this isolation permitted the Indian geographical race to develop separately from the Asian geographical race.

Anthropologists used the term *local races* to describe

The geographical-race theory

Geographical races were believed to exist because of the isolation created by oceans, mountains, and deserts. This map shows the races that were recognized by one popular classification system.

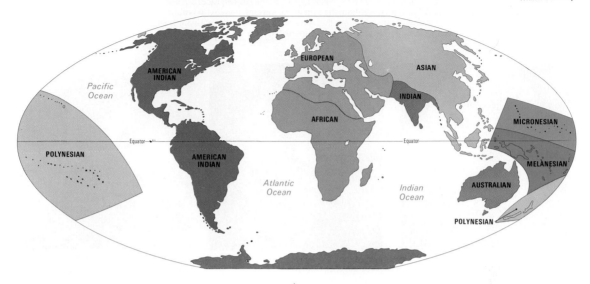

distinct subcategories of geographical races. Some local races had millions of members. For example, the Northwest European local race included the populations of Scandinavia, Germany, Belgium, Luxembourg, the Netherlands, Great Britain, and Ireland. It also included peoples who emigrated—or whose ancestors emigrated—from those areas. Local races containing much smaller numbers of people included the Lapps of extreme northern Europe and the Basques, who live in the mountains between France and Spain.

Some anthropologists used the term *microraces* to describe the subpopulations that existed within local races. But microraces—and even local races—could not always be clearly defined. Within a given geographic area, the members of different subpopulations often intermarried, so the physical features used to define these groups blended together.

This expanded, detailed classification system represented a major change in the view of human races. The geographical-race system took into account the theory of evolution as well as heredity, recognizing that populations are shaped by their environment. However, many anthropologists believed it did not eliminate the problems of the older systems. Because members of different races could possess the same physical characteristics, the racial criteria could not be clearly identified.

Alternatives to racial classification

In the past, scholars based racial classifications on clusters of physical characteristics that supposedly represented the "typical" member of that race. But many of the individuals categorized in a particular race did not reflect all the characteristics attributed to that race. In addition, the scholars who constructed classification systems did not always agree on which traits—or how many—should be considered.

To see the problems involved in defining races by means of "typical" characteristics, consider skin color. A pigment called *melanin* determines skin color. Dark skin contains more melanin than light skin does. Skin color has been used as a major classifying characteristic in all racial systems. For example, a light brown skin color was considered "typical" for the members of the European geographical race. But some members of the race had skin that was far lighter than the "typical" color, and others had skin that was much darker. Similarly, the members of the African geographical race "typically" had brownish-black skin. But again, many individuals classified in this race had skin that was lighter than the "typical" shade, and many others had skin that was darker.

To further confuse matters, some of the darker-skinned members of the European geographical race had skin as dark as some of the lighter-skinned members of the African geographical race. In view of these complications, it has become extremely difficult to assign people to a race based solely on skin color.

Increasing the number of identifying traits only added more problems. The shape and fullness of the lips, for example, varied widely among people who were considered members of the same race. Furthermore, lip shape demonstrated the same kind of overlap among members of supposedly different races as did skin color.

These problems have led many anthropologists to conclude that classification based on physical characteristics is not scientifically valid and serves no useful purpose. They find the study of human variation to be more productive than the assignment of racial labels. As a result, they have adopted alternate approaches to traditional systems of racial classification. Chief among these alternatives are (1) the clinal approach and (2) the population approach.

The clinal approach. The geographical distribution of a physical characteristic can be shown on a map by zones called *clines*. Clines are formed by drawing lines to connect points of the same or similar frequency. For example, in the case of skin color, each cline includes

The problem of skin color in racial classification

According to the geographical-race theory, the individuals in the top row of photos would belong to the European race. The individuals in the bottom row would belong to the African race. But skin color varies widely within each racial group. In addition, the skin of the Kuwaiti man—who would be assigned to the European geographical race—is about the same color as that of the woman from southern Chad, who would be assigned to the African geographical race.

© Gerard, Photo Researchers

Woman from Norway

© Blaine Harrington, The Stock Market

Woman from Germany

© David Hundley, The Stock Market

Man from Kuwait

© Jacques Jangoux from Peter Arnold

Woman from southern Chad

© Martha Cooper from Peter Arnold

Woman from Kenya

© Gerd Ludwig, Woodfin Camp, Inc.

Woman from Togo

locations at which populations demonstrate the same average skin color. As variations from dark to light are plotted on a map, certain distribution patterns begin to emerge. A clinal distribution does not associate specific traits with traditional racial categories, nor does it associate different traits with one another. For example, skin color and blood type would be plotted on separate maps and show different patterns of distribution.

The clinal approach has been used extensively to examine the worldwide distribution of blood types. Scientists classify human blood into groups according to proteins on the membranes of the red blood cells. The presence or absence of these proteins is determined by heredity. Studies show differences in the frequencies of some blood groups throughout the world.

The best-known blood-group system is called the ABO system. In this blood-group system, type O is the most common. Type O is followed by types A, B, and AB. Other systems that are used in comparing blood-group frequencies include the Kell, Kidd, Lutheran,

MNS, P, and Rh systems. See **Blood** (Blood groups).

Clines of blood-type distribution help anthropologists consider possible explanations for the geographic variations they observe. For instance, clinal mapping shows that central Asia has the lowest frequencies of type O blood. One possible explanation for this has to do with the deadly epidemic disease bubonic plague—a disease that has long been present in central Asia. The surface proteins that characterize type O red blood cells resemble the surface proteins found on the infectious bacteria that cause bubonic plague. Normally, the body can produce disease-fighting chemicals that recognize and attack cells that carry the bubonic-plague surface proteins. But if a person has type O blood, the body is less likely to make these disease-fighting substances because they would damage its own red blood cells. During a plague epidemic, central Asians with type O blood would have been at greater risk of dying from the disease than were those with other blood types. Over the centuries, this disadvantage could have led to the comparatively low frequency of type O blood in central Asia.

The population approach is used to study patterns of variation among human populations. Anthropologists define a population as a group of similar people who are more likely to mate with one another than with outsiders. Anthropologists using the population approach investigate clusters of physical traits but make no assumptions about race on the basis of those clusters. Instead, they see each population as the product of a unique set of circumstances, including adaptation, genetic change, isolation, and history of migration. These researchers then attempt to explain the similarities and differences among the populations. They do not try to fit the populations into racial categories.

The population approach assumes that groups of people who have lived in similar environments for a long period will demonstrate similar adaptations. This can happen even if the location of these similar environments is far apart. For example, populations living at very high altitudes must adjust to extreme conditions. Temperatures can get extremely hot during the day and very cold at night. Also, the air pressure is so low that less oxygen is available, making breathing more difficult. Throughout the world, populations living at high altitudes show specific traits in response to similar environmental conditions. For instance, their lungs can hold more air than those of people at lower altitudes, enabling them to inhale more oxygen with each breath.

How human populations develop and change

The characteristics studied by physical anthropologists—such as eye color, nose shape, blood type, body height, and susceptibility to genetic diseases—are determined by both heredity and the environment. The inherited aspects of a trait are determined by tiny biochemical structures in cells, called *genes.* Genes contain chemical instructions for the formation of hereditary

characteristics. Children inherit half their genes from their father and half from their mother. The underlying genetic makeup of a trait is called the *genotype.* The actual appearance of the trait is called the *phenotype.* The phenotype results from the environment and heredity.

Members of the same population of human beings tend to have more genes in common than do members of different populations. Closely related populations also share more genes than do distantly related groups, just as cousins have more genes in common than do members of different families. All the genes in a population are called the group's *gene pool.* The degree to which a gene is present in a population is called the *gene frequency.* For more information on how characteristics are inherited, see **Heredity; Cell; Gene.**

Scientists have shown that the gene pools of human populations can change over time. The presence of some genes increases, while the presence of other genes declines. As gene frequencies change, the frequencies of physical characteristics in a population may also change. Such changes can result from a number of different factors, including (1) natural selection, (2) mutation, (3) genetic drift, (4) the founder effect, and (5) migration and gene flow.

Natural selection is the process that enables some organisms or individuals to live and reproduce while others do not survive. Those who reproduce pass their genetic characteristics on to their offspring. Natural selection is the force that drives Darwinian evolution. For example, certain individuals within a population might possess a genetic characteristic that provides resistance to a local disease. As a result, those individuals tend to survive longer and to produce more offspring than the other members of the population. Moreover, their children who inherit the favorable characteristic will likewise tend to live longer and leave more descendants. Over time, individuals who possess the favorable trait

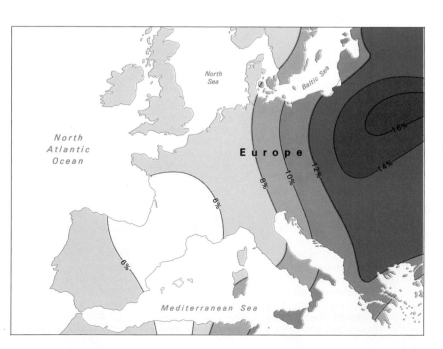

A clinal map shows the geographical distribution of a physical characteristic. Zones called *clines* indicate where the trait occurs with similar frequency. This map shows the distribution of a trait called the *B allele* in the ABO system of blood classification. People with the B allele have type B or type AB blood. It is more common in eastern Europe than in western Europe.

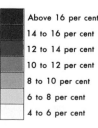

Above 16 per cent
14 to 16 per cent
12 to 14 per cent
10 to 12 per cent
8 to 10 per cent
6 to 8 per cent
4 to 6 per cent

WORLD BOOK map

will tend to outnumber those who do not, and the gene frequencies of the population will have changed.

As a result of natural selection, a population that lives in a certain area for many generations tends to exhibit distinctive genetic traits or clusters of traits. Scientists have shown that differences in skin color, body build, and other physical characteristics represent adaptations to environmental factors. See **Natural selection.**

Climatic adaptations. The genetic makeup of populations may change over time to adjust to climate. For example, dark and light skin and eye color represent adaptations to different amounts of sunlight. The color of our skin, hair, and eyes is determined by the pigment melanin. The amount of melanin in the skin, hair, and eyes can differ greatly from one person to another. Large amounts of melanin in the skin help protect it from sunburn and reduce the risk of skin cancer. Dark pigment in the eyes improves vision in bright sunlight. Therefore, dark skin and dark eyes represent adaptations of people whose ancestors have lived for many generations in sunny climates.

Sunlight also affects skin color in another way. Our bodies need vitamin D to help us absorb calcium. The absorption of sunlight enables our bodies to make vitamin D. In climates with long winter nights, it can be difficult for our bodies to absorb the sunlight needed to make enough vitamin D. People whose ancestors have lived in these climates for generations have adapted to reduced sunlight by developing light-colored skin that will absorb the little sunlight that is available. Therefore, skin colors in humans result from adaptations to the environments in which our ancestors have lived.

Human populations also differ in response to cold. Among Inuit (also called Eskimos), for instance, the body maintains a high temperature by burning large amounts of fat and protein. It also keeps large amounts of blood flowing to the arms, legs, fingers, and toes, to prevent frostbite. The Australian Aborigines, who live in a generally warm climate but traditionally slept in below-freezing temperatures with little clothing or shelter, have adapted to cold in a different way. The temperature in their legs and feet drops during sleep, and they burn less energy. But their bodies maintain warmth in the trunk, where the vital organs are.

The Australian Aborigines and the Inuit of the Arctic have both adapted to cold. The Aborigines have a limited food supply. They have no extra food to burn for body heat when the temperature drops. Instead, their adaptation enables them to save body energy. But this method would not work in the Arctic, where the climate is cold day and night. The Inuit are adapted to extreme cold—temperatures as low as −40 to −60 °F (−40 to −51 °C). Their adaptation depends on the availability of food to supply energy and body heat.

Susceptibility to genetic diseases. Many of the diseases that afflict human beings have some genetic basis. Human populations differ in the frequency of the genes that cause certain genetic diseases and disorders. For this reason, a number of genetic diseases are distributed differently throughout the world and affect some populations more than they do others. The fact that certain populations are plagued by particular genetic diseases can be explained in terms of natural selection.

The frequency of a hereditary blood disorder called *sickle cell anemia* varies widely in different populations. Individuals who inherit the sickling gene from both parents suffer from sickle cell anemia. Most cases of this disease are fatal. *Carriers*—people who inherit the defective gene from only one parent—may have almost no problems or experience only mild symptoms. But they can transmit the abnormal gene to their children. See **Sickle cell anemia.**

Scientists have found that carriers of the sickling gene have a higher resistance than noncarriers to *malaria,* a dangerous disease transmitted by certain mosquitoes. Sickle cell anemia is a rare disorder, but it occurs more often among populations of western Africa, the Middle East, southern Europe, and the Caribbean, most of whom live in areas threatened by malaria. Thus, the sickling gene—despite its negative effects—represents an important advantage for people in these areas.

Another genetic disease, *cystic fibrosis,* is more common among European populations and their descendants than among other populations. This rare and incurable disease affects the lungs and other organs. Like sickle cell anemia, cystic fibrosis results from the inheritance of a disease-causing gene from both parents. Carriers of the gene do not contract cystic fibrosis, but they can pass it on to their offspring. Some scientists believe that carriers are more resistant than other individuals to *tuberculosis*, an infectious disease affecting the lungs. Tuberculosis swept through Europe from the 1700's to the early 1900's. People who acted as carriers of the cystic fibrosis gene may have been more likely to survive these epidemics, which would explain the relatively high frequency of the cystic fibrosis gene in these populations. See **Cystic fibrosis.**

Mutation. A mutation is a change in genetic material. A changed gene often produces a different inherited trait that can be passed on to future generations. Mutations result from a chemical change in *DNA* (deoxyribonucleic acid), the chief chemical compound of genes. Mutations may also result from a change in the number or arrangement of *chromosomes,* the threadlike structures that contain the genes. Scientists know of many agents that can cause mutations, such as certain types of radiation, chemical treatments, and heat, but they cannot tell in advance which genes or chromosomes will mutate or how the trait controlled by that gene or chromosome will change.

Many mutations are harmful, causing mental or physical disorders. But other mutations are neutral, and some are favorable. A favorable mutation may provide the raw material for natural selection by making a person better suited to the environment. For example, a mutation that enhances the body's ability to make vitamin D from sunlight would be advantageous to a person living in the Far North, where the earth receives less sunlight. Such beneficial genes will increase in frequency from generation to generation. On the other hand, individuals possessing harmful mutations may be selected against, so the trait will not tend to increase in a population. In this way, mutation sometimes works together with natural selection to produce changes in gene frequencies. See **Mutation; Heredity** (Sources of genetic variation); **DNA; RNA.**

Genetic drift refers to chance fluctuations in the gene frequencies of a population from generation to generation. The genes of each generation represent only a sample of the previous generation's gene pool. As a result, the gene frequencies of each generation of individuals tend to vary randomly within the limitations of the preceding generation's gene pool. The smaller the population, the stronger the impact of these fluctuations is likely to be. Such changes are not likely to have much effect in very large populations, but they can lead to significant genetic changes in small populations.

The founder effect. When a small number of people from a large population establish a new population in a different place, it is unlikely that the founders represent the full range of diversity in their parent population's gene pool. When these founders produce offspring, a smaller, more limited gene pool is created. This phenomenon is called the *founder effect.* In future generations, the members of a population influenced by the founder effect are likely to resemble one another more closely than they do the members of the larger, more diverse parent population.

The founder effect may explain the increased incidence of certain traits or diseases in a population. For example, a hereditary brain disorder called *Tay-Sachs disease* occurs mainly among Jewish children of eastern European ancestry. People with one Tay-Sachs gene do not have the disease but may transmit the gene to their children. Children who inherit the gene from both parents have the disease. The Jews of eastern Europe made up a small population with a limited gene pool, so the incidence of the disease remains higher among their descendants than in other populations. See **Tay-Sachs disease.**

A similar limitation on a population's gene pool may occur if the genes of one person or family in a small population are passed to a large number of offspring. For example, if one man in a small, isolated group married several women and fathered many children, his genes would appear in future generations with more frequency than would the genes of other members of the population.

Migration and gene flow. When migration occurs between separate populations, new genes or combinations of genes are likely to be introduced into each group through interbreeding. As a result, the gene pool of each group comes to include genes from the gene pools of the other populations. In this manner, migration may cause the gene frequencies of populations to change over time. In modern times, easy access to transportation has greatly increased gene flow.

Since earliest times, people have moved from one place to another and have chosen mates from other groups. The greatest amount of gene flow occurs between populations that live next to one another. Mixture may also occur as a result of various cultural practices. Throughout history, such practices as exploration, colonization, bride capture, and enslavement have brought individuals of various genetic makeups together. The result in many cases has been change in the gene frequencies of the populations affected by these practices.

The social significance of race

As we have seen, most physical anthropologists have abandoned the idea of classifying human beings into biological races. In many societies, however, people continue to identify themselves and others as members of a particular race, often based on skin color. Thus, whatever its shortcomings on a biological basis, racial classification remains an important sociological factor. Social scientists must recognize the way a society defines racial categories if they hope to understand human behavior. It would, for instance, be difficult to analyze American society without taking into account the commonly used division of that society into "white," "black," "Hispanic," and other races. Yet these categories themselves reveal problems with the concept of race. "White" and "black" represent categories traditionally used to identify biological races. But "Hispanic" refers to the language group of Spanish-speaking people, not to any one biological group. Unfortunately, many social distinctions between races result from racial prejudice and misunderstanding.

Race and ethnic or national identity. The biological concept of race is sometimes confused with the idea of ethnicity or nationality. People identify themselves as members of certain ethnic or national groups based on certain geographical, cultural, or religious characteristics. However, these identifications are not based on physical differences. For instance, people sometimes incorrectly speak of the "Arab race," the "German race," the "Irish race," or the "Jewish race." But these labels

Bettmann

Migration can lead to changes in the gene frequencies of populations over time. The photograph at the left shows newly arrived European immigrants on Ellis Island, a United States immigration station in New York Harbor, about 1900.

refer to ethnicity or nationality and have nothing to do with the biological concept of race.

Race and discrimination. History includes many episodes in which the members of one group of people deemed themselves superior to another group. Such beliefs were long used to rationalize the enslavement and persecution of people viewed as inferior. For example, the ancient Romans viewed the Germanic tribes as a "race" of barbarians who were barely human. Europeans who settled in America claimed superiority over the American Indians to justify their expansion into the New World. In the 1930's, the leaders of Nazi Germany preached that Germans belonged to the "superior Aryan race," and that Jews and all other non-Aryan peoples were inferior.

Experts have not discovered any scientific basis for such claims of superiority. But many people still view other groups in terms of *stereotypes.* That is, they have oversimplified, preconceived, and generalized beliefs about the members of these groups. At various times, for example, certain groups have been described as dirty, dishonest, sly, humorless, or dull. These judgments have often been confused with racial traits, though they have nothing to do with the biological concept of race. Many such judgments have nothing to do with culture either, but only with the opinions or prejudices of those who make them. Discrimination can result from these stereotypes. As a result of these beliefs, members of minority groups in many societies have fewer educational and job opportunities than do members of the majority group.

The belief that some groups are more intelligent than others has been used to justify discrimination. Scientists have shown that a person's intelligence is partly inherited and partly determined by the environment. The use of intelligence to compare groups of people is extremely difficult, because few such comparisons can be considered equal. A better-educated group, for example, will score higher on tests that measure education. Groups that value mathematical skills or technical ability will do better on tests involving such skills.

Many experts believe it is impossible to design an intelligence test that is not influenced by a person's experiences. Nevertheless, scientists are trying to develop *culture-fair* or *culture-free* tests that reduce the effects of cultural differences on test scores.

The differences among human beings make the world a fascinating place in which to live. But when people focus on these differences, they often fail to appreciate how similar all human beings are. Most of the distinctions people make between themselves and others have much more to do with culture than with biology.

Alan Swedlund

Related articles. See the separate *World Book* articles listed under "People" at the end of **Africa** and **Asia.** See also:

Adaptation	Indian, American
Africa (People)	Inuit
African Americans	Latin America (People)
Aleuts	Maori
Asia (People)	North America (People)
Australia (The Aborigines)	Pacific Islands (People)
Dayaks	Prehistoric people (How
Europe (People)	*Homo sapiens* developed)
Evolution	Racism
Heredity	

Outline

I. **Systems of racial classification**
  A. The three-race theory
  B. Evolutionary theory
  C. The geographical-race theory
II. **Alternatives to racial classification**
  A. The clinal approach
  B. The population approach
III. **How human populations develop and change**
  A. Natural selection
  B. Mutation
  C. Genetic drift
  D. The founder effect
  E. Migration and gene flow
IV. **The social significance of race**
  A. Race and ethnic or national identity
  B. Race and discrimination

Questions

How do mutations lead to changes in human populations?
Why might the disease cystic fibrosis affect mainly members of European populations and their descendants?
Why do most physical anthropologists doubt that "pure" races ever existed?
Why were natural barriers considered important in the geographical-races theory?
What are difficulties in using intelligence as a basis for comparing groups of people?
What is a *nonadaptive* trait?
How can large amounts of melanin be helpful under some conditions and harmful under others?
What is natural selection? How does it cause human populations to change?
How do anthropologists use clines to study human variations?
How does a race differ from a species?

Additional resources

Birdseye, Debbie H. and Tom. *Under Our Skin: Kids Talk About Race.* Holiday Hse., 1997. Younger readers.
Kottak, Conrad P. *Anthropology: The Exploration of Human Diversity.* 7th ed. McGraw, 1997.
Lewontin, Richard C. *Human Diversity.* 1982. Reprint. W. H. Freeman, 1995.
Molnar, Stephen. *Human Variation.* 4th ed. Prentice Hall, 1998.

Rachel, *RAY chuhl,* in the Old Testament, was the favorite wife of Jacob. Jacob served Rachel's father, Laban, seven years in order to win her, and his love was so great, "they seemed to him but a few days" (Genesis 29:20). But Laban tricked Jacob and gave him Rachel's older sister, Leah, instead. Jacob married Rachel a week later, but had to work another seven years for her. Rachel's first child, Joseph, became his father's favorite. At the end of a journey from Mesopotamia to Canaan (later called Palestine), Rachel died after giving birth to Benjamin.

Rachel was considered the ancestress of the northern Israelite tribes of Ephraim and Manasseh, which claimed descent from Joseph. A century after the Assyrians deported part of the tribes in 722 or 721 B.C., Jeremiah described Rachel as mourning over her lost children (Jeremiah 31:15).   J. Maxwell Miller

See also Jacob.

Rachmaninoff, *rahk MAH nuh NAWF,* **Sergei Vassilievich,** *sehr GAY vahs SEE lyuh vihch* (1873-1943), was a Russian composer and conductor and one of the greatest pianists in history. His compositions generally carry the late romantic style of Russian composer Peter Ilich Tchaikovsky into the early 1900's. Even Rachmaninoff's last works from the 1930's are hardly affected by modern trends. His music is strongly influenced by the chants and church bells of the Russian Orthodox Church. These musical influences appear in Rachmaninoff's severely simple melodies and rich, full keyboard sounds. He combined these native Russian materials with his own passion and intensity of expression.

Rachmaninoff gained his greatest international reputation for his piano compositions. His most famous work is the Prelude in C-sharp minor for piano. He composed it in 1892, at the age of 19. The second (1901) of his four piano concertos shows the melancholy lyricism of his mature style and his skillful writing of virtuoso piano compositions. His other work for piano and orchestra is the *Rhapsody on a Theme of Paganini* (1934).

Rachmaninoff's major works for orchestra are his three symphonies (1897, 1908, and 1936), the symphonic poem *The Isle of the Dead* (1909), *Symphonic Dances* (1941), and the choral symphony *The Bells* (1913). The composer based *The Bells* on a Russian translation of the poem by the American author Edgar Allan Poe.

Rachmaninoff's main works for solo piano appear in the collections *Moments musicaux* (1896), two sets of *Preludes* (1903, 1910), and two sets of *Études-tableaux* (1911, 1917). He also wrote over 80 songs, all to Russian texts, for solo voice and piano accompaniment. He composed three operas, but none are widely performed.

Rachmaninoff was born on his family estate near Novgorod. In 1885, he entered the Moscow Conservatory to study piano and to begin courses in composition, orchestration, and counterpoint. Rachmaninoff completed his piano studies at the conservatory in 1891. He graduated in composition the next year, winning the conservatory's highest award for his one-act opera *Aleko*.

In 1902, Rachmaninoff married his cousin Natalya Satina. He was conductor of the Bolshoi Opera in Moscow from 1904 to 1906 and made his first tour of the United States in 1909 as a pianist and conductor. Rachmaninoff left Russia with his wife and two daughters in 1917. Eventually, he settled in the United States late in 1918.

In America, Rachmaninoff concentrated on concert performances rather than composing. He gained enormous popularity in America and Europe for his compositions and as a piano soloist. He lived in Switzerland for much of the 1930's but returned to the United States in the late 1930's. He died in the United States shortly after he received his American citizenship.   Edward V. Williams

Racial segregation. See Segregation.

Racine, Jean (1639-1699), ranks among the greatest French playwrights. Racine wrote during the French Classical Age. He followed the classical rules for composition, including the use of a single concentrated plot. The outstanding feature of Racine's art is its simplicity. He used a limited vocabulary and his plots contain little explicit action. He said his artistic ideal was "to construct something out of nothing."

Almost all of Racine's important plays are tragedies. Many of his tragic heroes and heroines follow the same pattern. They are victims of violent passions and try unsuccessfully to impose their wills on other people. In the process, most of them cause the death of those they love. They finally recognize their illusions and accept the misery of the human condition as unavoidable. In this respect, Racine is close in spirit to the Greek playwright Sophocles. Racine's tragedies have much in common with the descriptions of tragedies in Aristotle's literary essay, *Poetics.* Both Racine and his rival Pierre Corneille wrote in 12-syllable couplets, but Racine's style often is more severe.

Racine was born in La Ferté-Milon, near Meaux, and was educated by the strict Jansenist religious sect. He showed promise of a literary career at an early age. In 1664, Racine staged *La Thébaïde,* his first tragedy to be produced. It met with little success. His next play, *Alexandre* (1665), received considerable acclaim.

With the production of *Andromache* (1667), Racine became known as one of the greatest dramatists of his time. His next seven plays are masterpieces. They are *Les Plaideurs* (1668), his only comedy; and the tragedies *Britannicus* (1669), *Bérénice* (1670), *Bajazet* (1672), *Mithridate* (1673), *Iphigénie* (1674), and *Phaedra* (1677). In 1677, Racine retired from the stage. Later, he wrote *Esther* (1689) and *Athalie* (1691), tragedies based on stories from the Bible.   Carol L. Sherman

See also **Drama** (Neoclassical playwrights); **French literature** (The classical age).

Racing is a contest of speed. People compete in running, swimming, and walking races. Such sports as horse racing and automobile racing involve people riding animals or operating machines. Trained animals compete against one another in dog racing and pigeon racing. Some races rank among the world's most popular spectator sports, attracting millions of people every year.

Racing includes both individual and team competition. In some races, winners are determined only by the fastest time. In other races, the winner is the individual who finishes ahead of the other competitors. Some races last only a few seconds. Some other races are very long and test endurance as well as speed. A well-known example is the marathon, a running race of 26 miles 385 yards (42.2 kilometers). Some ocean yacht races and bicycle road races last for weeks.

Racing events have been popular throughout human history. A footrace was the only event in the first recorded Olympic Games held in ancient Greece in 776 B.C. More recently, racing has contributed to improvements in design and performance in airplanes, bicycles, and automobiles.   William F. Reed

Related articles in *World Book* include:

Automobile racing	Horse racing	Roller skating
Bicycle racing	Ice skating (Speed	Rowing
Bobsledding	skating)	Sailing (Sailboat
Canoeing (Canoe	Iceboating	racing)
racing)	Kart racing	Skiing
Dog racing	Motorboat racing	Swimming
Harness racing	Motorcycle	Track and field
Homing pigeon	Olympic Games	Walking

Racism is the belief that human beings can be divided into races and that members of some races are inferior to members of other races. Usually, this attitude also involves the belief that one's own race is superior to other races. People who believe in racism are called *racists*. They claim that members of their own race are mentally, physically, morally, or culturally superior to those of other races. Because racists assume they are superior, they feel they deserve special rights and privileges.

Groups, as well as individuals, differ. But there is no scientific evidence to support claims of superiority or inferiority for these differences. Social scientists emphasize that no two groups have exactly the same environment. As a result, many group differences are largely the result of different environments. Scientists have long debated the relative importance of heredity and environment in determining these differences. But most scientists believe that heredity and environment interact in complex ways. In addition, most anthropologists today reject the idea that human beings can be divided into biologically defined races. For a discussion of these ideas, see **Intelligence** (The roles of heredity and environment) and **Races, Human** (Race and discrimination).

Racism is widespread and has caused major problems, even though no scientific proof supports racist claims. Claims of racial superiority have been used to justify discrimination, segregation, colonialism, slavery, and even *genocide* (extermination of an entire people).

Racism is a form of prejudice. Many people tend to consider their own appearance and behavior as normal and therefore desirable. They may distrust or fear people who look or act differently. When differences are obvious—such as in skin color or religious worship—the distrust becomes greater. Such attitudes can lead to the belief that people who look or act differently are inferior. Many people do not bother to look for the same qualities in other groups that they admire in their own. Also, they do not recognize the different but equally good qualities that members of other groups possess.

Most racism in the United States has been directed by a white majority against ethnic minorities. Such groups include African Americans, American Indians, Hispanic Americans, and Asian Americans. These minorities have been discriminated against in such areas as housing, education, and employment. See **Segregation; Minority group; Ethnic group; Asian Americans; African Americans; Hispanic Americans;** and **Indian, American.**

Individual and institutional racism. In the United States, sociologists distinguish between individual and institutional racism. Individual racism refers chiefly to the prejudicial beliefs and discriminatory behavior of individual whites against minority groups. It is based on racial assumptions of superiority and inferiority.

Institutional racism refers to the policies of communities, schools, businesses, and other groups that restrict the opportunities of minority groups. Institutional racism may or may not have been intentionally set up to practice discrimination. Yet it has produced harmful results. For example, a company may hire only college graduates for work that does not require a college degree. But a far smaller number of blacks than whites have had the opportunity to earn a degree. Thus, the company policy lessens the job opportunities of blacks even though the firm might not have intended to do so.

Another example of institutional racism is the reported use of *racial profiling* in law enforcement. Racial profiling refers to the practice of using skin color as a basis for stopping citizens for police encounters, such as traffic checks. Complaints of racial profiling have led several states to pass laws against the practice.

History. Racism has existed since the beginning of history. More than 2,000 years ago, the ancient Greeks and Romans made slaves of people whom they regarded as inferior. Jews have long been persecuted on religious and cultural grounds.

Between the 1700's and early 1900's, Europeans gained control of large parts of Asia and Africa. These colonialists justified their domination on the grounds that the black-, brown-, and yellow-skinned "races" had to be "civilized" by the "superior" whites. This civilizing mission came to be called the "white man's burden." By the mid-1900's, most colonialism had ended. But its effects on the world are still felt today. For details, see the articles on **Africa** (History) and **Asia** (Results of colonialism; The spread of Communism).

From the 1600's to the mid-1800's, many whites in the United States held blacks in slavery. Slavery was a major cause of the American Civil War (1861-1865). The slaves were freed during the 1860's, but segregation and discrimination against blacks continued. In the mid-1900's, the U.S. government passed laws designed to give equal opportunities to blacks. Even so, racial problems continue to plague the United States.

Genocide is the most extreme result of racial hatred. Adolf Hitler, the ruler of Nazi Germany, preached that Germans belonged to the "superior Aryan race," and that Jews and other non-Aryan peoples were inferior. Hitler's belief in German superiority and his hatred of Jews resulted in Nazi policies that brought the murder of about 6 million Jews during the 1930's and 1940's. See **Jews** (Beginnings of Nazi persecution).

In the late 1940's, the South African government established a racial policy called *apartheid,* one of the world's most complete systems of racial separation. It called for separate institutions and residences for whites and nonwhites. In 1991, South Africa repealed the last of the laws that formed apartheid's basis. But blacks were not allowed to vote in national elections until 1994. Blacks and other nonwhites still face unofficial segregation and discrimination in South Africa.   Thomas F. Pettigrew

Related articles in *World Book* include:

Anti-Semitism	Hate crime	Prejudice
Apartheid	Oriental exclusion	Races, Human
Genocide	acts	Slavery

Additional resources

Dudley, William, and Cozic, Charles, eds. *Racism in America: Opposing Viewpoints.* Greenhaven, 1991.
Garg, Samidha, and Hardy, Jan. *Racism.* 1996. Reprint. Raintree Steck Vaughn, 1997.

Racketeering is any of several types of illegal activities usually associated with organized crime groups, such as the Mafia. There are three main types of rackets: (1) protection rackets, (2) labor rackets, and (3) business rackets. In a protection racket, an organization uses threats, also called *extortion,* to force businesses to pay it money. In a labor racket, the offenders steal union funds or use a union's power to force companies to give them money. In a business racket, a firm tries to prevent other businesses from competing against it.

In the United States, racketeering is prohibited under RICO, a section of the federal Organized Crime Control Act of 1970. RICO is an abbreviation of the section's title, "Racketeer Influenced and Corrupt Organizations Act." Under RICO, people convicted of racketeering can be given up to 20 years in prison for each offense.

After RICO took effect, a number of U.S. states and many other countries adopted similar laws. The countries with such laws include Belgium, Germany, Italy, and South Africa.   Howard Abadinsky

Rackham, Arthur (1867-1939), an English artist, won wide recognition for his illustrations for children's

A Rackham illustration from 1907 shows the artist's detailed style. In this scene from *Alice's Adventures in Wonderland,* Alice and the Gryphon listen to the Mock Turtle's sad life story.

books. His illustrations were filled with such figures as gnomes, elves, witches, and fairies, as well as with kindly human creatures.

Rackham drew and painted these figures with delicacy and rich detail. He made such details as wood grain, tree bark, and lines in faces and hands important parts of the whole design. He even gave his trees personalities. Rackham's imaginative and skillful pictures brought to life the characters in many favorite stories, including *Rip Van Winkle* (1905), *Peter Pan in Kensington Gardens* (1906), *Alice's Adventures in Wonderland* (1907), *Mother Goose, the Old Nursery Rhymes* (1913), *Some British Ballads* (1919), and *The Arthur Rackham Fairy Book* (published in 1950, after his death).

Rackham was born in London. He became interested in drawing when he was a boy and entered the Lambeth School of Art in 1884. He supported himself by working in an insurance office from 1885 to 1892. Rackham first gained recognition for his illustrations in an edition of *Grimm's Fairy Tales* that was published in 1900.

Marilyn Fain Apseloff

Racquetball is a fast, exciting game in which the players hit a ball with a short racket (or racquet) that resembles a small tennis racket. They play with a hollow rubber ball about the size of a tennis ball. Most racquetball games are played on indoor courts that are 20 feet (6.1 meters) high, 40 feet (12.2 meters) long, and 20 feet wide. The game can be played with one or two players on a side. In cut-throat racquetball, three players compete against each other.

A racquetball game starts with a *serve*. The server stands between the *service line* and the *short line* with the receiver standing behind the short line. In doubles play, the server's partner stands in the *service box* with his or her back to the wall. The server drops the ball on the floor and hits it on the first bounce. The ball must strike the front wall and rebound behind the short line. The players or teams then take turns hitting the ball. Each player must return the ball before it bounces twice on the floor. A player can return the ball by hitting it against any wall or the ceiling. But the ball must strike the front wall before it touches the floor.

The server or serving team scores points if an opponent fails to return the ball properly. The side continues the serve after each point until it makes an error on its serve or fails to win the point. The other side then serves. Originally, games were played to 21 points. Most games now go to 15 points. The first side to win either two or three games wins the match.

The American Amateur Racquetball Association governs the sport at the amateur national level. The International Racquetball Tour governs professional play.

Critically reviewed by the American Amateur Racquetball Association

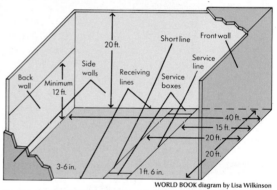

WORLD BOOK diagram by Lisa Wilkinson

A racquetball court has four walls. The server stands between the *short line* and the *service line.* During the serve, the ball must hit the front wall and bounce behind the short line. The opponent waits for the serve behind the *receiving lines.*

WORLD BOOK photo by Dan Miller

Racquetball is an exciting, fast-paced sport played in a four-walled court. Players, using rackets, take turns hitting a ball off the walls and ceiling of the court.

Hughes Aircraft Company

Radar enables an air traffic controller to track and guide planes in flight. Radio waves reflected from the planes appear as small spots on the controller's screen, *above.* The flight path of every plane in the area can be determined by following the movements of the spots.

Radar

Radar is an electronic instrument used to detect and locate moving or fixed objects. Radar can determine the direction, distance, height, and speed of objects that are much too far away for the human eye to see. It can find objects as small as insects or as large as mountains. Radar can even operate effectively at night and in heavy fog, rain, or snow.

The ability of radar to do so many tasks makes it useful for a wide variety of purposes. Pilots rely on radar to land their airplanes safely at busy airports. In bad weather, ship navigators use it to steer their ships clear of nearby vessels and dangerous objects. The United States, Canada, and many other countries use radar to guard against surprise attacks from enemy aircraft or missiles. Radar enables weather forecasters to keep track of approaching storms. Scientists use radar to in-

vestigate the upper atmosphere of the earth and also to study the other planets and their moons.

The word *radar* comes from *ra*dio *d*etection *a*nd *r*anging. Almost every radar set works by sending radio waves toward an object and receiving the waves that are reflected from the object. The time it takes for the reflected waves to return indicates the object's *range*—how far away it is. The direction from which the reflected waves return tells the object's location.

Radar sets vary in size and shape, but they all have the same kinds of basic parts. Every set has a transmitter to produce radar waves and an antenna to send them out. In most types of radar, the same antenna collects the waves bounced back from an object. The reflected waves, commonly called *echoes,* are strengthened by a receiver so they can be seen on a *display.* The typical radar display resembles the picture tube of a television set. It shows the echoes as spots of light or as an image of the object observed.

The uses of radar

In aviation. Radar is an important tool in aviation. Its use both at airports and in airplanes has contributed greatly to aviation safety.

G. D. Thome, the contributor of this article, is a consulting scientist for the Raytheon Company, which manufactures radar systems and other electronic equipment.

Air traffic near large airports is extremely heavy. Specially trained *air traffic controllers* at all the world's major airports use radar to direct the continuous flow of incoming and outgoing planes. Radar shows the controllers the position of every plane in the air within at least 50 miles (80 kilometers) of the airport. This information enables them to prevent collisions by selecting the safest routes for pilots to follow. The controllers also depend on radar to enable them to direct landings from the ground when bad weather makes approach lights and runways difficult for pilots to see.

Most modern aircraft have various types of radar to aid pilots. For example, the *radar altimeter* shows how high a plane is flying and so helps pilots maintain the proper altitude. Another device, *weather radar,* detects nearby storms and thus enables pilots to change course to avoid rough weather whenever possible.

In ship navigation. Radar is widely used as a navigation aid on all kinds of boats and ships, from small pleasure craft to huge oil tankers. When visibility is poor, a ship's radar can spot other vessels, reefs, and icebergs in time to prevent an accident. When a ship is near shore, the navigator can determine the vessel's position by the radar echoes from special reflector buoys, islands, and other landmarks.

Harbor masters use radar to control ship traffic in crowded seaports. They follow the movements of all ships in a harbor on a radar display that provides a maplike picture of the harbor. By means of radio communication, harbor masters can guide ships into and out of a port safely in any weather.

Some United States Coast Guard stations keep track of vessels in their vicinity through radar observations. The Coast Guard also uses radar to search for ships that are reported missing.

In the military. Radar has a variety of military uses. The major uses include (1) air defense, (2) missile defense, (3) space surveillance, (4) intelligence gathering, (5) range instrumentation, and (6) weapon fire control.

Air defense requires long-range radar that can detect and track approaching enemy aircraft at great distances and so give the earliest possible warning. Vast networks of radar stations form the heart of most nations' air defense systems. The North Warning System, a network of radar stations across northern North America, protects the United States and Canada from attack from the north. The United States also has built *over-the-horizon radar* stations to detect attacks from the east, south, and west.

In addition to land radar stations, the United States and several other countries use aircraft equipped with radar for protection against surprise air attacks. Airborne radar can spot low-flying enemy bombers that may escape detection by ground-based radar.

Missile defense consists of radar networks like those used for early warning of hostile aircraft. But more powerful radar is needed to detect guided missiles because they fly faster and much higher than planes. The main radar network developed by the United States for missile defense is the Ballistic Missile Early Warning System (BMEWS). This system has installations at Clear, Alaska; Thule, Greenland; and Fylingdales Moor, England. Radar units at these places can spot long-range missiles up to 3,000 miles (4,800 kilometers) away.

Another major radar network is the Sea-Launched Ballistic Missile Detection System (SLBMDS). Its radar stations guard the east and west coasts of the United States against missiles launched from enemy submarines and surface vessels.

Space surveillance involves the use of extremely powerful radars to detect and track artificial satellites and other objects put into orbit around the earth. For this purpose, the United States and Canada operate a network called the United States Air Force (USAF) Spacetrack network. The network includes the three BMEWS installations and other facilities throughout the

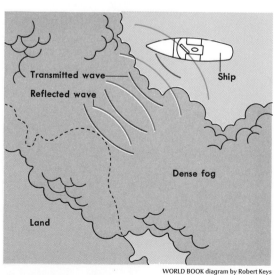

Stan Schrero

WORLD BOOK diagram by Robert Keys

Boats and ships use radar as a navigation aid, especially to avoid obstacles when visibility is poor. Small vessels, such as the tugboat at the left, use a compact radar set with a rotatable antenna on top of the cabin. The diagram at the right shows how radar waves can penetrate dense fog. Their echoes enable a ship's navigator to detect land, reefs, or other vessels hidden by the fog.

Radar is vital to the defense of the United States and Canada. Powerful BMEWS radars warn against long-range missiles. Radars of the North Warning System detect aircraft approaching from the north, and over-the-horizon radars protect against attack from other directions. The United States Air Force (USAF) Spacetrack Network keeps track of artificial satellites orbiting the earth.

 BMEWS–Ballistic Missile Early Warning System

North Warning System (selected sites)

USAF Spacetrack Network

Over-the-horizon radars

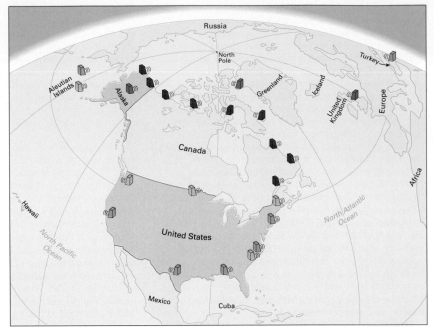

WORLD BOOK map

world. Each day, the USAF Spacetrack network provides more than 20,000 observations of hundreds of orbiting objects. Data from these observations can help identify *reconnaissance satellites,* which are used for spying.

Intelligence gathering. Radar is used to collect information about the preparations that other countries might be making for war. A *mapping radar* in a plane can produce detailed maps of the ground and show military installations and equipment. Other types of radar

can obtain important information about another country's missile systems by monitoring its missiles during test firings.

Range instrumentation. Radar is often used at test ranges to check the performance of military equipment. For example, *range instrumentation radars* can accurately track the flight of a new missile. If the missile does not perform as well as expected, the tracking data might help the designer determine what went wrong.

U.S. Air Force

U.S. Air Force

A long-range radar has a huge dome, *left,* which houses an antenna structure, *right,* that stands about 65 feet (20 meters) high. The radar shown here is part of the North Warning System, which protects the United States and Canada from attack from the north.

Weapon fire control. Radar can locate objects so precisely that it is used to aim and fire many kinds of weapons. Radar controls the firing of antiaircraft guns on tanks and warships. It directs guided missiles from jet fighters and from land-based launching sites. In addition, planes with radar bombsights can drop bombs accurately on targets at night or in bad weather.

In controlling automobile speed and traffic. Police in many areas of the United States and Canada use radar to enforce speed laws by checking the speed of motor vehicles on streets and highways. Their portable radar sets can detect speeding vehicles up to $\frac{1}{2}$ mile (0.8 kilometers) away.

In weather observation and forecasting. Radar has an important role in short-range forecasts of local weather conditions. Radar echoes can be detected from raindrops and ice particles in clouds up to about 250 miles (400 kilometers) away. In many cases, the intensity of these echoes reveals what type of storm is approaching. For example, strong echoes are produced by hailstones in a thunderstorm. Radar echoes also indicate the direction in which a storm is moving and its speed.

By analyzing radar observations, weather forecasters can predict when a storm will pass over a certain area. In many cases, they can give advance warning to communities in the path of a hurricane, tornado, or other violent storm. The United States National Weather Service operates hundreds of ground and airborne radar units that keep close track of such storms. Most major airports also have weather radar. If a severe storm is sighted along a particular flight path, air traffic is redirected to avoid it.

In scientific research. Scientists rely on radar in conducting various kinds of studies. They use high-

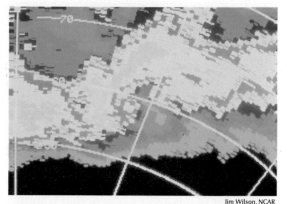

Jim Wilson, NCAR

Weather radar can detect the formation and movement of storms by registering echoes bounced off raindrops and ice particles. This display shows a tornado forming in Oklahoma.

powered radars to investigate the earth's upper atmosphere. At altitudes of 60 miles (100 kilometers) and higher, the air reflects radio waves. This air is in a part of the upper atmosphere known as the *ionosphere.* In this region, the sun's radiation is so strong that it breaks air molecules into electrically charged particles called *electrons* and *ions.* As a result, it can be studied by radar from the earth's surface. Radar observations help scientists determine the temperature of the upper atmosphere and the kinds of gases in the air. Radar observations also indicate how fast winds blow at such high altitudes during different periods of the day.

Radar equipment and techniques contribute much to the study of the solar system. Astronomers have made

How radar helps police catch speeders

Police use *Doppler radar* to detect speeding motorists. The radar antenna is mounted on the outside of a police car, *bottom left.* It launches a continuous radio wave of a certain frequency. When this wave strikes a moving car, it is reflected at a different frequency, as shown in the diagram. The radar set measures the frequency difference to find the car's speed and records it, *bottom right.*

WORLD BOOK diagram by Robert Keys

Transmitted wave   Reflected wave

Milt and Joan Mann

Jet Propulsion Laboratory

A radar image of a volcano on Venus was made by a computer using data from a scan by the space probe Magellan. Heights in the image are exaggerated 10 times to show detail.

radar observations of the moon, the sun, and the planets closest to the earth. They have even collected radar echoes from several of Jupiter's largest satellites. Such radar observations provide extremely accurate measurements of the distances to these objects. They also show how rapidly the objects rotate. Astronomers have obtained detailed radar maps of the moon and Mars by recording radio waves bounced off their surfaces. By using the same technique, astronomers have succeeded in penetrating the thick clouds that surround Venus and discovered enormous mountains and valleylike features on its surface. See **Telescope** (Radio telescopes).

The study of bird migrations is another area of scientific research that has benefited from radar. Zoologists depend on radar to trace the flight patterns of birds that migrate at night or that are too small to be seen from the ground. Radar can also be used to measure and map currents on the ocean surface within about 45 miles (72 kilometers) from shore. Such information is useful for research in marine biology and for planning offshore oil-drilling projects.

In space travel. Radar is vital to the success of missions into outer space. The first step in such a mission is to launch a manned or unmanned spacecraft into orbit around the earth. During the launching, mission controllers use a system of ground-based radars and other radio equipment to track the vehicle. As soon as the spacecraft enters its orbit, the radars measure the orbit's size and shape. Computers take the measurements and calculate when the craft's remaining rocket engines should be fired and for how long to send the vehicle from earth orbit into outer space.

Spacecraft designed to land on the moon or on another planet carry *landing radar.* This instrument measures the height of the spacecraft above the landing site and the rate of descent. Such information is used to regulate the engines of the craft so that it lands at the correct speed. If the vehicle descends too fast, it will crash.

If it lands too slowly, it will burn too much fuel. In addition, radar is used to select safe landing sites for spacecraft. For example, radar maps of the moon helped U.S. scientists choose landing areas where rugged rock formations would not damage the Apollo lunar modules.

A mission may call for a spacecraft to dock with another space vehicle. The astronauts in the spacecraft locate the other vehicle with radar. They then use the radar data to adjust the direction and speed of their own craft to perform the docking maneuver.

How radar works

Radar sets differ in design and purpose, but they all operate on the same general principles. All radars produce and transmit signals in the form of *electromagnetic waves*—that is, related patterns of electric and magnetic energy. Radar waves may be either radio waves or light waves. Almost all radar sets transmit radio waves. But a few called *optical radars* or *laser radars* send out light waves.

When the electromagnetic waves transmitted by a radar set strike an object, they are reflected. Some of the reflected waves return to the set along the same path on which they were sent. This reflection closely resembles what happens when a person shouts in a mountain valley and hears an echo from a nearby cliff. In this case, however, sound waves are reflected instead of radio waves or light waves.

The waves transmitted by radar have a definite frequency. The frequency of such a wave is measured in units called *megahertz* (MHz). One megahertz equals 1 million *hertz* (cycles per second). Radio waves have lower frequencies than light waves have. Most radars that transmit radio waves operate at frequencies of about 5 to 36,000 MHz. Optical radars operate at much higher frequencies. Some generate light waves with frequencies up to 1 billion MHz.

In many cases, radar sets designed for different purposes operate at different frequencies. Radars that transmit at lower frequencies are more effective than high-frequency radars in penetrating clouds, fog, and rain and so are widely used on planes and ships. On the other hand, high-frequency radars provide precise direction measurements with much smaller antennas than those used by lower frequency radars. An optical radar, for example, can produce an extremely narrow signal beam with an antenna only about $\frac{1}{2}$ inch (1.3 centimeters) in diameter. Optical radars are especially useful for surveying rough terrain where distant points have to be measured between such objects as large rocks and trees. Over-the-horizon radars use relatively low-frequency radio waves between 3 and 30 MHz. These waves reflect from an upper layer of the atmosphere called the *ionosphere* and can reach beyond the horizon to detect ships and planes at great distances. Radars of the North Warning System use relatively high-frequency radio waves called *microwaves,* which pass through the ionosphere.

Radar sets also differ in how they transmit signals. On this basis, they are usually classified into two general types: (1) pulse radar and (2) continuous-wave radar. Pulse radar is the more common type.

Pulse radar sends out signals in powerful bursts, or pulses. These pulses last only a few millionths of a second. A pulse radar set has one antenna, which alternately transmits the pulses and receives their echoes.

The distance to an object is found by measuring the time it takes a radar wave to reach the object and return. Radar waves, like all other electromagnetic waves, travel at the speed of light—186,282 miles (299,792 kilometers) per second. Therefore, a radar wave that returns after two seconds would have traveled 372,564 miles (599,584 kilometers)—186,282 miles to the object and 186,282 miles back. A pulse radar set automatically converts the time required for the round trip into the distance to the object.

The antenna transmits the pulses of waves in a narrow beam, which enables the set to determine an object's direction. Only an object within the area of the beam can reflect the waves. Thus the direction from which the waves are reflected to the antenna indicates the location of the object.

Pulse radar can track an object by continuously transmitting signal pulses and by measuring the object's distance and direction at regular intervals. It also can be used to make radar maps from an airplane. Radar maps are produced by scanning a beam of pulses over an area and plotting the strength of the echoes from each direction. The echoes appear as images on the radar display and are recorded on photographic film. Such objects as buildings, bridges, and mountains produce especially bright images because they reflect strong echoes.

Continuous-wave radar sends out a continuous signal rather than short bursts. There are two kinds of continuous-wave radar. They are (1) Doppler radar and (2) frequency-modulated (FM) radar.

Doppler radar is used chiefly to make precise speed measurements. It works on the basis of the *Doppler ef-*

fect, which is a change in observed wave frequency caused by motion. Doppler radar transmits a continuous wave of a constant frequency and uses the same antenna for transmitting and receiving. When the outgoing wave strikes an object that is approaching the radar set, the wave is reflected at a higher frequency than the frequency at which it was sent out. When an object is moving away from the set, the wave is bounced back at a lower frequency. The faster an object moves in either direction, the greater the difference in frequency between the transmitted and reflected waves. By measuring the difference in frequency, Doppler radar determines the speed of the object observed.

Police use Doppler radar to detect speeding motorists. Military personnel often use it to measure the velocity of targets for directing weapon fire.

Frequency-modulated (FM) radar also transmits a continuous signal, but it rapidly increases or decreases the frequency of the signal at regular intervals. As a result, frequency-modulated radar, unlike Doppler radar, can determine the distance to a moving or stationary object. By the time a radar signal reaches an object and returns, the frequency of the transmitter has changed. The difference between the frequency of the echo and that of the transmitter is measured and converted into the distance to the object that produced the echo. The farther away an object is located, the greater the difference in frequency.

Frequency-modulated radar, like pulse radar, can be used for mapping and tracking. It also serves as an altimeter for airplanes.

The parts of a radar set

Radar sets vary widely in size. The size of a unit depends mainly on its use. For example, the sets used by

Goodyear Aerospace Corporation

Radar mapping can be done from an airplane. The radar map of Flagstaff, Ariz., at the left, was made from an altitude of about 40,000 feet (12,000 meters). The city appears as a cluster of yellow images. The enormous landform to the left of the city is Elden Mountain.

How pulse radar works
Pulse radar is the most widely used type of radar. The diagram below shows the principal parts of a typical pulse radar set and illustrates how it detects a distant object.

WORLD BOOK diagram by Robert Keys

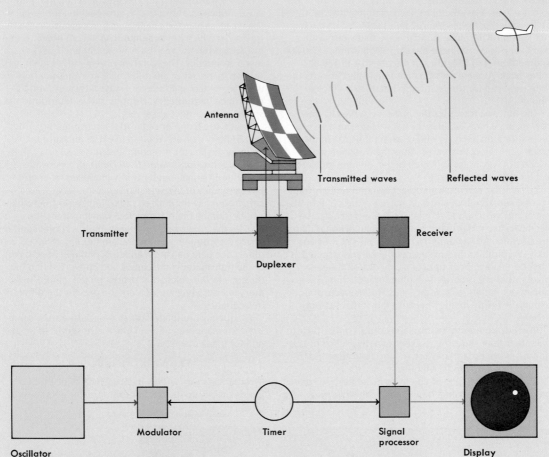

Antenna

Transmitted waves | Reflected waves

Transmitter | Duplexer | Receiver

Oscillator | Modulator | Timer | Signal processor | Display

Transmitting radar waves. The oscillator of a pulse radar set generates a low-power electric signal of a constant frequency. A modulator turns the transmitter on and off, causing the transmitter to produce short bursts of electromagnetic waves. The transmitter produces these high-power waves by amplifying the electric signal generated by the oscillator. A duplexer routes the waves from the transmitter to an antenna. After the waves have been released through the antenna, the duplexer connects the receiver to the antenna, which then collects the waves reflected from an object.

Receiving reflected waves. The switching action of the duplexer enables the receiver to pick up the echoes collected by the antenna. The receiver amplifies the reflected waves and filters out much of the accompanying noise and interference. A signal processor takes the incoming waves from the receiver and combines them, which improves their quality. A display shows the echoes as spots of light or as an image of the object detected. A timer automatically turns the signal processor and the modulator on and off at the right time and so coordinates the operations of the radar set.

motorcycle police to detect nearby speeding cars can be held in the hand. They weigh only about 4 pounds (1.8 kilograms). Many of the huge radar units used to study planets and other distant objects occupy large buildings. One radar unit is built into a valley and has an antenna that measures 1,000 feet (300 meters) in diameter.

Although radar sets differ in size, most have similar parts. These parts include (1) the oscillator, (2) the modulator, (3) the transmitter, (4) the duplexer, (5) the antenna, (6) the receiver, (7) the signal processor, (8) the display, and (9) the timer.

The oscillator is a device that generates a low-power electric signal of a constant frequency. The frequency of the oscillator determines the operating frequency of a radar set.

The modulator. In pulse radar, the modulator is an electronic switch that rapidly turns the transmitter on and off. It causes the transmitter to produce short bursts of waves. In frequency-modulated radar, the modulator varies the frequency of the continuously transmitted wave. Doppler radar has no modulator.

The transmitter serves as an amplifier. It takes the low-power electric signal generated by the oscillator and produces a high-power electromagnetic wave. For example, the transmitter of a pulse radar used in air traffic control may produce wave pulses with a peak power of several million watts.

The duplexer makes it possible to use one antenna for both transmitting and receiving. The duplexer routes the electromagnetic waves from the transmitter to the antenna and prevents them from flowing into the receiver. The powerful waves from the transmitter would damage the sensitive receiver if they flowed into it. After the waves have been released through the antenna, the duplexer connects the receiver to the antenna. This switching action enables the receiver to pick up incoming echoes.

The antenna sends out radar waves in a narrow beam. It also collects the reflected echoes. Because most modern radar units have a duplexer, they use the same antenna for transmitting and receiving.

The most common type of antenna consists of a horn attached to the front of a large reflecting dish called a *reflector.* The horn launches the radar waves, and the reflector focuses them into a narrow beam. The antenna rotates so that the beam sweeps around the radar station, scanning for objects in all directions.

Other types of antennas are used in radar sets that operate either at extremely low frequencies or at extremely high frequencies. Radars that transmit low-frequency radio waves have an antenna made of metal tubes or rods. Such antennas resemble the outdoor aerials of TV sets. Radars that operate at optical frequencies use a device called a *laser,* which generates an intense beam of light. In optical radars, lenses control the size of the transmitted laser beam and capture the light waves returning from the target.

The receiver takes the weak echoes collected by the antenna and greatly amplifies them. It is so sensitive that it can easily detect echoes of less power than a millionth of a millionth of a watt. The receiver also filters out much of the noise and other interference picked up by the antenna.

The signal processor. In most radar sets, the incoming waves from the receiver pass through a signal processor before going to the display. The signal processor performs different tasks in radars used for different purposes. In many radar units, it blocks out echoes from large, fixed objects and allows only echoes from small, moving targets to reach the display. By doing so, the signal processor enables the operator of a radar set to see an airplane, for example, even though the echoes from the plane arrive at the same time as much stronger echoes from a mountain. A computer serves as the signal processor in most modern radars.

The display presents radar operators with information obtained about an object. Some sets have a simple display. The portable Doppler radars used by police, for example, have a meter that indicates the speed of a car or truck. However, most radar sets have a more complex display that consists of a *cathode-ray tube* (CRT). A CRT is a type of vacuum tube with a fluorescent screen like that of a TV set (see **Vacuum tube**). A CRT display can present radar data in several forms. The most common form is the *Plan Position Indicator,* generally called the *PPI.*

The PPI provides a circular, maplike picture of the area scanned by the radar beam. The center of the picture corresponds to the location of the radar set. The screen has a compass scale around its edge for direction readings. The screen might also have rings spreading out from the center of the picture to mark distance in miles or kilometers. Radar echoes appear as bright spots. The position of a spot with respect to the compass scale shows the direction of the object. The distance of the spot from the center indicates how far away the object is. The speed of a moving object can be determined by noting the time it takes a spot to cover a certain distance on the radar screen.

Other forms of a CRT display show the elevation of an object. Such types of presentation are used with radar sets designed to help direct aircraft landings.

The timer ensures the smooth, efficient operation of a radar set. This device automatically turns the other major parts of the radar set on and off at precisely the right time. The timer does so by sending control signals to the various parts of the system in the proper sequence.

The development of radar

The theories and experiments of many scientists led to the development of radar. James Clerk Maxwell, a British mathematician and physicist, made the first major contribution. During the 1860's, Maxwell said that there existed then-undiscovered kinds of electromagnetic waves that travel at the speed of light—186,282 miles (299,792 kilometers) per second. He also proposed that devices might be developed to generate such waves. In the late 1880's, Heinrich R. Hertz, a German physicist, proved Maxwell's ideas correct by producing radio waves. In addition, Hertz demonstrated that such waves could be reflected from solid objects.

Hertz's discovery promoted widespread efforts to find ways of using radio waves for communication. Some scientists realized that radio waves might also be used for detecting distant objects. However, little research could be done in this area until basic radio equipment was developed. Devices for sending and receiving radio signals over long distances became available by the early 1900's.

The first uses of radar. In 1925, two American physicists, Gregory Breit and Merle A. Tuve, bounced short radio pulses off the ionosphere. They determined the height of the ionosphere by measuring the time taken by the reflected signals to return. Many scientists consider this experiment to have been the first practical use of radar. The success of the experiment encouraged researchers in many countries to conduct further scientific studies of the ionosphere with similar equipment and techniques.

Scientists also began experimenting with radio echoes to detect airplanes and ships. Much early work in this area was done by Robert A. Watson-Watt, a Scottish engineer and physicist. In 1935, he and a team of British scientists refined the pulse techniques used in ionospheric studies to locate aircraft at distances up to about 17 miles (27 kilometers). During this time, researchers in France, Germany, and the United States also developed experimental radars that could detect planes and ships within a limited range. These early radars were unreliable and lacked the sensitivity needed for many tasks.

But they provided information useful for military and navigational purposes.

The growing threat of a world war stimulated efforts to improve radar technology during the late 1930's. Before World War II began in September 1939, the British had built a chain of radar stations along the east and south coasts of England for defense against air and sea attacks. By 1940, the United States was producing pulse-type radar for tracking planes and for controlling antiaircraft guns. Germany also had similar kinds of radar by about the same time. Japan and the Soviet Union developed radar-warning systems a few years later.

Advances during World War II. The radar sets available at the beginning of the war proved extremely valuable for military operations. As a result, scientists were urged to develop even better equipment.

American and British radar experts cooperated closely during the war and produced important advances. The British were working to improve a special kind of vacuum tube called the *magnetron.* By late 1939, their version of the magnetron could generate pulses of microwave energy at high enough power levels to be used in radar systems. In 1940, the British turned it over to the Americans for further development and manufacturing.

The magnetron contributed greatly to the development of modern radar. This vacuum tube generates *microwaves*—that is, short radio waves with frequencies of more than 1,000 MHz. These high-frequency waves can be concentrated into narrow beams without the use of a huge radar antenna. Microwaves thus made it possible to design radar units small enough for aircraft, patrol boats, and mobile ground stations.

Before the war ended in 1945, British and American researchers had also developed methods of making enemy radar less effective. The Germans produced similar countermeasures. In one widely used method,

planes on bombing missions dropped countless numbers of metal foil strips called *chaff.* Each strip reflected radio signals like a radar target. The bombers filled the air with so many strips that enemy radar operators had difficulty recognizing echoes from the planes.

In another countermeasure, planes and ships carried high-powered radio transmitters. These transmitters produced enough interference to prevent enemy radar from receiving echoes from the planes and ships. Engineers also designed equipment that received pulses from enemy radar and sent them back at an increased power level after a short pause. As a result, false targets appeared on the display of the enemy radar and drew attention from the real targets.

Continued progress. During the early 1950's, American scientists worked on a type of vacuum tube called the *klystron.* They succeeded in developing a high-powered klystron, which is well-suited for radars that require little variation in microwave frequency from one pulse to the next. Scientists later improved the klystron so that it could generate microwaves at extremely high power levels. This development helped increase the accuracy of radar. Scientists also worked to improve radar sensitivity. By the late 1960's, they had designed receivers that produced little internal noise, which interferes with the reception of faint echoes.

The rapid development of the electronic computer after World War II contributed much to radar technology. Computers make effective signal processors. They can analyze echoes efficiently at high speeds and present the information obtained in a form most useful to radar operators.

Radar also benefited from the invention of the transistor in 1947 and of related solid-state devices during the 1950's and 1960's. These devices enabled engineers to build lighter and more reliable radar sets. In addition, engineers used a solid-state device called a *phase*

Hewlett-Packard
(WORLD BOOK photo)

Ron Phillips

An optical radar is often used to survey rough terrain where distant points must be accurately measured between brush and large rocks, *above.* A tiny solid-state device called a *lasing diode, above right,* enables this type of radar to transmit light waves in an extremely narrow beam.

shifter to develop a new kind of radar. This radar, which is known as a *phased array radar*, moves its signal beam electronically rather than by rotating an antenna. Phased array radars are especially useful when a signal beam must be moved rapidly from one target to the next.

In the late 1960's, physicists perfected the laser. Their work led to the development of optical radars, which operate at the high frequencies of laser light. This type of radar uses an antenna only about the size of a thumbtack to send out an extremely narrow signal beam.

Radar in the future. Researchers today are seeking ways to reduce the size of microwave radars and to manufacture them at low cost. Pocket-sized radar units could be widely used as aids for blind people and as collision-warning devices in cars. Researchers have discovered that over-the-horizon radars can monitor weather over large areas of the ocean that could not be observed previously. These radars might be used to make weather predictions more accurate. In addition, microwave radars built into a single artificial satellite might one day track ship and aircraft traffic over most of the earth.   G. D. Thorne

Related articles in *World Book* include:

Airport	North Warning	Shoran
DEW line	System	Watson-Watt, Sir
Guided missile	Radio	Robert A.
Laser	Rain (Measuring	Weather (Measur-
Microwave	rainfall)	ing the weather)
Navigation	Range finder	

Outline

I. **The uses of radar**
    A. In aviation
    B. In ship navigation
    C. In the military
    D. In controlling automo-
        bile speed and traffic
    E. In weather observation
        and forecasting
    F. In scientific research
    G. In space travel

II. **How radar works**
    A. Pulse radar
    B. Continuous-wave radar

III. **The parts of a radar set**
    A. The oscillator
    B. The modulator
    C. The transmitter
    D. The duplexer
    E. The antenna
    F. The receiver
    G. The signal processor
    H. The display
    I. The timer

IV. **The development of radar**

Questions

What are some uses of radar in scientific research?
Why was the magnetron important in the development of radar?
How does pulse radar find the distance to an object?
What is a Plan Position Indicator?
What are some military uses of radar?
What is the special feature of phased array radar?
How does radar help weather forecasters?
What is Doppler radar? How is it used?
Why is radar an effective aid in ship navigation?
What is a duplexer? Why is it important?

Additional resources

Barton, David K., and others. *Radar Technology Encyclopedia.* Artech Hse., 1997.
Buderi, Robert. *The Invention That Changed the World.* Simon & Schuster, 1996.
Skolnik, Merrill I. *Radar Handbook.* 2nd ed. McGraw, 1990.

Radcliffe-Brown, A. R. (1881-1955), a British anthropologist, helped develop present-day American and British anthropological theories. Alfred Reginald Radcliffe-Brown was born in England and graduated from Cambridge University. After years of research and teaching in London, Australia, and the Union of South Africa, he taught at the University of Chicago from 1931 to 1937. Radcliffe-Brown then became the first professor of social anthropology at Oxford University.   David B. Stout

Radcliffe College was a private liberal arts college for women in Cambridge, Massachusetts. It was an independent institution with close ties to Harvard University. Radcliffe was founded in 1879. At that time, it delegated to the Harvard faculty responsibility for the instruction of Radcliffe students.

Radcliffe was a separate institution with its own administration; board of trustees; and mission, designed to advance society by advancing women. In addition to regular college classes, Radcliffe offered programs of special interest to undergraduate women. It later added programs of continuing education, advanced scholarship and research, and public policy. Beginning in the mid-1970's, women students were admitted jointly to Harvard and Radcliffe, although Radcliffe remained an independent college for undergraduate women. In 1999, Radcliffe College and Harvard University merged, and the Radcliffe Institute for Advanced Study was established, offering a wide range of advanced scholarship and research with a special focus on women, gender, and society.   Critically reviewed by Radcliffe College

See also **Harvard University**.

Radford, Arthur William (1896-1973), an admiral in the United States Navy, served from 1953 to 1957 as chairman of the Joint Chiefs of Staff. Born in Chicago, he graduated from the U.S. Naval Academy, and served during World Wars I and II. Radford won recognition as an expert on naval aviation and aircraft-carrier warfare. He was commander in chief of the U.S. Pacific Fleet from 1949 to 1953.   Donald W. Mitchell

Radian is a metric unit used to measure angles. Engineers and scientists frequently measure angles in radians because the unit simplifies many of their calculations. Navigators, surveyors, and most other people measure angles in degrees. One radian equals an angle of 57.29578 degrees.

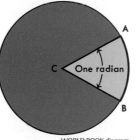

A radian. To draw an angle that equals 1 radian, first measure the radius of a circle. On the circumference of the circle, measure an arc that is the same length as the radius. In the diagram at the left, the arc AB equals the radius. Connect the ends of the arc with the center of the circle. The angle between lines AC and BC equals 1 radian.

WORLD BOOK diagram

An angle of 1 radian is formed between two radii of a circle if they mark off an arc equal to the length of the radius of the circle. Circles and arcs may represent angles and may be measured in radians. For example, the circumference of a circle equals 2 times *pi* (π) times the radius of a circle. Thus, there are 2π radians in a circle.   Colin C. Graham

See also **Degree**.

Radiant energy. See **Sun** (Energy output).
Radiant heating. See **Heating**.

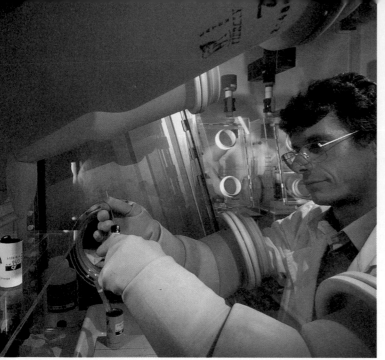
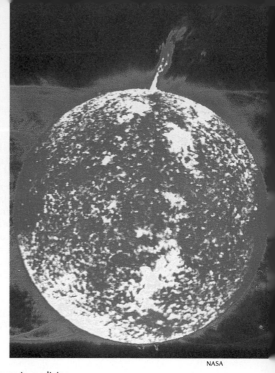

Radiation is a vital form of energy. Artificially produced radiation has many uses in medicine and other fields. A medical worker handles radioactive iodine, *left,* with special gloves through a protective shield. All life on earth depends on natural radiation from the sun, *right.*

Radiation

Radiation is energy given off in the form of waves or small particles of matter. Radiation is found throughout the universe and comes in many forms. Most people have heard of X rays, gamma rays, and radiation from nuclear reactors. These types of radiation are often mentioned as possible health hazards, though X rays and gamma rays also have valuable uses in medicine. But there are many other forms of radiation as well. The most familiar is probably the light we see, such as the light from the sun or a flashlight. The sun's ultraviolet rays, which cause suntan and sunburn, are another form of radiation. Heat from a fireplace, radio signals bringing music, the intense light from a laser, and the microwaves used to cook food are still others.

Radiation is present whenever energy moves from one place to another. Atoms and molecules give off radiation to dispose of excess energy. When the radiation strikes a substance, it may transfer some or all of its energy to the substance. Often, the energy takes the form of heat, raising the temperature of the material. Except for light, most kinds of radiation are invisible.

There are two chief types of radiation. One type, called *electromagnetic radiation,* consists only of energy. The other type, known as *particle radiation* or *particulate radiation,* consists of tiny bits of matter.

There are many sources of electromagnetic radiation. All materials that have been heated act as sources of

---

Douglas John Crawford-Brown, the contributor of this article, is Professor of Radiation Physics in the Department of Environmental Science and Engineering, University of North Carolina.

such radiation. The sun produces electromagnetic radiation from nuclear reactions in its core. This energy heats the sun's outer layer until the hot gases glow, giving off light and other radiation. This solar radiation travels through space to the earth and other planets.

Particle radiation comes from radioactive substances. Radium, uranium, and many other heavy elements found in rocks and soil are naturally radioactive. In addition, scientists can create radioactive forms of any element in a laboratory by bombarding the element with *atomic particles,* the tiny bits of matter that make up atoms.

All life on earth depends on radiation, but some forms of radiation can be dangerous if not handled properly. X rays, for example, allow doctors to locate and diagnose hidden diseases. But X rays also can damage cells, causing them to become cancerous or die. Light from the sun enables plants to grow and warms the earth, but it also causes sunburn and skin cancer. Gamma radiation is used to treat disease by killing cancer cells, but it also can cause birth defects. Nuclear power plants produce electric energy, but the same facilities create radioactive waste that can kill living things.

Uses of radiation

In medicine, radiation and radioactive substances are used for diagnosis, treatment, and research. X rays, for example, pass through muscles and other soft tissue but are stopped by dense materials. This property of X rays enables doctors to find broken bones and to locate cancers that might be growing in the body. Doctors also find certain diseases by injecting a radioactive substance and monitoring the radiation given off as the substance moves through the body.

In communication. All modern communication systems use forms of electromagnetic radiation. Variations in the intensity of the radiation represent changes in the sound, pictures, or other information being transmitted. For example, a human voice can be sent as a radio wave or microwave by making the wave vary to correspond to variations in the voice.

In science, researchers use radioactive atoms to determine the age of materials that were once part of a living organism. The age of such materials can be estimated by measuring the amount of radioactive carbon they contain in a process called *radiocarbon dating.* Environmental scientists use radioactive atoms known as *tracer atoms* to identify the pathways taken by pollutants through the environment.

Radiation is used to determine the composition of materials in a process called *neutron activation analysis.* In this process, scientists bombard a sample of a substance with particles called *neutrons.* Some of the atoms in the sample absorb neutrons and become radioactive. The scientists can identify the elements in the sample by studying the radiation given off.

In industry, radiation has many uses. Food processing plants employ low doses of radiation to kill bacteria on certain foods, thus preserving the food. Radiation is used to make plastics because it causes molecules to link together and harden. Industry also uses radiation to look for flaws in manufactured materials in a process called *industrial radiography.*

Nuclear power plants obtain energy from *nuclear fission,* the splitting of the nucleus of an atom into the nuclei of two lighter elements. Fission releases large amounts of radiation, including infrared radiation that is used to turn water into steam. This steam then runs a turbine that produces electric energy.

The opposite process, *nuclear fusion,* occurs when the nuclei of two lighter elements join to form the nucleus of a heavier one. Fusion, like fission, releases vast amounts of radiation. Fusion creates the heat and light of the sun and other stars, and the explosive force of the hydrogen bomb. Scientists are learning how to harness fusion to produce electric energy.

In military operations, radio waves are used in radar systems to locate aircraft and ships. Microwaves and the light from lasers have been used both for communication and to guide "smart" missiles to their targets. Heat-sensing devices for night detection rely on the infrared radiation given off by living bodies.

Radiation and radioactivity

Scientists distinguish radiation from *radioactivity,* which is a property of some types of matter. Radioactivity causes matter to release certain forms of radiation as the result of changes in the nuclei of the atoms that make up the matter.

To understand radiation and radioactivity, it is necessary to understand how an atom is constructed and how it can change. An atom consists of tiny particles of negative electric charge called *electrons* surrounding a heavy, positively charged nucleus. Opposite electric charges attract each other, and like charges *repel* (push away) each other. The positively charged nucleus therefore attracts the negatively charged electrons and so keeps them within the atom.

The nucleus of every element except the most common form of hydrogen consists of particles called *protons* and *neutrons.* (A normal hydrogen nucleus is made up of a single proton and no neutrons.) Protons carry a positive charge, and neutrons have no charge. The most common form of helium, for example, has two protons and two neutrons in the nucleus and two electrons outside the nucleus. Protons and neutrons consist of even smaller particles called *quarks.*

Within the nucleus, the positively charged protons repel one another because they have like charges. The protons and neutrons remain together in the nucleus only because an extremely powerful force holds them together. This force is called the *strong nuclear force* or the *strong interaction.* See **Atom** (Forces in the nucleus).

An atom can change the number of protons and neutrons in its nucleus by giving off or taking in atomic particles or bursts of energy—that is, by giving off or taking in radiation. But any change in the number of protons in the nucleus produces an atom of a different element. Radioactive atoms spontaneously release radiation to take on a more stable form. The process of giving off atomic particles is called *radioactive decay.* As radioactive elements decay, they change into different forms of the same element or into other elements until they finally become stable and nonradioactive.

Radioactive decay takes place at different rates in different elements or different forms of the same element. The rate of decay is measured by the *half-life,* the length of time needed for half the atoms in a sample to decay. For example, the half-life of cesium 137, a radioactive form of the metal cesium, is about 30 years. After about 60 years, approximately a fourth of the original cesium 137 remains. After another 30 years, only an eighth remains, and so on. The half-life of radon 222 is about 3.8 days. Half-lives vary from fractions of a second to billions of years.

Electromagnetic radiation

Electromagnetic radiation consists of electric and magnetic energy. Every electrically charged body is surrounded by an *electric field,* a region where the body's electric force can be felt. Every magnetic body is surrounded by a similar region known as a *magnetic field.* An electric current or a changing electric field creates a magnetic field, and a changing magnetic field creates an electric field. Electric and magnetic fields act together to produce electromagnetic radiation.

Electromagnetic radiation moves through space as a wave, but it also has properties of particles. Atoms release electromagnetic radiation in the form of a tiny packet of energy called a *photon.* Like a particle, a photon occupies a fixed amount of space. Like waves, however, photons have a definite frequency and wavelength, which can be measured. The number of times each second that a wave passes through one cycle is called its *frequency.* The distance a wave travels in the time it takes to pass through one cycle is called the *wavelength.* The energy of a photon of electromagnetic radiation varies according to the frequency and wavelength. If the radiation has a high frequency and a short wavelength, its photons have high energy. If the radiation has a low frequency and a long wavelength, its photons have low energy.

In a vacuum, all electromagnetic radiation moves at the speed of light—186,282 miles (299,792 kilometers)

Kinds of electromagnetic radiation

Electromagnetic radiation travels through space in waves, which vary in *frequency* (how quickly a wave passes through a cycle) and *wavelength* (how far the wave travels during one cycle). The kinds of radiation range in wavelength from short gamma rays to long radio waves.

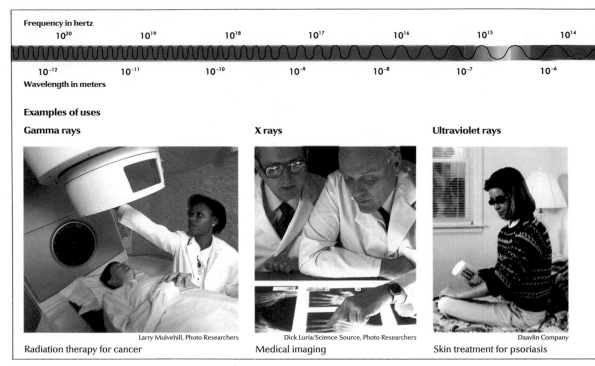

Frequency in hertz

10^{20} 10^{19} 10^{18} 10^{17} 10^{16} 10^{15} 10^{14}

10^{-12} 10^{-11} 10^{-10} 10^{-9} 10^{-8} 10^{-7} 10^{-6}

Wavelength in meters

Examples of uses

Gamma rays   **X rays**   **Ultraviolet rays**

Larry Mulvehill, Photo Researchers   Dick Luria/Science Source, Photo Researchers   Daavlin Company

Radiation therapy for cancer   Medical imaging   Skin treatment for psoriasis

per second. The various kinds of radiation differ, however, in their frequency and wavelength. They are classified according to an arrangement called the *electromagnetic spectrum.* In order of increasing wavelength, the kinds of electromagnetic radiation are gamma rays, X rays, ultraviolet rays, visible light, infrared (pronounced *IHN fruh REHD)* rays, microwaves, and radio waves. Gamma rays and X rays are high-energy forms of radiation. Radio waves, on the other end of the spectrum, have relatively low energy.

Particle radiation

Particle radiation consists of protons, neutrons, and electrons, the tiny particles that are the building blocks of an atom. All types of particle radiation have both mass and energy. Most such radiation travels at high speeds but slower than the speed of light. A type of particle called a *neutrino,* however, has an undetermined mass and travels at or near the speed of light.

Scientists have discovered that protons, neutrons, and electrons, which we usually think of as particles, also behave like waves. These waves, called *matter waves,* have wavelengths. The faster a particle is moving, the shorter its wavelength. This means that particle radiation, like electromagnetic radiation, has characteristics of both particles and waves. There are four common types of particle radiation: (1) alpha particles, (2) beta particles, (3) protons, and (4) neutrons.

Alpha particles consist of two protons and two neutrons and are identical with the nuclei of helium atoms. Alpha particles have a positive electric charge. The mass

of an alpha is about 7,300 times larger than the mass of an electron. Alpha particles are given off by the nuclei of some radioactive atoms. Most alpha particles eventually gain two electrons and become atoms of helium gas.

Beta particles are electrons. Most beta particles are produced when a radioactive nucleus creates and releases an electron. In the process, a neutron in the nucleus changes into a proton and a beta is released.

Most beta particles are negatively charged, but some are positively charged particles called *positrons* produced when an atom changes a proton into a neutron. Positrons are a form of *antimatter,* matter which resembles ordinary matter except that its electric charge is reversed. When a positron collides with a negatively charged electron, the two particles destroy each other, and two or three gamma ray photons are produced. This collision is called *pair annihilation* (pronounced *uh NY uh LAY shuhn).*

Two other small particles, *neutrinos* and *antineutrinos,* accompany beta radiation. When a nucleus produces a positron, it also releases a neutrino, which has no charge and an undetermined mass. When a nucleus creates and releases a negatively charged beta particle, it also gives off an antineutrino, the antimatter form of a neutrino.

Protons and neutrons can also be released from some radioactive nuclei. Each has a mass about 1,850 times larger than the mass of an electron. The mass of a neutron is slightly larger than the mass of a proton. Neutron radiation is more common than proton radiation, which rarely is produced naturally on the earth.

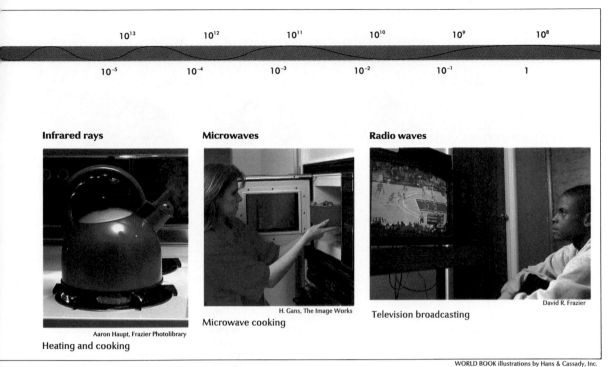

10^{13}	10^{12}	10^{11}	10^{10}	10^{9}	10^{8}

10^{-5}	10^{-4}	10^{-3}	10^{-2}	10^{-1}	1

Infrared rays

Aaron Haupt, Frazier Photolibrary

Heating and cooking

Microwaves

H. Gans, The Image Works

Microwave cooking

Radio waves

David R. Frazier

Television broadcasting

WORLD BOOK illustrations by Hans & Cassady, Inc.

Sources of radiation

Natural sources of radiation include the sun and other stars, and naturally radioactive elements. There are also many artificial sources of radiation.

The sun and other stars give off both electromagnetic and particle radiation. This radiation results from the fusion of hydrogen nuclei in the star. The hydrogen changes into helium and releases a large amount of energy, producing electromagnetic radiation across the entire spectrum. Besides visible light, a star gives off everything from radio waves to high-energy gamma radiation. However, the gamma radiation, which is produced when new elements form deep in the core of the star, does not reach earth directly.

Stars also produce alpha and beta particles, protons, neutrons, and other forms of radiation. The high-energy particles released by stars are called *cosmic rays.* Even the sun puts on brief displays called *solar flares,* bathing the earth in cosmic rays strong enough to interfere with communications.

Naturally radioactive substances. Most naturally radioactive substances belong to one of three sequences of change called *radioactive decay series:* (1) the uranium series, (2) the thorium series, and (3) the actinium series. In each of these series, heavy *isotopes* (forms of the same element that have different numbers of neutrons) decay into various lighter isotopes by giving off radiation until they eventually become stable.

The uranium series begins with uranium 238, the heaviest isotope of uranium, which has 92 protons and 146 neutrons. After losing an alpha particle, which consists of 2 protons and 2 neutrons, the nucleus has 90 protons and 144 neutrons. It is no longer uranium but a radioactive isotope of thorium. Scientists call this process of changing into another element *transmutation.* The thorium, in turn, breaks down in several steps to radium 226. The radium 226 decays into radon, a naturally occurring radioactive gas. Radon may become a health hazard if it accumulates in certain buildings, especially poorly ventilated ones. The series continues until the isotope becomes a stable form of lead.

The thorium series begins with thorium 232, an isotope of thorium. The actinium series begins with uranium 235, also called U-235, another isotope of uranium. These two series also end with lead.

A fourth group of naturally radioactive substances includes a wide variety of materials that do not belong to a radioactive series. Many of these elements, including carbon 14, potassium 40, and samarium 146, are produced by cosmic radiation striking the earth's atmosphere. Carbon 14 and potassium 40 are also present in the human body.

Artificial radioactive substances are made by human activities, such as the fission that takes place in nuclear weapons and nuclear reactors, or in laboratories. When fission splits a nucleus, it releases several types of radiation, including neutrons, gamma radiation, and beta particles. Fission also produces new radioactive atoms called *fission products.* For example, atomic bomb tests in the 1950's and 1960's covered the earth with a fission product called cesium 137, a radioactive

Particles given off by radioactive atoms

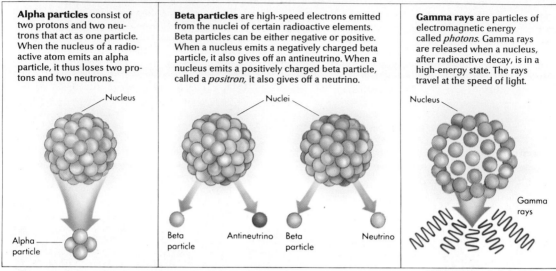

Alpha particles consist of two protons and two neutrons that act as one particle. When the nucleus of a radioactive atom emits an alpha particle, it thus loses two protons and two neutrons.

Beta particles are high-speed electrons emitted from the nuclei of certain radioactive elements. Beta particles can be either negative or positive. When a nucleus emits a negatively charged beta particle, it also gives off an antineutrino. When a nucleus emits a positively charged beta particle, called a *positron,* it also gives off a neutrino.

Gamma rays are particles of electromagnetic energy called *photons.* Gamma rays are released when a nucleus, after radioactive decay, is in a high-energy state. The rays travel at the speed of light.

WORLD BOOK illustration by Sarah Woodward

isotope of cesium. Used fuel from nuclear power plants also contains many fission products, such as plutonium 239, strontium 90, and barium 140. This used fuel, called nuclear waste, remains radioactive and dangerous for thousands of years.

In addition, nuclear plants create new radioactive elements known as *activation products.* Activation products form when the pipes and other materials in a nuclear reactor absorb neutrons and other types of radiation, becoming radioactive.

Many other types of radiation are created by human activities. Physicists use powerful devices called *particle accelerators* to speed up the movement of electrically charged particles, including electrons, protons, and entire nuclei. The physicists then bombard stable, nonradioactive atoms with beams of these high-speed particles. The resulting collisions produce new radioactive

atoms and help scientists learn more about the structure and properties of atoms.

Causes of radiation

Within an atom, electrons are confined to regions called *electron shells* at various distances from the nucleus according to how much energy they have. Electrons with less energy travel in inner shells, and those with more energy are in outer shells. Protons and neutrons in the nucleus are also arranged according to their energy levels in layers known as *nuclear shells.* All the protons, neutrons, or electrons in a shell have almost the same amount of energy.

Just as water always seeks its lowest possible level, electrons seek the state of lowest energy. When an electron shifts from an outer shell to one closer to the nucleus, the electron releases a packet of energy called a

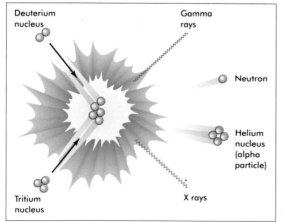

WORLD BOOK illustration by Mark Swindle

Nuclear fusion releases large amounts of radiation. Fusion occurs when the nuclei of two lightweight elements join to form the nucleus of a heavier one. In the example above, nuclei of deuterium and tritium unite and form a helium nucleus.

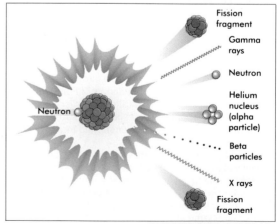

WORLD BOOK illustration by Mark Swindle

Nuclear fission releases several types of radiation, including neutrons, alpha and beta particles, gamma rays, and X rays. Fission involves using a neutron to split a nucleus of a heavy element, such as uranium, into two fission fragments.

photon, which escapes from the atom. The energy of the photon equals the difference in energy between the original shell of the electron and the new one. If the energy difference is small, as in a light bulb, the atom will give off visible light, infrared radiation, or both. If the difference is large, the atom might produce X rays.

When a proton or neutron moves from one nuclear shell to another, the nucleus releases gamma radiation. Most atoms that release particle radiation in the course of radioactive decay also produce gamma radiation because their protons and neutrons are shifting into new shells. The radiation produced by nuclear reactions also results from protons, neutrons, and electrons moving to new shells. In nuclear fission, for example, the particles are moving to the shells of new nuclei created when a nucleus splits into two smaller nuclei.

Electromagnetic radiation also is produced if an electrically charged particle changes direction, speed, or both. A particle that enters an electric or magnetic field, for example, slows down and changes course. As a result, the particle releases radiation. X rays are produced whenever electrons suddenly decelerate, such as when they collide with atoms of metal to create the X rays in an X-ray machine. Electrons also produce X rays if they pass near a large nucleus. The negatively charged electrons are attracted by the positively charged nucleus. As the electrons change direction, they produce X rays called *bremsstrahlung* (pronounced *BREHM shtrah lung*), a German word that means *braking radiation.*

Effects of radiation

Radiation produces two main effects in atoms or molecules: (1) excitation and (2) ionization. In *excitation,* an atom or molecule absorbs energy from radiation. Its electrons move to higher-energy shells. In most cases, the excited atom can hold the extra energy for only a fraction of a second before it releases the energy as a photon and falls back to a state of lower energy. In *ionization,* the radiation transfers enough energy to the electrons in an atom that they leave the atom and move through space. Atoms that have lost electrons become positively charged particles called *positive ions.* The electrons may then join other atoms.

Excitation and ionization also affect living tissues. The body's cells contain molecules, many of which are held together by electrons. When radiation excites or ionizes the molecules in cells, chemical bonds may be broken and the shape of a molecule may be changed. These changes disrupt the normal chemical processes of the cells, causing the cells to become abnormal or die.

If radiation affects molecules of DNA (deoxyribonucleic acid), the hereditary material in living cells, it may cause a permanent change called a *mutation.* In rare cases, mutations caused by radiation may pass on undesirable traits to offspring. Even low-energy photons, particularly ultraviolet light from the sun, may produce damage by excitation. If the injury is severe, the cell becomes cancerous or dies while trying to divide. The effect produced depends on the radiation's ionizing ability, the dose received, and the type of tissue involved.

Ionizing ability. Radiation may be classified as *ionizing* or *non-ionizing.* Ionizing radiation is the most dangerous. Some types of ionizing radiation have enough energy to directly strip electrons from any atoms near their path. Such radiation includes alpha and beta particles and protons. Other types of ionizing radiation, including X rays, gamma radiation, and neutron radiation, must first transfer energy to an atom. The added energy then causes the atom to lose an electron.

Non-ionizing radiation consists of photons with too little energy to cause ionization. Radio waves, microwaves, infrared radiation, and visible light are all non-ionizing radiation. Each will cause only excitation.

Dose. Scientists use two systems for measuring the amount, or *dose,* of radiation absorbed by a substance. The older system, still commonly used, measures doses in units called *rads. Rad* stands for *radiation absorbed dose.* One rad is produced when 1 gram of material absorbs 100 ergs. (An *erg* is an extremely small unit of energy.) The newer system, introduced in 1975, measures dosage in units called *grays,* named after Louis H. Gray, a British radiation biologist. One gray is equal to 100 rads or 1 joule per kilogram of material. A *joule* is a unit of energy equal to 10 million ergs. A typical dental X ray, for example, exposes the patient to about 0.25 rad (0.0025 gray).

Radioactive decay

A radioactive decay series is the process by which a radioactive atom releases radiation and changes into different forms of the same element or into other elements. The uranium series, shown at the right, begins with uranium 238. Losing an alpha particle, the atom changes into radioactive thorium 234. The series continues through many more steps of decay until the atom becomes a stable form of lead.

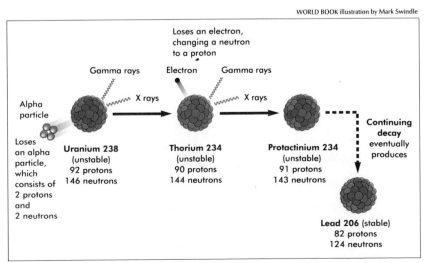

Loses an electron, changing a neutron to a proton

Gamma rays   Electron   Gamma rays

Alpha particle   X rays   X rays

Loses an alpha particle, which consists of 2 protons and 2 neutrons

Uranium 238 (unstable) 92 protons 146 neutrons

Thorium 234 (unstable) 90 protons 144 neutrons

Protactinium 234 (unstable) 91 protons 143 neutrons

Continuing decay eventually produces

Lead 206 (stable) 82 protons 124 neutrons

Different types of radiation produce different effects at the same dose. To account for this, scientists have developed the *quality factor.* The quality factor indicates how much the radiation damages living tissue compared with an equal dose of X rays. For example, a dose of alpha particles causes about 10 times as much damage as the same dose of X rays, so alpha particles have a quality factor of 10. X rays, gamma radiation, and beta particles have a factor of 1. Neutrons range from 2 to 11.

Multiplying the dose by the quality factor gives a measure of damage called the *dose equivalent.* If the dose is given in rads, the dose equivalent will be in *rems.* A rem, which stands for *r*oentgen *e*quivalent in *m*an, is the amount of radiation necessary to cause the same effect on a human being as 1 rad of X rays. If the dose is reported in grays, the dose equivalent will be in *sieverts,* named for Swedish radiologist Rolf M. Sievert. Grays and sieverts are part of the metric system of measurement, officially called the Système International d'Unités (International System of Units).

Large doses cause a combination of effects called *radiation sickness.* Doses above 100 rems damage red and white blood cells. This damage is known as the *hematopoietic effect.* At doses above 300 rems, death may follow in several weeks. Above 1,000 rems, the cells lining the digestive tract die and bacteria from the intestines invade the bloodstream. This effect, known as the *gastrointestinal effect,* may lead to death from infection within a week. At doses of several thousand rems, the brain is injured and death can come within hours.

Deaths from radiation sickness are extremely rare. People have only suffered such large doses in reactor accidents, in a few cases where radioactive material was mishandled, and in the 1945 bombings of Hiroshima and Nagasaki, Japan, during World War II. The worst reactor accident in history was a 1986 explosion and fire at the Chernobyl nuclear power plant in Ukraine, then part of the Soviet Union. Thirty-one workers died.

Robert Gale, Sygma
The worst radiation accident in history was a 1986 explosion and fire at the Chernobyl plant in Ukraine. Hundreds of workers suffered radiation sickness, *above,* and 31 died.

Small doses. The doses received in daily life, sometimes called *background doses,* are much smaller. Some scientists believe that the average background dose is 0.3 to 0.4 rem per year. About half of this amount comes from breathing radon gas released by radioactive rocks and soil. Medical and dental X rays add another 0.04 rem per year. Other sources, such as nuclear power plants and waste disposal sites, typically account for less than 0.01 rem per year. Smokers take in much higher doses from radioactive isotopes in smoke.

An accumulation of small doses of radiation increases the risk of developing a condition, but not the severity of the condition. The chief effects of repeated small doses of radiation are cancer and birth defects.

To protect people from the effects of radiation, the International Commission on Radiological Protection, a panel of experts from many countries, sets guidelines for exposure. This group recommends that nuclear workers receive a maximum permissible dose (MPD) of no more than 5 rems per year. The commission also urges that the general public receive no more than 0.5 rem in any year. Other agencies, including the National Council on Radiation Protection and Measurements in the United States and the Atomic Energy Control Board in Canada, set similar guidelines.

History

Early theories and discoveries. Scientists have studied radiation since ancient times. In the 300's and 200's B.C., the Greek philosopher Epicurus wrote of particles "streaming off" from the surface of bodies. Euclid, a Greek mathematician of the same time, thought the eye sent out radiation to allow an object to be seen.

Robert Grosseteste, an English bishop and scholar of the 1200's, thought of light as the root of all knowledge. He believed that understanding the laws controlling light would uncover all the laws of nature.

The composition of light was debated in the 1600's by the followers of the English scientist Sir Isaac Newton and the Dutch physicist Christiaan Huygens. Newton insisted that light consisted of tiny particles, while Huygens suggested it was composed of waves. Scientists argued about these two theories for more than 100 years. Then, in the early 1800's, the British physicist Thomas Young showed that light had properties similar to those of sound and water waves. A few years later, the French physicist Augustin Fresnel provided more evidence. By 1850, most scientists accepted Young's and Fresnel's findings as proof of the wave nature of light.

In 1864, the British scientist James Clerk Maxwell suggested that light consisted of electromagnetic waves. Maxwell also predicted that other, invisible forms of electromagnetic radiation would be discovered. Maxwell's predictions came true with the work of two German physicists, Heinrich R. Hertz and Wilhelm C. Roentgen. Hertz discovered radio waves in the late 1880's, and Roentgen discovered X rays in 1895.

Discovery of radioactivity. In 1896, the French physicist Antoine Henri Becquerel discovered that crystals of a uranium compound would darken photographic plates even if the plates were not exposed to light. He proposed that uranium gave off energy in the form of radiation. Later experiments by the British physicist Ernest Rutherford showed that this radiation consisted of particles he named *alphas* and *betas*.

In 1898, the French physicists Marie and Pierre Curie found other substances that produced radiation, naming them *polonium* and *radium*. A few years later, Rutherford showed that radioactive substances could change into new elements in the process of transmutation.

The work of Rutherford and the Curies led to great interest in the structure of the atom. Rutherford, his colleagues, and other scientists soon proved that the atom had a nucleus of high mass and positive electric charge surrounded by negatively charged electrons.

The quantum theory. In 1900, the German physicist Max Planck studied radiation from hot objects. He suggested that objects could only emit and absorb this radiation in packets of energy called *quanta,* a name later changed to *photons.* Another German physicist, Albert Einstein, used Planck's theory in 1905 to explain a phenomenon known as the *photoelectric effect.* Earlier scientists had discovered this effect, in which a bright beam of light striking a metal causes the metal to release electrons. Einstein proposed that the energy supplied by a single photon could free an electron from an atom in the metal. To produce the photoelectric effect, photons act in a localized manner characteristic of particles rather than waves. Thus, Einstein's ideas revived the particle theory of light. Scientists now know that radiation has features of both particles and waves.

The Danish physicist Niels Bohr used the quantum theory in 1913 to explain the structure of the hydrogen atom. Bohr proposed that electrons can have only certain values of energy. He showed that atoms release photons of radiation when their electrons drop from a high-energy level to a lower one. In 1924, the French physicist Louis de Broglie predicted that electrons themselves might act as waves, called matter waves.

The nuclear age began in 1942, when Italian-born physicist Enrico Fermi and his co-workers at the University of Chicago produced the first artificial nuclear chain reaction. Since then, many scientists have turned their attention from understanding what causes radioactivity and radiation to finding uses for them. Nuclear weapons based on fission—the atomic bomb—and fusion—the hydrogen bomb—were developed. The first full-scale nuclear power plant began operation in 1956. Radiation from across the entire electromagnetic spectrum was harnessed for communication, medicine, industry, and research.   Douglas John Crawford-Brown

Related articles in *World Book* include:

Kinds of radiation

Alpha particle	Gamma rays	Radio (How radio programs are broadcast)	Sun (Energy output)
Beta particle	Infrared rays		Ultraviolet rays
Cosmic rays	Light (The nature of light)		X rays
Electromagnetic waves	Microwave		

Radioactive substances

Actinium	Element 111	Nobelium	Radon
Americium	Einsteinium	Pitchblende	Rutherfordium
Astatine	Fermium	Plutonium	Seaborgium
Berkelium	Francium	Polonium	Technetium
Bohrium	Hassium	Promethium	Thorium
Californium	Lawrencium	Protactinium	Transuranium element
Curium	Meitnerium	Radiocarbon	Uranium
Dubnium	Mendelevium	Radium	
Element 110	Neptunium		

Other related articles

Atom	Nuclear energy
Cancer (Genes damaged by substances in the environment; Cancer treatment)	Nuclear physics
	Nuclear weapon
	Particle accelerator
Energy	Particle detector
Environmental pollution (Hazardous waste)	Phosphorescence
	Photon
Fallout	Plasma (physics)
Fluorescence	Quantum mechanics
Geiger counter	Radiochemistry
Ion	Radiogeology
Irradiation	Radiology
Isotope	Subatomic particle
Luminescence	Transmutation of elements

Outline

I. Uses of radiation
  A. In medicine
  B. In communication
  C. In science
  D. In industry
  E. In military operations
II. Radiation and radioactivity
III. Electromagnetic radiation
IV. Particle radiation
  A. Alpha particles
  B. Beta particles
  C. Protons and neutrons
V. Sources of radiation
  A. The sun and other stars
  B. Naturally radioactive substances
  C. Artificial radioactive substances
VI. Causes of radiation
VII. Effects of radiation
  A. Ionizing ability
  B. Dose
VIII. History

Questions

What is radioactivity?
How does ionizing radiation damage living cells?
What is the final product of uranium decay?
How are positive ions produced?
What are some natural sources of radiation?
How do physicists create radioactive forms of elements?
Who first suggested that radiation came in packets of energy called *quanta* or *photons?*
Why do atoms give off gamma radiation?
What are the chief health risks caused by repeated low doses of radiation?
What is the difference between electromagnetic radiation and particle radiation?
What are the chief types of electromagnetic radiation?

Additional resources

Kevles, Bettyann H. *Naked to the Bone: Medical Imaging in the Twentieth Century.* Rutgers, 1996.
Mather, John C., and Boslough, John. *The Very First Light.* Basic Bks., 1996.
Nilsson, Annika. *Ultraviolet Reflections: Life Under a Thinning Ozone Layer.* Wiley, 1996.
Taylor, Jack H. *Radiation Exchange.* Academic Pr., 1990.
Wolfson, Richard. *Nuclear Choices: A Citizen's Guide to Nuclear Technology.* Rev. ed. MIT Pr., 1993.

Radiation belt. See Van Allen belts.
Radiation detector. See Geiger counter.
Radiation sickness is the term for a variety of symptoms that follow a person's exposure to damaging amounts of certain types of radiation. The radiation may come from nuclear explosions and the resulting fallout, from medical and industrial uses of radioisotopes, or from particle accelerators or X-ray machines. Ionization

from the radiation causes a series of reactions in tissue that results in damage to the body's cells (see **Radiation** (Effects of radiation)). Exposures to high levels of radiation may cause lasting injury or even death.

Some types of cells are more easily injured by radiation than others. The most sensitive cells are those of the blood-forming bone marrow and lymphoid tissues and those of a human embryo. Adult muscle and brain cells are the least sensitive to radiation.

Scientists use a unit called the *rem* as a measure of radiation exposure. Over a lifetime, a person typically receives 7 to 14 rems from natural sources of radiation, such as cosmic rays. A single exposure of 5 to 75 rems produces few observable symptoms. Vomiting, fatigue, and loss of appetite accompany exposures of 75 to 200 rems, and recovery takes a few weeks. Severe changes in blood cells and hemorrhage occur with exposures of more than 300 rems. Above 600 rems, additional symptoms include loss of hair and loss of the body's ability to fight infection, usually resulting in death.

Doctors can treat only the symptoms of radiation sickness. Blood transfusions and the use of antibiotics to fight infection are common treatments.

W. Emmett Bolch

See also **Fallout.**

Radiator is a set of pipes or tubes that gives off heat to its surroundings. Steam or hot-water radiators in homes transfer heat to the air in a room. When warmed, the air next to the pipes expands, becomes lighter, and rises. Cooler air from the room streams in to take its place, creating a constant circulation of air. This process is called *convection,* and certain types of radiators are called *convectors.* Radiators also heat room air by direct *radiation.* See **Heat** (How heat travels).

An automobile radiator works in the same way. Water carries heat from the engine to tubes at the front of the radiator. Air rushing past the tubes absorbs heat from the water and cools it. An engine-driven or electric fan helps move air through the radiator when the car is stopped or moving at low speed.   Evan Powell

See also **Automobile** (The cooling system); **Heating** (Central heating systems).

Radical, in chemistry, is a group of two or more charged or neutral atoms that have at least one unpaired electron. Molecular oxygen, O_2, has two unpaired electrons and is a common radical. Most radicals are extremely reactive and combine with other atoms or radicals to form compounds or ions. However, some radicals, called *free radicals,* may exist for relatively short times unbound to any other group. Radicals play a major role in certain chemical reactions of commercial significance, including the formation of polymers. They are also important in understanding atmospheric reactions caused by sunlight.   Mark S. Wrighton

Radical Republican. See **Reconstruction** (The radicals and the moderates).

Radicalism is a political philosophy that emphasizes the need to find and eliminate the basic injustices of society. The word *radicalism* comes from the Latin word *radix,* meaning *root.* Radicals seek what they consider the roots of the economic, political, and social wrongs of society and demand immediate and sweeping changes to wipe them out.

In the United States, many people regard radicals as political extremists of either the left or right wing. But the meaning of the word *radical* varies from country to country and from time to time. For example, in the West, radicals often support some variety of socialism. In Eastern Europe, on the other hand, radicals oppose the existing socialist regimes. In addition, the people whom one generation considers radicals may differ greatly in viewpoint from the radicals of the previous or next generation.

In Europe, the term *radical* came into general use in Britain during the early 1800's. It described reform demands by such political leaders as Charles James Fox. In 1797, Fox had demanded what he called "radical reform" to make Britain's political system more democratic. During the 1800's, the British philosopher Jeremy Bentham led a group called "philosophical radicals." He believed all legislation should aim to provide the greatest happiness for the greatest number of people.

Radicalism developed in France after the French Revolution (1789-1799) had made that nation a republic. During the 1800's, many European radicals took the French Revolution as their model and tried to establish republics in their own countries.

Several European radicals established the socialist movement and demanded the total reconstruction of society. During the late 1800's, the movement split into moderate and radical factions. The moderate socialists sought change through gradual reform. The radical socialists insisted that only revolution could reform society. In Russia, the moderates were called *Mensheviks* and the radicals *Bolsheviks.* The Bolsheviks seized power in 1917 and set up a Communist government.

In the United States, the followers of Alexander Hamilton, the first secretary of the treasury, opposed the French Revolution. They used the term *radicals* for the pro-French followers of Thomas Jefferson.

In the years before and during the Civil War (1861-1865), radical abolitionists called for an immediate end to slavery. Other radicals demanded cheap land, prohibition of alcoholic beverages, voting reforms, and women's rights. After the Civil War, Radical Republicans sought a "hard peace" for the defeated South (see **Reconstruction**). During the late 1800's and early 1900's, left wing radical groups included the Knights of Labor, the Populists, and the Socialists.

American radicals, unlike European radicals, have never been able to establish a major political party. However, radicals in the United States have influenced national politics through their writings and speeches. They also have organized third parties that have often gained enough support to force the major parties to pass reform legislation. Such legislation has included the income tax, government regulation of industry, and social welfare programs.

During the 1960's and early 1970's, supporters of "black power" condemned the civil rights movement on the ground that its goals and tactics were too moderate. During the 1970's and 1980's, the women's movement also split into radical and moderate wings. Radical feminists urged the overthrow of male-dominated institutions. The moderates sought equal pay for equal work, passage of an Equal Rights Amendment, and federal support for day-care centers.   Christopher Lasch

See also **Left wing; Right wing.**

© Brent Jones

Dennis Hallinan, FPG

WORLD BOOK photo by Steven Spicer

Radio broadcasting originates in a studio and can be heard almost anywhere. A disc jockey at a radio station, *above left,* announces and plays recorded music. Many people use small, lightweight portable radios, *above, above right,* to receive broadcasts.

Radio

Radio is one of our most important means of communication. It enables people to send words, music, codes, and other signals over long distances. People on ships and in aircraft keep in contact with others on land by using radio. People also use radio to communicate far into space.

The most widespread and familiar use of radio is for the form of one-way communication known as broadcasting. Radio broadcasts feature music, news, discussions, interviews, descriptions of sports events, drama, reviews of cultural events, religious programs, and advertising. People wake up to clock radios and listen to radios while in their automobiles. Many also enjoy listening to radio programs during their leisure hours.

Radio broadcasting once had much the same entertainment role as television has today. From the 1920's to

The contributors of this article are Patrick D. Griffis, Digital Television Strategist for Microsoft Corporation, and Michael C. Keith, Senior Lecturer in Communication, Boston College.

the early 1950's, millions of families gathered around their radios every night. They listened to dramas, light comedies, variety shows, live music, and other kinds of programs. This period, which is sometimes called the Golden Age of Broadcasting, ended with the rise of television during the 1950's.

Radio has many uses in addition to broadcasting. People in many occupations use radio for two-way, wireless communication. Scientists send radio waves into the sky to learn about the weather. Telephone companies send messages across the ocean by radio. Many people operate amateur radio stations.

Radio works by changing sounds or other signals into radio waves, a form of energy called *electromagnetic radiation.* Radio waves travel through the air and through space. They also go through some solid objects, such as the walls of buildings. A radio receiver changes them back into the original sounds.

Many people contributed to the development of radio, and no one individual can be called radio's inventor. Guglielmo Marconi of Italy sent the first radio communi-

Radio terms

Adlib means to speak without a script.

AM stands for *amplitude modulation,* a broadcasting method in which the strength of the carrier waves is varied to match changes in the audio-frequency waves.

Amplitude is the strength of a wave.

Audio-frequency waves are electric waves that represent the sounds of a radio broadcast.

Automatic Frequency Control (AFC) is an electric circuit in an FM receiver that automatically remains locked on to the frequency of the selected transmission.

Bandwidth is the frequency range occupied by a transmitter signal.

Broadcast band is a group of radio frequencies. One band is for AM broadcasting, and one is for FM broadcasting.

Call letters are the initials that identify a radio station, such as station KRKO in Everett, Washington.

Carrier waves are radio waves that "carry" the sounds of a program by being combined with audio-frequency waves.

Channel is the radio frequency assigned to a station.

Digital Audio Broadcasting (DAB) is a system for transmitting sound and other information as a numeric code.

Detector is an electronic circuit that recovers the portion of a radio signal that represents the program.

FM stands for *frequency modulation,* a broadcasting method in which the frequency of the carrier waves is varied to match changes in the audio-frequency waves.

Frequency is the number of times a wave vibrates each second.

Ground waves consist of the radio waves that spread along the ground away from a broadcasting antenna.

Ham is a name for the operator of an amateur radio station.

Hertz is a unit used to measure frequency. One hertz equals one vibration per second.

Kilohertz means 1,000 hertz.

Line-of-sight refers to the direct line in which FM waves travel, without "bending" over mountains or the curve of the earth.

Live broadcast consists of sounds made at the moment of the broadcast, without having been prerecorded.

Long-wave band is the frequency band ranging from 148 to 283.5 kilohertz. It is used for radio broadcasts in Europe and in parts of Asia and northern Africa.

Medium-wave band is the frequency band ranging from 535 to 1,705 kilohertz used for AM radio broadcasts throughout the world.

Megahertz means 1 million hertz.

Multiplexing means sending two or more signals on a shared channel, as in stereophonic transmissions.

Network is an organization that provides radio programming for a group of stations that belong to it.

Oscillator is an electrical device which vibrates to produce a frequency.

Prerecorded means recorded on phonograph records, tapes, or audio compact discs for broadcast at a later time.

Radio data system (RDS) is a FM-based method for transmitting data along with an audio program.

Radio waves are electromagnetic waves in the radio frequency band.

Selectivity is a radio's ability to pick a desired radio signal from among the many received by the antenna.

Short-wave band is the frequency band ranging from 3 to 30 megahertz. It is used worldwide for radio broadcasts and other services.

Sky waves consist of the radio waves that come from a transmitting antenna and go into the sky.

Stereophonic sound comes from at least two radio speakers to match as closely as possible the sounds people would hear with their two ears.

Superheterodyne is a tuning method in which the desired incoming radio station signal is converted to an intermediate frequency before a detector recovers the signal.

---

cation signals in 1895. Today, radio waves that are broadcast from thousands of stations, along with waves from other sources, fill the air around us continuously. Many radio stations broadcast over the Internet, the worldwide computer network.

Uses

Broadcasting ranks as the most familiar use of radio by far. Every day, millions of people throughout the world listen to radio programs that are broadcast for their entertainment and information. But people also use radio in dozens of other ways. Many uses involve *two-way communication,* in which radio equipment is used both to send and to receive messages. In broadcasting and in most two-way communication, radio transmits sounds, such as voice and music. But in other uses, radio sends communication signals other than sounds. Such signals include the radio beams used in navigation and the remote control signals used in operating certain kinds of equipment.

Broadcasting. Radio broadcasts originate at radio stations. There is at least one radio station in every country in the world, and altogether there are more than 28,000 stations. The people of the world own about 2 billion radios, or an average of about 1 for every 3 people. The United States has more radio stations and more radios than any other country. The nation has more than a third of the world's radio stations and about a fourth of its radios. Other leading countries in number of radios include China and the United Kingdom.

Some radios are powered by current from electrical outlets. These radios are usually kept in the home, where electrical outlets are readily available. But many radios are powered by batteries. People listen to these radios almost everywhere—in homes and yards, at beaches and picnics, and even while strolling down the street. In addition, nearly all modern automobiles have a radio.

In some parts of the world, radios provide the people with one of the few links they have to the world outside their village or town. In some places, there is no electric power and batteries are too scarce or expensive for people to buy them. People in such communities sometimes use a special wind-up radio that requires no other source of power.

In most of Asia and Africa, radio listening is not as widespread as it is in Europe, the Americas, and Australia. Many people do not own radios, and they listen to radio programs in public gathering places instead.

Two-way communication. Two-way radio provides communication in an almost endless variety of jobs—whenever there is a need for wireless contact between one point and another. Some of the most important of these uses are in (1) public safety, (2) industry, (3) defense, and (4) private communication.

In public safety. Police officers and firefighters use two-way radios in their patrol cars and fire engines. They also carry small, portable two-way radios called *walkie-talkies.* They use these radios to get directions from their headquarters and to communicate with one another (see **Walkie-talkie**). Airplanes and ships use two-way radios for safe operation and for rescue missions. Special ambulance teams use radio to help save lives after rushing to the scene of an accident. These specialists radio the details of a victim's condition to a doctor in a hospital. The doctor then directs the emergency treatment of the victim by radio.

In industry. Two-way radio has become a standard tool of the transportation industry. Taxi drivers receive radioed instructions on where to pick up customers. Airplane pilots receive landing and take-off instructions by radio. Ships, trains, and many trucks and buses are equipped with two-way radios.

Radio also helps save time, money, and work in many other industries. Construction workers use it to communicate from street level to the top of a skyscraper. With the aid of two-way radio, farmers, ranchers, and lumber workers receive information when they need it and get equipment delivered where they want it.

In defense, radio plays a key role by linking a country's defense units. Military personnel use radio equipment in planes and tanks and on ships. Large communications centers and handy walkie-talkies help provide instant contact between military units.

In private communications. Many licensed radio operators called *hams* send and receive long-distance messages by radio as a hobby. Children play with walkie-talkies that broadcast over short distances. Many people use two-way radios in such places as cars and pleasure boats. Radio used by private citizens for short-distance, two-way communication is called *citizens band radio.* Radio signals also enable people to communicate using portable cellular telephones.

Other uses. Radio waves can carry many more kinds of information than just sounds. Radio signals make possible the operation of navigational aids, remote control devices, and data transmission equipment. In addition, radio has several highly specialized uses.

Navigation. Radio beams made up of special navigation signals help airplane pilots stay on the proper flying course. Many ships have devices for mapping their position with the aid of signals radioed from shore. Air-

planes and ships also rely on radar—a special form of radio—for their safe operation (see **Radar**).

Remote control by radio can be used to guide the flight of a model airplane or a real plane that has no pilot. Radio-controlled devices also direct railroad cars in switching yards. In addition, radio-controlled devices do such jobs as opening garage doors or changing television channels (see **Remote control**).

Data transmission. Radio equipment can send large quantities of information at great speeds. Data transmission usually occurs between one electronic device and another. For example, radio equipment on the ground may transmit data to a computer in a spacecraft orbiting the earth.

Special uses. Criminals and law enforcement officials sometimes use hidden radio devices called *bugs* to listen in on conversations in attempt to gather information. High-energy radio waves cook food in microwave ovens.

Radio programming

Radio programming varies from country to country. In most countries, a majority of programs broadcast are designed for entertainment. The rest provide some type of information. Advertisements are broadcast during and between the programs of commercial stations. Non-commercial stations, also called *educational* or *public* stations, have no commercials. Radio stations compete with one another for listeners. Most stations choose programs to appeal to a specific audience. For example, stations in the United States that play rock music try to attract teen-age and young adult listeners.

Entertainment. Recorded music is the chief kind of radio entertainment. Most stations specialize in one kind of music, such as rock, classical, country and Western, or jazz. Some stations broadcast several kinds of music.

Most radio stations that broadcast music have *disc jockeys* who introduce and comment on the music. They play an important role. Commercial stations try to hire disc jockeys whose announcing styles and personalities appeal to the station's largest audience.

Entertainment programs also include comedy shows,

An airplane pilot radios the control tower for instructions. During flight, radio beams help pilots stay on course.

Paramedics load an ambulance with supplies according to instructions transmitted by two-way radio from a hospital.

A police officer uses a handheld two-way radio called a *walkie-talkie* to communicate with other police officers.

serials, and plays that are performed live or recorded in a studio by actors. Some plays are written especially for radio.

Information. Programs that provide information include newscasts, talk shows, and live broadcasts of sports events. Newscasts are broadcast at regular times—every half-hour or hour on some stations. In addition, radio stations present on-the-spot news coverage of such events as political conventions, disasters, and speeches by national leaders. Radio stations also broadcast such specialized news as weather forecasts, traffic reports, and stock market information. Other information features include public service announcements about community events and government services. A few stations broadcast only news.

Talk shows present discussions on a variety of topics and interviews with people from many professions. Each show has a host or hostess who leads the discussion or does the interviewing. The subject of a program may be a current political topic, such as an election or a government policy, or it may deal with a social issue, such as crime, pollution, poverty, racism, or sexism. Many talk shows allow listeners to take part in the program. Listeners are invited to telephone the station to ask questions or give their opinions about the topic.

Sports events, like news, have always been an important part of radio programming. Sports announcers try to capture a game's action and excitement for the listeners. Games in many professional sports, such as baseball, basketball, cricket, football, hockey, and soccer, are broadcast locally on radio. Radio stations also broadcast many college and some high school sports contests.

How radio programs are broadcast

Radio stations are places where radio broadcasts begin. Many stations are located in office buildings.

The *studio* is the part of the radio station from which programs are broadcast. It is soundproofed so that no outside sounds can interfere with the broadcasts. Many studios have two separate areas—the *main studio* and the *control room.* The main studio is the place where the performers do their jobs. The control room contains the equipment needed to prepare and broadcast programs. This equipment includes the *control board,* a panel with the switches, knobs, buttons, and other devices used to regulate the sounds of the broadcasts. A large window in the wall between the main studio and the control room enables people in each area to see one another.

Putting a show on the air involves such jobs as script writing, announcing, and controlling the broadcasting equipment. At a small station, the same person may write scripts, announce, play recordings, and even operate the controls. A large station has a staff that plans programs, including the writing of news and other scripts. An announcer may use a script or may simply *adlib* (speak without a script).

During the Golden Age of Broadcasting, the production of some radio programs was a complex process involving many people. Writers wrote scripts for comedies, dramas, and variety shows. A director guided actors and actresses, who stood around a microphone reading their lines. An announcer introduced the show, closed it, and read the commercials. Sound-effects spe-

cialists created such sounds as thunder, footsteps, creaking doors, and galloping horses. An orchestra played appropriate music. Many radio shows were broadcast *live* (while they were being performed). These shows were often performed on a stage of a theaterlike studio in front of an audience.

Today, the production of most radio programs is less complicated. Most programs consist of conversation and recorded music. In addition, many radio stations use computers to do much of the work formerly done by people, such as operating technical equipment, recording program information, and even running the control board. Automation saves money by reducing the number of employees needed to run the station.

From sound waves to electric waves. A radio program consists of speech, music, and other sounds. These sounds may either be live or *prerecorded.* Prerecorded sounds are not broadcast when first produced. Most are stored on tapes or audio compact discs (CD's) and broadcast later. Almost all the music and commercials heard on radio are prerecorded.

To understand how radio broadcasting works, it is necessary to know what sound is. All sounds consist of vibrations. The number of vibrations each second is the *frequency* of the sound. For example, the sound of a person's voice consists of vibrations of the air that are caused by the person's vibrating vocal cords. The faster the vocal cords vibrate, the higher the frequency. The slower the vocal cords vibrate, the lower the frequency. Sound travels through the air in the form of waves called *sound waves.*

During a live radio broadcast, a microphone picks up speech and other sounds that make up the program. When sound waves enter the microphone, they cause an electric current that runs through the microphone to vary. The variations in the current form *audio-frequency waves* that match the program's sound waves. Prerecorded sounds are also changed into audio-frequency electric waves before being broadcast.

From electric waves to radio waves. The electric waves representing the live and prerecorded sounds of the program travel over wires to the control board. A technician uses switches on the control board to select, adjust, and mix the material to create the *program signal* that will be broadcast. The program signal travels from the control board to the transmitter, either by wire or by a special beam of radio waves.

Low-power transmitters may be in the studio. High-power transmitters are generally far away from the studio, at the site of the *transmitting antenna,* the device that sends radio waves through the air. A special beam of radio waves called *microwaves* is sometimes used to send the program signal from the studio to a distant transmitter.

In the transmitter, the program signal is combined with electric waves called *radio-frequency waves.* Radio-frequency waves have a much higher frequency than do the audio-frequency waves that make up the program signal. Radio-frequency waves are also known as *carrier waves* because they "carry" the program signal from the transmitter to radios. The frequency of the carrier waves produced in the transmitter is the radio station's *broadcast frequency*—that is, the frequency to which a radio must be tuned to hear that station.

Transmitting radio waves. After the program signal is combined with the carrier waves, the transmitter *amplifies* (strengthens) the combined radio signal and sends it to the antenna. The antenna then broadcasts the radio signal through the air.

Radio waves travel at the speed of light. This speed is 186,282 miles (299,792 kilometers) per second. By contrast, sound waves move through the air at the speed of only about $\frac{1}{5}$ mile (0.3 kilometer) per second.

A radio broadcast is transmitted in one of two ways, depending on how the carrier waves and program signal are combined. These two kinds of radio transmission are *amplitude modulation* (AM) and *frequency modulation* (FM). In AM transmission, the *amplitude* (strength) of the carrier waves is varied to match changes in the program signal coming from the radio studio. In FM transmission, the amplitude of the carrier waves remains constant. But the frequency of the carrier waves is varied to match changes in the program signal.

Transmitting AM signals. An AM antenna sends out two kinds of radio waves—*ground waves* and *sky waves.* Ground waves spread out horizontally from the transmitting antenna. They travel through the air along the earth's surface and follow the curve of the earth for a short distance. Sky waves spread up into the sky. When they reach a layer of the atmosphere called the *ionosphere* or the *Kennelly-Heaviside layer,* they are reflected back down to earth (see **Ionosphere**). AM broadcasts are thus reflected beyond the curve of the earth. The ionosphere rises at night and so reflects AM waves farther than it does during the day. As a result, radios can receive broadcasts from distant stations more clearly at night.

Transmitting FM signals. An FM radio antenna sends out waves that travel in the same directions as AM waves, but FM waves that travel skyward are not reflected. Instead, they pass through the atmosphere and go into space. The FM waves that spread horizontally travel in what is called *line-of-sight.* This means that FM waves cannot be received farther than the horizon as seen from the antenna. FM programs are not affected by static as much as AM programs are.

Transmitting short-wave signals. Many broadcasting stations operate in the short-wave bands. Short-wave broadcasts travel over long distances, and in some sparsely populated areas of the world they are the only broadcasts that can be received. Nearly every country operates at least one short-wave station. Generally, programs transmitted by these stations are addressed to audiences far away.

Most short-wave broadcasting stations transmit on several frequencies to ensure worldwide reception at different times of the day and year. Programs consist mainly of international and national news, commentaries, interviews, music and other cultural programs, sports events, radio plays, and language courses. The governments of some countries jam short-wave broadcasts during periods of political unrest.

The ionosphere reflects short waves best when solar activity is greatest. Thus, short-wave transmissions travel farther during the day than at night. They also travel farther in the winter, when the sun is farther away. However, eruptions on the sun's surface called *solar flares* may disturb the ionosphere enough to interfere with communication or even cause total blackouts of short-wave reception.

Digital Audio Broadcasting (DAB). Beginning in the early 1990's, several countries began experimenting with Digital Audio Broadcasting (DAB). For DAB broadcasts, sound is *sampled* by taking thousands of segments of sound per second and translating each into *digital* (numeric) code. The digital data are compressed by eliminating parts of the signal that do not change from sample to sample, and the signal is transmitted.

DAB can deliver sound of the same quality provided by a compact disc. DAB can also deliver data services. Some AM and FM radio transmitters must be modified to broadcast DAB. Special receivers are required to receive DAB.

Broadcasting power and frequency. Another factor that influences the distance a radio program can be broadcast is the power of the transmitter. The strongest AM stations have a power of 50,000 watts. They can be heard far away, especially at night when reflected waves

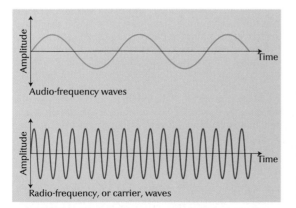

Broadcast waves are a combination of two kinds of electric vibrations. Audio-frequency waves represent voice and other sounds. Radio-frequency waves "carry" audio waves after being combined with them in one of the ways shown at the right.

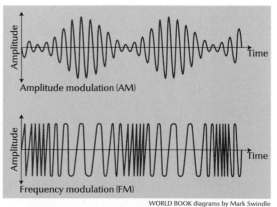

WORLD BOOK diagrams by Mark Swindle

AM and FM. In AM, the *amplitude* (strength) of the radio-frequency waves is varied to match the audio waves. In FM, the *frequency* (number of vibrations per second) of the radio-frequency waves is varied to match the audio waves.

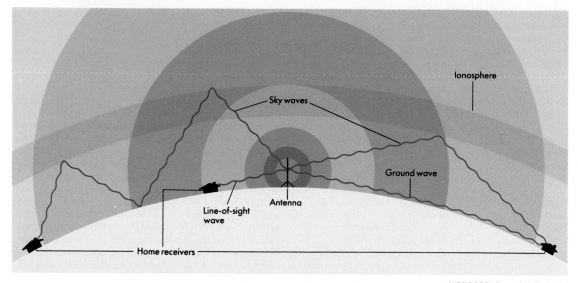

WORLD BOOK diagram by Sally Wayland

Radio waves. An AM antenna radiates *ground waves,* which may extend a short distance beyond the horizon, and *sky waves,* which bounce off the ionosphere and may also bounce off the earth. An FM antenna radiates *line-of-sight waves,* which cannot be picked up beyond the horizon.

travel farther. For example, 50,000-watt stations in Chicago can be heard at night by listeners in Florida, about 1,000 miles (1,600 kilometers) away. The weakest AM stations operate at 250 watts and usually serve only one or two towns.

The power of FM stations ranges from 100 watts, which can broadcast about 15 miles (25 kilometers), to 100,000 watts, which can broadcast about 65 miles (105 kilometers). Some noncommercial FM educational stations operate at as little as 10 watts and reach an area of only a few miles or kilometers.

Each station broadcasts on a different *channel,* also called an *assigned frequency.* The use of different frequencies keeps stations from interfering with one another's broadcasts. Frequency is measured in units called *hertz* (vibrations per second). One kilohertz equals 1,000 hertz, and one megahertz equals 1,000,000 hertz. AM stations transmit within the medium-wave band, which ranges from 535 to 1,705 kilohertz. FM stations transmit within a very high frequency (VHF) band that ranges from 88 to 108 megahertz. The short-wave band ranges from 3 to 30 megahertz. The L-band, within which most DAB signals are broadcast, ranges from 1,452 to 1,492 megahertz.

How radio programs are received

Radios pick up radio-frequency signals, separate the program signals from the carrier waves, and then change the program signals into sound waves. Different types of radios can receive different broadcast bands. Many radios can receive both AM and FM, the most popular broadcast bands. *Multiband radios* can pick up AM, FM, and other bands, such as police, marine, aviation, and short-wave bands.

One of the simplest radio receivers is the *crystal radio.* This type of receiver uses an electronic device called a *crystal rectifier* to detect changes in the strength of an

AM signal. These changes in signal strength represent the program's original sound waves. A crystal radio works on just the power of the radio waves it receives and needs no electric power source. However, a listener must use earphones because a crystal radio can produce sound only at a low volume. Furthermore, this type of radio does not receive FM broadcasts well. Because of such limitations, most radios made today are electrically powered.

The electric power for a radio can come from batteries or from an electrical outlet in a house or other building. A typical radio that runs on household power has a component called a *power transformer* that lowers the household voltage to the level the radio requires.

The main parts of an electrically powered radio include (1) the antenna, (2) the tuner, (3) the intermediate-frequency amplifier and detector, (4) the audio-frequency processor and amplifier, and (5) the speaker. A radio that can receive more than one type of signal also has a switch for selecting the band.

The antenna, also called the *aerial,* is a length of wire or a metal rod that picks up radio waves. The antenna may be entirely inside the radio, or part of the antenna may be outside the radio but connected to it, as is the case in automobile radios. When radio waves strike the antenna, they produce an extremely weak electric current in it. An antenna receives radio waves from many stations at the same time.

The tuner is the part of the radio that can be adjusted to particular frequencies. A display on the radio shows the frequencies, or channels, of the stations that may be tuned in. For example, station WQAM in Miami, Florida, broadcasts on a frequency of 560 kilohertz. To tune in WQAM, a listener selects number 560 (abbreviated as 56 or 5.6 on some radio displays).

Today, most radio receivers use the *superheterodyne* tuning method because of the advantages it offers. The

Main parts of an AM/FM transistor radio

Emerson Radio Corp. (WORLD BOOK photo)

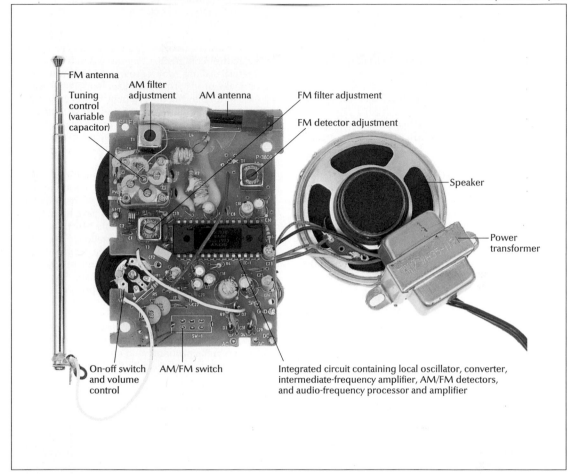

FM antenna

AM filter adjustment

Tuning control (variable capacitor)

AM antenna

FM filter adjustment

FM detector adjustment

Speaker

Power transformer

On-off switch and volume control

AM/FM switch

Integrated circuit containing local oscillator, converter, intermediate-frequency amplifier, AM/FM detectors, and audio-frequency processor and amplifier

tuner of a superheterodyne radio consists of three main parts: (1) an amplifier, (2) a local oscillator, and (3) a mixer/converter. The amplifier strengthens the antenna signal. The local oscillator generates a frequency, which the mixer/converter combines with the amplified antenna signal. The combined signal, called the *intermediate frequency,* contains a particular radio program. When a listener adjusts the tuning control, the local oscillator frequency changes and a different radio program is selected to be on the intermediate frequency. The intermediate frequency is 10.7 MHz for FM and 455 KHz for AM. Use of the same intermediate frequency to process many radio frequencies simplifies the radio's design. It also allows for improved *selectivity*—that is, the radio's ability to pick a desired radio signal from among the many received by the antenna.

The intermediate-frequency amplifier and detector receive the intermediate-frequency signal produced by the tuner. The amplifier strengthens the signal, which then enters the detector. The detector removes the intermediate frequency from the signal and leaves only the *audio-frequency signal*—the part that represents the program.

The audio-frequency processor and amplifier strengthen the audio-frequency portion of the signal. Volume, bass, and treble controls can be used to adjust the loudness and tone of the sound before it goes to the speaker.

The speaker is the final link between the broadcasting studio and the listener. It changes the electric signal back into the original program sounds. The basic parts of a speaker are a magnet and a coil of wire called the *voice coil.* The voice coil is attached to a cone, which is usually made of paper. The electric current from the amplifier passes through the coil and exerts varying push and pull against the magnet's field. The cone vibrates in time with the electric current flowing through the coil. The cone's vibrations create sound waves that match those that first went into the microphone or were recorded earlier, and the original program sounds come out of the speaker.

Stereophonic receivers can detect *stereophonic,* or *stereo, multiplex* signals. These signals are formed by sending two separate audio-frequency signals on a single carrier frequency at the same time. The two audio-frequency signals are called the *right channel* and the *left channel.* Stereo multiplex signals better re-create for the listener the sensation of hearing live sounds than do *monophonic* signals, which transmit only one channel.

Both stereo and monophonic receivers have a super-heterodyne circuit. However, stereo receivers have an additional circuit called a *demultiplexer.* This circuit changes the multiplex signal back into its original left and right channels. The two parts of the signal then enter separate audio-frequency processors and amplifiers. Stereo receivers have at least two speakers, one for each channel.

DAB receivers are required to pick up DAB signals. Such receivers recombine a DAB signal's components and restore the original sound even if reception has been affected by interference.

Radio data system (RDS) receivers pick up special signals that provide data in addition to audio broadcasts. Radio stations around the world have adopted an FM-based multiplex system for such signals. The additional data provide listeners with new features, including the ability to find stations based on type of program, such as classical music, rock and roll, or news. A special demultiplexer circuit is needed in the radio to receive and use the information. RDS radios are popular in cars in many countries.

The radio industry

Radio has several important industrial roles. Broadcasting stations provide jobs for thousands of workers around the world. Radio commercials help other businesses sell every kind of product and service—from dog food to automobiles to insurance. The recorded music played by disc jockeys is probably the most important factor affecting the sale of tapes and CD's. Stores throughout the world sell millions of radio receivers each year.

Stations and networks. There are two main types of radio stations—commercial stations and public stations. Commercial stations, which are owned by private companies, make profits from advertisements. Public stations are funded by the government. However, in some countries, public stations also take advertisements. Some countries also have nonprofit radio stations, many of which are operated by educational institutions. A radio station may employ only a few workers or as many as several hundred.

The organization of radio broadcasting varies from country to country. In the United States, for example, almost all commercial radio stations are privately owned businesses. Most European countries have both commercial stations and nonprofit stations. Most countries have at least one commercial radio station.

Commercial radio stations broadcast programs to attract listeners. They sell broadcasting time to advertisers who want to reach these listeners. Sponsors pay the stations for time during and between the programs to advertise their products. Stations that attract the largest audiences receive the highest fees. Many commercial stations have an *affiliation* (working agreement) with a national *network.* A network is an organization that provides some of the programming for its affiliated radio stations. It may also sell some of the stations' advertising

Cameramann International, Ltd.

The manufacture of radios provides job opportunities for a variety of skilled workers, from technicians to electronics engineers. The technician shown here is assembling radio parts.

Radios in the world and in the United States

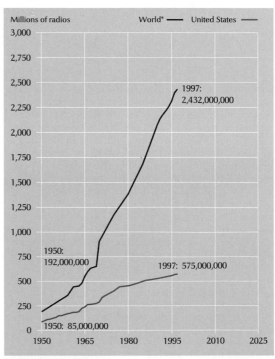

Millions of radios   World* ——   United States ——

1997: 2,432,000,000

1950: 192,000,000

1997: 575,000,000

1950: 85,000,000

*Excluding China before 1977.
Source: UNESCO.

time. Networks send radio signals to their affiliates using communications satellites.

Careers. The radio industry offers a variety of career opportunities. Stations and networks need program planners and announcers, news reporters and newscasters, technicians, and maintenance workers. Other personnel write scripts, sell advertising time, and work in such general business activities as accounting and public relations. An employee of a small radio station may be called on to do any of these jobs at one time or another. Therefore, a job with a small station provides excellent experience for a person starting a radio career. Most people who hold a key job at a large station first gained experience by working at small stations.

Employees of large stations or networks generally specialize in one of four kinds of work. These kinds of work are (1) programming, (2) engineering, (3) sales, and (4) general administration.

The programming department is headed by a program director. This department includes journalists who gather the news and write news reports and other material to be broadcast. Other members of the programming department include announcers, copywriters, and production personnel. The engineering department includes the technicians who operate and maintain the broadcasting equipment. Members of the sales department are responsible for selling broadcasting time to sponsors. The general manager of the station or network heads the department of general administration and has overall responsibility for the organization's operation. The general administration department also includes accountants, secretaries, and other general office workers.

Careers outside of broadcasting are available to people trained in the operation and repair of radio equipment. Many people skilled in radio repair go into business for themselves.

Government regulation of radio

The government of every country regulates the use of radio in some way. Without regulation, radio stations and other radio users would broadcast signals that would interfere with one another and make it impossible for communications to be understood. Another reason for regulation is to ensure that stations adhere to the terms of their broadcast licenses. Many governments regulate radio in a way that enables them to use the medium to promote their own ideas and policies. They also effectively prevent the broadcast of ideas that government leaders oppose.

A large number of countries have both private and government-owned stations. In most other countries, the government owns all the stations. The United States is the only nation in which the federal government does not control any radio stations that broadcast to the general public.

In general, a country allows radio broadcasters the same degree of freedom it allows its citizens. Most democratic countries allow wide freedom in broadcasting. Many totalitarian governments severely regulate and censor broadcasting for political purposes.

In the United States, the Federal Communications Commission (FCC) regulates all nonmilitary communication by radio. The FCC assigns frequencies and call letters for various types of radio operations, including broadcasting, amateur radio operation, and marine and aviation radio. In addition, the FCC issues licenses to stations and certain other users of transmitting equipment. The FCC does not censor radio programs or tell stations what programs they should broadcast. But it can impose a fine on or revoke the license of a station that violates broadcasting rules. Every station must apply to the FCC every seven years to have its license renewed.

In Canada, the Canadian Broadcasting Corporation (CBC) provides the programs for the government stations. The Canadian Radio-television and Telecommunications Commission supervises government and private stations. In the United Kingdom, the British Broadcasting Corporation (BBC) regulates the government-owned stations. The Radio Authority, a government agency, regulates privately owned stations.

History

The development of radio in the late 1800's revolutionized communication. At that time, people had two other means of quick, long-distance communication—telegraph and telephone. But the signals sent by both these devices had to travel through wires. As a result, telegraph and telephone communication was possible only between places that had been connected by wires. Radio signals, on the other hand, passed through the air. Thus, radio enabled people to communicate quickly between any two points on land, at sea, and—later—in the sky, and even in space.

Radio broadcasting, which began on a large scale during the 1920's, caused major changes in the everyday lives of people. It brought a tremendous variety of entertainment into the home for the first time. It also enabled people to learn about news developments as they happened or shortly afterward.

Early development. Radio, like many other inventions, developed from the theories and experiments of many people. Joseph Henry, a professor at the College of New Jersey (now Princeton University), and a British physicist, Michael Faraday, discovered one of the first important ideas in the early 1830's. The two men had experimented with electromagnets. Working separately, they each developed the theory that a current in one wire can produce a current in another wire, even though the wires are not connected. This idea is called the *induction theory.*

In 1864, James Clerk Maxwell, another British physicist, helped explain the induction theory by suggesting the existence of electromagnetic waves that travel at the speed of light. In the 1880's, the German physicist Heinrich Hertz performed experiments that proved Maxwell's theory.

In 1891, Nikola Tesla, an American inventor from Austria-Hungary, invented the Tesla coil, a type of high-frequency transformer. This device has become a vital component of radio transmitters.

In 1895, Guglielmo Marconi, an Italian inventor, combined earlier ideas and his own ideas and sent the first radio communication signals through the air. He used electromagnetic waves to send telegraph code signals a distance of more than 1 mile (1.6 kilometers). In 1901, Marconi's radio equipment sent code signals across the Atlantic Ocean from England to Newfoundland, Canada.

During the early 1900's, electrical engineers developed devices called *vacuum tubes* that could be used to detect and to amplify radio signals. Lee De Forest, an American inventor, patented a vacuum tube called a *triode* or *audion* in 1907. This tube became the key element in radio reception.

There are many claims for the first broadcast of human speech over the air. Most historians give credit to Reginald A. Fessenden, a Canadian-born physicist. In 1906, Fessenden spoke by radio from Brant Rock, Massachusetts, to ships offshore in the Atlantic Ocean. The American inventor Edwin H. Armstrong did much to improve radio receivers. In 1918, he developed the superheterodyne circuit. In 1933, he discovered how to make FM broadcasts.

The first practical use of the "wireless," as radio was then called, was for ship-to-ship and ship-to-shore communication. Radio helped save the lives of thousands of victims of sea disasters. The first sea rescue involving the use of radio took place in 1909, after the S.S. *Republic* collided with another ship in the Atlantic Ocean. The *Republic* radioed a call for help that brought rescuers who saved almost all the passengers.

Dozens of new uses were soon found for radio. By the 1930's, airplane pilots, police officers, and military personnel were using radio for wireless communication.

The start of broadcasting. Experimental radio broadcasts began about 1910. In that year, Lee De Forest produced a radio program from the Metropolitan Opera House in New York City. The program starred the famous opera singer Enrico Caruso.

Many people consider radio station WWJ, in Detroit, the first commercial radio station. It began regular broadcasts on Aug. 20, 1920. Others claim the distinction for station KDKA in Pittsburgh. KDKA grew out of an experimental station that began in 1916 in Wilkinsburg, a suburb of Pittsburgh. The station's broadcast of the 1920 U.S. presidential election results on Nov. 2, 1920, is generally considered the beginning of professional broadcasting. The first license to broadcast regularly went to station WBZ in Springfield, Massachusetts. The United States government issued the license on Sept. 15, 1921.

Culver

Guglielmo Marconi invented a way of sending telegraph signals by radio in 1895. His invention helped lead to the development of broadcasting. This photograph shows him with some of his wireless equipment.

Network broadcasting began as early as October 1922. At that time, WJZ in New York City and WGY in Schenectady, New York, broadcast the World Series. The two stations formed a simple network connected by telephone lines. Network broadcasting—or, as it was called, *chain broadcasting*—soon included stations across the United States. The Radio Corporation of America (RCA) formed the National Broadcasting Company (NBC), which was the first permanent national network, in 1926.

In the 1920's, radio stations began operating in many other countries as well. The British Broadcasting Corporation (BBC) began broadcasting in 1922. Stations began operations in Australia in 1923 and in Japan in 1925.

The Golden Age of Broadcasting began in the United States about 1925 and lasted until the early 1950's.

Bettmann

A "crystal" radio of the early 1920's worked without batteries or other source of power, but a listener needed earphones to hear it.

Culver

A radio of the mid-1920's was powered by electricity and had a trumpetlike loudspeaker.

Bettmann

By the early 1940's, radios had become "streamlined." Members of a family often got together to listen to programs.

During this period, radio was a major source of family entertainment. Every night, many families gathered in their living rooms to listen to comedies, adventure dramas, music, and other kinds of radio entertainment. Children hurried home from school to hear afternoon adventure shows. In the daytime, millions of women listened to dramas called *soap operas* because soap manufacturers sponsored many of them.

Radio brought to the home the music of famous band leaders, including Tommy Dorsey, Duke Ellington, Benny Goodman, Harry James, Guy Lombardo, and Glenn Miller. Exciting radio dramas of the Golden Age included "Buck Rogers in the 25th Century," "Gangbusters," "The Green Hornet," "Inner Sanctum," "Jack Armstrong, the All-American Boy," "The Lone Ranger," "The Shadow," and "Superman." Some radio soap operas were "The Guiding Light," "John's Other Wife," "Just Plain Bill," "Ma Perkins," "One Man's Family," "Our Gal Sunday," and "Stella Dallas."

Radio's famous comedians included Fred Allen, Jack Benny, Eddie Cantor, and Bob Hope. The ventriloquist Edgar Bergen and his dummy, Charlie McCarthy, hosted a weekly comedy program with famous stars as guests. Situation comedies included "Fibber McGee and Molly," "The Great Gildersleeve," "Duffy's Tavern," "Henry Aldrich," and "Our Miss Brooks." The husband-and-wife comedy team of George Burns and Gracie Allen gained fame in radio.

The popularity of "Amos 'n' Andy," a situation comedy, and the impact of a dramatic program called *The War of the Worlds* help illustrate the enormous influence radio entertainment had on people. "Amos 'n' Andy" was broadcast each weekday throughout the 1930's. While the program was being broadcast—from 7:00 to 7:15 p.m. Eastern Standard Time—many movie theaters stopped their films and turned on radios so the audiences could listen to the program. Some stores and restaurants played radios over public address systems so that customers would not miss it. The actors and actresses on the "Amos 'n' Andy" show were whites who portrayed blacks. Many people have criticized the program for portraying African Americans as a stereotyped group to be laughed at.

The War of the Worlds, broadcast on Oct. 30, 1938, was one program in a series of dramas put on by Orson Welles's Mercury Theater on the Air. The program was adapted from the science-fiction novel of the same name by the British author H. G. Wells. It took the form of on-the-spot news reports describing an invasion of New Jersey by aliens from Mars. The announcer told the radio audience that the show was fictional. Even so, large numbers of listeners believed the invasion was actually taking place, and widespread panic resulted. Thousands of people called the police and other authorities for instructions on what to do. Many people fled their homes, some taking furniture with them. Still others were treated in hospitals for shock.

Some radio news reporters of the Golden Age became almost as well known as the top entertainers. They included Elmer Davis, Gabriel Heatter, H. V. Kaltenborn, Fulton Lewis, Jr., Edward R. Murrow, Lowell Thomas, and Walter Winchell. Newscasts became especially important during World War II (1939-1945). Millions of people turned to radio every day for latest news on the war. The governments of countries that fought in the war made widespread use of broadcasts to their own and other countries for propaganda purposes. The Voice of America, an agency of the United States government, began broadcasting overseas in 1942 to inform the world of America's role in the war.

Franklin Delano Roosevelt, president of the United States from 1933 to 1945, used radio very effectively. He held informal talks called "fireside chats." The talks did much to help Roosevelt gain support for his policies.

NBC

A sound-effects expert used odd-looking equipment to create realistic sounds for Golden Age dramas. This picture shows water being sprayed into a bucket to make the sound of rain.

Culver

George Burns and Gracie Allen were famous radio performers during the Golden Age. The husband-and-wife team starred in a popular weekly situation comedy from 1932 to 1950.

Earlier presidents, beginning with Woodrow Wilson in 1919, had spoken on radio. But Roosevelt was the first to fully understand the great force of the medium and the opportunity it provided for taking government policies directly to the people. Other political leaders, including Winston Churchill of the United Kingdom and Charles de Gaulle of France, made use of radio to address their nations.

Broadcasting today. The rise of television in the 1950's ended the Golden Age of radio broadcasting. People turned to TV for comedies, dramas, and variety shows, and these kinds of shows all but disappeared from radio. Many people believed television would cause radio broadcasting to become an unimportant communication medium with a small audience. Instead, radio's audience has continued to grow, in spite of its competition from television.

After the Golden Age of Broadcasting, music became the major form of radio entertainment. Rock music, which was a new form of music in the 1950's, became an important kind of music on radio. Broadcasts of rock music gained many listeners—especially teen-agers—for radio. Talk shows and stations that broadcast only news also helped radio gain listeners. Thorough coverage of a topic or news event continues to be an important feature of such programs.

Portable radios also helped increase radio's popularity. Such devices, including tiny *personal radios* with headphones, have made radio a source of individual, rather than family, enjoyment. In addition, automobile radios are now commonplace.

Brown Bros.

President Franklin Delano Roosevelt broadcast "fireside chats" to the nation during the 1930's and 1940's. These talks helped him gain popular support for his government policies.

Important dates in radio

1864 James Clerk Maxwell predicted the existence of electromagnetic waves that travel at the speed of light.
1880's Heinrich Hertz proved Maxwell's theory.
1895 Guglielmo Marconi became the first person to send radio communication signals through the air.
1906 Reginald A. Fessenden broadcast voice by radio.
1909 Passengers of the S.S. *Republic* were saved in the first sea rescue using radio.
1918 Edwin H. Armstrong developed the superheterodyne circuit.
1919 Woodrow Wilson became the first U.S. president to make a radio broadcast. He spoke from a ship to World War I troops aboard other vessels.
1920 Two U.S. stations, WWJ of Detroit and KDKA of Pittsburgh, made the first regular commercial broadcasts.
1922 The British Broadcasting Company, later the British Broadcasting Corporation, made its first broadcast.
c. 1925-1950 Radio was a major source of family home entertainment, during the Golden Age of Broadcasting.
1934 The Telecommunications Act created the Federal Communications Commission (FCC) in the United States.
1947 Scientists at Bell Telephone Laboratories (now part of Lucent Technologies) developed the transistor.
1960 John F. Kennedy and Richard M. Nixon held the first radio and television debates between two U.S. presidential candidates.
1961 Soviet space officials held the first radio talks with a man in space, cosmonaut Yuri Gagarin.
1960's Stereophonic radio broadcasting began.
1969 Radio signals carried to earth the first words spoken by astronauts on the moon.
1982 AM radio stations in the United States began broadcasting in stereo.
1998 The world's first commercial digital audio broadcasting (DAB) service began in the United Kingdom.

Still another aid to radio's growth has been the development of stereophonic broadcasting. Stereo broadcasts began on a large scale in the 1960's. In 1961, the FCC allowed only FM stations to broadcast in stereo in the United States to help them compete with AM stations. FM's better sound quality enabled it to surpass AM in popularity by the late 1970's. The FCC authorized AM stereophonic broadcasting in 1982.

In the late 1980's and early 1990's, researchers developed *digital audio broadcasting* (DAB), a system that converts sounds to *digital* (numeric) code before transmission. DAB was introduced at a world conference in Spain in 1992. In 1998, the first commercial DAB operation began in the United Kingdom. Because DAB can carry multiple signals, radio programs similar to those broadcast today may be supplemented by images, text, graphics, and other data. For example, information about local traffic problems could be transmitted over a DAB data channel. Drivers might receive this information as text, synthesized speech, or maps. An LCD (liquid crystal display) on the receiver might display the name and composer of any music played, the radio station's telephone number, or an electronic program guide.

Patrick D. Griffis and Michael C. Keith

Related articles in *World Book* include:

Biographies

Armstrong, Edwin H.
De Forest, Lee
Hertz, Heinrich R.
Lodge, Sir Oliver J.
Marconi, Guglielmo
Maxwell, James Clerk
Sarnoff, David

Parts of a radio

Antenna	Speaker
Headphones	Transistor
Microphone	

Radio equipment

Cellular telephone
Citizens band radio
Communications satellite
Fax machine
Radar
Radiosonde
Remote control
Telephone (Telephones that
use radio)
Television
Walkie-talkie

Other related articles

Advertising
Airplane (Air navigation)
Australia (picture: Schools of the air)
British Broadcasting Corporation
Canadian Broadcasting Corporation
Corporation for Public Broadcasting
Electronics
Federal Communications Commission
Frequency modulation
Invention
Ionosphere
Journalism (Radio; Radio journalism)
Kilohertz
Monitoring station
Public opinion (Radio and television)
Radio, Amateur
Radio Free Europe/Radio Liberty
Railroad (Traffic control)
Reflection
Ship (A ship at sea)
Short waves
Soap opera
Static
Stereophonic sound system
Telescope (Radio telescopes)
Voice of America

Outline

I. Uses
  A. Broadcasting
  B. Two-way communication
  C. Other uses
II. Radio programming
  A. Entertainment
  B. Information
III. How radio programs are broadcast
  A. Radio stations
  B.. Putting a show on the air
  C. From sound waves to electric waves
  D. From electric waves to radio waves
  E. Transmitting radio waves
  F. Broadcasting power and frequency
IV. How radio programs are received
  A. The antenna
  B. The tuner
  C. The intermediate-frequency amplifier and detector
  D. The audio-frequency processor and amplifier
  E. The speaker
  F. Stereophonic receivers
  G. DAB receivers
  H. Radio data system (RDS) receivers
V. The radio industry
  A. Stations and networks
  B. Careers
VI. Government regulation of radio
VII. History

Questions

What are the basic steps in all kinds of radio communication?
What were the contributions of James Clerk Maxwell, Heinrich Hertz, and Guglielmo Marconi to the development of radio?

What is a radio network? An affiliate?
In what ways did radio programming change after the rise of television?
What are some important applications of radio?
Why must broadcasting be regulated by an agency of the government?
What was the Golden Age of Broadcasting? Why did this period end?
In what ways is the radio industry important to a country's economy?
How do AM and FM broadcasting differ?

Additional resources

Level I
Barr, Roger. *Radios*. Lucent Bks., 1994.
Crisfield, Deborah. *Radio*. Crestwood, 1994.
Finkelstein, Norman H. *Sounds in the Air: The Golden Age of Radio*. Scribner, 1993.
Stwertka, Eve and Albert. *Tuning In: The Sounds of Radio*. Messner, 1993.

Level II
Dunning, John. *On the Air: The Encyclopedia of Old-Time Radio*. Oxford, 1998.
Godfrey, Donald G., and Leigh, F. A., eds. *Historical Dictionary of American Radio*. Greenwood, 1998.
Hilliard, Robert L. *The Federal Communications Commission*. Focal Pr., 1991.
Keith, Michael C. *The Radio Station*. 4th ed. Focal Pr., 1997.
Nachman, Gerald. *Raised on Radio*. Pantheon, 1998.

Radio, Amateur, is a popular hobby in which an individual operates his or her own radio station. Amateur radio is often called *ham radio,* and the operators are frequently referred to as *hams.* Hams can send radio messages by voice or by International Morse Code to other radio amateurs throughout the world. About a million people participate in amateur radio. Boys and girls younger than 7 years old have operated their own amateur radio stations.

Amateur radio differs from a type of radio operation called *citizens band,* or *CB, radio.* Citizens band carries fewer channels than amateur radio and is more limited in the power and range of its signal. For more information on CB, see **Citizens band radio.**

Many hams enjoy talking with other radio amateurs in faraway places. When contacting hams in other countries, they have little difficulty with language barriers. Many amateur-radio operators around the world speak English.

When communicating by means of International Morse Code, amateur-radio operators may use an internationally accepted set of three-letter signals. These signals are called *Q signals* because they all begin with the letter Q. For example, the signal *QTH?* means "What is your location?" Q signals enable amateur-radio operators without a common language to understand each other.

Uses of amateur radio. Hams have a long history of providing communications assistance in times of emergency. Floods, fires, tornadoes, and hurricanes can interrupt telephone service and other common means of communication. Radio amateurs often have used their equipment during such disasters to reestablish vital communication links. This kind of voluntary work in emergencies has won hams the praise of governments around the world.

Some radio amateurs have developed special equipment for sending television pictures over radio waves.

Other radio amateurs send messages all over the world by bouncing their signals off the moon. Hams even use their sets to send information between computers.

One technically challenging activity involves building and using an amateur radio communications satellite. Many nations have allowed amateur radio communications satellites to "hitchhike" into orbit as part of the launch of other satellites. Most of these communications satellites have been called *Oscars.* The word *Oscar* comes from *O*rbiting *S*atellite *C*arrying *A*mateur *R*adio. Many schools tune in Oscars to provide students with firsthand experience in space science.

Equipment. Some amateurs design and build their own stations. Others assemble radios from do-it-yourself kits or buy assembled equipment. A complete amateur radio station includes an antenna, a transmitter, and a receiver. Many amateurs use a transceiver, which combines a transmitter and a receiver in a single unit. By purchasing used equipment, hams can assemble their own station for less than $100. Highly sophisticated stations may cost many thousands of dollars.

Licenses. Unlike most other hobbies, amateur radio requires a license. Amateurs share short-wave radio *frequencies* (channels) with such users as airlines, armed forces, police, ships, and television broadcasters (see **Short waves**). It is thus important that everyone follow regulations aimed at avoiding interfering with other users. Amateurs must pass a licensing test to assure that they know these regulations and that they can operate their equipment properly. Countries license amateurs in accordance with an international treaty.

In the United States, the Federal Communications Commission (FCC) issues amateur radio licenses. There are six levels of radio licenses: (1) novice, (2) technician, (3) technician plus, (4) general, (5) advanced, and (6) amateur extra. Starting with the novice level, each license gives greater privileges and requires greater knowledge and abilities.

Many local ham radio clubs offer courses that prepare amateurs to take the *novice* license test. The novice license does not require much technical knowledge of radio. Applicants must be able to send and receive International Morse Code at a rate of five words a minute. They also must demonstrate a basic understanding of FCC regulations. Novices are limited in the power of their stations and in the number of frequencies they may use. The novice license, like other amateur licenses, is good for 10 years and may be renewed.

The *technician* and *general* licenses require greater technical knowledge and familiarity with FCC rules. One type of technician license requires only a written examination, but restricts the frequencies available to the technician. Another type of technician license requires the ability to copy code at a rate of five words a minute. It allows the use of code and voice transmission on very high frequencies where short-range and experimental communications are possible. This license also allows the use of the novice frequencies. The general license requires the ability to copy code at a rate of 13 words a minute. It provides the amateur with a wide variety of privileges, including the increased use of voice and code transmission.

The *advanced* and *extra class* licenses provide successively greater frequency privileges and require progressively more detailed knowledge. The code speed requirement is 13 words a minute for the advanced license and 20 words a minute for the extra class license.

Amateur organization. In addition to local ham radio clubs, radio amateurs also have their own national organization, the American Radio Relay League (ARRL). Its headquarters are in Newington, Connecticut. The League provides information for beginners and publishes *QST,* a monthly amateur radio magazine. The ARRL also sponsors contests and operating activities. In one contest, amateurs try to contact as many different stations as they can in a limited period of time. An annual Field Day is one of the most popular activities sponsored by the ARRL. Each June, groups of amateurs with portable equipment meet in remote areas and practice sending emergency messages to one another. This exercise helps them develop skills that would be useful during an actual emergency.

History. Amateur radio began during the early 1900's. In 1901, the Italian inventor Guglielmo Marconi successfully transmitted radio signals across the Atlantic Ocean from England to Newfoundland. Marconi's feat encouraged many people to set up their own radio stations and begin communicating with each other over the airwaves. By 1912, there were so many radio stations on the air that a radio law became necessary to prevent interference. Amateur and other private stations were restricted to short-wave frequencies, which were considered of little value. But amateurs were soon sending messages from coast to coast, showing the value of short-wave radio for long-distance transmission.

Amateurs pioneered the development of radio in many other important ways. In 1919, a ham named Frank Conrad used his station in Wilkinsburg, Pennsylvania, to transmit recorded music for the entertainment of people in the area, who listened on small crystal sets. This use of an amateur station helped lead to commercial radio broadcasting. In the late 1930's, a United States radio amateur named Grote Reber built the first radio telescope with a dish antenna and received radio noise from outer space. In 1961, the first amateur radio satellite, *Oscar 1,* was launched. This was also the first non-

WORLD BOOK photo by Odyssey Productions

An amateur radio station may use a transceiver, shown here. The operator sends messages by speaking into a microphone and listens to other hams through headphones or a speaker.

governmental, noncommercial satellite. The first direct satellite communication between the Soviet Union and the United States took place via the *Oscar 4* amateur radio satellite in 1965.   William I. Dunkerley, Jr.

See also **Radio; Morse code; Marconi, Guglielmo.**

Additional resources

ARRL Handbook for the Radio Amateur. Am. Radio Relay League, published annually.
Gibilisco, Stan. *Amateur Radio Encyclopedia.* TAB, 1994.
Laster, Clay. *The Beginner's Handbook of Amateur Radio.* 3rd ed. TAB, 1993.

Radio control. See Remote control.

Radio Free Europe/Radio Liberty (RFE/RL) is a nonprofit corporation made up of two radio networks that broadcast to countries in eastern Europe and the former Soviet Union. The United States established the networks to oppose attempts by Communist governments to isolate their citizens from information about the world. In the late 1980's and early 1990's, Communists lost control of nearly all these governments of eastern Europe and, in 1991, the Soviet Union was replaced by a non-Communist Commonwealth of Independent States.

Today, Radio Free Europe broadcasts in a number of languages to European nations, including Bulgaria, Estonia, Latvia, Lithuania, Romania, and Slovakia. Radio Liberty broadcasts to Russia, Ukraine, and other former Soviet republics. RFE/RL is funded by grants from the U.S. government.

People from the audience areas write and produce most RFE/RL programs. Many of the programs consist of news and news analysis, and they focus on current events in the audience countries. Other RFE/RL programs describe cultural and religious activities and offer background information about economic, historical, and political matters.

Radio Free Europe began broadcasting to eastern Europe in 1950, and Radio Liberty started broadcasting to the Soviet Union in 1951. In 1976, the networks merged and formed RFE/RL, Inc. From 1985 to 1993, Radio Liberty broadcast to Afghanistan. RFE/RL broadcasting headquarters are in Prague, Czech Republic.

Critically reviewed by Radio Free Europe/Radio Liberty

Radio telescope. See Telescope (Radio telescopes).
Radio wave. See Electromagnetic waves; Radio (How radio programs are broadcast; diagrams).
Radioactivity. See Radiation.
Radiocarbon, or Carbon 14, is a radioactive isotope of carbon. It has an atomic weight of 14 and is heavier than ordinary carbon, which has an atomic weight of 12.011. Radiocarbon is used to determine the age of fossils and other kinds of ancient objects. In addition, researchers use radiocarbon to study certain biological processes.

In nature, radiocarbon forms when high-energy atomic particles called *cosmic rays* smash into the earth's atmosphere. Cosmic rays cause atoms in the atmosphere to break down into electrons, neutrons, protons, and other particles. Some neutrons strike the nuclei of nitrogen atoms in the atmosphere. Each of these nuclei absorbs a neutron and then loses a proton. In this way, a nitrogen atom becomes a radiocarbon atom.

All living things contain radiocarbon. In the atmosphere, there is about one atom of radiocarbon for every

trillion molecules of carbon dioxide gas. Plants absorb radiocarbon from the carbon dioxide in the air. Human beings and other animals take in radiocarbon chiefly from the food provided by plants.

Radiocarbon dating is a process used to determine the age of an ancient object by measuring its radiocarbon content. This technique was developed in the late 1940's by Willard F. Libby, an American chemist. Archaeologists and geologists have used it extensively. They have learned much about prehistoric human beings, animals, and plants that lived up to 50,000 years ago.

Radiocarbon atoms, like all radioactive substances, *decay* (break down by releasing particles) at an exact and uniform rate. Half of the radiocarbon disappears after about 5,700 years. Therefore, radiocarbon is said to have a *half-life* of that period of time. After about 11,400 years, a fourth of the original amount of radiocarbon remains. After another 5,700 years, only an eighth remains, and so on.

The radiocarbon in the tissues of a living organism decays extremely slowly, but it is continuously renewed as long as the organism lives. After the organism dies, it no longer takes in air or food, and so it no longer absorbs radiocarbon. The radiocarbon already in the tissues continues to decrease at a constant rate. This steady decay at a known rate—a half-life of approximately 5,700 years—enables scientists to determine an object's age.

In one method of radiocarbon dating, scientists burn

Radiocarbon dating

Scientists determine the age of an ancient object by measuring its radiocarbon content. This process is called *radiocarbon dating.* Two methods of radiocarbon dating are described here.

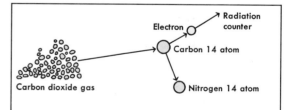

In the traditional method, a piece of the object is burned and converted to carbon dioxide gas. Radiocarbon (carbon 14) atoms in the gas release electrons as the radiocarbon changes into nitrogen 14. *Radiation counters* detect the number of electrons given off, which determines the object's radiocarbon content.

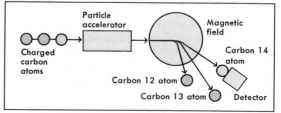

WORLD BOOK diagrams by Arthur Grebetz

In a newer method, a *particle accelerator* fires charged atoms originally from a small piece of the object into a magnetic field. The field deflects and separates the various carbon atoms by their weight. Then a *detector* counts individual carbon 14 atoms to determine the object's radiocarbon content.

Radiocarbon half-life

Half the radiocarbon in an object *decays* (breaks down by releasing particles) about every 5,700 years. This period is the *half-life* of radiocarbon. Newly cut wood retains most of its radiocarbon. After 5,700 years, half the radiocarbon disappears. After about 11,400 years, a fourth remains.

Newly cut wood

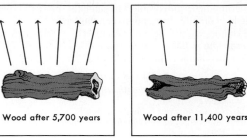

Wood after 5,700 years

Wood after 11,400 years

WORLD BOOK diagrams by Jean Helmer

a piece of the object and convert it to carbon dioxide gas. The carbon dioxide is purified, and the amount of radiocarbon in the purified carbon dioxide is measured with *radiation counters*. These instruments detect the electrons released by the radiocarbon atoms as the atoms change back into nitrogen atoms. The number of electrons emitted indicates the radiocarbon content.

Another method of radiocarbon dating involves the use of certain types of *particle accelerators* instead of radiation counters (see **Particle accelerator**). An accelerator enables scientists to detect and count directly the individual radiocarbon atoms in an extremely small portion of an object. After scientists measure an object's radiocarbon content, they compare it with the radiocarbon in tree rings whose ages are known (see **Tree** [diagram: How a tree reveals its history]). This technique enables them to compensate for small variations of radiocarbon content in the atmosphere at different times in the past. By doing so, scientists can convert an object's radiocarbon age to a more precise date.

Radiocarbon in biology. Radiocarbon is used as a "tracer" to study various complex biological processes. In such research, scientists substitute a radiocarbon atom for an atom of a carbon molecule. Then they use a radiation counter to trace the path of the radiocarbon atom through a chemical reaction in an organism.

The radiocarbon used as a tracer is produced artificially in nuclear reactors. Artificial radiocarbon was first discovered in 1939 by two American chemists, Martin D. Kamen and Samuel Ruben.   Rainer Berger

See also **Archaeology** (Dating).

Radiochemistry is a field of chemistry that involves the study of radioactive elements. It also deals with the production, identification, and use of such elements and their isotopes. Radiochemistry has benefited archaeology, biochemistry, and other scientific fields. Radiochemical techniques are often used in medicine to help diagnose disease and in various environmental studies.

A few radioactive elements, such as thorium and uranium, occur in nature. Others are created artificially. They can be produced in devices called *particle accelerators* by bombarding nonradioactive elements with high-energy particles. Elements also can be made radioactive in nuclear reactors by exposing them to large numbers of neutrons.

The isotopes of radioactive elements are called *radionuclides* or *radioisotopes*. They are widely used as *tracers* in certain kinds of research, especially the study of complex biological processes. This type of study involves tracing radionuclides through chemical reactions in organisms. The tracing is done with Geiger counters,

proportional counters, and other detection devices.

A radionuclide is produced in minute quantities, and so it tends to *plate out* (accumulate) on the walls of its container before it can be used. Radiochemists prevent this by adding a small, precisely measured amount of a *carrier element* (nonradioactive element) to it.

Another important radiochemical technique is called *neutron activation analysis*. In this method, an object is exposed to neutrons, causing some of the elements in the object to become radioactive. These elements then emit radiation of certain energies. One of the uses of this method is the verification of the authenticity of old paintings. The paint used in old works of art differs in composition from the paint in recent paintings, and so it gives off different radiations.   Raymond P. Borkowski

Radiogeology is the science that deals with the relation of radioactivity to geology. Geologists can determine the age of rocks, fossils, and other objects by measuring the radioactive elements in them.

The earth, the waters of the oceans, the air we breathe, and all living things contain small amounts of radioactivity. This radioactivity is caused by (1) the radioactive elements uranium and thorium, and their decay products; (2) radioactive potassium; (3) small amounts of less abundant radioactive elements, such as samarium and rubidium; and (4) radiocarbon, which forms when high-energy particles called *cosmic rays* strike nitrogen in the earth's atmosphere.

The rocks of the earth's surface contain an average of five parts of uranium per million parts of rock. Uranium has been in the earth since the earth was formed. It decays over time to become lead and helium. The rate at which a radioactive isotope decays is measured by its *half-life*—that is, the time required for half the atoms in the isotope to decay into another isotope. Lead isotope 206 is formed from uranium isotope 238, which has a half-life of about $4\frac{1}{2}$ billion years. Lead-207 is formed from uranium-235, which has a half-life of 700 million years. Scientists can measure the amounts of these isotopes in a rock sample and then calculate the rock's age from the ratio of lead-206 to uranium-238, the ratio of lead-207 to uranium-235, and the ratio of lead-206 to lead-207. Similar calculations can be made using other radioactive isotopes.

On the basis of lead-to-uranium ratios, scientists estimate that the age of the solar system is about $4\frac{1}{2}$ billion years. This figure agrees with the ages of meteorites and the oldest moon rocks as measured by the decay of other radioactive elements.

The decay of long-lived radioactive isotopes is like a great clock that measures time in millions or billions of years. The clock also has a "second hand" that measures time in thousands of years. This is radiocarbon, which has a half-life of 5,700 years. Analysis of radiocarbon content makes it possible to determine the age of wood, bone, and other once-living materials.

G. Brent Dalrymple

See also **Radiation; Radiocarbon.**

Radioisotope. See Isotope; Radiochemistry.

Radiolaria. See Protozoan (Sarcodines).

Radiological warfare. See Chemical-biological-radiological warfare.

Radiology, *ray dee AHL uh jee,* is the field of medicine that uses X rays and other means to create images of structures and processes inside the body. These images aid in diagnosis and treatment of diseases and other disorders. Radiology includes the use of such imaging techniques as computed tomography (CT), fluoroscopy, magnetic resonance imaging (MRI), and positron emission tomography (PET). Medical procedures that involve *ultrasound* (high-frequency sound waves) are also part of radiology. Doctors who specialize in radiology are called *radiologists.*

Radiological imaging techniques help doctors to diagnose disorders by providing a view of the patient's bones, organs, and other internal structures. For example, a *radiograph* (X-ray picture) of the leg can reveal a fractured bone. A CT scan of the brain can detect a tumor or blood clot. In examinations of certain organs, including the intestines and the urinary tract, the radiologist may give a substance called a *contrast agent* to the patient. The contrast agent may be a barium mixture given orally to coat the lining of the bowel so it is more clearly seen. A contrast agent consisting of an iodine mixture may be injected into a blood vessel to study arteries or veins.

Radiological procedures also aid in the treatment of certain disorders. For example, doctors use fluoroscopy, CT, or ultrasound imaging to guide *catheters* (small tubes) into a patient's body. This technique is used to drain obstructed ducts in the urinary tract and for many other treatments. P. Andrea Lum

See also **Fluoroscopy; Magnetic resonance imaging; Positron emission tomography; Ultrasound; X rays.**

Radiosonde, *RAY dee oh SAHND,* is an instrument meteorologists use to take *soundings* (measurements) of the upper air. A radiosonde consists of devices that measure temperature, relative humidity, and air pressure, combined with a radio transmitter. The measuring devices and transmitter are in a small, lightweight box carried aloft by a balloon filled with helium or hydrogen.

The radio transmits the information recorded by the measuring instruments to ground stations. In addition, a radio direction finder tracks the radiosonde to determine the speed and direction of the wind at various levels of the atmosphere.

Donald T. Acheson

See also **Weather** (Weather balloons, airplanes, and ships); **Balloon** (Scientific uses).

© David R. Frazier

A radiosonde is used by meteorologists to measure atmospheric conditions.

Radiotelephone. See Cellular telephone.

Radiotherapy. See Cancer (Radiation therapy).

Radish is a plant grown for its fleshy root. The roots, also called *radishes,* are crisp and sharp-tasting. Radishes are eaten raw in salads or as an appetizer.

Custom Medical Stock Photo

Radiologists use X rays and other techniques to create images of the body. The radiologists in this photograph are examining an X-ray picture during a surgical operation.

WORLD BOOK illustration by Jill Coombs

Radishes are plants with crisp, sharp-tasting roots. Several varieties of radishes are shown above. They are, *from left to right,* French Breakfast, Cherry Belle, Scarlet Globe, and White Icicle.

There are many *cultivars* (varieties) of radishes. Some are round or oblong, and others are shaped like icicles. They range in weight from less than 1 ounce (28 grams) to more than 2 pounds (1 kilogram). Their colors include white, red, yellow, pink, purple, black, and a combination of red and white.

Radishes grow best in cool weather, and they are able to withstand frost. The plants are ready for harvest 20 to 60 days after planting, depending on the cultivar. Most radishes grown in the United States are harvested in March, April, and May. Florida, California, and Ohio lead the states in commercial production. In addition, many people plant radishes in home gardens.

Scientific classification. The radish plant belongs to the mustard family, Brassicaceae or Cruciferae. Its scientific name is *Raphanus sativus.*   George R. Hughes

Radisson, *ra dee SAWN,* **Pierre Esprit,** *pyair ehs PREE* (1640?-1710?), was a French explorer and fur trader. He and his brother-in-law, Médard Chouart, Sieur des Groseilliers, were probably the first white people to explore the area north and west of the Great Lakes.

Radisson was born in France. He came to what is now Canada as a boy. Iroquois Indians captured him about 1651, but he escaped from them about two years later. About 1660, Radisson and Groseilliers explored the Lake Superior area. After quarreling with the French over fur-trading rights, the two men went to England in 1665. They persuaded a group of English merchants to support a trading expedition to Hudson's Bay. This trip led to the establishment of the Hudson's Bay Company, an English fur-trading firm, in 1670. Radisson worked for the company from 1670 to 1675. He then returned to France. In 1684, he rejoined the Hudson's Bay Company. Radisson settled in England in 1687.   P. B. Waite

See also **Groseilliers, Sieur des; Minnesota** (Exploration); **Wisconsin** (Exploration and settlement).

Radium, *RAY dee uhm,* is a highly radioactive, metallic element. It occurs chiefly in uranium and thorium ores. The French physicists Marie and Pierre Curie and a coworker, Gustave Bémont, discovered radium in 1898 while processing pitchblende, a uranium ore. See **Curie, Marie S.; Curie, Pierre.**

Before the mid-1950's, radium was widely used for treating cancer. It also was a key ingredient in fluorescent paint used for watch and instrument dials. Today, safer and cheaper sources of radiation have replaced radium for most medical and industrial uses. These sources include the isotope cobalt 60, particle accelerators, and X-ray machines.

Radium releases large amounts of high-energy radiation, which can be harmful to human health. The element resembles calcium chemically, and so it tends to accumulate in the bones after being absorbed by the body. The radiation given off by radium bombards the bone marrow and destroys tissue that produces red blood cells. It also can cause bone cancer. In the past, some workers who handled radium in factories that produced fluorescent watch dials died because they had absorbed the radioactive material. However, under normal conditions, there is almost no danger of absorbing hazardous amounts of radium because it occurs in such tiny quantities in the environment.

Properties. Radium is silver-white. Its chemical symbol is Ra, and its atomic number is 88. Radium is the heaviest member of the group of elements called *alkaline earth metals* (see **Element, Chemical** [Periodic table of the elements]). Radium has at least 26 isotopes, all of which are radioactive. Radium has a mass number of 226.025. Radium melts at 700 °C and boils at 1140 °C. It has a density of 5 grams per cubic centimeter at 20 °C.

How radium forms and breaks down. Radium is constantly being formed in nature by the *radioactive decay* of uranium. During radioactive decay, uranium 238, the heaviest isotope of uranium, emits radiation in the form of *alpha particles, beta particles,* and *gamma rays.* In doing so, uranium 238 becomes uranium 234, which later changes into thorium 230. This *unstable* (radioactive) isotope, in turn, breaks down into radium 226.

Concentrations of radium in nature are low because its isotopes disintegrate continually. Radium 226 decays into an unstable isotope of a gas called radon and eventually into a stable isotope of lead.   Duward F. Shriver

Related articles in *World Book* include:

Cobalt	Pitchblende	Transmutation of
Particle	Radiation	elements
accelerator	Radon	X rays

Radon, *RAY dahn,* is a radioactive chemical element that occurs naturally as a gas. The gas is produced by the radioactive *decay* (breakdown) of radium, a metallic element found in nearly all soil and rocks. Radon gas is colorless and odorless. It is classified as a *noble gas,* or an *inert gas,* because its atoms do not combine readily with other atoms. Radon gas may become a health hazard in certain buildings.

The main sources of radon in buildings are the soil and rocks beneath basements. Minor sources include water that comes from wells and building materials such as granite and gypsum that come from the ground. Some areas have a high concentration in the ground.

The gas seeps from soil and rocks into water and air. Radon may enter a basement through cracks or other openings. If the building is in a high-radon area, the gas may build up inside to an unhealthy level.

Radon decay. Radon atoms decay by giving off a form of radiation called an *alpha particle.* When a radon atom decays, it becomes an atom of the radioactive element polonium. Further decay produces atoms of other elements. Atoms produced by one or more decays of what were originally radon atoms are called *radon daughters,* also known as radon *progeny* (children).

How radon affects health. Radon daughters cling to airborne dust particles and can catch in the lungs when people breathe them. When well water contains high levels, turning on faucets or showers may release radon and its daughters into the air. Some radon may also enter the body when people drink water containing the gas.

Alpha particles released by radon and its daughters in the body disrupt the normal genetic or chemical processes of living cells, causing cells to grow abnormally or to die. Over time, such cell damage may lead to cancer.

During the 1960's and 1970's, studies of uranium miners, who breathed large amounts of radon in the air of mines, showed unusually high rates of lung cancer. Smokers who are exposed to high radon levels are also at increased risk. The United States Environmental Protection Agency (EPA) estimates that radon may cause as many as 10 percent of cancer deaths in the country.

Protection against radon. Test kits that people can use to check the radon levels in their homes are available from stores and mail-order sources. The EPA recommends corrective action if the radioactivity due to radon exceeds 4 *picocuries* per liter of air (4 pCi/L). A picocurie is one-trillionth of a *curie,* a unit of radioactivity. The EPA estimates that 6 percent of U.S. homes exceed 4 pCi/L. Some experts believe that the EPA threshold is too low, and that 4 pCi/L of radon does not threaten health significantly.

Most radon leaks can be fixed by coating the basement floor and walls with a flexible sealant. Increasing the ventilation in a building also helps lower the radon level.

In 1988, Congress passed the Indoor Radon Abatement Act to help reduce the threat from radon. The act set a goal of reducing radon until all home air was as pure as outdoor air. In outdoor air, the radioactivity due to radon is usually less than $\frac{1}{2}$ pCi/L.

Chemical properties. Radon's chemical symbol is Rn, and its atomic number is 86. Radon freezes at $-71\ °C$ and boils at $-61.7\ °C$. Friedrich E. Dorn, a German chemist, discovered radon in 1900.

Douglas John Crawford-Brown

Raeburn, *RAY buhrn,* **Sir Henry** (1756-1823), was the leading Scottish portrait painter of his day. Raeburn painted straightforward portraits that captured the character of the subject. Most of his subjects were fashionable and upper-class Scottish people. Raeburn rarely sketched his subjects before painting them. Instead, he worked directly on the canvas, using bold, vigorous

brushstrokes. Many of his portraits show strong color contrasts and dramatic lighting effects.

Raeburn was born in Edinburgh and lived there most of his life. He was largely a self-taught artist. In 1785, Raeburn met Sir Joshua Reynolds, an English portrait artist. He was influenced by Reynolds's style but painted in a more romantic manner.   Douglas K. S. Hyland

Raffia, *RAF ee uh,* is a fiber made from the leafstalks of certain varieties of palm trees. One of these palms, the

WORLD BOOK photo

Raffia is a fiber made from the leafstalks of certain palm trees. The basket shown above is woven from raffia.

Raphia ruffia, grows abundantly on the northeastern coast of Madagascar. Another, the *Raphia taedigera,* grows on the islands of Japan. Residents of Madagascar make clothes from raffia fiber and weave baskets, mats, and small fancy bags from it. Raffia was once used in greenhouses to protect plants from cold and to tie buds and grafts. But today, artificial fibers are often used in greenhouses in place of raffia. Raffia is used in schools for weaving baskets and other products. See also **Basket making.**   Robert A. Barnhardt

Rafflesia, *ra FLEE zhuh,* is the name of a small genus of plants which have huge flowers but no leaves or stems. The flowers grow as parasites on the stems and roots of several Cissus shrubs in Southeast Asia.

The giant rafflesia bears the largest flowers known. They can grow more than 3 feet (90 centimeters) wide.

Quentin McAdam (about 1810), an oil painting on canvas; Yale Center for British Art, Paul Mellon Collection

A Raeburn portrait shows the bold brushstrokes and dramatic lighting effects that are typical of the Scottish painter's style.

Kjell B. Sandved, Photo Researchers

The giant rafflesia produces the world's largest known flowers. They can grow more than 3 feet (90 centimeters) wide.

The stamens and pistils of the rafflesia grow on separate flowers. They require some agent to pollinate them. The flowers have five wide, fleshy lobes and usually have a bad odor.   Thomas B. Croat

Scientific classification. The rafflesia belongs to the rafflesia family, Rafflesiaceae. The giant rafflesia is classified as *Rafflesia arnoldii.*

See also **Flower** (picture: The rafflesia).

Rafsanjani, *ruhf sehn JAN ee,* **Ali Akbar Hashemi,** *AH lee AHK bahr HASH uh mee* (1934-   ), served as president of Iran from 1989 to 1997. He succeeded Ali Khamenei, who became Iran's spiritual leader after the death of Ayatollah Ruhollah Khomeini. Rafsanjani was considered a moderate president. He was succeeded by Mohammad Khatami in 1997.

© Eslami Rad, Gamma/Liaison
Hashemi Rafsanjani

Rafsanjani was born in a village near Kerman in eastern Iran. He became a follower of Khomeini in the 1950's, while studying theology in Qom.

During the 1960's and 1970's, Rafsanjani partici-pated in a campaign organized by Iran's clergy against the government of Shah Mohammad Reza Pahlavi. In 1979, Khomeini became the chief political figure of Iran after his followers had overthrown the shah. He appoint-ed Rafsanjani to the Revolutionary Council, which gov-erned Iran until 1980. Rafsanjani was elected to parlia-ment in 1980 and served as its speaker until 1989. During the 1980's, he also was minister of the interior and acting commander in chief of the armed forces.

Michel Le Gall

Raft is one of the simplest kinds of watercraft. It may be made of logs lashed together with ropes, or of any other material that floats. Rafts are usually square or rectangu-lar. Poles, paddles, or sails can be used to help propel a raft across the water. Sometimes river and ocean cur-rents alone move a raft to its destination. Most modern rafts used for recreational purposes are inflatable and are made of nylon fabric coated with a synthetic rubber called *neoprene* (see **Rafting**).

Early people built rafts of logs, bundles of reeds, or inflated animal skins lashed together with vines or twist-ed animal hides. Such rafts provided a means of using the currents of waterways for transportation. A raft drift-ing with a river's current could carry passengers and goods downstream to the sea. For this reason, ancient seaports were frequently located at the mouths of rivers, where they could easily receive goods from areas far-ther inland. During the 1800's, *flatboats* (large rafts) served as an important means of transportation on the Ohio and Mississippi rivers (see **Flatboat**).

In 1947, Thor Heyerdahl of Norway and five compan-ions drifted on the balsa-wood raft *Kon-Tiki* for about 4,300 miles (6,920 kilometers). They sailed from Peru to the Tuamotu Islands in the central Pacific (see **Heyer-dahl, Thor**). In 1963 and 1964, 70-year-old William Willis of the United States sailed for 10,850 miles (17,461 kilo-meters) on the *Age Unlimited,* a steel pontoon raft. He went from Peru to Australia—with a stop in the Samoa Islands for repairs—in 204 days.   Octavia N. Cubbins

Rafting is an outdoor recreational activity in which small groups of people float down a river on rafts. Raft-ing provides an opportunity to enjoy scenic wilderness areas in a fresh way. Many people enjoy the adventure and challenge of rafting on rivers that have *white water* (rapids). A raft trip can last for hours, or it can be com-bined with a camping trip that lasts for days.

Most rafts are inflatable, 12 to 16 feet (3.7 to 5 meters) long, and made of nylon fabric coated with *neoprene* (synthetic rubber). The shape resembles a rectangle with rounded corners. Most crews consist of six people, who sit on the sides of the raft and steer it with paddles. The raft is one of the oldest forms of transportation. But raft-ing did not become a popular leisure-time activity until the 1960's.   Critically reviewed by the American Rafting Association

Ragtime is a type of rhythmic music that was highly popular in the United States around 1895 to 1915. Rag-time (from "ragged time"), or simply *rag,* probably

Phil Degginger from E. R. Degginger

Rafting on *white water* (rap-ids) is an exciting challenge. The crew uses paddles to steer the craft through the swirling waters. A raft trip can last for hours, or it can be combined with a camping trip that lasts for days.

developed from military marches and from music that accompanied minstrel show dances.

Ragtime is characterized by melodies that are highly *syncopated* (irregularly accented) combined with accompaniments that have regular accents. Ragtime pieces also have clear-cut thematic sections. Rags were played either on piano or by small bands with various combinations of instruments and became an early influence on jazz.

Although improvised rags were common in the early years, formally composed versions soon became widely published. Among the earliest published rags were Tom Turpin's "Harlem Rag" (1897) and Scott Joplin's "Maple Leaf Rag" (1899). Joplin became known as the "King of Ragtime." Other important ragtime composers included Joseph F. Lamb and James Scott.   Thomas W. Tunks

See also **Jazz** (The roots of jazz); **Joplin, Scott; Popular music** (Ragtime, jazz, and blues).

Ragweed is the name of several weeds that grow in the United States and Canada. These weeds grow along roadsides, and in pastures, fields, and vacant lots. Many people are allergic to ragweed pollen. It is produced in great amounts and spread by the wind. People who are allergic to ragweed pollen may get symptoms of hay fever when there are about 25 grains of pollen per cubic yard (33 grains per cubic meter) of air. The air may contain more pollen than this when the plants bloom.

The *common ragweed,* also called *bitterweed* and *hogweed,* is a coarse annual plant with finely divided leaves. It usually grows 1 to 3 feet (30 to 91 centimeters) high. Its small, hard fruit has short, sharp spines near the end. *Giant ragweed,* sometimes called *kinghead,* is also an annual. It commonly grows 3 to 6 feet (0.9 to 1.8 meters) tall but may grow to 10 feet (3 meters). Its leaves usually are divided into three broad parts. *Perennial ragweed* grows from long, spreading roots. It looks something like the common ragweed but its fruit has blunt *tubercles* (small projections) instead of spines.

Ragweed grows quickly in any untended spot. It is so ordinary looking and its flowers are so inconspicuous that efforts to eliminate it have failed.

Scientific classification. Ragweeds are in the composite family, Compositae. The scientific name for the common ragweed is *Ambrosia artemisiifolia.* The giant ragweed is *A. trifida.* Perennial ragweed is *A. psilostachya.*   Anton A. Reznicek

See also **Hay fever.**

Raikes, Robert (1735-1811), an English publisher, first developed Sunday schools on an extensive scale. Many children in his home city, Gloucester, worked six long days in the factories and had no chance for education. He opened his first Sunday school there in 1780. Sunday schools helped train children in reading and arithmetic as well as in the Bible, because there were no public schools. Before Raikes died, his system had spread throughout England.   F. A. Norwood

Rail is the common name of a family of marsh birds that live throughout most of the world. The family includes the rails proper, the gallinules, and the coots or mud hens. The birds called rails live in grassy marshes.

John H. Gerard, DPI

The Virginia rail is a swift, slender bird that lives in marshes. The rail's coloring helps it blend into the vegetation.

They run swiftly over the mud, seeking worms, insects, snails, floating seeds, and plant sprouts to eat. Rails vary in length from 5 to 25 inches (13 to 64 centimeters). They have long, narrow bodies, short wings and tails, long legs and toes, and loose plumage of mixed black, brown, and gray feathers. A rail's shape helps it slip through reeds and grasses. The expression "thin as a rail" may come from their appearance. Rails migrate long distances. However, the birds are seldom seen in flight except when chased from cover. They build nests of grasses on the ground or among rushes over water. They lay from 6 to 15 buffy-white eggs, speckled with reddish-brown.

The rails most common in Europe are the *water rail* and the *corn crake,* or *land rail,* which frequents fields. The *king rail, yellow rail, black rail, clapper rail, Virginia rail,* and *sora* (or *sora rail*) are found in America. The clapper rail is hunted in the southern United States.

Scientific classification. Rails make up the rail family, Rallidae. The scientific name for the king rail is *Rallus elegans;* the clapper is *R. longirostris;* the Virginia, *R. limicola.* The yellow rail is *Coturnicops noveboracensis;* the sora, *Porzana carolina;* the black, *Laterallus jamaicensis.*   James J. Dinsmore

See also **Coot; Gallinule.**

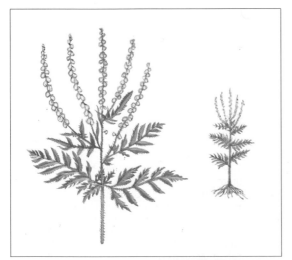

WORLD BOOK illustration by James Teason

The common ragweed usually grows 1 to 3 feet (30 to 91 centimeters) high. Ragweed sprouts quickly along roadsides and in fields. Many people are allergic to ragweed pollen.

Gamma/Liaison

The world's fastest passenger train is France's TGV *(train à grande vitesse)*. The TGV shown here travels between Paris and other cities in France and Belgium at up to 186 miles (300 kilometers) per hour. Trains once carried most of the passenger traffic between cities. But today more people use cars or airplanes, and most railroads get most of their income from hauling freight.

Railroad

Railroad is one of the most important means of transportation. Every day, thousands of trains speed along railroad tracks throughout the world. Some trains carry passengers. Others haul coal, grain, lumber, machinery, and other products on which people depend. Only ships carry heavier cargoes for longer distances. And only airplanes provide a faster means of public transportation than do railroads. A freight train can haul thousands of tons of goods across a continent. The fastest passenger trains in regular service travel at speeds of up to 186 miles per hour (mph), or 300 kilometers per hour (kph). In test runs, these trains have reached speeds of more than 250 mph (400 kph). In many parts of the world, railroads are also called *railways.*

Railroads use a two-railed track to guide trains of cars along a permanent route. Trains therefore are not steered, unlike airplanes, automobiles, and ships. Powerful diesel-electric or electric locomotives move most trains along the track. However, older steam locomotives still haul a few trains in some parts of the world, such as China and India.

Almost every country has at least one railroad. The world's longest rail line is in Russia. It extends about 5,600 miles (9,000 kilometers) and connects Moscow and

Vladivostok. Laid end-to-end, the tracks of the world's main railroad routes would stretch about 750,000 miles (1,200,000 kilometers)—about $3\frac{1}{4}$ times the distance from the earth to the moon.

The word *railroad* may refer not only to a method of transportation, but also to an organization that provides rail transportation. In many countries, a government agency or government-owned corporation operates the railroads. In other countries, including the United States, private companies own and operate all or most of the main railroads.

The first public railroads began in the United Kingdom in the 1820's and 1830's. These railroads used steam locomotives to haul wagons loaded with freight or coaches carrying passengers. By the mid-1800's, other countries also had steam-powered railroads. During the late 1800's and early 1900's, thousands of steam trains made their way across the U.S. countryside, carrying most of the nation's freight and long-distance passengers. The first railroad across western North America was completed in 1869 and so helped open the American West to settlers.

Over the years, railroads have faced ever-increasing competition from other forms of transportation. In most countries, the central government supports the railroads. But in a few countries, including the United States, freight railroads get little government aid. Private railroads generally face greater financial risks than do government-owned ones.

William L. Withuhn, the contributor of this article, is Curator of Transportation at the Smithsonian Institution.

How railroads serve the public

Railroads provide two main types of service: (1) passenger service and (2) freight service. The importance of each type of railroad service varies from country to country.

Passenger service. Railroads operate two main types of passenger trains: *commuter trains* and *intercity trains.* Commuter trains carry passengers between large cities and the surrounding suburbs. Most of these trains are made up of a locomotive and a number of *coaches.* Coaches provide seats for passengers but do not ordinarily offer any extra services, such as meals or refreshments. Intercity trains make longer runs than most commuter trains do. The longest intercity runs cover great distances and take several days to complete. As a result, many intercity passenger trains have special cars, such as *dining cars* and *sleeping cars,* in addition to coaches.

Since the 1940's, the number of rail passengers has declined sharply in many industrial countries, as more and more people travel by automobile and airplane. For example, railroads in the United States now carry less than 1 percent of all intercity passenger traffic. In some countries, however, passenger trains have not faced such strong competition from other forms of transportation. People in China, India, Japan, and most European countries still rely heavily on trains for intercity transportation. And even in the United States, thousands of

people who live in suburban areas ride commuter trains into major cities.

Commuter trains. A majority of rail passengers ride commuter trains. Each working day, these trains carry great numbers of suburban residents to and from work in such large cities as London and New York City. Commuter trains also serve many other cities throughout the world, including Berlin, Chicago, Johannesburg, Moscow, New Delhi, Paris, São Paulo, Tokyo, and Toronto. Some intercity trains also serve commuters.

It takes up to 1,000 automobiles to carry as many commuters as one commuter train can carry. Commuter trains thus help relieve rush-hour traffic jams on city highways. By reducing the number of automobiles in use, commuter trains help conserve fuel. They also help reduce air pollution caused by exhaust fumes.

Intercity trains. Some countries have unusually fast, efficient intercity passenger trains. The fastest passenger trains in the world operate in France and Japan. Trains in both countries travel up to 186 mph (300 kph) between stops. They may average more than 160 mph (260 kph). High-speed trains also serve cities in Germany, the United Kingdom, and other European countries. Some of the Japanese and European high-speed trains offer a number of luxury services, including gift shops, telephones, and meals served at the passengers' seats.

Some Canadian intercity trains, called *Corridor Trains,* also provide luxury service. One of these trains carries

Carol Brozman

A commuter train carries passengers between cities and suburbs. Many commuter trains have double-deck coaches.

Photo Trends

Refrigerator cars are equipped to keep fruits, vegetables, and meats at the right temperature.

Michael K. Nichols, Magnum

Container shipping speeds the loading and unloading of freight trains. The containers are large boxes loaded with freight. The double-stack car, *shown here,* can carry two large containers. A crane is about to stack the container at the rear on top of the container in the car.

passengers between Toronto and Montreal—a 335-mile (539-kilometer) journey—at an average speed of about 80 mph (130 kph).

In the early 1900's, there were thousands of passenger trains in the United States, linking almost all U.S. cities. Today, only about 125 daily intercity trains serve the entire country. *Metroliners,* the electric-powered trains that run between New York City and Washington, D.C., are among the fastest U.S. trains in commercial service. They can achieve a top speed of about 130 mph (210 kph). Amtrak is developing *Acela,* which will connect New York City, Washington, D.C., and Boston. The Acela are scheduled to replace Metroliners and may reach 150 mph (240 kph).

Freight service. In many countries, most of the income earned by railroads comes from hauling freight. Railroads provide the most inexpensive method of land transportation over long distances. Trains are used extensively to carry such bulk goods as chemicals, coal, grain, iron ore, and petroleum. They also carry such manufactured goods as automobiles and television sets, and such agricultural products as fruits, vegetables, and meats. Some of the cars on a freight train are empty cars being moved to various points for reloading.

Railroads use many types of cars and freight-handling equipment. Bulk materials, such as coal and ores, travel in open cars with *hatches* (doors) underneath. Such cars can be emptied quickly through these doors. Powdered materials, such as cement, travel in cars that are pressurized steel containers. The cars are loaded and unloaded using air pressure that pumps the material in or out through pipes. Chemicals, gasoline, milk, and other liquids are carried in tank cars. Refrigerated cars transport fruits, vegetables, and meats. Special railroad cars with two or three decks are used to carry automobiles.

The longest freight trains have 200 or more cars. In the United States, a typical freight train has about 80 cars and carries about 5,000 tons (4,500 metric tons) of goods.

Railroads in many countries carry more freight today than ever before. However, railroads haul a smaller share of the total freight traffic than in the past. For example, in 1929, railroads handled almost 75 percent of all the freight carried between U.S. cities. Today, they carry about 40 percent of all intercity commercial freight.

To attract more customers, railroads in many countries have tried to improve their freight service. In the 1950's, for example, U.S. railroads introduced *piggyback* service—the use of flatcars to carry truck trailers loaded with freight. Piggyback service attracted shippers because one train could carry many truck trailers for a fraction of what it cost to haul them individually by highway. Today, U.S. railroads carry hundreds of thousands of truck trailers each year. Another type of service uses flatcars to haul large containers loaded with freight. The containers are transferred to the flatcars from specially designed ships or trucks (see **Containerization**). The *Freight operations* section of this article discusses other improvements in freight service.

What makes up a railroad

A railroad consists basically of a track along which locomotives pull trains of cars. The track is made up of

Railroad passenger routes

This map shows the major railroad passenger routes in North America. The National Railroad Passenger Corporation (Amtrak), created in 1970, provides most of the passenger service in the United States. In Canada and Mexico, passenger service exists along with freight service on many minor routes not shown on the map. The cities shown are important rail passenger terminals.

———— Amtrak route

- - - - Other passenger railroad

0   500 Miles
0   500 Kilometers

WORLD BOOK map

Atchison, Topeka and Santa Fe Railway

Diesel-powered trains make up the backbone of U.S. railroads. Many diesel locomotives consist of several power units at the head of the train, all under the control of one engineer.

two steel rails fastened lengthwise to a series of wooden or concrete *crossties,* called *sleepers* in some countries. The wheel-and-axle assemblies on locomotives and cars are specially designed to run on the track. Each wheel has a *flange* (raised edge) around its rim. The flanges on each pair of wheels guide the wheels along the track. *Switches*—short movable rails—are built into a track where it meets other tracks. By turning a switch, a train can be made to run from one track to another. A railroad also includes signal and communications systems to control train traffic, stations to handle passengers and freight, *yards* to make up trains, and *shops* to repair locomotives and cars.

Rolling stock is a term that refers to railroad locomotives and cars.

Locomotives. Most trains are pulled by a locomotive at the head of the train. But some locomotives push as well as pull. These locomotives are especially useful on commuter lines because they eliminate the need to turn a train around for a return trip at the end of a run.

Locomotives can be classified into two groups by the work they do. *Road locomotives* haul freight or passenger trains. *Switching locomotives,* sometimes called *shunting locomotives* or *switch engines,* move cars from track to track in rail yards.

Almost all locomotives can also be classified into three groups according to how they are powered. *Diesel-electric locomotives* use oil-burning diesel engines to turn electric generators. The electric power produced by the generators runs the motors that turn the locomotive's wheels. *Electric locomotives* work much as diesel-electrics do. But instead of producing their own electric power, they get it from wires suspended above the track or from an electrified third rail. *Steam locomotives* burn coal or fuel oil to produce steam. The force of the steam powers the locomotive.

A few trains are hauled by two other kinds of locomotives. *Gas-turbine electric locomotives* use the force of hot gases to run turbines, which in turn operate electric generators. Power produced by the generators runs the locomotives. *Diesel-hydraulic locomotives* use diesel engines to produce energy that is transmitted to the driving mechanisms by means of fluids under pressure. See **Locomotive** and **Electric railroad.**

Railroads in most industrial countries operate both diesel-electric and electric locomotives. Almost all locomotives operated by U.S. railroads are diesel-electric. No large, commercial U.S. railroads use steam locomotives. Steam locomotives are still used in a few parts of China and India.

Passenger and freight cars. Railroad cars are grouped in two general categories, passenger cars and freight cars. Each car has a *coupler* at each end. This device links the cars together. Cars also have *air brakes,* which are connected to a master control in the locomotive (see **Brake** [Air brakes]).

On most passenger trains, the cars consist mainly of coaches. A typical coach has seats for 50 to 90 passengers. Double-deck coaches on commuter trains seat from 150 to 170 people. Some passenger-train cars, such as club cars or lounge cars, provide card tables, refreshments, or other services that are not generally available on coaches. Other passenger-train cars include baggage

Pulse Electronics, Inc.

An end-of-train device, mounted next to a coupler (yellow), senses the train's motion and monitors the air pressure for the brakes. A radio transmits data to the locomotive cab.

cars, dining cars, and sleeping cars.

Freight cars differ in shape and size according to the freight they are designed to haul. They range from box-cars for carrying general freight to specially designed cars for new automobiles. Many newer freight cars are longer and have been designed to carry different kinds of freight. For example, piggyback cars are flatcars designed to carry truck trailers.

Since the early 1980's, railroads have eliminated *ca-booses,* which once commonly served as the end cars on freight trains. Monitoring devices called *end-of-train devices* now perform duties once handled by crew members riding in the caboose.

Railroad companies are exploring the idea of *integral trains* for use in freight transport. An integral train consists of cars permanently coupled in units of various lengths. The train moves as a unit to its destination and back.

Railroads have greatly improved the safety of railroad cars over the years. One of the chief improvements has been to reduce the danger from overheated *journal boxes,* also called *axle boxes.* On older cars, each end of an axle turns on solid surfaces enclosed in an oil-filled journal box. On modern cars, the use of roller bearings rather than solid surfaces at the ends of axles has practically eliminated overheated axles, called "hotboxes." Railroads have electronic devices called *hotbox detectors* installed at various points alongside railroad tracks. As trains pass by, the devices detect any hotboxes. This information is transmitted to a control station. The station radios the train crew to stop the train and to remove cars with hotboxes.

Railroad cars with built-in power units do not need a locomotive. Such cars, sometimes called *railcars,* may be diesel-electric, electric, or gas-turbine electric.

Some railcars are equipped to carry passengers. These cars have seats and windows located behind the power unit. Some passenger railcars haul one or more passenger cars to form *railcar trains.* Well-known railcar trains include the Docklands Light Railway of London.

Some self-propelled cars are designed for use in railroad maintenance. Each carries equipment to do a particular job along a railroad line. For example, some have track-laying machinery or machinery for inspecting or repairing tracks. Others carry such equipment as snow-plows or weed cutters.

Tracks. The rails and crossties that make up railway track are laid along a *roadbed*—that is, land that has been prepared as a foundation for the track. The roadbed follows the route planned for a railroad. *Main-line* routes link major cities. *Branch lines* extend between main lines and various places not served by main lines, such as small communities or mining sites. Many main lines consist of two or more tracks laid side by side. Such *multiple tracks* enable trains to travel in opposite directions on the same line at the same time. Single-track lines must be equipped with *sidings* at various points along the route. A siding is a short track along-side a main or branch line to which one of two meeting trains is switched until the other train passes.

The track and roadbed, together with such other railway structures as tunnels and bridges, are sometimes referred to as the *roadway.* In addition to the roadway, railways own a certain amount of land on both sides of

Kinds of railroad cars The illustrations below show major kinds of passenger and freight cars. Not all the illustrations are drawn to the same scale.

Amtrak Superliner: Double-deck, long-distance coach carries 75 passengers on two levels; baggage on lower level; 85 feet (26 meters) long.

Amtrak Viewliner: Single-level sleeping car contains 12 sleeping compartments, including 2 deluxe bedrooms and 1 handicapped-accessible deluxe bedroom; 85 feet (26 meters) long.

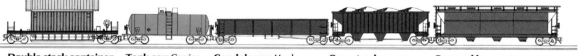

Double-stack container car: Hauls general freight in stacked containers; 51 feet (16 meters) long.

Tank car: Carries oil and other liquids; 50 feet (15 meters) long.

Gondola car: Hauls metal products and bulk freight; $52\frac{1}{2}$ feet (16 meters) long.

Open-top hopper car: Hauls such bulk freight as coal; length varies.

Covered hopper car: Protects bulk freight from the weather; 54 feet (16.5 meters) long.

Enclosed rack car: May have two or three enclosed decks for transporting vehicles safely; holds up to 18 automobiles; 90 feet (27 meters) long.

Piggyback flatcar: Common flatcar can hold two truck trailers or containers; 92 feet (28 meters) long.

Refrigerator car: Cooled car; hauls fresh and frozen produce and meats; 60 feet (18 meters) long.

Center-beam car: Has open sides for carrying lumber and other large goods; 73 feet (22 meters) long.

the roadway. This land and the roadway make up a railroad's *right of way.*

The crossties and rails. Most crossties, or *ties,* are spaced about 21 inches (53 centimeters) apart. The ties average about 3,000 per mile (1,900 per kilometer). There are two types of ties—wood ties and concrete ties.

When wood ties are used, two steel *tie plates* are placed on top of each tie, one plate near each end of the tie. Each plate has a wide groove that is shaped to hold the bottom of the rail. Steel spikes are driven through holes in the plates. The spikes hook over the bottom of the rail and keep it firmly fastened to the tie.

Concrete ties do not have plates and spikes. Instead, plastic pads replace the plates, and two steel bolts with spring clips hold the base of the rail firmly to the tie.

The spikes or bolts must be the same distance apart on each tie so that they hold the rails the same distance apart all along the track. This uniform distance between rails is called the *gauge.* Every country has a *standard gauge* for all its main rail lines. Most countries also have this same standard gauge for most branch lines. In this way, any locomotive or car can travel on almost any track in the country. But the standard gauge varies from country to country. Australia, Canada, Mexico, the United States, and most European nations have a standard gauge of 4 feet 8 $\frac{1}{2}$ inches (1.44 meters).

In the United States, steel mills produce rails in 39-foot (12-meter) or 78-foot (24-meter) lengths. Little new track is laid, and so new rails are used mainly to replace existing track. Much existing track consists of 39-foot lengths of rail joined end to end by pieces of steel called *joint bars* or *fishplates.* The joint bars are fastened to the rails by bolts that pass through holes in the bars and in the sides of the rail.

Railroads in the United States have replaced most of the old short-length rail with new lengths of rail. A majority of this rail measures about $\frac{1}{4}$ mile (0.4 kilometer) long. Shorter rail lengths are welded together to make the $\frac{1}{4}$-mile lengths. Welded rails have fewer gaps and so produce a smoother ride than do rails joined in many places. Such continuous rail is also easier for railroad work crews to maintain.

The roadbed and route. In building a roadbed, civil engineers use special instruments and machinery to make the land as smooth and level as possible. This process is called *grading.* Most roadbeds are then covered with a layer of *ballast,* which consists of such materials as gravel or crushed stone. Ballast holds the ties in place and so helps keep the track stable. Ballast also helps distribute the weight of passing trains and gives them a degree of cushioning. Trains thus ride more easily than they would over bare ground. Ballast also promotes drainage of rain water and slows the growth of weeds.

Before constructing the roadbed, engineers plan a route with the least possible *grade* and *curvature.* Grade refers to the steepness of the land. Curvature refers to the number and sharpness of curves along the route. The ideal railroad route lies across perfectly flat land. Track laid along such a route has little or no grade or curvature. Freight trains can easily carry heavy loads along the track, and passenger trains can travel at top speed. Steep grades, on the other hand, make it difficult for a train to carry heavy loads or travel at a high speed. If a route passes through hilly or mountainous country, engineers lay track around steep grades instead of over them. The track thus has many curves. Curves reduce a train's speed but do not prevent it from carrying heavy loads.

A route through a mountain range might require so many curves that travel along the route would be extremely slow. Engineers therefore sometimes build railroad tunnels through mountains. They also construct railroad bridges to span chasms and rivers. Tunnels and bridges are also built to extend railroad routes under or across bays and other bodies of water.

Freight operations

Freight trains are assembled in *classification yards,* also called *sorting yards* or *marshaling yards,* at various railroad terminals. A terminal may also have facilities for loading and unloading cars and for repairing locomotives and cars. After trains of freight cars arrive at a classification yard, the cars are sorted into groups according to their destinations. All the cars in a group must be headed for destinations along the same route or along branches of this route. After a locomotive has been coupled to such a group of cars, the cars become a freight train. Cars headed for destinations off the main route

Train wheels and tracks

Trains ride on *flanged* wheels. A flange is a rim on a wheel's inner edge that guides the wheel along the track. The track consists of two rails supported by *ties.* On wood ties, steel *tie plates* are spiked to the ties. A groove in the plates helps hold the rails in place. The ties are anchored in *ballast* (gravel or crushed stone). On concrete ties, steel rail clips hold the rails to the ties. The clips fit through steel parts that are bolted to the ties.

WORLD BOOK diagrams by Linda Kinnaman

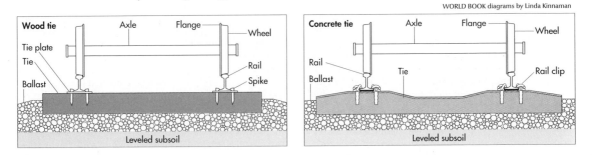

Jon Bentz, West Stock

A unit train is a freight train whose cars all carry the same kind of freight and are all headed for the same destination. This unit train is made up of open-top hopper cars loaded with coal.

must be switched to other trains along the way.

In the past, railroad freight shipments frequently met long delays at classification yards. They also met delays at *interchanges*—that is, at rail junctions where cars are switched from one railroad to another.

To speed freight shipments, railroads have improved their freight-handling methods in three main ways. First, they have consolidated and modernized classification yards. Second, they have simplified the work performed at interchanges. Third, and perhaps most important, the railroads have developed computer systems for planning and monitoring their operations. In one such system, the computer generates a specific "trip plan" for each car. As the car moves in trains from its origin to its destination, its plan is checked continually to see that the car is moving on schedule. The shipper and the receiver of the car are then notified of the car's delivery time.

At classification yards. A classification yard consists mainly of a number of closely spaced parallel tracks. Each track is reserved for cars assigned to a particular route. Incoming trains approach the yard along a main track at one end. Newly assembled trains leave the yard along a main track at the other end. There are two chief types of classification yards: *flat yards* and *hump yards.*

Flat yards are the older type of classification yard. In these yards, switching locomotives haul cars from incoming trains onto the proper tracks, from which de-

parting trains are made up. A switching locomotive must travel back and forth many times to make up a train. In addition, the track switches and car brakes in these yards are operated by hand. The work requires many employees and proceeds only as fast as the workers can do their jobs. As a result, classification often takes a long time.

Hump yards speed the work of classification. These yards make use of gravity. In hump yards, switching locomotives push incoming trains along a single track to the top of a low hill, or *hump.* On the other side of the hump, the track branches out into a number of classification tracks. As each car reaches the top of the hump, it is uncoupled and the proper track switches are opened. Devices called *retarders* control the car's speed, and the car rolls down the hump onto its assigned track. The retarders regulate a car's speed so that it meets the other cars on its track with just enough force to engage its coupler. Operators in a control tower use computers to control most of the yard operations.

At interchanges. Automated hump yards help speed interchange by *preblocking* cars on a freight train—that is, by arranging all the cars on the train into groups according to their final destination. Cars on such a *block train* do not have to be reclassified at interchanges or yards.

Unit trains further reduce the number of switchings or eliminate switching entirely. Unit trains have a single type of freight car loaded with a single type of freight, such as coal or wheat. The cars all have the same destination and remain together until they reach it. Many unit trains make regular nonstop runs between the same two terminals—for example, between a coal mine and an electric power plant. Some unit trains change or add locomotives when they change from one rail line to another.

Trains of flatcars carrying highway trailers or freight containers are called *intermodal trains.* Such trains require their own specialized yards. Special flatcars carry containers stacked two high. Heavy forklifts or other lifting machines pick up the containers and trailers. Trucks carry the containers between the yard and their final destinations over highways. Use of containers greatly speeds freight movement.

Traffic control

Railroads use signals and various other means to control train traffic. The chief purpose of traffic control is to prevent accidents. But it also helps make railroad operations speedier and more efficient.

Most railroad signals consist of colored lights alongside or over the track. Each color has a different meaning. For example, red means *stop,* and green means *proceed.* Yellow alerts the train to reduce speed, to stop at the next signal, or to maintain a lower speed.

The signals and other means a railroad uses to control traffic are part of its signal system. Most railroads have adopted some form of the *block signal* system. This system is designed chiefly to keep a safe distance between trains traveling on the same track. In block signal systems, a railroad line is divided into lengths of track

How freight trains are made up

Freight trains are made up at *classification yards,* which consist mainly of groups of parallel tracks. Each track is reserved for cars that will make up a particular train. Most large classification yards are *hump yards,* which use a low hill, or *hump,* in sorting cars onto the proper tracks.

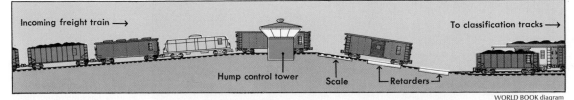

Incoming freight train →

To classification tracks →

Hump control tower   Scale   Retarders

WORLD BOOK diagram

The hump has a single track up one side, *left.* Partway down the other side, the track branches out into the classification tracks. A switch engine pushes an incoming train up the hump. As each car reaches the top, it is uncoupled and the proper switches are opened. The car is weighed and rolls onto its assigned track. Most hump yards are automated.

Atchison, Topeka and Santa Fe Railway   Atchison, Topeka and Santa Fe Railway   Gerry Souter, Van Cleve Photography

Sorting cars. A computer, *left,* uses information about each car's destination and weight to open the switches leading to the car's assigned track and to operate *retarders* in the downhill track, *center.* The retarders slow the car so that when it reaches the classification tracks, *right,* it is traveling just fast enough to couple automatically with the car ahead on the proper track.

called *blocks.* Most blocks range from 1 to 2 miles (1.6 to 3.2 kilometers) long. Only one train may be in a block at a time. Colored-light signals control entry to the block. When a train is in the block, the signals warn other trains to stop. No train may proceed from one block to the next without an all-clear signal. Block signals may be either *automatic* or *manual* (hand-operated).

Automatic block signal systems are the most common type of block systems used today. In an automatic block system, the signals are operated by an electric current, also called a *track circuit,* that flows through the rails. A train entering a block short-circuits this current, causing the signal that guards the block to turn red. As soon as the train leaves the block, the signal returns to yellow, meaning "all clear." Many automatic block systems also have *interlocking* controls. Interlocking controls set multiple track switches at one time to ensure a safe path for the train to follow through complex junctions.

A remotely controlled signal system is called Centralized Traffic Control (CTC). Signals and switches on the

line are controlled from a central dispatch station. This station has one or more electronic diagrams that show the present location of every train on a line. CTC operators study the diagrams to decide how to route the trains as safely, speedily, and efficiently as possible. The operators direct train traffic by setting the necessary signals and switches. Modern forms of CTC, with advanced computers and safety systems, are referred to as *centralized dispatching.* Such dispatching makes it possible for railroads to use single tracks efficiently for two-way traffic. If two trains are headed toward one another on the same track, a dispatcher switches one of the trains to a siding until the other passes. CTC also makes use of interlocking controls.

In the United States, the federal government requires automatic block systems on all tracks where passenger trains travel at 60 mph (97 kph) and over and where freight trains travel at 50 mph (80 kph) and over.

Manual block signal systems require operators at various points along the line to control the signals. Each operator is responsible for the movement of trains

A dispatching center, *shown here,* coordinates the flow of rail traffic in a 9,000-mile (14,500-kilometer) system. This center at Jacksonville, Florida, has illuminated displays that cover the walls of a circular building. Dispatchers seated at consoles talk by radio with train crews throughout the system.

Trans Pix from CSX Corporation

within one or two blocks and informs other operators by telephone whether a block is occupied or clear. The possibility of human error makes manual signal systems less reliable than automatic systems.

Some manual block systems have interlocking controls. These controls ensure that switches in complex combinations can only be set safely. They also give signals to approaching trains to prevent derailment or collision.

Other train controls. Many railroads are experimenting with *advanced train control systems,* also known as *positive train control,* to improve safety and efficiency. In addition to signal lights alongside their tracks, some railroads have signals providing the same information on panels in their locomotives. These signals may also work in connection with safety devices. One such device is the *automatic train stop* (ATS). The ATS puts on a train's brakes automatically if the engineer fails to notice a stop signal. Another safety device, called *automatic train control* (ATC), automatically controls a train's speed. If the engineer fails to notice a caution signal, the ATC puts on the brakes to slow the train to the required speed. The device also stops the train if necessary.

Many railroads use advanced communications systems to help control the movement of trains. Two-way radio systems on trains enable crew members to communicate from one end of the train to the other. Train crews also use two-way radio systems to communicate with distant dispatching centers. Railroads trace the exact locations of their trains and of individual cars by using *transponders* (electronic transmitting devices) as tags. Track-side equipment sends and then receives radio signals from the transponders. Satellite-based tracking of trains using the Global Positioning System (GPS) also helps railroads improve train control (see **Global Positioning System**).

Railroad systems

In the United States. The United States has about 450 railroad companies. All but two of the major railroad companies are owned by private investors. The exceptions are the Alaska Railroad, which is owned by the Alaska state government, and Amtrak Corporation, a passenger railroad financed by the U.S. government.

Categories of railroads. The federal government *categorizes* (classes) U.S. railroads as either *line-haul* or *switching and terminal.* Line-haul companies own the nation's main rail lines. Switching and terminal companies own tracks and other facilities in and around certain large railroad stations and classification yards. The largest U.S. line-haul companies in terms of miles of track operated include the Burlington Northern Santa Fe; CSX Corporation; Norfolk Southern Corporation; and the Union Pacific Railroad.

Automatic block signaling

Automatic block signals allow trains to follow one another safely on the same track. The track is divided into *blocks* about 1 to 2 miles (1.6 to 3.2 kilometers) long. An electric current flows through the rails and is short-circuited when a train is in a block. The short circuit causes the signal for that block to turn red and the preceding block signal to turn yellow. Other signals show green. A train may proceed through a green signal but must slow down at a yellow signal and stop at a red one.

WORLD BOOK diagram, adapted courtesy of Westinghouse Air Brake Company and Pulse Electronics, Inc.

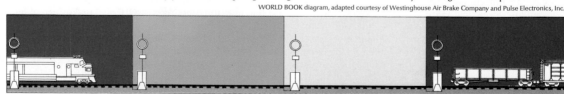

| **Occupied block** Stop signal | **Unoccupied block** All-clear signal | **Unoccupied block** Caution signal | **Occupied block** Stop signal |

The United States government further classifies railroads according to *operating revenue* (money earned from operations). Companies whose operating revenue is $250 million or more a year are *Class I railroads*. Only a few line-haul companies and Amtrak fall in this group. Firms with operating revenue between $20 million and $250 million are *Class II railroads*. Companies whose operating revenue is less than $20 million are *Class III railroads*. Some Class II and Class III railroads are owned by Class I railroads. Some Class I railroads are owned by conglomerates. Many Class I railroads have resulted from the *merger* (union) of smaller railroads.

Many railroads have been formed from line segments sold by other railroads because they were unprofitable. They include *short line railroads*, which have from a few to several hundred miles or kilometers of track, and larger companies called *regional railroads*. One regional railroad, the Wisconsin Central Ltd., has more than 2,000 miles (3,200 kilometers) of track.

Cooperation among railroads. The Association of American Railroads, an organization sponsored by the railroads, deals with matters of concern to the entire industry. Its membership includes railroads in Canada and Mexico as well as in the United States.

Railroad companies also cooperate with one another in various other ways. For example, most U.S. rail routes are owned by separate companies. Much of the freight traffic handled by a railroad originates on lines owned by other companies. In the past, every company required that its own locomotives and train crews be used on all trains run on its tracks. Today, a number of railroads share the use of their lines. Each of these companies operates *run-through trains* over lines owned by the other companies. A run-through train changes only its crew when it moves to another line.

Railroad workers range from dispatchers and switch operators to salespeople and clerks. Many railroad jobs require training in electronics, computer operations, marketing, and other fields.

Perhaps the best-known railroad jobs are those of the train crew. Most crews consist of a *conductor* to supervise the train's operation, an *engineer* to run the locomotive, and possibly a *brakeman* to uncouple cars and do various other tasks. In the days of steam locomotives, a *fireman* tended the locomotive boiler.

Rail unions. United States railroad workers belong to about 15 different labor unions. One of the most important is the United Transportation Union. Some of the unions include only railroad workers, but others also include workers in other industries. The Brotherhood of Locomotive Engineers, founded in 1863, is the oldest labor union in the United States. Over the years, the rail unions and the railroads have agreed to certain *work rules.* Unions have generally opposed changing most work rules, but they have agreed to change certain rules to improve safety. The Railway Labor Act, passed by Congress in 1926, establishes the rules for settling railroad labor disputes (see **Railway Labor Act**).

The role of the federal government. The Surface Transportation Board (STB), an independent government body, regulates some of the economic activities of railroads in the United States. For example, a railroad must receive board approval to merge with another railroad. The Federal Railroad Administration (FRA) sets railroad safety standards and inspects locomotives, cars, tracks, and signal systems. Both the FRA and the STB are part of the United States Department of Transportation. Amtrak operates as a semipublic corporation partly financed by the federal government. The Department of Transportation and Amtrak work with Congress and local governments to decide Amtrak's routes and the number of trains on each route.

Railroad finances. The federal government provides less financial aid for railroads than for any other form of transportation. In 1980, deregulation of U.S. railroads began, and many pricing controls were removed. Since that time, the major railroads have become profitable.

The railroads have become more competitive with other forms of transportation. Many railroads have speeded up freight shipments and improved service by operating container trains and unit trains. Railroads have also increased their ability to handle a variety of freight. They earn much of their income by hauling bulk cargoes, such as coal and grain. But many railroads have redesigned equipment so that they can handle more manufactured goods. The use of freight cars designed to carry new automobiles has proved especially successful. The railroads' share of new-automobile shipments has risen from about 10 percent in the 1950's to about 50 percent today. Manufactured goods account for a growing share of freight railroad income.

In Canada. Canada has two major freight railway systems. One system, Canadian National Railway Corporation (CNR), is a privately owned company. The other system, Canadian Pacific Railway Company, is owned by a conglomerate. Both systems own and operate extensive rail lines across the southern half of Canada. CNR has a line as far north as the Northwest Territories. Both systems also operate lines in the United States. Canada's major passenger railway is VIA Rail Canada, a government-funded company. A number of smaller, privately owned railroads also operate in Canada.

The Canadian Transport Commission regulates most Canadian railways. It operates within the Ministry of Transport. The commission sets and enforces rail safety standards and makes decisions on requests by railroads to drop unprofitable schedules or to abandon unprofitable track.

In other countries. Most countries have a single national rail system, which the government owns and operates. Some countries have a number of small, privately owned railroads in addition to the national railroad.

Most of the world's railroads make little or no profit. In most countries, the government provides the additional funds needed to keep the railroads running. These governments believe the services the railroads provide are worth the additional money. Other governments have *privatized* their railroads—that is, they have sold them to private companies.

In Latin America. Mexico has a large railroad network. It is made up of several privately owned companies. Some Central American countries have short lines that operate in coastal regions. Railroads in Peru and Bolivia were originally built to carry materials mined from the

Andes Mountains. The railroads are the world's highest, rising to nearly 19,700 feet (6,000 meters) above sea level. Argentina's railroad system links to those of Uruguay and Paraguay. The vast majority of Brazil's extensive railroad system is less than 300 miles (500 meters) from the coast.

In Australia and New Zealand. Australia's railroads are operated by the national government and four state-run railway administrations. Most lines use the standard gauge of 4 feet 8 $\frac{1}{2}$ inches (1.44 meters). However, a few lines, such as those that operate in Queensland's sugar plantations, use other gauges. New Zealand's private system of railroads uses a gauge of 3 feet 6 inches (1.07 meters). Ferries carry rail vehicles between the North and South Islands.

In Asia. China has an efficient railroad system that is quickly expanding. Most of the system is in the east, and vast areas in the western part of the country have no rail service. Because China has little of the petroleum need-

Leading countries in railroad transportation

Passenger service

Country	Passenger-miles*	Passenger-kilometers*
India	221,838,000,000	357,013,000,000
China	220,185,000,000	354,353,000,000
Japan	153,884,000,000	247,652,000,000
Russia	72,229,000,000	116,241,000,000
France	38,260,000,000	61,573,000,000
Egypt	37,666,000,000	60,617,000,000
Germany	37,051,000,000	59,628,000,000
Ukraine	33,890,000,000	54,540,000,000
Italy	30,758,000,000	49,500,000,000
United Kingdom	21,390,000,000	34,424,000,000

Freight service

Country	Ton-miles†	Ton-kilometers†
United States	1,348,926,000,000	1,969,394,000,000
China	893,607,000,000	1,304,641,000,000
Russia	660,187,000,000	963,855,000,000
Canada	193,489,000,000	282,488,000,000
India	190,118,000,000	277,567,000,000
Ukraine	109,888,000,000	160,433,000,000
Kazakhstan	72,895,000,000	106,425,000,000
Germany	49,737,000,000	72,614,000,000
Poland	46,356,000,000	67,679,000,000
France	36,888,000,000	53,855,000,000

Length of track††

Country	Miles	Kilometers
United States	149,100	240,000
Russia	95,700	154,000
Canada	45,300	73,000
China	40,300	64,900
India	38,900	62,700
Germany	27,300	44,000
Australia	24,000	38,600
Argentina	23,600	37,900
France	19,900	32,000
Brazil	16,700	26,900

*A passenger-mile is one passenger carried one mile. A passenger-kilometer is one passenger carried one kilometer.
†A ton-mile is one ton carried one mile. A ton-kilometer is one metric ton carried one kilometer.
††Mainline routes, not counting double tracks, sidings, or branch lines.
Figures are for 1997.
Sources: International Union of Railways; Statistics Canada; U.S. Central Intelligence Agency.

ed to run diesel locomotives, it has historically operated mainly steam locomotives. Today, China is rapidly converting its railroad lines to electric operation. In India, more than 10 million people ride passenger trains every day. The railroad system is important to the support of India's tremendous freight traffic. Most of India's trains run on a gauge of track 5 feet 6 inches (1.68 meters) wide. In Japan, a higher percentage of people ride the train daily than in any other country. Many trains run on a gauge of 3 feet 6 inches (1.07 meters). The country's high-speed *Shinkansen*—also known as "bullet trains"—travel on standard-gauge track.

In Europe, most countries use standard-gauge track. The exceptions are Finland and Russia, which use a gauge of 5 feet (1.52 meters), and Spain and Portugal, which use a gauge of 5 feet 6 inches (1.68 meters). Western European railroads cooperate to improve train service between countries. Nine Western European countries belong to the Trans-Europ Express Group (TEE). The group operates trains throughout much of Western Europe. Each train is owned by one of the member countries. But the train moves freely across national boundaries onto the tracks of other members of the railroad group. Several European countries, including France, Germany, Italy, and the United Kingdom, operate high-speed trains. Such trains also carry passengers and freight between the United Kingdom and France through the Channel Tunnel.

In Africa. South Africa has Africa's best railroad system. The system primarily handles freight, but it has many passenger trains, including the famous *Blue Train.* The system operates on a gauge of 3 feet 6 inches (1.07 meters). It links to a line in Namibia and to one in Zimbabwe through Botswana. A good network of tracks links parts of northern Africa. Rail lines in other parts of the continent are mainly single-track routes that are used to ship freight from mines and farms to seaports that handle international trade.

History

Several European countries had a few primitive railroads as early as the mid-1500's. But they were used mainly to bring up wagonloads of coal or iron ore from underground mines. The mining railroads consisted of two wooden rails that extended down into the mines and across the mine floors. Laborers or horses pulled wagons with *flanged* wheels—that is, wheels made with a protective rim—along the rails. The wagons moved more easily along the rails than they did over the rutted or muddy entrances and floors of the mines.

In the early 1700's, English coal-mining companies began building short wooden railroads to carry coal aboveground as well as underground. Horses pulled the trains of wagons along the rails. In the mid-1700's, workers began nailing strips of iron to the wooden rails to make them last longer. English ironmakers also began making all-iron rails. The rails were flanged to carry wagons with ordinary wheels. By the end of the 1700's, ironmakers were producing all-iron rails without flanges. These all-iron rails carried wagons with flanged wheels.

Invention of the locomotive. Meanwhile, inventors had been developing the steam engine. About 1800, the English inventor Richard Trevithick experimented with the first engines capable of using high-pressure steam. He mounted one of the engines on a four-wheeled undercarriage designed to roll along a track. In 1804, Trevithick used this vehicle to pull 10 tons (9 metric tons) of iron, 70 men, and 5 wagons along 9 1/2 miles (15 kilometers) of track. Trevithick's invention thus became the world's first successful railroad locomotive. Soon, other English inventors had also built successful locomotives.

An English railway engineer named George Stephenson constructed the world's first public railroad, the Stockton and Darlington, which opened in 1825. The line operated between the towns of Stockton and Darlington, a distance of about 20 miles (32 kilometers). It was the first railroad to run steam freight trains on a regular schedule. Stephenson's second railroad opened in 1830. It ran 30 miles (48 kilometers) from Liverpool to Manchester. It was the first railroad to run steam passenger trains on a regular schedule.

Stephenson also originated the idea that a country's railroads should all have a standard gauge. The gauge he selected for the railroads he built—4 feet 8 1/2 inches (1.44 meters)—corresponded to the length of the axles on many horse-drawn wagons. This gauge was eventually adopted by most European railroads and then by railroads in other parts of the world.

Developments in the United States. A few horse-powered railroads began operating in the eastern United States in the early 1800's. In 1815, an American engineer named John Stevens obtained a charter from the state of New Jersey to build a steam-powered railroad across the state. Although Stevens could not raise enough money for this project, he still wanted to apply steam locomotion to railway track. He constructed a circular track near his estate in Hoboken, New Jersey, and built a small steam-powered wagon to run on it. In 1825, this vehicle made a successful run.

In the late 1820's, the Delaware and Hudson Canal Company of Pennsylvania decided to build a railroad. In 1829, the company ran an English-built locomotive along a section of wooden track. This locomotive, called the *Stourbridge Lion,* became the first full-sized locomotive to run on a track in North America.

In 1830, the Baltimore and Ohio Railroad began service over 13 miles (21 kilometers) of track between Baltimore and Ellicott's Mills (now Ellicott City). The railroad's first cars were drawn by horses. These horse-powered cars were the first railroad cars in the United States to carry passengers. The Baltimore and Ohio also experimented with a car equipped with sails. In the summer of 1830, New York manufacturer Peter Cooper built a steam-powered locomotive, later called the *Tom Thumb,* for the Baltimore and Ohio. But it was too small for regular service. In 1831, the railroad began regular passenger service with a locomotive called the *York.*

Meanwhile, the West Point Foundry of New York had built a steam locomotive for the South Carolina Canal and Railroad Company. In 1830, this locomotive, called the *Best Friend of Charleston,* pulled a train of cars along 6 miles (10 kilometers) of track. This event marked the first run of a steam-powered train in the United States. The *Best Friend* began making regular runs between Charleston and Hamburg, South Carolina, in 1831. The South Carolina Canal and Railroad Company thus became the first U.S. railroad to provide regular steam-powered passenger and freight service.

The number of locomotives and railroads multiplied rapidly in the United States after 1830. Historic first runs of locomotives included those of the *De Witt Clinton* on the Mohawk and Hudson Railroad in New York in 1831; the *John Bull* on the Camden and Amboy Railroad in New Jersey in 1831; *Old Ironsides* on the Philadelphia, Germantown, and Norristown Railroad in Pennsylvania in 1832; and the *Pontchartrain* on the Pontchartrain Railway in Louisiana in 1832. By 1835, more than 200 railroad charters had been granted in 11 states, and over 1,000 miles (1,600 kilometers) of track had been laid.

Meanwhile, builders were developing locomotives especially suited to the eastern United States, where roadbeds had many curves. These locomotives had an independent wheeled undercarriage called a *leading truck.* The leading truck was attached to the locomotive by a *center pin,* which allowed the truck to swivel. A truck gave a locomotive more flexibility on curves. Most of the new locomotives had a four-wheeled truck and four driving wheels. These eight-wheeled locomotives, known as the *American-type,* became the most popular type of U.S. locomotive during the second half of the 1800's.

Canada's first steam-powered railway, the Champlain and St. Lawrence Railroad, was started in the province of Quebec. The line opened for business as a horse-powered railroad in July 1836, and began steam-powered service later that year. The railway operated between the towns of Laprairie and Saint-Jean, a distance of about 16 miles (26 kilometers). Other small railroads began operating in Canada soon after 1836.

Expansion in the United States. Railroads were under construction in all states east of the Mississippi River by 1850. Most of the lines were concentrated in the Northeast, and many of them ran only short distances. A network of lines radiated from Boston, New York City, and Philadelphia. Railroads also linked cities in the Southeast.

Competition for trade spurred railroad construction in the East. By the early 1850's, four railroads had built rail lines that enabled them to haul freight between the Great Lakes region and the East Coast. New York's Erie Railroad opened between Piermont and Dunkirk on Lake Erie in 1851. In 1853, 10 small railroads along the Erie Canal merged to form the New York Central Railroad, which provided service between Albany and Buffalo. By 1852, the Pennsylvania Railroad and the Baltimore and Ohio had opened lines to the Ohio River, one of the most important trade routes in the country. The large railroads took over many smaller lines and so expanded rapidly.

During the 1850's, railroad lines connected Chicago with the Mississippi River, which was a major trade route. The Baltimore and Ohio reached St. Louis on the Mississippi in 1857. Both Chicago and St. Louis thrived as transportation centers.

The "Lightning Express" Trains (about 1863), a lithograph by Currier & Ives

Powerful steam locomotives hauled passengers and freight throughout the United States as rail transportation became a nationwide industry during the last half of the 1800's.

In 1850, Congress began granting federal land to develop railroads. Government leaders knew that railroads would help attract settlers to undeveloped regions of the Midwest and the South. The railroad companies kept some of the land for right of way and sold the rest to help pay railroad construction costs. The first grant helped build the Illinois Central Railroad from the Great Lakes at Chicago to Cairo, Illinois. Settlers poured into the area along the route after the railroad's completion. The success of the experiment persuaded Congress to grant federal lands for railroad development in the western United States. In return, all U.S. railroads agreed to carry government troops and property at half the standard rates and United States mail at four-fifths the standard rates. These rates remained in effect until the mid-1940's.

The railroads continued to expand during the 1860's. They played a major role in the American Civil War (1861-1865) by moving troops and supplies to battle. The South was at a disadvantage because it had far fewer railroad tracks and locomotives than the North had. After the war, iron and steel railroad bridges were built

across such major rivers as the Ohio, the Mississippi, and the Missouri.

The first transcontinental rail lines. In the early 1860's, the United States government decided to extend rail lines across the country. The proposed route roughly followed the 42nd parallel from Omaha, Nebraska, to Sacramento, California. Eastern rail lines were to be extended westward from Chicago to meet the new railroad at Omaha. Congress passed the Pacific Railroad Act in 1862. The act gave two companies responsibility for building the railroad. The Union Pacific was to start laying track westward from a point near Omaha. The Central Pacific Railroad was to lay track eastward from Sacramento. Congress granted both railroads large tracts of land and millions of dollars in government loans.

Work began on the Central Pacific track in 1863 and on the Union Pacific in 1865. The railroads faced the gigantic task of crossing the rugged Rockies and the towering Sierra Nevada. To obtain skilled labor, the Central Pacific hired thousands of Chinese immigrants to work on the railroad. Thousands of European immigrants and former Civil War soldiers worked on the Union Pacific. On May 10, 1869, the tracks of the two railroads finally met at Promontory, Utah. North America became the first continent to have a rail line from coast to coast.

By the end of the 1800's, the United States had five transcontinental rail lines. The Canadian Pacific Railway completed Canada's first transcontinental line in 1885. It extended from Montreal, Quebec, to Vancouver, British Columbia. The completion of these rail lines opened vast regions of the continent to town development, farming, and trade.

Worldwide development. Railroad building spread rapidly, first in England and then throughout Europe. By 1870, most of Europe's major rail systems had been built. Other lines were built in the late 1800's and early 1900's. Some of these lines required that tunnels be blasted through the Alps to connect France, Switzerland, and Italy. The *Orient Express,* one of the most famous European passenger trains, began operation be-

Important dates in railroading

1804	Richard Trevithick of England invented the steam locomotive.
1825	The Stockton and Darlington Railway, built in England by George Stephenson, became the first railroad to offer regularly scheduled steam-powered train service.
1831	The South Carolina Canal and Railroad Company began the first regularly scheduled steam-powered train service in the United States.
1836	The Champlain and St. Lawrence Railroad began operating Canada's first regularly scheduled steam-powered trains in Quebec.
1850	Congress made the first federal land grants for the development of U.S. railroads.
1859	The first Pullman sleeping car went into service between Chicago and Bloomington, Illinois.
1869	The world's first transcontinental rail line was completed across the United States.
1885	The first transcontinental rail line across Canada was completed.

1887	Congress passed the Interstate Commerce Act to control certain economic practices of U.S. railroads.
1893	The American steam locomotive *No. 999* made the world's first 100-mph (160-kph) run.
1895	The Baltimore and Ohio Railroad started the world's first electric main-line service in Baltimore.
1925	The first commercial diesel-electric locomotive in the United States began service as a switch engine.
1934	The Burlington *Zephyr,* the first streamlined passenger train powered by a diesel-electric locomotive, began service in the United States.
1964	Japanese passenger trains began operating between Tokyo and Osaka at speeds up to 130 mph (209 kph).
1970	Congress authorized the creation of Amtrak to operate U.S. intercity passenger trains.
1980	The Staggers Rail Act eased some of the regulations imposed by the Interstate Commerce Act.
1990's	Many countries privatized their railroad systems, including Mexico, the Netherlands, and the United Kingdom.

The meeting of two railroads at Promontory, Utah, in 1869 marked the completion of the world's first transcontinental rail line. Officials of the Central Pacific and Union Pacific railroads drove in the last spike.

Union Pacific Railroad

tween Paris, France, and Istanbul, Turkey, in 1883.

As they had done for the western United States, railroads opened up other parts of the world to development and trade. Argentina and Brazil developed rapidly after they built extensive rail networks in the late 1800's. Railroads were also built across South America's towering Andes Mountains. One such railroad, the Central Railway of Peru, was begun in 1870. It is the world's highest standard-gauge railroad, climbing to more than 3 miles (5 kilometers) above sea level.

Also in the late 1800's, France, Germany, and the United Kingdom built railroads in their African and Asian colonies. The United Kingdom, for example, helped construct nearly 25,000 miles (40,200 kilometers) of railroad track in India during the late 1800's. Russia started work on its 5,600-mile (9,000-kilometer) Trans-Siberian railroad in 1891 and completed it in 1916. The Trans-Siberian is the world's longest continuous railroad line. Australia started building a railroad across its southern plains in 1912. The line, completed in 1917, extends 1,108 miles (1,783 kilometers) from Port Pirie to Kalgoorlie.

Engineering improvements. Beginning about the 1870's, railroads started to use steel for rails and cars. Steel rails last up to 20 times longer than iron rails, and so they gradually replaced iron rails. Early freight and passenger cars were made largely of wood. All-steel passenger cars were first put into regular service in 1907 and gradually replaced most wooden cars. All-steel freight cars had replaced most wooden freight cars by the late 1920's.

Several important inventions after the mid-1800's helped improve railroad safety. In 1869, the American inventor George Westinghouse patented a railroad air brake. The brake automatically stopped a train if air pressure was lost. In 1873, an American amateur inventor named Eli Janney patented an automatic car coupler. Before Janney's invention, coupling had to be done manually. Many brakemen and switchmen lost fingers or hands while coupling cars. But fail-safe air brakes and automatic couplers were not widely used until after

Railroad freight traffic

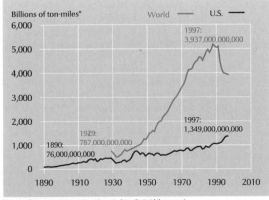

Billions of ton-miles*
World —— U.S. ——

6,000
5,000
4,000
3,000
2,000
1,000
0

1890 1910 1930 1950 1970 1990 2010

1997: 3,937,000,000,000
1997: 1,349,000,000,000
1929: 787,000,000,000
1890: 76,000,000,000

*A ton-mile is 1 ton (0.9 metric ton) carried 1 mile (1.6 kilometers).
Sources: International Union of Railways; Statistics Canada; United Nations.

Railroad passenger traffic

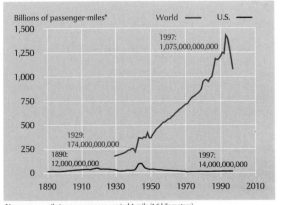

Billions of passenger-miles*
World —— U.S. ——

1,500
1,250
1,000
750
500
250
0

1890 1910 1930 1950 1970 1990 2010

1997: 1,075,000,000,000
1929: 174,000,000,000
1890: 12,000,000,000
1997: 14,000,000,000

*A passenger-mile is one passenger carried 1 mile (1.6 kilometers).
Sources: International Union of Railways; United Nations.

1893. That year, Congress passed the Railroad Safety Appliance Act, which required air brakes and automatic couplers on all trains.

The building of electric telegraph lines in the mid-1800's made block signaling possible. Manual block systems became common before the end of the 1800's. American engineer William Robinson patented the track circuit used in automatic block signaling in 1872. In 1887, American inventor Granville T. Woods patented an *induction telegraph*. This system allowed communication between stations and moving trains by sending a signal through the track.

Meanwhile, more and more people traveled by train. The railroads themselves did much to attract passengers. In 1867, an American businessman named George Pullman organized the Pullman Palace Car Company. The company manufactured a sleeping car that Pullman had designed. Other sleeping cars were already in use, but Pullman's car improved greatly on the others. By 1875, about 700 Pullman sleeping cars were in service. Railroads also introduced luxurious parlor cars and elegant dining cars.

Designers gradually increased the power and speed of steam locomotives. By the 1890's, many trains easily reached speeds of 50 to 70 mph (80 to 113 kph). In 1893, a train pulled by the American steam locomotive called *No. 999* was the first to exceed 100 miles (160 kilometers) per hour.

In 1879, Werner von Siemens, a German inventor, introduced the first functional electric train. In 1895, the Baltimore and Ohio Railroad became the first U.S. railroad to provide electric main-line service. It operated an electric train through a $3\frac{1}{2}$-mile (5.6-kilometer) tunnel under the city of Baltimore. Many European railroads electrified their main lines after 1900. But almost all U.S. railroads continued to use steam locomotives.

Regulation and control of U.S railroads. A financial panic in 1873 cut deeply into the profits of U.S. railroads. Financial leaders battled for control of the richest companies. Dishonest promoters made fortunes selling worthless railroad stock. The companies themselves fought bitterly for freight business. Some railroads combined to eliminate competition and raise prices, also called *rates*. Others offered bargain rates to favored shippers. These and other unfair practices led Congress to pass the Interstate Commerce Act in 1887. The act set up guidelines to regulate competition between railroads and to ensure reasonable railroad rates. The act also established the Interstate Commerce Commission (ICC). For more information, see **Interstate commerce** (The Interstate Commerce Act).

The United States entered World War I in 1917. In December 1917, the federal government took over wartime control of U.S. railroads. The war ended in November 1918, but the government kept control of the railroads until after Congress passed the Esch-Cummins Act of 1920. This legislation, also called the Transportation Act, increased the ICC's control over railroad rates. It also encouraged railroads to merge if mergers would increase their operating efficiency. The government returned the railroads to private control in March 1920.

The 1920's and the Great Depression. Railroads in the United States made record profits during the 1920's. Up to 80 percent of long-distance freight and passengers moved by rail. But there were signs of approaching trouble. Automobiles, buses, and trucks began carrying traffic once carried by trains. Disputes with labor also troubled the railroads during the early 1920's. The Railroad Shopmen's strike of 1922 was one of the largest strikes in U.S. history. Labor disputes led Congress to pass the Railway Labor Act in 1926. The act set up means to settle disputes.

Like most other industries, the railroads lost huge sums of money during the Great Depression of the 1930's. Many companies went into bankruptcy. But others spent large sums of money to win back passenger business with sleek, new diesel-electric trains.

Diesel-electric locomotives were more fuel-efficient and much easier to maintain than steam locomotives. The first commercial diesel-electric locomotive in the United States began service in 1925. It was used as a switch engine. The stainless steel *Zephyr,* the world's first streamlined passenger train powered by a diesel-electric locomotive, began regular service on the Burlington railroad in 1934. It traveled between Denver and Chicago and could maintain an average speed of 78 mph (125 kph). No other train had ever maintained so high a speed over such a long, nonstop run. Also in 1934, a streamlined, aluminum-bodied passenger train, the Union Pacific's *City of Salina,* began operation. Other railroads soon put diesel trains into service. These trains included the Santa Fe's *Super Chief* and the New York, New Haven, and Hartford's *Comet.* The Santa Fe put the first regularly scheduled diesel-electric freight trains into service in 1940.

Economic recovery—and decline. After the United States entered World War II in 1941, the nation's railroads handled more traffic than ever before. Rubber and gasoline rationing limited highway travel. Passenger and freight trains ran day and night, and almost every train was packed to capacity. During the war, the government left the railroads under private control.

After the war ended in 1945, railroads in many countries faced financial difficulties. Much railroad equipment was nearly worn out from overuse. During the late 1940's and early 1950's, the world's railroads spent billions of dollars to replace worn-out equipment. At the same time, they faced serious competition from other forms of transportation. In the 1950's, most industrialized countries phased out steam locomotives in favor of more economical diesel-electric models.

In 1958, Congress passed legislation enabling railroads to discontinue hundreds of unprofitable passenger runs. But some railroads continued to lose money during the 1960's.

Until 1970, the U.S. government required U.S. railroads to provide intercity passenger service even though most passenger trains lost money year after year. To relieve the railroads of this financial burden, the government formed Amtrak in 1970. This semipublic corporation, partly financed by the federal government, took over the operation of almost all U.S. intercity passenger trains in 1971 (see **Amtrak**).

Although the formation of Amtrak helped U.S. railroad companies reduce their losses, the financial condition of some railroads—especially those in the Northeast—continued to worsen. The Railroad Reorganization Act of 1973 was designed to help reverse the huge losses of several railroads and to guarantee continued rail service. In 1976, six bankrupt Northeastern railroads were reorganized by the federal government as a private corporation called the Consolidated Rail Corporation (Conrail). At first, the federal government was Conrail's chief stockholder, but the government sold its stock to private investors in 1987.

Railroads today. In 1980, Congress passed the Staggers Rail Act, which was designed to help railroads increase their profits. The law greatly reduced regulation of prices and various other aspects of railroad operations. It helped railroads become more competitive with other forms of transportation, and the financial health of major U.S. railroads improved dramatically in the 1990's. During the 1990's, railroad services were privatized in many countries to improve competition and profitability. Mexico, the Netherlands, and the United Kingdom were among the countries that had railroad services transferred from public to private control.

In 1998, the U.S. government authorized the breakup of Conrail, which had by that time become profitable. CSX Corporation and Norfolk Southern Corporation purchased Conrail's holdings.

Today, many people view railroads as essential to relieving highway traffic congestion. Many also point out the environmental benefits of trains, which produce a much lower amount of pollution per traveler than automobiles do. Some railroads are looking to high-speed trains to replace airplanes for travel over distances up to about 500 miles (800 kilometers).   William L. Withuhn

Related articles. See the *Transportation* section of the various state, province, country, and continent articles. See also:

Biographies

Other related articles

Outline

I. How railroads serve the public
   A. Passenger service   B. Freight service
II. What makes up a railroad
   A. Rolling stock   B. Tracks
III. Freight operations
   A. At classification yards   B. At interchanges
IV. Traffic control
   A. Automatic block signal systems
   B. Manual block signal systems
   C. Other train controls
V. Railroad systems
   A. In the United States   C. In other countries
   B. In Canada
VI. History

Questions

What is a *flange?* What does it do?
Who built the first public railroad? When did it open?
How do U.S. railroads earn most of their income?
When was the first transcontinental rail line completed?
What is a *piggyback car?* A *siding? Ballast?*
How did World War II affect U.S. railroads?
How does ownership of U.S. railroads differ from that in most other countries?
What is railroad *gauge? Standard gauge?*
What is a *classification yard?* A *hump yard?*
How are trains on the same track kept safely apart?

Additional resources

Level I
Blumberg, Rhoda. *Full Steam Ahead: The Race to Build a Transcontinental Railroad.* National Geographic Soc., 1996.
Coiley, John. *Train.* Knopf, 1992.
Elish, Dan. *The Transcontinental Railroad.* Millbrook, 1993.
Laughlin, Rosemary. *The Great Iron Link: The Building of the Central Pacific Railroad.* Morgan Reynolds, 1996.
Wormser, Richard. *The Iron Horse: How Railroads Changed America.* Walker, 1993.
Young, Robert. *The Transcontinental Railroad.* Dillon Pr., 1997.

Level II
Dale, Rodney. *Early Railways.* Oxford, 1994.
Jackson, Alan A. *The Railway Dictionary.* Alan Sutton Pub., 1992.
Jane's World Railways. Jane's, published annually.
Riley, C. J. *The Encyclopedia of Trains and Locomotives.* Michael Friedman, 1995.
Vance, James E., Jr. *The North American Railroad: Its Origin, Evolution, and Geography.* Johns Hopkins, 1995.

Railroad, Electric. See Electric railroad.
Railroad, Elevated. See Elevated railroad.
Railroad, Model, is a small railroad that copies the appearance and operation of a full-sized railroad. Model railroading is the hobby of building and operating model railroads. It is a favorite pastime for thousands of people.

A model railroad can include all the major features of a real railroad, such as locomotives, cars, switches, signals, stations, and bridges. Hobbyists can also build miniature towns and natural scenery as settings. Model railroad cars, engines, and other equipment can be bought ready-made. But most model railroad enthusiasts enjoy designing and assembling their own systems. They build models from kits or make them from parts and raw materials. Model railroaders lay down tracks according to their own layout designs, and they wire their railroads to operate in a realistic way.

Model railroading offers a variety of activities in addition to modelmaking, such as carpentry, wiring electrical circuits, and making scenery. Model railroaders can concentrate on building only those parts of the system that they enjoy most, because the other parts can be purchased ready-made.

Model railroading differs from the hobby of operating toy trains. Model railroads are made to represent real trains in accurate detail. In building their systems,

Railroad models are divided into two categories, *toy trains* and *model trains.* Each category is built to *scale,* which is the comparison between its size and the size of a real train. Most toy trains are built to *O* scale, *right.* The most popular model train scales are *HO, center,* and *N, left.*

model railroaders copy as closely as possible the appearance and operation of a real railroad. Toy trains are larger than most model trains, and they are built to withstand rougher handling. Toy trains do not have much of the fine detail and realism that model trains have. Toy train enthusiasts may put together large and highly complicated railroad systems. However, most toy locomotives, cars, and other equipment are purchased completely assembled.

Scale and size. Railroad models are built to *scale.* The scale is the comparison between the size of the model and the full-sized railroad, called the *prototype.* In the most common model railroad scale, called *HO,* each part of the model is $\frac{1}{87}$ the size of the prototype. HO uses a *gauge* (track width) of 16.5 millimeters, or about $\frac{5}{8}$ inch. This represents the standard track gauge of 4 feet 8 $\frac{1}{2}$ inches (1.44 meters) on a real railroad.

The most popular scale after HO is *N* scale, in which models are $\frac{1}{160}$ the size of the prototype. N scale models run on N gauge tracks that are 9 millimeters, or about $\frac{1}{3}$ inch wide. Most toy trains are built in *O* scale, which is $\frac{1}{48}$ the size of the prototype. They run on O gauge tracks that are $1\frac{1}{4}$ inches (3.2 centimeters) wide.

A layout built in N scale will take up less space than the same layout in HO scale. But a modeler can build an N scale layout in a larger space and devote more of that space to scenery and buildings. A model railroad may cover as little as 9 to 12 square feet (0.8 to 1.1 square meters). Many are built on tabletops made from a plywood sheet measuring 4 feet (1.2 meters) wide and 8 feet (2.4 meters) long. Bigger systems can occupy most or all of a basement or attic. The largest scale is *G* scale. It is $\frac{1}{22.5}$ of the prototype and is often used outdoors in *garden railways.* The smallest is *Z* scale, $\frac{1}{220}$ the size of the prototype, and it can operate on a small layout.

Track can be purchased in short sections or in

longer flexible strips. Sectional track comes in straight or curved pieces, which are put together to form the desired layout. Sectional model railroad track resembles toy train track. But model railroad track has more ties per section so it looks more realistic. Flexible track, often called *flextrack,* comes in either 3-foot or 1-meter strips. The strips can be put down either straight or curved to fit the layout design. Some model railroaders buy rails separately and spike them down by hand on individual wooden ties for greater realism.

Most model railroads use the two rails to carry electrical current to and from the locomotive. The rails form the sides of an electrical circuit, and the locomotive completes the circuit through its wheels and motor. Some model railroads represent prototypes of electrically powered trains. Some of these models are powered through an overhead wire, as in a trolley car. Other models receive power through an outside third rail, as in the elevated and subway trains operating in many cities.

Toy trains have a third rail running down the middle of the tracks. This rail and the side rails carry current to and from the toy train locomotive.

Locomotives for model railroads are purchased already assembled, or they are built from kits. Their power comes from household current that first passes through a separate electrical unit called a *power pack.* The power pack reduces the voltage of the household current from 110 volts to 12 volts. It also changes the type of current from *alternating current,* which continually reverses direction, to *direct current,* which flows in one direction. Most toy trains use alternating household current. The current first passes through a transformer that reduces the voltage. Both power packs and transformers include switches by which the operator controls the speed and direction of the locomotive.

Most model locomotives are made in one of two engine prototypes—steam or diesel.

Steam locomotives are especially popular with model railroad enthusiasts, though they are no longer used on real railroads. A great variety of steam locomotives were custom built for different railroad companies. Each steam locomotive prototype has unique features that model builders value. Many hobbyists enjoy building steam locomotives because the locomotives have many visible moving parts. In a steam locomotive model, the motor is usually located in the firebox behind the boiler. A set of gears connects the motor to the axles of the large drive wheels.

Diesel locomotives are simpler in appearance and easier to build than steam models. They are popular with hobbyists who want to create a more modern looking system. Diesel locomotive models have a more standard appearance than steam locomotives, but they have a variety of paint and lettering designs that represent the different railroad companies. Most diesel locomotive models have the motors in the middle of the body. The wheels are mounted on swiveling pieces called *trucks* attached to the bottom of the body. Gears connect the motor to the wheels of the locomotive. Many diesel models use two or more locomotive units to copy the makeup of real diesel locomotives. One of the model units might be a *dummy,* without motor or gears, which will still create the appearance of the real locomotive but at less expense.

Cars for model railroads usually come in kits that can be assembled with a few simple tools. Most are made of plastic pieces that snap together. More challenging kits, called *craftsman kits,* include a combination of materials, such as wood, metal, and plastic. The pieces of the model must be cut to size and fitted together. In many kits, the cars are already painted with the designs of prototype railroads. In others, the model builders paint the cars themselves with their own designs. Some model builders combine parts from two or more kits, a practice that is called *kitbashing.*

Buildings and scenery. Much of the realism of a model railroad depends on how creatively the builder designs the scenery of the system. The builder may send the train over a complicated route through tunnels and small towns, over rivers and highways, and into freight yards or passenger terminals.

There are a variety of kits for making buildings. Buildings can also be constructed from raw materials. Hobbyists build most scenery by shaping screen wire or cardboard webbing into the contours of hills, valleys, streams, and other landforms. They cover this shell with plaster. Builders then apply paint and texture materials to represent earth and grass, and add miniature trees and shrubs to complete the landscape.

Other systems and equipment can be as simple or complex as the builder wishes. The basic wiring system for a model railroad allows only one train to run at a time. More complicated wiring permits several trains to run at once. Signals reproduce the functions of their prototype systems and add additional realism. Sound effects systems re-create the sounds of steam and diesel locomotives. Some hobbyists build working models of such equipment as drawbridges and coal dumpers. However, such accessories are more common in toy

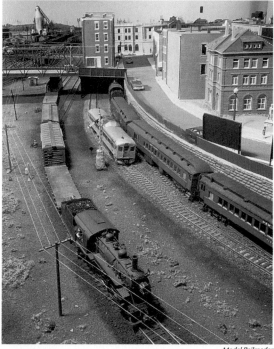
Model Railroader

Lifelike scenery adds realism and variety to a model railroad layout. Hobbyists can create scenes depicting a highly detailed miniature town, shown here.

train systems. Advanced model railroaders may operate their railroad systems by radio control or by computer.

History. Model railroading became a well-known hobby as a result of the model railroads shown at the Century of Progress Exposition in Chicago during 1933 and 1934. Public interest in these models encouraged manufacturers to produce model railroad kits and parts. In 1935, model railroad hobbyists and manufacturers organized the National Model Railroad Association to establish uniform standards for tracks, wheels, and other model railroad equipment.

Hundreds of thousands of adults operate model railroads as a hobby. Many belong to model railroad clubs. Members of clubs work as a group to build larger and more elaborate model railroads than they could do as individuals.   Andy Sperandeo

Additional resources

Level I
Goodman, Michael E. *Model Railroading.* Crestwood Hse., 1993.
Mallerich, Dallas. *Greenberg's Guide to Toy Trains.* Wallace-Homestead, 1990.
Townsley, John. *Getting Started with Model Trains.* Sterling Pub., 1991.

Level II
Friberg, Rutger. *Model Railroad Electronics 1.* 2nd ed. Marklin, 1997.
McGuirk, Martin. *Realistic Track Plans for O Gauge Toy Trains.* Kalmbach, 1997.
Selby, Rick. *HO Railroad from Set to Scenery.* Kalmbach, 1995.

Railroad Retirement Board (RRB) is a United States government agency that administers a retirement pension system for retired railroad employees, their spouses, and their survivors. It also administers an unemployment-sickness benefit system, together with a reemployment service. The board was established by the Railroad Retirement Act of 1935. The president appoints the three members of the board, with the consent of the Senate. The national headquarters of the RRB are located in Chicago.

Critically reviewed by the Railroad Retirement Board

Railroad worm. See **Apple maggot; Insect** (picture: The gorgeous colors).

Railway is the term used in the United Kingdom and other Commonwealth countries for a railroad. See **Railroad.**

Railway brotherhoods were unions of railroad workers in the United States and Canada. Many persons used the term for the "big four" railroad labor unions. These were the Brotherhood of Locomotive Engineers, the Brotherhood of Locomotive Firemen and Enginemen, the Brotherhood of Railroad Trainmen, and the Order of Railway Conductors and Brakemen. In 1969, the latter three unions merged with the Switchmen's Union of North America to form the United Transportation Union. This union has about 160,000 members.

Railroad unions did not develop as other unions did. They started as insurance agencies for their members. Insurance companies considered railroading so hazardous that they would not insure the workers. Locomotive engineers formed the first brotherhood in 1863. They were followed by the railway conductors in 1868, the firemen and engineers in 1873, and the railroad trainmen in 1883.

The railway brotherhoods did not operate in the same way as other labor unions. The railroads were subjected to strict government controls, and the unions usually used collective bargaining, rather than strikes, to achieve their goals. The brotherhoods remained independent of the organized labor movement until the late 1950's. Then the trainmen and the firemen and enginemen groups joined the American Federation of Labor and Congress of Industrial Organizations (AFL-CIO).

Robert C. Post

Railway Labor Act is a United States federal law that deals with labor disputes between railroad and airline companies and their employees. Its main purpose is to prevent strikes that might endanger the economy or create a national emergency.

The act was designed to bring about settlements through negotiation, mediation, arbitration, or, if necessary, through the investigation and recommendations of an emergency fact-finding board appointed by the president. The act has no provision that can force the parties to reach an agreement. However, it does require that employees not strike for a period of 60 days after the appointment of a fact-finding board. If the employees reject the board's recommendations, they are then free to go on strike after the 60 days.

Two federal agencies administer the Railway Labor Act. The three-member National Mediation Board can invoke the act on its own or upon the request of employers or employees. The board also handles disputes concerning railroad and airline employee representation and negotiation of new contracts. The 36-member National Railroad Adjustment Board decides disputes involving grievances or the interpretation of existing agreements. This board has jurisdiction only over railroads and their employees.

The Railway Labor Act was passed by Congress in 1926, and it has since been amended several times. The original act applied only to railroads. The railway industry received early congressional attention because its unions were strong, and it was feared that a series of railroad strikes might be dangerous for the nation's economy. In 1936, the act was amended to make it apply also to labor relations between airlines and their employees.

The Railway Labor Act proved successful in helping avoid major strikes until the early 1940's. In 1941, the railroads prevented a strike by granting wage increases that were much higher than the emergency board's recommendations. It soon became common for companies and unions to reject board recommendations. Since the early 1960's, most railroad and airline strikes have been prevented by emergency actions outside the Railway Labor Act. During a railroad dispute in 1963, Congress passed an emergency measure demanding compulsory arbitration. There has since been increasing pressure for revision of this act, which was once considered a model labor law.   David Brody

See also **National Mediation Board; Strike** (Kinds of strikes).

Rain is precipitation that consists of drops of water. Raindrops form in clouds when microscopic droplets of water grow or when particles of ice melt before reaching the ground. Rain falls throughout most of the world. In the tropics, almost all precipitation is rain. But in the inland areas of Antarctica, all precipitation is snow.

Rain is a part of an unending process known as the *hydrologic cycle.* This process begins with the evaporation of water from the surface of the earth—mostly from the ocean. The resulting *water vapor*—the gaseous state of water—then condenses, forming clouds of liquid droplets. Some of the droplets may freeze, forming particles of ice. The droplets and particles then undergo a variety of changes in the clouds. Eventually, however, they fall to the surface as precipitation. Much of the precipitation that falls on continents eventually flows in rivers into the ocean. The process then repeats itself.

When ocean water evaporates, the salt in the ocean water remains in the ocean. As a result, rain and frozen precipitation, such as snow, hail, and sleet, are made up of fresh water. Human beings and most other creatures that live on land depend on the fresh water produced by the hydrologic cycle.

Rain cleans the air by washing away dust and chemical pollutants. But too much rain may cause flooding that destroys property and threatens lives. Heavy rainfall can also damage crops and speed up the loss of soil.

Characteristics of rain

Raindrops vary greatly in their size and in the speed of their fall. The diameter of most raindrops ranges from about 0.02 to 0.25 inch (0.5 to 6.35 millimeters). Rates of fall for these sizes range from $6\frac{1}{2}$ feet (2 meters) per second for the smallest to about 30 feet (9 meters) per second for the largest. *Drizzle* is rain with drops less than about 0.02 inch in diameter and falling speeds of less than about $6\frac{1}{2}$ feet per second.

Raindrops smaller than about 0.04 inch (1 millimeter)

How rain forms   Raindrops develop within clouds by means of two processes. The different stages of development occur in overlapping zones, as shown in these greatly simplified diagrams.

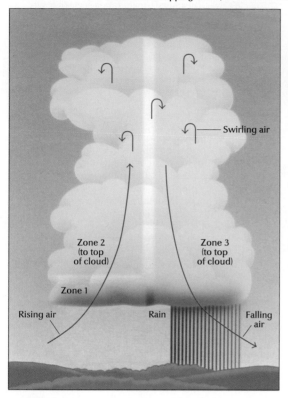

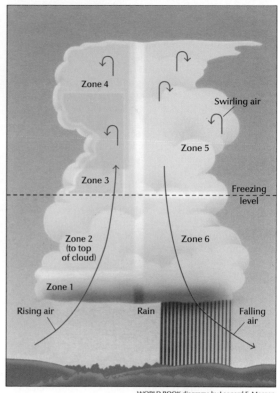

WORLD BOOK diagrams by Leonard E. Morgan

The coalescence process begins at the cloud base, zone 1. There, *water vapor* (the gaseous form of water) condenses on tiny particles called *cloud condensation nuclei*, creating water droplets. In zone 2, droplets grow as more vapor condenses on them. As droplets fall through zone 3, larger ones strike smaller ones and *coalesce* (combine) with them, forming raindrops.

The ice-crystal process begins when water droplets form and grow in zones 1 and 2. A tiny fraction of the droplets freeze in zone 3. In zone 4, water vapor freezes on the frozen droplets, forming snow crystals. As the crystals fall through zone 5, liquid droplets freeze onto them, creating hailstones or ice particles called *graupel*. These objects melt in zone 6 and fall as raindrops.

in diameter are round. Larger drops are somewhat flat, due to the force of the air flowing around them. The largest raindrops alternate between a flattened shape and a stretched-out shape.

Most rain comes from *convective clouds,* in which currents of air usually rise 10 to 100 feet (3 to 30 meters) per second. Within the currents, the air undergoes many sudden changes in speed and direction. Because of the currents, the growing raindrops take complicated paths within the clouds.

It takes about 10 to 30 minutes for rain to form. The time rain takes to fall to the ground depends on the height of the cloud in which it forms and the size of the raindrops. This time ranges from a few seconds for large drops falling from low clouds to about 15 minutes for small drops falling from high clouds. In dry areas, rain from high clouds may not even reach the ground. Instead, it evaporates completely as it falls.

The intensity of rainfall varies widely. Rainfall that is too light to measure is called a *trace* of rain. Rain that falls at a measurable rate of up to 0.10 inch (2.5 millimeters) per hour is a *light rain*. A *moderate rain* falls at a rate of 0.11 to 0.30 inch (2.8 to 7.6 millimeters) per hour. Rain that is even more intense is *heavy rain*.

Acid rain is the term for rain, snow, sleet, or other precipitation that is polluted by such acids as sulfuric acid and nitric acid. The acid in acid rain forms when chemical compounds known as nitrogen oxides and sulfur dioxide react within growing droplets and raindrops. These compounds are released by motor vehicles, factories, and certain power plants. Acid rain pollutes lakes and streams. It also damages buildings and other structures and is suspected of harming forests and soil.

Formation of rain

The "life" of a raindrop begins when molecules of water vapor in a cloud condense on a tiny particle of matter called a *cloud condensation nucleus*. This particle can be a speck of dust or soot. However, it is usually a very tiny droplet known as a *haze droplet*. This consists of a concentrated solution of sea salt or of a chemical compound such as ammonium sulfate or magnesium sulfate. The compound may have formed when gases in the air interacted chemically, or it may have been given off by a motor vehicle or a factory.

Continuing condensation enlarges the droplet, which grows as long as the air is rising. But it will grow by condensation to a diameter of only a few thousandths of an inch—less than 0.1 millimeter, too small to be a raindrop. To become a raindrop, a droplet must undergo one of two processes—(1) the *coalescence process* or (2) the *ice-crystal process.*

The coalescence process produces much of the rain that forms over the oceans and in the tropics. This process occurs as droplets fall. The larger droplets fall faster than the smaller ones. The larger droplets thus collide with the smaller ones and *coalesce* (combine) with them, becoming larger yet. A large droplet that falls 1 mile (1.6 kilometers) through a cloud may coalesce with 1 million small droplets.

The ice-crystal process accounts for much of the rainfall in the two *temperate zones*—(1) the area between the Tropic of Cancer and the Arctic Circle and (2) the area between the Tropic of Capricorn and the Antarctic Circle. In both zones, the temperature of the clouds is usually below the freezing point of water, 32 °F (0 °C).

The clouds consist of droplets of *supercooled water,* water that is colder than the freezing point, but still liquid. But some of these droplets eventually freeze because they contain, or come into contact with, microscopic particles called *freezing nuclei* or *ice nuclei.* Most freezing nuclei are dust particles or tiny specks of plant debris raised by the wind.

When a supercooled droplet freezes, it turns into an ice crystal. The crystal then grows by collecting water vapor. This growth produces the complicated shapes of snow crystals. As a crystal grows, it falls faster and collides with supercooled droplets, which immediately freeze onto it. This process produces soft ice pellets called *graupel* or small hailstones. When these ice particles fall into air that is warmer than 32 °F, they melt. Such particles produce almost all the raindrops in thunderstorms.

Rain in long-lasting, steady storms forms in a slightly different way. The ice crystals continue to grow by collecting water vapor. The resulting snow crystals may then collide with one another and stick together as snowflakes. Snow crystals and snowflakes become raindrops when they fall into air that is warmer than 32 °F and melt.

Scientists have been trying to develop reliable methods of *cloud seeding* to make more rain fall from clouds. In the technique investigated the most, aircraft drop artificial freezing nuclei into clouds. The usual seeding material has been silver iodide, whose crystals have a structure much like that of ice.

Rainfall distribution

The earth as a whole receives abundant rainfall. If rain fell evenly, all the land would receive 34 inches (86 centimeters) a year. But rainfall is unevenly distributed over the earth's surface. Distribution is especially uneven over the continents because of mountain ranges. Heavy rain often drenches slopes where the air rises, leaving dry the slopes where the air descends. For example, *southerly winds* (winds from the south) rising over the Himalaya range in Asia deposit 200 to 600 inches (510 to 1,500 centimeters) of rain annually on their southern slopes. But the northern slopes of the range average less than 10 inches (25 centimeters) of rain a year.

Rainfall is generally heavy along the equator because of the high humidity and because surface winds *con-*

Some rainfall records

The earth's average annual precipitation (including rain, snow, and hail) is about 34 inches (86 centimeters).
Greatest rainfall in the world occurs at Mount Waialeale in Hawaii. An average of about 460 inches (1,168 centimeters) of rain falls there yearly.
Least rainfall in the world is recorded at Arica, Chile, a desert town that receives an average of 0.03 inch (0.76 millimeter) a year.
Least rainfall in the United States occurs in Death Valley, California. An average of 1.63 inches (4.14 centimeters) falls there annually.

Source: *Weather and Climate Extremes,* U.S. Army Topographic Engineering Center.

verge (come together) there. The convergence causes the air to rise, producing clouds and rain.

Certain regions alternate between rainy and dry seasons due to shifting winds. In regions near the tropics, winds known as *monsoons* blow in one direction in the winter and in the opposite direction in the summer. Monsoon winds bring extremely heavy rain to southern Asia in the summer.

On both sides of the equator, generally along the Tropic of Cancer and the Tropic of Capricorn, are regions where the air usually sinks to the surface. Rainfall is therefore light in those areas, and so deserts have formed in them. Sinking air is responsible for the Sahara and the Kalahari Desert in Africa and a band of deserts in the western and central parts of Australia.

Away from the tropics, the western coasts of large land masses have more rainfall than their central regions. For example, along the west coast of North America, moist winds from the Pacific Ocean produce as

World distribution of precipitation

much as 150 inches (381 centimeters) of rain and snow a year. To the east lies the Great Basin, a desert area that covers parts of Oregon, California, Nevada, Idaho, Utah, and Wyoming. The eastern side of North America receives moisture largely from southerly and southwesterly winds from the warm Gulf of Mexico.

Polar regions are dry partly because their cold air cannot hold much water vapor. In addition, relatively little evaporation occurs in those regions, and the wind blows away from the poles.

Measuring rainfall

People measure rainfall with a variety of devices, including simple funnel gauges and sophisticated radar systems.

A funnel gauge consists of a funnel connected to the top of a narrow cylindrical tube. The diameter of the mouth of the funnel is much larger than the diameter of the tube. Rain falls into the funnel and collects in the tube. Markings on the side of the tube indicate the amount of rainfall. This design makes the depth of the rain easy to measure. A small amount of water falling into the mouth of the funnel will fill the tube to a considerable—and easily readable—level.

Radar systems. Networks of gauges can measure rainfall over large regions, such as river basins, states and provinces, and even countries. However, a network can produce an inaccurate result if the rainfall is unevenly distributed across a region.

A radar system can provide a more complete picture of rainfall. In a radar system, an antenna sends out radio waves that reflect from raindrops and return to the antenna. Electronic devices connected to the antenna measure the strength of the returning waves. The strength of the reflection indicates the amount of rainfall—the stronger the waves, the heavier the rainfall.

This method of measurement avoids the limited coverage of gauge networks. However, radar may provide inaccurate results if the raindrops are unusually large or if hail is mixed with the rain. In this case, the radar waves may appear to have been reflected from a storm that is much heavier than the actual storm. A combination of radar and rain gauges usually provides the most accurate results. Charles Knight

Related articles. See the *Climate* section of the articles on the continents, countries, states, and provinces. See also:

Acid rain	Desert	Humidity	Rainmaking
Climate	El Niño	Rain gauge	Storm
Cloud	Evaporation	Rainbow	Water
Cloudburst			

Rain dance is a ceremony performed by American Indians of the southwestern United States to ask spirits to send rain for their crops. The Indians ask the spirits to send the rain in the proper amounts and at the right times. Indians hold most rain dances during the spring planting season and in the summer while the crops are growing. Each tribe has its own particular ceremonies for bringing rain. For example, participants in the rain ceremony of the Tohono O'odham tribe sing and dance and drink wine made from cactus juice. The Hopi dance with live rattlesnakes in their mouths to encourage the gods to send rain (see **Snake dance**). Michael D. Green

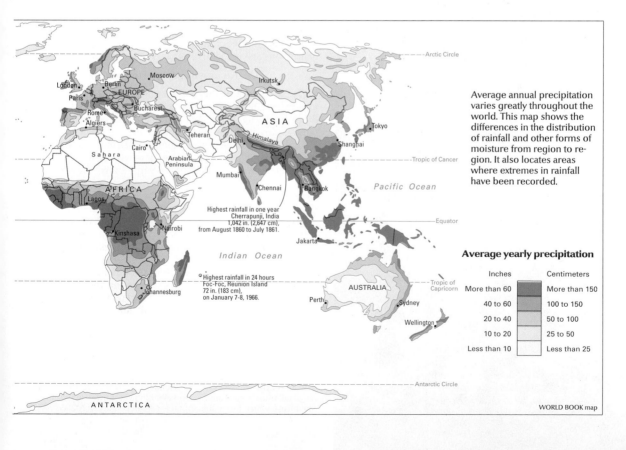

Average annual precipitation varies greatly throughout the world. This map shows the differences in the distribution of rainfall and other forms of moisture from region to region. It also locates areas where extremes in rainfall have been recorded.

Highest rainfall in one year
Cherrapunji, India
1,042 in. (2,647 cm),
from August 1860 to July 1861.

Highest rainfall in 24 hours
Foc-Foc, Reunion Island
72 in. (183 cm),
on January 7-8, 1966.

Average yearly precipitation

	Inches		Centimeters
	More than 60		More than 150
	40 to 60		100 to 150
	20 to 40		50 to 100
	10 to 20		25 to 50
	Less than 10		Less than 25

WORLD BOOK map

Rain forest

Rain forest is a woodland of tall trees growing in a region of year-round warmth and abundant rainfall. Almost all rain forests lie at or near the equator. They form an evergreen belt of lush vegetation that encircles the planet. German botanist Andreas F. W. Schimper first coined the term *rain forest*—in German, *Regenwald*—in 1898.

Tropical rain forests occupy only 6 to 7 percent of the earth's surface. However, they support more than half of the world's plant and animal *species* (kinds). More kinds of frogs and other amphibians, birds, insects, mammals, and reptiles live in rain forests than in any other area. Scientists believe millions more rain forest species remain undiscovered.

The rain forest provides people with many benefits. Its plants produce timber, foods, medicines, and such industrial products as dyes, fibers, gums, oils, and resins. Rain forests help regulate the earth's climate and maintain clean air. The forests' lush, green beauty and rich wildlife offer a special source of enjoyment.

In addition, rain forests provide homes to millions of people. Such groups as the Yanomami of South America, the Dayaks of Southeast Asia, and the Pygmies of central Africa have lived in rain forests for centuries. They make their living by hunting, fishing, collecting forest products, and farming. Traditional forest peoples have acquired much knowledge about the rain forest's plants and animals.

In spite of these benefits, people cut down thousands of square miles or square kilometers of rain forest each year. This destruction eliminates thousands of species of animals. A number of governments and conservation organizations are working to preserve the rain forests.

Characteristics of rain forests

Climate and soil. The temperature in a tropical rain forest varies little. It rarely rises above 95 °F (35 °C) or drops below 64 °F (18 °C). In many regions, the average temperature in the hottest month is only 2 to 5 °F (1 to 3 °C) higher than the average temperature in the coldest month. Most rain forests receive more than 80 inches (203 centimeters) of rain annually. Some areas may receive more than 250 inches (635 centimeters) of rain each year. Thundershowers can occur more than 200 days a year.

Rain forest soils vary greatly from place to place. In many areas, the soil is acidic and infertile because years of heavy rains have washed out most of the *nutrients* (nourishing substances). Most rain forest nutrients are part of living plants. Small amounts of nutrients occur in a thin layer of topsoil that contains decaying vegetation.

Rain forest trees have developed several ways of capturing nutrients. For example, they obtain nourishment from rainwater that collects in their leaves or along their trunks and branches. They also withdraw nutrients from their old leaves before they shed them. The roots of most rain forest trees grow close to the surface and

The lush rain forest houses an abundance of plant life. A variety of tall trees, dense shrubs, and climbing vines grow in this rain forest, which lies in the Southeast Asian country of Malaysia.

quickly absorb soil nutrients before they wash away. Special fungi called *mycorrhizae* grow in or on many of the roots and help them absorb minerals from the soil.

Structure and growth. Rain forests grow in four major layers: (1) the *canopy,* or top layer; (2) the *sub-canopy,* a layer of trees just below the canopy; (3) the *understory,* a shady lower area; and (4) the *floor.* The tallest trees, known as *emergents,* grow more than 165 feet (50 meters) tall. The *crowns* (tops) of these trees dominate the canopy. Emergents receive the greatest amount of sunlight, but they must endure high temperatures and strong winds. The crowns of other trees in the canopy usually form a nearly continuous covering of leaves 65 to 165 feet (20 to 50 meters) above the ground. Some tall trees have large growths called *buttresses* that extend from the base of the trunk and help support the tree.

More than 70 percent of rain forest animal and plant species reside in the canopy and sub-canopy. Many tree branches have a dense covering of *epiphytes,* plants that grow on other plants and obtain nourishment from the air and rain. Vines called *lianas* often climb on or around the trunks and branches of trees.

The shady understory shelters small palms, young trees, and *herbaceous* (nonwoody) plants that can grow in dim light. Many popular house plants, such as philodendrons, dieffenbachia, and ferns, are developed from species that live in this area. Some scientists believe only 1 percent of the sunlight available to emergent trees reaches the understory.

A thin layer of fallen leaves, seeds, fruits, and branches covers the forest floor. This layer quickly decomposes and is constantly replaced.

The layers of a rain forest continually change. Large old trees die and fall to the ground, leaving a gap in the canopy. Direct sunlight penetrates through to the understory and stimulates the growth of seedlings, saplings, and small trees below. The small trees slowly stretch upward into the canopy. As they branch and expand their crowns, they fill the gaps in the canopy. A mature rain forest consists of a mixture of closed canopies, gaps, and patches of growing trees where the canopy is being rebuilt. The regeneration of many rain forest trees depends on gaps developing regularly in the canopy.

Plants and animals. About 45 percent of the world's plant species occur in tropical rain forests. Scientists have counted over 250 species of trees in small areas of Asian and South American rain forests. A similar plot of land in a northern temperate forest would have only about 10 to 15 tree species. In addition to trees, rain forests support a great variety of bamboos, herbs, and shrubs. Climbing vines, ferns, mosses, and orchids grow directly on the trunks and branches of large trees.

Because of continual moisture and warmth, tropical rain forests stay green all year. Most rain forest trees continually lose old leaves and grow new ones. Only a few species lose all of their leaves for a brief period.

Fish, amphibians, reptiles, birds, and mammals abound in the rain forest and its rivers. However, insects rank as the most plentiful rain forest animals. An individual tree in a South American rain forest may support more than 40 species of ants. Scientists have counted about 1,200 species of beetles living in only 19 tree crowns from Panama.

Plants and animals in the rain forest depend on one another for survival. Many animal groups, especially insects and birds, pollinate the flowers of rain forest trees. Such animals receive food from the flowers' nectar. In return, they pollinate the next flowers they visit. Some

The Sepik River winds through dense rain forest on the island of New Guinea in Papua New Guinea. Many rain forest peoples and animals live along rivers.

© Jean-Paul Ferrero, Explorer

Rain forests of the world

The largest rain forests occur in tropical parts of the Americas, Asia, and Africa. Smaller areas of rain forest exist on many Pacific Islands and in parts of Australia's northeastern coast. These forests lie chiefly near the equator, in regions that receive some of the world's heaviest rainfall.

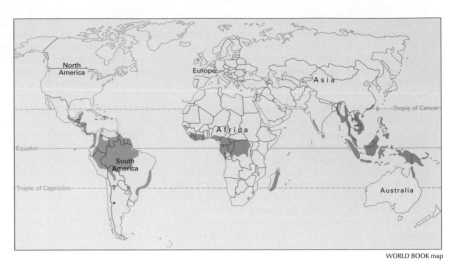

WORLD BOOK map

trees rely on only one species of insect for pollination. Many rain forest trees also depend on animals to disperse their seeds. In the Amazon rain forest, fish disperse the seeds of some trees.

Rain forests around the world

The world's largest rain forests occur in tropical regions of the Americas, Asia, and Africa. Smaller areas of rain forest exist on many Pacific Islands and in parts of Australia's northeastern coast. People have also applied the term *rain forest* to such woodlands as those in North America's Pacific Northwest. However, the plant life in these forests is much less diverse than that found in tropical rain forests. For example, only a few species of large *conifers* (cone-bearing trees) dominate Pacific Northwest forests.

The Americas. About half of the world's rain forests grow in the American tropics. The largest expanse of forest—about 2 million square miles (5.2 million square kilometers)—lies in the Amazon River basin. Rain forests also occur in coastal areas from Ecuador and Brazil to southern Mexico, and in patches on many of the Caribbean islands.

American tropical rain forests support a rich assortment of plant species. More than 500 kinds of large plants may inhabit only 5 acres (2 hectares) of forest. Valuable hardwood trees include mahogany and rosewood. Over 150 species of trees produce edible fruits. Avocados, cocoa, rubber, and vanilla also grow there.

The rain forests of tropical America support more than 1,500 species of birds, 500 species of mammals, and 2,000 species of butterflies. More bats live there than live anywhere else. Monkeys, sloths, and toucans feed in the forest canopy and sub-canopy. Capybaras, the world's largest rodents, as well as ocelots and tapirs, forage along the forest floor. Emerald tree boas and arrow-poison frogs hide among foliage in the understory. The Amazon River contains more than 2,000 species of freshwater fish, including the dangerous piranha.

American rain forests provide homes to a variety of peoples. They include the Kuna of Panama, the Maya of Mexico and Central America, the Shipibo of Peru, and the Yanomami of Brazil and Venezuela. Such forest groups survive primarily by farming, but they also hunt animals and gather edible wild plants from the forest.

Asia. Rain forests cover about 1 million square miles (3 million square kilometers) of the Asian tropics. The forests grow in western and southern India and extend eastward through Vietnam. Large blocks of forest also occur in Indonesia, Malaysia, and the Philippines.

A single family of trees, the *dipterocarps*, forms a dominant part of the Asian rain forest canopy. About 380 species of dipterocarps grow in these forests. Dipterocarp trees produce valuable wood and *resins*. Resins are sticky substances that people use for varnishing and *caulking* (making objects watertight). Other important plants include the *pitcher plants,* which feed on animal life, and the *rafflesia,* the world's largest flower. A single rafflesia may grow more than 3 feet (90 centimeters) wide. Such fruits as bananas, durians, litchis, and mangoes also flourish in Asian rain forests.

Some of the best-known rain forest mammals in Asia include elephants, gibbons, orangutans, and tigers. The forests also support hundreds of reptile and amphibian species and thousands of bird and beetle species.

Rain forest peoples of Asia include the Penan of Borneo. They rely on rain forest plants and animals for subsistence and rarely farm the land. Another Bornean group, the Lun Dayeh, clear small areas of forest to make rice farms. The T'in people of Thailand and Laos harvest hundreds of wild plant species from the rain forest for food and other purposes.

Africa. Africa's tropics have about 810,000 square miles (2.1 million square kilometers) of rain forest. The forested area extends from Congo (Kinshasa) westward to the Atlantic Ocean. Patches of rain forest also occur on the east coast of Madagascar.

African rain forests do not house as many plant species as do the forests of South America or Asia. Small areas of African rain forest support from 50 to 100 species of trees. Many of these trees have their fruits dispersed by elephants. A number of valuable woods, including ebony, mahogany, and sipo, flourish in the African tropics. Other well-known plants from the region include oil palms and coffee plants.

Diverse animal life characterizes Africa's tropical rain forests. Squirrels and monkeys share the canopy and sub-canopy with other small mammals, including galagos and golden pottos, as well as hundreds of species of birds. The mandrill, a brightly colored relative of the baboon, and the okapi, a horselike relative of the giraffe, roam the forest floor. Congo peacocks and wild hogs called bush pigs also dwell on the ground. Gorillas and chimpanzees live on the ground and in trees. The forests of Madagascar support animals found almost nowhere else, including long-tailed, monkeylike lemurs.

Forest-dwelling people in the African tropics are collectively known as Pygmies. Traditionally, they have survived by hunting and gathering wild animals and plants. Pygmies live in such countries as Burundi, Cameroon, Congo (Brazzaville), Congo (Kinshasa), Gabon, and Rwanda.

Australia and the Pacific Islands. Tropical rain forests cover about 145,600 square miles (377,000 square kilometers) in northeast Australia and on many Pacific Islands. Rain forest trees of these regions include several kinds of figs, as well as the smaller lilly-pilly and brush cherry. The lacewood and Queensland maple trees produce valuable hardwoods. Coachwood and Moreton Bay chestnut trees develop brilliantly colored flowers.

Rain forests of Australia and New Guinea house unique wildlife. Such marsupials as cuscuses, sugar gliders, and tree kangaroos make their homes in the trees. Several kinds of parrots and numerous species of snakes also reside in the forests.

Rain forest peoples of this area include Australian Aborigines and Melanesian peoples from such islands as New Guinea, the Solomon Islands, and Vanuatu. Many of these cultures hunt and gather food from the rain forest. They also raise crops.

The value of rain forests

Rain forests benefit people in four major ways. They provide (1) economic, (2) scientific, (3) environmental, and (4) recreational value.

Economic value. Wood ranks as the most important rain forest product. Foresters harvest millions of trees from rain forests each year. People use about 80 percent of rain forest wood for fuel and about 20 percent for timber. International trade in tropical hardwoods averages billions of dollars a year.

Other valuable rain forest resources include fibers, fruits, nuts, oils, and resins. Indonesia and the Philippines export millions of dollars in furniture and other products made from *rattan,* a kind of palm. Amazon rain forests provide thousands of tons of Brazil nuts and rubber. Mexican and Central American forests yield various types of *chicle,* an ingredient used in chewing gum.

Scientific value. Tropical rain forests have much to teach people. Many scientists study the rain forest as an *ecosystem*—that is, they investigate the relationships among all its living things and the environment that supports them. Because of its great diversity of life, the rain forest ranks as the most complex ecosystem on land. Biologists have discovered and classified only a small percentage of the organisms believed to live there. As scientists learn more about rain forests, they can better understand how to conserve these and other ecosystems.

Rain forests provide a wealth of foods and medicines. The forest peoples of Borneo use hundreds of different plant species for food. Most of these plants have not been grown outside Borneo. About 85 wild relatives of the common avocado exist in forests of Central America. Commercial avocado growers are working with scientists to develop ways of using these species to breed avocados that are more resistant to disease.

Several important medicines come from rain forest plants. These include *quinine,* used to treat malaria; *tubocurarine,* a muscle relaxant sometimes used in heart surgery; and *pilocarpine,* used to treat the eye disease glaucoma. The rosy periwinkle plant from Madagascar yields important anticancer drugs. Scientists believe many more potential medicines may exist in rain forests.

Environmental value. Tropical rain forests help regulate the earth's environment in several ways. For example, tropical trees help control the amount of rain water that reaches the ground. These trees absorb an enormous quantity of rain. In a process called *transpiration,*

Jaguar

© Luiz Claudio Marigo, Bruce Coleman Ltd.

Tussock moth

© George D. Dodge, Bruce Coleman Inc.

Keel-billed toucan

© MPL Fogden, Bruce Coleman Ltd.

Wild orchid

© Corel

Rain forest life includes an astonishing variety of colorful animals and plants. More kinds of birds, flowers, insects, mammals, and reptiles live in the rain forests than in any other region. Biologists believe millions more rain forest species remain undiscovered. Because people are clearing the world's rain forests so quickly, many forest species may become extinct before scientists can discover them.

Carpet chameleon

© Gail Shumway, FPG

Rafflesia

© Alain Compost, Bruce Coleman Ltd.

much of this water evaporates from the trees' leaf pores and reenters the atmosphere as vapor. Eventually, the vapor condenses into water and falls to the earth again as rain. Transpiration may account for as much as half of the rainfall in some rain forests. By regulating rainfall, rain forest trees keep floods and droughts from becoming too severe. The dense rain forest vegetation also reduces soil erosion.

Rain forests help control temperatures in their own regions and in other parts of the world. Rain forest trees absorb light and heat. This absorption keeps tropical climates from becoming too hot or too cold. The forests also take in and store massive amounts of carbon dioxide, preventing the build-up of this gas in the atmosphere. Scientists believe the accumulation of carbon dioxide and other gases in the atmosphere increases temperatures around the world. By absorbing carbon dioxide, tropical rain forests may help keep worldwide temperatures from becoming too warm.

Recreational value. Rain forests offer great beauty, lush vegetation, and unique wildlife for tourists. A growing number of people travel to rain forests each year. Tourism has helped increase awareness of the need to preserve these environments.

The future of rain forests

People are rapidly destroying the world's rain forests. In 1950, rain forests covered about 8,700,000 square miles (22,533,000 square kilometers) of the earth. This area would cover about three-fourths of Africa. Today, less than half the original extent of the earth's rain forest remains. In such regions as Madagascar, Sumatra, and the Atlantic coast of Brazil, only small patches still stand.

Few rain forest species can adjust to severe disturbance of their habitat. Most perish when people clear large areas of forest. Scientists estimate that tropical *deforestation* (clearing of trees) wipes out about 7,500 species per year.

Causes of deforestation. Commercial logging and the expansion of agriculture have damaged or wiped out extensive areas of rain forest. Huge mining projects, the construction of hydroelectric dams, and government resettlement programs have also taken their toll.

A complex mix of social, political, and economic factors has triggered these destructive activities. Rapid population growth and poverty often intensify the pressure to clear rain forest for short-term economic benefits. Brazil, Indonesia, and other nations have cut down huge expanses of rain forest to create new settlements that allow people to move out of overcrowded cities. Moreover, the governments of many tropical countries are deeply in debt. This debt provides a strong motivation to gather as much as possible from the rain forest as quickly as possible. After clearing the forest to harvest wood and other products, people then commonly use the land to grow crops.

Deforestation usually displaces forest peoples. When denied access to the forest, these peoples often lose important knowledge about rain forest species and their uses. Loss of such knowledge further threatens the survival of the forests.

Saving rain forests. Many conservation organizations, including the World Wildlife Fund, Conservation International, and the Nature Conservancy, are working

© Philippe Guignard

Deforestation wipes out large areas of rain forests each year, threatening the wildlife in those regions. This picture shows a partially deforested area of Gabon, a country in western Africa.

with governments to conserve rain forests. Such efforts include (1) establishing protected areas, (2) promoting intelligent management of rain forests, and (3) increasing public awareness about the importance of the forests.

In the 1980's and 1990's, hundreds of protected areas were established in tropical forests. These areas included nature reserves, wildlife sanctuaries, and national parks. However, such efforts affected only a small percentage of the total area of rain forest. Moreover, many conservation areas remain only "paper parks," with little protection or enforcement on the ground.

Governments and conservation organizations also promote sound management of tropical forests by the people who use them. For example, certain organizations certify timber from loggers that harvest rain forest wood in a sustainable fashion. Certified timbers may bring a higher price on the international market. Areas of some rain forests have been set aside as *extractive reserves*. Local populations manage these reserves and practice sustainable harvesting of many forest products.

Increasing public awareness about the plight of rain forests may also aid the struggle to conserve them. Awareness has grown due to greater exposure of rain forest issues in the media, and to an increasing number of tourists who travel to rain forests.   Charles M. Peters

Related articles in *World Book* include:

Rain forest animals

Cuscus	Loris	Parrot	Tarsier
Flying lemur	Mandrill	Sloth	Titi
Gorilla	Okapi	Tamarin	Toucan
Lemur	Orangutan	Tapir	

Rain forest plants

Anthurium	Cinchona	Litchi	Rattan
Baobab	Ebony	Mahogany	Rosewood
Brazil nut	Epiphyte	Mango	Rubber
Brazilwood	Kapok	Orchid	Sapodilla
Cacao	Kola nut	Palm	Tamarind
Cashew	Liana	Rafflesia	Teak

Rain forest peoples

Dayaks	Pygmies	Yanomami Indians

Other related articles

Amazon rain forest
American Samoa, National Park of
Forest (Tropical rain forest)
Jungle
Olympic National Park

Additional resources

Collins, N. Mark, and others, eds. *The Conservation Atlas of Tropical Forests.* 2 vols. Simon & Schuster, 1991-1992. Tropical forests in Africa, Asia, and the Pacific.
Terborgh, John. *Diversity and the Tropical Rain Forest.* Scientific Am. Lib., 1992.

Rain gauge is an instrument used to measure the amount of rain that falls in a certain place during a specific period of time. The National Weather Service uses a rain gauge that is shaped like a cylinder and has a removable cover. Inside the cylinder is a long narrow tube, where the rainfall is measured. The top of the tube is connected with a funnel. The rain falls into the funnel and flows into the tube. The mouth of the funnel has an area 10 times that of the tube. Therefore, if an inch of rain falls into the funnel, it would fill 10 inches of the tube. The rain in the tube is measured by a "ruler." With this ruler, a depth of 10 inches gives a reading of 1 inch of rainfall. Rain gauges that use the metric system measure in millimeters.

If the rainfall is so heavy that the water in the tube overflows, this extra rain flows into the space between the outside of the cylinder and the tube. After the rain in the tube is measured, it is poured out and the extra rain is placed in the tube and measured. The total rainfall equals the sum of these two measurements. A gauge is usually placed on the ground away from buildings and trees to ensure accuracy.

Some rain gauges can record the amount and the rate of rainfall. A *tipping bucket rain gauge* has a small bucket that tips and empties after it fills with rain. Each tip of the bucket activates an electrical switch that records the amount of rain. A *weighing rain gauge* collects water in a bucket that stands on a platform attached to a scale. As the bucket fills, the weight of the rain water pushes down the platform. This movement is recorded on a tape and processed by a computer.

Some rain gauges can be used to measure snowfall. But they do not provide very accurate measurements when used for this purpose. David D. Houghton

Rain tree, also called *cenizero,* is a shade tree that grows in tropical climates. Rain trees have short, stout trunks and long spreading branches. Some trees measure more than 100 feet (30 meters) across. The trees are called rain trees because moisture that looks like rain often drips from them. The liquid is really a discharge from insects feeding on the trees.

Rain trees have pink and white flowers that grow in clusters. The seeds are contained in star-shaped, brown pods. A freshly cut tree has moist wood that is easy to carve and keeps its shape as it dries. The wood has a golden to dark brown color and is used to make bowls, trays, furniture, and paneling. The tree is native to Central America and northern South America. In the United States, it is grown in Hawaii and Florida. Alwyn H. Gentry

Scientific classification. The rain tree belongs to the family Fabaceae or Leguminosae. It is *Samanea saman.*

Rainbow is a circular arc of colors that appears in the sky when raindrops are illuminated by sunlight. A rainbow is not a physical object. Rather, it is a pattern of light to which a great number of raindrops contribute. A rainbow may spread across the entire sky, and its ends may seem to rest on the earth. Not all rainbows form complete arcs, however, because a rainbow cannot appear in a part of the sky where there is no rain.

You are at the center of the rainbow you see. A person standing next to you would be at the center of a different rainbow—that is, a rainbow to which a different set of raindrops contributes. Thus, no two people ever see the same rainbow.

How to find a rainbow. A rainbow in the form of a complete arc attracts our attention. Sometimes, however, only patches of a rainbow are visible. Knowing when and where to look will help you find them.

Rainbows are most likely to be seen toward the end of the day, especially where local thunderstorms build up during hot summer days, yield rain in the late afternoon, and break up by evening. To locate a rainbow, turn your back to the sun. Next, locate your *antisolar point,* which will be in the direction of the shadow of your head. Scan the sky in an arc about 42° above the antisolar point. A rainbow at this location is called a *primary rainbow.* It will be red on its outer edge and violet on its inner edge—with many other colors in between.

Alistair B. Fraser

A rainbow appears in the sky when sunlight illuminates raindrops. The center of the rainbow is directly opposite the sun. Thus, as in the photo shown here, shadows of objects near the observer point toward the center of the rainbow. A rainbow is an image of sunlight, not a physical object.

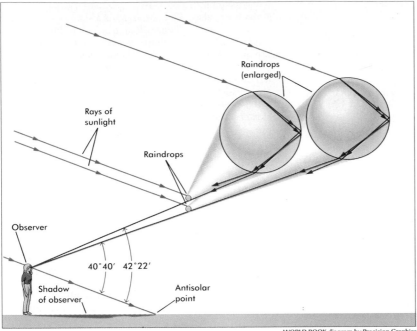

A rainbow forms when raindrops bend and reflect sunlight, *as shown here.* As this light bends, it breaks up into rays of various colors—red and violet as shown and, between them, orange, yellow, green, and blue. The rays reflect off the inner surface of the drops, then bend again as they exit the drops. As a result, a rainbow appears about 42° above an observer's *antisolar point,* the point directly opposite the sun. The rainbow's outer edge is red, and its inner edge is violet.

WORLD BOOK diagram by Precision Graphics

If you scan about 9° above this rainbow, you may see a less bright *secondary rainbow* with its color order reversed. Between the rainbows will be a relatively dark region called *Alexander's dark band.*

How rainbows appear. To understand some of the general features of rainbows, it helps to pretend that sunlight can be divided into many parallel rays. The rays are uniformly spaced when they arrive at the surface of a raindrop. It also helps to know about the wave nature of light, and how a prism bends sunlight.

The wave nature of light. Light is a form of energy that behaves in some ways like waves. Light waves have a range of *wavelengths.* A wavelength is the distance between any point on one wave and the corresponding point on the next wave. Visible light of different wavelengths appears as different colors. Light with the longest wavelengths appears red. Light with the shortest wavelengths appears violet.

Sunlight has a mixture of wavelengths. We see this mixture as white light. People often specify the colors in sunlight, from the longest wavelength to the shortest, as red, orange, yellow, green, blue, and violet. Other people also mention the color indigo, which is closely related to blue, between blue and violet. All these colors shade into their neighboring colors, however, and each shading is itself a color. Nature produces many more colors than people have ever named.

How a prism bends sunlight. When light passes through a prism, the light is *refracted* (bent). Light of a given wavelength bends at only one angle. Therefore, when sunlight—with its mixture of wavelengths—passes through a prism, it separates into a rainbowlike band of colors. Light with the longest wavelengths bends the least and appears red. Light with the shortest wavelengths bends the most and appears violet.

How droplets form a rainbow. When uniformly spaced rays of white light enter a raindrop, the raindrop acts as a prism. Thus, each ray of white light is separated into many rays corresponding to all the colors in sunlight. Each ray of colored light bends at a different angle.

Some of the rays of colored light reflect once off the inside surface of the raindrop, then exit the drop. As they exit, they bend again. The exiting rays are highly concentrated at angles of about 42° relative to the paths of entry of the original rays of white light.

Such concentrations of rays exit from many raindrops. These rays reach an observer who is scanning the sky about 42° above the antisolar point. As a result, the observer sees a primary rainbow with its colors in the following order, from outer edge to inner edge: red, orange, yellow, green, blue, violet.

Other rays of colored light reflect twice off the inside surface of raindrops. The rays then exit the drops concentrated at angles of about 51°. An observer therefore sees a secondary rainbow at about 51° above the antisolar point.

Other kinds of bows. People sometimes use the term *rainbow* to refer to colored arcs formed in sea spray or the spray of waterfalls, garden hoses, or lawn sprinklers. You may see such bows even when the sun is high in the sky.   Craig F. Bohren

See also **Color** (The relationship between color and light); **Light** (The nature of light); **Prism.**

Rainbow Bridge National Monument, in southern Utah, has one of the world's best-known natural bridges. This bridge is 290 feet (88 meters) high, and has a 275-foot (84-meter) span. There are two hiking trails to the bridge. The area was established as a national monument in 1910. See also **Utah** (Places to visit [picture]).

Rainbow for Girls is an international organization for girls from the ages of 11 through 19. Its official name is the Supreme Assembly, International Order of the Rainbow for Girls. An applicant must be (1) a daughter of a Master Mason from the fraternal society of Masons, (2) a daughter of a member of the Order of Eastern Star, an organization associated with the Masons, or (3) a girl recommended by a member of either of these orders. But an applicant need not be related to a Mason.

Rainbow for Girls encourages church membership, reverence for the Bible, patriotism, love of family, and service to the community. The local chapters, called *assemblies,* hold fund-raising events for charitable causes. They also sponsor recreational outings for their members, such as trips to amusement parks and theaters.

The organization was founded in McAlester, Oklahoma, in 1922 by an American clergyman and Mason named W. Mark Sexson. Today, Rainbow for Girls has about 100,000 active members throughout the world. The members are divided into approximately 3,000 assemblies.

The central governing board of the organization, called the Supreme Assembly, issues the bylaws for all Rainbow assemblies. Each assembly also has its own advisory board headed by a Mother Adviser. The organization's headquarters are in McAlester.

Critically reviewed by Rainbow for Girls

See also **Masonry.**

Rainier, Mount. See Mount Rainier.

Rainier III, *ray NEER* (1923-   ), became prince of Monaco in 1949. His full name is Rainier Louis Henri-Maxence Bertrand de Grimaldi. Rainier's marriage to actress Grace Kelly in 1956 aroused international interest. The birth of their daughter Princess Caroline the next year delighted Monaco. As long as the royal family continues, Monaco remains independent from France. The couple also had a son, Prince Albert, and a daughter, Princess Stephanie Marie Elisabeth. Rainier's wife died in 1982 following an automobile accident near Monaco. As prince, Rainier has provided low-cost housing, expanded schools, and tried to balance the budget of his government.   Janet L. Polasky

See also **Kelly, Grace; Monaco.**

Rainmaking, also called *cloud seeding,* is a process that makes rain fall from a cloud. People use the process chiefly to increase an area's general water supply or its supply of water for irrigation or for generation of electric power by hydroelectric plants. But they also use it to prevent heavy rainfall in areas where rain can damage crops. By seeding clouds before they reach such areas, experts can sometimes reduce the strength of a storm. Several United States scientists, working independently, developed rainmaking procedures during the 1940's.

Rainmaking methods. Rain occurs when the water vapor in a cloud forms ice crystals or water drops large and heavy enough to fall to the earth. In some cases, the chance of rain can be increased by adding substances called *seeding agents* to clouds. The seeding process works best in clouds from which rain is almost ready to fall. The substance used for seeding depends on the cloud's temperature.

At temperatures above 32 °F (0 °C), the chief seeding agent is a liquid composed of ammonium nitrate and urea. Particles of this substance cause water vapor to form raindrops around them. The seeding agent is sprayed from an airplane into the bottom of a cloud.

At temperatures below 32 °F, clouds may contain *supercooled water.* This form of water may remain unfrozen in temperatures as low as −40 °F (−40 °C). Supercooled water must form ice crystals in order to become heavy enough to fall to the earth. Ice crystals can be produced by using such seeding agents as dry ice or crystals of silver iodide. When the ice crystals form, they fall toward the earth as snowflakes. As the flakes enter a region that is warmer than 32 °F, they melt into rain.

Dry ice, which is frozen carbon dioxide, has a temperature as low as −112 °F (−80 °C). When dropped into a cloud from an airplane, pellets of dry ice reduce the temperature of supercooled water. The lower temperature makes the water form ice crystals. Silver iodide crystals resemble crystals of ice and cause supercooled water to form ice crystals around them. Devices called *flares* and *generators* are used to produce and distribute a vapor containing silver iodide crystals. The vapor is made by burning silver iodide with other substances. It is usually distributed from an airplane, though generators also may be used to distribute it from the ground.

Arguments about rainmaking. Cloud seeding has caused much debate because scientists have not been able to demonstrate its effectiveness in all cases. In addition, some people believe increased rainfall in certain areas might cause shortages of rain elsewhere. Many states of the United States have imposed regulations on rainmaking, and some states have even prohibited it.

Wayne M. Wendland

See also **Snow** (Artificial snow).

Rainy Lake lies on the boundary between Ontario and Minnesota, about 125 miles (201 kilometers) north of Duluth, Minnesota. For location, see **Minnesota** (physical map). It covers about 350 square miles (906 square kilometers) and is shaped roughly like a capital L. Each arm is about 40 miles (64 kilometers) long and from 3 to 8 miles (5 to 13 kilometers) wide. Thousands of islands lie scattered throughout the lake. The longest stretch of open water is only about 1 mile (1.6 kilometers) wide. The CN North America railroad crosses the lake almost at its center on bridges that link islands.

Stands of spruce and pine cover the rocky shores of Rainy Lake. Many of these trees are cut for paper mills at Fort Frances and International Falls, located at the west

Three methods of rainmaking

WORLD BOOK diagram

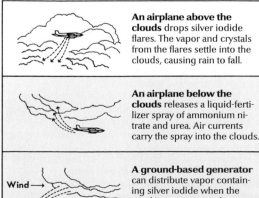

An airplane above the clouds drops silver iodide flares. The vapor and crystals from the flares settle into the clouds, causing rain to fall.

An airplane below the clouds releases a liquid-fertilizer spray of ammonium nitrate and urea. Air currents carry the spray into the clouds.

A ground-based generator can distribute vapor containing silver iodide when the wind is strong enough to carry the vapor into the clouds.

end. A dam at Fort Frances harnesses water for power. Pike, pickerel, and other kinds of fish are caught in Rainy Lake. Whitefish taken from the lake are sold commercially. Bear, moose, and other wild game roam around the lake. The Rainy River carries overflow waters westward to Lake of the Woods.   Thomas J. Baerwald

Raisa, *rah EE suh,* **Rosa** (1893-1963), a dramatic soprano, was especially popular for many years with audiences in Italy and Chicago. Born in Białystok, Poland, she fled from there at the age of 14. She went to Italy and studied singing at the Conservatory of Naples. She was trained by opera singer Eva Tetrazzini. Raisa made her European and American opera debuts in 1913.

    Martin Bernheimer

Raisin is a dried grape. The word *raisin* comes from a French term meaning *dry grape.* Varieties of white grapes that have tender skin, rich flavor, and high sugar content are especially suited for making raisins. Raisins are used in puddings, cakes, candies, cookies, and bread. They are also sold as sweets in small boxes.

Raisins have been a food delicacy since ancient times. The Egyptians first discovered that drying fruit preserved it, made it sweeter, and improved its flavor. The Bible mentions that an Israelite brought cheese and raisins to pay his taxes to King David. Wealthy Romans served raisins at feasts.

Spanish missionaries planted grapevines in California during the 1700's. Soon after the Civil War ended in 1865, former gold hunters discovered that the region of California now called the Central Valley had an ideal climate for producing raisins. The dry, hot summers allowed for grapes to ripen, and the low chance of rain after the harvest meant that the grapes could be sun-dried in the vineyard. Commercial raisin production began in California in the 1870's.

Today, California leads the world in raisin grape production. It is the only U.S. state that produces raisins commercially. California produces about 670 million pounds (300 million kilograms) annually. Other leading producers include Australia, Greece, Iran, and Turkey.

Varieties of raisins. Four main varieties of grapes are used in raisin production. The most common is the Thompson Seedless. Seedless grapes used to make raisins first came from Turkey. In 1872, William Thompson introduced seedless grape cuttings to California. Thompson Seedless today make up more than 95 per cent of the grapes used to make raisins in California. Other varieties include Muscat of Alexandria, Black Corinth, and Sultana. The Muscat is a large, seed-bearing grape brought to America by Spanish missionaries. Grapes from Black Corinth vines are used to make Zante currants—tiny, seedless raisins used mainly to flavor baked goods. Raisins made from Sultana grapes, which are seedless and have a distinctive flavor, are used mainly in baked goods.

Growing grapes. Almost all the raisins produced in California come from vines grown within 100 miles (160 kilometers) of Fresno. Grapevines start growing there in March, and the fruit is harvested about the first week of September. The vineyards must be irrigated because little rain falls in the area during the period when the vines grow. Vines used for raisins generally are planted in rows that run in an east-west direction. They must be spaced far enough apart to allow room for drying the

fruit and to permit cultivation. Grapevines begin bearing fruit in three years. With proper care, they may continue to produce fruit for 100 years. About $4\frac{1}{2}$ pounds (2 kilograms) of grapes produce 1 pound (0.5 kilogram) of raisins.

Preparation for market. Seedless grapes ripen on the vine until sugars account for more than 20 per cent of their weight. The grapes are then harvested by hand or machine and placed on trays of heavy, brown paper between the rows of vines. The fruit may be turned over after about eight days so that grapes on the bottom can dry faster. The east-west direction of the rows allows the sun to dry the grapes in 10 to 14 days. The raisins are then stored in large bins, called *sweat boxes,* to equalize their moisture content. Next, the fruit is sent to packing houses, where workers stem and grade the raisins by passing them over screens. Machines remove stem caps. A machine whirls the raisins through a fine spray of water to give them a final cleaning. The raisins are then pressed into sealed packages.

Raisins with seeds go through a slightly different process. Muscat raisins are larger and softer than the seedless types after drying. They are passed through the stem-removal machine and are washed in hot water to soften them further. They are then fed between rubber rollers that press the seeds to the surface. A saw-tooth roller catches the seeds between its teeth and removes them.

Sun-dried raisins are called *natural raisins.* Most raisins are natural. However, golden seedless or golden raisins, made from Thompson Seedless grapes, are dried in large machines. The grapes are first treated with sulfur dioxide to preserve their golden color.

Because of their high sugar content, raisins need no preservatives to keep them fresh. If raisins are kept cool and stored in a sealed container, they will retain their flavor, color, and nutritional value for up to 15 months. They may also be frozen.

Food value. Raisins are a good source of vitamin A, the B_1 vitamins thiamine and riboflavin; and such minerals as calcium, iron, and potassium. The sugars in raisins give quick energy because the body absorbs them immediately.   Larry E. Williams

See also **Grape.**

Raisin River Massacre. See War of 1812 (Chief battles of the war).

Rajah, *RAH juh,* is a title taken from the Sanskrit word *rajan,* which means *king.* Ruling princes of native states in India were once the only persons known as rajahs. But under the British Empire the title of rajah was also given to certain other high-ranking Hindus. Native princes who kept some authority under British rule were called *maharajah* (great king).

Rake is a machine used to gather mowed hay and place it in long piles called *windrows.* The windrows are then gathered by a hay loader or baler. The first rakes were wooden hand rakes. People still use hand rakes to rake leaves from lawns. Modern rakes are usually pulled by, or mounted on, a tractor. Rakes can also be used to gather straw, green forage, and seed crops.

The dump rake consists of curved steel teeth mounted on an axle between two wheels. The teeth slide over the ground and rake hay as the machine moves forward. The operator dumps the hay in a wind-

Case IH

A dual rake consists of two rakes hitched to a tractor. As the dual rake is pulled along by the tractor, it gathers mowed hay and deposits it into long rows called *windrows*.

row by pulling a lever that causes the teeth to lift from the ground.

The side-delivery rake leaves the hay in a continuous windrow at the side of the vehicle carrying the rake. In one type of side-delivery rake, the teeth are attached to cylinders that roll along at an angle to the direction traveled. The teeth just clear the ground as the cylinder rotates. As the machine moves ahead, the teeth brush the hay to the side, leaving it in a windrow. A *dual rake* consists of two side-delivery rakes, which deposit two windrows together at one time.

The *finger-wheel rake* consists of several wheels with spikes on the rim. The wheels are set at an angle to the direction traveled, and move the hay sideways to form a windrow. The *drag-type rake* has no moving parts. It has curved fingers that move the hay to one side, much as a snowplow moves snow.   Gerald E. Rehkugler

Raleigh, *RAW lee* or *RAH lee* (pop. 207,951), is the capital of North Carolina and an educational, research, and trade center of the state. It lies in east-central North Carolina, where the hilly Piedmont region meets the flat coastal plain. For location, see **North Carolina** (political map). Raleigh, Durham, and Chapel Hill form a metropolitan area with a population of 855,545.

Raleigh's major industries include the manufacture of electronic products, electrical machinery and equipment, and food products. Research Triangle Park, a complex of scientific laboratories, is near the city. More than 60 corporations and agencies of the federal government operate research facilities in the complex.

Cultural attractions in Raleigh include the North Carolina Museum of Art and the North Carolina Symphony Orchestra. The city is the home of Meredith College, North Carolina State University, Peace College, St. Augustine's College, and Shaw University. The Andrew Johnson House, the birthplace of the 17th President of the United States, also is in Raleigh.

Tuscarora Indians lived in what is now the Raleigh area before white settlers arrived there. The state legislature founded Raleigh in 1792 after choosing the site for the state capital. The city was named for Sir Walter Raleigh, a famous English soldier and explorer.

Raleigh's chief growth occurred after World War II ended in 1945, especially following the opening of Research Triangle Park in 1959. A new Civic Center, which includes a convention center, opened in downtown Raleigh in 1977. That same year, the city completed a project in which part of its main street was converted into a shopping mall. The mall, which is called the Fayetteville Street Mall, connects the Civic Center with the Capitol. Raleigh is the county seat of Wake County. The city has a council-manager form of government.   Ted Vaden

See also **North Carolina** (Climate; pictures).

Raleigh, *RAW lee* or *RAH lee,* **Sir Walter** (1552?-1618), is one of the most colorful figures in English history. He was a soldier, explorer, writer, and businessman. He spelled his last name *Ralegh.*

Raleigh was born at Hayes Barton, a family home in Devonshire, and attended Oxford University. He left school before graduating to join a band of gentlemen volunteers who were helping the Huguenots in France (see **Huguenots**). In 1578, he returned to England and joined his half brother, Sir Humphrey Gilbert, on a voyage of discovery and piracy.

Raleigh and Elizabeth I. In 1580, Raleigh became a captain in the army in Ireland. There he distinguished himself by his ruthlessness at the siege of Smerwick. The next year, he went to Queen Elizabeth's court with dispatches (see **Elizabeth I**). There is a famous story about his meeting with Elizabeth. The queen was out walking, and stopped before a large mud puddle. Raleigh removed his coat and placed it over the puddle for her to walk on. It is doubtful that this story is true. But Raleigh did become the queen's favorite. She granted him an estate of 12,000 acres (4,860 hectares) in Ireland. She also gave him trade privileges and the right to colonize in America. In 1585, she made him a knight.

His expeditions. Raleigh became deeply interested in exploration, like many prominent English people of his day. He sent several expeditions to America, and spent a fortune trying to establish an English colony there. His settlers landed in what is now the state of North Carolina and explored the coast as far as present-day Florida. Raleigh and Elizabeth, who was known as "The Virgin Queen," named much of what is now the Eastern United States *Virginia,* in honor of the queen.

Raleigh's first colonizing expedition left Plymouth in April 1585. It established a colony on Roanoke Island in Pamlico Sound. But sickness and fear caused the survivors of this first English colony in North America to go home with Sir Francis Drake in 1586.

In 1587, Raleigh sent a second expedition. A group of 117 colonists, including 17 women, landed on Roanoke Island. On Aug. 18, 1587, the first English child was born in North America (see **Dare, Virginia**). John White, the governor, went back to England for supplies. He was delayed by war with Spain, and when he returned to Roanoke in 1590, the settlers had mysteriously disappeared (see **Lost Colony**).

Raleigh also took part in the victory over the Spanish Armada in 1588. He led other expeditions against Spanish possessions and returned with much booty. During the 1590's, his power reached its height, and he had

Oil painting on canvas (1588) by an unknown artist
(Granger Collection)

Sir Walter Raleigh tried to establish an English colony in North America. He failed, but his efforts aided later colonists.

much influence and many enemies. Raleigh, who was also a poet, obtained a pension for the English poet Edmund Spenser and helped Spenser publish *The Faerie Queene* (see **Spenser, Edmund**). Raleigh also helped introduce the potato plant and tobacco use to Ireland.

His fall. Raleigh lost the queen's favor by marrying one of her attendants. Hoping to recover his position and the money he had spent, he led an expedition to Guiana, in South America, to search for El Dorado, a legendary land of gold. However, the expedition failed.

Elizabeth died in 1603, and the new king, James I, distrusted and feared Raleigh. He charged Raleigh with treason and imprisoned him in the Tower of London. There Raleigh lived comfortably for 12 years with his family and servants, and wrote his *History of the World.* He was released in 1616 to lead an expedition to search for gold in South America. The king ordered him not to invade Spanish territory. But Raleigh's men attacked the Spaniards. Raleigh's son Wat was killed in the attack, and Raleigh was forced to abandon the project.

Upon his return to England, he was sentenced to death for disobeying orders. Raleigh met his fate bravely. He joked with the executioner and even gave the signal for the ax to fall.   Stephen Greenblatt

Additional resources

Lacey, Robert. *Sir Walter Ralegh.* Atheneum, 1973.
May, Steven W. *Sir Walter Ralegh.* Twayne, 1989.

Ram. See **Sheep** (The body of the sheep); **Aries; Battering ram**.

Rama is a popular god in Hinduism. He is the seventh *avatar* (physical form) of the god Vishnu. Rama is usually shown as a king carrying a bow and arrow.

Rama's story is told in many books. A complete version of the story appears in the epic the *Ramayana.* Rama was the oldest of four sons of the king of Ayodhya, and the heir to the throne. One of his father's wives wanted her son Bharata, Rama's half brother, to rule instead. She made the king exile Rama to a forest for 14 years. Rama was accompanied by his wife, Sita, and brother Lakshmana.

While in the forest, Sita was abducted by the 10-headed demon Ravana. The demon took Rama's wife to his island kingdom of Lanka (now Sri Lanka). Rama defeated Ravana in a war and rescued Sita with the aid of troops led by the monkey god Hanuman.

After 14 years of exile, Rama returned to Ayodhya and assumed the throne. He ruled as a righteous king over a land known for peace and prosperity. Today, Ayodhya in northern India is a popular pilgrimage site, with many temples dedicated to Rama.   David L. Haberman

See also **Ramayana; Vishnu.**

Ramadan, *ram uh DHAN,* is an Islamic holy month when Muslims may not eat or drink from morning until night. Ramadan is the ninth month of the Islamic year. Because the Islamic calendar is lunar, Ramadan falls at different times of the year. Muslims celebrate Ramadan as the month during which the prophet Muhammad received the first of the revelations that make up the Quran, the holy book of Islam.

Fasting during Ramadan is the fourth of the five Pillars of Faith, the chief religious duties of a Muslim (see **Islam** [The Five Pillars of Islam]). All Muslims must fast if they have reached puberty and are of sound mind. Exceptions are made for some groups, such as the sick, the elderly, pregnant women, and travelers. Those who are able, however, must make up the missed fast days at a later time. A Muslim who deliberately breaks the fast must atone by fasting for two continuous months or feeding the poor.

Fasting begins at dawn and lasts until sunset. During this time, Muslims cannot take food or drink, inhale tobacco smoke or perfume, or engage in sexual activity. Believers may not even swallow their own saliva. The daily fast is broken by a light meal called the *iftar,* followed by the evening prayer. The preferred food for the iftar is dates and water.

Ramadan is also a time for other religious activities. The nights are often devoted to special prayers and to recitations from the Quran. During the last 10 days, some Muslims seclude themselves in a mosque to give full time to religious contemplation. The end of Ramadan is celebrated by a great festival.   Charles J. Adams

Raman, *RAH muhn,* **Sir Chandrasekhara Venkata,** *CHUHN druh SHAY kuhr uh VEHNG kuh tuh* (1888-1970), an Indian physicist, discovered that when a beam of light passes through a liquid or a gas, it is scattered and the frequency of some of the scattered light is changed. This change, which is called the *Raman effect,* provides a way for studying the structure of the scattering molecules. For his discovery, Raman was knighted in 1929 and received the 1930 Nobel Prize for physics.

Raman was born in Trichinopoly (now Tiruchchirappalli). He founded the *Indian Journal of Physics* and the Indian Academy of Sciences. After 1930, he mainly studied the structure of crystals.   Robert H. March

Ramayana, *rah MAH yuh nuh,* is one of the two great epic poems of India. The other is the *Mahabharata.* Rama, the hero of the *Ramayana,* is a human form of the god Vishnu. In the *Ramayana,* he is the son and heir of an Indian king. Rama serves as a model for Hindu men. He is handsome and brave and a devoted husband. Sita, his beautiful wife, represents the Hindu ideal of devotion to duty and husband.

In the story, Rama lives in the kingdom of Ayodhya in northern India. His father exiles him for 14 years because of a dispute over the throne. The main plot concerns the conflict between Rama and Ravana, a demonking. Ravana kidnaps Sita and takes her to his kingdom on the island of Lanka, now known as Sri Lanka. Rama rescues his wife and kills Ravana with an arrow. At the end of Rama's exile, Rama and Sita return home in triumph and Rama becomes king.

The poet Valmiki supposedly wrote the first version of the *Ramayana* in Sanskrit about 500 B.C. or earlier. It has 24,000 couplets. Translated or rewritten versions appear in other Indian languages. The Hindi version, written by the poet Tulsidas (also spelled Tulsi Das) in the late 1500's, became the most popular. The *Ramayana* remains popular today because of its characters, who set high standards for human behavior and inspire devotion to God. Readers also enjoy the beautiful language and exciting plot of the *Ramayana.*   Charles S. J. White

See also **Mahabharata; Rama; Vishnu.**

Rameau, *ra MOH,* **Jean-Philippe,** *zhahn fee LEEP* (1683-1764), was a French composer and musical theorist of the baroque period. Rameau worked as an organist for about 20 years in several cities before settling in Paris in about 1722. He became famous that year with the publication of a book of music theory called *Treatise on Harmony.* The book became a landmark in the history of harmony and was the first of several works he wrote on harmony.

At the age of 50, Rameau began a new career as an opera composer. He wrote more than 25 operas and opera-ballets, beginning with the opera *Hippolyte and Aricie* (1733). His major opera-ballets included *Les Indes galantes* (1735) and *Les Fêtes d'Hébé* (1739). His operas include *Castor and Pollux* (1737) and *Dardanus* (1739, 1744). Rameau's operas were controversial because of their unconventional use of orchestral color, vivid harmonies, and speechlike singing called recitative. Rameau engaged in a quarrel with the philosopher Jean-Jacques Rousseau, largely over the preferred style of opera. Rameau favored the French style, and Rousseau supported opera in the Italian fashion.

Rameau was born in Dijon. In addition to his theoretical writings and compositions for the stage, he wrote many suites for an early keyboard instrument called the harpsichord. In 1745, Rameau was appointed chamber music composer to King Louis XV.   Joscelyn Godwin

See also **Opera** (French opera).

Rameses II. See **Ramses II.**

Ramie, *RAM ee,* is a perennial plant grown chiefly for its fiber. It is native to Asia and is grown chiefly in India, China, and Taiwan. Ramie is one of the oldest known sources of fiber. There are over 30 known varieties of ramie. The most common kinds come from China and Japan. The thick, broad leaves of the ramie plant are dark green on top, and white and woolly underneath. Grow-ers plant pieces of the roots, which grow into plants in about three months. The stalks grow from 3 to 7 feet (0.9 to 2 meters) high.

In Asia, workers strip the tough ramie fiber from the stalks by hand. The fiber at this stage is often called *China grass.* Then it is washed and dried several times to remove the gums, pectins, and waxes. In the United States, ramie is grown mainly in Florida. Machines harvest it and strip it of its bark and core. Chemicals remove gummy material and impurities from the fiber.

Ramie's strength increases greatly when it is wet, so it is suitable for life rafts, ropes, canvas, and nets. Other uses include surgical dressings, towels, air-conditioning filters, and fabrics. However, synthetic fibers have largely replaced ramie fibers in these products, especially in industrialized nations. Farmers in Central America have used ramie as a high-protein fodder for pigs.

Robert A. Barnhardt

Scientific classification. Ramie is in the nettle family, Urticaceae. It is classified as *Boehmeria nivea.*

See also **Boehmeria.**

Ramjet. See **Jet propulsion** (Ramjet).

Ramp, or *wild leek,* is a wild onion that grows in moist woodland areas in the eastern United States. The flat leaves grow from the ground in spring and disappear by summer. Then a leafless flowering stem appears, bearing several greenish-white flowers at its tip. The plant smells and tastes like onions. Some people believe that the Indian word *checagou,* from which the city of Chicago got its name, refers to the smell of the ramp.

Hugh C. Price

Scientific classification. Botanists consider the ramp a member of either the amaryllis family, Amaryllidaceae, or the lily family, Liliaceae. The plant's scientific name is *Allium tricoccum.*

See also **Onion; Leek.**

Rampolla, *rahm POHL lah,* **Mariano Cardinal,** *mah RYAH noh* (1843-1913), Marchese del Tindaro, became a cardinal of the Roman Catholic Church and papal secretary of state in 1887. He shared responsibility for Pope Leo XIII's policy of reconciling French Catholics to their country's republican form of government. His efforts displeased not only the French monarchists, but also Emperor Francis Joseph of Austria-Hungary. The emperor took extraordinary action in 1903, when the College of Cardinals met to elect a new pope. He registered a veto of Cardinal Rampolla. The exact effect of the emperor's veto cannot be known, because popes are elected by secret vote. However, it seems likely that the veto prevented the choice of Rampolla, whose ability was well known.

Rampolla was born at Polizzi, Italy. He was ordained a priest in 1866. During his education at the Vatican seminary, he showed such ability, particularly in Asian languages, that he was chosen for a career in Vatican diplomatic service.   Marvin R. O'Connell

Ramsay, *RAM zee,* **Sir William** (1852-1916), was a Scottish chemist who, with English physicist Lord Rayleigh, isolated the rare atmospheric gas argon. Ramsay also discovered helium, neon, krypton, and xenon gases. The five gases are called *noble gases* because they do not readily react with other elements. For this work, Ramsay received the 1904 Nobel Prize for chemistry. His explanation of the nature of these elements led to important ideas about atomic structure. Each of these elements has a separate article in *World Book*.

Ramsay was born in Glasgow. He taught at Glasgow and Bristol, and at University College in London. He was knighted in 1902, and in 1911, he became president of the British Association for the Advancement of Science.

Bruce R. Wheaton

See also **Element, Chemical**.

Ramses II, *RAM seez,* was a famous Egyptian *pharaoh* (king) who reigned from about 1290 to 1224 B.C. Ramses came to the throne at an early age. He served as *core-gent* (co-ruler) with his father, Seti I, for a short time before he began his own long reign.

During the early part of his reign, Ramses tried to end Hittite control of Syria. About 1285 B.C. he fought an indecisive battle against the Hittites at Kadesh and claimed a great victory. But about 1269 B.C., Ramses made a treaty with the Hittite king that divided Syria between them (see **Hittites**).

During the rest of his long reign, Ramses devoted his energies to a vast building program. He built a new capital in the Nile Delta. He completed the *hypostyle* (col-

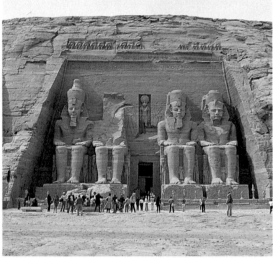

© Robert Azzi, Woodfin Camp, Inc.

Statues of Ramses II guarded the Abu Simbel temple near the Nile for more than 3,000 years. Construction of the Aswan High Dam made it necessary to move the temple to higher ground.

umned) Great Hall of the Temple of Amon-Re at Karnak. He also built the mighty rock temples at Abu Simbel, and other temples in nearly every major Egyptian city. He also took credit for many buildings of his ancestors.

Ramses was probably the pharaoh spoken of in the Biblical book of Exodus. His mummy is preserved in the Egyptian Museum in Cairo.   Leonard H. Lesko

See also **Cleopatra's Needles; Abu Simbel, Temples of**.

Ramsey, Alexander. See **Minnesota** (Territorial days; table: The governors of Minnesota).

Rancheria. See **Indian reservation**.

Ranching usually means raising cattle and sheep on large farms. Some fruit farms and farms that raise such small fur animals as mink are also called *ranches*. So are

many places of 5 to 10 acres (2 to 4 hectares) in California. But this article deals with cattle and sheep ranching. For information on *dude ranches,* the resorts where tourists get an idea of what life in the Old West was like, see **Dude ranch**.

Cattle and sheep ranches are very large because it generally takes many acres of grassland to feed a herd. An average ranch in the Western United States covers nearly 3,350 acres (1,356 hectares).

Most American ranches are found in the western United States and Canada. There are some in the Southeastern States along the Gulf of Mexico. Australia, Argentina, Mexico, New Zealand, and African countries also have large ranches. But Australians and New Zealanders call them *stations.*

Most early U.S. ranchers raised cattle on unfenced land called *open range.* Workers called *cowboys* or *cowhands* rode herd on the cattle. Today, ranchers generally own much of the land in their ranch, and they and members of their family do most of the work. Neighbors help each other when extra help is needed on the ranch. Only the largest ranches employ cowhands.

Life on a cattle ranch centers on raising calves that can be sold as *stocker cattle* or as *feeder cattle.* After the animals are fattened, they are called *slaughter cattle.* The fattened stock are shipped to a *stockyard* (market), where they are sold and slaughtered for meat. The rancher usually keeps some of the *heifer* (female) calves to replace older cows.

Ranchers start their year in the fall after selling their calves. They prepare for winter by buying or harvesting a hay crop and such feed grains as barley, corn, oats, or sorghum. When snow covers the ground in the winter, the cattle cannot find food by themselves. Ranchers then carry feed to their cattle in trucks or helicopters, spreading it on the ground for them to eat.

Many of the cows give birth to calves in early spring, and the rancher must watch them closely then. If a calf gets ill, the rancher may move it and its mother in from the fields to the ranch headquarters to treat the calf.

A month or two later, when the calves are active and strong, neighbors help the rancher round up the cattle and herd them into a small fenced area called a *corral.* There the calves are *branded* (marked) with a hot iron to show who owns them. They may also be ear tagged at this time. They are given medicine to prevent diseases. Male calves may be *castrated* (have their sex glands removed). During the rest of the spring and summer, the herd *grazes* (eats grass) on the range.

The cattle follow a daily routine on the range. They graze very early in the morning, eating rapidly. They chew their food only enough to moisten it and then swallow it. In the middle of the day, the cattle rest in a shady place. The food is returned to their mouths in the form of a *cud,* and they chew it again to aid in its digestion. In late afternoon, most cattle go to the watering hole or stock tank to drink. They then graze until dusk.

During the day, ranchers mend fences, repair machinery, and make sure watering holes store enough water. They also put out blocks of salt mixed with other minerals that the cows can lick, because cattle need such minerals in their diet. In the fall, neighbors help each other round up cattle. Then the calves that are old enough to be *weaned* (taken from their mothers) are sold.

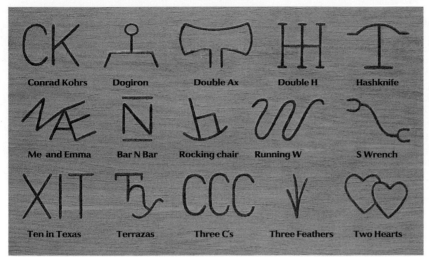

Conrad Kohrs	Dogiron	Double Ax	Double H	Hashknife
Me and Emma	Bar N Bar	Rocking chair	Running W	S Wrench
Ten in Texas	Terrazas	Three C's	Three Feathers	Two Hearts

Famous ranch brands of the Old West. Branding cattle was very important in the 1800's, when cattle roamed on *open* (unfenced) range. The brand on each animal showed who owned it. Branding also made it difficult for *rustlers* (thieves) to steal cattle and sell them as their own.

WORLD BOOK illustration by Walter Maslon

Ranch life once was lonely. But the automobile, truck, and good roads have brought the rancher closer to other people. Most ranch children ride school buses to school in nearby towns. Ranch families now live in comfortable homes that have electric power, plumbing, a telephone, and other modern conveniences.

Life on a sheep ranch is different from life on a cattle ranch because sheep produce two crops—lambs and wool. In the spring, crews of workers use power clippers to *shear* (cut off) the sheep's wool, and the rancher sells it. Lambs are usually born in spring. They and the freshly sheared *ewes* (mother sheep) are then branded with paint or are ear tagged. In the fall, most of the lambs are weaned, shipped to feeders or stockyards, and sold for slaughter.

History. Ranching in the United States began in the mid-1800's. Ranchers raised cattle on the open range, and hired cowhands to help guard and herd the cattle.

When the cattle were almost ready for slaughter, the ranchers formed big herds and drove them overland to the nearest railroad, in Kansas. A single herd had several thousand cattle and moved from 10 to 15 miles (16 to 24 kilometers) each day. In Kansas, the cattle were sold to buyers who shipped the cattle to the East.

During the 1870's and early 1880's, large ranches developed in the West. One, the XIT ranch in northern Texas, was 200 miles (320 kilometers) long, 25 miles (40 kilometers) wide, and had 150,000 cattle. Many cowhands worked on these big ranches, and they lived in buildings called *bunkhouses.* But in the mid-1880's, bad weather killed thousands of cattle, and ruined many ranchers. Many big ranches were sold and divided.

Range wars. Some of the best land was *homesteaded.* That is, people moved onto federal land under the

Werner Stoy, Camera Hawaii; Ernst Peterson, Publix

Life on cattle ranches has changed greatly since they were founded in the 1800's in the American Southwest. Ranchers still use cow ponies occasionally to rope calves and do other work. But now some also use helicopters to check on herds in a ranch's distant areas.

terms of the Homestead Act, which gave a person up to 160 acres (65 hectares) of land if the individual promised to live on it and farm it. Homesteaders built fences to protect their crops from cattle. Sheep ranching also began to develop. Sheep ranchers moved sheep from one range to another, and the sheep occasionally grazed on ranges that cattle used. Soon, cattle ranchers, homesteaders, and sheep ranchers began to fight for the land and watering holes. Many of these disputes developed into bloody *range wars.* Unlimited use of the open range ended in 1934. Since then, ranchers have needed permits to graze herds on federal land.

Since the 1940's. Land prices increased in the 1940's, so ranchers had to develop new ways to make their land more productive. They developed more watering holes, cleared brush, planted better grasses for their cattle and sheep to eat, and rotated their animals from one grazing area to another to allow the grass to grow back. Ranchers also began to use new methods of handling livestock with less help. Horses are still necessary, but ranchers now also use jeeps, trucks, and even helicopters to get the most production. Doreen H. D. Swakon

Related articles in *World Book* include:

Australia (Agriculture)	King Ranch
Cattle	Sheep
Chuck wagon	Western frontier life in America (Life in the country)
Cowboy	

Additional resources

Ewing, Sherm. *The Ranch.* Mountain Pr. Pub. Co., 1995. *The Range.* 1990.

Marrin, Albert. *Cowboys, Indians, and Gunfighters: The Story of the Cattle Kingdom.* Atheneum, 1993.

Witney, Dudley. *Ranch.* Doubleday, 1983.

Rand, Ayn, *eyen* (1905-1982), was an American author and social critic. Her books serve mainly as a means of expressing her philosophies. Literary critics tend to see them as marred by a tendency to instruct the reader.

Rand's best-known novels are *The Fountainhead* (1943) and *Atlas Shrugged* (1957). Both present a moral and economic philosophy, called Objectivism, based on individualism and self-interest. These novels express the belief that original ideas are the main force in the world and that creative individuals deserve to profit from their ideas. The heroes represent disciplined, rational people of action who reject organized religion. In *The Fountainhead,* an architect destroys a housing project in which his ideas had been altered. In *Atlas Shrugged,* one of the central characters calls a *mind strike,* during which all creative people withhold their ideas from the rest of the world. The strike reveals that society cannot exist without creative genius.

Rand was born in St. Petersburg, Russia. She moved to the United States in 1926 and became a U.S. citizen in 1931. Her novels *We the Living* (1936) and *Anthem* (1938) reflect her early life in Russia. Both novels express her revolt against socialist forms of government. Rand also wrote

NYT Pictures

Ayn Rand

about her philosophies in such works of nonfiction as *For the New Intellectual* (1961), *The Virtue of Selfishness* (1964), and *Capitalism, the Unknown Ideal* (1966).

Arthur M. Saltzman

Rand Corporation is a nonprofit research organization that studies policy problems of the United States, especially those involving national defense. The United States Air Force began Project RAND (*Research ANd Development*) in 1946 to conduct long-range studies of intercontinental warfare by forces other than armies. RAND became an independent corporation in 1948, but the Department of Defense still finances most of its work.

The Rand Corporation investigates such subjects as the military and economic strength of Russia and China, and the air defenses of the United States. It also studies international terrorism, nuclear arms control, defense resource management, weapon design, uses of earth satellites, and military and political conditions throughout the world. Since 1967, the corporation has increased its research on such nonmilitary problems as city transportation, criminal justice, educational management, health care delivery, water supplies, and housing.

Most of the Rand Corporation's reports on military matters are secret and are given directly to the Air Force or the Department of Defense. The corporation also operates an Army research center and a graduate program that grants doctor's degrees in policy analysis. Its headquarters are in Santa Monica, California, but it also maintains a branch in Washington, D.C.

Allan R. Millett

Randolph, A. Philip (1889-1979), played a leading role in the struggle for black rights from the 1920's through the 1960's. He also became an important figure in the American labor movement. In 1925, Randolph founded the Brotherhood of Sleeping Car Porters (now part of the Brotherhood of Railway and Airline Clerks), a union he headed until 1968. He became a vice president of the American Federation of Labor and Congress of Industrial Organizations (AFL-CIO) in 1957.

Asa Philip Randolph was born in Crescent City, Florida, but moved to New York City as a young man. He held odd jobs during the day and attended City College of New York at night. A Socialist during World War

Wide World

A. Philip Randolph

I, Randolph later believed unions offered African Americans the best hope for a fair wage. A group of Pullman car porters asked him to organize and lead a union for them. In 1941, Randolph threatened a march on Washington, D.C., to demand jobs for blacks in defense industries. The threat was one reason why President Franklin D. Roosevelt set up the Fair Employment Practices Committee. Randolph won the Spingarn Medal in 1942. He helped organize the march in Washington, D.C., in 1963 to protest injustice to blacks.

Richard Bardolph

Randolph, Edmund (1753-1813), a Virginia states-man, presented the famous *Virginia Plan* to the Constitu-tional Convention in 1787. The plan favored the large states by calling for representation in Congress based on population or the tax contribution made by each state. Randolph refused to sign the Constitution because he thought it would create dangerously powerful presi-dents. Nevertheless, he supported its adoption at Vir-ginia's ratifying convention.

In 1789, President George Washington appointed Randolph the nation's first attorney general and, in 1794, named him secretary of state. However, Randolph re-signed as secretary of state in 1795 after he was unjustly accused of trying to sell diplomatic secrets to France.

Randolph was born near Williamsburg, Virginia, and was educated at the College of William and Mary. Dur-ing the Revolutionary War in America (1775-1783), he served as then General George Washington's *aide-de-camp* (assistant). Randolph became attorney general of Virginia in 1776 and later served as a member of the Continental Congress and as governor of Virginia. Ran-dolph also was one of Aaron Burr's attorneys when Burr was tried for treason in 1807 (see **Burr, Aaron** [Tried for treason]).   Robert A. Becker

Randolph, Edward (1632?-1703), was a British agent in colonial New England. In 1676, he carried royal in-structions for the colonial governments to Boston. Curtly treated there, he returned to England and wrote two strongly critical reports. As a result, the British separated New Hampshire from Massachusetts.

Randolph took charge of customs for New England in 1679, and he started the new royal government of New Hampshire the next year. When Massachusetts resisted his authority, he had its charter annulled in 1684. In 1686, Massachusetts and New Hampshire became part of the newly formed Dominion of New England. Randolph served the royal governor of the dominion, Sir Edmund Andros, until 1689, when both were jailed during a re-bellion in Boston. Randolph became surveyor general of customs for Britain in North America in 1691. He was born in Canterbury, England.   John W. Ifkovic

Randolph, John (1773-1833), was a Virginia politician noted more for his colorful personality than for his achievements. He had a cruel, biting tongue, and was one of the most feared orators of his time. He is also known as John Randolph of Roanoke.

Randolph served a number of terms in the United States House of Representatives, where he became a champion of lost causes and opposed many popular measures. He led the Democratic-Republican Party in the House and supported President Thomas Jefferson's purchase of the Louisiana Territory in 1803. But later, he broke with the president over the intended purchase of Florida. Thereafter, Randolph was almost always in the opposition. He upheld states' rights against expanding federal powers. He opposed the War of 1812 and tariffs on imports. He led Southern opposition to the Missouri Compromise in 1820 and became a bitter enemy of Hen-ry Clay, one of its chief supporters.

Randolph was born in Prince George County, Virginia. He served in the U.S. House of Representatives from 1799 to 1813, 1815 to 1817, 1819 to 1825, and 1827 to 1829. He was a member of the U.S. Senate from 1825 to 1827.   James C. Curtis

Randolph, Peyton (1721?-1775), was an Amer-ican lawyer who served as president of both the First and the Second Continen-tal Congresses in 1774 and 1775. Those two meetings of colonial lead-ers at first sought fair treatment from Britain for the American Colonies but eventually declared independence. Randolph himself held moderate political views. He per-suaded extreme patriots and those with more cautious views to work together.

Culver
Peyton Randolph

Randolph was born in Williamsburg into one of Vir-ginia's most respected families. He graduated from the College of William and Mary and then studied law at the Inns of Court in London. In 1748, Randolph became at-torney general of Virginia. That year, he won election to the House of Burgesses, Virginia's legislature. In 1766, he became speaker of the House.

The British governor of Virginia dissolved the House of Burgesses in 1774. Its members then met in a series of revolutionary conventions. Randolph was elected to preside over the conventions in 1774 and 1775. He head-ed Virginia's delegates to the First and Second Conti-nental Congresses. He was elected as the first president of both meetings. He died in October 1775, five months after the Second Continental Congress began.

James Kirby Martin

See also **Continental Congress.**

Range is an appliance that provides heat for cooking. A range has a cooktop with several heating areas, and one or two ovens. Ranges are sometimes called *stoves.* At one time, stoves were widely used to provide heat for warming rooms. Today, heating stoves are again be-coming popular in the United States and Canada.

There are two chief kinds of ranges: (1) electric ranges and (2) gas ranges. For information about microwave ovens, see the article on **Microwave oven.**

Electric ranges have *heating units,* in which an elec-tric current generates heat. Most electric ranges have four circular heating units on the cooktop and one or two rectangular units in each oven. In some ranges, the heating units are placed under a smooth ceramic cook-ing surface.

Most heating units have an outer surface that consists of a metal tube in two parts. Each part has a spiral shape and encloses a coil of wire. Electric current passes through the coil and heats the coil and the metal tube. An insulating material prevents electric current in the coil from reaching the surface of the tube.

The amount of heat produced by a heating unit can be regulated easily. Some cooktop units have controls that regulate which one of two possible voltages of elec-tric current is supplied to the coil. The coil becomes hot-ter at the higher voltage. Controls may also regulate whether both of the coils heat up or whether only one heats up. Another kind of cooktop unit control turns the current on and off at intervals that vary with the heat de-sired. The longer the current flows through the unit, the

WORLD BOOK photo by Dan Miller

Amana Refrigeration, Inc.

Ranges cook with gas or electric power. The gas range in which the woman is baking cookies has burners on the cooktop and in the oven beneath it. The electric range shown here has four heating units covered by a smooth ceramic cooking surface.

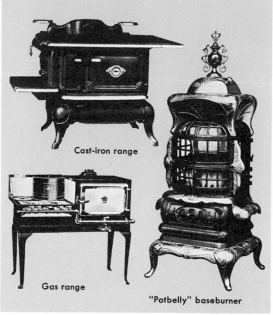

Chambers Corporation; Crown Stove Works

Stoves of the past. A cast-iron range of the late 1800's burned coal, coke, or wood. A 1925 gas range had an oven next to the cooktop. A "potbelly" baseburner of the late 1800's burned hard coal to heat a room.

The Franklin Institute

The Franklin stove was built from plans that the American statesman and inventor Benjamin Franklin drew in 1744.

higher the heat. Most oven units are regulated by thermostats, and some cooktop units also have thermostatic controls (see **Thermostat**).

Gas ranges have *burners* on the cooktop and in each oven. A burner mixes air with natural gas, synthetic natural gas, or *LP-gas* (liquefied petroleum gas). The resulting mixture flows through small holes in the burner. The mixture is ignited by a spark produced by a built-in electric device or a *pilot light* near the burner. A pilot light is a small flame that burns continuously.

The heat that is produced by a burner depends mainly on the amount of gas flowing to the burner. A valve regulates the gas flow to each burner. Hand-operated valves control most cooktop burners. Thermostats operate the valves of most oven burners and some cooktop burners.

History. People in northern China used earthenware stoves for heating as early as the 700's. Europeans began to use such stoves in the 1400's.

The first stoves produced in the American Colonies were made in Lynn, Massachusetts, in 1642. They were little more than cast-iron boxes with lids. The American statesman and inventor Benjamin Franklin developed the Franklin stove in the early 1740's. This stove, a cast-iron enclosure, fitted into a fireplace. It extended into the room so that three sides gave off heat. The first practical cooking stove was designed in the 1790's by Ben-

jamin Thompson, Count Rumford, a British statesman and inventor. This stove, a boxlike brick structure, had holes in the top to hold pots.

Until the early 1800's, most people in Canada and the United States used fireplaces for cooking and heating. During the 1830's, advances in ironmaking and transportation made cast iron widely available. As a result, iron cookstoves and heating stoves became popular. Most of these early stoves burned wood. The first practical coal stove, called a *baseburner*, was patented in 1833 by Jordan L. Mott, an American inventor. It had ventilation so it could burn coal efficiently. In 1855, Robert W. Bunsen, a German chemist, invented the first practical gas burner. In the 1860's, ranges based on Bunsen's burner became popular in cities that had gas piped into homes for use in gaslights. People who lived in rural areas began to use gas ranges after 1910, when gas became available in pressurized containers.

Electric ranges were first sold in 1909. The early models of electric ranges cooked extremely slowly, and few people purchased them. After the modern cooking unit was developed in 1930, electric ranges gained in popularity.

Microwave ovens were introduced in the mid-1950's. Microwave ovens heat food by using radio waves that penetrate the food and vibrate its molecules. Friction among the moving molecules produces heat, which cooks the food. In the early 1980's, sales of *convection,* or *hot-air, ovens* increased. Such ovens, which may be either electric or gas, have blowers that circulate hot air around the food. The ovens cook faster, more evenly, and at a lower temperature than regular ovens.

Evan Powell

Range finder is a device for measuring distances. The military uses range finders to determine the distance to a target.

The basis of a military range finder is a long tube with eyepieces at the center and an arrangement of lenses and prisms at each end. By adjusting the prisms, the operator can sight the target simultaneously from both ends of the tube. The difference in direction of the two lines of sight is called the *parallactic angle.* This angle will be large at short distances, and small at long distances. The parallactic angle is measured on a dial from which the range in yards can be read directly.

There are two principal types of range finders. The operator of a *coincidence* instrument looks through a single eyepiece and sees two distinct images of the target. By turning a knob, the operator can make these two images merge. When this happens, the distance can be read on the range dial. The operator of a *stereoscopic* instrument looks through a pair of eyepieces like binoculars and sees a single image of the target. The instrument's operator also sees a marker that appears to be floating in space near the target. The operator moves a knob until the marker and the target appear to be at the same distance. Then the distance is read on the range dial.

Since World War I (1914-1918), range finders have been used in naval gunnery as a part of *director systems* that aim the guns automatically. During World War II (1939-1945), some armies adopted director systems for antiaircraft fire. But radar, which can measure ranges more accurately, largely replaced the range finder in World War II.

Since the early 1970's, the armies of many nations have equipped their tanks and other large weapons with *laser range finders.* These instruments measure the time needed for a light pulse to travel to and from a target. Laser range finders work during the day and at night. Some can measure the distance to a target up to 12 miles (20 kilometers) away. Frances M. Lussier

See also **Photography** (Range finder cameras); **Radar.**

Ranger, Forest. See Forestry; Forest Service.

Rangers are specialized U.S. Army infantry units. They get much tougher training than other infantrymen. The Rangers were organized in 1942, during World War II, under Colonel William O. Darby. The first regiment of 2,000 men was formed in Britain. It consisted of volunteers from the American Commando School. About 9 out of 10 of the first regiment lost their lives opening up enemy defenses before invasions.

A group called *Rogers's Rangers* fought with the British and American armies during the French and Indian wars of the 1750's. They adopted and improvised on the stealthy, daredevil tactics of the American Indian. Their tactics have since been associated with the name ranger.

Joel Slackman

See also **Commando; Rogers's Rangers.**

Rangers, Texas. See Texas Rangers.

Rangoon. See Yangon.

Ranjit Singh, *RUHN jiht sihng* or *RUHN jiht SIHN huh* (1780-1839), known as the *Lion of the Punjab,* was one of the most important figures in the history of India. He became the first Indian ruler to create a great Sikh kingdom (see **Sikhism**).

Ranjit was the son of an important chief in the Punjab, a region in northwest India. His father died when he was 12. At first, Ranjit ruled only a small state. But he gradually conquered neighboring states and threw off the control of the powerful Afghans.

Ranjit wanted to unite all Sikhs in a great nation. He expanded to the north and west, and made his state the largest in the Indus valley. But the British prevented him from uniting all Sikhs. He signed treaties with the British that kept the peace. T. Walter Wallbank

Rank, Military, indicates a person's authority and standing. The terms *rank* and *grade* are usually synonymous, but officers are said to hold rank, and enlisted men and women to hold ratings or grades. Grade also refers to the authorized level of pay. These terms indicate rights, powers, and duties fixed by law. In the United States, Congress creates ranks and grades and regulates appointments and promotions.

Under the U.S. Constitution, the president holds the rank of *commander in chief* of the armed forces. A *commissioned* officer holds a commission granted by the president with the advice and consent of the Senate. A *warrant* officer, a specialist in a particular field, holds a warrant granted by the secretary of the Army, Navy, or Air Force. *Noncommissioned* officers are enlisted personnel who hold their grades based on skill and long service.

A person is appointed to, or commissioned in, a rank or grade. Among people who hold the same grade, length of service and date of appointment to the grade determine who ranks higher. One colonel outranks another if he or she has been in grade one day longer. If a group without a designated commander faces a situation that requires command decisions, the highest ranking person takes command. This person may later have to prove the right to command others.

Rank is a right granted to an officer by law. It cannot be withdrawn except through legal processes. An officer's rank is not a guarantee of the right to exercise command or hold employment, but it normally indicates that the officer will do so. The president or a military superior in the chain of command may relieve an officer of command.

During the 1800's, the Army used an honorary title called *brevet* in order to recognize superior service by officers. The brevet, a temporary rank, gave an officer a rank higher than his regular one. Brevet rank sometimes

Grades for United States armed services personnel

Commissioned officers

Grade	Air Force, Army, and Marine Corps	Navy
O-10	General	Admiral
O-9	Lieutenant general	Vice admiral
O-8	Major general	Rear admiral (upper half)
O-7	Brigadier general	Rear admiral (lower half)
O-6	Colonel	Captain
O-5	Lieutenant colonel	Commander
O-4	Major	Lieutenant commander
O-3	Captain	Lieutenant
O-2	First lieutenant	Lieutenant junior grade
O-1	Second lieutenant	Ensign

Warrant officers

Grade	Army, Marine Corps, and Navy
W-4	Chief (commissioned) warrant officer
W-3	Chief (commissioned) warrant officer
W-2	Chief (commissioned) warrant officer
W-1	Warrant officer

Enlisted personnel

Grade	Air Force	Army
E-9	Chief master sergeant	Sergeant major
E-8	Senior master sergeant	First sergeant; master sergeant
E-7	Master sergeant	Sergeant first class
E-6	Technical sergeant	Staff sergeant
E-5	Staff sergeant	Sergeant
E-4		Corporal; specialist
E-3	Airman first class	Private first class
E-2	Airman	Private 2
E-1	Airman basic	Private

Grade	Marine Corps	Navy
E-9	Sergeant major; master gunnery sergeant	Master chief petty officer
E-8	First sergeant; master sergeant	Senior chief petty officer
E-7	Gunnery sergeant	Chief petty officer
E-6	Staff sergeant	Petty officer first class
E-5	Sergeant	Petty officer second class
E-4	Corporal	Petty officer third class
E-3	Lance corporal	Seaman
E-2	Private first class	Seaman apprentice
E-1	Private	Seaman recruit

allowed officers to command other officers of higher regular rank. During and after World War I and World War II, army officers held both *temporary* and *permanent* ranks. The permanent rank was normally two or three grades lower than the temporary one.

Promotion to the next higher rank for officers is usually based on length of service in the grade they hold, satisfactory performance of their duties, and a vacancy in the next higher grade. Promotion boards consider officers for promotion. Boards usually consider officers within a certain *zone* (based on their time in grade), but outstanding officers below the zone may be promoted. A person "passed over" for promotion twice while in the zone may be discharged or retired. In wartime, promotions may be given "on the battlefield."

Enlisted men and women must spend some time in a grade before they can be considered for advancement. All the services use both written tests and performance evaluations to determine fitness for promotion.

Rank and pay. Officers and enlisted personnel are paid according to their rank and length of service. In-creases are added to minimum basic pay after certain years of service are completed. These increases are called *longevity pay.* Most personnel begin to receive such pay after two years of service. Officers above the rank of major general or rear admiral receive a personal allowance. The armed services also grant *proficiency pay* to people with much needed skills. Allan R. Millett

Related articles in *World Book* include:

Air Force, U.S. (pictures)	General
Army, U.S. (pictures)	Marine Corps, U.S. (pictures)
Commission, Military	Mate
Flag officer	Navy, U.S. (pictures)

Ranke, *RAHNG kuh,* **Leopold von,** *LAY oh pohlt fuhn* (1795-1886), a German historian, persuaded historians to use critical methods and examine history scientifically. He introduced the seminar method of teaching. After 1840, his methods were largely used in teaching German historians. Ranke was born at Wiehe, in Thuringia. His first book, *History of the Romance and Teutonic Nations,* appeared in 1824. His other published works include a three-volume *History of the Popes* (1834-1836), and a nine-volume *World History* (1881-1888) that covers events up to the end of the 1400's. See also **History** (Modern times; picture). Joseph Martin Hernon, Jr.

Rankin, Jeannette (1880-1973), was the first woman to be elected to the United States Congress. A Republican, she served from 1917 to 1919 as congresswoman at large from Montana. In 1940, she was elected to the House of Representatives for one term. She voted against U.S. participation in World War I (1914-1918), and was the only member of the House to vote against entering World War II in 1941. She also opposed U.S. involvement in the Korean War (1950-1953) and the Vietnam War (1957-1975).

Harris & Ewing
Jeannette Rankin

Rankin was born near Missoula, Montana. A statue of her represents Montana in the United States Capitol in Washington, D.C. James S. Olson

Ransom, John Crowe (1888-1974), was an American poet, critic, and editor. In his writing, Ransom criticized what he considered a materialistic, spiritually barren society brought about by science and technology. He expressed nostalgia for the rural and feudalistic values he associated with the Old South.

Ransom's poems seem to be quiet and gentle, but they are toughened by his ironic wit, complexity of thought, and awareness of human frailty. Ransom helped lead the New Criticism movement, which emphasized close analysis of the language of a work rather than discussing its author or social significance.

Ransom was born in Pulaski, Tennessee. While teaching at Vanderbilt University, he led a group of conservative Southern writers called the Fugitives. From 1937 to 1958, he taught at Kenyon College. There, he founded and edited the *Kenyon Review,* a literary magazine. Steven Gould Axelrod

Ransome, Arthur (1884-1967), was a British author and journalist. Ransome became best known for his series of children's outdoor adventure novels. The first book, *Swallows and Amazons* (1931), is a classic story about a group of young people camping and sailing. Ransome wrote 11 other novels in the series, ending with *Great Northern?* (1947).

Ransome was born in Leeds, England. He became a free-lance writer of articles and stories at the age of 17. He went to Russia in 1913 and stayed as a correspondent for English newspapers until 1919. Ransome wrote books about Russia and fishing in addition to his children's books. *The Autobiography of Arthur Ransome* was published in 1976.

Rao, *ROW,* **P. V. Narasimha,** *nah rah SIHM HAH* (1921-   ), a Congress-I Party politician, was prime minister of India from 1991 to 1996. As prime minister, he introduced economic reforms designed to encourage foreign investment and to increase economic development. However, his government was hampered by conflicts between the country's religious and ethnic groups.

Rao, whose full name is Pamulaparti Venkata Narasimha Rao, was born in Karimnagar, near Warangal. He studied at Bombay and Nagpur universities. Rao became active in the Congress Party in the 1940's. In 1969, the party split into one group that supported Prime Minister Indira Gandhi and another that opposed her. Indira Gandhi's group became the Congress-I Party in 1978. Rao remained loyal to Gandhi and her son Rajiv, who succeeded her in 1984. In the 1980's, Rao held several cabinet positions, including foreign affairs minister and minister of defense. In May 1991, the Congress-I Party chose Rao as its head after party leader Rajiv Gandhi was assassinated. Rao became prime minister in June, after his party won the most seats in parliamentary elections. The Congress-I Party failed to win a majority of seats in elections held in April and May 1996, and Rao was replaced as prime minister. He resigned as leader of the Congress-I Party in September.   Robert LaPorte, Jr.

AP/Wide World

P. V. Narasimha Rao

Rap music is a form of popular music that is generally spoken or chanted at a fast pace rather than sung. Rap is performed over musical accompaniment that emphasizes rhythm rather than melody. Often this accompaniment consists of short segments of earlier recorded music combined in new patterns.

Rap music first developed in the mid-1970's in New York City, and soon in other urban areas, primarily among African American teen-agers. The style soon spread throughout the United States and much of the world. Some critics believe rap replaced rock music as the creative force in music of the 1980's and 1990's. But the lyrics of some rap songs have caused controversy. Critics have charged that such lyrics promote racism and violence and show contempt for women.

The biggest inspiration for rap came from disc jockeys in Jamaica who would talk, or *toast,* over recorded music they played in clubs. The style, known as *dub,* produced popular records that featured disc jockeys talking over instrumental backing and electronic effects. A Jamaican-born disc jockey known as DJ Kool Herc is often credited with introducing rap into New York City. He and other disc jockeys used records playing on two turntables, switching rapidly from one to the other to mix and match beats between two songs.

The first rap hit was "Rapper's Delight" (1979) by the Sugar Hill Gang. "The Breaks" (1980) by Kurtis Blow helped to spread rap's popularity among a wider audience. Much early rap was primarily concerned with a dance and party spirit. However, "The Message" (1982) by Grandmaster Flash and the Furious Five took a harder look at social issues in its portrayal of black inner-city life. Such acts as Public Enemy and Ice Cube have popularized styles of rap that are even more militant and radical. A style known as *gangster rap* or *gangsta rap* has emphasized gunplay and other outlaw aspects of urban life. Popular rappers have included Hammer, Dr. Dre, Ice-T, Run-DMC, the Beastie Boys, and Arrested Development.   Don McLeese

See also **Rock music** (New directions and old).

Rapanui. See Easter Island.

Rape is the crime of forcing sexual intercourse upon a person against the person's will. Women or men may be the victims. This article discusses the rape of women.

A man may force a woman to submit to him by beating her or threatening her verbally or with a weapon. *Statutory rape* refers to sexual intercourse with a female who is under the legal age of consent. The age of consent is the age at which the law considers a female fully responsible for her sexual actions. The legal age ranges from 12 to 16 in most states of the United States.

Some experts believe rape is one of the nation's most underreported crimes. Officials estimate that the actual number committed may be two or more times the number reported. Many rape victims do not report the crime to police because of shame or fear. Some victims dread the possible humiliation of media publicity or being asked embarrassing questions by police or, later, in a courtroom. Also, many rapists threaten to kill their victims if the women go to the police.

Only about 2 percent of all rapists are convicted and imprisoned and, on average, convicted rapists serve only half of their original sentence. The low conviction rate results from the difficulty of proving rape under most state laws. Some states require evidence from witnesses or evidence of bodily injury to the woman. Some states also require proof that a woman struggled to resist her attacker. In most of the states, the law demands evidence from a physician proving that a woman has had recent sexual intercourse. For such proof, a woman must be examined within 24 hours after the rape. In some cases, a defense lawyer may try to cast doubt on a woman's story by asking about her past sex life. The jury may conclude that a woman willingly consented to sexual intercourse if she had sexual experiences with several men in the past.

Some states have changed their laws on rape. Many of the new laws have provisions that make it more difficult for the defendant to argue that the victim consented. A few states have eliminated laws that require evidence from witnesses or evidence of bodily injury. Most states have limited the introduction of information on a woman's previous sexual experience.

Some states have also allowed women to prosecute their husbands for raping them. However, convictions for this kind of rape, called *marital rape,* are difficult to obtain.

During the 1970's, because of the alarming increase in rape, local communities created rape crisis centers to offer counseling to rape victims, most of whom feel great anxiety and depression after being attacked. Rape crisis centers also encourage women to report the crime to the police. In addition, various groups and universities offer instruction on rape prevention.

Few men commit rape for sexual pleasure. In most cases, rape is an antisocial act in which men who fear and hate women want to prove their power and domination by humiliating and hurting them.

Susan Gluck Mezey

Additional resources

Allison, Julie A., and Wrightsman, L. S. *Rape.* Sage, 1993.
Bode, Janet. *The Voices of Rape.* Watts, 1990. First-person accounts of rape victims and offenders.
Hall, Rob. *Rape in America: A Reference Handbook.* ABC-Clio, 1995.
Parrot, Andrea. *Coping with Date Rape & Acquaintance Rape.* Rev. ed. Rosen Pub. Group, 1993.

Rape is a flowering herb of the mustard family. It is grown commercially in Asia, Canada, Europe, New Zealand, and the United States. Some varieties of rape are called *rutabagas* in the United States and *swedes* in Europe. They have an edible turniplike root. Farmers grow other varieties of rape as pasture crops. Varieties called *rapeseed* are grown for their oilbearing seeds, which are processed into livestock feed, vegetable oil, and industrial lubricants.

Canola is a variety of rapeseed from which canola oil is obtained. Food-processing companies use canola oil to make cooking oil and such products as margarine and salad dressings. Canola oil is popular because it is lowest in *saturated fat* among vegetable oils. Saturated fats seem to increase the amount of *cholesterol* in blood and thus may contribute to heart disease (see **Cholesterol**).

The rape plant grows from about 2 to 6 feet (61 to 183 centimeters) tall. It has slender, branched stems with bluish-green leaves. It bears pale yellow flowers about $\frac{1}{2}$ inch (1.3 centimeters) long.

WORLD BOOK illustration by John D. Dawson
The rape plant

Some varieties of the plant live only one year. Others live for two years.   Richard C. Keating

Scientific classification. Rape plants are members of the mustard family, Brassicaceae or Cruciferae. All varieties belong to either of two species, *Brassica napus* and *B. campestris.*

See also **Canola oil.**

Raphael, *RA fih uhl* or *RAY fee uhl* (1483-1520), was one of the greatest and most influential painters of the Italian Renaissance. His graceful figures and skillful compositions influenced artists up to the early 1900's. The period of his activity is called the *High Renaissance.*

Raphael painted altarpieces, *frescoes* (paintings on damp plaster) of historical and mythological scenes, and portraits. His most popular works include his gentle paintings of the Madonna and Child. Raphael was also an architect. From 1514 until his death, he directed the construction of St. Peter's Basilica in Rome.

His life. Raphael was born in Urbino. His real name was Raffaello Sanzio. His father served as court painter to the Duke of Urbino. About 1494, Raphael went to Perugia to study with Perugino, an important painter. Perugino introduced Raphael to the latest ideas in Italian art and greatly influenced his student's style.

Raphael settled in Florence in 1504. In Florence, Raphael studied the paintings of the great Italian artist Leonardo da Vinci. Leonardo da Vinci's balanced compositions and idealized figures had a strong influence on all

Oil painting on wood panel (1504); Brera Gallery, Milan (SCALA)

Raphael's *Marriage of the Virgin* is one of his earliest masterpieces. This painting is particularly noteworthy for its graceful figures and expert use of perspective.

Fresco (1510-1511); The Vatican, Rome (SCALA)

Raphael's *School of Athens* shows a gathering of ancient Greek philosophers and scientists in a Roman architectural setting. Standing in the center are Plato, *left*, and Aristotle, *right*. The harmony and balance of the composition are typical of the period called the *High Renaissance*.

Renaissance painters, including Raphael.

Late in 1508, Pope Julius II asked Raphael to work for him in Rome. Julius wanted to rebuild and redecorate Rome to reflect its ancient glory. He gathered together the most illustrious architects, painters, and sculptors from all parts of Italy. Raphael created his finest work while in the service of Julius and his successor, Pope Leo X. With the assistance of a large workshop, Raphael produced religious paintings, tapestry designs, palace decorations, and portraits. He remained in Rome until he died, after a short illness.

His works. A masterpiece of Raphael's early career is the *Marriage of the Virgin* (1504), reproduced on the previous page. It shows the influence of Perugino's sentimental style. However, Raphael's own style can be seen in the dignified figures and the emphasis on perspective. The painting shows a gentle Virgin Mary receiving a ring from an ideally handsome Joseph.

Perhaps Raphael's greatest achievement was the series of frescoes that decorate the pope's private quarters in the Vatican. Raphael painted several of these frescoes in a room called the Stanza della Segnatura. Each wall in the room has an arch to support the curved ceiling. Raphael brilliantly incorporated this architectural feature into his compositions.

Raphael's *School of Athens,* shown above, covers one wall of the Stanza and captures the classical spirit of the High Renaissance. Three painted arches serve as a background for the ancient Greek philosophers and scientists in the front of the scene. In the center of the painting, beneath the arches, stand Plato and Aristotle, the leading philosophers. These powerful and expressive figures were influenced by Michelangelo's paintings on the Sistine Chapel ceiling. But Raphael harmonized and clarified the arrangement of figures in space, achieving the perfect balance for which he is noted.

In his final works, such as *The Transfiguration* in the Vatican, Raphael began to move toward a style of greater emotion and movement that would characterize the next generation of Italian artists.

For other examples of Raphael's works, see the pictures with the articles on **Painting; Plato;** and **Renaissance.**   Eric M. Zafran

Additional resources

Hersey, George L. *High Renaissance Art in St. Peter's and the Vatican.* Univ. of Chicago Pr., 1993.
Labella, Vincenzo. *A Season of Giants: Michaelangelo, Leonardo, Raphael, 1492-1508.* Little, Brown, 1990.
Mulhberger, Richard. *What Makes a Raphael a Raphael?* Viking, 1993. Younger readers.

Rapid City (pop. 54,523; met. area pop. 81,343) is the second largest city in South Dakota. Only Sioux Falls has more people. Rapid City is a center of education, health care, tourism, and trade for western South Dakota. It lies just east of the scenic Black Hills, about 25 miles (40 kilometers) from Mount Rushmore National Memorial. For location, see **South Dakota** (political map).

The chief industries in Rapid City make cement, computer parts, jewelry, meat products, and particle board. The South Dakota School of Mines and Technology is located there. Ellsworth Air Force Base lies nearby.

Sioux Indians lived in the Black Hills before white settlers arrived there. Prospectors founded Rapid City in 1876, during the Black Hills gold rush. They named it after Rapid Creek, which flows through the city.

In 1972, Rapid Creek overflowed. The flood killed 238 people and caused about $165 million in damage in Rapid City and the surrounding area. The city then created a *floodway*—a path for drainage of excess water—by clearing land on both sides of the creek. The floodway, 7 miles (11 kilometers) long, involved removal of about 240 businesses and 800 homes. Other projects included a civic center, opened in 1977 and expanded in 1985, and the Rushmore Mall, a shopping mall completed in 1978. Rapid City has a mayor-council form of government.   Ronald Bender

Rappahannock River, *RAP uh HAN uhk,* is a waterway in Virginia. Much Civil War fighting took place along this river. It rises in the Blue Ridge Mountains and flows southeast for 185 miles (298 kilometers) into Chesapeake Bay (see **Virginia** [physical map]). The Rapidan River is its main branch.   Michael P. O'Neill

Rare earth is any one of a group of metallic elements with atomic numbers 58 through 71. The name *rare earth* is really incorrect, since they are neither rare nor earths. They received this name because chemists first isolated them in their oxide forms. These oxides somewhat resemble calcium, magnesium, and aluminum oxides, sometimes called *common earths.*

Rare earths have three electrons in the outer shells of their atoms that take part in valence bonding. Because of this structure, all rare earths have similar properties in water solutions, and all can exist in the *trivalent* (three electric charges per atom) state. The elements scandium, yttrium, lanthanum, and actinium also have three valence electrons. They are sometimes called rare-earth elements, but they have somewhat different electronic structures. The rare-earth elements are also called the *lanthanides* because they follow lanthanum in the periodic chart of elements. The elements following actinium are called the *actinides.*

The true rare earths are silver-colored metals. In nature, they are always found together in combination with nonmetallic elements in the form of phosphates, carbonates, fluorides, silicates, and tantalates. The minerals monazite and bastnasite are the chief sources of the rare earths. The rare earths are not really rare. Even the scarce rare earths, such as europium and lutetium, are more common than the platinum-group metals. Promethium does not occur naturally, but forms as a result of atomic reactions. Many rare earths form during the fission of uranium and plutonium (see **Fission**).

The rare earths have many scientific and industrial uses. Separated rare earths are used in lamps, lasers,

The rare earths

Element	Chemical symbol	Atomic number	Atomic weight
Cerium	Ce	58	140.12
Praseodymium	Pr	59	140.907
Neodymium	Nd	60	144.24
Promethium	Pm	61	145.00
Samarium	Sm	62	150.35
Europium	Eu	63	151.96
Gadolinium	Gd	64	157.25
Terbium	Tb	65	158.924
Dysprosium	Dy	66	162.50
Holmium	Ho	67	164.930
Erbium	Er	68	167.26
Thulium	Tm	69	168.934
Ytterbium	Yb	70	173.04
Lutetium	Lu	71	174.97

Each element listed in this table has a separate article in *The World Book Encyclopedia.*

magnets, phosphors, and X-ray intensifying screens. Unseparated rare earths are added to various metals, including aluminum and magnesium, to make them stronger. The carbon electrodes used in motion-picture projectors have rare-earth cores. A mixed rare-earth alloy called *misch metal* is combined with iron to make flints for cigarette lighters. Rare-earth compounds are widely used as catalysts in the production of various petroleum and synthetic products.

Until 1945, processors had to use long and complicated chemical processes to obtain significant amounts of pure rare earths. This made them scarce and costly. Today, *ion-exchange* and *solvent extraction* processes have made possible a rapid separation that gives highly pure, low-cost rare earths.   Larry C. Thompson

See also **Berzelius, Jöns Jakob; Element, Chemical** (tables); **Scandium; Yttrium.**

Ras Tafari. See **Rastafarians; Haile Selassie I.**

Raskin, Ellen (1928-1984), was an American author and illustrator. She won the 1979 Newbery Medal for her children's novel *The Westing Game* (1978). This book is a mystery about 16 people who compete for a millionaire's fortune by trying to solve a puzzle in his will. Raskin wrote and illustrated many other children's books. Raskin was born in Milwaukee.   Virginia L. Wolf

Raspberry is a thorny bush that produces small, round, tasty fruit. Each fruit, also called a *berry,* consists of a cluster of cells, called *drupelets,* that look like tiny beads. Drupelets are partly hard and partly fleshy and grow around a core known as a *receptacle.* The receptacle remains on the bush after the fruit is picked. Most commercially grown raspberries are red, but some are black, purple, white, or yellow. Raspberries are eaten fresh or used to make jams and jellies. Frozen raspberries are also popular.

Raspberries grow best in cool regions of North America and Europe. The countries of Eastern Europe produce more than three-fourths of the world's raspberries. In the United States, the leading raspberry-growing states are Oregon and Washington. In Canada, British Columbia ranks first in production.

Growing raspberries. Growers begin new red raspberry bushes from raspberry *suckers* obtained from healthy plants. Suckers are underground shoots that grow from the roots of the plants. The suckers are raised in a nursery for one growing season and then

WORLD BOOK illustration by Kate Lloyd-Jones, Linden Artists Ltd.

Raspberries are tasty fruits that grow on thorny bushes. Each berry consists of a cluster of tiny, beadlike *drupelets*. Most raspberries are red, but some are purple or black.

transplanted outdoors. During the first growing season after they have been transplanted, the suckers produce only *canes* (stems) and branches. Fruit and flowers develop the following year.

Growers produce new black and purple raspberries by bending the tips of raspberry plants over and covering them with soil. The tips develop roots, which are transplanted the next season. They produce fruit the second growing season after transplanting. Most raspberry plants produce fruit for about six years. The bushes thrive in deep, fertile, well-drained soil.

Various *training systems* are used to grow raspberries. These systems ensure the proper development of the raspberry plants and allow growers to care for them easily. The three most common systems are the *hedgerow, staked hill,* and *trellis* systems. In the hedgerow system, raspberry bushes are planted in rows that are about 3 feet (0.9 meter) apart. Growers using the staked hill system plant the bushes in mounds about 6 feet (1.8 meters) apart. In the trellis system, plants grow on three to five wires attached to stakes. Raspberries are harvested by machine, or they are picked by hand.

Diseases and pests. Raspberries are attacked by a number of diseases, including mosaic disease and other virus diseases, as well as the fungus diseases anthracnose and orange rust (see **Fungal disease; Mosaic disease**). Growers control these diseases by spraying the bushes with fungicides and by clearing patches of dead wood away from the plants. They also destroy the canes after the fruit has been harvested.

Raspberry plants are also attacked by such insects as the crown borer, the cane borer, the raspberry sawfly, and the rose chafer. Growers guard against these pests by spraying the bushes with insecticides.   Paul Eck

Scientific classification. The raspberry belongs to the rose family, Rosaceae. The American red raspberry is *Rubus strigosus.* The European red raspberry is *R. icaeus.* The purple raspberry is *R. neglectus,* and the black raspberry is *R. occidentalis.*

Raspe, Rudolph Erich. See Munchausen, Baron.
Rasputin, ra SPYOO tihn, **Grigori Efimovich,** grih

GAW rih ih FEE muh vihch (1864?-1916), was a Siberian peasant, healer, and holy man. He served as an adviser to the last Russian czar, Nicholas II, and contributed to his downfall.

Rasputin impressed Russian church and society leaders with his peasant wisdom and religious teachings. In 1905, he met Nicholas and his wife, Czarina Alexandra. Rasputin was able to stop the bleedings of their son, Alexis, who was a hemophiliac. Rasputin's standing with the royal couple gave him influence over appointments to church and state offices. Businessmen bribed Rasputin to gain government contracts and favors.

Rasputin had common sense, but he was selfish, greedy, and immoral. During World War I (1914-1918), he was unjustly thought to be a German spy and the czarina's lover. Many people resented his influence over ministerial appointments. A group of the czar's supporters feared that this resentment would lead to the czar's overthrow. In December 1916, they poisoned and shot Rasputin and threw him into the Neva River, where he drowned. But the Russian Revolution broke out in less than three months, and Nicholas was deposed. Rasputin was born in Pokrovskoye, near Tyumen.   Joseph T. Fuhrmann

Culver

Grigori Rasputin

See also **Russia** (The February Revolution).

Rastafarians are members of a religious and political movement that began in Jamaica in the late 1920's. They are perhaps best known as the originators of a musical style called *reggae;* for their use of marijuana (which they call *ganja*); and for wearing their hair in long, ropelike braids called *dreadlocks.*

The name *Rastafarian* comes from *Ras Tafari,* a title held by Emperor Haile Selassie I of Ethiopia from 1916 to 1974. Ethiopia is a country in northeastern Africa. Many early Rastafarians believed Haile Selassie was a god. However, Haile Selassie did not consider himself a god, and when he visited Jamaica in 1966, he was puzzled by Rastafarians who tried to worship him.

Today, Rastafarianism is a worldwide movement. Members live not only in Jamaica but also in the United States, Canada, Australia, New Zealand, South Africa, and many European countries. Although Rastafarians today belong to many races and nationalities, the religion began as a black nationalist movement.

Early Rastafarians taught that all Africans are descendants of the ancient Hebrews. According to this teaching, God made many black Africans the slaves of whites as punishment for disobedience. The Rastafarians believed Haile Selassie would arrange for all people of African descent to return to Africa. After Haile Selassie's death in 1975, Rastafarians changed some of their beliefs. Today, many look forward to a return to African spirituality rather than to actually living in Africa.   Stephen D. Glazier

See also **Haile Selassie I; Jamaica** (People); **Reggae.**
Rat is a furry mammal that looks like a mouse but is larger. The smallest kinds of rats grow longer and weigh

John Markham, Bruce Coleman Inc.

Rats are small, furry mammals that have plagued human beings for centuries. The black rat, *above*, causes disease and widespread property damage in the seaports of North America.

more than the largest mice. Rats, like mice, beavers, and squirrels, are *rodents*. All such animals have chisellike front teeth especially suited for gnawing.

There are about 120 kinds of rats, of which the best known are the *black rat* and the *brown rat.* Both these species live in all parts of the world. Most other kinds of rats live in areas not inhabited by people.

Black rats and brown rats rank among the most serious animal threats to people. They carry the germs of several diseases, including plague, food poisoning, and typhus. Rats also damage or destroy crops and other food products, and they kill poultry, lambs, and baby pigs. On the other hand, scientists use rats in research projects that have benefited people.

The word *rat* is often used for any long-tailed rodent that is larger than a mouse. But most of these animals are not true rats. They include the *cotton rat,* the *rice rat,* the *kangaroo rat,* and the *woodrat.*

The body of a rat. All species of rats have a slender, scaly tail and long, sharp claws. But black rats and brown rats differ in several ways besides color.

Black rats grow 7 or 8 inches (18 or 20 centimeters) long, not including their tail, and weigh about 10 ounces (280 grams). The tail is longer than the rest of the body. These rats have large ears, a pointed snout, and soft fur. The fur of a black rat may be black, grayish-brown, or smoky-gray. Gray, white, or yellow fur covers the animal's underside. Black rats are also called *roof rats* or *ship rats.*

Brown rats measure from 8 to 10 inches (20 to 25 centimeters) long, not including their tail, and weigh up to 16 ounces (485 grams). The tail is shorter than the rest of the body. Brown rats have small ears, a blunt snout, and coarse fur. They vary in color from brownish-gray to reddish-gray. Other names for the brown rat include *barn rat, gray rat, house rat, Norway rat,* and *sewer rat.*

The life of a rat. Black rats and brown rats originally lived in Asia. They reached Europe by ship or overland. From Europe, they spread to North and South America on ships. More brown rats than black rats live in North America. Some black rats live near coastal seaports in

the Northern United States, but most dwell in the Gulf states, such as Louisiana and Texas. Brown rats live throughout the United States.

Both black and brown rats live in large groups, with certain rats *dominating* (having control over) others. Most members of both species build a nest in or near buildings. Black rats live in the upper stories of buildings or in trees. Brown rats are found under floors, within walls, in piles of garbage, or in the ground. If the two species live in the same building, black rats usually occupy the upper levels, and brown rats dwell on the ground level. Rats are cautious creatures and generally avoid anything unfamiliar in their environment. They have a keen sense of smell and can quickly detect approaching danger.

Both black and brown rats eat almost any kind of plant or animal—even other rats of the same or a different species. The brown rat is fierce and aggressive, compared with the milder black rat. Rats feed mostly at night, and sometimes they band together and attack such animals as chickens and pigs. Most rats live within an area that may be no more than 150 feet (46 meters) in diameter. But if a food shortage occurs, rats may travel long distances in search of food.

Most black and brown rats mate the year around, and the females give birth to three to six litters annually. A female rat carries her young in her body for about three weeks before they are born. Most black rat litters consist of six or seven babies. Most brown rat litters have eight or nine babies. Newborn rats are blind and deaf. They remain in the nest for about three weeks.

Few rats live more than a year in their natural surroundings because they have so many enemies. Animals that prey on rats include cats, dogs, hawks, owls, snakes, and weasels. In captivity, some rats live more than three years.

Rats and people. Rats cause damage totaling hundreds of millions of dollars a year in the United States alone. Both black and brown rats destroy eggs, fruits, stored grain, vegetables, and other foods and attack various farm animals. Rats also cause considerable addi-

The skeleton of a rat

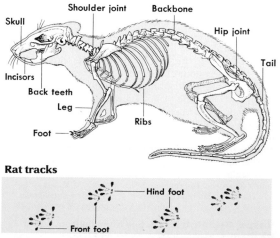

Rat tracks

WORLD BOOK illustration by Marion Pahl

WORLD BOOK photo

White rats play an important role in scientific research. In the picture above, a drug company researcher measures weight changes in a rat that has been given an experimental medicine.

tional damage by gnawing on such objects as furniture and lead pipes. They sometimes cause fires by chewing the insulation off electric wires. In addition to spreading disease, rats sometimes attack human beings, including babies in cribs. Their bite may cause a disease called rat-bite fever.

Some people fight rats by destroying the food sources or homes of the animals. Others kill rats by poisoning, shooting, or trapping them. Rat poisons must be used carefully to prevent accidental poisoning of human beings or of other animals.

Rats may also be controlled by placing specially treated food in areas where they live. Such food contains chemicals called *antifertility drugs*. These drugs make the rats incapable of reproducing.

Domesticated varieties of brown rats, especially the *white rat,* play an important role in many research projects. Researchers use white rats in studies of disease, drug effects, heredity, nutrition, and learning and other aspects of behavior. They also use rats in the preparation and testing of new drugs. Many zoos maintain colonies of rats as food for snakes and other animals. Some people keep domesticated rats as pets.

Clyde Jones

Scientific classification. Rats belong to the family, Muridae. Black rats are *Rattus rattus.* Brown rats are *R. norvegicus.*

See also **Mouse; Rodent; Kangaroo rat; Mole-rat; Woodrat.**

Additional resources

Barnett, S. A. *The Rat: A Study in Behavior.* Rev. ed. Univ. of Chicago Pr., 1981.
Fox, Susan. *Rats.* T. F. H., 1983.
Himsel, Carol A. *Rats: A Complete Pet Owners Manual.* Barron's, 1991.
Zinsser, Hans. *Rats, Lice and History.* 1935. Reprint. Black Dog & Leventhal, 1996. A classic history of rats as carriers of disease.

Ratchet, *RACH iht,* is a wheel or bar that can move in only one direction. It often consists of a notched wheel and a *pawl* (metal bar hung from a pivot). The pawl is attached to a lever. As the lever is moved, the free end of the pawl locks into a tooth of the wheel, causing the wheel to rotate. A second pawl may be used to prevent the wheel from turning backwards while the lever is being returned to begin another stroke.

A mechanical counter is a simple device that uses the ratchet-and-pawl combination. A ratchet-and-pawl mechanism locks a machine, such as a hoisting winch, so that it does not slip.   Alva H. Jared

Rate of exchange. See Exchange rate.

Ratel, *RAY tuhl,* is a badgerlike animal that lives in Saudi Arabia, India, Nepal, and much of Africa. The ratel is also called *honey badger* because it often feeds on honey. The ratel is about $2\frac{1}{2}$ feet (76 centimeters) long. It has white or dark-gray fur on its upper body and black fur on its underside. Ratels have long claws. The animals also have thick, loose skin that protects them from stings or bites. In addition, ratels have special glands that give off a foul-smelling liquid that helps to discourage their enemies.

Ratels live in holes in the ground, among rocks, or in hollow logs, stumps, or trees. They may travel alone or in pairs. Ratels feed chiefly on honey, insects, small mammals, lizards, and both poisonous and nonpoisonous snakes. The animals also eat plants, roots, and fruit. The ratel often looks for honey with the assistance of a bird called the *honey guide.* The honey guide's call leads

Mark N. Brultan, Photo Researchers

The ratel, unlike most fur-bearing mammals, is light on top and dark below, reversing the usual coloration.

the ratel to a beehive. The ratel then uses its claws to break open the hive, and both animals feed.

Gary A. Heidt

Scientific classification. The ratel belongs to the weasel family, Mustelidae. It is classified as *Mellivora capensis.*

Rating, in television. See **Television** (The national networks).

Ratio, *RAY shee oh* or *RAY shoh,* is an ordered pair or set that represents a relationship between numbers or quantities. The numbers in a ratio are called the *terms* of the ratio.

The ratio of two numbers or quantities represented by the letters *a* and *b* may be written as *a:b, (a,b), a/b,* or $\frac{a}{b}$. All fractions and percentages are ratios. The expression "40 percent" may be restated as $\frac{40}{100}$ or 40:100. Two ratios are equal when each term of one ratio can be multiplied by a certain number to produce the terms of the other ratio. The expressions 2:3, 4:6, and 6:9 represent equal ratios. Two equal ratios make up a *proportion* (see **Proportion**).

Ratios may be used to describe a variety of relationships. For example, a ratio may express the relationship between the amounts of two ingredients in a liquid mixture. If a mixture contains 5 gallons of syrup and 15 gallons of water, the relationship, or ratio, of syrup to water is 5:15 or 1:3. A ratio may also indicate the rate at which something occurs, such as the use of gasoline by an automobile. The rate of gasoline-use for an automobile that travels 30 miles on a gallon of gas is expressed by the ratio 30:1. Such a ratio may also be stated as "30 miles per gallon." A ratio may also describe the probability of the occurrence of an event. For example, the probability of drawing an ace from a well-shuffled deck of cards is described by the ratio 4:52 or 1:13. The terms of this ratio are derived from the number of aces (4) and the total number of cards (52) in the deck.

Ratio ranks as one of the most widely used mathematical concepts. It plays an important role in the physical sciences, the social sciences, and the arts. In physics, for example, ratio provides a basis for the concepts of speed and acceleration.   Thomas E. Kieren

See also **Fraction; Percentage; Trigonometry.**

Rational number, *RASH uh nuhl,* is any number that can be expressed in the form $\frac{a}{b}$, where *a* is any integer and *b* is any integer except zero. Integers are whole numbers greater than, less than, or equal to zero. Rational numbers include such positive numbers as $\frac{3}{4}$ and $\frac{2}{3}$ and such negative numbers as $-\frac{1}{3}$ and $-\frac{5}{2}$.

Integers are rational numbers because they can be expressed as fractions ($\frac{a}{b}$). For example, the integers 3 and -5 can be written as the fractions $\frac{3}{1}$ and $-\frac{5}{1}$. *Terminating decimals* and *repeating decimals* are also rational numbers. Terminating decimals are decimals that have a limited number of digits. For instance, .75 is a terminating decimal. When expressed in the form $\frac{a}{b}$, .75 becomes $\frac{3}{4}$. Repeating decimals repeat the same digit or a series of digits. In the repeating decimal .$\overline{6}$, the digit 6 repeats indefinitely. When expressed in the form $\frac{a}{b}$, .$\overline{6}$ becomes the fraction $\frac{2}{3}$.

Numbers that cannot be expressed as $\frac{a}{b}$ are called *irrational numbers. Pi (π),* for example, can be written as a decimal with an approximate value of 3.14159. However, the decimal continues indefinitely, does not repeat, and cannot be converted into a fraction. Pi is therefore an irrational number.   Thomas E. Kieren

Rationalism, *RASH uh nuh ᴌɪᴢ uhm,* is an outlook that emphasizes human reason and its ability to answer basic questions. *Philosophical rationalism,* in the 1600's, stressed the power of reason as opposed to sense experience. René Descartes, Gottfried Leibniz, and Baruch Spinoza developed philosophical systems based on the idea that, through reason, people have direct access to the nature of reality. *Cultural rationalism,* in the 1700's, relied on reason rather than on faith in creating a theory of human beings and their destiny. Voltaire and Thomas Paine were prominent figures in this movement. See also **Age of Reason; Philosophy** (Modern philosophy).

Margaret D. Wilson

Rationing, *RASH uh nihng* or *RAY shuh nihng,* is a system used by a government to distribute scarce products among the people of a country. Rationing is generally used only during a war or some other emergency. During a war, for example, people usually earn more money and so want to buy more products than they did before. But the armed forces need many of these products. Thus, manufacturers cannot produce enough of the products to satisfy the people's demand.

When people want to buy more products than manufacturers can supply, *inflation,* a period of rising prices, usually results. A government can try to fight inflation by using a system of *price controls* to limit the amount of money that manufacturers can charge for their products. Through rationing, the government also tries to assure a fair distribution of the scarce products to all the people.

The two most common types of rationing are *specific rationing* and *point rationing.* Specific rationing uses a coupon for each type of rationed product. The government gives each household a certain number of coupons for the rationed goods. A person must submit the correct coupon and the cash value of each rationed item being purchased. Specific rationing generally is used to control the sale of scarce products that vary little in value and quality, such as gasoline and sugar. To use this rationing system for such goods as meat and clothing, which differ greatly in value and quality, there would have to be coupons for every variety of the products. For such products, the government uses point rationing, giving each rationed item a point value. The government also gives each individual or family a certain number of points to use when buying products that have point values.

The stages involved in creating an effective ration program may be difficult to carry out. A large government organization must be set up to decide which products will be rationed and what price controls will be put into effect. Also, laws must be established and enforced to prohibit *black marketing,* the selling of rationed products without proper coupons or points. Black markets operate because people want to buy larger amounts of certain products than the government allows and are willing to pay a high price for the products.

During World War II (1939-1945), the United States and other countries involved in the war rationed a wide variety of products, including automobiles, coffee, sugar, and tires. Today, periods of rationing are common for certain items that are in short supply in a number of developing nations, including India and Sri Lanka.

Gary Jay Dorman

See also **Black market; Price control; World War II** (On the home front).

Rattan, *ra TAN,* is a tough, stringy material. It comes from the reedy stems of different kinds of palms that grow in Africa and southeast Asia. These trees belong to the genus of palms known as *Calamus.* The stems of rattan palms may grow to lengths of more than 500 feet (150 meters). The plants climb over other trees by means of hooks on the stems.

In the countries where these palms grow, natives use the rattan stem to make ropes and mats. American and European countries import the stems. Manufacturers use them to make umbrella handles, walking sticks, furniture, baskets, ship cables, and chair bottoms. Rattan is strong, bends easily, and lasts long. The finest grades of rattan come from the island of Borneo. Other good rattans grow in Burma, Malaysia, Sri Lanka, and Sumatra.

Workers prepare the stems for shipment by cutting them into lengths of 5 to 20 feet (1.5 to 6 meters). They remove the leaves and outer covering by pulling the stems through a notch in a tree or board. Some rattan palms have a fruit that can be eaten. The young shoots of others are eaten like vegetables.   David S. Seigler

See also **Basket making.**

Rattlesnake is any one of the poisonous snakes of the Western Hemisphere with a rattle on the end of the tail. The rattle is used to warn enemies to stay away. Rattlesnakes sometimes give no warning sound with the rattle before they bite.

The rattlesnakes are classed among the pit vipers. There are about 30 species of rattlesnakes. They live from southern Canada to Argentina. By far the greatest number of rattlesnakes live in the dry region of the southwestern United States and northern Mexico. One species is found over a large part of South America. Only one kind of rattlesnake lives in almost the whole of the northern United States west of the Mississippi Valley. A few other kinds appear in the valley and east of it.

It is easy to recognize a rattlesnake by its rattle, which

is a set of horny pieces loosely joined together. It makes a buzzing sound when the snake shakes it. Many other snakes also have the habit of vibrating the tail. Certain harmless snakes, often mistaken for rattlesnakes, can make a sound with their tails in dry grass or leaves. But a careful observer can quickly tell whether a snake is a real rattler. The rattlesnake always lifts its tail when it sounds. The harmless snake moves its tail back and forth on top of dry leaves or grass.

There are large and small kinds of rattlesnakes. The diamondback rattler of the southeastern United States is the heaviest of all poisonous snakes, though not the longest. It gets its name because diamond-shaped blotches edged with yellow cover its body. Diamondbacks rarely grow over $7\frac{1}{3}$ feet (2.2 meters) long. A few other rattlers grow almost as large. Several small kinds of rattlers ordinarily grow only 2 feet (61 centimeters) long. The horned rattlesnake, or sidewinder, found in desert regions, belongs to this group. The ridge-nosed rattlesnake and the pygmy rattlesnake are even shorter.

Females of the eastern diamondback, the timber rattlesnake, and the northern Pacific rattlesnake have young when they are 3 years old. The females then give birth every two to three years. The young are born in late summer. All rattlesnakes bear live young instead of laying eggs. The newborn snakes can take full care of themselves and give painful bites.

Naturalists know very little about the life span of rattlesnakes. Many people falsely believe that they can tell the age of a rattler by the number of segments, or "rattles," in its rattle. Two to four new segments are added each year, one every time the skin is shed. But when about 10 segments accumulate on the end of a rattlesnake's tail, they begin to fall off. The segments look like hollow rings, each one partly fitting over the one behind it. A young snake has a single small segment. Each new rattle is a little larger. Segments that develop on a fullgrown snake are all about the same size.

Most rattlesnakes eat birds and small mammals. A few also eat amphibians and reptiles. They destroy rodents and other animals that are harmful to crops.

The larger rattlers rank among the most dangerous of snakes. They should be carefully avoided. They do not always rattle before striking.

The rattlesnake sends out poison through two long hollow teeth, or fangs, in its upper jaw. The poison forms in a pair of glands behind each eye on the upper jaw. The rattlesnake's fangs are folded back in the mouth

Some common varieties of rattlesnakes

WORLD BOOK illustrations by Richard Lewington, The Garden Studio

Sidewinder rattlesnake

Ridge-nosed rattlesnake

Northern Pacific rattlesnake

Timber rattlesnake

Zig Leszczynski, Animals Animals

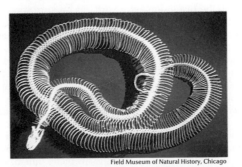

Field Museum of Natural History, Chicago

Charles Palek, Animals Animals

A rattlesnake has a forked tongue, *left,* that helps it detect odors. Its backbone, *center,* has about 200 flexible joints. The rattle on its tail, *right,* is a set of loosely interlocking segments.

when not in use. When an angry rattlesnake strikes, the fangs are erected and the mouth opened wide.

Scientific classification. Rattlesnakes belong to the viper family, Viperidae. The pygmy rattlesnake is *Sistrurus miliarius.* The ridge-nosed is *Crotalus willardi.* The eastern diamondback is *C. adamanteus;* the sidewinder is *C. cerastes;* the northern Pacific is *C. viridis oreganus;* and the timber is *C. horridus.*

D. Bruce Means

See also **Snake** (pictures: Male rattlesnakes battle; Some poisonous snakes); **Snakebite.**

Rattner, Abraham (1895-1978), was an American painter who is best known for his religious works. His paintings are noted for their brilliant color, rich texture,

Oil painting on composition board (1958); Whitney Museum of American Art, New York City

Rattner's *Song of Esther* shows the artist's use of vibrant colors and geometric forms, which create a stained-glass effect.

and symbolism. They have been compared to stained-glass windows because of their glowing colors and bold black lines. Rattner often used words and inscriptions in his works. He painted many familiar Biblical themes, including the Crucifixion and the Last Judgment. He also painted less familiar Biblical subjects, such as the Valley of Dry Bones. He developed personal symbolic themes. For example, he painted a window cleaner removing dirt from a window. This is a symbol of the way God clears human vision to enable people to see the brilliance and beauty of the divine. Rattner was born in Poughkeepsie, N.Y.   Pamela A. Ivinski

Rauschenberg, *ROW shuhn burg,* **Robert** (1925-
   ), is an American artist famous for experimenting with a variety of materials, techniques, and styles. His search for new forms of expression has inspired many artists in the United States and other countries.

Rauschenberg was born in Port Arthur, Tex. He studied art at Black Mountain College in North Carolina. He

Nelson Atkins Museum, Kansas City, Mo.

Rauschenberg's *Tracer* reproduces unrelated realistic images with oil paint and the silk-screen printing process to achieve an unusual effect. The artist completed the picture in 1963.

first attracted attention in the early 1950's with all-white and all-black paintings. He then invented the *combine,* an assemblage with everyday objects, often joined with painted canvases. One combine called *Bed* (1955) consists of a real quilt, sheet, and pillow, all splattered with paint.

Starting in the early 1960's, Rauschenberg experimented with printmaking techniques, often combining them with printing and drawing. He selected images from the media and ordinary objects from his environment and reproduced them through silk-screen printing. Rauschenberg's works, in subject and technique, anticipate the *pop art* movement of the 1960's (see **Pop art**). His random combinations of imagery illustrate the contradictions of modern life.

In 1966, Rauschenberg co-founded Experiments in Art and Technology (EAT), a project that advanced the incorporation of new interests, such as electric light and motion in art. During the 1980's, the Rauschenberg Overseas Cultural Exchange was formed. It includes work in painting, photography, graphic media, and sculptural form. In this project, Rauschenberg works with artists from 20 nations.   Charles C. Eldredge

Ravel, *ruh VEHL,* **Maurice,** *moh REES* (1875-1937), was a French composer. Ravel's music is finely crafted, and his piano music is especially brilliant. Some critics classify him as an impressionist along with Claude Debussy. Indeed, Ravel's piano works *Mirrors* (1906) and

Gaspard de la nuit (1909) fall into the impressionist category. However, Ravel's music is generally less experimental than Debussy's and relies more on the forms and mannerisms of earlier periods.

Ravel used classical forms in his early String Quartet (1904) and *Sonatine* for piano (1906) and in his late Piano Concerto in G (1932). *The Tomb of Couperin* (1919) takes the form of a baroque keyboard suite. His orchestral suite *La Valse* (1920) paints an exaggerated portrait of the Viennese waltz of the 1800's. A more modern influence, jazz, can be found in portions of the Concerto for Left Hand (1932) for piano. Ravel was especially known for his skill as an orchestrator. In addition to his own compositions, his orchestration in 1922 of Modest Mussorgsky's *Pictures at an Exhibition* is a standard symphonic work.

Joseph Maurice Ravel was born in Ciboure, near the Spanish border. A Spanish influence appears in such works as the orchestral *Spanish Rhapsody* (1907), the comic opera *The Spanish Hour* (1911), and Ravel's famous ballet music *Boléro* (1928).   Steven E. Gilbert

Raven is a type of large all-black bird that belongs to the crow family. Ravens live throughout the Northern

WORLD BOOK illustration by Trevor Boyer, Linden Artists Ltd.
The raven has black feathers with a purple luster. Ravens are often mentioned in myths and legends as magical birds.

Hemisphere. The *common raven* and the *chihuahuan raven* are found in North America. The common raven ranges from the Arctic south to Nicaragua in the west and New England in the east. It also lives in the Appalachians as far south as eastern Kentucky and western Virginia. The chihuahuan raven ranges from western Kansas and central Texas west to south-central Arizona.

A raven is 22 to 27 inches (56 to 69 centimeters) long and has a wingspread of 36 inches (90 centimeters). Its black feathers have a bluish-green luster on the head, wings, and underparts. Feathers elsewhere have a purplish-blue luster. A raven's voice is a deep, rumbling croak with variations in tone and length that seem meaningful to other ravens. Ravens feed on insects, worms, young birds, frogs, and other small animals. They also eat fruits, grains, and *carrion* (the flesh of dead animals).

Ravens build their nests in late winter on cliffs or in

trees. The nest's outer part is made of sticks reinforced with lumps of earth and grass. The deep inner cup is lined with fine strands of wool, hair, and plant fibers.

The female raven lays 3 to 6 spotted eggs that may vary widely in color. The female *incubates* (sits on and warms) the eggs. The eggs hatch after about 18 days. Both parents feed the young. They prepare the food by crushing insects and by removing the hair, feathers, and bones from birds and other small animals. Young ravens can fly at about 6 weeks of age, but the parents continue to care for them for another five months.

The raven is one of the first birds mentioned in mythology. In Norse mythology, the god Odin had two sacred ravens that flew about the world each day and returned at evening to tell Odin all they had seen. In American literature, the bird was immortalized by Edgar Allan Poe in his famous poem "The Raven."

Edward H. Burtt, Jr.

Scientific classification. Ravens belong to the crow family, Corvidae. The common raven is *Corvus corax.* The chihuahuan raven is *C. cryptoleucus.*

Ravenna, *ruh VEHN uh* (pop. 135,844), is a city in northern Italy, famous for its art treasures and architecture. It is also an agricultural and manufacturing center. A 6-mile (10-kilometer) canal connects Ravenna with the Adriatic Sea. For location, see **Italy** (political map).

Ravenna's Mausoleum of Galla Placidia, built about A.D. 440, is one of the oldest examples of early Christian architecture. It has some of the most beautiful mosaics in Ravenna. The famous churches of San Vitale, Sant' Apollinare Nuovo, and Sant' Apollinare in Classe, built in the 500's, also contain beautiful mosaics.

Ravenna served as the capital of the West Roman Empire from about 402 until the barbarian leader Odoacer seized the empire in 476. Then Theodoric, king of the Ostrogoths, murdered Odoacer and took over the city. Ravenna was part of the Byzantine Empire from about 540 until the 700's. It was one of the Papal States for many years, and it became part of the Kingdom of Sardinia in 1860. Ravenna became part of the Kingdom of Italy in 1861.   Anthony James Joes

See also **Clothing** (picture: Clothing of early Byzantine times); **Mosaic** (pictures: An early Christian mosaic).

Rawlings, Jerry John (1947-   ), has been the head of Ghana for all but two years since 1979, when he seized control of the government in a military coup. He was elected president of Ghana in multiparty elections held in 1992 and was reelected in 1996. Rawlings became known for his efforts to end government corruption and to improve the Ghanaian economy.

Rawlings was born in Accra. He joined the air force in 1967 and rose through the ranks. He was promoted to flight lieutenant in 1978. Rawlings tried to overthrow Ghana's military government on May 15, 1979. The coup failed, and Rawlings was jailed. But he gained nationwide attention for the speeches against corruption that he made during his trial. On June 4, Rawlings was freed from prison as he and fellow officers staged a successful coup. As head of the government, Rawlings allowed scheduled elections to go ahead as planned. In September 1979, he turned control over to the elected civilian government. Angered by what he saw as continued corruption, however, Rawlings retook control of the government on Dec. 31, 1981.   Mark W. DeLancey

Rawlings, Marjorie Kinnan (1896-1953), was an American novelist who wrote about the conflict between people and nature in the Florida backwoods. In 1928, Rawlings gave up a journalism career to settle on a farm in Cross Creek, Florida. Her difficult life there gave her the setting and theme for her novels. Her best-known work, *The Yearling,* won the 1939 Pulitzer Prize for fiction. The novel is set in rural Florida in the 1870's. It tells the story of a 12-year-old boy whose father must kill the boy's pet fawn because the animal was eating the family's scanty crops.

Marjorie Kinnan was born in Washington, D.C., and married Charles Rawlings in 1919. Her other novels include *South Moon Under* (1933) and *Golden Apples* (1935). Her stories were collected in *When the Whippoorwill* (1940). Rawlings humorously described her life in Florida in *Cross Creek* (1942).   Barbara M. Perkins

Ray is any of a group of more than 400 species of fishes. These fishes include eagle rays, guitarfish, manta rays, sawfish, skates, stingrays, and electric rays.

Most rays live on the sea floor. They feed on such bottom-dwelling creatures as clams, oysters, shellfish, and certain fishes. Many species dwell in coastal waters, but a few live at great depths. Manta rays live in the upper waters of the open sea and feed on small sea animals and on tiny organisms called *plankton.*

Rays, like sharks, have a boneless skeleton made of a tough, elastic substance called *cartilage.* Rays also resemble sharks in having slotlike body openings called *gill slits* that lead from the gills. But a ray's gill slits lie under the *pectoral fins* (fins behind the gill openings), and a shark's are on the sides of the head. Most rays have a flat, disklike body. Among many species, the pectoral fins form large "wings." Guitarfish and sawfish have a more sharklike, torpedo-shaped body.

Ray eggs, unlike those of most other fishes, are fertilized inside the female's body. Female skates lay the fertilized eggs. The eggs of all other rays hatch inside the female. The young are born alive.   John D. McEachran

Scientific classification. Rays make up the order Rajiformes.

See also **Electric ray; Sawfish; Skate; Stingray; Fish** (pictures: Fish of coastal waters).

Ray, Dixy Lee (1914-1994), was governor of the state of Washington from 1977 to 1981. She had been chairman of the United States Atomic Energy Commission from 1973 until it was dissolved in 1975. From January to June 1975, Ray served as assistant secretary of state for oceans and international environmental and scientific affairs. In 1973, when the nation faced serious fuel shortages, President Richard M. Nixon asked Ray to prepare a plan to develop new sources of energy. She proposed a $10-billion research and development program. It included such projects as the development of new forms of nuclear power generation and new ways to manufacture gaseous and liquid fuels from coal. Ray also started a campaign to eliminate defects in nuclear power plants.

Ray was born in Tacoma, Washington. From 1945 to 1972, she served as a marine zoologist on the faculty of the University of Washington. She became an AEC commissioner in 1972.   Robert Gillette

Ray, James Earl. See **King, Martin Luther, Jr.**

Ray, Man (1890-1976), was an American painter, sculptor, photographer, and filmmaker. Early in his career, Ray painted in a fairly realistic style. In 1913, he began to

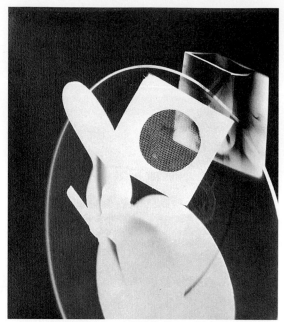

Untitled gelatin-silver print (1927); The Museum of Modern Art, New York City. Abby Aldrich Fund ©The Museum of Modern Art

A Man Ray photo called a *rayograph, shown here,* was made without a camera. Ray placed objects directly on sensitized paper and exposed them to light, producing abstract images.

experiment with Cubist and Expressionist styles that were modern at the time. By 1916, he was affiliated with an experimental art movement called Dadaism, which encourages use of unconventional materials and chance occurrences. Ray incorporated found objects, called *ready-mades,* into his Dada sculptures and paintings.

Ray worked in many mediums simultaneously but concentrated on filmmaking in the 1920's. Most of his films reflect the style of the Surrealism movement, in which the imagery is inspired by dreams and the subconscious. In the early 1920's, he developed a cameraless technique called *rayograph,* in which objects are placed on photographic paper and exposed to light. Ray continued to work mostly in photography in the 1930's, combining portraiture, nude studies, and abstraction.

Ray was born in Philadelphia. His real name was Emmanuel Radnitzky.   Deborah Leveton

Ray, Satyajit (1921-1992), was the first internationally famous Indian motion-picture director. He wrote the screenplays for all of his films. Ray gained fame for his *Apu trilogy.* The three films deal with a poor young man from rural India as he grows into manhood. The trilogy consists of *Pather Panchali* (1955), *Aparajito* (1956), and *The World of Apu* (1959). The films won acclaim for their realism, humanity, and sensitivity. Ray's other major motion pictures include *The Big City* (1963), *The Lonely Wife* (1964), *The Hero* (1966), *The Chess Players* (1977), and *The Stranger* (1991). Ray was born in Calcutta.   Dan Zeff

Rayburn, Sam (1882-1961), a Democrat, served longer as speaker of the United States House of Representatives than any other person. He was speaker from 1940 to 1947, from 1949 to 1953, and from 1955 until his death—nearly 17 years. Rayburn also served 49 consecutive years as a member of the House of Representatives.

Samuel Taliaferro Rayburn was born in Roane County, Tennessee. At age 5, he moved to Texas with his family.

He studied at East Texas College and at the University of Texas Law School. He served in the Texas state legislature from 1907 to 1913 and was speaker of the Texas House of Representatives from 1911 to 1913. He was elected to

UPI/Bettmann Newsphotos
Sam Rayburn

the U.S. House in 1912 and quickly became a leader in Congress, though he seldom made speeches. He presided over the 1952 and 1956 Democratic national conventions. Alonzo L. Hamby

Raymond, Henry Jarvis (1820-1869), brought political independence and moderation to American journalism through the newspaper he and two associates founded, *The New York Times*. He had two careers, one in journalism, the other in politics. As a journalist, he worked as an assistant to Horace Greeley, editor of the *New York Tribune*. After Raymond helped found the *Times*, they became political and journalistic rivals. The *Times* avoided sensationalism and concentrated on facts, and it soon became a leading newspaper. Raymond held public offices in New York, and served a term as a Republican member of Congress from 1865 until 1867. But he supported President Andrew Johnson's Reconstruction policies and soon lost political power. Raymond was born near Lima, New York.

I. W. Cole

Rayon is a manufactured fiber produced from wood or cotton. It is widely used to make industrial materials and knit and woven textiles for clothing and decorating fabrics. Some rayon fabrics are made heat resistant and used in certain spacecraft parts.

How rayon is made. Rayon is manufactured from the cellulose fiber of wood pulp or cotton (see **Cellulose**). Various chemical processes change the cellulose into a thick liquid. This liquid is then forced through extremely small openings in devices called *spinnerets* to form *filaments*, or tiny threads. There are two chief methods for making rayon: the viscose process and the cuprammonium process.

The viscose process is the usual method of making rayon. The process begins by soaking sheets of white pulp in a solution of sodium hydroxide. The soaked sheets are put through presses that squeeze out the ex-

cess solution. The sheets then pass through shredding machines where they are made into fine pieces called *crumbs*. The crumbs of cellulose are aged at high temperatures for about a day. Aging helps determine what type of yarn will be produced.

After aging, the crumbs are treated with carbon disulfide, which turns them to *cellulose xanthate*, a deep orange substance. Then the crumbs are dissolved in a weak solution of sodium hydroxide. This turns the mixture into *viscose,* a thick, molasseslike solution, which "ripens" for one to two days at a low temperature. When the solution has ripened, it is pumped to spinning machines and forced through the tiny holes in spinnerets to form filaments.

The cuprammonium process is a method of dissolving cotton cellulose in a copper-ammonia solution. A special spinning process produces yarns of ultrafine *denier*, or weight.

Spinning. All rayon-making centers on the spinneret, which contains a plate with tiny holes. Pumps force the cellulose through these holes. The threadlike cellulose then flows into a chemical bath that hardens the liquid into threads. The threads are twisted together to form rayon yarn. The yarns are woven into fabrics that look like cotton, wool, or spun silk.

Properties of rayon. Viscose and cuprammonium rayons have much the same chemical properties. Both dye easily, and both lose their strength when wet. They regain their original strength when dry. The wet strength of rayon can be considerably improved by varying the chemical bath composition.

History. In 1884, the French inventor and industrialist Hilaire Chardonnet patented the first practical manufactured fiber. He called it *artificial silk*. The fiber was first commercially produced in the United States in 1910. In 1924, it was named *rayon,* the *ray* indicating the sheen of the fiber, and the *on* showing that it was a cottonlike fiber. John H. Cosgrove

See also **Fiber** (Manufactured fibers); **Flannel**.

Razor is a cutting instrument used to remove hair from the skin. There are three chief kinds of razors: (1) safety razors, (2) straight-edged razors, and (3) electric razors.

Safety razors have blades that are shielded by metal or plastic holders. The holders make it difficult for a person to be cut deeply while shaving. The blade may have a cutting edge on one side or on both. It may be made of stainless steel and have chromium or platinum edges to prolong sharpness. After the blade becomes dull, it is replaced by a new one. Some razors use two replaceable blades, positioned one on top of the other. Others have a replaceable metal band that can be unwound to

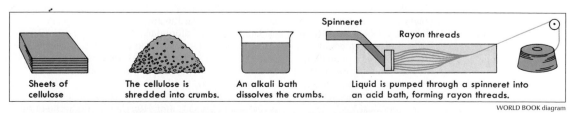

Spinneret

Rayon threads

Sheets of cellulose

The cellulose is shredded into crumbs.

An alkali bath dissolves the crumbs.

Liquid is pumped through a spinneret into an acid bath, forming rayon threads.

WORLD BOOK diagram

In the viscose process of making rayon, cellulose fibers from wood pulp or cotton are formed into sheets and treated with sodium hydroxide. The cellulose is then shredded into crumbs, treated with carbon disulfide, and dissolved in an alkali bath. Next, pumps force the liquid through the tiny holes of a device called a *spinneret* and into an acid bath to form rayon threads.

expose a fresh cutting edge. Disposable safety razors do not have replaceable blades. These inexpensive razors are thrown away after the blade becomes dull.

Straight-edged razors have specially tempered steel blades about 3 or 4 inches (8 to 10 centimeters) long. The blade has a rounded back and slopes to a fine edge. It is usually fastened by a rivet to a handle of two pieces of metal, ivory, or bone. The blade rests in the handle when not in use. It closes like a springless knife. The best blades were formerly made in Sheffield, England, but a number of factories now make blades as fine as the best Sheffield razors.

A good straight razor will last a long time if given good care. The razor wears well if the shaver soaks his face with lather before shaving. When a person shaves, the edge of the blade actually bends, causing it to become dull. The cutting edge should be smoothed with a leather strop before it is used. The blade must be *honed* (sharpened) regularly.

Electric razors are widely used. These little machines are powered by small electric motors. The cutting head passes over the skin and clips the hair. The head may become dull after continued use and may need either sharpening or replacing. The heads of many electric shavers can be adjusted for different beards. Some shavers have built-in auxiliary clippers that can trim long hairs and sideburns. Most cutting heads must be cleaned from time to time.   Robert Mugnai

RCMP. See **Royal Canadian Mounted Police**.

RDX is a powerful explosive also known as *cyclonite* and *hexogen*. During World War II (1939-1945), RDX was widely used as the chief explosive charge in bombs. It is still an important military explosive and also has wide use in detonators and fuses. RDX is made by the action of nitric acid on hexamethylene-tetramine, a product of formaldehyde and ammonia. Mixing RDX with liquid TNT forms an explosive called *Composition B*. This explosive is more powerful than TNT and has replaced it in most artillery shells.   James E. Kennedy

Re, *ray,* also known as *Ra (rah),* was the sun god in Egyptian mythology. He was a popular god often merged with other Egyptian deities, so he is often portrayed in various forms. The sun god was often shown as a simple sun disk. He also appeared as a child rising from a lotus, a falcon, a cat, and a scarab.

There are more myths and legends about Re than about any other Egyptian god. Some myths tell about the creation of the world and descriptions of his daily rebirth and perilous journey through the sky and the underworld. Other myths tell about Re's ruling on earth as king and about his becoming the father of three pharaohs.

Heliopolis was an early center for the worship of the sun god. There Re assumed many of the characteristics of Atum, an early sun god who created the world. By Dynasty V (2494-2345 B.C.), Egyptians regarded the sun god as their chief deity. From that time, every Egyptian king was given the title "son of Re." When other gods were later considered universal rulers, they absorbed Re's solar nature and had his name joined to theirs, as in Amon-Re and Sobek-Re.   Orval Wintermute

See also **Amon; Egypt, Ancient** (Gods and goddesses; The New Kingdom); **Mythology** (Egyptian mythology).

REA. See **Rural Electrification Administration**.

Reaction, in physics. See **Rocket** (How rockets work).

Reaction, Chemical. See **Chemical reaction**.

Reactionary. See **Conservatism**.

Reactor, Nuclear. See **Nuclear energy**.

Read, *reed,* **George** (1733-1798), a lawyer and statesman from Delaware, was one of six people who signed both the Declaration of Independence and the Constitution of the United States. At the Constitutional Convention of 1787, Read was a chief spokesman for the interests of small states, such as Delaware. He also supported the establishment of a strong presidency. Read led the movement for *ratification* (approval) of the Constitution by Delaware.

Read was born near North East in Cecil County, Maryland. Soon after his birth, his family moved to New Castle in the Delaware region. In 1754, Read began practicing law in New Castle. He served as attorney general of Delaware from 1763 to 1774 and as a state legislator from 1765 until about 1777.

Read served in the First and Second Continental Congresses from 1774 to 1777. He first voted against the Declaration of Independence, but he eventually signed the document.

Read served as a United States senator from 1789 to 1793. In 1793, he was appointed chief justice of the Delaware Supreme Court. He held this position until his death.   Barbara E. Benson

Reading, *REHD ihng* (pop. 78,380; met. area pop. 336,523), is a city on the Schuylkill River in southeastern Pennsylvania. For the location of Reading, see **Pennsylvania** (political map). The city lies in the heart of the Pennsylvania Dutch region. It is surrounded by fertile valleys that are noted for fruit growing, poultry producing, and dairy farming.

Reading is a center for agriculture-related businesses, including the farming of mushrooms and the production of pretzels and candy. Other products of the city include electronic components, specialty steels, truck and car frames, batteries, optical goods, paints, bricks, textiles, precision machinery and machine tools, and foundry products. In addition, the Reading area is a regional center for banking, insurance, and engineering services.

The Schuylkill River, the Schuylkill Canal, and the Reading Railroad played an important role in the development of Reading as a regional transportation center in the early 1800's. Today, the city receives rail freight service from the Norfolk Southern Railway. Commuter airplanes link Reading Municipal Airport with East Coast airports. An extensive system of highways, including the Pennsylvania Turnpike, serves the area.

Reading was designed in 1748 under the direction of two sons of William Penn. It was named for Reading, England, which was the ancestral home of the Penn family. During the Revolutionary War in America (1775-1783), military supplies for the Continental Army were stored in Reading. The city also was a hospital center and prison camp. Reading became a borough in 1783 and a city in 1847.

The city has a mayor-council form of government and is the seat of Berks County. Reading is the home of Albright and Alvernia colleges, Reading Area Community College, and the Berks Campus of Pennsylvania State University.   Joseph N. Farrell

© Richard Gross, The Stock Market

© David R. Frazier Photolibrary

WORLD BOOK photo

Reading is important at school, at work, and during leisure time. Students may read information from a computer disk for a class project. An executive may read a financial report or business plan. People may read magazines on home decorating or many other topics that interest them.

Reading

Reading is the act of getting meaning from printed or written words. It is basic to learning and one of the most important skills in everyday life. Reading provides the key to all kinds of information. It enables us to learn how to build or fix things, to enjoy stories, to discover what other people believe, and to develop ideas and beliefs of our own.

People may read hundreds or thousands of words a day without even looking at a book, newspaper, or magazine. For example, they read their mail, street signs, traffic directions, billboards, the printing on television commercials, package labels, and many other things that contain words.

In the simplest sense, reading means recognizing letters and groups of letters as symbols that stand for particular sounds. The sounds, in turn, form words that express ideas in written or printed form. A broader definition of reading links it more closely with other

Roger Farr, the contributor of this article, is Director of the Center for Reading and Language Studies at Indiana University at Bloomington.

uses of language and with thinking. According to that definition, reading first depends on a reader's memory and experience to understand what is read. It then involves how well the reader remembers, uses, and reacts to the material.

In most cases, the teaching of reading stresses certain skills, such as word recognition, vocabulary development, and *comprehension* (understanding of reading matter). However, the best way to learn to read may simply be just to read. Adults, especially parents, teachers, and librarians, can help children become good readers by reading to them and by encouraging them to read many kinds of materials—and to read often.

The importance of reading

Reading plays an essential role in the daily lives of most people. People read road signs, maps, recipes, labels on medicine bottles, and directions for operating new appliances. They read and fill out forms to file their income tax, to apply for jobs, and to request credit. The ability to perform such useful activities is sometimes called *functional reading* or *functional literacy.*

A special kind of functional reading, *learner literacy,* has always been important to students. All elementary school subjects, such as mathematics, science, social studies, and spelling, require students to read. In high school and college, learner literacy becomes even more vital. Older students must read to gain an understanding of a wide variety of topics. Learner literacy also requires the ability to read special kinds of materials, including charts, graphs, maps, and tables. People learn throughout their lives, and so such reading skills remain useful after a person has completed school.

Another kind of functional literacy, *workplace literacy,* concerns the ability to read written materials necessary for doing a job. Such materials include manuals on how to operate computers, robots, and other technical devices. In addition, being promoted often involves special training classes and workshops that call for particular reading skills. This is one way that a person's ability to read directly influences job success.

Besides reading in the classroom and on the job, people read books, magazines, and other printed materials for personal information and recreation. Many people read to learn more about their special interests, such as sports, science, current events, history, health, flowers, or painting. Millions of people read novels, adventure stories, biographies, and other books for fun. Recreational reading helps people understand others, takes readers on journeys to unknown parts of the world, and enables them to share the experiences of people throughout history.

As television became a major part of modern life, some experts predicted that people would not need or want to read as much as before. However, books, magazines, and newspapers still fill shelves in bookstores, drugstores, and supermarkets, as well as in libraries. Some experts believe that the information and entertainment provided by TV and related technologies have exposed people to new ideas and interests and so have created additional reasons to read.

Kinds of reading

People differ in reading ability. For example, those who have been reading a long time tend to understand what they read more quickly and more automatically than do new readers. In addition, older readers bring more background experiences to their reading. They can use their experiences to fill in important information that is not clearly stated in the text.

Regardless of age, training, and other experiences, reading abilities and habits vary from person to person. Some people read remarkably fast, while understanding the main points and remembering key examples. Others read at a snail's pace as they try to absorb every word—sometimes without evaluating the worth of the information.

A good reader uses various reading techniques. The technique depends on the type and difficulty of the material, the purpose for reading it, and the reader's own language development and familiarity with the subject.

Reading can be classified into three main kinds: (1) recreational reading, (2) study-type reading, and (3) survey reading. Good readers can easily shift from one kind to another, depending on their purpose for reading and on the material itself.

Recreational reading can provide hour after hour of enjoyment. When reading a story purely for pleasure, most people read at a relaxed, uneven speed. They may skim through a tale until they come to a scene, a description, or even a phrase that is especially pleasing or satisfying. That portion may be read slowly and then reread to be enjoyed, appreciated, or considered.

Study-type reading usually requires the reader to pay close attention to the text. A good reader looks for significant ideas and details. The reader then tries to understand how those ideas and details relate to one another and how they fit into the general topic. Reading speed tends to be slower the first time study-type material is read, and the reader may need to reread portions of the text to understand it fully. Reading speed may be much faster when the material is reviewed.

Survey reading involves covering a large amount of text to get a general idea of its content. In such cases, the person may first skim the material to understand the main point. The reader may then look for details that reinforce or illustrate that point. If the purpose is to find a particular fact or example, the reader may begin by skimming the text. The person may then read some sections carefully to make sure that the desired information has been found.

Shifting among kinds of reading. Most people use different reading techniques for different reading situations. For example, a mystery enjoyed simply for entertainment may be read rapidly. But a classic Russian novel may call for slow, careful reading. Technical texts that could lead to job advancement or that tell how to fix something usually require thoughtful reading.

Good readers can easily shift from one kind of reading to another. For instance, a student collecting information to write a paper might begin surveying articles to see if they fit the topic. One article may lead the student to consider changing the topic, and so the article is studied thoroughly and another topic chosen. While surveying for the new topic, the student looks for information to create an outline. During the survey reading, the student may see an entertaining article and read it for pleasure.

Reading flexibility improves with experience. Beginners may tend to read everything somewhat awkwardly, advancing slowly word by word because they doubt their ability to recognize words. By reading materials that follow their own *language patterns*—that is, familiar words and sentences they use—even beginning readers can read with both speed and understanding. In time, they learn that different reading materials make different demands on their abilities.

How we read

Reading depends first on our *perceiving* (seeing and recognizing) written or printed letters and words. We must then be able to comprehend what we perceive.

Perceiving reading matter. The process of reading begins as our eyes see *visual stimuli*—that is, the printed or written symbols that make up what is to be read. Eye movements across the symbols capture the stimuli. Eye movements called *saccadic movements* take place as our eyes move across a page, pausing briefly to take in groups of words. As our eyes move across a line, they alternately pause and move on. The pauses are called *fixations.* Another type of eye movement, *regression,* occurs when our eyes shift back to reread a word or group of words. To move from one line of type to the next, our eyes use a movement called a *return sweep.* However, good readers are unaware of their eye movements as they read.

Nerve cells in our eyes change the visual stimuli into electrical impulses that travel to the vision center of the brain. The vision center then sends the impulses to the specific areas of the brain responsible for thought organization, memory storage, and reasoning. Those areas identify the printed and written symbols and translate them into meaning. The physical process of reading also includes the storage of the sounds, meanings, and pictorial representations of what we read.

Comprehending what is perceived. Reading involves far more than simply seeing visual stimuli. You must first choose a particular text to satisfy some purpose. That purpose not only determines the selection of the text but also helps you decide which experiences and reading skills to use to comprehend the material. Your purpose may also suggest how you might use any new knowledge or understanding that you gain from the material.

While reading, you draw on numerous ideas and feelings stored in your memory. Those ideas and feelings make up your *background.* You also rely on *verbal memory*—that is, an understanding of how words come together and form more complex ideas.

Your background and verbal memory change and grow with each reading experience. Information in new material blends with your past experiences and may correct misunderstandings, provide fresh knowledge, broaden interests, or help solve problems.

In many cases, readers lack the background and verbal memory needed to comprehend a text quickly and easily. Such readers may use techniques called *word-recognition strategies.* The more experienced a reader becomes, the more automatically the reader applies these strategies to comprehend unfamiliar words.

Readers can use several general types of word-recognition strategies. For example, a reader who does not know the meaning of a particular word may look for *context clues* in the surrounding text. These clues may be either *semantic* or *syntactic.* When using semantic clues, the reader tries to relate the word to other information or illustrations in the material. Semantic clues include comparisons and contrasts, definitions, descriptions, and the placement of new words near familiar words that help explain their meaning. A reader may also rely on syntactic clues—that is, the word's position and grammatical use in the text. For example, deciding whether a word is functioning as a noun, verb, adjective, or adverb can help a reader figure out its meaning.

In a word-recognition strategy called *structural analysis,* a reader uses clues within the word itself to guess what the word means. The reader relies on knowledge of the meanings of prefixes, suffixes, *roots* (word bases), compound words, and inflectional endings such as *ed* and *ing,* and of how they are combined. For example, the adverb *undoubtedly* has the prefix *un,* the root *doubt,* the inflectional ending *ed,* and the suffix *ly.* Knowing the meanings of the parts of the word leads the reader to decide that the word means *without*

doubt. Some methods of teaching reading drill students on prefixes, suffixes, and the meaning of Latin and Greek roots. But the best way for readers to add such knowledge to verbal memory is to encounter words made of those parts in text they find meaningful, and to use the words in conversation and writing.

A word-recognition strategy called *phonics* uses the relationships between spoken sounds and letters. The word *phonics* comes from a Greek word meaning *sound.* Many beginning readers are taught to "sound out" a word, which they may then recognize if they have heard it before. In that way, a reader learns to associate printed symbols with spoken sounds. For more information on phonics, see the section *The teaching of reading* in this article. See also **Phonics.**

Readability. Reading success is determined not only by how well a person reads, but also by how readable the material is. Important factors that influence the readability of any printed material include (1) the average number of words in sentences, (2) the number of commonly understood words, (3) the average number of syllables in the words, (4) the number of long complex sentences, (5) the number of abstract ideas, and (6) the use of prepositional phrases.

Textbooks, reference books, newspapers, government publications, and informational brochures for consumers can be written at predetermined grade levels by controlling these factors. A number of formulas have been developed for estimating readability. The approximate reading level of the people who will read the material must be known. However, there is no formula or procedure to predict the attitudes and interests of readers, or to predict their previous knowledge about the subject. These three factors may lead people to read at lower or higher levels than might be predicted by a formula. Today many publishers reject rigid readability formulas, but they continue to design materials to the reading levels of the intended audience.

The teaching of reading

The complexity of the reading process makes it difficult to teach reading by only one method. Instead, most reading teachers use a combination of techniques determined by their own preferences, students' needs, and the instructional materials available. Commonly used teaching programs include (1) the developmental method, (2) the whole-language philosophy, (3) the language-experience method, (4) phonics instruction, (5) sight words and look-and-say instruction, and (6) individualized reading programs.

The developmental method uses a series of textbooks called *basal readers.* They serve as the basic reading materials in many schools. Basal readers gradually introduce the skills considered important for new readers, especially word-recognition strategies. The textbooks also give students opportunities to apply and practice the various skills.

The typical basal reader series consists of textbooks for each level of reading instruction. Publishers of these textbooks try to present stories, essays, and other writings to which children can relate. A book may include selections from award-winning literature and classics. In addition to student textbooks, basal programs provide teacher manuals, student workbooks, tests, and supplementary materials for each grade level. Teachers who use basal readers generally separate the children into groups according to reading abilities and instructional needs. They can then select the teaching materials that most closely match their teaching goals and the students' needs.

In developmental programs, most reading lessons involve answering in writing questions about the assignment and completing workbook pages that enable students to practice concepts presented in the reading lesson. A large number of lessons and activities also focus on the development of comprehension and analytical thinking. In addition, many programs help students determine their purpose for reading and encourage them to select additional reading materials.

Developmental programs are planned in great detail and enable schools to adjust their reading courses for all grade levels. However, some experts believe that the programs emphasize word-recognition strategies over comprehension, especially for beginning readers.

The whole-language philosophy tries to teach children that language is an effective and enjoyable way to communicate. Children learn new words in the reading material itself, where the meanings and uses of the words can be best understood.

The relationships between reading, writing, listening, and speaking are essential to the whole-language philosophy. The method defines writing as speaking in print, reading and listening as means of learning, and writing and reading as two ways of thinking with language. Whole-language teachers introduce children to both oral language and written language at as young an age as possible, sometimes as early as preschool.

The whole-language method states that the best way to learn to read is to read meaningful materials. Whole-language teachers emphasize the purpose for reading and student selection of reading matter. Instead of reading copies of the same textbook, students read materials that reflect their individual interests. They may often choose their own materials from their classroom, school, library, and home collections.

Reading in a whole-language classroom does not fol-low lessons that foresee reading strategy needs for a particular text. Nor do teachers drill students after reading a particular text on the reading skills used for that text. Instead, practice comes from simply reading more.

Whole-language theory claims that students cannot interpret a text correctly or incorrectly. Teachers encourage students to bring meaning to a text on the basis of their own backgrounds. The teachers assist students in the process by engaging them in conversation, asking thought-provoking questions, and suggesting examples of how they might interpret or respond to the text. A student learns through experience that inappropriate interpretations may lead to unsuccessful applications of what has been read. At the same time, the student learns that fresh, creative interpretations may be effective. Teachers accept any reasonable ideas that result from trying to construct meaning.

Educators who favor the whole-language method believe that reading cannot be analyzed in terms of specific strategies or skills. They argue that such analysis detracts from what reading really and simply is—the attempt of a reader to get meaning from a text. However, other educators believe that children learn reading more effectively through more structured programs that teach various strategies essential to reading.

The language-experience method seeks to develop reading skills by having learners use their own experiences and language abilities. It is based on the belief that "What I can say, I can write. What I can write, I can read." The method helps students understand that written language is simply oral language in printed form. The teacher uses the children's own language patterns and ideas to help them improve skills in reading, writing, listening, and speaking. The method is commonly used in whole-language classrooms and in some developmental programs.

In language experience, beginning readers create their own texts by dictating story ideas to the teacher. The students base the ideas on their own experiences at home or school. The teacher writes the story ideas on a chalkboard or on large sheets of paper, creating what are sometimes called *experience charts*. The teacher

© T. A. Etter

The language-experience method of reading instruction encourages beginning readers to tell their own stories to a teacher. The teacher writes the stories on large sheets of paper.

then goes over the experience chart with the class, having individual students read various sentences, reviewing material the class has already learned, or teaching any new words the chart contains. More experienced readers may also write and illustrate the stories themselves to create books for others to read.

Some educators believe that the language-experience method might limit students' learning of different ideas and cultures. But in most cases, teachers soon combine language experience with other methods. Experts who favor language experience believe that it is especially effective in giving children a solid grasp of what reading is—the process of getting meaning from written words.

Phonics instruction teaches children to relate letters to sounds. Phonics is actually a word-recognition strategy that becomes a teaching method only through heavy emphasis. Using phonetic principles, youngsters learn to associate the correct sound with each part of a word and to recognize and pronounce words.

Teachers of phonics assume that children know certain words from hearing them. They also assume that children can learn that the various sounds of spoken language, called *phonemes,* are represented by specific letters and letter combinations, called *graphemes.* Phonics instruction generally begins with teaching the sounds of initial consonants in words and of some vowel sounds. It moves on to consonants at the end of words, additional vowel sounds, and consonant combinations, such as *ch* in *chair* and *sh* in *wish.* Students also learn certain rules for sounding out words. For example, they are taught that when a word contains two vowels and one of them is a final *e,* as in *hole,* the final *e* is silent while the sound of the first vowel is long and so sounds like the name of the letter.

Phonics can be taught in two general ways. *Synthetic,* or *deductive, phonics* deals with the relationships between individual letters and sounds. Children then learn to split graphemes and to blend the phonemes they represent into words. They *synthesize* (sound out) the sounds that form unfamiliar words. Synthetic phonics has helped some people with severe reading problems. But it may limit a reader's ability to quickly grasp the ideas represented by groups of words. In *analytic,* or *inductive, phonics,* children analyze words for their sounds. Instruction begins by teaching the relationships between letters and sounds by referring to words the students know by sight. The teacher may then present other words that begin or end with the same letter and sound. Consonant and vowel combinations are also taught that way. Beginning readers eventually learn to recognize the sounds of new words.

The great irregularity in the relationships between letters and sounds in the English language presents difficulty if reading instruction heavily emphasizes phonics. Many sounds may be spelled in several ways. For example, the words *beat* and *beet, size* and *sighs,* and *eight* and *ate* sound the same but have different spellings and meanings. In addition, the same letters and letter combinations can stand for several sounds. For instance, the word *tear* is pronounced one way if it means to rip and another way if it means a drop of water from the eye. Some phonics instruction tries to deal with such irregularities through numerous complex exceptions to the rules of sounding out words.

A knowledge of phonics enables a person to determine the sounds of many unfamiliar words. Phonics can also help children in the early elementary grades learn to read. But the majority of experts believe that phonics becomes most effective when combined with other methods which stress meaning and comprehension.

Sight words and look-and-say instruction. If a reader recognizes a series of letters as soon as they are seen as a word, it is considered a *sight word.* Such a word communicates its meaning to the reader so fast that the process seems automatic. Sight-word instruction grew out of the assumption that children probably learn to identify words first by either their appearance or the context in which they appear. They learn to recognize the form of many words from simple books, program titles and commercials on television, and labels on various products. The beginning reader must acquire a basic sight vocabulary that includes the words used most frequently in spoken language. The same words also occur often in written language. Children can be helped to recognize basic sight words by practicing them.

Some reading authorities believe that new words can be taught as sight words, without any analysis of the sounds they require. Children learn many common words that way. In the 1930's, an extension of the practice led to a method called *look-and-say instruction* or *whole-word identification.* The technique stresses word recognition. Phonetic principles may unconsciously aid word recognition in the method. Reading teachers no longer emphasize look-and-say learning, but the development of a vocabulary of sight words remains part of the reading instruction in many classrooms.

Individualized reading programs take into account the wide range of reading abilities and needs. Such a program adjusts instruction and reading materials to the reading achievement, interests, and ability of each student. The classrooms and school libraries have books and other reading matter that cover many grade levels and fields of interest. An individualized reading program requires careful supervision by the teacher, who must check each child's progress in skills, attitudes, and interests. Individual children progress as rapidly as they can. These programs may include elements of other teaching methods, such as the whole-language philosophy or the language-experience method.

Computer-assisted instruction may play an important role in individualized reading programs, though it can also supplement other teaching methods. Computer instruction includes text material followed by questions that test the student's comprehension. In addition, word-processor programs enable students to create their own stories. Such programs are also common in language-experience and whole-language classrooms.

Developing good readers

For many years, educators tried to determine *reading readiness*—that is, when children were ready to learn how to read. They believed that visual and listening abilities, personality development, interests and experiences, emotional stability, language achievement, and certain other characteristics indicated reading readiness. The experts generally agreed that by the time boys and girls reached $6\frac{1}{2}$ years of age, the various charac-

A visit to the library enables students to select books on subjects that interest them. Reading about topics they enjoy, or want to know more about, helps children develop their reading abilities.

Oak Park Elementary Schools (WORLD BOOK photo by Dan Miller)

teristics had developed enough for children to learn to read. As a result, most schools offered formal reading instruction to youngsters beginning at that age.

Today, most educators question the idea of reading readiness at precisely age $6\frac{1}{2}$. They point out that being $6\frac{1}{2}$ years old does not automatically assure that a child will profit from reading instruction. Some children do not fully develop the skills traditionally associated with reading readiness until age 8. Others have them by age 4. In addition, many experts now believe that learning to read depends mainly on whether a child can focus the mind on letters and words as symbols of meaning. The development of that capacity has come to be called *emergent literacy*—that is, the beginning of the ability to read. The amount of experience a child has had with oral and written language—rather than the child's age—appears to be a key to emergent literacy.

Research shows that children begin to associate sounds with the symbols they stand for at an early age. Very young children with no reading experience may astound their parents with the first words they read, such as a department store sign announcing Big Sale. If children who cannot write are asked to write the story they have been telling orally, they tend to scribble in patterns across a page. Such children show an understanding of what writing is and how it is put on a page.

Research thus demonstrates that children begin to understand language from the time they first listen to adults talk to them. Children try, in turn, to express their needs to adults with a variety of sounds. Emergent literacy suggests that children of all ages can learn from language-related experiences. Children's experiences at home and at school greatly influence how well they learn to read.

Learning in the home. At home, parents and other adults can promote the growth of a child's language-related abilities in many ways. First, they should make sure that the child is physically able to read by watching for vision or hearing problems that could be treated or corrected. Adults should also spend much time talking to the young child in an appealing and clear voice. Such

attention will likely arouse the youngster's interest in language and provide opportunities to distinguish various sounds and to build vocabulary. Some adults move attractive objects before a baby's eyes to encourage alertness and to exercise developing *motor skills* (controlled movements) of the eyes and head.

As children begin to use language, parents and other adults should try to converse with them. In so doing, grown-ups should respect a child's interests and ideas and be patient with the youngster's attempts to express them. Adults thereby teach the value of language as a means of communication. They also become a chief source of information for a curious child. Adults can help a child grasp basic ideas and how they relate to one another, such as the difference between *up* and *down* and between *under* and *over*.

Letting a child assist with cooking or building something serves as an excellent way to introduce measurements and an understanding of sizes and proportions. In helping sort the laundry, the youngster can learn to group or classify objects. Such activities aid the development of logical-thinking skills and teach the young girl or boy how to follow a sequence of directions.

By reading aloud to a child regularly, an adult can help a child learn to love books and reading. Even a child too young to understand the words will enjoy the closeness of the activity. In selecting reading materials for older children, adults should consider the child's maturity and interests. The youngster can become involved in a story by asking questions or by trying to guess what will happen next. Above all, frequent reading aloud to the child enables the adult to demonstrate the enjoyment that language and reading can provide. Adults can also show how much they like to read by setting aside time to read for their own enjoyment.

Working with the school. Schools build on the language learning begun in the home. Teachers encourage reading development by reading to children, telling them stories, discussing childhood experiences, and providing them with new experiences. Teachers can also give children many opportunities to express themselves orally, and they can write or type simple stories the children dictate. Reading programs in the early elementary grades stress basic skills essential to gaining independence in recognizing and understanding new words. Such programs also help children use the words in meaningful sentences and develop interests and attitudes toward reading as a satisfying experience.

A child's progress in becoming an independent reader depends heavily on cooperation between parents and teachers. Parents can reinforce the school's reading instruction by learning about their youngster's school experiences. As the child learns to read, adults should continue to show that they view reading as important, enjoyable, and worthwhile. For example, they can read often and regularly themselves. They can also provide interesting and appealing reading matter in the home.

Parents and other adults should find out which topics and school subjects especially interest a child. The information will help them determine how well the school's reading materials serve—or could serve—the youngster's particular interests. Adults themselves may then be led to provide reading matter that the child would gladly turn to. For example, the parent of a teen-ager might mention what a critic said about a new pop singer in a magazine. A copy of the magazine just happens to be on the coffee table, where the teen-ager can later discover it and verify or challenge the critic's comments.

Children who care little about school and perform poorly might not have developed the necessary reading abilities to succeed, or they may simply lack interest in the subjects covered. Forcing a youngster to read seldom provides a lasting solution and almost certainly

© Superstock

Reading aloud to a child is an enjoyable activity for both the adult and the youngster. In selecting reading materials, adults should consider the child's maturity and interests.

does not contribute to developing a good reader. But appealing to young people's interests and showing how reading can serve them have proved to be successful.

Reading problems

Researchers have long tried to identify the specific reasons some people do not learn to read as well as others. But the more that researchers have realized how complex the reading process is, the more they have concluded that it is more important to treat the reading problems that arise in an individual child than to find the precise cause of the problems. Some specialists use the term *dyslexia* to cover most reading problems. Narrowly defined, dyslexia refers to a problem in which a reader sees letters or words reversed or upside down. However, such reversals occur fairly often among inexperienced readers. The term has generally lost favor because it came to be used to describe a broad range of reading problems, which led to confusion about its meaning. See **Dyslexia.**

Most specialists prefer the term *reading disability* to describe a lack of the reading development that could be expected in a person with normal vision, normal hearing, and normal or above normal intelligence. Many experts now believe that reading problems have a combination of causes. Many of the causes are so closely interwoven that it is extremely difficult to separate them. In addition, no two readers have exactly the same difficulties. All reading problems should be therefore diagnosed and treated by a specialist. For more information on reading problems, see **Learning disabilities.**

Signs of reading problems. Parents, teachers, and other adults should watch for signs of reading difficulty in children. They should suspect a possible disability if a child dislikes reading, school, and homework. Instead, the child may prefer activities that require little or no use of language. Poor grades and teacher concern may result. The youngster may seek out friends who are not particularly involved or successful at school.

Adults should also consider the possibility of a reading problem if a child has an unusually small vocabulary. A youngster who does not speak well, resists talking with adults, or avoids situations that might involve writing may have trouble understanding both oral language and written language.

Causes of reading difficulties. Reading problems can be classified into four general types. They are (1) aliteracy, (2) failure to concentrate, (3) insufficient experience, and (4) physical disabilities.

Aliteracy means the lack of desire to read. Aliterate people can read, but they tend to avoid the activity. Aliteracy reinforces itself—that is, people who do not read much do not develop their reading skills. People usually dislike doing things they do poorly, and so aliterate people tend to read less and less. Such reinforcement becomes especially true in the classroom, where the aliterate student sits among skilled readers.

A solution to aliteracy lies in capturing the student's interest with attractive, meaningful reading materials. The student who learns obviously beneficial things through reading may become a frequent reader.

Failure to concentrate. To get meaning from reading matter, a person must focus the mind on the text. Almost all readers occasionally fail to understand the text their

Oak Park Elementary Schools (WORLD BOOK photo by Dan Miller)

Reading disabilities require special teaching methods. This teacher is using individualized reading materials to help a student improve her ability to recognize letters and words.

eye movements perceive. Some readers—particularly young ones dealing with assigned material—often try to read that way, as though the process were so automatic as to require no thought. But for comprehension to occur, readers must bring their knowledge and experience to the act of gaining meaning from words. Obviously, comprehension demands paying attention to the topic and what the text appears to say about it.

Readers can work to improve comprehension in several ways. First, they should understand the reason for reading a particular text. Readers should then make assumptions and predictions regarding the text to be read based on such things as its title, author, and structure. While reading, they should summarize and evaluate the material. Consulting other resources—such as a dictionary, another text, or a teacher or other adult—can help clarify difficult material.

Insufficient experience. All readers bring their experiences to the comprehension process. Youngsters from homes where conversation, ideas, and printed materials are valued have a broad base of experience and thus an advantage in developing as readers. Children whose experiences have been limited may have more difficulty with reading. In addition, readers may bring considerable background to some topics but little experience to others.

Adults can help children become successful readers by providing them with many varied experiences, especially language-related experiences. The act of reading itself enriches the child's background, and so experience and reading reinforce each other.

Children who speak a language or dialect that differs from the one used in their school may require language-development programs. Such programs teach that children can learn more than one language or dialect to take part in mainstream society—and still have

pride in their own culture. Many schools in the United States teach English as a second language and provide special instruction for children who speak two languages.

Physical disabilities. Inadequate brain development or vision or hearing defects can cause reading difficulties. However, they account for only a small percentage of all reading problems. Adults will almost certainly notice major brain-development abnormalities in a child long before concerns about the youngster's reading abilities arise. Parents may thus already have been receiving help with the child. However, lesser abnormalities may not appear until the child begins to learn to read. Teachers who notice a large difference between a child's expected reading performance and the youngster's actual achievement may recommend that a pediatrician evaluate the child.

A vision or hearing problem does not by itself cause poor reading. However, correction of such a problem aids reading development. Vision or hearing defects may not become obvious until a child takes screening tests at school, but parents or teachers may notice them earlier. Signs of possible vision problems include frequent rubbing or squinting of the eyes, holding pictures and print close to the face or too far away, and complaining of headaches. Children who do not pay attention, who misunderstand directions or ask to have them repeated, or who have unusual speech habits may experience hearing difficulties. In most cases, vision or hearing problems can be corrected with eyeglasses or a hearing aid. But for some children, special help with reading is also necessary.

Reading and society

The way of life in any country reflects in large part the percentage of its people who can read and write—and

Reading Is Fundamental®; illustrated by Tracy Bailey, winner of the RIF National Poster Contest

A poster promoting the joy of reading was created by a schoolgirl for Reading Is Fundamental, one of various groups that work to increase awareness of the importance of reading.

© J. R. Holland, Stock, Boston

Eliminating illiteracy is an important part of the educational program of developing nations. The teacher shown above is teaching students in Libya how to read Arabic.

the percentage who can read and write well. The higher the percentage of literate people, the more technologically, scientifically, and economically advanced the way of life.

Most societies therefore value the ability to read and write well. Skilled readers contribute to creating a prosperous, productive society. At the same time, they themselves enjoy fuller, more satisfying lives.

In every society, some people have only basic reading and writing skills. They can read simple signs, package labels, and similar matter. Such functionally literate people can read and write just enough to get by. That limited ability may be adequate in a remote village of a developing country but not in a major city of a modern industrial nation. On the other hand, even highly developed nations have functionally illiterate people. They cannot handle the reading and writing that may be required on the job. They may also be unable to use language well enough in other ways to meet the demands of their society.

Figures on literacy around the world are based on estimates made in each country. Not all countries define literacy the same way. But most try to describe some very basic level of reading and writing ability. In the early 1990's, about three-fourths of the world's population 15 years old or older could read and write. That means about 1 billion of the world's people were illiterate.

In a number of countries, including Australia, Germany, and Japan, 99 percent or more of the people age 15 or older can read and write. However, functional illiteracy remains a problem in advanced nations. For example, about one-fifth of all adult Americans are functionally illiterate.

Africa, Asia, and Latin America have the greatest percentages of illiterate people. The world literacy rate,

however, has been increasing. In Latin America, for example, the literacy rate rose from about 70 percent in 1960 to about 85 percent in the early 1990's. See **Literacy** (table: Literacy rates for selected countries).   Roger Farr

Related articles in *World Book* include:

Book	Learning disabilities
Curriculum	Library
Dictionary	Literacy
Dyslexia	Literature for children
Elementary school	Perception
Encyclopedia	Phonics
Guidance	Speed reading
Kindergarten	Study
Language	Vocabulary

Outline

I. The importance of reading
II. Kinds of reading
  A. Recreational reading
  B. Study-type reading
  C. Survey reading
  D. Shifting among kinds of reading
III. How we read
  A. Perceiving reading matter
  B. Comprehending what is perceived
  C. Readability
IV. The teaching of reading
  A. The developmental method
  B. The whole-language philosophy
  C. The language-experience method
  D. Phonics instruction
  E. Sight words and look-and-say instruction
  F. Individualized reading programs
V. Developing good readers
  A. Learning in the home
  B. Working with the school
VI. Reading problems
  A. Signs of reading problems
  B. Causes of reading difficulties
VII. Reading and society

Questions

How can teachers encourage reading development?
Why do most people use different reading techniques for different reading situations?
What is *emergent literacy*?
Why has the ability to read well always been important to students?
How can *context clues* help a reader figure out the meaning of a word?
Why do most societies value reading ability?
What is *aliteracy*? How can it be solved?
In the language-experience method of instruction, how do beginning readers create their own texts?
How can parents and other adults promote language development in children at home?
How do the two general types of phonics instruction differ?

Additional resources

Anderson, Walter. *Read with Me.* Houghton, 1990. Concerns adult literacy.
Carruth, Gorton. *The Young Reader's Companion.* Bowker, 1993.
Cullinan, Bernice E. *Read to Me: Raising Kids Who Love to Read.* Scholastic, 1992.
Fox, Barbara J. *Rx for Reading.* Penguin, 1989.
Hauser, Jill F. *Growing Up Reading: Learning to Read Through Creative Play.* Williamson, 1993.
Itzkoff, Seymour W. *How We Learn to Read.* Paideia Pubs., 1986.
Leonhardt, Mary. *Parents Who Love Reading, Kids Who Don't.* Crown, 1993.
Lyman, Donald E. *Making the Words Stand Still.* Houghton, 1986. Presents techniques for overcoming reading and learning disabilities.
Rosenthal, Nadine. *Teach Someone to Read: A Step-By-Step Guide for Literacy Tutors.* David S. Lake, 1987.

**40th President of
the United States 1981-1989**

Carter
39th President
1977-1981
Democrat

Reagan
40th President
1981-1989
Republican

Bush
41st President
1989-1993
Republican

**George H. W.
Bush**
Vice President
1981-1989

Michael Evans,Gamma/Liaison

Reagan, *RAY guhn,* **Ronald Wilson** (1911-   ), was
elected President of the United States in 1980 and won a
second term in 1984. Reagan, a Republican, had served
two terms as governor of California before he became
President. In 1980, Reagan defeated President Jimmy
Carter, the Democratic candidate. In 1984, Reagan defeated former Vice President Walter F. Mondale, the
Democratic nominee, in a landslide. The President won
525 electoral votes, more than any other presidential
candidate in the nation's history. Before Reagan entered
politics, he had been an actor nearly 30 years. He appeared in more than 50 movies.

When Reagan became President, the nation faced serious foreign and domestic problems. Relations between the United States and the Soviet Union had
reached their lowest point in years following a Soviet invasion of Afghanistan in late 1979 and early 1980. Reagan
strengthened the military systems of the United States
and its allies in Western Europe. This angered the Soviet
Union. The Reagan Administration also increased U.S. involvement in Central America. It gave military equipment
to troops fighting Communist-supported forces in El Salvador and Nicaragua. In 1987, Reagan and Soviet leader
Mikhail Gorbachev signed a treaty that led to a reduction of certain U.S. and Soviet nuclear arms.

At home, Reagan had to deal with high inflation, a recession, and high unemployment. He won congressional
approval of large federal income tax cuts to help stimulate the economy. By the end of Reagan's first term, rapid

inflation had ended, unemployment had fallen, and the
economy had made a strong recovery. But federal expenses so greatly exceeded income that budget *deficits*
(shortages) reached record levels.

Reagan was a skillful campaigner and a gifted speaker.
He stressed such traditional values as work, the family,
patriotism, and self-reliance. At the age of 69, Reagan
was the oldest man ever elected President. But he
looked far younger and was vigorous and athletic. Reagan listed his chief interests as drama, politics, and
sports. Reagan especially enjoyed horseback riding at
his weekend ranch, Rancho del Cielo, near Santa Barbara, Calif.

Early life

Boyhood. Reagan was born on Feb. 6, 1911, in Tampico, Ill. His parents were John Edward Reagan, a shoe
salesman, and Nelle Wilson Reagan, a homemaker and
occasional shop clerk. When Ronald was a baby, his father nicknamed him Dutch. The boy had one brother,
John Neil (1909-1996), nicknamed Moon, who was an advertising executive.

Nelle Reagan loved the theater and took part in many
amateur productions. As a result, Dutch became interested in acting at an early age. The Reagans lived in several small towns in western Illinois. Dutch's father moved
the family from town to town as he searched for work.
Reagan later wrote about his boyhood, "I realize now
that we were poor, but I didn't know it at the time."

Education. When Dutch was 9 years old, he and his
family settled in Dixon, Ill., where the boy finished elementary school and went to high school. In high school,
he played football and basketball and took part in track
and swimming meets. He appeared in several school

*Bill Boyarsky, the contributor of this article, is a columnist for
the* Los Angeles Times *and the author of* Ronald Reagan: His Life
and Rise to the Presidency.

Sandra Day O'Connor, *left,* became the first woman justice of the Supreme Court of the United States. Reagan appointed O'Connor during his first term to fill a vacancy created by the retirement of Justice Potter Stewart in 1981.

A terrorist bombing of U.S. Marine headquarters in Beirut, Lebanon, in 1983 killed 241 U.S. troops. They were part of a peacekeeping force sent by the Reagan Administration.

The world of President Reagan

The first permanent artificial heart implantation took place at the University of Utah Medical Center in 1982. Surgeons implanted the mechanical heart in 61-year-old Barney Clark, who survived for 112 days after the surgery.

Terrorism became a growing international concern, as political extremists from various countries used such tactics as bombings, hijackings, and kidnappings to call attention to their causes.

A "computer revolution" took hold in the United States during the 1980's. Computers became common in schools, banks, offices, libraries, supermarkets, and other places.

Famine in Africa caused thousands of deaths in the early 1980's, as one of the worst droughts in history spread across Ethiopia and other nations. Worldwide relief efforts included an all-day televised rock music concert, called "Live Aid," that raised millions of dollars for the famine victims in 1985.

A volcanic eruption in Colombia in 1985 triggered mud slides and floods that killed about 25,000 people.

The space shuttle *Challenger*'s destruction in an accident in January 1986 stunned the nation and brought the United States manned space program to a halt. The country mourned the deaths of the seven crew members on board.

South Africa's apartheid system of racial segregation became the target of widespread protests in the United States and elsewhere during the mid-1980's.

The Statue of Liberty centennial was celebrated in New York City in July 1986. The extravaganza included fireworks, parades of ships, and outdoor musical performances.

© Owen Franken, Sygma; © Frank Dougherty, Camera 5

plays and was elected president of the student council. During the summers, he worked as a lifeguard.

In 1928, following graduation from high school, Reagan entered Eureka College in Eureka, Ill. He paid his college expenses with a partial scholarship, savings from the lifeguard job, and money he earned washing dishes at a fraternity house. In college, Dutch majored in economics and sociology. He played football, joined the track team, and served as captain of the swimming team. He had leading roles in many college plays and became president of the student body.

Acting career

Motion-picture star. After graduating from Eureka College in 1932, Reagan became a sports announcer for radio station WOC in Davenport, Iowa. That year, he moved to station WHO in Des Moines, Iowa. He broadcast play-by-play accounts of major league baseball games, Big Ten football games, and other sports events.

Important dates in Reagan's life

1911 (Feb. 6) Born in Tampico, Ill.
1932 Graduated from Eureka College.
1937 Made film debut in *Love Is On the Air.*
1940 (Jan. 25) Married Jane Wyman.
1942-1945 Served in the U.S. Army Air Forces.
1948 Divorced from Jane Wyman.
1952 (March 4) Married Nancy Davis.
1966 Elected governor of California.
1970 Reelected governor of California.
1980 Elected President of the United States.
1984 Reelected President.

In 1937, Reagan traveled to southern California to report on the spring training season of the Chicago Cubs baseball team. There, he made a screen test for Warner Brothers, one of the largest motion-picture studios. The studio signed him to an acting contract.

Reagan made his film debut in *Love Is On the Air*

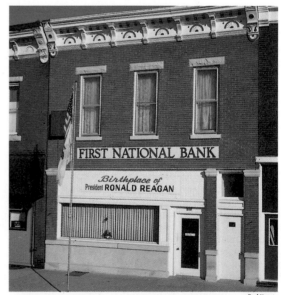

Earl Krantz

Reagan's birthplace was an apartment above a bakery, later a bank, in this brick building in Tampico, Ill. Reagan finished elementary school and attended high school in nearby Dixon, Ill.

(1937), in which he played a radio announcer. He soon became a star and was known for his roles as a wholesome, likable young man. He portrayed Western heroes in such films as *Santa Fe Trail* (1940), *Law and Order* (1953), and *Tennessee's Partner* (1955). He also played American servicemen in many movies, including *International Squadron* (1941), *The Voice of the Turtle* (1947), and *The Hasty Heart* (1949). In *Knute Rockne—All American* (1940), Reagan played one of his best-known roles, that of college football star George (the Gipper) Gipp. Reagan won praise from critics for his performance as a young man whose legs were amputated in *Kings Row* (1942). In 1965, Reagan used a line he spoke in that film—"Where's the rest of me?"—as the title of his autobiography. Altogether, Reagan appeared in more than 50 feature films between 1937 and 1964, most of them for Warner Brothers.

Reagan entered the U.S. Army Air Forces in 1942, during World War II. He was disqualified from combat duty because of poor eyesight. Instead, he spent most of the war in Hollywood, where he helped make training films. He was discharged in 1945 as a captain.

Union leader. In 1947, Reagan became president of the Screen Actors Guild (SAG), a union that represents film performers. He was elected to five consecutive terms, serving until 1952. During that time, which was a period of strong anti-Communist feeling in the United States, Reagan worked to remove suspected Communists from the movie industry. In 1949 and 1950, he served as chairman of the Motion Picture Industry Council, a public relations organization devoted to improving the public image of the film business.

Reagan served a sixth term as president of SAG in 1959 and 1960. During that period, he led a long and finally successful strike against the movie studios. The strike won payments to the actors for sales of their old films to television. Part of the money was used for a pension fund.

Family life. Reagan met actress Jane Wyman while they both were appearing in Warner Brothers films. They were married on Jan. 25, 1940. The couple had a daughter, Maureen Elizabeth (1941-   ), and adopted a son, Michael Edward (1945-   ). The marriage ended in divorce in 1948.

In 1951, while Reagan was president of SAG, he met actress Nancy Davis (July 6, 1923-   ). Davis had complained to SAG that she was receiving unwanted Communist literature in the mail. She and Reagan were married on March 4, 1952. The couple had two children, Patricia Ann (1952-   ) and Ronald Prescott (1958-   ).

Television star. From 1954 to 1962, Reagan hosted "The General Electric Theater," a weekly dramatic series on television. He also starred in several episodes in the series, which was sponsored by the General Electric Company, a leading manufacturer of electrical products. Between TV appearances, Reagan toured the country as a public relations representative for General Electric. He visited the company's plants and made speeches before chambers of commerce and other civic groups. In his talks, Reagan stressed such conservative ideas as the importance of free enterprise and the dangers of too much government.

From 1962 to 1965, Reagan hosted and performed in a Western series called "Death Valley Days." He also made

Culver

A popular movie actor, Reagan appeared in more than 50 feature films from 1937 to 1964. The scene above is from *Tennessee's Partner* (1955), one of many Westerns that starred Reagan.

commercials for the sponsor, United States Borax & Chemical Corporation, a maker of cleaning products.

Political career

Entry into politics. Reagan had long taken an active interest in politics. At first, he held liberal views and belonged to the Democratic Party. In the 1948 presidential election, he campaigned for President Harry S. Truman, the Democratic candidate. During the 1950's, Reagan's views became more conservative. He campaigned as a Democratic supporter of several Republican candidates, including presidential nominees Dwight D. Eisenhower in 1952 and 1956 and Richard M. Nixon in 1960. In 1962, Reagan became a Republican.

Reagan first gained nationwide political attention during the 1964 presidential campaign, when he made a stirring TV speech in behalf of the Republican candidate, Barry M. Goldwater. In the speech, Reagan attacked high taxes, wasteful government spending, the growth of government agencies, the rising crime rate, and soaring welfare costs. The speech drew record numbers of contributions for the Goldwater campaign.

Governor of California. Reagan first won public office in 1966, when he was elected governor of California. He defeated the state's Democratic governor, Edmund G. (Pat) Brown, by a landslide.

Reagan began his term as governor in January 1967. Once in office, he worked to slow the growth of government spending. He put a freeze on the hiring of state employees. He also persuaded state lawmakers to pass a welfare reform program. During his campaign, Reagan had criticized high taxes. Upon taking office, however, he found that there was a deficit in the state treasury. Reagan then sponsored three tax increases, one of them the largest in the state's history. But after the tax hikes had produced a surplus in the treasury, Reagan distributed much of the excess money to taxpayers.

Reagan was reelected governor of California in 1970 and served until 1975. As governor, he made major policy decisions himself but relied on others to handle the details.

Presidential candidate. In 1968, Reagan had campaigned briefly for the Republican presidential nomination but did not win. In 1976, he tried again. He attracted much support among conservatives and won many delegates in the South and West. In an attempt to appeal to more liberal and Eastern delegates, he announced that his choice for Vice President would be Senator Richard S. Schweiker of Pennsylvania. Schweiker was known for his liberal Senate record. But Reagan lost the nomination to President Gerald R. Ford by a narrow margin.

Reagan soon began to plan his campaign for the 1980 nomination. By November 1979, when he announced his candidacy, he had a huge lead in the polls over his Republican rivals. Six other Republicans sought the nomination. Reagan's chief opponents were Representative John B. Anderson of Illinois; George Bush, former U.S. ambassador to the United Nations (UN); and John B. Connally, former governor of Texas.

In February 1980, Reagan won the year's first presidential primary election in New Hampshire. His popularity continued to grow during the spring. In March, he won important primary victories over Connally in South Carolina and over Anderson and Bush in Illinois. By the end of May, Reagan had won 20 of the 24 primaries so far held, and the other Republican candidates had withdrawn from the race. Anderson, however, decided to run as an independent.

In July 1980, Reagan easily won the nomination for President on the first ballot at the Republican National Convention in Detroit. At his request, Bush was nominated for Vice President. The Democrats renominated President Jimmy Carter and Vice President Walter F. Mondale. Anderson chose former Governor Patrick J. Lucey of Wisconsin as his running mate.

The 1980 election. In the presidential campaign, Reagan charged that Carter had failed to deal effectively with inflation and unemployment. During the first half of 1980, the inflation rate was about 15 per cent, and about $7\frac{1}{2}$ per cent of the nation's workers had no jobs. Reagan called for a lowering of the minimum wage law in the

© Shelly Katz, Black Star

Reagan and his running mate, George Bush, easily won the 1980 presidential election. They were reelected in 1984.

Reagan's first election

Place of nominating convention	Detroit
Ballot on which nominated	1st
Opponents	Jimmy Carter (Democratic Party)
	John B. Anderson (independent candidate)
Electoral vote	489 (Reagan) to 49 (Carter) and 0 (Anderson)
Popular vote	43,904,153 (Reagan) to 35,483,883 (Carter) and 5,719,437 (Anderson)
Age at inauguration	69

case of teen-agers to reduce unemployment among young people. To stimulate the economy, he proposed to slash federal income taxes by up to 30 per cent. He pledged to boost military spending and to reduce government regulation of business. He also promised to balance the federal budget, claiming that a tax cut would increase economic activity so much that tax revenues would rise, not fall. This emphasis on tax reductions to stimulate business activity was known as the *supply-side theory* of economics.

Carter argued that Reagan's plans would lead to still more inflation. He also questioned whether Reagan could balance the budget, reduce taxes, and increase defense spending all at the same time. In the election, Reagan defeated Carter and Anderson by a wide margin. He received about 44 million popular votes to about 35 million popular votes for Carter and about $5\frac{1}{2}$ million for Anderson. Reagan carried 44 states for a total of 489 electoral votes, while Carter carried only 6 states and the District of Columbia for 49 electoral votes.

Reagan's first Administration (1981-1985)

Events at home. Reagan's first major domestic programs dealt with the economy. The President quickly took steps to fulfill his campaign pledges to stop rapid inflation and stimulate business.

Early economic programs. In February 1981, Reagan proposed an economic plan that combined tax cuts with wide reductions in welfare and unemployment programs and in many other areas of the budget. The plan included a large increase in defense spending. Reagan also worked to curb federal agencies that he felt went too far in regulating business. Newspapers and magazines called his economic policies *Reaganomics.*

By August, Congress had approved nearly all of Reagan's proposed tax and spending cuts. The main law, called the Economic Recovery Tax Act of 1981, reduced individual and corporation income taxes by about $33 billion for the 1982 fiscal year, with more cuts scheduled later. It was the largest income tax cut in U.S. history.

Recession and recovery. A recession struck in mid-1981 and ended Reagan's hope for rapid improvement in the economy. The rate of inflation slowed, but thousands of companies went bankrupt and unemployment soared. The rising joblessness contributed to a sharp loss of tax revenue. This decline and increased defense spending helped produce a growing federal budget deficit.

To reduce the deficit, Congress adopted tax increases

totaling about $91 billion in 1982. This was the largest tax increase in U.S. history. The deficit for the 1982 fiscal year, however, reached a record $110.7 billion. By late 1982, about 11 percent of the labor force had no jobs—the highest unemployment rate since 1941.

The economy began to recover rapidly in 1983. But the federal budget deficit reached another record level in the 1983 fiscal year—about $195 billion. The economy thrived in 1984, and the rate of inflation remained low. But the deficit rose rapidly.

Public criticism of many of Reagan's appointments and domestic policies grew steadily. The President's major critics included blacks, women, and environmentalists. Millions of Americans, especially blacks, suffered from unemployment and reductions in social programs. Numerous blacks charged that the President's policies discriminated against them. Many people contended that Reagan's chief goal was to aid the rich. But a number of wealthy Americans criticized the President for supporting the tax increases. In addition, many business executives objected to the record deficits.

A number of women's groups claimed that Reagan did not name enough women to important government posts. But Reagan became the first President to appoint a woman to the Supreme Court of the United States. In 1981, he chose Sandra Day O'Connor to fill a vacancy on the court. Reagan was the first President to have three women serving in Cabinet-level posts at the same time. These women were Margaret M. Heckler, secretary of health and human services; Elizabeth H. Dole, secretary of transportation; and Jeane J. Kirkpatrick, U.S. representative to the United Nations.

Reagan and Secretary of the Interior James G. Watt came under heavy criticism from conservation and wildlife preservation groups. These groups opposed the Administration's efforts to weaken a number of laws designed to protect air and water quality, endangered species, and wildlife refuges. Reagan argued that the laws blocked industrial and mineral development needed to create jobs and help the economy. Continued criticism of Watt led to his resignation in 1983.

Important legislation approved during Reagan's first Administration included bills dealing with banking, job training, and social security. The Garn-St. Germain Depository Institutions Act of 1982 helped banks and savings and loan associations compete with money market funds for savings (see **Bank** [A boom in money market funds]). The Job Training Partnership Act of 1982 provided job training for unskilled, disadvantaged youths and for needy adults. The Social Security Amendments of 1983 were designed to solve short- and long-term financing problems. One of the amendments raised the system's traditional retirement age (see **Social security** [Developments since 1970]).

An attempted assassination of Reagan occurred in March 1981 in Washington, D.C. Reagan was shot in the chest, but surgeons removed the bullet , and the president made a full recovery. Three other people, including Reagan's press secretary, James S. Brady, also were shot. John W. Hinckley, Jr., of Evergreen, Colorado, was charged with the shooting. In 1982, a jury declared that Hinckley was insane at the time of the attempted assassination and, therefore, found him not guilty of the attempted murder charge. A federal judge later ordered that Hinckley be placed in a mental institution.

Foreign affairs. Reagan showed much political skill when he won a struggle with Congress over his defense program. The plan called for a large build-up of missiles, bombers, and other weapons. Critics charged that the build-up was unneeded and too expensive. Reagan insisted that the Soviet Union held a military advantage over the United States. The United States and the Soviet Union held talks to reduce nuclear arms, but they failed to reach an agreement. Reagan then supplied nuclear missiles to U.S. allies in Western Europe. This action further worsened U.S.-Soviet relations.

The Reagan Administration attempted to reduce the level of fighting in Lebanon in the early 1980's. In June 1982, Israel had invaded Lebanon to attack military bases of the Palestine Liberation Organization (PLO). The PLO is the political representative of Palestinian Arabs, many of whom fled from Israeli-controlled territory during the Arab-Israeli War of 1948 and became refugees in Lebanon. PLO forces in Lebanon had been attacking settlements in Israel. In August 1982, the United States helped arrange for the withdrawal of PLO units from Lebanon. It later sent several U.S. Marine Corps units to join a peacekeeping force in Lebanon.

In October 1983, explosives set off by a terrorist collapsed a four-story Marine headquarters building at the airport of Beirut, Lebanon's capital. A total of 241 U.S. troops died as a result of the explosion. In early 1984, the level of fighting between Lebanese groups in Beirut increased. In February, the United States began moving its troops stationed in Beirut to offshore ships.

Rebellions in Nicaragua and El Salvador also became a major concern in the early 1980's. Cuba and the Soviet Union were giving war materials to the government of Nicaragua and the rebels in El Salvador. The United States, in turn, sent advisers and arms to the rebels in Nicaragua and the government of El Salvador.

In October 1983, Reagan ordered the invasion of the Caribbean island of Grenada after Grenadian rebels overthrew the island's government. Soldiers from six other Caribbean nations helped defeat the rebels. Reagan said the invasion was needed to protect Americans in Grenada, including almost 600 students at St. George's University School of Medicine. Reagan also said Cuba planned to use Grenada as a military base.

Life in the White House. The Reagans took great pleasure in hosting official receptions and other formal functions in the White House. They created a warm and elegant atmosphere and restored much of the traditional pageantry that President Jimmy Carter had ended. The Reagans brought back the trumpeters who announced the President and the first lady and welcomed foreign visitors. A color guard once again preceded the entrance of the presidential family and its guests of honor. At state dinners, military social aides accompanied members of the official party. The Reagans often sat at separate tables with their own special guests.

The Reagans's children lived in California and New York and occasionally visited the White House. When the Reagans were not entertaining, they sometimes had their meals on trays as they watched television. They both liked to watch movies in the White House theater. Mrs. Reagan took a special interest in supporting activities that called attention to the problems of drug and alcohol abuse among young people. In October 1987, she underwent surgery for breast cancer.

The 1984 election. Reagan and Bush easily won renomination at the 1984 Republican National Convention in Dallas, Tex. The Democrats nominated former Vice President Walter F. Mondale for President and Representative Geraldine A. Ferraro of New York for Vice President. In the campaign, Reagan stressed the nation's economic growth, the decline in unemployment, and the low rate of inflation. Mondale charged that Reagan's economic policies had greatly favored the wealthy and that the President's foreign policies had increased tension between the United States and the Soviet Union. In the election, Reagan and Bush won in a landslide. For the electoral vote by states, see **Electoral College** (table).

Reagan's second Administration (1985-1989)

The President's health became a national concern early in his second term. A cancerous tumor was found

Reagan's second election

Place of nominating convention	....Dallas, Tex.
Ballot on which nominated	.........1st
Democratic opponent	...............Walter F. Mondale
Electoral vote	........................525 (Reagan) to 13 (Mondale)
Popular vote	........................54,455,075 (Reagan) to 37,577,185 (Mondale)
Age at inauguration	73

Vice President and Cabinet

Vice President	.................*George H. W. Bush
Secretary of state	..............*Alexander M. Haig, Jr. *George P. Shultz (1982)
Secretary of the treasury	...... Donald T. Regan *James A. Baker III (1985) *Nicholas F. Brady (1988)
Secretary of defense	..........*Caspar W. Weinberger Frank C. Carlucci III (1987)
Attorney general	.... William French Smith Edwin P. Meese III (1985) Richard L. Thornburgh (1988)
Secretary of the interior	.... James G. Watt William P. Clark (1983) Donald P. Hodel (1985)
Secretary of agriculture	.... John R. Block Richard E. Lyng (1986)
Secretary of commerce	.... Malcolm Baldrige, Jr. C. William Verity (1987)
Secretary of labor	.... Raymond J. Donovan William E. Brock III (1985) Ann Dore McLaughlin (1987)
Secretary of health and human services	.... Richard S. Schweiker *Margaret M. Heckler (1983) Otis R. Bowen (1985)
Secretary of housing and urban development	..........*Samuel R. Pierce, Jr.
Secretary of transportation	.... Andrew L. Lewis, Jr. *Elizabeth H. Dole (1983) James H. Burnley IV (1987)
Secretary of energy	.... James B. Edwards Donald P. Hodel (1982) John S. Herrington (1985)
Secretary of education	.... Terrel H. Bell William J. Bennett (1985) *Lauro Cavazos (1988)

* Has a separate biography in *World Book.*

© Dennis Brack, Black Star

Reagan debated Walter Mondale, the Democratic presidential nominee, on national television during the 1984 campaign. In the election, Reagan won in a landslide.

in Reagan's colon, and a surgical team removed the tumor on July 13, 1985. Reagan made a rapid recovery.

Domestic affairs. The President hoped to reduce the huge federal budget deficit, but slow economic growth contributed to another record deficit exceeding $200 billion in the 1986 fiscal year. In 1986, Congress followed up on Reagan's request to create a new, simplified tax system that included lower tax rates on individual and corporate income taxes. The tax reform and a thriving economy helped reduce the deficit to $148 billion for the 1987 fiscal year. But after a U.S. stock market crash on Oct. 19, 1987, Reagan and Congress agreed on tax increases for 1988. Most of the increases affected corporations and wealthy individuals. In the mid-1980's, Reagan expanded the Strategic Defense Initiative, a controversial research program designed to develop a space-based missile defense system (see **Strategic Defense Initiative**). The press called the program "Star Wars."

Foreign events. Reagan met with Soviet leader Mikhail Gorbachev several times during his second Administration. In Geneva, Switzerland, in 1985, the first

Bill Fitz-Patrick, The White House

Reagan and Soviet leader Mikhail Gorbachev signed a treaty in 1987 that led to reductions of U.S. and Soviet nuclear arms. Reagan met with Gorbachev several times.

David Wells, Gamma/Liaison

Reagan and his wife, Nancy, liked to spend time at their ranch near Santa Barbara, Calif.

meeting between the two men led to agreements for educational, scientific, and cultural exchanges. The two leaders met again at Reykjavík, Iceland, in 1986. In 1987, Gorbachev visited the United States. During the visit, he and Reagan signed a treaty to eliminate all U.S. and Soviet ground-launched nuclear missiles with ranges of 500 to 5,500 kilometers (310 to 3,420 miles). The treaty took effect in 1988. That year, Reagan met with Gorbachev in the Soviet Union.

Terrorism increased in the mid-1980's, and Reagan acted boldly to combat it. In October 1985, he ordered U.S. Navy jets to intercept an Egyptian airliner carrying a small group of Palestinian terrorists. The terrorists had hijacked the Italian cruise ship *Achille Lauro* and killed an American passenger before surrendering to Egyptian authorities. The United States jets forced the airliner to land in Sicily, where the hijackers were arrested. Egypt had planned to give the terrorists to the PLO. In April 1986, a U.S. serviceman was killed and others injured when terrorists bombed a disco in West Berlin. United States officials claimed Libyan agents were involved. Reagan ordered U.S. air strikes against military and suspected terrorist centers in the Libyan cities of Tripoli and Benghazi.

The Iran-contra affair. Reagan and his Administration lost prestige because of sales of United States weapons to Iran and use of the profits to help Nicaraguan rebels, known as *contras.* Both activities were secret operations but became widely known to the public in November 1986.

The arms sales were chiefly designed to win the freedom of Americans who were held hostage by Lebanese terrorists friendly to Iran. Reagan supported the arms sales. At the time, however, the United States had a policy that prohibited the sale of weapons to Iran and other nations considered to be supporters of terrorism. The arms sales led to the release of three hostages.

The transfer of funds to the contras took place in the mid-1980's. Congress had banned military aid to the con-

tras during that period. Reagan said he knew nothing about the fund diversion. Both that action and the arms sales had been carried out by the National Security Council (NSC), a White House advisory agency.

In 1987, televised congressional hearings into what became known as the *Iran-contra affair* revealed deep conflict among members of the Reagan Administration. The hearings also exposed attempts by the NSC to deceive Congress about the arms sales and contra aid. Later in 1987, Reagan was strongly criticized in a joint report of the congressional committees investigating the affair. Most committee members blamed Reagan for failing to meet the constitutional obligation to "take care that the laws be faithfully executed" and said he was chiefly responsible for wrongdoing by his aides.

Marine Lieutenant Colonel Oliver L. North, an NSC aide, was the person most closely involved with the day-to-day management of the undercover operation. In 1989, a federal court convicted North on three charges related to the Iran-contra affair, including altering and destroying documents related to Congress's investigation. In 1990, however, an appeals court overturned North's conviction.

During the Iran-contra operations, North worked under national security advisers Robert C. McFarlane and John M. Poindexter. In 1989, McFarlane pleaded guilty of withholding information from Congress during its investigation. In 1990, Poindexter was convicted of conspiracy and of lying to and obstructing Congress in its investigation. An appeals court overturned Poindexter's conviction in 1991. In 1992, Caspar W. Weinberger, Reagan's secretary of defense, was charged with lying to Congress and government investigators in connection with the Iran-contra affair. Later that year, President George Bush pardoned Weinberger, McFarlane, and several other former federal officials for any crimes they may have committed in relation to the Iran-contra affair.

Persian Gulf conflicts. In 1987, Iran laid mines to disrupt shipping in the Persian Gulf and fired on United States vessels and helicopters there. Reagan ordered military responses to these actions and ended U.S.-Iranian trade. In May 1987, two missiles from an Iraqi warplane hit the U.S.S. *Stark,* a warship that was patrolling the gulf. Thirty-seven American crew members were killed. Iraqi officials said the attack was a mistake. In July 1988, the U.S.S. *Vincennes* shot down an Iranian civilian airliner that it mistook for a warplane, killing all 290 people on board.

Later years

In 1990, Reagan gave videotaped testimony in the Iran-contra trial of former national security adviser John Poindexter. But it had little effect on the trial's outcome. Later in 1990, Reagan published his autobiography, *An American Life.* In 1991, the Ronald Reagan Presidential Library opened in Simi Valley, California. It contains documents and other items related to Reagan and his presidency.

In 1994, Reagan revealed that he was suffering from the early stages of Alzheimer's disease. The disease causes an increasing loss of memory and other mental processes.   Bill Boyarsky

Related articles in *World Book* include:
Bush, George H. W.   Carter, Jimmy

Iran-contra affair   Republican Party
President of the United States

Questions

What were some problems the nation faced when Reagan became president?
How did Reagan serve in World War II?
What was Reagan's career before he entered politics?
When was Reagan first elected to public office?
How did Reagan gain national political attention?
How did life in the White House change under Reagan?
Why was Reagan's health a national concern in 1985?
What was the *Iran-contra affair*?
When did Reagan become a Republican?

Additional resources

Berman, Larry, ed. *Looking Back on the Reagan Presidency.* Johns Hopkins, 1990.
Hill, Dilys M., and others, eds. *The Reagan Presidency.* St. Martin's, 1990.
Morris, Jeffrey B. *The Reagan Way.* Lerner, 1996.
Reagan, Ronald. *An American Life.* Simon & Schuster, 1990. The autobiography of Ronald Reagan.
Schaller, Michael. *Reckoning with Reagan.* Oxford, 1992.

Real estate is land and all the things permanently attached to it, such as trees, buildings, and minerals beneath the surface. A house is *real estate,* but the rugs and furniture in it are *chattels* (personal property).

The basic real estate vocation is that of a *broker,* who markets real property on behalf of owners. Typically, *salespeople* are associated with and responsible to the broker. A career in real estate usually begins with sales work that may involve long, irregular hours. But success may bring an excellent income.

More than 1,800,000 people in the United States are actively employed as real estate brokers or salespeople. Many more people work in building, mortgage finance, and related fields. All states require real estate agents and brokers to be licensed. Applicants must pass a test on real estate principles. Fields of specialization in real estate include *appraisal, property management,* and *counseling* on such real estate problems as industrial sites and farm purchases and sales. Other specialized fields in real estate are *mortgage lending, financial analysis,* and *market analysis.*

About 375 universities and colleges now offer real estate courses for credit, and more than 360 two-year colleges offer such courses. Some universities and colleges offer courses leading to a master's degree in real estate. Real estate organizations encourage formal training by offering seminars on such topics as finance, appraisal, and market analysis.

The National Association of Realtors coined the term *Realtor* to designate its active members who subscribe to the Code of Ethics of the association. The term may not lawfully be used by others.   John M. Clapp

Related articles in *World Book* include:

Air rights	Fixture	Lien	Title
Appraisal	Heir	Mortgage	Torrens system
Deed	Joint tenancy	Primogeniture	
Depreciation	Lease	Property	Will

Realism, in the arts, is the attempt to portray life as it is. To the realist, the artist's main function is to describe as accurately and honestly as possible what is observed through the senses.

Realism began as a recognizable movement in the arts in the 1700's. By the mid-1800's, it was a dominant art form. In part, realism has been a revolt against *classicism* and *romanticism*—artistic movements characterized by works that idealize life. The works of classicists show life as being more rational and orderly than it really is. Romanticists' works show life as being more emotionally exciting and satisfying than it normally is.

Realists try to be as objective as possible. They try not to distort life by forcing it to agree with their own desires or with the formulas of art. However, in the process of selecting and presenting their material, they cannot help being influenced by what they feel and think. Even the most thoroughgoing realism, therefore, is the result of observation and personal judgment.

In fiction. Realistic fiction has been primarily a revolt against the sentimentality and melodrama of romantic idealism. Characters in realistic fiction tend to be less extraordinary than those in romantic fiction. Settings are more familiar, styles are plainer, and plots have fewer twists. Most realistic fiction deals with probable, com-

The Washerwoman (1863), an oil painting on a wood panel; The Louvre, Paris (SCALA/Art Resource)

A realistic painting by the French artist Honoré Daumier shows ordinary people in everyday surroundings.

Egg tempera painting on canvas (1930); Whitney Museum of American Art, New York City

Realistic art is an attempt to portray life as accurately as possible. The American artist Reginald Marsh painted *Why Not Use the "L"?, left,* and other realistic scenes of everyday life in New York City.

monplace events and believable people. Much realistic fiction presents dreary, and even ugly, subject matter. This sordid quality is especially associated with *naturalism,* an outgrowth of realism.

The growing popularity of realism has been more than simply a reaction against the pretty worlds of romantic fiction. More fundamentally, its popularity has been due to two factors. One is the development of modern science, with its emphasis upon detailed reporting. The other is an increasing desire of writers and readers for a realistic understanding of social problems.

In English literature, realism first became important in the 1700's with the work of Daniel Defoe. In the 1800's, realism became much more important in the works of Jane Austen, George Eliot, Thomas Hardy, George Moore, William Makepeace Thackeray, and Anthony Trollope. Honoré de Balzac, Gustave Flaubert, and Stendhal of France; and Leo Tolstoy and Ivan Turgenev of Russia were other outstanding European realists of the 1800's. See **Russian literature** (The age of realism).

Henry James, William Dean Howells, and, to some extent, Mark Twain were the first acknowledged realists in American literature. Stephen Crane, Frank Norris, and Theodore Dreiser were the first American naturalists. In their fiction, and in that of later writers such as Sinclair Lewis, F. Scott Fitzgerald, Ernest Hemingway, John Steinbeck, and Saul Bellow, realism became so accepted as to make romantic fiction seem outdated.

In drama. As in fiction, realism in drama is an attempt to show life as it is. Realistic drama first developed in Europe as a reaction to the melodramas and sentimental comedies of the early and middle 1800's. It has taken many forms, from the light realism of the comedy of manners to the heavy tragedy of naturalism.

Realistic drama first became important in Europe with the plays of Henrik Ibsen of Norway. Ibsen examined the social issues of his time in such plays as *Pillars of Society* (1877) and *A Doll's House* (1879). Anton Chekhov de-

scribed Russia's fading aristocracy in *The Cherry Orchard* (1904). The English theater was slow to accept realism. George Bernard Shaw finally brought the movement to life with his long series of witty plays dealing with social problems, starting with *Widowers' Houses* in 1892. In Ireland, John Millington Synge blended realism and poetry in *Riders to the Sea* (1904). In a similar manner, Sean O'Casey explored the issues of Ireland's struggle for independence from England in *Juno and the Paycock* (1924) and other plays.

Realism did not make a permanent impact on the American theater until the production of Eugene O'Neill's *Beyond the Horizon* in 1920. Since then, most American drama has been realistic.

In painting. Realistic painting developed as a reaction to two influential styles of the early 1800's—neoclassicism and romanticism (see **Painting** [The 1800's]). Aspects of realism can be seen in the work of Spanish painter Francisco Goya in the 1700's. Realism gained dominance in European painting in the 1800's with the work of such French artists as Camille Corot, Gustave Courbet, and Honoré Daumier. The French *impressionists* of the late 1800's developed a modified form of realism. In their paintings, realism was narrowed to the brightly lighted but restricted reality that can be seen at a momentary glance (see **Impressionism**).

Leading American realists of the late 1800's included Thomas Eakins and Winslow Homer. They were followed in the early 1900's by a group called the *Ashcan School* or *The Eight.* This group opposed the sentimentality and academic quality then popular in American art (see **Ashcan School**). It included William Glackens, Robert Henri, and John Sloan. They painted realistic street scenes, portraits, and landscapes. Other realists include George Bellows, John Steuart Curry, Edward Hopper, Reginald Marsh, and Grant Wood.

Realism today. In fiction and drama, realism has become so widespread it scarcely has identity as a distinct movement. Common realistic themes include the importance of upbringing, the oppression of minorities, and the search for values in a hostile world. During the early 1900's, painters began rejecting realism in favor of non-representational and abstract styles. By the 1980's, realism was often associated with photography rather than with painting.   Lawrence Lipking

There is a separate biography in *World Book* for each author and painter discussed in this article.

Additional resources

Furst, Lilian R., ed. *Realism.* Longman Pub. Group, 1992.
Lucie-Smith, Edward. *American Realism.* Abrams, 1994.
Martin, Alvin. *American Realism.* Abrams, 1986.
Shi, David E. *Facing Facts: Realism in American Thought and Culture, 1850-1920.* Oxford, 1995.

Reaney, *RAY nee,* **James** (1926-   ), is a Canadian poet and playwright. He seeks to express the allegorical patterns behind the sights, sounds, and customs of rural Ontario, where he grew up. His plays combine rapidly shifting scenes, organized more by patterns of images than by plot.

Reaney won three Governor General's Awards for poetry for *The Red Heart* (1949), *A Suit of Nettles* (1958), and *Twelve Letters to a Small Town* (1962). The best of his poetry has been collected in *Selected Shorter Poems* (1975) and *Selected Longer Poems* (1976). Reaney founded the literary magazine *Alphabet* and was its editor from 1960 to 1971. He has also written more than 20 plays, including many for children. His play *Wacousta* (1979) is based on an early Canadian novel by John Richardson. Reaney's best dramatic writing is found in the three related plays *Sticks and Stones* (1973), *St. Nicholas Hotel* (1974), and *Handcuffs* (1975). Reaney was born near Stratford, Ont.   Laurie R. Ricou

Reaper is a machine that farmers once used to harvest grain. Horse-drawn reapers took the place of sickles and cradle scythes, which farmers had used for centuries. With a reaper, farmers could harvest larger crops with fewer workers than ever before.

Several reapers were developed during the early 1800's. But none of them became as commercially successful as the reaper developed by the American inventor Cyrus Hall McCormick (see **McCormick, Cyrus Hall**). His reaper had a straight blade linked by gears to a drive wheel. As the wheel turned, the blade moved back and forth and sawed through the stalks of grain. Projecting rods caught and held the stalks while the blade cut through them. The stalks fell onto a platform and a worker raked them onto the ground.

McCormick first offered his reaper for sale in 1840. He continued to improve it, and sales grew. The reaper was well suited for the Midwest, where farmers grew wheat and other small grains on fairly level land. But 8 to 10 workers were needed to bring in the crop. One drove the horse, a second raked the platform, and 6 to 8 workers bound the sheaves. Inventors worked on reducing the number of workers needed.

During the mid-1850's, *self-rake reapers* came into use. On these reapers, a rake swept across the platform. In the early 1870's, the American inventor Sylvanus D. Locke produced a *binder.* This reaper bound the sheaves and dropped them on the ground. By the early 1920's, many farmers used tractors to pull binders. Since the 1920's, reapers have been replaced by combined

harvester-threshers that are called *combines* (see **Combine**).   R. Douglas Hurt

Reapportionment. See Apportionment.

Reason usually has three different meanings. (1) It can signify the mind, or an agency used in thinking. For example, we may ask someone to use reason rather than emotions. (2) Reason also refers to the evidence for a belief, opinion, or judgment. We may demand a reason for a person's belief that someone is a thief. (3) Reason may refer to a process of arriving at a decision or a conclusion. For instance, we may say that a jury was reasoning correctly when it decided a defendant was guilty.

Reasoning can be inductive or deductive. People use *inductive reasoning* when they see a puddle of water and infer that it has rained recently. Inductive reasoning is not conclusive. The evidence only makes the conclusion probable. See **Inductive method.**

People use *deductive reasoning* when they assert that oxygen is present in a place because life is present there and because life requires oxygen. Deductive reasoning shows what else must be true if the initial beliefs are true. See **Deductive method.**   Morton L. Schagrin

See also **Fallacy; Geometry** (Geometry as a logical system); **Human being; Logic; Philosophy** (Logic).

Reason, Age of. See Age of Reason.

Reasoning. See Logic.

Rebate, *REE bayt,* in mercantile law, is a discount, or reduction of the amount to be paid. Giving a certain percentage off for cash is a rebate. Many manufacturers of such items as television sets, household appliances, and automobiles offer rebates to improve sales. Sometimes a rebate is given to obtain favors or good will. It is unlawful for transportation companies to give rebates to shippers. Those who do are subject to heavy fines. See also **Roosevelt, Theodore** (Domestic problems).

Jay Diamond

Rebecca. See Isaac.

Rebellions of 1837 were revolts against British rule in the North American colonies of Upper Canada and Lower Canada. Both colonies had an elected Legislative Assembly. But a British governor and a Legislative Council appointed by the British government still had much control over local affairs. The rebel leaders, Louis J. Papineau in Lower Canada and William Lyon Mackenzie in Upper Canada, attempted to win independence for their colonies from Britain. However, both revolts were easily defeated.

In Lower Canada, French-speaking professionals and small merchants held a majority of seats in the Legislative Assembly. But many of them felt that the Legislative Council favored the interests of the colony's large landowners over those of the French-Canadian, middle-class majority. Papineau was especially concerned with the English-speaking minority's growing opposition to the traditional French civil law and landholding system in the colony. He called for the establishment of an elected Legislative Council, knowing that such a council would protect the interests of the French-Canadian people.

However, the British rejected Papineau's proposal. He then helped organize a French-Canadian protest group called the Sons of Liberty. Increasing tension led to an uprising in late 1837. Armed rebels won a battle with government forces at St. Denis but lost clashes at St.

Charles and St. Eustache. Another uprising broke out in late 1838, but British troops quickly crushed it. Altogether, about 8,000 colonists joined the revolt.

In Upper Canada, many members of the Legislative Assembly had difficulty dealing with powerful members of the Legislative Council who belonged to a group known as the *Family Compact.* This group consisted of officials and Anglican religious leaders who supported the policies of the Church of England. However, most of the colonists did not belong to that church and strongly opposed its influence.

In 1837, Mackenzie became convinced that moderate reformist members of the Legislative Assembly had no chance of winning British approval of their proposals for major democratic reforms. He urged the colonists to revolt. In December 1837, a few hundred rebels tried to capture government military supplies in Toronto, but were defeated. Mackenzie fled to the United States. His followers in Canada attracted little support, and the uprising ended late in 1838.

Results. Largely as a result of the uprisings, the British Parliament passed the Act of Union in 1840. This act, which took effect in 1841, united the colonies of Upper and Lower Canada into a single colony, the Province of Canada.   Fernand Ouellet

See also **Mackenzie, William L.; Union, Act of.**

Rebus, *REE buhs,* is a word game in which the placement or size of letters, numbers, or words indicates names, phrases, or other words. A rebus can also have

Bettmann Archive

Benjamin Franklin used rebuses along with script writing in a short tract called "The Art of Making Money Plenty."

pictures, or words and pictures. For example, a picture of an eye, followed by "CA," followed by a picture of a dog, could stand for "I see a dog." Or, using words and figures:

stand   you   my
I   charged   4   shoes

for "I understand you overcharged for my overshoes." AL could be *altogether* (*A L* together).   Will Shortz

Recall enables voters to remove a person from office before a term is completed, and to elect a new public official. A special election is held for this purpose.

Before a recall election can be held, a petition must be filed that has been signed by a certain number of voters. Usually the number must equal from 10 to 25 percent of the votes cast for this particular office during the previous election. The individual in question may give up the office voluntarily. If the individual does not do this, candidates for the office may file petitions in the usual way. The special election then becomes a contest between the new candidates and the officer whose recall is sought. The person receiving the largest vote in the election serves the rest of the term.

The movement to provide for recall of state and local officials came with efforts to provide for more direct popular control over government generally. The modern use of recall in the United States began with the

charter of Los Angeles in 1903. Several hundred cities and 15 states have since adopted it. The states include Oregon (1908), California (1911), Colorado, Washington, Idaho, Nevada, and Arizona (1912), Michigan (1913), Louisiana and Kansas (1914), North Dakota (1920), Wisconsin (1926), Alaska (1960), Montana (1976), and Georgia (1979). Some states that use the recall do not apply it to judges. Mayors have often been recalled. The recall of a state officer is unusual, but North Dakota removed a governor by recall in 1921.

People who favor the recall argue that voters should have a direct way of removing an officer whom they consider dishonest, incompetent, or heedless of public opinion. Most state constitutions provide for the removal of an officer by impeachment. But people sometimes wish to remove from office someone who is not guilty of an impeachable offense.

Opponents of recall point out that the practice may be abused. They say that able men and women may be unwilling to risk taking an office from which the voters may later remove them for no fault except the failure to go along with the public sentiment of the moment.
          Robert Agranoff

Recall, in psychology. See **Memory** (Measuring memory).

Receipt is a written statement showing that one person has paid money to another. It may also be a written statement showing that goods, or property, has passed from the ownership or responsibility of one person to another. The receipt is proof that a transaction has taken place. Three kinds of receipts are *receipts in full, receipts on account* (when some of the amount due is paid), and *receipts to apply on special accounts.*

A receipt should always show whether payment is made in full, on account, or on the special account to which payment is made, when there is more than one account between two persons. A receipt should always be given when an account is paid. A bill that has been properly signed and marked *paid* serves as a receipt. A canceled check would also show that payment was made.   Jay Diamond

Receiver. See **Radio** (How radio programs are received); **Telephone** (How a telephone works); **Television** (Receiving television signals).

Receiver is an individual, a bank, or a trust company appointed by a court to hold, manage, or dispose of property. A receiver may also be called a *trustee* or an *assignee.* The most common reason for appointing a receiver is bankruptcy (see **Bankruptcy**). If a person or company does not have enough assets to cover all debts, the court may name a receiver to protect the people or companies to whom the debts are owed. A receiver also may manage property involved in a lawsuit, such as a mortgage foreclosure.

Receivers are officers of the court. They are limited in their authority and actions by the decree appointing them, and by the laws of the state and the nation. Ordinarily, receivers must have no direct interest in the business or estate they handle. They also must administer the estate in the best interests of all parties concerned. In some states, receivers may be appointed to take charge of the property of a husband who fails to support his wife or his children. After receivers have finished their work, they are discharged by the court.

The court pays receivers for their services. The fees of receivers and the expenses of the receivership must be paid before any other obligations. The court requires receivers to furnish bond.   James E. Krier

Recession is a decline in overall business activity. During a nationwide recession, a country suffers a drop in buying, selling, and production, and a rise in unemployment. A recession may also hit an industry or a region. Historically, nationwide recessions have also brought an end to severe inflation or even a fall in prices. During the 1970's, however, prices in the United States continued to rise rapidly in spite of several recessions. A recession hurts countless people, especially the workers who lose jobs.

Recessions, also known as *contractions,* are part of the *business cycle,* a recurring rise and fall in economic activity. Many economists consider a nation's economy to be in a recession if the output of goods and services falls for six consecutive months. A recession lasts an average of about a year. A recession that grows worse and lasts longer becomes a *depression.*

Causes of recession. Most recessions occur because the total amount of spending in the economy drops. For example, if sales rise more slowly than usual, businesses may reduce their orders for new goods. The manufacturers that supply the goods cut back on production. They need fewer workers, and so layoffs and unemployment increase. Workers have less money to spend, which further decreases the demand for goods. As this pattern spreads, a recession begins.

Government action may trigger the drop in spending. For example, cuts in government spending could reduce the nation's total spending enough to start a recession. Reduced spending also may result if the government conducts a *tight money* policy, which makes bank loans more expensive and harder to obtain.

People's expectations also play an important role in the decline of economic activity. If manufacturers or consumers believe conditions will worsen, they may cut back on their buying. By doing so, they could help bring on the slump they were trying to avoid. This process is called *self-realizing expectation.*

Some recessions result from shortages of vital products. For example, interruptions in oil shipments have caused recessions in many Western countries.

Fighting recession. A government tries to end a recession chiefly by means of its *fiscal policy* and *monetary policy.* Fiscal policy deals with a government's spending and taxing. Monetary policy refers to how a government influences such economic factors as interest rates and the availability of money and loans. To halt a recession, a government may boost its own spending or reduce income taxes. It may also reduce interest rates so that loans are less expensive and easier to obtain. These actions give people more money to spend, increasing the demand for goods and services and creating more jobs.

Many nations also have built-in stabilizers that work to stimulate the economy without any special government action. One such stabilizer is a progressive income tax system, which taxes higher incomes more heavily than lower ones. If a taxpayer's income falls, his or her taxes drop by an even greater percentage. As a result, the person has a larger share of his or her income to

spend. Another automatic stabilizer is unemployment insurance, which provides benefit payments from the government for workers who lose their jobs.   Clair E. Morris

See also **Business cycle; Depression; Unemployment.**

Additional resources

Hall, Thomas E. *Business Cycles: The Nature and Causes of Economic Fluctuations.* Praeger, 1990.
Shilling, A. Gary. *After the Crash: Recession or Depression? Business and Investment Strategies for a Deflationary World.* Lakeview Economic Services, 1988.

Recife, *ruh SEE fuh* (pop. 1,375,404; met. area pop. 2,814,795), in northeastern Brazil, is the capital of the state of Pernambuco (see **Brazil** [political map]). Recife lies at the mouths of the Capibaribe and Beberibe rivers, partly on the mainland and partly on an island in the Atlantic Ocean.

Factories and mills of Recife produce alcohol, ceramics, paper and leather goods, textiles, and vegetable oils. The city's chief source of wealth comes from the exportation of bananas, coffee, cotton, hides, and sugar. Recife has four universities.

The Portuguese established permanent settlements in the Recife region in 1535. During Dutch invasions of Brazil (1630-1654), Recife was the center of Dutch operations. It became a Brazilian town in 1710, and a city in 1823.   J. H. Galloway

Reciprocal trade agreement, *rih SIHP ruh kuhl,* is a pact between two or more nations to lower tariffs or other trade barriers on certain goods or services. Reciprocal trade agreements form the basis of most nations' foreign trade policies.

Most reciprocal trade agreements begin as pacts between two governments to lower specific tariffs or other trade restrictions. Such pacts are called *bilateral trade agreements.* Since 1947, most bilateral trade agreements have been expanded to include other countries. That year, 23 countries, including the United States and Canada, signed the General Agreement on Tariffs and Trade (GATT). They received tariff reductions on goods specified in various bilateral trade agreements. The GATT provision that grants the reductions is called a *most-favored-nation clause.* See **General Agreement on Tariffs and Trade.**

As an example of how a reciprocal trade agreement might be arranged, suppose that one nation produces more wheat than it needs—but not enough shoes. Another country may produce too many shoes but not enough wheat. The two governments would negotiate a bilateral trade agreement. The first country would reduce by a certain percentage its tariff on shoes imported from the second country. The second country would similarly reduce its tariff on wheat imported from the first country. Under the most-favored-nation clause of the GATT, each country would extend its tariff reductions to all GATT countries. These nations could then trade under the lower tariff even if they had not signed a trade agreement with that country. Most nations have subscribed to the GATT.

In 1995, the World Trade Organization (WTO) was set up to administer the GATT and to reduce barriers to trade in services and in other areas not covered by the GATT. As a result, the most-favored-nation clause began to be applied to trade in services and other areas.

Reciprocal trade agreements have been an important part of U.S. foreign trade policy since 1934. That year, Congress passed the first Reciprocal Trade Agreements Act. Since then, periodic legislation has allowed the government to continue such trade policies.

Today, some reciprocal trade agreements are designed to encourage economic growth in developing countries. For example, industrial nations may agree to import manufactured products from developing countries at a lower tariff rate than is charged for the same products made by other industrial nations. At the same time, the developing countries may keep their own tariffs high to encourage expansion of their domestic industries. Robert M. Stern

See also **World Trade Organization.**

Reclamation, *REHK luh MAY shuhn,* **Bureau of,** is a United States government agency that works to manage and protect water resources in the Western States. It plans projects that create more efficient use of water for cities and industries, hydroelectric power generation, irrigation, and outdoor recreation. It also works to preserve water quality and to create habitats for fish and other animals that live in water.

The agency was established in 1902. It planned the construction of dams, hydroelectric power plants, reservoirs, and water distribution systems. It also maintained the projects after they were completed. In 1987, the Bureau of Reclamation announced that it would no longer plan such large-scale construction projects.

The original name of the agency was the Reclamation Service. Its name was changed in 1923 to the Bureau of Reclamation, in 1979 to the Water and Power Resources Service, and in 1981 back to its present name. The Bureau of Reclamation is part of the United States Department of the Interior.

Critically reviewed by the Bureau of Reclamation

See also **Irrigation** (History); **Rio Grande Project.**

Recombinant DNA. See **Genetic engineering.**

Reconstruction was the period in United States history that followed the Civil War. The word also refers to the process by which the Union restored relations with the Confederate states after their defeat. Reconstruction lasted from 1865 to 1877 and was one of the most controversial periods in the nation's history. Scholars still debate its successes and failures.

The South faced enormous problems in rebuilding itself after the Civil War. Such cities as Atlanta, Georgia, and Richmond, Virginia, lay in ruins. Much of the South's railroad system, as well as its few factories, had been destroyed. The North, on the other hand, had suffered relatively little damage during the war. Farms and industries in the North had prospered.

Political leaders of the North and South faced many difficult questions during Reconstruction. For example, how should the 11 states that had *seceded* (withdrawn) from the Union be readmitted? How, if at all, should the Confederate leaders be punished? What rights should be granted to the approximately 4 million freed slaves, and how should these rights be protected? How should the war-torn South be rebuilt?

Some of the problems were solved during Reconstruction. The Confederate states eventually met various requirements for readmission, and all rejoined the Union by 1870. Congress passed laws and proposed constitutional amendments to protect the rights of the former slaves and to give them the vote. Newly formed state governments in the South began to rebuild the ruined regions.

Other problems remained, however. Most Southern whites refused to accept blacks as equals, and the living and working conditions of the blacks improved only slightly. The Reconstruction governments also failed to win enough support from Southern whites to survive without aid from the North. Most Southern whites considered these governments illegal, and some whites used violence to prevent blacks from voting.

The North gradually lost interest in Reconstruction. In time, Southern whites regained control of their state governments and took away many of the rights that blacks had won during Reconstruction.

Detail of *Back Home: April 1865* (1939), an oil mural on canvas by Tom Lea; Pleasant Hill (Missouri) Post Office

The Reconstruction period followed the American Civil War. It marked the beginning of efforts to rebuild the war-torn South. Thousands of Southerners, such as the ones shown to the left, faced the problem of finding enough food to stay alive until they could cultivate the land again.

The debate over Reconstruction

Soon after the Civil War began in 1861, Northerners started to debate how the Confederate states should be brought back into the Union. These states were Alabama, Arkansas, Florida, Georgia, Louisiana, Mississippi, North Carolina, South Carolina, Tennessee, Texas, and Virginia. Some Northerners believed these states should be treated as territories. Others insisted that, because secession was illegal, the South still belonged to the Union. Still others declared that the Southern leaders—but not the states—should be punished.

Lincoln's plan. In December 1863, President Abraham Lincoln announced his plan for Reconstruction. It offered a pardon to every Southerner who took an oath to support the Union. Lincoln proposed that if 10 percent of a state's voters took the oath, the state could form a new government and adopt a new constitution. The 10 percent would be based on the number of people who had voted in the 1860 presidential election. The state's new constitution had to prohibit slavery.

Early congressional reaction. Many Northerners considered Lincoln's plan too mild. In 1864, Congress proposed that Reconstruction wait until half the voters in a state had taken an oath of loyalty. A national debate then developed over whether Congress or the President should establish Reconstruction policy.

In January 1865, Congress proposed the 13th Amendment to the U.S. Constitution. This amendment called for the abolition of slavery throughout the nation. In March, Congress created the Freedmen's Bureau to protect the interests of Southern blacks. Most blacks had no homes or money. They also lacked education because Southern laws had barred them from receiving instruction. The bureau obtained jobs and set up hospitals and schools for blacks in the South. See **Freedmen's Bureau**.

The Civil War ended on April 9, 1865. Less than a week later, Lincoln was assassinated by John Wilkes Booth. Vice President Andrew Johnson, a former Democratic U.S. senator from Tennessee, succeeded Lincoln as President. The Republicans had added Johnson to their ticket in 1864 to attract Southern support.

The start of Reconstruction

Johnson's plan. In May 1865, Johnson announced his own Reconstruction plan. It offered pardons to all Southern whites except the main Confederate leaders and wealthy Confederate supporters. The defeated Southern states were to hold conventions and form new state governments. These governments had to abolish slavery and vow loyalty to the nation in order to qualify for readmission to the Union. Johnson's plan did not offer blacks a role in the process of Reconstruction. The Southern states were to determine that role themselves. During the summer and fall of 1865, new state governments were organized throughout the South under Johnson's plan.

Most Northerners hoped the nation could be reunified quickly. They expected the South to renew its loyalty to the Union, and they insisted that the basic rights of the former slaves be protected. The 13th Amendment was ratified in December 1865.

The black codes. The status of the blacks soon became the most crucial issue of Reconstruction. The state governments that were established under Johnson's plan passed a series of laws called the *black codes*. One of these codes forced blacks to sign labor contracts requiring them to work at a job for a full year. Another permitted employers to whip black workers. Other codes allowed states to jail unemployed blacks and hire out their children. See **Black codes**.

Violence against blacks. The former slaves also suffered from attacks by whites. In 1865 and 1866, whites murdered about 5,000 Southern blacks. During race riots in 1866, white mobs killed 46 blacks in Memphis and 34 in New Orleans.

In 1865 or 1866, a secret white organization called the Ku Klux Klan was founded in Tennessee. Klan members wore white robes and hoods and draped white sheets over their horses. The Ku Klux Klan grew rapidly and spread terror across the South. Klan members beat and even murdered blacks and their white sympathizers to keep them from exercising their rights. See **Ku Klux Klan**.

The Newberry Library, Chicago

Schools for blacks were opened throughout the South by the Freedmen's Bureau. This federal agency was established in 1865 to help blacks make the change from slavery to freedom. The sketch at the left appeared in *Frank Leslie's Illustrated Newspaper* in 1866.

Granger Collection

The impeachment of President Andrew Johnson took place in 1868. The ticket shown above was required for admission to Johnson's impeachment trial in the United States Senate.

The struggle over Reconstruction

Congress was in recess during the summer and fall of 1865, when Johnson's plan took effect. When Congress reassembled in December, many newly elected Southern congressmen came to take their seats.

Many of the Southern newcomers had been Confederate officials, and few of the others had remained loyal to the Union during the Civil War. The election of such lawmakers, plus the passage of the Black Codes, helped convince Republicans in Congress that Johnson's plan had failed. Congress, which had a Republican majority, refused to seat any of the Southerners who had been elected from Confederate states. Congress wanted to control Reconstruction, and it started to develop its own policies for the South.

The Radicals and the Moderates. When the Civil War ended, the Republican Party included two main groups. They were the *Radicals* and the *Moderates.*

The Radicals in Congress vigorously demanded a new Reconstruction policy. Their leaders were Senator Charles Sumner of Massachusetts and Representative Thaddeus Stevens of Pennsylvania. The Radicals felt the federal government should take strong action to protect the rights of blacks and loyal whites in the South. They also thought that giving blacks the vote was the only way to establish Southern governments that were loyal to the Union and controlled by Republicans. See **Stevens, Thaddeus; Sumner, Charles**.

The Moderates made up the largest group of Republicans, and so they controlled the party. They agreed with Johnson that the states should decide whether to give blacks the vote. But the Moderates also agreed with the Radicals that the rights of blacks needed greater protection. And they supported the Radicals in demanding that Congress, rather than Johnson, should determine Reconstruction policy.

The Civil Rights Act. Early in 1866, Congress passed the Civil Rights Act, which guaranteed various legal rights of the former slaves. Johnson vetoed the bill because he opposed federal protection of the rights of blacks. Congress then repassed the Civil Rights Act, which was the first major law in U.S. history to be approved over a President's veto.

The 14th Amendment. In June 1866, Congress proposed the 14th Amendment to the Constitution, which gave citizenship to blacks. It also guaranteed that all federal and state laws would apply equally to blacks and whites. In addition, the amendment barred former federal and state officeholders who had supported the Confederacy from holding high political office again.

None of the defeated Southern states had yet been readmitted into the Union, and Congress declared that none could rejoin until it ratified the 14th Amendment. Johnson urged the states to reject the amendment, and all the former Confederate states except Tennessee did so. Tennessee then became the first of the 11 defeated Southern states to be readmitted into the Union. The 14th Amendment was finally ratified by the required number of states in 1868.

The Reconstruction Acts. The stubbornness of Johnson and his Southern supporters helped move the Moderates toward the Radical position. Early in 1867, Congress passed a series of laws called the Reconstruction Acts. These laws abolished the Southern state governments formed under Johnson's plan. They also divided all the states that had seceded from the Union—except Tennessee—into five military districts. A major general commanded each area. Federal troops stationed in each district helped enforce the Reconstruction Acts.

The Reconstruction Acts also outlined the process of readmission for the 10 Southern states that still had not rejoined the Union. Election boards in each state would register as voters all adult black males and all qualified adult white males. The voters would elect a convention, which would adopt a new state constitution. This constitution had to give black men the right to vote. The voters then would elect a governor and state legislature. Finally, the state had to ratify the 14th Amendment.

Johnson vetoed the Reconstruction Acts. But the Republican-controlled Congress easily repassed them over his vetoes.

The impeachment of Johnson. Congress passed two other measures in 1867 that challenged Johnson's authority. The Tenure of Office Act prohibited the President from firing Cabinet members and certain other officials without the Senate's approval. The Command of the Army Act prevented the President from dismissing any general commanding one of the new Southern military districts without Senate approval. Johnson believed that the acts were unconstitutional. In February 1868, he violated the Tenure of Office Act by dismissing Secretary of War Edwin M. Stanton, a supporter of the Radicals. Partly as a result, the Radicals demanded that Johnson be removed from office.

On Feb. 24, 1868, the House of Representatives voted 126 to 47 to impeach the President. About three weeks later, his impeachment trial began in the Senate. On May 16, the Senate voted 35 to 19 to remove Johnson from office. This tally was one vote short of the two-thirds majority required for removal, and Johnson remained President. See **Johnson, Andrew** (Johnson's Administration).

In 1869, Congress proposed the 15th Amendment to the Constitution. This amendment, which was ratified by the states in 1870, made it illegal to deny citizens the right to vote because of their race.

The Reconstruction governments

New state governments were established under the Reconstruction Acts. Many Southern whites protested against the acts by refusing to vote in the elections that set up these governments. The Republicans, who had little strength in the South before the Civil War, won control of every new state government.

By 1870, all the former Confederate states had been readmitted to the Union. Six of them—Alabama, Arkansas, Florida, Louisiana, North Carolina, and South Carolina—had met the requirements of the Reconstruction Acts by 1868. Georgia, Mississippi, Virginia, and Texas took longer to ratify the 14th Amendment and were not readmitted until they had ratified the 15th Amendment.

The Republicans in the South consisted of three chief groups: (1) blacks; (2) former Northerners, who became known as *carpetbaggers;* and (3) Southern whites, who were called *scalawags* by their opponents.

Blacks formed the largest group of Southern Republicans. Thousands of blacks voted in the elections to form the new Reconstruction governments. These voters helped the Republicans win power throughout the South. Opponents charged that blacks dominated the new state governments. But no state elected a black governor, and only 17 blacks won election to Congress during Reconstruction. South Carolina, where blacks made up more than half the population, was the only Southern state with a black majority in its legislature.

The carpetbaggers were largely former Union soldiers who had been attracted by economic opportunities in the South. Many carpetbaggers bought cotton land or opened businesses in the cities. More than 60 carpetbaggers won election to Congress, and 9 served as governors. Others included missionaries and teachers who wanted to help blacks. Southern whites made up the term *carpetbagger* to suggest these Northerners could fit all their possessions in a *carpetbag* (suitcase) when they came south. See **Carpetbaggers.**

Most scalawags were poor whites who lived in the hilly areas of the South. They resented the plantation owners who had dominated Southern politics before the Civil War. These people looked to the new state governments for education and jobs. See **Scalawags.**

New state programs and policies. The Reconstruction governments established the first public, tax-supported school systems in most states of the South. Only one Southern state, North Carolina, had such a system before the war. Many historians consider the school programs to be the most significant achievement of the new state governments. The states took over the schools established by the Freedmen's Bureau and built many more. Blacks, both young and old, flocked to these schools. At first, many whites refused to attend. Most of the Southern states then attracted white students by segregating the schools by race, even though many laws prohibited this action.

Major economic problems troubled the Southern state governments. Agriculture, the basis of the South's economy before the war, recovered slowly. And few Southerners had enough money to launch new industries. The state governments attempted to fight the South's economic backwardness by offering aid to railroads and various industries. State officials also worked to attract investment money from the North.

The Reconstruction governments opened the political process to Southern blacks. The new governments not only banned racial discrimination, but also guaranteed blacks the right to vote and to hold political office. In addition, the governments held elections for offices previously filled by appointment.

White resistance. Most Southern whites refused to support the Reconstruction governments. Many of these Southerners considered the governments illegal because the 14th Amendment prevented many former Southern leaders from holding political office. Some whites had land and other property taken from them because they were unable to pay taxes. Corruption in the new governments also angered many whites. A number of Southern legislators accepted bribes from railroad officials. Other political leaders often sold public land in return for favors, or they awarded business contracts unfairly. Southern whites were also concerned about rapidly rising taxes and public expenses. But much of the increased state spending was needed to pay for the new schools and other public facilities.

The basic reason for white opposition to the Reconstruction governments was that most Southern whites could not accept the idea of former slaves voting and holding office. Many whites stayed away from elections. Others turned to violence. U.S. Army regiments tried to stop the attacks against blacks and their white sympathizers. But these troops had little success in preventing the Ku Klux Klan and similar groups from terrorizing blacks and keeping them from voting.

The end of Reconstruction

The Republicans lose power. Southern Democrats began to regain control of the South in 1869, when they defeated the Republicans in Tennessee and Virginia. Reconstruction—and Republican control—ended in North Carolina in 1870 and in Georgia in 1871.

The use of violence to keep blacks from voting, despite attempts by President Ulysses S. Grant to stop it, played a large part in the Democratic victories. Also during the early 1870's, many Northerners lost interest in Reconstruction, and U.S. troops aiding the Reconstruction governments were gradually withdrawn. Alabama, Arkansas, and Texas came under the control of the Democratic Party in 1874, and Mississippi in 1876.

The 1876 presidential election led to the end of Reconstruction. In this election, Rutherford B. Hayes, the Republican candidate, opposed Democrat Samuel J. Tilden. The outcome depended on disputed returns from the three states that still had Reconstruction governments—Florida, Louisiana, and South Carolina. A compromise, which included agreement to withdraw the remaining federal troops, resulted in Hayes's election as President. Hayes carried out the agreement after he took office in 1877. See **Hayes, Rutherford B.** (The election dispute; The end of Reconstruction).

Effects of Reconstruction

During Reconstruction, the Union was restored and the rebuilding of the South was started. The public school systems that were established in the South had lasting importance for the region.

However, Reconstruction failed to solve the economic problems of either the blacks or the South as a whole. Few blacks acquired land and so lacked the economic independence that it provided. Instead, most blacks continued to pick cotton on land that was owned by whites, the same labor they had performed as slaves. State governments helped develop the South's natural resources and expand its railroad network. But the South long remained the poorest, most backward section of the country.

In politics, Reconstruction made most Southern whites firm supporters of the Democratic Party and created what became known as the "Solid South." For more than 40 years after Reconstruction, no Republican presidential candidate received a majority of the votes in any Southern state.

Reconstruction also failed to bring racial harmony to the South. Whites refused to share important political power with blacks. In turn, blacks set up their own churches and other institutions rather than attempt to join white society. After Reconstruction ended, the blacks gradually lost all the rights they had gained. By the early 1900's, every Southern state had passed laws limiting voting rights. These laws gave the vote only to males who could pass certain educational tests or pay special taxes called *poll taxes.* Such laws effectively prevented most blacks from voting. See **Grandfather clause; Poll tax.**

The Southern States continued to violate the rights of blacks for many years after the end of Reconstruction. Yet, perhaps the most lasting effect of the period resulted from the 14th and 15th amendments to the Constitution. These amendments established a national system of legal protection of equality before the law. The guarantees of these amendments, though often broken through the years, remained part of the United States Constitution. And, starting in the mid-1900's, the 14th and 15th amendments became the legal basis of the civil rights movement, the struggle of black Americans for equality.   Eric Foner

See also **African Americans** (The first years of freedom); **Civil War; Constitution of the United States** (Amendments 13, 14, 15); **Force Bill; Grant, Ulysses S.** (Reconstruction policies).

Additional resources

Mettger, Zak. *Reconstruction: America After the Civil War.* Lodestar, 1994. Younger readers.
Richter, William L. *The ABC-Clio Companion to American Reconstruction, 1862-1877.* ABC-Clio, 1996.
Stalcup, Brenda, ed. *Reconstruction: Opposing Viewpoints.* Greenhaven, 1995.

Record player. See Phonograph.

Recorder is a type of flute that has a whistle mouthpiece. The instrument consists of a wooden or plastic tube with a row of seven finger holes and a thumb hole. A recorder is held almost vertically, and the holes are covered or uncovered to play different notes. The instrument has a soft, mellow tone. The most popular sizes of recorders are, from smallest to largest, soprano, alto, tenor, and bass.

The recorder was invented during the Middle Ages and has remained basically unchanged. It became popu-

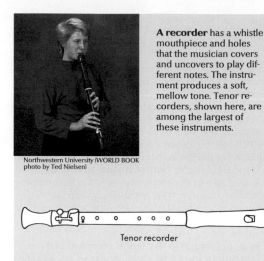

A recorder has a whistle mouthpiece and holes that the musician covers and uncovers to play different notes. The instrument produces a soft, mellow tone. Tenor recorders, shown here, are among the largest of these instruments.

Northwestern University (WORLD BOOK photo by Ted Nielsen)

Tenor recorder

WORLD BOOK illustration by Oxford Illustrators Limited

lar during the 1500's and 1600's and was an important part of the music of the Renaissance. By the mid-1700's, the modern flute had largely replaced the recorder. Since about 1920, however, a revival of interest has developed in the recorder and in recorder music of the Renaissance and baroque periods of music history.

André P. Larson

Recording industry is the group of businesses involved in the production and sale of such sound recordings as compact discs (CD's) and cassette tapes. Hundreds of companies in the United States, and many more in other countries, make up the recording industry.

Each year, millions of musical recordings are made and sold throughout the world. Such recordings enable people to listen to a wide variety of musical styles, including classical, country and western, jazz, blues, rap, and rock. They also enable musicians around the world to learn about one another's musical styles, instruments, and songs. A number of spoken-word recordings, such as instructional records, comedy albums, and dramatic readings, are also made and sold. For information on the impact of recordings on musical styles, see **Popular music** (The recording era).

Several companies dominate the manufacture and distribution of popular recordings. These companies, called the "majors," include BMG Entertainment, EMI Group, Sony Music Entertainment, Universal Music Group, and Warner Music Group. Many well-known record companies, such as Atlantic, Chrysalis, Geffen, MCA, and Motown, are administered by the larger recording companies. In addition, small independent companies are important in certain segments of the industry, including bluegrass, folk, and gospel music.

Making a musical recording

The procedure used to make a musical recording varies. This section describes how a popular recording, such as a rock song or rap performance, is made.

Before recording. Performers who do not write their own music obtain a composition from a composer. Composers protect their interest in a song by copyrighting it and by assigning it to a publisher (see **Copyright**). The publisher promotes the song for the composer.

After an artist has decided to record a song, a copy of it is given to an arranger. The arranger adds instrumental or vocal parts, changing the music to suit the artist's performing style. An *artist and repertoire* (A & R) executive, who works for the record company, oversees artists and their recordings. The responsibilities of an A & R executive also include listening to demonstration, or "demo," tapes from new artists, deciding which artists to hire, and choosing which songs to record.

In a recording studio. A recording session involves the work of musicians and technicians, and their assistants. These individuals are directed by the recording engineer and the producer. The recording engineer oversees all technical aspects of the recording session, such as choosing the recording equipment and arranging the placement of microphones. The producer makes artistic decisions about the overall sound of the recording based on the tastes of the music-buying public. The producer's duties also include reserving the studio and hiring musicians.

Popular recordings are usually made in two basic steps. First, the song is recorded part by part. Next, the parts are edited and combined into a single performance.

Recording. The singers and the drummers, guitarists, and other instrumentalists needed for a song are recorded with separate microphones. These recordings may be made with professional *multitrack recorders,* which can record dozens of separate *tracks* (channels of sound). The tracks may be recorded on magnetic tape as *analog* patterns, which are similar to the wave patterns

of the original sound. Or they may be recorded as a *digital* (numeric) pattern that represents the sound, on digital audiotape or on a computer hard disk. Each musician is usually recorded on a separate track. The tracks can be played back alone or in any combination.

The parts of a popular recording are often recorded at different times. A process called *overdubbing* enables engineers to add one musical part after another. The background sounds of a song, such as drums and rhythm guitars, are usually recorded first. As the remaining parts are recorded, the musicians use headphones to listen to what has already been taped. Vocal tracks are usually recorded last, though a rough vocal track may be made first to guide the instrumentalists.

The mixdown. Once all the parts have been recorded, the tracks are edited and combined on tape or on a computer's hard disk using a device called a *mixer.* This process, called the *mixdown,* reduces tracks to the required number. Two tracks are needed for stereophonic sound. Surround-sound recordings using a DVD-Audio (digital versatile disc) format require six tracks.

With a mixer, an engineer can control the overall sound of the song. For example, mistakes in the recording can be corrected by erasing unnecessary or undesirable parts. Various aspects of sound quality, such as loudness and tone, can be adjusted for each track. The mixing engineer can even rearrange vocal and instrumental segments of the recording. The mixing engineer tries to find a sound balance that will work well on home, car, and portable stereo playback systems, and over the radio. Many mixers have computer controls that can "remember" the way in which the engineer has organized and manipulated the tracks. This feature al-

De Laubier, Gamma/Liaison

In a recording studio, a vocalist sings while an engineer adjusts sound levels with a mixer and records the performance. A soundproof glass window separates the performing studio from the control room. The engineer hears the singer through speakers in the control room.

lows engineers to experiment until they achieve the desired sound effects.

More than one version of a recording may be made. Recording companies often remix popular recordings to make them better for dancing.

Mastering refers to the processes used to create copies of the recording for use in the mass production of such products as compact discs and cassette tapes.

The mixdown process produces a new recording called the *master.* The sound information on the master is eventually transferred to a number of *production masters,* tapes or digital files that are used to quickly duplicate the information onto blank tapes or discs. Different mastering techniques are required for each type of product. For information on how sound is stored on various products, see **Compact disc; Tape recorder; Phonograph.**

Live recording involves installing portable recording equipment at a concert site. Actual live recordings do not have the excellent sound quality of those made in studios, where an engineer can carefully record the elements of a performance. Most recordings that are labeled "live" are actually combinations of parts from several live performances, often with studio recording segments mixed in.

Releasing the recording

The release of a new recording is often promoted by a music video or by a concert tour. In addition, it is important that new songs are played over the radio, because that is how many people first hear new music.

A company can release a recording for sale whenever it wishes. Sometimes a company reissues an old recording because the public seems interested in it again.

An artist receives a *royalty* payment from the record company for every recording sold. A royalty is a percentage of the price of the recording. Composers and publishers receive *mechanical royalties* for allowing a song to be recorded. In addition, the owner of the song's copyright receives a *performance royalty* whenever the music is used on radio or television. Performance royalties are collected by several large societies, including the American Society of Composers, Authors and Publishers (ASCAP) and Broadcast Music, Incorporated (BMI).

The sale of *pirated* recordings costs recording companies and artists billions of dollars annually. Pirated products include *bootleg* records made by secretly recording a live performance and records and tapes copied from an original recording without permission.

Recording industry awards

Several organizations present awards for artistic and commercial achievement within the recording industry. For example, Grammy Awards are given annually by the National Academy of Recording Arts and Sciences for artistic achievement in a broad range of categories. Grammy winners are determined by members of the academy, which includes musicians, engineers, and producers. In Canada, the Canadian Academy of Recording Arts and Sciences annually gives the Juno Awards.

The Recording Industry Association of America presents awards to artists who sell a specific number of recordings. When 500,000 copies of an album have been sold, an artist receives a *gold record.* A *platinum record* is awarded when sales of an album reach 1 million copies, and a *multi-platinum* record is given for sales of 2 million or more.

History

The history of the recording industry has been dictated by technological developments. In 1877, Thomas Edison invented the phonograph, which could record and play back sounds on tin-wrapped cylinders. Edison's invention was later improved by recording on wax cylinders. By the late 1890's, the flat disc record had been introduced by the Victor Talking Machine Company of Camden, New Jersey. During the mid-1920's, discs became widespread, and cylinder recordings began to disappear.

During the 1940's, recording tape was invented. As a result, the length of recordings was no longer determined by the wax disc blanks of three or four minutes duration that were being used at the time. The long-playing (LP) record was then introduced. Stereo records and recorded tapes were first sold during the 1950's and 1960's.

In the 1980's, music videos became a popular means for promoting songs and artists. CD's were introduced in 1982. By the 1990's, they had largely replaced phonograph records. In the early 1990's, the Minidisc was introduced. This product provides near-CD quality sound. In Minidisc recording, sounds that cannot be heard by the human ear are sifted out electronically. This enables more music to be stored on the disc. Manufacturers introduced surround-sound recordings on the DVD-Audio format in 2000.

The growth of the Internet, the worldwide network of computers, in the 1990's inspired the distribution of music recordings as digital data files. The smaller a data file is, the more quickly and easily it can be transferred over the Internet. Using data compression methods, the size of digital music data files can be reduced. *MP3* is a common compressed music data format. In some cases, a computer user *downloads* (copies) a file before it is played. In other cases, music is *streamed*—that is, it begins to play while the file is being downloaded. Music pirates have posted illegal recordings on the Internet. In the late 1990's, record labels began using the Internet to sell music. Purchasers can download songs and record them directly to their computer's hard disk or to a device that records CD's.   Ken C. Pohlmann

See also **Compact disc; Phonograph; Popular music; Stereophonic sound system; Tape recorder.**

Recreation is an activity that people voluntarily pursue for personal enjoyment or satisfaction, usually during their free time. Recreation takes a wide variety of forms and occurs in many different places, depending on the choice of the individual. Some recreation is passive, such as watching television. Many people enjoy extremely active forms of recreation, such as jogging or participating in sports.

Since the 1940's, recreation has become an important element in modern life. Higher incomes and improvements in working conditions and transportation have given many people more money, time, and mobility for recreation. Today, recreation is a major industry. By the early 1980's, Americans were spending more than $200 billion annually on recreation. Many companies provide facilities and equipment for commercial recreational use. Popular facilities include motion-picture theaters, bowling lanes, campgrounds, resorts, golf courses, tennis centers, and theme parks. A number of companies manufacture merchandise for recreation, such as sports equipment and camping supplies.

Recreation provides pleasure for millions of people, but it may also make an important contribution to an individual's mental and physical health. For example, hospitals often organize recreational activities under trained supervisors as therapy for patients.

Kinds of recreation. The most popular kind of recreation is watching television. On the average, a TV set in an American home is in use about seven hours a day.

Hobbies are an important form of recreation for millions of people. A large number of families engage in gardening. Stamp collecting is a very popular hobby. Games such as bridge and chess are a common type of recreation.

Many people concentrate on outdoor forms of recreation. The 10 most popular types of recreation in the United States are (1) visiting zoos, aquariums, fairs, and carnivals; (2) picnicking; (3) automobile driving for pleasure; (4) walking or jogging; (5) swimming; (6) travel; (7) watching sports events; (8) participating in sports and games; (9) fishing; and (10) taking nature walks.

For many people, attending cultural events is a favorite form of recreation. Such people may attend museum exhibits, theater performances, or concerts.

Opportunities for recreation. Private businesses, service organizations, and government agencies all provide opportunities for recreational activities. Many companies offer organized recreation for their employees, such as softball leagues and bowling tournaments. Community recreation services are provided by boys clubs, scouting organizations, and religious groups.

Local, state or provincial, and national government agencies provide many recreational services. Most local governments have a recreation and parks department responsible for maintaining facilities and offering programs. These services are financed by taxes and fees.

At the state or provincial and national levels, opportunities for recreation are primarily provided through parks.   Roger A. Lancaster

Related articles in *World Book.* See **Sports** and its list of *Related articles.* See also the *Visitor's guide* section of the state and provinces articles. Other related articles include:

Amusement park	Jogging	Safety (Safety in
Camping	Motion picture	recreation)
Carnival	Museum	Sports car
Circus	National park	Storytelling
Colonial life in	National Park	Television
America (Recre-	System	Theater
ation)	Park	Trampoline
Dance	Photography	Video game
Fair	Play	World's fair
Game	Radio	Zoo
Handicraft	Reading	
Hobby		

Recreational vehicle (RV) provides temporary living quarters for year-round travel, camping, or recreation. Some RV's have an engine and can be driven. Others are towed by an automobile, a van, or a truck. Still other RV's are carried on the bed of a pickup truck. All can

Popular recreational vehicles

Recreational vehicles provide living quarters for people who are camping or traveling. Many models have a bathroom, kitchen, areas for sleeping, and other facilities of permanent homes.

WORLD BOOK illustrations by Robert Keys and Ronald L. Kempke

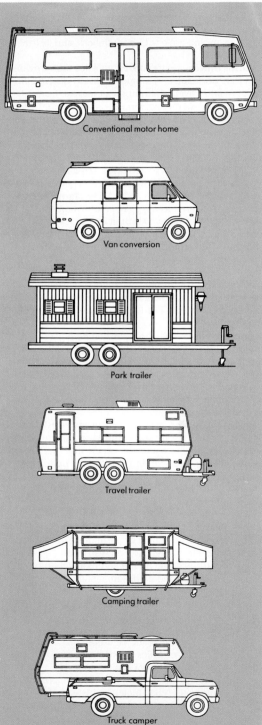

Conventional motor home

Van conversion

Park trailer

Travel trailer

Camping trailer

Truck camper

be moved easily and travel almost anywhere on land.

Early models of the recreational vehicle appeared in the 1920's. During the 1960's, RV's came into wide use as a means of comfortable and economical travel. In the early 1990's, about 10 percent of the households in the United States that had a motor vehicle owned an RV. Today, the basic types of recreational vehicles are (1) motor homes, (2) van conversions, (3) travel trailers, (4) folding camping trailers, (5) park trailers, and (6) truck campers.

Motor homes are motorized vehicles that provide both transportation and temporary living quarters for camping and travel. Motor homes measure from 17 to 40 feet (5.2 to 12.2 meters) long and up to $8\frac{1}{2}$ feet (2.6 meters) wide. They can sleep 2 to 10 people. Motor homes contain conveniences similar to those found in permanent homes, including a kitchen, a bathroom, heat, air conditioning, and a television set. Lighting and appliances are powered by electricity, a 12-volt battery, or propane gas. Separate storage tanks carry fresh water to the bathroom and kitchen and hold waste water and sewage. There are three types of motor homes. The *conventional motor home* is built on a truck frame. The *mini-motorhome* is built on a van frame. The *van camper* is a van with motor home conveniences added.

Van conversions are vans that have been modified after manufacture for travel and recreational use. Changes may include special windows, carpeting, custom seats, fold-down sofa beds, and a television set. Van conversions can seat 7 to 12 people and sleep 2 to 4 people.

Travel trailers have the same conveniences as motor homes but are towed by a hitch attached to an automobile, van, or pickup truck. They measure from 10 to 40 feet (3 to 12 meters) long and from 6 to 8 feet (1.8 to 2.4 meters) wide. Some travel trailers can sleep up to eight people. A *fifth-wheel trailer* has a raised forward section that creates a two-level floor plan.

Folding camping trailers measure from 10 to 25 feet (3 to 8 meters) long and about $6\frac{1}{2}$ feet (2 meters) wide. They unfold into a tentlike enclosure that provides kitchen, dining, and sleeping facilities for up to eight people. They offer many of the same conveniences as other RV's, including electricity, running water, appliances, and toilets.

Park trailers, the largest of all RV's, can measure up to 400 square feet (37 square meters) in floor area. They can be towed to a seasonal or permanent location and connected to electricity, gas, and water lines.

Truck campers ride on the bed of a pickup truck. Many have kitchen and bathroom facilities, electricity, air conditioning, microwaves, and other conveniences. They can sleep two to six people. Truck campers are available in many sizes and floor plans.

Critically reviewed by the Recreation Vehicle Industry Association

See also **Trailer** (Recreational trailers).

Rectifier. See **Electronics** (Diodes).

Rectum. See **Alimentary canal; Colon.**

Recycling is a process designed to collect, process, remanufacture, and reuse materials instead of throwing them away. Commonly recycled wastes include aluminum and steel cans, glass containers, newspapers, and office paper. Recycling programs also collect plastics, used motor oil, and magazines. Recycling helps conserve raw materials and energy that manufacturers would otherwise use to make new products. Recycling keeps materials out of *landfills* (areas where wastes are deposited and covered with earth or other material), saving scarce landfill space. Recycling also helps reduce the pollution that may result from waste disposal.

Uses for recycled materials. Recycled wastes provide basic raw materials, sometimes called scrap or *feedstocks*, for manufacturing a variety of products. Recycling has been an important source of feedstocks for the iron and steel industry and for papermaking since the early 1900's. Manufacturers use aluminum from recycled cans to make new cans and other products. Recycled paper is used not only in paper and cardboard but also in such materials as insulation and animal bedding. Manufacturers grind up waste glass and use it to make new glass containers and as a substitute for sand in concrete. Some plastic containers can be melted and molded into new plastic products. Recycled motor oil can be used as industrial fuel oil.

Such *organic waste* as plant material and food scraps can be recycled through *composting*. In this process, the collected waste is allowed to decay into a substance that can be added to soil to improve it.

Collecting materials. Recyclable materials have the most value if they are not mixed with garbage but are sorted before the garbage is sent for disposal. This sorting keeps materials from becoming contaminated, which lowers their usefulness and value. Separating recyclable materials can be more complicated when done at a waste-processing plant. Such special equipment as conveyor belts, screens, and magnets is used to separate large quantities of waste mechanically.

Recyclable materials are collected from consumers mainly through (1) buy-back centers, (2) drop-off centers, and (3) curbside collection programs. Buy-back centers pay people for materials they bring in. People are asked to separate recyclables by type and to separate glass by color. Drop-off centers are usually open longer hours than buy-back centers but do not offer money for the materials. An increasing number of communities require residents to participate in curbside collection programs. In these programs, residents of a community separate their materials and put them on the curb by their homes. Trucks pick up the materials and bring them to a central plant for processing. Curbside recycling usually recovers the greatest quantity of materials.

Many businesses and industries also take part in recycling efforts. Offices can recycle such wastes as paper and cardboard. Manufacturers who reuse recycled materials build plants near cities or industrial regions that produce large quantities of recyclable waste. Many countries have laws that require or encourage the purchase of products made from recycled materials, such as office paper. These laws provide incentives for businesses to invest in recycling equipment.

Prices paid for recycled waste usually depend on local demand, the quantity a seller can guarantee to the market, and the degree of contamination of the material. Buyers often reject loads of recyclables that are too dirty. The demand for recyclable paper and metal is strong in most areas. The demand for other materials, such as magazines and plastics, is growing as processing technologies improve.

Recycling has been most successful where it is less expensive than other methods of waste management. For example, recycling programs work well in many European countries and in Japan. In these countries, such conditions as high population density, plentiful recyclable materials, low transportation costs, and a shortage of landfill space contribute to the success of recycling.   Patrick Walsh

Related articles in *World Book* include:
Aluminum (Recycling)
Compost
Conservation (Mineral conservation: picture)
Environmental pollution
Industry (picture)
Plastics (Plastics and the environment)
Waste disposal

Additional resources

Fifty Simple Things Kids Can Do to Recycle. EarthWorks, 1994. Younger readers.
Lund, Herbert F., ed. *The McGraw-Hill Recycling Handbook.* McGraw, 1993.
Parker, Steve. *Waste, Recycling and Re-Use.* Raintree Steck-Vaughn, 1998. Younger readers.
Stein, Kathy. *Beyond Recycling: A Re-Users Guide.* Clear Light Pubs., 1997.

Red. See Color.
Red Baron. See Ace.
Red Beard. See Frederick I.
Red blood cell. See Blood.
Red Cloud (1822-1909) was one of the greatest warriors and chiefs of the Oglala, a band of the Teton Sioux Indians. During the 1860's, Red Cloud and his followers fought to keep the whites out of Sioux territory in what are now Montana, South Dakota, and Wyoming. A number of historians have called this struggle Red Cloud's War.

During the 1860's, white settlers began to travel the Bozeman Trail to gold fields in Montana (see **Bozeman Trail**). This trail crossed
northeastern Wyoming, a main hunting area of the Sioux. Red Cloud's band continually attacked travelers on the trail. In 1866, to keep the route open, the U.S. Army built Fort Phil Kearny and Fort Reno in Wyoming and Fort C. F. Smith in Montana. Red Cloud and his allies kept these forts under siege for almost two years.

Smithsonian Institution, Washington, D.C.
Red Cloud

In 1868, the United
States government
agreed to abandon the three forts and not build any more roads through Sioux territory. Because of this victory, Red Cloud has been called the only Indian who ever won a war against the U.S. government. He lived at peace with the whites after 1868.   Beatrice Medicine

Red Cross is an organization that works to relieve human suffering. More than 135 nations have Red Cross societies. Each national Red Cross society carries on its own program. However, Red Cross workers in all parts of the world are united in their aims. They try to prevent misery in time of war or peace, and serve all peoples, regardless of race, nationality, or religion.

The name *Red Cross* comes from the organization's flag, a red cross on a white background. The flag honors Switzerland, where the Red Cross was founded in 1863. The Swiss flag is a white cross on a red field. Societies in most Muslim countries use a red crescent on a white field, and call themselves Red Crescent societies. See **Flag** (pictures: Flags of world organizations).

The American Red Cross

In the United States, the work of the Red Cross is carried out by the American Red Cross and its more than 10 million volunteers, including blood donors and students. The programs and services of the American Red Cross are funded by voluntary contributions.

Services to the armed forces and veterans. Red Cross services are available to U.S. military personnel and veterans wherever they are. The Red Cross helps solve personal and family problems and provides counseling, emergency communications, and other assistance. Red Cross volunteers serve in military medical facilities and in veterans' hospitals.

Disaster services programs begin long before disaster strikes. Local Red Cross chapters help their communities develop year-round preparedness for disaster situations. Volunteer groups are trained to provide food, clothing, emergency first aid, and nursing and medical service; and to operate shelters for homeless families. All aid to disaster sufferers is free.

The blood and tissues program of the Red Cross collects and distributes about half the blood drawn in the United States yearly. It collects more than 6 million units of blood annually from voluntary donors. The program also makes blood products for hospitals and provides blood and blood products to the United States Department of Defense on request or during a national emergency. In 1984, the Red Cross began a national transplant service. The service provides bone, skin, and organs to the needy.

Safety programs. The Red Cross offers courses in first aid and in cardiopulmonary resuscitation (CPR). These courses include information on accident prevention. Other courses taught by the Red Cross include swimming, swimming for disabled individuals, and water and boating safety. The Red Cross also trains lifeguards and prepares instructors to teach first aid, water safety, and skills in the use of small boats. Local Red Cross chapters provide demonstrations, exhibits, films, talks, and radio and television broadcasts on safety training. Certificates of merit are awarded to people who use skills that they have learned in Red Cross courses to save lives.

Nursing and health programs include courses on health in the home, preparation for parenthood, child raising, education about AIDS, and lifestyle and nutrition. Nursing students, registered professional nurses, and licensed vocational nurses are enrolled for service in Red Cross and community activities, and in disasters.

Red Cross youth and service programs. Elementary and secondary school students serve in the Red Cross. Youth activities, which are designed to develop leadership skills, range from volunteer hospital service to such international friendship projects as gift exchanging.

The Red Cross works to relieve human suffering. During a fire, *far left,* a Red Cross volunteer helps a child to safety. Through the Red Cross disaster services program, *left,* volunteers help provide food, clothing, shelter, and medical aid to disaster victims.

Photographs by American Red Cross

International services. The American Red Cross maintains relations with national societies in other countries. It provides emergency help to disaster victims and refugees in other countries through its affiliation with the League of Red Cross Societies, Red Crescent societies, and the International Committee of the Red Cross. It also helps reunite families separated by war, disasters, or other emergencies.

Organization. Volunteers and career staff members form the backbone of Red Cross activities in the United States. Most Red Cross workers belong to about 2,500 chapters that serve every county in the United States. The members elect a volunteer board of directors to administer chapter programs. Volunteers make up the entire staffs of about 1,600 chapters. Some chapters have only one paid professional worker, who serves as executive secretary.

Three area offices give general guidance and technical assistance to the local chapters. They also direct field staff members assigned to armed forces installations in their areas. These offices are in Alexandria, Virginia.; St. Louis; and Burlingame, California. Overseas area offices supervise work for military personnel abroad.

The American Red Cross has national headquarters in Washington, D.C. A 50-member board of governors, made up of volunteers, develops national policies of the organization. The President of the United States is honorary chairman of the American Red Cross. The President appoints the organization's chairman and seven other board members. The board itself elects 12 more members. Chapter representatives elect 30 additional members at the organization's annual convention. The board selects the president of the American Red Cross.

The Canadian Red Cross

The Canadian Red Cross Society operates nearly 9,000 clinics and has the support of about $2\frac{1}{2}$ million volunteers, including blood donors. Its clinics collect about 6,000 units of blood or blood products a day. The Cana-

dian Red Cross offers a variety of other services.

Health services. The Red Cross in Canada has pioneered in many nursing projects. It has a number of outpost hospitals and nursing stations that serve remote areas. Hundreds of communities benefit from the free use of sickroom supplies provided by the Sickroom Equipment Loan Service. Registered nurses volunteer to teach basic home nursing.

Until 1998, the National Blood Transfusion Service was a major project of the Canadian Red Cross. In 1998, a new national agency called Canadian Blood Services officially took over collection and distribution of blood in Canada.

Aid to veterans. Red Cross volunteers visit veterans' hospitals and institutions to cheer sick and disabled veterans. They also help veterans learn various craft skills, such as macramé, weaving, and leatherwork. Red Cross lodges provide homelike surroundings for patients near veterans' hospitals.

Welfare services. Trained Canadian Red Cross volunteers visit homes where parents are ill. They feed and care for the children and perform other tasks. The Canadian Red Cross Corps, a uniformed group of volunteers, helps veterans and performs community services. The Tracing and Reunion Bureau obtains health and welfare reports on people throughout the world. This bureau of the Canadian Red Cross also traces missing persons.

Relief work. All provincial divisions of the Canadian Red Cross are prepared to give emergency disaster relief. They provide services that include food, shelter, clothing, medical assistance, registration of disaster victims, and answers to welfare inquiries during the emergency period.

The Canadian Red Cross supplies clothing and other items to national societies in countries throughout the world. It also sends professional and technical personnel to international disaster areas when requested to do so by the League of Red Cross Societies or the International Committee of the Red Cross.

The Canadian Red Cross Youth, made up of Canadians up to the age of 25, raises money to support international development and relief projects. The money also provides hospital and medical care for children with disabilities.

Organization. Volunteers perform more than 90 per cent of Canadian Red Cross work. The society has over 435 branches in 10 provinces. An office directs the work in each province and supervises each provincial division.

A Central Council of not more than 75 volunteers governs the national organization. The 10 provincial divisions elect four members each to the council. These 40 representatives appoint not more than 35 other members. The council elects the officers of the society and the members of a national executive committee.

The Red Cross in other lands

The American and Canadian Red Cross societies belong to the International Red Cross and Red Crescent Movement, made up of over 135 national Red Cross and Red Crescent societies in all parts of the world. Each society conducts humanitarian services according to its country's needs. All societies operate under the basic principles of Red Cross, and most carry on extensive medical and health programs. Nearly all of the societies have junior divisions and youth activities.

National Red Cross societies cooperate internationally through their federation, the *League of Red Cross Societies,* which has headquarters in Geneva, Switzerland. The league encourages its members to work together, represents them in international discussions, and helps them develop their programs. The *International Committee of the Red Cross,* also located in Geneva, serves as a neutral intermediary during conflicts between nations for the protection of war victims. It works for the continual improvement of the Geneva Conventions, the treaty that provides for the humane treatment of prisoners during war. It also grants recognition to new Red Cross societies. The League and the International Committee shared the 1963 Nobel Peace Prize. The *International Red Cross Conference* is the highest deliberative body of the international Red Cross. Delegates from Red Cross groups and representatives of governments that signed the Geneva Conventions attend the conference every four years to discuss the Geneva Conventions and world humanitarian problems involving cooperation between the Red Cross and governments.

History

Beginnings. Jean Henri Dunant, a Swiss philanthropist, founded the international Red Cross. He was touring Italy in 1859 during the Austro-Sardinian War. Dunant saw the field at Solferino the day after 40,000 people had been killed or wounded in a battle. Horrified at the suffering of the wounded, he formed a group of volunteers to help them.

In 1862, Dunant published a pamphlet called *Un Souvenir de Solferino (Recollections of Solferino).* It ended with the plea, "Would it not be possible to found and organize in all civilized countries permanent societies of volunteers who in time of war would give help to the wounded without regard for their nationality?" The ap-

peal won favorable response. On Oct. 26, 1863, delegates from 16 nations and several charitable organizations met in Geneva to discuss Dunant's idea. This conference laid the groundwork for the Red Cross movement and chose the organization's symbol.

Delegates from 12 European nations met in Geneva in August 1864, on invitation from the Swiss Federal Council. Two U.S. observers attended. Out of this meeting came the *First Geneva* (or Red Cross) *Convention.* Later treaties amended and improved it.

In the United States, Congress did not ratify the Geneva Convention for 18 years, fearing foreign entanglements. The American Association for the Relief of Misery on the Battlefields was organized during this time. It adopted the red cross as its emblem. This group disbanded in 1871 because the United States had not yet ratified the Geneva Convention. Clara Barton worked to have the treaty ratified, and helped establish the American Association of the Red Cross in 1881. President Chester A. Arthur finally signed the treaty on Mar. 1, 1882. The Senate accepted it a few days later without a dissenting vote. The Red Cross association was later reorganized, and in 1905 Congress granted it a new charter that established the basic organization of today's American Red Cross.

The American Red Cross grew during World War I (1914-1918). It met the welfare needs of rapidly expanding military forces. Red Cross field directors and other workers served troops in the United States and overseas. In 1917, Home Service was set up in many communities to provide a link between military personnel and their families. The Red Cross also organized and equipped 58 base hospitals, 54 of which went overseas. The Junior Red Cross, founded in 1917, gave U.S. schoolchildren a chance to help the war effort.

After the war, the Red Cross aided millions of veterans and helped relieve war-caused suffering in many lands. During the 1920's, the Red Cross established 2,400 public health nursing services throughout the United States.

During World War II (1939-1945), the Red Cross Army-Navy Blood Donor Service collected more than 13 million pints (6,150,000 liters) of blood. Whole blood was flown from the United States to a warfront for the first time during the Korean War (1950-1953). Also during the 1950's, the Red Cross aided refugees of Algerian and Hungarian revolts.

The Red Cross spent nearly $146 million during the 1960's for disaster relief and rehabilitation. The organization provided assistance for survivors of earthquakes in Chile (1960), Yugoslavia (1963), and Alaska (1964). The Red Cross also directed the shipment of $53 million worth of donated food and drugs to Cuba for the release of about 1,100 prisoners and refugees (see **Cuba** [The Bay of Pigs invasion]).

In the late 1960's and early 1970's, the Red Cross provided hospital and recreational programs for U.S. armed forces in Vietnam. In 1973, the Red Cross assisted released American prisoners of war. It also worked with the U.S. government in 1975 on the resettlement of refugees from Southeast Asia in the United States. Major foreign relief efforts by the American Red Cross followed the earthquakes in Nicaragua in 1972, Guatemala in 1976, and several other nations in the 1980's.

The American Red Cross also took part in the Cambodian refugee relief operation in 1979 and 1980, the medical and food relief effort in Poland in 1982, the drought relief operation in Africa in 1985, and the volcanic eruption effort in Colombia in 1985. In 1990, the Red Cross began refugee relief operations in Jordan as a result of the events that led to the Persian Gulf War (1991). After the war, it aided Kurdish refugees in camps in Kuwait, Iraq, and Turkey.

In Canada. George S. Ryerson, an army doctor, founded the Red Cross movement in Canada. He first flew a flag with a red cross on a white background while serving in the Canadian Army Medical Services during the North West Rebellion of 1885. In 1896, Ryerson organized a Canadian branch of the British Red Cross. This branch developed into the Canadian Red Cross Society and was incorporated by an act of the Canadian Parliament in 1909. The International Committee of the Red Cross recognized the Canadian Red Cross in 1927.

Critically reviewed by the American Red Cross

Related articles in *World Book* include:

Barton, Clara	Geneva Conventions
Dunant, Jean Henri	Social work
First aid	Swimming (Water safety)

Additional resources

Moorhead, Caroline. *Dunant's Dream: War, Switzerland and the History of the Red Cross.* Carroll & Graf, 1998.
Pollard, Michael. *The Red Cross and the Red Crescent.* New Discovery Bks., 1994.

Red deer is the common name for a species of deer that lives in forests of Europe, Asia, and northern Africa. There are several subspecies of red deer. Scientists classify the *American elk,* also called *wapiti,* as a subspecies of red deer (see **Elk**).

Red deer have smooth coats that range in color from rich, reddish-brown in summer to grayish-brown in winter. The *hart* (adult male) grows stately, branched antlers that are shed each year. A hart weighs from 250 to 350 pounds (113 to 159 kilograms) and stands $3\frac{1}{2}$ to $4\frac{1}{2}$ feet (1 to 1.4 meters) high. Most *hinds* (adult females) are shorter than the harts and have no antlers. American elk are much larger than other red deer. Males may weigh as much as 1,000 pounds (500 kilograms).

Gregory K. Snyder

Scientific classification. Red deer belong to the deer family, Cervidae. They are *Cervus elaphus.*

See also **Deer**.

Red drum. See **Redfish**.

Red gum. See **Sweet gum**.

Red Jacket (1750?-1830) was a Seneca Indian leader and noted orator. He strongly opposed attempts by whites to force their culture on the Seneca.

Red Jacket and his tribe aided the British during the Revolutionary War in America (1775-1783). A British officer rewarded him with a red jacket, the source of his name. Red

Thomas Gilcrease Institute of American History and Art, Tulsa, Oklahoma

Red Jacket

Jacket served as an official spokesman of the Iroquois Confederacy, which included the Seneca, in dealings between the Indians and the United States government after the war.

The Seneca leader encouraged his tribe to live in peace with the whites. He also resisted efforts by Christian missionaries, other whites, and even the Seneca prophet Handsome Lake to change some traditional Seneca ways of life.

Red Jacket was born in what is now Seneca County in New York. At the height of his influence, he was called Sagoyewatha (He Keeps Them Awake). Red Jacket died of cholera on the Buffalo Creek Reservation in New York. A monument of the Seneca leader stands in Buffalo, New York.   Robert E. Powless

Red pepper. See **Cayenne pepper**.

Red River, so named because of the red-colored sediment it carries, forms much of the boundary between Oklahoma and Texas. It is about 1,300 miles (2,090 kilometers) long. Its drainage basin covers about 90,000 square miles (230,000 square kilometers). The Red River rises in northern Texas. Its north fork has its source east of Amarillo, Texas, and the Prairie Dog Town fork rises south of it. The river flows through southwestern Arkansas and into Louisiana. It joins the Atchafalaya River about 5 miles (8 kilometers) north of Simmesport, Louisiana. For location, see **Louisiana** (physical map). See also **Lake Texoma**.   Daniel D. Arreola

Red River of the North, also called Red River, is a major waterway of the United States and Canada. It flows north 545 miles (877 kilometers) and empties into Lake Winnipeg in the Canadian province of Manitoba. The Red River of the North forms part of Canada's Saskatchewan-Nelson river system. It runs through a level plain that was formerly the bed of Lake Agassiz, a glacial lake (see **Lake Agassiz**). The Red River Valley is one of the richest farming areas in the world.

The Red River of the North is formed by the union of the Otter Tail and Bois de Sioux rivers at Wahpeton, North Dakota, opposite Breckenridge, Minnesota. The Red forms the boundary between North Dakota and Minnesota. The Otter Tail rises in west-central Minnesota, just west of the headwaters of the Mississippi River. The Bois de Sioux begins in Lake Traverse. The Red River flows northward into Lake Winnipeg.

WORLD BOOK map

Location of the Red River of the North

Farmers in the Red River Valley raise wheat, oats, flax, barley, potatoes, sugar beets, sunflowers, hogs, and poultry. Cities along the Red River of the North include Fargo and Grand Forks, in North Dakota; Moorhead, Minn.; and Winnipeg, Man. Boats carried large amounts of goods on the river between Winnipeg and Fargo until 1878, when a railway began to serve the valley. Winnipeg is now protected from flooding by the Red River Floodway, a channel that directs the flow of the river around the city.   John S. Brierley

Red River Rebellion occurred in 1869 and 1870, when settlers of the Red River Valley of what is now Manitoba resisted steps to put the valley under Canadian government control. The region had long been governed by the Hudson's Bay Company. The uprising is sometimes called the First Riel Rebellion, after its leader, Louis Riel.

The Hudson's Bay Company had allowed the valley's residents much independence. In 1869, however, the company surrendered its rights in Rupert's Land, including the Red River Valley, to Britain. The British decided to transfer Rupert's Land to the Canadian government, which paid the company for the land. The Canadian government planned to develop the region for farmers from what is now eastern Canada.

In 1869, the population of the Red River Valley consisted of Indians, settlers, and a few fur traders. Most of the settlers were *métis* (people of mixed white and Indian ancestry). The settlers farmed land to which they held no formal title. They feared that the transfer of the valley to the Canadian government would threaten their land rights and their distinctive culture.

The revolt. Shortly before the transfer of Rupert's Land to the Canadian government, roadbuilders, surveyors, and officials of all kinds from the east descended upon the valley. One of their chief aims was to divide the land into townships and sections in advance of incoming settlers. This activity angered the residents.

A leader arose among the métis. He was Louis Riel, a young man of French, Irish, and Indian descent who came from a prominent local family. The Canadian government then sent out William McDougall as the first governor of the new territory. When the métis heard of McDougall's approach, they determined to prevent him from entering the territory. A group of métis met McDougall at the border of Rupert's Land and forced him to turn back. Riel then led the métis in a successful attempt to capture Fort Garry, at what is now Winnipeg, and set up a *provisional* (temporary) government there.

As a result of the rebellion, the Canadian government decided not to take control of the area on Dec. 1, 1869, as it had planned. Early in 1870, a group of métis with much popular support in the valley decided to negotiate with the Canadian government. But before any negotiations began, settlers loyal to Canada launched an unsuccessful attack on Fort Garry. Riel's provisional government imprisoned several of them. One of the prisoners was an English Canadian named Thomas Scott. The provisional government condemned Scott as a traitor and had him shot. Scott's death inflamed the people of eastern Canada against the provisional government.

End of the conflict. After the killing of Scott, the Canadian government ordered troops under Colonel Garnet Wolseley to the Red River Valley. But before the force could start westward, Riel's provisional government opened negotiations with the government of Canada. The Canadian government agreed to admit the Red River area to the Canadian Confederation as a self-governing province. It also set aside 1,400,000 acres (567,000 hectares) of land for the métis. But many of the métis moved westward into what is now Saskatchewan. In addition, the Canadian government refused to pardon Riel for actions taken by the provisional government, including the killing of Scott. As a result, Riel fled to the United States. In 1885, he returned to Canada to lead another métis uprising, known as the North West Rebellion. But he was captured and hanged for treason later that year.   J. M. Bumsted

See also **North West Rebellion; Riel, Louis; Manitoba** (History); **Métis.**

Red Sea is a long, narrow arm of the Indian Ocean that separates the Arabian Peninsula from northeastern Africa. The sea ranks as one of the world's busiest waterways. Much of the trade between Europe and Asia passes through the Red Sea, which is connected with the Mediterranean Sea by the Suez Canal. Scholars are uncertain about the origin of the sea's name. One widely held theory is that the Red Sea is so named because a type of algae forms a reddish-brown scum on its surface during the summer.

The Red Sea covers about 176,000 square miles (456,000 square kilometers), an area larger than the state of California. The sea is about 1,400 miles (2,200 kilometers) long and about 220 miles (350 kilometers) wide at its widest point. Its average depth is 1,765 feet (538 meters). Its deepest point is 9,974 feet (3,040 meters).

At its northern end, the Red Sea branches into the Gulf of Suez on the west and the Gulf of Aqaba on the east. The Sinai Peninsula lies between the two gulfs. The Gulf of Suez, a major offshore oil-producing area, leads into the Suez Canal. The Gulf of Aqaba leads to the Israeli port of Elat and the Jordanian port of Aqaba. At the southern end of the Red Sea, a narrow waterway called the Strait of Bab el Mandeb flows into the Gulf of Aden, which, in turn, leads into the Indian Ocean.

The Red Sea lies in the Great Rift Valley system, a series of valleys that cut through much of eastern Africa and part of southwestern Asia. High cliffs tower above both banks of the sea. In most places, narrow coastal

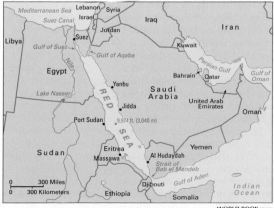

WORLD BOOK map

Location of the Red Sea

plains lie between the cliffs and the sea. The Red Sea has large numbers of coral reefs. The reefs, together with irregular currents and strong winds, make navigation in the Red Sea difficult for small vessels.

In summer, the water temperature at the surface of the Red Sea averages 85 °F (29 °C). The waters are among the saltiest in the world. Extreme heat in the region produces a rapid rate of evaporation, resulting in the high salt concentration. Some salt is collected in evaporation pans for local use. Many varieties of fish live in the Red Sea. But the number of fish of each variety is too small to make commercial fishing profitable.

The Red Sea was probably formed millions of years ago when the Arabian Peninsula and the African continent drifted apart. One of the most famous stories in the Bible describes the parting of the waters of the Red Sea, which enabled the Israelites to escape from Egypt (Exodus 14). However, because the Hebrew text actually says "sea of reeds," most modern scholars believe the body of water was actually the marshy lands east of the Nile Delta, well to the north of the Red Sea.

The Red Sea has served as an important trade route since ancient times. Before the opening of the Suez Canal in 1869, goods were transported overland by camel or donkey between the Mediterranean and Red seas.   Bernard Reich

Red snapper. See Snapper.

Red tape is an unfavorable term used to describe the inefficiency of any large bureaucracy, public or private. The term originated in England during the 1700's. People used red string to tie legal and official documents together. Later, the term came to mean official routine in general. *Red tape* may describe an official's rigid observance of rules and regulations; the routing of requests and orders through channels, resulting in delay; or excessive paperwork associated with the administration of a program. See also **Bureaucracy.**   Charles O. Jones

Red tide is a term used for brownish or reddish areas of ocean, river, or lake water. The color comes from the presence of millions of microscopic organisms in the water. The discolored areas may range from less than a few square yards or meters to over 1,000 square miles (2,600 square kilometers). They may last from a few hours to several months. Red tides appear in waters in most parts of the world. In the United States, they are often seen off the coasts of Florida, Texas, and California.

Many red tides are harmless. But some kill fish and other water animals, which then may float on the water or wash ashore in great numbers. The decaying bodies cause an unpleasant odor. Still other red tides do not kill sea life, but they make the shellfish that feed on them poisonous to eat. Harmful red tides are caused by several species of *dinoflagellates* (one-celled organisms). Some dinoflagellates produce a poison that paralyzes and kills fish. Dinoflagellates may also kill fish during red tides by using up nearly all the oxygen in the water.

Scientists do not fully understand why the dinoflagellate population suddenly increases, causing red tides. It is known that dinoflagellates accumulate when the nutrients, temperature, amount of sunlight, water currents, and other conditions in the water suit their needs. Red tides may decrease when other sea organisms eat the dinoflagellates.   David L. Garrison

See also **Dinoflagellate; Pfiesteria.**

Red-winged blackbird. See Blackbird.

Redbird is the common name for all birds with red or mostly red plumage. In the United States, the name is often applied to the cardinal and occasionally to the scarlet tanager and summer tanager. See also **Cardinal** (bird); **Tanager.**

Redbreast. See Robin.

Redbud is the name for a group of trees and shrubs native to Asia, North America, and southern Europe. Redbuds are particularly beautiful early in spring when they are covered with delicate blossoms, each about 1 inch (2.5 centimeters) long. The flowers, which may be pink, purplish-pink, or white, reach full bloom before the leaves appear. Redbud trees have smooth, reddish-brown bark and heart-shaped leaves. The trees bear many seeds in flat, thin pods. The seeds are a valuable source of food for animals.

Redbuds grow best in fertile, sandy soil. Some grow 40 feet (12 meters) high. People cultivate the trees from seeds or from cuttings. Redbuds are widely planted as ornamental trees because of their colorful blossoms and graceful form.

One species of redbud is called the *Judas tree* be-

© Irvin L. Oakes, Photo Researchers

A redbud tree has spreading branches with reddish-brown bark. Gardeners use redbuds as decorative shrubs.

Grant Heilman

Clusters of redbud blossoms cover the tree's branches in the early spring, before the leaves begin to unfold.

cause of the belief that Judas Iscariot, the betrayer of Jesus Christ, hanged himself on this kind of tree. The Judas tree grows in southern Europe and western Asia.   Linda B. Brubaker

Scientific classification. Redbuds belong to the pea family, Fabaceae or Leguminosae. The Judas tree is *Cercis siliquastrum.*

See also **Tree** (Familiar broadleaf [picture]).

Redcoat. See **Revolutionary War in America.**

Redfish is a name applied to several kinds of fish, but particularly to the *red drum,* also called *channel bass.* This game fish lives along the Atlantic Coast of North America from Massachusetts to northern Mexico. It has a gray skin with a reddish sheen. The fish grows to 5 feet (1.5 meters) long and may weigh up to 75 pounds (34 kilograms), but red drums of over 40 pounds (18 kilograms) are rare. This popular food fish has been caught in large numbers, and fishery agencies have restricted the catching of red drums in the Gulf of Mexico.

The term *redfish* is also applied to the *California sheepshead,* a red fish of southern California. This richly colored fish has a thick, crimson body with blackish-purple fins. It weighs up to 15 pounds (7 kilograms) and is sometimes called the *fathead,* because of the fatty lump on its blunt forehead. Its flesh is prized, especially by the Chinese, who dry and salt it. *Redfish* is also the name given in Alaska to the *red salmon,* also called *sockeye salmon* (see **Salmon**).   William J. Richards

Scientific classification. The red drum is a member of the drum family, Sciaenidae. Its scientific name is *Sciaenops ocellatus.* The California sheepshead is a member of the wrasse family, Labridae. It is *Semicossyphus pulcher.*

Redford, Robert (1937-   ), is an American motion-picture actor and director. Redford has played a wide variety of characters, but he is best known for his good looks and his understated acting style. He won the 1980 Academy Award as best director for *Ordinary People.* Redford also directed the popular films *A River Runs Through It* (1992) and *Quiz Show* (1994). He directed and starred in *The Horse Whisperer* (1998).

Charles Robert Redford, Jr., was born in Santa Monica, California. He first won acclaim in 1963 in the Broadway comedy *Barefoot in the Park.* He also starred in the film version in 1967. Redford became a movie star as a Western outlaw in *Butch Cassidy and the Sundance Kid* (1969) and as a successful screenwriter in *The Way We Were* (1973).

George Rodriguez, Shooting Star
Robert Redford

Redford has also starred in political films, most notably *The Candidate* (1972) and *All the President's Men* (1976). His other films include *Jeremiah Johnson* (1972), *The Sting* (1973), *The Great Gatsby* (1974), *Three Days of the Condor* (1975), *The Electric Horseman* (1979), *The Natural* (1984), *Out of Africa* (1985), *Sneakers* (1992), and *Indecent Proposal* (1993).   Louis Giannetti

Redgrave, Michael (1908-1985), was an English actor who became known for his roles in the plays of William Shakespeare. Redgrave made more than 50 motion pictures and played a wide variety of parts ranging from comic to tragic. He was also a noted stage director.

Redgrave made his stage debut in 1934 in *Counsellor-at-Law.* He began his movie career in 1938 in *The Lady Vanishes,* a famous suspense film directed by Alfred Hitchcock. Redgrave's other movies include *The Stars Look Down* (1939), *Dead of Night* (1945), *Fame Is the Spur* (1947), *The Browning Version* (1951), *The Importance of Being Earnest* (1951), and *The Loneliness of the Long Distance Runner* (1963).

Michael Scudamore Redgrave was born in Bristol and graduated from Cambridge University. He was knighted in 1959. He was married to Rachel Kempson, a famous stage actress. Their daughters, Vanessa and Lynn, are noted stage and film actresses. Vanessa Redgrave also became known for her radical left-wing political and social views.   John F. Mariani

Redpoll is the name of two species of small songbirds found in North America, Asia, and Europe. Redpolls are 5 to 5$\frac{1}{2}$ inches (12.7 to 14 centimeters) long. The *common redpoll* has a patch of red feathers on the forehead, a black chin, and whitish underparts, with dark streaks

WORLD BOOK illustration by Trevor Boyer, Linden Artists, Ltd.
The redpoll, a member of the finch family, has a reddish crown. The adult male has rosy-pink breast feathers.

on the sides. The adult male has a rosy-pink breast. The *hoary redpoll* looks much like the common redpoll but is paler in color.

Redpolls breed in Arctic regions. They build grassy nests on the ground or in small trees or bushes. The females lay from three to seven pale blue eggs speckled with reddish-brown. Redpolls eat plant buds, seeds, and some insects. In North America, common redpolls sometimes migrate as far south as the central United States for the winter.   Martha Hatch Balph

Scientific classification. Redpolls belong to the subfamily Carduelinae in the finch family, Fringillidae. The scientific name for the common redpoll is *Carduelis flammea.* The hoary redpoll is *C. hornemanni.*

Redshift is a stretching of the wavelengths of visible light or similar radiation sent out by a cosmic object. Wavelength is the distance between successive crests of a wave. Redshift occurs in the radiation *emitted* (sent out) by an object moving away from the observer. It occurs in all the kinds of radiation known as *electromagnetic radiation.* From the longest wavelengths to the shortest, these kinds of radiation are radio waves, infrared rays, visible light, ultraviolet rays, X rays, and gamma rays. *Redshift* is sometimes spelled as *red shift.*

The amount of redshift is related to the speed at which the emitting object is moving away from the observer. An object with a large redshift is receding more rapidly than an object with a small redshift.

In 1929, American astronomer Edwin Hubble discovered that the farther a galaxy is from Earth, the larger its redshift and thus the faster it is moving away. Hubble's discovery indicated that the universe is expanding. The expansion of the universe is a key part of the *big bang theory,* the modern theory of the beginning of the universe. According to this theory, all space expanded from a hot, dense, pointlike concentration called a *singularity.*

Astronomers originally measured a galaxy's redshift by breaking up its visible light into a rainbowlike band of colors called a *spectrum.* They displayed the spectrum horizontally and identified dark, vertical lines that indicated the presence of certain substances in the galaxy. The scientists then compared this spectrum with spectra of stars in our home galaxy, the Milky Way. (The plural of *spectrum* is *spectra.)* The lines in the galaxy's spectrum were nearer the red end of the spectrum than were the corresponding lines in the spectra of the stars. The term *redshift* comes from the fact that such lines are displaced toward the red end of the spectrum.

Today, astronomers analyze galactic spectra electronically. The dark "lines" appear as low points in a graph that shows how brightness varies with wavelength.

An effect related to redshift, *blueshift,* occurs in the radiation emitted by an object moving toward the observer. Blueshift is a compression of wavelengths.In a spectrum of visible light, the dark lines are displaced toward the blue end. An effect similar to redshift and blueshift also occurs in sound waves. Known as the *Doppler effect,* it involves a change in the frequency of sound waves caused by motion of the source of sound. See **Sound** (diagram: The Doppler effect).   Wendy Freedman

See also **Cosmology; Electromagnetic waves; Light** (Electromagnetic waves); **Spectrometer.**

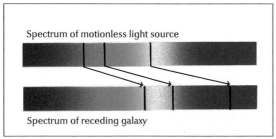

WORLD BOOK diagram by Ernest Norcia

Redshift causes a displacement of lines in the *spectrum* (band of colors) sent out by a galaxy that is moving away from Earth. If the galaxy were motionless relative to Earth, those lines would appear in the positions shown in the upper diagram. The cause of the displacement is known as *redshift* because the lines are displaced toward the red end of the spectrum.

Redstart is the name of several species of small woodland birds. The *American redstart* breeds throughout most of North America. The male is black with vivid salmon-red or orange-red markings. The female and young are brown with dull yellow markings. The female lays four or five creamy white eggs. The bird feeds chiefly on insects. The *painted redstart* breeds from the southwestern part of the United States to Central America. The male is black, with a bright red breast and white marks on the wings and tail. The female usually lays three or four eggs.   Sandra L. Vehrencamp

Scientific classification. Redstarts belong to the subfamily Parulinae in the emberizid family, Emberizidae. The scientific name for the American redstart is *Setophaga ruticilla.* The painted redstart is *Myioborus pictus.*

See also **Bird** (pictures: Birds of forests and woodlands; Birds' eggs).

Redstone Arsenal, near Huntsville, Alabama, serves as headquarters of the United States Army Aviation and Missile Command. The Aviation and Missile Command designs, develops, and purchases army aviation and missile systems. Redstone Arsenal covers about 38,000 acres (15,000 hectares) and received its name from the red soil in the area. It includes two free-flight rocket ranges and facilities for testing liquid and solid propellant missiles. Redstone Arsenal was established in 1941 by combining the Chemical and Ordnance arsenals located there. The George C. Marshall Space Flight Center at the arsenal manages the research and development of high-power rocket boosters. See also **Alabama** (The mid-1900's; picture).   Steve E. Dietrich

Reduction is a chemical reaction in which a substance gains electrons. The term originally referred to any chemical process in which a substance either combines with hydrogen or loses oxygen. Reduction is the opposite of *oxidation,* a chemical reaction in which a substance gives up electrons. Reduction and oxidation always occur together. These two combined reactions are known as *redox reactions.* See **Oxidation.**

Many kinds of processes involve reduction. For example, metal plating occurs when metal *ions* (electrically charged atoms) in a solution are reduced to form neutral atoms. When a piece of copper is placed in a solution containing silver ions (Ag^+), it slowly becomes coated with silver. In this process, each positively charged silver ion gains an electron given up by a copper atom and becomes electrically neutral. The chemical equation for the reduction of silver is written as follows:

$$Ag^+ + 1e^- \rightarrow Ag.$$

An example of the original meaning of reduction is the combining of nitrogen and hydrogen gases in the production of ammonia (NH_3). Another example is the removal of oxygen from zinc oxide (ZnO) to form metallic zinc. Zinc may be extracted from its ore in this manner.   Cathleen J. Hapeman

See also **Corrosion; Electrolysis.**

Redwood is a magnificent forest tree that grows along the West Coast of the United States from central California to southern Oregon. It thrives in the foggy climate alongside the mountains that face the Pacific Ocean and only rarely occurs over 50 miles (80 kilometers) inland.

Many redwood forests have been set aside as state or national parks in order to preserve these impressive trees. The redwood is also called *coast* or *California redwood* to distinguish it from the giant sequoia to which it is related (see **Sequoia**).

Redwoods are the world's tallest living trees. They commonly grow 200 to 275 feet (61 to 84 meters) high

Gerald French, Photofile

Redwoods are the tallest living trees. They commonly stand 200 to 275 feet (61 to 84 meters) tall, and they grow so close together that little sunlight reaches the forest floor.

and often have trunks that are 8 to 12 feet (2.4 to 3.7 meters) in diameter. A redwood in northern California is the tallest known living tree in the world. It is about 368 feet (112 meters) high.

In a typical redwood forest, the massive trees grow close together, shutting out most of the sunlight. There is little underbrush, for few plants can survive in the cool, dim conditions on the ground beneath these tall trees. Often tight circles of young redwoods grow from the roots of old stumps, completely enclosing them. The lowest branches of old trees may be 80 to 100 feet (24 to 30 meters) above the ground. However, the lowest branches of the young redwoods grow all the way to ground level.

The redwood tree has green needles that grow about 1 inch (2.5 centimeters) long and remain on the tree for several years. The tree's globe-shaped cones are also

about 1 inch long. Tightly packed under each scale of a cone are several reddish-brown seeds. Each seed is about $\frac{1}{16}$ inch (1.6 millimeters) long. It would take about 123,000 of these tiny seeds to weigh a pound, or about 271,000 to weigh a kilogram.

Redwood bark has a deeply fissured appearance and may be 12 inches (30 centimeters) thick. The thick bark makes the tree fire resistant. The wood is soft, red, and weak. However, it is also remarkably resistant to decay, disease, or insect enemies. Lumber manufacturers prize the wood for siding or interior finish in buildings, and for other nonstructural uses when durability is important.

Great *burls* (lumps) often grow on trunks of older redwoods. These burls are highly valued for their beautiful grain and are often used for veneer. Small burls are sold for table decorations because of their ability to sprout when placed in water.   Linda B. Brubaker

Scientific classification. Redwood belongs to the taxodium family, Taxodiaceae. It is *Sequoia sempervirens.*

See also **Conifer; Tree** (Familiar broadleaf and needle-leaf trees [picture]).

Additional resources

Murray, Peter. *Redwoods.* Child's World, 1996. Younger readers.
Rohde, Jerry and Gisela. *Redwood National & State Parks: Tales, Trails, and Auto Tours.* MountainHome, 1994.
Weaver, Harriet E. *Redwood Country.* Rev. ed. Chronicle, 1983.

Redwood National Park, in northern California, is in the huge forest of redwood trees that grows along the Pacific Coast from central California to southern Oregon. For location, see **California** (political map). The world's tallest living tree, a redwood about 368 feet (112 meters) high, is in the park. The park has 40 miles (64 kilometers) of scenic coastline. Three state parks lie within its boundaries. Congress established Redwood National Park in 1968. For the park's area, see **National Park System** (table: National parks).

Critically reviewed by the National Park Service

See also **Redwood.**

Reed is a common name for many kinds of tall, slender grass plants. The word may also refer to the stems of these plants, which are often jointed in many places. The

Bob Fitch, Black Star

The massive trunk of a redwood dwarfs a curious sightseer. Redwoods grow along the West Coast of the United States from central California to southern Oregon.

stems may be as slender and fragile as straw, or as thick and sturdy as bamboo. The pith that fills the center of the reed can usually be removed, leaving a hollow, jointed tube. The hollow stems of the reed have been used to make musical instruments.

The reed musical instruments have a mouthpiece with a vibrating strip once made only of reed. Plastic, wood, glass, and metal are now used to make the "reed." Farmers in Europe thatch houses with other types of reeds.

Reeds grow in almost all countries of the temperate and warm regions. They are found in a variety of habitats, from low upland meadows to wet lowlands and shallow lakes and ponds. Straw is sometimes called reed in the United Kingdom. The American Indians often made the roots, young leaves, and stems of various kinds of reeds a part of their diet.   David A. Francko

Reed, John (1887-1920), was an American journalist and revolutionist. He is best known for his book *Ten Days That Shook the World* (1919), an eyewitness account of the Russian Revolution of 1917. He also helped organize the first Communist party in the United States.

Reed was born in Portland, Oregon. He graduated from Harvard University in 1910 and the next year moved to New York City. There, he became an editor of *The Masses,* a socialist journal of politics and culture. Reed gained national attention for his reporting of the revolt led by Pancho Villa of Mexico in 1914. He served as a reporter in Europe later in 1914 and in 1915, during World War I. In 1917, Reed and his wife, the journalist Louise Bryant, went to Russia. Reed became a supporter of V. I. Lenin, leader of a group of Russian Communist revolutionists known as the *Bolsheviks.* Reed observed the Bolsheviks' victory in the Russian Revolution.

After returning to the United States, Reed helped form the Communist Labor Party. In 1919, he went to Russia on business for the party. While trying to return to the United States, Reed was arrested in Finland and imprisoned for 13 weeks. Then he returned to Russia, and he died there of typhus. He was buried in front of the Kremlin in Moscow.   Robert A. Rosenstone

Reed, Thomas Brackett (1839-1902), served as speaker of the United States House of Representatives from 1889 to 1891 and from 1895 to 1899. He was sometimes called *Czar Reed* because of the blunt way he controlled the House. A Maine Republican, Reed served in the House from 1877 to 1899. In 1890, he won adoption of "Reed's Rules," which increased the speaker's power but made the House more effective. The House still uses many of these rules. Reed was born in Portland, Maine.

Edward A. Lukes-Lukaszewski

Reed, Walter (1851-1902), a medical officer in the United States Army, helped show how to control typhoid fever and yellow fever. During the Spanish-American War in 1898, he directed a commission to study the origin and spread of typhoid fever in Army camps. Experiments showed that flies were the main carriers of the infection and that dust and uncleanliness helped spread it.

In 1900 and 1901, Reed headed a commission to investigate an epidemic of yellow fever among American troops in Cuba. He and the other doctors, including James Carroll and Jesse Lazear, carried on a series of daring experiments. Several doctors, as well as some soldiers, volunteered to be infected by yellow fever germs to study the course of the disease. All of them

contracted the disease but survived. Two others, who were not volunteers, became infected accidentally and died as a result. The experiments established that the bite of certain mosquitoes transmits yellow fever. In addition, the experiments showed how the disease might be controlled. See **Yellow fever**.

Reed was born in Gloucester County, Virginia. He studied medicine at the University of Virginia and at Bellevue Hospital Medical College in New York City. He entered the U.S. Army in 1875. Walter Reed Army Medical Center in Washington, D.C., is named for him.   Audrey B. Davis

U.S. Army

Walter Reed

Reef. See **Atoll; Coral.**

Reference book. See **Almanac; Atlas; Dictionary; Encyclopedia; Library; Publishing** (Reference books).

Referendum. See **Initiative and referendum.**

Reflection is the return of a wave of energy, such as light, heat, sound, or radio, after it strikes a surface. Reflection can be compared to the action of a ball rebounding from a wall. A ball thrown at right angles to the wall will bounce back in the same line. If the ball is thrown along a path that makes less than a right angle with the wall, its path on rebounding will make the same angle with the wall, but on the opposite side of the point where the ball hit the wall. Imagine a line drawn to make a 90-degree angle with the wall at the point where the ball struck. The angle formed by the path of the thrown ball and this line is called the *angle of incidence.* The corresponding angle made by the rebounding ball is known as the *angle of reflection.* These angles are equal.

The principle of reflection has many applications in daily living. A mirror (a glass coated with silver) reflects most of the light that strikes it. The best example of the reflection of sound waves is the echo. Radar uses the reflection of radio waves.   Joseph A. Muscari

Related articles in *World Book* include:

Echo	Mirror
Kaleidoscope	Parabola
Light (Reflection, refraction,	Radar
and absorption; Science	Sound (Reflection)
project: How light behaves)	Telescope

Reflex action. If you accidentally touch a hot stove, you jerk away before you have time to think what you are doing. Actions of this kind, which are not planned or decided beforehand, are called reflex actions. Each reflex involves some stimulus that causes a response. In the above example, the hot stove was the stimulus and the jerking away was the response.

Reflex actions are quite common and easy to notice. If light is directed at a person's eye, the pupil of the eye will become smaller. When the light is removed and the person's eye is shaded, the pupil becomes larger again. The light acts as a stimulus, and the reaction of the pupil is the eye's response. Doctors often test a person's reflex actions. Frequently they test the *patellar reflex,* or knee jerk. The patient sits with her or his knees crossed, and the doctor strikes a point just below the kneecap. This causes the patient's foot to kick suddenly.

Scientists call these kinds of reflexes *unconditioned reflexes.* They occur in all normal persons and many animals. Unlike most of human behavior, unconditioned reflexes occur with no specific learning or experience. They are considered involuntary acts, because a response always occurs when a stimulus is presented.

How reflex action occurs. Most reflex acts are very complicated. But in the simplest forms, four events are involved. Briefly, these events could be called (1) reception, (2) conduction, (3) transmission, and (4) response. Stimulation is received by *receptors,* or sensitive nerve endings. These may be in the eye, ear, nose, tongue, or skin. Energy from the stimulus is changed into nerve impulses and conducted from the receptor to the central nervous system. From there, the nerve impulses are transmitted to the motor nerves, which control muscle action. The motor nerves conduct the impulses to the muscles and glands, causing them to respond, or act.

Most reflex acts are much more complicated than this. They often involve other parts of the nervous system, such as the brain. Reflex acts are quicker than voluntary acts. You jerk your hand away from a hot stove before you feel pain. You do not have to take the time to decide exactly what you are going to do.

People have many reflex reactions to emotional stimuli. These include changes in blood pressure and respiration. A lie detector measures certain body reactions to emotional stimuli. A person telling a lie usually has small emotional reactions that can be detected because of these reflex reactions. See **Lie detector.**

Conditioned reflex, another kind of reflex action, works by association. For example, a dog's mouth begins to water when the animal smells food. The Russian physiologist Ivan P. Pavlov showed that the flow of saliva—though originally an automatic reaction to the smell of food—can become a conditioned reflex. Pavlov rang a bell each time he brought food to a dog. Eventually, the dog's mouth began to water when Pavlov merely rang the bell—with no food being present. The dog associated the ringing of the bell with the food, just as it associated the odor with the food.　　Daniel S. Barth

See also **Nervous system.**

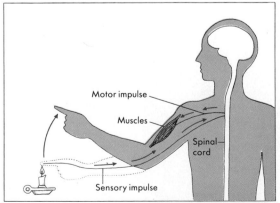

WORLD BOOK diagram by Patricia Wynne

A reflex action occurs automatically. When a person touches a candle flame, impulses travel along a nerve to the spinal cord. The message is relayed to the muscles, which jerk the arm back.

Reform Party was a conservative political party in Canada. Based in Alberta, it gained much support in Canada's Western provinces. In general, the Reform Party favored extensive federal budget cuts to reduce the national debt, greater equality among Canada's provinces, and lower immigration. It also supported amending Canada's constitution to provide for an elected and more powerful Senate.

The Reform Party was established in 1987. Preston Manning, an Alberta business consultant and son of a former premier of Alberta, became its leader. Manning claimed Canada's traditional parties had lost touch with voters' concerns. The Reform Party received strong support from Alberta's oil industry, which claimed it had been hurt by federal government policies.

In 1989, one Reformer won a seat in Canada's House of Commons. In 1990, a Reformer was appointed to the Canadian Senate. In 1992, the party helped defeat the Charlottetown accord, a set of constitutional amendments proposed by leaders of the federal and provincial governments. The plan included recognizing French-speaking Quebec as a distinct society within Canada. In 1993, Reformers captured 52 House seats. In the 1997 general election, the Reform Party won 60 of 301 House seats—more than any other party except the Liberal Party—and became Canada's official opposition party. In 2000, Reform members voted to dissolve their party and join a new national conservative party called the Canadian Reform Conservative Alliance. The new party is commonly known as the Canadian Alliance.　　J. L. Granatstein

See also **Manning, Preston.**

Reform Party is a political party in the United States that promises to reform national politics. Ross Perot, a wealthy Texas businessman, founded the Reform Party in 1995. It quickly became the most successful third party since Theodore Roosevelt's Progressive or "Bull Moose" Party of 1912.

The Reform Party's platform calls for balancing the federal budget, repaying the national debt, and simplifying the nation's tax code. The platform urges stricter laws to regulate campaign financing and limit gifts to officeholders "to ensure that our elected officials owe their allegiance to the people whom they are elected to serve." The party also supports term limits, which would prevent elected officials from serving more than a specified number of terms. For example, U.S. senators would serve no more than two terms, or 12 years.

The Reform Party also urges elimination of the United States trade deficit. It calls for trade policies that would protect home industries from outside competition, and it opposes free-trade agreements.　　James I. Lengle

See also **Perot, Ross.**

Reformation was a religious movement of the 1500's that led to Protestantism. It had a tremendous impact on social, political, and economic life, and its influences are still felt today. The movement began in 1517 when Martin Luther, a German monk, protested certain practices of the Roman Catholic Church. About 40 years later, Protestantism was established in nearly half of Europe.

Before the Reformation, Europe had been held together religiously by the Catholic Church. After the Reformation, Europe had several large Protestant churches and some smaller Protestant religious groups. All of these churches competed with the Catholic Church—

and with each other—for the faith and allegiance of the people.

Causes of the Reformation

Religious causes. During the late Roman Empire and the early Middle Ages, missionaries had converted many European peoples to Christianity. The pope gradually assumed greater importance and authority in the church and in relation to the secular rulers. In the early 1200's, Pope Innocent III claimed that "Ecclesiastical liberty is nowhere better preserved than where the Roman church has full power in temporal as well as spiritual matters." But about 100 years later, in 1303, King Philip IV of France humiliated Pope Boniface VIII by having him arrested (see **Philip** [Philip IV]). The secular rulers were growing in power, and the church was no longer a serious threat to them.

In the 1300's and 1400's, the church suffered several serious setbacks. In 1309, a French pope, Clement V, moved the papacy from Rome to Avignon, a city on the border of France, where it remained for about 70 years. This period was called the *Babylonian Captivity,* in remembrance of the 70 years that the Biblical prophet Jeremiah predicted the Jews would spend as captives in ancient Babylon. In 1378, after Pope Gregory XI moved the papal residence back to Rome, a small group of French cardinals elected another pope, called an *antipope* (see **Pope** [The troubles of the papacy]). For nearly 30 years, there were two popes. After 1409, there was a third pope, who resided in Pisa, Italy. This split caused great confusion in the church. Some Catholic leaders believed that the church should be ruled by church councils rather than by a pope. Such councils met in Constance, Germany, from 1414 to 1418 and in Basel, Switzerland, from 1431 to 1449. The councils called for a "reform in head and members."

Serious abuses also had appeared in the church. The large administrative structure of the church required a great deal of money to finance it. To obtain this money, the church used many devices that hurt its spiritual nature. These devices included selling important positions

Wood engraving of the early 1500's by Jorg Breu the Elder; The Newberry Library, Chicago

The sale of indulgences caused Martin Luther to attack the church. This picture shows three enemies that threatened Germany with financial ruin. Indulgences are represented in the center by an indulgence letter that hangs on the cross in place of Jesus. Greedy merchants are portrayed on the left, and expensive imported foreign fashions are shown on the right.

in the church. In Italy, the popes and higher clergy lived like secular princes. They built lavish palaces and indulged in corrupt financial practices. The religious life of the church suffered. The sacraments were often celebrated mechanically, and the church's spiritual message about God's mercy was weakened by an emphasis on a person's good works.

Critics of the church included the religious reformers John Wycliffe in England, John Hus in Bohemia, and Girolamo Savonarola in Italy. These men protested the abuses but could not stop them. Some thinkers within the church, including Johannes Eckhart and Thomas à Kempis, emphasized a mystical approach to Christianity. But no one could restore the church's spiritual health and moral purity.

Cultural causes. Beginning in the 1300's, a great revival of learning and art called the Renaissance developed in Italy and, to a lesser extent, elsewhere in Eu-

Engraving of the 1500's by M. Herz and G. Köler; Bibliothèque Nationale, Paris

The Augsburg Confession summarized the religious teachings of Martin Luther. In this picture, the confession is being read to Charles V, Holy Roman emperor, at the Diet of Augsburg in 1530.

rope. Between 1300 and 1500, universities more than tripled in number. The Italian author Petrarch pioneered in the revival of classical studies—the literature, history, and philosophy of ancient Greece and Rome. Renaissance humanists believed that by returning to the classics, they could begin a new golden age of culture.

The interest in ancient civilizations encouraged by the Renaissance had an important effect on religion. The study of Hebrew and Greek enabled scholars to read the Holy Scriptures in the languages in which they originally had been written. Also, in studying early Christian times, scholars saw how the church had changed through the centuries. The invention of movable type in Europe in the mid-1400's helped spread learning and criticism through printed books. As a result, an increasing number of people outside the clergy gained an education during the Renaissance and Reformation.

Political causes. During the Middle Ages, the Holy Roman emperor claimed to be the secular head of Christianity within the Holy Roman Empire. Most of the nobility ranked beneath the emperor. But the broad authority of the emperor never really existed, and by the end of the Middle Ages, the empire consisted chiefly of the German territories of central Europe. Even there, the princes of a large number of areas were independent. An imperial *diet* (council), which consisted of the princes and representatives of the nobility and of the cities, helped the emperor govern.

In western Europe, the kings were increasing their power over their own people and against the pope. The monarchies in England, France, and Spain were growing stronger, organizing their finances, and building their armies. Some people regarded the pope as a political leader of a foreign state and opposed his control and influence in their own countries. After the Reformation began, some monarchs broke away from the pope.

Economic causes. During the Middle Ages, Europe had an agricultural economy. Most people were peasants who lived in villages and tilled the soil with simple tools. Beginning in the 1100's, cities began to increase in size, especially in Italy and the Netherlands. Merchants traded woolen cloth, glassware, iron implements, and other manufactured goods for raw materials such as furs, wood, and wool. As the cities grew wealthy and independent, they threw off the control of local lords and prince-bishops. Many turned to kings or the emperor for protection.

Development of the Reformation

Martin Luther. The Reformation began within the Catholic Church itself. On Oct. 31, 1517, Martin Luther, a monk and professor of theology, wrote his Ninety-Five Theses and, according to tradition, posted them on the door of the Castle Church in Wittenberg, Germany. The theses were a series of statements that attacked the sale of *indulgences* (pardon from some of the penalty for sins). Luther later criticized what he considered other abuses in the church.

Luther believed that people could be saved only through faith in Jesus Christ, in whom alone righteousness sufficient for salvation could be found. His view of religion placed a person directly before God, trusting Him and relying on His forgiving grace. Luther taught that God *justifies* human beings. By that he meant that

God makes them righteous through His kindness to them. This doctrine of justification by faith in Christ alone was the heart of Luther's belief. It contradicted the church's teaching of grace and good works as a way to salvation.

In January 1521, Pope Leo X excommunicated Luther and declared him a heretic. Emperor Charles V and members of the imperial diet ordered Luther to appear before the diet in Worms, Germany, in April. There, Luther was ordered to *recant* (take back) what he had said and written. Luther replied in a famous speech: "Unless I am convinced by the testimony of the Scriptures or by clear reason (for I do not trust either in the pope or in councils alone, since it is well known that they have often erred and contradicted themselves), I am bound by the Scriptures I have quoted and my conscience is captive to the Word of God. I cannot and I will not retract anything, since it is neither safe nor right to go against conscience."

In May 1521, the emperor signed the Edict of Worms, a document that declared Luther to be an outlaw whom anyone could kill without punishment. However, Frederick the Wise, Prince of Saxony, feared a revolt and protected Luther. Luther continued to lead the Protestant movement until his death in 1546.

The word *Protestant* (one who protests) dates from the diet of Speyer, Germany, in 1529. There, princes who supported Luther protested the anti-Lutheran actions forced on them by the emperor and the Catholic nobility. In 1530, the Lutherans presented the *Augsburg Confession* to the diet of Augsburg, Germany. The main author of the confession was Philipp Melanchthon, Luther's chief colleague in the Reformation. The confession became the basic statement of Lutheran doctrine. In the Peace of Augsburg, signed in 1555, the Lutheran churches were officially recognized in the Holy Roman Empire. Each ruler was allowed to choose the religious faith of his land. See **Augsburg Confession**.

The introduction of Lutheranism into Scandinavia was largely the work of the Swedish and Danish kings. In the 1520's, King Gustavus I of Sweden took over much church property and introduced Lutheranism in Sweden and in Finland, which was then under Swedish control. In 1536, King Christian of Denmark and the National Assembly made Lutheranism the state religion. They also established it in Norway, which was then a Danish province.

Zwingli and the Anabaptists. In Switzerland, Huldreich Zwingli, a priest in Zurich, led the movement for religious reform. Zwingli was an eloquent preacher and a great Swiss patriot. Long after his death in 1531 in a war against Catholic forces, his ideas of reform continued to inspire the Swiss Protestant churches. In 1529, Zwingli and Luther met in Marburg, Germany, to discuss their disagreement over the interpretation of Christ's presence in the Lord's Supper. Luther regarded this sacrament as a means by which God gave people His grace. He believed in a real presence of Christ in the bread and wine. Zwingli considered the sacrament a thanksgiving to God for grace already given in other ways, especially through the Gospel. He believed the bread and wine were powerful symbols of Christ's body and blood. The quarrel between Luther and Zwingli led to the first major split in Protestantism.

In Zurich during the 1520's, a group known as the Swiss Brethren, led by Conrad Grebel, decided that the Scriptures did not teach infant baptism. The Swiss Brethren favored adult baptism and were called *Anabaptists* (rebaptizers). The Anabaptists were not satisfied with Protestant efforts to reform Christianity, so they withdrew from religious and secular life and formed their own communities. The Anabaptists were the ancestors of the modern-day Amish and Mennonites. The Anabaptists were persecuted by both Catholic and Protestant authorities. See **Anabaptists**.

John Calvin helped establish Protestantism in Geneva, Switzerland. From there, he directed efforts to convert the people of France and other countries of western Europe. Calvin, a refugee from France, had studied law and the classics before becoming a Protestant. He had an iron will and a great gift for organization. Calvin's *Ecclesiastical Ordinances* (1541) established the structure of a *presbyterian* form of church government in which a council of elders rules each church. His influential *Institutes of the Christian Religion,* first published in 1536, offers a clear, systematic presentation of Protestant teachings.

Calvin's followers in France were called *Huguenots*. They came from all classes of society, including some influential noble families such as the Bourbons. Supported by Spain, France's Catholic kings attempted to suppress the Huguenots in a series of religious wars from 1562 to 1598. Beginning on Saint Bartholomew's Day, Aug. 24, 1572, the pro-Catholic party murdered thousands of Huguenots in Paris and in the French provinces. But Protestantism survived as a minority religion, even in France. See **Saint Bartholomew's Day, Massacre of.**

In England, as in Scandinavia, the Reformation was established by an act of state. But its success was due in part to anticlericalism among the people. The immediate cause for England's break with the Catholic Church was the refusal of Pope Clement VII to *annul* (cancel) King Henry VIII's marriage to his first wife, Catherine of Aragon. Catherine had not borne Henry a son, and the king wanted to marry Anne Boleyn in the hope that the marriage would produce a male heir to the throne.

In 1534, Parliament passed the Act of Supremacy, which made the monarch the head of the church in England. Henry VIII remained basically a Catholic. However, Protestantism made great advances under his son, Edward VI. Queen Mary I succeeded Edward in 1553. She restored Catholicism as the state religion of England, and she suppressed the Protestants.

Queen Elizabeth I, who reigned from 1558 to 1603, established a moderate form of Protestantism that became known as *Anglicanism*. The Thirty-Nine Articles, issued in 1563 and approved by Parliament in 1571, presented the teachings of Anglicanism. English people who followed John Calvin were called *Puritans*. They opposed Anglicanism because it was *episcopal* (governed by bishops). The Puritans preferred the presbyterian form of church government. Catholicism was officially banned. See **England** (The English Reformation).

In Scotland, John Knox introduced Calvin's teachings and presbyterian system. In 1560, the Scots made Protestantism their state religion. England forced Ireland to adopt Protestantism as the state religion, but the Irish people remained loyal Catholics. Protestants colonized northern Ireland, also known as Ulster, and the conflict there between Catholics and Protestants is still a serious problem today.

Results of the Reformation

Religious influences. As a result of the Reformation, Europe was divided between the Catholic countries of the south and the Protestant countries of the north. Many Protestant denominations developed, and they were organized in a variety of ways. In many parts of Europe, this diversity of religious life created the necessity of religious toleration and a respect for the importance of the individual conscience. The Reformation also stimulated reforms within the Catholic Church. The church gained new purity and strength from the middle 1500's into the 1600's in a movement called the Counter Reformation, also known as the Catholic Reformation (see **Counter Reformation**).

Political and social influences. The establishment of state churches, as occurred in England, reflected the growth of nationalism. Lutheran regions tended to be conservative and supported strong central governments. Calvinist areas, where Protestants were often in the minority, tended to support democracy and argued for a citizen's right to oppose tyranny by monarchs.

Luther and other Protestants regarded life in the world as the "sphere of faith's works." They opposed the celibate life of monks and nuns and idealized family life and participation in community activities. The Protestant stress on the holiness of a person's daily life encouraged industriousness, thrifty living, and careful management of material things. This attitude became known as the *Protestant ethic*. It may have contributed to the growth of industry and commerce during the 1700's and 1800's. See **Protestant ethic**.

Protestant leaders also emphasized education. They promoted literacy, an educational curriculum based on ancient Greek and Roman literature, and a high respect for teachers and learning.   Steven Ozment

Related articles in *World Book* include:

Biographies

Calvin, John	Knox, John	Ridley, Nicholas
Cranmer, Thomas	Latimer, Hugh	Tetzel, Johann
Eck, Johann	Luther, Martin	Tyndale, William
Erasmus,	Mary I	Wycliffe, John
Desiderius	Melanchthon,	Zwingli, Huldreich
Henry VIII	Philipp	
Hus, John		

Reform groups

Albigenses	Covenanters	Lutherans	Puritan
Anabaptists	Huguenots	Presbyterians	Waldenses
Anglicans	Lollards		

Other related articles

Augsburg Confession	Pope (Renaissance and Reformation)
Church and state (The Reformation)	Protestantism
Education (The Reformation)	Schmalkaldic League
England (The English Reformation)	Scotland (The Scottish Reformation)
France (Religious wars)	Thirty-Nine Articles
Germany (The Reformation; The Thirty Years' War)	Thirty Years' War
Nantes, Edict of	Toleration Act
Peasants' War	Worms, Edict of

Additional resources

Hillerbrand, Hans J., ed. *The Oxford Encyclopedia of the Reformation.* 4 vols. Oxford, 1996.
Mackenney, Richard. *Sixteenth Century Europe.* St. Martin's, 1993.
Ozment, Steven. *Protestants: The Birth of a Revolution.* Doubleday, 1992.
Thompson, Stephen P., ed. *The Reformation.* Greenhaven, 1998.

Reformatory is a correctional institution for lawbreakers over the age of 18 who do not need maximum security. Reformatories are often used to separate young adult offenders from older prisoners. The institutions provide counseling, education, vocational training, and other improvement programs. In the United States, state or local government authorities or private agencies operate reformatories.

Institutions for most lawbreakers under the age of 18 are called *training schools.* Most inmates of training schools are held from 6 to 9 months. Institutions at which youthful offenders stay for a shorter time are called *juvenile detention centers.*

The first reformatories in the United States were established during the early 1800's in New York City, Boston, and Philadelphia. These institutions received some state funds but were mainly supported and operated by private citizens. In 1847, Massachusetts opened the first state-controlled reformatory.

By 1900, reformatories had been established throughout the United States. These institutions originally attempted to reform and educate the youths rather than to punish them. However, early reformatories operated much like prisons and lacked effective programs.

Anthony P. Travisono

Reformed Church in America is incorporated as The General Synod of the Reformed Church in America, a Protestant organization. The doctrines of the Reformed Church have their origin in the teachings of John Calvin. The minister, elders, and deacons are collectively designated the *Consistory* in each local church, and they run the local churches. A group of churches make up a *Classis,* and a group of Classes make up a *Synod.* The *General Synod* is the highest judicial body of the church.

The Reformed Church in America is an offspring of the Dutch Reformed Church in the Netherlands. The Reformed Church was organized on Manhattan Island in 1628 by Dutch and Walloon colonists. It received a charter from King William III of England in 1696.

The Reformed Church founded Hope College in Holland, Michigan; Central College (now Central University of Iowa) in Pella, Iowa; and Northwestern College in Orange City, Iowa. In addition, the Reformed Church has seminaries in New Brunswick, New Jersey; and in Holland, Michigan.

Critically reviewed by the Reformed Church in America

Refraction is a change in the direction in which waves travel when they pass from one kind of matter into another. Waves are *refracted* (bent) when they pass at an angle from one medium into another in which the velocity of light is different. A pencil standing in water looks broken at the water line because light travels slower in water than it travels in air. The amount that a ray of a certain wavelength bends in passing from one medium into another is indicated by the *index of refraction (n)* between the two mediums for that wavelength. Finding *n*

is a problem in trigonometry. It is a function of the sines of the angles of incidence and refraction:

$$n = \frac{\sin i}{\sin r}$$

This formula is also called Snell's Law after the Dutch mathematician Willebrord Snell van Royen, who formulated the law in the early 1600's.

Common indexes of refraction depend on the relationship of a ray's angle in air to its angle in such mediums as glass, quartz, or plastic. The different colors in light are not refracted to the same extent. Because of this characteristic of light, refracted light beams often break up into the colors of the spectrum. A prism works on this principle.

WORLD BOOK photo by Odyssey Productions

A pencil in a glass of water appears to be broken at the water's surface as a result of light refraction.

Joseph A. Muscari

See also **Lens; Light** (How light behaves; Science project: How light behaves); **Mirage; Prism; Rainbow; Sound** (Refraction).

Refractory is any nonmetallic material or object that can withstand high temperatures without becoming soft. Refractories are used to line furnaces for melting metals and glass, in crucibles for inducing chemical reactions and for melting materials, as insulation in the walls of furnaces and kilns, and in other places where resistance to temperature and corrosion is required. A common refractory called *firebrick* contains aluminum silicates and minor amounts of titanium and iron oxides. Other refractory substances include alumina, magnesia, silica, zirconia, silicon carbide, and graphite.

James S. Reed

Refrigeration is the process of producing low temperatures. It takes place when heat is removed from a substance. Cooling can be achieved with ice or snow, or by machines. For thousands of years, people have used some kind of refrigeration to cool beverages and preserve food. Since the mid-1800's, refrigeration has been widely used to keep food from spoiling.

Today, people store foods in home refrigerators and freezers. Grocery stores and food companies use refrigerated display cases. They also have freezing rooms and cold-storage warehouses. Fresh foods are carried long distances in refrigerated trucks, refrigerated railway cars, and refrigerated compartments of ships. People on camping trips can keep food fresh for days with portable refrigerators installed in their vehicles.

Refrigeration has many uses besides preserving food. Air conditioning depends on refrigeration to cool homes, offices, theaters, stores, and automobiles. Refrigeration makes it possible to store serums, vaccines, blood plasma, and other lifesaving medical supplies. Drug companies use refrigeration to make penicillin and other drugs. Cleaners and fur companies store furs in refrigerated vaults to protect them from moths and to keep the furs in good condition. Florists refrigerate cut flowers to preserve their fresh appearance. Drinking fountains supply cold water, and ice machines provide blocks, cubes, flakes, and chips of ice. Ice plants and skating rinks use refrigerating machines to manufacture ice. Industry uses refrigeration in the processing of rubber, lubricants, and steel. Refrigeration is also used in commercial production of frozen fruit juices, candy, photographic films, ice cream, chemicals, and many other products.

Principles of refrigeration

Refrigeration removes heat from solids, liquids, and gases. It is based on the second law of thermodynamics (see **Thermodynamics**). This law states that heat flows only from warmer bodies to colder bodies, or from a substance at a certain temperature to a substance at a lower temperature. Heat cannot go from a colder substance to a warmer substance of its own accord. The flow of heat from warmer bodies to colder bodies is called *heat transfer*. During refrigeration, heat transfer occurs when we place the substance we wish to cool near a *refrigerant* (cooling agent).

Heat transfer. Simple heat transfer takes place when a colder substance comes in contact with a warmer substance. The temperature rises in the colder substance and decreases in the warmer substance as heat is transferred. This simple type of refrigeration occurs when we cool a warm bottle of water in a running stream. The stream acts as a refrigerant. It absorbs heat and rises in temperature as it flows over the bottle.

All substances have the ability to absorb heat. But refrigerants absorb heat quickly and in large quantities. The most common types of refrigerants include air, water, brine, ice, ammonia, carbon dioxide, sulfur dioxide, and such specially prepared substances as chlorofluorocarbons (CFC's), hydrofluorocarbons (HFC's), and methylene chloride.

Effects of heat transfer. Heat transfer produces several effects. It both cools the warmer body and heats the body that absorbs the heat. Heat transfer may also change the physical state of a substance. For example, removing sufficient heat causes a gas to change to a liquid. This process is called *condensation*. The reverse of condensation is *vaporization* (the process of a liquid changing to a gas). Gases lose heat when they condense. Liquids absorb heat when they vaporize. The temperature at which a substance condenses or vaporizes at a given pressure is its *boiling point*. Removing enough heat from a liquid causes it to *freeze* (become solid). The temperature at which a substance freezes is called its freezing point. The reverse of freezing is *melting*. Melting is the process of changing a solid to a liquid. Liquids lose heat when they freeze. Solids gain heat when they melt.

All refrigeration systems depend on gains or losses of heat that occur during condensation, vaporization, freezing, or melting. The heat gained or lost is called *latent heat* (see **Heat** [Changes in state]).

Ice refrigeration

People cool with ice if they lack convenient power to produce other methods of refrigeration. Natural ice, cut from lakes and ponds in winter, has long provided refrigeration during warm seasons. Some campers and farmers cool food in iceboxes similar to those used before the development of mechanical refrigeration. Railroad refrigerator cars and some refrigerated motor trucks carry ice to keep foods cool during shipment.

Ice is one of the oldest methods of refrigeration. The Chinese cut and stored ice as long ago as 1000 B.C. Ice refrigerates because it absorbs heat when it melts. For example, this absorption happens when we cool a warm drink by putting ice cubes in the glass. Ice makes a useful refrigerant because it has a constant melting temperature of 32 °F (0 °C). It absorbs large quantities of heat as it melts. However, the unmelted ice always maintains the same temperature. Ice is used to cool foods in iceboxes or to freeze liquids by *endothermic reactions*. These chemical reactions enable ice to produce temperatures below freezing.

Iceboxes work because warm air rises. A cake of ice in the upper part of an icebox absorbs heat from the warm air. This cools the warm air and increases its density. The heavier air flows downward to the food compartments. The air becomes warmer and lighter as it absorbs heat from the food. The warmer, lighter air rises and again loses heat to the ice.

Endothermic reactions. By itself, ice could never absorb enough heat to reduce the temperature of a substance below its own melting point of 32 °F (0 °C). But endothermic reactions enable ice to produce freezing temperatures. Certain chemical compounds, particularly salts, produce a freezing action when mixed with ice or snow, or even other compounds (see **Salt, Chemical**). Such combinations are called *endothermic mixtures.* Some mixtures produce temperatures of −40 °F (−40 °C) or lower. They include calcium chloride and snow; ice, sodium chloride, and ammonium nitrate; and sodium sulfate, ammonium chloride, potassium nitrate, and diluted nitric acid. All these substances absorb heat during their chemical reactions.

The hand-operated ice-cream freezer is an example of the use of endothermic mixtures. Ice cream begins to freeze at about 28 °F (−2 °C). To freeze ice cream, the ingredients are mixed in a container surrounded by crushed ice and salt. The endothermic reaction of the ice and salt absorbs latent heat from the ingredients, causing them to freeze.

WORLD BOOK photo

Refrigeration keeps food from spoiling in a supermarket. Refrigeration prevents spoilage by keeping foods at temperatures near or below freezing. These low temperatures slow down or stop the growth of microorganisms that ruin food.

Ice was the only form of home refrigeration until mechanical refrigerators became widespread during the 1920's. Blocks of ice were delivered to home iceboxes several times a week.

Using chemicals to reduce temperature is not new. About 1550, the Italians found that a mixture of potassium nitrate (saltpeter) and water could be used to cool bottled liquors.

Dry ice is solid carbon dioxide. As a refrigerant, it has two important advantages over ice made from water. Like water ice, dry ice undergoes change at a constant temperature. But, instead of changing to a liquid, dry ice *sublimes* (vaporizes) directly to a gas (see **Sublimation**). For this reason boxes containing food packed in dry ice do not leak fluid as they would if packed with water ice. This characteristic gives dry ice its name.

Dry ice sublimes at $-109.3\ °F\ (-78.5\ °C)$, which is much lower than the melting temperature of water ice. Food processors find dry ice especially valuable for maintaining a freezing temperature in foods and ice cream, because it produces much lower temperatures than water ice. Dry ice must be handled carefully, because it can cause frostbite and severe burnlike injuries. See **Dry ice.**

Mechanical refrigeration

Mechanical refrigeration works on the principle that liquids absorb heat when they vaporize. You can demonstrate this by wetting your hands and waving them rapidly. The water evaporates quickly and causes a cooling sensation by lowering the skin temperature. A fan cools you because it evaporates the natural moisture on your skin. Mechanical refrigeration includes three principal systems. They are (1) compression, (2) absorption, and (3) steam-jet.

Compression and absorption systems refrigerate by changing a refrigerant from a liquid to a gas and back to a liquid again. These repeated operations make up the *refrigeration cycle.* In a compression system, a compressor brings about the refrigeration cycle. This system is widely used in industry and in most home electric re-

frigerators. In the absorption system, the refrigeration cycle is caused by the direct application of heat from gas, steam, or some other source. All home and camper gas refrigerators, and some industrial units, use the absorption system. Jacob Perkins, a Massachusetts inventor, developed the first compression machine in 1834. During the 1850's, Ferdinand Carré, a French engineer, developed the first absorption system using ammonia. Carl von Linde of Germany introduced the first successful compression system using ammonia between 1873 and 1875.

Electric and gas home refrigerators are hermetically sealed, or airtight and leakproof, refrigeration units that maintain cooling temperatures between 32 °F (0 °C) and 40 °F (4 °C). Most have freezing compartments with temperatures between 0 °F (-18 °C) and 10 °F (-12 °C).

Steam-jet refrigeration uses water as a refrigerant. High-velocity steam brings about the refrigeration cycle. Steam-jet refrigeration is less common than the compression system because its temperature is limited to about 36 °F (2 °C) and above.

The electric refrigerator is a compression-type refrigeration unit powered by an electric motor. A home electric refrigerator consists of five basic parts: (1) the receiver, (2) the refrigerant-control device, (3) the evaporator, (4) the compressor, and (5) the condenser.

At the beginning of the refrigeration cycle, the refrigerant leaves the *receiver* (storage tank) under high pressure. The refrigerant travels through pipes to the *refrigerant-control device.* This mechanism reduces the pressure of the refrigerant as it enters the *evaporator.* The evaporator is the coldest spot in the refrigerator and serves as the freezing unit. It consists of pipes or coils on the walls or sides of the cabinet, or surrounding the ice-tray compartment. At a low pressure, the liquid refrigerant evaporates inside these coils and absorbs heat. This causes refrigeration to take place. The *compressor* pumps the refrigerant from the freezing unit as a vapor, and raises its pressure. It then discharges high-pressure gas into the air-cooled *condenser.* There the gas loses the heat it gained in the evaporator and condenses into a liquid at the high pressure, which flows back to the storage tank.

The gas refrigerator works on the absorption principle. It uses heat energy as a source of power, and has no moving parts. A home gas refrigerator consists of five basic parts: (1) the generator, (2) the separator, (3) the condenser, (4) the evaporator, and (5) the absorber. Liquid ammonia serves as the refrigerant in most gas refrigerators.

During the refrigeration cycle, heat from a gas flame is applied to the *generator.* This tank contains a strong solution of ammonia gas dissolved in water. The heat causes the solution to boil. Ammonia vapor and some of the solution rise to the *separator,* which removes the liquid. The hot gas continues its rise to the *condenser,* where it is cooled and liquefied. Since the water has been separated from the ammonia, the liquid is now almost pure ammonia. The liquid ammonia flows through a tube into the *evaporator,* or freezing unit, where it vaporizes with hydrogen gas. The hydrogen equalizes the pressure between the condenser and the evaporator. The vapor absorbs heat and produces refrigeration. The heavy mixture passes downward into the air-cooled *ab-*

sorber, where the ammonia is absorbed by water. The light hydrogen gas separates from the solution, rises through a pipe above the absorber, and returns to the evaporator. The cool ammonia-water solution flows back to the generator.

Steam-jet refrigeration uses only water as a refrigerant. Steam-jet refrigeration systems work on the principle that water vaporizes easily when it is under low pressure. As the water evaporates, its temperature goes down. The lower the pressure on the water, the faster the evaporation and, as a result, the lower the temperature produced.

The water flows through a chamber with an opening, across which a high-speed jet of steam passes. The steam creates suction within the space above the water, and lowers the pressure in the chamber. Some of the water evaporates and absorbs heat from the liquid in the chamber. The cool water is pumped out through pipes that carry it to wherever it is to be used. The water vapor rising from the chamber combines with the steam and is removed from the system.

Steam-jet systems produce practically no noise or vibration, occupy little space, and have no moving parts except a pump. Such mechanical refrigeration systems require a constant supply of steam, but this supply may come from the exhaust of other machinery. Steam-jet refrigeration has wide use in industrial and shipboard cooling. In addition, numerous brewers and distillers make use of this type of mechanical refrigeration.

Low-temperature refrigeration works very much like other compression systems, except that it uses different refrigerants. Low-temperature refrigerators are called *cryogenic refrigerators* or *cryocoolers.* They can produce temperatures as low as −459 °F (−273 °C), very near absolute zero. Cryogenic refrigerators have important uses in science and industry. For example, physicians use them to freeze living parts of the body for future use. Manufacturers use them to cool miniature electronic systems. See **Cryogenics.**

A cryogenic refrigerator uses helium, nitrogen, or other gas as a refrigerant. It works by changing the refrigerant from a gas to a liquid and back to a gas again. Helium is used as the refrigerant in the lowest-temperature refrigeration because it is the only substance that can remain liquid below −435 °F (−259 °C). A simple cryogenic refrigerator consists of four basic parts: (1) the compressor, (2) the heat exchanger, (3) the expansion valve, and (4) the evaporator.

During the refrigeration cycle, the gas leaves the compressor under high pressure and moves through a tube to the heat exchanger. There, it transfers some of its heat to a stream of cooler gas. The refrigerant then passes through an expansion valve. This process greatly reduces the pressure of the gas. As the gas expands, its temperature drops until part of the gas condenses. The liquid refrigerant then flows through a tube into the evaporator, which serves as the refrigerating unit. As it goes through the evaporator, the refrigerant absorbs

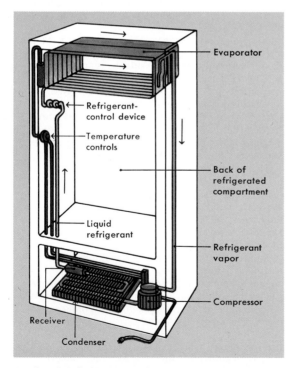

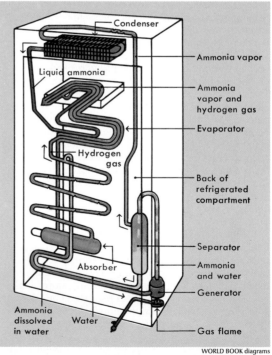

WORLD BOOK diagrams

An electric refrigerator circulates a refrigerant through pipes with an electrically-driven compressor. The liquid refrigerant picks up heat in the evaporator inside the refrigerator. The compressor then pumps the refrigerant vapor into the condenser, where it gives up its heat outside the refrigerated compartment.

A gas refrigerator circulates an ammonia refrigerant, using heat from a gas flame, and an absorber, a generator, and a separator. The ammonia vapor loses heat in the condenser and becomes a liquid. It then picks up heat from the refrigerated compartment and becomes a vapor again in the evaporator.

heat and becomes a gas again. The gas returns through the heat exchanger, and the cycle repeats.

Defrosting

Defrosting is probably the most important part of refrigerator care. The coating of frost that collects on the freezing unit acts as insulation and interferes with the refrigerator's cooling ability. Because of this, the refrigerator should be defrosted regularly. The process of defrosting may be automatic, semiautomatic, or manual.

Automatic defrosting works by means of clocks or by means of devices that count the number of times the door opens. It takes place at a certain time each day, or after the door has been opened a certain number of times. The controls open a valve that allows hot gas from the compressor to flow through the coils and melt the frost. During this time, refrigeration is stopped. In some refrigerators, the controls activate an electric heater near the coils. In many automatic-defrosting refrigerators, the drip water from the coils drains from the cabinet through an opening near the compressor. Heat from the compressor evaporates the water. Other automatic-defrosting refrigerators, and most semiautomatic and manual units, have drip pans under the freezing unit. Water collects in the pans and must be emptied after defrosting. Automatic defrosting takes little time, so food will not spoil while refrigeration stops.

Semiautomatic and manual defrosting. Refrigerators can be defrosted by turning them off. In a manual type, a hand-operated switch turns off the freezing unit and starts it again after defrosting. A semiautomatic refrigerator must be turned off manually, but it starts again automatically when defrosting is completed. Defrosting can be speeded by putting hot water in the ice trays.

Randall F. Barron

Related articles in *World Book* include:

Air conditioning	Food, Frozen	Melting point
Ammonia	Food preservation	Railroad (pictures:
Chlorofluorocarbon	Freezing point	Refrigerator
Cold storage	Heat	cars; Kinds of
Cryogenics	Ice	railroad cars)
Dry ice		

Refugee is a person forced to flee from his or her country of origin and seek safety elsewhere. Most refugees flee to escape persecution because of religion, nationality, membership in a social group, or political belief. The term *refugee* comes from the French word *refugie,* which was used to describe Protestant Huguenots who fled Roman Catholic France in 1685.

The term *displaced person,* or DP, was originally applied to the millions of European refugees who were forcibly moved from their homes during and immediately after World War II (1939-1945). Since then, the terms displaced person and refugee have sometimes been used interchangeably. Both terms refer to people who are uprooted and homeless. But refugees also lack national protection and status.

Just before and during World War I (1914-1918), there were many Jewish refugees fleeing from *pogroms* (persecutions) in Russia. Over $1\frac{1}{2}$ million refugees fled from Russia during the Russian Revolution from 1917 to 1920. There were also many Greek and Armenian refugees from Asia Minor (now Turkey) both during and after World War I. Europe had so many refugees after World War I that in 1921 the League of Nations appointed the famous Norwegian explorer and scientist Fridtjof Nansen as a special commissioner to help the refugees. After Nansen died in 1930, the League established the Nansen International Office for Refugees.

The number of refugees increased again before and during World War II. Between 1933 and 1941, hundreds of thousands of Jews and other opponents and victims of the Nazis fled Germany and German-controlled areas. During World War II, the Allied nations set up the United Nations Relief and Rehabilitation Administration (UNRRA) to help people uprooted by the war.

At the war's end in 1945, there were over 12 million uprooted people in Europe. In 1946, the United Nations established the International Refugee Organization (IRO) to take over the work of UNRRA. The IRO aided many displaced persons in Europe. It also helped millions of people who fled as a result of the *partition* (division) of India in 1947, the partition of Palestine in 1947, and the Arab-Israeli War in 1948.

Wars and revolutions have continued to create large numbers of refugees. About 2 million people fled Cambodia, Laos, and Vietnam between 1975, when Communists took over those countries, and the early 1990's. More than $3\frac{1}{2}$ million fled Afghanistan after the Soviet Union invaded that nation in 1979. By the early 1990's, millions had also left China and Palestine, as well as countries in Africa, Central America, and Eastern Europe. In the mid-1990's, more than 2 million people left Rwanda because of civil war. Also during the 1990's, about 5 million people in Yugoslavia and its former republics became refugees or displaced persons as a result of civil war in that region.

International programs have helped some refugees. Millions of people have been moved to new homes by the Intergovernmental Committee for European Migration (now Intergovernmental Committee for Migration) and the UN Office of the High Commissioner for Refugees.   Frank J. Coppa

See also **Asia** (picture: Arab refugees); **Asian Americans** (History of Asian immigration); **Asylum; Nansen, Fridtjof; United Nations** (Aid to refugees).

Regelation, *REE juh LAY shuhn,* is the process in which ice melts under pressure and refreezes as soon as the pressure is taken away. If two blocks of ice near 32 °F (0 °C) are pressed together for a while, they will be found frozen together when the pressure is taken off. At 32 °F (0 °C), water is denser than ice. Therefore, ice when compressed changes into water. When the pressure is removed, the water expands and refreezes.

A skate passing over ice places pressure on the ice and melts a thin film of water. The skater glides on this water. A heavy object placed on ice will gradually sink into the ice and bury itself as the ice melts under the object and refreezes above it.

A glacier moving along slowly melts and refreezes, slipping a little under pressure each day. In the most recent ice age, which ended about 11,500 years ago, regelated ice in central Canada pushed continental glaciers as far as 2,400 feet (730 meters) up the sides of the Rocky Mountains.   Satish Ramadhyani

Regeneration, in plants and animals, is the capacity to replace lost or damaged parts by growing new ones. Regeneration is common in plants. If a tree or shrub is cut off near the ground, new shoots may spring up from the stump. Among animals, the sponges, cnidarians, and the simpler worms show remarkable power of regeneration. They can be cut in pieces, and each piece can grow into a new animal. Starfishes can grow new arms. Crayfishes can grow new claws, eyes, and legs.

Animals with a backbone—called *vertebrates*—have only limited powers of regeneration. But a reptile called the *glass lizard* escapes from its enemies by breaking off the end of its tail. The glass lizard later grows a new one. Salamanders can regenerate lost limbs. People and other mammals can regenerate only hair, nails, skin, and a few other tissues. In some cases, a different sort of tissue grows over the damaged area and forms a scar.

George B. Johnson

See also **Animal** (Regeneration); **Crustacean** (Growth and development); **Flatworm; Planarian; Sponge** (Regeneration).

Regent, *REE juhnt,* is a person who rules a country when the rightful ruler cannot, either because he or she is too young, out of the country, or ill. In some countries, a member of the royal family acts as regent. In others, a council may exercise duties of the ruler.

The British had no special arrangements providing for a regency until the Regency Act of 1937 was passed. This law provides for the appointment of a regent if the monarch is unable to rule. A council of state can act as regent for short periods of time. This council is composed of the husband or wife of the ruler and the next four persons in succession to the crown.

In the United States, members of the governing body of libraries, museums, school systems, and universities and colleges are called *regents.*   I. J. Sanders

Reggae, *REHG ay* or *RAY gay,* is a type of popular music that developed in Jamaica in the 1960's. At first it was primarily performed by and for poor Jamaicans. It later became popular throughout Jamaica and also in England and the United States. Reggae has influenced soul, rhythm and blues, and rock music.

The words in most reggae songs deal with the social concerns and religious beliefs of poor Jamaicans. The songs are in 4/4 time and feature strong accents off the beat. Short rhythmic patterns are repeated many times by electric guitars and drums. They are also sometimes repeated with organ or piano. The rhythms in reggae are sometimes complex, but the harmonies are simple.

As with rock music, the volume of reggae is loud.

Reggae has its roots in traditional African music, Jamaican folk music, and North American popular music. It developed from two other types of Jamaican popular music—*ska* and *rock steady.* Reggae began to gain popularity outside Jamaica in the late 1960's through the recordings of a number of reggae musicians. The most important was Bob Marley, who grew up in the slums of Kingston, Jamaica. Marley led a group called the Wailers, founded in 1964. He was the most famous reggae star internationally until his death in 1981 at the age of 36. Songs that became hits in the United States include Eric Clapton's "I Shot the Sheriff" and Johnny Nash's "Stir It Up" (both written by Marley) and Desmond Dekker's "The Israelites."   Valerie Woodring Goertzen

Regina, *rih JY nuh,* is the capital and second largest city of Saskatchewan. Only Saskatoon is larger. Regina is located on a plain in southern Saskatchewan, and is about 100 miles (160 kilometers) north of the Canadian-United States border. The Latin word *regina* means *queen,* and Regina is sometimes called the *Queen City of the Plains.*

Regina is the commercial, financial, and industrial center of Saskatchewan. The city lies in the heart of Canada's richest wheat-growing region. Until the 1960's, Regina served mainly as a marketing and supply center for this region. Since then, it has become a manufacturing center as well.

Before white settlers came, the Cree Indians often camped on a site near what is now Regina. They butchered buffalo there, and the bones piled up. The Indians called the place *Oskunah-kasas-take,* which the whites translated as *Pile o' Bones*, and the stream that ran by it became known as Wascana Creek. In 1882, the Canadian government chose a small settlement on the creek as the new capital of what was then the North West Territories. At the time, the settlement was also called Pile o' Bones. The site was only a treeless plain, but it lay near the new Canadian Pacific Railway (now CP Rail System). This railroad, which linked eastern and western Canada, attracted the first settlers to Pile o' Bones. In 1882, they renamed the settlement Regina, in honor of Queen Victoria of England.

The city. Regina covers 43 square miles (111 square kilometers). Wascana Creek winds through the city. Southeast of the downtown area, a dam widens the

Saskatchewan Economic Development

Regina is Saskatchewan's capital and commercial, financial, and industrial center. It lies on a plain in the southern part of the province. High-rise buildings of downtown Regina rise in the background at left.

City of Regina

Regina, the capital of Saskatchewan, is the chief industrial and market center of the southern plains area of the province. The city map shows Regina and its major landmarks.

WORLD BOOK maps

- ▬▬ City boundary
- ═══ Expressway
- ── Other road
- ── Railroad
- ▪ Point of interest
- ▬ Park

SASKATCHEWAN

Regina

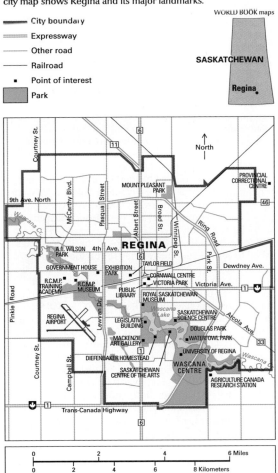

| 0 | 2 | 4 | 6 Miles |
| 0 | 2 | 4 | 6 | 8 Kilometers |

yards, a flour mill, a printing and publishing plant, and a farm supplies service.

The oil fields of southern Saskatchewan have helped make Regina an important oil center. The city has oil refining facilities. The petroleum pipeline that links the Alberta oil fields with ports on the Great Lakes runs through Regina.

Regina is the trade and distribution center for the surrounding region. Almost a fourth of the city's workers have jobs in wholesale or retail trade. Nearly a seventh of the workers have jobs with the city, provincial, or federal government. The Royal Canadian Mounted Police has its training headquarters there.

The Canadian Pacific Railway and CN North America (formerly Canadian National Railways) connect Regina with the East and West coasts. Regina lies on the Trans-Canada Highway, and Regina Airport is just west of the city.

Education and cultural life. Regina's public school system includes about 90 elementary schools, and 13 high schools. The city also has more than 30 private and parochial schools. The University of Regina is a coeducational school that grants bachelor's, master's, and doctor's degrees. The Saskatchewan Indian Federated College in Regina is the only North American Indian college that is part of a university.

The Regina Public Library operates a main library and 10 branch libraries. The Saskatchewan Provincial Library is also in the city. Regina has a daily newspaper, *The Leader-Post.*

The Saskatchewan Centre of the Arts includes the Centennial Theatre Concert Hall, the Jubilee Theatre, and a convention facility called Hanbidge Hall. The Regina Symphony Orchestra performs at the center. The Globe Repertory Theatre stages productions in the Globe Theatre in downtown Regina.

Wascana Waterfowl Park features hundreds of water birds and animals. The Royal Saskatchewan Museum features galleries that trace the human history and geological history of Saskatchewan.

The MacKenzie Art Gallery displays paintings and sculpture. The Royal Canadian Mounted Police Museum features exhibits that show how the Mounties brought law and order to Canada's frontier. The Mounties' chapel, called the "Little Chapel on the Square," ranks as one of Regina's oldest buildings. Part of it dates from 1885.

Buffalo Days, an annual festival held in late July and early August, celebrates Regina's frontier days. The festival includes parades, rodeos, and square dances. The Saskatchewan Roughriders of the Canadian Football

creek into an artificially created lake, Wascana Lake. Wascana Centre, a 2,500-acre (1,000-hectare) belt of parks and public buildings, surrounds the lake. Buildings in Wascana Centre include the Legislative Building, where the Saskatchewan legislature meets; the University of Regina; the Royal Saskatchewan Museum; and the Saskatchewan Centre of the Arts. See **Saskatchewan** (picture: The Legislative Building).

About 40 percent of Regina's people have some English ancestry. Other large ethnic groups, in order of size, are people of German, Scottish, or Irish descent.

Economy. Regina has more than 250 manufacturing plants. They account for more than a third of Saskatchewan's industrial production. The city's chief manufactured products include cement, fertilizer, and steel.

The rich agricultural region around Regina makes the city a center for the distribution of farm machinery. The Saskatchewan Wheat Pool, the largest grain-handling cooperative in the world, has its headquarters there. About 60,000 farmers belong to the pool. The members of the cooperative operate grain elevators, livestock

Facts in brief

Population: 180,400. *Metropolitan area population*—193,652.
Area: 44 sq. mi. (114 km²). *Metropolitan area*—1,321 sq. mi. (3,422 km²).
Altitude: 1,890 ft. (576 m) above sea level.
Climate: *Average temperature*—January, 2 °F (−17 °C); July, 67 °F (19 °C). *Average annual precipitation* (rainfall, melted snow, and other forms of moisture)—15 in. (38 cm). For the monthly weather in Regina, see **Saskatchewan** (Climate).
Government: Council-manager. *Terms*—3 years for the mayor and 10 aldermen.
Founded: 1882. Incorporated as a city in 1903.

League play at Taylor Field. The Lawson Aquatic Centre features an Olympic-sized swimming pool. Nearby Exhibition Park includes a horse racing track and a casino.

Government. Regina has a council-manager form of government. The voters elect a mayor and 10 council members to the city council. The council establishes city policies and appoints a professional administrator called a city manager to carry them out. The mayor and council members serve three-year terms. The city gets more than half its revenue from property taxes.

History. The Cree Indians hunted buffalo in what is now the Regina area before whites arrived. In 1857, the British explorer John Palliser visited the site and reported that it was unfit for farming. But in 1880, a Canadian botanist named John Macoun realized the Regina plains would make fertile wheatlands. He persuaded the Canadian Pacific Railway Company to build its transcontinental railroad across the area.

The railroad reached Regina in 1882, and the Canadian government chose it for the new capital of the North West Territories. Regina actually became the new capital in 1883. Battleford, the former capital, lay more than 225 miles (362 kilometers) north of the railroad and was too hard to reach. Also in 1882, the North-West Mounted Police (now the Royal Canadian Mounted Police) established its headquarters in Regina. By 1903, when Regina was incorporated as a city, it had 3,000 people.

In 1905, the province of Saskatchewan was created with Regina as its capital. Settlers from eastern Canada, Europe, and the United States poured into the area's rich wheatlands. The city grew into an important trade and supply center for the surrounding farms. By 1911, Regina's population had reached 30,000.

A cyclone destroyed much of Regina in 1912, but the city was quickly rebuilt. During World War I (1914-1918), the Regina area produced huge quantities of wheat for the Allies. But the demand for wheat dropped after the war, and falling wheat prices created a depression in Saskatchewan. Regina farmers formed the Saskatchewan Wheat Pool in 1924 to fight the depression.

The city's economy continued to slump during the Great Depression of the 1930's, and many workers were unemployed. By 1937, about a fifth of the population was receiving welfare payments.

In 1933, the Co-operative Commonwealth Federation (CCF), a socialist political party, held its first national convention in Regina. The CCF adopted a statement, known as the *Regina Manifesto,* that called for the end of capitalism. In 1944, the CCF gained control of the provincial government, which thus became the first socialist government in Canada. Regina served as CCF headquarters from 1933 until the party merged with the New Democratic Party in 1961.

During the 1950's and 1960's, the discovery of underground resources—chiefly potash, used for fertilizer, and petroleum—strengthened the region's economy. Many new industries came to Regina, and the city's economy became less dependent on a good annual wheat crop. Regina's population nearly doubled during this period, rising from 71,000 in 1951 to 139,000 in 1971.

A construction boom changed Regina's skyline during the 1960's. Three of the city's tallest structures went up—the 16-story Avord Tower, the 16-story Canadian Imperial Bank of Commerce, and the 13-story Saskatchewan Power Building.

Regina faced financial problems in the 1970's. Taxes failed to provide enough money to run the city government, and the public transportation system operated at a loss. Regina's population grew during the 1970's. It reached 162,613 by 1981. Another construction boom in Regina began in the mid-1970's. A new City Hall opened in 1976. Two provincial government buildings were constructed in 1979—the sprawling T. C. Douglas Building and the Saskatchewan Government Insurance Tower.

In 1980, a huge, enclosed shopping mall called the Cornwall Centre was completed. In 1983, the Bank of Montreal Building opened near the Cornwall Centre. Regina's tallest building, the 25-story Ramada Renaissance Centre, was completed in 1988.   A. D. Rosseker

Regina Medal, *rih JEE nuh,* is an award honoring a person for a lifetime contribution to children's literature. The award is sponsored by the Catholic Library Association, and is given regardless of nationality or creed. The

Saskatchewan Centre of the Arts

The Saskatchewan Centre of the Arts stands on Wascana Lake in Regina. It includes two theaters and a convention hall.

Winners of the Regina Medal

Year	Winner	Year	Winner
1959	Eleanor Farjeon	1981	Augusta Baker
1960	Anne Carroll Moore	1982	Theodor Geisel
1961	Padraic Colum		(Dr. Seuss)
1962	Frederic G. Melcher	1983	Tomie dePaola
1963	Ann Nolan Clark	1984	Madeleine L'Engle
1964	May Hill Arbuthnot	1985	Jean Fritz
1965	Ruth Sawyer	1986	Lloyd Alexander
1966	Leo Politi	1987	Betsy Byars
1967	Bertha Mahony Miller	1988	Katherine Paterson
1968	Marguerite de Angeli	1989	Steven Kellogg
1969	Lois Lenski	1990	Virginia Hamilton
1970	Ingri and Edgar d'Aulaire	1991	Leonard Everett
1971	Tasha Tudor		Fisher
1972	Meindert DeJong	1992	Jane Yolen
1973	Frances Clarke Sayers	1993	Chris Van Allsburg
1974	Robert McCloskey	1994	Lois Lowry
1975	May McNeer and	1995	Gary Paulsen
	Lynd Ward	1996	Russell Freedman
1976	Virginia Haviland	1997	Eve Bunting
1977	Marcia Brown	1998	Patricia C. and Fredrick
1978	Scott O'Dell		L. McKissack
1979	Morton Schindel	1999	Eric Carle
1980	Beverly Cleary	2000	Milton Meltzer

face of the medal bears a crown superimposed on an *M*, signifying *Mary*, for whom the medal is named. The words "Regina Medal, Continued Distinguished Contribution to Children's Literature," encircle the symbols. On the reverse side, names of the winner, the sponsor, and the year encircle a shield that bears a quotation from Walter de la Mare's collection of poems, *Bells and Grass*. The quotation reads: "… only the rarest kind of best in anything can be good enough for the young."

Critically reviewed by the Catholic Library Association

Regression is a characteristic sign of certain mental illnesses. It comes from a Latin word meaning *to go backward*. Doctors use the word to mean a return to a way of thinking or behaving that would normally be characteristic of an earlier period of life. For example, if a 4-year-old child, after the birth of a baby brother or sister, began to act like a baby, doctors would call the child's behavior regression. However, mentally healthy persons sometimes exhibit regression, as when they play games or daydream. Nancy C. Andreasen

Regulus, *REHG yuh luhs,* **Marcus Atilius,** *uh TIHL ee uhs* (? -249? B.C.), was a Roman general who became a national hero. His life story was repeated as an example of true patriotism. As *consul* (chief government official) in 256 B.C., he commanded the Roman invasion of Africa against Carthage in the First Punic War (see **Punic Wars**). He was victorious and demanded harsh peace terms. But the Carthaginians raised more troops and hired Xanthippus, a Spartan general, who defeated the Romans and captured Regulus.

Carthage sent Regulus to Rome about 249 B.C. with its own peace terms. He promised to return if the Romans refused to make peace. Regulus urged the Roman Senate to reject the terms, though he knew this meant his death when he returned to Carthage. Romans later said he was killed by torture by the Carthaginians, but this story may have been made up by his family. Regulus, an aristocrat, was not rich. Before the war, he lived a simple life on his farm. Arthur M. Eckstein

Rehnquist, *REHN kwihst,* **William Hubbs** (1924-), became chief justice of the United States Supreme Court in 1986. President Ronald Reagan nominated him to succeed Chief Justice Warren E. Burger, who retired.

Rehnquist had served as an associate justice of the court since 1972. He was nominated to the court by President Richard M. Nixon. Nixon's nomination of Rehnquist sparked a debate in the Senate. The debate centered on Rehnquist's philosophy, which his opponents termed "ultraconservative." During Senate hearings on the nomination, several civil rights groups and liberals objected to positions Rehnquist had taken on such issues as school desegregation and police surveillance. As an associate justice, Rehnquist continued to reflect the conservative viewpoint on almost every issue and was the most conservative justice on the court. When Reagan nominated him to be chief justice, debate again broke out in the Senate over Rehnquist's conservatism.

As chief justice, Rehnquist led a group of conservative Supreme Court justices. The group gained strength from court appointments made by Reagan and President George Bush. The court issued many conservative rulings under Rehnquist, especially regarding *criminal procedures* (methods for arresting, prosecuting, and punishing people accused of crimes), abortion, and affirmative action (see **Affirmative action**). In the early 1990's, however, several of the court's conservatives broke with Rehnquist to uphold some earlier key Supreme Court rulings that many conservatives felt had been too liberal on abortion and other issues. In early 1999, Rehnquist presided over the Senate impeachment trial of President Bill Clinton that ended in Clinton's acquittal.

Rehnquist was born in Milwaukee. He attended Stanford University and graduated the top student in his class from Stanford Law School in 1952. That year, Supreme Court Justice Robert H. Jackson appointed Rehnquist his law clerk. Rehnquist was a U.S. assistant attorney general from 1969 to 1971. Sheldon Goldman

See also **Supreme Court of the United States** (picture).

Reich, *ryk,* is a German word meaning *empire* or *state*. Adolf Hitler, the German dictator, called his government the *Third Reich*. The first was the Holy Roman Empire. The second was the German Empire that lasted from 1871 to 1918 (see **Germany** [History]).

Reichstag. See **Germany** (History); **Hitler, Adolf** (The New Order).

Reid, *reed,* **Whitelaw** (1837-1912), was an American journalist and diplomat. He bought control of the New York *Tribune* in 1872. From 1905 until his death he served as ambassador to Britain.

Reid was born in Xenia, Ohio. During the Civil War (1861-1865), he was war correspondent for the Cincinnati *Gazette*. In 1892, Reid was the Republican nominee for Vice President of the United States, but he was defeated.

Joseph P. McKerns

See also **Harrison, Benjamin** (Bid for reelection).

Reign of Terror. See **French Revolution** (Terror and equality).

Reims, *reemz* (pop. 185,164; met. area pop. 206,362), is a fortified city of northern France. It is on the Vesle River about 98 miles (158 kilometers) northeast of Paris. For location, see **France** (political map). The beauty of Reims

SEF/Art Resource

The Cathedral of Notre Dame in Reims, France, is a beautiful example of Gothic architecture. It was completed in 1430.

centers on a cathedral, which was begun in the 1200's and completed in 1430. This cathedral towers high above the surrounding homes.

During World War I, Reims was bombed daily for nearly four years. After the war ended in 1918, the people rebuilt many homes and buildings. World War II brought more suffering to the city. The Germans occupied Reims from 1940 to 1944. Reims later became an important supply base for Allied troops. The Germans signed their surrender at Reims on May 7, 1945.

Reims lies in one of the important wine regions of France, and leads in French champagne production. It is also France's most important wool market. Other products made in Reims include machinery, chemicals, soap, paper, and wine bottles and casks.

Lovers of art and architecture have long admired the Cathedral of Notre Dame at Reims, one of the most beautiful examples of Gothic architecture. Nearly all the French kings were crowned in the cathedral. Heavy bombing during World War I badly damaged the cathedral, but it was repaired by 1937.   William M. Reddy

Reincarnation, *REE ihn kahr NAY shuhn,* is the belief that the soul survives after death and is reborn in the body of another person or some other living thing. The word *reincarnation* means *coming back into the flesh.* This concept is also called *transmigration of the soul.*

The ancient Greeks and some primitive peoples believed in reincarnation. The concept is an important part of Buddhism, Hinduism, Jainism, Sikhism, and other religions that originated in India. It also is a doctrine of some modern *spiritualist* movements (see **Spiritualism**).

In the religions of India, reincarnation is related to the law of *karma.* According to this law, a person's actions determine the type of body that the soul will enter during reincarnation. If a person leads a good life, his or her soul will be reborn in a higher state, such as the body of a priest. If a person leads a bad life, the soul will be reborn in a lower state, such as the body of a dog.

Other religions explain reincarnation in different ways. Some teach that the soul may be reborn in the body of a descendant of the person.   Nancy E. Auer Falk

Related articles in *World Book* include:

Buddhism	Pythagoras
Hinduism (Reincarnation and karma)	Religion (A doctrine of salvation)
Jainism	Sikhism
Karma	Theosophy
Plato (Immortality of the soul)	

Reindeer is a kind of large deer that lives in the northernmost regions of Europe, Asia, and North America. The reindeer, which is closely related to the caribou, is often herded and tamed by nomadic peoples.

Reindeer differ from most other forms of deer in several ways. For example, reindeer have larger antlers, larger and wider hoofs, and a heavy coat that is grayish-brown to almost white. These features help reindeer survive in the cold Arctic. The large hoofs, for example, prevent the reindeer from sinking into the snow during winter. Female reindeer are the only kind of female deer except caribou to have antlers. Reindeer often make a variety of noises. When frightened, adults snort and young reindeer bawl. When reindeer walk, their feet make a clicking sound.

In summer, reindeer may eat grasses and leaves from

Bruce Coleman Inc.

The reindeer lives in Arctic regions of Europe, Asia, and North America. Nomadic peoples of these far northern lands herd and tame these animals. They drink reindeer milk, eat reindeer meat, and make clothing and tents from reindeer hide.

willows and birches. In winter, they paw through the snow to find lichens to eat. In the short Arctic summers, plants grow slowly and cannot stand much grazing. So reindeer move frequently to a new place when their food becomes scarce. They may migrate several hundred miles or kilometers in a year. They are excellent swimmers and can cross rivers. During migration, several thousand reindeer may gather into one herd. By traveling in herds, individual reindeer are protected from their enemies. Animals that prey on reindeer include wolves, lynxes, wolverines, and grizzly bears.

A male reindeer is known as a *bull.* The female is called a *cow.* In the fall, the bulls fight with one another to gather their own group of cows, called a *harem.* A bull then mates with the cows in its harem, and later the harem breaks up. In the spring, a cow usually will bear one offspring, called a *calf.* After a few days, the calf is strong enough to join the herd. Adult reindeer stand about 3 to 4 feet (90 to 120 centimeters) high and weigh up to 400 pounds (180 kilograms).

Reindeer are very useful to the Lapps of northern Scandinavia. The Lapps are one of the nomadic peoples well known for developing much of their way of life around the migrating herds of reindeer. They have trained reindeer to serve as pack animals and to pull sleds and sleighs. They use reindeer skin for boots, clothing, and tents. They also drink reindeer milk and kill wild reindeer for meat. In some areas, snowmobiles, trucks, helicopters, and two-way radios are used to capture and herd the reindeer. But nomads in extreme northern Siberia still herd the reindeer in the old way, following the herds, with their possessions carried on a reindeer-pulled sled.

Scientific classification. Reindeer belong to the deer family, Cervidae. They are subspecies of *Rangifer tarandus.*

L. David Mech

See also **Deer; Caribou; Tundra.**

Reindeer Lake covers 2,444 square miles (6,330 square kilometers) in central Canada. It lies on the border between northern Saskatchewan and Manitoba.

For location, see **Saskatchewan** (physical map). The waters of Reindeer Lake drain south, into Reindeer River and the Churchill river system.   Adrian A. Seaborne

Reindeer moss is a type of lichen that grows in the Arctic and sometimes farther south. It is an important food for the caribou and reindeer of the Arctic. People sometimes eat reindeer moss. In Scandinavia, it has been used to make bread. See also **Lichen.**

Scientific classification. Reindeer moss belongs to the kingdom Fungi. Its scientific name is *Cladina rangiferina.*

Joe F. Ammirati

Reiner, *RY nuhr,* **Fritz** (1888-1963), was one of the great symphony orchestra and operatic conductors of his time. He became especially noted for his heroic performances of music of central European composers. He valued precision and balance, yet he never neglected the monumental passions of romantic music. He specialized in the operas and tone poems of Richard Strauss.

Reiner was born and educated in Budapest, Hungary. From 1914 to 1921, he served as musical director of the Dresden Royal Opera in Germany. He came to the United States in 1922 as director of the Cincinnati Symphony Orchestra and held that position until 1931. Reiner then taught at the Curtis Institute of Music in Philadelphia until 1941. From 1938 to 1948, he conducted the Pittsburgh Symphony. Reiner served as a major conductor at the Metropolitan Opera in New York City from 1949 to 1953. He served as musical director of the Chicago Symphony Orchestra from 1953 until his death in 1963.   Martin Bernheimer

Reinforcement, in psychology. See **Learning** (Classical conditioning; Instrumental conditioning).

Reinhardt, *RYN hahrt,* **Max** (1873-1943), was a theatrical producer and director. He became a leader of the German-speaking theater during the early 1900's.

Reinhardt was born in Baden, near Vienna. His given and family name was Max Goldmann. Beginning in 1917, he helped found and plan the famous Salzburg music and theater festival. He directed the festival's first production in 1920. Reinhardt staged such classics as *Faust* and *Everyman* as well as productions of such modern playwrights as George Bernard Shaw, August Strindberg, and Henrik Ibsen. Reinhardt became famous for his imaginative productions. He staged the Greek tragedies *Oresteia* and *Oedipus Rex* as mass spectacles. For the pageant *The Miracle,* Reinhardt rebuilt the inside of theaters to resemble a Gothic cathedral. He moved to the United States in 1934.   Daniel J. Watermeier

Relapsing fever is an infectious disease that occurs chiefly in the tropics, often as an epidemic. It is caused by bacteria called *spirochetes.* A person with relapsing fever develops chills, fever, headache, and muscular aches and pains. Vomiting also may occur. These symptoms may last for several days or a week. Then the patient seems to return to good health for about a week. Suddenly, however, the symptoms return, and if the patient is not treated, he or she may have as many as 10 relapses. Doctors advise bed rest and use antibiotics.

Lice and ticks transmit the bacteria to human beings. Like typhus, louse-borne relapsing fever is found in regions with poor living conditions (see **Typhus**). The two diseases often occur together. Tick-borne relapsing fever is found in the Western United States as well as in other parts of the world.   Thomas J. Gill III

Relativity. Einstein's theory of relativity has caught the imagination of the average person more than any other physical theory in history. Yet the theory of relativity, unlike many other results of physical science, is not easily understood by the average person. We can understand the relativity theory fully only by means of the mathematical formulas which make it up. Without mathematics, we can only state some of its basic ideas and quote, but not prove, some of its conclusions.

The relativity theory deals with the most fundamental ideas which we use to describe natural happenings. These ideas are time, space, mass, motion, and gravitation. The theory gives new meaning to the old ideas that these words represent. It is basically made up of two parts. One is the special, or restricted, relativity theory, published by Albert Einstein in 1905. The general relativity theory was put forward by Einstein in 1915.

Special theory of relativity

This theory is called the special relativity theory because it refers to a special kind of motion. This is uniform motion in a straight line, that is, with constant *velocity.*

Suppose we are on a smoothly running railroad train which is moving at a constant velocity. In this train you may drop a book, play catch, or allow a pendulum to swing freely. The book will appear to fall straight down when it is dropped; the ball will travel directly from the thrower to the catcher. All these activities can be carried on in much the same way and with the same results on the ground outside the train. So long as the train runs smoothly, with constant velocity, none of our mechanical activities will be affected by its motion.

On the other hand, if the train stops or speeds up abruptly, our activities may be changed. A book may be jarred from a seat and fall without being dropped. A ball will travel differently.

One way of stating the principle of this theory is to say that the laws of mechanics are the same for an observer in a smoothly moving train as for the observer on the ground. Physicists would say: *If two systems move uniformly relative to each other, then all the laws of mechanics are the same in both systems.* This principle may be called the classical relativity principle. This principle is as old as the ideas of mechanics and physics.

Suppose we have a long train much like the train in the previous example. But instead of rolling along at a normal speed, it will be moving uniformly at a speed of, let us say, 20,000 miles (32,000 kilometers) a second. Instead of having two persons playing catch on the train, we will have a radio antenna on the train sending out radio waves, or a flashlight sending out light signals. Observers on the train will measure the velocity of the radio waves and light signals. On the ground we will also have an antenna or flashlight, and observers measuring the velocity of the signals. Is the velocity of the radio or light waves the same for those on the ground as it is for those on the train? Physicists in the late 1800's would have answered, "No." They would have said the classical relativity principle holds true for mechanical activities, but not for those of electromagnetic waves—that is, not for radio or light waves.

A physicist would have said that radio and light waves travel through *ether* at a velocity of 186,282 miles

(299,792 kilometers) per second. Ether was a substance that scientists imagined to fill all space, to account for the transmission of light in outer space. The physicist would have said that the stars, sun, planets, and our imaginary moving train move through the ether sea at different speeds. Thus, the velocity of light will be different for an observer on the sun, on the earth, and on the train. Just as the earth changes velocity during the year in which it completes its journey around the sun, the speed of light for the observer should change too.

Scientists believed that the ether through which all objects of the universe were believed to move provided a nonmoving frame of reference. All other motions could be judged from this frame of reference. Ether was looked upon as a fluid or elastic solid. It was believed to occupy the spaces between the atoms that made up matter. It offered no resistance to the earth's movement.

Among the many experiments which helped destroy the ether theory, the most famous is that of Michelson and Morley in 1887. Their measurements of the speed of light showed that the motion of the earth as it moved around the sun had no influence upon the velocity of light. Therefore, light has a uniform velocity, regardless of the frame of reference. This experimental result seemed strange, since normally we expect the speed of an object to depend on how fast the observer is moving.

Einstein asserted that the relativity principle was true for all phenomena, mechanical or electromagnetic. In other words, there was no special, or nonmoving, frame of reference for electromagnetic phenomena.

The basic ideas of the special relativity theory are found in a mathematical formulation of two postulates. The first is that the relativity principle is valid for all phenomena. The second postulate is that the velocity of electromagnetic waves, or light, in empty space is constant, and furthermore is independent of the velocity of its source or observer.

The following deductions have been made from these postulates by mathematical means.

According to the special relativity theory, a material body can only move with a velocity lower than that of light.

If a conductor on a fast-moving train compared his clock with the many clocks in the stations he passed, he would find that the rhythm of his clock is faster than the rhythm of the clocks on the ground. On the other hand, it will appear to the stationmasters that the rhythms of their clocks are faster than the rhythm of the conductor's clock on the train passing the station. This effect is small, and could be detected only if the velocity of the one clock that passes many others were not very small compared with the speed of light.

Two events judged as taking place at the same time by the observer in the train may not be simultaneous for the observer on the ground.

The length of every object resting in the train appears to the observer outside to be shortened in the direction in which the train is moving.

Perhaps the most important of these deductions is the fact that mass is not unchangeable. The mass of an object increases with its velocity. Theoretically, the mass of an object would become infinite if its velocity became the velocity of light. This mass increase has been observed with experiments. A small particle of matter ac-

celerated to 86 per cent of the speed of light has twice as much mass as it does when it is at rest.

The theory also shows a relation between a body's mass and its energy ($E = mc^2$). This relation has great practical importance in the liberation of the energy in the nucleus of an atom. When energy is liberated from the nucleus of the uranium atom and atoms of other elements are formed, the total mass of these atoms is less than the total mass of the uranium atom. This means that some of the mass of the nucleus of the uranium atom has been transformed into energy. The $E = mc^2$ law shows that the energy in a single uranium nucleus is 220,000,000,000 electronvolts, providing that all its mass could be converted to energy. However, splitting the uranium nucleus, a process known as *fission,* releases only 0.1 per cent of the total energy content. This amount is still about a million times greater than the energy released in the burning of chemical fuels.

Various experiments have proved the truth of many of these conclusions about relativity. In 1938, H. E. Ives used a hydrogen atom as a moving clock. He found that a fast-moving hydrogen atom does slow down in its rhythm, just as Einstein predicted the moving clock would do. This slowing down could be shown by a change in the frequency of the line given off in its spectrum. The changes of mass as predicted by the special theory of relativity are observed in machines that are used to accelerate electrons and nuclear particles to the high speeds necessary to study nuclear properties.

The mathematician H. Minkowski gave a mathematical form to the special relativity theory in 1907. A line involves only one dimension. We can locate any point on a sheet of paper by measuring from that point to any two sides of the paper that are perpendicular to each other. Therefore, we can say that any point on a sheet of paper involves two dimensions. All points in space involve three dimensions: height, length, and breadth. But there is one other important fact involved. In physics as well as history we must deal with events. When and where did the French Revolution start, for example? When and where does the earth have the smallest velocity in its movement about the sun? Events must be characterized by four numbers, bringing in the idea of a fourth dimension. Three of these numbers answer the question *where;* one must answer the question *when.* Answering the question *when* involves the idea of time. Then we consider things in terms of four dimensions.

This question of answering when and where an event took place becomes more complicated, according to the theory of special relativity, because rods can change their lengths, and clocks change their rhythms, depending on the speed at which they operate when they are in motion. Therefore, we must answer the questions *when* and *where* an event took place in terms of a definitely moving system, or in terms of the relationships between two moving systems. For example, if we know when and where an event took place for an observer on our swiftly moving train, and if we know the velocity of the train, we can find out when and where the same event took place for an observer on the ground. The mathematical formulation of the theory of special relativity tells us how to find these four numbers, characterizing an event in one system from an event in another. It tells us that the question *when* has no absolute meaning, that

Relativity and time

According to the theory of relativity, a clock moving relative to an observer appears to run slower than a stationary clock. This effect can be observed if the clock travels almost as fast as the speed of light, 186,282 miles (299,792 kilometers) per second. The illustrations below show a clock experiment performed in an imaginary train traveling 150,000 miles (241,000 kilometers) per second.

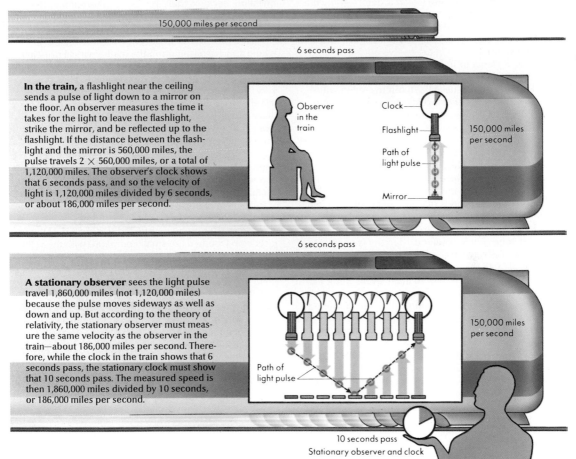

150,000 miles per second

6 seconds pass

In the train, a flashlight near the ceiling sends a pulse of light down to a mirror on the floor. An observer measures the time it takes for the light to leave the flashlight, strike the mirror, and be reflected up to the flashlight. If the distance between the flashlight and the mirror is 560,000 miles, the pulse travels 2 × 560,000 miles, or a total of 1,120,000 miles. The observer's clock shows that 6 seconds pass, and so the velocity of light is 1,120,000 miles divided by 6 seconds, or about 186,000 miles per second.

Observer in the train

Clock

Flashlight

Path of light pulse

Mirror

150,000 miles per second

6 seconds pass

A stationary observer sees the light pulse travel 1,860,000 miles (not 1,120,000 miles) because the pulse moves sideways as well as down and up. But according to the theory of relativity, the stationary observer must measure the same velocity as the observer in the train—about 186,000 miles per second. Therefore, while the clock in the train shows that 6 seconds pass, the stationary clock must show that 10 seconds pass. The measured speed is then 1,860,000 miles divided by 10 seconds, or 186,000 miles per second.

Path of light pulse

150,000 miles per second

10 seconds pass
Stationary observer and clock

WORLD BOOK illustrations by Sarah Woodward

the answer to the question depends on the system we choose.

General relativity theory

The mathematical formulas which make up this general theory are much more difficult than those which are concerned with special relativity. The general relativity theory changes the old ideas about gravitation that have dominated physics since the days of Isaac Newton. According to Newton, two bodies attract each other with a force depending upon their mass and their distance apart. The gravitational influence of a star is felt at the same moment throughout the entire universe, even though it decreases with the distance from the star. But for electromagnetic waves, action spreads through space with great but perfectly definite velocity, that of light. Because of our knowledge of electromagnetic radiation, we tend to reject ideas that disturbances and actions that travel through space have infinite speed. We tend to believe that though they may travel at a very high speed, that speed is not limitless.

Einstein illustrated the basic idea of general relativity

with an imaginary experiment. Suppose an elevator is at rest in space. If a ball is released within the elevator, it will float in space and not fall. If the elevator accelerates upward, an observer within the elevator will see the ball fall to the floor exactly as it would under the pull of gravity. The ball appears to fall because the floor of the elevator—as seen from outside the elevator—accelerates upward toward the ball. All the effects we associate with gravity would be seen by the observer in the elevator. Einstein called the phenomenon shown in this experiment the *Principle of Equivalence*. This principle states that it makes no difference whether an object is acted on by a gravitational force or is in an accelerated frame of reference. The result in both cases will be the same. From this principle, Einstein reasoned that matter in space distorts or "curves" the frame of reference of space. The result of this curvature is what we experience as gravity. Euclidian or "flat" geometry cannot describe curved space. Thus, Einstein used geometries called *Riemannian geometries* to describe the effects of gravitation.

According to Newton's theory, a planet moves around

the sun because of the gravitational force exerted by the sun. According to the theory of general relativity, the planet chooses the shortest possible path throughout the four-dimensional world, which is deformed by the presence of the sun. This may be compared to the fact that a ship or an airplane crossing the ocean follows the section of a circle, rather than a straight line, in order to travel the shortest route between two points. In the same way, a planet or light ray moves along the "shortest" line in its four-dimensional world.

So far, three things have been discovered in which Einstein's theory of general relativity receives experimental proof as opposed to the theories of Newton. These differences are not great, but are measurable. In the first place, according to Newton's theory, the planet Mercury moves in an ellipse about the sun. According to Einstein's theory, Mercury moves along an ellipse, but at the same time the ellipse rotates very slowly in the direction of the planet's motion. The ellipse will turn about forty-three seconds of an arc per century (a complete rotation contains 360 degrees of an arc and $360 \times 60 \times 60$ seconds of an arc). This effect is rather small, but it has been observed. Mercury is nearest to the sun and the relativistic effect would be still smaller for other planets.

If we take a picture of part of the heavens during an eclipse of the sun and near the eclipsed sun, and then take another picture of the same part of the heavens a little later, the two photographs will not show identical positions for all the stars. This is so because, according to general relativity, a light ray sent by a star and passing near the rim of the sun is deflected from its original path because the sun's gravity curves space.

Physicists have known for more than a hundred years that when some elements are heated to incandescence they give off a pattern of colored lines which can be examined through a spectroscope. According to the Einstein theory, if we examine the spectral lines of an element on our earth with the spectral lines given off by the same element on the sun or on a star, the spectral lines of the element on the sun or star should be very slightly shifted toward the red end of the spectrum, compared with the spectral lines of the same element on our earth. Experiment has confirmed this shift. In 1960, two American physicists, R. V. Pound and G. A. Rebka, Jr., detected the red shift resulting from the earth's gravitational field. They measured the effect of altitude in the frequency of gamma rays.

Many scientists are doing research in general relativity and studying possible improvements on Einstein's theory. For example, the general theory predicts the existence of waves that "carry" the force of gravity, just as electromagnetic waves carry light. Experimenters have not yet been able to detect these *gravitational waves*. Scientists are also trying to combine electromagnetic and gravitational forces in a theory called the *unified field theory*.

Relativity and other ideas

The ideas of relativity form a framework which can embrace all laws of nature. Relativity has changed the whole philosophical and physical notions of space and time. It has influenced our views and speculation of the distant worlds and stars and of the tiny world of the atom. Some of this speculation is still going on. Does our universe, regarded as a whole, resemble a plane surface or a sphere? It is not possible to answer this question, because there are many different theories and much uncertainty about the distribution of matter in the universe.

All the theories try to describe the universe as a whole and are based upon the mathematical principles of general relativity. According to some theories, a light ray sent from an arbitrary point in space returns, after a very long time interval, to the point of departure, like a traveler in a journey around our earth. Thus, if you were to start from your home and travel into space along a straight line, you would eventually return to the point from which you started. According to other theories, however, a light ray or a traveler would continue an endless journey through space.

Such theories about the universe are developed to explain the motion and distribution of distant nebulas.

In spite of all these successes of the relativity theory, it is not right to say that Newtonian physics is wrong. Newtonian physics holds true if the velocities of the objects being studied are small compared with the velocity of light. Such objects are found every day in our own experience, and therefore classical physics can still be applied to our daily problems. Astronomers have found that Newton's theory of gravitation still holds true in their calculations. But the relativity theory does limit the area to which the Newtonian physics can be successfully applied.

The relativity theory is, like all our theories, an invention of the human mind. New theories may eventually show limitations of the relativity theory and deal with problems that the relativity theory does not cover. But no physicist doubts that the relativity theory has brought much scientific progress.   William B. Case

Related articles in *World Book* include:

Einstein, Albert	Interferometer
Electromagnetism	Physics (Einstein and
Fourth dimension	relativity)
Gravitation	Tachyon

Relaxation. See Health (Rest and sleep).

Relaxin. See Hormone (Other hormones).

Relief, in art, is sculpture in which the figures or designs project from their background. It differs from *sculpture in the round,* in which the figures stand alone and have three full dimensions. In relief sculpture, the figures are only partly modeled, but they give an illusion of being fully modeled. They may stand out from the background surface, or they may be carved into it. If they are carved into it, the sculpture is called *hollow relief* or *intaglio.*

Relief sculpture may be of three types: high relief; low relief; and half relief, or semirelief. Some relief sculpture combines two or more types.

High relief. Figures modeled in high relief project from their background more than half of their implied thickness. High relief is often called by its Italian name, *alto-rilievo.*

Low relief. Figures that stand out from their background less than half of their suggested thickness are in low relief. When the work is well done, they appear to stand out more than they actually do. The frieze of the Parthenon is the most famous example of low-relief

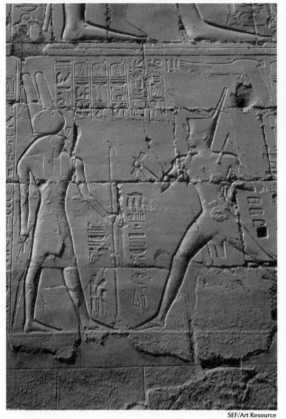

A low relief shows a pharaoh offering gifts to Horus, the Egyptian god of light and heaven. Reliefs portraying gods and royalty decorated many ancient Egyptian structures.

Half-relief figures appear in panels on the marble pulpit of the Baptistery of Pisa, Italy. The pulpit, completed by sculptor Nicola Pisano in 1260, also includes realistic carved figures in high relief, extending above the pillars.

Bronze panel (1425 to 1452) by Lorenzo Ghiberti
from the east doors of the baptistery
in Florence, Italy (SCALA/Art Resource)

High-relief figures in the foreground add drama to a scene from the Old Testament story of Joseph. Italian sculptor Lorenzo Ghiberti designed the background in low relief.

sculpture (see **Parthenon**). Sometimes low relief may be nearly flat, as in the design on a coin. Low relief is also known by its French name, *bas-relief*.

Half relief, or semirelief. Figures in half relief stand out half their thickness. Half relief is a little higher than low relief, but lower than high relief. It is often called by its Italian name, *mezzo-rilievo*.

History. Sculptors have carved figures in relief for thousands of years. Peoples of the stone ages often carved or scratched figures and designs in relief. The Assyrians, Egyptians, and Greeks used all forms of relief sculpture in their palaces and temples.

Relief sculpture is used in many ways today. It is almost the only form used in making coins and medals. As in all sculpture, the subject matter, design, and execution of relief reflect the development of civilization, the religious trends, and the art of the time in which it is made.   Harold L. Enlow

See also **Cameo; Engraving; Sculpture** (Kinds of sculpture).

Relief. See Welfare.

Relief Corps, National Woman's. See Woman's Relief Corps, National.

The mass is the most important act of worship in several Christian churches. These worshipers are American Roman Catholics.

A Buddhist prays in a South Korean temple. The center statue represents Siddhartha Gautama, Buddhism's chief teacher.

Religion

Religion. No simple definition can describe the numerous religions in the world. For many people, religion is an organized system of beliefs, ceremonies, practices, and worship that center on one supreme God, or the Deity. For many others, religion involves a number of gods, or deities. Some people have a religion in which no specific God or gods are worshiped. There are also people who practice their own religious beliefs in their own personal way, largely independent of organized religion. But almost all people who follow some form of religion believe that a divine power created the world and influences their lives.

People practice religion for several reasons. Many people throughout the world follow a religion simply because it is part of the heritage of their culture, tribe, or family. Religion gives many people a feeling of security because they believe that a divine power watches over them. These people often ask the power for help or protection. Numerous people follow a religion because it promises them salvation and either happiness or the chance to improve themselves in a life after death. For many people, religion brings a sense of individual fulfillment and gives meaning to life. In addition, religion pro-

Walter Holden Capps, the contributor of this article, is Professor of Religious Studies at the University of California, Santa Barbara and the author of Ways of Understanding Religion.

vides answers to such questions as What is the purpose of life? What is the final destiny of a person? What is the difference between right and wrong? and What are one's obligations to other people? Finally, many people follow a religion to enjoy a sense of kinship with their fellow believers.

There are thousands of religions in the world. The eight major ones are Buddhism, Christianity, Confucianism, Hinduism, Islam, Judaism, Shinto, and Taoism. Of these eight religions, Hinduism, Shinto, and Taoism developed over many centuries. Each of the other religions traditionally bases its faith on the life or teachings of specific individuals. They are Prince Siddhartha Gautama, who became known as Gautama Buddha, for Buddhism; Jesus Christ for Christianity; Confucius for Confucianism; Muhammad for Islam; and Abraham and Moses for Judaism.

The religions that trace their history to individuals follow a general pattern of development. During the individual's lifetime or soon after his death, a distinctive system of worship ceremonies grew up around his life and teachings. This system, called a *cult,* became the basis of the religion. The heart of the cult is the individual's teachings. In addition to inspiring worship, the individual represents an ideal way of life that followers try to imitate.

The teachings of religions have shaped the lives of people since prehistoric times. Judaism, Islam, and especially Christianity have been major influences in the formation of Western culture. These three faiths, particularly Islam, have also played a crucial role in the development of Middle Eastern culture. The cultures of Asia

Edward S. Ross

The San of Africa go into a trance while dancing near a sacred fire. They believe the fire's heat gives them power to heal.

have been shaped by Buddhism, Confucianism, Hinduism, Shinto, and Taoism.

Religion has been a supreme source of inspiration in the arts. Some of the most beautiful buildings in the world are houses of worship. Much of the world's greatest music is religious. Religious stories have provided countless subjects for paintings, sculptures, literature, dances, and motion pictures.

This article describes the chief characteristics of religion. It also examines the origin of religion in prehistoric times. In addition, the article describes the organization of the world's eight major religions and briefly relates the history of each. Many separate *World Book* articles provide information on topics related to religion. For a list of these articles, see the *Related articles* at the end of this article.

Chief characteristics of religion

Most of the leading religions throughout history have shared characteristics. The chief characteristics include (1) belief in a deity or in a power beyond the individual, (2) a *doctrine* (accepted teaching) of salvation, (3) a code of conduct, (4) the use of sacred stories, and (5) religious *rituals* (acts and ceremonies).

The essential qualities of a religion are maintained and passed from generation to generation by sources, called *authority,* which the followers accept as sacred. The most important religious authorities are writings known as *scriptures.* Scriptures include the Bibles of Christians and Jews, the Koran of Muslims, and the Vedas of Hindus. Religious authority also comes from the writings of saints and other holy persons and from

decisions by religious councils and leaders. Unwritten customs and laws known as *traditions* also form a basic part of authority.

Belief in a deity. There are three main philosophical views regarding the existence of a deity. *Atheists* believe that no deity exists. *Theists* believe in a deity or deities. *Agnostics* say that the existence of a deity cannot be proved or disproved. Most of the major religions are theistic. They teach that deities govern or greatly influence the actions of human beings as well as events in nature. Confucianism is the most important atheistic religion.

Religions that acknowledge only one true God are *monotheistic.* Judaism, Christianity, and Islam are examples of monotheistic religions. A religion that has a number of deities is *polytheistic.* The ancient Greeks and Romans had polytheistic religions. Each of their many gods and goddesses had one or more special areas of influence. For example, Aphrodite was the Greek goddess of love, and Mars was the Roman god of war. In *henotheistic* religions, the worship of a supreme Deity does not deny the existence and power of other deities. For example, Hinduism teaches that a world spirit called Brahman is the supreme power. But Hindus also serve numerous other gods and goddesses. Many tribes in Africa and the Pacific Islands also worship a supreme power as well as many other deities.

The followers of some religions worship deities that are or were people or that are images of people. The ancient Egyptian people considered their pharaohs to be living gods. Before World War II (1939-1945), the Japanese honored their emperor as divine. Taoists believe in deities that look and act like human beings. They also worship some deities that were once human beings and

T. S. Satyan, Black Star

Honoring the saint Gommateswara, followers of Jainism bathe a huge granite figure with a sacred liquid. Jain pilgrims travel to Mysore, India, for the ceremony every 12 years.

Fresco (1536-1541) by Michelangelo in the Sistine Chapel, The Vatican, Rome; © Nippon Television Network Corporation Tokyo 1991

Salvation from eternal punishment is the goal of many religions. This painting represents the Christian belief in the Last Judgment, when every person will either be granted happiness in heaven or be condemned to suffering in hell.

became gods or goddesses after death.

Many people worship nature deities—that is, deities that dwell in or control various aspects of nature. The Chinese in particular have worshiped gods of the soil and grain. Followers of Shinto worship *kami,* spirits that live in nature. Many American Indian tribes worshiped a *spirit power,* a mysterious, magic force in nature.

A doctrine of salvation. Among the major religions, Christianity, Islam, Buddhism, and Hinduism teach a doctrine of salvation. They stress that salvation is the highest goal of the faithful and one that all followers should try to achieve. Religions differ, however, in what salvation is and in how it can be gained.

A doctrine of salvation is based on the belief that individuals are in some danger from which they must be saved. The danger may be the threat of physical misfortune in this world, such as a disease. Christianity and several other major religions teach that the danger is spiritual, is centered in each person's soul, and pertains mainly to life after death. If a person is saved, the soul enters a state of eternal happiness, often called heaven. If the person is not saved, the soul may spend eternity in a state of punishment, which is often called hell.

Most religions teach that a person gains salvation by finding release from certain obstacles that block human fulfillment. In Christianity, the obstacles are sin and its effects. In most Asian religions, the obstacles are worldly desires and attachment to worldly things. Salvation in these religions depends on whether believers can free themselves from the obstacles with the aid of a savior. The savior may be the individual on whose teachings the religion is based, a god, or some other divine figure. People must accept the savior. They must also accept certain teachings, perform certain ceremonies, and abide by certain rules of moral conduct—all of which were inspired by the savior.

Some religions consider salvation to be a gift from the Deity or deities. For example, many Christian denominations believe that individuals are saved by the grace of God and not by their own merit.

Most religions teach that salvation comes only once and is eternal. According to Buddhism and Hinduism, the soul lives on after the death of the body and is reborn in another body. This cycle of rebirths is called *reincarnation.* The doctrine of *karma* is closely related to reincarnation. According to this doctrine, a person's actions, thoughts, and words determine the kind of animal or human body the soul will live in during the next reincarnation. The process of reincarnation continues until, through good deeds and moral conduct, a person finally achieves a state of spiritual perfection, which is salvation. Buddhists call this state *nirvana,* and Hindus call it *moksha.*

A code of conduct is a set of moral teachings and values that all religions have in some form. Such a code, or *ethic,* tells believers how to conduct their lives. It instructs them how to act toward the deity and toward one another. Religious codes of conduct differ in many ways, but most agree on several major themes. For example, they stress some form of the *golden rule,* which states that believers should treat others as they would like to be treated themselves. A religion's code of conduct also may determine such matters as whom believers may marry, what jobs they may hold, and what kinds of foods they may eat.

The use of sacred stories. For thousands of years, followers of religions have believed in sacred stories, called *myths.* Religious leaders often used these stories to dramatize the teachings of their faith.

Originally, people told myths to describe how the sacred powers directly influenced the world. As the stories developed, they showed how some feature or event in the world was indirectly caused by the sacred powers. Many stories described the creation of the world. Others told how the human race or a particular people began. Some of the stories tried to explain the cause of natural occurrences, such as thunderstorms or the changes in seasons.

Today, there are scientific explanations for many of the subjects dealt with in sacred stories. But some religious groups still insist that the stories are true in every

Hindus bathe in the Ganges River, *left,* to purify their bodies. Millions of Hindus make periodic pilgrimages to their holy city of Varanasi, India, to be purified in the sacred river.

detail. Other groups believe only in the message contained in the stories, not in the specific details. Still other religious groups regard sacred stories as symbolic expressions of the ideals and values of their faith.

Religious rituals include the acts and ceremonies by which believers appeal to and serve God, deities, or other sacred powers. Some rituals are performed by individuals alone, and others by groups of worshipers. Important rituals are performed according to a schedule and are repeated regularly. The performance of a ritual is often called a *service.*

The most common ritual is prayer. Through prayer, a believer or someone on behalf of believers addresses words and thoughts to an object of worship. Prayer includes requests, expressions of thanksgiving, confessions of sins, and praise. Most major religions have a daily schedule of prayer. Meditation, a spiritual exercise much like prayer, is important in Asian religions. Buddhist monks try to be masters of meditation.

Many religions have rituals intended to purify the body. For example, Hindus consider the waters of the Ganges River in India to be sacred. Every year, millions of Hindus purify their bodies by bathing in the river, especially at the holy city of Varanasi.

In some religions, *pilgrimages* are significant rituals. Pilgrimages are journeys to the sites of holy objects or to places credited with miraculous healing powers. Believers also make pilgrimages to sacred places, such as the birthplace or tomb of the founder of their faith. All devout Muslims hope to make a pilgrimage to Mecca, the birthplace of Muhammad.

Many rituals are scheduled at certain times of the day, week, or year. Various religions have services at sunrise, in the morning, at sunset, and in the evening. The different religions have special services to mark the beginning of a new year. Many religions celebrate springtime, harvesttime, and the new or full moon.

Many rituals commemorate events in the history of

Jews celebrate the Passover in memory of the ancient Israelites' escape from Egyptian slavery. The highlight of this annual festival is a ceremonial feast called the *Seder, left.*

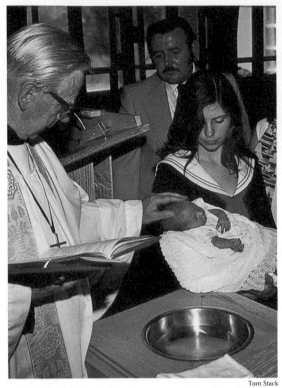

Tom Stack

The ceremony of baptism marks the entrance of a person into Christianity. The Lutheran minister shown above has baptized the baby by placing a small quantity of water on its head.

religions. For example, the Jewish festival of Passover recalls the meal the Israelites ate just before their departure from slavery in Egypt. Various Christian celebrations of Holy Communion are related to the last meal Jesus shared with His disciples before His death.

Rituals also mark important events in a person's life. Various ceremonies make sacred occasions of birth, marriage, and death. Rituals accept young people into the religion and into religious societies. In Judaism, the ritual of circumcision is performed on male infants. Some Christians baptize babies soon after birth. Other Christians baptize only youths or adults.

How the major religions are organized

The organization of the world's major religions ranges from simple to complex. Many religions have spiritual leaders, often called the *clergy*. These leaders have the authority and responsibility to conduct religious services, to advise or command believers, and to govern the religious organization at various levels. In some religions, the *laity*—that is, the believers who are not members of the clergy—also have important organizational roles.

In many countries, there is a *state* (official or favored) religion. For example, Islam is the state religion of Iran. Lutheranism is the state religion of Sweden, and Buddhism is the state religion of Thailand.

Judaism has no one person as its head. Each local congregation supervises its own affairs, usually under the leadership of a rabbi. Israel and a few other countries have chief rabbis. These rabbis are scholars who serve as the top judges of religious law.

Christian *denominations* (groups) are organized in various ways. In the Roman Catholic Church, believers are organized into districts called *parishes,* which belong to larger districts called *dioceses.* Dioceses, in turn, belong to *provinces.* The main diocese in each province is called an *archdiocese.* Pastors preside over parishes, bishops over dioceses, and archbishops over archdioceses. The pope presides over the entire Roman Catholic Church with the advice and assistance of high officials called *cardinals.* Some Protestant denominations are governed by similar patterns of *hierarchies* (levels of authority). Others are governed by boards of the clergy and laity or by local congregations.

Confucianism and Islam have no clergy. Leadership is provided by scholars who interpret the teachings of the faith. In Shinto and Taoism, the basic organizational unit is the priesthood. In Buddhism, the chief organizational unit is an order of monks called the *sangha.* The monks serve as advisers and teachers and play a vital part in everyday life in Buddhist countries. In some Buddhist countries, the head of state is also the leader of the national order of monks.

Hinduism has no consistent pattern of organization. There are no congregations or parishes. Hindus tend to worship individually or in families. Services in temples are performed by the Brahmans, members of the highest Hindu *castes* (social classes). In some regions, the Brahmans occasionally serve as a kind of royal priesthood.

The origin of religion

The earliest recorded evidence of religious activity dates from only about 60,000 B.C. However, anthropologists and historians of religion believe that some form of religion has been practiced since people first appeared on the earth about 2 million years ago.

Experts think prehistoric religions arose out of fear and wonder about natural events, such as the occurrence of storms and earthquakes and the birth of babies and animals. To explain why someone died, people

Religious beliefs of the world

Percentage of the world that follows each religious belief.

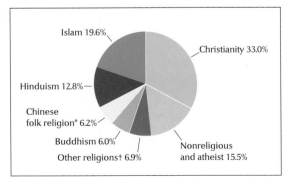

Islam 19.6%

Christianity 33.0%

Hinduism 12.8%

Chinese folk religion* 6.2%

Buddhism 6.0%

Other religions† 6.9%

Nonreligious and atheist 15.5%

*A system of beliefs that includes Confucianism and Taoism.
†Includes Judaism, Shinto, and other religions. Each of these religions is followed by less than one-half of one percent of the world's people.
Figures are for 1997.
Source: David B. Barrett, editor, *World Christian Encyclopedia.*

Drawing based on engravings on the wall of a cave
in southern France; Musée de l'Homme, Paris

Prehistoric people performed religious ceremonies to ensure a
sufficient food supply. The prehistoric artist who drew this scene
may have believed that it would bring success in hunting.

credited supernatural powers greater than themselves
or greater than the world around them.

Prehistoric people centered their religious activities
on the most important elements of their existence, such
as the prosperity of their tribe and getting enough food
to survive. They often placed food, ornaments, and tools
in graves. They believed that these items would be useful to or desired by dead people. Prehistoric people
drew pictures and performed dances that were intended to promote the fertility of women and animals and to
ensure good hunting. They also made sacrifices for the
same reasons.

Certain scholars have developed theories that attempt
to explain how religion began. No single theory has
been accepted by all scholars, but each major theory
has contributed to an understanding of the subject.
Leading theories were developed by Sir Edward Burnett
Tylor, Friedrich Max Müller, and Rudolf Otto.

Tylor's theory. Tylor was a British anthropologist of
the 1800's. According to Tylor's theory, early people believed that spirits dwelled in and controlled all things in
nature. For example, they thought that spirits lived in
such objects or forces as plants, the wind, volcanoes,
and the sun. Tylor called the spirits *animae,* and his theory became known as *animism.*

Prehistoric people, Tylor said, explained such occurrences as windstorms and the change from day to night
as the actions of the spirits. Because many of the objects
and forces were impressive or very powerful, people
started to worship their spirits. According to Tylor, religion originated in this worship.

Müller's theory. Müller, a German-born language
scholar of the 1800's, is often considered the first historian of religion. Müller agreed with Tylor that religion began as spirit worship. But he rejected Tylor's view that
the earliest people believed spirits dwelled in nature.
Instead, Müller suggested that prehistoric people
thought that the forces of nature themselves had human
qualities, such as good or bad temper. People thus
transformed these forces into deities. In this way,
Müller explained the earliest belief in gods.

Otto's theory. Otto was a German scholar of religion
of the early 1900's. Otto believed that an awareness of
holiness and mystery lies at the heart of religious experience and is therefore the basis for all religions. In his
view, all human beings possess the capacity for awe
and recognize the power of the sacred. For Otto, the
holy is the true, the good, and the beautiful, a representation of a basic and universal aspect of being human.

History of the world's major religions

The eight major religions practiced in the world today were either founded or developed their basic form
between about 600 B.C. and A.D. 600. The following discussion traces the history of each of these religions.

Judaism began among the ancient Israelites in the
Middle East. Jewish tradition traces the roots of the religion back to Abraham, who lived between about 1800
and 1500 B.C. His grandson Jacob, who was also called
Israel, had 12 sons. They founded the 12 tribes that became the Israelites.

Over a period of time, many Israelites settled in
Egypt, where they eventually became slaves. In the
1200's B.C., the great lawgiver Moses led them out of
Egypt to Canaan (Palestine). Jewish tradition also says
Moses received from God the first five books of the
Bible, which are called the Pentateuch or the Torah.
These books, sometimes known as the Mosaic Law,
have been the basis of the Jewish religion.

Judaism was the first religion to teach the belief in
one God. Some scholars say that the Jews became
monotheistic during the time of Moses. But most scholars believe that Jewish *prophets* (religious teachers and
thinkers) converted the Jews to monotheism by about
600 B.C.

Illustration (about 1300) by an unknown German artist from the Birds' Head Hag-
gadah; Collection of the Israel Museum, Jerusalem (photo © the Israel Museum)

The Ten Commandments contain the basic laws of Judaism
and Christianity. In this picture, the Jewish leader Moses gives
the commandments to the Jews, after getting them from God.

Giant Buddha in the Ling Yin Temple, Hang-chou, China; Artstreet

Buddha preached that people can gain *nirvana,* or salvation, by freeing themselves from worldly attachments and desires. Buddhism began in India and spread to China and other Asian lands.

During Biblical times, first the Assyrians, then the Babylonians, and finally the Romans conquered the Israelites. Many Jews were driven into exile. Over the centuries, the Jewish people settled in various parts of the Middle East and in European countries. Everywhere, they were always a religious minority, and they were often persecuted for their faith.

After about 1800, Jews divided into three general groups—Orthodox, Conservative, and Reform. Orthodox Jews observed rituals in traditional ways. Conservative and Reform Jews modernized certain practices. Most eastern European Jews followed Orthodox Judaism, and most western European and North American Jews followed Conservative or Reform Judaism.

In the 1930's, the German dictator Adolf Hitler and his Nazi Party began a vicious campaign against Jews. By 1945, the Nazis had killed about 6 million of the 8 million to 9 million Jews in Europe. Many of the survivors joined Jews living in Palestine. Together, they established the state of Israel in 1948 under the sponsorship of the United Nations (UN). It was the first homeland Jews had known since Biblical times.

Hinduism began about 1500 B.C. At that time, a central Asian people called the Aryans invaded and conquered India. The Aryan culture gradually combined with the culture of a native people known as the Dravidians. Hinduism developed from a blend of the two cultures.

The oldest Hindu scriptures are the Vedas. They were composed over a period of nearly 1,000 years, beginning about 1400 B.C. This stage in Hindu history is often called the Vedic period. During Vedic times, believers worshiped a number of nature deities. At the end of the period, the doctrines of reincarnation and karma were adopted.

By the 500's B.C., Hinduism was splitting into various schools of thought. Two of these schools—Buddhism and Jainism—became new religions. The Hindu schools

further split into smaller *sects.* Today, Hinduism includes a great number of schools and sects. Many of the sects were formed by saints or *gurus* (spiritual teachers). Each sect has its own philosophy and form of worship. But they all accept basic Hindu doctrines.

Buddhism developed in India during the late 500's B.C. from the teachings of a prince named Siddhartha Gautama. Gautama became known as Gautama *Buddha,* meaning *Enlightened One.* Buddhism was partly a rebellion against certain features of Hinduism. Buddhism opposed the Hindu worship of many deities, the Hindu emphasis on caste and the supernatural, and the power of the Hindu priest class.

Buddha taught that people should devote themselves to finding release from the suffering of life. Through this release, people would gain *nirvana,* a state of perfect peace and happiness. To achieve nirvana, they had to free themselves from all worldly desires and attachments to worldly things. Buddha taught that nirvana could be gained by following the *Middle Way* between the extremes of severe self-denial and uncontrolled passion. As Buddha preached, he attracted a growing number of followers. By the time of his death, about 483 B.C., Buddhism was firmly established in India.

Buddhism spread into central Asia. By the end of the A.D. 100's, it had been introduced into China. Buddhism swept through much of China from the 300's to the 500's, challenging the native Chinese religions of Confucianism and Taoism in popularity. In the 500's, Chinese Buddhism spread to Korea and Japan. Buddhism became the chief Japanese religion for the next 1,000 years.

Early in its history, Buddhism divided into two forms, Theravada and Mahayana. Today, Theravada Buddhism is strongest in Cambodia, Laos, Myanmar, Sri Lanka, and Thailand. Most Mahayana Buddhists live in Japan, Korea, Mongolia, Nepal, Tibet, Vietnam, and scattered parts of India and Russia.

Confucianism is a Chinese religion based on the teachings of Confucius, a philosopher who died about 479 B.C. Confucianism has no organization or clergy. It does not teach a belief in a deity or in the existence of life after death. Confucianism stresses moral and political ideas. It emphasizes respect for ancestors and government authority and teaches that rulers must govern according to high moral standards.

Confucianism, Buddhism, and Taoism have been the major religions in China. However, Confucianism has had the greatest impact on Chinese society. Confucianism was the state religion of China from the 100's B.C. until the A.D. 1900's. Chinese rulers approved of its emphasis on respect for authority and dedication to public service. Confucian scriptures called the Five Classics and Four Books served as the foundation of the Chinese educational system for centuries. Candidates applying for government jobs had to pass examinations based on these scriptures.

Beginning in the 1000's, a more philosophical approach to Confucianism known as Neo-Confucianism became widely popular. Neo-Confucianism also influenced Japanese moral codes and philosophy from the 1600's through the 1800's.

In 1949, the Chinese Communists gained control of China. The government officially condemned Confucianism, as well as other religions. As a result, most follow

Confucius' birthday is a holiday in Taiwan. The men in the temple shown at the left help perform special birthday ceremonies. Followers of Confucius placed the food offerings before the altar.

ers lived outside mainland China, especially in Taiwan. In the late 1970's, however, the Communist government relaxed its policy against religion, and so Confucianism has enjoyed a revival on the mainland.

Taoism, like Confucianism, is a native Chinese religion. Its roots go back to the earliest history of China. However, Taoism did not begin to develop as an organized religion until the 100's B.C.

Taoism teaches that everyone should try to achieve two goals, happiness and immortality. The religion has many practices and ceremonies intended to help people. They include prayer, magic, special diets, breath control, meditation, and recitation of scriptures. Taoists also believe in astrology, fortunetelling, witchcraft, and communication with the spirits of the dead.

Taoists worship more deities than do the followers of almost any other religion. Some deities are ancestors, and others are the spirits of famous people.

During its early history, Taoism borrowed heavily from Buddhism. Many Taoist deities, temples, and ceremonies show the influence of Buddhism. By the A.D. 1000's, Taoism had divided into many sects. The members of some of these sects withdrew from everyday life to meditate and study in monasteries. Other sects were based in temples. The temple priests passed their positions on to their children. The members of this hereditary priesthood lived among the common people. They gained a reputation as highly skilled magicians who could tell the future and protect believers from illness, accidents, and other misfortune.

Chinese governments of the early and mid-1900's opposed Taoism, claiming it was based on superstition. Today, the Chinese government permits the practice of the religion and followers are gradually increasing in number. In addition, Taoists remain active in Chinese societies outside China, especially in Taiwan.

Detail of a fresco (late 1200's or early 1300's) by an unknown Chinese artist; Royal Ontario Museum, Toronto

Taoist deities outnumber those of almost every other religion. They include the Jade Emperor, *center,* who rules the earth, and the Empress of Heaven, *left,* who rules heaven. The figure at the right is Laozi, an ancient Chinese philosopher who is considered a founder of Taoism.

A Shinto festival attracts thousands of believers to the Meiji shrine in Tokyo. Parents visit the shrine with their children to thank the gods for their children's good health. They also pray for good fortune for their children. The large wooden gate, or arch, called a *torii,* is the symbol of Shinto.

Milt and Joan Mann

Shinto is the native religion of Japan. According to Shinto mythology, deities created Japan and its people. Until the mid-1900's, the Japanese worshiped their emperor as a direct descendant of Amaterasu-Omikami, the sun goddess and most important Shinto deity.

Shinto developed from native folk beliefs. Followers worship spirits and demons that live in animals and in mountains, trees, and other parts of nature. In early Japanese history, Shinto was devoted chiefly to this form of nature worship. Beginning in the A.D. 500's, Buddhism influenced the development of Shinto. Confucianism became influential in the A.D. 600's. Both of these religions helped shape Shinto rituals and doctrines. Buddhist and Shinto services have occasionally been held in the same temples. But unlike Buddhism, Shinto never developed strong doctrines on either salvation or life after death.

During the late 1800's, the Japanese government sponsored a form of Shinto called State Shinto. State Shinto stressed patriotic religious ceremonies and the divine origins of the emperor. In 1882, the government officially separated Shinto into State Shinto and Sectarian Shinto. The government administered State Shinto. Sectarian Shinto was popular among the common people. After World War II, the government abolished State Shinto and the doctrine of a divine emperor.

Christianity is based on the life and teachings of Jesus Christ. Most Christians believe God sent Jesus to the world as the Savior. Christianity teaches that humanity can achieve salvation through Jesus.

After Jesus' Crucifixion, a number of His followers spread His teachings. One of the most important of these followers was Saint Paul. After Paul's death, about A.D. 67, Christianity continued to grow in spite of persecution by the Romans, whose empire covered most of Europe, the Middle East, and northern Africa. In the early 300's, the Roman emperor Constantine the Great became a Christian. By the late 300's, Christianity was widely practiced throughout the empire.

During the Middle Ages, Christian missionaries converted many European barbarian tribes, which led to the Christian church's dominant influence on European life for centuries. For many years, a split had been developing between Christians in western Europe and those in eastern Europe and western Asia. The split finally occurred in the 1000's. The churches in Greece, Russia, and other parts of eastern Europe and western Asia became known as the Eastern Orthodox Churches. The church in western Europe became known as the Roman Catholic Church.

In the 1500's, a religious movement called the Reformation divided western Christianity into several bodies. Most southern Europeans remained Roman Catholics. A great number of northern Europeans, known as Protestants, formed new churches. The largest included the Baptist, Congregationalist, Episcopal, Lutheran, Methodist, and Presbyterian churches.

Beginning in the 1500's, Catholic missionaries converted many people in Africa, Asia, and the Americas to Christianity. Protestant missionaries became active in the 1600's and made converts in the Far East, Africa, and North America.

Islam is based on the life and teachings of the prophet Muhammad, who lived in Arabia during the early A.D. 600's. Before Muhammad's time, the people in the region worshiped Allah (God) as well as other deities. But Muhammad said Allah was the only God.

According to Islamic tradition, Muhammad had the first of several visions about 610. The vision occurred while Muhammad was meditating in a cave on Mount Hira, a hill near his birthplace of Mecca. The vision commanded Muhammad to preach the message of Allah to the people of his country. He began preaching in Mecca. A tribe called the Quraysh controlled Mecca and opposed Muhammad. To avoid persecution by the Quraysh, Muhammad fled to the city of Medina. Muhammad's journey from Mecca to Medina is called the *Hegira* and is one of the central events in the founding of Islam.

In 630, Muhammad led an army to Mecca. He offered the people of the city generous peace terms. As a result, his forces were able to take the city with little resistance. He made Mecca the sacred city and center of Islam.

After Muhammad's death in 632, his friend and disciple Abu Bakr became the first *caliph* (leader) of Islam. Abu Bakr defeated a rebellion against his rule by Arabian tribes and began a campaign of religious conquest outside Arabia. Succeeding caliphs continued Abu Bakr's conquests. Within 100 years of Muhammad's death, Islam had spread throughout the Middle East, across northern Africa, and into Spain. In 732, Muslim and Christian armies fought a major battle near Tours, France. The Muslims were defeated, and western Europe remained Christian.

Muslim missionaries and traders carried Islam to India and other parts of Asia. From the 1000's to the 1200's, Islam spread into western Africa. Today, Islam is the major religion of nearly all countries in northern Africa and the Middle East. It is also the chief religion in Bangladesh, Indonesia, Malaysia, and Pakistan.

Religion today

Religion in the West was severely criticized in the 1900's. Numerous critics charged that many religious doctrines had become dry and uninspiring and no longer satisfied spiritual needs. Critics also claimed that traditional religions failed to deal with current social issues and that they supported outdated moral attitudes.

Some religious groups have tried to meet society's needs and problems. For example, most religions have traditionally prohibited the ordination of women as clergy and from other leadership positions. For many women, these limitations left their spiritual needs unfulfilled. Many Christian denominations and groups in Judaism now allow women roles equal to those of men.

Many people see the *ecumenical movement* in Christianity as a positive step toward bringing a spirit of cooperation and renewal to Western religion. The ecumenical movement seeks to unify Christians worldwide. It began in the early 1900's and was almost exclusively confined to Protestantism for many years. Many Protestant groups combined and formed new denominations. In the mid-1900's, the Roman Catholic Church began to take a more active part in the movement. A document issued by Vatican Council II (1962-1965), a meeting of Catholic leaders, endorsed the movement's goals. Leaders of the Eastern Orthodox Churches and the Roman Catholic Church also met during the mid-1900's to investigate ways to bring the denominations closer together.

Many people in the West have turned to new religions or movements, or to religions whose origins are in the East. A large number of people have sought fulfillment in the teachings of Asian religions. Some of these people have been attracted to Zen, a form of Buddhism that emphasizes meditation. Others follow the teachings of Hinduism. Islam has also gained many followers in the Western world.

Within Christianity, a movement called *charismatic Christianity* has attracted millions of followers. The movement began with the founding of Pentecostalism in the United States in 1901. Pentecostalism is a highly emotional form of religious worship and behavior that emphasizes praying. *Christian fundamentalism* is a conservative religious movement that has had great social and political influence in the United States. Christian fundamentalist leaders include such television evangelists as Jerry Falwell and Pat Robertson. Islam and Judaism

Elkoussy, Sygma

A Muslim reads the Quran in Mecca, the holiest city of Islam. The Islamic religion is based on the teachings of Muhammad, a prophet who preached during the A.D. 600's.

also have developed strong fundamentalist movements since the mid-1900's, both in the West and in the Middle East.

Some Westerners have turned to other kinds of beliefs or faiths. For example, some people have been attracted to the *occult*—mysterious forms of supernatural teachings, such as astrology and spiritualism. Astrology is based on the belief that the planets and other heavenly bodies influence human affairs. Spiritualists believe that it is possible to communicate with the spirits of the dead.   Walter Holden Capps

Related articles. See the *Religion* section of the articles on various countries, such as **Canada** (Religion); **Israel** (Religion). See also the following articles:

Christianity

See the following articles and their lists of *Related articles:*

Bible	Eastern Orthodox	Religious life
Cardinal	Churches	Roman Catholic
Christianity	Missionary	Church
Eastern Catholic	Pope	Saint
Churches	Protestantism	

Other religions

Bahá'ís	Islam	Shinto
Buddhism	Jainism	Sikhism
Confucianism	Judaism	Taoism
Hinduism	Rastafarians	Zoroastrianism

Founders of religions

Bahá'u'lláh	Confucius	Muhammad
Buddha	Jesus Christ	

Bob Fitch, Black Star

Charismatic Christianity became a flourishing movement in the 1900's. Followers of the movement emotionally declare their faith in Jesus during prayer meetings, such as the one shown here.

Deities

For lists of articles on deities of early religions, see the *Related articles* with **Mythology**. See also the following articles:

Allah	God	Mithra
Brahman	Jehovah	Shiva
Elohim	Krishna	Vishnu

Beliefs and doctrines

Agnosticism	Heaven	Polytheism
Ancestor worship	Hell	Predestination
Atheism	Immaculate Conception	Purgatory
Creationism	ception	Resurrection
Deism	Immortality	Spiritualism
Devil	Liberation theology	Theism
Ethics	gy	Theology
Faith healing	Messiah	Theosophy
Foreordination	Pantheism	Transfiguration
Free will	Philosophy (Philosophy and religion)	Transubstantiation
Gnosticism	ophy and religion)	Trinity
Golden rule	gion)	

Sacred writings

Bhagavad-Gita	Quran	Talmud
Bible	Ramayana	Vedas
Mahabharata		

Officials and organization

Abbot	Friar	Monk
Archbishop	High priest	Nun
Bishop	Levite	Patriarch
Cardinal	Magi	Pope
Deacon	Metropolitan	Priest
Dervish	Minister	Rabbi
Fakir	Missionary	Sanhedrin

Religious practices

Anointing of the sick	Drama (Religious plays)	Hymn
Baptism	plays)	Kosher
Bar mitzvah	Exorcism	Liturgy
Bat mitzvah	Fast	Marriage
Catechism	Feasts and festivals	Mass
Celibacy	Funeral customs	Prayer
Communion	Grace	Ramadan
Confirmation	Hajj	Sacrament
Coronation		

Ancient and traditional religions

Animal worship	Devil worship
Animism	Egypt, Ancient (Religion)
Assyria (Religion)	Fetish
Aztec (Religion)	Fire worship
Babylonia (Religion)	Greece, Ancient (Religion)

Inca (Religion)	Pacific Islands (Religions)
Indian, American (Religion)	Persia, Ancient (Religion)
Inuit (Religion)	Phoenicia (Religion)
Maya (Religion)	Rome, Ancient (Religion)
Mysteries	Sun worship
Mythology	Voodoo

Other related articles

Astrology	Idolatry
Church and state	Magic
Cult	Mysticism
Dance (Why people dance)	Occultism
Druses	Painting (pictures)
Education (Religion and early Western education)	Religious education
Western education)	Revivalism
Evolution (Acceptance of evolution; Evolution and religion)	School prayer
lution; Evolution and religion)	Scientology
gion)	Taboo
Freedom of religion	Theocracy
Heresy	Witchcraft (Witchcraft as a religion)
Hermit	ligion)

Outline

I. Chief characteristics of religion
 A. Belief in a deity
 B. A doctrine of salvation
 C. A code of conduct
 D. The use of sacred stories
 E. Religious rituals
II. How the major religions are organized
III. The origin of religion
 A. Tylor's theory   C. Otto's theory
 B. Müller's theory
IV.History of the world's major religions
 A. Judaism   E. Taoism
 B. Hinduism   F. Shinto
 C. Buddhism   G. Christianity
 D. Confucianism   H. Islam
V. Religion today

Questions

How long have people practiced some form of religion?
What is the Pentateuch? The Quran? The Five Classics and Four Books?
Who founded Buddhism? Islam?
What is *charismatic Christianity*?
What are the doctrines of *reincarnation* and *karma*?
What are some reasons people practice religion?
How do *monotheistic, polytheistic,* and *henotheistic* religions differ?
What is the theory of *animism*?
Who is the most important Shinto deity?
What is the most common religious ritual?

Additional resources

For additional resources on specific religions, see the lists that are at the end of such *World Book* articles as **Buddhism** and **Judaism**.

Level I

For books on religion for younger readers, see **Literature for children** (Information books/Religion).

Level II

Breuilly, Elizabeth, and others. *Religions of the World.* Facts on File, 1997.

Eliade, Mircea, ed. *The Encyclopedia of Religion.* 16 vols. Macmillan, 1987.

Ellwood, Robert S., Jr. *Many Peoples, Many Faiths.* 5th ed. Prentice Hall, 1995.

Green, William S., and Neusner, Jacob, eds. *The Religion Factor: An Introduction to How Religion Matters.* Westminster John Knox, 1996.

Hall, T. William, and others. *Religion.* Harper San Francisco, 1986.

Hinnells, John R., ed. *A New Handbook of Living Religions.* Rev. ed. Blackwell, 1997. Original title was *A Handbook of Living Religions.*

Paden, William E. *Religious Worlds: The Comparative Study of Religion.* 2nd ed. Beacon Pr., 1994.

Smart, Ninian. *The Religious Experience.* 5th ed. Macmillan Coll., 1995.

Smith, Jonathan Z., and others, eds. *The HarperCollins Dictionary of Religion.* Harper San Francisco, 1995.

Wilson, Colin. *The Atlas of Holy Places & Sacred Sites.* D K Pub., 1996.

Religion, Freedom of. See Freedom of religion.

Religious education involves instruction in the beliefs of a particular religion. This type of education is the work of organized religions, through their school and religious organizations. Religious education may also be defined as general education that follows religious instructions and ideals.

Public schools in the United States have sometimes offered religious instruction to students through various arrangements. But many people feel that such instruction violates the principle of the separation of church and state.

Various court decisions have affected religious education in the public schools. In the 1948 case of *Illinois ex rel. McCollum v. Board of Education,* the Supreme Court of the United States ruled that religious instruction could not be conducted within public school buildings. In the 1962 case of *Engel v. Vitale,* the court forbade public schools to require the recitation of prayers. A year later, in *School District of Abington Township, Pennsylvania v. Schempp,* the court banned school prayers and Bible readings even if they were voluntary (see **School prayer**).

All three of these Supreme Court rulings held that religious activities in public schools violate the First Amendment to the United States Constitution. This amendment guarantees freedom of religion and separation of church and state (see **Freedom of religion**). However, the Supreme Court said that public schools could teach about religion if they did so without favoring some beliefs over others. As a result, many schools in the United States introduced courses in *comparative religion,* the study of various faiths. Other courses dealt with the role of religion in history or with the Bible and other religious writings as literature.

Since the late 1940's, there has been new interest in religious education given during school hours in classes held outside the school. Churches or religious organizations pay the cost of such instruction, called *release-time* instruction. The school merely arranges for the time. Some communities release pupils from regular school hours so that they may attend such classes in the faith of their choice. These classes are taught by special teachers provided by the religious groups. These groups also provide the lesson materials. However, this practice is declining in popularity.

There are differences of opinion as to the merits of this system. Some parents say their children are embarrassed by it. If they belong to no particular church, they may not wish to attend these classes. In that case, their classmates may point to them as "different." Other parents feel it is not the function of the school to teach the doctrines of the church, or to provide the time for such instruction.

Private education. Many religious groups have their own educational buildings. Roman Catholic and some Protestant groups maintain grade schools, high schools, and colleges. Such schools offer both secular and religious courses. Some Jewish elementary schools, high schools, and colleges have been established. Jewish synagogues and temples offer instruction in religious subjects and Hebrew to children after school hours and on Sunday mornings. The various religious groups educate their own leaders for teaching their doctrines. See **Parochial school.**

The Roman Catholic Church conducts religion classes at least once a week for students attending non-Catholic schools. The classes present oral and written instruction in the doctrines of the Catholic faith. Many Protestant churches offer similar classes. Some of these classes, held in a series, are concluded by a ceremony called *confirmation.*

In Protestant churches, one of the chief methods for religious education is the Sunday school. The modern Sunday school uses specially prepared programs and lessons, such as the International Sunday School Lessons. These courses present graded lesson materials. Other material includes religious history and background, problems in living, and ideals as taught in the Bible and interpreted today. Some churches also sponsor *vacation Bible schools.* These schools offer religious education for one or more weeks during summer vacation.

Children who do not attend church seldom receive any formal religious education. However, their parents may educate them in their own religious beliefs and teach them from the Bible.

Career opportunities. The clergy and various religious orders offer the best opportunities for religious education. Churches may give training for students interested in this type of work. Most students attend college for a general background and continue specific study at a seminary. There, they study religion and related subjects, as well as educational techniques. With this training, they can preach, instruct, and counsel, as well as perform other duties that are connected with the field of religious education.

Persons serving in religious education may teach religion classes in colleges, lead educational programs for such organizations as the YMCA, or teach in missionary schools. Some churches have a director of religious education who is responsible for planning and directing the church's overall program of religious education. These officials usually work with the pastor of the church. They direct and supervise the Sunday school and other activities, such as adult classes, teacher training classes, club programs, family life education, and home Bible classes. Most people holding such positions have studied religious education. Some of them have attended a seminary and have graduated as ordained ministers.

Educators in religious education may also work with young people. The director of children's work handles the religious program of children up to the age of 12. A director of youth work plans and guides the study, worship, and recreation of junior and senior high-school students. Other religious education that is directly connected with the church includes supervising or teaching in weekday church schools and instructing Sunday school classes.

Religious education also includes such work as publishing, editing, or writing religious literature. Many churches and religious organizations sponsor regular publications. Some may be magazines or newspapers on a national level. Others may be intended for local or parish work. Some groups publish books and pamphlets for general use or for educational purposes. So-called "inspirational" novels may also form part of educational programs. Many newspapers and magazines publish articles and columns written by religious educators.   Kenneth O. Gangel

See also **Catechism.**

Religious festivals. For examples, see **Feasts and festivals** and its list of *Related articles.*

Religious freedom. See **Freedom of religion.**

Religious life is a term for a life bound by vows and may also include service to others. *Religious* is a name for monks and nuns dedicated to a life of prayer and for sisters, priests, and brothers actively engaged in teaching and nursing.

Most followers of the religious life are members of organizations called *orders.* The members follow a *rule* (program of life). The rule may require that they live cloistered lives of prayer. Such religious are known as *contemplative religious.* Some orders send members out to do pastoral, educational, missionary, medical, or social work. These people are called *active religious.* Other orders follow a "mixed life" that combines community prayer with external work.

Most members of orders live together in a community, or congregation, which trains them. After admission, an *aspirant* (candidate) serves as a *postulant* for several months. If members of the community approve, the individual is admitted as a *novice* for an additional year or more of training. *Profession,* the taking of vows, marks the entry of the new religious into full membership. Most orders have temporary profession for several years, followed by *life,* or *solemn,* final profession. After profession, some religious continue to live in a community. Others live alone or in small groups.

This article deals only with the religious life in Christianity. For information on religious life in other religions, see **Buddhism** (The sangha) and **Hinduism.**

Religious life in early Christianity. Some early Christian men and women chose to remain unmarried, or, if widowed, not to remarry, in order to serve God and their fellow Christians. In the late A.D. 200's, Christianity became socially acceptable in Roman society. At this time, many Christians chose to withdraw from their families to devote themselves to prayer and the recitation of Scripture. These people lived in seclusion in the deserts of Egypt, in the wilderness of Syria and Palestine, in city monasteries, or in the forests of Europe. Some lived as hermits and some lived in groups. Eventually, all came to be called monks or nuns.

In the early 300's, Saint Pachomius, a monk from Egypt, organized the first religious community in southern Egypt. He wrote a rule for monks who wished to live together under a superior. Later in the 300's, Saint Basil of Caesaria adopted the rule of Pachomius and made his monasteries in Asia Minor homes of charity. Today, Eastern Orthodox religious still look to the writings of Saint Pachomius and Saint Basil for inspiration.

In the mid-300's, Saint Athanasius introduced Eastern Christian monasticism to Western Christianity through his writings on the life of Saint Anthony of Thebes, a hermit. This model influenced the entire Christian community of Athanasius' time and today remains the classic model.

Religious life in the Middle Ages. In the 500's, Saint Benedict drew upon the writings of Saint Basil and of John Cassian, a monk, when he wrote the Benedictine rule. This document included instructions for the formation, government, and administration of a monastery and for the daily lives of its monks.

From the 300's to the 900's, the Benedictines provided missionaries to such remote areas as Germany and northern England. The Benedictine missionaries provided the liturgical and devotional standards of European Christendom. In many countries, they were the only people who could read and write, and so they became the record keepers in these societies.

In the late 1000's and early 1100's, several new orders were formed that placed more emphasis on solitude than had been customary in large Benedictine abbeys. These new orders included the Cistercians and the Carthusians. Men who followed the rule of Saint Augustine became prominent teachers at universities and cathedral schools throughout Europe.

During the 1200's, the growth of the cities produced often violent social change. Society became more divided between the poor and the wealthy. New orders of religious sprang up to take the Christian message to poor people and to heretics. Prominent orders that developed during this time were the Franciscans and the Dominicans.

The Franciscans were founded by Saint Francis of Assisi. Francis left a well-to-do merchant family to embrace a life of poverty. He attracted a group of followers, who eventually became the Franciscans. The Franciscans vowed poverty, chastity, and obedience. Their poverty originally forbade them from owning anything, either as individuals or as a group. The Dominicans were founded by Saint Dominic to preach doctrine to those who had fallen under the influence of heretical ideas. Both the Franciscan and the Dominican orders soon emphasized study in preparation for preaching. Many members of these orders became professors at universities across Europe.

Religious life in the 1500's and 1600's. During the Protestant Reformation of the 1500's, Protestant leaders did not encourage religious life under vows. Following the Reformation, several new Roman Catholic orders were founded with the goal of winning Protestants back to the church. The Jesuits, founded by Saint Ignatius Loyola, trained their men in theology and secular subjects. The Discalced Carmelites, founded in Spain by Saint Teresa of Avila, stimulated a widespread spiritual renaissance. Saint Angela Merici and her companions established a fellowship of teachers that later became the Ursuline order. In 1610, Saint Francis de Sales and Saint Jane Frances de Chantel founded the Visitation Nuns, an order of nuns devoted to visiting the sick in their homes. The Trappists, a strict branch of the Cistercians, were formed in 1664.

Religious life in the 1700's and 1800's. The Age of Reason and the French Revolution led to a period in which governments dissolved many orders (see **Age of Reason; French Revolution**). Some governments did tolerate those religious who cared for the sick or who taught. A revival of religious life began in the 1800's. The Jesuit order was restored in 1814, and both active and contemplative orders were reestablished throughout Europe.

By the mid-1800's, several Protestant denominations began to establish religious communities. Communities of deaconesses were organized in Germany to provide Lutheran and Calvinist women with support and discipline in their lives of service. In the Church of England, a group for men was founded in 1842, and another for women in 1845. These were the first such groups formed since the Church of England had closed all monasteries during the Reformation.

Religious life in the 1900's. From the early to the mid-1900's, several new Protestant communities formed throughout the world. Lutheran and Calvinist communities appeared in Germany, France, Africa, and the Scandinavian countries. In the 1940's, the Taizé community of men and the Grandchamp community for women were formed in France under Lutheran and Reformed sponsorship.

Vatican Council II (1962-1965) called on members of monastic and religious orders to rediscover the ideals of their founders. As a result, many active followers of the religious life have discontinued monastic customs that had been introduced into their societies. Monastic orders have, in turn, reexamined regulations that were not originally part of their religious tradition.

The Eastern Orthodox Churches regard monasticism as an essential feature of their tradition. All Eastern Christian religious look to Saint Basil as their spiritual guide, though they do not have a rule in the same sense as do Western monks and nuns. Several forms of monastic life have developed in Eastern Christianity. The *cenobitic* follows community life. The *idiorrhythmic* gives religious the freedom to choose their own life style. *Eremetical* religious live as hermits.

In the 1900's, a few active religious associations similar to Western orders began to appear in Eastern churches. The most famous monastic center in the Orthodox world is Mount Athos, a collection of about 20 monasteries of various nationalities located on a rocky peninsula in Greece. As Eastern Christians moved into Europe, North America, Australia, and New Zealand, they established monasteries in these areas.

E. Rozanne Elder

Related articles in *World Book* include:

Religious orders

Benedictines	Dominicans
Capuchins	Franciscans
Carmelites	Jesuits
Carthusians	Knights Hospitallers
Cistercians	Knights Templars

Some leading Christian religious orders

Popular name	Official name	Religion	Founder	Place founded	Date
Benedictines	Order of St. Benedict	Roman Catholic	St. Benedict	Italy	529?
Carmelites	Order of Our Lady of Mount Carmel	Roman Catholic	St. Berthold	Palestine	1100's
Christian Brothers	Brothers of the Christian Schools	Roman Catholic	St. Jean Baptiste de la Salle	France	1680
Cowley Fathers	Society of St. John the Evangelist	Anglican	R. M. Benson	England	1866
Dominicans	Order of Friars Preachers	Roman Catholic	St. Dominic	France	1216
Franciscans	Order of Friars Minor	Roman Catholic	St. Francis of Assisi	Italy	1209
Irish Christian Brothers	Brothers of the Christian Schools of Ireland	Roman Catholic	Edmund Ignatius Rice	Ireland	1802
Jesuits	Society of Jesus	Roman Catholic	St. Ignatius Loyola	France	1534
Monastic Brotherhood	None	Eastern Orthodox	Sts. Pachomius, Basil, Theodore, and Athanasius	Egypt, Asia Minor, and Greece	300's-1000's
Redemptorists	Congregation of the Most Holy Redeemer	Roman Catholic	St. Alphonsus Liguori	Italy	1732
Salesians	Society of St. Francis de Sales	Roman Catholic	St. John Bosco	Italy	1859
Sisters of Charity	Many branches	Roman Catholic	Sts. Vincent de Paul and Louise de Marillac	France	1633
Trappists	Order of Cistercians of the Strict Observance	Roman Catholic	St. Robert of Molesme	France	1664
Wantage Community	Community of St. Mary the Virgin	Anglican	William J. Butler	England	1848

Little Sisters of the Poor
Paulists

Saint Lazarus, Order of
Trappists

Other related articles

Abbot
Anthony of Thebes, Saint
Asceticism
Benedict of Nursia, Saint
Celibacy
Convent

Friar
Hermit
Monasticism
Monk
Nun

Religious Society of Friends. See Quakers.

Religious tolerance. See Freedom of religion.

Remarque, *rih MAHRK,* **Erich Maria** (1898-1970), a German-American author, wrote realistic, suspenseful novels about the horrors and effects of war. His *All Quiet on the Western Front* (1929) is among the most famous of all war stories. This story relates the shattering experiences of a group of German soldiers in World War I (1914-1918).

Remarque followed this success with *The Road Back* (1931) and *Three Comrades* (1937), stories of the confusion in postwar German society and the hardships faced by combat veterans. He continued the war theme in *Arch of Triumph* (1946), a novel about a German doctor who fled to Paris to escape the Nazis at the beginning of World War II. *Spark of Life* (1952) is a story of human suffering and courage in a Nazi concentration camp. *The Night in Lisbon* (1964) also describes human suffering during World War II (1939-1945).

Remarque was born in Osnabrück, Germany. He fought in World War I, and was wounded several times. In 1933, the Nazis publicly burned his books because of their antigovernment and antimilitarist themes. The Nazis took away his citizenship in 1938. Remarque lived in Switzerland from 1931 to 1939. Remarque moved to the United States in 1939, but often returned to Switzerland. He became a United States citizen in 1947.

Werner Hoffmeister

Rembrandt, *REHM brant* (1606-1669), was the Netherlands' greatest artist. Rembrandt's output of works of art was tremendous. Some scholars credit him with about 600 paintings, 300 etchings, and 1,400 drawings, though several of his paintings are now attributed to his students. Many other works have been lost. Unlike some other great artists, Rembrandt wrote almost nothing about his art.

The range of Rembrandt's subjects is extraordinary. His works depict stories inspired by the Bible, history, and mythology. He also painted portraits, landscapes, nudes, and scenes of everyday life. Throughout his career, Rembrandt also made about 100 known self-portraits, in which he portrayed himself in various roles and contexts.

Rembrandt's reputation rests on his power as a storyteller, his warm sympathy, and his ability to show the innermost feelings of the people he portrayed. His use of light and shadow and warm colors creates an atmosphere that enables us to share his profound understanding of the individual's inner life. Few artists match his genius for showing the human aspect of Biblical characters, which he conveys through moving facial expressions and gestures.

Early years. Rembrandt was born in Leiden on July 15, 1606. His full name was Rembrandt Harmenszoon van Rijn. Rembrandt first studied art with an obscure

National Gallery of Art, Washington, D.C., Widener Collection

The Descent from the Cross shows how Rembrandt used strong contrasts in light and shadow for dramatic effect. The painting also reveals the artist's genius for portraying people from the Bible in a powerful yet human manner.

Leiden painter from about 1621 to 1624. Then he studied with the Dutch artist Pieter Lastman in Amsterdam. About 1625, Rembrandt returned to Leiden to paint on his own.

Leiden years: 1625-1631. Most of Rembrandt's early works are small, precisely finished pictures of Biblical and historical subjects. The influence of Lastman can be seen in the lively gestures and expressions of his figures and in his vivid colors and glossy paint. It can also be seen in his often crowded compositions and in his frequent use of less well known Biblical or historical sub-

Maurithaus Museum, The Hague, Netherlands;
© The Frick Collection, New York City

Rembrandt's self-portraits form a vivid record of his life. The portrait at the left was completed in 1629. The portrait at the right was finished in 1658, after he declared bankruptcy.

jects. However, Rembrandt rapidly surpassed his teacher's ability to tell a story. He used light and shadow to heighten the drama of his works.

Rembrandt quickly achieved local success. He began to teach in 1628, and his strong personality continued to attract students and followers throughout his career.

Early Amsterdam years: 1632-1640. About 1632, Rembrandt moved to Amsterdam, where he painted portraits of wealthy middle-class patrons. He remained there for the rest of his life, except for a few short trips within the Netherlands. In 1634, he married Saskia van Uylenburgh. They had four children, but only one, Titus (1641-1668), survived infancy.

In 1632, Rembrandt painted the *Anatomy Lesson of Professor Tulp.* The painting was a group portrait of eight men that showed a sense of integrated activity at the same time he portrayed each person as an individual. The painting immediately established Rembrandt's reputation as the most fashionable portrait painter in Amsterdam. See **World, History of the** (picture: The study of the body). Rembrandt became wealthy and eagerly collected works of art. In 1639, he bought a large, heavily mortgaged house.

Rembrandt's paintings *Blinding of Samson, Danae,* and *Rape of Ganymede* show the exciting subjects he favored during these years. They, like most of his other works during this period, emphasize dramatic movement, emphatic gestures, sharp contrasts of light and shadow, and striking color accents.

The last years: 1640-1669. Rembrandt's most famous picture, *The Night Watch,* was painted in 1642. The painting represents a civic militia group of Amsterdam preparing to march. Such guards had only a social function in the 1600's, but Rembrandt brilliantly captured a sense of their original active and heroic role from an earlier time. Rembrandt received a high price for *The Night Watch,* and he continued to receive important public and private commissions during the last years of his life.

However, tragedy did strike Rembrandt in 1642 when his beloved wife, Saskia, died. Also, the mature Rembrandt did not enjoy the wide popularity he had as a young painter. Although he still ranked as one of his country's leading artists, he ran short of money. The house he purchased in 1639 was too expensive. Rembrandt also collected works of art on a scale he could not afford. Most important, he began to paint more and more for himself. His late majestic Biblical paintings were not commissioned works. An example of these works, *Jacob Blessing the Sons of Joseph,* was painted in 1656.

During this period, Rembrandt's art gained steadily in spiritual depth and pictorial richness. His wonderful light now seemed to glow from within his works. The shadows became more intense and vibrant. Rembrandt reduced his palette to warm colors, such as browns, reds, and oranges, and applied paint thickly to create texture. In place of earlier sensational effects, his work shows solemn restraint, calmness, and tenderness. When humanity is represented, the thoughtful rather than active side of human nature is stressed. A detail of *The Return of the Prodigal Son,* an example from this period, is reproduced in the **Painting** article.

Rembrandt was forced to declare bankruptcy in 1656.

The British Museum, London, England

Rembrandt's etching *The Ratkiller* was completed in 1632, the year he established his reputation as a leading artist in the Netherlands. The etching shows Rembrandt's ability to portray common people and scenes from everyday life dramatically.

His house and possessions were sold at auction in 1657 and 1658. But when he died on Oct. 4, 1669, he left his surviving relatives a fairly large inheritance.

For other examples of Rembrandt's paintings, see the pictures with the articles **Aristotle** and **Jesus Christ.**

Linda Stone-Ferrier

See also **Painting** (The 1600's and 1700's).

Additional resources

Schwartz, Gary. *Rembrandt.* Abrams, 1992.
Silver, Larry. *Rembrandt.* Rizzoli, 1992.
Tümpel, Christian. *Rembrandt.* Rev. ed. Fonds Mercator, 1993.
White, Christopher. *Rembrandt.* Thames & Hudson, 1984.

Remembrance Day is a holiday that honors the memory of the men and women who died in World Wars I and II and later conflicts. It is observed in a number of countries on November 11 each year. The countries include Canada, Australia, and New Zealand. In the United Kingdom, the holiday is observed on the Sunday nearest November 11. The red poppy serves as the symbol of Remembrance Day.

Remington, Frederic (1861-1909), was an American artist best known for his action-filled paintings, drawings, and sculptures of cowboys and Indians. His works became famous for capturing the vitality and spirit of the West.

Remington was born in Canton, New York. He loved horses and outdoor life as a child and often sketched Western characters and dramatic battle scenes. He studied art at Yale University from 1878 to 1880. His first published drawing appeared in the campus paper.

In 1881, Remington traveled to Montana on the first of many Western trips. He decided in 1885 to become an artist and to devote his art to portraying the rapidly van-

Bronze sculpture (1895); Frederic Remington Art Museum, Ogdensburg, N.Y.

The *Bronco Buster* by Frederic Remington shows the action-filled style he used in his sculptures of life in the Old West.

ishing soldiers, cowboys, Indians, and open lands of the West. He lived in the East, but traveled throughout the West to gather material for his pictures.

Remington's early works were precisely drawn and full of detail. His illustrations for Henry Wadsworth Longfellow's poem *The Song of Hiawatha* (1891) show his technique of this period. Remington later painted with less detail, but he expressed more moods and emotions. He used broader brushstrokes and became more concerned with color and the effects of light. *Downing the Nigh Leader* (1907) illustrates his late dramatic style. It appears in **Western frontier life in America.** He also gained praise for his quietly romantic night scenes. In his sculptures, Remington made dynamically balanced figures, as in *Bronco Buster* (1905).

Remington illustrated many of his own books, including *Pony Tracks* (1895) and *The Way of an Indian* (1906). Many of his works are in the Remington Art Memorial in Ogdensburg, N.Y., and the Whitney Gallery of Western Art in Cody, Wyo.   Sarah E. Boehme

For other examples of Remington's paintings, see the pictures with the articles on **Cavalry** and **Pony express.** An example of his sculptures appears in **Sculpture** (American sculpture).

Additional resources

Manley, Atwood. *Frederic Remington and the North Country.* Dutton, 1988.
Samuels, Peggy and Harold. *Frederic Remington.* Doubleday, 1982. *Remington: The Complete Prints.* Crown, 1990.
Shapiro, Michael E., and Hassrick, P. H. *Frederic Remington: The Masterworks.* Abrams, 1988.

Remora, *REHM uhr uh,* is a fish with a sucker at the top of its head that it uses to attach itself to larger marine animals. Remoras live in warm to tropical seas. They measure about 7 inches (17 centimeters) to $3\frac{1}{2}$ feet (110 centimeters) long.

The remora's sucker is a modified *dorsal fin* (back fin) that resembles the sole of a rubber boot. Slatlike structures on the sucker open and close to create powerful suction. Remoras attach themselves to a variety of animals, which are called the *hosts.* These animals include sharks, rays, and other large fish; sea turtles; and whales. Certain types of remoras are found almost exclusively on specific host animals. For example, a species of remora called the *whalesucker* attaches itself only to whales. A remora receives a "free ride" from its host and also may eat scraps of food left by this animal. In turn, the remora rids its host of external parasites. Some remoras attach to the hulls of ships or other floating objects.

Scientific classification. Remoras belong to the remora family, Echeneidae. The scientific name for the whalesucker is *Remora australis.*   Samuel H. Gruber

See also **Fish** (picture: Three remoras).

Remote control is the control of a system from a distance. The system may range from a television set to a guided missile or satellite, and the distance may be a few feet or thousands of miles. Remote control improves the ease and efficiency of operating various mechanisms. It also helps perform certain tasks that otherwise would be too difficult or dangerous.

Remote control requires a device called a *command unit,* by which the human operator sends signals that control the system. As the system performs, the operator checks it and may send additional signals to keep it working correctly. In simple remote control systems, the operator can check the performance of the system merely by observing it. Complex systems may include instruments that provide information on performance.

Kinds of remote control can be grouped according to the way the command unit sends signals to the system. Some command units send signals by radio waves. Others use infrared light beams, ultrasonic waves, a device called a *laser,* electric wires, the human voice, or even mechanical hands.

Radio remote control has many uses. For example, it is used to fly some model airplanes. A command unit transmits a radio signals to a radio receiver in the plane. The receiver decodes the signals and gives the information to electric motors that control the plane's movements. Model cars and other model toys are operated in the same way. Some radio control systems work with the aid of a computer. These radio control systems help operate automated machines, guided missiles, and many other mechanisms. Controllers on the ground use radio signals to position antennas and operate other equipment on artificial satellites in earth orbit. See **Airplane, Model** (Radio control models).

Infrared remote control is used to operate such devices as TV sets and videocassette recorders (VCR's). A device called a *photodetector* receives the beam of infrared rays from the command unit. The photodetector converts the rays into electronic signals, which control the on-off switch, channel selector, and volume.

Ultrasonic remote control is used to operate such devices as telephone answering machines and some TV sets. Microphones in these devices convert the waves into electronic signals that go to electric switches. The switches control the operation of the devices.

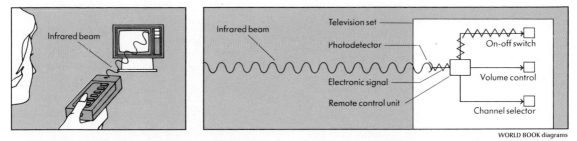

WORLD BOOK diagrams

A remote control television set has a device that sends a beam of infrared rays to the set, *above left*. A photodetector converts the rays to an electronic signal and sends it to a remote control unit, *above right*. This unit controls the on-off switch, volume, and channel selector.

Laser remote control may be used to steer guided missiles. Guidance signals are transmitted from a laser to a missile along a beam of light that tracks the missile during flight. See **Laser**.

Electrical remote control may be used to pay bills or transfer money from one account to another. The electric signals travel by telephone line from a home computer to a bank or other firm. Automated teller machines also send electric signals to banks over telephone lines.

Human voice control is used to operate light switches and other devices. A microphone in the remote control unit detects a loud voice or a hand clap and converts the sound into signals that go to the light switch.

Mechanical remote control provides a safe method of handling radioactive materials and other dangerous substances. A technician uses a pair of mechanical hands to work with the hazardous material while viewing it from behind a thick protective screen.

History. The first machines operated by remote control were radio-controlled motorboats. They were developed by the German Navy to ram enemy ships during World War I (1914-1918). Radio-controlled bombs and other remote control weapons were developed during World War II (1939-1945). After the war, United States scientists began to experiment with nonmilitary uses of remote control. Manufacturers introduced automatic garage door openers in the late 1940's, and remote control TV became available in the mid-1950's.

Today, robots operated by remote control are used to perform tasks in dangerous areas. For example, such robots performed much of the cleanup of the Three Mile Island nuclear power plant near Harrisburg, Pa., after an accident in 1979 released radioactive materials.

Joseph F. Kasper, Jr.

See also **Automation; Guided missile.**

Remote sensing is a technique used to gather information about an object without actually touching it. We practice remote sensing with our eyes, ears, and even our skin. These *sensors* obtain information about the size, color, location, and temperature of objects.

Television also is a form of remote sensing. A TV camera acts as a sensor when it picks up an image and transmits it to a studio. The image is then relayed by cable, broadcasting station, or satellite into viewers' homes. Sensors similar to TV cameras are flown in aircraft and satellites. They relay images of the earth to stations on the ground. Cloud maps used on TV weather forecasts are created from images relayed by satellites

about 22,300 miles (35,900 kilometers) above the earth.

Some sensors detect invisible forms of energy, especially *infrared rays* (heat rays) that the earth sends out. A computer converts the data into images for study on TV screens or in photographs. The colors created by computer are called *false colors* because they do not correspond to the colors we normally see. Radar is a sensor that uses radio waves to make images of the planets (see **Radar**). Sonar uses sound waves to map the ocean floor and search for sunken ships (see **Sonar**).

Remote sensing is useful for obtaining information about the earth. Images from satellites are used for estimating crop yields and searching for mineral and petroleum deposits. Remote sensing also helps scientists understand how human activity affects the environment. For example, sensors monitor the health of forests threatened by pollution, map the destruction of tropical rain forests, and measure the warming of the earth's atmosphere known as the *greenhouse effect* (see **Greenhouse effect**). We can even learn about past environments. Imaging radar has mapped stream channels under the Sahara in southern Egypt, showing that this desert once had a wetter climate.   Alexander F. H. Goetz

Remus. See **Romulus and Remus.**

NASA

Remote sensing can provide information about the earth's environment. This aerial view from a satellite reveals the extent of a flood in Australia. Water and wet land appear blue or black, vegetation is red, and dry land ranges from brown to white.

Detail of *Family and Court of Ludovico Gonzaga II* (1474), a fresco by Andrea Mantegna; Ducal Palace, Mantua (SCALA/Art Resource)

The ruling families of the Italian city-states strongly supported the Renaissance. Like the Gonzaga family of Mantua, *above,* they employed many leading artists and scholars at their courts.

Renaissance

Renaissance, *REHN uh sahns*, was a great cultural movement that began in Italy during the early 1300's. It spread to England, France, Germany, the Netherlands, Spain, and other countries in the late 1400's and ended about 1600.

The word *Renaissance* comes from the Latin word *rinascere* and refers to the act of being reborn. During the Renaissance, many European scholars and artists, especially in Italy, studied the learning and art of ancient Greece and Rome. They wanted to recapture the spirit of the Greek and Roman cultures in their own artistic, literary, and philosophic works. The cultures of ancient Greece and Rome are often called *classical antiquity*. The Renaissance thus represented a rebirth of these cultures and is therefore also known as the *revival of antiquity* or the *revival of learning*.

The Renaissance overlapped the end of a period in European history called the Middle Ages, which began in the 400's. The leaders of the Renaissance rejected many of the attitudes and ideas of the Middle Ages. For example, European thinkers in medieval times believed that people's chief responsibility was to pray to God and concentrate on saving their souls. They thought that so-

Painted terra-cotta statue (about 1485) by Andrea del Verrocchio; National Gallery of Art, Washington, D.C., Samuel H. Kress collection, 1939

Lorenzo de' Medici was the political and cultural leader of Florence when the city was the center of the Italian Renaissance in the 1400's. Lorenzo was called "the Magnificent" because of his achievements as a ruler, supporter of the arts, and author.

Anthony Molho, the contributor of this article, is Professor of History at Brown University.

ciety was filled with evil temptations. Renaissance thinkers, on the other hand, emphasized people's responsibilities and duties to the society in which they lived. They believed that society could civilize people rather than make them wicked.

During the Middle Ages, the most important branch of learning was *theology* (the study of God). However, many Renaissance thinkers paid greater attention to the study of humanity. They examined the great accomplishments of different cultures, particularly those of ancient Greece and Rome.

Medieval artists painted human figures that looked stiff and unrealistic and which often served symbolic religious purposes. But Renaissance artists stressed the beauty of the human body. They tried to capture the dignity and majesty of human beings in lifelike paintings and sculptures.

The changes brought about by the Renaissance happened gradually and did not immediately affect most Europeans. Even at the height of the movement, which occurred during the late 1400's and early 1500's, the new ideas were accepted by relatively few people. But the influence of the Renaissance on future generations was to prove immense in many fields—from art and literature to education, political science, and history. For centuries, most scholars have agreed that the modern era of human history began with the Renaissance.

The Italian Renaissance

Political background. Italy was not a unified country until the 1860's. At the beginning of the Renaissance, it consisted of about 250 separate states, most of which were ruled by a city. Some cities had only 5,000 to 10,000 people. Others were among the largest cities in Europe. For example, Florence, Milan, and Venice had at least 100,000 people each in the early 1300's.

At the dawn of the Renaissance, much of Italy was supposedly controlled by the Holy Roman Empire. However, the emperors lived in Germany and had little power over their Italian lands. The popes ruled central Italy, including the city of Rome, but were unable to extend political control to the rest of Italy. No central authority was thus established in Italy to unify all the states.

During the mid-1300's and early 1400's, a number of major Italian cities came under the control of one family. For example, the Visconti family governed Milan from the early 1300's until 1447, when the last male member died. Soon after, the Sforza family took control of Milan and governed the city until the late 1400's. Other ruling families in Italy included the Este family in Ferrara, the Gonzaga family in Mantua, and the Montefeltro family in Urbino.

The form of government established by the ruling families of the Italian cities was called the *signoria*, and the chief official was known as the *signore*. All power was concentrated in the signore and his friends and relatives. An elaborate court slowly grew up around each signorial government. At the court, the area's leading artists, intellectuals, and politicians gathered under the sponsorship of the signore.

Other Italian cities had a form of government known as *republicanism*. In republican cities, a ruling class controlled the government. Members of the ruling class considered themselves superior to the other residents

of the city. The most important examples of republican government were in Florence and Venice.

In the republican government of Florence, about 800 of the city's wealthiest families made up the ruling class. The members of these Florentine families intermarried and lived in large, beautiful palaces built by Renaissance architects. They paid for the construction of great religious and civic buildings and impressive monuments throughout Florence. They also supported artists and intellectuals. In addition, the ruling class encouraged the study of ancient Greek and Roman authors in the desire to have their society resemble the cultures of classical antiquity.

By the 1430's, the Medici family dominated the ruling class of Florence. The family controlled the largest bank in Europe and was headed by a series of talented and ambitious men. Under Medici domination, the government of Florence resembled a signorial government.

About 180 families controlled the republican government of Venice. All government leaders came from these families. A law passed in 1297 restricted membership in the Great Council, the principal governing body, to descendants of families that had already sat in the council. Like Florence, Venice became a leading center of Renaissance art under the support of the ruling class.

Humanism was the most significant intellectual movement of the Renaissance. It blended concern for the history and actions of human beings with religious concerns. The humanists were scholars and artists who studied subjects that they believed would help them better understand the problems of humanity. These subjects included literature and philosophy. The humanists shared the view that the civilizations of ancient Greece and Rome had excelled in such subjects and thus could serve as models. They believed that people should un-

WORLD BOOK map

Renaissance Italy consisted of about 250 states, most of which were ruled by a city. The Renaissance began during the 1300's in the *city-states* of northern Italy. Early centers of the Renaissance included the cities of Florence, Milan, and Venice.

derstand and appreciate classical antiquity to learn how to conduct their lives.

To understand the customs, laws, and ideas of ancient Greece and Rome, the humanists had first to master the languages of classical antiquity. The Greeks had used a language foreign to Italians, and the Romans had used a form of Latin far different from that used in the 1300's and 1400's. To learn ancient Greek and Latin, the humanists studied *philology* (the science of the meaning and history of words). Philology became one of the two principal concerns of the humanists. The other was history, which the humanists saw as the study of great actions taken by courageous, noble, or wise men of classical antiquity.

The interest of the humanists in ancient Greece and Rome led them to search for manuscripts, statues, coins, and other surviving examples of classical civilization. For example, they combed monastery libraries throughout Europe, locating on dusty shelves long neglected manuscripts by classical authors. The humanists carefully studied these manuscripts, prepared critical editions of them, and often translated them.

Petrarch and Giovanni Boccaccio were the first Renaissance humanists. During the mid-1300's, the two friends recovered many important but long ignored ancient manuscripts. Petrarch discovered the most influential of these works. It was *Letters to Atticus*, a collection of letters on Roman political life by the statesman and orator Marcus Tullius Cicero.

As Petrarch and Boccaccio studied the rediscovered classical writings, they tried to imitate the styles of the ancient authors. They urged that people express themselves accurately and elegantly, characteristics they saw in classical literary style. Petrarch said, "The style is the man." He meant that careless expression reflected careless thought.

Petrarch became known for his poetry, and Boccaccio for his collection of stories called the *Decameron* (about 1349-1353). In their works, they tried to describe human feelings and situations that people could easily understand. Petrarch and Boccaccio insisted that the duty of intellectuals was to concentrate on human problems, which they believed were more important than an understanding of the mysteries of nature or of God's will. They thought that people could learn how to deal with their problems by studying the lives of individuals of the past.

The ideal courtier. Some Italian humanists spent most of their time in signorial courts. During the late 1400's, these humanists began to develop ideas about the proper conduct of *courtiers*—the noblemen and noblewomen who lived in a royal court. About 1518, an author and diplomat named Baldassare Castiglione completed *The Book of the Courtier*. Castiglione based the work on his experiences at the court of Urbino. It was translated into several European languages and influenced the conduct of courtiers throughout Europe. *The Courtier* also strongly influenced educational theory in England during the Renaissance.

Castiglione wrote that the ideal male courtier is re-

Detail of *The Madonna Enthroned with Angels* (about 1285), an oil painting on wood panel by Cimabue; Uffizi Palace, Florence, Italy (SCALA/Art Resource)

Detail of *The Small Cowper Madonna* (1505), an oil painting on wood panel by Raphael; National Gallery of Art, Washington, D.C., Widener collection, 1942

Medieval and Renaissance art differed in the portrayal of the human figure. The medieval painting at the left has unlifelike figures that represent religious ideas, not flesh-and-blood people. The Renaissance painting at the right shows realistic figures in a natural setting.

fined in writing and speaking and skilled in the arts, sports, and the use of weapons. He willingly devotes himself to his signore, always seeking to please him. The courtier is polite and attentive to women. Whatever he does is achieved with an easy, natural style, which reflects his command of every situation. An ideal court woman knows literature and art and how to entertain the court. She exhibits the highest moral character and acts in a feminine manner.

The fine arts. During the Middle Ages, painters and sculptors tried to give their works a spiritual quality. They wanted viewers to concentrate on the deep religious meaning of their paintings and sculptures. They were not concerned with making their subjects appear natural or lifelike. But Renaissance painters and sculptors, like Renaissance writers, wanted to portray people

Bronze statue (1430's); Bargello, Florence, Italy (SCALA/Art Resource)

Donatello's *David* was the first large free-standing nude since classical antiquity. The sculptor's emphasis on the subject's physical beauty greatly influenced other Renaissance artists.

SCALA/Art Resource

The Pazzi Chapel in Florence, Italy, was one of the first buildings designed in the Renaissance style. The chapel was begun in 1429 and completed in 1461. The architect, Filippo Brunelleschi, incorporated arches, columns, and other elements of classical architecture into his design. Both the exterior, *above,* and the interior, *right,* have been praised for the beauty and harmony of their proportions.

SCALA/Art Resource

and nature realistically. Architects of the Middle Ages designed huge cathedrals to emphasize the majesty and grandeur of God. Renaissance architects designed buildings on a smaller scale to help make people aware of their own powers and dignity.

Arts of the 1300's and early 1400's. During the early 1300's, the Florentine painter Giotto became the first artist to portray nature realistically. He produced magnificent *frescoes* (paintings on damp plaster) for churches in Florence, Padua, and Assisi. Giotto attempted to create lifelike figures showing real emotions. He portrayed many of his figures in realistic settings.

A remarkable group of Florentine architects, painters, and sculptors worked during the early 1400's. They included the architect Filippo Brunelleschi, the painter Masaccio, and the sculptor Donatello.

Brunelleschi was the first Renaissance architect to revive the ancient Roman style of architecture. He incorporated arches, columns, and other elements of classical architecture into his designs. One of his best-known buildings is the beautifully and harmoniously proportioned Pazzi Chapel in Florence. The chapel, begun in 1429, was one of the first buildings designed in the new Renaissance style. Brunelleschi also was the first Renaissance artist to use *linear perspective*, a mathematical

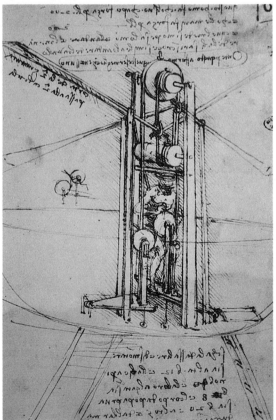

Pen-and-ink drawing (about 1488); Bibliothèque Nationale, Paris (Art Resource)

The drawings of Leonardo da Vinci reveal the inquiring mind of perhaps the greatest intellect of the Renaissance. Leonardo was fascinated by the possibility of human flight. He designed a flying machine that used revolving paddles, *above*.

system in which painters could show space and depth on a flat surface.

Masaccio's finest work was a series of frescoes he painted about 1427 in the Brancacci Chapel of the Church of Santa Maria del Carmine in Florence. The frescoes realistically show Biblical scenes of emotional intensity. Masaccio created the illusion of space and depth in these paintings by using Brunelleschi's mathematical calculations.

In his sculptures, Donatello tried to portray the dignity of the human body in realistic and often dramatic detail. His masterpieces include three statues of the Biblical hero David. In a version completed in the 1430's, Donatello portrayed David as a graceful, nude youth, moments after he slew the giant Goliath. The work, which is about 5 feet (1.5 meters) tall, was the first large free-standing nude created in Western art since classical antiquity.

Arts of the late 1400's and early 1500's were dominated by three men. They were Michelangelo, Raphael, and Leonardo da Vinci.

Michelangelo excelled as a painter, architect, and poet. In addition, he has been called the greatest sculptor in history. Michelangelo was a master of portraying the human figure. For example, his famous statue of the Israelite leader Moses (1516) gives an overwhelming impression of physical strength and spiritual power. These qualities also appear in the frescoes of Biblical and classical subjects that Michelangelo painted on the ceiling of the Sistine Chapel in the Vatican. The frescoes were painted from 1508 to 1512 and rank among the greatest achievements of Renaissance art.

Raphael's paintings are softer in outline and more poetic than those of Michelangelo. Raphael was skilled in creating perspective and in the delicate use of color. He painted a number of beautiful pictures of the Madonna (Virgin Mary) and many outstanding portraits. One of his greatest works is the fresco *School of Athens* (1511). The painting was influenced by classical Greek and Roman models. It portrays the great philosophers and scientists of ancient Greece in a setting of classical arches. Raphael was thus making a connection between the culture of classical antiquity and the Italian culture of his time.

Leonardo da Vinci painted two of the most famous works of Renaissance art, the fresco *The Last Supper* (about 1497) and the portrait *Mona Lisa* (about 1503). Leonardo had one of the most searching minds in all history. He wanted to know the workings of everything he saw in nature. In more than 4,000 pages of notebooks, he drew detailed diagrams and wrote down observations. Leonardo made careful drawings of human skeletons and muscles, trying to discover how the body worked. Because of his inquiring mind, Leonardo has become a symbol of the Renaissance spirit of learning and intellectual curiosity.

The Renaissance outside Italy

During the late 1400's, the Renaissance spread from Italy to such countries as France, Germany, England, and Spain. It was introduced into those countries by visitors to Italy, who included merchants, bankers, diplomats, and especially young scholars. The scholars acquired from the Italians the basic tools of humanistic study—history and philology.

Detail of a fresco (1510-1511); The Vatican, Rome (SCALA/Art Resource)

Raphael's *School of Athens* portrays an imaginary gathering of ancient Greek philosophers and scientists, including the mathematician Euclid, *bending forward, foreground.* The painting shows the Renaissance respect for classical culture.

A series of invasions of Italy also played a major role in the spread of the Renaissance to other parts of Europe. From 1494 to the early 1500's, Italy was repeatedly invaded by armies from France, Germany, and Spain. The invaders were dazzled by the beauty of Italian art and architecture and returned home deeply influenced by Italian culture.

In Italy, evidence of classical antiquity, especially Roman antiquity, could be seen almost everywhere. Ruins of Roman monuments and buildings stood in every Italian city. This link between the present and the classical past was much weaker elsewhere in Europe. In ancient times, Roman culture had been forced upon northern and western Europeans by conquering Roman armies. But that culture quickly disappeared after the Roman Empire in the West fell in the A.D. 400's.

The relative scarcity of classical art affected the development of European art outside Italy during the 1400's. Painters had few examples of classical antiquity to imitate, and so they tended to be more influenced by the northern Gothic style of the late Middle Ages. The first great achievements in Renaissance painting outside Italy appeared in the works of artists living in Flanders. Most of the Flanders region lies in what are now Belgium and France. Flemish painting was known for its precise details. The human figures were realistic but lacked the sculptural quality that was characteristic of Italian painting.

Political background. During the Renaissance, the political structure of northern and western Europe differed greatly from that of Italy. By the late 1400's, England, France, and Spain were being united into nations

under monarchies. These monarchies provided political and cultural leadership for their countries. Germany, like Italy, was divided into many largely independent states. But Germany was the heart of the Holy Roman Empire, which tended to unify the various German states to some extent.

The great royal courts supported the Renaissance in northern and western Europe much as the cities did in Italy. For example, the French king Francis I, who ruled from 1515 to 1547, tried to surround himself with the finest representatives of the Italian Renaissance. The king brought Leonardo da Vinci and many other Italian artists and scholars to France. In England, the House of Tudor became the most important patron of the Renaissance. The Tudors ruled from 1485 to 1603. Henry VII, the first Tudor monarch, invited numerous Italian humanists to England. These men encouraged English scholars to study the literature and philosophy of ancient Greece and Rome.

Christian humanism. Renaissance scholars in northern and western Europe were not as interested as the Italians in studying classical literature. Instead, they sought to apply humanistic methods to the study of Christianity. These scholars were especially concerned with identifying and carefully editing the texts on which Christianity was based. These texts included the Bible, the letters of Saint Paul, and the works of such great early church leaders as Saint Ambrose, Saint Jerome,

Oil painting on wood panel (about 1460); Uffizi Palace, Florence, Italy (SCALA/Art Resource)

Mythological subjects were popular with Italian artists. Antonio del Pollaiuolo painted the Greek hero Hercules killing a monster called the Hydra, *above.* His portrayal of the human body in vigorous action inspired other Renaissance artists.

Detail of *The Madonna and Child with Chancellor Rolin* (about 1436),
an oil painting on wood panel; the Louvre, Paris (SCALA/Art Resource)

A northern Renaissance painting by the Flemish artist Jan
van Eyck emphasizes lighting, perspective, and details. Van Eyck
was one of the first major Renaissance artists outside Italy.

and Saint Augustine. The scholars became known as
Christian humanists to distinguish them from those humanists who were chiefly involved with the study of
classical antiquity.

Desiderius Erasmus and Saint Thomas More were
the leading Christian humanists. They were close friends
who courageously refused to abandon their ideals.

Erasmus was born in the Netherlands. He was educated in Paris and traveled throughout Germany, England, and Italy. He was an excellent scholar, with a thorough knowledge of Latin and Greek.

Erasmus refused to take sides in any political or religious controversy. In particular, he would not support
either side during the Reformation, the religious movement of the 1500's that gave birth to Protestantism. Both
Roman Catholics and Protestants sought Erasmus' support. He stubbornly kept his independence and was
called a coward by both sides. However, Erasmus did attack abuses he saw in the church in a famous witty work
called *The Praise of Folly* (1511). In this book, Erasmus
criticized the moral quality of church leaders. Erasmus
also accused them of overemphasizing procedures and
ceremonies while neglecting the spiritual values of
Christianity.

Saint Thomas More was born in England and devoted
his life to serving his country. He gained the confidence
of King Henry VIII and carried out a number of important missions for him. In 1529, the king appointed More
lord chancellor, making him England's highest judicial
official.

Throughout his career, More dedicated himself to the
principles that had inspired Erasmus. Like Erasmus, he
believed it was important to eliminate the abuses, inequalities, and evils that were accepted as normal in his
day. More's best-known work is *Utopia* (1516). In this
book, More described a society in which the divisions

between the rich and the poor and the powerful and the
weak were replaced by a common concern for the
health and happiness of everyone.

More's strong principles finally cost him his life. He
objected to Henry VIII's decision to divorce the queen,
Catherine of Aragon, and remarry. More then refused to
take an oath acknowledging the king's authority over
that of the pope. In 1535, More was beheaded for treason.

The heritage of the Renaissance

The Renaissance left an intellectual and artistic heritage that still remains important. Since the Renaissance,
scholars have used Renaissance methods of humanistic
inquiry, even when they did not share the ideas and
spirit of the Renaissance humanists. In literature, writers
have tried for centuries to imitate and improve upon the
works of such Renaissance authors as Petrarch and Boccaccio.

The influence of Renaissance painters, sculptors, and
architects has been particularly strong. The artists of
Florence and Rome set enduring standards for painting
in the Western world. For hundreds of years, painters
have traveled to Florence to admire the frescoes of
Giotto and Masaccio. They have visited Rome to study
the paintings of Raphael and Michelangelo. The works
of Donatello and Michelangelo have inspired sculptors
for generations. The beautifully scaled buildings of Brunelleschi and other Renaissance architects still serve as
models for architects.

Since the Renaissance, people have also been inspired by the intellectual daring of such men as Petrarch
and Erasmus. Leaders of the Renaissance seemed to be

Detail of an oil painting on wood panel (about 1523)
by Hans Holbein the Younger; the Louvre, Paris (Art Resource)

Desiderius Erasmus, a Dutch priest and scholar, became a
leading Christian humanist during the Renaissance. He often attacked religious superstition and abuses he saw in the church.

breaking out of intellectual boundaries and entering unknown territories.

Perhaps it is no accident that some of the greatest explorers of the late 1400's and early 1500's were Italians exposed to the traditions of the Renaissance. Christopher Columbus was a sailor from Genoa and an expert navigator. For his voyage to the New World, Columbus consulted the same scientist who taught mathematics to the architect Filippo Brunelleschi. Columbus—like such other Italian explorers as John Cabot, Giovanni da Verrazzano, and Amerigo Vespucci—was willing to take enormous risks to achieve results that people had never dreamed of. In a sense, Columbus's arrival in America in 1492 was one of the greatest achievements of the Renaissance.   Anthony Molho

Related articles in *World Book* include:

Architects

Alberti, Leon Battista
Bramante, Donato
Brunelleschi, Filippo
Jones, Inigo
Palladio, Andrea

Painters

Angelico, Fra
Bellini, Gentile
Bellini, Giovanni
Bellini, Jacopo
Botticelli, Sandro
Bruegel, Pieter, the Elder
Campin, Robert
Caravaggio, Michelangelo Merisi da
Corregio
Cranach, Lucas, the Elder
Dürer, Albrecht
Ghirlandajo, Domenico
Giorgione
Giotto
Greco, El
Grünewald, Matthias
Holbein, Hans, the Elder

Holbein, Hans, the Younger
Leonardo da Vinci
Lippi, Filippino
Lippi, Filippo
Mantegna, Andrea
Masaccio
Michelangelo
Piero della Francesca
Pollaiuolo, Antonio del
Raphael
Schongauer, Martin
Tintoretto
Titian
Uccello, Paolo
Van der Goes, Hugo
Van der Weyden, Rogier
Van Eyck, Jan
Veronese, Paolo

Political leaders

Borgia, Cesare
Borgia, Lucrezia
Francis I (of France)
Machiavelli, Niccolò
Medici
Medici, Cosimo de'
Medici, Lorenzo de'

Sculptors

Cellini, Benvenuto
Della Robbia, Luca
Donatello
Ghiberti, Lorenzo
Michelangelo
Pisano, Giovanni
Pisano, Nicola
Verrocchio, Andrea del

Writers

Ariosto, Ludovico
Boccaccio, Giovanni
Bruno, Giordano
Castiglione, Baldassare
Cervantes, Miguel de
Du Bellay, Joachim
Erasmus, Desiderius
Marlowe, Christopher
Marot, Clement
Montaigne, Michel de

More, Saint Thomas
Petrarch
Rabelais, François
Ronsard, Pierre de
Shakespeare, William
Spenser, Edmund
Surrey, Earl of
Tasso, Torquato
Vega, Lope de
Wyatt, Sir Thomas

Other related articles

See the section on the *Renaissance* in the various articles on national literatures, such as **French literature** (The Renaissance). See also the following articles:

Architecture
Ballet (The birth of ballet)

Classical music (The Renaissance period)
Democracy (The Renaissance and the Reformation)
Drama (Italian Renaissance drama)
Education (The Renaissance)
Exploration (The great age of European exploration)
Florence
Fresco
Furniture (The Renaissance)

Humanism
Italy (History)
Jewelry
Mural
Painting (The Renaissance)
Perspective
Philosophy (Modern philosophy)
Poetry (Renaissance poetry)
Reformation
Science (The rebirth of science)
Sculpture (Italian Renaissance sculpture)

Outline

I. **The Italian Renaissance**
    A. Political background
    B. Humanism
    C. The fine arts
II. **The Renaissance outside Italy**
    A. Political background
    B. Christian humanism
    C. Desiderius Erasmus and Saint Thomas More
III. **The heritage of the Renaissance**

Questions

What was the most significant intellectual movement of the Renaissance?
What is meant by *classical antiquity*?
How did the Renaissance spread from Italy?
What are some lasting achievements of the Renaissance?
How did many attitudes and ideas of the Renaissance differ from those of the Middle Ages?
What three men dominated Italian arts during the late 1400's and early 1500's?
How did the signorial and republican governments of the Italian cities promote the Renaissance?
Why was *philology* studied during the Renaissance?
What was *The Book of the Courtier* and why was it important?
Who were the *Christian humanists*?

Additional resources

Level I
Caselli, Giovanni. *The Renaissance and the New World.* Bedrick, 1985.
Clare, John D., ed. *Italian Renaissance.* Harcourt, 1995.
Howarth, Sarah. *Renaissance People.* Millbrook, 1992. *Renaissance Places.* 1992.
Walker, Paul R. *The Italian Renaissance.* Facts on File, 1995.

Level II
Aston, Margaret, ed. *The Panorama of the Renaissance.* Abrams, 1996.
Burckhardt, Jakob C. *The Civilization of the Renaissance in Italy.* 2 vols. First published in 1860 and available in many editions. First important modern analysis of the Renaissance as a historical period.
Burke, Peter. *The Italian Renaissance.* Rev. ed. Princeton, 1987.
Hale, John. *The Civilization of Europe in the Renaissance.* 1993. Reprint. Atheneum, 1994.
Hartt, Frederick. *History of Italian Renaissance Art.* 4th ed. Abrams, 1994.
Kelley, Donald R. *Renaissance Humanism.* Twayne, 1991.
Porter, Roy, and Teich, Mikuláš, eds. *The Renaissance in National Context.* Cambridge, 1992.
Rabb, Theodore K. *Renaissance Lives.* Pantheon, 1993.
Schmitt, Charles B., and others, eds. *The Cambridge History of Renaissance Philosophy.* Cambridge, 1988.

Reno, *REE noh* (pop. 133,850; met. area pop. 254,667), is a major tourist center and the second largest city in Nevada. Only Las Vegas has more people. Reno lies on the Truckee River in western Nevada at the foot of the Sierra Nevada (see **Nevada** [political map]).

Reno is the second largest city in Nevada. Its many gambling casinos and nightclubs make the city a major tourist attraction.

David R. Frazier

Reno has many popular gambling casinos and nightclubs. Many famous entertainers perform in Reno. Recreational attractions near Reno include boating, downhill skiing, fishing, and water-skiing. A branch of the University of Nevada is in Reno.

Paiute and Washoe Indians lived in what is now the Reno area before white settlers arrived there. Reno was founded in 1868 as a station on the Central Pacific Railroad. Railroad officials named the city for Jesse Lee Reno, a Union general killed in the American Civil War (1861-1865). The city grew rapidly after Nevada legalized gambling in 1931. Its population rose from about 21,300 in 1940 to about 133,850 in 1990. Reno has a council-manager form of government and is the county seat of Washoe County.   Lenita Powers

See also **Nevada** (picture: The Reno skyline).

Reno, Janet (1938-   ), was the first woman to serve as attorney general of the United States. Reno, appointed by President Bill Clinton, held the Cabinet post from 1993 to 2001. Before her appointment, Reno had served 15 years as state attorney for Florida's Dade County (now Miami-Dade County), which included the city of Miami.

As U.S. attorney general, Reno faced the problem of deciding when to order independent investigations of charged wrongdoing by government officials rather than having her Department of Justice do the investigating. In some cases, she approved independent investigations. For example, she did so for charges against Cabinet heads; and she appointed an independent special prosecutor to look into charges about Whitewater, a business deal in which Clinton was involved before he became president. She also approved an investigation into whether Clinton had lied under oath and committed other offenses related to an alleged affair with a former White House intern. For more details, see **Clinton, Bill** (Domestic events). But Reno rejected demands by Republican leaders for an independent investiga-

U.S. Department of Justice
Janet Reno

tion of charges about Democratic fund-raising practices. As state attorney, she had earned a reputation as a tough but compassionate crime fighter who worked to reform the criminal justice system.

Reno was born in Miami. She earned a bachelor's degree from Cornell University and a law degree from Harvard University. She became a lawyer in Miami. In 1972, Reno ran for a seat in the Florida legislature, but lost. She then joined the Dade County state attorney office as a prosecutor. She was appointed state attorney in 1978. Reno was elected to the office in November of that year and was reelected four times.   Don Van Natta, Jr.

Reno, *REE noh,* **Marcus Albert** (1834-1889), was a United States Army officer who became known for his role in the Battle of the Little Bighorn in Montana Territory in 1876. During this battle, often called "Custer's Last Stand," Indians killed Lieutenant Colonel George A. Custer and all the men of the Seventh Cavalry under his direct command.

News of Custer's defeat led to a bitter dispute. Supporters of Custer accused Major Reno of cowardice for failing first to attack the Indian village and then to rejoin Custer. Reno claimed he had tried to attack the village but that the Indians outnumbered his unit, forced it to retreat, and kept it from helping Custer. Reno asked the Army to investigate his conduct, and a military court cleared him of blame in 1879. But later that year, a court-martial convicted Reno of drunkenness and conduct unbecoming an officer. The Army gave him a dishonorable discharge in 1880. In 1967, Reno's case was reopened and the Army changed his record to show he had been honorably discharged.

Reno was born in Carrollton, Illinois. He graduated from the U.S. Military Academy in 1857 and served in the cavalry in the American Civil War.   Brian W. Dippie

See also **Custer, George Armstrong** (The battle).

Renoir, *REHN wahr* or *ruh NWAHR,* **Jean** (1894-1979), was a French motion-picture director. Many of his films expose human faults and ridicule social attitudes. They also show compassion for people and their failings.

Renoir directed 36 films, including two of the most acclaimed movies ever made. One of them, *Grand Illusion* (1937), attacks the futility of war. The other, *The Rules of the Game* (1939), satirizes relationships among upper-class people at a weekend house party.

Renoir's first film was *A Life Without Joy* (1924). His other films include *Nana* (1926), *Boudu Saved from Drowning* (1932), *The Crime of Monsieur Lange* (1935), *Toni* (1935), and *La Bête Humaine* (1938). His last film, *The Little Theatre of Jean Renoir* (1970), was made for French television.

Renoir was born in Paris. His father was the French painter Pierre Auguste Renoir. After World War II began in 1939, Jean Renoir fled France. He settled in the United States in 1941. Renoir made several films in the United States, including *Swamp Water* (1941) and *The Southerner* (1945). He became a U.S. citizen in 1944.

John F. Mariani

Renoir, *REHN wahr* or *ruh NWAHR,* **Pierre Auguste,** *pyair oh GOOST* (1841-1919), a French impressionist painter, is famous for his pictures of young girls and children, and intimate portraits of French middle-class life. He loved to show lively groups in sensuous surroundings, and often used his friends as models. Renoir frequently painted his wife and children.

In the 1870's, Renoir and Claude Monet together developed the broken color technique of the Impressionists. Instead of mixing paints completely, they left small dabs of color in a sketchy manner. But Renoir was more interested in rich color effects and a sense of volume than Monet. Renoir also preferred figure painting to landscapes. During the 1870's, he painted a large number of portraits on commission. Perhaps his most famous is *Mme. Charpentier and Her Children.* While many Impressionists brought Japanese qualities into their work, Renoir revived the rococo style of such artists as François Boucher and Jean Honoré Fragonard.

Renoir traveled to Italy in 1880, and his study of Renaissance painters there led him to a new appreciation of the importance of line. He returned to France, where he gave up his broad, coloristic manner and spent several years concentrating on drawing. Renoir painted a famous series, *The Bathers,* during this time.

The happy quality of Renoir's later work does not show the agony he suffered from arthritis, which finally crippled his hands. He had brushes tied to his hands and developed a final style of painting in broad brush strokes and vivid colors.

Renoir was born in Limoges, France. He was apprenticed to learn porcelain painting after he showed an early talent for drawing. He painted window shades and fans in Paris. He studied at Charles Gleyre's studio, where he met Monet and other young painters who were to form the Impressionist group. He was influenced also by Edouard Manet and the color methods of Eugène Delacroix.   Richard Shiff

See also **Delacroix, Eugène; Manet, Edouard; Monet, Claude; Impressionism.**

Additional resources

Gaunt, William. *Renoir.* 3rd ed. 1982. Reprint. Phaidon, 1994.
Renoir. Abrams, 1985. Exhibition catalog.
Renoir. Gramercy Bks., 1994.
White, Barbara E. *Renoir.* 1984. Reprint. Abrams, 1988.

Reorganized Church of Jesus Christ of Latter Day Saints. See Latter Day Saints, Reorganized Church of Jesus Christ of.

Repeal means wiping out a law already on the books. A legislative body has the power not only to pass new laws, but also to do away with laws that have been passed earlier. Sometimes, the legislature may pass an act which directly states that an earlier law is repealed. Such an act is known as an *express repeal.* Sometimes, a new law may simply make it quite clear that an older one no longer applies. In this case, the repeal is known as a *repeal by implication.* A new law will sometimes conflict only with a certain portion of an earlier one. The new law is understood to repeal by implication those parts of the earlier law that are inconsistent with it.

Oil painting on canvas (1881); the Phillips Collection, Washington, D.C.   Brown Bros.

Pierre Auguste Renoir, a master of impressionist painting, became famous for his luminous colors and cheerful scenes of everyday life. In such works as *The Luncheon of the Boating Party, left,* he portrayed a carefree group of people at an informal moment. The woman holding the dog is Renoir's wife.

To avoid confusion, legislatures often enact an *express repeal* of a law which has already been repealed by implication. For example, the passage by Congress of the Kansas-Nebraska Bill had the effect of repealing the Missouri Compromise. But Congress later passed a second bill specifically declaring the Missouri Compromise "void and inoperative."   Peter Woll

Repetitive strain injury is any of a group of painful medical disorders caused by performing a similar activity over and over again. Such injuries, often called RSI's, are responsible for more than half of all workplace illnesses. Other names for such disorders include *cumulative trauma disorders* (CTD's) and *repetitive stress injuries,* also shortened to RSI's.

Anyone who regularly performs a repetitive task is at risk of developing an RSI. Computer users, meat cutters, and assembly-line workers often develop such problems. The number of RSI sufferers increased greatly during the late 1900's, possibly due to increased computer use. Dentists, cashiers, and musicians also frequently complain of symptoms.

Carpal tunnel syndrome, a wrist disorder, is the most common RSI. Others include *de Quervain's disease* (inflammation of the tendon sheaths in the thumb) and *lateral epicondylitis* (tennis elbow). Workers may also suffer from numbness in the fingers; pain in the arms, neck, and back; and aching muscles.

Prevention is the best treatment. An expert in *ergonomics* (the study of the relationship between people and their workplace) can recommend changes to the work area. Employees should be taught proper posture and use of tools and machines. They also should be encouraged to maintain a reasonable pace and take rest breaks. Medical treatment may be necessary in some cases. Anti-inflammatory drugs or steroid injections may be prescribed. Surgery may be necessary if other treatments fail.   Gordon H. Derman

See also **Backache; Carpal tunnel syndrome.**

Reporter. See Foreign correspondent; Journalism; Newspaper (Gathering the news); **War correspondent**.

Representative is the name for a member of the lower house of the Congress of the United States (the House of Representatives), or of the lower house of a state legislature. See also **Address, Forms of; Congressman; House of representatives.**

Representative government. See Democracy; Republic.

Representatives, House of. See House of representatives.

Reprieve, *rih PREEV,* is the temporary suspension of a sentence passed on a criminal. The sentence is postponed for a definite period of time. Reprieves are sometimes granted to permit consideration of new evidence, or a further investigation of the case. The chief executive of a state or country usually grants reprieves.

A reprieve is not a pardon (see **Pardon**). A reprieve makes no change in the sentence, but merely changes the date when the sentence goes into effect. A delay or reprieve granted to a prisoner by the court which passed the sentence is often called a *stay of execution.*
    James O. Finckenauer

Reproduction is the process by which living things create more of their own kind. All types of living creatures reproduce, from the tiniest bacteria to the largest plants and animals. Without reproduction, all forms of life would die out.

Organisms can produce offspring like themselves because they possess *genes.* Genes are tiny segments of DNA (deoxyribonucleic acid), the substance that determines an organism's essential traits. Genes are contained in each cell of an organism and are transferred to the organism's offspring during reproduction.

There are two general types of reproduction—*sexual* and *asexual.* In sexual reproduction, a new organism is formed by the joining of a *gamete* (sex cell) from one organism with a gamete from another organism. Human beings and almost all other animals reproduce sexually. In asexual reproduction, a new organism develops from parts of, or parts produced by, one organism. Living things that reproduce asexually include bacteria and other simple organisms. Many organisms can reproduce both sexually and asexually. They include most plants and fungi and certain simple animals, such as sponges.

Scientists believe that the first living things lived in the sea and reproduced asexually. Sexual reproduction also *evolved* (developed gradually) in the sea. After organisms began to live on land, they evolved increasingly complex methods of sexual reproduction.

This article describes reproduction in living things other than human beings. For a discussion of human reproduction, see **Reproduction, Human.**

How genes are transferred

During reproduction, an organism transmits a copy of its genes to its offspring. Genes are contained in thread-like structures called *chromosomes.* Bacteria, which are one-celled organisms, have only one chromosome, consisting of a single strand of DNA. In more complex organisms, each body cell contains two copies of each chromosome, and the two copies are arranged in pairs. Cells with pairs of chromosomes are called *diploid cells.* Cells that contain only one copy of each chromosome are called *haploid cells.*

Through sexual reproduction, the offspring inherits genes from two parents. The genes are transmitted by the two gametes that form the new individual. Sexual reproduction involves a cycle of two processes, *meiosis* and *fertilization.* In meiosis, diploid cells produce gametes, which are haploid cells. The male gamete is called a *sperm,* and the female gamete is called an *egg.* Fertilization is the union of these gametes. It produces a diploid cell, the fertilized egg. The fertilized egg develops into the new organism. Because it receives genes from each parent, the offspring has a unique genetic makeup and traits that differ from those of either parent.

Through asexual reproduction. Although many diploid organisms reproduce sexually, others reproduce asexually. For example, sponges are diploid animals that can reproduce by a process called *budding.* In this process, a small portion of the sponge breaks off and gives rise to a new individual. There is no meiosis and no fertilization. A similar process, called *vegetative propagation,* occurs in many plants (see **Plant** [Vegetative propagation]).

Another form of asexual reproduction occurs in bacteria and other one-celled organisms. Such organisms simply divide when they grow to a certain size. This process is called *binary fission*. Before dividing, the organism makes a copy of its chromosomes, which contain the genes. The cell splits between the two copies so that each of the resulting cells gets one of the copies. Thus, in asexual reproduction, every cell of the new organism has the same genes as the parent, and the offspring and the parent are identical.

How reproduction has evolved

Most scientists believe that life arose on earth about $3\frac{1}{2}$ billion years ago. The first living things probably were microscopic, one-celled organisms that lived in the sea and reproduced asexually. Sexual reproduction also evolved in the sea. Sea animals reproduce sexually by means of *external fertilization*. In this process, the female releases eggs into the water. Fertilization occurs after a male releases sperm into the water and the sperm unite with the eggs.

About 400 million years ago, some organisms left the sea to inhabit land. The new, dry environment presented problems for existing methods of reproduction. Organisms that reproduced sexually could not simply release their gametes near one another on land since the gametes would dry up and die. Thus, organisms evolved new reproduction methods suitable to land conditions.

Plants evolved seeds, watertight structures that enclose the plant's *embryo* (fertilized egg). The seed keeps

© M.D. Phillips, Phototake

In sexual reproduction, a new organism forms from the union of a sperm from the male parent and an egg from the female parent. In this photograph, the whiplike sperm of a hamster penetrates a round hamster egg.

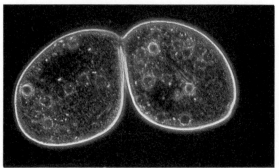

© M.I. Walker from Photo Researchers

In asexual reproduction, a new organism develops from a single parent organism. This photograph shows a paramecium splitting into two individuals, a process called *binary fission*.

the embryo from drying out until enough water is available for it to grow.

Fungi developed a form of reproductive cell called the *spore*. Like the seeds of plants, the spores of fungi only begin to grow when water is available.

Amphibians, such as frogs and toads, fertilize their eggs externally in a puddle or pond. The fertilized egg of an amphibian does not contain enough nutrients for the offspring to develop completely by the time the egg hatches. As a result, an amphibian goes through a *larval stage* after it hatches and before it becomes an adult. During the larval stage, the animal gathers and eats the food it needs to reach full maturity.

Insects developed eggs with shells that retain water. The female can lay the eggs on twigs and other places exposed to air without their loss of moisture. In most insects, the eggs are fertilized as they leave the female's body by sperm stored in her abdomen.

Reptiles and birds. Reptiles evolved *internal fertilization,* a process in which the male releases sperm into an opening in the female's body. The egg is fertilized within the female's body, where it is completely protected from drying out. Most scientists believe that birds evolved from reptiles. The eggs of reptiles and birds contain a large amount of nutrients and are within a watertight shell, so they can be laid in dry places. The offspring develops within the egg, eventually using up all the nutrients and developing into a miniature adult before it hatches.

Mammals. Reproduction in mammals involves internal fertilization. Like reptiles, the earliest mammals laid eggs. Only two such mammals, the echidna and the platypus, survive today. In all other mammals, the young are born alive.

Certain mammals, called *marsupials,* give birth to extremely underdeveloped young. The young continue their development in a pouch on the mother's body, where they feed on the mother's milk. Marsupials include kangaroos, opossums, and koalas.

The great majority of mammals, however, give birth to well-developed offspring. While in the body of the mother, the young of these mammals receive nourishment from the mother's blood through a specialized organ called the *placenta* (see **Placenta**). Such mammals are called *placentals*.   George B. Johnson

Related articles in *World Book* include:

Animal (How animals reproduce)
Alternation of generations
Bacteria (How bacteria reproduce)
Biogenesis
Bird (Laying and hatching eggs)
Cell (Cell division)
Clone
Dinosaur (Reproduction and growth)
Egg
Estrous cycle
Evolution

Fertilization
Fish (How fish reproduce)
Fungi
Genetics
Heredity
Insect (Reproduction)
Mammal (How mammals reproduce)
Plant (How plants reproduce)
Reptile (Reproduction)
Seed
Sponge (How sponges reproduce)

Additional resources

Catton, Chris, and Gray, James. *Sex in Nature.* Facts on File, 1985.
Farley, John. *Gametes and Spores: Ideas About Sexual Reproduction, 1750-1914.* Johns Hopkins, 1982.
Twist, Clint. *Reproduction to Birth.* Gloucester Pr., 1991. Younger readers.

Copyright © Lennart Nilsson, 1990. From *A Child Is Born,* Dell Publishing Company

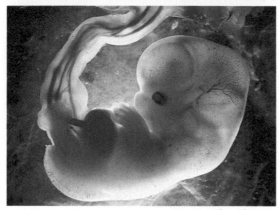

Lennart Nilsson, *Life* Magazine

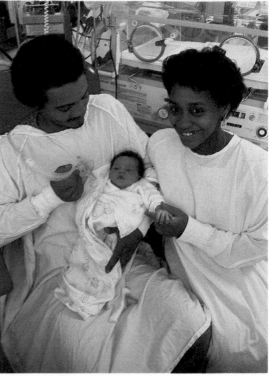

© Dan McCoy, Rainbow

Human reproduction begins when a sperm from the father unites with and fertilizes an egg from the mother. The egg divides rapidly, *top left,* and soon becomes an embryo, *above left,* that develops and grows within the mother's body. After about nine months, a baby is born, *right.*

Human reproduction

Reproduction, Human, is the process by which human beings create more of their own kind. Human beings reproduce sexually. That is, a new individual develops from the joining together of two sex cells, one from a female parent and one from a male parent. The union of these cells is called *fertilization.*

Biologists refer to sex cells as *gametes.* Females produce gametes called *eggs* or *ova.* Male gametes are called *sperm.* Fertilization may occur after a male delivers sperm to the female's egg by means of sexual intercourse. Fertilization begins a remarkable period of development in which the egg develops into a fully formed baby within the body of the female. This period of development, called *pregnancy,* takes about nine months.

At the beginning of pregnancy, the fertilized egg is smaller than the period at the end of this sentence. The egg develops into a growing mass of cells called an *embryo.* Gradually, the cells rearrange themselves to form tissues. By the end of the second month of pregnancy, all the major body organs and organ systems have

Lynn J. Romrell, the contributor of this article, is Associate Dean for Education and Professor of Anatomy and Cell Biology at the University of Florida College of Medicine.

formed and the embryo looks distinctly human. During the rest of pregnancy, the embryo is called a *fetus.* The fetus grows while its systems prepare for the day when they must function outside the mother's body. Pregnancy ends when the new baby passes out of the mother's body at birth.

This article discusses the biological aspects of reproduction in humans. For a discussion of some of the moral and social issues related to human reproduction, see such articles as **Abortion, Baby, Birth control** and **Family.** For information on reproduction among other living things, see **Reproduction.**

The human reproductive system

Human beings are born with the body organs needed for reproduction. But reproduction cannot actually occur until these organs mature. This maturation process takes place during *puberty,* a period in which a boy or girl goes through dramatic physical changes. These changes are regulated by certain *hormones* (chemicals produced by the body). Puberty begins during or just before the early teen-age years.

The reproductive systems of females and males differ greatly in shape and structure. But both systems are specifically designed to produce, nourish, and transport the eggs or sperm.

In females, the reproductive system consists primarily of a group of organs located within the pelvis. A woman or girl has external organs called the *vulva* between her legs. The outer parts of the vulva cover the opening to a narrow canal called the *vagina.* The vagina leads to the *uterus,* a hollow, pear-shaped, muscular organ in which a baby develops. Two small, oval organs called *ovaries* lie to the right and left of the uterus. The ovaries produce, store, and release eggs. These organs also produce two types of hormones—*progesterone* and *estrogens.* Eggs from the ovaries reach the uterus through tubes called *fallopian tubes* or *oviducts.*

Females produce eggs as part of a monthly process called the *menstrual cycle,* which begins during puberty. Each menstrual cycle, the female reproductive system undergoes a series of changes that prepares it for fertilization and pregnancy. If the egg is not fertilized, a shedding or loss of tissue in the uterus called *menstruation* occurs. Bleeding is associated with this process and lasts three to seven days. Menstruation marks the beginning of each menstrual cycle. Each cycle lasts about 28 days. See **Menstruation.**

Other changes during a menstrual cycle involve cells in the ovaries called *oocytes.* Eggs develop from these cells. At birth, each ovary has about 400,000 oocytes. These cells remain inactive until the first menstrual cycle. Thereafter, many oocytes grow and begin to mature each month. Normally, only one oocyte in either of the ovaries reaches full maturity. This fully developed cell— the mature egg—is released from the ovary in a process called *ovulation.* This process occurs at about the midpoint of the menstrual cycle. After ovulation, the egg travels toward the uterus through one of the fallopian tubes by means of wavelike contractions of muscles and the beating of *cilia* (hairlike structures) located on cells in the walls of the oviduct. Fertilization may occur in one of the tubes. An unfertilized egg lives for about 24 hours after it leaves the ovary.

Important changes also occur in the *endometrium* (lining of the uterus). During the first half of the menstrual cycle, the ovaries release relatively large amounts of estrogens, which cause the endometrium to thicken. The endometrium reaches its maximum thickness at about the time of ovulation. After ovulation, the ovaries release relatively large amounts of progesterone. This hormone maintains the thickness of the endometrium, so that a fertilized egg can attach to the uterus.

If fertilization occurs, the endometrium continues to develop. If fertilization does not occur, the egg breaks down and the production of progesterone decreases. The thickened endometrium also breaks down and passes out of the body during menstruation.

Most women produce eggs until the ages of about 45 to 55, when the menstrual cycles become increasingly infrequent and then stop. This period of a woman's life is called *menopause.* The completion of menopause marks the end of a woman's natural childbearing years.

In males, the reproductive system includes the *testicles,* a *duct system, accessory glands,* and the *penis.* The testicles, also called *testes,* are the organs that produce sperm. The duct system, which includes the *epididymis* and the *vas deferens,* transports the sperm. The accessory glands, mainly the *seminal vesicles* and the *prostate gland,* provide fluids that lubricate the duct system and nourish the sperm. The sperm leave the body through the penis, a cylindrical organ that is located between the legs.

The testicles are contained in the *scrotum,* a pouch behind the penis. The location of the scrotum keeps the testicles about 4 to 5 Fahrenheit degrees (2.2 to 2.8 Celsius degrees) cooler than the normal body temperature of 98.6 °F (37.0 °C). Unlike other cells of the body, sperm cells cannot develop properly at normal body temperature. In addition to producing sperm, the testicles also produce hormones, particularly *testosterone.*

Sperm develop in the testicles within a complex system of tubes called *seminiferous tubules.* At birth, a

The human reproductive system
The reproductive systems of males and females are specifically designed to produce, nourish, and transport the sperm or egg. After sperm are deposited in the vagina, they pass through the uterus and into the fallopian tubes, where fertilization usually occurs.

WORLD BOOK diagrams by George Suyeoka

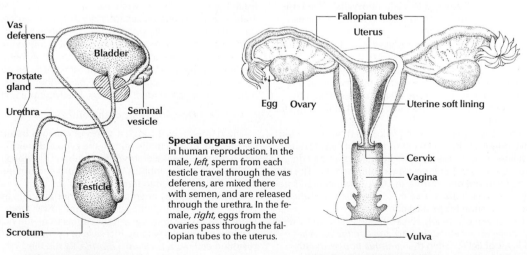

Special organs are involved in human reproduction. In the male, *left,* sperm from each testicle travel through the vas deferens, are mixed there with semen, and are released through the urethra. In the female, *right,* eggs from the ovaries pass through the fallopian tubes to the uterus.

Male reproductive system

Female reproductive system

male baby's tubules contain only simple round cells. But during puberty, the testicles begin to produce testosterone and other hormones that make the round cells divide, and undergo changes to become slender cells with a tail. A sperm cell uses its tail, called a *flagellum,* to propel itself forward. Sperm pass from the testicles into the epididymis, where they complete their development in about 12 days and are stored.

A healthy adult male normally produces about 200 million sperm per day. Although sperm production begins to decline gradually at about 45 years of age, it normally continues throughout life.

From the epididymis, sperm move to a long tube that is called the vas deferens. The seminal vesicles and prostate gland produce a whitish fluid called *seminal fluid.* This fluid mixes with sperm to form *semen.* The vas deferens leads to the *urethra,* a tube that runs through the penis.

Semen, which contains the sperm, is expelled from the body through the urethra. This process is called *ejaculation.* The penis usually hangs limp. But when a male becomes sexually excited, special tissues in the penis fill with blood, and the organ becomes stiff and erect. When the erect penis is stimulated, muscles around the reproductive organs contract. This contraction forces fluid from the glands and propels the semen through the duct system and the urethra. The amount of semen ejaculated varies from 2 to 6 milliliters (0.07 to 0.2 fluid ounce). Each milliliter has about 100 million sperm.

Fertilization

A pregnancy begins when a sperm fertilizes an egg. Fertilization, also called *conception,* normally occurs by means of sexual intercourse. Sexual intercourse takes place when the man's erect penis is inserted in the woman's vagina. When a man ejaculates, semen containing the millions of sperm is deposited in the vagina.

Scientists have developed techniques of achieving fertilization without sexual intercourse. In a process called *artificial insemination,* sperm are collected from a man and later injected into a woman's uterus. In another technique, called *in vitro fertilization,* collected sperm are used to fertilize eggs in a laboratory dish. The fertilized eggs are then inserted into the woman's uterus. See **Infertility** (Treatment).

After ejaculation, the sperm pass from the vagina into the uterus and then into the fallopian tubes. Most sperm die along the way. In each tube, only a few thousand sperm reach the *ampulla,* a section that makes up one-half to two-thirds of the tube's length. If a sperm fertilizes an egg, it usually does so in the part of the ampulla near the uterus.

Some sperm may reach the fallopian tubes in as little as five minutes. Others take hours. Sperm can survive in the fallopian tubes for up to 48 hours. It takes an egg about 72 hours to pass through a fallopian tube. The egg can be fertilized only during the first 24 hours of this period. Therefore, intercourse must take place near the time of ovulation for fertilization to occur.

The surface of a newly released egg is covered with a jellylike layer of cells called the *zona pellucida.* A second layer of cells, called the *cumulus oophorus,* surrounds the zona pellucida. A sperm must pass through both layers to fertilize the egg. The *acrosome* (tip) of the

sperm releases special enzymes that scatter the cells of both layers. Although several sperm may begin to penetrate the zona pellucida, usually only one can fertilize the egg. After the first sperm enters, the egg releases substances that prevent other sperm from entering.

How sex is determined. Fertilization is complete when the *chromosomes* of the sperm unite with the chromosomes of the egg. Chromosomes are threadlike structures that contain *genes,* the units of heredity that determine each person's unique traits. Most body cells have 46 chromosomes that occur in 23 pairs. However, as each egg or sperm develops, it undergoes a special series of cell divisions called *meiosis.* As a result, each sperm or egg cell contains only one member of each chromosome pair, or 23 unpaired chromosomes. During fertilization, the chromosomes pair up so that the fertilized egg has the normal number of 46 chromosomes. The fertilized egg is called a *zygote.*

Special *sex chromosomes* determine whether the zygote will develop into a boy or a girl. Each body cell contains a pair of sex chromosomes. In females, the two sex chromosomes are identical. Each of the chromosomes is called an *X chromosome.* The cells of males have one X chromosome and a smaller chromosome called the *Y chromosome.*

After meiosis, each sperm or egg cell has only one sex chromosome. All egg cells carry one X chromosome. Half the sperm cells carry an X chromosome, and the other half have a Y chromosome. At fertilization, a sperm with an X chromosome uniting with an egg will develop into a girl baby because the fertilized egg will have two X chromosomes. A sperm with a Y chromosome uniting with an egg will form a boy baby because the fertilized egg will have the X and Y combination. See **Heredity** (Chromosomes and genes).

Multiple birth. In most cases, a single egg is fertilized and develops into one baby. Occasionally, however, two or more infants develop and are born at the same time. The birth of more than one baby from the same pregnancy is called *multiple birth.*

Multiple births can result from separate zygotes or from a single zygote. For example, if two eggs are released during ovulation, each may be fertilized by a separate sperm, producing separate zygotes. The two zygotes develop into *dizygotic twins,* also called *fraternal twins.* Monozygotic twins develop from a single zygote that divides into separate cells, with each cell developing independently. The infants born have the same genetic makeup and usually resemble each other. Such twins are also called *identical twins.* See **Multiple birth.**

Development of the embryo

The zygote goes through a series of changes before it reaches the uterus. In the uterus, the zygote develops into a form called the embryo. The embryo develops rapidly. Within two months, all the tissues and organs of the body have begun to form.

The first days of pregnancy. After fertilization, the zygote travels through the fallopian tube toward the uterus. Along the way, the zygote begins to divide rapidly into many cells with no increase in overall size. The resulting cell mass is called a *morula.* By the third or fourth day after fertilization, the morula enters the uterus. At that time, the morula is still surrounded by the

The development of a human embryo

During the first two months of pregnancy, an embryo develops from a single cell to a recognizably human shape about $1\frac{1}{4}$ inches (3 centimeters) long. After this period, the embryo is called a *fetus*.

WORLD BOOK illustrations by Barbara Cousins

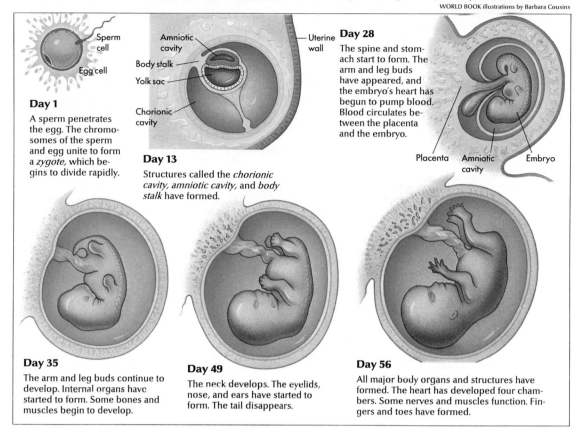

Day 1

A sperm penetrates the egg. The chromosomes of the sperm and egg unite to form a *zygote*, which begins to divide rapidly.

Day 13

Structures called the *chorionic cavity, amniotic cavity*, and *body stalk* have formed.

Day 28

The spine and stomach start to form. The arm and leg buds have appeared, and the embryo's heart has begun to pump blood. Blood circulates between the placenta and the embryo.

Day 35

The arm and leg buds continue to develop. Internal organs have started to form. Some bones and muscles begin to develop.

Day 49

The neck develops. The eyelids, nose, and ears have started to form. The tail disappears.

Day 56

All major body organs and structures have formed. The heart has developed four chambers. Some nerves and muscles function. Fingers and toes have formed.

zona pellucida and consists of about 12 to 16 cells.

The embryo develops from the central cells of the morula. These cells are called the *inner cell mass*. The outer cells of the morula are called the *outer cell mass*. They develop into the *placenta*, a special organ that enables the embryo to obtain food and oxygen from the mother.

After the morula enters the uterus, it continues to divide. A fluid-filled cavity forms between the inner cell mass and the outer cell mass, and the zona pellucida begins to disintegrate. At this stage, the ball of cells is called a *blastocyst* or *blastula*. The cells of the blastocyst divide as it floats in the uterus for one or two days.

About the fifth or sixth day of pregnancy, the blastocyst becomes attached to the internal surface of the uterus. The outer cells of the blastocyst, called the *trophoblast*, secrete an enzyme that breaks down the lining of the uterus. The trophoblast begins to divide rapidly, invading the uterine tissue. The process of attachment to the uterine wall is called *implantation*. By the 11th day of the pregnancy, the blastocyst is firmly implanted in the uterus.

Nourishing the embryo. Various structures develop in the uterus to help the embryo grow. These structures include the placenta and certain membranes.

By the 13th day of pregnancy, a space called the *chorionic cavity* has formed around the embryo. Two membranes surround the chorionic cavity. The outer membrane is called the *chorion*, and the inner membrane is called the *amnion*. The chorion interacts with tissues of the uterus to form the placenta. The chorion pushes into the wall of the uterus with fingerlike projections called *chorionic villi*. The chorionic villi contain the embryo's first blood vessels. The chorion is attached to the embryo by a structure called the *body stalk*. The body stalk develops into the *umbilical cord*, which joins the embryo to the placenta.

The amnion forms a sac around the embryo and is filled with fluid. The embryo floats in this fluid, called *amniotic fluid*. The amniotic fluid protects the embryo by absorbing jolts to the uterus. It also allows the embryo to move without damaging the amnion and other tissues.

About the 21st day of pregnancy, blood begins to circulate between the placenta and the embryo. The blood vessels of the mother and those of the embryo exchange substances through a thin layer of cells called the *placental barrier*. Waste products from the embryo are carried away through the barrier. Likewise, nutrients and oxygen from the mother's blood pass through the thin walls of the barrier and enter the embryo's blood. However, such organisms as viruses and bacteria, as well as chemical substances, including drugs, also may cross the placental barrier and harm the embryo.

Origin of tissues and organs. At about the same time that the placenta begins to form, the inner cell mass flattens and develops into three layers of cells in what is called the *embryonic disc*. The three types of cell layers are the *ectoderm,* the *mesoderm,* and the *endoderm.* In a process called *differentiation,* cells from each layer move to certain areas of the embryonic disc and then fold over to form tubes or clusters. These tubes and clusters develop into various tissues and organs of the body.

Cells from the ectoderm form the brain, nerves, skin, hair, nails, and parts of the eyes and ears. Cells from the mesoderm form the heart, muscles, bones, tendons, kidneys, glands, blood vessels, and reproductive organs. The linings of the digestive and respiratory systems develop from cells of the endoderm.

Development of organs and organ systems. The body's organs and organ systems grow rapidly from the third through eighth weeks of pregnancy. The major structures include the central nervous system and the circulatory system, as well as such organs as the eyes, ears, and limbs. Defects in the development of these structures often occur during these weeks. Such defects sometimes are caused by substances introduced from the mother's body through the placental barrier. These substances are called *teratogens.* They include medications taken by the mother, as well as viruses, bacteria, and other infectious organisms. Other teratogens include nonmedicinal drugs, alcoholic beverages, and cigarette smoke.

The central nervous system, which consists of the brain and spinal cord, starts to develop in the middle of the third week of pregnancy. It begins as a flattened strip of cells within a long cylinder of cells called the *neural tube.* At about the 25th day of pregnancy, one end of the neural tube closes. The brain develops from three sacs formed in this end of the tube. The other end of the tube closes two days later. Failure of the tube to close can result in birth defects, especially *spina bifida,* a disorder of the spine.

The circulatory system also begins to develop in the third week of pregnancy. Two tubes of cells combine to form a single tube that becomes the heart. By the fourth week, a simple circulatory system is functioning and the heart has begun to pump blood. During the fourth to seventh weeks of pregnancy, the heart tube divides into four chambers. Any irregularity in the normal pattern of development during this period can produce a defect in the heart.

The eyes and ears begin to develop in the fourth week of pregnancy. Both these organs form rapidly. The external parts of the ears appear by the sixth week. Defects in the eyes or ears often stem from abnormalities that occur during the fourth to sixth weeks.

The arms and legs appear as buds of tissue during the fifth week of pregnancy. The arms develop a few days ahead of the legs. The fingers and toes become recognizable in the sixth week. They form when certain cells die and leave spaces in the remaining tissue.

The structures of the mouth, such as the lips and palate, begin to form during the fourth and fifth weeks of pregnancy. The lips and palate form during the sixth to ninth weeks. Each forms from paired structures that gradually move from the sides toward the middle of the face and *fuse* (join). If anything interferes with normal development during this period, a split in the upper lip or palate may develop. Such a defect is called *cleft lip* or *cleft palate.* See **Cleft palate.**

Growth of the fetus

From the ninth week of pregnancy until birth, the developing baby is called a fetus. In the first three months of this period, the fetus increases rapidly in length. It grows about 2 inches (5 centimeters) in each of these months. In the later months of pregnancy, the most striking change in the fetus is in its weight. Most fetuses gain about 25 ounces (700 grams) in both the eighth and ninth months of pregnancy.

Stages of growth. Physicians commonly divide pregnancy into three, three-month parts called *trimesters.* At the end of the first trimester, the fetus weighs about 1 ounce (28 grams) and is about 3 inches (7.6 centimeters) long. At the end of the second trimester, the fetus weighs about 30 ounces (850 grams) and measures about 14 inches (36 centimeters) long. At the end of the third trimester, the fetus measures about 20 inches (50 centimeters) and weighs about 7 pounds (3.2 kilograms).

The mother can feel movements of the fetus by the fifth month of pregnancy. By this time, fine hair called *lanugo* covers the body of the fetus. Hair also appears on the head. Lanugo disappears late in pregnancy or shortly after birth. The eyelids open by the 26th week of pregnancy. By the 28th week, the fingernails and toenails are well developed.

Until the 30th week of pregnancy, the fetus appears reddish and transparent because of the thinness of its skin and a lack of fat beneath the skin. In the last six to eight weeks before birth, fat develops rapidly and the fetus becomes smooth and plump.

The mother also experiences many physical changes during pregnancy. For example, a pregnant woman gains weight and her breasts increase in size. For more information on such changes, see **Pregnancy.**

Checking the fetus. Physicians can use several procedures to monitor the development of the fetus in the mother's uterus. Two of the most commonly used techniques are *ultrasonography* and *amniocentesis.*

Ultrasonography, also called *ultrasound,* involves the use of high-frequency sound waves to produce an image of the fetus on a screen. By viewing the shape and body features of the fetus, a physician can measure its growth and detect malformations. Fetal abnormalities also can be detected through amniocentesis. This technique involves the removal of a sample of the amniotic fluid, which contains cells of the fetus. The fluid and cells are then analyzed and examined. See **Amniocentesis; Ultrasound.**

Birth

The process of giving birth is called *parturition* or *labor.* By this process, the fetus and the placenta are pushed out of the uterus. Scientists believe that labor is triggered by the release of certain hormones from the adrenal glands of the fetus.

A fetus that undergoes the normal period of development before labor begins is considered to have reached *term.* Labor occurs at term if it begins during the 38th to 41st week of pregnancy. Labor that starts before the 38th week is called *preterm labor.* Labor that begins after the 41st week is called *postterm labor.* Babies born at

The birth of a baby   Before birth (1), the head of the baby lies near the opening of the uterus. As muscle action forces the baby out of the uterus (2), the head turns and (3) the baby passes through the vagina.

WORLD BOOK illustrations by Joann Harling

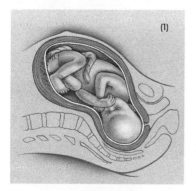

(1)

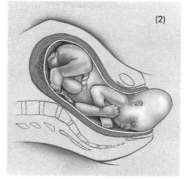

(2)

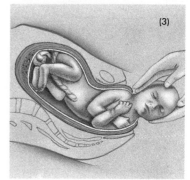

(3)

term or postterm have the best chance for survival. Most babies born from the 26th to 36th weeks of pregnancy also will live, but some of these babies may experience serious health problems because their respiratory and central nervous systems are not fully developed at birth. Babies born before the 26th week have a poor chance of surviving.

The stages of labor. Labor has three stages. The first stage begins with an alternating tensing and relaxing of muscles in the uterus. These muscle contractions are called *labor pains.* When labor begins, the fetus lies within its protective membranes and is held in place by the *cervix* (neck of the uterus). During the first stage of labor, the cervix begins to *dilate* (open). This stage ends when the cervix has fully dilated to a diameter of about 4 inches (10 centimeters). The first stage of labor is the longest, averaging about 14 hours in women giving birth for the first time. In women who have had children before, this stage normally takes 8 hours or less.

The second stage of labor begins at full dilation of the cervix and ends with the delivery of the baby. This stage may last from one to five hours. The muscle contractions of the uterus and abdomen help push the baby through the cervix and out the vagina. Most babies are born headfirst, but some are born with their shoulders or buttocks first. After the head comes out, the rest of the baby follows easily.

The third stage of labor starts after the baby's delivery and ends when the placenta, now called the *afterbirth,* is expelled from the uterus. This stage lasts about 30 minutes. A few minutes after the baby is born, the umbilical cord is clamped and cut. The placenta then detaches from the uterus and passes out the vagina.

Sometimes, the smallness of a woman's pelvis or some other condition makes it difficult to deliver a child through the vagina. In these situations, doctors may perform surgery to remove the baby through the mother's abdomen. This procedure is called a *cesarean section.* See **Childbirth.**

The newborn infant. At birth, most babies weigh about 7 pounds (3.2 kilograms) and measure about 20 inches (50 centimeters) long. The newborn infant is fed with the mother's breast milk or with a formula of milk and other nutrients. The baby can now survive outside its mother's body but needs constant care.

Lynn J. Romrell

Related articles in *World Book* include:

Abortion	Hormone (Other	Pregnancy
Baby	hormones)	Prostate cancer
Birth control	Infertility	Prostate gland
Birth defect	Medical ethics	Sexuality
Cervical cancer	Menstruation	Sexually transmit-
Childbirth	Miscarriage	ted disease
Embryo	Multiple birth	Sterility
Fallopian tube	Ovary	Testicle
Fertilization	Penis	Uterus
Genetics	Placenta	Vagina
Heredity		

Outline

I. **The human reproductive system**
   A. In females
   B. In males
II. **Fertilization**
   A. How sex is determined
   B. Multiple birth
III. **Development of the embryo**
   A. The first days of pregnancy
   B. Nourishing the embryo
   C. Origin of tissues and organs
   D. Development of organs and organ systems
IV. **Growth of the fetus**
   A. Stages of growth
   B. Checking the fetus
V. **Birth**
   A. The stages of labor
   B. The newborn infant

Questions

What are the three stages of labor?
How many chromosomes does a fertilized egg have?
What is *lanugo?*
How long does an egg survive after being released by a woman's ovary?
Where in a woman's body does fertilization usually occur?
What is *menopause?* When does it occur?
How long does pregnancy last?
What are *dizygotic twins? Monozygotic twins?*
How does a sperm propel itself?
What are *teratogens?*

Additional resources

Cooper, Susan L., and Glazer, E. S. *Beyond Infertility.* Lexington Bks., 1994.
Jones, Richard E. *Human Reproductive Biology.* Academic Pr., 1991.
Macmillan Health Encyclopedia, Vol. 6: Sexuality and Reproduction. Macmillan, 1993.
Parramón, Mercè. *The Miracle of Life.* Chelsea Hse., 1994. Younger readers.

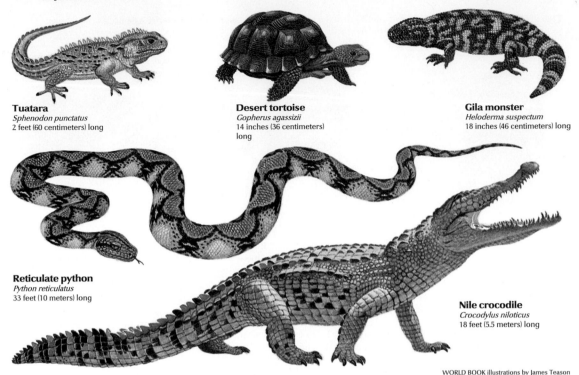

Tuatara
Sphenodon punctatus
2 feet (60 centimeters) long

Desert tortoise
Gopherus agassizii
14 inches (36 centimeters)
long

Gila monster
Heloderma suspectum
18 inches (46 centimeters) long

Reticulate python
Python reticulatus
33 feet (10 meters) long

Nile crocodile
Crocodylus niloticus
18 feet (5.5 meters) long

WORLD BOOK illustrations by James Teason

Reptiles vary greatly in size, shape, and color. However, they all have skin that consists of dry, tough scales. There are more than 7,100 species of reptiles. Most of these animals live on land, but some make their home in the ocean and others dwell in fresh water.

Reptile is an animal that has dry, scaly skin and breathes by means of lungs. There are more than 7,100 species of reptiles, and they make up one of the classes of *vertebrates* (animals that have a backbone). Reptiles include alligators, amphisbaenians, crocodiles, lizards, snakes, tuataras, and turtles.

Reptiles are cold-blooded—that is, their body temperature stays about the same as the temperature of their surroundings. To stay alive, these animals must avoid extremely high or low temperatures. Most reptiles that are active during the day keep moving from sunny places to shady spots. Many species of reptiles that live in hot climates are active mainly at night. Reptiles in regions that have harsh winters hibernate during the winter.

Reptiles vary greatly in size. For example, pythons grow more than 30 feet (9 meters) long, and leatherback turtles may weigh more than 1 short ton (0.9 metric ton). On the other hand, some species of lizards measure no more than 2 inches (5 centimeters) long.

Many reptiles live a long time, and some turtles have lived in captivity for more than 100 years. For lifespans of other reptiles in captivity, see **Animal** (table: Length of life of animals).

Reptiles live on every continent except Antarctica and in all the oceans except those of the polar regions. They are most abundant in the tropics. Many kinds of lizards and snakes thrive in deserts. Other reptiles, such as rat snakes and box turtles live in forests. Still others, including marine iguanas and sea turtles, spend much of their life in the ocean. Some sea snakes live entirely in water.

Many people fear reptiles, but most species are harmless and avoid human beings if possible. The Nile crocodile and the saltwater crocodile may attack and kill people. The Gila monster, the Mexican beaded lizard, and numerous snakes, including the rattlesnake, have *venomous* (poisonous) bites.

Many people eat reptiles and reptile eggs. Some reptiles, including alligators, crocodiles, lizards, and snakes, are hunted for their skin. Manufacturers use the skin as leather for belts, shoes, and other products. The United States government prohibits the import of the hides of those reptiles classified as endangered species.

Kinds of reptiles

Zoologists divide reptiles into four main groups: (1) lizards, amphisbaenians, and snakes, (2) turtles, (3) crocodilians, and (4) tuataras.

Lizards, amphisbaenians, and snakes make up the largest group of reptiles. There are more than 4,000 species of lizards, over 100 species of amphisbaenians, and about 2,700 species of snakes. Most lizards have four legs, long tails, movable eyelids, and external ear openings. A few species, such as glass snakes and slow worms, have no legs. Lizards thrive in regions that have a hot or warm climate and are common in deserts.

Amphisbaenians resemble worms. Most species have no limbs, but a few kinds possess very small front legs. Amphisbaenians live in many warm regions, inhabiting underground tunnels that they burrow themselves.

Snakes have tails that vary in length, depending on

the species. But snakes have no legs, eyelids, or ear openings. An unmovable covering of transparent scales protects their eyes. Snakes live mostly in the tropics and in warm regions. However, the European viper lives north of the Arctic Circle, in Finland and Sweden.

Turtles are the only reptiles with a shell. They pull their head, legs, and tail into the shell for protection. There are more than 250 species of turtles. They live on land, in fresh water, and in the ocean.

Crocodilians include alligators, caymans, crocodiles, and gavials. There are more than 20 species of crocodilians, all of which live in or near water. These reptiles have a long snout, strong jaws, and webbed hind feet. They use their long, powerful tail to swim. All except a few crocodilians dwell in the fresh waters and lowlands of the tropics. Alligators live in the Southeastern United States and in Southern China.

Tuataras inhabit several islands off the coast of New Zealand. The two species look like lizards but are more closely related to extinct dinosaurs.

The body of a reptile

Reptiles vary greatly in size, shape, and color, but all of them share certain physical characteristics. These characteristics, in addition to the animals' being cold-blooded, include various features of the skin, skeleton, internal organs, and sense organs.

Skin of a reptile consists of scales. Lizards and snakes have a single sheet of overlapping scales. The scales of turtles, crocodilians, and tuataras grow in the form of individual areas called *plates*. Crocodilians and some lizards have pieces of bone called *osteoderms* within scales. Such skin serves as protective armor.

Many reptiles shed their skin several times a year. New scales form under the old layer of scales, and chemicals called *enzymes* loosen this old layer. Among snakes, the skin on the snout is forced loose first. The snake pushes this skin backwards against a rock or plant stem. The animal then crawls out of the old skin and sheds it in one piece. Most lizards shed their skin in large strips, and crocodilian skin wears away gradually.

Skeleton of reptiles provides a framework for the head, trunk, and tail. Most reptiles have hip and shoulder bones called *girdles* that support the legs. The majority of snakes do not have girdles. The hip and shoulder girdles of turtles, unlike those of any other animal, are inside the ribcage. The ribs and vertebrae make up the inner layer of the turtle's shell.

Internal organs. Reptiles breathe by means of lungs. Most species have two lungs, but some snakes have only one. The digestive system of reptiles varies among the species, according to the kind of food the animal eats. Reptiles that feed mainly on animals or on such animal products as eggs have a fairly simple stomach and a short intestine. Such reptiles include boa constrictors and Gila monsters. Species that eat plants, including iguanas and most tortoises, have a more complicated stomach and long intestines. Crocodilians have very large stomach muscles that grind flesh into tiny pieces.

Poisonous reptiles produce their venom by means of venom glands on the sides of the head. The venom affects a victim's circulatory system or nervous system.

Sense organs. Most reptiles have good vision. Species active during the day have eyes with round pupils.

Interesting facts about reptiles

Cold-blooded animals. Reptiles are cold-blooded—that is, their body temperature rarely differs much from the temperature of their surroundings. Reptiles that are active on hot, sunny days cool off by moving to shady spots.

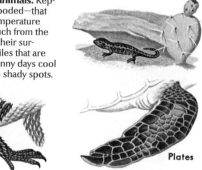

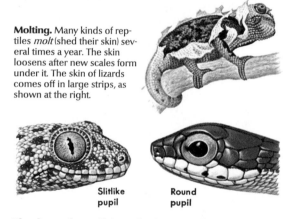

The skin of reptiles. Lizards and snakes have a single sheet of overlapping scales, *left.* Other reptiles grow *plates* (separate areas of scales), *right.* The main function of the skin is to keep water in the animal's body. Reptiles can go without water for long periods, and many species thrive in deserts.

Overlapping scales

Plates

Molting. Many kinds of reptiles *molt* (shed their skin) several times a year. The skin loosens after new scales form under it. The skin of lizards comes off in large strips, as shown at the right.

Slitlike pupil

Round pupil

The shape of a reptile's pupil indicates whether the animal is active at night or during the day. Most reptiles active at night have slitlike pupils that can be closed almost completely in bright light. Reptiles active in daytime have round pupils. Most reptiles have good vision, and some can tell the difference among colors.

Egg-laying reptiles include most of the species. The eggs are laid in decayed wood, a nest of leaves and moist soil, or elsewhere on land. Heat from the sun causes the eggs to hatch.

WORLD BOOK illustrations by James Teason

WORLD BOOK illustration by John F. Eggert

Dinosaurs, the most spectacular reptiles, dominated land animals for millions of years. These creatures died out about 65 million years ago. The Diplodocus, *above,* a plant-eating dinosaur that measured about 90 feet (27 meters) long, was one of the largest animals that ever lived.

Most species active at night have slitlike eye pupils, which can be closed almost completely in bright light.

The hearing of reptiles varies among the species, but most can hear at least low-pitched sounds. The majority of reptiles have an eardrum, a middle ear, and an inner ear. However, snakes lack a middle ear and cannot hear most sounds carried through the air. They "hear" by sensing vibrations from the ground.

Snakes and lizards have two tiny cavities called the *Jacobson's organ* in the roof of the mouth. The animals pick up particles from the air and the ground with their tongue and put them into this organ. The cavities are lined with sensitive tissue that aids the sense of smell. Pit vipers have special nerves in two depressions near the snout. The nerves are sensitive to heat—including the body heat of birds and mammals—and help the snakes hunt these animals as prey.

Ways of life

Reproduction. Most reptiles reproduce sexually. The male releases *sperm* (male sex cells) into the female opening that leads to the reproductive organs. In a process called *fertilization,* the sperm unite with *eggs* (female sex cells) within the female's body. The fertilized eggs then develop into new animals. In some lizards and snakes, females can reproduce without mating. This process is called *parthenogenesis.*

Most reptiles mate in the spring, and the young are born in summer. All turtles, crocodilians, tuataras, and some lizards and snakes are *oviparous*—that is, the female lays eggs that have shells. She lays her eggs in rotten wood, a hole in the ground, or elsewhere on land. Heat from the sun—and, in some cases, from rotting plant matter—*incubates* (warms) the eggs, causing them to hatch. Some snakes and lizards are *ovoviviparous.* Among these species, the female protects the eggs within her body until they hatch. A few species of snakes and lizards are *viviparous.* The unborn young of these species receive nourishment through the *placenta,* a structure that attaches them to the female's body. Young of ovoviviparous and viviparous reptiles are born alive.

Only a few species of reptiles provide care for their eggs or young. Among pythons, mud snakes, and some skinks, the female wraps her body around the eggs and protects them. A female alligator carries her newly hatched young to water in her mouth.

Food. Most reptiles eat other animals, and they prey on almost any creature they can catch. However, some lizards and turtles eat mainly plants. Other reptiles eat only certain animals or animal products. For example, map turtles eat freshwater clams and snails, and African egg-eating snakes feed on birds' eggs.

Most reptiles simply grab their food and either chew it or swallow it whole. Crocodilians may drown prey before eating it. Venomous reptiles paralyze victims by biting them. Pythons, king snakes, and rat snakes suffocate prey by wrapping themselves tightly around it. Reptiles can go without food for long periods. After a snake eats a large meal, it might not feed again for several weeks.

Protection. The chief enemies of reptiles include birds, mammals, and other reptiles. Most of the enemies prey on small or young reptiles. Large adult reptiles generally are safe from all attackers except people.

Reptiles avoid their enemies in a variety of ways.

Many reptiles have protective coloration that blends with their surroundings and makes them hard to see. Several kinds of lizards can change color to match their surroundings. Other reptiles bluff or play tricks to avoid attack. For example, if a hognose snake is approached, it rolls over on its back and lies completely motionless. The snake plays dead until the attacker goes away.

Most reptiles fight by biting and scratching, and some of the larger species inflict deep wounds. Crocodilians and large lizards strike sharp blows with their powerful tail, which they use as a whip. The bite of a venomous reptile can be fatal.

Hibernation. Reptiles that hibernate in winter do so by burrowing into the ground or slipping into a crack between two rocks. They stay there until the weather warms up. Before hibernating, a reptile eats a lot of food, which forms a layer of fat in its body. The fat serves as food during hibernation. Reptiles that live in the tropics sometimes enter an inactive state during dry periods, when food becomes scarce. This type of inactivity, called *estivation,* resembles hibernation.

The evolution of reptiles

The oldest fossils of reptiles date back to the Pennsylvanian Period—from 325 million to 286 million years ago. Reptiles *evolved* (developed slowly) from amphibians, which live near water because their eggs must be laid in a moist place. The eggs of amphibians dry up quickly on land. Reptiles developed eggs with thick shells and membranes, which prevent loss of moisture. As a result, reptiles can live away from water.

Reptiles became the earth's dominant animals during the Mesozoic Era—about 248 million to 65 million years ago. This period is called the *Age of Reptiles.* Mesozoic reptiles included fishlike ichthyosaurs and birdlike pterodactyls. But the most spectacular ancient reptiles were dinosaurs. Huge plant-eating dinosaurs, such as *Seismosaurus,* ranked as the largest land animals that ever lived. Ferocious *Tyrannosaurus* was a powerful land-dwelling meat eater. Most scientists believe modern birds evolved from small meat-eating dinosaurs.

Dinosaurs died out at the end of the Mesozoic. Scientists do not know why they became extinct. Many believe gradual changes in climate may have altered the food supply of plant-eating dinosaurs. As plant eaters died out, the flesh-eating dinosaurs that preyed on them also disappeared. Other scientists believe a giant asteroid hit the earth, causing catastrophic environmental damage and wiping out the dinosaurs relatively quickly.

Through the centuries, more and more species of reptiles became extinct. Today, the future of wild reptiles is threatened by the continual need of people for more farmland and living space. This need may destroy the habitats of many species of reptiles and thus wipe out the animals themselves. Other species are endangered by continued hunting and egg collecting. The survival of a number of species depends on conservation action by governments and individuals.　　D. Bruce Means

Related articles in *World Book* include:

Reptiles

See **Lizard** and **Snake** with their *Related articles.* See also:

Alligator	Gavial	Tortoise
Crocodile	Terrapin	Tuatara
Dinosaur		Turtle

Other related articles

Cold-blooded animal
Evolution (picture: The evolution of mammals from reptiles)
Fossil

Heart (Amphibians and rep-
  tiles)
Herpetology
Hibernation

Additional resources

Level I

McCarthy, Colin. *Reptile.* Knopf, 1991.
Ricciuti, Edward R. *Reptiles.* Blackbirch Pr., 1993.
Snedden, Robert. *What Is a Reptile?* Sierra Club, 1995.

Level II

Cogger, Harold G., and Zweifel, R. G., eds. *Reptiles and Amphib-
  ians.* Smithmark, 1992.
Halliday, Tim R., and Adler, Kraig, eds. *The Encyclopedia of Rep-
  tiles and Amphibians.* Facts on File, 1986.
Smith, Hobart M., and Brodie, E. D., Jr. *Reptiles of North America:
  A Guide to Field Identification.* Golden Pr., 1982.

Republic is any form of government whose leader or
leaders are elected, usually for a specific term of office.
The word *republic* also refers to a country that has an
elective form of government.

In the United States, the idea of a republic is widely
associated with the notion of a *democratic republic.* In a
democratic republic, the people as a whole exercise important controls over their elected leaders through elections, lobbying, and other processes. The leaders are expected to represent the interests of the people who
elected them. If the voters believe that their interests
have not been represented well enough, they may decide not to reelect the leaders. In this way, the voters in
a democratic republic have some control over their government.

There are many other kinds of republics besides democratic republics. In some republics, the leaders are
elected by a relatively small number of people and may
be reelected more or less automatically. Communist nations traditionally allowed only candidates approved by
the Communist Party to run for election, and there was
only one candidate for each post. As a result, voters had
no real choice of candidates when they went to the
polls. These practices are still in effect in China and a
few other Communist countries.

In some countries that are republics according to
their constitutions, elections typically are not free, open,
or honest. In some Latin American republics, for example, widespread charges of vote fraud accompany nearly every election.

The most important early republic was the one that
was established in ancient Rome in 509 B.C. This republic lasted until 27 B.C., when the political and military
leader Augustus declared himself emperor. When the
United States was founded in 1776, it became the only
major country at the time that had a republican form of
government.

Today, many of the countries of Western Europe are
republics, including Austria, Finland, France, Germany,
Italy, and Switzerland. Many of the newer African and
Asian nations are republics, as are all Latin American
countries. The Commonwealth of Nations, an association of nations that includes Britain and many of its former possessions, has numerous members that are republics (see **Commonwealth of Nations** [table:
Independent members]).   Alexander J. Groth

See also **Democracy; Government.**

Republic, The. See Plato.

Republican Party is one of the two principal political
parties of the United States. The other is the Democratic
Party. The Republican Party is often called the *G.O.P.,*
which stands for *Grand Old Party,* a nickname Republicans gave their party in the 1880's.

The Republican Party has greatly influenced the nation's history and politics. It won 14 of the 18 presidential elections from 1860, when Abraham Lincoln was
elected, to 1932. From 1932 through 2000, it won 8 of the
18 presidential elections.

The policies of the Republican Party, like those of other political parties, have changed through the years. At
first, Republican candidates got most of their support
from people who opposed slavery. To gain wider support, the party passed land legislation that appealed to
farmers. Republicans won the backing of business leaders by endorsing sound money policies and high tariffs.
By the late 1800's, the Republican Party represented a
firm alliance of the agricultural West and the industrial
East.

The Republican Party dominated American politics in
the 1920's. The economy boomed during much of the
decade, and the party became known as the "party of
prosperity." But the Republicans fell out of power in the
1930's, when the Great Depression, the worst economic
downturn in U.S. history, hit the nation.

The Republican Party includes both strongly conservative members and less conservative members called
moderates. During the 1950's, the party prospered under the moderate leader Dwight D. Eisenhower. Eisenhower won two terms as president—in 1952 and 1956.
He was the first Republican to do so since William
McKinley in 1896 and 1900. The conservatives of the Republican Party gained strength during the 1980's under
the leadership of Ronald Reagan. Reagan also won two
terms as president—in 1980 and 1984.

This article describes chiefly the history of the Republican Party. For information about the party's national
convention and organization, see **Political convention**
and **Political party.**

Origin of the Republican Party dates back to the
strong antislavery opposition to the Kansas-Nebraska
Bill of 1854. As passed by Congress in May 1854, the bill
permitted slavery in the new territories of Kansas and
Nebraska if the people there voted for it.

The Republican Party grew out of a series of antislavery meetings held throughout the North to protest the
Kansas-Nebraska Bill. One such meeting was held by Al-
van E. Bovay, a leading Whig, on Feb. 28, 1854, in Ripon,
Wisconsin. This meeting passed a resolution declaring
that a new party—the Republican Party—would be organized if the United States Congress passed the
Kansas-Nebraska Bill.

Bovay held a second meeting in Ripon on March 20,
after the Senate had passed the Kansas-Nebraska Bill.
The 53 men at this meeting appointed a committee to
form the new party. On July 6, 1854, at a party meeting in
Jackson, Michigan, the delegates formally adopted the
name *Republican.*

The new party had chiefly sectional appeal. Few
Southern voters supported the Republicans, because almost all Southerners wanted to expand slavery, not restrict it. Many Northerners supported the party. But

some feared that the extreme antislavery views of such Republican leaders as Senator Charles Sumner of Massachusetts threatened the Union.

The election of 1856. As their first presidential candidate, the Republicans chose John Charles Frémont, a dashing young explorer and soldier. During the campaign, antislavery and proslavery groups fought in Kansas. The chief campaign issue became "bleeding Kansas." Democrats predicted that the South would secede from the Union if the antislavery Frémont won.

The voting reflected the sectional appeal of the Democratic and Republican parties. Frémont won 11 Northern states. His Democratic opponent, James Buchanan, carried 19 states—including every Southern state except Maryland—and won.

Changes in party policy. After the Republican defeat in 1856, party leaders realized that they could not win the presidency on just the slavery issue. To broaden their appeal, Republicans endorsed construction of a transcontinental railroad system and federal aid to improve harbors and rivers. They also promised to open Western land for settlement, to raise U.S. tariff rates, and to permit slavery where it already existed.

In 1860, the Republicans chose Abraham Lincoln, a lanky, self-educated Illinois lawyer, as their presidential candidate. Lincoln had received national attention by expressing moderate antislavery views in his debates with Illinois Senator Stephen A. Douglas, a Democrat.

Lincoln easily won the election, even though he received less than 40 percent of the popular vote. The Democrats had split over the slavery issue. Northern Democrats nominated Douglas, and Southern Democrats chose Vice President John C. Breckinridge.

The Civil War began in April 1861. Most Southerners believed the election of Lincoln justified secession. In 1860 and 1861—both before and after the shooting started—11 Southern states left the Union.

Above all, Lincoln wanted to save the Union. But many Republicans—the so-called Radical Republicans—

made the abolition of slavery their main goal. Many Northern Democrats supported Lincoln and the war and were called War Democrats.

Lincoln tried to bring all groups of both parties together, but he succeeded only partly. By 1864, Lincoln's chances of reelection looked doubtful. To stress the national character of the war—and to gain more supporters—the Republican Party used the name *Union Party* in the 1864 election. It nominated Andrew Johnson, a War Democrat, for vice president. With the help of Northern victories just before the election, Lincoln won a second term.

On April 9, 1865, shortly after Lincoln's second term began, the war ended when General Robert E. Lee surrendered to General Ulysses S. Grant. Five days later, Lincoln was assassinated.

The Radical Republicans and Reconstruction. Johnson hoped to follow Lincoln's moderate plan of Reconstruction. But the Radical Republicans in Congress favored harsh punishment for the South.

The Radicals dominated Congress after the congressional elections of 1866. They divided the South into five military districts, deprived former Confederate soldiers of the vote, and gave the vote to former slaves.

The dispute over Reconstruction hardened political loyalties along sectional lines. Most Northern Republicans supported the Radical Republicans who, by 1868, felt strong enough to drop the Union Party label. Many Northern Democrats also backed Republican policies. But Southerners rejected Republican leadership. As a result, Reconstruction led to the birth of the Democratic "Solid South." See **Reconstruction.**

The Republicans nominated Grant, the great Union war hero, for president in 1868, and he won an easy victory. Grant won reelection in 1872, but by this time many voters had become alarmed over corruption in both business and government. A depression in 1873 helped the Democrats win a sweeping victory in the congressional elections of the next year.

From *Thomas Nast* by Albert Bigelow Paine, permission of Harper & Row

The elephant as a Republican symbol first appeared in this 1874 cartoon by Thomas Nast in *Harper's Weekly.* The elephant in the cartoon represented the Republican vote. Nast used the elephant many times as a Republican symbol, and it soon came to stand for the Republican Party.

In 1876, the Republicans nominated a cautious reformer, Rutherford B. Hayes. A group of conservative Republicans called *Stalwarts* opposed Hayes because he favored civil service reform and friendly relations with the South. Hayes and his followers became known as *Half-Breeds*. Samuel J. Tilden, the Democratic candidate, won more popular votes than Hayes, but the electoral vote was disputed. A special commission declared Hayes the winner by one vote. The Democrats accepted the verdict only because the Republicans had promised to end Reconstruction and withdraw federal troops from the South. Hayes kept the promise.

Political inactivity marked the 1880's and 1890's. Both major parties failed to face the problems resulting from the rapid industrialization that followed the Civil War. Many industrial monopolies set high prices for their products and services. Economic power became centered with a few wealthy business leaders, and farmers and wage earners suffered increasingly hard times.

In 1880, Republican James A. Garfield won the presidency. He was assassinated in 1881, only a few months after taking office, and Vice President Chester A. Arthur, a Stalwart, succeeded him. Arthur surprised his fellow Stalwarts by supporting civil service reform. In 1883, Congress passed the Pendleton Act, which established the merit system in the civil service.

In 1884, the Republican candidate, James G. Blaine, narrowly lost to Grover Cleveland. The party made the protective tariff its chief campaign issue in 1888 and won the presidency with Benjamin Harrison. In 1890, the McKinley Tariff pushed tariffs higher than they had ever been before. Dissatisfaction with the tariff helped Cleveland defeat Harrison in 1892.

The money issue dominated the election of 1896. A third party, the Populist Party, had appeared during the early 1890's. The Populists demanded that the government increase the amount of money in circulation by permitting unlimited coinage of silver. They believed such action would help farmers and wage earners and improve the nation's economy. Many Democrats joined the Populists in their demand for silver coinage. In 1896, the Democratic Party nominated William Jennings Bryan, the leading silver spokesman, for president. The Republican presidential candidate, William McKinley, supported a currency backed by gold and won the election.

Republican presidential and vice presidential candidates

Year	President	Vice President	Year	President	Vice President
1856	John C. Frémont	William L. Dayton	1932	Herbert Hoover	Charles Curtis
1860	*Abraham Lincoln*	*Hannibal Hamlin*	1936	Alfred M. Landon	Frank Knox
1864	*Abraham Lincoln*	*Andrew Johnson*	1940	Wendell L. Willkie	Charles L. McNary
1868	*Ulysses S. Grant*	*Schuyler Colfax*	1944	Thomas E. Dewey	John W. Bricker
1872	*Ulysses S. Grant*	*Henry Wilson*	1948	Thomas E. Dewey	Earl Warren
1876	*Rutherford B. Hayes*	*William A. Wheeler*	1952	*Dwight D. Eisenhower*	*Richard M. Nixon*
1880	*James A. Garfield*	*Chester A. Arthur*	1956	*Dwight D. Eisenhower*	*Richard M. Nixon*
1884	James G. Blaine	John A. Logan	1960	Richard M. Nixon	Henry Cabot Lodge, Jr.
1888	*Benjamin Harrison*	*Levi P. Morton*	1964	Barry M. Goldwater	William E. Miller
1892	Benjamin Harrison	Whitelaw Reid	1968	*Richard M. Nixon*	*Spiro T. Agnew*
1896	*William McKinley*	*Garret A. Hobart*	1972	*Richard M. Nixon*	*Spiro T. Agnew*
1900	*William McKinley*	*Theodore Roosevelt*	1976	Gerald R. Ford	Robert J. Dole
1904	*Theodore Roosevelt*	*Charles W. Fairbanks*	1980	*Ronald W. Reagan*	*George H. W. Bush*
1908	*William Howard Taft*	*James S. Sherman*	1984	*Ronald W. Reagan*	*George H. W. Bush*
1912	William Howard Taft	James S. Sherman	1988	*George H. W. Bush*	*Dan Quayle*
1916	Charles Evans Hughes	Charles W. Fairbanks	1992	George H. W. Bush	Dan Quayle
1920	*Warren G. Harding*	*Calvin Coolidge*	1996	Robert Dole	Jack Kemp
1924	*Calvin Coolidge*	*Charles G. Dawes*	2000	*George W. Bush*	*Richard B. Cheney*
1928	*Herbert Hoover*	*Charles Curtis*			

Names of elected candidates are in italics.
Each candidate has a separate biography in *World Book*.

Administrations in office

WORLD BOOK graph

Democratic Party   Republican Party

1857 1861 1865 1869 1873 1877 1881 1885 1889 1893 1897 1901 1905 1909 1913 1917 1921

1921 1925 1929 1933 1937 1941 1945 1949 1953 1957 1961 1965 1969 1973 1977 1981 1985

1985 1989 1993 1997 2001 2005 2009 2013 2017 2021

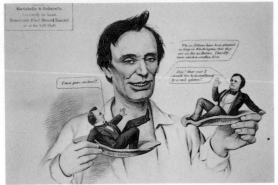

Lithograph (1860) by Currier & Ives (Granger Collection)

Abraham Lincoln is about to devour his Democratic opponents, Stephen A. Douglas and John C. Breckinridge, in a political cartoon published during the 1860 presidential race.

Granger Collection

In the Republican Party split of 1912, "Teddy" Roosevelt and William Howard Taft pulled apart. The division of the party helped Woodrow Wilson, the Democratic candidate, win the presidency with about 40 percent of the popular vote.

Economic conditions improved rapidly during the late 1890's. The United States victory in the Spanish-American War also gained support for the Republicans. McKinley defeated Bryan again in 1900. Six months after beginning his second term, however, McKinley was assassinated. Vice President Theodore Roosevelt succeeded him.

The party splits. "Teddy" Roosevelt supported much reform legislation. He brought suits against several large monopolies and crusaded for honesty in government. Roosevelt also sponsored a conservation policy, laws to protect the American public from impure food

and drugs, and legislation to regulate railroad rates.

In 1908, Roosevelt chose his friend, Secretary of War William Howard Taft, to succeed him and continue his policies. Taft easily beat Bryan, who ran for the third time as the Democratic nominee.

Taft brought many more suits against monopolies than Roosevelt had. But Taft, by nature quieter and more conservative than Roosevelt, lost favor with Republican progressives. He faced open hostility from the progressives after signing into law the high Payne-Aldrich Tariff in 1909. By 1912, Taft no longer led a united party, and the progressives turned to Roosevelt, who wanted to be president again. After the Republicans renominated Taft, Roosevelt left the party and formed the Progressive, or "Bull Moose," Party. The Republican split helped Woodrow Wilson, the Democratic candidate, win the election.

The Republicans began to reunite after their defeat, and in 1916, most of them supported the party candidate, Charles Evans Hughes. But some backed Wilson because he had promoted progressive legislation and had kept the nation out of World War I, which had begun in 1914. Wilson won reelection by a close margin. A month after he took office for the second time, the United States went to war against Germany.

By the congressional elections of 1918, the Republicans had reunited, and they gained control of Congress. After the war, the Republican-controlled Senate rejected American membership in the League of Nations (see **League of Nations**).

During the Roaring 20's, the Republicans won every presidential and congressional election. In 1920, the party's candidate, Warren G. Harding, promised a return to "normalcy." Americans, weary of wartime controls and world problems, wanted just that—and Harding won in a landslide.

The nation's economy boomed during the 1920's as business and industry expanded. Successive Republican administrations helped big business by keeping government spending and taxes low and by raising tariffs.

After Harding's death in 1923, congressional investigations revealed corruption in several government departments during his Administration. But the exposures did not prevent Harding's successor, Vice President Calvin Coolidge, from easily winning the 1924 election. Coolidge's conservative Administration seemed to reflect the largely antiforeign, anti-immigration, antilabor mood of the nation.

In 1928, the Republicans turned to Herbert Hoover, Coolidge's secretary of commerce. Hoover easily defeated his Democratic opponent, Alfred E. Smith, but Smith carried most of the largest cities.

Soon after Hoover took office in 1929, the worst stock-market crash in the nation's history occurred. The Great Depression followed. Hoover tried to stop the depression but could not do so, and he lost badly in 1932 to the Democratic candidate, Franklin D. Roosevelt. Hoover's defeat reduced the Republican Party to a hard core of business leaders, Midwestern farmers, and conservative workers.

From 1933 to 1953, the Republican Party was the minority party. Roosevelt led the nation through the Great Depression with a massive federal program called the New Deal (see **New Deal**). The Republicans, far outnumbered in both houses of Congress, took little action against his policies. The 1936 Republican Party platform criticized the New Deal, but Roosevelt won reelection by a landslide over Alfred M. Landon.

By the election of 1940, World War II (1939-1945) had started. The Republicans nominated Wendell L. Willkie and continued to attack the New Deal, but Roosevelt easily won a third term. The United States entered the war in 1941. Roosevelt defeated Thomas E. Dewey in 1944 and became the only candidate to be elected president four times.

In the 1930's and 1940's, many Republicans accepted the idea of federal welfare programs and of U.S. leadership in world affairs. They also accepted U.S. membership in the United Nations, formed in 1945. Vice President Harry S. Truman became president after Roosevelt's death in 1945. The Republicans expected to win the 1948 election easily, and they nominated Dewey again. But Truman won a surprise victory.

The Eisenhower years. Dwight D. Eisenhower easily won the 1952 election for the Republicans, defeating Adlai E. Stevenson. Eisenhower, a World War II hero, carried four Southern states and broke the Democratic Solid South for the first time in more than 20 years. Great numbers of voters turned to Eisenhower for reasons other than his popularity. Many voted Republican because of dissatisfaction with the government's conduct of the Korean War (1950-1953). Others believed charges that the Democrats had harbored Communists in high government posts. Eisenhower won reelection in 1956 by a landslide, again over Stevenson.

Eisenhower, a moderate Republican, won support from his own party and from many Southern Democrats. His administration encouraged private enterprise, and during his presidency, Congress extended Social Security benefits and passed the first civil rights act since Reconstruction.

Defeat, then victory. Vice President Richard M. Nixon won the Republican presidential nomination in 1960. He narrowly lost the election to his Democratic opponent, John F. Kennedy. After Kennedy's assassination in 1963, Vice President Lyndon B. Johnson succeeded to the presidency. In 1964, the Republicans nominated Barry M. Goldwater, who stood for an extreme form of conservatism. Johnson defeated him overwhelmingly.

At Johnson's urging, Congress passed additional civil rights legislation and other laws to help disadvantaged Americans. Conservative Republicans and conservative Southern Democrats joined forces to oppose many of Johnson's programs.

For the 1968 presidential election, the Republicans turned to Nixon again. The Democrats nominated Vice President Hubert H. Humphrey. A third party, the American Independent Party, nominated George C. Wallace, a Southern Democrat who strongly opposed civil rights legislation. Nixon won even though he received only about 43 percent of the popular vote. In 1972, the Republicans renominated Nixon. The Democrats nominated George S. McGovern. Nixon received over $17\frac{3}{4}$ million more popular votes than McGovern—the widest margin of any United States presidential election.

The Watergate scandal. In 1973, Nixon helped end U.S. involvement in the Vietnam War. His administration suffered a loss of public confidence later that year, however, because of the Watergate scandal and an unrelated criminal investigation that led to the resignation of Nixon's vice president, Spiro T. Agnew (see **Watergate; Agnew, Spiro T.**).

House Minority Leader Gerald R. Ford replaced Agnew as vice president. In July 1974, the House Judiciary Committee recommended that Nixon be impeached on charges related to the Watergate scandal. Nixon resigned in August, before the House voted on impeachment, and Ford became president. In 1976, Ford was defeated by Jimmy Carter, his Democratic opponent.

Victories in the 1980's. The Republicans won every presidential election during the 1980's. In 1980, they chose Ronald Reagan for president. The Democrats renominated Carter, and Representative John B. Anderson of Illinois ran as an independent. Reagan won by a wide margin. The Republicans also won control of the Senate. In the 1984 presidential election, Reagan defeated his Democratic opponent, Walter F. Mondale. In the 1986 elections, the Democrats regained control of the Senate. In 1988, Vice President George H. W. Bush won the Republican presidential nomination. He defeated his Democratic opponent, Michael S. Dukakis.

Control of Congress. In 1992, the Republicans renominated Bush for president. The Democrats nominated Bill Clinton, and Texas businessman Ross Perot ran as an independent. Bush and Perot lost the election to Clinton. In 1994, the Republicans won control of both houses of Congress. The party had not controlled both houses since 1955. In 1996, Senator Robert Dole of Kansas won the Republican presidential nomination. The Democrats renominated Clinton. Dole lost the election to Clinton. But the Republicans retained control of both houses of Congress in 1996 and 1998.

Mixed results. In 2000, the Republican candidate was Texas Governor George W. Bush, son of former President George H. W. Bush. He defeated the Democratic candidate, Vice President Al Gore, in an extremely close election. The Republicans kept control of the House, but the election left the Senate with 50 Republican members and 50 Democratic members.   George H. Mayer

Related articles in *World Book* include:

Christian Coalition	President of the United States
Free Soil Party	Progressive Party
Liberal Republican Party	Reconstruction (The struggle
Mugwumps	over Reconstruction)
Nast, Thomas	United States, History of the
Political convention	Whig Party
Political party	

Additional resources

Connelly, William F., Jr., and Pitney, J. J., Jr. *Congress' Permanent Minority? Republicans in the U.S. House.* Rowman & Littlefield, 1994.
Foner, Eric. *Free Soil, Free Labor, Free Men: The Ideology of the Republican Party Before the Civil War.* 1970. Reprint. Oxford, 1995.

Research. See Science (How scientists work). See also *A Guide to Research Skills* in the Research Guide/Index, Volume 22.

Reserpine, *REHS uhr pihn* or *ruh SUR pihn,* is a drug used to treat mild *hypertension* (high blood pressure). It is obtained from a shrub called *Rauwolfia serpentina,* which grows in India and Southeast Asia. Extracts from this plant have been used for centuries in that part of the world to treat such disorders as hypertension, insomnia, mental illness, and poisoning from snakebite.

In the 1950's, physicians in Western countries used reserpine to treat hypertension and to calm emotionally ill patients. Since the 1960's, it has been used mainly to lower the blood pressure of people with mild hypertension. Other, more effective drugs have largely replaced reserpine in the treatment of emotional illness.

Reserpine may produce harmful reactions. Small doses can cause drowsiness, severe depression, and peptic ulcers. Larger doses of the drug may result in abnormally low blood pressure and loss of consciousness.

N. E. Sladek

Reservation, called *reserve* in Canada. See **Indian reservation.**

Reserve Officers Training Corps (ROTC) trains students in schools, colleges, and universities to become officers in the United States armed services. It seeks to develop students for positions of military leadership. Qualified students take ROTC training in addition to their regular school or college work. All such training is given on campus, except for field training during the summer.

Students enrolled in an ROTC unit are organized along military lines. One student serves as cadet commander, and others hold staff or command positions. The commissioned officer directing the unit usually has the title of professor of military science (for Army units), naval science (for Navy units), or aerospace studies (for Air Force units). The staff includes officers and enlisted personnel who teach courses, and others who handle the administration of the unit.

Army ROTC consists of two divisions. *Junior* units provide three years of basic military training in high schools. *Senior* units enroll students for two to four years in military schools, colleges, and universities. Course work includes drills, lectures, demonstrations, and field trips. The first two years of the senior course may be required for qualified students. The last two years are voluntary. In the Advanced ROTC Course program, students may enter in their junior year. Instead of the regular first two-year program, they attend a qualifying basic training course in the summer before entering the advanced course. Students receive pay and allowances in their junior and senior year training. The Army grants commissions as second lieutenant in the Army reserve to students who complete the four-year program and a summer of field training. It offers regular Army commissions to students designated as *Distinguished Military Graduates*. Upon graduation, the new officers serve two to four years on active duty in the U.S. Army. They serve for shorter periods if they go into the Army Reserve or Army Guard. The Army has ROTC units in more than 300 colleges and universities and about 800 high schools. In addition, students at many other educational institutions may enroll in ROTC units at extension centers or at host universities. Women are admitted to ROTC units at coeducational universities and colleges.

Navy ROTC has units in about 65 colleges and universities and about 230 high schools. Women are admitted in the program at coeducational universities and colleges. The senior course level has two types of training. The *scholarship NROTC* program provides a four-year education paid for almost entirely by the government. These students must take three summer cruises as part

of their ROTC course work. Upon graduation, they receive commissions as ensigns in the Navy or as second lieutenants in the Marine Corps. Under the Navy's *college NROTC* program, participating college students have the same course work as do those in the regular program but they have only one summer training cruise. They also pay their own tuition and receive a monthly allowance during their last two years in the program. They serve three years of active duty after receiving commissions as ensigns in the Naval and Marine Corps reserve. Graduates of the scholarship NROTC must serve for four years.

Air Force ROTC operates in about 150 universities and colleges and about 300 high schools. It has both junior and senior programs that resemble those of Army ROTC. College students who participate in Air Force ROTC take two years or four years of part-time military training, and one summer of field training at an Air Force base. They may apply for a scholarship and allowances. Special programs are available for students who seek assignments as pilots, navigators, or missile officers, or as medical or legal personnel. Newly appointed second lieutenants in the Air Force reserve must serve four years of active duty. Distinguished Military Graduates are offered commissions in the regular Air Force. The Air Force admits women to ROTC programs at coeducational universities.

History. The ROTC has its origin in the Morrill, or Land-Grant, Act of 1862. The act authorized grants of public land to state colleges. In return, it required those colleges to offer military training for all able-bodied male students. The first actual reserve commissions were granted to students in 1908. The National Defense Act of 1916 established the first Army ROTC units. It set up an Officers Reserve Corps to be composed of men trained in the ROTC and in training camps. By the fall of 1916, the Army had enrolled about 40,000 students. In 1926, the Navy established its ROTC program, and set up units at six colleges and universities. The Air Force began its ROTC program in 1947, when it became an independent military service.   Allan R. Millett

Reserves. See **Air Force, United States** (Air Force reserves); **Army, United States** (Organization of the Army); **Navy, United States** (Regulars and reserves).

Reservoir is a place where large quantities of water are stored to be used for irrigation, power generation, water supply, and recreation. Reservoirs may also serve as a means to control flooding. A reservoir may be either natural or artificial. Natural lakes form reservoirs from which some cities obtain their water supply.

Engineers build artificial reservoirs by constructing a dam across a narrow valley or by digging a basin in a level tract of land. Examples of reservoirs that are made by building dams are those of the Tennessee Valley Authority; Lake Mead, which is *impounded* (confined) by Hoover Dam; and Franklin D. Roosevelt Lake, which is impounded by Grand Coulee Dam. The capacity of a reservoir is measured in acre-feet or cubic meters. An acre-foot of water represents a volume of water that covers an area of one acre and has a depth of one foot. An acre-foot equals 1,233 cubic meters and contains 325,829 gallons (1,233,482 liters).

Some small cities store their water in large tanks supported on a high framework or in small *holding reser-*

Largest reservoirs in the United States

Reservoir	Location	Capacity		Year completed
		In thousands of acre-feet*	In millions of cubic meters	
Lake Mead	Arizona-Nevada	28,250	34,850	1936
Lake Powell	Arizona-Utah	27,000	33,300	1966
Lake Sakakawea	North Dakota	22,630	27,920	1953
Lake Oahe	North Dakota-South Dakota	22,240	27,430	1958
Fort Peck Lake	Montana	17,930	22,120	1937
Franklin D. Roosevelt Lake	Washington	9,560	11,790	1942
Lake Koocanusa	Montana	5,810	7,170	1973
Lake Francis Case	South Dakota	4,620	5,700	1952
Shasta Lake	California	4,550	5,610	1945
Toledo Bend Lake	Louisiana	4,480	5,520	1968

*An acre-foot equals one acre of water one foot deep.
Source: U.S. Committee on Large Dams.

Largest reservoirs in the world

Reservoir	Location	Capacity		Year completed
		In thousands of acre-feet*	In millions of cubic meters	
Lake Victoria†	Kenya, Tanzania, Uganda	166,000	204,800	1954
Bratsk	Russia	137,000	169,000	1964
Lake Nasser	Egypt, Sudan	131,300	162,000	1970
Kariba Lake	Zambia, Zimbabwe	130,000	160,400	1959
Lake Volta	Ghana	120,000	148,000	1965
Manicouagan	Canada	115,000	141,900	1968
Guri	Venezuela	109,400	135,000	1986
Krasnoyarsk	Russia	59,400	73,300	1967
Williston Lake	Canada	57,000	70,300	1967
Zeya	Russia	55,500	68,400	1978

*An acre-foot equals one acre of water one foot deep.
†Enlarged natural lake.
Source: U.S. Committee on Large Dams.

voirs. The tanks or reservoirs are built at an elevation above the highest buildings to create enough pressure to force the water to the tops of the buildings. Such tanks are often called *standpipes.* Larry W. Mays

See also **Aqueduct; Dam; Irrigation** (Surface water); **Water; Water power.**

Resin, *REHZ uhn,* is any one of a class of natural substances used in varnishes, medicines, soaps, paints, and other applications. Natural resins have largely been replaced by synthetic resins. Natural resins may be divided into three main groups: (1) those that flow from plants as the result of wounds; (2) those extracted from wood by solvents; and (3) fossil resins found with the preserved remains of animals and plants. A scale insect of the acacia tree also produces a resin, called *lac.*

Gum resins, such as asafetida, aloe, and the gum of the balsam tree, often have been used in medicines. However, recent developments in pharmacology question the use of resins in medicine. *Rosin,* a resin obtained from several varieties of pine trees, is used in paints, varnishes, and printing inks. *Oleoresins* are resins combined with essential oils that are used in turpentine and tar. Roger D. Barry

Related articles in *World Book* include:
Amber
Lac
Mastic
Resin, Synthetic
Rosin

Resin, *REHZ uhn,* **Synthetic,** is any one of a large group of chemical compounds that includes most of our common plastics. These resins may be made as fibers or films, or molded into a great variety of shapes, ranging from pocket combs to automobile bodies. Manufacturers use these compounds in paints and adhesives and as coatings for cloth, paper, and metal.

Synthetic resins are made up of many simple molecules linked together to form large, complex ones. Scientists call them *high polymers. Polymer* comes from the Greek words *poly,* meaning *many,* and *meros,* meaning *part.* The nature of synthetic resins is determined by the chemicals they contain and by the patterns of the new molecules. If long, fibrous molecules form, the substance is tough but softens when heated. If the molecules form long chains with many cross-links, the resin is hard, brittle, and sets when it is heated. If few cross-links form, the resin usually is elastic. Resins with short chainlike molecules are gummy or waxlike.

Manufacturers use coal, natural gas, petroleum, wood, salt, air, and water to make synthetic resins. Complicated chemical processes change these common materials into a variety of chemicals such as alcohol, formaldehyde, glycerol, phenol, ethylene, ammonia, and urea. These substances are then combined in many ways to form the complex molecules of the resins.

Synthetic polymers vary greatly in composition, properties, and uses. Manufacturers often alter the original properties before making them into marketable items. They do this by combining or compounding the substances with fillers, colors, lubricants, and other materials and by heat treatment. Richard F. Blewitt

Related articles in *World Book* include:
Molecule
Painting (Materials and techniques)
Plastics
Polymer
Silicone
Urea

Resistance. See **Electric circuit** (Circuit mathematics).
Resistor. See **Electronics** (Passive components).
Resonance. See **Sound** (Resonance).
Resorcinol, *rehz AWR suh nahl,* is a compound used in making ointments, dyes, and other useful chemical compounds. It is a colorless, crystalline phenol with the chemical formula $C_6H_4(OH)_2$ and is also known as *meta-dihydroxybenzene.* Resorcinol is prepared by fusing benzenedisulfonic acid with sodium hydroxide.

Resorcinol is added to ointments used to treat skin diseases such as acne and eczema. Hexylresorcinol is a general antiseptic. Chemists use resorcinol to make dyes such as *eosin,* a dye used in red ink. It is also important in the preparation of resins and adhesives.
Patrice C. Bélanger

Resources, Natural. See **Natural resources.**
Respighi, *reh SPEE gee,* **Ottorino,** *oh toh REE noh* (1879-1936), was one of the most successful Italian composers of the early 1900's. His studies with the Russian composer Nikolai Rimsky-Korsakov influenced his vividly colorful orchestrations. The symphonic poems *The Fountains of Rome* (1917) and *The Pines of Rome* (1924), his most famous compositions, also show the influence of the composers Maurice Ravel and Richard Strauss. Respighi's interest in older music is reflected in the use of medieval Gregorian themes. Respighi was born in Bologna. Vincent McDermott

Respiration is the process by which human beings and other living things obtain and use oxygen. Except for certain microorganisms, all living things require oxygen to live. Respiration also involves the elimination of carbon dioxide, a gas produced when cells use oxygen.

Respiration may be divided into two processes: (1) organismic respiration and (2) cellular respiration. Organismic respiration is the process by which animals take in oxygen from the environment and carry it to the cells of their tissues. Carbon dioxide is carried away from the cells and delivered to the environment. In cellular respiration, oxygen is used in chemical reactions within the cells. These reactions release energy and produce carbon dioxide and water as waste products.

Organisms carry out organismic respiration in various ways, depending on their size and environment. For example, single-celled organisms, such as diatoms and amebas, exchange oxygen and carbon dioxide directly with the environment through their cell membranes. In higher animals, however, each cell lacks direct contact with the environment. A system of specialized structures or organs is required to carry out organismic respiration in these animals.

This article deals chiefly with respiration in humans and other mammals. Respiration in other animals with lungs—such as birds, reptiles, and most adult amphibians—is carried out in similar ways. These animals all exchange gas with the environment by breathing.

Breathing

Structures of breathing. The lungs are the organs of breathing. They are elastic structures in the chest cavity. Each lung contains millions of small air chambers called *alveoli.* A network of tiny blood vessels called *capillaries* lies within the walls of each alveolus.

Other important structures are the *chest wall* and the *diaphragm.* The chest wall includes the bones that form a protective cage around the chest cavity, the muscles associated with these bones, and the abdominal muscles. The diaphragm is a dome-shaped sheet of muscle that separates the chest cavity from the abdomen.

Gas enters and leaves the body through the nose and mouth. The *pharynx* (back of the nose and mouth), the *larynx* (voice box), and the *trachea* (windpipe) are the passages that connect the nose and mouth with the lungs.

The process of breathing. Breathing consists of two acts, *inspiration* (breathing in) and *expiration* (breathing out). During inspiration, also called *inhalation,* air from the atmosphere is drawn into the lungs. During expiration, or *exhalation,* gas is expelled from the lungs.

Inspiration occurs when the diaphragm and the muscles of the chest wall contract. This action lifts the ribs and makes the chest cavity longer and wider, causing the lungs to expand. The expansion of the lungs lowers the pressure in the alveoli, drawing fresh air into the lungs. Oxygen makes up about 20 per cent of the volume of this fresh air. Almost all the rest of it is nitrogen. Only about 0.03 per cent is carbon dioxide.

Expiration results when the diaphragm and other muscles relax, allowing the lungs to retract. This action causes the pressure of the gas in the alveoli to become greater than the atmospheric pressure. As a result, gas flows out of the lungs. Carbon dioxide makes up about 5 per cent and oxygen about 15 per cent of this gas.

Oxygen and carbon dioxide are exchanged between

Breathing   Breathing is the process by which the body takes in oxygen from the atmosphere and releases carbon dioxide into the atmosphere. This exchange of gases takes place in the lungs. Breathing is controlled by an area of the brain called the *respiratory center.*

WORLD BOOK diagrams by Leonard E. Morgan

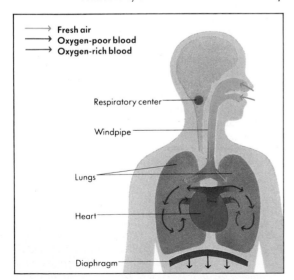

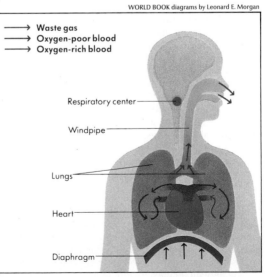

Inspiration—the act of drawing air into the lungs—occurs when the inspiratory muscles contract. Contraction of the *diaphragm,* the chief inspiratory muscle, makes the chest volume larger and thus expands the lungs. This expansion lowers the pressure in the lungs, and air flows in from the atmosphere.

Expiration—the act of letting gas out of the lungs—takes place when the inspiratory muscles relax. The relaxation of these muscles removes the force expanding the lungs, which become smaller. Because of the smaller lung volume, gas pressure inside the lungs increases, and gas flows out into the atmosphere.

the gas and the blood in the lungs through the thin walls of capillaries in the alveoli. Blood entering these capillaries is low in oxygen and high in carbon dioxide. Oxygen that has been inhaled passes into the blood, while carbon dioxide moves from the blood into the alveoli. Between breaths, when the respiratory system is "at rest," the lungs still contain almost half the gas they are capable of holding. This gas provides a reserve so exchange of oxygen and carbon dioxide can continue between breaths.

Control of breathing. Breathing is regulated by the *respiratory center,* groups of nerve cells in the brain stem. Every few seconds, these cells send bursts of impulses to the muscles involved in inspiration. These signals determine the rate and depth of breathing. The average rate in adult human beings is 12 to 15 breaths per minute. Another group of special cells, called *chemoreceptors,* sense the oxygen and carbon dioxide levels in the blood and the acidity of *cerebrospinal fluid* surrounding the brain. Slight increases or decreases in carbon dioxide cause changes in the acidity of body fluids. These changes may affect various body functions. Chemoreceptors send signals to the respiratory center to adjust the rate and depth of breathing. When necessary, such as during exercise, muscles in the chest wall can be stimulated to speed up expiration. In this way, the respiratory center maintains normal levels of oxygen and acidity in the body.

Gas transport between the lungs and tissues

The circulatory system transports oxygen to body tissues and carries carbon dioxide away from them. Red blood cells play an essential role in this process. They contain *hemoglobin,* a molecule that can carry much oxygen. The cells also contain an enzyme called *carbonic anhydrase.* This enzyme helps change carbon dioxide into *bicarbonate ion,* a form that is easily carried in blood.

Red blood cells pick up oxygen as they pass through the lungs. The heart then pumps this oxygen-rich blood through the arteries to capillaries in the body tissues. There, oxygen is released from the hemoglobin and passes through the capillary walls to the tissue cells. At the same time, carbon dioxide produced by the tissue cells enters the blood.

Carbonic anhydrase in the red blood cells helps change most of the carbon dioxide to bicarbonate ions. Most of these bicarbonate ions move out of the red blood cells and are carried in blood plasma. The rest of the carbon dioxide entering the blood becomes associated with hemoglobin molecules or stays dissolved in plasma. When the blood reaches capillaries in the alveoli, these reactions reverse and the released carbon dioxide enters the gas in the alveoli.

Cellular respiration

Respiration in cells involves a series of chemical reactions that occur in the presence of oxygen. These reactions release energy from food substances and make it available so that the cells can function.

Cells can obtain some energy without oxygen by a chemical process called *glycolysis.* Glycolysis converts molecules of *glucose* (a simple sugar) into smaller molecules called *pyruvic acid.* This action releases energy, which is captured in a compound known as *adenosine triphosphate* (ATP). ATP is very important because it supplies energy to all cells. However, glycolysis produces only a small amount of ATP.

Cells require oxygen to obtain large amounts of ATP. When oxygen is present in a cell, pyruvic acid enters a series of chemical reactions called the *Krebs cycle.* During the cycle, energy is captured and passed on to a series of reactions called the *electron transport chain.* As a result of these reactions, carbon dioxide and water are formed and a great deal of energy is stored as ATP.

Breathing in animals without lungs

Many animals that live in water, including fish and shellfish, have gills for exchanging oxygen and carbon dioxide with their environment. When water comes in contact with the gills, oxygen dissolved in the water moves through the thin membrane that separates the animal's blood from the water. At the same time, carbon dioxide moves from blood to water. Fish take in water through the mouth and force it out over the gills.

Other animals that lack lungs also have special ways of breathing. For example, insects have a system of tiny air tubes called *tracheae.* These tubes carry air from the environment directly to all parts of the body.

Some animals, such as amphibians, use more than one organ of respiration during their life. Frogs, for example, breathe through gills while they are tadpoles. Mature frogs breathe chiefly with lungs and also exchange gas with the environment through their skin.

Respiration in plants

In higher plants, oxygen and carbon dioxide move into and out of the roots and stems through the outer layers of cells. The majority of gas exchange in plants, however, takes place through small openings in the leaves called *stomata.*

Like animal cells, plant cells obtain energy through chemical reactions that break down glucose. Green plants also produce energy through a "reverse respiration" process called *photosynthesis.* In photosynthesis, the plant uses energy from light to make glucose. During this process, the plant takes in carbon dioxide from the environment and produces oxygen as a waste product. Certain bacteria also perform photosynthesis.

Harold I. Modell and Jack Hildebrandt

Related articles in *World Book* include:

Additional resources

Kittredge, Mary. *The Respiratory System.* Chelsea Hse., 1989.
Silverstein, Alvin, and others. *The Respiratory System.* 21st Century Bks., 1994. Younger readers.

Respirator is a machine that helps a person breathe. A respirator may be used if illness or an accident causes breathing to become difficult or to stop. It also can be used to administer oxygen or to treat a patient with a mist containing medications. Respirators are often called *ventilators* or *resuscitators.* There are two basic types—*positive-pressure respirators* and *negative-pressure respirators.*

A positive-pressure respirator forces air into the lungs under pressure. After the lungs are filled, the machine cuts off the pressure, and the natural elasticity of the lungs expels the air. Such machines operate as either *assist respirators* or *automatic respirators.* Assist respirators are triggered by the patient's breathing. They help extremely weak people inhale. Automatic respirators control respiration completely and aid people whose breathing muscles are paralyzed.

Negative-pressure respirators include the *iron lung,* which encloses the entire body except for the head, and the *chest cuirass,* which covers only the chest. These machines create a vacuum that causes the patient's chest to expand, drawing air into the lungs. They then destroy the vacuum, allowing the patient's chest to contract and expel the air.   Brian J. Sproule

See also **Iron lung.**

Respiratory distress syndrome. See Hyaline membrane disease.

Respiratory system. See Respiration.

Response. See Learning (How we learn); **Reflex action.**

Rest. See Health (Rest and sleep); **Sleep.**

Rest. See Music (Indicating time values).

Restaurant is a business establishment that serves food and beverages to the public. The first restaurants operated along roadsides, where travelers stopped to rest and to restore their energy. The word *restaurant* comes from the Latin word *restaurare,* meaning *to restore.* Today, restaurants may be found almost everywhere. The United States has more than 350,000 restaurants. They serve a total of about 150 million meals daily.

Restaurants make up the largest part of the *food service* industry. All places that prepare food outside the home are part of this industry, including food operations in schools, hospitals, factories, and prisons. The

WORLD BOOK photo by Odyssey Productions

Restaurants include full-service restaurants and fast-service restaurants that offer quick service and inexpensive food.

food service industry ranks as one of the chief U.S. retail industries. It is the country's largest employer of women and minorities.

Kinds of restaurants. There are two main kinds of restaurants: (1) full-service restaurants and (2) fast-service restaurants.

Full-service restaurants. In most of these restaurants, customers are seated at a table and given a menu. The menu offers a variety of choices. A server usually takes the customer's order and brings food to the table. The largest number of full-service restaurants are family restaurants, which offer foods at moderate prices.

Other types of full-service restaurants include ethnic restaurants and gourmet restaurants. Ethnic restaurants serve the food of a specific country, such as Mexico or China. Gourmet restaurants offer menus that change daily and feature somewhat unusual menu choices. Some also feature classical dishes prepared from recipes created by great chefs. Meals served in gourmet restaurants usually cost more than those served in other restaurants.

Some full-service restaurants offer a buffet. Various dishes are placed on a table and customers serve themselves. A server may bring beverages. In some restaurants, the server brings the main course, and diners serve themselves from a salad bar or a dessert bar.

Cafeterias display a wide variety of plated food on a counter or in heated trays. Customers move along a counter with a tray and serve themselves. A cashier is located at the end of the counter. Cafeterias are the most common type of food service in institutional operations such as schools and business offices.

Fast-service restaurants provide inexpensive food and quick service. Many of these restaurants serve only such foods as hamburgers, fried chicken, pizza, tacos, or ice cream. Because these foods do not provide a balanced variety of nutrients, many fast-service restaurants also offer salads and other nutritional foods.

In addition to sit-down services, fast-service restaurants offer *drive-through, carry-out,* and *home-delivery* services. In a drive through, customers place orders from their cars by means of a parking lot microphone and then drive to a restaurant window to pick up their food. Carry-out services enable customers to pick up prepared food and take it out of the restaurant to eat. Home-delivery service allows customers to have food delivered to their homes. Home-delivery is most common with restaurants offering pizza, Chinese, and fried chicken menus, though some restaurants deliver full gourmet meals.

Chains and franchises. A restaurant *chain* consists of two or more restaurants owned by one person or company. Most chains are formed by a person who operates a successful restaurant and wishes to expand the business. Usually, all restaurants in a chain look alike and serve the same food.

In most *franchise* agreements, a restaurant owner grants another person or company the right to use the name of his or her restaurant. This right also includes use of the original owner's patented products, building designs, and trademarks. In return for this right, called a *franchise,* the original owner receives a fee. In addition, the franchise buyer (called *franchisee*) usually pays a percentage of the restaurant's income to the original owner. The franchisee receives services from the original owner, including financial advice, computer programs, and training programs. In most cases, if the franchisee does not maintain standards of food quality, service, and cleanliness in the restaurant, the original owner can cancel the franchise agreement.

Career opportunities. Employment opportunities in restaurants range from part-time jobs to full-time careers. Restaurant employees include bartenders; servers; cashiers; chefs; cooks; food *prep* (preparation) workers; dishwashers; buspersons, who set and clear tables; and counter workers, who serve fast food. In addition, every restaurant has a manager. Restaurant chains employ district managers and regional managers to oversee several operations.

Many restaurant employees learn their jobs while working. In many cities and states, restaurant workers must complete a course in sanitation. Schools, colleges, and unions prepare people for restaurant careers through food service courses. Special cooking schools provide chef's training. Restaurants also hire people trained in such fields as advertising, marketing, design, engineering, economics, and nutrition. Jane Y. Wallace

Restaurant Employees International Union.
See Hotel Employees and Restaurant Employees International Union.

Restigouche River, *REHS tih GOOSH,* forms part of the boundary between Quebec and New Brunswick. It is over 100 miles (160 kilometers) long (see **New Brunswick** [physical map]). The Restigouche ranks among the world's most famous trout and salmon streams.

The Indian word *Restigouche* means *the river which divides like a hand.* The name refers to the five branches of the river, the Matapédia (meaning *musical),* Upsalquitch *(blanket),* Kedgwick *(large),* Patapédia *(little),* and Wagan *(knife).* T. W. Acheson

Restoration was the period in English history that followed the return of the royal family, the House of Stuart, to the throne. The Puritan leader Oliver Cromwell, who had ruled as Lord Protector, died in 1658. His son Richard, who succeeded him, was a weak ruler, and civil war threatened the country. But General George Monck seized control of the government and led Parliament in restoring the Stuart Prince Charles to the throne. The prince had lived in exile after the execution of his father, Charles I, in January 1649. A new Parliament, elected in 1660, abolished Cromwell's government and, in May 1660, restored the monarchy in the name of Charles II.

The English welcomed Charles back to the throne. His reign was dated back to the execution of Charles I, instead of the actual year of the restoration. Parliament reestablished the Anglican Church as England's official church and returned property that had been taken from it. Parliament also passed many laws against the Puritans. Their worship was restricted, and their political rights were limited. During the Restoration period, extreme reaction set in against the strict morality of the Puritans. The court of Charles II became known for immorality and loose living. People were valued not for their wisdom or integrity, but for their cleverness and wit.

The Restoration marked the return of royal power, but governmental power actually was divided between the monarch and Parliament. When King James II, who succeeded Charles II, refused to maintain this division of power, he was deposed in the Glorious Revolution of 1688. This revolution limited the king's power and gave Parliament greater power. Charles Carlton

See also **Charles II** (of England); **Cromwell, Oliver; England** (The Restoration); **English literature** (Restoration literature); **Monck, George.**

Résumé. See Careers (Getting a job; picture).

Resurrection, *REHZ uh REHK shuhn,* is a religious belief that a dead person will return to life through the power of God. The person will be restored to life in his

The Resurrection (about 1597-1604), an oil painting on canvas; The Prado, Madrid (MAS)

The Resurrection of Jesus Christ is a central doctrine of Christianity. The artist El Greco painted a Resurrection scene of a serene Jesus rising above figures overcome by awe and fear.

or her physical body and individuality, but in perfected form. Most believers expect resurrection to occur at the end of time and be accompanied by God judging people based on the good and evil of their lives.

The belief in resurrection is important in Judaism, Christianity, and Islam. The first references in Jewish literature to the resurrection of individuals at the end of time appear in the Book of Daniel (probably composed in the 160's B.C.). Belief in final resurrection and judgment is also a major doctrine in Islam.

In Christianity, the resurrection of believers to eternal life at the Last Judgment is linked to the Resurrection of Jesus. Christians have traditionally believed that God defeated death through Jesus's Crucifixion and Resurrection. The story of Jesus's Resurrection is told in all four Gospels. Saint Paul discusses the resurrection of believers in I Corinthians 15. Resurrection is a topic of sermons in the Acts of the Apostles. During the first 300 years of Christianity, Easter Sunday gradually developed as a major celebration of Jesus's return to life.

Stanley K. Stowers

See also **Easter; Jesus Christ** (The Resurrection); **Mormons** (Church doctrines).

Resurrection plant, *REHZ uh REHK shuhn,* is the name of several different plants that can be dried but turn green again when watered. The dried stems curl into a tight ball but spread out when the plant is put into water. A common plant of this type, called the *rose of Jericho,* belongs to the mustard family. It grows from seeds and is native to northern Africa and many regions of the Middle East. The mature plant loses its leaves, curls up with its seed pods inside, and blows across the land. Another resurrection plant, also called *rose of Jericho,* is in the selaginella family. It reproduces by means of microscopic cells called *spores.*   Thomas B. Croat

Scientific classification. The rose of Jericho of the mustard family, Brassicaceae or Cruciferae, is *Anastatica hierochuntica.* The rose of Jericho of the selaginella family, Selaginellaceae, is *Selaginella lepidophylla.*

Resuscitator. See Respirator.

Retailing consists of all the activities that result in the offering for sale of merchandise or services to con-

sumers for their own use. Retailing is the final step in bringing goods to consumers. Not all retailers sell merchandise. For instance, a shop that rents tools for home use sells the service of having tools available. It does not sell the tools themselves. Many retailers sell both goods and services. A clothing store, for example, may perform alterations as well as sell clothes. Retailers sell to consumers for use, rather than to producers or other firms for resale. When an automobile manufacturer needs tires for the cars it builds, it does not buy from a retailer. But individuals who need tires for their cars buy them from a retail tire dealer. Some retailers do not operate from a store. Instead, they sell goods by such techniques as door-to-door selling and selling through catalogs.

Retailers perform several functions as part of the marketing system. They assume risk by buying merchandise without any guarantee that they will be able to sell it and by extending credit to consumers who purchase their goods. Retailers bring buyers and merchandise together by purchasing products in large lots and dividing them up for sale in smaller quantities that are more convenient for consumers. Retailers stock a variety of goods to provide customers with a wide range of choice and quick delivery.

Through advertising and other types of promotion, retailers help attract consumers to a producer's goods. Also, because of their day-to-day contact with customers, retailers are in a good position to know what consumers want. They can therefore provide producers with information on consumers' buying habits. Careers in retailing include such positions as salesperson, credit manager, fashion coordinator, merchandise buyer, manager, and owner.

Retail firms can be classified according to the products that they sell and in a number of other ways. Some stores are located in downtown areas, but others are in shopping malls. Some firms are owned by individual proprietors, and others are belong to large, national chains. Some retail businesses are cooperatives and are owned by the people who use their services (see **Cooperative**). This article discusses (1) specialty stores, (2) de-

A resurrection plant differs in appearance depending on whether it is dry or wet, as shown here. A dry resurrection plant has shriveled, brownish stems. After the plant receives water, the stems open and become green.

partment stores, (3) discount stores, (4) supermarkets, (5) chain stores, (6) service retailing, and (7) nonstore retailing.

Specialty stores normally sell a single type of merchandise, such as clothing, books, or jewelry. They may also carry a few closely related lines of merchandise.

Department stores have separate departments devoted to selling a particular line of goods. Such *hard goods* as furniture and appliances are sold in one section of the store, and such *soft goods* as clothes and sheets are sold in other areas. Many department stores also have separate areas that provide such services as gift wrapping and credit. The first department stores were established in the 1850's in Europe and in the 1860's in the United States. See **Department store**.

Discount stores operate largely on a self-service basis. They sell hard and soft goods, beauty aids, and other general merchandise at low prices. They became important after World War II ended in 1945. Today, there are over 9,000 discount stores in the United States.

Supermarkets are large retail food stores that have annual sales of $2 million or more. They account for about 75 percent of all food-store sales in the United States. Supermarkets began operating in the United States during the 1930's. At first, they sold only food. Today, supermarkets sell many other products as well.

Chain stores are groups of 11 or more stores with a common, central management. In some chains, all the stores are owned by one company. In others, each store is owned by an individual who pays a fee for the franchise (see **Franchise**). Historians consider the Great Atlantic and Pacific Tea Company (A&P) to be the first retail chain in the United States. It began in 1859 as the Great American Tea Company. Today, many department and discount stores, drugstores, and supermarkets belong to chains. Chain stores account for about one-third of all U.S. retail sales. See **Chain store**; **Walton, Sam**.

Service retailing is the selling of services. These services include hair styling, lawn care, photography, car rental, and many other activities.

Nonstore retailing is selling that does not take place in a store building. It includes such methods as selling via the Internet, mail order, vending machine, telephone, and door-to-door visits. Most large retail stores offer their products for sale online, as well as in their retail shops. Other companies, such as Amazon.com and eToys, do not have stores, but only sell their products online. Selling products online is known as electronic commerce, or e-commerce. See **Mail-order business; Telemarketing; Vending machine**.   William H. Bolen

See also **Salesmanship; Sears, Roebuck and Co.**

Retainer is a formal agreement between a lawyer and a client in which the lawyer agrees to take the client's case. This type of agreement is called a *special* retainer. There is also a *general* retainer, in which the lawyer agrees to act for the client when needed. Usually, a client retains a lawyer by paying a *retaining fee,* which may also be called a retainer. After a lawyer has entered into a retainer agreement with a client, the lawyer is legally bound to represent that client in the case. The lawyer cannot agree to represent any other party in the case. A lawyer who accepts a general retainer cannot perform services for anyone else that would be against the client's best interests.   Sherman L. Cohn

Retardation. See Mental retardation.
Retina. See Eye.
Retinol. See Vitamin (Vitamin A).
Retirement. See Old age (Ways of life of the elderly); Pension; Social security.
Retrieval system. See Information retrieval.
Retriever, *rih TREE vuhr,* is a hunting dog trained to *retrieve* (find and bring back) game that has been shot. The dog's coat protects it from water and cold. Retrievers are fine swimmers and have a fine sense of smell. They take training easily. Dog breeders in the United States classify retrievers as sporting dogs. The five recognized breeds of retrievers are the *Chesapeake Bay,* the *curlycoated,* the *flat-coated,* the *golden,* and the *Labrador.* Each breed has an article in *World Book.*
Critically reviewed by the American Kennel Club
See also **Dog** (pictures; table: Sporting group).
Retting. See Flax (Growing and processing fiber flax); Hemp; Jute.
Return, Law of. See Citizenship (Naturalization); Immigration (Asia).
Reunion, *ree YOON yuhn* or *ray oon YAWN,* is an island in the Indian Ocean, about 400 miles (640 kilometers) east of Madagascar. For location, see **Indian Ocean** (map). Of volcanic origin, it covers 970 square miles (2,512 square kilometers). Saint-Denis (pop. 109,072) is the capital. Reunion's important products are vanilla, tobacco, tea, sugar cane, perfumes, and corn. The population of 515,814 consists largely of French Creoles, with some Indians and Chinese. Discovered by the Portuguese in the early 1500's, it was not settled until the French took possession in 1642. They named it *Bourbon.* The island received its present name in 1848. Since 1946, it has been an overseas department of France. Reunion is governed by a 36-member council that is elected by the people.   Hartmut S. Walter
Reuter, *ROY tuhr,* **Baron de** (1816-1899), founded Reuters, one of the world's leading news services. Reuters was one of the first services to furnish financial, political, and general news to European newspapers.

In 1849, Reuter began a service that used pigeons to carry stock quotations between the terminal points of the telegraph lines in Belgium and Germany. In 1851, he established Reuters in London to relay European financial news. He entered the general news business in 1858. Reuter started a cooperative effort among several news agencies that expanded the worldwide distribution of news. He directed the operations of Reuters until 1878 and worked as an adviser to the agency until his death. Reuter's full name was Paul Julius Reuter. He was also called Baron Von Reuter. He was born in Kassel, Germany. See also **Reuters**.   Michael Emery
Reuters, *ROY tuhrz,* is one of the world's largest news services. Reuters serves more than 150 countries and has bureaus in about 75 nations. In the United States, newspapers subscribe to Reuters through an arrangement with the Associated Press (see **Associated Press**). Reuters's coverage of the financial world is particularly strong. Reuters provides information to banks, brokers, and corporations. Controlling interest in the service is held by newspapers from a number of nations, including Britain, Ireland, Australia, and New Zealand.

Reuters was founded in London in 1851 by Baron de Reuter, a German journalist (see **Reuter, Baron de**). It started as a financial service and expanded in 1858 to furnish general news as well. The first major news event covered by Reuters was the Civil War in the United States (1861-1865). Jean Gaddy Wilson

Reuther, *ROO thuhr,* **Walter Philip** (1907-1970), was president of the United Automobile Workers (UAW) from 1946 until his death in 1970. He began his work in the union when it was formed in 1935. Under him, it pioneered in negotiated welfare and pension programs, guaranteed employment, and wage increases tied to productivity. Reuther became an important labor spokesman.

© Chase, AFL-CIO

Walter P. Reuther

Reuther was president of the Congress of Industrial Organizations (CIO) from 1952 to 1955. He led CIO negotiations in the no-raiding and merger agreement with the American Federation of Labor. After the merger in 1955, he was head of the AFL-CIO Economic Policy Committee and a member of the executive committee and executive council. He left these posts in 1967. The UAW withdrew from the AFL-CIO in 1968 but rejoined it in 1981. In 1969, the UAW and the Teamsters formed the Alliance for Labor Action to organize nonunion workers. Reuther was born in Wheeling, West Virginia. Jack Barbash

See also **Labor movement** (Reunification of the AFL and the CIO; picture).

Revelation, *REHV uh LAY shuhn,* **Book of,** is the last book of the New Testament. It is also called the *Apocalypse,* from a Greek word translated as *revelation.* The book was written by a man named John while he was in exile on the island of Patmos in the Aegean Sea, probably about A.D. 95. Many scholars believe that this was not the apostle John, but another person of that name.

The Book of Revelation is an example of *apocalyptic literature.* The only other example of this type of literature in the Bible is the Book of Daniel. Like other apocalyptic literature, Revelation is addressed to people undergoing persecution. It encourages them to withstand the persecution, principally by predicting the rapidly approaching end of the world, when God will rescue them by destroying the powers of evil. The author presented this prediction in symbolic language. To the original readers of the book, the meaning of these symbols was clear. To modern readers the symbols seem obscure, and close study is required to understand the original meaning of the book. Terrance D. Callan

See also **Four Horsemen of the Apocalypse; Bible** (Books of the New Testament).

Revels, Hiram Rhodes (1822-1901), was the first African American to serve in the United States Senate. He was a Republican senator from Mississippi in 1870 and 1871. He completed the unfinished term of Jefferson Davis, the former president of the Confederacy. In the Senate, Revels supported civil rights for blacks.

Revels was born free in Fayetteville, North Carolina. He was educated at seminaries in Indiana and Ohio and attended Knox College. In 1845, he became a minister of the African Methodist Episcopal Church. Revels helped establish black churches and schools in the Midwest and the South. During the American Civil War (1861-1865), he recruited black soldiers for the Union Army. In 1866, he settled in Natchez, Mississippi. He became an alderman and later served as a state senator. After completing his term in the U.S. Senate, he

Historical Pictures Service

Hiram Revels

was named president of Alcorn University (now Alcorn State University). Nancy J. Weiss

Revenue, Internal. See Internal revenue.

Revenue sharing was a special form of United States government aid to state and local governments. The program began in 1973 and ended in 1986. Under revenue sharing, Congress authorized aid without specifying how the money should be spent, or with only broad restrictions on its use.

The federal government had always made grants to the states and to local communities. But these grants had to be spent for specific purposes, such as low-cost housing, medical programs, vocational training, and highways. States could use their revenue-sharing funds any way they wished. Local communities had to spend their funds for such general purposes as environmental protection, health, libraries, public safety, recreation, social services, and transportation.

Revenue sharing was controversial. Supporters of the program believed that state and local governments are more aware of the people's needs than is the federal government, and can therefore spend public funds more wisely. Opponents claimed revenue sharing simply meant additional government spending.

President Richard M. Nixon first proposed a revenue-sharing program in 1969. In 1972, Congress passed the State and Local Fiscal Assistance Act, which authorized revenue sharing. The act created a trust fund for use by state and local governments. State governments received one-third of the funds, local governments two-thirds. Under 1980 legislation, state revenue sharing was discontinued from Oct. 1, 1980, to Sept. 30, 1981. Then it was resumed for five years. Irving Morrissett

Revere, *rih VEER,* Massachusetts (pop. 42,786), is a residential and resort city 6 miles (10 kilometers) northeast of Boston. Its beach and greyhound race track attract thousands of visitors. At the time of its settlement, shortly before 1630, it was known as Rumney Marsh and was part of Boston. It separated from Boston in 1739 and was named Revere in 1871. It has a mayor-council government. Robert L. Turner

Revere, Paul (1734-1818), was an American patriot who, in April 1775, carried news to Lexington of the approach of the British. He warned the patriot leaders Samuel Adams and John Hancock of their danger and called the citizens of the countryside to arms. His exploit inspired Henry Wadsworth Longfellow's "Paul Revere's Ride," one of the most popular poems in American literature. Revere made other contributions during the Rev-

Oil painting on canvas by John Singleton Copley (about 1769); Museum of Fine Arts, Boston, gift of Joseph W. Revere, William B. Revere, and Edward H. R. Revere

Paul Revere was a noted American craftsman who won fame for his patriotic activities at the time of the Revolutionary War.

olutionary War and aided the nation's industrial growth.

His early life. Paul Revere was born in Boston, a silversmith's son. There are no official records of his birth, only of his baptism. It is believed he was born in December 1734. He was baptized on Jan. 1, 1735 (Dec. 22, 1734, on the Old Style Calendar then in use; see **Calendar**).

Revere's family was of French Huguenot descent, and his father changed the family name from Rivoire "merely on account that the Bumpkins should pronounce it easier." Paul studied at North Grammar School in Boston and learned the silversmith's trade. In 1756, he served briefly in the French and Indian War. Then he married

Sarah Orne and entered his father's silversmith business.

The patriot. Revere soon became interested in supporting American liberty. He engraved a number of political cartoons that received wide attention. As the leader of the Boston craftworkers, he cooperated closely with such revolutionary leaders as Samuel Adams and John Hancock. Revere took part in the Boston Tea Party on Dec. 16, 1773. Revere also served as a special messenger for the Boston patriots. He was so familiar to the British in this role that his name appeared in London journals before his famous ride. Two days before the ride took place, he galloped to Concord to warn patriots there to move their military supplies.

Paul Revere's ride. In 1775, King George III instructed General Thomas Gage, the British commander in chief in North America, to enforce order among the rebellious colonists. Gage sent 700 troops from Boston under Lieutenant Colonel Francis Smith to seize or destroy the supplies at Concord. Smith and his soldiers were also to arrest Adams and Hancock for treason.

Smith assembled his force on Boston Common on the evening of April 18. His orders were secret, but the patriots knew about them. Patriot leader Joseph Warren sent Revere and William Dawes by separate routes to warn Adams and Hancock in Lexington and the patriots in Concord. Revere arranged for a signal to be flashed from the steeple of Boston's Old North Church. Two lanterns would mean the British were coming by water, and one, by land. Contrary to Longfellow's account, the signal was not sent to Revere. Instead, Revere directed that the signal be sent to friends in Charlestown.

Revere left Boston at about 10 p.m. and arrived in Lexington about midnight, riding a borrowed horse. Shortly after 1 a.m., Revere, William Dawes, and Dr. Samuel Prescott left for Concord. A British cavalry patrol surprised them on their way. Prescott and Dawes escaped, but Revere was captured. Only Prescott got through to Concord. The British released Revere and let him return to Lexington without his horse. There he joined Adams and Hancock, and they fled to safety in Burlington. But Revere returned to Lexington to rescue valuable papers in Hancock's trunk. When the British arrived in Lexington on April 19, they found the minutemen waiting.

Ivan Massar, Black Star

Paul Revere's house, built about 1670, is the oldest building in downtown Boston. Revere lived in this home from 1770 to 1800. Visitors may see some of its original furnishings, plus mementos of Revere.

Templeman Tea Service; The Minneapolis Institute of Arts, Minneapolis, Minnesota, gift of Mr. and Mrs. James Ford Bell

A silver tea set made by Paul Revere in 1792 featured decorated grooves on, *left to right,* a teapot, a sugar bowl, a creamer, and a tea caddy. The set included sugar tongs and a tea scoop, *foreground.* The noted silversmith's trademark is enlarged at the right.

Museum of Fine Arts, Boston

Revolutionary soldier. During 1778 and 1779, Revere commanded a garrison at Castle William in Boston Harbor. In 1779, he commanded artillery in the disastrous Penobscot Expedition, an attempt to regain control of British-held territory in Maine. The Penobscot Expedition cost Massachusetts virtually its entire trading fleet. Revere was accused of cowardice and insubordination, but a court-martial cleared him of wrongdoing in 1782. Meanwhile, Revere had left the service in some disrepute.

Craftsman and industrialist. When the war started, Revere learned to manufacture gunpowder. He designed and set up a mill at Canton, Massachusetts. He also designed and printed the first issue of Continental paper currency, and he made the state seal still used by Massachusetts. Revere cast bronze cannon for the army.

During and after the war, Revere continued his silversmith trade in Boston. Craftworkers still copy the graceful lines of his work. He marked his own work with the name *Revere* in a rectangle or with the initials *P.R.* He developed considerable skill in making copper plates for printing and engraving. He cast cannon and bells in bronze, and many of his bells are still used in New England. He made the copper fittings for the frigate U.S.S. *Constitution* ("Old Ironsides").

Revere was the first American to discover the process of rolling sheet copper, and he built the first copper-rolling mill in the United States. Before that time, all sheet copper had to be imported.   James Kirby Martin

Related articles in *World Book* include:

Boston (illustration: Boston's Freedom Trail)	Harvard University (picture)
Boston Massacre (picture)	Prescott, Samuel
Dawes, William	Revolutionary War in America (Lexington and Concord)

Additional resources

Fischer, David H. *Paul Revere's Ride.* 1994. Reprint. Oxford, 1995.

Forbes, Esther. *Paul Revere and the World He Lived In.* 1942. Reprint. Peter Smith, 1992. The standard biography.

Triber, Jayne E. *A True Republican: The Life of Paul Revere.* Univ. of Mass. Pr., 1998.

Reversing Falls of Saint John is a waterfall located in the St. John River at Saint John, New Brunswick, just before the river enters the Bay of Fundy. The name refers to the fact that the river's current sometimes runs backwards up the falls.

The waterfall is formed as the river valley becomes a narrow gorge. At low tide, the river falls 14 feet (3.7 meters) in going through this gorge to the harbor below. At high tide, a *bore* (rushing tide) sweeps in from the bay and makes the level of the harbor water 14 feet (3.7 meters) higher than the level of the river. The current through the gorge then flows upstream and up over the falls.   T. W. Acheson

Revivalism is an approach to religion that emphasizes individual religious experience rather than church doctrines. In the United States, revivalism has been associated with frontier camp meetings, outdoor religious services, and fervent, emotional forms of preaching.

Periods of revivalism occurred in Europe among German Pietists and English Methodists during the 1700's. The first major revival movement in the United States was the Great Awakening, which began in the 1730's. This movement took place primarily within Congregational and Presbyterian denominations along the East Coast (see **Great Awakening**). A second Great Awakening occurred from about 1790 to about 1820. During the mid-1800's, the Baptists and Methodists were the chief denominations that used revivalistic methods. The leading revivalists of this period included Peter Cartwright and Charles G. Finney.

During the late 1800's and early 1900's, many preachers, including Dwight L. Moody and Billy Sunday, brought frontier revivalism to growing U.S. cities. In the late 1900's, the revivalist tradition was carried on by such preachers as Billy Graham and by such organizations as the men's group Promise Keepers. Charles H. Lippy

See also **Graham, Billy; Moody, Dwight L.; Sunday, Billy; Tennent, William.**

Revolution is a term that generally refers to a fundamental change in the character of a nation's government. Such a change may or may not be achieved through violent means. Revolutions may also occur in other areas, including cultural, economic, and social activities. People who work to replace an old system with a new one are called revolutionaries.

Kinds of revolution. A political revolution may change various ways of life in a country, or it may have no effect outside the government. For example, the Russian Revolution of 1917 not only deposed the czar but also began major social changes, such as the elimination of private property. On the other hand, the Revolutionary War in America (1775-1783) changed a political system without causing basic social changes.

Some revolutions last for many years. The Chinese Communists fought for 22 years before defeating the Nationalist Chinese government in 1949. This revolution involved widespread guerrilla warfare, a popular form of combat among modern revolutionaries. See **China** (History); **Guerrilla warfare.**

Some political movements that appear to be revolutions only change a country's rulers. Many Latin American political uprisings have replaced dictators without making fundamental changes in governmental systems. Political scientists call such movements *rebellions* rather than revolutions. But a rebellion sometimes leads to a political or social revolution. See **Coup d'état; Junta.**

Many revolutions involve illegal uprisings, but some occur after a legal transfer of power within the existing system. For example, Adolf Hitler took power as dictator of Germany soon after the country's president had appointed him chancellor.

Some of history's most widespread revolutions did not have political beginnings. The Industrial Revolution of the 1700's and early 1800's changed the basic nature of Western society from rural to urban (see **Industrial Revolution**). The invention of the telephone and other advances in technology since the late 1800's have also caused revolutions in industry and everyday life.

Causes of revolution. Most revolutions occur because of widespread dissatisfaction with an existing system. Poverty and injustice under cruel, corrupt, or incapable rulers may contribute to revolution. But in most cases, social problems alone do not cause revolutions. They lead to despair rather than a will to fight for something better. Revolutions need strong leaders who can use unsatisfactory conditions to unite people under a program that promises improvements.

Many revolutions occur after rulers begin to lose confidence in themselves and yield to various demands from their rivals. Such compromises by rulers, or rapidly improving social conditions, create a *revolution of rising expectations* as people begin to see hope for a better life. If changes do not keep pace with their expectations, the people lose faith in their rulers and start listening to revolutionary leaders. The French Revolution of 1789 and the Russian Revolution both began after the rulers

agreed to the people's demands for representative assemblies. The Hungarian Revolution of 1956 occurred after the government released some of its strongest opponents from prison.

Not all revolutions have led to improved conditions. Some revolutionaries have worked for change only to gain political power for themselves. A number of conservative rulers have called themselves revolutionaries simply to convince the public that they support social and economic changes. Guenter Lewy

Related articles in *World Book* include:

French Revolution	Russia (History)
Lenin, V. I.	Terrorism
Revolution of 1848	Union of Soviet Socialist Re-
Revolutionary War in America	publics (History)

Additional resources

Almond, Mark. *Revolution.* De Agostini, 1996.
Goldstone, Jack A., ed. *The Encyclopedia of Political Revolutions.* Congressional Quarterly, 1998.
Greene, Thomas H. *Comparative Revolutionary Movements.* 3rd ed. Prentice Hall, 1990.
Van Creveld, Martin L., ed., *The Encyclopedia of Revolutions and Revolutionaries.* Facts on File, 1996.

Revolution of 1848 involved a series of uprisings in France, Germany, and the Austrian Empire, including parts of Italy. Causes of the revolution included demands for constitutional government; increasing nationalism among Germans, Italians, Hungarians, and Czechs; and peasant opposition to the manorial system in parts of Germany and in the Austrian Empire (see **Manorialism**).

The revolution began in France in February 1848 as a protest against voting restrictions, political corruption, and poor economic conditions. Soon afterward, the French king, Louis Philippe, abdicated. Liberal politicians then set up a new government called the Second Republic.

The revolution quickly spread to the Austrian Empire and Germany. In the Austrian Empire, students and workers rioted in Vienna. Elsewhere in the empire, Hungarian and Czech nationalists rebelled against Austrian authority. In addition, Italians tried to drive their Austrian rulers from northern Italy. In Germany, liberal uprisings swept through the German Confederation, which consisted of Prussia and 38 other independent states. Workers in German cities demanded social reform. Representatives of various parts of Germany assembled in Frankfurt to try to unify the states into a single nation.

The Revolution of 1848 quickly failed. In France, Louis Napoleon Bonaparte, who had been elected president, declared himself emperor. Protests by French workers were brutally put down. In the Austrian Empire, troops crushed the nationalist uprisings and defeated the Italian rebels. In Germany, monarchies became more firmly established in the major German states. In addition, the assembly at Frankfurt broke up without achieving German unity. However, one major goal of the revolution was achieved—the ending of the manorial system in Germany and the Austrian Empire. Also as a result of the revolution, European rulers became more sensitive to the demands of nationalists and began experimenting with more liberal forms of government. Peter N. Stearns

See also **Austria** (Metternich and revolution); **France** (The revolutions of 1830 and 1848); **Germany** (The Revolution of 1848); **Italy** (Italy united).

WORLD BOOK illustration by Robert Addison

The Battle of Bunker Hill (1775), actually fought on Breed's Hill, was the first major battle of the Revolutionary War. The Americans twice drove back the British with musket fire from the hilltop fortifications. The Americans then ran out of gunpowder and were driven from the hill.

Revolutionary War in America

Revolutionary War in America (1775-1783) led to the birth of a new nation—the United States. The war, which is also called the American Revolution, was fought between Great Britain and its 13 colonies that lay along the Atlantic Ocean in North America. The war began on April 19, 1775, when British soldiers and American patriots clashed at Lexington, Mass., and at nearby Concord. The war lasted eight years. On Sept. 3, 1783, Britain signed the Treaty of Paris, by which it recognized the independence of the United States.

Tension had been building between Great Britain and the American Colonies for more than 10 years before the Revolutionary War began. Starting in the mid-1760's, the British government passed a series of laws to increase its control over the colonies. Americans had grown used to a large measure of self-government. They strongly resisted the new laws, especially tax laws. Fierce debate developed over the British Parliament's right to tax the colonies without their consent.

The disobedience of the American Colonies angered the British government. In 1775, Britain's Parliament declared Massachusetts—the site of much protest—to be in rebellion. The British government ordered its troops in Boston to take swift action against the rebels. The Revolutionary War broke out soon afterward.

The American Colonies were unprepared for war.

James Kirby Martin, the contributor of this article, is Professor of History at the University of Houston and the author of In the Course of Human Events: An Interpretive Exploration of the American Revolution.

They lacked a central government, an army, and a navy. Delegates from the colonies formed the Continental Congress, which took on the duties of a national government. The Congress directed the war effort and voted to organize an army and a navy. It appointed George Washington, a wealthy Virginia landowner and former military officer, commander in chief of the Continental Army. On July 4, 1776, the Congress adopted the Declaration of Independence, in which the colonies declared their freedom from British rule.

Great Britain launched a huge land and sea effort to crush the revolution. Britain had a far larger and better-trained army than did the Americans. However, Britain had to transport and supply its army across the Atlantic Ocean. Although the British won many battles, they gained little from their victories. The American patriots could always form new forces and fight on.

In 1777, the Americans won an important victory at Saratoga, N.Y. The victory convinced France that the Americans could win the war. As a result, France went to war against Britain, its long-time enemy. France provided the Americans with the money and military equipment they badly needed to fight the war.

In October 1781, a large British force surrendered to Washington at Yorktown, Va. That defeat led the British government to begin peace talks with the Americans. The Treaty of Paris formally ended the war in 1783.

The Revolutionary War in America stood as an example to peoples in many lands who later fought to gain their freedom. In 1836, the American author Ralph Waldo Emerson referred to the first shot fired by the patriots at Concord as "the shot heard round the world."

Great Britain's power in North America was at its height in 1763, only 12 years before the Revolutionary War began. Britain had just defeated France in the French and Indian War (1754-1763). The treaty that ended the war gave Britain almost all of France's territory in North America. That territory stretched from the Appalachian Mountains in the east to the Mississippi River and included much of Canada. Most American colonists took pride in being part of the British Empire, which was then the world's most powerful empire.

Yet in 1775, the American Colonies rebelled against British authority. The dramatic turnabout resulted from disagreements over the proper relationship between Great Britain and its colonies. As the "mother country," Britain expected obedience from its "children," the colonies. The colonists, on the other hand, believed that they had certain rights which Britain should respect. They wished to be treated like adults, not children. Each side refused to yield, which led to a military showdown and eventual independence for the colonies.

Life in the American Colonies during the 1700's resembled life in the most advanced European nations. Wealthy merchants and planters formed a small upper class, known as the "better sort." A large middle class, or "middling sort," consisted mainly of farmers who owned their land, shopkeepers, and craftworkers. Unskilled workers and farmers who rented their land ranked among the poor, or "lower sort."

Farming was by far the main occupation in the American Colonies. It provided a living for nearly 90 per cent of the people. Most farmers owned their land. The rest rented farmland from large landholders. In addition, black slaves worked on Southern plantations. Only about 10 per cent of the colonists lived in towns or cities. Philadelphia, with about 40,000 people, was the largest American city in 1775. The next largest cities were New York City and Boston.

The opportunity to own land had drawn many settlers to the American Colonies. Owning property gave a person a chance to get ahead. It also gave men the right to vote, though some colonies denied that right to Roman Catholics and Jews. In each colony, voters elected representatives to a legislature. Colonial legislatures passed laws and could tax the people. However, the governor of a colony could veto any laws passed by the legislature. The king appointed the governor in most colonies.

Great Britain expected the American Colonies to serve its economic interests, and it regulated colonial trade. In general, the colonists accepted British regulations. For example, they agreed not to manufacture goods that would compete with British products. For more information, see **Colonial life in America.**

British policy changes. Great Britain had largely neglected the administration of the American Colonies while it fought France in a series of wars during the 1700's. But after the French and Indian War ended in 1763, the British government sought to tighten its control over the colonies. The war had drained Britain's treasury and left a huge debt. Most British leaders did not expect the colonists to help pay off the debt. However, Britain planned to station troops in America to defend the colonies' western frontier. It wanted the colonists to help pay for those troops.

Relations between the colonies and the mother country steadily worsened from 1763 to 1775. During that time, Parliament passed a number of laws to increase

Important dates in the Revolutionary War

1775
April 19 Minutemen and redcoats clashed at Lexington and Concord.
June 15 The Congress named George Washington commander in chief of the Continental Army.
June 17 The British drove the Americans from Breed's Hill in the Battle of Bunker Hill.

1776
Feb. 27 The patriots defeated the Loyalists at Moore's Creek Bridge.
March 17 The British evacuated Boston.
July 4 The Declaration of Independence was adopted.
Aug. 27 The redcoats defeated the patriots on Long Island.
Sept. 15 The British occupied New York City.
Dec. 26 Washington mounted a surprise attack on Hessian troops at Trenton.

1777
Jan. 3 Washington gained a victory at Princeton.
Aug. 6 Loyalists and Indians forced the patriots back at Oriskany, but then withdrew.
Aug. 16 The patriots crushed the Hessians near Bennington.
Sept. 11 The British won the Battle of Brandywine.
Sept. 19 Gates's forces checked Burgoyne's army in the First Battle of Freeman's Farm.
Sept. 26 The British occupied Philadelphia.
Oct. 4 Washington's forces met defeat in the Battle of Germantown.
Oct. 7 The patriots defeated the British in the Second Battle of Freeman's Farm.
Oct. 17 Burgoyne surrendered at Saratoga.
Dec. 19 Washington's army retired to winter quarters at Valley Forge.

1778
Feb. 6 The United States and France signed an alliance.
June 28 The Battle of Monmouth ended in a draw.
Dec. 29 The redcoats took Savannah.

1779
Feb. 25 British defenders of Vincennes surrendered to George Rogers Clark.
June 21 Spain declared war on Great Britain.
Sept. 23 John Paul Jones's ship, the *Bonhomme Richard,* captured the British ship *Serapis.*

1780
May 12 Charleston fell after a British siege.
Aug. 16 The British defeated the Americans at Camden.
Oct. 7 American frontiersmen stormed the Loyalist positions on Kings Mountain.

1781
Jan. 17 The patriots won a victory at Cowpens.
March 15 Cornwallis clashed with Greene at Guilford Courthouse.
Sept. 5 A French fleet inflicted great damage on a British naval force at Chesapeake Bay.
Oct. 19 Cornwallis' forces surrendered at Yorktown.

1782
March 20 King George's chief minister, Lord North, resigned.
Nov. 30 The Americans and British signed a preliminary peace treaty in Paris.

1783
April 15 Congress ratified the preliminary peace treaty.
Sept. 3 The United States and Great Britain signed the final peace treaty in Paris.

Great Britain's income from the colonies. The colonists reacted angrily. They lived far from Britain and had grown increasingly self-reliant. Many Americans believed that the new British policies threatened their freedom. In late 1774, Britain's King George III declared, "The die is now cast, the colonies must either submit or triumph." A few months later, the Revolutionary War broke out.

The Proclamation of 1763 was issued by King George to halt the expansion of the American Colonies beyond the Appalachian Mountains. Before the French and Indian War, France had helped prevent colonists from settling on Indian hunting lands west of the Appalachians. But settlers began crossing the frontier soon after Britain defeated France. To preserve Indian hunting grounds, an Ottawa chief named Pontiac led an uprising in the spring of 1763. Indian tomahawks killed hundreds of colonists along the western frontier.

Britain feared a long and bloody Indian war, which it could not afford. To prevent future uprisings, King George issued the Proclamation of 1763. The document reserved lands west of the Appalachians for Indians and forbade white settlements there. Britain sent soldiers to guard the frontier and keep settlers out. The colonists deeply resented the Proclamation of 1763. They felt that Britain had no right to restrict their settlement. In addition, many Americans hoped to profit from the purchase of western lands.

The Sugar Act. George Grenville became King George's chief cabinet minister in 1763. Grenville was determined to increase Britain's income from the American Colonies. At his urging, Parliament passed the Revenue Act of 1764, also known as the Sugar Act. The act placed a three-penny tax on each gallon of molasses entering the colonies from ports outside the British Empire. Several Northern colonies had thriving rum industries that depended on imported molasses. Rum producers angrily protested that the tax would eat up their profits. However, the Stamp Act—an even more unpopular British tax—soon drew the colonists' attention

away from the Sugar Act. In 1766, Parliament reduced the tax on molasses to a penny a gallon.

The Quartering and Stamp acts were passed by Parliament in 1765, again with Grenville's support. The laws were intended to make the colonists pay part of the cost of stationing British troops in America. The Quartering Act ordered the colonies to supply the soldiers with living quarters, fuel, candles, and cider or beer.

Massachusetts Historical Society

A tax stamp placed on certain items showed that colonists had paid taxes on them.

The Stamp Act required the colonists to pay for tax stamps that had been placed on newspapers, playing cards, diplomas, and various legal documents.

Most colonies half-heartedly obeyed the Quartering Act, often providing fewer supplies than requested. But the Stamp Act resulted in riots. Angry colonists refused to allow the tax stamps to be sold. Merchants in port cities agreed not to order British goods until Parliament abolished the act.

In October 1765, delegates from nine colonies met in New York City and prepared a statement protesting the Stamp Act. The objections of that so-called Stamp Act Congress stemmed from the colonists' belief that the right of taxation belonged only to the people and their elected representatives. The delegates argued that Parliament had no power to tax the colonies because the colonies had no representatives in Parliament. The meeting of the Stamp Act Congress was the first united action by the colonies against an unpopular British law.

Parliament abolished the Stamp Act in 1766. But at the same time, it passed the Declaratory Act, which stated that the king and Parliament had full legislative authority over the colonies in all matters.

Detail of *The Bloody Massacre Perpetrated in King Street* (1770); American Antiquarian Society, Worcester, Mass.

The Boston Massacre took place on March 5, 1770, when British soldiers fired into a mob, killing five Americans. Patriot propaganda like this engraving by Paul Revere called the incident a massacre to stir up feeling against the British government.

The Townshend Acts. Many members of the British government disliked giving in to the disobedient colonies over the Stamp Act. They included the Chancellor of the Exchequer Charles Townshend, who developed a new plan for raising money from the colonies. Townshend convinced Parliament that the colonists would find a *duty,* or indirect tax placed on imported goods, more agreeable than the Stamp Act, which taxed them directly. In 1767, Parliament passed the Townshend Acts. One act placed duties on glass, lead, paint, paper, and tea imported into the colonies. Another act set up a customs agency in Boston to collect them efficiently.

The Townshend Acts led to renewed protests in the American Colonies. The colonists accepted Britain's right to regulate their trade. But they argued that the Townshend duties were taxes in disguise. To protest the duties, Americans stopped buying British goods. British merchants, hurt by the boycott, pressured the government to back down. In 1770, Parliament withdrew all the Townshend duties except the one on tea. It kept the tea duty to demonstrate its right to tax the colonies.

Protests against what the colonists called "taxation without representation" were especially violent in Boston. On March 5, 1770, soldiers and townspeople clashed in a street fight that became known as the Boston Massacre. During the fight, frightened British soldiers fired into a crowd of rioters. Five men died as a result, including a black patriot named Crispus Attucks. They were the first colonists to lose their lives in protest against British policies.

Patriots spread news of the Boston Massacre to turn public opinion in America against Great Britain. In 1772, political leaders in Boston formed the Committee of Correspondence to explain to other communities by such means as letters how British actions threatened American liberties. Other committees of correspondence were soon set up throughout the colonies. The committees helped unite the colonies in their growing struggle with the British government.

The Tea Act. To avoid paying the Townshend duty on tea, colonial merchants smuggled in tea from the Netherlands. Britain's East India Company had been the chief source of tea for the colonies. The smuggling hurt the company financially, and it asked Parliament for help. In 1773, Parliament passed the Tea Act, which enabled the East India Company to sell its tea below the price of smuggled tea. Lord North had become the king's chief minister in 1770. North believed that the colonists would buy the cheaper British tea and thereby acknowledge Parliament's right to tax them. In the process, the colonists would lose their argument against taxation without representation.

Samuel Adams, a Boston patriot, led the resistance to the Tea Act. On the evening of Dec. 16, 1773, Bostonians disguised as Indians raided British ships docked in Boston Harbor and dumped their cargoes of tea overboard. The so-called Boston Tea Party enraged King George, Lord North, and the king's other ministers. They wanted the Bostonians punished as a warning to all colonists not to challenge British authority.

The Intolerable Acts. Britain responded to the Boston Tea Party in 1774 by passing several laws that became known in America as the Intolerable Acts. One law closed Boston Harbor until Bostonians paid for the de-

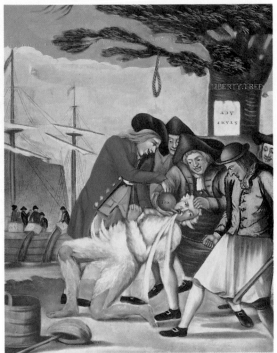

Detail of *The Bostonians Paying the Excise Man* (1774), a color engraving by an unknown artist; John Carter Brown Library at Brown University, Providence, R.I.

British propaganda showed unruly colonists forcing a tax collector they had tarred and feathered to drink scalding tea. The colonists in the background are dumping British tea overboard.

stroyed tea. Another law restricted the activities of the Massachusetts legislature and gave added powers to the post of governor of Massachusetts. Those powers in effect made him a dictator. King George named Lieutenant General Thomas Gage, the commander in chief of British forces in North America, to be the new governor of Massachusetts. Gage was sent to Boston with troops.

Committees of correspondence throughout the colonies warned citizens that Britain could also disband their legislatures and take away their political rights. Several committees called for a convention of delegates from the colonies to organize resistance to the Intolerable Acts. The convention was later to be called the Continental Congress.

The First Continental Congress met in Philadelphia from Sept. 5 to Oct. 26, 1774, to protest the Intolerable Acts. Representatives attended from all the colonies except Georgia. The leaders included Samuel Adams and John Adams of Massachusetts and George Washington and Patrick Henry of Virginia. The Congress voted to cut off colonial trade with Great Britain unless Parliament abolished the Intolerable Acts. It also approved resolutions advising the colonies to begin training their citizens for war.

None of the delegates to the First Continental Congress called for independence from Great Britain. Instead, the delegates hoped that the colonies would regain the rights which Parliament had taken away. The Congress agreed to hold another Continental Congress in May 1775 if Britain did not change its policies before that time.

Detail of an engraving (1775) by Amos Doolittle based on a painting by Ralph Earl; Albany Institute of History and Art

The fighting began on April 19, 1775, at Lexington, Mass., and nearby Concord. This engraving of 1775 shows the Americans turning back British redcoats at North Bridge near Concord.

Fighting broke out between American patriots and British soldiers in April 1775. The Americans in each colony were defended at first by the members of their citizen army, the *militia.* The militiamen came out to fight when the British neared their homes. The patriots soon established a regular military force known as the Continental Army. Britain depended chiefly on professional soldiers who had enlisted for long terms. The British soldiers were known as *redcoats* because they wore bright red jackets.

The patriots won several victories in New England and the Southern Colonies during the early months of the Revolutionary War. As the fighting spread, many Americans became convinced of the need to cut their ties with Great Britain. In July 1776, more than a year after the start of the Revolutionary War, the colonies adopted the Declaration of Independence.

Lexington and Concord. In February 1775, Parliament declared that Massachusetts was in open rebellion. This declaration made it legal for British troops to treat troublesome colonists as rebels and shoot them on sight. The king and his ministers hoped to avoid a war by crushing the disorder in Boston. In April, General Gage received secret orders from the British government to take military action against the Massachusetts troublemakers and arrest their principal leaders.

Boston patriots learned about the secret orders before Gage did. The leaders of the rebellion fled Boston to avoid arrest. Gage decided to capture or destroy arms and gunpowder stored by the patriots in the town of Concord, near Boston. On the night of April 18, 1775, about 700 British soldiers marched toward Concord. Joseph Warren, a Boston patriot, discovered that the British were on the march. He sent two speedy couriers, Paul Revere and William Dawes, to ride to Concord and warn the people about the approaching redcoats.

The redcoats reached the town of Lexington, on the way to Concord, near dawn on April 19, 1775. Revere's ride had alerted volunteer soldiers called *minutemen,* members of the militia who were highly trained and prepared to take up arms on a minute's notice. About 70 minutemen waited for the redcoats in Lexington. No one knows who fired the first shot. But 8 minutemen fell dead, and 10 more were wounded. One British soldier had been hurt.

The British continued on to Concord, where they searched for hidden arms. One group of redcoats met minutemen at North Bridge, just outside Concord. In a brief clash, 3 redcoats and 2 minutemen were killed. The British then turned back to Boston. Along the way, patriots fired at them from behind trees and stone fences. British dead and wounded for the day numbered about 250, and American losses came to about 90.

Word spread rapidly that fighting had broken out between British troops and the Americans. Militiamen throughout New England took up arms and gathered outside Boston. The Americans prepared to pounce on Gage's troops if they marched out of Boston. Three British officers—Major Generals John Burgoyne, Henry Clinton, and William Howe—arrived in Boston with more troops in late May 1775.

Bunker Hill. The British and the Americans each hoped to gain an advantage by occupying hills overlooking Boston. The Americans moved first. They had intended to fortify Bunker Hill. Instead, they dug in on Breed's Hill, closer to the city.

On June 17, 1775, British troops led by Howe attacked

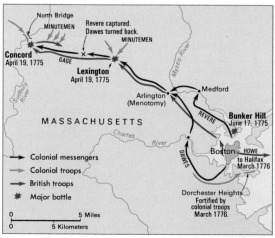

WORLD BOOK map

Clashes at Lexington and Concord opened the Revolutionary War. In March 1776, the British evacuated Boston. This map locates major battles and troop movements in and around Boston.

American positions on Breed's Hill. To save ammunition, the patriots were ordered: "Don't fire until you see the whites of their eyes." The Americans drove back two British charges before they ran out of ammunition. During a third charge, British bayonets forced the Americans to flee. The fighting, usually called the Battle of Bunker Hill, was the bloodiest battle of the entire war. More than 1,000 British soldiers and about 400 Americans were killed or wounded.

The Continental Army. The Second Continental Congress began meeting in Philadelphia in May 1775, soon after the battles at Lexington and Concord. Patriot leaders in Massachusetts urged the Congress to take charge of militia units outside Boston and raise an army strong enough to challenge the redcoats. On June 14, the Congress established the Continental Army. The next day, George Washington was made the army's commander in chief. The Congress named 13 more generals soon afterward. It then had to figure out how to recruit troops, supply an army, and pay for a war.

Washington took command of the military camps near Boston on July 3, 1775. He immediately worked to establish order and discipline in the army. The militia units were poorly trained and undisciplined. They lacked weapons and overall organization. Their camps were filthy. Most soldiers had volunteered for service to defend their families and farms. They expected to return home after a few months. Washington issued a flood of orders and dismissed junior officers who failed to enforce them. Soldiers who disobeyed were punished.

The evacuation of Boston. Soon after Washington took charge of the Continental Army, he sought to drive the British from Boston. To accomplish that task, the Americans needed artillery. In May 1775, Colonels Ethan Allen and Benedict Arnold had seized Fort Ticonderoga, a British post in the colony of New York. Shortly afterward, their troops captured another British post at nearby Crown Point. The two victories provided the Americans with much-needed artillery.

In November 1775, Colonel Henry Knox, Washington's chief of artillery, proposed a plan to move the heavy guns by sled from Ticonderoga across the snow-covered Berkshire Mountains to Boston. The guns reached Framingham, near Boston, by late January 1776.

The arrival of the artillery enabled the patriots to fortify a high ground south of Boston known as Dorchester Heights. The work was completed during the night of March 4, 1776. General Howe had taken command of the British army several months earlier. Howe realized that his soldiers could not hold Boston with American cannons pointed at them. By March 17, the British troops had been loaded onto ships. They soon sailed to Canada. But the evacuation of British troops from Boston was only a temporary victory for the Americans. Howe and his troops landed at New York City in July.

The invasion of Canada. To prevent British forces from sweeping down from Canada into New York, the Continental Congress ordered an invasion of Canada. Some delegates also hoped that Canada might join the colonies in their rebellion against Great Britain.

In the fall of 1775, two American expeditions marched northward into Canada. Benedict Arnold led one force along rivers and over rugged terrain toward the city of Quebec. Disease and hunger caused many of his men to

Details of an oil painting on canvas (about 1930) by Thomas Lovell; Fort Ticonderoga Museum and the John Dixon Crucible Company

Artillery captured from the British was dragged from Fort Ticonderoga, N.Y., to Boston in late 1775 and early 1776. The Americans needed cannons to drive the British from Boston.

turn back. The other expedition, under Brigadier General Richard Montgomery, headed toward Montreal. Montgomery captured Montreal on November 13. He then joined Arnold outside Quebec.

On Dec. 31, 1775, under cover of a blizzard, the Americans stormed Quebec. But they failed to take the city. Montgomery died in the attack, and Arnold was seriously wounded. Major General Guy Carleton, governor of the colony of Quebec, commanded the British forces in Canada. The Americans retreated to New York in the spring, after British reinforcements reached Canada. The invasion of Canada had ended in failure for the patriots.

Fighting in the Southern Colonies. Some Southern planters feared that a rebellion against Great Britain in the name of liberty might inspire black slaves to rise up against them. Those colonists hesitated to support the war at first. For that reason, Britain expected to restore its authority more easily in the Southern Colonies than in the North. However, the patriots enjoyed great success in the South at the start of the Revolutionary War. In urging his fellow Virginians to arm, Patrick Henry reportedly uttered the stirring words, "I know not what course others may take, but as for me, give me liberty or give me death."

In November 1775, the British governor of Virginia, Lord Dunmore, offered to free black slaves who took up arms on Britain's side. From 1,000 to 2,000 blacks joined Dunmore. In December, the patriots defeated a force led by Dunmore at Great Bridge, south of Norfolk. Dunmore fled Virginia the following summer.

North Carolina's governor, Josiah Martin, also hoped to crush the rebellious colonists by force. He urged North Carolinians loyal to Great Britain to join him. More than 1,500 colonists answered Martin's call and marched toward the coast to join British troops arriving by sea. But on the way, these colonists took a beating from patriot forces at Moore's Creek Bridge, near Wilmington. British troops under General Clinton had

Detail of an oil painting on canvas (1921), by J. L. G. Ferris; Archives of 76, Bay Village, Ohio

The Declaration of Independence was adopted on July 4, 1776. The statesmen shown working on a draft are, from left to right, Benjamin Franklin, John Adams, and Thomas Jefferson.

sailed southward from Boston. However, they failed to arrive in time to prevent the defeat at Moore's Creek Bridge on Feb. 27, 1776.

The British warships continued on to Charleston, S.C., the chief port in the South. They opened fire on a fort outside the city on June 28, 1776. However, the attack was called off later that day, after gunfire from the fort damaged several ships. Clinton soon rejoined British forces in the North.

The Declaration of Independence. When the Second Continental Congress opened in May 1775, few delegates wanted to break ties with the mother country. John Dickinson of Pennsylvania led the group that urged a peaceful settlement with Great Britain. Dickinson wrote the Olive Branch Petition, which the Congress approved in July 1775. The document declared that the colonists were loyal to the king and urged him to remedy their complaints. However, George III ignored the petition. On August 23, he declared all the colonies to be in rebellion. A few months later, Parliament closed all American ports to overseas trade. Those actions convinced many delegates that a peaceful settlement of differences with Britain was impossible.

Support for American independence continued to build early in 1776. In January, the political writer Thomas Paine issued a sensational pamphlet titled *Common Sense*. Paine attacked George III as unjust, and he argued brilliantly for the complete independence of the American Colonies.

In June 1776, Richard Henry Lee of Virginia introduced the resolution in the Congress "That these United Colonies are, and of right ought to be, free and independent States. . . ." The Congress appointed a committee to draft a declaration of independence in case Lee's resolution was adopted. On July 2, the Congress approved Lee's resolution. It adopted the Declaration of Independence on July 4, and the United States of America was born. See **Declaration of Independence**.

Major battles of the Revolutionary War

Name	Place	Date	Commander		Dead and wounded*		Results
			American	British	American	British	
Bennington	New York, near Bennington, VT.	Aug. 16, 1777	Stark	Baum, Breymann	80	200	British defeat encouraged the patriots in their campaign against Burgoyne.
Brandywine	Pennsylvania	Sept. 11, 1777	Washington	Howe	700	540	An American retreat enabled the British to occupy Philadelphia.
Bunker Hill	Massachusetts	June 17, 1775	Prescott	Howe	400	1,000	The patriots were driven from their positions overlooking Boston.
Camden	South Carolina	Aug. 16, 1780	Gates	Cornwallis	1,000	300	The British crushed an American army.
Cowpens	South Carolina	Jan. 17, 1781	Morgan	Tarleton	70	330	Patriot victory encouraged Southern militiamen to come out and fight.
Freeman's Farm (First Battle)	New York	Sept. 19, 1777	Gates	Burgoyne	300	600	The British advance from Canada was halted.
Freeman's Farm (Second Battle)	New York	Oct. 7, 1777	Gates	Burgoyne	150	600	The patriots turned back a second attack.
Germantown	Pennsylvania	Oct. 4, 1777	Washington	Howe	650	550	An American attack turned into a loss and a retreat.
Guilford Courthouse	North Carolina	March 15, 1781	Greene	Cornwallis	250	650	The British decided to give up most of North Carolina.
Kings Mountain	South Carolina	Oct. 7, 1780	Campbell	Ferguson	100	300	The British advance into North Carolina was delayed.
Lexington and Concord	Massachusetts	April 19, 1775	Parker and others	Smith	90	250	The Revolutionary War in America began.
Long Island	New York	Aug. 27, 1776	Washington	Howe	250	400	The British forced the Americans from Long Island.
Monmouth	New Jersey	June 28, 1778	Washington	Clinton	250	400	A patriot attack ended in a draw.
Princeton	New Jersey	Jan. 3, 1777	Washington	Cornwallis	50	100	The British withdrew from western New Jersey.
Quebec	Quebec	Dec. 31, 1775	Arnold, Montgomery	Carleton	100	18	The Americans failed to seize the city of Quebec.
Trenton	New Jersey	Dec. 26, 1776	Washington	Rall	10	100	The patriots crushed the Hessians in a surprise assault.
Yorktown	Virginia	Oct. 6-19, 1781	Washington	Cornwallis	100	600	The British surrendered in the war's last major battle.

*Approximate totals. The figures listed are a compromise between several conflicting estimates.

Revolutionary War battles and campaigns British strategy at first called for crushing the American Revolution in the North. After 1778, the fighting shifted to the South. In 1781, an American and French force defeated the British at Yorktown in the last major battle of the war. This map locates important battles and campaigns

WORLD BOOK map

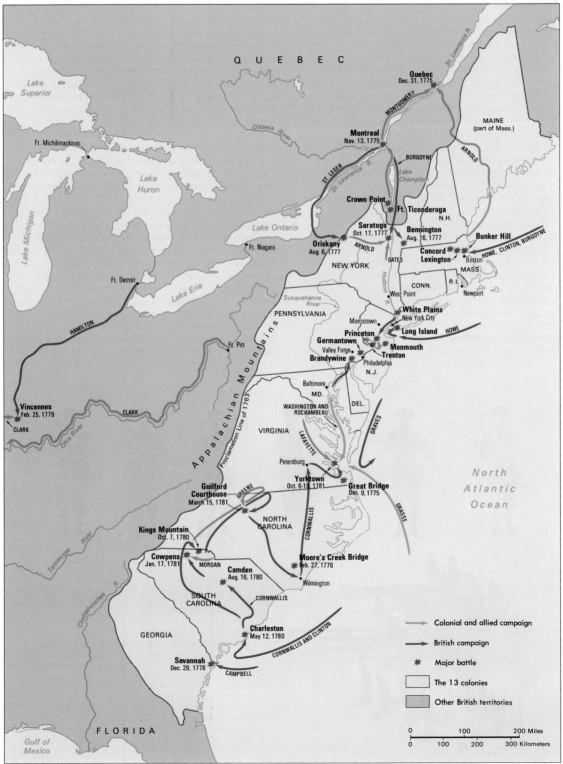

Colonial and allied campaign

British campaign

Major battle

The 13 colonies

Other British territories

After the Americans declared their independence, they had to win it by force. The task proved difficult, partly because the people never fully united behind the war effort. A large number of colonists remained unconcerned about the outcome of the war and supported neither side. As many as a third of the people sympathized with Great Britain. They called themselves Loyalists. The patriots called them Tories, after Britain's Tory Party, which strongly supported the king. Victory in the Revolutionary War depended on the patriots, who made up less than a third of the population.

Although the patriots formed a minority of the colonial population, they had many advantages over the British in the Revolutionary War. They had plenty of manpower, if they could only persuade citizens to come out and fight. Unlike the British, they did not have to supply their army across an ocean. In addition, the patriots fought on familiar terrain and could retreat out of reach of the British. In time, Britain's chief rivals, France and Spain, joined the war. Their aid enabled the patriots to win independence.

The American patriots also benefited from British blunders. The British expected an easy victory. They thought that the patriots would turn and run at the sight of masses of redcoats. Yet British military leaders were cautious in their battle plans. American military leaders were less experienced and less assured than British officers. But they were more willing to take chances. In the long run, daring leadership provided the Americans with a valuable advantage.

The fighting forces. The American Colonies entered the Revolutionary War without an army or a navy. Their fighting forces consisted of militia units in the various colonies. The militias were made up of white men from 16 to 60 years old. Those citizen-soldiers were ready to defend their homes and families when danger threatened. The colonies could call up militiamen for periods of service ranging from a few days to a few months.

Great Britain had an army of well-trained and highly disciplined soldiers. Britain also hired professional German soldiers. Such soldiers were often called Hessians because most of them came from the German state of Hesse-Kassel. American Loyalists and Indians also joined British fighting forces during the war. At its peak, the British military force in North America numbered about 50,000.

George Washington and other patriot leaders doubted that part-time militias could defeat the British in a long war. Washington worked to build an army made up of disciplined soldiers who had enlisted for several years. However, recruitment for the Continental Army remained a constant problem. Most citizens preferred to serve in local militias and support the Continental Army when a major battle threatened nearby.

Washington rarely commanded as many as 15,000 soldiers at a time, and he frequently commanded far fewer. Soldiers often went without pay, food, and proper clothing because the Continental Congress was so poor and transportation in the colonies was so bad. Yet many poor soldiers stayed in the army because they had been promised free land after the war. They fought as much for economic gain as for political liberty. In time, most states permitted blacks to serve in the Continental Army. In all, about 5,000 blacks fought on the pa-

WORLD BOOK illustration by David A. Cunningham

The flintlock musket was the chief firearm of the Revolutionary War. Loading a musket required careful drill, as demonstrated by the Continental Army soldier above. First, he bites open a paper cartridge to release the gunpowder. He next pours powder into the firing pan. More gunpowder and a lead ball are then rammed down the barrel. After the flintlock is cocked, the musket is ready to fire. The British soldiers at the left are lined up shoulder to shoulder in firing formation. Soldiers fired in massed formations because of the musket's inaccuracy.

Artillery took part in attacks and defense. Cannons fired slowly because soldiers had to swab the barrel after each round as these British gunners demonstrate.

A rifle fired more accurately than a musket and was handled skillfully by American frontiersmen. The sharpshooter above takes aim at a British officer.

WORLD BOOK illustration by David A. Cunningham

A bayonet fastened to a musket was used in hand-to-hand combat. A German soldier hired by the British, *left,* clashes with an American infantryman, *right.*

triot side in the war. Many were slaves who had been promised freedom in exchange for military service.

Britain's powerful navy loosely blockaded America's Atlantic coast and at times raided port towns. The Americans had a small navy, which was too weak to challenge large British warships. However, the Continental Navy sank or captured many smaller British vessels, especially cargo ships. Privately owned American vessels known as *privateers* also captured enemy cargo ships. The stolen cargoes were then sold, with the profits going to investors, the ship captains, and the crews.

Weapons and tactics. The most important weapons of the Revolutionary War were the flintlock musket, the rifle, and the cannon. The musket discharged a large lead ball and could fire three or four rounds a minute. A bayonet could be fastened over the muzzle of a musket. Rifles had much greater accuracy than muskets. But rifles took longer to reload, which made them less efficient in battle. American frontiersmen improved the rifle's value by their skill at rapid loading. Cannons hurled shells long distances and blasted soldiers at closer range.

On the battlefield, soldiers lined up shoulder to shoulder, two or three rows deep. Their muskets had little accuracy beyond about 60 yards (55 meters). For that reason, the attackers advanced as far as possible before shooting. After firing several rounds, the two sides closed in for hand-to-hand combat with bayonets. The battle ended when one side broke through enemy lines or forced the other side to retreat. In the early years of the war, the Americans had few bayonets, which gave the redcoats an enormous advantage.

Patriot governments. The Continental Congress provided leadership for the 13 former British colonies during most of the Revolutionary War. After the Declaration of Independence was adopted, each former colony called itself a state. The Congress drew up a plan called the Articles of Confederation to unify the states under a central government. The Articles left nearly all powers to the states because many delegates distrusted a strong central government. By March 1781, all 13 states had approved the Articles.

Each state formed a government to replace its former British administration. In most states, an elected legislature drafted a new constitution that defined the powers of the government. In 1780, Massachusetts became the last state to introduce a new constitution.

Patriot committees in each state stirred support for the war effort. Such committees tormented citizens suspected of sympathizing with Great Britain. Many Loyalists left the colonies rather than submit to the demands of patriot committees. By the end of the war, as many as 100,000 Loyalists had fled to Canada, England, the Bahamas, and other British territories.

Financing the war. The Continental Congress had to pay for the Revolutionary War. But it had no power to tax the people. Late in 1775, the Congress began to issue paper currency known as Continental dollars. However, it issued so many Continentals that they became nearly worthless. The Congress received some money from the states, but never enough. Loans and gifts of cash from other nations—especially from France, the Netherlands, and Spain—saved the patriots. The Congress also obtained loans from patriot merchants and other Americans who had cash or goods to spare. Those citizens received certificates that promised full repayment of their loans with interest.

Diplomatic triumphs. Vital support for the American cause in the Revolutionary War came from France, Spain, and the Netherlands. Benjamin Franklin represented the Americans in France and played a key role in obtaining French support for the patriots.

Before the Revolutionary War began, French leaders had watched with interest the widening split between Great Britain and the American Colonies. France still smarted from its defeat by Britain in the French and Indian War. France's foreign minister, the Count de Vergennes, believed that a patriot victory would benefit France by weakening the mighty British Empire. France agreed to aid the patriots secretly. But France refused to ally itself openly with the Americans before they had proved themselves in battle.

From 1776 to 1778, France gave the patriots loans, gifts of money, and weapons. In 1778, treaties of alliance were signed, making France and America "good and faithful" allies. Thereafter, France also provided the patriots with troops and warships. Spain entered the war as an ally of France in 1779. The Netherlands joined the war in 1780. With so much support, the patriots were at last able to win their independence.

The war in the North

The Revolutionary War battles of 1775 convinced the British that defeating the American Colonies required a major military effort and an effective strategy. As a result, Britain sent additional troops and a large naval force to America. British strategy called for crushing the rebellion in the North first. Once New England was knocked out of the war, Britain expected resistance to crumble in the remaining colonies.

Britain nearly conquered the patriots several times during the fighting in the North, which lasted from 1775 to 1778. But British generals failed to carry out British strategy effectively. In 1777, a British army surrendered to the Americans at Saratoga in New York. Soon afterward, France entered the Revolutionary War on the patriot side.

The campaign in New York. Immediately after the British evacuated Boston in March 1776, General Howe began to plan his return from Canada to the American Colonies. In July, he landed on Staten Island in New York Harbor. Howe was joined by General Clinton's men, following their defeat in South Carolina, and by Hessian troops from Europe. Howe commanded a total force of more than 45,000 experienced soldiers and sailors. They faced about 20,000 poorly trained and ill-equipped Americans.

Washington had shifted his forces to New York City after the redcoats withdrew from Boston. He did not expect to hold New York City, but he wanted to make the British fight for it. To defend the city, patriot troops fortified Brooklyn Heights, an area of high ground on the western tip of Long Island.

Howe saw an opportunity to trap large numbers of patriot troops in Brooklyn. In August 1776, British troops landed on Long Island in front of the American lines. Howe surrounded the patriots' forward positions in the Battle of Long Island on August 27. However, the slow-moving Howe paused before attacking again, enabling the remainder of the Americans to escape. In September, Washington sent Captain Nathan Hale behind British lines to obtain information about British positions on Long Island. Hale was caught and hanged for spying. Before being hanged, he reportedly said, "I only regret that I have but one life to lose for my country."

By mid-September 1776, Howe had driven Washington's troops from New York City. Howe slowly pursued the Americans as they retreated toward White Plains,

Detail of an oil painting on canvas (about 1834) by Edward Hicks; collection of Nina Fletcher Little (Fernand Bourges, *Life* Magazine, © Time Inc.)

George Washington led his troops across the Delaware River on the stormy night of Dec. 25, 1776. The next day, he directed a surprise attack at Trenton, N.J. Washington's victory at Trenton, which followed a string of American defeats, lifted patriot morale.

The Battle of Princeton, which took place on Jan. 3, 1777, resulted in a brilliant victory for the Americans. This painting shows Washington, on horseback in the foreground, rallying his troops shortly before they drove the redcoats from the field.

Detail of an oil painting on canvas (about 1790) by William Mercer; Historical Society of Pennsylvania, Philadelphia

N.Y. His hesitation cost the British a chance to crush Washington's army. But another patriot force remained on Manhattan Island to defend Fort Washington. The fort fell to Howe in November, and Britain captured nearly 3,000 Americans. New York City remained in British hands until the war ended.

During the summer and fall of 1776, General Carleton led a British force southward from Canada. British strategy called for Carleton to link up with Howe in the Hudson River Valley, thereby cutting New England off from the rest of the colonies. But Carleton met heavy resistance from patriot forces under Brigadier General Benedict Arnold in a naval battle near Valcour Island on Lake Champlain. In November, Carleton turned back to Canada for the winter.

Trenton and Princeton. The patriot situation appeared dark at the end of 1776. Washington's discouraged forces had withdrawn to New Jersey. In late November, British troops led by Major General Charles Cornwallis poured into New Jersey in pursuit of Washington. The patriots barely escaped to safety by crossing the Delaware River into Pennsylvania on December 7.

Washington's forces were near collapse, and New Jersey militiamen had failed to come to their aid. Yet Howe again missed an opportunity to destroy the Continental Army. He decided to wait until spring to attack and ordered his troops into winter quarters in Trenton, Princeton, and other New Jersey towns. Clinton was assigned to capture Newport, R.I.

Howe believed he had broken the patriot rebellion. But he was quite mistaken. Although Washington had few troops, he decided to strike at Trenton. The town was defended by Hessians. On the stormy and bitterly cold night of Dec. 25, 1776, Washington and about 2,400 troops crossed the Delaware River. They landed 9 miles (14 kilometers) north of Trenton and marched through the night. The next morning, they surprised the Hessians and took more than 900 prisoners.

On Jan. 2, 1777, Cornwallis advanced toward Trenton. He planned to attack the Americans the next day. But

during the night, Washington's troops silently stole away and marched past Cornwallis' army. The following morning, Washington attacked at Princeton. He won a brilliant victory over redcoats on their way to join Cornwallis. Washington then moved his troops northward to winter headquarters near Morristown, N.J. He soon began to rebuild his army.

The victories at Trenton and Princeton revived patriot hopes. The Continental Army had almost been destroyed. But it had kept going and regained most of New Jersey. In spite of superior strength, the British had again failed to defeat the rebels.

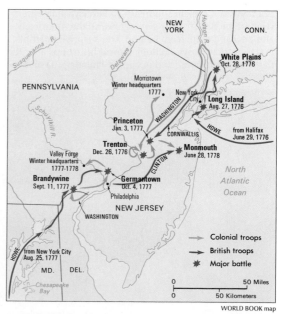

WORLD BOOK map

In the North, Washington and the redcoats fought a seesaw campaign. The patriots lost several battles but kept on fighting. British generals acted cautiously and failed to cooperate.

Detail of an oil painting on canvas (1786), by John Trumbull; Yale University Art Gallery

Britain's surrender at Saratoga on Oct. 17, 1777, marked a turning point in the war. In this painting, defeated General John Burgoyne, *left,* offers his sword to General Horatio Gates.

Brandywine and Germantown. Washington's successful maneuvering at Trenton and Princeton had embarrassed Howe. In the spring of 1777, Howe sought to lure Washington into battle and destroy his army. After failing to draw Washington into battle in New Jersey, Howe set out to take Philadelphia, the patriot capital.

In the summer of 1777, Howe's redcoats sailed from New York City to the top of Chesapeake Bay, about 50 miles (80 kilometers) southwest of Philadelphia. Washington had rebuilt his army during the spring, and he had received weapons from France. He positioned his troops between Howe's forces and Philadelphia.

The opposing armies clashed on Sept. 11, 1777, at Brandywine Creek in southeastern Pennsylvania. One wing of the British army swung around the Americans and attacked them from behind. The surprised patriots had to retreat. Howe skillfully moved his troops after the Battle of Brandywine and occupied Philadelphia on Sep-

tember 26. The Continental Congress had fled to York, Pa., where it continued to direct American affairs.

On Oct. 4, 1777, Washington struck back at British forces camping at Germantown, north of Philadelphia. But his complicated battle plan created confusion. In a heavy fog, patriot forces fired on one another. The Americans again had to retreat.

Victory at Saratoga. While Howe won victories at Brandywine Creek and Germantown, another British force became stranded near Saratoga, N.Y. That force had advanced southward from Canada under Lieutenant General John Burgoyne.

Burgoyne had a successful start against the Americans. On July 6, 1777, he recaptured the British post of Fort Ticonderoga in New York from the Americans without a struggle. A second British expedition, led by Lieutenant Colonel Barry St. Leger, marched up the Mohawk River Valley to meet Burgoyne. In August, St. Leger ambushed militiamen outside Oriskany, N.Y. In the bloody Battle of Oriskany, the British beat back patriot forces. General Arnold stopped St. Leger soon afterward. By then, conditions favored the patriots.

As Burgoyne advanced southward, patriot forces destroyed bridges and cut down trees to block his path. Riflemen fired on British soldiers from the woods. Burgoyne ran short of food and other supplies. In August 1777, the Congress appointed Major General Horatio Gates to command the Northern Department of the Continental Army. Gates was popular with New England patriots, and they poured out to support him and his Continentals. On August 16, militiamen overwhelmed two groups of Hessians and Loyalists searching for horses and food near Bennington, Vt.

Burgoyne trudged slowly through the wilderness along the Hudson River. His poor progress gave the Americans time to fortify a wooded area along the Hudson about 40 miles (64 kilometers) north of Albany. On Sept. 19, 1777, British troops attacked the fortifications. But they were met by patriot forces in a clearing on a nearby farm. Nightfall and the bravery of Hessian soldiers saved Burgoyne's troops from destruction in what became known as the First Battle of Freeman's Farm.

Detail of an oil painting on canvas (1883) by William B. Trego; Valley Forge Historical Society

A ragged and hungry Continental Army was reviewed by General Washington, mounted on the white horse, as it marched toward winter quarters at Valley Forge, Pa., in December 1777. The army suffered from a severe shortage of food, shoes, and warm clothing that winter, and many soldiers died or deserted as a result.

Although the patriot forces greatly outnumbered his army, Burgoyne decided not to retreat toward Canada. On Oct. 7, 1777, Burgoyne attacked again. Arnold's daring leadership won the Second Battle of Freeman's Farm for the patriots. Burgoyne finally began to retreat. But he soon found himself encircled by the Americans at Saratoga. On October 17, Burgoyne surrendered to Gates. The Americans took nearly 6,000 prisoners and large supplies of arms.

The victory at Saratoga marked a turning point in the Revolutionary War. It revealed the failure of British strategy. More important, the great victory at Saratoga helped convince France that it could safely enter the war on the American side.

Valley Forge. Washington's army of about 10,000 soldiers spent the winter camped at Valley Forge, about 20 miles (32 kilometers) northwest of Philadelphia. Many of the troops lacked shoes and other clothing. They also suffered from a severe shortage of food. By spring 1778, nearly a fourth of the soldiers had died of malnutrition, exposure to the cold, and such diseases as smallpox and typhoid fever. Many soldiers deserted because of the horrid conditions.

In February 1778, a Prussian soldier called Baron Friedrich von Steuben arrived at Valley Forge. He convinced Washington that he could train the Continental Army in European military formations and bayonet charges. By late spring, Steuben had created a disciplined fighting force. The Marquis de Lafayette, a young French soldier, also spent part of the winter at Valley Forge. Fired with enthusiasm for the revolution, Lafayette had joined Washington's staff as a major general without pay.

France's entry into the Revolutionary War in 1778 forced Great Britain to defend the rest of its empire. The British expected to fight the French in the West Indies and elsewhere, and so they scattered their military resources. As a result, Britain no longer had a force strong enough to battle the Americans in the North.

In May 1778, General Clinton became commander in chief of British forces in North America. He replaced Howe, who had been occupying Philadelphia since September 1777. Clinton received orders to abandon Philadelphia and go to New York City. He was also told to send troops to the West Indies and other areas.

Monmouth. Clinton left Philadelphia on June 18, 1778, and marched across New Jersey toward New York City. The Continental Army followed him. On June 28, the patriots attacked near Monmouth Court House, N.J. Clinton soon counterattacked. After early confusion, the Americans held their ground, and the battle ended in a draw. During the night, Clinton's exhausted forces limped off the battleground and continued the march toward New York. The Battle of Monmouth was the last major Revolutionary War battle in the North.

Stalemate in the North. Washington hoped to drive the British from New York City in a joint operation with the French. In July 1778, a French fleet under Admiral Charles Hector d'Estaing reached America. But the French warships were unable to cross a sandbar at the mouth of New York Harbor. Later that summer, a combined French and American effort to take Newport, R.I., also failed. In November, d'Estaing sailed southward to protect the French West Indies from British attack.

Problems along the western frontier also troubled Washington in 1778. That year, Loyalists and Iroquois Indians massacred frontier settlers in Pennsylvania and New York. Washington sent Major General John Sullivan to take revenge in 1779. Patriot troops burned Iroquois villages and destroyed crops. Many Iroquois starved to death as a result.

The war in the West, at sea, and in the South

Great Britain changed its strategy after France entered the Revolutionary War. Rather than attack in the North, the British concentrated on conquering the colonies from the South. British leaders believed that most Southerners supported the king. Although the British failed to find as much Loyalist support as they expected, they defeated the Americans in several important battles. The patriots were forced onto the defensive in the South. But they attacked successfully in the West and at sea.

Fighting in the West broke out because land-hungry colonists crossed the Appalachian Mountains and settled on Indian territory. During the Revolutionary War, Indians raided white settlements in the wilderness with British encouragement. In 1778, Virginia sent militiamen led by Lieutenant Colonel George Rogers Clark to strike back at the British. Clark captured several settlements in what are now southern Illinois and southern Indiana. The British recaptured the settlement at Vincennes in Indiana. Clark and his men fought their way back to Vincennes across flooded countryside and took its British and Indian defenders by surprise in February 1779.

Fighting at sea. Congress established the Continental Navy in 1775. Its few ships had little effect on the war's outcome. However, one American naval officer carried the war to British waters. In April 1778, Captain John Paul Jones raided the coast of England. The following year, Jones engaged in battle the heavily armed British warship *Serapis.* Jones captured the *Serapis,* though his own ship, the *Bonhomme Richard,* was badly damaged and later sank. When the British demanded his surrender during the battle, Jones reportedly replied: "I have not yet begun to fight."

Savannah and Charleston. The first stage of Great Britain's Southern strategy called for the capture of a major Southern port, such as Charleston, S.C., or Savannah, Ga. Britain would then use the port as a base for rallying Southern Loyalists and for launching further military campaigns. After its army moved on, the British expected Loyalists to keep control of the conquered areas. Britain assumed it could more easily retake the North after overcoming resistance in the South.

Britain's Southern campaign opened late in 1778. On December 29, a large British force that had sailed from New York City easily captured Savannah. Within a few months, the British controlled all Georgia.

The Congress named Major General Benjamin Lincoln commander of the Southern Department of the Continental Army. In October 1779, Lincoln and Admiral d'Estaing failed to drive the British from Savannah. After-

A naval battle between the *Bonhomme Richard,* commanded by John Paul Jones, and the British warship *Serapis* took place off the coast of England in September 1779. The two ships were lashed together much of the time, and the crews fought in hand-to-hand combat. Jones captured the *Serapis* though his own ship was badly damaged.

Detail of an oil painting on canvas (1789) by William Elliott; U.S. Naval Academy Museum

ward, d'Estaing returned to France, and Lincoln retreated to Charleston. A joint operation by French and American forces had again ended in failure, and Georgia remained in British hands.

Success at Savannah led the British to invade South Carolina. Early in 1780, British forces under General Clinton landed near Charleston. They slowly closed in on the city, trapping its defenders. On May 12, General Lincoln surrendered his force of about 5,500 patriots—almost the entire Southern army. Clinton placed General Cornwallis in charge of British forces in the South and returned to New York City.

The loss of Charleston and so many patriot soldiers badly damaged American morale. However, the British victory had an unexpected result. Soon afterward, bands of South Carolina patriots began to roam the countryside, battling Loyalists and attacking British supply lines. The rebels made it risky for Loyalists to support Cornwallis. The chief rebel leaders included Francis Marion, Andrew Pickens, and Thomas Sumter.

Camden. In July 1780, the Continental Congress ordered General Gates, the victor at Saratoga, to form a new Southern army to replace the one lost at Charleston. Gates hastily assembled a force made up largely of untrained militiamen. The rest of his men consisted of disciplined Continentals. He rushed to challenge Cornwallis at a British base in Camden, S.C.

On Aug. 16, 1780, the armies of Gates and Cornwallis unexpectedly met outside Camden and soon went into battle. The militiamen quickly panicked. Most of them turned and ran without firing a shot. The Continentals fought on until heavy casualties forced them to withdraw. The British had defeated a second American army in the South.

The disaster at Camden marked the low point in the Revolutionary War for the patriots. They then received a

Detail of an oil painting on canvas (about 1845) by William Ranney; State Capitol, Columbia, S.C. (Victor Tutte)

The Battle of Cowpens was fought in a cattle-grazing area of South Carolina in January 1781. It ended in victory for the patriots. In the clash shown here, a young black bugler shoots a British officer who was about to stab an American cavalry commander.

further blow. In September 1780, the patriots discovered that General Arnold, who commanded a military post at West Point, N.Y., had joined the British side. The Americans learned of Arnold's treason just in time to stop him from turning West Point over to the enemy.

Kings Mountain. Cornwallis' victory at Camden in August 1780 led him to act more boldly. In September, he charged into North Carolina before the Loyalists had gained firm control of South Carolina. After Cornwallis' departure, rebels in South Carolina terrorized suspected Loyalists. In addition, patriot frontiersmen turned out to fight the British.

In October 1780, the left wing of Cornwallis' army, which was made up of Loyalist troops, was surrounded and captured on Kings Mountain, just inside South Carolina. After the defeat at Kings Mountain, Cornwallis temporarily halted his Southern campaign and retreated to South Carolina.

Cowpens and Guilford Courthouse. In October 1780, the Continental Congress named Major General Nathanael Greene to replace Gates as commander of the Southern army. Greene was a superb choice because he knew how to accomplish much with extremely few resources. Greene divided his troops into two small armies. He led one army and put Brigadier General Daniel Morgan in charge of the other. Greene hoped to avoid battle with Cornwallis' far stronger force while he rebuilt the Southern army. Instead, Greene planned to let the British chase the Americans around the countryside.

Cornwallis set out to trap Morgan's army. Just before the British caught up with him, Morgan prepared for battle in a cattle-grazing area known as the Cowpens in northern South Carolina. On Jan. 17, 1781, Morgan's sharpshooting riflemen quickly killed or captured nearly all the onrushing redcoats.

The patriot victory at Cowpens enraged Cornwallis, and he pursued Morgan with even greater determination. Greene rushed to join Morgan, hoping to crush Cornwallis' weakened force. On March 15, 1781, a bloody exchange occurred at Guilford Courthouse in North Carolina. Although Cornwallis drove Greene from the battlefield, the British had taken a battering. Cornwallis halted the chase after the Battle of Guilford Courthouse. He moved to Wilmington, N.C., where he gave his exhausted army a brief rest.

Greene challenged British posts in South Carolina during the spring of 1781. The patriots fought several small battles but failed to win clear victories. Yet the fact that a rebel army moved freely about the countryside proved that Britain did not control the Carolinas.

The end of the war

The fighting in the Revolutionary War centered in Virginia during 1781. In January, the traitor Benedict Arnold began conducting raids in Virginia for the British, who had made him a brigadier general. Arnold's troops set fire to crops, military supplies, and other patriot property. General Washington sent Lafayette with a force of Continentals to rally Virginia's militia and go after Arnold. But Lafayette had too few troops to stop Arnold.

Cornwallis rushed into Virginia in the spring of 1781 and made it his new base in the campaign to conquer the South. However, Cornwallis had violated Britain's Southern strategy by failing to gain control of North and South Carolina before advancing northward. General Clinton believed that the Southern campaign was therefore doomed. He also feared an American attack on his base at New York City. Clinton ordered Cornwallis to adopt a defensive position along the Virginia coast and prepare to send his troops north. Cornwallis moved to Yorktown, which lay along Chesapeake Bay.

Surrender at Yorktown. The last major battle of the Revolutionary War was fought at Yorktown. French and American forces cooperated to deliver a crushing defeat to British forces under Cornwallis.

About 5,500 French soldiers had reached America in July 1780. They were led by Lieutenant General Jean Rochambeau. Washington still hoped to drive the British from New York City in a combined operation with the French. In August 1781, however, Washington learned that a large French fleet under Admiral François de Grasse was headed toward Virginia. De Grasse planned to block Chesapeake Bay and prevent Cornwallis from escaping by sea. Washington and Rochambeau rushed their forces southward to trap Cornwallis on land. A British naval force sailed from New York City and battled de Grasse at the mouth of Chesapeake Bay in early September. But after several days, the British ships returned to New York for repairs.

By late September 1781, Cornwallis knew that he was in trouble. A combined French and American force of about 18,000 soldiers and sailors surrounded him at Yorktown. The soldiers slowly and steadily closed in on the trapped British troops. Cornwallis made a desperate attempt to ferry his forces across the York River to safety on the night of October 16. But a storm drove them back. Cornwallis asked for surrender terms the next day.

The surrender at Yorktown took place on Oct. 19, 1781. More than 8,000 men laid down their arms as a British band reportedly played a tune called "The World Turned Upside Down." They represented about a fourth of Britain's military force in America.

Britain's defeat at Yorktown did not end the Revolutionary War. The fighting dragged on in some areas for two more years. However, British leaders feared they might lose other parts of Britain's empire if they continued the war in America. Cornwallis' defeat at Yorktown brought a new group of British ministers to power early in 1782. They began peace talks with the Americans.

The Treaty of Paris. Peace discussions between the Americans and the British opened in Paris in April 1782. Richard Oswald, a wealthy merchant, represented the British government. The statesmen Benjamin Franklin, John Adams, and John Jay negotiated for the United States.

The Congress instructed the American delegates to consult with the French before they took any action. But the Americans disregarded the instructions and concluded a preliminary peace treaty with Great Britain on Nov. 30, 1782. The Congress approved the treaty on April 15, 1783, and it was signed on Sept. 3, 1783.

The Treaty of Paris recognized the independence of

Detail of an oil painting on canvas (about 1790) by Henri van Blarenberghe; Musée de Versailles (Giraudon/Art Resource)

The siege of Yorktown in October 1781 was the last major battle of the Revolutionary War. Britain began peace talks with the Americans several months after its defeat at Yorktown.

the United States and established the new nation's borders. United States territory extended west to the Mississippi River, north to Canada, east to the Atlantic Ocean, and south to about Florida. Britain gave Florida to Spain. The treaty also granted the Americans fishing rights off the coast of Newfoundland and Nova Scotia. In addition, it instructed the Congress to recommend that the states restore property taken from Loyalists during the war. The last British soldiers were withdrawn from New York City in November 1783.

Results of the war

As a result of the Revolutionary War, the 13 British colonies threw off royal rule. In its place, they established governments ruled by law and dedicated to the guarantee of certain basic rights, including life, liberty, and the pursuit of happiness. Admiration for the principles that guided the revolution led peoples elsewhere to demand political reforms. Thomas Paine declared that the Revolutionary War "contributed more to enlighten the world, and diffuse a spirit of freedom and liberality among mankind, than any human event . . . that ever preceded it."

War losses. Most historians estimate that about 7,200 Americans were killed in battle during the Revolutionary War. Approximately 8,200 more were wounded. About 10,000 others died in military camps from disease or exposure. Some 8,500 died in prison after being captured by the British. American military deaths from all causes during the war thus numbered about 25,700. In addition, approximately 1,400 soldiers were missing. British military deaths during the war totaled about 10,000.

Many soldiers in the Continental Army came out of the war penniless. They had received little or no pay while they served. Soldiers who had enlisted for the entire war received certificates for Western land. But many veterans had to sell the certificates because they needed money before Western lands became available. In 1818, Congress agreed to pay pensions to needy veterans.

Costs of the war. The 13 states and the Congress went deeply into debt to finance the Revolutionary War. A new Constitution, approved in 1788, gave Congress the power of taxation. Largely through taxes, Congress paid off much of the war debt by the early 1800's.

The Revolutionary War severely strained Britain's economy. The king and Parliament feared the war might bankrupt the country. But after the war, greatly expanded trade with the United States helped the economy recover. Taxes on that trade reduced Britain's debt.

Of all the warring nations, France could least afford its expenditures on the Revolutionary War. By 1788, the country was nearly bankrupt. France's financial troubles helped bring on the French Revolution in 1789.

James Kirby Martin

WORLD BOOK map

The borders of the United States were set by the Treaty of Paris, which ended the Revolutionary War. The new nation extended from the Atlantic Ocean west to the Mississippi River.

Related articles in *World Book.* See the *History* section of the articles on the states that fought in the Revolutionary War, such as **Massachusetts** (History). See also the following:

Background and causes of the war

Boston Massacre	Committees of	Intolerable Acts
Boston Port Act	safety	Minutemen
Boston Tea Party	Continental	Navigation Acts
Committees of	Congress	Stamp Act
correspond-	Declaration of In-	Writ of assistance
ence	dependence	

American military leaders

Allen, Ethan	Hale, Nathan	Putnam, Rufus
Arnold, Benedict	Jones, John Paul	Saint Clair, Arthur
Barry, John	Knox, Henry	Schuyler, Philip J.
Clark, George R.	Lee, Charles	Stark, John
Clinton, George	Lee, Henry	Warner, Seth
Dearborn, Henry	Marion, Francis	Washington,
Gates, Horatio	Moultrie, William	George
Greene, Nathanael	Putnam, Israel	Wayne, Anthony

American civilian leaders

Adams, John	Jay, John	Morris, Robert
Adams, Samuel	Jefferson, Thomas	Otis, James
Dawes, William	Lee, Richard	Prescott, Samuel
Deane, Silas	Henry	Randolph, Peyton
Franklin, Benjamin	Livingston,	Revere, Paul
Hancock, John	Robert R.	Salomon, Haym
Henry, Patrick	Mason, George	Warren, Joseph

British leaders

André, John	Cornwallis,	Howe, Richard
Burgoyne, John	Charles	Howe, William
Burke, Edmund	Gage, Thomas	North, Lord
Carleton, Sir Guy	George III	Saint Leger, Barry
Clinton, Sir Henry		

Other biographies

Attucks, Crispus	Jouett, Jack	Pulaski, Casimir
Brant, Joseph	Kalb, Johann	Rochambeau,
Corbin, Margaret	Kościuszko,	Comte de
Cochran	Tadeusz	Ross, Betsy
De Grasse,	Lafayette,	Rutledge, John
François J. P.	Marquis de	Salem, Peter
Forten, James	Ludington, Sybil	Sampson,
Girty, Simon	Mazzei, Philip	Deborah
Galloway, Joseph	Paine, Thomas	Steuben, Baron
Gálvez,	Pitcher, Molly	von
Bernardo de		

Other related articles

Army, U.S.	Flag (Flags in Unit-	Navy, U.S. (History)
(History)	ed States his-	Privateer
Brother Jonathan	tory; pictures)	Sons of Liberty
Bunker Hill,	Fort Ticonderoga	Sons of the Ameri-
Battle of	Green Mountain	can Revolution
Cabal	Boys	United States,
Cincinnati, Society	Hessians	History of the
of the	Marine Corps, U.S.	Valley Forge
Concord, Battle of	(History)	Wyoming Valley
Constitution of	National Park	Massacre
the U.S.	System	Yankee Doodle
Daughters of the		
American Revo-		
lution		

Outline

I. Background and causes of the war
  A. Life in the American Colonies
  B. British policy changes
  C. The Proclamation of 1763
  D. The Sugar Act
  E. The Quartering and Stamp acts
  F. The Townshend Acts
  G. The Tea Act
  H. The Intolerable Acts
  I. The First Continental Congress

II. The beginning of the war
  A. Lexington and Concord
  B. Bunker Hill
  C. The Continental Army
  D. The evacuation of Boston
  E. The invasion of Canada
  F. Fighting in the Southern Colonies
  G. The Declaration of Independence

III. Conduct of the war
  A. The fighting forces   D. Financing the war
  B. Weapons and tactics   E. Diplomatic triumphs
  C. Patriot governments

IV. The war in the North
  A. The campaign in New York
  B. Trenton and Princeton
  C. Brandywine and Germantown
  D. Victory at Saratoga
  E. Valley Forge
  F. France's entry into the Revolutionary War

V. The war in the West, at sea, and in the South
  A. Fighting in the West   D. Camden
  B. Fighting at sea   E. Kings Mountain
  C. Savannah and   F. Cowpens and Guil-
    Charleston   ford Courthouse

VI. The end of the war
  A. Surrender at Yorktown
  B. The Treaty of Paris

VII. Results of the war
  A. War losses   B. Costs of the war

Questions

How did British military forces differ from patriot forces at the outbreak of the Revolutionary War?

What pamphlet built support for American independence?

Which defeat marked the low point of the Revolutionary War for the patriots?

Where was the last major battle of the Revolutionary War fought?

Why did colonists object to the Stamp Act?

How did Britain change its strategy after France entered the Revolutionary War?

What advantages did the patriots have in the Revolutionary War over the British?

How did France help the patriots during the Revolutionary War?

Why did the Continental Congress order an invasion of Canada in 1775?

Which patriot victory marked a turning point in the Revolutionary War?

Additional resources

Level I

Brenner, Barbara. *If You Were There in 1776.* Bradbury, 1994.
Carter, Alden R. *The American Revolution: War for Independence.* Watts, 1992.
Dolan, Edward F. *The American Revolution: How We Fought the War of Independence.* Millbrook, 1995.
Wilbur, C. Keith. *The Revolutionary Soldier, 1775-1783.* Chelsea Hse., 1997.
Zeinert, Karen. *Those Remarkable Women of the American Revolution.* Millbrook, 1996.

Level II

Blanco, Richard L., ed. *The American Revolution, 1775-1783: An Encyclopedia.* 2 vols. Garland, 1993.
Bobrick, Benson. *Angel in the Whirlwind: The Triumph of the American Revolution.* Simon & Schuster, 1997.
Dudley, William, ed. *The American Revolution: Opposing Viewpoints.* Greenhaven, 1992.
Ward, Harry M. *The American Revolution: Nationhood Achieved, 1763-1788.* St. Martin's, 1995.
Zall, Paul M. *Becoming American: Young People in the American Revolution.* Linnet, 1993.

Rex cat. See Cat (Short-haired breeds; picture).

Rexroth, *REHKS rawth,* **Kenneth** (1905-1982), was an American poet. He called for freedom from traditional styles in poetry, which he considered artificial. Many critics called Rexroth the forerunner of the *beat* movement of the 1950's. Beat writers attacked the use of what they considered outmoded traditions in art.

Rexroth's poems generally show he had a more complex, interesting, and informed mind than most beat writers. *The Dragon and the Unicorn* (1952) is a book-length story poem that explores the nature of love. *In Defense of the Earth* (1956) contains love poetry, poems directed toward young people, and translations of Japanese poetry. *The Collected Shorter Poems* (1967) and *The Collected Longer Poems* (1968) confirmed Rexroth's reputation as a leader of many poetry movements on the West Coast. Rexroth was a painter and essayist and also translated Chinese, Greek, and Latin poetry. *The World Outside the Window: The Selected Essays of Kenneth Rexroth* was published in 1987. He was born in South Bend, Ind.   Bonnie Costello

Reye's syndrome, *ryz SIHN drohm,* is a rare childhood disease of the liver and central nervous system. Advanced cases can result in brain damage or death. The disease kills about 3 to 5 percent of its victims.

Most patients with Reye's syndrome are from 4 to 15 years old. The majority of them develop the disease while recovering from a mild viral illness, such as chickenpox or influenza. For some unknown reason, the virus apparently triggers Reye's syndrome. Studies indicate that many Reye's syndrome patients had been given aspirin during the viral illness. Based on these studies, experts and government health agencies have cautioned against using aspirin to treat chickenpox, influenza, or various other viral illnesses in children.

The first symptom of Reye's syndrome is repeated vomiting. In mild cases, the patient recovers with no aftereffects. But if the disease progresses, convulsions and alternating states of excitation and confused sleepiness may occur. In the final stages of the disease, brain cells swell and pressure builds in the skull, followed by a coma and possible brain damage or death.

The cause of Reye's syndrome has not been determined. Physicians treat the disease by giving the patient glucose and other nutrients, and by reducing the body's production of ammonia. They use drugs or surgery to lower the pressure within the skull if it reaches dangerous levels. This treatment has saved many patients. Reye's syndrome was first described by R. D. K. Reye, an Australian pathologist, in 1963.   Henry L. Nadler

Reykjavík, *RAY kyuh VEEK* (pop. 99,623; met. area pop. 145,098), is the capital and largest city of Iceland. It is a seaport on the southwest coast, at the head of Faxaflói, a bay (see **Iceland** [map]). The city is Iceland's trading center and its center of government and education. It has many schools, a university, an observatory, a theater, a national museum, and a national library.

Water from nearby hot springs is used to heat all buildings in Reykjavík. The water is first piped to large concrete tanks on a hill outside the city. It is then piped into the buildings by flow of gravity.

Reykjavík was settled in A.D. 877. In World War II, British and American troops protected Reykjavík and all Iceland from possible attack by Germany. Today, U.S. troops are stationed at a North Atlantic Treaty Organization (NATO) base in nearby Keflavík.   George W. Rich

See also **Iceland** (pictures).

Reynolds, *REHN uhldz,* **Sir Joshua** (1723- 1792), was a great English portrait painter. Reynolds' portraits show his skill in capturing the likeness of his subjects, as well

Icelandic Photo & Press Service

Reykjavík is the capital and largest city of Iceland. It lies on the country's southwest coast. More than half the people of Iceland live in or near Reykjavík. Rugged land lies beyond a residential area of the city, *left.*

Reynolds' *The Age of Innocence* shows the artist's skill in painting sensitive and appealing portraits of young children.

Oil painting on canvas (1788); Tate Gallery, London (John Webb)

as his keen understanding of human nature. Among Reynolds' masterpieces are the portraits *Hon. Augustus Keppel* (1754), *William Robertsen* (1772), and *Sarah Siddons as the Tragic Muse* (1784). Reynolds wrote 15 essays on art education called *Discourses* that stressed the importance of grandeur in art and rigid academic training. His writings influenced generations of artists.

Reynolds became the most fashionable painter of his time. His close friends included James Boswell, Edmund Burke, Samuel Johnson, and other leading intellectual figures of the late 1700's. Reynolds helped found the Royal Academy of Arts in 1768 and became its first president. In 1784, he was appointed painter to the king.

Reynolds was born in Plympton-Earl's, near Plymouth. In 1740, he was apprenticed to Thomas Hudson, a leading London portrait painter. Reynolds later studied the works of Sir Anthony Van Dyck, the most famous portrait painter of the 1600's. In 1749, Reynolds traveled to Italy. There he was influenced by the warm colors and sculptural clarity he saw in paintings of such Renaissance artists as Tintoretto, Titian, and Paolo Veronese.

Reynolds returned to England in 1753. He soon became a favorite portrait painter of the wealthy and the leaders of society. He also painted charming and sensitive portraits of children. In 1781, Reynolds visited Flanders and the Netherlands where he was influenced by the rich colors of the Flemish artist Peter Paul Rubens.

Douglas K. S. Hyland

For other examples of Reynolds' paintings, see the pictures with **Blackstone, Sir William; Boswell, James; Johnson, Samuel.**

Reza Shah Pahlavi, *rih ZAH SHAH pah lah VEE* (1878-1944), ruled Persia, which he renamed Iran, from 1925 to 1941. His main goals as *shah* (king) were to make his nation self-reliant and respected, as well as to unify and modernize it. He built railroads and factories, promoted education, increased job and educational opportunities for women, and reformed the legal system.

Reza was born in Alasht, a village northeast of Teheran, Iran's capital. His original name was Reza Khan, also spelled *Riza Khan.* He enlisted in the armed forces, rose through the ranks, and eventually commanded the principal military unit of Iran. In 1921, he led his troops into Teheran and overthrew the government. He became prime minister in 1923 and forced the shah, Ahmad Shah, to give up the throne. In 1925, Reza became shah and changed his family name to Pahlavi, also spelled *Pahlevi.* He named his oldest son, Mohammad Reza Pahlavi, crown prince. During World War II (1939-1945), Allied troops wanted to use Iran as a supply route. However, Reza Shah refused to cooperate. As a result, British and Soviet troops invaded the country and forced him to resign. He died in exile in South Africa and was succeeded by his oldest son.   Malcolm C. Peck

See also **Iran** (History).

Rh factor is a substance in the red blood cells of most people. Red blood cells that contain the Rh factor *agglutinate* (clump) if they come into contact with an antibody called *anti-Rh.* This reaction can produce serious illness or death. People who have the Rh factor are known as Rh-positive. Those lacking it are Rh-negative. Karl Landsteiner, Philip Levine, and Alexander Wiener discovered the factor in rhesus monkeys in 1940. They named it *Rh* for the monkey.

Anti-Rh does not occur naturally in the blood. But if an Rh-negative person receives a transfusion of Rh-positive blood, anti-Rh may build up in the blood plasma. By the time the antibody has been produced, the donor blood usually is so diluted that no serious reactions take place. But if the patient receives later transfusions of Rh-positive blood, the anti-Rh will attack the Rh-positive red blood cells and cause agglutination.

The Rh factor is inherited. The child of an Rh-negative mother and an Rh-positive father may be Rh-positive. Before birth, some of the baby's blood cells may enter the mother's blood. Then the mother may build up anti-Rh. Most of the antibody does not form until after the baby is born, however, so it seldom causes any problems with the first child. But if the mother becomes pregnant with another Rh-positive baby, she now has a ready-made supply of anti-Rh. The flow of large amounts of her anti-Rh into the child's blood can cause clumping and destruction of the infant's red blood cells. This condition, which is called *erythroblastosis fetalis,* can result in severe anemia, brain damage, and even death. Such severe reactions take place in only about 1 of 20 cases in which the mother is Rh-negative and the father is Rh-positive. Even among these couples, physicians can usually prevent erythroblastosis fetalis by injecting the mother with a serum shortly after she gives birth to an Rh-positive child. The serum contains anti-Rh, which destroys any of the baby's cells in her blood before her body has time to produce its own anti-Rh. When erythroblastosis fetalis does occur, doctors treat the condition by replacing the baby's blood with fresh blood. In most cases, this procedure eliminates any long-term effects of the disease.   Joseph V. Simone

See also **Landsteiner, Karl; Blood transfusion.**

Rhapsody is a term used for a musical composition of a generally epic, heroic, or nationalistic nature. A rhapsody is not a particular musical form. It refers to musical pieces of an emotional nature, often characterized by marked changes of mood. Many rhapsodies are based on folk material. Most are instrumental compositions, but some have been written for voice. Some well-known rhapsodies of the 1800's are the 19 Hungarian Rhapsodies by Franz Liszt and Antonín Dvořák's 3 Slavonic Rhapsodies. The best-known rhapsodies of the 1900's include *Rhapsody on a Theme of Paganini* by Sergei Rachmaninoff and *Rhapsody in Blue* by George Gershwin.

In ancient Greece, a rhapsody was part of an epic poem, such as Homer's *Iliad,* sung by a professional singer. In modern literature, the term has come to mean a highly emotional work.   Thomas W. Tunks

Rhea, *REE uh,* is a large South American bird that cannot fly. It looks like a small ostrich, and it is often called the *South American ostrich.* However, it has three toes on each foot, while the ostrich has two. The rhea also has larger wings and more feathers on its neck and head than the ostrich (see **Ostrich**). The common rhea stands about 5 feet (1.5 meters) tall and weighs about 50 pounds (23 kilograms).

Rheas live on the plains of southern Brazil, Uruguay, Paraguay, and Argentina. They usually live in flocks of 5 to 30, generally in brush-covered land near water where they can bathe and swim. They eat leaves, roots, and insects. Rheas have unusual nesting habits. The male scrapes a shallow hole in the ground, lines it with dry grass, and leads several hens to the nest. Each hen lays an egg. This process may be repeated several times, and a nest may have up to 30 eggs. The male then hatches the eggs and cares for the young.

Scientific classification. Rheas belong to the order Rheaformes. Two species make up the rhea family, Rheidae. The common, larger species is *Rhea americana.*   John W. Fitzpatrick

WORLD BOOK illustration by Trevor Boyer, Linden Artists Ltd.

The rhea, a bird that cannot fly, resembles a small ostrich. Rheas live on the grasslands of South America.

Rhea, *REE uh,* in Greek mythology, was the wife and sister of Cronus, ruler of the race of gods and goddesses called *Titans.* Her mother was Gaea, the earth, and her father was Uranus, the sky. She became queen of the gods when Cronus overthrew Uranus. In many parts of Asia, Rhea was known as Cybele.

According to myth, Rhea and Cronus had six children—the goddesses Demeter, Hera, and Hestia; and the gods Hades, Poseidon, and Zeus. Cronus swallowed five of the children when they were born to prevent them from deposing him. However, Rhea deceived Cronus by tricking him into swallowing a stone wrapped in baby clothes in place of their youngest child, Zeus. Rhea then hid Zeus in a cave on the island of Crete. After Zeus was grown, he returned and tricked Cronus into vomiting up his other children. They helped Zeus defeat Cronus and the other Titans in a 10-year battle called the *Titanomachy.*   Nancy Felson-Rubin

See also **Mythology** (Greek mythology); **Titans.**

Rhea Silvia. See Romulus and Remus.

Rhee, *ree,* **Syngman,** *SIHNG muhn* (1875-1965), a Korean statesman, served as the first president of the Republic of Korea from 1948 to 1960. He resigned in 1960, soon after his election to a fourth term, because of widespread riots following unfair election practices.

Rhee was born in Hwanghae province and was educated in Seoul. Imprisoned from 1897 to 1904 for leading student demonstrations for independence, he wrote the book *Spirit of Independence* (1904). He then studied in the United States at George Washington, Harvard, and Princeton universities. Rhee lived in exile in Honolulu for 20 years. He returned to Korea after Japan surrendered in World War II (1939-1945), but went back to Hawaii following his resignation.   George E. Taylor

Rhenium, *REE nee uhm,* is a rare, costly, silvery-white metal. It is found in small amounts in such minerals as *gadolinite* and *molybdenite.* Rhenium has one of the highest melting points of the chemical elements. Because it withstands high temperatures, rhenium is a valuable ingredient in certain *alloys* (mixtures of metals). It is sometimes mixed with tungsten or platinum to make heat-resistant electrical equipment. It is also used in making *filaments* (fine wires) for instruments called *mass spectrometers* that measure the mass of atoms and molecules.

The German scientists Walter Noddack, Ida Tacke, and Otto Berg discovered rhenium in 1925. It has the chemical symbol Re. Its atomic number is 75, and its atomic weight is 186.207. Rhenium melts at 3180 °C and boils at 5627 °C.   S. C. Cummings

Rheostat, *REE uh stat,* is a device that increases or decreases the amount of resistance in an electric circuit. It regulates the flow of current through a circuit. Many kinds of rheostats are used with motors, radio transmitters, generators, and other electrical equipment.

A simple rheostat consists of a metal resistance wire wound around a cylindrical piece of insulating material. A metal arm that can be moved along the turns of the resistance wire touches each turn as it moves. The current passes through the resistance wire and then into the movable arm. The more turns of wire on the rheostat, the greater its resistance will be, and the smaller the amount of current that will flow through the circuit it controls.   Douglas M. Lapp

George H. Harrison from Grant Heilman

Rhesus monkeys are among the most popular monkeys exhibited in zoos. These monkeys have also served a valuable purpose as research animals in scientific experiments.

Rhesus monkey, *REE suhs,* is a monkey noted for its usefulness in medical and behavioral research. Scientists have learned much about the behavior and ecology of rhesus monkeys because these monkeys are easy to find and to follow in the wild. Research on the rhesus monkey led to the discovery of the *Rh factor,* a substance in the red blood cells of most human beings (see **Rh factor**). Scientists named the substance for the animal. Rhesus monkeys are also popular zoo animals.

The rhesus monkey lives in many regions of southern and southeastern Asia, from Afghanistan in the west to Thailand and southern China in the east. It is the most widespread of a group of monkeys called *macaques* (see **Macaque**). Rhesus monkeys measure from 18 to 25 inches (48 to 64 centimeters) long, not including a 7- to 12-inch (18- to 30-centimeter) tail. They weigh from 9 to 22 pounds (4 to 10 kilograms) and have dull yellow to brown fur. They live both on the ground and in trees in groups of about 5 to more than 100 animals. Rhesus monkeys inhabit a variety of surroundings, including deserts, farm areas, forests, mountains, and swamps. These monkeys also live in villages and in crowded bazaars of large cities. Their food includes buds, fruit, insects, leaves, roots, and various crops.

Many Hindus once regarded rhesus monkeys as sacred. But religious tolerance of the animals declined because rhesus monkeys destroy crops and property. Until 1978, about 200,000 rhesus monkeys a year were exported from India to laboratories around the world. However, India stopped exporting them that year. Today, most rhesus monkeys used by scientists are bred in captivity. Destruction of the monkey's natural habitat endangers the animal's survival in the wild.   Randall L. Susman

Scientific classification. Rhesus monkeys belong to the genus *Macaca* in the Old World monkey family, Cercopithecidae. They are classified as *M. mulatta.*

See also **Monkey** (picture).

Rhetoric. See Oratory.

Rheumatic fever, *roo MAT ihk,* is a disease that occurs primarily in children from 5 to 15 years old. It also strikes younger children and adults. Rheumatic fever gets its name from its most common symptoms— *rheumatism* (inflammation of the joints) and fever. The disease may last several weeks or months. Rheumatic fever can cause permanent damage to the heart valves.

Rheumatic fever is caused by bacteria called *streptococci.* People who develop the disease have had a recent streptococcal infection, such as strep throat. The streptococci subsequently trigger the immune system to attack the body's own tissues.

Before antibiotic drugs were developed in the mid-1900's, rheumatic fever with its resulting valve damage was a leading cause of heart disease throughout the world. Today, prompt treatment of streptococcal infections with penicillin and other antibiotics usually prevents rheumatic fever, and the disease has become rare in industrialized countries. However, rheumatic fever remains a problem in many developing nations.

The first symptoms of rheumatic fever usually occur a few weeks after the streptococcal infection. Common symptoms include fever; with pain and swelling in such joints as the elbows, wrists, knees, or ankles. Nodules (lumps) may develop under the skin over bony areas and a mild rash sometimes occurs. Some patients develop *chorea,* a condition marked by jerky, involuntary movements (see **Chorea**).

Mild to severe *carditis* (inflammation of the heart) occurs in many cases of rheumatic fever. Severe carditis can lead to heart failure. Both mild and severe carditis can cause permanent damage to the heart valves resulting in the condition called *rheumatic heart disease.* In rheumatic heart disease, the damaged valves no longer open and close properly, and the resulting turbulent passage of blood produces a sound called a heart murmur (see **Heart murmur**). Severe rheumatic heart disease can lead to heart failure. Surgical replacement of badly damaged valves may prevent this outcome.

Toby R. Engel

See also **Heart** (Valve disease).

Rheumatism, *ROO muh tihz uhm,* is a general term for disorders involving stiffness or pain in the muscles or joints. Physicians do not use the term. They refer to the disorders by more specific names. Common conditions that are frequently called rheumatism include *arthritis, bursitis, myalgia,* and *tendinitis.*

See also **Arthritis; Bursitis; Rheumatic fever.**

Rheumatology is the study of diseases affecting the body's joints and their associated tissues, including the bones, muscles, tendons, cartilage, and ligaments. Such diseases are called *rheumatic diseases.* Doctors who specialize in the care of patients with rheumatic diseases are called *rheumatologists.*

Diseases most commonly treated by rheumatologists include various forms of arthritis, particularly osteoarthritis, rheumatoid arthritis, gout, and disorders of the body's connective tissues, such as scleroderma and systemic lupus erythematosus. Rheumatologists also care for patients with general back pain and aching muscles, bones, and joints. In addition, other doctors often consult rheumatologists for help in treating patients with nonrheumatic diseases that involve the joints, muscles, and bones. Rheumatologists do not perform surgery, but they often work closely with orthopedic surgeons and specialists in rehabilitation medicine.

To become a certified rheumatologist in the United States, a doctor must study rheumatology for two to three years after completing medical school and residency training. The doctor must then pass a series of examinations conducted by an authorized medical board.

Research in rheumatology often involves specialists from other fields, such as biochemistry, cell biology, genetics, immunology, and molecular biology. Some researchers search for the causes and cures of rheumatic diseases, and others study how a rheumatic disease progresses.   Michael D. Lockshin

Rhine River, *ryn,* is the most important inland waterway in Europe. It is about 820 miles (1,320 kilometers) long and drains an area of about 86,700 square miles (224,600 square kilometers). The river rises in eastern Switzerland. It forms part of the borders of Switzerland, Liechtenstein, Austria, France, and Germany. It flows through Germany and the Netherlands into the North Sea. To Germans, the Rhine is a symbol of national history. Many German legends relate to the river.

The course of the Rhine. Two glacier-fed mountain torrents rise and flow eastward in the high Alps of eastern Switzerland, close to the Italian border. One is the *Vorder* Rhine, and the other is the *Hinter* Rhine. From their union, the Rhine flows along the western borders of Liechtenstein and Austria to Lake Constance, 1,306 feet (398 meters) above the sea. This lake sends the river westward to tumble over a fall 70 feet (21 meters) high at Schaffhausen. From there the Rhine flows between Germany and Switzerland to Basel. This city serves as landlocked Switzerland's principal port.

North of Basel, the Rhine flows between the Black Forest on the east and Vosges Mountains on the west. It

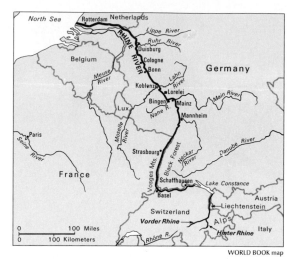

WORLD BOOK map

The Rhine River flows from the Alps to the North Sea.

follows a course down the middle of a plain that is about 20 miles (32 kilometers) wide and 180 miles (290 kilometers) long. In the southern part of the plain, the Rhine serves as the boundary between France and Germany.

From Basel, the river gradually widens, and at Bingen, it leaves the plain and plunges into a narrow gorge through the Rhenish Slate Mountains. Here is the cliff called the Lorelei where the legendary nymph also called Lorelei lures boatmen to destruction with her song. The legends of the heroic Roland, Siegfried, and other historic and mythical figures also developed in this region (see **Lorelei**). At Bonn, the river and valley

Shostal

The Rhine River in Germany winds past a cliff called the Lorelei, *center.* According to legend, the lure of a nymph also called Lorelei dooms sailors at the cliff.

Dennis Hallinan, FPG

Stately castles overlook the Rhine Valley. They were built for protection during the Middle Ages, when the countries of Europe were frequently at war with one another. Today, the historic castles attract large numbers of sightseers.

widen again as the Rhine enters the North German Plain on its journey to the Netherlands and its broad delta leading into the North Sea.

Along its course, the Rhine receives the waters of the Neckar, Main, Lahn, Ruhr, and Lippe rivers from the east. The Nahe and Moselle rivers flow into the Rhine from the west. Canals connect the Rhine to the Danube, Elbe, Ems, Marne, Oder, Rhône, and Weser rivers and so make the Rhine part of a great inland navigation system. North of Basel, major Rhine ports are Strasbourg, Mannheim, Cologne, Duisburg, and Rotterdam. Duisburg is the gateway to the industrial Ruhr Valley.

The Rhine in history. The Rhine has been important in European history ever since Julius Caesar built a timber bridge across it. For 400 years, the Rhine was the boundary between the Romans and the Germanic tribes. On the west bank of the Rhine grew up the Roman cities of Cologne, or Köln (Colonia Agrippinensis), Bonn (Bonna), Koblenz (Confluentes), Mainz (Mogontiacum), all in Germany; Strasbourg (Argentoratum), in France; and Basel (Basilia), in Switzerland. During the Middle Ages, the Rhine was under German rule from Basel to the Netherlands. But when France gained a foothold on its western shore, in 1648, at the close of the Thirty Years' War, a struggle began. The struggle lasted into the 1900's.

King Louis XIV made gains in the Rhine Valley, and Napoleon restored the old Roman boundaries of France. Even after Napoleon was defeated, Alsace, which borders the Rhine from Switzerland to beyond Strasbourg,

was left in French hands. But Germany gained almost all of Alsace in 1871.

The same territory was battled over in World War I. The Treaty of Versailles returned Alsace and Lorraine to France, again extending that country's domain to the Rhine. Germany signed an agreement not to fortify the Rhineland. In 1936, German dictator Adolf Hitler repudiated this agreement and began to militarize the region. During World War II, heavy fighting occurred along the Rhine in the last part of the European struggle. After the war, the river again became one of the world's busiest waterways.   Frank Ahnert

Rhineland is a historic area in what is now western Germany. It lies along the Rhine River and extends west to the borders of Belgium, France, Luxembourg, and the Netherlands. For the location of the Rhineland, see **Germany** (terrain map).

The Rhineland was settled during ancient times. Through the years, it was ruled by the Celts, the Romans, the Huns, and the Franks. About 800, such Rhineland cities as Cologne, Mainz, and Trier began to grow in importance, and in time became religious and political centers of the Holy Roman Empire. The Rhineland was made part of France during the Napoleonic Wars of the late 1790's. The region became part of the German state of Prussia in 1815.

The Rhineland's rich mineral resources and location on the Rhine River led to the growth of important industrial centers there, including the Ruhr coal-mining district. After World War I (1914-1918), Germany signed treaties agreeing not to fortify the region or station troops there. But German troops occupied the Rhineland in 1936 and used it for military purposes during World War II (1939-1945). Today, the area is one of Germany's major industrial districts. Tourists visit the Rhineland to see its picturesque towns, historic castles, and extensive vineyards.   J. A. Hellen

Rhinitis, *ry NY tihs,* is an inflammation of the mucous membranes that line the nose. The inflammation increases the production of nasal mucus and can make breathing through the nose difficult. Rhinitis can result from infections, allergic reactions, and unknown causes. It occurs most frequently as part of the common cold, a viral infection. Many other cases result from hay fever. Certain *chronic* (long-lasting) forms of rhinitis can cause the mucous membranes to thicken or to wear away. See also **Cold, Common; Hay fever.**   Neil R. Blacklow

Rhinoceros is a huge animal that ranks as one of the largest land creatures. The rhinoceros has an immense, solid body, and short, stocky legs. Its thick skin appears to lie in folds but is actually just creased at the joints. Most species have little hair. Depending on the species, the rhinoceros has one or two slightly curving horns that project from its long nose. The horns continue to grow throughout the life of the rhinoceros. The horn consists of a fiberlike material similar to a mixture of hair and fingernails. It appears to be permanently joined to the rhinoceros's nose but can be torn out during fighting. The name *rhinoceros* comes from two Greek words and means *nose-horned.*

The animal has three toes on each foot. Each toe ends in a separate hoof. On each front foot is a fourth toe that is *rudimentary,* or no longer used. The rhinoceros differs from the hippopotamus, which has four developed

African rhinoceroses. The white rhinoceros, *left,* is the largest kind of rhinoceros. All rhinoceroses like to rest in the water after drinking. A charging black rhinoceros, *right,* is a frightening sight. Rhinoceroses have poor vision and often attack things that they do not recognize.

toes. The hippopotamus is a relative of the hog, camel, and cow, and the rhinoceros is more nearly related to the horse.

The rhinoceros eats grass, leafy twigs, and shrubs. In captivity, it is fed hay and special protein and mineral biscuits. Wild rhinoceroses live in Africa, in southeastern Asia, and on a few large islands near the Asiatic coast. In prehistoric times, they also roamed over Europe, North America, and northern Asia. Baluchitherium, a prehistoric relative of the modern rhinoceros, was larger than any land mammal that lives today. This animal reached over 16 feet (5 meters) in height. Rhinoceroses have been known to live almost 50 years.

Kinds of rhinoceroses. There are five species of rhinoceroses. Three of them live in Asia and two in Africa.

The *Indian rhinoceros* is the largest of the three Asian species. It stands about 5 feet 8 inches (1.7 meters) high at the shoulder and weighs about 2 short tons (1.8 met-

ric tons). It has one great blue-black horn, very thick at the base and about 1 foot (30 centimeters) long. In rare cases, the animal may stand up to $6\frac{1}{2}$ feet (2 meters) with a horn 2 feet (61 centimeters) long. The skin of the Indian rhinoceros is sprinkled with round knobs. It hangs in such definite folds that the animal looks as though it were wearing armor plate. But the hide can be pierced by a knife or bullet. The animal lives in marshy jungles among reeds and tall grass, on which it feeds morning and evening. Ancient peoples of Asia knew this rhinoceros well. It was even used in the circus games in Rome before the time of Christ.

The similar one-horned *Javan rhinoceros* once ranged from eastern Bengal into Burma, and southward to Java, Borneo, and Sumatra. It is now nearly extinct.

The *Sumatran* species is smaller than any other rhinoceros and has two horns. It stands about $4\frac{1}{2}$ feet (1.4 meters) tall and weighs about 1 short ton (0.9 metric ton).

The Indian rhinoceros has skin that resembles a suit of armor. Its hide includes large folds of skin and bumps that look like rivets. This rare animal lives in northeast India, Bhutan, and Nepal.

It is hairy, especially on the tail and ears. The young have more body hair than the adults. This species lives in Sumatra, Borneo, and on the Malay Peninsula. It too is nearing extinction. Both the Javan and Sumatran rhinoceroses are found in forested hills. Less than 2,000 rhinoceroses live in the wild in Asia.

The two African species are two-horned. They are known as the *black rhinoceros* and the *white rhinoceros,* though they are almost the same bluish-gray color. *Hook-lipped* (for the black) and *square-lipped* (for the white) are better names for them.

The black rhinoceros has a front horn that is sometimes as much as $3\frac{1}{2}$ feet (107 centimeters) long. It uses this horn to defend itself and to dig. The rear horn may be the same length or shorter. The digging horn is so strong that the animal can easily uproot bushes and small trees with it. Then it feeds on the leaves and twigs. Although it appears clumsy, the black rhinoceros can move swiftly. The black rhinoceros is almost extinct in the wild. About 200 of these animals live on nature preserves in Africa.

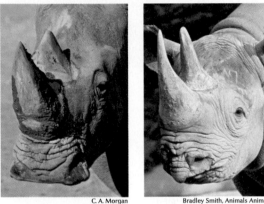

C. A. Morgan   Bradley Smith, Animals Animals

The mouth of a rhinoceros is suited for the animal's food. The white, or *square-lipped,* rhinoceros uses its flat lips, *left,* to break off grass. The black, or *hook-lipped,* rhinoceros uses its pointed upper lip, *right,* to grasp small branches. The two species have almost the same bluish-gray color.

J. C. Stevenson, Animals Animals

A baby rhinoceros begins to grow horns soon after birth. This 3-month-old white rhinoceros has a small horn. Rhinoceroses have three toes on each foot. Each toe has a hoof.

The white rhinoceros is the largest of all rhinoceroses. It stands about 5 feet 8 inches (1.7 meters) tall. In some cases, it may be over 6 feet (1.8 meters) tall and 15 feet (4.6 meters) long. It weighs about $3\frac{1}{2}$ short tons (3.2 metric tons). The horns of the female are longer but more slender than those of the male. This is also true for the black rhinoceros. Less than 6,000 white rhinoceroses remain in the wild.

Protecting the rhinoceros. All species, especially the Javan, Sumatran, and black rhinoceroses, are nearly extinct. The growth and spread of the human population has destroyed much of the animal's habitat. Rhinoceroses are greatly threatened by *poachers*—people who illegally hunt animals. Poachers kill rhinoceroses and sell their horns and skin. Many Asian people believe the powdered horn of the rhinoceros has healing qualities and can be used to cure lung and chest illnesses. Some people believe the horn has magical powers. Asian people also use the skin, blood, and urine of rhinoceroses to cure illnesses. For all these reasons, thousands of rhinoceroses have been needlessly killed.

Laws of many countries and international trade treaties are designed to protect the rhinoceros from poachers. In the African nations of Kenya and Zimbabwe, special teams of rangers are on constant watch over the animals. Almost all remaining wild rhinoceroses in Zimbabwe have been captured and placed in nature preserves. Some of the preserves have high, electrified fences and are closely patrolled by rangers. In Zimbabwe and two other African nations, Namibia and Swaziland, wildlife officials have further attempted to reduce poaching by cutting off the horns of some rhinoceroses. Many scientists, however, believe this approach puts the animals in even greater danger. Hornless rhinoceroses are less able to protect themselves against such predators as lions and hyenas. Also, poachers may kill hornless rhinoceroses for other body parts, including the horn root.

In addition to antipoaching efforts, attempts have been made to increase the population of certain species of rhinoceroses. For example, black and white rhinoceroses have been sent to Australia and the United States to form breeding colonies for future repopulation. But despite these efforts, the future of wild rhinoceroses remains bleak.

Scientific classification. Rhinoceroses make up the family Rhinocerotidae. The Indian rhinoceros is *Rhinoceros unicornis;* the Javan is *R. sondaicus;* the Sumatran is *Dicerorhinus sumatrensis;* the black is *Diceros bicornis;* the white is *Ceratotherium simum.*   Harry John Herbert

See also **Animal** (pictures: Animals of the grasslands); Poaching.

Rhizoid. See Moss (The structure of mosses).

Rhizome, *RY zohm,* is a horizontal stem that grows at or just below the soil surface. Rhizomes produce leaves and flowers that rise above the soil, and small roots below. They can also produce buds that develop into branches. Some nonwoody perennial plants, such as iris, ginseng, wild ginger, and bloodroot, have rhizomes. Ginger root, which is used in Asian cooking, is a rhizome. In many plants, rhizomes can be thick and can function as an organ for the storage of food.

Joseph E. Armstrong

See also **Bulb; Orrisroot; Perennial.**

Cliff Walk winds past *The Breakers,* the beautiful estate of Cornelius Vanderbilt in Newport. Rhode Island's scenic Atlantic coast and water sports attract thousands of vacationers each year.

Rhode Island   *The Ocean State*

Rhode Island is the smallest state in the United States. It covers only 1,213 square miles (3,142 square kilometers), and is a little more than half the size of Delaware, the second smallest state. In spite of its size, Rhode Island is an important industrial state. It ranks high among the states in the production of jewelry. Rhode Island's official nickname is *The Ocean State.* But because of its size, the state has traditionally been called *Little Rhody.* Providence is the capital and largest city of Rhode Island.

Rhode Island lies on beautiful Narragansett Bay, an arm of the Atlantic Ocean. The bay makes the state a leading vacationland. Hundreds of thousands of tourists come to Rhode Island each summer to enjoy boating, fishing, and other water sports. Naval installations along Narragansett Bay include the Newport Naval Underwater Systems Center and the Naval War College.

Narragansett Bay almost cuts Rhode Island in two. The bay extends 28 miles (45 kilometers) inland from southern Rhode Island. The state has 36 islands, most of which are in the bay. Aquidneck, the largest island, was officially named *Rhode Island* in 1644. Towns on the

---

The contributors of this article are Stanford E. Demars, Professor and Director of the Department of Geography at Rhode Island College; and Michael R. H. Swanson, Professor of Historic Preservation in the Center for Historic Preservation, School of Architecture, at Roger Williams University.

---

mainland were called *Providence Plantations.* As a result, Rhode Island's official name is *State of Rhode Island and Providence Plantations.* Thus, the smallest state has the longest official name.

About a sixth of Rhode Island's people live in the city of Providence. The Providence-Fall River (Mass.)-Warwick metropolitan statistical area extends into Massachusetts. About nine-tenths of the state's people live in this metropolitan area.

The people of Rhode Island have played important parts in the history and industrial development of the United States. Roger Williams, who founded Providence in 1636, worked for religious and political freedom. Under his leadership, Rhode Islanders gained fame for their love of personal liberty. In 1776, Rhode Island became the first of the 13 original colonies to formally declare independence from Britain. But it was the last of these colonies to ratify the U.S. Constitution. Rhode Island delayed ratification for three years—until 1790—when the Bill of Rights was ready to be added to the Constitution.

Samuel Slater, an English machinist who settled in Rhode Island, helped establish the American textile industry. In the late 1700's, he built the country's first cotton spinning machines driven by water power. Nehemiah and Seril Dodge, Rhode Island brothers, started the jewelry industry in America. Rhode Islanders also were prominent in the boatbuilding, fishing, shipping, and whaling industries.

Interesting facts about Rhode Island

The first quonset hut was built in 1941 at the Quonset Point Naval Air Station near Davisville. United States troops used the huts during World War II for barracks, storage rooms, medical facilities, and many other purposes. The quonset hut is a prefabricated sheet-metal structure in the shape of a half cylinder with the flat side forming the floor. Most huts were built about 50 to 100 feet (15 to 30 meters) long and 20 to 40 feet (6 to 12 meters) high. They were designed for easy shipment, assembly, and disassembly.

First quonset hut

The Rhode Island Red is the chicken that made the raising of poultry a major industry in the United States. The breed was developed in 1854 on a farm in Little Compton. It became famous for its delicious meat and for the outstanding quality and quantity of its eggs.

The first free republic in the New World was Rhode Island. The Rhode Island General Assembly formally declared the colony's independence from Great Britain on May 4, 1776. This action was enthusiastically supported by the other 12 colonies exactly two months later.

The oldest Jewish synagogue still standing in the United States is located in Newport. It was built in 1763, and the congregation dates back to 1658.

Rhode Island Reds

Historic Bowen's Wharf in Newport has restaurants and shops in restored buildings dating back to the 1700's. Newport was the East Coast's busiest port before the Revolutionary War.

Downtown Providence includes the Kennedy Plaza, *left,* set among office buildings. Providence is the capital, largest city, and chief manufacturing center of Rhode Island.

Rhode Island in brief

Symbols of Rhode Island

On the state flag, adopted in 1897, 13 stars represent the original 13 colonies. The state motto, *Hope,* appears on a ribbon below an anchor, a symbol of hope. The state seal, adopted in 1896, has a design similar to that of the flag. The date 1636 is the year Roger Williams founded Providence, Rhode Island's first permanent European settlement.

State flag

State seal

Rhode Island (brown) ranks as the smallest of all the states. It is one of the New England States (yellow).

General information

Statehood: May 29, 1790, the 13th state.
State abbreviations: R.I. (traditional); RI (postal).
State motto: *Hope.*
State song: "Rhode Island." Words and music by T. Clarke Brown.

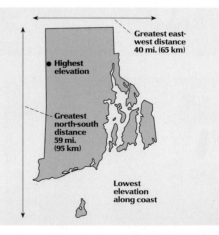

The State House is in Providence, the capital since 1900. Rhode Island had five capitals from 1663 to 1854. Newport and Providence were co-capitals from 1854 to 1900.

Land and climate

Area: 1,213 sq. mi. (3,142 km²), including 168 sq. mi. (436 km²) of inland water but excluding 18 sq. mi. (47 km²) of coastal water.
Elevation: *Highest*—Jerimoth Hill, 812 ft. (247 m) above sea level. *Lowest*—sea level along the Atlantic coast.
Coastline: 40 mi. (64 km).
Record high temperature: 104 °F (40 °C) at Providence on Aug. 2, 1975.
Record low temperature: −23 °F (−31 °C) at Kingston on Jan. 11, 1942.
Average July temperature: 71 °F (22 °C).
Average January temperature: 29 °F (−2 °C).
Average yearly precipitation: 44 in. (112 cm).

Greatest east-west distance 40 mi. (65 km)

Highest elevation

Greatest north-south distance 59 mi. (95 km)

Lowest elevation along coast

Important dates

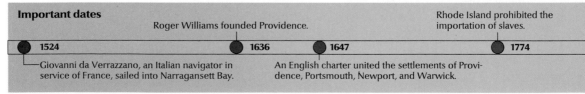

Roger Williams founded Providence.

Rhode Island prohibited the importation of slaves.

| 1524 | 1636 | 1647 | 1774 |

Giovanni da Verrazzano, an Italian navigator in service of France, sailed into Narragansett Bay.

An English charter united the settlements of Providence, Portsmouth, Newport, and Warwick.

State bird
Rhode Island Red

State flower
Violet

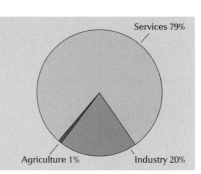

State tree
Red maple

People

Population: 1,005,984 (1990 census)
Rank among the states: 43rd
Density: 829 persons per sq. mi. (320 per km²), U.S. average 69 per sq. mi. (27 per km²)
Distribution: 86 percent urban, 14 percent rural
Largest cities in Rhode Island

Providence	160,728
Warwick	85,427
Cranston	76,060
Pawtucket	72,644
East Providence	50,380
Woonsocket	43,877

Source: U.S. Bureau of the Census.

Population trend

Millions

(line graph of population from 1800 to 2000, rising from near 0 to about 1 million)

Source: U.S. Bureau of the Census.

Year	Population
1990	1,005,984
1980	947,154
1970	949,723
1960	859,488
1950	791,896
1940	713,346
1930	687,497
1920	604,397
1910	542,610
1900	428,556
1890	345,506
1880	276,531
1870	217,353
1860	174,620
1850	147,545
1840	108,830
1830	97,199
1820	83,059
1810	76,931
1800	69,122
1790	68,825

Economy

Chief products

Agriculture: greenhouse and nursery products.
Fishing industry: lobster, clams, squid.
Manufacturing: jewelry and silverware, fabricated metal products, scientific instruments.

Gross state product

Value of goods and services produced in 1997: $26,226,000,000.
Services include community, business, and personal services; finance; government; trade; and transportation, communication, and utilities. *Industry* includes construction, manufacturing, and mining. *Agriculture* includes agriculture, fishing, and forestry.

Source: U.S. Bureau of Economic Analysis.

Services 79%
Agriculture 1%
Industry 20%

Government

State government

Governor: 4-year term
State senators: 50; 2-year terms
State representatives: 100; 2-year terms
Cities and towns: 39 with local governments (no county governments).

Federal government

United States senators: 2
United States representatives: 2
Electoral votes: 4

Sources of information

Tourism: Rhode Island Tourism Division, 7 Jackson Walkway, Providence, RI 02903
Economy: Department of Economic Development, 7 Jackson Walkway, Providence, RI 02903
Government: Office of the Secretary of State, Room 220, State House, Providence, RI 02903
History: Office of the Secretary of State, Room 220, State House, Providence, RI 02903

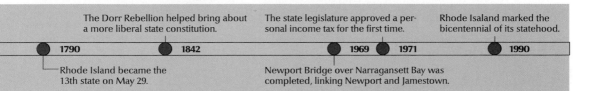

The Dorr Rebellion helped bring about a more liberal state constitution.

The state legislature approved a personal income tax for the first time.

Rhode Isaland marked the bicentennial of its statehood.

1790   1842   1969   1971   1990

Rhode Island became the 13th state on May 29.

Newport Bridge over Narragansett Bay was completed, linking Newport and Jamestown.

Population. The 1990 United States census reported that Rhode Island had 1,005,984 people. The state's population had increased 6 percent from the 1980 census figure, 947,154. According to the 1990 census, Rhode Island ranks 43rd in population among the 50 states.

Rhode Island has eight cities. The state's other communities are called towns. The cities, in order of size, are Providence, Warwick, Cranston, Pawtucket, East Providence, Woonsocket, Newport, and Central Falls.

About a sixth of Rhode Island's people live in Providence. More than nine-tenths of the people live in metropolitan areas (see **Metropolitan area**). For the names and populations of these metropolitan areas, see the *Index* to the political map of Rhode Island.

Most of the people in Rhode Island were born in the United States. A number of Rhode Islanders who were born in other countries came from Portugal.

Schools. In colonial times, many Rhode Island ministers established schools to teach boys. Girls and very young boys attended *dame schools,* which were taught by women. In 1640, the people of Newport founded a free school to educate poor children. Rhode Island's first statewide law establishing public schools was passed in 1800. The law was discontinued in 1803, but was adopted again in 1828. Also in 1828, the Rhode Island legislature set up the state's first permanent public school fund. The Barnard Law of 1845, named for the state's first commissioner of education, established the basis for the current public education system.

A commissioner of education and an 11-member board of regents direct Rhode Island's public elementary and secondary education system. The governor appoints nine of the board members to three-year terms. The other two members are the chairpersons of the House and Senate finance committees. The regents appoint the commissioner. School committees and superintendents head the local school districts.

Rhode Island children are required to attend school from age 5 through 15. For the number of students and teachers in Rhode Island, see **Education** (table).

Population density

Eastern Rhode Island is far more heavily populated than the west. About nine-tenths of the state's people live in the Providence-Fall River-Warwick metropolitan area.

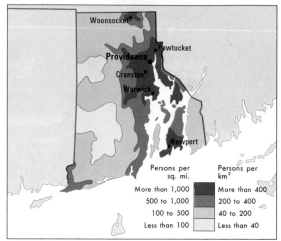

Persons per sq. mi.	Persons per km²
More than 1,000	More than 400
500 to 1,000	200 to 400
100 to 500	40 to 200
Less than 100	Less than 40

WORLD BOOK map; based on U.S. Bureau of the Census data.

Libraries. Thomas Bray, an English minister, founded Rhode Island's first library in Newport in 1700. The Redwood Library and Athenaeum was established in Newport in 1747. It is the oldest operating library in Rhode Island. Today, Rhode Island has about 45 public libraries, about 18 university and college libraries, and about 50 special libraries. The Providence Public Library has eight branches. The library's collections include the George W. Potter and Alfred M. Williams Memorial on Irish Culture and the Harris Collection on the Civil War and Slavery.

The libraries of Brown University house over a million volumes. The John Hay Library of the university has one of the world's most complete collections of writings by

Rhode Island Department of Economic Development

A crowded ferry takes passengers to Block Island, a popular Rhode Island resort and recreation area. The island lies about 10 miles (16 kilometers) off the mainland.

Tennis is a tradition at the Newport Casino, the site of the United States Tennis Championships from 1881 to 1915. Lawn tennis in America began at the Casino, which now houses the International Tennis Hall of Fame.

© John T. Hopf

and about Abraham Lincoln. The John Hay Library also includes the famous Harris Collection of American Poetry and Plays.

The Rhode Island State Library in Providence includes a special law collection that may be used by government officials and the public. Other special libraries include those of the Newport Historical Society and the Rhode Island Historical Society in Providence.

In 1964, Rhode Island established a Department of State Library Services. This department administers both state and federal funds for libraries in Rhode Island and administers the Rhode Island Library Network.

Museums. The Museum of Art at the Rhode Island School of Design in Providence displays water colors and oils by many famous artists. The Roger Williams Park Museum, also in Providence, has science displays, exhibits of animals and plants, and a planetarium. It also owns a large collection of Indian relics. The South County Museum near Wickford displays tools used by American colonists. Other museums in the state include the Haffenreffer Museum of Anthropology in Bristol, the Museum of Primitive Cultures in Peace Dale, the Children's Museum in Pawtucket, the Betsey Williams Cottage in Providence, and the Westerly Museum and Art Gallery.

Universities and colleges

This table lists the universities and colleges in Rhode Island that grant bachelor's or advanced degrees and are accredited by the New England Association of Schools and Colleges.

Name	Mailing address
Brown University	Providence
Bryant College	Smithfield
Johnson and Wales University	Providence
Naval War College	Newport
Providence College	Providence
Rhode Island, University of	Kingston
Rhode Island College	Providence
Rhode Island School of Design	Providence
Roger Williams University	Bristol
Salve Regina University	Newport

Jim Daniels

Brown University in Providence is one of the oldest colleges in the United States. It was chartered in 1764. Sayles Hall, *above,* stands in the center of the campus.

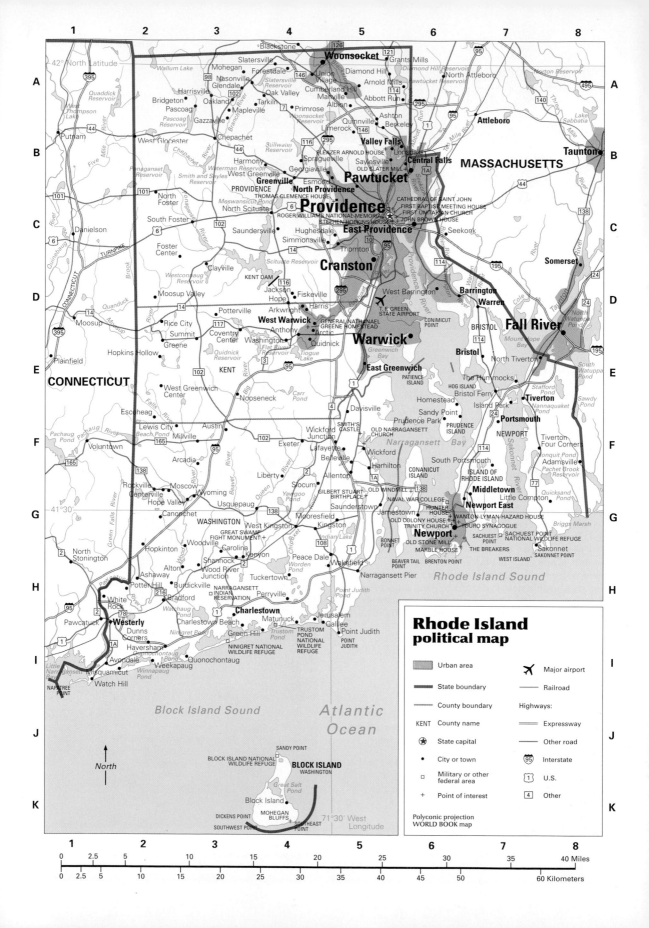

Rhode Island political map

Urban area	✈ Major airport
State boundary	— Railroad
County boundary	Highways:
KENT County name	Expressway
✪ State capital	Other road
• City or town	95 Interstate
▫ Military or other federal area	1 U.S.
+ Point of interest	4 Other

Polyconic projection
WORLD BOOK map

North

Block Island Sound

Atlantic Ocean

Block Island Sound

71°30' West Longitude

Scale
| 0 | 2.5 | 5 | 10 | 15 | 20 | 25 | 30 | 35 | 40 Miles |
| 0 | 2.5 | 5 | 10 | 15 | 20 | 25 | 30 | 35 | 40 | 45 | 50 | 60 Kilometers |

Rhode Island map index

Metropolitan areas

New London-
  Norwich 290,734
  (262,256 in Conn.;
  28,478 in R.I.)
Providence-
  Fall River-
  Warwick 1,134,350
  (909,606 in R.I.;
  224,744 in Mass.)

Counties

Bristol ....48,859 ..D 7
Kent ....161,135 ..E 4
Newport ....87,194 ..F 6
Providence ...596,270 ..C 3
Washington ....110,006 ..G 2

Cities, towns, and other populated places

Adamsville ....F 8
Albion ....A 5
Allenton ....F 5
Alton ....H 2
Anthony ....D 4
Arcadia ....F 3
Arctic ....D 4
Arkwright ....D 4
Arnold Mills ....A 5
Ashaway ....1,584 ..H 2
Ashton ....B 5
Austin ....F 5
Avondale ....I 2
Barrington▲ .....15,849 ..D 6

Belleville ....F 5
Berkeley ....B 5
Block Island ....K 4
Bradford† ....1,604 ..H 2
Bridgeton ....A 2
Bristol▲ ....21,625 ..E 7
Bristol Ferry ....E 7
Burdickville ....H 2
Burrillville*▲ ..16,230 ..A 3
Canonchet ....G 2
Carolina ....G 3
Centerville ....G 2
Central Falls ....17,637 ..B 6
Charlestown▲ .....6,478 ..H 3
Chepachet ....B 3
Clayville ....D 3
Coventry*▲ ....31,083 ..E 5
Coventry Center ....D 3
Cranston ....76,060 ..D 5
Cumberland*▲ ..29,038 ..A 5
Cumberland
  Hill† ....6,379 ..A 5
Davisville ....F 5
Diamond Hill ....A 5
Dunns Corner ....I 2
East
  Greenwich▲ ..11,865 ..E 5
East
  Providence ...50,380 ..C 6
Esmond ....B 5
Exeter▲ ....5,461 ..F 4
Fiskeville ....D 4
Forestdale ....A 4
Foster*▲ ....4,316 ..C 2
Foster Center ....C 2
Galilee ....H 4
Georgiaville ....B 4
Glendale ....G 2
Glocester*▲ .....9,227 ..B 3
Grants Mills ....A 5
Green Hill ....I 4

Greene ....E 2
Greenville† ......8,303 ..B 4
Hamilton ....F 5
Harmony ....B 4
Harris ....D 4
Harrisville† .....1,654 ..A 3
Haversham ....I 2
Homestead ....E 6
Hope ....D 4
Hope Valley† .....1,446 ..G 3
Hopkins Hollow ....E 2
Hopkinton▲ .....6,873 ..G 2
Hughesdale ....C 5
Hummocks, The ....E 7
Island Park ....E 7
Jackson ....D 4
Jamestown▲ .....4,999 ..G 6
Jerusalem ....H 4
Johnston*▲ ....26,542 ..C 5
Kenyon ....H 3
Kingston† ....6,504 ..G 4
Lafayette ....F 5
Lewis City ....E 2
Liberty ....E 4
Limerock ....B 5
Lincoln*▲ .....18,045 ..B 5
Little Compton▲ ..3,339 ..G 8
Lonsdale ....B 5
Manville ....A 5
Mapleville ....A 4
Matunuck ....H 4
Melville*† ....4,426 ..F 6
Middletown▲ ...19,460 ..G 7
Misquamicut ....I 2
Mohegan ....A 3
Mooresfield ....G 4
Moosup Valley ....D 2
Moscow ....G 2
Narragansett† ...14,985 ..H 5
Narragansett
  Pier ....3,721 ..H 5

Narragansett
  Indian
  Reservation .....31 I 1
Nasonville ....A 3
New Shoreham*▲ ..836 ..K 4
Newport ....28,227 ..G 6
Newport East† ...11,080 ..G 6
Nooseneck ....E 3
North Foster ....C 2
North
  Kingstown▲ ...23,786 ..F 5
North
  Providence▲ ..32,090 ..C 5
North Scituate ....C 4
North
  Smithfield*▲ ..10,497 ..A 4
North Tiverton ....E 7
Oak Valley ....A 4
Oakland ....A 3
Pascoag† ....5,011 ..A 3
Pawtucket ....72,644 ..B 6
Peace Dale ....H 4
Perryville ....H 4
Point Judith ....I 5
Portsmouth▲ ....16,857 ..F 7
Potter Hill ....I 2
Potterville ....D 3
Primrose ....A 3
Providence .....160,728 ..C 5
Prudence Park ....F 6
Quidnick ....E 4
Quinnville ....B 5
Quonochontaug ....I 3
Rice City ....D 2
Richmond*▲ .....5,351 ..H 2
Rockville ....G 2
Sakonnet ....G 7
Saunderstown ....G 5
Saylesville ....B 5
Scituate*▲ ....9,796 ..D 3
Shannock ....H 3

Simmonsville ....C 4
Slatersville ....A 4
Slocum ....G 4
Smithfield*▲ ...19,163 ..B 4
South Foster ....C 3
South
  Kingstown*▲ ...24,631 ..H 4
Spragueville ....B 4
Summit ....E 3
Tarkiln ....A 4
Thornton ....C 5
Tiverton† 7,259
                ▲14,312 ..E 7
Tuckertown ....H 4
Union Village ....A 4
Usquepaug ....G 3
Valley Falls† .....11,175 ..B 5
Wakefield ....H 5
Wakefield-
  Peacedale*† .....7,134 ..H 5
Warren▲ ....11,385 ..D 7
Warwick ....85,427 ..E 5
Watch Hill ....I 1
Weekapaug ....I 2
West Barrington ....D 6
West Glocester ....B 2
West Greenville ....B 4
West
  Greenwich*▲ ....3,492 ..E 2
West Greenwich
  Center ....E 2
West Kingston ....G 4
West
  Warwick▲ .....29,268 ..D 4
Westerly† 16,477
                ▲21,605 ..H 2
White Rock ....H 1
Wickford ....F 5
Wickford Junction ....F 5
Woonsocket ....43,877 ..A 4
Wyoming ....G 3

*Does not appear on map; key shows general location.
†Census designated place—unincorporated, but recognized as a significant settled community by the U.S. Bureau of the Census.

▲Population is for entire town (township), including rural areas.
Places without population figures are unincorporated.
Source: 1990 census.

© John T. Hopf

The Newport Bridge, New England's longest suspension bridge, opened in 1969. It replaced the Jamestown ferry, providing a more direct route between Newport and western Rhode Island.

Thousands of vacationers visit the coastal resorts of Rhode Island each year. The resorts in the state offer swimming, boating, fishing, and beautiful scenery. Rhode Island's leading resort centers include Block Island, Narragansett, Newport, and Watch Hill. In addition, tourists can visit the many historic sites, colonial buildings, and old churches in Rhode Island. Many of Rhode Island's most popular annual events include boat races, fishing contests, and tennis tournaments. The annual Newport Music Festival is held in July. This event features internationally known classical artists performing in Newport mansion settings.

© J. H. Peterson, Marine Photographic Services

A yacht race off the coast of Newport

Places to visit

Following are brief descriptions of some of Rhode Island's most interesting places to visit.

The Arcade, in Providence, is the oldest indoor shopping mall in the United States. It was built in 1828 and is now a National Landmark. The Arcade features three levels of shops.

Blithewold Gardens and Arboretum, in Bristol, is set on a large estate overlooking Narragansett Bay. The gardens feature many old and exotic plants and trees.

Block Island and Southeast Lighthouse lie about 10 miles (16 kilometers) off the Rhode Island mainland. The Mohegan Bluffs, which rise about 200 feet (60 meters) above the ocean, add to the island's spectacular scenery. The famous Southeast Lighthouse stands on Mohegan Bluffs.

Cliff Walk, in Newport, is a 3-mile (5-kilometer) path along the rocky coast of the Atlantic Ocean. It passes several famous Newport mansions. It is a National Recreation Trail.

Colonial buildings rank among Rhode Island's most interesting landmarks. They include the Gilbert Stuart Birthplace, built in North Kingstown in 1751, and the General Nathanael Greene Homestead, built in Coventry in 1770. Stuart was the foremost painter of portraits of George Washington. Greene was a great patriot leader of the Revolutionary War. Other Rhode Island colonial buildings, with the location and original completion date, include White Horse Tavern (Newport, 1673); Wanton-Lyman-Hazard House (Newport, 1675); Smith's Castle (near Wickford, 1678); Old Narragansett Church (North Kingstown, 1707); Trinity Church (Newport, 1726); Hunter House (Newport, 1748); Touro Synagogue (Newport, 1763); First Baptist Meeting House (Providence, 1775); John Brown House (Providence, 1786); and Old Windmill (Jamestown, 1787).

Newport mansions also rank among Rhode Island's points of interest. Many of these beautiful mansions were built as summer houses for wealthy American families. The Breakers, the estate of Cornelius Vanderbilt, is among the most famous. Its 70-room mansion was built in 1895. A nearby mansion called Marble House is one of the most ornate buildings in the United States. It was built for William K. Vanderbilt in 1892. Other famous Newport mansions include Chateau-sur-Mer (1852), The Elms (1901), Kingscote (1839), and Rosecliff (1902).

Rhode Island State House, in Providence, has one of the world's few self-supporting marble domes. Construction of the State House began in the late 1800's.

Slater Mill Historic Site, in Pawtucket, includes one of the first successful textile mills in North America. This mill was built in 1793 by Samuel Slater, the founder of the American textile industry. The mill is now a museum.

State parks. Rhode Island has 20 state parks. For information on these parks and other Rhode Island attractions, write to Rhode Island Tourism Division, 7 Jackson Walkway, Providence, RI 02903.

Jim Daniels

Old Narragansett Church in North Kingstown

Annual events

January-June

New Year's Day Plunge swimming events In Newport, Wickford, and Jamestown (January); Irish Heritage Month in Newport (March); May Breakfasts, statewide (May); Festival of Historic Houses in Providence (June); Gaspee Days Colonial Encampment in Warwick (June).

July-August

Bristol Fourth of July Parade (July 4); Wickford Art Festival (July); Hall of Fame Tennis Championships in Newport (July); Newport Music Festival (July); Black Ships Festival in Newport (July); Ben & Jerry's Folk Festival in Newport (August); Charlestown Chamber Seafood Festival (August); JVC Jazz Festival in Newport (August).

September-December

Annual Tuna Tournament near Galilee and Narragansett (September); Providence Waterfront Festival (September); Scituate Art Festival (October); Autumnfest in Woonsocket (October); International Quahog Festival in North Kingstown (October); First Night Providence, an arts and entertainment celebration (December).

Mohegan Bluffs on Block Island

Jim McElholm

Rhode Island Tourism

The Arcade in Providence

Rhode Island Tourism

Slater Mill Historic Site in Pawtucket

Land regions. Rhode Island has two main land regions. These regions are, from east to west, (1) the Coastal Lowlands, and (2) the Eastern New England Upland.

The Coastal Lowlands cover more than half the Rhode Island mainland, the islands in Narragansett Bay, and the land east of the bay. The Coastal Lowlands are part of a larger land region of the same name that covers the entire New England coast.

Many sandy beaches and plains line the shores of Rhode Island's lowlands. The shore west of Point Judith has sandy beaches, lagoons, and salt ponds. Rocky cliffs are found on the islands and the shore along the bay. Inland, the land rises to form higher elevations. East of Narragansett Bay, the slopes are low, round, and have few trees. West of the bay, the slopes are rugged and forested.

The Eastern New England Upland covers the northwestern third of Rhode Island. The entire Eastern New England Upland extends from Maine to Connecticut. The portion in Rhode Island is often called the *Western Rocky Upland.* It has sloping hills and a higher elevation than the Coastal Lowlands. The land of the Western Rocky Upland rises from about 200 feet (60 meters) above sea level in the east to over 800 feet (240 meters) in the northwest.

Lakes, reservoirs, and ponds nestle among the region's many hills. These hills include 812-foot (247-meter) Jerimoth Hill, the state's highest point. The state has no mountains.

Islands. Rhode Island includes 36 islands. They range in size from Aquidneck Island (officially named Rhode Island) with an area of 45 square miles (117 square kilometers), to Despair, a clump of rocks in Narragansett Bay. Block Island (officially New Shoreham) covers about 11 square miles (28 square kilometers). It lies in the Atlantic, about 10 miles (16 kilometers) south of the Rhode Island mainland. Bridges and ferry service connect the largest islands and the mainland.

Coastline. Rhode Island has a 40-mile (64 kilometer) general coastline. If the tidal shoreline of the state's bays and islands were included, the coastline would measure 384 miles (618 kilometers). The largest bay, Narragansett Bay, extends 28 miles (45 kilometers) inland. The many arms of Narragansett Bay include Greenwich and Mount Hope bays.

Rivers and lakes. Three of Rhode Island's chief rivers—Providence, Sakonnet, and Seekonk—are really saltwater arms of Narragansett Bay. Several freshwater rivers flow into the bay. These include the Pawtuxet, Pettaquamscutt, Potowomut, and Woonasquatucket. One river, the Blackstone, becomes the Pawtucket and then the Seekonk before flowing into the bay. The Pawcatuck River flows through southwestern Rhode Island and

Rhode Island Department of Economic Development

A farm in Lincoln is part of the Coastal Lowlands region that stretches along the entire New England coast. The lowlands of Rhode Island include many plains and sandy beaches.

Land regions of Rhode Island

EASTERN NEW ENGLAND UPLAND

COASTAL LOWLANDS

BLOCK ISLAND

WORLD BOOK map

Map index

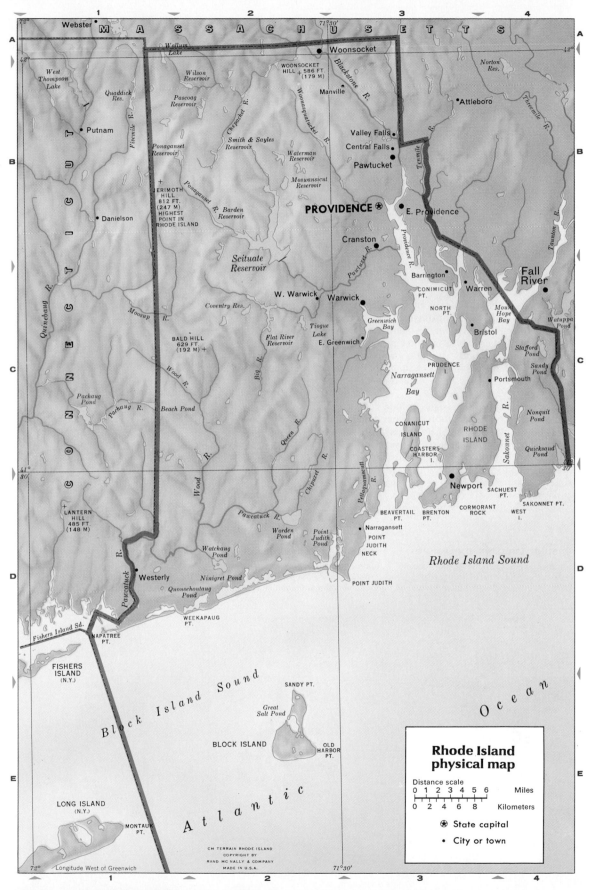

Rhode Island physical map

Distance scale

0 1 2 3 4 5 6 Miles

0 2 4 6 8 Kilometers

✪ State capital

• City or town

CM TERRAIN RHODE ISLAND
COPYRIGHT BY
RAND MC NALLY & COMPANY
MADE IN U.S.A.

Specially created for *The World Book Encyclopedia* by Rand McNally and World Book editors

forms part of the Rhode Island-Connecticut border. Other important rivers include the Chepachet, Ponaganset, and Wood.

Most of the state's inland rivers are small but swift. Many of the rivers have waterfalls. Water was once the major source of power for Rhode Island's mills and factories.

Many lakes, ponds, and reservoirs dot the Rhode Island countryside. Scituate Reservoir, the largest inland body of water in the state, supplies water for Providence and nearby communities. Other large bodies of water in Rhode Island include Watchaug Pond and Worden Pond.

Plant and animal life. Forests cover about three-fifths of Rhode Island. The state's trees include ashes, birches, cedars, elms, hickories, maples, oaks, pines, poplars, and willows. Pin and post oaks are found near the north shore of Wickford harbor. Paper birches, also called canoe birches, thrive in the northern part of the state.

Asters and cattails bloom in the marshlands of Charlestown and South Kingstown. Scarlet pimpernels grow on the cliffs of Newport. Red deer grass, white daisies, and wild carrots are found in meadows. Dogwoods, mountain laurels, rhododendrons, trilliums, and violets grow in the woodlands. A variety of freshwater and saltwater seaweeds grow in the waters of Rhode Island.

Wild animals in Rhode Island include deer, foxes, minks, muskrats, otters, rabbits, raccoons, and squirrels. Barred owls, blue jays, catbirds, flickers, robins, ruffed grouse, and screech owls live in the woodlands. Gulls, loons, ospreys, terns, and other shore birds make their homes along the coast. Game birds found in Rhode Island include partridges, pheasants, quails, wild ducks, and woodcocks.

Freshwater fish in the state's waters include bass, eels, perch, pickerel, and trout. Saltwater fish include bluefish, butterfish, flounder, mackerel, menhaden, sea bass, striped bass, swordfish, and tuna.

Climate. Warming winds from Narragansett Bay help give Rhode Island a mild climate. January temperatures average 29 °F (−2 °C), and July temperatures average 71 °F (22 °C). The state's highest temperature, 104 °F (40 °C), was recorded at Providence on Aug. 2, 1975. The lowest temperature, −23 °F (−31 °C), was recorded at Kingston on Jan. 11, 1942.

Yearly *precipitation* (rain, melted snow, and other forms of moisture) in Rhode Island averages about 44 inches (112 centimeters). Snowfall averages about 31 inches (79 centimeters) a year. The state has a growing season of about 200 days. Hurricanes and huge, destructive waves called *tsunamis* sometimes lash the Rhode Island coast. The most destructive hurricanes in the state occurred in 1815, 1938, 1944, and 1954.

Average monthly weather

	Block Island Temperatures F°	Block Island Temperatures F°	Block Island Temperatures C°	Block Island Temperatures C°	Block Island Days of rain or snow		Providence Temperatures F°	Providence Temperatures F°	Providence Temperatures C°	Providence Temperatures C°	Providence Days of rain or snow
	High	Low	High	Low			High	Low	High	Low	
Jan.	38	26	3	−3	12	Jan.	37	21	3	−6	12
Feb.	37	25	3	−4	11	Feb.	37	20	3	−7	10
Mar.	43	31	6	−1	12	Mar.	45	29	7	−2	12
Apr.	51	39	11	4	11	Apr.	55	37	13	3	12
May	61	48	16	9	11	May	66	47	19	8	11
June	69	57	21	14	9	June	75	56	24	13	10
July	75	63	24	17	9	July	80	62	27	17	10
Aug.	75	63	24	17	9	Aug.	79	60	26	16	9
Sept.	70	57	21	14	8	Sept.	72	53	22	12	8
Oct.	61	48	16	9	9	Oct.	62	43	17	6	8
Nov.	51	39	11	4	10	Nov.	51	34	11	1	10
Dec.	41	29	5	−2	11	Dec.	39	24	4	−4	11

Average January temperatures

Warming winds from the Atlantic Ocean keep the coastal areas of Rhode Island warmer in winter than the inland areas.

Average July temperatures

Summer temperatures are generally even throughout the state. The southern and central sections are slightly warmer.

Average annual precipitation

There is little variation in precipitation throughout the state, but the southwest is generally the wettest section.

WORLD BOOK maps

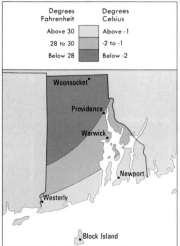

Degrees Fahrenheit	Degrees Celsius
Above 30	Above -1
28 to 30	-2 to -1
Below 28	Below -2

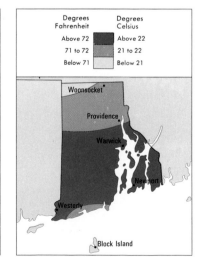

Degrees Fahrenheit	Degrees Celsius
Above 72	Above 22
71 to 72	21 to 22
Below 71	Below 21

Inches	Centimeters
More than 48	More than 122
46 to 48	117 to 122
Less than 46	Less than 117

Service industries, taken together, account for the largest portion of Rhode Island's *gross state product—* the total value of all goods and services produced in a state in a year. They also employ about three-fourths of the state's workers. Tourist activities supply about $1¼ billion a year to the state's economy.

Natural resources. Rhode Island has few large mineral deposits or other natural resources.

Soil. Rhode Island's richest soil is found along Narragansett Bay. Miami stony loam covers the bay's basin and tableland. This firm brown soil holds moisture for an entire growing season. Glocester stony loam is the state's least fertile soil. This light brown sand covers much of western and northern Rhode Island.

Minerals. Westerly granite is Rhode Island's best-known mineral. Its hardness and fine grain make it an excellent building material. Deposits of this granite lie mainly in southwestern Rhode Island, near the town of Westerly. The Coastal Lowlands have large sand and gravel deposits. Other mined products found in Rhode Island include limestone and sandstone.

Service industries account for the greatest portion of Rhode Island's gross state product. Service industries are concentrated in the Providence metropolitan area.

Community, business, and personal services constitutes Rhode Island's leading service industry. This group contributes more to the gross state product and employs more people than any other industry. Community, business, and personal services consists of a variety of businesses, including private health care, law firms, computer programming companies, and repair shops.

Finance, insurance, and real estate ranks second among Rhode Island's service industries. Real estate is important because of the large sums of money involved in the development of homes, office buildings, and other property. Providence is one of New England's leading financial centers. Fleet/Norstar, one of the nation's biggest banking companies, is headquartered in the city. So are a large insurance company and a major savings and loan.

Wholesale and retail trade ranks third among the state's service industries in terms of the gross state product. The wholesale trade of automobiles, groceries, jewelry, and petroleum products is important in Rhode Island. Major retail businesses include department stores, automobile dealerships, and food stores.

Government is the state's fourth-ranking service industry. Government services include the operation of public schools, public hospitals, and military bases. The public school system employs many people. Several U.S. Navy facilities lie along Narragansett Bay.

Transportation, communication, and utilities ranks fifth among Rhode Island's service industries. Several shipping and trucking firms are based in Providence. Telephone companies make up the largest part of the communications sector. Utilities provide electric, water, and gas service. More information about transportation and communication appears later in this section.

Manufacturing. Goods manufactured in Rhode Island have an annual *value added by manufacture* of approximately $5 billion. Value added by manufacture represents the increase in value of raw materials after they become finished products.

The production of jewelry and silverware is Rhode Island's most important manufacturing activity. The Providence area ranks among the nation's leading centers of this industry. The production of costume jewelry is especially important in the state.

Fabricated metal products rank second in terms of value added by manufacture. Factories in Rhode Island make structural metal, nuts and bolts, and pipe fittings.

Scientific instruments rank third among the state's manufactured products. Major products in this category include instruments that measure electric current and medical and surgical instruments.

Other products manufactured in Rhode Island include electrical equipment, machinery, and primary metals. Light bulbs and lighting fixtures are among the leading types of electrical equipment made in Rhode Island. Machine tools are the state's major type of machinery prod-

Production and workers by economic activities

Economic activities	Percent of GSP* produced	Employed workers Number of people	Percent of total
Community, business, & personal services	23	194,700	35
Finance, insurance, & real estate	22	42,700	8
Manufacturing	17	83,000	15
Wholesale & retail trade	14	114,100	20
Government	12	75,100	13
Transportation, communication, & utilities	7	18,900	4
Construction	4	24,400	4
Agriculture	1	7,500	1
Mining	†	300	†
Total	100	560,700	100

*GSP = gross state product, the total value of goods and services produced in a year.
†Less than one-half of 1 percent.
Figures are for 1997.
Sources: *World Book* estimates based on data from U.S. Bureau of Economic Analysis and U.S. Bureau of Labor Statistics.

Swarovsky Jewelry U.S. Limited

Crystal stones are set by hand in beautiful jewelry by a Rhode Island jeweler. The production of jewelry and silverware ranks as Rhode Island's most important manufacturing activity.

Farm and mineral products

This map shows the areas where the state's leading farm and mineral products are produced. The major urban areas (shown in red) are the state's important manufacturing centers.

WORLD BOOK map

BLOCK ISLAND

uct. Foundries in many of Rhode Island's towns produce wire.

Agriculture. Rhode Island has about 700 farms. Farmland covers less than 10 percent of the state's land area.

Greenhouse and nursery products are the leading source of agricultural income in Rhode Island. Sales of sod, ornamental trees and shrubs, and other nursery products earn about two-thirds of the state's agricultural income.

Milk ranks as the second most important source of agricultural income in Rhode Island. Milk is produced in many parts of the state. Potatoes are the leading crop. Farmers grow potatoes mainly in the southern part of the state. Hay is the second leading crop. Apples are the most valuable fruit crop in Rhode Island. The state's farmers also raise chickens, eggs, and turkeys. The Rhode Island Red, a famous breed of chicken, was developed in the town of Little Compton.

Fishing industry. The annual fish catch in Rhode Island is valued at about $70 million. The catch is made up of a variety of fish, mollusks, and shellfish. Lobster is the state's most valuable catch. Anglerfish, clams, cod, flounder, scup, squid, whiting, and yellowfish are also important catches.

Mining accounts for less than one-half of 1 percent of the gross state product. Stone and sand and gravel are the most valuable mined products in Rhode Island.

Electric power. Steam turbine plants produce all of Rhode Island's electric power. The steam used to drive the turbines comes from water that is heated by burning natural gas or petroleum.

Transportation. Newport and Providence were international shipping centers from colonial days until the 1830's. Their importance as shipping centers declined with the development of railroads.

Rhode Island's first railroad began operating between Providence and Boston in 1835. Today, the Providence and Worcester Railroad provides freight service in the state.

Roads and highways total about 6,000 miles (9,600 kilometers), and most are surfaced. The Rhode Island portion of Interstate Highway 95 extends from the Connecticut border, near Ashaway, to Pawtucket. Interstate 295 skirts Providence to the north and west. The biggest airport in Rhode Island is the Theodore Francis Green State Airport in Warwick.

Communication. About 35 newspapers and about 50 periodicals are published in Rhode Island. The state's leading daily newspapers, in order of circulation, include *The Providence Journal-Bulletin, The* (Pawtucket) *Times,* and *The* (Woonsocket) *Call.*

Rhode Island's first newspaper, the *Rhode Island Gazette,* began publication in 1732. Its publisher, James Franklin, was the brother of Benjamin Franklin.

Rhode Island's first radio stations, WEAN and WJAR, began broadcasting from Providence in 1922. The state's first television station, WJAR-TV, started operating there in 1949. Rhode Island now has about 25 radio stations and 5 television stations. Cable television systems serve several communities.

Government

Constitution of Rhode Island was adopted in 1842. It became effective on May 2, 1843. Until then, a royal English charter of 1663 served as the constitution of Rhode Island.

An *amendment* (change) to the state Constitution may be proposed by the Rhode Island legislature or by a constitutional convention. To become law, amendments proposed in the legislature need the approval of a majority of the legislators twice—once before and once after an election. The amendments are then submitted to the people in a regular election. Three-fifths of those voting must approve the amendments. To call a constitutional convention, a majority vote by the legislators and voters is needed. Amendments that are proposed by a constitutional convention require the approval of a majority of the voters in a regular election.

Executive. The governor of Rhode Island is elected to a four-year term and may be reelected no more than twice. Rhode Island has no official residence for its governor. Rhode Island voters also elect the lieutenant governor, attorney general, secretary of state, and state treasurer to four-year terms.

The governor, with the Senate's approval, appoints most other key executive officials. These executive officials include the directors of administration, business regulation, environmental management, health, labor and training, and transportation and human resources.

Legislature of Rhode Island is called the General Assembly. It consists of a 50-member Senate and a 100-member House of Representatives. Voters in each of Rhode Island's 50 senatorial districts elect one senator. Voters in each of the state's 100 representative districts elect one representative. Senators and representatives serve two-year terms. The legislature meets annually, beginning on the first Tuesday of January. Regular and special legislative sessions have no time limit.

In 1966 and again in 1992, the legislature *reapportioned* (redivided) the Senate and the House of Representatives. For a discussion of reapportionment in Rhode Island, see *The Mid-1900's* section of this article.

Courts. The Supreme Court of Rhode Island has a chief justice and four associate justices. The General Assembly elects the justices to life terms and chooses a chief justice from among the associate justices.

Other Rhode Island courts include a district court, a family court, and a superior court. The district court has a chief judge and 12 associate judges. The family court has 11 judges, including a chief judge. The superior court has a presiding justice and 18 associate justices. The governor, with the consent of the Senate, appoints district, family, and superior court judges to life terms. Rhode Island also has approximately 40 probate judges.

City and town councils appoint these judges.

Local government. Seven of Rhode Island's 8 cities and 25 of its 31 towns have *home rule*. That is, they can write and amend their charters without permission from the legislature. Rhode Island *towns* are similar to *townships* in other states. They are geographic districts that may include rural areas and several unincorporated villages under one government. Rhode Island and Connecticut are the only states that have no county governments. The two states do have geographical areas called counties, however.

Most large Rhode Island cities have the mayor-council form of government. These cities include Central Falls, Cranston, Newport, Pawtucket, Providence, Warwick, and Woonsocket. East Providence and Middletown are some cities that use the council-manager form of government.

The town meeting is the most common form of government in Rhode Island towns. Dating from colonial days, the town meeting is one of the purest examples of democracy. Voters at annual town meetings participate directly in governmental decisions. They elect officials, approve budgets, pass laws, and decide other town business.

Revenue. Taxation provides almost half of the state government's *general revenue* (income). Other major

The state governors of Rhode Island

	Party	Term		Party	Term
Nicholas Cooke	None	1775-1778	George P. Wetmore	Republican	1885-1887
William Greene	None	1778-1786	John W. Davis	Democratic	1887-1888
John Collins	None	1786-1790	Royal C. Taft	Republican	1888-1889
Arthur Fenner	Anti-Federalist	1790-1805	Herbert W. Ladd	Republican	1889-1890
Henry Smith	Unknown	1805	John W. Davis	Democratic	1890-1891
Isaac Wilbur	Unknown	1806-1807	Herbert W. Ladd	Republican	1891-1892
James Fenner	* Dem.-Rep.	1807-1811	D. Russell Brown	Republican	1892-1895
William Jones	Federalist	1811-1817	Charles W. Lippitt	Republican	1895-1897
Nehemiah R. Knight	* Dem.-Rep.	1817-1821	Elisha Dyer	Republican	1897-1900
William C. Gibbs	* Dem.-Rep.	1821-1824	William Gregory	Republican	1900-1901
James Fenner	* Dem.-Rep.	1824-1831	Charles D. Kimball	Republican	1901-1903
Lemuel H. Arnold	†Nat. Rep.	1831-1833	Lucius F. C. Garvin	Democratic	1903-1905
John Brown Francis	Democratic	1833-1838	George H. Utter	Republican	1905-1907
William Sprague	Democratic	1838-1839	James H. Higgins	Democratic	1907-1909
Samuel Ward King	Rhode Island Party	1840-1843	Aram J. Pothier	Republican	1909-1915
James Fenner	Law and Order	1843-1845	R. Livingston Beeckman	Republican	1915-1921
Charles Jackson	Liberation	1845-1846	Emery J. San Souci	Republican	1921-1923
Byron Diman	Law and Order	1846-1847	William S. Flynn	Democratic	1923-1925
Elisha Harris	Whig	1847-1849	Aram J. Pothier	Republican	1925-1928
Henry B. Anthony	Whig	1849-1851	Norman S. Case	Republican	1928-1933
Philip Allen	Democratic	1851-1853	Theodore F. Green	Democratic	1933-1937
Francis M. Dimond	Democratic	1853-1854	Robert E. Quinn	Democratic	1937-1939
William W. Hoppin	Whig and Know-Nothing	1854-1857	William H. Vanderbilt	Republican	1939-1941
Elisha Dyer	Republican	1857-1859	J. Howard McGrath	Democratic	1941-1945
Thomas G. Turner	Republican	1859-1860	John O. Pastore	Democratic	1945-1950
William Sprague	Democratic & Conservative	1860-1863	John S. McKiernan	Democratic	1950-1951
			Dennis J. Roberts	Democratic	1951-1959
William C. Cozzens	Democratic	1863	Christopher Del Sesto	Republican	1959-1961
James Y. Smith	Republican	1863-1866	John A. Notte, Jr.	Democratic	1961-1963
Ambrose E. Burnside	Republican	1866-1869	John H. Chafee	Republican	1963-1969
Seth Padelford	Republican	1869-1873	Frank Licht	Democratic	1969-1973
Henry Howard	Republican	1873-1875	Philip W. Noel	Democratic	1973-1977
Henry Lippitt	Republican	1875-1877	J. Joseph Garrahy	Democratic	1977-1985
Charles C. Van Zandt	Republican	1877-1880	Edward D. DiPrete	Republican	1985-1991
Alfred H. Littlefield	Republican	1880-1883	Bruce Sundlun	Democratic	1991-1995
Augustus O. Bourn	Republican	1883-1885	Lincoln C. Almond	Republican	1995-

*Democratic-Republican   †National Republican

sources of revenue are federal grants, municipal bonds, and charges for government services.

The largest source of tax revenue in Rhode Island is a personal income tax. A general sales tax is the second largest source of tax revenue. Other important sources of tax revenue include taxes on corporate profits, insurance premiums, motor fuels, tobacco products, and utility bills. The state also receives income from taxes on motor vehicle licenses and other licenses.

Politics. Rhode Island became a Republican state shortly before the Civil War (1861-1865). Most voters in Rhode Island favored the antislavery and pro-Northern policies of the Republican Party. The growth of cities, usually favorable to the Democratic Party, helped Rhode Island become a two-party state during the 1920's.

Rhode Island voters supported the Republican presidential candidate in every election from 1856 to 1908. They voted for Woodrow Wilson, a Democrat, in 1912, but supported Republicans in the next three elections. Since 1928, the state has voted Democratic in all presidential elections except 1952, 1956, 1972, and 1984. For the state's electoral votes and voting record in presidential elections, see **Electoral College** (table).

In state and congressional elections, the people of Rhode Island usually voted for Republicans from the 1860's to the 1920's. Since the 1920's, they have generally favored Democratic candidates for the state legislature, the governorship, and the U.S. Congress.

The Rhode Island Senate meets in the State House in Providence. The 50 senators are elected to two-year terms.

Rhode Island Department of Economic Development

History

Indian days. A few thousand Indians lived in what is now Rhode Island before white people came. The Indians belonged to five tribes of the Algonquian Indian family—the Narragansett, Niantic, Nipmuck, Pequot, and Wampanoag. The Narragansett Indians were the most numerous tribe in the Rhode Island area. They were peaceful people who hunted, fished, and farmed.

Exploration. Miguel de Cortereal, a Portuguese navigator, may have sailed along the Rhode Island coast in 1511. Giovanni da Verrazzano, an Italian navigator working for France, explored Narragansett Bay in 1524. Some historians believe Verrazzano named Rhode Island when he wrote that it resembled the Island of Rhodes in the Mediterranean Sea. Other historians believe the Dutch navigator Adriaen Block named the region. In 1614, Block called an island in Narragansett Bay *Roodt Eylandt* (Red Island). Block used this name because of the red clay on the island's shore.

Settlement. In 1636, Roger Williams established Rhode Island's first permanent white settlement, at Providence. Williams, a minister, had been driven out of Massachusetts because he called for increased religious and political freedom. Massachusetts leaders feared him as a threat to their colony's security. Williams founded Providence on land he bought from Canonicus and Miantonomo, two Narragansett Indian chiefs. He established a policy of religious and political freedom.

In 1638, William Coddington, John Clarke, Anne Hutchinson, and others left Massachusetts in search of religious freedom. They founded the settlement of Pocasset on Aquidneck Island (now officially called Rhode Island). The settlers separated after political and religious differences developed among them. Hutchinson and her followers stayed at Pocasset and renamed it Portsmouth. Coddington, Clarke, and their followers moved south and founded Newport in 1639.

In 1643, Samuel Gorton, John Greene, and others founded a fourth Rhode Island settlement, Warwick. They had left Providence because they believed true liberty was possible only under established English law. Providence was largely independent of English law.

Williams proposed that the four Rhode Island settlements unite for protection against neighboring colonies. He obtained a charter from the English Parliamentary Commission in 1644, and the four settlements united under this charter in 1647. In 1663, King Charles II of England granted Rhode Island a second charter, called the *Charter of Rhode Island and Providence Plantations.* It remained the law of Rhode Island until 1843.

King Philip's War. Roger Williams respected the rights of Indians and maintained peace with them. But trouble began in nearby Massachusetts Bay Colony and Plymouth Colony when young Indian chiefs replaced older ones. The young chiefs feared further English settlement as a threat to their lands. In 1675, the Wampanoag chief King Philip (Metacomet) began killing New England colonists. The same year, troops from Massachusetts, Plymouth, and Connecticut defeated the Indians in the Great Swamp Fight near Kingston, R.I. The Indians then burned towns and murdered colonists in Rhode Island. The colonists killed King Philip in 1676 near Mount Hope (present-day Bristol). The war ended in southern New England that year, but fighting continued in Maine and New Hampshire until 1678. See **Indian wars** (King Philip's War).

The early 1700's was a period of great prosperity in Rhode Island. The fertile coastal regions and the islands in Narragansett Bay made excellent farm and grazing land. Many Rhode Islanders developed large plantations somewhat like those of the South. Slaves worked the land and took care of cattle, horses, and sheep. The plantations also produced great quantities of cheese. Plantation owners developed a fine breed of saddle horse called the Narragansett Pacer.

During the 1700's, Newport merchants owned large fleets of ships. These vessels were used to export plantation products to the other English colonies in America and to the West Indies. The plantation owners and merchants increased their profits by investing in the rum trade and the African slave trade. In spite of the profitable slave trade, Rhode Island was the first colony to prohibit the importation of slaves. It did so in 1774.

The Revolutionary War. During the 1760's, Great Britain passed a series of laws that caused unrest in Rhode Island and the other American colonies. Most of these laws either imposed severe taxes or restricted colonial trade. The people of Rhode Island were among the first colonists to take action against British rule. Their many acts of rebellion included the burning of the British ship *Liberty* at Newport in 1769.

After the Revolutionary War began in Massachusetts in 1775, hundreds of Rhode Islanders joined the patriot forces. Stephen Hopkins and other Rhode Island men were among the chief organizers of the Continental Navy. Esek Hopkins became the first commander in chief of the navy. Nathanael Greene rose to fame as one of the great leaders of the Continental Army.

British troops occupied Newport from December 1776 to October 1779. The British also raided other Rhode Island communities during the war. But no major battles took place on Rhode Island soil.

On May 4, 1776, Rhode Island became the first colony to declare its independence from Great Britain. New Hampshire had adopted an independent constitution in January 1776. But New Hampshire did not sign its declaration of independence until July.

Rhode Island ratified the Articles of Confederation (the forerunner of the United States Constitution) on July 9, 1778. On May 29, 1790, Rhode Island became the last of the 13 original colonies to *ratify* (approve) the U.S. Constitution. Rhode Island delayed ratification until the amendments called the Bill of Rights were ready to be added to the Constitution. These amendments placed limits on the powers of the federal government and guaranteed individual liberties. Even with the Bill of Rights, many Rhode Islanders opposed joining the Union. The Rhode Island convention ratified the Constitution by a slim 34 to 32 vote.

Industrial growth began in Rhode Island during the late 1700's. Textile manufacturing was the state's first important industry. The nation's first hand-operated cotton spinning jenny was built in Providence in 1787. The first water-powered spinning machines were built in Pawtucket in 1790 by Samuel Slater. Power spinning had begun in England, but the English kept the process secret. They wanted to prevent people in other countries from manufacturing cloth and thread by machine. Textile workers were forbidden to leave England. Slater, who had worked with textile machines in England, escaped to the United States disguised as a farmer. He was hired by Moses Brown, a Providence businessman. Slater built the power machines from memory.

The Rhode Island textile industry grew rapidly for several reasons. The textile makers had power spinning, an abundance of water power, nearby markets in Boston and New York City, and excellent transportation. The Jefferson Embargo of 1807, which prohibited importing textiles, also aided the industry.

Other Rhode Island industries also began and grew during the late 1700's. In 1794, Nehemiah Dodge of Providence found a way to cover cheap metals with precious metals. Dodge and his brother Seril founded the United States jewelry industry, and Rhode Island became the country's jewelry-making center. Newport, Providence, and Warren were leading whaling centers from 1775 to 1850. Whale oil and candles made from the head oil of sperm whales became profitable products. The fishing industry was another important business of the period.

The Dorr Rebellion. Rhode Island cities grew rapidly during the early 1800's. Thousands of Canadians, Europeans, and Rhode Island farmers came to the cities to work in textile mills. But Rhode Island laws did not keep pace with the growth of cities. For example, most city people were denied the right to vote. Rhode Island was still governed by its 1663 charter, which restricted voting to landholders or their eldest sons. Rural areas had the greatest representation in the state legislature, even though cities had the largest populations. These conditions led to a political struggle and an uprising called the *Dorr Rebellion.* Thomas Dorr and his followers tried to form their own government. Their revolt failed, but it was partly responsible for the adoption of a more liberal state constitution in 1842. The new constitution became effective in 1843. It gave voting rights to native-born Rhode Island men of legal age who paid taxes of $1 a year or served in the militia. It also increased city representation in the legislature. See **Dorr Rebellion.**

The late 1800's. More than 24,000 Rhode Islanders served in the Union Army and Navy during the Civil War (1861-1865). The most famous one was Major General Ambrose E. Burnside, who commanded the Army of the Potomac for a brief period. He later served as governor of Rhode Island and as a U.S. senator.

Prosperity continued in Rhode Island after the war. The state's population almost doubled between 1870 and 1900. The textile industry developed worldwide markets, and other industries also expanded. Newport became the home of the Newport Naval Station in 1883 and of the Naval War College in 1884. The college is the navy's highest educational institution. Also in the late 1800's, Newport won fame as the summer home of many wealthy railroad and banking families.

Historic Rhode Island

Roger Williams founded Rhode Island's first permanent white settlement at Providence in 1636.

The *Liberty,* a British ship docked at Newport, was burned by Rhode Islanders in 1769 in one of the first acts of rebellion by the colonists.

The Slater Mill, built in Pawtucket in 1793, was one of the first successful textile mills in North America.

Rhode Island shipyards built hundreds of merchant and whaling vessels from the mid-1600's to the late 1800's.

The slave trade thrived in Rhode Island until 1774, when the colony prohibited the importation of slaves.

WORLD BOOK illustrations by Kevin Chadwick

Important dates in Rhode Island

1524 Giovanni da Verrazzano sailed Narragansett Bay.

1636 Roger Williams founded Providence.

1638 William Coddington, John Clarke, Anne Hutchinson, and others settled on Aquidneck Island.

1647 The settlements of Providence, Portsmouth, Newport, and Warwick were united after England granted Roger Williams a charter in 1644.

1663 England granted Rhode Island its second charter.

1774 Rhode Island prohibited the importation of slaves.

1776 Rhode Island declared its independence from England.

1790 Rhode Island became the 13th state when it ratified the U.S. Constitution on May 29.

1842 The Dorr Rebellion helped bring about a more liberal state constitution.

1938 A disastrous hurricane struck Rhode Island.

1969 Newport Bridge over Narragansett Bay was completed, linking Newport with Jamestown.

1971 The state legislature approved a personal income tax for the first time.

1990 Rhode Island celebrated the *bicentennial* (200th anniversary) of its statehood.

The early 1900's. During World War I (1914-1918), Rhode Island's factories made chemicals, munitions, and other war materials. Shipyards in Newport and Providence built combat and cargo ships.

The Rhode Island textile industry began a decline during the 1920's. Many plants moved to the South, where labor and transportation costs were low. The increased manufacture of machine tools, machinery, and metal products helped make up the loss. But then the Great Depression of the 1930's further slowed Rhode Island's economic growth. Conditions improved as the depression eased in the late 1930's.

In 1938, Rhode Island suffered one of its worst natural disasters. A hurricane and tidal wave struck the state, killing 258 people and causing $100 million in property damage.

The mid-1900's. During World War II (1939-1945), war industries helped stimulate the state's recovering economy. The U.S. Navy established Quonset Point Naval Air Station in 1941, creating many jobs. Quonset huts, a famous type of World War II shelter, were first built at Quonset Point that year.

Rhode Island's economy lagged after the war. Employment fell as wartime industries closed and textile mills continued to move to the South. By 1949, more than 17 per cent of the state's workers were unemployed. Rhode Island revived its economy during the 1950's and 1960's by expanding the electronics, chemical, machinery, and plastics industries. By the end of the 1960's, the state had a varied economy, and unemployment had dropped to about 3 per cent. The textile industry remained important, but Rhode Island's economy no longer depended largely on it.

During the 1960's, the tourist industry became increasingly important to Rhode Island's economy. New roads and freeways opened much of the state to tourists. In 1969, a $71-million bridge was completed across Narragansett Bay between Jamestown and Newport. Completion of the Rhode Island section of Interstate Highway 95, also in 1969, allowed motorists to travel across the state from Connecticut to Massachusetts without a traffic light along the way.

Also during the 1960's, the University of Rhode Island began to develop a scientific research center at Saunderstown. The United States Public Health Service has a shellfish laboratory at the center, and the United States Bureau of Sports Fisheries and Wildlife has a biological laboratory there. The center is also the site of the nation's first state-owned nuclear reactor.

Destructive hurricanes struck Rhode Island again in the 1940's and 1950's, though none was so severe as the 1938 hurricane. During the 1960's, the U.S. Army Corps of Engineers built a large hurricane barrier across the Providence River. This dam, completed in 1966, protects downtown Providence from hurricanes.

The Rhode Island legislature passed many new laws in the mid-1900's. The state held its first direct primary election in 1948. In 1951, the legislature repealed the poll tax and gave home rule to Rhode Island's cities and towns. A 1963 law provided for lending textbooks to students in private schools. In 1964, Rhode Island set up a program to help pay medical bills for needy persons over 65.

The Rhode Island Supreme Court ruled in 1962 that

Jim Daniels

Water-pollution testing is one of the many projects conducted at the University of Rhode Island's Graduate School of Oceanography located in Narragansett.

the state House of Representatives must be *reapportioned* (redivided) to provide equal representation based on population. A constitutional convention met in 1964 to act on reapportionment of both the house and the senate and to consider other issues. In 1965, the legislature appointed a special commission to draw up a temporary reapportionment plan. The legislature used this plan to reapportion itself in 1966. In 1967, the constitutional convention proposed a new constitution. The constitution, which included a new reapportionment plan, was rejected by the state's voters in 1968.

Recent developments. In the early 1980's, the United States federal government deregulated the nation's savings and loan industry, which provides loans for construction. The deregulation helped cause a real estate boom in Rhode Island. In the late 1980's and early 1990's, however, a sharp decline in real estate values, mismanagement, and other factors led to major problems for financial institutions. The Rhode Island state government had to restore funds to uninsured, failing financial institutions at a large cost to the taxpayers of the state.

Rhode Island industries shared in a national defense build-up in the 1980's. But with the end of Cold War tensions in the late 1980's, United States defense spending began to decline. Rhode Island faced the need to convert from defense-related projects to other industrial activities. Many members of Rhode Island's labor force are employed in low-paying positions in the jewelry and textile industries. These industries face much competition from foreign companies.

Tourism has continued to grow and to contribute heavily to Rhode Island's economy. Also, Rhode Island has become an important center for oceanographic research. The oceanographic research program of the University of Rhode Island is recognized as one of the finest in the United States.

Stanford E. Demars and Michael R. H. Swanson

Study aids

Related articles in *World Book* include:

Biographies

Burnside, Ambrose E.
Cohan, George M.
Ellery, William
Gray, Robert
Green, Theodore F.
Greene, Nathanael
Hopkins, Stephen
Hutchinson, Anne M.
Philip, King
Slater, Samuel
Williams, Roger
Woodcock, Leonard

Cities

Newport
Pawtucket
Providence
Warwick

History

Colonial life in America
Dorr Rebellion
Flag (picture: Flags in United States history;
    New England flags)
Indian wars
Narragansett Indians
Revolutionary War in America

Outline

I. **People**
  A. Population
  B. Schools
  C. Libraries
  D. Museums
II. **Visitor's guide**
  A. Places to visit
  B. Annual events
III. **Land and climate**
  A. Land regions
  B. Islands
  C. Coastline
  D. Rivers and lakes
  E. Plant and animal life
  F. Climate
IV. **Economy**
  A. Natural resources
  B. Service industries
  C. Manufacturing
  D. Agriculture
  E. Fishing industry
  F. Mining
  G. Electric power
  H. Transportation
  I. Communication
V. **Government**
  A. Constitution
  B. Executive
  C. Legislature
  D. Courts
  E. Local government
  F. Revenue
  G. Politics
VI. **History**

Questions

What American industries began in Rhode Island?
What is *The Breakers*?
What were the conditions that led to the Dorr Rebellion? What
  were the results of the rebellion?
What is Rhode Island's leading manufacturing activity?
Why did Roger Williams move to Rhode Island?
What are Rhode Island's two main land regions?
What is an unusual feature of Rhode Island's system of local
  government?
What is often called the *Cradle of American Industry*?
Why did Rhode Island wait so long to ratify the U.S. Constitu-
  tion?
What is Rhode Island's official name? How did Rhode Island get
  this name?

Additional resources

Level I
Aylesworth, Thomas G. and V. L *Southern New England: Con-
  necticut, Massachusetts, Rhode Island.* Chelsea Hse., 1996.
Fradin, Dennis B. *The Rhode Island Colony.* Childrens Pr., 1989.
Fradin, Dennis B. and J. B. *Rhode Island.* Childrens Pr., 1995.
Heinrichs, Ann. *Rhode Island.* Childrens Pr., 1990.
Thompson, Kathleen. *Rhode Island.* 2nd ed. Raintree Steck
  Vaughn, 1996.
Warner, J. F. *Rhode Island.* Lerner, 1993.

Level II
Conley, Patrick T. *An Album of Rhode Island History, 1636-1986.*
  Donning, 1986. *Democracy in Decline: Rhode Island's Consti-
  tutional Development, 1776-1841.* R. I. Hist. Soc., 1977.
Curley, Robert P. *Rhode Island: Off the Beaten Path.* Globe Pe-
  quot, 1996. A travel guide.
Withey, Lynne. *Urban Growth in Colonial Rhode Island: Newport
  and Providence in the Eighteenth Century.* State Univ. of N. Y.
  Pr., 1984.
Wright, Marion I., and Sullivan, R. J. *The Rhode Island Atlas.* R. I.
  Pubns. Soc., 1982.

Rhode Island, University of, is a state-supported,
coeducational institution. The university's main campus
is located in Kingston, Rhode Island. In addition to the
main campus, the University of Rhode Island also has
three additional campuses. These campuses are located
in the towns of Providence, Narragansett, and West
Greenwich.

The University of Rhode Island offers curricula in the
following colleges: arts and sciences, business administration, engineering, human science and services, nursing, pharmacy, and resource development. It also has a
graduate school, a graduate school of library and information studies, and a graduate school of oceanography.
The school grants bachelor's, master's, and doctor's degrees.

The University of Rhode Island was founded in
Kingston in 1888. It was originally chartered as the
Rhode Island College of Agriculture and Mechanic Arts.
It changed its name to Rhode Island State College in
1909. The University of Rhode Island took its present
name in 1951.

Critically reviewed by the University of Rhode Island

See also **Rhode Island** (picture: Water-pollution testing).

Rhodes, *rohdz,* is the largest of the Dodecanese Islands in the Aegean Sea. It lies 12 miles (19 kilometers)
off the southwestern coast of Turkey (see **Greece** [ter-
rain map]). Rhodes (also referred to as Ródhos) has a total area of 540 square miles (1,398 square kilometers).
Rhodes has a population of about 91,000. One of its
chief physical features is a mountain range that runs
lengthwise across the island, rising to a height of 3,986
feet (1,215 meters) above the sea. Tourism is the chief industry. Other products are cigarettes, food products,
machinery, and textiles. The major crops of Rhodes in-

clude citrus fruits, olives, tobacco, and vegetables.

In early days, Rhodes was a wealthy and independent state of Greece. Rhodes was the home of numerous poets, artists, and philosophers. A great statue of Helios, called the *Colossus of Rhodes,* was one of the Seven Wonders of the Ancient World (see **Seven Wonders of the Ancient World**). In 1310, the Knights Hospitallers occupied Rhodes. In 1522, the Turks captured it. Then Rhodes declined in glory and grandeur.

Italy occupied Rhodes during the Turko-Italian War of 1911-1912. Italy held Rhodes and the rest of the Dodecanese Islands until 1947. It then ceded them to Greece. The capital of the island is the city of Rhodes (or Ródhos). It is a major tourist attraction.   John J. Baxevanis

Rhodes, *rohdz,* **Cecil John** (1853-1902), was a British businessman and statesman. He made a fortune in the diamond industry and probably did more than anyone else of his time to enlarge the British Empire in Africa. Rhodes used his wealth and his ability as a statesman to gain control of most of southern Africa. He spent his fortune freely when he thought he could advance the empire. But he was often ruthless and racist in pursuing his goals. Rhodes left much of his fortune to Oxford University for the establishment of the Rhodes Scholarship (see **Rhodes Scholarship**).

Early life. Rhodes was born in the county of Hertfordshire in England. In 1870, he went to Natal (then a British colony in what is now South Africa), where one of his brothers was a cotton grower. In 1871, he became a supervisor in a diamond mine his brother had opened at Kimberley, also in present-day South Africa. By 1873, Rhodes had taken control of the mine. Rhodes enrolled at Oxford University in 1873 and spent half of each year there until he graduated in 1881. He also gained control of more diamond mines at Kimberley.

Gains Rhodesia. In 1881, Rhodes was elected to the assembly of Britain's Cape Colony in what is now South Africa. Aided by his wealth, he set out to advance British imperial authority in southern Africa. He forced the annexation of Bechuanaland (now Botswana) to the British Empire in 1885. By 1888, when he combined all his mines into the De Beers Consolidated Mines, Rhodes had become extremely rich and powerful. In 1889, he forced the Shona and Ndebele (often called Matabele) peoples to surrender most of their land to Britain. This huge territory later became the state of Southern Rhodesia (now Zimbabwe). Rhodes also arranged the annexation of what later became Northern Rhodesia (now Zambia). The British South Africa Company, which Rhodes had created, effectively ruled both territories.

In 1890, Rhodes became prime minister of the Cape Colony. He dreamed of building a railroad from the colony to Egypt and of extending British power over much of Africa. He also sought cooperation between English-speaking white colonists and moderate *Boers* (now called Afrikaners), especially in the Cape Colony. The Boers

Culver Pictures
Cecil Rhodes

were white settlers, mainly of Dutch descent.

In 1892, Rhodes approved the Franchise and Ballot Bill, which denied almost all the colony's blacks the right to vote. In 1894, he enacted the Glen Grey Act, which restricted the amount of land blacks could own.

Conflict with the Boers. Rhodes saw that British rule in southern Africa could only be expanded at the expense of the Boers, who had large possessions in the region. Rhodes interfered in the politics of the Transvaal area (in what later became South Africa). The area was settled by the Boers. Rhodes was largely responsible for the Jameson Raid of 1895, in which Rhodesian troops attacked the Transvaal. This incident was badly planned and widely criticized. After the raid, Rhodes resigned as prime minister of the Cape Colony and withdrew into Rhodesia.

Rhodes was at Kimberley in 1899 when the Boer War finally broke out between Britain and the Boers (see **Boer War**). He assisted in the defense of the city and helped direct the course of the war. But he had a fatal heart attack before the war ended.   Denis Judd

Rhodes, *rohdz,* **John Jacob** (1916-   ), an Arizona Republican, served as minority leader of the United States House of Representatives from 1973 to 1981. He succeeded Gerald R. Ford after Ford replaced Spiro T. Agnew as Vice President. Rhodes supported conservative financial policies and worked for government-sponsored projects to increase the water supply in Arizona.

Rhodes was born in Council Grove, Kans. He graduated from Kansas State College (now Kansas State University) and then from Harvard Law School. Rhodes served in the Army Air Forces from 1941 to 1945, during World War II. He then practiced law in Mesa, Ariz. In 1952, Rhodes became the first Republican elected to the U.S. House of Representatives from Arizona. He served as chairman of the Republican House Policy Committee from 1965 to 1973.   Guy Halverson

Rhodes Scholarship, *rohdz,* is an award that enables students from many countries to study at Oxford University in England. The scholarship pays the student's tuition and fees directly to the university. It also provides an allowance to cover living expenses. Scholarships are awarded for two years, but may be extended for a third year.

The scholarships were established in the will of Cecil J. Rhodes, a British colonial statesman who died in 1902. Rhodes's aim was to strengthen ties among the English-speaking peoples. He also wanted to provide potential leaders of many nations with an opportunity to study at Oxford. The scholarship program began full operation in 1904. At first, Rhodes scholars came to Oxford from the United States, Germany, and several nations of the British Empire. Since then, the program has expanded to include several additional nations.

About 90 Rhodes Scholarships are awarded yearly. The United States receives 32; Canada, 11; South Africa, 9; Australia, 17; India, 13; New Zealand, 2; and Germany, 2. Zambia and Zimbabwe send three scholars each every two years. Bermuda, Jamaica, Pakistan, Hong Kong, Malaysia, Singapore, Kenya, Nigeria, and the British Caribbean, which includes the Bahamas, Barbados, and Trinidad and Tobago, are each offered one Rhodes Scholarship each year.

The committees who select Rhodes scholars seek

people with superior scholastic records. Candidates also must display qualities of character, leadership, and personal vigor.

Applicants from the United States must be unmarried U.S. citizens who are at least 18 years old and not older than 24. They must have lived in the country at least five years. They also must have completed enough college to ensure that they will receive a bachelor's degree before they arrive in Oxford.

Candidates from the United States apply to state committees. The committee in each state nominates two candidates to the district competition. The nation is divided into eight districts for this competition. Each district committee selects four Rhodes scholars from the state nominees who appear before it.

Critically reviewed by the Rhodes Trust

See also **Oxford University; Rhodes, Cecil J.**

Rhodesia. See Zimbabwe.

Rhodesia and Nyasaland, *roh DEE zhuh, ny AS uh LAND,* **Federation of,** was a federated territory in central Africa from 1953 to 1963. It belonged to Britain. The federation consisted of the self-governing colony of Southern Rhodesia and the protectorates of Northern Rhodesia and Nyasaland. Britain created the federation in 1953. Black Africans opposed the Federation of Rhodesia and Nyasaland because the whites controlled the government even though they were in the minority there.

Britain agreed to dissolve the federation on Dec. 31, 1963. In 1964, Nyasaland became the independent nation of Malawi and Northern Rhodesia gained independence as Zambia. Southern Rhodesia became the self-governing area of Rhodesia, which is now the independent nation of Zimbabwe. See **Zimbabwe** (History) for details on the area since the federation ended.

Hibberd V. B. Kline, Jr.

See also **Malawi; Zambia; Zimbabwe.**

Rhodesian ridgeback, *roh DEE zhuhn,* is a medium-sized hound that originated in southern Africa. It is also called the *African lion hound* because it was bred to find and hold off lions so that hunters could get a good shot at their prey. The dog has a ridge of hair on the back that grows in a direction opposite to the rest of the coat. The coat has a light to reddish-wheatlike color. The ridgeback stands 24 to 27 inches (61 to 69 centimeters) high at the shoulder. It makes an excellent watchdog and is good with children.

Critically reviewed by the Rhodesian Ridgeback Club of the United States

See also **Dog** (picture: Hounds).

Rhodium is a rare, silver-white, metallic element that serves mainly as a *catalyst,* a substance which increases the speed of a chemical reaction. Rhodium is a catalyst in the production of nitric acid and various organic compounds and medicinal drugs. It is also used in *catalytic converters,* which reduce pollutants in automobile exhausts. Rhodium *alloys* (metal mixtures) are used in aircraft turbine engines, electric connections, and reflective surfaces of mirrors and searchlights.

Rhodium has the chemical symbol Rh. Its atomic number is 45, and its atomic weight is 102.906. Rhodium melts at $1963 \pm$ °C and boils at 3697 ± 100 °C. William H. Wollaston, an English chemist, first isolated rhodium in 1803. Rhodium occurs in Brazil, Canada, Colombia, Russia, South Africa, and Sri Lanka. Emily Jane Rose

See also **Element, Chemical** (Periodic table).

Rhododendron, *ROH duh DEHN druhn,* is the name of a group of trees and shrubs that belong to the heath family. The name means *rose tree.* The group includes several species which are known for the beauty of their flowers and for their evergreen leaves. One of the best known is the *great rhododendron,* which is also called *great laurel* and *rosebay.* It grows widely in the Allegheny Mountains. There, the interlocking branches form

© E. R. Ricciuti, Photo Researchers

WORLD BOOK photo by Ken Love

The Rhodesian ridgeback is a powerful hunting dog that originated in southern Africa. It is an excellent watchdog.

© Dale Athenas, Photo Researchers

The rhododendron has large clusters of colorful flowers that make this evergreen plant a popular ornamental shrub. The showy blossoms, *right,* appear in the spring. Rhododendrons generally grow in cool, mountainous regions.

almost impassable thickets. This rhododendron rarely grows higher than 35 feet (11 meters). Its white or rose-colored flowers grow in a large cluster.

Another species, the *mountain rosebay,* is a common shrub in Virginia. It produces brilliant, lilac-purple flowers. Other species are found in the Pacific Coast region. Some magnificent rhododendrons grow in the mountainous regions of India. The leaves of most rhododendrons are poisonous.

Scientific classification. Rhododendrons belong to the heath family, Ericaceae. The scientific name for the great rhododendron is *Rhododendron maximum.* The mountain rosebay is *R. catawbiense.*   James L. Luteyn

See also **West Virginia** (picture: State flower).

Rhomboid, *RAHM boyd,* is a plane figure with two parallel sides of equal length, and the other two sides a different, but also equal, length. Its sides are not at right angles to each other. See also **Rhombus.**

Rhombus, *RAHM buhs,* is a plane figure with two pairs of straight, parallel sides, all of equal length. The parallel sides of a rhombus make it a parallelogram. A square is a rhombus with sides at right angles to each other. See **Quadrilateral.**

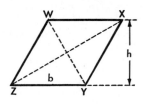

The area of a rhombus is found by multiplying base by altitude, or $A = bh$. The area of a rhombus can also be found by determining the product of its diagonals, WY and XZ in the figure, then dividing this product in half.   Mary Kay Corbitt

Rhône River, *rohn,* is an important commercial waterway of France. The river has become famous for the beauty of its valley.

The river rises in the Rhône glacier of Switzerland, at an altitude of over 5,000 feet (1,500 meters). Glacial clay picked up by the river in the Swiss Alps makes the water of the Rhône almost milky. But during the Rhône's course through Lake Geneva, it loses most of the glacial clay at the bottom of that lake. The clear blue of the river, after leaving Lake Geneva, inspired the English poet Lord Byron to describe it as "the blue rushing of the arrowy Rhône."

After the Rhône leaves Switzerland and enters France, it flows southwestward to Lyon. It then winds south and empties through a large delta into the Gulf of Lion, an arm of the Mediterranean Sea.

The Rhône is over 500 miles (800 kilometers) long, and navigable for about 300 miles (480 kilometers). Chief branches are the Saône, the Isère, and the Durance. Hydroelectric power plants along the Rhône generate electricity. Canals feed irrigation projects along the lower course of the river. A canal near the mouth of the Rhône connects the river with France's largest Mediterranean port, Marseille.

Greek and Latin civilizations followed the Rhône Valley to Lyon, and up its tributaries.   Hugh D. Clout

Rhubarb, *ROO bahrb,* is one of the few perennial vegetables. It is also called *pieplant.* Rhubarb originally came from Mongolia, but is grown both in Europe and America. The plant forms a large, yellow storage root and a mass of feeder roots underground. Its *rhizome* (underground stem) produces buds from which grow long, thick leafstalks with large leaves. People use the reddish, juicy stalks for food. A person may become ill from eating the leaves because they contain poisonous oxalic acid salts (see **Oxalic acid**).

Although rhubarb is technically a vegetable, people usually prepare it as a dessert food, often as pie fillings and sauces. Stores sell rhubarb packaged frozen and in cans. However, many people prefer to cook the fresh stalks. Rhubarb contains some vitamin C, and has laxative qualities.

Rhubarb plants produce many seeds, but plants from the seeds are not always like the parent plant. Growers plant pieces of the big storage root that have several buds from which new plants grow. Each plant lasts 5 to 8 years. Rhubarb is relatively free from insect attack and suffers from few diseases.

Scientific classification. Rhubarb belongs to the buckwheat family, Polygonaceae. Its scientific name is *Rheum rhaponticum.*
Hugh C. Price

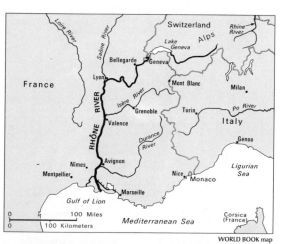

WORLD BOOK map
Location of the Rhône River

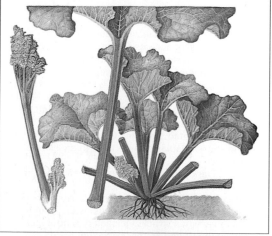

WORLD BOOK illustration by Jill Coombs
The rhubarb plant has juicy, reddish stalks with a tangy flavor. Rhubarb, though a vegetable, is popular as a dessert.

Rhumb line. See Great-circle route.

Rhumba. See Rumba.

Rhyme, also spelled *rime,* means echoing or repeating sounds at the end of words. In poetry, rhyme usually occurs at the end of lines, as in this quotation from the Irish poet William Butler Yeats:

O body swayed to music, O brightening glance,
How can we know the dancer from the dance?

This is an example of *end rhyme. Glance* in the first line rhymes with *dance* in the second. *Internal rhyme* refers to the rhyming of two or more words within a line, such as *seared, bleared,* and *smeared* in this line by the English poet Gerard Manley Hopkins: "And all is seared with trade; bleared, smeared with toil."

In *single rhyme,* the final vowel and consonant sounds of the rhyming words are repeated, as in *glance* and *dance.* In *double rhyme,* the last two syllables of the rhyming words are repeated, as in *staples* and *maples.* Less frequently, rhymes involve many syllables, as in *Tennyson* and *venison.*

In *near rhyme,* also called *slant rhyme,* the words almost rhyme. The words repeat either (1) the final consonant sounds after the last stressed vowel sound, as in *have* and *grave,* or (2) the final stressed vowel sound but not the final consonant sounds, as in *wake* and *late.* In *visual rhyme,* also called *eye rhyme,* the words are connected by the eye, not by the ear, as in *tough* and *through.*

Poets often use a rhyme pattern to create an overall form for a poem, as in a sonnet. In addition, they may use individual rhymes for various effects of sound and meaning. However, rhyme is not necessary in poetry. Blank verse and much free verse do not use rhyme.

Paul B. Diehl

See also **Alliteration; Blank verse; Free verse; Poetry** (Sounds); **Sonnet.**

Rhyolite. See Granite.

Rhythm is the regular repetition of a beat, accent, or rise and fall in dance, music, and language. The word comes from the Greek word *rhythmos,* meaning *measured motion.* In dancing, rhythmic patterns and variations are created by physical motions of shorter or longer duration and of greater or lesser emphasis. In music, rhythmic figures and phrases come from an arrangement of tones, organized according to their duration and stresses, or accents. Rhythm is the most primitive element of music. Unlike the other elements, it can exist independently. Any sound, even noise, can establish a rhythm. In language, rhythm is the rise and fall of sounds according to syllables, vocal inflections, physical speech accents, and pauses. Modern English and German are of the language type that has physically stressed, or accented, syllables. Greek and Latin use long and short syllables or inflections to give stress.

Stewart L. Ross

See also **Dance; Language; Meter** (Poetry); **Music** (Rhythm; Musical notation).

Rhythm band describes a group of performers playing *percussion instruments* (instruments that produce musical tones when struck). Elementary school music teachers in the United States use rhythm bands as a method of teaching children about basic rhythm in music. Children learn to sing, tap, or play the characteristic rhythm of a melody. The purpose of these bands is to develop a feeling and response to rhythms of all kinds. Some instruments played in rhythm bands include rhythm sticks, maracas, claves, wood blocks, triangles, and tambourines.

Stewart L. Ross

Rhythm method. See Birth control (Methods of birth control).

Rial, *ree AWL,* is the basic monetary unit of Iran (formerly Persia), Oman, Qatar, Saudi Arabia, and Yemen. The rial is sometimes called the *riyal.* The value of the rial varies in each country that uses it. The name *rial* comes from the old French and Spanish words for *royal.* The monetary unit is sometimes incorrectly called *real,* which was the name for a silver coin of Spain.

Burton H. Hobson

Rib is any one of the 24 bones that enclose the chest in the human body. There are 12 ribs on each side of the body, each connected to the *vertebral column* (backbone) by small joints called *costovertebral joints.* In the front of the body, the uppermost seven ribs on each side are connected directly to the breastbone by a tough, elastic material called *cartilage.* These are called the *true ribs.* The five lower ribs, called *false ribs,* are not linked directly to the breastbone. Each of the upper three false ribs is attached to the rib above by cartilage. The lowest two ribs are attached only to the backbone. They are known as *floating ribs.* The spaces between the ribs, called *intercostal spaces,* contain arteries, veins, muscles, and nerves.

Most *vertebrates* (animals with backbones) have ribs, but the number of ribs varies considerably. In mammals the number of ribs varies from 9 pairs, as in some whales, to 24 pairs, as in two-toed sloths.

The ribs perform two functions in the body. They form a cage around the chest cavity that protects the heart and lungs. They also move up and down and, together with the diaphragm, control the movement of air in and out of the lungs. When the ribs move up, the chest cavity enlarges and air is sucked into the lungs. When they move down, air is forced out of the lungs.

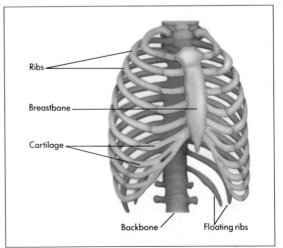

WORLD BOOK illustration by Leonard Morgan

The ribs are connected to the backbone, from which they curve downward and forward to form a protective cage around the heart and lungs. The human body has 24 ribs, 12 on each side.

A hard blow on the chest can fracture a rib. Fractured ribs cause sharp pain when the injured person breathes, and tenderness when pressure is applied to the fracture area. A person who has an injured chest should call a doctor.   Bruce Reider

See also **Human body** (Trans-Vision color picture).

Ribaut, *REE BOH,* **Jean** (1529-1565), a French colonizer, took part in attempts to establish French colonies in South Carolina and Florida. In 1562, he led the expedition that built Fort Charles, where Port Royal, South Carolina, now stands. He then returned to France. The garrison of 26 soldiers he left behind later deserted. In 1565, Ribaut led an expedition to the French Protestant settlement of Fort Caroline in Florida. He arrived safely, but the fort was later destroyed by the Spanish. Ribaut himself was shipwrecked, captured by the Spanish, and executed. He was born in Dieppe, France.   D. Peter MacLeod

Ribbentrop, *RIHB uhn TROHP,* **Joachim von,** *YOH ah khihm fuhn* (1893-1946), was Adolf Hitler's top diplomatic agent. He served as foreign minister of Germany from 1938 to 1945. He helped engineer the seizure of Austria, the partition of Czechoslovakia, and alliances with Italy and Japan. In August 1939, he made a deal with Joseph Stalin of the Soviet Union in which Germany and the Soviet Union agreed to divide Poland and much of the rest of Eastern Europe between them. After World War II ended in 1945, Ribbentrop was tried and hanged for war crimes and crimes against humanity and peace.

Ribbentrop was born in Wesel, Germany. His familiarity with different languages helped him greatly in diplomacy. In 1935, he gained from England a naval treaty that gave Germany equality in submarines and the right to expand its fleet of surface ships to 35 percent the size of Britain's surface fleet.   Donald M. McKale

Ribbon Falls is a beautiful waterfall that looks like a narrow ribbon as it drops 1,612 feet (491 meters) in the Yosemite Valley in California's Yosemite National Park. It is one of the highest waterfalls in the world. Ribbon Falls is fed by a creek that rises in the mountains above the Yosemite Valley. The water drops down a narrow gorge into the Merced River, which flows through the valley. Ribbon Falls goes dry in early August during the California summer. It becomes a torrent during May and June. See also **Waterfall** (picture; chart).   Tom L. McKnight

Ribbon worm is any of a group of worms with a slender, often flattened body and a long *proboscis* (snout). The proboscis lies above the mouth and can be thrown out quickly and wrapped around the prey. In some ribbon worms, the proboscis has daggerlike *stylets.* In others, it has *nematocysts* (fine stinging threads). A ribbon worm has a complete digestive tract, with openings at the mouth and anus. Ribbon worms feed on other worms and mollusks, both living and dead. They are not harmful to people.

Most ribbon worms live in the ocean, but a few live in moist earth and fresh water. They range in size from less than 1 inch (2.5 centimeters) to 100 feet (30 meters) long. Some ribbon worms are brilliantly colored.

David F. Oetinger

Scientific classification. Ribbon worms make up the phylum Nemertea, also called Rhynchocoela.

Ribera, *ree BAY rah,* **Jusepe de,** *hoo SAY pay day* (1588-1652), was a Spanish painter. Many of his paintings show Christian martyrdoms and saints doing penance.

Until 1635, Ribera's style showed the influence of the Italian painter Michelangelo Caravaggio. Ribera then used somber colors and placed realistic figures in simple, diagonal compositions. Between 1635 and 1639, influenced by the Italian painters Correggio and Titian, he used brighter colors and more complex compositions. Elements of these styles are found in his work after 1639.

Ribera was born in Játiva, near Valencia, Spain. In 1616, he settled in Naples, Italy, then a Spanish territory. He became very successful and never returned to Spain. The Italians nicknamed him *Lo Spagnoletto* (Little Spaniard).   Marilyn Stokstad

Ribicoff, *RIHB uh KAWF,* **Abraham A.** (1910-1998), a Connecticut Democrat, served in many high government posts. He served in the United States Senate from 1963 to 1981. Ribicoff was secretary of health, education, and welfare under President John F. Kennedy in 1961 and 1962. He also served in the Connecticut House of Representatives from 1938 to 1942 and in the U.S. House of Representatives from 1949 to 1953. Ribicoff was governor of Connecticut from 1955 to 1961.

Ribicoff was born in New Britain, Connecticut, and graduated with honors from the University of Chicago Law School in 1933. He practiced law and served as a police court judge before entering politics. As governor, he led a traffic safety program. As a senator, he called for legislation to require certain safety features on automobiles.   James I. Lengle

Riboflavin. See **Vitamin; Nutrition** (Vitamins).

Ricardo, *rih KAHR doh,* **David** (1772-1823), was the leading British economist of the early 1800's. He helped establish the theories of *classical economics,* which stresses economic freedom through free trade and free competition. In his book *Principles of Political Economy and Taxation* (1817), Ricardo defined the conditions that would enable a nation's economy to reach its greatest potential. He believed that the accumulation of capital was the key to rapid economic growth. He argued that allowing businesses to seek high profits would bring about a rapid accumulation of capital.

Ricardo considered labor to be the most important source of wealth. But he also thought that population growth would push wage rates down to a level that would barely support the people. As the economy expanded and the population continued to grow, land rent would rise. This would reduce profits, the accumulation of capital would slow down, and economic growth would end. But Ricardo believed that by this time industrialization would have spread throughout the world and peak production would be a reality.

Ricardo's theories influenced other economists. His theory of comparative advantage is still the basis for the modern theory of international trade (see **International trade**). Karl Marx was influenced by Ricardo's *labor theory of value,* which held that the value of a commodity is determined by the amount of labor needed in its production. Henry George, a land reformer, developed Ricardo's theory of rent into a detailed study of progress and poverty. John Stuart Mill, a British philosopher and economist, used Ricardo's ideas as the basis for a philosophy of social reform.

Ricardo was born in London, and made a fortune on the stock exchange while still in his 20's. He served in Parliament from 1819 until his death.   Daniel R. Fusfeld

E.R. Degginger, Bruce Coleman Inc.   W.E. Ruth, Bruce Coleman Inc.

Farmers cultivate rice on many kinds of land. In hilly areas, farmers build terraces and *dikes* (dirt walls) to catch rainfall for growing rice, *left.* In lowland regions, farmers plant rice in fields that are surrounded by dikes and then flooded, *right.* Rice is one of the world's most important food crops.

Rice

Rice is one of the world's most important food crops. More than half of the people in the world eat this grain as the main part of their meals. Nearly all the people who depend on rice for food live in Asia. In some Asian languages, the same word means *eat* and *eat rice.* Most rice is eaten as boiled, white grain.

Rice is a cereal grain. Like other cereal grains, including wheat, corn, and oats, rice belongs to the grass family. But unlike other grains, rice grows best in shallow water. Rice thrives in many tropical areas because of their warm, wet climate. Farmers usually flood rice fields to supply the growing plants with moisture and to kill weeds and other pests. China and India are the world's leading rice-producing countries. Together, they produce more than half of the world's yearly rice harvest.

A type of grass called *wild rice* grows in central Canada and parts of the Northern United States. In spite of its name, this grain is not closely related to rice.

The rice plant

Young rice plants have a bright green color. As the grain ripens, the plants turn golden-yellow. The grain becomes fully ripe from 110 to 180 days after planting.

J. Neil Rutger, the contributor of this article, is a research geneticist specializing in rice at the United States Department of Agriculture.

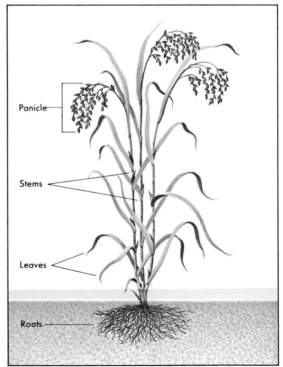

WORLD BOOK diagram by James Teason

The rice plant grows from 31 to 72 inches (80 to 180 centimeters) tall and has several stems. At the end of each stem is a *head,* or *panicle,* which holds the kernels of rice. Each panicle bears from 60 to 150 kernels.

Structure. The main parts of a mature rice plant are the roots, stems, leaves, and head. A system of slender roots supports the plant's hollow stems. Each stem has at least five or six joints from which the long, narrow leaves grow. The head, also known as the *panicle,* grows from the top joint. The panicle holds the kernels—that is, the seeds or grains—of the rice plant. Each panicle carries from 60 to 150 kernels.

A typical rice kernel is $\frac{1}{4}$ to $\frac{3}{8}$ inch (6 to 10 millimeters) long. The kernel has a hard covering called a *hull* that is not good to eat. Underneath the hull are the *bran layers,* the *endosperm,* and the *embryo.* Several bran layers provide a tough coat for the kernel. They contain many of the kernel's nutrients. The starchy endosperm makes up most of the kernel. It is the part of the kernel most often eaten. The tiny embryo is the part of the kernel from which a new plant grows.

Growth and reproduction. A new rice plant develops from the embryo inside the seed. The seed begins to sprout a few days after it is exposed to warm temperatures and plentiful moisture. The first *tiller* (shoot) appears 5 to 10 days after planting. Some rice plants may send out as many as 50 tillers, but most grow far fewer. More leaves appear as the tillers grow taller. The panicle grows from the top of the tiller. Older varieties of rice grow from 48 to 72 inches (120 to 180 centimeters) tall. But some newer varieties stand from 31 to 39 inches (80 to 100 centimeters) high.

Rice plants begin to develop flowering parts 6 to 10 weeks after planting. The panicle forms inside the *sheath*—a tubelike, leafy covering that surrounds the stem. After about 4 weeks, the panicle emerges from the sheath and bears flowers. Pollination must occur for grains of rice to develop. Rice can pollinate itself because each flower has both male and female reproductive parts (see **Pollen**). The flowers give rise to mature grains of rice 4 to 6 weeks after pollination.

Uses of rice

Food. Nearly all the rice produced in the world provides food for people. Rice supplies about half the calories in the daily diet of many people in Asia. It is an excellent source of *carbohydrates*—nourishing substances that provide the body with energy. Although low in protein, rice becomes an important source of protein if eaten in large amounts. Rice also has small amounts of the B vitamins—niacin, riboflavin, and thiamine—and the minerals iron, phosphorus, potassium, and sodium. Rice has very little fat and is easy to digest.

Most rice is eaten as *milled white rice*—rice that has had both its hull and bran layers removed during milling. *Brown rice* has had its hull removed but not its bran layers. Brown rice is more nutritious than white rice because the bran layers contain most of the kernel's vitamins and minerals. However, most people prefer white rice because it is less chewy than brown rice and takes about half as long to cook.

White rice may be treated in various ways to make it more nutritious. For example, much white rice is *enriched* with vitamins and minerals to replace the nutrients lost in removing the bran. In areas where rice is the main food, enrichment helps prevent *beriberi,* a disease caused by lack of thiamine (see **Beriberi**).

Rice may also be steamed under pressure with the

hulls on before milling. This process, called *parboiling,* makes the kernels less likely to break during milling. In addition, parboiled rice keeps many of the vitamins and minerals usually lost during milling because these nutrients spread throughout the grain during parboiling. *Quick-cooking rice* is partially cooked after milling. The kernels become more absorbent in the process and need less time for final cooking.

Other uses. Rice appears in many processed foods, including certain breakfast cereals, soup, baby food, snack foods, frozen foods, and flour. Breweries use broken rice kernels to make *mash,* an important ingredient in beer (see **Brewing** [Mashing]). In Japan, rice kernels are used to make an alcoholic drink called *sake,* or rice wine.

Farmers may use rice hulls for fertilizer and add bran layers to livestock feed. In industry, hulls are sometimes used as an ingredient in such products as insulation, cement, and the liquid chemical *furfural* (see **Furfural**). A few producers extract cooking oil from the bran. Many people in Asia use the *straw* (dried stalks) from rice plants to thatch roofs and weave sandals, hats, and baskets.

Kinds of rice

Scientists have identified 20 species of rice. But only two species are cultivated today—Asian rice and African rice. Nearly all cultivated rice is Asian rice. A small amount of African rice is grown, mostly in west Africa.

Cross section of a grain of rice

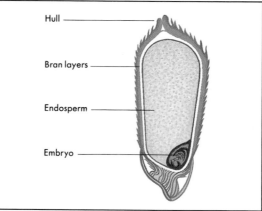

WORLD BOOK diagram by James Teason

Food value of white rice

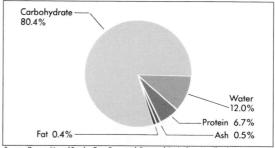

Source: *Composition of Foods—Raw, Processed, Prepared,* Agriculture Handbook No. 8, Agricultural Research Service, U.S. Department of Agriculture. Data are for uncooked white rice.

Leading rice-growing countries

Tons of rice produced in a year

China
●●●●●●●●●●●●●●●●●
222,050,000 tons (201,440,000 metric tons)

India
●●●●●●●●●●(
138,903,000 tons (126,011,000 metric tons)

Indonesia
●●●(
54,141,000 tons (49,116,000 metric tons)

Bangladesh
●●(
31,722,000 tons (28,778,000 metric tons)

Vietnam
●●
31,152,000 tons (28,261,000 metric tons)

Thailand
●(
25,385,000 tons (23,029,000 metric tons)

Myanmar
●(
19,170,000 tons (17,391,000 metric tons)

Japan
(
12,872,000 tons (11,677,000 metric tons)

Philippines
(
12,017,000 tons (10,902,000 metric tons)

Brazil
(
10,433,000 tons (9,465,000 metric tons)

Figures are for a three-year average, 1997-1999.
Source: Food and Agriculture Organization of the United Nations.

Leading rice-growing states

Tons of rice produced in a year

Arkansas
●●●●●●●●●●●●●●●●
3,993,000 tons (3,622,000 metric tons)

California
●●●●●●●(
1,878,000 tons (1,704,000 metric tons)

Louisiana
●●●●●(
1,351,000 tons (1,226,000 metric tons)

Texas
●●●
809,000 tons (734,000 metric tons)

Mississippi
●●(
703,000 tons (638,000 metric tons)

Figures are for a three-year average, 1996-1998.
Source: U.S. Department of Agriculture.

Asian rice can be divided into three main groups: Indica, Japonica, and Javanica. Indica rice is grown in India and other tropical regions. Japonica rice is cultivated in the cooler areas of Asia, including China, Japan, and Korea. It is also grown in Europe, North America, and Australia. Javanica rice is grown in Indonesia. Within these three groups, agricultural researchers have identified more than 70,000 varieties, but only a few hundred varieties are grown.

For marketing purposes, growers classify rice into three types by the length of its grain. Short grain rice is less than $\frac{1}{5}$ inch (5 millimeters) long. Medium grain rice ranges in length from $\frac{1}{5}$ to $\frac{1}{4}$ inch (5 to 6 millimeters); and long grain rice, from $\frac{1}{4}$ to $\frac{5}{16}$ inch (6 to 8 millimeters). Long grain rice contains a large amount of *amylose,* a starch that makes the rice dry and fluffy when cooked. Both short and medium grain rice have less amylose and so become moist and sticky when cooked. Most tropical varieties have long grains. Most varieties grown in milder climates have short or medium grains.

Rice also may be classified by how it is cultivated. *Lowland rice* is grown in flat fields that are flooded by irrigation. Banks of earth enclose the land into fields called *paddies.* About a third of the world's rice, including all rice grown in the United States, is lowland rice. *Upland rice* grows in areas too hilly for flooding. Such rice depends on rainfall for moisture. Upland rice accounts for about a sixth of the total rice production. The remaining half, called *rainfed paddy* rice, combines features of lowland and upland cultivation. It grows in paddies watered by rainfall rather than irrigation.

Researchers produce *hybrids* by crossing (mating) different varieties. Hybrids have improved yields. Some farmers in China grow hybrid rice. But few other farmers cultivate hybrids because they need too much work.

Where rice is grown

Farmers grow rice in more than 100 countries. In all, they plant about 360 million acres (145 million hectares) of rice each year and harvest about 640 million tons (580 million metric tons). Rice grows best in areas with warm temperatures and with plentiful moisture from rainfall or irrigation. Such favorable growing conditions occur mainly in many tropical regions and the valleys and deltas of certain rivers. These rivers include the Yangtze in China, the Ganges in India, and the Mekong in Vietnam.

Asian farmers grow about 90 percent of the world's

WORLD BOOK map

Rice-producing areas of the world

China and India produce more than half of the world's rice. Other major rice-producing countries include Bangladesh, Indonesia, Japan, Myanmar, Thailand, and Vietnam.

Major rice-producing area

Other rice-producing area

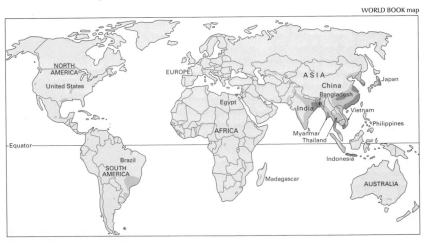

rice. China and India are the leading producers. Together, they grow more than 50 percent of the world's rice. Other top producers include Bangladesh, Indonesia, Japan, Myanmar, Thailand, and Vietnam.

The United States produces about 1 percent of the world's rice. The country's chief rice-producing regions lie along the Mississippi River in Arkansas and Mississippi, the Sacramento River in California, and the Gulf of Mexico in Texas and Louisiana.

Nearly all rice is eaten in the country where it is grown. Only about 5 percent of the world's rice crop is traded internationally. A few countries regularly import rice. Other nations import rice if their crop fails.

The chief exporters of rice include India, Thailand, and the United States. The United States exports about half of its crop each year. California-grown rice is sent mainly to Asia. Rice from the Southern States is sent to Western Europe, the Middle East, and Africa.

How rice is grown

Methods of growing rice vary, depending on the labor supply and the level of *mechanization* (work done by machinery). In Southeast Asia and other developing areas, labor is plentiful, and most work is done by hand. Some farmers have oxen or water buffaloes for pulling plows. In the United States and other developed countries, farmers use machinery for most production stages.

Most rice grows in areas of the world with a yearly rainfall of at least 40 inches (100 centimeters). But farmers can cultivate rice in drier regions by irrigating the land. Rice needs an average temperature of at least 70 °F (21 °C) throughout its growing season. It grows best in heavy, slightly acid soils that contain fine particles of clay. Such soils hold water well.

Growing rice involves four main steps: They are (1) preparing the ground, (2) planting, (3) controlling diseases and pests, and (4) harvesting.

Preparing the ground. Rice grows best in a field covered with shallow water. Farmers build low dirt walls called *dikes* or *levees* to hold water in the paddies. Many Asian farmers flood their fields before leveling them. They work the soil into a soft mud to make it easi-

© V. Rastelli, Woodfin Camp, Inc.

Planting rice seeds along dirt ridges may be done by hand, as shown here, or by machine. Many Asian farmers plant small seedbeds and later transplant the seedlings to a flooded field.

er to plow and to bury weeds. The practice of working flooded land is called *puddling*.

In the United States, most rice growers level the ground with large earth movers. They make sure the land slopes slightly so it can drain quickly before the harvest. Farmers use special machines to *till* (plow) the land and build dikes. Before planting, they may add mineral fertilizers to the soil to enrich it. Commonly applied fertilizers include nitrogen, phosphorus, and potassium.

Planting. In developing countries, farmers sometimes plant rice seeds directly in the ground. But more commonly they sow seeds thickly in small seedbeds and transplant the seedlings to a flooded field after several weeks. This method reduces the length of time rice occupies the main field by about 15 to 20 days. This is important in areas where several crops are grown on the same land each year. Transplanting seedlings also permits better weed control. Fewer weeds are able to grow in the thickly sown seedbeds. In addition, farmers

Leon V. Kofod   John Launois, Black Star   Norman Myers, Bruce Coleman Inc.

Most rice farming in Asia is done by hand. Seedlings are transplanted from beds into flooded fields, *left.* At harvest, farmers cut the rice stalks with knives or sickles and tie the stalks into bundles to dry, *center.* The dried stalks are then beaten against "screens" to separate the grain, *right.*

Grant Heilman

Rice growers in developed countries use crop-duster airplanes and other machines. This plane is spraying weedkillers.

can remove weeds more easily in the main rice fields when the plants are larger.

Farmers transplant clumps of 3 to 6 seedlings into the muddy soil. The clumps are spaced 4 to 8 inches (10 to 20 centimeters) apart and may be lined up in rows.

In industrialized nations, many rice growers use a machine called a *drill* to place the seeds directly in the soil. After planting if the soil's moisture is low, they may flood the field briefly and then drain it so that the seeds can sprout and grow. The field may be flooded and drained a few more times before the plants reach a height of 3 to 6 inches (8 to 15 centimeters). A layer of water 2 to 8 inches (5 to 20 centimeters) deep is then left in the field until a few weeks before harvest. Some rice growers scatter seeds onto a flooded field from a small, low-flying airplane. The seeds are allowed to sprout before they are sown to help speed their growth and to ensure that they sink in the water. Fertilizers also may be sprayed on the plants from an airplane.

Controlling diseases and pests is an important part of growing a good rice crop. Fungi, bacteria, and viruses infect rice plants with diseases. Weeds compete with rice plants for nutrients in the soil. Such destructive

insect pests as leaf hoppers and stem borers also attack rice. Farmers use chemicals to control many of these enemies. However, since many of these chemicals may be harmful to people and the environment, farmers must use care in applying them. Rice growers can best protect their crop from damage by planting varieties that can resist diseases and pests.

Harvesting. Farmers drain the rice fields two to three weeks before the harvest. The grain is ready for harvesting when moisture makes up 18 to 25 per cent of its weight. The wet rice must be dried after harvesting, before storage and milling.

In developing countries, farmers harvest the rice by hand. They usually cut the stalks with sickles or knives, tie the stalks in bundles, and dry them in the sun. The crop is then ready for *threshing,* the process of separating the grain from the rest of the plant. The farmers may thresh the grain by beating the panicles against a slatted bamboo screen and letting the grain fall between the slats. Some farmers put the bundles of rice through a gasoline-powered thresher. In some areas, farm animals walk over the bundles to thresh the grain. If the grain needs further drying after threshing, it is spread out on mats in the sun.

In industrialized countries, large self-powered machines called *combines* harvest and thresh rice in one operation. The wet grain is then dried by heated air.

How rice is processed

Harvested rice, still in its hull, is called *rough rice* or *paddy rice.* Most rough rice is processed in mills and sold as milled white rice. Millers use machines for most of the work, even in developing countries. There are three basic steps in processing harvested rice: (1) cleaning and hulling, (2) removing the bran layers, and (3) grading.

Cleaning and hulling. Cleaning removes dirt, straw, weeds, and other impurities from the rough rice. The cleaning equipment uses screens to sift out unwanted materials and fans to blow away lightweight debris.

After cleaning, the rice is placed in a machine called a *sheller* for hulling. In the sheller, the grains pass be-

Grant Heilman

Powerful machines called *combines, left,* are used to harvest rice in the United States and other developed countries. Combines also thresh the grain as they harvest it.

Charles Moore, Black Star

Hulling rice separates the shell-like hulls from the grain. The machine shown above loosens the rice hulls but does not remove the bran coats from the kernels.

tween rubber rollers or stone disks that loosen the hulls without breaking the kernels. The hulls are separated from the grain by suction. A screen then separates the hulled grain from any remaining unhulled rice. Some hulled rice may be packaged as brown rice. But most of it is processed into white rice. Rice may be treated by parboiling or other methods to improve its food value.

Removing the bran layers. After hulling, the brown rice passes through a series of machines that rub off its bran layers and embryo. The remaining endosperm becomes the white rice we eat. In many Asian countries, a single machine called a *huller mill* strips off both the hull and most of the bran. After milling, the kernels are packaged for sale. Most of the bran removed during milling is used in livestock feed.

Grading. Millers sort the processed rice into different grades for marketing. In the United States, the Department of Agriculture sets standards for grading rice. It bases these grades on such qualities as the size of the kernels, the moisture content of the kernels, and the number of chalky or damaged kernels. These grades range from U.S. No. 1, for the highest quality rice, to U.S. No. 6, which is a lower quality rice. U.S. Sample is the lowest grade of rice.

History

No one knows exactly when or where rice originated. But it probably first grew wild and was gathered and eaten by people in Southeast Asia thousands of years ago. Archaeologists have found evidence that people cultivated rice for food by about 5000 B.C. in southern China and the northern part of Thailand, Laos, and Vietnam. From there, rice spread northward in China and to Japan and Korea; westward to India; and southward to Indonesia.

Traders and explorers carried rice from Asia to other parts of the world. Rice cultivation had spread to Persia (now Iran) and Syria by 300 B.C. Europeans first learned of rice from Greek soldiers who accompanied Alexander the Great's military expedition to India in the 320's B.C. But rice was not cultivated in Europe until the Moors of northwestern Africa conquered Spain about A.D. 700 and brought rice with them. Rice was brought from Spain to Italy several hundred years later and afterward spread to southeastern Europe. Spanish explorers

introduced rice to the West Indies and South America on voyages during the 1400's, 1500's, and 1600's.

Rice reached the American Colonies during the 1600's. Colonists first grew it commercially in South Carolina about 1685. Rice soon thrived in the Carolinas and Georgia. After the Civil War (1861-1865), rice production shifted westward. By 1900, farmers in Louisiana were growing about 70 per cent of the rice in the United States. Rice became established as a crop in California in the early 1900's.

In 1960, government agencies and private foundations set up the International Rice Research Institute in the Philippines. The institute worked to improve rice production as part of a worldwide effort to increase food production in developing countries. This successful effort was an important part of what became known as the Green Revolution. In the 1960's, researchers at the institute developed new varieties of rice that produce more grain than older varieties, especially when fertilized. Traditional rice plants often grow so tall that they fall over and destroy their panicles. The new high-yield varieties have shorter, sturdier stalks and are less likely to topple. Since the 1960's, scientists have worked to develop varieties that can better resist diseases and insects and can grow without irrigation.

Today, farmers in some developing countries increasingly use machines for plowing and other work once done by hand. Computers help some farmers plan production and control irrigation, especially in developed countries.

Scientific classification. Rice belongs to the grass family, Gramineae. Asian rice is *Oryza sativa,* and African rice is *O. glaberrima.*   J. Neil Rutger

See also **Agriculture** (picture: Intensive agriculture); **Grain weevil; Wild rice.**

Outline

I. **The rice plant**
  A. Structure   B. Growth and reproduction
II. **Uses of rice**
  A. Food   B. Other uses
III. **Kinds of rice**
IV. **Where rice is grown**
V. **How rice is grown**
  A. Preparing the ground
  B. Planting
  C. Controlling diseases and pests
  D. Harvesting
VI. **How rice is processed**
  A. Cleaning and hulling
  B. Removing the bran layers
  C. Grading
VII. **History**

Questions

Which two countries produce the most rice?
Why is brown rice more nutritious than white rice?
What are the chief rice-growing areas in the United States?
What are the four main parts of a rice plant?
How can farmers best protect rice crops from diseases and insects?
How do rice planting methods in developing countries differ from those in developed countries?
Why do rice farmers usually flood their fields?
What are some advantages of new varieties of rice?
Which part of a rice kernel is most often eaten?
How does the cultivation of lowland rice differ from that of upland rice?

Additional resources

Bray, Francesca. *The Rice Economies: Technology and Development in Asian Societies.* 1986. Reprint. Univ. of Calif. Pr., 1994.
Owen, Sri. *The Rice Book: The Definitive Book on the Magic of Rice, with Hundreds of Exotic Recipes from Around the World.* St. Martin's, 1994.

Rice, Elmer (1892-1967), was an American dramatist who championed moral, social, and personal freedom. His many plays reflect his belief that it is better to love than to hate, to question than to accept, to be free than to be bound.

Rice is best known for two plays. *The Adding Machine* (1923) is an expressionistic satire on the growing mechanization of humanity. Rice used distorted settings and nonrealistic acting to show the tortured mind of the chief character, Mr. Zero. *Street Scene* (1929), a Pulitzer Prize winner, gives a naturalistic picture of life in a crowded big-city apartment house. Rice's other plays include *Counsellor-at-Law* (1931); *We, the People* (1933); and *Dream Girl* (1945). Rice also wrote novels and an autobiography, *Minority Report* (1963).

Rice was born Elmer Leopold Reizenstein in New York City. He studied law, but became a playwright after his *On Trial* (1914) became a hit.   Mardi Valgemae

See also **Expressionism** (Expressionist drama).

Rice, Grantland (1880-1954), was the first United States newspaperman to gain fame by writing about sports. He wrote about Bobby Jones, Jack Dempsey, Bill Tilden, Helen Wills, and other sports champions during the 1920's. His autobiography, *The Tumult and the Shouting,* was published in 1954. Grantland Rice was born in Murfreesboro, Tennessee.   Pat Harmon

Rice, Henry Mower (1817-1894), was a frontier Indian trader, an Indian commissioner, and one of the first United States senators from Minnesota. He was born in Waitsfield, Vermont. In 1839, he moved to Minnesota as an Indian trader, and became a partner in various frontier trading firms. His knowledge of Indians led to his appointment as commissioner to make treaties with them. Through his treaties, the Chippewa tribes gave up most of the state of Minnesota. Rice was a U.S. senator from 1858 to 1863. He represents Minnesota in Statuary Hall in Washington, D.C.   Jerome O. Steffen

Rice, Jerry (1962-   ), ranks among the greatest pass receivers in football history. Rice combines speed, strength, the ability to get open for passes, and skill at making difficult catches. Rice holds the National Football League (NFL) record for touchdowns scored. He also holds the NFL records for career passes caught, yards gained by a pass receiver, and most consecutive games catching at least one pass.

Jerry Lee Rice was born in Starkville, Mississippi. He played at Mississippi Valley State University, setting 18 college records. In 1985, the San Francisco 49ers of the NFL drafted Rice. In the 1987-1988 season, he scored a record 22 touchdowns on pass receptions and led the league in scoring. He was awarded the Jim Thorpe Trophy as the NFL's Most Valuable Player that season.

Rice helped the 49ers win Super Bowls in 1989, 1990, and 1995 while setting game records for receiving yardage and touchdowns.   Bob Carroll

Rice weevil. See **Grain weevil.**

Rich, Adrienne (1929-   ), is one of the leading American poets of her generation as well as a major voice in the women's movement. Rich has attacked what she sees as the male-dominated structure of society. Rich holds this system responsible for the oppression of women. She advocates replacing the male-dominated structure with a set of values derived from the experiences and insights of women.

Rich anchors her larger political concerns in individual lives, her own and those of other women. Her poetry is attentive to particular situations and concrete circumstances. At the same time, she shows how those circumstances participate in broader historical patterns. Rich's poetry reflects her willingness to admit and wrestle with contradictions—for example, her awareness that anger can be both destructive and creative. Such contradictions often give her poems a charged, dramatic quality, as though the poet were struggling to make up her mind before our eyes.

Rich was born in Baltimore. Her poems have been published in many collections, including *Collected Early Poems: 1950-1970* (1993), *The Will to Change* (1971), *The Fact of a Doorframe* (1984), and *An Atlas of the Difficult World* (1991). She has also written *What Is Found There* (1993) and other books of prose.   Roger Gilbert

Richard I (1157-1199) was king of England from 1189 to 1199. He is known in history as Richard the Lion-Hearted, or Richard Coeur de Lion. He was a son of Henry II, the first king of the Plantagenet dynasty, and Eleanor of Aquitaine. After becoming king, he joined Philip II of France in a crusade to the Holy Land, which was under Muslim control. Richard captured Acre (now called Akko) but saw that Jerusalem could not be recovered.

During the crusade, Richard aroused the hatred of Leopold V, Duke of Austria. In 1192, while Richard was on his journey home, Leopold seized him. Leopold kept Richard in a castle as a prisoner of the Holy Roman emperor, Henry VI. Richard was later taken to Henry, who released him in 1194 after a ransom was paid.

As a Plantagenet, Richard had inherited not only England but also most of northern and western France. While Richard was in prison, Philip II seized some of the Plantagenet lands in France. Richard spent the rest of his reign fighting to get the lands back. He left efficient ministers in charge of England while he concentrated on the war with Philip. In 1199, Richard was killed during the siege of a castle, and his brother John became king.

Richard was born in Oxford, England, but spent nearly all of his life in France. In 1183, Richard's older brother died. However, their father, Henry II, refused to recognize Richard as the heir to the throne of England. Richard rebelled against his father several times. Richard finally defeated Henry II in 1189.

John Gillingham

See also **Flag** (picture: Historical flags of the world [English and French]); **Plantagenet.**

Richard II (1367-1400) was king of England from 1377 to 1399. He ascended the throne at the age of 10 when his grandfather King

Detail of an engraving (1743) by George Vertue; The Newberry Library, Chicago

Richard I

Edward III died.

During the first four years of Richard's reign, a council ruled England on his behalf, and Richard's uncle John of Gaunt exercised much influence. However, the council could not agree on a consistent governing policy. One result was Wat Tyler's Rebellion of 1381, which the young king courageously put down. For the next few years, Richard tried to increase his control over the government with the help

Detail of an illuminated manuscript (about 1389) by an unknown artist; St. John's College, Cambridge, England

Richard II

of favorite advisers. But many of his favorites were imprisoned or executed by the "Merciless Parliament" of 1388. In 1389, Richard began to rule on his own.

Richard ruled well in the early 1390's. But through his control of the "Revenge Parliament" of 1397, he began to punish many of his enemies. He became increasingly tyrannical and angered the English people with such measures as forced loans and loyalty oaths.

In 1399, Richard led an expedition to Ireland. While he was there, John of Gaunt's son Henry of Bolingbroke led a revolt against Richard in England. The revolt resulted in Richard's removal from the throne. Bolingbroke became King Henry IV. Richard died in early 1400. He was probably murdered.

Richard was born in Bordeaux, France. His father was Edward, the Black Prince, a famous English warrior. Richard supported the arts and the famous English writer Geoffrey Chaucer.   George B. Stow

See also **John of Gaunt; Wat Tyler's Rebellion.**

Richard III (1452-1485) was king of England from 1483 to 1485. Richard's reign brought on the revolt that ended the Wars of the Roses. These wars were fought between the two branches of the royal family—the House of Lancaster and the House of York. Richard belonged to the House of York.

Richard was born in Northamptonshire, England, a son of Richard, Duke of York. In 1461, young Richard's oldest brother became King Edward IV. Richard was made Duke of Gloucester the same year.

Years later, in 1483, Edward IV died, and his elder son became King Edward V at the age of 12. The government was put in the care of Richard, who was named protector of the realm. The Woodvilles, the family of the young king's mother, attempted to seize power. In crushing their conspiracy, Richard sought to become king himself. He was crowned early in July 1483, after Parliament had declared him king. Edward V and his younger brother Richard were put in the Tower of London. Some scholars believe that King Richard had the boys

National Portrait Gallery

Richard III

killed. But no proof of such a crime exists.

Richard tried to govern well, but he lacked widespread support. Powerful Yorkist and Lancastrian nobles plotted against him. With their help, Henry Tudor, Earl of Richmond, a kinsman of the House of Lancaster, invaded England from his exile in France. His forces won the Battle of Bosworth Field in 1485, killing Richard. Henry Tudor became king as Henry VII.   Ralph A. Griffiths

See also **Wars of the Roses.**

Richard, *REE shahrd,* **Maurice** (1921-2000), ranks among the leading goal scorers in National Hockey League (NHL) history. During his career, Richard scored 544 goals and 421 assists for a total of 965 points in 978 regular-season games. Richard's explosive skating speed and high-powered offensive skills earned him the nickname "Rocket."

Richard played right wing for the Montreal Canadiens from the 1942-1943 season through the 1959-1960 season, helping the Canadiens win eight Stanley Cup championships. In the 1944-1945 season, Richard became the first player in NHL history to score 50 goals in one season. He won the Hart Trophy (now the Hart Memorial Trophy) in 1947 as the NHL's most valuable player. He was inducted into the Hockey Hall of Fame in 1961. Richard was born in Montreal.   Larry Wigge

Richard the Lion-Hearted. See Richard I.

Richards, I. A. (1893-1979), was an influential English literary critic and poet. His criticism was mainly concerned with the differences between ordinary language and poetry. Richards argued that ordinary language is made up of statements that relate to and can be tested against matters of fact. Poetry, by contrast, consists of statements that cannot be verified, but which arouse or quiet our feelings. He discussed his theories in *Principles of Literary Criticism* (1924).

Richards became one of the founders of the New Criticism, a critical movement of the mid-1900's that shifted the direction of literary criticism from historical scholarship to interpretation (see **Criticism**). He became interested in the close reading of a text partly through his studies in psychology and semantics. His ideas on this subject appear in *The Meaning of Meaning* (1923), co-written with English scholar Charles Kay Ogden; and in *Practical Criticism* (1929).

Ivor Armstrong Richards was born in Sandbach, near Crewe. He was also a distinguished poet. A selection of his poems and two verse plays were collected in *Internal Colloquies* (1971).   David H. Richter

See also **Semantics.**

Richards, Laura Elizabeth Howe (1850-1943), an American author, wrote books for adults and nonsense verse and stories for children. She won the Pulitzer Prize in 1917 for *Julia Ward Howe,* a biography of her mother. She also wrote an autobiography, *Stepping Westward* (1931). Richards had a genius for writing nonsense verses, collected under such titles as *Tirra Lirra* (1932) and *The Hottentot and Other Ditties* (1939). She was born in Boston, Massachusetts.   Virginia L. Wolf

Richards, Sir William Buell, *BOO uhl* (1815-1889), a Canadian lawyer and statesman, served as the first chief justice of the Supreme Court of Canada from 1875 to 1879. His judicial career began in 1853 when he was appointed to the Court of Common Pleas. He rose to become chief justice of this court in 1873, and then was called to head the newly established Supreme Court. He also served as attorney general of Canada, holding that office from 1851 to 1853. Richards was born in Brockville, Ontario.   J. E. Hodgetts

Richardson, Bill (1947-   ), was United States secretary of energy from 1998 to 2001, under President Bill Clinton. From January 1997 until he became energy secretary, he was United States ambassador to the United Nations. He was the first Hispanic American to hold that post. Richardson, a New Mexico Democrat, had served in the U.S. House of Representatives from 1983 to 1997. After Clinton became president in 1993, he sent Congressman Richardson on several diplomatic missions. Richardson's diplomatic achievements included negotiating the release of Americans held hostage in North Korea, Iraq, and Sudan.

Richardson was born in Pasadena, California. His full name is William Blaine Richardson. His mother was Mexican, and his father was a non-Hispanic banker from Boston who worked in Mexico. The family lived in Mexico City from the time Bill was 1 until he was 13. They moved to Concord, Massachusetts, in 1961. Richardson earned a B.A. degree from Tufts University in 1970 and an M.A. from the Fletcher School of Law and Diplomacy at Tufts in 1971. He moved to New Mexico in 1978 and was elected to Congress there in 1982.   Jackie Koszczuk

Richardson, Elliot Lee (1920-1999), held four Cabinet offices, more than any other person in United States history. Richardson, a Republican, served as secretary of health, education, and welfare from 1970 until January 1973, when he became secretary of defense. From May to October 1973, he was attorney general. He served as secretary of commerce in 1976 and 1977.

Richardson resigned as attorney general in protest against President Richard M. Nixon's order to fire Archibald Cox. Cox was the chief prosecutor in the investigation of the Watergate scandal (see **Watergate**). Richardson had appointed Cox to head the investigation and had promised that Cox would have complete independence in the case. But in October, a dispute over the investigation arose between Nixon and Cox. President Nixon ordered Richardson to dismiss Cox. But Richardson refused to do so and resigned as attorney general. Richardson served as U.S. ambassador to the United Kingdom from March 1975 to January 1976 and as ambassador at large from 1977 to 1980.

Richardson was born in Boston. He graduated from Harvard Law School in 1947. From 1959 to 1961, he served as U.S. attorney in Massachusetts. He was lieutenant governor of Massachusetts from 1964 to 1967 and Massachusetts attorney general from 1967 to 1969. In 1969, Richardson became undersecretary of state in the Nixon administration.   Clark R. Mollenhoff

Richardson, Henry Hobson (1838-1886), was the first American architect to achieve international fame. He introduced the Romanesque Revival style to the United States and dominated American architectural practice during the 1870's and 1880's.

In his buildings, Richardson united a highly developed sense of craftsmanship with the subdued grandeur of the Romanesque style. He used stone and wood for public buildings, and wood and wood shingles for many of his houses. His work, notably the Marshall Field Wholesale Store (1887) in Chicago, profound-

© Odyssey Productions

Richardson's Glessner House shows the influence of Romanesque architecture in its massiveness and rough stone surface.

ly influenced Louis H. Sullivan and other architects. *Richardsonian Romanesque* is a term used loosely to describe buildings in stone or shingle with large round-arched openings. See **Architecture** (Early modern architecture in America; Romanesque architecture).

Richardson was born on a plantation near New Orleans. He was educated at Harvard University and in Paris and settled in Brookline, Massachusetts, in 1874. His first major work, the Trinity Church (1877) in Boston, contained the basic elements of Richardson's style. It was built of monumental cut stone with an asymmetrical plan and French Romanesque forms. Richardson designed several public libraries in the Boston area as well as buildings for the Harvard campus. His other commissions include the Glessner House (1887) in Chicago and the Allegheny County Courthouse and Jail (1888) in Pittsburgh, Pennsylvania.   Nicholas Adams

Richardson, Samuel (1689-1761), an English writer, is considered one of the founding fathers of the novel. He wrote three novels: *Pamela; or, Virtue Rewarded* (1740), *Clarissa; or, The History of a Young Lady* (1748), and *Sir Charles Grandison* (1754). These works are too long to be much read today, but their influence on literature has been enormous. Richardson's books brought various important, and in some ways new, elements to the novel. Each of his novels has a genuinely unified plot rather than disconnected episodes. The characters maintain a consistent point of view, without interference by the author. The works established the theme of courtship leading to marriage as a basic plot of the novel.

All three novels are written in the form of letters. Indeed, the idea for the form of *Pamela* originated from a manual of model letters written by Richardson. *Pamela* was published anonymously and was a sensational success. All the novels have a breathless quality that sweeps the reader along from letter to letter.

It is easy to mock the somewhat dubious, often priggish morality of these novels. Indeed, *Pamela* inspired witty parodies by writers of his time. Still, Richardson set the novel firmly in what became its main direction: a detailed description of real people in common situations of domestic life. In particular, Richardson's novels treat women's concern for security, marriage, and a proper social role. This reflects how, with the rise of the new middle class, women with conscious individual identities and problems were coming to the forefront. This tendency has grown since Richardson's time, and in him, as in many later novelists, women have found a sympathetic and sensitive voice.

Richardson was born in Derbyshire. He started his own printing business in 1719 and later became one of London's most successful publishers.   Ian Watt

Richelieu, *RIHSH uh LOO* or *REE sheh LYU,* **Cardinal** (1585-1642), served as prime minister of France from 1624 to 1642. He and King Louis XIII worked closely to govern the country. Richelieu strengthened the king's rule and helped make France the most powerful country in Europe.

Rise to power. Richelieu was born in Paris. His given and family name was Armand Jean du Plessis. He took the title of Richelieu from the name of his family's estate. In 1607, Richelieu became the Roman Catholic bishop of Luçon, near La Rochelle in western France. In 1614, he was elected to France's Estates-General, a legislative body consisting of representatives of three *estates* (groups)—the clergy, the nobility, and the common people. Richelieu was chosen as spokesman for the clergy. In 1616, he became a member of Louis XIII's royal council. But this appointment lasted only a short time.

Pope Gregory XV named Richelieu a cardinal in 1622. In 1624, Richelieu regained his post on the royal council and soon headed the council. As the council's head, he became known as *prime minister.* In the council, Richelieu demonstrated a deep understanding of politics and great skill at helping to put the king's policies into effect. Soon, Richelieu became the dominant power in the French government.

Strengthening the monarchy. When Richelieu rose to power, Louis XIII had not yet firmly established his own authority in France. The Huguenots, a Protestant group, exercised much political and religious power even though most of France was Roman Catholic. The independence of the nobility and unreliability among government officials also threatened the monarchy's rule. Richelieu wanted to ensure that the king's will would be obeyed.

In 1627, Richelieu directed a siege of the French city of La Rochelle, where the Huguenots maintained self-rule. After 14 months of fighting, La Rochelle surrendered in October 1628. The royal forces then attacked other cities controlled by the Huguenots. In 1629, the Huguenots and the French government signed the Peace of Alais. This treaty eliminated the Huguenots' right to maintain military forces in the cities they governed, a right granted by the Edict of Nantes in 1598. As a result, the Huguenots could no longer wage civil war or act as a state within the state.

To control the nobles, Richelieu severely punished people who plotted against the king. Richelieu ordered the destruction of all fortresses controlled by the nobility, except those protecting the French borders. Many nobles who rebelled were executed or exiled.

By 1631, Richelieu had replaced his enemies in the government with officials he could trust. Marie de Médicis, the king's mother, was forced into exile for plotting against Richelieu. In addition, Richelieu expanded the king's control over local governments by sending royal agents called *intendants* into the provinces.

Thirty Years' War. During Richelieu's service as prime minister, Europe fought a series of religious and political wars called the Thirty Years' War (1618-1648).

Members of the Habsburg (or Hapsburg) royal family ruled Spain and the Holy Roman Empire. Lands controlled by Spain included what are now Belgium and parts of Italy. The Holy Roman Empire included what are now Austria, the Czech Republic, Germany, the Netherlands, Switzerland, and part of Italy. To stop the growth of Habsburg power, Richelieu supported others fighting the Habsburgs. For example, he gave Sweden funds to continue fighting. But the Habsburgs grew stronger.

In 1635, France declared war on Spain. At first, the war went poorly for France. Spanish armies quickly penetrated French borders, and tax revolts and uprisings by French nobles distracted Richelieu. France regained its position against Spain in later years and eventually won the war. But Richelieu died before the war ended.

Historical reputation. Many historians have admired Richelieu for his extraordinary intelligence and energy. He promoted the growth of royal authority and helped France become Europe's leading power. Richelieu's work also led to the building of a French navy and expansion of French ports. He helped establish French colonies in Africa, Canada, and the West Indies. However, Richelieu concentrated on France's foreign affairs and, as a result, failed to resolve many domestic problems and even aggravated some of them.

Richelieu took great interest in the arts and made lasting investments in them. He rebuilt the Sorbonne, the theological college of the University of Paris. He also supported promising writers and founded the French Academy, an organization of France's leading writers and other thinkers.   Donald A. Bailey

Related articles in *World Book* include:

French Academy	La Rochelle	Sorbonne
Huguenots	Louis XIII	Thirty Years' War

Richler, *RIHCH luhr,* **Mordecai,** *MAWR duh ky* (1931-   ), is a Canadian novelist. As a boy, Richler lived in a poor Jewish district of Montreal, where he was born. His experiences there provided the background for *Son of a Smaller Hero* (1955) and *The Apprenticeship of Duddy Kravitz* (1959).

From 1954 to 1972, Richler lived mainly in England. In *Cocksure* (1968) and *St. Urbain's Horseman* (1971), he wrote about Canadians living in Europe. These novels and *Joshua Then and Now* (1980) are character studies that satirize sophisticated, urban society. *Solomon Gursky Was Here* (1989) is a comic satire about four generations of a family. Richler has also written short stories, motion-picture and television scripts, and children's books about a boy called Jacob Two-Two. The best of his essays and articles were published as *Notes on an Endangered Species and Others* (1974) and *Broadsides* (1990). He described his impressions of Canada in *Home Sweet Home* (1984) and *Oh Canada! Oh Quebec: Requiem for a Divided Country* (1992). Richler reported on a trip he made to Israel in 1992 in *This Year in Jerusalem* (1994).   Laurie R. Ricou

Richmond. See Staten Island.

Metropolitan Richmond Chamber of Commerce

Monuments to Confederate leaders line Monument Avenue in Richmond. The men honored include Major General Jeb Stuart, *foreground,* and General Robert E. Lee, *center.*

Richmond, Virginia (pop. 203,056; met. area pop. 865,640), is the state capital and a major commercial, cultural, educational, and historical center. It also ranks as one of Virginia's largest cities. Richmond is a leading producer of cigarettes and other tobacco products. It was the capital of the Confederate States of America during most of the Civil War (1861-1865).

Richmond lies on the James River, in east-central Virginia (see **Virginia** [political map]). In the mid-1600's, English colonists chose the site because of its natural advantages for trade and transportation. Richmond was named for a suburb of London, England.

The city. Richmond covers 63 square miles (163 square kilometers) on both sides of the James River. About 55 percent of the city's people are African Americans. The Richmond metropolitan area covers 3,029 square miles (7,845 square kilometers).

A government area in downtown Richmond includes the city hall and a federal office building. The State Capitol stands in Capitol Square. Thomas Jefferson, before he became president, designed the building. Jefferson modeled it after a Roman temple in Nîmes, France. The capitol has influenced the architecture of many public buildings in the United States.

A famous marble statue of George Washington stands beneath the dome of the Capitol. The statue was completed in 1791 by the French sculptor Jean Antoine Houdon. Busts of seven other presidents who were born in Virginia are displayed in the encircling wall. The presidents are William Henry Harrison, Jefferson, James Madison, James Monroe, Zachary Taylor, John Tyler, and Woodrow Wilson. See **Virginia** (picture: The State Capitol).

A bronze statue of Washington on horseback stands in Capitol Square. Six bronze figures of important Virginia statesmen flank its stone base. Statues of Jefferson

Davis, Stonewall Jackson, Robert E. Lee, Jeb Stuart, and other Confederate leaders stand along Richmond's Monument Avenue. In 1996, a statue of tennis star Arthur Ashe, who was born in Richmond, was added to Monument Avenue.

Educational and cultural life. Richmond's public school system includes nine high schools and about 50 elementary and middle schools. These schools have a total of about 27,000 students. The Richmond area has more than 30 private and parochial schools. Richmond is the home of the University of Richmond, Virginia Commonwealth University, and Virginia Union University. Virginia Commonwealth University includes the Medical College of Virginia. Also in the city is Union Theological Seminary and Presbyterian School of Christian Education.

The Virginia Museum of Fine Arts owns a valuable collection of paintings, and Russian imperial jewels and jeweled Easter eggs designed by the Russian jeweler Peter Carl Fabergé. The Science Museum of Virginia has science education exhibits and a planetarium theater. The Valentine Museum features exhibits that illustrate the history of Richmond. Battle Abbey, headquarters of the Virginia Historical Society, displays Confederate military equipment and a series of murals of Confederate scenes. The Virginia State Library and Archives houses materials on early Virginia history.

The Richmond Symphony Orchestra performs in the Carpenter Center for the Performing Arts. Many athletic events and musical concerts take place in the Richmond Coliseum.

Other interesting places to visit include:

St. John's Church, built in 1741. It is one of the oldest wooden buildings in the state. There, in 1775, the Virginia orator and statesman Patrick Henry delivered his famous speech that, according to tradition, ended with the words, "Give me liberty or give me death!"

Museum of the Confederacy houses a large collection of Confederate items. Exhibits include General Robert E. Lee's sword, General Stonewall Jackson's sword and cap, and the original Great Seal and provisional Constitution of the Confederacy. Next to the museum is the White House of the Confederacy, the home in which Jefferson Davis lived as president of the Confederate States of America.

John Marshall House, occupied by the fourth chief justice of the United States from about 1790 until his death in 1835.

Edgar Allan Poe Museum, a group of four buildings that form a shrine to the famous American author. Poe lived in Richmond as a child and later as editor of the *Southern Literary Messenger,* a magazine. One of the buildings, the Old Stone House, is believed to date from about 1737 and is probably Richmond's oldest house.

Hollywood Cemetery, the burial place of Confederate President Davis and United States Presidents James Monroe and John Tyler.

Economy. Many of Richmond's people are employed by the local, state, and federal governments. Manufacturing and banking, education, trade, and other service industries are also important to the economy. Richmond is the headquarters for about 30 companies. The metropolitan area is second only to Atlanta, Georgia, as a corporate headquarters in the Southeastern United States. The city's chief products include tobacco products, machinery for manufacturing and packaging tobacco products, chemicals, food products, and paper. Industrial research concerning tobacco and other products takes place in Richmond.

Airlines use nearby Richmond International Airport. Railroads provide freight service to Richmond, and passenger trains also serve the city. In addition, bus and truck lines connect Richmond with other cities. Ocean-going freighters use Richmond's port on the James River.

The *Richmond Times-Dispatch* ranks among the South's most influential newspapers. The Richmond area has 7 television stations and approximately 30 radio stations.

Government. Richmond has a council-manager government. Voters elect the nine members of the city council to two-year terms. The council members choose one of their group to serve as mayor and preside over council meetings. The council also appoints the city manager. The government of Richmond gets most of its revenue from real estate taxes and from state and federal sources.

History. Before white settlers arrived, Indian tribes of the Powhatan Confederacy lived in what is now the Richmond area. The city's history began in 1607, when Captain Christopher Newport led an exploring party of English settlers to the site of what became Richmond. Two early attempts to establish a settlement there failed. The construction of Fort Charles at the site in 1644 attracted new settlers, and their community grew into a trading post for furs, hides, and tobacco.

In 1742, when Richmond was established as a town, it had a population of 250. In 1780, Virginia moved its capital from Williamsburg to Richmond, which had a more central location. Richmond had only 684 people at that time. It was incorporated as a city in 1782.

In 1781, during the Revolutionary War in America, British troops led by Benedict Arnold raided Richmond. Arnold was an American general who turned traitor and joined the British. His soldiers looted Richmond and burned several important buildings.

After the war ended in 1783, Richmond entered a period of growth. Its population increased to 3,761 by 1790 and reached 5,737 by 1800. The city developed around the tobacco trade, the slave trade, and trade to the west over the James River Canal. With the coming of the railroads in the mid-1800's, Richmond grew rapidly as a commercial and industrial center. By 1860, it had a population of about 38,000. From the 1830's until the start of the Civil War in 1861, Richmond was one of the most important slave markets in the United States. Slave traders in the city bought and sold thousands of slaves each year.

In May 1861, a month after the outbreak of the Civil War, Richmond replaced Montgomery, Ala., as the capital of the Confederacy. The capture of Richmond became a prime goal of the Union forces, especially during the campaigns of 1862 and 1864. In April 1865, the Confederate government moved from Richmond to Danville, Va. Richmond's people burned part of their city so it would not fall undamaged to the Union. The task of rebuilding the city began immediately after the end of the Civil War.

During the early 1900's, the city attracted many industries. By 1950, it had a population of 230,310. In 1970, Richmond annexed 23 square miles (60 square kilometers) from neighboring Chesterfield County. A civil rights leader sued the city. He charged that the primarily white population of the annexed area would injure the rights of Richmond's black voters. A federal court approved the annexation in 1976. The city was divided into nine districts, each of which elects one member to the city council.

In 1977, blacks won races for five of the nine seats on the city council. The council then elected Richmond's first black mayor, Henry L. Marsh III.

Richmond completed several major construction projects during the late 1900's. They included the 6th Street Marketplace, a glass-enclosed pedestrian bridge and shopping mall built over the city's main street, and Richmond Centre, a convention center and exhibition hall.   Henry S. Chenault, Jr.

The Edgar Allan Poe Museum in Richmond, built about 1737, is said to be the city's oldest house. It holds many papers and relics of the famous poet, who once lived in Richmond.

The White House of the Confederacy in Richmond was the home of Jefferson Davis during the Civil War. A museum next door exhibits General Lee's sword and other Confederate relics.

Richmond, University of, is a private, liberal arts university in Richmond, Va. The university has two coordinate undergraduate colleges—Richmond College for men and Westhampton College for women. Students pursue their degrees in the schools of arts and sciences (which includes a graduate school), business, law, and leadership studies; and in the University College for evening, summer, and continuing education. Courses lead to bachelor's and master's degrees, and the J.D. degree in law. The University of Richmond was founded as Dunlora Academy in 1830. It was chartered as Richmond College in 1840 and received its present name in 1920.

Critically reviewed by the University of Richmond

Richmond Town is a historic area of Staten Island in New York City. The first settlement of Europeans in what is now Richmond Town dates from the 1690's. Richmond Town became the county seat of Richmond County in 1729. The county became one of the five boroughs of New York City in 1898, and the city took over the administration of the Richmond County government.

In 1939, the Staten Island Historical Society began a project called the Richmond Town Restoration. The project includes moving, rebuilding, and restoring 28 buildings constructed during the 1600's, 1700's, or 1800's. One building, the Voorlezer's House, was built about 1695 and is the oldest elementary school building in the United States. New York City and private individuals and organizations are financing the project. Brian J. Laline

Richter, *RIHK tuhr,* **Conrad** (1890-1968), was an American author known for his novels about pioneer life. His work celebrates such pioneer virtues as endurance, independence, and self-discipline. In addition, Richter wrote about the close relationship between individuals and nature. Richter's historical novels display his knowledge and appreciation of the traditional tales of the American West.

Richter wrote 14 novels, 3 books of essays, and 5 collections of essays. He is best known for *The Awakening Land,* a *trilogy* (three related novels) about a pioneer

family in Ohio. It consists of *The Trees* (1940), *The Fields* (1946), and *The Town* (1950). Richter won the 1951 Pultzer Prize for fiction for *The Town.* He also wrote three novels about Southwest pioneer life. They are *The Sea of Grass* (1937), his first novel; *Tacey Cromwell* (1942); and *The Lady* (1957). He won the National Book Award for fiction in 1961 for *The Waters of Kronos* (1960), an autobiographical novel. Richter's short stories were collected in *The Rawhide Knot and Other Stories* (1978).

Richter was born in Pine Grove, Pennsylvania. He lived in Albuquerque, New Mexico, from 1928 to 1950.

Samuel Chase Coale

Richter, *RIHK tuhr,* **Hans** (1843-1916), was a famous German orchestra conductor who helped popularize the operas of Richard Wagner. Richter was conductor of the Wagner Bayreuth Festival in Germany from 1876 to 1912. At Bayreuth in 1876, he conducted the first complete performance of Wagner's opera cycle *The Ring of the Nibelung.* Richter was a leading interpreter of German music, especially that of Wagner, Johannes Brahms, Ludwig van Beethoven, and Anton Bruckner. In addition, Richter was a supporter of the music of English composer Sir Edward Elgar and Czech composer Antonín Dvořák.

Richter was born in Györ, Hungary. He began conducting in Munich, Germany, in 1868. Richter conducted both the Vienna Philharmonic and the Vienna Opera from 1875 to 1898. He made his conducting debut in England in 1877. Richter conducted the London Symphony Orchestra from 1904 to 1911. He also conducted the Covent Garden Opera beginning in 1882. Richter led the Hallé Orchestra in Manchester from 1897 until 1911.

John H. Baron

Richter magnitude, *RIHK tuhr,* is a number that indicates the strength of an earthquake. It is based on data obtained by a *seismograph,* an instrument that records ground movements. Charles F. Richter, an American *seismologist* (scientist who studies earthquakes), developed the magnitude numbering system in 1935.

© Jim Anderson, Woodfin Camp, Inc.

WORLD BOOK photo by Bill Higgins

Richmond Town has been restored to its original appearance in early colonial times. Visitors can learn about daily colonial life through demonstrations and tours of authentic craft shops, *left.* The streets of Richmond Town, *right,* are lined with carefully preserved homes and other buildings.

The system is sometimes called the *Richter scale.*

Each number on the scale represents a tenfold increase in the *amplitude* of waves of ground motion recorded on a seismograph. The seismograph measures the back-and-forth movement of the ground beneath it. Amplitude is the distance this ground moves from its original position during the passage of a wave. Thus, each number represents ground motion 10 times greater than that represented by the next lower number. In an earthquake of magnitude 7, the ground moves 10 times as much as it moves in a quake of magnitude 6.

Calculations based on the Richter scale can show the amount of energy released by an earthquake. Each number represents a release of about 30 times the energy represented by the next lower number. Thus, an earthquake of magnitude 7 releases about 30 times the energy released by a quake of magnitude 6.

To measure the largest earthquakes, seismologists now use another system, the *moment magnitude scale.* Moment magnitude is based on data recorded by instruments that are more sensitive than those available in Richter's time. Moment magnitude and Richter magnitude are about the same for earthquakes up to magnitude 7. The highest recorded moment magnitude was 9.5, for an earthquake in the Pacific Ocean near Chile in 1960. The Richter magnitude of this quake was 8.5.

Over 1,000 earthquakes with a Richter magnitude of at least 2 occur daily. But few earthquakes of magnitude 5 or less cause serious damage. An earthquake of magnitude 7 or more can cause much damage and kill many people.   Sean C. Solomon

See also **Earthquake; Seismograph; Seismology.**

Rickenbacker, Eddie (1890-1973), was the leading United States air ace in World War I (1914-1918). He shot down 22 enemy planes and 4 balloons.

Rickenbacker was born Edward Rickenbacher in Columbus, Ohio. In 1918, he changed the spelling of his family name to *Rickenbacker.* Before World War I, he became a professional automobile racer and won an international reputation as a racing-car driver. Rickenbacker enlisted in the Army in 1917, after the United States had entered the war. He served as a staff driver and as an engineering officer before becoming a pilot.

After the war, Rickenbacker worked with several automobile firms and was co-owner of the Indianapolis Speedway from 1927 to 1945. He served as president of Eastern Airlines from 1938 to 1959 and chairman of its board of directors from 1954 to 1963.

During World War II (1939-1945), Rickenbacker was a civilian inspector of American air bases abroad. On an inspection trip in 1942, his plane was forced down in the Pacific Ocean. Rickenbacker and six others survived on rubber rafts for 24 days before being rescued. Rickenbacker wrote about his wartime experiences in *Fighting the Flying Circus* (1919) and *Seven Came Through: Rickenbacker's Full Story* (1943).   Christopher R. Gabel

Rickets is a bone disease that occurs mostly in children. It may be caused by a lack of calcium, phosphate, or vitamin D. Rickets also may be caused by the inability of the body to use those substances properly. In rickets, bones are so soft they bend into abnormal shapes and may develop bumps called *knobs.* Rickets results in conditions called rosary ribs, knobbed forehead, and funnel chest. As the child grows, bones harden, but the abnor-

mal shape usually remains. In severe rickets, bones may be so deformed a child's normal height is greatly reduced. Symptoms of rickets are sweating, weakness, pain in the bones, general body tenderness, and misshapen bones.

Eating foods rich in calcium and vitamin D usually prevents rickets. Milk and green vegetables are good sources of calcium. The best sources of vitamin D include vitamin-D enriched milk, sunlight, and fish oils.

Rickets in children usually can be stopped by supplying them with plenty of vitamin D and calcium. A disease similar to rickets occurs in adults and is called *osteomalacia.*

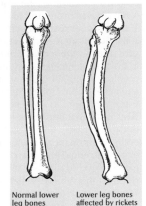

Normal lower leg bones

Lower leg bones affected by rickets

Madison B. Cole, Jr.

See also **Cod-liver oil; Vitamin (Vitamin D).**

Rickettsia, *rih KEHT see uh,* is any of a group of microorganisms that cause certain infectious diseases in human beings. Rickettsias were once classified as viruses, but they are now usually regarded as a special kind of bacteria. They differ from most bacteria in two major ways. They are smaller, and they cannot reproduce outside of living cells.

Rickettsias live primarily in the cells of certain insects and other arthropods, such as mites and ticks. A few species can infect human cells and cause such diseases as epidemic typhus, Rocky Mountain spotted fever, scrub typhus, and Q fever.

Epidemic typhus is spread among people by the bite of infected body lice. This disease occurs in the colder regions of the world, particularly those where people have poor sanitary facilities. The rickettsia that causes Rocky Mountain spotted fever lives in ticks and wild rodents and is spread to people by tick bites. This disease occurs most frequently in the Southeastern United States. Scrub typhus is common in southern and Southeast Asia, northern Australia, and Japan. Rodents and chigger mites carry the rickettsia that causes this disease, and it is spread to people by mites.

Unlike other rickettsias, the Q-fever organism infects people by being inhaled. Q fever is common in many livestock-raising regions. Cattle and sheep bitten by infected ticks pass Q-fever rickettsias in their urine and in the fluids lost while giving birth. The rickettsias may infect people who inhale dust from livestock pens.

The symptoms of rickettsial diseases include chills, fever, headaches, and rashes. Untreated rickettsial diseases—particularly epidemic typhus and Rocky Mountain spotted fever—are often fatal. However, these diseases can be treated effectively with antibiotics. Rickettsias were named for Howard Taylor Ricketts, an American pathologist who first identified the organisms in 1909.   Thomas P. Monath

Rickover, Hyman George (1900-1986), an American naval officer, pioneered in developing the U.S.S. *Nautilus,* the first nuclear-powered submarine. In 1965, he received the Enrico Fermi Medal, the highest United

States atomic science award. Rickover stated his views on education in *Education and Freedom* (1959).

In 1947, Rickover became head of the Naval Reactors Branch of the U.S. Atomic Energy Commission. He also served as head of the Nuclear Power Division of the U.S. Navy. He was promoted to the rank of vice admiral in 1959. Rickover reached compulsory retirement age in 1964, but his active duty was extended. In 1973, he was promoted to the rank of admiral. He continued to serve in the Navy's nuclear propulsion program until his retirement in 1982. Rickover was born in Warsaw, Poland, and came to the United States with his family when he was 4 years old.   Kenneth J. Hagan

Ricksha. See Jinrikisha.

Riddle is a question or statement that contains a deliberately hidden meaning. Riddles today are usually meant to be amusing. They often take the form of a *conundrum*, a kind of riddle that depends on puns. A typical riddle of this type is: "What has four wheels and flies?" The answer, "A garbage truck," makes sense when we realize that the word *flies* has two meanings.

Another popular type of riddle depends on possible but unexpected assumptions in a given question. The answer to the riddle, "Where does an elephant go when he wants to lie down?" is "Anywhere he pleases." That answer is both humorous and surprising because the question seems to concern the habits of elephants, but it is really about the intimidating size of elephants.

For many centuries, the riddle was often regarded as a kind of coded message that came from divine inspiration. People believed the message could be understood only by persons equipped with special knowledge. In ancient Greece, priests and priestesses called *oracles* frequently expressed their messages in the form of riddles (see **Oracle**). The most celebrated riddle in Greek mythology was asked of the citizens of Thebes by the Sphinx: "What has one voice and becomes four-footed, two-footed, and three-footed?" The hero Oedipus solved the riddle. He correctly answered, "Man, who crawls on all fours as a baby, then walks on two legs as an adult, and finally needs a cane in old age."

During the Middle Ages, poets in Europe seem to have particularly enjoyed composing riddles. The so-called *Exeter Book* contains nearly 100 examples of riddles. They were written in an early form of English called Old English, probably in the early 700's. These riddles dealt with such subjects as storms, ships, beer, books, and falcons. The answers to some of these riddles are obvious, but other riddles are extremely difficult to understand. However, they are valuable for the insights they provide into the way people of that period regarded events of nature and everyday life.

Collections of riddles were among the first books ever printed for popular entertainment. A book of riddles called *Amusing Questions* was published in England in 1511 by a printer called Wynkyn de Worde. Many standard nursery rhymes, such as "Humpty Dumpty," are actually riddles that were invented centuries ago.   Marcus Klein

See also **Nursery rhyme** (Rhyming riddles); **Rebus**; **Sphinx** (The Greek sphinx).

Ride, Sally Kristen (1951-   ), was a United States astronaut who became the first American woman to travel in space. In June 1983, she and astronauts Robert L. Crippen, John M. Fabian, Frederick H. Hauck, and Norman E. Thagard made a six-day flight on the space shuttle *Challenger.* During the mission, Ride and Fabian launched communications satellites for the Canadian and Indonesian governments and conducted experiments involving the production of pharmaceuticals. In addition, they tested the shuttle's *remote manipulator arm.*

NASA
Sally Ride

They used the arm to release a satellite and then retrieve it and place it in the shuttle's cargo area.

Ride made her second shuttle flight in October 1984. On this mission, she used the remote manipulator arm to launch a satellite designed to measure the sun's effect on the earth's weather.

Ride was born in Los Angeles. In 1978, she received a Ph.D. degree in physics from Stanford University and became an astronaut candidate. On Jan. 28, 1986, *Challenger* broke apart shortly after take-off, killing all seven members of its crew. In February, Ride was appointed to the presidential commission that was established to investigate the accident. Ride resigned from the astronaut program in 1987 in order to accept a fellowship at the Stanford University Center for International Security and Arms Control. In 1989, she became a professor of physics at the University of California at San Diego and the director of the California Space Institute.
James E. Hannigan

Rideau Canal, *rih DOH,* is a Canadian waterway connecting the Ottawa River at Ottawa with Lake Ontario at Kingston. It consists of the Rideau and Cataraqui rivers, several lakes, and some short canals. It is 123 miles (198 kilometers) long, and has 47 locks, each 134 feet (41 meters) long, 33 feet (10 meters) wide, and 5 feet (1.5 meters) deep. One branch of the canal, known as the Tay branch, extends to the town of Perth, and has two locks. The Rideau Canal was completed in 1832. It was designed to offer a safe route for gunboats and military supplies between Montreal and the Great Lakes. The canal is a national historic site of Canada.   Roger Nadeau

See also **Ottawa.**

Ridgway, Matthew Bunker (1895-1993), became the first United States Army officer to hold supreme commands in both the Pacific and Atlantic areas. In 1951, he succeeded General Douglas MacArthur as supreme commander for the Allied Powers in Japan, and as supreme commander for the United Nations forces in the Far East. The following year, Ridgway succeeded General Dwight D. Eisenhower as supreme commander of Allied forces in Europe. From 1953 to 1955, Ridgway was United States Army Chief of Staff.

Ridgway was born in Fort Monroe, Va., and was graduated from the U.S. Military Academy in 1917. He served in China, Nicaragua, the Panama Canal Zone, and the Philippines. Ridgway was with the War Department War Plans Division when World War II began. He led the 82nd Airborne Division in the invasions of Sicily, Italy, and Normandy, and later commanded the 18th Airborne

Corps in Europe. After the war, Ridgway became commander of the Mediterranean theater and the Caribbean command. In 1949, he went to Washington, D.C., as army deputy chief of staff. The next year Ridgway was appointed commander of the United States Eighth Army in Korea.

In 1955, Ridgway retired. He became chairman of the Mellon Institute of Industrial Research in Pittsburgh, Pa., serving until 1960.   Maurice Matloff

Riding. See Horse (How to ride).

Riding Mountain National Park. See Canada (National parks).

Ridley, Nicholas (1500?-1555), an English bishop, was a martyr of the Protestant Reformation. Many regarded him as the master spirit among the English reformers. He helped compile the first Book of Common Prayer of 1549, and the Forty-Two Articles of Religion in 1553. The Forty-Two Articles later served as the basis for the Thirty-Nine Articles (see **Thirty-Nine Articles**). Ridley supported Lady Jane Grey's unsuccessful claim to the throne, and in 1553 Queen Mary imprisoned him in the Tower of London. In 1554 Ridley was condemned for heresy, and the following year he was burned at the stake at Oxford.

Ridley was born in Northumberland and graduated from Cambridge University. In 1547 he became bishop of Rochester, and in 1550, bishop of London.

Peter W. Williams

Riel, *ree EHL,* **Louis** (1844-1885), led uprisings against the Canadian government in 1869-1870 and 1885. He led protesting *métis* (people of mixed white and Indian ancestry), who feared the land they had settled would be taken over by new settlers. Riel was hanged as a traitor after the second revolt.

The first uprising began after the Canadian government decided to buy Hudson's Bay Company land in what is now Manitoba and open the land to new settlers. The métis in the Red River Valley feared they would lose their land to the settlers. Riel protested in vain. In 1869, métis led by Riel captured Fort Garry (present-day Winnipeg). Government troops put an end to the revolt of the métis in 1870. Riel fled and was classed as an outlaw. But the government set aside land for the métis, and established the Province of Manitoba.

Riel was elected to the Canadian House of Commons in 1873 and 1874, but was denied his seat. He was given a pardon in 1875 on the condition that he leave Canada for five years. But Riel suffered a mental breakdown in 1875 and was in insane asylums from 1876 until 1878. Then he moved to Montana. He became a United States citizen in 1883.

During this time, hundreds of métis had moved from the Red River Valley to what is now Saskatchewan. In 1884, the métis again feared they would lose their land to new settlers. Riel helped the métis form a provisional government in March 1885. Fighting broke out, and government troops defeated the

Glenbow Museum, Calgary
Louis Riel

métis. Riel surrendered, was convicted of treason, and was hanged. His death caused an outburst of racial hatred between French Canadians and English Canadians that weakened Canadian unity. Riel was born in St. Boniface, Manitoba.   P. B. Waite

See also **Red River Rebellion; North West Rebellion; Dumont, Gabriel; Manitoba** (The Red River Rebellion); **Métis; Saskatchewan** (picture).

Riemenschneider, *REE muhn SHNY dur,* **Tilman** (1460?-1531), was one of the best-known sculptors of his day in Germany. Riemenschneider carved in both stone and wood. He was the first German woodcarver to leave the surfaces of his works unpainted. Riemenschneider worked in a late Gothic style, with elaborate drapery and weightless figures. Most of his sculpture is concerned with religious subjects. Riemenschneider's work is noted for its quiet religious feeling.

Riemenschneider was born in Thuringia. He studied his trade in several German cities before settling in Würzburg. He spent most of his life there, becoming a prominent citizen and a member of the Würzburg city council.   Alison McNeil Kettering

Rienzi. See Cola di Rienzo.

Herrgottskirche, Creglingen, Germany (Erick Lessing from Art Resource)
A Riemenschneider altarpiece was completed about 1505 for a German church. The central panel shows the Assumption of the Virgin Mary into heaven. The wings portray scenes from Mary's life. The altarpiece stands 32 feet (9.75 meters) high.

Rifle is a gun with spiral grooves in its long barrel that spin the bullet as it is shot. Rifles are usually held against the shoulder when firing. Soldiers use rifles in battle. People also use rifles to hunt game and to compete in shooting matches.

Military rifles and sporting rifles differ greatly. Military rifles are ruggedly built and are designed to work under the harshest conditions. Most military rifles are *automatic* or *semiautomatic.* An automatic rifle can fire bullets rapidly one after another with one squeeze of the trigger. A semiautomatic rifle fires and reloads one bullet with each squeeze of the trigger. Most hunting and target rifles are operated by hand after each firing and are designed for beauty as well as accuracy.

The parts of a rifle

All rifles have four basic parts: (1) the barrel, (2) the stock, (3) the action, and (4) the sights.

The *barrel* is a strong steel tube with spiral grooves called *rifling* cut along the inside. The front end of the barrel is called the *muzzle,* and the rear end is the *breech.*

The *stock* of a rifle helps keep the rifle steady when firing. The butt of the stock is placed against the shoulder when firing. The front end extends under the barrel. Stocks of military rifles are made of wood, plastic, or fiberglass. Many sporting rifles have stocks made of expensive wood with decorative or grip-aiding carving called *checkering.*

The *action* is the basic machinery of the rifle. The action includes the parts that feed a *cartridge* into the *firing chamber.* A cartridge is a metal case that holds an explosive charge and a bullet. The firing chamber, which holds the cartridge, is a widened hole at the breech. The action also includes the parts that fire the bullet and *eject* (force out) the used cartridge.

The *sights* are used to aim the rifle. When aimed properly, the rear sight, the front sight, and the target should be in a straight line. Some rifles have *telescopic sights* that make distant targets appear closer.

How a rifle works

A rifle is ready to be fired when a cartridge has been fed into the firing chamber. Then the rifle is aimed and the trigger squeezed. The rifle's *hammer* or *firing pin* strikes the rear end of the cartridge and ignites the *primer.* The primer in turn ignites the propellant powder in the cartridge. The powder burns rapidly, creating pressure that drives the bullet down the barrel.

The rifling in the barrel makes the bullet spin. Without spin, a bullet would not stay pointed forward in flight, but would tumble over and over. The spinning motion increases the accuracy of a bullet.

Kinds of rifles

Rifles are classified by type of action (manually operated, automatic, or semiautomatic); by the name of the designer or manufacturer (for example, Remington or Winchester); or by *caliber.* Caliber may refer to the inside diameter of the barrel or the diameter of the bullet. The caliber is measured in *millimeters* or in decimal fractions of an inch.

There are three kinds of repeating rifles with hand-operated actions—*bolt-action, lever-action,* and *slide-action.* These rifles have *magazines* (cartridge holders) that feed cartridges into the firing chamber. The action on two other kinds of rifles—automatic and semiautomatic—is operated by forces caused by the burning of the propellant powder in the firing chamber.

Bolt-action rifles have an action that resembles a bolt used to lock a door. When the bolt on the rifle is pulled back, the used cartridge is thrown out and the hammer is cocked. When the bolt is moved forward, it pushes a new cartridge into the firing chamber.

Lever-action rifles are loaded by moving a lever under the breech down and back up. The down move-

Parts of a rifle

A bolt-action rifle is generally used for hunting or target shooting. The weapon is fired by first pulling the bolt back to throw out the used cartridge and to cock the firing pin. Moving the bolt forward pushes a new cartridge into the firing chamber. When the trigger is squeezed, the firing pin strikes and ignites the cartridge's primer.

WORLD BOOK diagram by Oxford Illustrators Limited

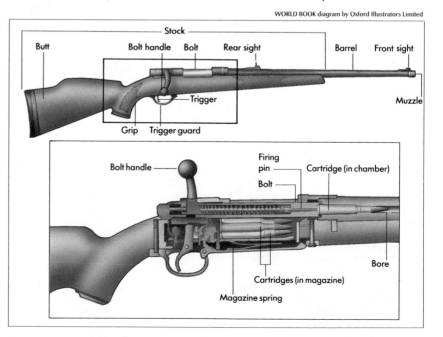

Stock — Butt — Bolt handle — Bolt — Rear sight — Barrel — Front sight — Trigger — Grip — Trigger guard — Muzzle

Bolt handle — Firing pin — Cartridge (in chamber) — Bolt — Cartridges (in magazine) — Magazine spring — Bore

ment throws out the used cartridge and cocks the hammer. The up movement inserts a new cartridge into the firing chamber.

Slide-action rifles, also called *pump-action rifles,* are loaded with a back-and-forth movement of a rod and handle beneath the front part of the barrel. When the handle is pulled back, the breech opens and the used cartridge is thrown out. A live cartridge is inserted when the handle is pushed forward.

Automatic and semiautomatic rifles are used mainly by soldiers and police officers. When a rifle is fired, gas is formed by the burning powder in the firing chamber. The expanding gas drives the bullet out of the barrel. In most modern automatic and semiautomatic rifles, some of this gas operates the action. When a cartridge is fired, a fresh cartridge is moved out of the magazine into the firing chamber, and the firing mechanism is cocked.

The M16A2 is the automatic rifle used by the U.S. armed forces. It weighs 8.9 pounds (4 kilograms) when loaded with a 30-cartridge magazine. The M16A2 can fire one shot at a time, or three shots in a single burst. It uses a 5.56-millimeter cartridge.

Rifle cartridges

Rifle cartridges are enclosed in a *casing* (metal covering) made of brass or steel. Cartridges vary in size according to the caliber of the rifle. The names of some cartridges include the year the cartridge was put into use. The .30-06 is a .30-caliber cartridge chosen for use by the U.S. Army in 1906. The classification of some cartridges includes the caliber and *velocity* (speed) of the bullet. The bullet from a .250-3000 cartridge has a velocity of 3,000 feet (910 meters) per second.

History

Modern rifles developed from the crude, muzzle-loading firearms of the 1400's. Rifling of barrels was invented in Europe about 1500. *Smooth-bore* firearms (weapons without rifling) could not be depended on to hit targets more than 100 steps away.

The jaeger rifle of central and northern Europe was

Famous rifles   Early rifles were used for hunting, target shooting, and warfare. The same type of rifle was used for all three purposes. Today's automatic and semiautomatic rifles are used mainly by the military, and repeating rifles with hand-operated actions are used for hunting and target shooting.

Garry James Collection (Roger Roland Fuhr, *ROLAND*esign)

The flintlock rifle had to be reloaded through the muzzle after each firing. This British military rifle—the Baker—was used during the first half of the 1800's.

Phil Spangenberger Collection (Roger Roland Fuhr, *ROLAND*esign)

The Sharps buffalo rifle was a long-range hunting rifle popular during the 1870's and 1880's. It could be fired by lightly touching one trigger after pulling the other.

Sherwood International Inc. (Roger Roland Fuhr, *ROLAND*esign)

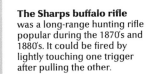

The Mauser 1898 was a bolt-action military rifle. It was the model for the American Springfield rifle used during World War I and many other military and sporting rifles.

Sherwood International Inc. (Roger Roland Fuhr, *ROLAND*esign)

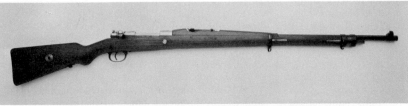

The M16A2 rifle is capable of firing one shot at a time, or three bullets in less than a second. The M16A2 is the official rifle of the United States armed forces.

the first accurate rifle. It was developed about 1665. German immigrants brought jaegers to Pennsylvania in the early 1700's and gave them new features, including longer barrels. The Pennsylvania-made Kentucky rifle developed from the jaeger. Some Kentucky rifles were used in the Revolutionary War in America (1775-1783).

Rifles used round bullets until the 1850's, when more accurate Minié bullets became popular. Minié bullets had hollow bases and pointed tips and were used in the U.S. Civil War (1861-1865). Improvements of the late 1800's included repeating rifles, smokeless explosive powder, and *jacketed* bullets, which have a tough metal cover over a lead or steel core.   Frances M. Lussier

Related articles in *World Book* include:

Ammunition	Firearm	Night vision sys-
Bullet	Garand rifle	tems
Carbine	Gunpowder	Shotgun
Cartridge	Musket	

Rift Valley. See Great Rift Valley.

Riga, *REE guh* (pop. 920,000.), is the capital and largest city of Latvia. The city lies at the south end of the Gulf of Riga, at the mouth of the Western Dvina (Daugava) River. For location, see **Latvia** (map).

Riga is a shipping center, and it accounts for more than half of Latvia's industrial output. Its products include chemicals, electronics, and industrial machinery. It also has been the cultural and political center of Latvia for hundreds of years. In the city, modern housing complexes rise near lovely churches and merchant houses that date from the Middle Ages.

Riga was founded by German crusaders in 1201. Latvia became an independent nation in 1918, with Riga as its capital. In 1940, the Soviet Union seized Latvia and made it part of the Soviet Union. In 1991, Latvia broke away from the Soviet Union and became an independent nation again.   Jaroslaw Bilocerkowycz

Rigging. See Sailing (Rigging).

Right-hand rule. See Electric motor (Basic principles).

Right of privacy. See Privacy, Right of.

Right of search. Under international law, a nation at war has the right to visit and search merchant ships of neutral nations. The search must be carried out by the officers of a warship. The purposes are to determine the true nationality of the vessel, and to find out whether the vessel is engaged in unneutral service or in carrying contraband of war (see **Contraband**). In peacetime, the right of search may be exercised to enforce revenue laws or prevent piracy.

When a search is made, the ship's papers are first examined. These papers name the ship, its master, or captain, the port it sailed from, and the port for which it is bound. The papers should describe the cargo and certify that the officers have met the customs regulations of the country from which the ship has sailed.

If the papers are correct, the search usually ends. But if suspicion is aroused, the cargo may be examined. Officers who refuse to stop their ship and allow it to be searched run the risk of having both ship and cargo confiscated. The Hague Peace Conference of 1907 and the London Conference of 1909 tried to set limits to the right of search. Conference members agreed that the mail of neutral nations should be free from search. However, all sides disregarded these agreements in wartime.

During Prohibition in the United States, some countries agreed to extend their territorial limits to the number of nautical miles that could be covered in one hour's sailing from their coasts. These agreements made it easier to search for smuggled articles, and they remain in force. For other purposes, the limits are 3 to 12 nautical miles, depending on the kind of search. For revenue purposes, the President may authorize a search up to 62 nautical miles from the U.S. coast.   Robert J. Pranger

Right of way. See Easement.

Right-to-work law provides that a person need not belong to a labor union to get or keep a job. It also provides that a person may not be denied a job because of union membership. About 20 states have such laws. Unions, which strongly oppose right-to-work laws, generally have little power in states with these laws.

Right-to-work laws have the effect of barring closed shop, union shop, and maintenance-of-membership agreements between employers and unions. In the *closed shop*, the employer can hire only members of the union. In the *union shop*, all employees must join the union after they have worked there for a certain period. *Maintenance-of-membership clauses* require that employees who are union members retain membership until the union contract expires.   Paul L. Burgess

Right whale. See Whale (Right whales; The early days of whaling; pictures).

Right wing refers to a conservative, traditional group or political party. In some legislative bodies, the conservatives sit to the right of the speaker. Radical and liberal groups form the *left wing*, with middle-of-the-road groups making up the *center*. This custom originated with the French National Assembly of 1789. In that assembly, nobles took the honored seats to the king's right. See also **Conservatism**.   Carl L. Davis

Rights, Bill of. See Bill of rights.

Rights of Man, Declaration of the, is a French document that sets forth the principles of human liberty and the rights of individuals. The document's full name is the Declaration of the Rights of Man and of the Citizen. The first two articles of the declaration state that all people are free and equal in rights, which include "liberty, property, security, and resistance to oppression." The other 15 articles of the declaration concern both the limitations of government and the rights and obligations of citizens.

The French National Assembly adopted the declaration on Aug. 26, 1789, during the French Revolution. The refusal of King Louis XVI to approve the declaration helped bring about increased revolutionary activity in October 1789.

The writers of the declaration were influenced partly by the United States Declaration of Independence, but above all by the circumstances of the revolution. The document was intended to be the statement of principle for the new regime.   Isser Woloch

Riis, *rees,* **Jacob August** (1849-1914), was an American journalist, photographer, and social reformer. During the late 1800's and early 1900's, he helped improve living conditions in New York City slums by exposing them to the public through his writings and photographs. Photographs taken by Riis were among the first to appear in newspapers.

Riis was born in Ribe, Denmark. He immigrated to the

United States in 1870. In 1877, Riis became a reporter for the *New York Tribune,* and in 1890, he moved to the *New York Evening Sun.* As a reporter, Riis worked for improvements in education, housing, and law enforcement and for child labor laws and playground construction. In 1888, he helped bring about the elimination of a notorious New York City slum district called Mulberry Bend.

Besides writing for newspapers, Riis wrote 12 books. They include *How the Other Half Lives* (1890), *The Children of the Poor* (1892), and *The Battle with the Slum* (1902). An autobiographical work, *The Making of an American* (1901), tells the story of his immigration to the United States.   Michael Emery

See also **Playground** (with picture); **United States, History of the** (picture: The lives of the poor and the rich).

Riley, James Whitcomb (1849-1916), won fame as the *Hoosier Poet.* He wrote much verse in pure English, but his most popular poems were those he wrote in the dialect of his home state of Indiana. They include "When the Frost Is on the Punkin'," "Out to Aunt Mary's," and "Little Orphant Annie." These works are characterized by light humor, pathos, and sentiment. Riley's poems were published in a number of collections, including *The Old Swimmin'-Hole and 'Leven More Poems* (1883), *Rhymes of Childhood* (1890), *Poems Here at Home* (1893), and *Book of Joyous Children* (1902).

Riley, the son of a lawyer, was born in Greenfield, Indiana. He left home after receiving a grammar school education and worked for a time as a sign painter. For a short period, he traveled with a medicine show. Riley had heard the dialect and learned the manners of the country folk of Indiana from his childhood, and he began to write poems about them.

Riley joined the *Indianapolis Journal* in 1877. He made his home in Indianapolis. He began to contribute poems to several papers under the name "Benj. F. Johnson of Boone." He became a celebrated platform reader and appeared throughout the United States, often with the humorist Bill Nye.   Marcus Klein

See also **Indiana** (Places to visit).

Rilke, *RIHL kuh,* **Rainer Maria,** *RY nuhr mah REE ah* (1875-1926), was an important lyric poet in German literature and a major representative of the symbolism movement. His poems are characterized by richness of imagery and melody and fine shades of meaning. They have a tone of self-examination and prophecy.

Rilke's cycle of poems *The Book of Hours* (1905) expresses a longing for a mystic union with God. *New Poems* (1907, 1908) contains works that try to express the essence, or "idea," of an object or experience. Rilke's novel *The Notebooks of Malte Laurids Brigge* (1910) is a highly innovative "modernist" work in style and structure. It portrays the loneliness and confusion of a young poet searching for identity in turbulent Paris. The *Duino Elegies* (1923) and *Sonnets to Orpheus* (1923) are poems that praise human existence.

Rilke was born in Prague. He spent much of his life wandering through Europe.   Werner Hoffmeister

Rillieux, *RIHL ee yoo,* **Norbert** (1806-1894), an American engineer, revolutionized the sugar industry by making the first practical multiple-effect vacuum evaporator. This machine used an improved process to remove water from sugar cane.

In one chamber of Rillieux's machine, the sugar cane juice was boiled until it became syrup. Then, in a connected chamber, the hot vapor from the first chamber boiled the syrup until it became grains of sugar. This double use of the same heat greatly reduced the cost and improved the quality of the final product. Other products, including soap, gelatin, some glues, and condensed milk, are now manufactured through a process based on Rillieux's invention.

Rillieux was born in New Orleans, the son of a French engineer and a free black woman. He studied in Paris and became an engineering teacher there in 1830. In the 1840's, he installed his invention on many sugar plantations in the United States. He returned to Paris permanently in the 1850's.   Douglas E. Bowers

Rimbaud, *ram BOH,* **Arthur,** *ar TEWR* (1854-1891), was a French poet of extraordinary originality. Rimbaud wrote his major verse between the ages of 15 and 20. He then abandoned his literary career and became a trader in what is now Ethiopia.

Rimbaud was born in Charleville, France. His first poems satirize the people of his hometown and celebrate the joys of youth, often in violent, colloquial language. In 1871, Rimbaud went to Paris to deliver his visionary poem, "Le Bateau ivre" ("The Drunken Boat") to the French poet Paul Verlaine. He quickly built a reputation as a wild poet of genius. He also became involved in a homosexual relationship with Verlaine.

Rimbaud's major work, *Une Saison en enfer (A Season in Hell,* 1873), is an autobiographical narrative that evokes his painful relationship with Verlaine. The poem describes Rimbaud's struggles with Christianity and French imperialism, and his experiments with hallucinatory poetry, the "verbal alchemy" which almost drove him insane. Verlaine published Rimbaud's prose poems, *Illuminations* (1886), after Rimbaud left France. These innovative works create a verbal universe almost entirely separate from the outside world.

Rimbaud's "Lettre du voyant" ("Visionary Letter," 1871) describes the "long, immense and calculated derangement of all the senses" required to reach truth. His statement in this letter that "The Self is other than myself" became a philosophical statement by the Surrealist movement of the 1920's.   Edward K. Kaplan

See also **Symbolism; Verlaine, Paul.**

Rimsky-Korsakov, *RIHM skih KAWR suh kawf,* **Nikolai** (1844-1908), was a celebrated Russian composer and teacher. He is especially known for his imaginative and colorful orchestral compositions, including *Spanish Capriccio* (1887), *Scheherazade* (1888), and the *Russian Easter Overture* (1888). Russian folk songs can be heard in his music, as can choral music and bell ringing of the Russian Orthodox Church.

In spite of his orchestral successes, Rimsky-Korsakov's main emphasis was on opera. He based many of his 15 operas on Russian history and folklore. Only two of them, however, have gained success outside Russia. They are *Sadko* (1898) and *The Golden Cockerel* (1909). But still popular today in Russia are *The Snow Maiden* (completed in 1881, revised about 1895), *The Tsar's Bride* (1899), and *The Tale of Tsar Saltan* (1900). His masterpiece, *The Legend of the Invisible City of Kitezh and the Maiden Fevroniia* (1907), is virtually unknown in the West. Two of his best-known pieces come from his operas—"Song of India" from *Sadko* and "The Flight of the Bumblebee" from *Tsar Saltan.*

Rimsky-Korsakov was born in Tikhvin, near Novgorod. In 1861, he met the composer Mily Balakirev and joined a group of his students who later became known as The Five. Balakirev encouraged them to draw upon their Russian heritage in their music.

In 1871, Rimsky-Korsakov joined the faculty of the St. Petersburg Conservatory. Realizing he knew almost no music theory, he began to teach himself counterpoint, harmony, and musical form. As a musical theorist and teacher, he had a decisive influence on the course of Russian music in the early 1900's. Several of his students became important composers, including Sergei Prokofiev and Igor Stravinsky. His book *Principles of Orchestration* (published in 1913, after his death) has become a standard work. He also wrote an autobiography, translated into English as *My Musical Life.*

Rimsky-Korsakov edited and revised compositions that his friends Alexander Borodin and Modest Mussorgsky had left unfinished at their deaths. Today, his version of Mussorgsky's opera *Boris Godunov* is usually performed. Borodin's opera *Prince Igor* is usually performed in the version completed by Rimsky-Korsakov and Russian composer Alexander Glazunov.

Edward V. Williams

Rinderpest, *RIHN duhr PEHST,* also called *cattle plague,* is a highly contagious, usually fatal disease of cattle and other members of the ox family. The disease is caused by a virus. Symptoms include sudden loss of milk in cows, fever, diarrhea, and ulcers in the mouth. The death rate is as high as 98 percent.

Rinderpest hindered the development of Western civilization for many hundreds of years. It swept over Europe from the East with every war. The last European outbreak occurred in Belgium following World War I (1914-1918). The disease has never reached the United States and is chiefly confined to Asian countries.

Lawrence D. McGill

Rinehart, Mary Roberts (1876-1958), was an American novelist and playwright. She was best known for her mystery stories with clever plots that mix horror and humor. She gained fame with her first two mystery novels, *The Circular Staircase* (1908) and *The Man in Lower Ten* (1909). With Avery Hopwood, she adapted *The Circular Staircase* into a popular mystery play, *The Bat* (1920). Most of Rinehart's mysteries are narrated by a heroine who solves the crime but must be rescued from the villain by a detective. Rinehart also wrote a series of comic stories about an eccentric spinster called Tish.

Mary Ella Roberts was born in Allegheny (now part of Pittsburgh) and studied nursing in Pittsburgh. She married Stanley M. Rinehart in 1896. *My Story* (1931, revised 1948) is her autobiography. Barbara M. Perkins

Ring is a circular band made of metal or other material worn as jewelry. Some rings are decorated with gems or engraving. Rings are commonly worn on the fingers, but they may also be worn on the ears, nose, or toes.

Rings also serve functional or symbolic purposes. For example, rings have long been a symbol of authority. Each pope gets a ring engraved with a picture of Saint Peter in a fishing boat. After the pope dies, the ring is destroyed and a new one is made for the next pope.

A ring is often used to symbolize an engagement or

Kinds of rings

Ancient Egyptian ring

Mycenaean gold ring

Grecian gold ring

Roman bronze ring

Key ring

Anglo-Saxon engagement ring

Papal ring, 1400's

Brahman signet ring

Jewish wedding ring

marriage. Engagement and wedding rings were probably first worn by the ancient Romans. Some of the early wedding rings may have been made of gold. The custom of decorating engagement and wedding rings with gems began about 1200. During the 1600's, many people exchanged *posey rings* as a sign of love or friendship. This ring was a simple band engraved with a short love poem.

Rings often indicate membership or rank in an organization, such as a fraternity or sorority. Many people wear class rings to represent the year they graduated from high school or college. Another popular type of ring has a gem that is associated with the month of a person's birth (see **Birthstone**).

In the past, people used *signets,* which were small seals attached to rings, to authenticate official documents. Rings were once used to indicate social status. In ancient Egypt, the wealthy wore heavy gold and silver rings. The poorer Egyptians wore rings made from bronze, glass, and glazed pottery. John S. Lizzadro

See also **Jewelry.**

Ring of Fire is a zone along the edge of the Pacific Ocean that has many volcanoes and earthquakes. This horseshoe-shaped belt stretches about 25,000 miles (40,000 kilometers) from New Zealand northwest to the Philippines, northeast to Japan, east to Alaska, and south to Oregon, California, Mexico, and the Andes Mountains of South America.

Scientists believe that the motion of *tectonic plates* (pieces that make up the strong outer shell of the earth) cause the Ring of Fire's earthquakes and volcanic eruptions. Tectonic plates move slowly on an underlying layer of weak rock that is so hot it flows, even though it remains solid. The edge of one plate sinks beneath the edge of a neighboring plate in a process called *subduc-*

WORLD BOOK map

The Ring of Fire is a zone of volcanic and earthquake activity located mostly along the rim of the Pacific Ocean. It has more than half the world's active volcanoes, many of which are shown here.

tion. The movements of subduction generate many earthquakes and usually a line of volcanoes along the upper plate's boundary. A volcano erupts where melted rock, hot gases, and fragments of solid rock burst through to the earth's surface.

The Ring of Fire is the site of thousands of earthquakes each year. The largest earthquake ever recorded occurred there, along the coast of Chile in 1960.

Although the Ring of Fire covers only about 1 percent of the earth's surface, it has more than half the world's active volcanoes. There are about 350 historically active volcanoes in the zone. Eruptions occurred in the late 1900's at Mount St. Helens in the United States and Mount Pinatubo in the Philippines. The hot gases of volcanic activity carry dissolved metals toward the surface, where they settle out. Geologists have found copper, gold, molybdenum, silver, tin, and tungsten where ancient volcanic activity occurred within the Ring of Fire.

Mark Cloos

See also **Earthquake; Plate tectonics; Volcano.**

Ringette, *rihng EHT,* is a team sport for girls and young women that is similar to ice hockey. The game was invented in Ontario, Canada, in 1963. It is now played in the northern United States and in several European countries as well as in Canada.

As in ice hockey, ringette teams have six players, all of whom wear ice skates. The game is played on a rink divided into three sections by blue lines. The object of the game is to score goals by shooting a hollow rubber ring into a net guarded by a goaltender. The ring has an outer diameter of 16.5 centimeters (6.5 inches), an inner diameter of 11.5 centimeters (4.5 inches), and a thickness of 2.7 centimeters (1.06 inches). Players use a straight stick that resembles a bladeless hockey stick to shoot and pass the ring. Most sticks are made of wood, but aluminum and plastic sticks are also used. Players must

wear knee and elbow pads and helmets with face masks. Players commonly wear a track suit as a uniform, sometimes combined with a hockey sweater.

A ringette team consists of a goaltender, a center, two forwards, and two defensive players. The center is the only player who can skate anywhere on the ice. Forwards may not skate closer to the net their team is defending than the blue line nearest the net. Defensive players may not come closer to the net their opponents are defending than the blue line nearest the net. Centers play with white sticks, forwards with blue sticks, and defensive players with red sticks. Ringette games consist of two 15-minute halves. Violations are similar to those of ice hockey. But unlike hockey, ringette prohibits body contact and requires passing over each blue line.

Jim Merrithew, Ringette Canada

Ringette is a team sport for girls and women that is similar to hockey. Players skate on an ice-covered rink, and use a straight stick to pass and shoot a hollow rubber ring.

Organized ringette in Canada features six major age groups: petites (age 10 and under), tweens (12 and under), juniors (14 and under), belles (17 and under), debs (18 and over), and ladies (20 and over). Teams compete for provincial and national championships in Canada each year.   Critically reviewed by Ringette Canada

Ringling brothers were five brothers who founded the most famous circus in American entertainment history. The brothers were Albert (1852-1916), Otto (1858-1911), Alfred (1861-1919), Charles (1864-1926), and John (1866-1936). Their dedication and organizational skills helped build a small group of performers into one of the greatest circuses in the world.

The Ringlings were the sons of a harness maker from Germany. Albert was born in Chicago, Otto in Baraboo, Wisconsin, and Alfred, Charles, and John in McGregor, Iowa. In 1884, the brothers started a traveling circus. At the time, there were a number of circuses touring the United States, including the huge Barnum show that traveled on 60 railroad cars. The Ringlings had little money for equipment or performers, so they did most of the work themselves. They held their first performance on May 19, 1884, in Baraboo. The brothers and 17

The five Ringling brothers built up the world's largest, most famous, and most spectacular circus in the early 1900's.

other employees sewed and pitched the tent, sold tickets, played in the band, and performed the acts.

Two other brothers, Henry and August, joined the Ringling circus later in the 1880's. Each of the seven brothers was responsible for one aspect of the circus management. The brothers invested almost all the profits back into the circus, which grew rapidly. At first, they took their show from town to town in wagons pulled by horses. By 1890, the circus traveled by railroad. The Ringlings soon became strong competitors of the Barnum & Bailey circus, the largest circus of the time. In 1907, the Ringlings purchased the Barnum & Bailey circus, but the two shows toured separately until 1919. That year, they merged to form the Ringling Brothers and Barnum & Bailey Circus. The Ringling family sold the circus in 1967, but the new owners kept the name.

Robert L. Parkinson

See also **Barnum, P. T.; Circus.**

Ringtail is a small North American mammal of the raccoon family. It is also called ring-tailed cat. The ringtail has a slender, grayish-tan body and a long, bushy tail with white and black bands. The animal measures 25 to 32 inches (64 to 81 centimeters) long, including the tail, which is 12 to 17 inches (30 to 43 centimeters) long. Ringtails have large eyes ringed with black; whitish facial fur; large, pointed ears; and catlike feet.

Ringtails inhabit woodlands, chaparrals, and deserts from southern Oregon and southwestern Wyoming south to central Mexico and east to Louisiana. A closely related species called the *cacomistle* lives in forests of southern Mexico and Central America. Ringtails make

nests of leaves and grass in caves, hollow tree trunks, tangled roots, cracks in rocks, abandoned burrows, and buildings. They feed on mice and other small mammals, insects, fruits, acorns, and birds. Ringtails are hunted by great horned owls and bobcats.

Ringtails mate in late winter or early spring. The female carries the young inside her body for about eight weeks and then gives birth to two to four babies. The parents bring food to the young until late summer, when the young begin to hunt. Ringtails occasionally live up to 10 years. They can be tamed as pets and are good at catching mice around mountain cabins.

Scientific classification. The ringtail is a member of the raccoon family, Procyonidae. Its scientfic name is *Bassariscus astutus*. The cacomistle is *B. sumichrasti.*   Charles A. Long

Ringworm is a general name for several kinds of skin diseases that are caused by tiny fungi. Itching may or may not be a symptom. Common ringworm of the skin is often seen on children. It begins as a small red area the size of a split pea. This grows larger, and sometimes reaches the size of a silver dollar. The inside of the area clears, and the eruption appears as a red, scaly ring. There may be one or several patches. This form of ringworm occurs on the non-hairy parts of the body.

Ringworm is highly infectious, but it can usually be easily cured if treated with local applications of fungicidal compounds as advised by a physician. The spots of this type of ringworm may disappear without treatment after a few weeks, or they may persist for months. Body ringworm may attack persons of any age. Flat yellowish or brownish patches may appear on the patient's neck, back, chest, or abdomen.

Ringworm of the hands and feet is another common ailment, and has three types. A soft, white area between the toes, especially the part next to the little toe, may be *interdigital* ringworm, commonly called *athlete's foot.* It may not cause discomfort, but is sometimes followed by the *vesicular* form, which causes eruptions of blisters on the hands and feet. *Keratotic* ringworm is less common but more persistent than these forms. This disease is usually limited to the palms of the hands and soles of the feet. The affected areas are dry, slightly thickened, and slightly reddened.

Ringworm may also occur on the hairy parts of the body. Children are especially susceptible to ringworm of the scalp, which they sometimes contract from other children or from dogs and cats. Epidemics of ringworm of the scalp may occur in schools. If ringworm appears in a family, affected people should use only their own combs and other personal items.   Paul R. Bergstresser

See also **Athlete's foot; Itch.**

Rio de Janeiro, *REE oh day zhuh NAIR oh,* Brazil (pop. 6,042,411; met. area pop. 11,205,567), is the second largest city of Brazil. Only São Paulo has more people. Rio de Janeiro, often called simply *Rio,* ranks as an important center of finance, trade, and transportation. The city also has one of the chief seaports of South America. Rio is the capital of the state of Rio de Janeiro in southeastern Brazil (see **Brazil** [political map]).

The exciting scenery of Rio de Janeiro makes the city one of the most beautiful in the world. Rio lies between forested mountains and the sparkling blue waters of the Atlantic Ocean and Guanabara Bay. Gleaming white beaches and graceful palm trees rim the shore. Sugar

Victor Englebert, Black Star

Rio de Janeiro lies on Guanabara Bay, on the Atlantic Ocean. Sugar Loaf Mountain, a landmark of Rio, rises above the bay.

Claus Meyer, Black Star

Small wooden homes crowd the hillsides of Rio de Janeiro. They provide housing for thousands of low-income families.

Loaf Mountain rises 1,325 feet (404 meters) from a peninsula in the bay.

Rio is a crowded city. But in spite of the crowded conditions, many of the city's people consider Rio the best place to live in Brazil. They especially enjoy Rio's sunny beaches, lively nightclubs, and colorful festivals.

Rio grew from a fort established by Portuguese soldiers in 1565 on what is now Guanabara Bay. The Portuguese built the fort during their attempt to drive French settlers out of the area. The French were expelled in 1567. They named their settlement for the bay, which at that time was called Rio de Janeiro (River of January). Historians believe that Gonçalo Coelho, a Portuguese explorer, had named the bay for the month in 1502 when he arrived there. Coelho thought the bay was the outlet of a great river.

The city covers about 452 square miles (1,171 square kilometers). The ocean shore forms Rio's southern boundary, and Guanabara Bay borders the city on the east. Mountains rise to the north and west, and the city itself includes many steep hills. A huge statue called *Christ the Redeemer* overlooks the city from atop Corcovado Mountain, the highest of these hills.

Rio has three main sections called the north, center, and south zones. The north zone, the largest of the zones, is located north of a line of hills that rises parallel to the ocean shore. This section, which lies along the shore of the bay, has many docks and factories and large, poor residential areas. The Rio-Niterói Bridge, which stretches about $8\frac{3}{4}$ miles (14 kilometers), connects the north zone of Rio with Niterói, a city east of the

bay. The water in parts of Guanabara Bay is polluted by sewage and industrial waste.

The small center zone, which includes the main business district, is situated on the bay, a short distance from the ocean. In downtown Rio, large modern office buildings stand near pastel churches built during the city's colonial period, which lasted from the 1500's to the 1800's. Automobiles crowd such broad boulevards as President Vargas and Rio Branco avenues. Other downtown streets are narrow and limited to pedestrians. Most of Rio's chief libraries, museums, and theaters are in the central zone.

The long, narrow south zone occupies the land between the coastal hills, the bay, and the ocean. This area includes a lake, Rodrigo de Freitas Lagoon. The nearby Botanical Garden features tropical plants. Hundreds of tall apartment buildings overlook the many beaches of the area. Copacabana Beach is famous for its elegant hotels and patterned sidewalks made of colored stone.

Slums called *favelas* form a sharp contrast to the luxury of Copacabana. Thousands of people live in shabby shacks on the steep hillsides and swampy shorelands of the bay. Suburban communities lie in valleys near Rio. Many low-income workers live in these towns.

People of Rio de Janeiro have long been called *Cariocas*. The Portuguese settlers may have taken this nickname from a South American Indian expression meaning *white man's house.* Today, Cariocas include people of American Indian, European, or African descent. Many have ancestors from two or three of these groups. Cariocas, like other Brazilians, speak Portuguese.

Most of the city's people belong to the Roman Catholic Church. But many of the Catholics also participate in *Macumba* religious ceremonies. Followers of Macumba pray to divine beings who are identified both with Christian saints and with the gods and goddesses of certain African religions. On New Year's Eve, hundreds of thousands of Cariocas crowd the beaches for candlelit Macumba ceremonies. These ceremonies honor the sea goddess Iemanjá.

Many Cariocas go to the beach to sunbathe, to swim, or to play volleyball. Crowds of as many as 200,000 fans cheer the soccer teams that play at Maracanã Stadium, one of the largest sports arenas in the world. In the evening, many people go to one of Rio's numerous nightclubs or chat with friends at a sidewalk cafe.

Rio has won fame for an annual festival called Carnival, which takes place just before Lent, the religious season that precedes Easter. Carnival features four days and nights of parades and dancing in the streets.

Education and cultural life. Rio's educational institutions, libraries, and museums make the city the leading cultural center of Brazil. The Federal University of Rio de Janeiro ranks as the largest of the several institutions of higher learning. The city's libraries include the National Library, which has about 3 million books. Many visitors view the exhibits at such museums as the National Museum of Fine Arts, the Folklore Museum, and the Indian Museum. The National Museum is located in a palace that was the home of Brazil's Portuguese royalty during the 1800's. It houses exhibits on natural history, archaeology, and minerals. Concerts and plays are presented at the Municipal Theater and other auditoriums.

Economy. Rio's banks and stock market make the city a center of Brazilian finance. The city's factories produce about 10 percent of the nation's industrial output. Products of Rio include, in order of value, processed foods, chemicals, drugs, and metals. The city has many large shipyards. Tourism is also an important industry.

Rio is a major transportation center. Highways and railroads link the city with other large Brazilian cities. Rio has two major airports and is one of Brazil's chief seaports. A ferry connects Rio with Paquetá Island in Guanabara Bay. A subway system and many buses provide local transportation.

History. Tupi Indians lived near what is now Guanabara Bay when Portuguese explorers first arrived there in 1502. Portugal had claimed the Brazil region as a colony in 1494. France established a settlement on the bay in 1555. Ten years later, Portuguese soldiers led by Captain Estácio de Sá established a fort there. They drove out the French in 1567. The fort grew into the city of Rio de Janeiro.

Portuguese prospectors found gold in southern Brazil during the 1690's, and ships began to carry the precious metal from Rio to Portugal. The gold trade attracted many settlers to Rio during the 1700's, and the city became the capital of Brazil in 1763.

The ruler of Portugal, Prince John (later King John VI), came to Rio in 1808 to escape a French invasion of Lisbon, the Portuguese capital. He made Rio the capital of the Portuguese Empire. Thousands of other wealthy Portuguese also fled to Rio. They established medical and military schools and a large city library. Lisbon again became the capital of the empire in 1821, when John re-

turned there. In 1822, Brazil became independent with Rio as its capital. Trade expanded with Europe and North America in the mid-1800's. Coffee became an important export. Rio had more than half a million people in 1890.

During the early 1900's, Rio was modernized. The port was redesigned and broad boulevards were built. Millions of people moved to the city from rural Brazil during the early and mid-1900's. Apartment buildings were erected to provide housing for the growing population. However, many of the newcomers could not afford to rent apartments and had to live in the favelas. Since the mid-1900's, the federal government has built a number of housing projects in Rio for low-income residents. The government has also granted financial aid to manufacturers in an effort to attract new industrial employers to Rio de Janeiro.

Brasília replaced Rio as the national capital in 1960. The federal government moved there during the 1960's and 1970's. In 1975, Rio annexed some of its suburbs and outlying areas. As a result, the city's area increased from 60 square miles (155 square kilometers) to 452 square miles (1,171 square kilometers). The population increased by about 20 percent. In the 1990's, housing for the poor and pollution were among the problems facing the government of Rio.   J. H. Galloway

Río de la Plata, REE *oh duh luh PLAHT uh,* is an estuary, or funnel-shaped bay, on the southeastern coast of South America between Argentina and Uruguay (see **Argentina** [terrain map]). It is formed by the Paraná and the Uruguay rivers. The bay extends northwest from the Atlantic Ocean for about 170 miles (270 kilometers). A great volume of water flows into the bay from the rivers, and there is a powerful current. Many dangerous shallows make sailing risky. The natural harbor of Montevideo, in Uruguay, lies near the bay's mouth, which is 140 miles (225 kilometers) wide. On the Argentine side, at Buenos Aires and La Plata, huge docks have been built and deep channels have been dredged.

In 1516, Juan Díaz de Solís became the first white person to enter the bay. It was named Río de la Plata (Silver River) by Sebastian Cabot, the Italian navigator. Cabot probably chose the name because of the silver ornaments worn by the Indian residents.   Richard W. Wilkie

Rio Grande, REE *oh GRAND,* one of the longest rivers in North America, flows for 1,885 miles (3,034 kilometers) through the Southwestern United States. It forms the international boundary between the United States and Mexico for about 1,240 miles (1,996 kilometers), or almost two-thirds of the common border. Early Spanish explorers gave the river its name. *Rio Grande* means *large river.* Mexicans call the river *Río Bravo* (*bold river*) or *Río Bravo del Norte* (*bold river of the north*).

Upper course. The Rio Grande rises on the Continental Divide in the southern Rocky Mountains in southwestern Colorado. It flows southeast through the San Luis Valley Reclamation Project. At Alamosa, the river turns south. It crosses into New Mexico, and flows from north to south through the center of the state. In northern New Mexico, the Rio Grande, fed by mountain streams, passes through a series of basins separated by narrow valleys. The Rio Grande's valley widens near Albuquerque, and the river flows out upon a dry plateau to the south. On the plateau, Elephant Butte Dam blocks the Rio Grande and forms the Elephant Butte Reservoir. Farther downstream is the Caballo Reservoir. Both of these reservoirs store water for the Rio Grande Reclamation Project at Las Cruces. The American Dam controls the waters of the Rio Grande north of El Paso at the Texas, New Mexico, and Mexico borders.

Middle course. From El Paso to the Gulf of Mexico, the Rio Grande forms the international boundary. The

Rio Grande

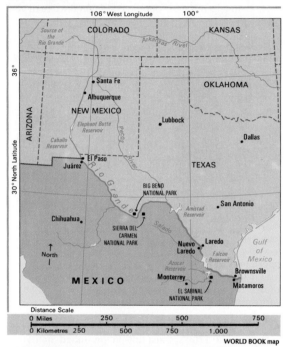

250 miles
250 kilometres

WORLD BOOK map

Joe Viesti

The Rio Grande forms most of the United States border with Mexico. It flows from Colorado to the Gulf of Mexico.

river flows southeast from El Paso. At Presidio, it is joined by the Rio Conchos, an important tributary from Mexico. At Big Bend National Park, the river turns north to pass around the mountainous Big Bend country. It then flows east until the Pecos River joins it. The Rio Grande turns southeast for the rest of its course. Amistad Dam spans the river about 12 miles (19 kilometers) northwest of Del Rio, Tex. The dam forms Amistad Reservoir, which extends upstream 86 miles (138 kilometers). During its middle course, the Rio Grande flows through very dry country. The river may be dry in late summer, because of little rainfall and the amount of water used for irrigation. Railroads cross the border at El Paso and Presidio.

Lower course. The Rio Grande widens between Eagle Pass and Laredo, both important railroad crossings. About 50 miles (80 kilometers) below Laredo, the Salado River, a major tributary from Mexico, joins the Rio Grande. Falcon Dam, about 20 miles (32 kilometers) below the mouth of the Salado River, forms Falcon Reservoir, which extends upstream more than 35 miles (56 kilometers). El Azúcar Reservoir lies across the Rio Grande at Camargo in Mexico. These reservoirs hold back floodwaters for the lower valley's irrigation projects. Between Rio Grande City and Brownsville, farmers grow citrus fruits, vegetables, and cotton in the irrigated valley.

In 1936, a 17-mile (27-kilometer) canal was built from Brownsville to Laguna Madre, which leads to the Gulf of Mexico. Most of the river is too shallow for boats.

Daniel D. Arreola

See also **Pecos River; Rio Grande Project.**

Rio Grande Project, *REE oh GRAND,* is a federal flood-control, power, and irrigation project that extends along the Rio Grande from Elephant Butte Reservoir in southern New Mexico into southern Texas. Congress authorized the project in 1905. Elephant Butte Dam, a major dam, was completed in New Mexico in 1916. The United States Bureau of Reclamation has built six diversion dams and more than 1,000 miles (1,600 kilometers) of canals and ditches at a cost of about $26 million. The project irrigates 178,000 acres (72,000 hectares) in New Mexico and Texas. Edward C. Pritchett

Rio Madeira. See Madeira River.

Río Muni. See Equatorial Guinea.

Riot is a noisy, violent outbreak of disorder by a group of people. Rioters often harm other persons and damage property. Rioting or urging people to riot is a crime in most countries and in all the states of the United States. However, the precise legal definition of a riot differs from place to place.

Rioting cannot always be easily distinguished from vandalism, disorderly conduct, or other similar offenses. But most riots involve hundreds or thousands of people, and follow an aggravation of already severe economic, social, or political grievances. A riot may break out spontaneously, or it may be carefully planned through conspiracy. Few riots—unlike revolts or rebellions—are aimed at overthrowing a government or removing specific leaders. However, a riot may set forces in motion that bring about such a result.

A riot may break out during a demonstration. In a demonstration, many people gather merely to protest publicly against some policy of the government, an industry, a university, or some other institution. But when passions run high, the massing together of thousands of persons and the efforts of police to keep order can lead to violence. In the United States, the Constitution guarantees everyone the rights to assemble in peace, to petition the government for grievances, and to *dissent* (disagree) as an individual or in a group (see **Freedom of speech**). But when dissent changes into disruption of order and is accompanied by violence that injures others or causes physical damage, it is a riot.

Causes of riots

Riots have occurred throughout the world since the beginning of history. In most societies, at one time or another, the poor have rioted to press their demands for food. But poverty and need are not the only reasons. For example, in Britain during the early 1800's, workers called *Luddites* staged riots in which they destroyed labor-saving machines, which they feared would replace them. In Mexico City in 1968, rioting students fought with police over various issues, including alleged police brutality during student demonstrations.

The specific issues that trigger riots vary. However, the underlying causes of many riots are similar. Many riots occur because some groups believe they do not have an equal chance for economic, political, or social advancement. Members of most minority groups live in this situation (see **Minority group**). Many people in such groups may feel they are mistreated by individuals or by government agencies or other organizations that influence their lives. They may become depressed because they feel they cannot help make decisions that affect themselves and their community. People who believe their grievances are being ignored often become defiant, and their feelings can erupt.

Members of a majority group may also become rioters if they fear a minority. They may attack members of the minority to keep them in an inferior social or economic position. Most lynch mobs in the Western and Southern United States were composed of members of dominant, majority groups (see **Lynching**).

Many social scientists classify riots into two groups: (1) *instrumental riots* and (2) *expressive riots.*

Instrumental riots occur when groups resort to violence because of discontent over specific issues. Most riots have been of this type. The violence results from attempts to change certain policies or to improve certain conditions. Most labor riots, especially those in the past, fall into this category. During the 1800's and early 1900's, for example, U.S. laborers fought to improve working conditions in mines, on railroads, and in factories. Union disputes with management often resulted in violence. Other instrumental riots include prison, antidraft, antiwar, and student riots.

Instrumental riots frequently indicate that the organizations being attacked have not listened effectively to or acted upon grievances previously voiced through orderly channels. But most people condemn the use of violence to achieve even the most desirable goals when peaceful means of change are available.

Expressive riots occur when many people in a minority group use violence to express dissatisfaction with their living conditions. Studies of urban riots of the 1960's show that African Americans in the riot areas had many grievances, including few job opportunities, bad housing, and inferior schools, and the use of what they felt was excessive force by the police. Several riots were triggered by arrests or other routine police actions that people of the black ghettos considered police provocation or brutality. These police actions brought crowds into the streets in protest. The small number of police at the scene could not control them.

The resulting riots became chiefly symbolic gestures of widespread discontent. For some rioters, however, they became opportunities to loot stores for personal gain. For others, the riots were little more than destructive play. In trying to restrain the rioters and promote a return to order, the police sometimes used more force than many people thought necessary. Such action caused many rioters to become even more violent. See **African Americans** (Unrest in the cities).

Major riots in the United States

During the 1700's, most riots in the United States were instrumental riots. High and unfair taxation was a leading cause of such riots. During the 1760's and 1770's, American colonists rioted against tax collectors and other British-appointed officials (see **Boston Tea Party; Revolutionary War in America** [Background and causes of the war]). For information on other riots resulting from taxation, see **Shays' Rebellion; Whiskey Rebellion**.

During the 1800's, anti-Catholic, anti-immigrant, and antiblack riots were common. Many native-born Americans strongly disliked immigrants, especially Irish

Labor riots broke out frequently in the United States during the late 1800's and early 1900's. In 1916, rioting during a steel strike in Youngstown, Ohio, *left,* caused extensive property damage.

Roman Catholics and Asians. In the mid-1850's, members of the Know-Nothing, or American, Party opposed the Catholic Church. The Know-Nothings feared rising Irish Catholic political power. They attacked Irish Catholics in several cities, including Baltimore, Louisville, New Orleans, and St. Louis. The uprisings took several lives. See **Know-Nothings**.

In 1863, during the Civil War, antidraft riots broke out in New York City. They were among the most destructive riots in U.S. history. Armed mobs swarmed through the downtown area to protest the drafting of men into the Union Army. Rioters looted, set buildings on fire, and shot blacks, policemen, and federal troops. More than 1,000 people were killed or wounded.

Race riots in the United States have been especially destructive. Violence aimed at blacks and abolitionists broke out in several Northern cities before the Civil War. After the war, in 1866, white Southerners attacked blacks in New Orleans and Memphis.

Many Chinese immigrants were victims of mob violence during a depression in the 1870's. Many native-born Americans believed the immigrants were taking their jobs and forcing down wages. Anti-Chinese riots in California and other states resulted in several deaths and the passage of laws prohibiting Asians from entering the United States. See **Oriental exclusion acts**.

Labor riots of the late 1800's caused great bloodshed. Dozens of people were killed in riots in several cities during the great railroad strikes of 1877 (see **Labor movement** [Opposition to unions]). The Haymarket riot of 1886 in Chicago erupted when someone threw a bomb during a meeting of anarchists who were protesting police tactics against strikers at an industrial plant (see **Haymarket riot**).

During the 1900's, labor and race riots continued to cause destruction. In 1919, efforts to unionize the steel industry led to riots at plants in Indiana, Ohio, and Pennsylvania. In 1934, a dispute between unions and management in the cotton-textile industry led to riots in Georgia, South Carolina, Alabama, Rhode Island, and other states. These riots took about 20 lives.

In the early 1900's, attempts to segregate Southern blacks and keep them from voting led to lynchings in rural areas and riots in cities. During World War I (1914-1918), many blacks moved to the North to work in defense plants. Whites feared blacks would take their jobs and move into their neighborhoods. Blacks claimed white law officers treated them unfairly. These grievances led to clashes between whites and blacks. The worst one occurred in 1917 in East St. Louis, Ill., where 39 blacks and 9 whites died in a riot. A riot in Chicago in 1919 caused 38 deaths. Racial violence broke out during World War II (1939-1945). The most destructive riot occurred in 1943 in Detroit, where 34 people died.

Many riots erupted in U.S. cities during the 1960's, largely because of the economic deprivation and social injustices suffered by ghetto blacks. They included those in the Watts section of Los Angeles in 1965, in Detroit and Newark in 1967, and in Cleveland in 1968. The Detroit riot was the most violent. It led to 43 deaths and property damage of about $45 million.

After the Detroit riot, President Lyndon B. Johnson established the National Advisory Commission on Civil Disorders—also known as the Kerner Commission—to study the causes of urban riots. The commission put much of the blame on the racial prejudice and discrimination of whites against blacks. In 1968, Johnson established the National Commission on the Causes and Prevention of Violence. It recommended such measures as better housing and increased economic opportunities for blacks and poor people.

In 1968, riots broke out during the Democratic National Convention in Chicago. Thousands of young people assembled downtown. Many were protesting the nation's part in the Vietnam War (1957-1975). Many supported the presidential nomination of Senator Eugene J. McCarthy of Minnesota, a critic of the war. Several bloody clashes took place between demonstrators and the police, but no one was killed. U.S. involvement in the war led to an increasing number of small riots and demonstrations across the country.

During the late 1960's and early 1970's, student riots occurred in many U.S. cities. Most of the rioters were middle-class students who demanded a greater voice in the administration of their schools. Militant black students also used violence in efforts to enforce their demands, which included the addition of Afro-American history and culture courses.

In 1971, one of the worst prison riots in the history of the United States occurred at the state prison in Attica, N.Y. The inmates, mostly black, charged that the white prison guards mistreated them. Rioters seized the prison and held it for four days. Finally, state troopers stormed the prison to regain control. This action resulted in the deaths of 11 guards and 32 prisoners.

In 1992, riots triggered by a court decision broke out in Los Angeles and some other U.S. cities. The riots erupted after a California jury decided not to convict four white Los Angeles police officers of assault and other charges that resulted from their beating of Rodney G. King, a black motorist, in 1991. No blacks had served on the jury. King had been stopped after a pursuit, and a local resident videotaped the beating. The videotape was then broadcast by television stations throughout the nation. The court decision set off several days of rioting, mainly in black areas of South-Central Los Angeles. The rioting in Los Angeles resulted in 53 deaths, about 2,400 injuries, and over $1 billion in property damage. Later in 1992, the federal government indicted the four police officers on charges that they had violated King's civil rights. In 1993, a federal jury convicted two of the officers on these charges.

In 1997, the Oklahoma Legislature created a commission to investigate a major riot that occurred in Tulsa in 1921. During the riot, more than 300 people were killed, mostly blacks, and 1,200 buildings were destroyed. In early 2000, the commission recommended that survivors of the riot and their descendants be paid to compensate for their losses during the riot.   M. Cherif Bassiouni

Rip Van Winkle is the title character of one of the most famous short stories in American literature. The author, Washington Irving, published "Rip Van Winkle" in his collection *The Sketch Book of Geoffrey Crayon, Gent.* (1819-1820). His story, based on a German folk tale, "Peter Klaus," is set in the Catskill Mountains of New York. Irving's picturesque descriptions of the Hudson River Valley help create the story's dreamy mood.

Rip, a cheerful but lazy man, is married to a nagging

wife in American colonial times. One day he takes his dog and gun into the mountains to hunt. He meets an odd little man in old-fashioned Dutch clothing who gets Rip to help him carry a keg of liquor up the mountain. Other little men are there playing a game of ninepins. Rip samples the liquor and falls asleep.

Rip awakens 20 years later and returns to his village. There he finds that his wife has died, his children have grown, and the American Colonies have become an independent nation. At first, everyone laughs at Rip's story. But his story seems confirmed when the oldest villager assures everyone that the ghosts of the English explorer Henry Hudson and his crew keep a watch on the Catskills. Rip becomes a popular storyteller.

The tale is outstanding comic literature. It also deals with such themes as change, aging, independence, and the importance of the imagination.   Sargent Bush, Jr.

See also **Irving, Washington; Jefferson, Joseph.**

Riparian rights, *rih PAIR ee uhn,* are the legal rights of a landowner whose property borders or forms the bed of a stream or river. Each riparian owner has a right to have access to the stream and to use or consume the water reasonably. In many jurisdictions, the owner's permission is required for any increase or decrease in the flow, any move to change the flow's direction, or any action that would make the water dirty. The owner may own the land extending to the center of the bed of a nonnavigable stream, or only to the ordinary high-water mark along a navigable stream or lake.

In Western states with scarce water supplies, riparian rights to consume water are either limited or do not exist. In these states, reasonable use of water by riparian owners has been replaced by the right of *prior appropriation.* This right gives legal use of the water to the person who takes it first. Other people may use any remaining water.   Linda Henry Elrod

Ripley, Robert LeRoy (1893-1949), was an American cartoonist who became internationally famous for his cartoon panel "Believe It or Not." The panel describes oddities and strange facts and occurrences from around the world. At its peak of popularity, "Believe It or Not" had an estimated daily newspaper readership of 80 million. The feature also provided material for lectures and personal appearances by Ripley, and for radio and television shows, books, motion pictures, and museums.

Ripley was born in Santa Rosa, California. His given and family name was LeRoy Ripley, and he later added Robert. He began his career as a sports cartoonist for the *Bulletin* and the *Chronicle* in San Francisco and the *Globe* in New York City. "Believe It or Not" first appeared in the *Globe* on Dec. 19, 1918.   Charles P. Green

Ritalin, *RIHT uh lihn,* is the trade name for the drug *methylphenidate (MEHTH uhl FEHN uh dayt).* It is the drug most often prescribed to treat attention-deficit/hyperactivity disorder (ADHD). ADHD is a behavior problem in which people have unusual difficulty paying attention, sitting still, or controlling their impulses. Because the disorder is common, millions of people worldwide take Ritalin. For most ADHD patients, the drug improves concentration and reduces restlessness.

Some medical experts worry that doctors may sometimes prescribe Ritalin for people who do not really need it. Although most doctors consider the drug safe, they caution that the benefits and risks of taking it for long periods are not yet fully known.

Ritalin improves attention by stimulating the brain. It provides stimulation by lengthening the time during which two brain chemicals called *dopamine (DOH puh meen)* and *norepinephrine (NAWR ehp uh NEHF rihn)* remain active. These chemicals are *neurotransmitters* that carry messages among nerve cells. Prolonging activity of these chemicals helps nerve cells in some parts of the brain function more efficiently.

Ritalin and similar drugs can also sharpen concentration less dramatically for people without ADHD. As a result, such drugs—called *stimulants*—can be abused. The United States and many other countries strictly regulate production and prescription of stimulants.

By itself, Ritalin cannot usually overcome all the symptoms of ADHD. Most patients also require treatment involving behavioral or psychological techniques. The most common side effects of Ritalin are decreased appetite and difficulty falling asleep.   F. Xavier Castellanos

See also **Attention deficit disorder.**

Rite of passage is a ceremony held by nearly all societies to observe a person's entry into a new stage of life. Rites of passage note such occasions as birth, graduation, or marriage. Most rites help people understand and accept their new roles in society, and help others learn to treat them in new ways.

Most rites of passage have three stages—*separation, transition,* and *incorporation.* First, a participant in the rite is temporarily separated from the rest of society and from his or her former role. During the transitional, or in-between, stage, the participant may learn the behavior appropriate to the new role. The participant is then formally incorporated, or admitted, into that role.

In many graduation ceremonies, for example, students sit in a special area, separate from friends and relatives. Then they walk across a stage to symbolize the transition. Finally, they switch the tassels on their caps from one side to the other to indicate their entry into society as graduates. In some African societies, boys who will soon become men are separated for days or months while they learn legends and technical skills.

Participants in most rites of passage wear special costumes to symbolize their temporary separation from society and the change they experience. Such costumes include wedding dresses and graduation gowns.

The term *rites of passage* was invented by French anthropologist Arnold van Gennep to describe such ceremonies as baptisms, weddings, and funerals. He used it in his book *Les Rites de Passage* (1909).   Jennie Keith

Each rite discussed in this article has a separate article in *World Book.* See also **Bar mitzvah; Bat mitzvah; Confirmation.**

Ritter, Tex (1907-1974), was an American country music singer and songwriter. Ritter also gained popularity as a radio actor and as a singing cowboy in motion-picture Westerns. His most popular recording was the theme song from the movie *High Noon* (1952).

Ritter was born on a farm in Panola County, Texas. His full name was Maurice Woodward Ritter.

Ritter became a radio actor in New York City in 1929 and eventually performed on such Western shows as "The Lone Ranger" and "Death Valley Days." He also appeared in several stage plays. Ritter moved to Hollywood, California, in the mid-1930's. He made his first movie in 1936 and appeared in approximately 80 Western films. Ritter spent the final years of his life in Nashville, where he often appeared on "The Grand Ole Opry" radio program. Lee Rector

Ritty, James (1836-1918), an American restaurant owner, invented the cash register. While traveling to Europe in 1878, he saw a device for counting the revolutions of the ship's propellers. When he came home, he devised a similar machine to record business transactions. In 1879, he and his brother John built and patented a gear-operated adding machine. They sold the business in 1881. James Ritty was born in Dayton, Ohio. George H. Daniels

Ritual. See Religion (Religious rituals).

River is a large, natural stream of water that flows overland within a channel. Most rivers begin in mountains or hills. A river ends where it flows into another river, desert basin, ocean, or lake. A river is the main part of a *river system,* which also includes all the smaller streams that supply water to the river. A region of land that is drained by a river system is known as a *drainage basin.*

The world's longest river is the Nile River in Africa, which flows for 4,160 miles (6,695 kilometers). The next longest is the Amazon River in South America, which is about 4,000 miles (6,437 kilometers) long. The Amazon carries more water than any other river—and more water than the Nile, the Mississippi River in the United States, and the Yangtze River in China combined.

Uses of rivers

For centuries, people have used rivers for transportation and trade. In North and South America, for example, early explorers, traders, and pioneers traveled on rivers. Later, they built towns along major rivers. Several of these towns grew into large cities. On the Mississippi River, for instance, Minneapolis, St. Louis, Memphis, and New Orleans became large cities.

Rivers are also valuable to agriculture. Farmers grow crops in the fertile land of river plains and the terraced surfaces above those plains. In dry regions, farmers use river water to irrigate their land. They dig irrigation ditches to carry water from rivers to farmland.

In addition, rivers serve as a source of power. The energy of flowing water at waterfalls and other steep places along a river can drive machines and generate electric power.

Sources of river water

Almost all river water comes from rain or melted snow. Most of the water reaches rivers indirectly. In some cases, water called *surface runoff* flows over the land to the river. In other cases, the water soaks into soil and rocks and becomes *ground water* (water beneath the surface of the earth). The ground water then moves slowly through the soil or underground rocks to the rivers. This subsurface supply of water can keep a river flowing between periods of rain. Other sources of river water include glaciers, springs, and overflowing lakes.

Where rainfall is seasonal, a river may be dry for part of the year. This kind of river is known as an *intermittent river.* A river that flows across a desert may also be intermittent. Such a river does not receive ground water. Rather, it gives up water to the ground beneath it. This loss, together with evaporation, may cause the river to dry up for part of the year.

Exotic rivers are large rivers that begin in a rainy area, then flow across a desert without drying up. The Nile River and the Colorado River, which is in the United States, are exotic rivers in parts of their channels.

River systems

A river system consists of the river itself and all the smaller streams that supply water to the river. A river is highest at its *headwaters,* where it begins. It is lowest at its *mouth,* where it ends.

A river *erodes* (wears away) a great deal of material from the land over which it flows. This material is called the river's *load* while it is flowing and *sediment* when it is deposited. In many rivers, most of the material is dissolved in the water and cannot be seen. This *invisible load* mixes with lake or ocean water at the mouth. A river also carries a *visible load* that consists of material ranging from tiny particles of clay to large boulders. The finer particles may determine the color of the water, which may range from red to brown or yellow.

Some rivers flow gradually from headwaters to mouth. Other rivers have irregular features, such as waterfalls, rapids, and canyons. Many rivers that empty into oceans have deep, broad mouths called *estuaries.*

Tributaries. Runoff collects in tiny, temporary channels called *rills.* Rills often flow into streams that eventually join to form rivers. Smaller streams that flow into larger ones are called *tributaries.*

Scientists often classify streams by *stream order.* For example, a stream with no permanent tributaries is a first order stream. Two first order streams meet to form a second order stream. Two second order streams join

© William E. Ferguson

A melting glacier near Furka Pass in the Swiss Alps is the source of the Rhône River. The Rhône flows from Switzerland through southern France and empties into the Mediterranean Sea.

to form a third order stream, and so on. Low order streams are commonly called *brooks* or *creeks,* while higher order streams are commonly called rivers. One river may be a tributary of another river. For example, the Missouri River is a tributary of the Mississippi.

Channels are passages in which river water flows. A river's channel extends from the headwaters to the mouth. The channel bottom is the river's *bed,* and the edges of the channel are the *banks.*

The slope of a channel tends to be steep near the source of a river and almost flat near the mouth. Channel width and depth typically increase downstream due to the increasing flow of water.

Waterfalls and rapids occur in the upper *courses* (segments) of many rivers. A waterfall occurs where a river crosses a layer of hard rock that resists erosion. The water erodes softer rock downstream, creating a steep drop in the channel. *Rapids* occur where water tumbles over large boulders or rock ledges.

Canyons. In the upper course of a river, the channel may occupy the full width of the valley floor. The river may undercut the sides of the valley from place to place, and it also deepens the valley. Valley sides are typically V-shaped above the valley floor. Rapid cutting can produce a canyon, a deep valley with cliffs above the floor.

Estuaries contain a mixture of salt water from the ocean and fresh water from the river. The Amazon River is an estuary for several hundred miles or kilometers upstream from its mouth.

Estuaries formed as a result of ancient changes in sea level. During the Pleistocene Epoch, which lasted from about 2 million to 11,500 years ago, sea level moved down and up several times. This movement occurred because vast ice sheets accumulated on the land and then melted away several times. At the end of the epoch, the sea level was low, and rivers near the ocean had cut their valleys down to the low level. Since then, many of the ice sheets have melted. As a result, sea level has

Famous rivers of the world

Name	Length* In miles	In kilometers	Location	Interesting facts
Amazon	4,000	6,437	South America	Carries more water than any other river; world's second longest river; only the Nile is longer.
Colorado	1,450	2,334	United States	River's current, combined with other agents of erosion, created the Grand Canyon.
Congo	2,900	4,667	Africa	Second longest river in Africa and second in the amount of water carried in the world.
Danube	1,770	2,850	Europe	Its beauty inspired Austrian composer Johann Strauss, Jr., to write the famous waltz "On the Beautiful Blue Danube."
Euphrates	1,700	2,736	Turkey-Syria-Iraq	Longest river in southwestern Asia; part of the Tigris-Euphrates river system, in which the world's first civilization developed.
Ganges	1,560	2,510	India-Bangladesh	Considered sacred by members of the Hindu faith.
Huang He	3,000	4,830	China	Name means *yellow river;* large amounts of yellow silt are deposited along its course; world's fourth longest river.
Indus	1,800	2,897	Tibet-Pakistan	Source of one of the largest irrigation systems in the world.
Jordan	200	320	Israel-Jordan	River mentioned most often in the Bible.
Lena	2,734	4,400	Russia	Russia's longest river.
Mackenzie	1,100	1,770	Canada	Canada's longest river.
Mekong	2,600	4,180	Asia	Largest river on the Indochinese Peninsula.
Mississippi	2,350	3,780	United States	Second longest river in the United States.
Missouri	2,565	4,130	United States	Longest river in the United States.
Murray	1,609	2,589	Australia	Longest permanently flowing river in Australia.
Niagara	34	55	United States-Canada	Famous for its spectacular Niagara Falls.
Niger	2,600	4,180	Africa	Its delta is the largest in Africa.
Nile	4,160	6,695	Northeast Africa	World's longest river.
Rhine	820	1,320	Europe	Most important inland waterway in Europe; one of the world's busiest rivers.
Rio Grande	1,885	3,034	United States-Mexico	Spanish name for *large river;* forms part of international boundary between United States and Mexico.
St. Lawrence	800	1,300	Canada-United States	Links the Great Lakes and the Atlantic Ocean.
Seine	480	770	France	Flows through the heart of Paris, where more than 30 bridges span it.
Thames	210	340	United Kingdom	Longest and most important waterway entirely within England; flows through the center of London.
Volga	2,300	3,700	Russia	Longest river in Europe.
Yangtze	3,900	6,275	China	China's longest river; third longest river in the world; only the Nile and the Amazon are longer.
Zambezi	1,700	2,736	Africa	Its Victoria Falls is one of the Seven Natural Wonders of the World.

*Refers only to the length of the river itself and not the length of the river system.

Parts of a river system

A river may drain water from a huge area. The source of the river in this diagram is a melting glacier high in the mountains. But all the water that flows into the river—and the river itself—make up the parts of the river system.

WORLD BOOK diagram
by Laura Lee Lizak

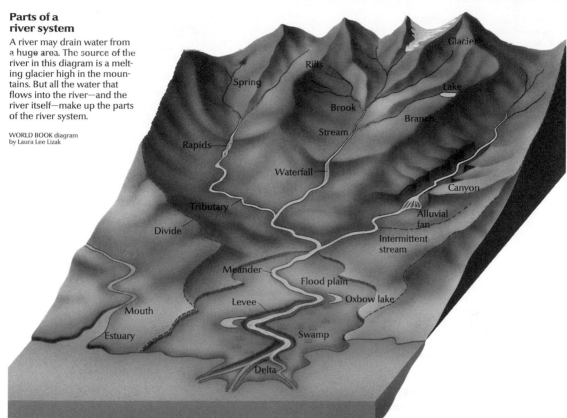

risen. Ocean water has flowed into the valleys that had been cut, forming the estuaries.

Drainage basins

A drainage basin consists of the region drained by a river system. The Amazon River has a drainage basin of about 2,700,000 square miles (7,000,000 square kilometers). The Mississippi River drains about 1,244,000 square miles (3,220,000 square kilometers) of land in North America. This land includes about 40 percent of the United States, except Alaska and Hawaii. A basin's waters make up a *drainage net.*

Divides. The rim of a drainage basin is called a *drainage divide.* One major drainage divide follows the crest of the Rocky Mountains. This divide splits the continent of North America into two large drainage regions. It is therefore known as the Continental Divide. Basins to the west of the divide carry water to the Pacific Ocean. To the east is the Mississippi River basin, which carries water to the Gulf of Mexico. Other eastern basins carry water to the Atlantic Ocean and the Arctic Ocean.

Flood plains are flat areas on one or both sides of the middle or lower course of a river. When the river overflows its banks, it floods these areas. A flood plain can be hundreds of miles or kilometers wide.

Floodwaters deposit sediment on the flood plain, particularly on the parts of the plain next to the channel. The deposits create banks called *natural levees.* Marshy areas called *back swamps* occupy the parts of flood plains beyond the natural levees.

A channel in a wide flood plain tends to curve from one side of the plain to the other. The snakelike bends in the channel are known as *meanders.* Meanders can form almost complete loops, with only a narrow neck of land separating the beginning and end of each loop. Eventually, floodwater flows across this neck, cutting off the loop and creating a new, straight channel for the river. The separated loop then fills with rain water or ground water. The loop may continue to exist for many years as a crescent-shaped *oxbow lake.*

Alluvial fans and deltas are land masses that build up where a flow of river water decreases quickly. The decrease in the flow causes the river to deposit its visible load rapidly, forming the land mass. An alluvial fan is a fan-shaped land mass that forms where a river flows from a steep mountain slope to a flatter plain next to the slope. The decrease in elevation slows the river down, causing some of the river's load to be deposited. River flow also slows down where a river reaches a lake or ocean, so most of the remaining load is deposited there.

A delta is a low plain that may form at a river's mouth. The Mississippi River and the Nile River have large deltas. David S. McArthur

Related articles in *World Book.* See the *Rivers and lakes* section in the various country, state, and province articles, such as **Alabama** (Rivers and lakes). See also:

Africa

Congo River	Nile River	Ubangi River
Limpopo River	Orange River	Zambezi River
Niger River		

Asia

Amur River	Indus River	Tigris River
Brahmaputra River	Irrawaddy River	Ural River
Euphrates River	Jordan River	Xi Jiang
Ganges River	Lena River	Yalu River
Hooghly River	Mekong River	Yangtze River
Huang He	Ob River	

Australia

Murray River	Torrens

Canada

Athabasca River	Niagara River	Saint Lawrence
Churchill River	Ottawa River	River
Columbia River	Peace River	Saint Marys River
Detroit River	Red River of the	Saskatchewan
Fraser River	North	River
Mackenzie River	Restigouche River	Skeena River
Miramichi River	Saguenay River	Winnipeg River
Nelson River	Saint John River	Yukon River

Europe

Aisne River	Mersey, River	Severn, River
Arno River	Meuse River	Shannon, River
Avon, River	Moselle River	Tagus River
Clyde, River	Neman River	Thames, River
Danube River	Oder River	Tiber River
Dnepr River	Po River	Torne River
Don River	Rhine River	Tweed, River
Dvina River	Rhône River	Ural River
Elbe River	Rubicon	Vistula River
Humber, River	Saône River	Volga River
Loire River	Seine River	Weser River
Marne River		

North America

See the articles listed under Canada and United States in this section.

South America

Amazon River	Paraguay River	São Francisco
Madeira River	Paraná River	River
Orinoco River		Uruguay River

United States

Allegheny River	Penobscot River
Arkansas River	Platte River
Colorado River	Potomac River
Columbia River	Rappahannock River
Connecticut River	Red River
Cumberland River	Red River of the North
Delaware River	Rio Grande
Detroit River	Sacramento River
Gila River	Saint Marys River
Housatonic River	Salt River
Hudson River	San Joaquin River
Illinois River	Savannah River
James River	Schuylkill River
Kanawha River	Shenandoah River
Kennebec River	Snake River
Merrimack River	Susquehanna River
Minnesota River	Suwannee River
Mississippi River	Tennessee River
Missouri River	Tombigbee River
Mobile River	Wabash River
Mohawk River	Willamette River
Monongahela River	Wisconsin River
Niagara River	Yellowstone River
Ohio River	Yukon River
Pecos River	

Other related articles

Alluvial fan	Bayou	Delta
Alluvium	Canyon	Divide
Basin	Dam	Erosion
Flood	Silt	World (graph:
Lagoon	Valley	Longest river
Levee	Water power	on each
Oxbow lake	Water wheel	continent)
Reservoir	Waterfall	

Additional resources

Ayer, Eleanor. *Our Great Rivers and Waterways.* Millbrook, 1994. Younger readers.
Bolling, David M. *How to Save a River.* Island Pr., 1994.
Calow, Peter, and Petts, G. E. *The Rivers Handbook.* 2 vols. Blackwell Science, 1992, 1994.
Palmer, Tim. *America by Rivers.* Island Pr., 1996. *Lifelines: The Case for River Conservation.* 1994. *The Wild and Scenic Rivers of America.* 1993.
Patrick, Ruth. *Rivers of the United States.* Wiley, 1994-. Multivolume work.
Sayre, April P. *River and Stream.* 21st Century Bks., 1996. Younger readers.

River . . . Some rivers, particularly those in the United Kingdom, have names starting with the word *River,* such as River Clyde. See the separate articles for these rivers under the name following the word *River,* for example, **Clyde, River; Thames, River.**

River dolphin is a type of dolphin that lives in fresh or slightly salty water. River dolphins inhabit warm rivers and lakes of Asia and South America.

Both river dolphins and marine dolphins belong to a group of mammals called *cetaceans.* But these two types of dolphins differ somewhat in appearance. For example, the snout of a river dolphin measures about 1 foot (30 centimeters) long, approximately four times as long as that of most marine dolphins. River dolphins have smaller eyes than marine dolphins, and their vision is poorly developed because they live in dark, muddy water. This environment also makes river dolphins less active than marine dolphins. River dolphins feed primarily on fish.

The largest river dolphins usually grow up to 8 feet (2.4 meters) long, but most of the animals are smaller. River dolphins may be white, pink, yellow, brown, gray, or black in color.

There are four species of river dolphins. The *bouta,* also called the *Amazon porpoise,* lives in rivers of northern South America. The *white fin dolphin* is found in Dongting Lake in China. The blind *Ganges dolphin* inhabits rivers of northern India and Pakistan. The *La Plata*

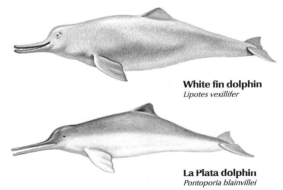

White fin dolphin
Lipotes vexillifer

La Plata dolphin
Pontoporia blainvillei

WORLD BOOK illustration by James Teason

River dolphins live in warm rivers and lakes of Asia and South America. They have a long snout and feed mainly on fish. Two of the four kinds of river dolphins are shown above.

Fresco (1942) by Diego Rivera; Giraudon

Paintings by Diego Rivera portray the culture and history of Mexico. The mural at the left shows the Zapotec Indians of southern Mexico making gold jewelry before Spain conquered Mexico in the 1500's. The mural is one of a series by Rivera in the National Palace in Mexico City.

dolphin, also known as *Franciscana,* lives in rivers and coastal waters of eastern South America. All species of river dolphins are seriously threatened by human activities that directly kill the animals or destroy their habitat.

Scientific classification. River dolphins belong to the family Platanistidae. The scientific name for the bouta is *Inia geoffrensis.* The white fin dolphin is *Lipotes vexillifer;* the Ganges dolphin, *Platanista gangetica;* and the La Plata dolphin, *Pontoporia blainvillei.*   Daniel K. Odell

See also **Cetacean; Dolphin.**

River horse. See Hippopotamus.

Rivera, Diego (1886-1957), was a Mexican artist. He became famous for murals that portrayed Mexican life and history. Rivera was a controversial figure because of his radical political beliefs and his attacks on the church and clergy.

Rivera was born in Guanajuato. In the 1920's, he became involved in the new Mexican mural movement. With such Mexican artists as José Clemente Orozco and David Siqueiros, he began to experiment with fresco painting on large walls (see **Fresco**). Rivera soon developed his own style of large, simplified figures and bold colors. Many of his murals deal symbolically with Mexican society and thought after the country's 1910 revolution. Some of Rivera's best murals are in the National Palace in Mexico City and at the National Agricultural School in Chapingo, near Mexico City.

Rivera painted several significant works in the United States, which he visited in the early 1930's and again in 1940. Perhaps his finest surviving United States work is a mural at the Detroit Institute of Arts. Frida Kahlo, Rivera's wife, was also a noted Mexican painter.

Judith Berg Sobré

See also **Aztec** (picture).

Rivers, Larry (1923-   ), is an American painter. Beginning in the early 1950's, Rivers chose American symbols as his subjects. They were either historical themes or images of commercial products, such as cigarette packages. Rivers' deliberately unidealistic works have an amusing, ironical nature. With his introduction of popular imagery as subjects, he is often considered a forerunner of the pop art movement (see **Pop art**).

Rivers' subjects emerge from loosely painted backgrounds with visible brushstrokes or sometimes bare canvas. Many paintings have an appearance of rapid execution and fragmentation, almost as if they were unfin-

Oil painting on canvas (1953); the Museum of Modern Art, New York City

Rivers' *Washington Crossing the Delaware* shows the artist's individual approach to traditional American subjects.

ished. Some works show parts of the same figure from several points of view. Rivers was born in New York City.

Deborah Leveton

Riveting is a method of joining two metal plates with threadless aluminum, iron, or steel bolts called *rivets.* A rivet has a rounded head at one end.

In riveting, a worker called a *rivet heater* heats rivets in a small portable forge. When the rivets become red hot, the rivet heater removes them from the forge with small tongs and passes them to another worker called the *riveter helper.* The riveter helper inserts the rivets in holes that have been drilled or punched in two metal plates. The rivets are long enough to extend through both plates. The riveter helper places an *anvil* or *bucking bar* against the rounded head of the bolt. Then another worker, called the *riveter,* uses a pneumatic hammer to close and shape the *tail,* or open end of the rivet. Rivets compressed and joined together in this way become double-ended bolts that hold the plates firmly together.

Ordinarily, only one row of rivets is used. This is called *single* riveting. Riveters sometimes use *double* riveting, or two rows of rivets, when extra strength is needed. Workers can punch holes in soft metals. But they must drill the rivet holes in thick pieces or in hard metals.

Sometimes devices other than pneumatic hammers are used to shape and close rivets. Machine shops often use large hydraulic presses for riveting. A *riveting machine* has the anvil and the hammer joined together by a hinge or solid yoke. The anvil holds the rivet in place, and the hammer closes and shapes the tail.

In *cold heading,* riveters use soft iron rivets that are shaped and closed while cold. The cold forming of the soft metal increases its strength. The aircraft industry commonly uses cold heading on the aluminum wing and body surfaces of airplanes.

Welding has replaced riveting for many uses. But riveting is still the accepted method in making boilers and erecting structural steel for buildings. It is also necessary in shipbuilding.   Melvin Bernstein

Riviera, *RIHV ee AIR uh,* is a narrow strip of land on the Mediterranean Sea. The region runs from Hyères in southern France to La Spezia in northwestern Italy. The Alps rise back of the Riviera. Each year, travelers from many parts of the world bask in the warm sunshine of the Riviera for both health and pleasure. Balmy southern breezes drift in from the Mediterranean Sea throughout the year, and the Alps shut off the cold north and east winds.

A chain of French and Italian towns lies on the Riviera. They are connected by an excellent road that follows an ancient Roman highway. A railroad also links the towns together. The towns are colorful with brightly painted houses and green, fragrant gardens. The people of the Riviera cultivate bananas, dates, flowers, pomegranates, and prickly pears.

The towns that are located along the Riviera include Antibes, Cannes, Hyères, Menton, Nice, and St. Tropez in France; Monte Carlo in Monaco; and Albenga, Genoa, La Spezia, Rapallo, San Remo, Savona, and Ventimiglia in Italy.   William M. Reddy

See also **France** (picture); **Cannes; Monaco; Nice.**

Riyadh, *ree YAHD* (pop. 2,776,096), is the capital and largest city of Saudi Arabia. Riyadh lies among oases on a dry, rocky plateau near the center of the country (see **Saudi Arabia** [political map]). Riyadh is a business center and serves as the administrative headquarters of Saudi Arabia's vast oil industry. The city is also the center of Wahhabism, a conservative form of Sunni Islam.

Since the mid-1970's, when Saudi Arabia's oil income increased dramatically, Riyadh has been one of the world's fastest-growing cities. Hundreds of thousands of people have moved from rural areas of Saudi Arabia and from other countries to Riyadh in search of employment.

High-rise office buildings and large homes of concrete, steel, and marble have replaced nearly all of Riyadh's old mud-brick buildings. Wide avenues and highways have taken the place of most narrow, unpaved streets. Many schools and hospitals have also been built in Riyadh. The Saudi government has laid a pipeline to help supply the city's residents with water. The pipeline extends 290 miles (467 kilometers) between Riyadh and Al Jubayl on the Persian Gulf coast. It delivers *desalinated* seawater—that is, seawater from which the salt has been removed. In the 1980's, a huge embassy complex,

© Marc Riboud, Magnum

Riyadh is the capital and largest city of Saudi Arabia. Oil income has made it one of the world's fastest-growing cities with modern skyscrapers and wide, busy streets.

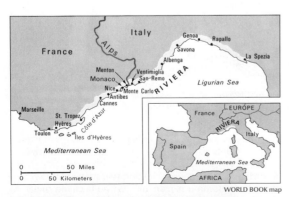
WORLD BOOK map

The Riviera lies on Europe's Mediterranean coast.

called the Diplomatic Quarter, was built in Riyadh to accommodate diplomatic missions to Saudi Arabia. Previously, such missions had their embassies in Jidda.

Riyadh has numerous public gardens, parks, children's playgrounds, and a zoo. A covered stadium in the city hosts international sports events. The Riyadh Museum displays objects from the country's past. King Saud University Museum in Riyadh exhibits items from the university's archaeological excavations. The university itself is the largest one in Saudi Arabia.

The Saudi government, which controls the country's oil industry, is Riyadh's largest employer. Factories there produce aluminum, chemicals, china, paper, plastics, prefabricated houses, and many other products. A railroad links Riyadh to Ad Dammam on the Persian Gulf. King Khalid International Airport serves the city.

Riyadh became the center of Wahhabism after Egyptian forces destroyed the nearby town of Dariyah, capital of the Wahhabi empire, in 1818. The Saud family controlled Riyadh from 1824 to 1891, when they were expelled by a rival group. They retook the town in 1902. Riyadh then became the capital of the growing Saudi territory, which was recognized as the Kingdom of Saudi Arabia in 1932.   Eleanor Abdella Doumato

See also **Saudi Arabia** (History).

Rizal, *ree ZAHL,* **José,** *hoh SAY,* (1861-1896), a Filipino doctor and novelist, became a national hero of the Philippines. He was an early leader of the Filipino movement for political and social freedom from Spain. The Spaniards, who ruled the Philippines at the time, executed Rizal for his activities.

José Mercado y Alonso Rizal was born in Calamba, the Philippines. After obtaining his qualifications in medicine in Madrid, Spain, Rizal traveled to Germany, England, and France, where he continued to study medicine. He wrote for *La Solidaridad,* a magazine published in Barcelona, Spain, that campaigned for reforms in the Philippines.

While living in Europe, Rizal gained worldwide attention with two novels. *Noli Me Tangere* (Latin for *Touch Me Not)* was published in Berlin in 1886. Rizal's second book, *El Filibusterismo (The Subversive),* was published in Belgium in 1891. Both novels exposed the ills of the Spanish colonial government and Filipino society.

While conducting research at the British Museum in London, Rizal came across an early history of the Philippines. The book was written by Antonio de Morga and was printed in Mexico in 1609. Morga, an early Spanish governor general of the Philippines, pointed out that Filipinos had a civilization of their own before the Spanish arrived. In 1890, Rizal printed a new edition of the history with his own notes added to the text.

In 1892, Rizal returned to Manila. He was arrested and exiled to the southern Philippine island of Mindanao.

In 1896, the Katipunan, a secret Filipino revolutionary society, tried to overthrow the Spanish government. Rizal was on his way back to Manila when the revolution broke out. Though he had no connection with the Katipunan or the uprising, a Spanish military court found him guilty of promoting the rebellion. On the morning of Dec. 30, 1896, Rizal was executed by firing squad.

Rizal was a man of numerous talents. A gifted linguist, he is said to have understood 22 languages. Rizal was not only a novelist but also a poet, essayist, historian, musician, painter, and sculptor.

RNA, also known as *ribonucleic acid,* is a complex molecule that plays a major role in all living cells. RNA molecules help produce substances called *proteins.* Proteins are chains of smaller organic molecules known as *amino acids.* The body uses proteins to build cells and to carry out the cells' work.

RNA is similar in structure to *DNA (deoxyribonucleic acid),* another important molecule found in cells. Like DNA, all RNA molecules contain hundreds of smaller chemical units called *nucleotides.* These nucleotides are bonded together chemically to form thin, chainlike molecules called *polynucleotides.* Unlike DNA, each RNA molecule consists of a single polynucleotide chain. A DNA molecule has two chains. In addition, RNA occurs throughout the cell, while DNA is found mainly in the cell's nucleus.

RNA nucleotides contain a compound called a *phosphate,* a sugar called *ribose,* and a compound called a *base.* The phosphate and sugar are the same in all RNA nucleotides, but the bases vary. There are four RNA bases: (1) *adenine,* (2) *guanine,* (3) *cytosine,* and (4) *uracil.*

Different types of RNA perform different jobs. One type, known as *messenger RNA* or *mRNA,* copies chemical instructions from DNA for making proteins. The mRNA then leaves the nucleus and carries the instructions to protein-making cell structures called *ribosomes.* These instructions tell the cell how to put amino acids together in the right order to make a specific protein. Some RNA molecules act as enzymes to speed up certain chemical reactions.

Another type of RNA is called *transfer RNA* or *tRNA.* A tRNA molecule collects amino acids and brings them to the ribosome. A third type of RNA, *ribosomal RNA* or *rRNA,* is an important physical component of ribosomes.
                          Irwin Rubenstein

See also **Cell; DNA; Heredity.**

Roach. See **Cockroach.**

Roach is a fish of the carp and minnow family that lives in slightly salty lowland rivers and lakes in Europe. It is caught both for sport and for food. The fish usually grows 6 to 8 inches (15 to 20 centimeters) in length, but may reach a length of 14 inches (36 centimeters). The roach is silvery, with a greenish back. The iris of the eye is bright red. The name *roach* is also given to a large American minnow called the *golden shiner.*
                          David W. Greenfield

Scientific classification. The roach belongs to the carp and minnow family, Cyprinidae. The scientific name for the roach is *Rutilus rutilus.*

Road is a strip of land that provides routes for travel by automobiles and other wheeled vehicles. Roads within towns and cities are often called *streets.*

Roads and highways are vital lifelines. Farmers use them to ship their products to market. Trucks can transport manufactured products from one area to another. Roads carry automobiles, buses, bicycles, and other vehicles on business and pleasure trips.

Kinds of roads and highways

Local and secondary roads. *Local roads* carry traffic within a local area. *Secondary roads* link small communities and connect local roads to main highways leading to more distant places.

Primary highways. The most important roads generally are those that carry the greatest number of automobiles, trucks, and buses. These main roads, called *primary highways,* connect the larger communities.

Major types of primary highways include *divided highways* and *controlled access highways.* Divided highways are roads with four or more traffic lanes divided in the center with a strip of land, called a *median strip.* This strip separates vehicles going in opposite directions and helps prevent collisions.

Controlled access highways are designed to achieve safety and smooth traffic flow through the principle of *controlled access.* On fully controlled access highways, a vehicle can enter or leave a main highway only at certain locations called *interchanges.* Most of these interchanges are at main crossroads. *Grade separations* are often used to separate crossing streams of traffic. In a grade separation, one of the intersecting highways crosses over the other on a bridge. The two are connected by sloping, curved roadways called *ramps.*

With controlled access, no driveways from homes or commercial establishments connect directly with the main highway. Minor roads and streets pass over or under the road without connecting to it. Minor roads may also dead-end at the highway or connect with a service road that runs parallel to the highway.

Freeways or *superhighways,* called *motorways* in some countries, are main highways with full access control and grade-separated interchanges. Those with four or more lanes are divided by a median strip. Freeways in congested parts of large cities are often *elevated* (built above surface streets) or *depressed* (built below surface streets). The term *freeway* refers only to the free flow of traffic. Motorists may have to pay a toll to travel on these roads. Roads that require a toll are called *tollways* or *toll roads.*

Expressways are similar to freeways but sometimes have only partial access control. *Parkways* are roads resembling freeways. But they are built in parklike surroundings with attractive landscaping and scenery. Most parkways are limited to passenger vehicles.

Freeways and other roads are numbered to help travelers. In some countries, roads are designated by a combination of numbers and letters. In the United Kingdom, for example, freeways are designated by the letter M and a number, while minor roads begin with the letter B. The letters and numbers that represent the roads appear on road signs and on maps.

Signs on freeways and expressways alert drivers to exits and indicate the distance to the next rest area or service area with fuel and restaurant facilities. Emergency warning signs may be posted to tell drivers to slow down when approaching road construction or some type of hazard.

How roads and highways are built

Planning. Highway planners study everything from the long-range needs of a region or an entire country to a particular section of a single route. This planning determines what the highway needs of the region are and how these needs can best be fulfilled and paid for.

Much road work involves improving existing roads. This may mean paving over a dirt road that is experiencing increasing traffic. New roads may be needed to cope with increasing traffic or to connect with a new town or development area.

In planning a system or a route, planners must learn: (1) where people live, (2) where they want to go, (3) by what means and route they get there, (4) where goods are produced, (5) what markets the goods are sent to, and (6) how the goods reach their final users. Traffic counts tell how many and what kinds of vehicles travel on a road, and when traffic is heaviest. From these and other facts about the past and present, planners try to predict future growth in population and industry, changes in land use, and how such growth and change will affect highway needs.

Public participation in road planning is essential. In many countries, planners hold public hearings on most major highway projects. These meetings enable citizens to present their views before a project begins.

Engineers have set standards for various kinds of roads, highways, and bridges. These standards govern the thickness and kind of foundation and surfacing for different kinds of traffic; the number of lanes needed; the sharpness of curves; and the steepness of hills.

Engineers run tests where a new road is to be built to find out how the soil's properties differ when it is wet or dry. Such tests help determine the weight of traffic the road can support.

In planning a new road or rebuilding an existing one, maps must be drawn if they are not already available. These maps show the location of other roads, railroads, towns, farms, houses, and other buildings. They also show such natural features as rivers, lakes, forests, hills, and the slope of the land. Soil types may be identified.

Using these maps, engineers locate new highways and make drawings called *plans,* which show the boundaries of the *right of way.* The right of way is land needed for road pavement, shoulders, ditches, and side slopes. The plans also show the location, grades, and curves of the pavement, and the location of bridges and culverts.

In the United States, highway planners must also prepare an *environmental impact statement* before beginning construction. The purpose of such a statement is to discover in advance all the possible good and bad effects that a new highway may have on the public and on the environment.

Bypasses are built to take motorists around cities. Motorists traveling some distance often do not want to drive through small towns or the centers of large cities that lie on their routes. Those traveling from one part of a city to another also usually prefer to avoid downtown traffic. The bypass helps these motorists avoid city traffic, and reduces traffic congestion for those who want to drive into town.

Bypasses are usually built as freeways, sometimes with service roads on one or both sides to serve local traffic. In large cities, a bypass may be called a *circumferential* or a *beltway.*

Intersections, called *junctions* in some countries, are crossings of one road by another. Most intersections are at the same level, so that vehicles going east and west have to take turns crossing with vehicles going north and south. Sometimes roads intersect at odd angles, and it is especially difficult to make a safe crossing. At such places, the traffic engineer may put *islands* in the paved

A typical design for a paved road

WORLD BOOK illustration by Oxford Illustrators Limited

Subgrade is the natural soil that forms the roadbed. The soil is either naturally firm, or is leveled off and packed by heavy machines.

Base provides support for the surface and prevents moisture from forming under it. Materials include sand, stone, and bitumen or portland cement.

Surface, or wearing course, is smooth, firm, and water-shedding. This pavement has a concrete surface. Many pavements have bituminous surfaces.

Shoulders are wide for safe emergency stopping, and sloped for proper drainage. They often have an asphalt surface and a gravel or soil-cement base.

area to keep traffic in the proper paths. The best and safest kind of intersection is the grade-separated interchange. One common type of interchange is called a *cloverleaf,* because its curved inner ramps form the pattern of a four-leaf clover. A simpler kind is called a *diamond* because its ramps form that shape. Diamonds often connect a major highway and a secondary road. When two freeways intersect, more complex interchanges are sometimes needed. These may require a number of bridges and many ramps.

Grading. The first job in building a new highway is to clear the right of way. There may be trees to cut down and stumps to pull up. Sometimes buildings must be torn down or moved. The right of way then is ready for rough grading. At this stage, huge machines called earth movers, which can dig up a roomful of dirt in one scoop, are used. They cut into the hills, carry the earth along, and drop it into the valleys to make a road with gentle grades. This method is known as *cut-and-fill construction.*

Sometimes, the right kind of earth to be used for the foundation of the road must be hauled in, perhaps from some distance away. While the grading is going on, *culverts* (pipes to carry away rain water) are put in place under the road or under driveway entrances. Ditches are cut at the roadsides to carry rain water to the culverts. After the right-of-way is shaped roughly for traffic lanes, shoulders, and ditches, it is smoothed and packed down to the required level and shape.

Paving begins after grading is completed. The pavement is of definite thickness and is of stronger materials than the earth underneath. The kind and thickness of pavements depend largely on the weight and amount of traffic expected to use them.

In some places, different kinds of earth or soil are mixed together to form a pavement. Certain chemicals, lime, cement, or *bitumens* (asphalts and tars) may also be mixed with soil to act as a binder and to make it harder and more durable. On most of the low-traffic surfaced

roads, however, the pavements are of gravel, crushed rock, or other mined materials. These types of pavements may be given a thin surfacing of bitumens known as *seal coat.*

Roads that carry heavy traffic must have a durable surface. An intermediate type of surfacing is called *bituminous macadam.* This is made by placing crushed stone or gravel on the roadbed, packing it down firmly, and filling the spaces with a bitumen. Better types of bituminous surfacing are made with sand, gravel, or crushed stone premixed with bitumens. These types of surfacing are laid with a paving machine, and then rolled hard and smooth. Bituminous pavement is sometimes referred to as *blacktop.*

Another hard surfacing material is portland cement concrete. It is made with sand, portland cement, water, and gravel or crushed stone. In both kinds of surfacing—bituminous and portland cement concrete—the *aggregate* (stone and sand) forms the body of the material and the bitumen or portland cement serves as a binder.

As roads are built, they are inspected continually, and tests are also made on the construction materials. After a road is finished, drilling machines take core samples of the paving and the base. Engineers use these samples to be sure that the finished paving is as thick and as strong as was planned.

Storm-water drainage. Storm-water runoff from paved highways and parking lots may contain oil, exhaust emissions, and other dangerous chemicals from vehicles. These chemicals once mixed with other storm water and entered rivers and streams. Many areas now require that highway projects include ditches or channels that direct storm water into temporary storage ponds. The water eventually evaporates or is absorbed into the ground. Storm-water storage facilities are also built near large parking areas.

Lighting. Good lighting helps reduce the number of accidents for both vehicles and pedestrians. On most roads and highways, nearly all the light comes from the headlights of the trucks and cars. But on busy streets and at dangerous rural locations, overhead lights are used. Reflectors for the lamps are designed specifically to shine most of the light down on the roadway without glaring into the eyes of drivers.

Noise control. The increased use of highways causes loud traffic noise, creating a problem for people who live nearby. For this reason, engineers have designed noise barriers made of concrete, wood, metal, plastic, and other materials that block sound. In some areas, trees, vegetation, or mounds of earth provide protection from traffic noise. Noise barriers are costly, but they successfully reduce highway noise in many areas.

Roadside improvement. Roadsides are often planted with special grasses or vines to keep the earth from washing into the ditches. In addition, many roadsides are beautified with trees and bushes. Such planting and landscaping help break the monotony of travel and make the countryside more attractive. Many areas have laws that prohibit putting billboards and other commercial signs close to the road. Many highways have turnouts of various types where travelers can stop to picnic, to refuel, or to admire a scenic view.

How roads and highways are maintained

Repairing damage and resurfacing. Roads and highways gradually wear out. The work of repairing and resurfacing is called *maintenance.* Maintenance also includes removing ice and snow, painting stripes on pavement, cutting grass, putting up signs, and caring for roadside shoulders, roadsides, and bridges.

Gravel and other similar type roads have to be smoothed quite often. Surfaces and edges of bituminous materials are repaired by patching with new material where worn spots develop from travel or because of weak spots in the ground underneath. Every 10 or 15 years, many roads with bituminous surfaces are resurfaced completely.

Workers repair concrete pavements by digging out broken sections and putting in new concrete. They often repair cracks by filling them with asphalt. Many older concrete pavements must be resurfaced completely.

Clearing ice and snow. Most roads and highways must serve the year around. So roads in cold regions must be kept free from snow and ice in the winter. In some places, *snow fences* are put up. These are thin pickets wired together and placed parallel to the road, on the side from which the storm winds usually blow, and about 50 to 100 feet (15 to 30 meters) from the road. Snowdrifts then form between the fence and the road instead of piling up in the road.

Trucks with V-shaped or straight-blade plows attached to the front clear the roads when it snows. In deep drifts, special snowplows are needed. Some of the most powerful snowplows are called *rotary plows.* Rotary plows have a big screw at the front that chews into the snowdrifts and pulls the snow back into a large fan. The fan shoots the snow to one side of the road. Often roads and highways that are slippery from ice and snow must have salt, chemicals, sand, or cinders spread on them to keep them passable.

How roads and highways are paid for

Roads and highways are built and maintained by local and national governments.

In the United States, local governments build and maintain most local and secondary roads, while state governments construct and care for primary highways. The federal government helps the states pay the cost of building and improving primary and secondary roads and streets. The routes are selected by the states.

State and local communities pay for roadbuilding and maintenance with tax receipts. Much of this money comes from taxes levied on highway and road users. Every state levies taxes on motor fuel and charges fees for registering motor vehicles. In some states, trucks and buses pay special fees. Some states levy a *weight-distance* or a *ton-mile* tax. This tax requires trucks to pay a set amount, based on the weight of the load and the distance it is carried.

Most highway-user taxes are spent only for roads and streets. Using this money for other purposes is called *diversion.* For example, some states set aside part of their motor fuel tax money for education. Constitutional amendments in many states prohibit such diversion.

Most states give part of the taxes they collect from highway users to local governments, to be spent on local roads. The local governments provide whatever additional money they need for roads, usually from general funds raised by property taxes.

State and local governments often borrow money to build roads. These loans, which are made by selling *bonds,* are repaid with tax money. Some state governments set aside part of their motor fuel tax money to repay these loans.

The cost of building many bridges and *turnpikes* (toll roads) is paid by the travelers who use them. Motorists pay a flat fee for crossing toll bridges. Fees for using turnpikes usually depend on how far the motorist travels. Large vehicles, such as trucks and trailers, usually pay more than passenger cars.

Since 1916, the federal government has aided states in building and improving the nation's highways. This aid reflects the federal government's interest in adequate roads for mail delivery, interstate commerce, national defense, and the general welfare of the country.

The federal-aid program was greatly expanded by legislation passed by Congress in 1956 and later years. Federal aid for primary and secondary roads and streets totals several billion dollars a year. The federal interstate highway system cost a total of about $100 billion over a period of about 40 years. The federal government paid 90 percent of the cost and the states 10 percent. To finance the interstate program, Congress established a highway trust fund. This fund receives money from taxes on motor fuel; tires; new trucks, trailers, and buses; and an annual tax on heavy vehicles. Construction or improvement of the roads is done by the states, with federal aid. The roads belong to the state or local governments, which must maintain them.

In other countries. Road and highway construction and maintenance in industrialized countries are financed in ways like those in the United States. In the United Kingdom, the national and local governments work together on issues concerning road improvement. In Australia, a part of a national gasoline tax, fees collected by the states for drivers' licenses, and local property taxes contribute to the funding for road construction and development.

Artstreet

Blacktopping a highway involves laying an asphalt mixture with a paving truck, *right.* The paver spreads the mixture to the desired thickness. A compacting machine, *left,* rolls the pavement hard and smooth. Workers heat and mix asphalt cement and crushed stone to make the paving material.

In less developed countries, funds for road construction may come from a development budget that is part of a country's total annual budget. The total budget is supported by customs duties, sales taxes, taxes on mined resources, and other revenues. Foreign investors often pay for the construction of roads in areas in which they operate businesses.

History of roads and highways

The first roads. Because roads are so old, experts are uncertain of the origin of the word *road.* Most think that it came from the Middle English word *rode,* meaning *a mounted journey.* This may have come from the Old English *rad,* from the word *ridan,* meaning *to ride.*

In England, hundreds of years ago, certain main roads were higher than the surrounding ground. This was because earth was thrown from the side ditches toward the center. Because they were higher, they were called *highways.* These roads were under protection of the king's men and were open to all travelers. Private roads were known as *byways.*

The first roads in the world probably followed trails and paths made by animals. These trails and paths led from feeding grounds to watering places. People followed these trails to hunt for animals. People also made their own trails and paths in searching for water, food, and fuel. Explorers followed these trails as they investigated new lands.

Early roads were built in the Near East about 3000 B.C., soon after the wheel was invented. As trade developed between villages, towns, and cities, other paths, or trade routes, were made. One such early system of roads was the Silk Road, which ran about 5,000 miles (8,050 kilometers), connecting China with Europe. Merchants used this ancient route to carry Chinese silk across Turkestan, India, and Persia.

The first road markers were piles of stones at intervals. Trails through forests were marked by *blazing* trees, or cutting a piece from the bark of the tree.

The Egyptians, Carthaginians, and Etruscans all built roads. But the first really great road builders were the Romans. They laid a solid base and gave the road a

pavement of flat stones. The Romans knew that the road must slope slightly from the center toward both sides to drain off water. This gave the road a *crown.* The Roman road builders knew also that there must be ditches along the sides of the road to carry water away. Roman roads were built mainly to get soldiers from one part of the empire to another. These roads ran in almost straight lines and passed over hills instead of cutting around them. The Romans built more than 50,000 miles (80,000 kilometers) of roads in their empire and some of them still are in use. See **Appian Way** (picture).

From the 500's to the 1800's, most roads in Europe were merely clearings in the forests. Cobblestone paving was used in some urban areas. There was not much reason to build good roads, because most of the travel was on horseback. The cleared way was sometimes quite wide, so that robbers hiding in the woods could not leap out suddenly upon unsuspecting travelers.

In South America, from the 1200's to the 1500's, the Inca Indians built a network of 10,000 miles (16,000 kilometers) of roads. The roads connected their cities.

The first highway department was established in France in 1716. This department built Europe's finest gravel and stone roads of the 1700's using methods developed by Pierre M. J. Tresaguet, an engineer.

In the early 1800's, the person who did more for European roadbuilding than anyone else up to that time was John Loudon McAdam, a Scottish engineer. McAdam is remembered for the surface he developed for roads. This kind of surface, called *macadam,* is still used today. McAdam also stressed the importance of proper drainage to keep roads on a solid foundation.

Early American roads. The first settlers in North America found a wilderness. They located their homes along the rivers and bays and used the water for transportation. As new settlers went inland, they usually built crude roads to the nearest wharf. Until after the War of 1812, people traveled mainly on foot or on horseback.

The first extensive hard-surfaced road was completed in 1794. This road was called the Lancaster (Pennsylvania) Turnpike. It measured 62 miles (100 kilometers) long and was surfaced with hand-broken stone and gravel. In the next 40 years, many turnpikes were built. Most surfaces were of earth, gravel, or broken stone. Some roads were covered with logs or planks, laid crosswise. Where logs were used, the roads were called *corduroy roads.* Both corduroy roads and plank roads were very bumpy.

In 1830, the steam locomotive was successfully operated and rapid development of railroads began. Many people became convinced that the railroad was the best means for travel over long distances. From 1830 to 1900, there was little change in the surfacing materials for roads and highways.

Modern roads. By 1900, there was a growing demand for good roads. Roads that extended a short distance were built in the United States to give farmers access to the railroads, which hauled farm products. The first freeway was completed in 1921 in the Grunewald, a forest area in Berlin, Germany. This road, which was 6 miles (10 kilometers) long, served as a route for suburban commuters and as a race track. Italy soon began building freeways. In 1925, the United States adopted its system of numbering highways, which was suggested by Wisconsin highway engineer A. R. Hirst in 1917.

In 1934, Germany began building its *Autobahn* (expressway) system. This extensive system featured divided highways, grade-separated interchanges, and well-designed service areas. A section of the Pennsylvania Turnpike, the first U.S. freeway, opened in 1940. It ran from Middlesex (near Carlisle) to Irwin. In California, the Arroyo Seco Parkway opened in 1940 between Pasadena and Los Angeles. This and similar roads opened new suburban areas to development, and population often grew quickly where freeways were built. Few other highways were built from the Great Depression of the 1930's to the end of World War II in 1945. After the war, road construction in industrialized countries increased, as more and more families purchased automobiles.

In the 1950's, many United States industry and civic groups joined in supporting highway improvement programs. The U.S. federal interstate highway system was begun in 1956. This system became part of the National Highway System in 1995.

The governments of many of the developing nations of Africa and Asia have begun modernization and industrialization programs that include the building of new roads. Industrialized nations continue to improve and expand their road systems. Engineers today continue to seek ways of increasing highway safety through better construction. They also seek to improve traffic flow by using computers to help plan road systems.

David Boyce

Related articles. See the *Transportation* section in the various state, province, and country articles. See also the following articles in *World Book:*

Some roads and highways

Alaska Highway	Oregon Trail
Appian Way	Pan American Highway
Boston Post Road	Pennsylvania Turnpike
Burma Road	Route 66
Dixie Highway	Simplon Pass and Tunnel
El Camino Real	Trans-Canada Highway
Lincoln Highway	United States (map: The U.S.
National Road	interstate highway system)

Construction and maintenance

Asphalt	Easement	Lighting
Bridge	Electric light	Traffic
Bulldozer	Eminent domain	Tunnel
Cement and con-crete	Gravel	Viaduct

Other related articles

Automobile	Safety (Safety in transportation)
Bus	
Gasoline tax	Telford, Thomas
Interstate commerce	Transportation
McAdam, John Loudon	Truck
Police	Turnpike
Rome, Ancient (Transportation and communication)	

Roadrunner is a swift, ground-dwelling bird found in the brushy deserts of the Southwestern United States and Mexico. Roadrunners can fly, but they are most at home on the ground. They can run as fast as 15 miles (24 kilometers) per hour. The name *roadrunner* comes from the bird's habit of racing down roads in front of moving vehicles and then darting to safety in the brush. Other names for the bird include chaparral cock, ground cuckoo, and snake killer. The roadrunner is the state bird of New Mexico.

Roadrunners measure nearly 2 feet (61 centimeters) in length, about half of which is tail. They have long, sturdy legs and a slender, pointed bill. The upper body is mostly brown with black streaks and white spots. The neck and upper breast are white or pale brown with dark brown streaks, and the belly is white. A crest of brown feathers sticks up on the head, and a bare patch of orange and blue skin lies behind each eye.

Roadrunners eat chiefly insects and small *vertebrates* (animals with backbones), including gophers, baby birds, mice, lizards, and snakes. Roadrunners kill their larger prey by beating it against a hard object and then swallowing it whole. Roadrunners build a cup-shaped nest of sticks in a low tree or a clump of cactuses. They line the nest with leaves, grass, and other soft materials. The female roadrunner lays from two to six white or yellowish eggs.   Sandra L. Vehrencamp

Scientific classification. The roadrunner belongs to the cuckoo family, Cuculidae. Its scientific name is *Geococcyx californianus.*

See also **Bird** (picture: Birds of the desert).

Roanoke, *ROH uh NOHK* (pop. 97,397; met. area pop. 224,477), is a city on the Roanoke River in Virginia. It lies between the Blue Ridge and Allegheny mountains (see **Virginia** [political map]). Roanoke is a railroad center and the major retail, financial, and health care center for the western part of the state. It also serves as a convention center.

Manufacturers in the Roanoke Valley produce electronic equipment, fiber optics, furniture, night vision goggles, robots, and textiles. Schools in the Roanoke area include Hollins College, Roanoke College, and Virginia Polytechnic Institute and State University. The city has a symphony orchestra. The Virginia Museum of Transportation is in Roanoke.

Roanoke was originally the small pioneer settlement of Big Lick, named after a large salt marsh where deer fed. In 1882, the Norfolk and Western and the Shenandoah railroads made a junction at Big Lick. The town was renamed Roanoke the same year and became a city in 1884. The name *Roanoke* comes from the Indian word *Rawenoke,* meaning *shell money.*

Roanoke has a council-manager form of government. For the monthly weather, see **Virginia** (Climate).

Donald J. Zeigler

Roanoke Island. See Lost Colony.

Roaring Twenties was the colorful decade of the 1920's in the United States. Other nicknames for this period included the *Jazz Age* and the *Dollar Decade.*

The restless era of the 1920's brought the United States spectacular economic growth, generally rising prosperity, and far-reaching social change. For about 20 years, many Americans had demanded reforms that would curb what they regarded as the control of society by big business. During World War I (1914-1918), husbands, sons, and sweethearts had died in answering President Woodrow Wilson's call to "make the world safe for democracy." After the war ended, large numbers of Americans wanted to forget about the troubles of Europeans. Instead, they simply wanted to enjoy life. They chose to amuse themselves with soaring stock profits, illegal liquor, short skirts, and what many looked upon as shocking morals.

Rising prosperity. During the Roaring Twenties, economic expansion created booming business profits and a rising standard of living for most Americans. From 1922 to 1929, the national income increased more than 40 per cent, from $60.7 billion annually to $87.2 billion. The increased use of labor-saving machinery in factories and on farms enabled workers to produce more goods faster and less expensively.

Several new major industries expanded in the 1920's. Even many low-income families could now afford to buy an inexpensive automobile called the Model T, which Henry Ford had developed in 1908. The number of passenger cars in the United States jumped from fewer than 7 million in 1919 to about 23 million in 1929. Traffic jammed the nation's highways and created a need for still more businesses, including gas stations, roadside restaurants, and tire manufacturers.

Radio also revolutionized the nation's economy. The value of radio sales in the United States jumped from $60 million in 1922 to almost $850 million in 1929. Popular network programs, such as "Amos 'n' Andy" and "The Philco Hour," provided an effective method of advertising products to a nationwide audience. Radio commercials persuaded listeners to spend a larger share of their rising income. Stores developed installment payment plans and urged customers to "Buy now, pay later." Higher wages and the use of credit enabled millions of Americans to purchase their first automobile, refrigerator, and washing machine.

Throughout the 1920's, most Americans regarded big business as the foundation of society. They agreed with President Calvin Coolidge that "The business of America is business." Coolidge's comment symbolized the spirit of the era. Republican candidates—Warren G. Harding, Coolidge, and Herbert Hoover—won all three presidential elections of the 1920's. Their policies reflected the belief that the economy can best regulate itself without government controls. Americans bought millions of copies of *The Man Nobody Knows* by Bruce Barton, the best-selling nonfiction book of 1925 and 1926. It called Jesus Christ the founder of modern business because

He "picked twelve humble men and created an organization that won the world."

John J. Raskob, vice president of the DuPont Company and the General Motors Corporation, declared that anyone who invested $15 a month in the stock market could make $80,000 in 20 years. Such promises of wealth convinced many Americans to buy stocks. Stock prices had risen gradually since the early 1920's, but they skyrocketed in 1927 and 1928. The average price of stocks on the New York Stock Exchange nearly tripled from 1925 to 1929. The high profits seemed to confirm President Hoover's pledge of a new era of abundance, in which "poverty will be banished from this nation."

Changing attitudes toward foreign relations, society, and leisure revolutionized American life in the 1920's. After World War I, many Americans demanded that the United States stay out of European political affairs. The Senate refused to approve the Treaty of Versailles, which officially ended the war with Germany and provided for the establishment of a League of Nations. Some senators argued that League membership could involve the United States in future European wars.

Distrust of foreigners also set off a nationwide panic called the Red Scare. Many Americans blamed what they regarded as an international Communist conspiracy for various protest movements and union activities in 1919 and 1920. More than 2 million rural Americans joined a secret organization called the Ku Klux Klan. The Klan terrorized not only foreigners but also blacks, Jews, and Roman Catholics.

Political corruption made front-page headlines during the Roaring Twenties. Albert B. Fall, secretary of the interior under President Harding, was convicted of accepting a $400,000 bribe from two oil companies. Fall had arranged to secretly lease these companies three government oil reserves, including one that was located at Teapot Dome, Wyo. (see **Teapot Dome**).

Breaking the law became fashionable after the 18th Amendment to the Constitution went into effect in 1920. This amendment prohibited the manufacture and sale of alcoholic beverages. Thousands of Americans began to make their own liquor at home. Gangsters bootlegged liquor from Canada, supplied it to illegal bars called *speakeasies,* and bribed the police not to interfere. More than 500 gangland murders occurred as various

Bettmann Archive

This fashionable couple wore raccoon coats for a drive in their 1928 Chrysler. The woman is sitting in an open compartment called a *rumble seat.*

John Held, Jr.

Fads of the 1920's helped Americans forget the hardships of World War I. The two couples shown here are doing the Charleston, a popular dance of the era, in a contest in 1925. The fashions shown in the drawing included short skirts and rolled silk stockings.

underworld mobs fought for control of the liquor traffic.

Many people feared that morality had crumbled completely. Before World War I, women had worn long hair, ankle-length dresses, and long cotton stockings. But in the 1920's, they wore short, tight dresses and rolled their silk stockings down to their knees. They cut their hair in a boyish style called the *bob* and wore flashy lipstick and other cosmetics. Couples danced cheek-to-cheek to blaring jazz music.

Most Americans kept busy having a good time. Charlie Chaplin, Mary Pickford, Rudolph Valentino, and other motion-picture stars attracted crowds to theaters. Sports fans jammed stadiums to watch such top athletes as home run slugger Babe Ruth and boxing champion Jack Dempsey. Charles A. Lindbergh, the "Lone Eagle," received a hero's welcome after making the first solo nonstop airplane flight across the Atlantic Ocean. And Alvin (Shipwreck) Kelly won nationwide fame by sitting on top of a flagpole for 23 days and 7 hours.

Cultural trends. The literature, art, and music of the 1920's reflected the nation's changing values. In his novel *Main Street* (1920), Sinclair Lewis attacked what he considered the dull lives and narrow-minded attitudes of people in a small town. Many American authors, including F. Scott Fitzgerald and Ernest Hemingway, lived in Paris during the period. Some of their finest works present the attitudes and experiences of the era's so-called Lost Generation. H. L. Mencken, in his witty magazine *The American Mercury,* ridiculed the antics of dimwitted politicians, prohibitionists, and others.

Artists and composers were inspired by both the traditions and changes in American life. Joseph Stella painted soaring lines and precise geometric patterns to represent skyscrapers, his favorite theme. The paintings of Edward Hopper show the loneliness experienced by some people—even among familiar surroundings. George Gershwin became the most popular composer of the 1920's. His best-known orchestral works, *Rhapsody in Blue* (1924) and *An American in Paris* (1928), feature many elements of jazz.

The end of an era. By 1929, the U.S. economy was in serious trouble despite the soaring profits in the stock market. Since the end of World War I in 1918, farm prices had dropped about 40 percent below their prewar level. Farm profits fell so low that many farmers could not pay their debts to banks. Partly as a result, about 550 banks went out of business between July 1928 and June 1929. Also, industrial production rose about four times as fast as wages. People could not afford to buy manufactured goods as fast as industry produced them.

The nation's illusion of unending prosperity was shattered on Oct. 24, 1929. Worried investors who had bought stock on credit began to sell it. A panic developed, and on October 29, stockholders sold a record 16,410,030 shares. By mid-November, stock prices had plunged about 40 percent. The stock market crash led to the Great Depression. It was a terrible price to pay for the false sense of prosperity and national well-being of the Roaring Twenties.   E. David Cronon

See also **Great Depression; Prohibition; United States, History of the** (A new place in the world).

Additional resources

Baughman, Judith S., ed. *American Decades, Vol. 3: 1920-1929.* Gale Research, 1996.

Olson, James S. *Historical Dictionary of the 1920s*. Greenwood, 1988.

Pietrusza, David. *The Roaring Twenties*. Lucent Bks., 1997.

Visual Education Corp. *The Twentieth Century, Vol. 2: The Roaring Twenties and an Unsettled Peace (1919-1929)*. Macmillan, 1992.

Rob Roy (1671-1734) was a famous Scottish outlaw whose real name was Robert MacGregor. *Roy* is a Gaelic word meaning *red*. MacGregor became known as Rob Roy because of his red hair and ruddy skin.

Rob Roy was born at Glengyle, near Loch Lomond. He inherited land from his father and was a nephew of a chieftain of the MacGregor clan. Rob Roy probably combined cattle trading with stealing cattle and with threatening to steal his neighbors' cattle if they did not pay him money for "protecting" them. But charges that, in 1711, he fled with money that various people had given him to purchase cattle for them were never supported.

Rob Roy participated in the Jacobite rebellion of 1715. The rebellion sought to restore the Scottish House of Stuart to the British throne after George I of the House of Hanover had gained the throne in 1714. The rebellion was easily crushed. In 1722, British authorities captured Rob Roy. He was imprisoned for participating in the rebellion and sentenced to exile. But he was later pardoned. The Scottish writer Sir Walter Scott gave a romantic, fictionalized account of Rob Roy's adventures in his novel *Rob Roy* (1817).   James Anthony Sharpe

Robbery means stealing money or goods from a person by violence or threats of immediate physical harm. This crime is classed as a *felony* and is punishable by imprisonment. The value of the property taken has little influence in determining the legal penalty, so long as the property is of value to its owner. Robbery with a gun is usually considered more serious than simple robbery. Robbery on a street or highway is often called *highway robbery. Carjacking* is a type of robbery in which the thief steals an automobile. Robbery occurs only when a thief uses force or threats to obtain something from a person. Stealing a person's possessions without using force or threats is called *larceny. Burglary* is the act of entering a home or business without permission for the purpose of committing a crime.   Charles F. Wellford

See also **Bandit; Burglary; Felony; Larceny; Pirate.**

Robbins, Jerome (1918-1998), was an American dancer and *choreographer* (dance creator). He became well known to dance audiences in 1944, when he created his first ballet, *Fancy Free*. He achieved more widespread fame as the director and choreographer of many Broadway musicals, including *The King and I* (1951), *West Side Story* (1957), and *Fiddler on the Roof* (1964). In these musicals, he blended the acting, singing, and dancing into a unified work of art. Robbins and Robert Wise shared the 1961 Academy Award as best director for *West Side Story*. He again began to focus primarily on the ballet with his creation of *Les Noces* in 1965. Many of Robbins's ballets are based on American subjects. Others are abstract in nature and modern in style. They often include jazz rhythms.

Robbins was born in New York City. He was a member of Ballet Theatre from 1940 to 1948 and associate artistic director of the New York City Ballet from 1949 to 1959. Robbins became ballet master of the New York City Ballet in 1969 and was ballet master in chief with Peter Martins from 1983 until Robbins's resignation in 1990.   Selma Landen Odom

Roberts, Sir Charles George Douglas (1860-1943), was a Canadian author. Roberts's finest work appears in his romantic poems of nature and country life. They display Roberts's sensitive feeling for the landscape and wildlife of his native New Brunswick.

Roberts's first book of verse was *Orion and Other Poems* (1880). His successful use of traditional poetic forms and themes in this book influenced many other young Canadian poets. Roberts's sonnet sequence *Songs of the Common Day* (1893) contains some of his finest poems of rural life. Roberts also wrote much prose, including *A History of Canada* (1897) and a number of historical novels. Several of these historical novels were romances set in colonial North America. He won international fame for animal stories, many of which were collected in *The Last Barrier and Other Stories* (published in 1958).

Roberts was born in Douglas, near Fredericton, New Brunswick. He was knighted in 1935.   Rosemary Sullivan

Roberts, Owen Josephus (1875-1955), served as a justice of the Supreme Court of the United States from 1930 to 1945. President Calvin Coolidge appointed Roberts to prosecute the "oil scandal" cases arising from the leasing of public lands to the oil industry in 1924 (see **Teapot Dome**). In 1930, President Herbert Hoover appointed Roberts to the Supreme Court. Roberts was born in Philadelphia. He graduated from the University of Pennsylvania in 1898.   Bruce Allen Murphy

Robertson, Oscar (1938-   ), became one of the greatest scorers and passers in basketball history. He played for the Cincinnati Royals of the National Basketball Association (NBA) from the 1960-1961 season through the 1969-1970 season and for the Milwaukee Bucks from the 1970-1971 season through the 1973-1974 season, after which he retired. During his professional career, Robertson had 9,887 *assists*—passes to teammates that result in field goals. This total was an NBA record until 1991, when Magic Johnson broke it. Robertson also became the second NBA player to score over 25,000 points. Wilt Chamberlain was the first. Robertson was the NBA's most valuable player in 1964.

Robertson was born in Charlotte, Tennessee. He is 6 feet 5 inches (196 centimeters) tall and was nicknamed the "Big O." He was an all-America guard for three seasons at the University of Cincinnati.   Bob Logan

Roberval, *raw behr VAL*, Sieur de, *syur duh* (1500?-1560), was a French nobleman and soldier and an explorer and colonizer in Canada. He made the first French effort to set up a permanent colony in America .

King Francis I appointed Roberval lieutenant general of Canada in 1541. The next year, Roberval sailed to Canada with about 200 colonists. In waters near Newfoundland, he met the French navigator Jacques Cartier. Cartier had spent the winter near what is now Quebec City and was returning to France. Roberval and the colonists reoccupied Cartier's settlement. They explored the St. Lawrence River from what is now the Montreal area to the mouth of the Saguenay River, in search of a fabled kingdom of gold. But the winter of 1543 was marked by famine, disease, and mutiny, and so later that year, Roberval returned to France with the few surviving colonists. Roberval's given and family name was Jean-François de La Rocque.   S. Dale Standen

Robeson, *ROHB suhn,* **Paul** (1898-1976), was a black American singer, actor, and political activist. He had significant impact on the United States and the world.

Robeson was born in Princeton, N.J. He attended Rutgers University, where he starred in four sports and twice was named an all-America end in football. Robeson was valedictorian of his class and a member of Phi Beta Kappa, the national college honor society.

In 1923, Robeson earned a degree from the Columbia University Law School. He then began a long and successful career as an actor and singer. He performed on the stage and on radio and made many motion pictures and phonograph records. Robeson gained international acclaim for his performances in such plays as *Othello* and *The Emperor Jones.* He also won praise for his moving interpretations of

Culver

Paul Robeson

black spirituals and the folk music of many countries.

In the late 1930's, Robeson became involved with national and international movements for peace, racial justice, and better labor conditions. He also supported independence for African colonies from their European rulers. This involvement, his friendship with the Soviet Union, and his association with Communists brought strong opposition from conservative groups in the United States. In 1950, the U.S. government canceled Robeson's passport. Although his musical and theatrical career declined sharply as the result of opposition, he continued his political work.

In 1958, Robeson regained his passport and moved to London, where he resumed his acting and singing career. He returned to the United States in 1963 because of ill health and lived there in retirement until his death. Robeson described his political beliefs in a book called *Here I Stand* (1958).   Eloise Greenfield

See also **Shakespeare, William** (picture: *Othello*).

Robespierre, *ROHBZ peer* or *ROHBZ pee air* (1758-1794), was the most famous and controversial leader of the French Revolution (1789-1799). In the name of democracy, he helped bring about the Reign of Terror, a period in which thousands of suspected opponents of the revolution were executed. In time, Robespierre met the same fate.

Maximilien Robespierre was born in Arras. He studied at the College of Louis-le-Grand in Paris and became a successful lawyer. Robespierre was greatly influenced by the philosopher Jean-Jacques Rousseau, who argued that the right to govern came from the people.

In 1789, Robespierre was elected to the Estates-General, an assembly that

Brown Bros.

Robespierre

the king called to deal with a financial crisis in France. There, Robespierre distinguished himself as a spokesman for the principle of equality and the rights of the common people. He wanted voting rights extended to all the people, including Protestants, Jews, and free blacks of the French colonies. Robespierre became a leader of the Jacobin Club of Paris, a radical political group. By 1792, most Jacobins wanted a democratic republic instead of a constitutional monarchy.

Revolutionary leader. In August 1792, the people of Paris took custody of King Louis XVI and his family and imprisoned them. Soon afterward, Robespierre was elected to the National Convention, a national assembly established to take over the government of France. The Convention declared that France was a republic, placed King Louis XVI on trial, and sentenced him to death as a traitor. Robespierre then led an attack in the Convention against moderate deputies known as the Girondists. He and his followers expelled the Girondists in June 1793 and took control of the Convention.

In July 1793, Robespierre was elected to the Committee of Public Safety, the Convention's governing body. He stressed the republic's need for a single center of opinion and viewed disagreement with the committee's policies as treachery. His speeches justified the Reign of Terror to defend and "purify" the revolution. By the end of July 1794, about 17,000 rebels and suspected "enemies of the republic" had been executed, including Robespierre's one-time friend and fellow deputy, Georges Danton.

His death and role. As a result of his policies, many members of the Convention became Robespierre's enemies. They feared for their lives and organized a plot against him. On July 26, 1794, Robespierre seemed to call for an end to the use of terror, but he also threatened unnamed deputies. The next day, a group of his opponents persuaded the Convention to order his arrest. The Convention sentenced him to die on the guillotine. He was executed on July 28, 1794.

Today, historians still argue over Robespierre's role. Some scholars regard him as cold-blooded, fanatical, and self-righteous. Others view him as "The Incorruptible," a totally dedicated patriot and democrat.

Isser Woloch

Related articles in *World Book* include:

Robin is a type of bird common to North America and Europe. The *American robin* grows about 9 to 11 inches (23 to 28 centimeters) long. The male has a brick-red breast, a brownish-gray back, and a black head and tail. Its white throat is streaked with black and its outer tail feathers are tipped with white. Its bill is yellow. The female robin generally is slightly smaller than the male and duller in color, with a gray head and tail. The American robin is the state bird of Connecticut, Michigan, and Wisconsin.

American robins breed throughout North America, from northern Canada and Alaska to central Mexico. They are among the last birds to migrate south from northern regions in autumn. American robins are also among the first birds to return north in spring. The first

An American robin tends her newly hatched young, *above.* American robins usually have three to five young in each brood. The young leave the nest about 15 days after hatching.

robin of spring is a popular sign that winter will soon be over.

From April to July, male American robins sing together for long periods at dawn and dusk and for shorter periods during the day. Their cheerful caroling song consists of repeated short notes that alternately rise and fall. The song sounds as if the robins were singing "cheerily cheery."

American robins frequently return to the same place each year to build their nests. The favorite nesting places of American robins are in trees, but they will also nest on a shelf or ledge on a barn or house. The female American robin forms a cup-shaped nest from such materials as grass stems, roots, twigs, rags, string, and paper. The male American robin often accompanies the female on trips to and from the nest, and he may help bring nest-building materials. The female typically lays 3 to 5 blue eggs that hatch after about 13 days. Both parents feed the newly hatched birds. The young robins leave the nest about 15 days after they hatch. The male robin then becomes the sole caretaker of the young robins. American robins may raise two or three broods during the spring and summer.

American robins eat chiefly fruit. In addition, American robins consume beetles, cutworms, earthworms, and wireworms.

The *European robin* lives throughout Europe. It is smaller than the American robin and has an orange-red forehead, throat, and breast. Its back, wings, and tail are olive-brown, and its belly is grayish-white. Males and females look alike. According to English legend, this bird mercifully picked a thorn from the crown of Jesus Christ as He was on His way to Calvary. As the bird carried the thorn in its beak, a drop of blood fell from the thorn to its breast, dyeing it red.   Edward H. Burtt, Jr.

Scientific classification. Robins are in the thrush subfamily, Turdinae, in the family Muscicapidae. The American robin is *Turdus migratorius.* The European robin is *Erithacus rubecula.*

Robin Hood was a legendary English outlaw who stole from the rich and gave to the poor. He is the subject of countless ballads and stories, some dating as far back as the 1300's. He treated poor people kindly and fought the sheriff of Nottingham, a corrupt official who persecuted the poor. Robin Hood thus became a hero of the common people and a symbol of "right against might."

Robin Hood lived with his merry band of followers in Sherwood Forest in Nottinghamshire. His best-known companions included Friar Tuck, Little John, and Maid Marian. Friar Tuck was a fat, jolly priest. Little John stood more than 7 feet (210 centimeters) tall and was known for his great skill with a bow and arrow. Maid Marian was Robin Hood's sweetheart.

No one knows whether the character of Robin Hood was based on a real person. According to one scholar, Robin Hood was actually the Earl of Huntingdon, and his real name was Robert Fitzooth. However, many other scholars believe that Robin Hood is a fictitious character.

Detail of an oil painting on canvas (1917) by N. C. Wyeth (Brandywine River Museum, Chadds Ford, Pa.)

Robin Hood and his men were legendary English outlaws who lived in Sherwood Forest. Stories claim that he and several of his followers were expert marksmen with a bow and arrow.

The oldest written reference to Robin Hood appears in the *Vision of Piers Plowman,* which is a long poem that was written about 1378. However, the earliest surviving stories of Robin Hood were ballads written a century later. The first detailed description of his activities was the *Lytell Geste of Robin Hood* (about 1500). Robin Hood also appears as the character Locksley in *Ivanhoe* (1819), by the Scottish novelist Sir Walter Scott.

Carl Lindahl

Robinson, Bill (1878-1949), was a popular black American tap-dancer. He was affectionately known as "Bojangles." Robinson became especially famous for a routine in which he tap-danced up and down a staircase.

Robinson performed in nightclubs, vaudeville, motion pictures, and on Broadway. He is probably best remembered for his scenes with child star Shirley Temple in four movie musicals— *The Little Colonel* (1935), *The Littlest Rebel* (1935), *Rebecca of Sunnybrook Farm* (1938), and *Just Around the Corner* (1938). He also starred in the Broadway musicals *Blackbirds of 1928* (1928), *Blackbirds of 1933* (1933), and *The Hot Mikado* (1939).

Robinson was born in Richmond, Virginia. His given name was Luther, but he later changed it to Bill. He began dancing for tips at an early age in the streets and taverns of Richmond.   Gerald Bordman

See also **Temple, Shirley** (picture).

Robinson, Eddie (1919-   ), coached his teams to more victories than any other coach in college football history. Robinson began his career in 1941 at Grambling State University (then called Louisiana Negro Normal and Industrial Institute). He coached there until he retired in 1997. In 1985, Grambling won its 324th game under Robinson, which broke the record of 323 coaching victories held by Paul Bryant. Robinson retired with a career record of 408 victories, 165 defeats, and 15 ties.

Grambling State University
Eddie Robinson

Edward Gay Robinson was born in Jackson, Louisiana. He attended Leland College near Baker, Louisiana, from 1937 to 1941. Robinson played quarterback, fullback, and tailback on the Leland football team. Following graduation, Robinson worked in a feed mill before being hired by Grambling. He was 22 years old when he began coaching. He also served as the school's athletic director from 1958 to 1989. His teams won or shared 17 Southwest Athletic Conference championships. More than 200 of Robinson's players went on to play professional football.   William F. Reed.

Robinson, Edwin Arlington (1869-1935), an American poet, became best known for short poems in which he presents character studies. Three of his 13 volumes of poetry won Pulitzer Prizes—*Collected Poems* in 1922, *The Man Who Died Twice* in 1925, and *Tristram* in 1928.

Robinson's characters are citizens of the imaginary community of Tilbury Town. Among the most familiar characterizations are those in "Richard Corey," "Miniver Cheevy," "Flammonde," and "Mr. Flood's Party." In these poems, the characters seem doomed to failure and suffering. Yet Robinson was not a pessimistic writer. He indicated clearly that his characters suffer because they ask too much from life and themselves.

Robinson's continuing theme of the need for humility and complete self-honesty also appears in his philosophical poem "The Man Against the Sky" (1916). Robinson also wrote long narrative poems. *Merlin* (1917) and *Lancelot* (1920), along with *Tristram,* form a connected series telling the legends of King Arthur.

Robinson was born in Head Tide, Maine. Through the assistance of President Theodore Roosevelt, who admired his poetry, Robinson became a clerk in the New York Custom House in 1905. Robinson resigned in 1909 in order to devote himself to writing.   Bonnie Costello

Robinson, Frank (1935-   ), became the first black manager of a major league baseball team when he managed the Cleveland Indians from 1975 to 1977. He later managed the San Francisco Giants from 1981 to 1984 and the Baltimore Orioles from 1988 to 1991. Robinson had also been a star outfielder. He was the first man to be named Most Valuable Player in both the National and American leagues. In his 21-year playing career, Robinson hit 586 home runs.

Robinson received the Rookie of the Year award in 1956 with the Cincinnati Reds. In 1961, he was voted the National League's Most Valuable Player. After the 1965 season, Cincinnati traded him to the Baltimore Orioles. He won the American League's Most Valuable Player award in 1966. Robinson played for the Los Angeles Dodgers in 1972 and the California (now Anaheim) Angels in 1973 before being sold to Cleveland in 1974. He retired as a player after the 1976 season. Robinson was elected to the National Baseball Hall of Fame in 1982. In 2000, Robinson was appointed vice president for on-field operations for major league baseball. He was born in Beaumont, Texas.   Dave Nightingale

Robinson, Jackie (1919-1972), was the first African American to play modern major league baseball. Robinson joined the Brooklyn Dodgers in 1947 and played all 10 years of his major league career with the Dodgers.

Robinson started as a first baseman for the Dodgers but gained his greatest fame playing second base. Robinson was an outstanding hitter and finished with a .311 lifetime batting average. He was also a superior runner and base stealer. In 1947, Robinson was named Rookie of the Year. In 1949, he won the National League's Most Valuable Player award, as well as the league's batting championship with a .342 average.

Jack Roosevelt Robinson was born in Cairo, Georgia. He starred in four sports at the University of California at Los Angeles (UCLA). In 1945, Robinson played with the Kansas City Monarchs of the Negro American League. In 1946, he played minor league baseball for the Montreal Royals. In 1956, Robinson received the Spingarn Medal.

National Baseball Hall of Fame (UPI)
Jackie Robinson was the first black player in modern major league baseball. He gained fame with the Brooklyn Dodgers for his fielding at second base and for his hitting and base running.

He was elected to the National Baseball Hall of Fame in 1962. Dave Nightingale

See also **Baseball** (picture).

Additional resources

Rampersad, Arnold. *Jackie Robinson.* Knopf, 1997.
Robinson, Jackie. *I Never Had It Made.* 1972. Reprint. Ecco Pr., 1995.

Robinson, Joan Violet (1903-1983), was a British economist whose theories have significantly influenced economic thought. She was a leader of the British school of Keynesian economics, which follows the doctrines of the British economist John Maynard Keynes (see **Keynes, John Maynard**).

Robinson helped Keynes develop his doctrines, which revolutionized economic policy during the 1930's. Like Keynes, she believed that government spending could prevent depressions and widespread unemployment. She extended Keynesian concepts to such long-term issues as economic growth and technical change.

Robinson believed capitalistic systems were unstable because of conflicts between business and labor over each other's share of income. She proposed that government policies be established to determine the distribution of income between the two groups.

Robinson was born near London. She graduated from Cambridge University in 1925, and she served as a professor of economics there until 1973. She wrote many books, including *The Economics of Imperfect Competition* (1933), *Marxian Economics* (1952), and *Economic Heresies* (1971). Carolyn Shaw Bell

Robinson, Joseph Taylor (1872-1937), was the Democratic candidate for vice president of the United States in 1928. He and presidential candidate Alfred E. Smith lost to Republicans Herbert C. Hoover and Charles Curtis. Robinson was elected to the U.S. House of Representatives in 1902. He was elected governor of Arkansas in 1912. Just after he took office, the state legislature elected him to the U.S. Senate. He served as Senate majority leader from 1933 until his death. He was born in Lonoke County, Arkansas. James S. Olson

Robinson, Mary (1944-), became the United Nations (UN) High Commissioner for Human Rights in 1997. She had long supported humanitarian causes, particularly women's rights. From 1990 to 1997, Robinson served as president of Ireland, the first woman to hold that post. The Irish presidency is a largely ceremonial office, but Robinson became one of Ireland's most popular and respected leaders. She used her office to draw attention to such problems as poverty and discrimination. For example, she helped persuade the UN to provide aid to starving people in Somalia in the early 1990's.

Mary Terese Winifred Bourke was born in Ballina, Ireland. She earned degrees in law from the University of Dublin (more generally called Trinity College) and from Harvard Law School. Bourke then practiced law in Dublin. In one important case, she won the right for Irish women to sit on juries. She married Nicholas Robinson, also a lawyer, in 1970. From 1969 to 1990, she taught law at Trinity College. Robinson served in Ireland's Senate from 1969 to 1989, where she campaigned for the legalization of divorce and birth control. Paul E. Gallis

Robinson, Sugar Ray (1921-1989), won fame as one of the greatest boxers in history. He got his nickname,

Wide World

Sugar Ray Robinson

"Sugar Ray," after a sportswriter described him as "a sweet fighter ... sweet as sugar." Robinson held the welterweight title from 1946 to 1951 and then won the middleweight championship five times.

Robinson defeated Jake LaMotta in 1951 to win the middleweight title for the first time. That same year, he lost it to Randy Turpin and then won it back. Robinson retired as champion in 1952 but returned to the ring in 1954. In 1955, he regained the title by defeating Bobo Olson. Gene Fullmer won the title in 1957. Robinson won it back and lost it to Carmen Basilio that same year. In 1958, he again regained the title. In 1959, the National Boxing Association stripped Robinson of the title because he failed to defend it within a year. But he retained the New York State Athletic Commission version of the championship, losing that title to Paul Pender in 1960. Robinson retired from boxing in 1965. He had won 174 of his 201 professional fights, 109 by knockouts.

Robinson was born in Ailey, Georgia. He grew up in New York City. Robinson's given and family name was Walker Smith, Jr. Bert Randolph Sugar

Robinson Crusoe is an imaginary story about a merchant-adventurer marooned on a desert island off the northern coast of South America. Daniel Defoe wrote this novel in 1719. He based the story partly on the experiences of a Scottish sailor, Alexander Selkirk. But Defoe's realistic account of Crusoe's life is much more interesting, and has become one of the most popular books in English.

The book explains how Crusoe cleverly manages to make himself at home while he lives on the island. After living alone for 26 years, Crusoe rescues a man from cannibals. He calls the man *Friday* because he met him on that day. Friday becomes Crusoe's trusted friend and servant. The term, "man Friday," has come to mean any trusted servant. Two years later, Crusoe and Friday board a passing ship and are taken to England.

Michael Seidel

See also **Defoe, Daniel.**

Robot is a mechanical device that operates automatically. Robots can perform a wide variety of tasks. They are especially suitable for doing jobs too boring, difficult, or dangerous for people. The term robot comes from the Czech word *robota,* meaning *drudgery.* Robots efficiently carry out such routine tasks as welding, drilling, and painting automobile body parts. They also produce plastic food containers and wrap ice cream bars. Some industrial robots can even assemble electronic circuits and watches. The science and technology that deals with robots is called *robotics.*

A typical robot performs a task by following a set of instructions that specifies exactly what must be done to complete the job. These instructions are entered and stored in the robot's control center, which consists of a computer or part of a computer. Robots vary in design and size, but few resemble the humanlike machines that

Arnold Zann, Black Star

Robots efficiently perform a wide variety of tasks that are boring, difficult, or dangerous for people, including welding automobile body parts, *above,* and assembling electronic circuits.

appear in works of science fiction. Most robots today are stationary structures with a single arm capable of lifting objects and using tools. But engineers are developing mobile robots equipped with television cameras for sight and electronic sensors for touch. These robots are controlled by both stored instructions and feedback they receive from the sensors. Such robots might be used for sea-floor and planetary exploration or some other scientific research.　　Thomas T. Liao

See also **Automation; Čapek, Karel; Computer.**

Additional resources

Berger, Fredericka. *Robots: What They Are, What They Do.* Greenwillow, 1992. For younger readers.
Bone, Jan. *Opportunities in Robotics Careers.* VGM Career, 1987.
Engelberger, Joseph F. *Robotics in Service.* MIT Pr., 1989.
Harrar, George. *Radical Robots: Can You Be Replaced?* Simon & Schuster, 1990. For younger readers.
Robotics. Rev. ed. Time-Life Bks. 1991.

Robusti, Jacopo. See Tintoretto.

Rochambeau, *row shahn BOH,* **Comte de,** *kawnt duh* (1725-1807), a French general, came to America in 1780 with French troops to serve under General George Washington in the Revolutionary War. In 1781, he helped plan the Battle of Yorktown and the defeat of Lord Cornwallis.

Rochambeau was born in Vendôme, the younger son of a French noble. His full name was Jean Baptiste Donatien de Vimeur. In 1742, he began a long and distinguished career as a soldier. Rochambeau's bravery and skill in the War of the Austrian Succession and Seven Years' War won him steady advancement. As inspector general of the army, Rochambeau made important military reforms later used successfully during the French Revolution and by Napoleon.

On his return from America in 1783, Rochambeau was appointed governor of Picardy and Artois. He served in the French Revolution, and was promoted to Marshal of France in 1791. He resigned after suffering defeats early in a war that France had begun fighting against Austria and Prussia in 1792. Imprisoned during the Reign of Terror, Rochambeau narrowly escaped being executed. Napoleon later restored his rank.　　Isser Woloch

Roche, Mazo De la. See De la Roche, Mazo.
Rochelle salt. See Tartaric acid.

Rochester, *RAHCH ehs tuhr,* N.Y. (pop. 231,636; met. area pop. 1,062,470), is a major manufacturing center of the United States. The city also is a leading cultural and commercial center of New York. Rochester ranks as one of the state's largest cities. It lies along the Genesee River, near the river's outlet into Lake Ontario. For the location of Rochester, see **New York** (political map).

Nathaniel Rochester, a businessman from Hagerstown, Md., founded Rochester in 1812. He and two associates had purchased 100 acres (40 hectares) of land on the Genesee River in 1803. The abundance of water power and rich soil attracted settlers to the area.

Description. Rochester, the county seat of Monroe County, covers 37 square miles (96 square kilometers). The Rochester metropolitan area covers 3,426 square miles (8,873 square kilometers). The Genesee River divides the city into two parts of almost equal size. Downtown Rochester has many buildings that have been erected since the early 1960's. They include the 30-story Xerox Tower and the 27-story marble and bronze Lincoln First Tower.

Rochester's public school system includes about 35 elementary schools and 10 high schools. The city is the home of the University of Rochester and its famous Eastman School of Music. Other institutions of higher learning in the city are Nazareth College of Rochester, Rochester Institute of Technology, and St. John Fisher College. The Rochester Public Library consists of a main library and 10 branches.

The Rochester Philharmonic Orchestra presents programs in the Eastman Theatre, part of the Eastman School of Music. Other attractions in the city include the International Museum of Photography and the Memorial Art Gallery. The Rochester Museum and Science Center includes the Strasenburgh Planetarium. The Margaret Woodbury Strong Museum houses one of the country's largest doll collections. The Monroe County Parks System consists of about 20 parks and includes the Seneca Park Zoo.

Economy. Rochester is a major producer of cameras and film. The Eastman Kodak Company, a leading manufacturer of cameras and film, ranks as the city's chief employer. Other Rochester products include dental and optical equipment; nonelectrical machinery, including copying devices; electronic equipment; food and food products; clothing and textile products; automobile engine parts; and tool and die equipment. Rochester has about 1,000 manufacturing plants.

Passenger and freight trains serve Rochester. The Rochester-Monroe County Airport is located in southwestern Rochester.

Government and history. Rochester has a strong-mayor form of government, in which the mayor appoints most department heads and has direct control over them. The voters elect the mayor and the nine members of the city council.

Ebenezer Allen, the first white settler in what is now Rochester, arrived in 1789. He built a flour mill on the Genesee River shore for the Seneca Indians. The first permanent settlers came in 1812, and the village was incorporated as Rochesterville in 1817. Its name was changed to Rochester in 1822.

Trade flourished after construction of the Erie Canal through Rochester in the mid-1820's. The canal reduced transportation costs and opened Eastern and Western markets to Rochester farmers and manufacturers. Flour mills multiplied along the Genesee, and Rochester became known as the *Flour City.* It received a city charter in 1834. By 1856, the population had grown to about 50,000, and Rochester was called the *Flower City* as well. One of the city's many plant nurseries covered 440 acres (178 hectares) and ranked among the largest in the world. In 1880, George Eastman established a photographic plate-making business in Rochester. His company began to sell Kodak cameras and film in 1888. The company's success gave Rochester a third nickname, *Film City.*

During the early 1900's, the city's harbor was deepened, and piers and a terminal were expanded. Rochester became an ocean port in 1959 when the St. Lawrence Seaway opened. The seaway lets ships sail inland from the Atlantic Ocean to ports on the Great Lakes.

Major redevelopment projects gave downtown Rochester a new look during the 1960's and 1970's. One project, Midtown Plaza, features the nation's first enclosed downtown shopping mall. The Genesee Crossroads Development, an urban renewal project, consists of two hotels, office buildings, and a public park. Xerox Square includes an office building and an auditorium. In 1985, the Rochester Riverside Convention Center opened. A third new downtown hotel was completed in 1992. The Third Ward, Southeast Loop, and Upper Falls urban renewal projects all lie just outside the downtown area.

Thomas P. Flynn

Rock is the hard, solid part of the earth. In many areas, the rock is covered by a layer of soil in which plants or trees may grow. Soil itself is made up of tiny bits of rocks usually mixed with organic materials from plants and animals. Rock also lies beneath the oceans and under the polar icecaps.

Where highways cut through hills, you can often see layers of rock in the exposed hillsides. Many rivers cut deep channels through rock to form canyons. Great cliffs of rock line the seashore in such places as Maine and Norway. In desert regions, rock cliffs and pinnacles may rise high above the sandy plains.

Most rocks are *aggregates,* or combinations, of one or more minerals. Basalt, for example, contains crystals of the minerals plagioclase and pyroxene. In some cases, the minerals are so small that the rocks appear to be dense and massive, with no mineral grains. But if you examine a very thin slice of such rock under a microscope, you can see grains of minerals.

Rocks and minerals are useful in a number of ways. Builders use granite, marble, and other rocks in construction work. Cement made from limestone and other rocks serves to bind crushed stone into strong, long-lasting concrete for buildings, dams, and highways.

Metals such as aluminum, iron, lead, and tin come from rocks called *ores.* Ores also supply such radioactive elements as radium and uranium. Ore deposits may lie close to the earth's surface, or deep underground. In some regions, deposits of iron or copper ores make up entire mountains.

Some rocks contain valuable nonmetallic minerals such as borax and graphite. All gems, except amber, coral, and pearl, come from rocks. Diamonds mined in Africa and Arkansas come from a rock called *peridotite.*

Emeralds are found in black limestone in Colombia.

Geologists trace the history of the earth by studying rocks (see **Geology**). They find oil deposits by studying the structure, age, and composition of rock layers. Other scientists study *fossils* (remains of plants and animals found in rock) to learn about the kind of life that existed millions of years ago (see **Fossil**).

Thousands of young people and adults enjoy collecting rocks and minerals as a hobby. The hobbyists call themselves "rock hounds." They trade rocks and minerals just as stamp collectors trade stamps. A collector in Los Angeles may trade with fellow hobbyists in his or her local rock and mineral club, or with other collectors as far away as New York City, Montreal, or Vienna. There are about a thousand rock and mineral clubs in the United States and Canada. These clubs hold regular meetings, sponsor study groups and exhibits, and organize field trips to collecting areas. Sometimes the clubs help develop collections for local museums.

The three main kinds of rocks are (1) igneous rocks, (2) sedimentary rocks, and (3) metamorphic rocks.

Igneous rock

Deep within the earth there exists *molten* (melted), rock material called *magma.* Magma is under great pressure and is extremely hot (1380 °F to 2280 °F, or 750 °C to 1250 °C). This hot material sometimes rises to the earth's surface through *fissures,* or cracks, caused by earthquakes and other deep movements of the earth's crust. Or, the intense heat and pressure of the magma weakens the rocks above it until they give way. *Igneous rocks* form when magma cools and solidifies. Scientists divide igneous rocks into two groups: extrusive rocks and intrusive rocks.

Extrusive rocks form when magma is *extruded,* or forced out, onto the surface of the earth. The magma emerges as streams of molten rock, as partially solid masses of hot lava, or as fine cinders and ash. When lava piles up and hardens around a fissure, it forms a volcano.

Exposure to the cooler surface temperatures causes the lava to harden in a few hours. The minerals it contains do not have time to form large crystals. It may harden so quickly that it forms *obsidian,* a smooth, shiny *volcanic glass; pumice,* a finely porous rock frothy with air bubbles; or *scoria,* a rough rock that looks like furnace slag. Lava that hardens more slowly forms rocks with tiny mineral crystals in them. These *finely crystalline* rocks include dark-colored *basalts* and light-colored *felsites.*

Sometimes a volcano throws lava into the air with great violence. The masses of lava form lumps of rock that range in size from tiny particles of *volcanic dust* to *volcanic bombs* more than 1 foot (30 centimeters) in diameter. Pieces bound together by natural cement are called *agglomerate* rocks or *volcanic breccias.*

Intrusive rocks form from magma that does not rise all the way to the surface of the earth. It may push up the surface rock in the shape of a huge blister. Sometimes it spreads out in sheets between layers of older rocks. The magma may also melt surrounding rocks to create an opening for itself. Beneath the surface, the molten rock cools and hardens slowly. Rocks formed in this way have coarse mineral grains that can be seen with the unaided eye. These *coarsely crystalline* rocks include the *granites, syenites,* and *gabbros.*

Sedimentary rock

Sedimentary rock consists of materials that once were part of older rocks or of plants and animals. These materials accumulate as *strata* (layers) of loose material. Most of the deposits occur on ocean floors, but some form on land and in fresh water. As time passes, the loose materials harden into solid rocks. Geologists divide these rocks into three groups, according to the type of material from which they are formed. These groups are (1) clastic sediments, (2) chemical sediments, and (3) organic sediments.

Clastic sediments are made from rock fragments that range in size from coarse boulders and cobbles, through pebbles and gravels, to fine grains of sand and particles of silt and clay. Rocks break into fragments by a natural process called weathering (see **Erosion** [How erosion occurs]). These fragments are carried about and deposited, chiefly by running water, but sometimes by wind and glaciers. In time, layers build up and then *lithification* (a stone-forming process) occurs. Sometimes, pressure *compacts* (squeezes) the water from the deposits. This locks the particles together and forms rocks called *siltstone* from silt, and *shale* from clay. Natural chemical substances *cement* (bind) grains of sand together to form *sandstone.* Sometimes, waterworn boulders, cobbles, and pebbles become cemented together to form *conglomerate* rocks. Angular fragments become cemented to form *breccias.*

Chemical sediments are deposits of minerals that were once dissolved in water. The evaporation of the water causes minerals to crystallize, leaving deposits of *rock salt* (sodium chloride), *phosphate rocks* (calcium phosphate), and *gypsum* (calcium sulfate). Many *limestone* beds form from calcite (calcium carbonate) crystals, and some deposits of *iron ore* form from the crystallization of dissolved iron oxide. Dissolved silica makes beds of flint rocks.

Organic sediments are the shells, skeletons, and other parts of organisms. Shellfish take calcite from water and use it to build their shells. Coral polyps use the same mineral to build coral reefs (see **Coral**). Coral reefs and piles of shells harden to form *fossiliferous limestone.* The shells of one-celled organisms called *foraminifera* make *chalky limestone* such as that found in the famous white cliffs of Dover, England. Coal formed from ferns and other plants that became buried in swamps and decayed. These deposits of organic matter hardened into beds of peat and coal (see **Coal** [How coal was formed]).

Metamorphic rock

Metamorphic rock is rock that has changed its appearance, and in many cases, its mineral composition.

Common rocks

Rocks are classified into three major groups. *Igneous rock* forms from hardened magma. Hardening of various plant, animal, and mineral materials results in *sedimentary rock. Metamorphic rock* forms when any kind of rock undergoes changes as a result of intense heat and pressure.

Igneous

A. W. Ambler, NAS/Photo Researchers
Basalt

Lee Boltin
Gabbro

WORLD BOOK photo
Granite

Lee Boltin
Obsidian

Sedimentary

L. S. Stepanowicz, Panographics
Bituminous coal

Lee Boltin
Breccia

L. S. Stepanowicz, Panographics
Flint

WORLD BOOK photo
Limestone

Metamorphic

L. S. Stepanowicz, Panographics
Amphibolite

Charles R. Belinky, Photo Researchers
Gneiss

L. S. Stepanowicz, Panographics
Pink marble

A. W. Ambler, NAS/Photo Researchers
Quartzite

These changes may be caused by hot magma or by pressure and heat due to deep burial or mountain-building movements in the earth's crust. All kinds of rock, including igneous and sedimentary, may go through such *metamorphism* to produce metamorphic rocks. Granite, for example, is an igneous rock that contains quartz, feldspar, and mica in a random arrangement. Metamorphism of granite causes feldspar and quartz crystals to form layers between which mica crystals often lie in wavy bands. The new rock is called *gneiss*. Metamorphism recrystallizes the calcite in limestone to form *marble*. The quartz grains in sandstone grow larger and form connecting crystals to create *quartzite*. Soft shales and clays harden to form *slate*, a rock that easily splits into smooth slabs. Felsites and impure sandstones, limestones, and shales change into *schists* that glisten with mica and other minerals such as hornblende and chlorite. Some minerals, including chlorite, garnet, and staurolite, occur only in metamorphic rocks.

Rocks as a hobby

Collecting rocks. You can find interesting rocks and minerals in many places near your home. Good "hunting grounds" include mines, quarries, building excavations, ocean cliffs and beaches, and the rocky sides of road cuts and riverbanks. Be very careful when working near steep rock walls, and always obtain permission to visit private property. You can easily start a collection by gathering loose rocks, but a few simple tools will help in obtaining specimens.

The most important tool is a *rock hammer* that has a square head and a pointed end for pounding and loosening specimens embedded in solid rocks. A chisel helps loosen crystals. By examining rocks through a low-power magnifying glass you can choose the most desirable specimens. Many collectors carry a pocket magnet to help identify rocks containing magnetite. A *streak plate* (piece of unglazed porcelain) aids them in recognizing minerals by streak colors. A pocketknife makes a handy tool for testing mineral hardness. All this equipment can be bought inexpensively at a hardware store or from a mineral dealer. A small backpack makes a good carrying case. All rock specimens should be wrapped in newspaper or tissue paper for protection.

As you collect specimens, identify each with a label. The label should tell the location and date of collection, and what kind of rock or mineral it may be. Later you can transfer the information about the rocks and minerals to a permanent record book.

Identifying rocks may seem hard at first. But it soon becomes easy to recognize common types. Books with good color pictures of rocks and minerals can be purchased. Many beginners buy inexpensive *reference collections* of rocks or minerals from rock and mineral dealers. These collections identify common rocks and

Lee Boltin
Peridotite

L. S. Stepanowicz, Panographics
Pumice

Igneous rocks

Rock	Color	Structure
Basalt	Dark greenish-gray to black.	Dense, microscopic crystals, often form columns.
Gabbro	Greenish-gray to black.	Coarse crystals.
Granite	White to gray, pink to red.	Tightly arranged medium-to-coarse crystals.
Obsidian	Black, sometimes with brown streaks.	Glassy, no crystals, breaks with a shell-like fracture.
Peridotite	Greenish-gray.	Coarse crystals.
Pumice	Grayish-white.	Light, glassy, frothy, fine pores, floats on water.

A. W. Ambler, NAS/Photo Researchers
Sandstone

A. W. Ambler, NAS/Photo Researchers
Shale

Sedimentary rocks

Rock	Color	Structure
Breccia	Gray to black, tan to red.	Angular pieces of rock, held together by natural cement.
Coal	Shiny to dull black.	Brittle, in seams or layers.
Flint	Dark gray, black, brown.	Hard, glassy, breaks with a sharp edge.
Limestone	White, gray, and buff to black and red.	Dense, forms thick beds and cliffs. May contain fossils.
Sandstone	White, gray, yellow, red.	Fine or coarse grains cemented together in beds.
Shale	Yellow, red, gray, green, black.	Dense, fine particles, soft, splits easily, smells like clay.

Lee Boltin
Schist

George Whitely, Photo Researchers
Slate

Metamorphic rocks

Rock	Color	Structure
Amphibolite	Light green to black.	Fine-to-coarse grains, hard, often sparkles.
Gneiss	Gray and pink to black and red.	Medium to coarse crystals arranged in bands.
Marble	Many colors, often mixed.	Medium to coarse crystals, may be banded.
Quartzite	White, gray, pink, buff.	Massive, hard, often glassy.
Schist	White, gray, red, green, black.	Flaky particles, finely banded, feels slippery, often sparkles with mica.
Slate	Black, red, green, purple.	Fine grains, dense, splits into thin, smooth slabs.

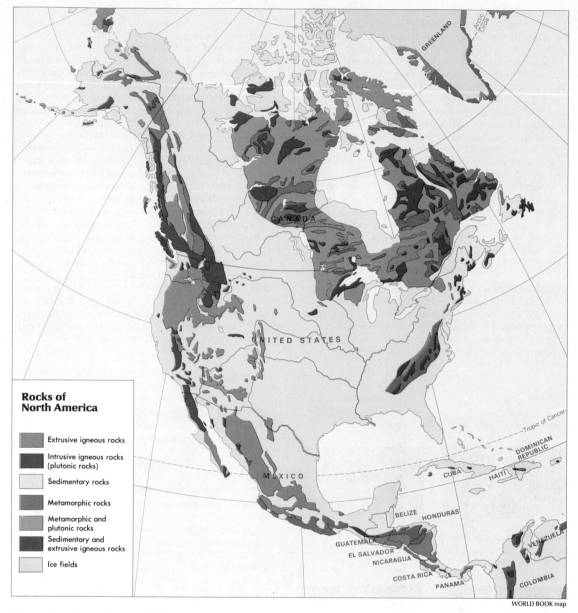

**Rocks of
North America**

- ◼ Extrusive igneous rocks
- ◼ Intrusive igneous rocks (plutonic rocks)
- ◻ Sedimentary rocks
- ◼ Metamorphic rocks
- ◼ Metamorphic and plutonic rocks
- ◼ Sedimentary and extrusive igneous rocks
- ◻ Ice fields

WORLD BOOK map

Interesting facts about rocks

Balanced Rock, in the Garden of the Gods near Colorado Springs, Colo., is an enormous block of sandstone delicately balanced on a small base.

Bendable rock. Most rocks cannot be bent or squeezed out of shape. But thin slabs of itacolumite, a rare kind of sandstone found in India and North Carolina, can be bent by hand because of their crystalline structure.

Eight elements make up more than 98 per cent of all the rocks in the world. These elements are found in about the following percentages: oxygen (46.5), silicon (27.6), aluminum (8.0), iron (5.0), calcium (3.6), sodium (2.8), potassium (2.6), and magnesium (2.0).

Floating rock. Pumice is a rock that floats on water. It was once volcanic lava filled with gases. When the gases escaped, they left millions of tiny holes that filled with air.

Rock of Gibraltar is a huge block of limestone near the southern tip of the mainland of Europe.

minerals. You can compare unknown rocks with pictures and with known specimens.

All minerals have characteristics, such as chemical composition, hardness, and streak color, that help identify them. Experienced collecters also study the formations in which rocks are found, and the physical characteristics of the rocks.

Chemical composition may be determined by certain chemical tests for the mineral elements. For example, a simple chemical test for calcite in limestone is to pour warm soda pop over the rock. The pop, a weak acid, fizzes vigorously on limestone.

Hardness is a measure of how easy it is to scratch a mineral. Soft minerals can be scratched with your fingernail. Harder minerals are scratched by a steel knife blade or pin, and the hardest resist scratching by all materials except diamond—the hardest mineral known.

Streak color is the color of the powder obtained by rubbing a mineral across a hard, rough surface such as unglazed porcelain or a file. The powder color often differs from the color of the mineral mass. For example, pyrite (ferrous sulfide) looks yellow in rocks. But its streak color is black. Many minerals have a typical streak color.

Formations and physical characteristics. You can often identify rocks by knowing where they are found and how they look. For example, you usually can recognize sedimentary rocks because they lie in *stratified,* or layered, formations. Sedimentary rocks often contain fossils, and many have markings, such as old mud cracks or ripple marks caused by waves. Except for volcanic glass, all igneous rocks are solid and crystalline. Some appear dense, with microscopic crystals. Others have larger, easily seen crystals. They occur in volcanic areas, and in intrusive formations that geologists call batholiths, laccoliths, sills, dikes, and stocks. Many metamorphic rocks have characteristic bands and can be split easily into sheets or slabs. See also **Mineral** (Identifying minerals).

Displaying rocks. The size of the rocks in your collection will depend on the available storage space. Some people collect small *micromounts,* that can be kept in small boxes and viewed under a low-power microscope. Other people prefer larger specimens of the size found in museum collections. Probably the best size for storage ranges from 2 by 3 inches (5 by 8 centimeters) to about 3 by 4 inches (8 by 10 centimeters). Crystals, of course, would be smaller. You can trim rocks to the desired size with a hammer. But be careful not to damage choice crystals. Dirty specimens can be cleaned by washing with soap and water and by brushing with a stiff brush. Specimens that contain rock salt cannot be washed, because the salt dissolves in water. Usually, you can brush or blow the dirt from such specimens.

After cleaning your specimens, you can catalog them by painting a small white spot on each rock and writing a number on the spot with waterproof ink. This allows you to refer to the corresponding number in your record book for information about each one.

A chest of drawers or a set of bookshelves makes an ideal storage unit. Put your rocks in shallow cardboard trays. You might keep very small specimens and crystals in cardboard boxes or trays that have partitions. Small exhibits of choice specimens make attractive displays on mantels or shelves, or in glass-front cases.

Rock collections. Many public museums in larger cities of the United States, Canada, and Europe exhibit excellent collections of rocks and minerals. Museums connected with state geological surveys, usually located at state capitals, have exhibits of fossils, minerals, and rocks found in the state. Some of the best-known rock and mineral collections are in the following places: American Museum of Natural History, New York City; British Museum (Natural History), London; California Academy of Sciences, San Francisco; Field Museum of Natural History, Chicago; Cranbrook Institute of Science, Bloomfield Hills, Michigan; Harvard University Museum, Cambridge, Massachusetts; National Museum of Natural History, Washington, D.C.; and Royal Ontario Museum, Toronto, Canada. Maria Luisa Crawford

David R. Frazier

Rock hunters search for specimens near a stream. The man is using a rock hammer to chip a sample from a larger stone.

Related articles in *World Book* include:

Famous rock formations

Garden of the Gods
Giant's Causeway
Gibraltar
Stone Mountain

Igneous rocks

Basalt	Lava	Pumice
Granite	Obsidian	

Metamorphic rocks

Gneiss	Quartzite	Slate
Marble	Schist	Soapstone

Sedimentary rocks

Chalk	Coral	Sandstone
Clay	Flint	Shale
Coal	Limestone	Travertine

Other related articles

Building stone	Gem	Mining	Pyroxene
Cliff	Geode	Moon (What	Quarrying
Corrosion	Geology	the moon is	Sand
Crystal	Gravel	made of;	Silt
Earth	Hardness	pictures)	Soil
Emery	Loess	Mountain	Taconite
Erosion	Metamor-	Ore	Tektite
Fossil	phism	Petrology	Volcano

Additional resources

Level I

Barrow, Lloyd H. *Adventures with Rocks and Minerals.* 2 vols. Enslow, 1991, 1995.
Pellant, Chris. *Rocks and Minerals.* Dorling Kindersley, 1992.
VanCleave, Janice. *Janice VanCleave's Rocks and Minerals.* Wiley, 1996.

Level II

Dickey, John S. *On the Rocks: Earth Science for Everyone.* Wiley, 1996.
O'Donoghue, Michael. *Illustrated Guide to Rocks and Minerals.* Smithmark, 1992.
Schumann, Walter. *Handbook of Rocks, Minerals, and Gemstones.* Houghton, 1993.

Rock climbing. See Climbing.

© Dave Benett, Gamma/Liaison

Rock music's energetic style is captured by Mick Jagger, *left,* and Ron Wood, *right,* of the Rolling Stones. Formed in 1962, the "Stones" have been one of rock's most enduring groups.

Rock music

Rock music is one of the world's most popular and adaptable musical forms. When it originated in the United States in the early 1950's, rock music was known as *rock 'n' roll* (also spelled *rock and roll*). From the start, it was party music, dance music, and music that appealed to young listeners. It often celebrated the joys of being young, and it occasionally expressed the frustrations of youth.

Many adults dismissed rock 'n' roll as a passing fad or condemned it as a threat to society. By the mid-1960's, however, rock 'n' roll had earned wide respect as a legitimate art form. The music's popularity spread internationally and among older listeners as well. By the end of the 1960's, the music had moved far from its roots in blues and country music, and it became known simply as *rock.*

In the 1970's, rock became a bigger business than ever. It not only dominated the music industry, but also influenced everything from film to fashion to politics. As rock music became increasingly accepted, it lost much of the rebelliousness that had originally given it its power.

Since the early 1980's, rock music has continued to defy musical barriers and has drawn much of its strength from international musical influences. Today,

Don McLeese, the contributor of this article, is Pop Music Critic for the Austin American-Statesman.

rock music is no longer only the music of young Americans. It is music of the world.

Characteristics of rock music

At first, rock music generally followed a $\frac{4}{4}$ beat and used only two or three chords in its melody. The songs were simple, repetitive, and easy to remember. Most of them were only two or three minutes long. The simplest rock continues to rely on a basic beat and a few chords. But some rock songs are more complex and sophisticated. Rock music has also expanded to include international influences. Traditional musical elements from Africa, Ireland, South America, and other places have become more widely used in rock music.

Rock lyrics express a wide range of emotions and ideas. Early rock songs dealt with such themes as cars, girls, boys, dances, and the joy of being young. Later, rock songwriters broadened their range to include everything from world politics to highly personal poetry.

Early rock music featured electric guitar or a blues-style boogie-woogie piano and drums. Today, musicians may use computers and electronic instruments called *synthesizers* as well as guitars, pianos, and drums. Some recordings include electronic drum machines instead of human drummers. Musicians also use electronic devices to manipulate the pitch, tempo, and duration of digitally recorded sounds. Today, many studio recordings are produced entirely by computer.

Many rock groups feature a vocal soloist, with other group members performing as a chorus. When groups perform, they usually use huge amplifiers and dozens of speakers. The music may be soft but is often extremely loud. Many groups specialize in highly theatrical concert performances. Some performers wear wild costumes and makeup. They may also add unusual stage effects, such as clouds of smoke or laser light shows.

Beginnings of rock music

Musical roots. Rock developed from a variety of different popular music styles. The roots of rock can be heard in the lyrics and electric guitar of the blues, in the rhythms of a form of blues known as *rhythm and blues,* and in the spirit of American country music. The squawking saxophone of dance-band jazz, and the melodies, choruses, and harmonies of popular (pop) music also added to the rock sound.

Many of the elements of rock music had been around long before rock developed as a musical form. In the 1950's, musicians combined these musical elements and created the revolutionary form of music called rock 'n' roll. It was louder and faster than the forms from which it drew. Its lyrics contrasted sharply with the sentimental lyrics of earlier pop songs. And it was generally performed in a wild and spontaneous manner with a more primitive and raw display of emotions.

The emergence of rock 'n' roll. Before rock 'n' roll became a musical category, such rhythm and blues hits as "Rocket '88" (1951) by Jackie Brenston had the spirit of rock 'n' roll. This and other similar records became increasingly popular with both black rhythm and blues audiences and white country music audiences.

The major rock 'n' roll explosion began with Elvis Presley. Although he was white, he had the style commonly associated with increasingly popular black music. The popularity of his black sound combined with his hip-shaking live performances and frequent radio play quickly made Presley a superstar. His first major success came with his 1956 recording of "Heartbreak Hotel" for RCA Victor.

Another important influence on rock music was St.

UPI/Bettmann

Chuck Berry helped define the rebellious spirit of rock 'n' roll in the 1950's. His rocking guitar rhythms and vivid lyrics effectively expressed the feelings and problems of youth.

Louis blues artist Chuck Berry. He was the first of the great rock songwriters. His lyrics effectively expressed the feelings and problems of youth. Berry's first hit record was a country-styled tune titled "Maybellene" (1955). Berry was a major influence on later rock performers, including the Beatles and the Rolling Stones.

Richard Penniman, known as Little Richard, helped influence rock performance styles. His vigorous and flamboyant stage performances provided a model for performers who followed. His first major success came in 1955 with "Tutti Frutti."

Bill Haley and the Comets became the first famous rock band. Their recording of "Rock Around the Clock" was the first international rock hit. It was used as the theme song for *The Blackboard Jungle,* a 1955 motion picture about juvenile delinquents. The song contributed to rock 'n' roll's reputation as music of rebellion.

Growing popularity. Radio played an important role in spreading rock music during the mid-1950's. Television had replaced radio as the chief producer of drama and variety entertainment, and many radio stations began to play rock to capture an audience. Disc jockeys who played the records became powerful forces in promoting the popularity of rock performers. Disc jockey Alan Freed helped popularize the name rock 'n' roll with his radio program, "Moondog Rock 'n' Roll Party."

Though the United States was racially divided, some people sensed a spirit of racial equality in rock 'n' roll. It featured black artists, such as Chuck Berry, who were influenced by white country music. It also presented white artists, such as Presley and songwriter-guitarist Buddy Holly, who adopted styles based on black rhythm and blues. In earlier times, the recordings of such Southern black artists as Bo Diddley and Fats Domino would have

Bettmann

Elvis Presley, *center,* became rock's first superstar. His tough, rebellious manner and suggestive movements are apparent in this scene from the movie *Jailhouse Rock* (1957).

been categorized as "race records" and sold primarily to black customers. With the rise of rock 'n' roll, these artists appealed to black and white audiences alike.

Most important for its young listeners, rock 'n' roll was the first music that was all their own. Rock 'n' roll proclaimed that being a teen ager was special. Although rock 'n' roll was extremely popular, its lyrics and the performance style that went with it were still considered indecent by many adults.

Artistic decline. As rock 'n' roll continued to grow in popularity, the major record companies and professional songwriters who had ignored the music started to recognize rock 'n' roll's profitability. By the late 1950's, much of what record companies released as rock 'n' roll was no longer wild, spontaneous, and rebellious. While rock continued to sell well, the music was much tamer than it had been just a few years earlier. Such popular artists as Frankie Avalon and Pat Boone had toned down the volume and the feel of the music. As a result, rock 'n' roll became just another form of popular music.

Rock 'n' roll also lost many of its stars and creative forces toward the end of the 1950's. In 1958, Elvis Presley was drafted into the United States Army and rocking pianist Jerry Lee Lewis caused a scandal by marrying his 13-year-old cousin. Then in 1959, Chuck Berry was arrested, Buddy Holly and singer-guitarist Ritchie Valens died in an airplane crash, and Little Richard left music to study for the ministry.

British Invasion and rock's revival

The Beatles and the British Invasion. The Beatles, a group from Liverpool, England, returned excitement to rock 'n' roll in the early 1960's. They made the music more popular than ever and more respected artistically. Their witty and sophisticated music made the sentimental rock of the time seem tame and old-fashioned.

The Beatles consisted of George Harrison, John Lennon, Paul McCartney, and Ringo Starr. Their first British hit was "Love Me Do" in 1962. Their American breakthrough came with "I Want to Hold Your Hand" in 1964. Both hits were written by Lennon and McCartney, who eventually established themselves as the most popular songwriting team in rock's history.

Beatlemania was the term generally used to describe the excitement generated by the Beatles. It affected society in a number of ways. Teen-age boys began growing their hair longer to copy the Beatles. Teen-age girls screamed so loudly during the band's concerts that it was impossible to hear the music. At first, many parents feared the effects of Beatlemania. But the personal charm and musical appeal of the band soon conquered older listeners.

The Beatles turned rock 'n' roll from an American-dominated musical style into an international phenomenon. Soon after the Beatles hit the United States, popular music charts became filled with songs by British bands that wrote and played their own music. The British bands replaced American solo singers, such as Fabian and Frankie Avalon, who relied primarily on outside songwriters and musicians.

The Rolling Stones were the most significant of the groups that followed the Beatles in the "British Invasion" of the United States. They represented a scruffier, more rebellious alternative to the more widely accepted Beatles. Their music also was more faithful to its roots in the blues. Other British bands that became popular in the United States included The Who, the Kinks, the Animals, the Dave Clark Five, and Herman's Hermits.

Expanding styles and sounds. In addition to the Beatles and the Rolling Stones, the third major force in the rock of the 1960's was Bob Dylan. The strong social message of Dylan's songs influenced many musicians. Dylan helped swing the balance of popularity away from the British and back to American musicians.

Dylan began his musical career in the early 1960's as a solo folk singer and follower of American folk singer Woody Guthrie. His popularity began among many fans of early rock 'n' roll who had dismissed the music of the early 1960's as uninspired. They began listening to folk music for its social significance. Folk music fans turned to Dylan for his "protest songs." These songs protested what many people considered the wrongs of society, such as racial prejudice, poverty, and war. Some Dylan songs, such as "Blowin' in the Wind" (1962) and "A Hard Rain's A-Gonna Fall" (1963), achieved wider popularity through versions by such artists as Peter, Paul, and Mary and Joan Baez. They helped make Dylan the leading writer of protest songs.

Following the example of the Beatles, Dylan began playing his material on electric guitar with a band that used electrically amplified instruments. Gradually, his songs became less political and more poetic and personal. Dylan had one of his first and biggest rock hits in 1965 with "Like a Rolling Stone." Dylan's ambitious, po-

UPI/Bettmann

The Beatles, shown here at a 1965 press conference, earned a huge international following with their witty, sophisticated songs and whimsical humor. Their sensational popularity—called *Beatlemania*—resulted in mobbing fans, Beatle fashions, and tremendous media coverage of the band.

The 1969 Woodstock Music and Arts Festival was a huge rock concert that celebrated the "hippie" culture. The event drew over 300,000 people and lasted for three days. Woodstock showed that rock music had become a focal point for social issues.

© Dan McCoy, Black Star

etic lyrics set to a rock beat produced a style known as *folk rock.* Folk rock was the first major challenge to rock's domination by the British.

The mid-1960's became a time of peak creativity for rock music. Rock artists explored new possibilities in lyrical content and form. Some began to examine the meaning of dreams in their lyrics. Others began to use *free-verse* poetry that did not rhyme. Some musicians also began to produce *concept albums,* which linked their songs together by story line or theme. One such album was *Sgt. Pepper's Lonely Hearts Club Band* (1967) by the Beatles. In addition, rock was featured in a number of popular stage works, including *Hair* (1967).

The 1960's also found instrumentalists exercising more creative freedom. American guitarist Jimi Hendrix extended the range of the electric guitar by manipulating its switches and pedals to create new sounds. In addition, such instrumentalists as Hendrix and British guitarist Eric Clapton began stretching a single song to about 10 or 20 minutes. Their extended solos were inspired by blues and jazz traditions. The music played by such bands as the Jimi Hendrix Experience and Clapton's Cream were sometimes categorized as *progressive rock.* Some of their music was also called *acid rock,* after the illegal drug LSD, or "acid," which was popular among some rock fans.

Another popular musical style of the 1960's was the California sound called *surf music.* The Beach Boys became the most popular surf music group. They sang of surfing, hot rods, and teen dreams. The Beach Boys became well known for their fine vocal harmonies, as well as the experimental production techniques of the band's Brian Wilson.

The 1960's was also the peak period for *soul music.* Soul music developed from the gritty, emotional rhythm and blues style, but it had a smoother sound and more widely pleasing melodies. It was recorded primarily by black artists, but it found wide popularity among both black and white listeners. Detroit's Motown label was the most popular and successful soul label. Leading Motown artists included Marvin Gaye, Diana Ross and the Supremes, and Stevie Wonder. The gritty soul styles of Otis Redding, Sam and Dave, and others from the Stax

label in Memphis were also popular with rock fans.

Growing social significance. The growing influence and popularity of rock music affected society in a number of ways. It produced new fashions, such as Beatle boots and longer hairstyles. Some rock music encouraged the use of illegal drugs. Other rock music inspired public protest against such social and political problems as racial prejudice and the Vietnam War.

Toward the end of the 1960's, rock's various styles came together at massive outdoor rock festivals. These festivals showed how popular and diverse the music had become. The most significant rock festival was the 1969 Woodstock Music and Arts Festival in upstate New York. Woodstock was a musical, communal celebration of the alternative "hippie" culture. It was dedicated to world peace. The event drew more than 300,000 fans and featured three days of top rock talent. It included such performers as the Grateful Dead, Jimi Hendrix, Jefferson Airplane, and blues singer Janis Joplin.

Rock music in the 1970's

Rock goes pop. Throughout the 1970's, almost all popular music contained elements of the rock style. The music's audience spanned from preteens to middle-aged adults. As the audience for rock grew, a variety of new musical categories developed. *Country rock* featured such groups as Poco and the Eagles, which emphasized country music roots. Musicians such as Chick Corea and the members of the group Chicago blended rock with the improvisation techniques of jazz to create a form called *jazz rock. Heavy metal rock* groups, such as Led Zeppelin, stressed screaming electric guitars. The *glitter rock* of David Bowie and others popularized flamboyant onstage visuals. Musical groups including King Crimson and Emerson, Lake, and Palmer combined a rock beat with the more complex melodies of classical music in a form called *art rock.* James Taylor, Joni Mitchell, and others popularized an acoustic singer-songwriter tradition by composing music with thoughtful, often autobiographical, lyrics.

The early 1970's found rock more profitable than ever. In terms of musical quality, however, the period was generally considered rock's lowest point since the pre-

Beatles 1960's. Through its attempt to appeal to a wide audience, rock lost much of the youthful energy and spirit of rebellion that had once powered it.

By the mid-1970's, the music started to reclaim some of the inspiration and energy associated with earlier rock. Bruce Springsteen and the E Street Band attracted an enthusiastic following with "Born to Run" (1975). Springsteen's music reflected the energetic rock 'n' roll and rhythm and blues music of the 1950's. He showed how rock might find a future by drawing from its past. The *reggae* music of Jamaica's Bob Marley and the Wailers injected fresh inspiration into the sounds of the mid-1970's with its slow, pulsing rhythms and soulful singing.

Disco and punk. Probably the most popular musical style of the mid-1970's was *disco.* Disco often combined Latin rhythms and elements of *funk,* a type of earthy blues, to produce a strong, steady dance beat. It was created primarily for dance clubs called *discothéques,* or *discos.* It was rarely performed live. Instead, discothéques played records and tapes of the music. Popular disco artists of the 1970's included Donna Summer and Chic. Although many people considered disco to be mindless formula music, disco returned dancing and the spirit of fun to popular music. At a time when many white rock radio stations were giving little exposure to black artists, disco appealed to a diverse audience with dance music recorded by both black and white artists.

The *punk rock* of the mid-1970's attempted to launch a rock revolution. Such British bands as the Sex Pistols and the Clash returned to the raw energy of earlier rock. They were fueled by an anger at the materialism of society and the lack of inspiration in much of the early 1970's rock music. Punk was not a big commercial success, but it had a number of important effects on rock music. It proved that new styles could develop outside the established rock industry. It also showed that young musicians could express themselves without expensive equipment and years of practice. Punk rock influenced many nonpunk musicians to make their music simpler, faster, and more energetic.

Such New York City bands as Talking Heads and the Patti Smith Group took an artier approach to punk rock. Their music was more poetic and conceptually original than punk. These groups became categorized as punk's *new wave* of rock. The music of punk and new wave bands represented an aggressive alternative to the more established musicians who dominated the rock industry.

At first, disco and punk were considered opposites. But they came together in the late 1970's. Blondie and other musical groups enjoyed hits that combined disco rhythms with the spirit of new wave rock.

Rock music in the 1980's and 1990's

New directions and old. The most popular new music to emerge from the 1980's was *rap music.* Rap is spoken rather than sung. Electronic rhythms and sounds of records being scratched provide background music. Rap's streetwise rhymes and chants reflect the concerns of urban youths living in a tough world. Public Enemy became one of the most successful rap groups.

Music from the 1960's inspired some of rock's most popular musicians of the 1980's. Among these musicians was the American band R.E.M., which drew heavily from 1960's folk rock. In addition, many artists who had begun their careers in the 1960's, such as singer Tina Turner, achieved greater popularity than ever before. Some bands from the 1960's, such as the Rolling Stones, Pink Floyd, and the Grateful Dead, were among the leading concert attractions of the 1980's. These bands remained popular not only with their original fans from the 1960's but with new and younger listeners as well.

Rock videos. In the 1980's, many rock performers began to feature their music in short films called *rock videos.* These films featured music, acting, dancing, striking visual images, and sometimes excerpts from rock concert performances. Rock videos were shown on television and at many dance clubs. Cable television's Music Television (MTV) network played rock videos 24 hours a day. The rise of rock video and MTV brought widespread exposure and massive popularity to a number of artists, including the Eurythmics, Madonna, and George Michael. Many songs became as popular for the visual element of the video as they did for the music. The popularity of rock videos continued into the 1990's.

The American singer and dancer Michael Jackson starred in several highly successful videos and became one of the most popular performers in the history of rock music. His *Thriller* (1982) became the largest-selling record album of all time.

Rock and society. In the 1980's, rock extended its importance as a force for social change through a broadening interest in international concerns and a reawakening of its social idealism. Several artists, including Peter Gabriel, Talking Heads, and Paul Simon, incorporated the music of Africa into their music. Such albums as Springsteen's *Born in the U.S.A.* (1984) and U2's *The Joshua Tree* (1987) dealt with socially relevant themes.

Rock's idealism and internationalism came together in such events as Live Aid, an all-day concert held in July 1985. Money raised by the event went to help feed starving people in Africa. The concert, held in both Philadelphia and London, was televised throughout the world and featured many of the biggest stars in rock.

The rise of *grunge rock* from Seattle represented perhaps the most revolutionary change in rock music in the 1990's. Such grunge bands as Nirvana, Pearl Jam, and Soundgarden rapidly became international superstars. The grunge style combined punk attitude with heavy metal dynamics and pop music influences. Grunge

© Giovanni Canitano, LGI

U2, a rock group from Ireland, has enjoyed worldwide popularity since the 1980's. Lead singer Bono, *second from left,* composes the lyrics to many of the group's songs.

© Alice Arnold, LGI

Rap music consists of spoken words over a rhythm accompaniment. It emerged from black inner city culture in the 1980's and quickly became popular among young people. Arrested Development, shown here, became one of rap's most successful groups in the 1990's.

songs reflected a detachment from the values of society. In the mid-1990's, an emerging style of rap music called *gangster rap* or *gangsta rap* stressed violence, sex, and street gang associations in its confrontational lyrics.

The rise of grunge, gangsta rap, and other forms of controversial music led to attacks from politicians and private groups. Critics charged that such music celebrated sex and violence. The artists defended the music as an accurate reflection of modern society.

Rock music today

Rock music today features more female singers and composers than at any time before. The success in the late 1990's of Alanis Morissette of Canada and of Courtney Love led to the emergence of many other women artists. Some of the most successful female performers appeal especially to younger listeners. These artists include Americans Jewel, Fiona Apple, Paula Cole, and Sheryl Crow; Sarah McLachlan of Canada; and the British group the Spice Girls. Another group with special appeal for young fans is Hanson, a trio of teen-aged brothers.   Don McLeese

Related articles in *World Book* include:

Beach Boys	Hendrix, Jimi	Rolling Stones
Beatles	Holly, Buddy	Simon, Paul
Berry, Chuck	Jackson, Michael	Springsteen,
Blues	Jazz (Fusion)	Bruce
Brown, James	Lennon, John	Synthesizer
Country music	Madonna	Townshend, Peter
Dance (introduc-	McCartney, Paul	Turner, Tina
tion; picture)	Popular music	Who, The
Dylan, Bob	Presley, Elvis	Wonder, Stevie
Electronic music	Rap music	Woodstock
Grateful Dead	Reggae	Festival

Outline

I. Characteristics of rock music
II. Beginnings of rock music
    A. Musical roots   C. Growing popularity
    B. The emergence of   D. Artistic decline
       rock 'n' roll
III. British Invasion and rock's revival
    A. The Beatles and the   C. Growing social
       British Invasion   significance
    B. Expanding styles and sounds
IV. Rock music in the 1970's
    A. Rock becomes pop
    B. Disco and punk
V. Rock music in the 1980's and 1990's
    A. New directions and old
    B. Rock videos
    C. Rock and society
IV. Rock music today

Questions

What kinds of rock music emerged during the 1970's?
Who were the Beatles? How did they affect rock music?

© John Roca, LGI

Madonna, one of rock's superstars of the 1980's and 1990's, gained fame for her recordings, videos, and live performances.

What is *rap music*?
Why was Elvis Presley popular?
What are the characteristics of early rock 'n' roll?
Why was Bob Dylan an important force in the music of the 1960's?
How did rock music contribute to social causes in the 1980's?
What are the roots of rock music?
Why was rock music seen as music of racial equality in the 1950's? In the 1970's?
What did Chuck Berry contribute to rock 'n' roll? Who did he influence?

Additional resources

Helander, Brock. *The Rock Who's Who.* 2nd ed. Schirmer Bks., 1996.
Powell, Stephanie. *Hit Me with Music: How to Start, Manage, Record, and Perform with Your Own Rock Band.* Millbrook, 1995.
Romanowski, Patricia, and others, eds. *The New Rolling Stone Encyclopedia of Rock & Roll.* Fireside Paperbacks, 1995.
Shirley, David. *The History of Rock & Roll.* Watts, 1997.

Rockefeller, John Davison (1839-1937), was an American businessman. He made a fortune in the petroleum industry and became famous for his *philanthropy* (charity). A number of his descendants have become prominent in the United States in a variety of fields.

Many people have criticized the business methods Rockefeller used in developing his vast industrial empire. But his contributions to the welfare of humanity form an equally important part of his record.

Early life. Rockefeller, the son of a peddler, was born in Richford, New York, near Ithaca. When he was 14 years old, his family moved to Cleveland. Rockefeller started work at 16 as a clerk in a small produce firm. He then formed a partnership in a grain commission house. He used the profits to enter the oil business at 23.

At that time, oil production and refining had little organization. Wide price variations and wasteful practices occurred frequently. Rockefeller set out to make the industry orderly and efficient. He realized that to do this he had to establish centralized control. Fifteen years later, he achieved his goal of having the flow of oil products from producer to consumer controlled by one company—the Standard Oil Company.

The Standard Oil Company, which was established in 1870, grew out of Rockefeller, Andrews & Flagler, a partnership owned by Rockefeller, his younger brother William, and some associates. By the end of the 1870's, the company owned the chief refineries in Cleveland,

New York City, Pittsburgh, and Philadelphia.

Rockefeller also concentrated on the transportation and distribution of crude petroleum and its refined products. He built tank cars and distribution systems. His dealings with railroads involved rebates and other types of privileged treatment (see **Rebate**). In 1882, Rockefeller organized the Standard Oil Trust. He then controlled almost all U.S. oil refining and distribution and much of the world's oil trade.

The vastness of Rockefeller's holdings—plus public criticism of his methods—caused the Ohio Supreme Court to dissolve the Standard Oil Trust in 1892. The Standard Oil Company (New Jersey), a holding company, replaced the trust. In 1911, the Supreme Court of the United States ordered the firm to dissolve. See **Antitrust laws; Standard Oil Company; Holding company**.

Philanthropic work. From 1895 to 1897, Rockefeller gradually retired. By then, he had started his philanthropic activities, to which he devoted the rest of his life.

Rockefeller donated about $520 million during his lifetime. Most of this money was donated through foundations that he established himself and through other organizations. He donated money to such institutions as the Rockefeller Foundation, Rockefeller University, the University of Chicago, the General Education Board, and the Laura Spelman Rockefeller Memorial (see **Rockefeller Foundation; Chicago, University of** [History]).

Rockefeller's descendants. Several of Rockefeller's male descendants became well-known figures in business, finance, and philanthropy. Several others became prominent in American politics and government. His only son, John D. Rockefeller, Jr., continued his father's philanthropic work. John D., Jr., had five sons—John D. III, Nelson, Laurance, Winthrop, and David. John D. III served as chairman of the Rockefeller Foundation from 1952 to 1971. Nelson was governor of New York from late 1958 to 1973 and Vice President of the United States from 1974 to 1977. Laurance was a noted conservationist. Winthrop served as governor of Arkansas from 1967 to 1971. David was chief executive officer of Chase Manhattan Bank from 1969 to 1980. John D. Rockefeller IV, the son of John D. III, served as governor of West Virginia from 1977 to 1985 and has been a member of the U.S. Senate since 1985.   Edward Nelson Akin

See also **Rockefeller, Nelson A.; Rockefeller, John D., Jr.; Rockefeller, John D., III; Rockefeller, John D., IV.**

Wide World

John D. Rockefeller, shown here with a young boy, became famous for his philanthropies. In his later years, Rockefeller often gave shiny new dimes as mementos to strangers he met. At his death, his heirs included, *left to right,* his son, John D., Jr., and his grandsons David, Nelson, Winthrop, Laurance, and John D. III.

Additional resources

Harr, John E., and Johnson, P. J. *The Rockefeller Century.* Scribner, 1988.

Hawke, David F. *John D.: The Founding Father of the Rockefellers.* Harper, 1980.

Nevins, Allan. *John D. Rockefeller.* 2 vols. 1940. Reprint. Kraus Reprint, 1969. The definitive biography.

Souker, Nancy. *John D. Rockefeller.* Silver Burdett, 1989.

Rockefeller, John Davison, Jr. (1874-1960), was the only son of the wealthy American businessman John D. Rockefeller. He became a business associate of his father's and devoted most of his life to extending the *philanthropic* (charitable) work that his father had started, especially his conservation efforts. John D. Rockefeller, Jr., donated $8 $\frac{1}{2}$ million to buy land for United Nations Headquarters in New York City. In addition, he built Rockefeller Center, a landmark of New York City; and provided the funds to restore the historic city of Williamsburg, Virginia. Rockefeller was born in Cleveland. Edward Nelson Akin

See also **New York City** (Manhattan; A visitor's guide); **Rockefeller, John D.; Williamsburg.**

Rockefeller, John Davison, III (1906-1978), served as chairman of the board of trustees of the Rockefeller Foundation from 1952 to 1971. Rockefeller helped found the Lincoln Center for the Performing Arts in New York City and later became its chairman. He also founded the Population Council, a group that conducts research on population problems throughout the world.

Rockefeller was born in New York City. He was the oldest son of John D. Rockefeller, Jr. (see **Rockefeller, John D., Jr.**). Edward Nelson Akin

Rockefeller, John Davison, IV (1937-), was elected a United States senator from West Virginia in 1984. Rockefeller, a Democrat, won reelection in 1990 and 1996. He served as West Virginia's governor from 1977 until 1985. He was secretary of state of West Virginia from 1969 to 1973 and president of West Virginia Wesleyan College from 1973 to 1975.

Rockefeller was born in New York City and graduated from Harvard University. He was the son of John D. Rockefeller III (see **Rockefeller, John D., III**). In the 1960's, John D. IV served as special assistant to the director of the Peace Corps and in the U.S. Department of State. Rockefeller was a member of the West Virginia House of Delegates from 1967 to 1969. Edward Nelson Akin

Rockefeller, Nelson Aldrich (1908-1979), served as vice president of the United States from 1974 to 1977. He filled a vacancy that was created when Vice President Gerald R. Ford succeeded Richard M. Nixon, who had resigned as president. Ford nominated Rockefeller for the vice presidency.

Rockefeller's nomination required the approval of both houses of Congress under the procedures that were established in 1967 by the 25th Amendment to the United States Constitution. Rockefeller was the second per-

Wide World
Nelson A. Rockefeller

son to become vice president under terms of the 25th Amendment. Ford became the first in 1973. Before adoption of the amendment, vacancies in the vice presidency stayed unfilled until the next presidential election.

Rockefeller, a Republican, had served as governor of New York from 1959 to 1973. Before he took office as governor, Rockefeller had held a number of posts in the federal government.

Early life. Rockefeller was born on July 8, 1908, in Bar Harbor, Maine. His grandfather, John D. Rockefeller, and father, John D. Rockefeller, Jr., became famous for their many contributions to American business and human welfare. Nelson graduated from Dartmouth College in 1930. During the 1930's, he took part in his family's business and philanthropic activities.

In 1930, Rockefeller married Mary Todhunter Clark. They had five children: Rodman, Anne, Steven, and the twins Mary and Michael. The Rockefellers were divorced in 1962. In 1963, Rockefeller married Margaretta (Happy) Fitler Murphy. The couple had two children: Nelson, Jr., and Mark.

Career in government. In 1940, President Franklin D. Roosevelt appointed Rockefeller coordinator of inter-American affairs. In 1944 and 1945, Rockefeller served as assistant secretary of state. He was undersecretary of health, education, and welfare in 1953 and 1954 and special assistant to President Dwight D. Eisenhower in 1954 and 1955.

Rockefeller was elected governor of New York in 1958 and won reelection in 1962, 1966, and 1970. He sought the Republican presidential nomination in 1964 and 1968. In 1973, he resigned as governor of New York and set up the Commission on Critical Choices for Americans, a group devoted to the study of world problems.

On Aug. 9, 1974, Nixon resigned the presidency while facing almost certain impeachment because of his role in the Watergate political scandal. Ford became president and nominated Rockefeller for vice president. Rockefeller took office on Dec. 19, 1974. As vice president, he helped develop U.S. domestic policies and headed a federal commission that investigated the Central Intelligence Agency. J. F. terHorst

See also **Ford, Gerald R.; Vice President of the United States; Watergate.**

Rockefeller Foundation is a philanthropic organization chartered in 1913. It sponsors programs to fight hunger, to improve health, to provide education and jobs, and to deal with problems of overpopulation and environmental degradation. It works to ensure that poor people share in the benefits of new technology and global changes. It also seeks to preserve and support the world's many forms of culture and creative arts.

In the United States, for example, some foundation programs work to provide equal opportunities for minority groups, to improve public education, and to encourage international and intercultural understanding through the arts and the humanities. Aid is given through grants to agencies and cooperative projects, and through fellowships.

John D. Rockefeller originally provided an endowment of $100 million for the foundation. Later, he increased it to more than $183 million. The foundation's offices are in New York City. For assets, see **Foundations** (table). Critically reviewed by the Rockefeller Foundation

Rocket

The giant Saturn 5 rocket that carried the first astronauts to the moon rises from its launch tower. Rockets are the only vehicles used for launching people and machines into space.

Rocket is a type of engine that can produce more power for its size than any other kind of engine. A rocket can produce about 3,000 times more power than an automobile engine of the same size. The word *rocket* is also used to mean a vehicle driven by a rocket engine.

Rockets are made in a variety of sizes. Some rockets that shoot fireworks into the sky are only 2 feet (61 centimeters) long. Rockets 50 to 100 feet (15 to 30 meters) long carry missiles that may be used to bomb distant targets during wartime. Larger and more powerful rockets lift artificial satellites into orbit around the earth. For example, the Saturn 5 rocket that carried astronauts to the moon stood about 363 feet (111 meters) high.

The rockets now in use produce their power by burning a fuel. These rockets are called *chemical rockets* because burning is a chemical reaction. In addition, researchers have experimented with rockets that produce power by heating a propellant so that it expands. The heat can come from an electrical unit or a small nuclear reactor.

A chemical rocket can produce great power, but it burns fuel rapidly. As a result, a rocket needs a large amount of fuel to work for even a short time. The Saturn 5 rocket burned over 560,000 gallons (2,120,000 liters) of fuel during the first $2\frac{3}{4}$ minutes of flight. Rockets become very hot as they burn fuel. The temperature in some rocket engines reaches 6000 °F. (3300 °C), about twice the temperature at which steel melts.

People use rockets chiefly for scientific research, space travel, and war. Rockets have been used in war for hundreds of years. In the 1200's, Chinese soldiers fired them against attacking armies. British troops used rockets to attack Fort McHenry in Maryland during the War of 1812 (1812-1815). After watching the battle, Francis Scott Key described "the rocket's red glare" in "The Star-Spangled Banner." During World War I (1914-1918), the French used rockets to shoot down enemy airplanes. Germany attacked London with rockets during World War II (1939-1945). In the Persian Gulf War (1991), the United States used Patriot missiles to intercept Iraq's Scud missiles.

Scientists use rockets for exploration and research in the atmosphere and in space. Rockets carry scientific instruments high in the sky to gather information about the air that surrounds the earth. Since 1957, rockets have lifted hundreds of satellites into orbit around the earth. These satellites take pictures of the earth's weather and gather other information for scientific study. Rockets also carry instruments far into space to explore and study other planets.

Rockets also power human space flights, which began in 1961. In 1969, rockets carried astronauts to the first landing on the moon. In 1981, rockets lifted the first space shuttle into orbit around the earth.

The contributor of this article, Eugene M. Cliff, is Reynolds Metals Professor of Aerospace and Ocean Engineering at Virginia Polytechnic Institute and State University.

A basic law of motion—discovered in the 1600's by the English scientist Sir Isaac Newton—describes how rockets work. This law states that for every action, there is an equal and opposite reaction (see **Motion** [Newton's laws of motion]). Newton's law explains why the flow of air from a toy balloon *propels* (drives forward) the balloon in flight. A powerful rocket works similarly.

A chemical rocket burns special fuel in a *combustion* (burning) chamber and creates rapidly expanding gas. This gas presses out equally in all directions inside the rocket. The pressure of the gas against one side of the rocket balances the pressure of the gas against the opposite side. The gas flowing to the rear of the rocket escapes through a nozzle. This exhaust gas does not balance the pressure of gas against the front of the rocket. The uneven pressure drives the rocket forward.

The flow of gas through the nozzle of a rocket is the *action* described in Newton's law. The *reaction* is the continuous *thrust* (pushing force) of the rocket away from the flow of exhaust gas.

Rocket propellant. Rockets burn a combination of chemicals called *propellant.* Rocket propellant consists of (1) a fuel, such as gasoline, kerosene, or liquid hydrogen; and (2) *an oxidizer* (a substance that supplies oxygen), such as nitrogen tetroxide or liquid oxygen. The oxidizer supplies the oxygen that the fuel needs to burn. This supply of oxygen enables the rocket to work in space, which has no air.

The thrust of a rocket depends upon the mathematical product of two qualities of the burned propellant: (1) its *mass* (quantity of matter) and (2) the velocity with which it leaves the engine. A large engine can release mass at a high rate, so the most powerful engines are gigantic. To achieve a high exhaust velocity, rocket designers select propellants that release tremendous amounts of energy when they burn.

A rocket burns propellant rapidly, and most rockets carry a supply that lasts only a few minutes. During the first minutes of flight, the rocket's speed is held down by air friction and gravity. Air friction drags on the rocket as long as the rocket travels through the atmosphere. As the rocket climbs higher, the air becomes thinner and the friction decreases. In space, no air friction acts on the rocket. Gravity pulls a rocket toward the earth, but the pull decreases as the rocket travels farther from the earth. As a rocket burns its propellant, the weight it must carry becomes less.

Jet engines also work by means of an action-reaction process. However, jet fuel does not contain an oxidizer. Instead, jet engines use the oxygen in the surrounding air. As a result, they cannot function outside the earth's atmosphere.

The thrust of a jet engine depends upon the difference between the *momentum* (mass times velocity) of the exhaust stream and the momentum of the incoming air relative to the engine. As a jet aircraft gains speed, the relative velocity—and therefore the relative momentum—of the incoming air increases. The difference between the momentums of the exhaust stream and the incoming air therefore decreases, and so does the thrust. See **Jet propulsion.**

In contrast, all the exhaust from a rocket comes from the onboard propellant. Thus, as a rocket gains speed, its thrust remains nearly constant.

Multistage rockets consist of two or more sections called *stages.* Each stage has a rocket engine and propellant. Engineers developed multistage rockets for long flights through the atmosphere and for flights into space. They needed rockets that could reach greater speeds than were possible with single-stage rockets. A multistage rocket can reach higher speeds because it lightens its weight by dropping stages as it uses up propellant. A three-stage rocket can reach about three times the speed of a single-stage rocket carrying the same amount of fuel.

The first stage, called the *booster,* launches the rocket. After the first stage has burned its propellant, the vehicle drops that section and uses the second stage. The rocket continues using one stage after another. Most space rockets have two or three stages.

How a multistage rocket works

A two-stage rocket carries a propellant and one or more rocket engines in each stage. The first stage launches the rocket. After burning its supply of propellant, the first stage falls away from the rest of the rocket. The second stage then ignites and carries the payload into earth orbit or even farther into space.

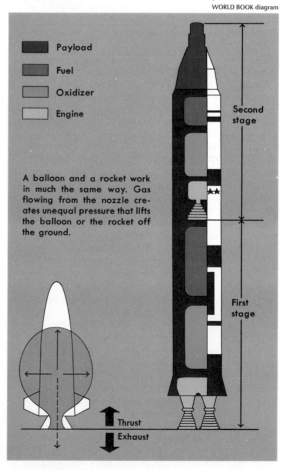

WORLD BOOK diagram

Payload

Fuel

Oxidizer

Engine

A balloon and a rocket work in much the same way. Gas flowing from the nozzle creates unequal pressure that lifts the balloon or the rocket off the ground.

Second stage

First stage

Thrust

Exhaust

People use rockets chiefly to provide high-speed transportation, both within the earth's atmosphere and in space. Rockets are especially valuable for (1) military use, (2) atmospheric research, (3) launching probes and satellites, and (4) space travel.

Military use. Rockets used by the military vary in size from small, battlefield rockets to giant guided missiles that can fly across an ocean.

The *bazooka* is a small rocket launcher carried by soldiers for use against armored vehicles. A person using a bazooka has as much striking power as a small tank (see **Bazooka**). Armies use larger rockets to fire explosives far behind enemy lines and to shoot down enemy aircraft. Fighter airplanes carry guided missiles to attack other planes and ground targets. Navy ships use guided missiles to attack other ships, land targets, and planes.

One of the most important military uses of rockets is to propel a type of long-range guided missile called an *intercontinental ballistic missile* (ICBM). Such a missile can travel as far as 9,200 miles (15,000 kilometers) to bomb an enemy target with nuclear explosives. A set of powerful rockets launches an ICBM and propels it during the early part of its flight. The ICBM coasts the rest of the way to its target. See **Guided missile.**

Atmospheric research. Scientists use rockets to explore the earth's atmosphere. *Sounding rockets,* also called *meteorological rockets,* carry such equipment as barometers, cameras, and thermometers high into the atmosphere. These instruments collect information about the atmosphere and send it by radio to receiving equipment on the earth. This method of collecting information and sending it great distances by radio is called *telemetry* (see **Telemetry**).

Rockets also provide the power for experimental research airplanes. Engineers use these planes in the development of spacecraft. By studying the flights of such planes as the rocket-powered X-15, engineers learn how to control vehicles flying many times faster than the speed of sound.

Launching probes and satellites. Rockets that carry research equipment on long voyages to explore the solar system are called *probes. Lunar probes* gather information about the moon. They may fly past the moon, orbit it, or land on its surface. *Interplanetary probes* take one-way journeys into the space among the planets. Interplanetary probes have explored Jupiter, Saturn, Uranus, and Neptune. *Planetary probes* collect information about the planets. A planetary probe travels in orbit around the sun with the planet it is exploring. Planetary probes have explored Mars and Venus.

Rockets lift artificial satellites into orbit around the earth. Some orbiting satellites gather information for scientific research. Others relay telephone conversations and radio and television broadcasts across the oceans (see **Satellite, Artificial**). The armed forces use satellites for communications and to guard against surprise missile attack. They also use satellites to observe enemy facilities and movements.

Rockets that launch probes and satellites are called *carrier rockets* or *launch vehicles.* Most of these rockets have from two to four stages. The stages lift a satellite to its proper altitude and give it enough speed—about

18,000 miles (29,000 kilometers) per hour—to stay in orbit. An interplanetary probe's speed must reach about 25,000 miles (40,200 kilometers) per hour to escape earth's gravity and continue on its voyage.

Space travel. Rockets provide the power for spacecraft that orbit the earth and travel to the moon and the planets. These rockets, like the ones used to launch probes and satellites, are called carrier rockets or launch vehicles.

The first space launch vehicles were military rockets

NASA

Sounding rockets, such as this Taurus-Nike-Tomahawk, collect information about the earth's upper atmosphere. Radio equipment in the rocket sends data to the earth for scientific study.

Photri

A military rocket called a TOW missile is fired by a crew of two. TOW stands for *T*ube-launched, *O*ptically tracked, *W*ire-guided missile. It can be fired from the ground or a vehicle.

or sounding rockets that engineers changed slightly to carry spacecraft. For example, they added stages to some of these rockets to increase their velocity. Today, engineers sometimes attach smaller rockets to the first stage of a launch vehicle. These *piggyback boosters* provide additional thrust to launch heavier spacecraft.

The Saturn 5 rocket, which carried astronauts to the moon, was the most powerful launch vehicle ever built by the United States. It is no longer in use. Before launch, it weighed more than 6 million pounds (2.7 million kilograms) and stood about 363 feet (111 meters) tall. It could send a spacecraft weighing more than 100,000 pounds (45,000 kilograms) to the moon. The Saturn 5 used 11 rocket engines to propel three stages.

Reusable space shuttles, which are used to launch satellites, can fly into space and return to the earth for repeated journeys. In the future, space shuttles may carry people and supplies to and from space stations that will orbit the earth. Also, smaller rocket-powered vehicles called *space tugs* someday may provide transportation over short distances, such as from a shuttle vehicle to a space station or from one satellite to another. Such vehicles may also provide power for space probes launched to the planets from earth orbit. See **Space exploration.**

Other uses. Rockets have been used for many years as distress signals from ships and airplanes and from the ground. Rockets also shoot rescue lines to ships in distress. Small rockets called *JATO (jet-assisted take-off) units* help heavily loaded airplanes take off. Rockets have long been used in fireworks displays (see **Fireworks**). Scientists even use rockets to "seed" clouds with chemicals in an effort to control the weather (see **Weather** [How people affect the weather]).

Sovfoto

A Soviet rocket sits on its pad before launching the Soyuz 6 spacecraft in 1969. Soyuz 6 was the first of three spacecraft with crews launched in three days by the Soviet Union.

NASA

An Orbiting Astronomical Observatory satellite is prepared by technicians for launch. Such satellites gather information about stars and galaxies that are deep in space.

NASA

An Atlas-Centaur rocket lights up its launch pad during liftoff. These rockets place such scientific satellites as those of the Orbiting Astronomical Observatory in orbit around the earth.

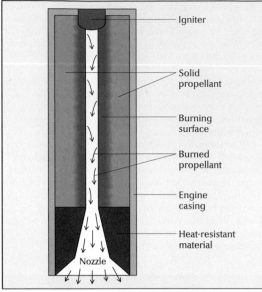

A solid-propellant rocket burns a solid material called the *grain*. Engineers design most grains with a hollow core. The propellant burns from the core outward. Unburned propellant shields the engine casing from the heat of combustion.

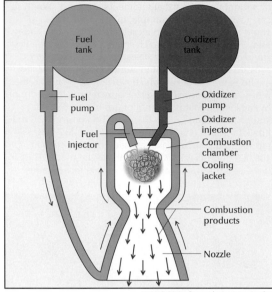

A liquid-propellant rocket carries fuel and an oxidizer in separate tanks. The fuel circulates through the engine's cooling jacket before entering the combustion chamber. This circulation preheats the fuel for combustion and helps cool the rocket.

Two kinds of chemical rockets are now in use: (1) solid-propellant rockets and (2) liquid-propellant rockets. In addition, researchers have built experimental electric rockets and nuclear rockets.

Solid-propellant rockets burn a rubbery or plastic-like material called the *grain*. The grain consists of a fuel and an oxidizer in solid form. Unlike some liquid propellants, the fuel and oxidizer of a solid propellant do not burn upon contact with each other. The propellant must be ignited in one of two ways. It may be ignited by the burning of a small charge of *black powder* (a mixture of saltpeter, charcoal, and sulfur) or other chemicals. The propellant also may be ignited by the chemical reaction of a liquid chlorine compound that is sprayed onto the grain.

The temperature in the combustion chamber of a solid-propellant rocket ranges from 3000 to 6000 °F. (1600 to 3300 °C). In most of these rockets, engineers use high-strength steel or titanium to build chamber walls that can stand the pressure created at such high temperatures. They also may use fiber glass or special plastic materials. Solid propellants burn faster than do liquid propellants. But they usually produce less thrust than an equal amount of liquid propellant burned in the same amount of time.

Solid propellants remain effective for long periods of storage and present little danger of exploding until ignited. Furthermore, they do not require the pumping and blending equipment needed for liquid propellants. On the other hand, it is difficult to stop and start the burning of a solid propellant. Astronauts on space flights must stop and start the burning of propellant to control the flight of their spacecraft. One method used to stop the burning of solid propellant involves blasting the entire nozzle section from the rocket. But this method prevents restarting.

Solid-propellant rockets are preferred to liquid-propellant rockets by the armed forces. Military rockets must be ready to fire instantly, and solid propellants can be stored better than other kinds of propellants. Solid-propellant rockets provide the power for ICBM's, including the Minuteman 2 and MX, and for such smaller missiles as the Hawk, Talos, and Terrier. Solid-propellant rockets are used as boosters for carrier rockets, as JATO rockets, and as sounding rockets. They are also used in fireworks displays.

Liquid-propellant rockets burn a mixture of fuel and oxidizer in liquid form. These rockets carry the fuel and the oxidizer in separate tanks. A system of pipes and valves feeds the two propellant elements into the combustion chamber. Either the fuel or the oxidizer flows around the outside of the chamber before blending with the other element. This flow cools the combustion chamber and preheats the propellant element for combustion.

Methods of feeding the fuel and oxidizer into the combustion chamber include using (1) pumps or (2) high-pressure gas. The most common method uses pumps. Gas produced by burning a small portion of the propellant drives the pumps, which force the fuel and oxidizer into the combustion chamber. In the other method, high-pressure gas forces the fuel and oxidizer into the chamber. The supply of high-pressure gas may come either from nitrogen or some other gas stored

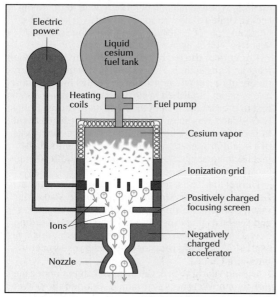

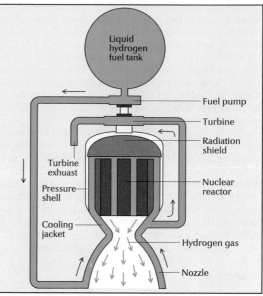

An ion rocket is a kind of electric rocket. Heating coils in the rocket change a fuel, such as cesium, into a vapor. A hot platinum or tungsten *ionization grid* changes the flowing vapor into a stream of electrically charged particles called *ions.*

A nuclear rocket uses the heat from a nuclear reactor to change a liquid fuel into a gas. Most of the fuel flows through the reactor. Some of the fuel, heated by the nozzle of the rocket, flows through the turbine. The turbine drives the fuel pump.

under high pressure, or from the burning of a small amount of the propellant.

Some liquid propellants, called *hypergols,* ignite when the fuel and the oxidizer contact each other. But most liquid propellants require an ignition system. An electric spark may ignite the propellant, or the burning of a small amount of solid propellant in the combustion chamber may do so. Liquid propellants continue to burn as long as the mixture of fuel and oxidizer flows into the combustion chamber.

Thin, high-strength steel or aluminum is used to construct most tanks that hold liquid propellant. Most combustion chambers in these rockets are steel or nickel.

Liquid propellants usually produce greater thrust than do equal amounts of solid propellants burned in the same amount of time. It also is easier to start and stop the burning of liquid propellants than that of solid propellants. The burning can be controlled merely by closing or opening valves. But liquid propellants are difficult to handle. If the propellant elements blend without igniting, the resulting mixture often will explode easily. Liquid propellants also require more complicated rocket construction than do solid propellants.

Scientists use liquid-propellant rockets for most space launch vehicles. For example, the main engines of the space shuttle are liquid-propellant rockets.

Electric rockets use an electric field to accelerate electrically charged particles called *ions* out the nozzle. In one design, electric heating coils turn liquid cesium into a vapor. The vapor flows over an electrical *ionization grid,* which removes electrons from the vapor molecules. Electrons are negatively charged, so the vapor

molecules become positive ions. A positively charged screen repels the ions, focusing them into a beam. The beam then enters a negatively charged device called an *accelerator.* The accelerator speeds up the ions and shoots them out the nozzle.

Such rockets can produce high exhaust velocities. However, the exhaust stream has a low mass. As a result, the rockets cannot produce enough thrust to launch themselves. But the low rate of mass flow has an advantage. The rockets can operate for a long time without running out of fuel. Small electric rockets using xenon ions have provided the thrust to keep communications satellites in position above the earth's surface. A xenon rocket has also powered the U.S. probe Deep Space 1, which was launched in 1998.

Nuclear rockets use the heat energy of a *nuclear reactor,* a device that releases energy by splitting atoms. Some proposed designs would heat hydrogen and shoot it out the nozzle. The rocket would store the hydrogen as a liquid. Heat from the reactor would boil the liquid, creating hydrogen gas. The gas would expand rapidly and flow out the nozzle.

The exhaust velocity of a nuclear rocket could be four times that of a solid-propellant rocket or a liquid-propellant rocket. By expelling a large quantity of hydrogen, a nuclear rocket could therefore achieve high thrust. However, the rocket would require shielding because a nuclear reactor uses radioactive materials. The shielding would have to be so heavy that the rocket would be impractical for use as a booster. More practical applications would use small engines with low, continuous thrust to decrease flight times to Mars or other planets.

Early rockets. Scientists believe the Chinese invented rockets, but they do not know exactly when. Historians describe "arrows of flying fire"—believed to have been rockets—used by Chinese armies in A.D. 1232. By 1300, the use of rockets had spread throughout much of Asia and Europe. These first rockets burned a substance called *black powder,* which consisted of charcoal, saltpeter, and sulfur. But for several hundred years, the use of rockets in fireworks displays outranked their military use in importance.

During the early 1800's, Colonel William Congreve of the British Army developed rockets that could carry explosives. Some of these rockets weighed as much as 60 pounds (27 kilograms) and could travel $1\frac{1}{2}$ miles (2.4 kilometers). British troops used Congreve rockets against the United States Army during the War of 1812. Austria, Russia, and several other countries also developed military rockets during the early 1800's.

An English inventor, William Hale, improved the accuracy of military rockets. He substituted three fins for

From *Rocketry and Space Exploration* by Andrew G. Haley
© 1958 by Litton Educational Publishing, Inc.

Chinese warriors fired rockets in battle during the A.D. 1200's. The use of rockets as weapons and fireworks spread from China throughout much of Asia and Europe during the next century.

the long wooden tail that had been used to guide the rocket. United States troops used Hale rockets in the Mexican War (1846-1848). During the American Civil War (1861-1865), each side used rockets.

Rockets of the early 1900's. A Russian high-school teacher, Konstantin E. Tsiolkovsky, first stated the correct theory of rocket power. He described his theory in a scientific paper published in 1903. Tsiolkovsky was also the first to present the idea of the multistage rocket. Robert H. Goddard, was an American pioneer of rocket science. In 1926, Goddard conducted the first successful launch of a liquid-propellant rocket. The rocket climbed 184 feet (56 meters) into the air at a speed of about 60 miles (97 kilometers) per hour.

During the 1930's, rocket research went forward in Germany, the Soviet Union, and the United States. Hermann Oberth led a small group of German engineers and scientists that experimented with rockets. Leading Soviet rocket scientists included F. A. Tsander and I. A. Merkulov. Goddard remained the chief researcher in the United States.

During World War II, German rocketeers under the direction of Wernher von Braun developed the powerful V-2 guided missile. Germany bombarded London and Antwerp, Belgium, with hundreds of V-2's during the last months of the war. American forces captured many V-2 missiles and sent them to the United States for use in research. After the war, von Braun and more than 200 other German scientists came to the United States to continue their rocketry work. Some other German rocket experts went to the Soviet Union.

High-altitude rockets. For several years after World War II, U.S. scientists benefited greatly by conducting experiments with captured German V-2's. These V-2's were the first rockets used for high-altitude research.

The first high-altitude rockets designed and built in the United States included the WAC Corporal, the Aerobee, and the Viking. The 21-foot (6-meter) WAC Corporal reached altitudes of about 45 miles (72 kilometers) during test flights in 1945. Early models of the Aerobee climbed about 75 miles (121 kilometers). In 1949, the U.S. Navy launched the Viking, an improved liquid-propellant rocket based chiefly on the V-2. The Viking measured more than 45 feet (14 meters) long, much longer

© National Geographic Society courtesy Esther C. Goddard

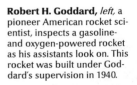

Robert H. Goddard, *left,* a pioneer American rocket scientist, inspects a gasoline- and oxygen-powered rocket as his assistants look on. This rocket was built under Goddard's supervision in 1940.

than the Aerobee. But the first models of the Viking rose only about 50 miles (80 kilometers).

Rockets developed by the U.S. armed forces during the 1950's included the Jupiter and the Pershing. The Jupiter had a range of about 1,600 miles (2,570 kilometers), and the Pershing could travel about 450 miles (724 kilometers). The U.S. Navy conducted the first successful launch of a Polaris underwater missile in 1960. United States space scientists later used many military rockets developed in the 1950's as the basis for launch vehicles.

Rocket-powered airplanes. On Oct. 14, 1947, Captain Charles E. Yeager of the U.S. Air Force made the first *supersonic* (faster than sound) flight. He flew a rocket-powered airplane called the X-1. A rocket engine also powered the X-15, which set an unofficial airplane altitude record of 354,200 feet (107,960 meters) in 1963. In one flight, the X-15 reached a peak speed of 4,520 miles (7,274 kilometers) per hour—more than six times the speed of sound. See **Airplane** (table: Altitude records).

The space age began on Oct. 4, 1957, when the Soviet Union launched the first artificial satellite, Sputnik 1, with a two-stage rocket. On Jan. 31, 1958, the U.S. Army launched the first American satellite, Explorer 1, into orbit with a Juno I rocket. On April 12, 1961, a Soviet rocket put a cosmonaut, Major Yuri A. Gagarin, into orbit around the earth for the first time. On May 5, 1961, a Redstone rocket launched Commander Alan B. Shepard, Jr., the first American to travel in space. On April 12, 1981, the United States launched the rocket-powered Columbia, the first space shuttle to orbit the earth. For more information about rockets in space, see **Space exploration.**   Eugene M. Cliff

Study aids

Related articles in *World Book* include:

American Institute of Aeronautics and Astronautics	Inertial guidance
Army, United States (Missiles)	Jet propulsion
Artillery	Rocket, Model
Bazooka	Satellite, Artificial
Congreve, Sir William	Space exploration
Goddard, Robert H.	Telemetry
Guided missile	Von Braun, Wernher
	Yeager, Charles E.

Outline

I. **How rockets work**
    A. Rocket propellant
    B. Multistage rockets
II. **How rockets are used**
    A. Military use
    B. Atmospheric research
    C. Launching probes and satellites
    D. Space travel
    E. Other uses
III. **Kinds of rockets**
    A. Solid-propellant rockets
    B. Liquid-propellant rockets
    C. Electric rockets
    D. Nuclear rockets
IV. **History**

Questions

What makes a rocket move?
Where does a rocket get the oxygen it needs?

What is a *multistage rocket?* A *booster?*
How do jet engines differ from rockets?
What was the contribution of Robert H. Goddard to rocket development? Of Konstantin E. Tsiolkovsky?
What is an *intercontinental ballistic missile (ICBM)?*
What is a *sounding rocket?* A *planetary probe?*
How might scientists use electric rockets?
Who probably invented rockets?
What are the two basic parts of rocket propellant?

Additional resources

Level I
Baird, Anne. *The U. S. Space Camp Book of Rockets.* Morrow, 1994.
Maurer, Richard. *Rocket!* Crown, 1995.
Miller, Ron. *The History of Rockets.* Watts, 1999.

Level II
Baker, David. *Spaceflight and Rocketry.* Facts on File, 1996.
Breuer, William B. *Race to the Moon: America's Duel with the Soviets.* Praeger, 1993.
Winter, Frank H. *Rockets into Space.* Harvard Univ. Pr., 1990.

Rocket was the first steam locomotive built along the lines of modern steam engines. The *Rocket* had a multitubular boiler and driving rods connecting the pistons directly to the wheels. Many earlier locomotives used gears to drive the wheels.

Two English engineers—George and Robert Stephenson, father and son—built the *Rocket* in 1829. It reached a speed of 29 miles (46 kilometers) per hour at the Rainhill Trials held by the Liverpool and Manchester Railway that year. The *Rocket's* success in the trials proved that steam locomotives were practical for railroads.

George H. Drury

See also **Locomotive; Stephenson, George.**

Rocket, Model, is a miniature rocket patterned after military or space rockets. Model rockets fly the same way as do the giant space rockets. But models weigh less than $3\frac{1}{2}$ pounds (1.5 kilograms), and many of them

WORLD BOOK photo by Steinkamp/Ballogg

Three kinds of model rockets can be built by hobbyists. A single-stage rocket, *left,* requires less skill and experience to make than a multistage rocket, *center,* or a glider rocket, *right.*

measure only 8 to 24 inches (20 to 61 centimeters) long. Model rockets are also known as *space models.*

The engine of a model rocket produces its power by burning a specially manufactured solid fuel. Model rockets can rise as high as 2,000 feet (610 meters) in a few seconds, traveling as fast as 300 miles (480 kilometers) an hour. Some kinds of model rockets carry a *payload.* A payload is any small cargo, such as a miniature camera or a radio transmitter. A few model rockets have two or more sections called *stages* assembled on top of one another. Each stage has an engine that starts to operate when the previous stage's engine burns out.

Large numbers of young people and adults build and fly model rockets as a hobby. Most rocketeers build their first rockets with kits sold by hobby stores.

Model rocketry is a safe hobby, but four main rules must be followed at all times. (1) Rockets must be powered by factory-made engines. (2) Rockets must be built of such lightweight materials as cardboard, plastics, and balsa wood, with no metal structural parts. (3) Rockets must be launched with electrical equipment from a distance of at least 15 feet (4.6 meters). (4) The launching device must be pointed within 30 degrees of vertical. In addition, payloads should never include a live animal or a flammable or explosive substance.

Parts of a model rocket

Every model rocket has seven basic parts: (1) the body tube, (2) the launch lug, (3) fins, (4) the engine holder, (5) the engine, (6) the nose cone, and (7) the recovery device. A rocket also has a launch system to get it into the air.

The body tube is a hollow cylinder to which all the other parts are attached. Most are made of cardboard.

The launch lug is a narrow paper or plastic tube fastened to the side of the body tube. It fits loosely over the *launch rod,* a long, vertical metal rod that is part of the launch system. During liftoff, the launch lug guides the rocket and keeps it vertical.

Fins help the rocket travel straight during flight. Most model rockets have three or four winglike fins on the bottom of the body tube. The fins are made of cardboard, plastics, or wood.

The engine holder, or *engine mount,* is a cardboard or plastics ring cemented inside the bottom of the body tube. The rocket's engine fits in the holder.

The engine of most rockets consists of a thick cardboard tube that contains the solid fuel. Such an engine can be used only once.

The nose cone forms the top of a model rocket. Its tip has a rounded point that reduces air resistance. Most nose cones are made of plastics or balsa wood.

The recovery device returns the rocket slowly to the ground. One such device is a small parachute made of paper, cloth, or plastics film. It is carried inside the body tube behind the nose cone. At the height of the flight, an ejection charge in the engine forces the nose cone forward and separates it from the body tube. This forward movement also releases the parachute.

The parachute is attached to the nose cone and the body tube by a strong *shock cord* made of rubber or other elastic. This cord prevents the parachute from tearing away from the rocket after the ejection. A wad of cotton or some other flame-resistant material is inserted

into the body tube between the parachute and the engine. It protects the parachute from the heat of the ejection charge.

The launch system consists of a launch pad and an engine ignition system with a battery. A typical launch pad is made up of a three-legged base, the launch rod, and a deflector. The deflector keeps the engine's hot exhaust gases from coming into contact with the launch pad or the ground.

The ignition system includes a switching device called the *launch controller* and a battery. Wires connect the launch controller to the *igniter,* a special wire inserted into the engine. When the operator presses the launch button of the controller, an electric current from the battery makes the igniter become hot. Heat produced by the igniter starts the engine.

Building and flying model rockets

The kits used by many model rocketeers include all parts except the engine and the launch system, which must be purchased separately. Other necessary materials include an adhesive, sandpaper for smoothing the rocket's surfaces, and a sharp knife for cutting out the fins or other parts. Many enthusiasts paint their completed models to make them look more realistic.

Before flying a model, a rocketeer should find out if model rocketry is regulated by any laws in his or her area. Next, the rocketeer selects a safe launch site. The site should be a large, open area away from power lines, tall buildings, and trees. It also should be free of anything that could burn easily, such as dead grass, dry

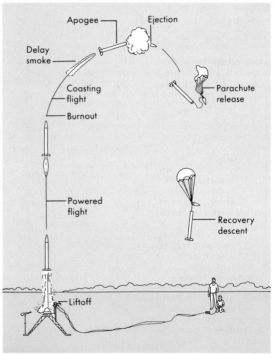

WORLD BOOK drawing by Art Grebetz

The flight pattern of a model rocket consists of several phases. The rocket's *apogee* (maximum altitude) can be varied by using engines of different sizes.

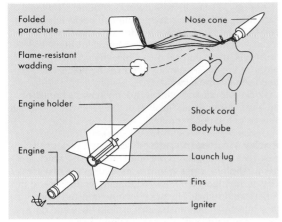

Folded parachute
Nose cone
Flame-resistant wadding
Engine holder
Shock cord
Body tube
Engine
Launch lug
Fins
Igniter

The basic parts of a model rocket are sold in kits by many hobby stores. The stores sell rocket engines separately, and a rocketeer can select from a variety of power capacities.

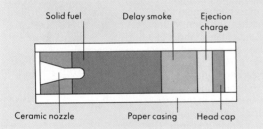

Solid fuel
Delay smoke
Ejection charge
Ceramic nozzle
Paper casing
Head cap

WORLD BOOK diagrams by Art Grebetz

A model rocket engine includes the solid fuel, which propels the rocket. The delay smoke allows it to slow down, and the ejection charge releases the parachute.

weeds, or wastepaper. The length of the shortest side of the site should measure at least a fourth of the highest altitude that the rocket will reach.

At the launch site, the rocketeer installs the engine and mounts the rocket on the launch pad. After making sure that all spectators are a safe distance from the rocket, the rocketeer calls out a 5-second countdown and presses the launch button. The rocket lifts off and soars into the air. At its maximum altitude, the rocket releases its recovery device and floats to the ground.

Model rocket clubs and competition

Local model rocket clubs may be formed among almost any group. For example, a club can be part of a church youth group program or a scouting activity. Model rocket clubs should have experienced advisers to help members with projects. The groups also may have their own launch systems and other equipment. Many clubs hold contests. One contest is *egg-lofting,* which involves launching a rocket that carries an egg. Each contestant sends a rocket as high as possible and tries to recover the egg unbroken.

Several countries have national model rocket organizations. They set up safety rules, certify model rocket engines, issue publications, and charter local clubs. The national organization in the United States is the National

Association of Rocketry in Altoona, Wisconsin. The Canadian Association of Rocketry is in Mississauga, Ontario. Through associations, rocketeers can set flight records and become national or world champions. The world championships are held every two years.

J. Patrick Miller

Rockford (pop. 139,426; met. area pop. 329,676) is a manufacturing center and the second largest city in Illinois. Only Chicago has more people. The city lies on the Rock River, 17 miles (27 kilometers) south of the Wisconsin border. It is about halfway between Chicago and Dubuque, Iowa (see **Illinois** [political map]).

Rockford is the largest *screw product* (fasteners, nuts, bolts) producer in the United States and a major manufacturer of a wide range of metal products and engine components. Parts for automobile engines, farm equipment, and aerospace uses are made in the city. Other manufacturers include tools, locks, and products for home remodeling. Three freight railroads and a number of truck lines have terminals there. The city is the home of Rockford College and Rock Valley College, a two-year school. The Burpee Museum of Natural History collection includes exhibits of stuffed birds, animals and their habitats, and Native American history.

Rockford was founded in 1834. In 1836, it received a town charter. It became a city in 1852. Its original settlers were chiefly from New England, but large numbers of Swedes moved there after 1850. Rockford has a mayor-council government. The city is the seat of Winnebago County. William D. Walters, Jr.

Rockne, *RAHK nee,* **Knute,** *noot* (1888-1931), was an American college coach. From 1918 until his death in an airplane crash in Kansas, he served as head coach at the University of Notre Dame. His teams' colorful style, emphasizing speed and deception, helped popularize football. An outstanding strategist, he was famous for his inspirational talks to his players. His "Win one for the Gipper" speech propelled Notre Dame to victory over Army in 1928. It was featured in the biographical film *Knute Rockne, All American* (1940), which starred Ronald Reagan as Notre Dame star George Gipp. Rockne's teams won 105 games, lost 12, and tied 5. His winning percentage of .881 is the highest in college football.

Knute Kenneth Rockne was born in Voss, Norway. His family immigrated to the United States in 1893 and settled in Chicago.

University of Notre Dame
Knute Rockne

Rockne studied chemistry at Notre Dame, graduating in 1914 with highest honors. As a player, his pass receiving was important in Notre Dame's 1913 upset of Army, a game that first brought national attention to Notre Dame and to the forward pass. Bob Carroll

Rockwell, Norman (1894-1978), was an American illustrator. His paintings of everyday, usually small-town people almost always tell stories, often humorous ones. They show careful observation and technical skill. Rockwell was a meticulous craftsman, whose works portray homely incidents, well-defined character, and a wealth of supporting detail.

Rockwell gained great popularity as a cover illustrator for *The Saturday Evening Post* and other magazines. He also did art work for many advertisers. He illustrated the "Four Freedoms" of the Atlantic Charter in a well-known series of paintings.

United Press International

Norman Rockwell

Rockwell was born in New York City. He studied at the Chase School of Art, the National Academy of Design, and the Art Students League. His work first appeared in *Boys' Life, St. Nicho-*

Oil painting on canvas (1950); Mr. and Mrs. Ken Stuart Collection

Rockwell's painting *Saying Grace* shows his detailed, realistic style. It is also an example of the artist's sentimental treatment of scenes from middle-class American life.

las, American Boy, and other magazines and books for children.   Sarah Burns

Rocky Mountain National Park, a mountain playground in northern Colorado, is one of the most magnificent sections of the Rocky Mountains. The federal government made it a national park in 1915. Some of the highest and most rugged mountain country in the United States is in the park. It has more than 100 peaks over 10,000 feet (3,050 meters) high. The highest, Longs Peak, rises 14,255 feet (4,345 meters). Rocky Mountain National Park has two main entrances, Estes Park on the east, and Grand Lake on the west. For the park's area, see **National Park System** (table: National parks).

Naturalist Enos Mills has been called "the father of Rocky Mountain National Park." It was through his efforts that the park was established. He built his log cabin in a valley that looked up to Longs Peak.

About 155 lakes lie within Rocky Mountain National Park. They reflect the snowy mountain peaks in summer, and become blocks of ice in winter. The park is noted for its wildlife, including Rocky Mountain sheep (bighorn), elk, deer, and coyotes. More than 200 varieties of birds and over 700 species of flowering plants have been seen in the park.

Rocky Mountain National Park once was a home for the Arapaho Indians. The area of the park was also a rich source of furs for trappers.

Critically reviewed by the National Park Service

Rocky Mountain spotted fever is a serious disease that is often fatal. One of the *rickettsias,* which are germs slightly larger than viruses, causes the disease. The germ infects the Rocky Mountain wood tick and the American dog tick. The ticks become infected when they bite small mammals, such as field mice and dogs, that are infected with the germ. When the tick bites a person, it transfers the rickettsia to that person's bloodstream. Doctors first discovered the fever in the Rocky Mountain area of the United States, but it occurs throughout the country. It is most common in the Southeastern and Middle Atlantic States. About 600 cases are reported every year, usually in late spring or early summer. It begins with chills and fever, and severe pains in the leg muscles and the joints. Then a rash develops. The fever resembles many of the typhus diseases (see **Typhus**).

WORLD BOOK illustration by Oxford Illustrators Limited

The American dog tick is one of two types of ticks that transmit Rocky Mountain spotted fever.

Tetracyclines, chloramphenicol, and other antibiotics are effective in treatment. Vaccines against the disease have proved relatively ineffective. Recovery from the fever gives complete immunity.   Thomas P. Monath

See also **Rickettsia.**

Rocky Mountain States are Colorado, Idaho, Montana, Nevada, Utah, and Wyoming. Arizona and New Mexico are also sometimes considered Rocky Mountain States, as well as Southwestern States. For more information on the region, see **United States** (Regions). See also the articles on the states that make up the region.

Rocky Mountains are the largest mountain system in North America. The Rocky Mountain Chain extends more than 3,000 miles (4,800 kilometers) through the United States and Canada. It is about 350 miles (563 kilometers) wide in some places. In the United States, the Rockies stretch through New Mexico, Colorado, Utah, Wyoming, Idaho, Montana, Washington, and Alaska. The Canadian Rockies spread through the provinces of Alberta and British Columbia, and the Northwest Territories and the Yukon Territory.

Visitors to the Rockies enjoy snow-capped peaks, sparkling lakes, and other magnificent scenery. Several U.S. and Canadian national parks are in the Rocky Mountains. The region is also famous for its ski resorts and wild game.

The Rockies form the Continental Divide, which separates rivers that flow west to the Pacific Ocean from those going east to the Atlantic Ocean (see **Divide**). The Canadian Rockies also separate rivers flowing north to the Arctic Ocean from those that empty into the Pacific Ocean to the southwest. A number of rivers, including the Arkansas, the Colorado, the Columbia, the Missouri, and the Rio Grande, begin in the Rockies.

Chief ranges of the Rockies include (1) the Southern Rockies, (2) the Middle Rockies, (3) the Northern Rockies, (4) the Canadian Rockies, (5) the Selwyn and Mackenzie mountains, and (6) the Brooks Range.

The Southern Rockies extend from the Sangre de Cristo Range in New Mexico to central Wyoming. They include the highest peaks in the Rocky Mountain System. Wheeler Peak, the highest peak in New Mexico, is 13,161 feet (4,011 meters) high. Colorado's tallest peak, Mount Elbert, rises 14,433 feet (4,399 meters). Colorado has about 55 peaks over 14,000 feet (4,270 meters) high.

The Middle Rockies, which include the Grand Tetons, run from northwestern Colorado and northern Utah to the upper Yellowstone River in Montana. The highest peaks in this range include King's Peak, 13,528 feet (4,123 meters) high, in Utah; Gannett Peak, 13,804 feet (4,207 meters) high, in Wyoming; and Granite Peak, 12,799 feet (3,901 meters) high, in Montana. Yellowstone National Park is in the Middle Rockies.

The Northern Rockies stretch from southern Idaho to the border between the United States and Canada. Borah Peak, the tallest mountain in Idaho, rises 12,662 feet (3,859 meters) in the Northern Rockies. Glacier National Park lies in this region.

The Canadian Rockies extend from the border north through British Columbia and Alberta. Some of the finest scenic areas of the Rockies lie in Alberta, including Banff and Jasper national parks.

The Selwyn Mountains extend beyond the Liard River in northern Canada. The Mackenzie Range lies east of the Selwyns. The Brooks Range crosses northern Alaska. Part of the range lies north of the Arctic Circle.

Plant and animal life. Forests of piñon pines and junipers cover the lower slopes of the Southern Rockies. Firs, pines, and spruces are abundant in the higher areas of the Rockies. Sagebrush dominates the Wyoming Basin and other valley regions of the Middle Rockies and the Southern Rockies.

Rocky Mountain goats and bighorn sheep live above the *timber line,* the elevation beyond which trees cannot grow. Bears, deer, hares, elk, minks, mountain lions, porcupines, squirrels, and other animals occupy the higher forested slopes. Chipmunks, coyotes, moose, and muskrats make their homes in the grassy valleys between the mountains. Rainbow trout, grayling, cutthroat trout, and other fishes swim in Rocky Mountain streams.

Agriculture and industry. Livestock raising is the main agricultural activity in the Rockies. Cattle and sheep are driven to mountain pastures for the summer and back to warmer valleys in winter. Farmers raise chili peppers and pinto beans in the Southern Rockies. Grains, potatoes, sugar beets, and truck vegetables are raised in Colorado, Idaho, Montana, and Utah.

The chief industrial activities of the Rocky Mountains are mining and lumbering. The Southern Rockies, especially the Leadville District of Colorado, produce gold, lead, molybdenum, silver, uranium, and zinc. The Wyo-

Rocky Mountains

The Rocky Mountains extend more than 3,000 miles (4,800 kilometers) across the western part of North America, from northern Alaska to northern New Mexico. The Rockies are famous for their scenic beauty.

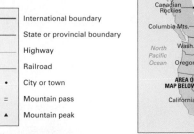

——	International boundary
——	State or provincial boundary
——	Highway
——	Railroad
•	City or town
=	Mountain pass
▲	Mountain peak

WORLD BOOK maps

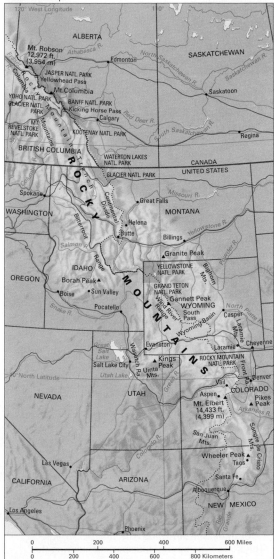

Glenn Tooke, Image Finders

The Rocky Mountains are famous for their majestic peaks and other beautiful scenery. The Canadian Rockies tower over the resort town of Banff in southwestern Alberta, *above.*

ming Basin, in southwestern Wyoming, is a coal, petroleum, and natural gas producing area. Lumbering and the mining of coal, copper, lead, silver, and zinc are important in the Northern and Canadian Rockies. Much of the coking coal used in Japan's iron and steel industry is exported from the Fernie, British Columbia, area.

Tourism contributes greatly to the economy of the Rocky Mountain states and provinces. Every year, millions of visitors enjoy the region's national parks, ski resorts, and many other attractions.

History. Most peaks of the Rockies were formed millions of years ago during a great upheaval of the earth's crust. The sides of the mountains contain fossils of animals that once lived in the sea, and rocks that were formed in the hot interior of the earth. The southern half of the Rockies includes mountains that were once volcanic plateaus. Through the centuries, the peaks of the Rockies have been cut into various formations by the forces of wind, rain, and glaciers.

Many Indian tribes lived along the flanks of the Rockies when Europeans first arrived in North America. They included the Coeur d'Alene, Flathead, Kalispel, Kutenai, Shoshone, and Ute. The first Europeans to reach the Rockies were Spanish explorers. They established a colony near what is now Santa Fe, New Mexico, in 1598.

The American explorers Meriwether Lewis and William Clark traveled through the Northern Rockies in 1805 and 1806. Another American, Zebulon M. Pike, explored the Southern Rockies during this period. Pikes Peak, in central Colorado, was named for him. In the early 1800's, the Rockies became the center of the American fur trade (see **Fur trade** [The 1800's]).

The Rockies hampered transportation during the Westward Movement of the 1800's. However, the Ore-

gon Trail, the longest overland route used by explorers and pioneers, wound through the Rockies (see **Oregon Trail**). The first railroad route through the Rockies was built in the Wyoming Basin in 1868. Today, Interstate Highway 80 runs through the Wyoming Basin. Major railroad routes also go through the Rockies.

The Eisenhower Memorial Tunnel, west of Denver, Colorado, is the highest motor-traffic tunnel in the world. The tunnel has an altitude of about 11,000 feet (3,400 meters). Moffat Tunnel, one of the longest railroad tunnels in the United States, cuts through James Peak, also west of Denver.   John Edwin Coffman

Related articles in *World Book* include:

Banff National Park   Pikes Peak
Bighorn   Teton Range
Glacier National Park   Wasatch Range
Grand Teton National Park   Yellowstone National Park
Jasper National Park

Additional resources

Kraulis, J. A., and Gault, John. *The Rocky Mountains*. 1986. Reprint. Key Porter, 1995.
Schmidt, Jeremy. *Adventuring in the Rockies*. Rev. ed. Sierra Club, 1993.

Rococo, *roh KOH koh,* is a style of art that flourished in western Europe from about 1700 to 1780. The term comes from a French word for a fanciful rock or shell design. It implies a refined, elegant feeling and style.

Rococo found its fullest expression in France, where the leading representatives were the painters François Boucher, Jean Honoré Fragonard, and Antoine Watteau. They worked primarily for royal and aristocratic clients. Their paintings differed greatly in style and subject matter from those of the preceding baroque period. A typical baroque painting was created on a heroic and grand scale, and usually presented Christian religious subjects. Rococo paintings were intimate in scale and delicate in manner. They often portrayed scenes from classical mythology. Rococo artists also created a new category of painting called the *fête galante.* Their paintings showed gatherings of elegantly dressed figures in parks and gardens.

Outside France, there were other artists during this period who worked in a bright, lively style characteristic of rococo. They included Giovanni Battista Tiepolo in Italy and Thomas Gainsborough in England.

The ornate and decorative style of rococo was also applied to architecture, furniture, porcelain, tapestries, and opera and theater scenery. In architecture, rococo reached its greatest splendor in the palaces, monasteries, and churches of southern Germany and Austria.

Eric M. Zafran

Related articles in *World Book* include:

Architecture (The 1700's)   Furniture (The rococo style;
Austria (picture: Historical revivals)
   Austrians attend Mass)   Painting (The 1600's
Baroque   and 1700's)
Boucher, François   Watteau, Antoine
Fragonard, Jean Honoré

Rod. See **Eye** (The retina; diagram).
Rod is a unit of distance in the inch-pound system of measurement customarily used in the United States. One rod equals $5\frac{1}{2}$ yards (5.029 meters).
Rodent, *ROH duhnt,* is an animal with front teeth especially suited to gnawing hard objects. Squirrels, beavers,

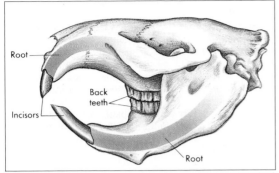

WORLD BOOK illustration by Sarah Woodward

All rodents have chisellike upper and lower front teeth called *incisors.* They can be seen in the beaver skull above.

and rats are rodents. Squirrels can break the shells of nuts with their front teeth. Beavers can gnaw through tree trunks, and rats can gnaw through some wood and plaster walls. The many kinds of rodents include gophers, hamsters, mice, and porcupines.

All rodents have two top and two bottom front teeth called *incisors.* They wear away at the tips, but do not wear out until late in the animal's lifetime because they keep growing until the animal is old. The incisors wear faster in the back than in front. As a result, they have a chisellike edge, well-suited to gnawing. Rodents also have back teeth consisting of molars and premolars that they use for chewing. The space between the incisors and back teeth is called the *diastema.*

Rodents are *mammals* (animals that feed their young milk). There are more individual rodents than there are individuals of all other kinds of mammals combined. Rodents live in almost all parts of the world.

Mice are the smallest rodents and capybaras of South America are the largest. Some capybaras are up to 4 feet (1.2 meters) long. Most rodents are *herbivorous* (plant eaters). But rats and other rodents eat almost any food.

Rodents are both helpful and harmful to people. Some rodents eat harmful insects and weeds, and some have valuable fur. Scientists use mice and rats in research. But some rodents damage crops and other property. Many rodents also carry serious diseases, such as plague and typhus.

Scientific classification. Rodents make up the order Rodentia in the class Mammalia and the phylum Chordata.

Clyde Jones

Related articles. See the following articles on rodents:

Agouti	Dormouse	Kangaroo rat	Paca
Animal (A	Flying squirrel	Lemming	Porcupine
table of	Gerbil	Marmot	Prairie dog
animal	Gopher	Mole-rat	Rat
intelligence)	Guinea pig	Mountain bea-	Springhare
Beaver	Hamster	ver	Squirrel
Capybara	Jerboa	Mouse	Vole
Cavy	Jumping	Muskrat	Woodchuck
Chinchilla	mouse	Nutria	Woodrat
Chipmunk			

Rodeo, *ROH dee oh* or *roh DAY oh,* is a sport that combines the skills of cowboys and cowgirls with the color and spirit of the Old West. The word *rodeo* also refers to a rodeo contest. Rodeos are held in many parts of the United States, Canada, and Australia.

In rodeo competition, the contestants match their riding and roping skills in rugged, exciting events. Contestants who rank high in an event receive prize money. Rodeo clowns provide additional entertainment.

Rodeo livestock are valuable and receive careful handling. The American Humane Association establishes or approves rules for the care of the livestock.

There are two main groups of rodeo events: (1) rough stock events and (2) timed events. Rough stock events feature cowboys or cowgirls trying to ride bucking horses or bulls for a specified number of seconds. The judges award points to the contestants, chiefly for their form and how well they spur the animals. Timed events are judged according to how quickly the contestants complete the required task.

Most rodeos have three rough stock events and five timed events. The rough stock events are bareback bronc riding, saddle bronc riding, and bull riding. The timed events are calf roping, steer wrestling, team roping, steer roping, and barrel racing. In most rodeos, only women compete in barrel racing, and only men compete in the other events. But all-girl rodeos include some events that only men enter in other rodeos.

Bareback bronc riding is an event in which the rider must remain mounted for 8 seconds while spurring the horse as it bucks. With one hand, the rider holds onto the *bareback rigging,* a device made of leather that is cinched to the horse like a saddle.

Saddle bronc riding is an event that resembles bareback bronc riding, except that the rider uses a saddle, a halter, and a single rein. The rider must hold the rein in one hand and spur the bucking horse as many times as possible while staying on for 8 or 10 seconds.

Bull riding does not require contestants to spur the animal. They try to remain seated for 8 seconds by holding onto an unknotted rope looped around the bull's belly. They hold the rope with one hand.

Calf roping calls for teamwork between contestants and their horses. A contestant chases the calf on horseback, ropes it, and dismounts. The horse keeps backing up so that the rope is held tight and the calf cannot break free. The contestant throws the calf to the ground and ties three of its legs together.

Steer wrestling, also called *bulldogging,* is one of two events in which the contestant may have a helper, called a *hazer.* The hazer keeps the steer running in a straight line so the cowboy can slide off his horse and grab the steer's horns. Then the cowboy wrestles the steer to the ground.

Team roping is the only event in which two contestants work together. One contestant ropes a steer's horns, and the other ropes its hind legs. The team finishes when both members have pulled their ropes tight at a 90-degree angle from the steer.

Steer roping is a major event in some rodeos. A contestant on a horse ropes a running steer around its horns from one side. Next, the rider races the horse behind the steer to the other side, causing the steer to trip over the rope. The contestant then dismounts and ties the animal's hind legs together.

Barrel racing is a regular women's event in most rodeos. Each contestant runs her horse in a cloverleaf pattern around three barrels. The judges add 5 seconds to a rider's time for each barrel she knocks over.

© Thomas Woodrich, Hillstrom Stock Photo

Barrel racing is a women's rodeo event in which a contestant rides her horse as fast as she can in a cloverleaf pattern around three barrels. She is penalized for each barrel she knocks over.

All-girl rodeos have some events designed specifically for women and some that resemble men's events at other rodeos. In all-girl rodeos, cowgirls compete in bareback bronc riding and bull riding. They have to remain mounted for 6 seconds and can hold on with two hands. A steer may be substituted for a bull.

Women also compete in barrel racing, team roping, and calf roping. In all-girl rodeos, calf roping is called *tie-down* roping. Cowgirls also compete in *break-away* roping. In this event, a rope is tied to the saddle horn with ribbon or string. After the rider ropes the calf, she stops her horse. The running calf breaks the tie, pulling the rope from the saddle horn.

Cowgirls also compete in *goat tying* and *steer undecorating*. In goat tying, a cowgirl rides up to a goat that is tied to a stake with a long rope. She must trip the goat to the ground and tie three of its legs together. In steer undecorating, a cowgirl on horseback chases a steer that has a ribbon taped to its back. She must get the ribbon while the steer is running in a straight line.

History. Rodeo developed from various ranching activities of the late 1800's. For example, after working on a trail drive or roundup, cowboys gathered together and competed in such skills as bronc riding and steer roping. The first rodeo to charge an admission fee to spectators and offer prizes was held in Prescott, Arizona, in 1888.

Cowboys formed the first professional rodeo organization in 1936. Today, professional rodeos are sponsored by the Professional Rodeo Cowboys Association, by the Girls Rodeo Association, and by the International Professional Rodeo Association. Rodeos for young people are supervised by the Little Britches, by the National High School Rodeo Association, and by the National Intercollegiate Rodeo Association.

Critically reviewed by the International Professional Rodeo Association

See also **Bronco**; and the *Annual events* section of **Alberta; Colorado; Montana; Nevada; North Dakota; Oregon; South Dakota; Texas;** and **Wyoming.**

Additional resources

Alter, Judy. *Rodeos.* Watts, 1996. Younger readers.

Fredriksson, Kristine. *American Rodeo.* 1985. Reprint. Texas A & M Univ. Pr., 1993.

Rodgers, Jimmie (1897-1933), was a country music performer. Rodgers developed a unique style of music called the "blue yodel," which blended Negro blues and country yodeling. Often called "the Singing Brakeman," Rodgers wrote and sang songs about trains that were among the first to call national attention to rural Southern music.

Rodgers was born near Meridian, Mississippi. He quit school at age 13 to work for the railroad. In 1924, he became sick with tuberculosis and turned to music as an occupation. In 1927, Rodgers recorded for Ralph Peer, a recording company executive, who was touring the South recording folk music. Rodgers recorded two songs, "Sleep Baby Sleep" and "The Soldier's Sweetheart." Under Peer's supervision, Rodgers recorded more than 100 songs during the next six years, until he died of tuberculosis. The songs included "T. for Texas," "TB Blues," "Mule Skinner Blues," and "Waitin' for a Train."   Lee Rector

Rodgers, Richard (1902-1979), became famous as a composer for the American musical theater. He worked chiefly with two great lyric writers, Lorenz Hart and Oscar Hammerstein II. Rodgers's songs include "The Lady Is a Tramp" and "Falling in Love with Love," written with Hart, and "People Will Say We're in Love" and "Some Enchanted Evening," written with Hammerstein.

Rodgers was born in New York City and attended Columbia University. He began to work with Hart on amateur shows in 1919. They achieved their first professional success with *The Garrick Gaieties* (1925). During the 1920's and 1930's, Rodgers and Hart helped make musical comedy into a well-developed art form. Two of their outstanding productions were *On Your Toes* (1936), which contained Rodgers's ballet "Slaughter on Tenth Avenue," and *Pal Joey* (1940). See **Hart, Lorenz.**

Shortly before Hart's death in 1943, Rodgers joined with Hammerstein to write *Oklahoma!,* one of the top musicals in history. Rodgers and Hammerstein also created several other shows that rank among the greatest musicals. These works include *Carousel* (1945), *South Pacific* (1949), *The King and I* (1951), and *The Sound of Music* (1959). They won a 1945 Academy Award for their song "It Might As Well Be Spring" from *State Fair.* See **Hammerstein, Oscar, II.**

Rodgers won a Pulitzer Prize in drama for *South Pacific* and a special Pulitzer citation for *Oklahoma!* In 1952, he composed the music for *Victory at Sea,* a documentary TV series. He also wrote the music and lyrics for *No Strings* (1962) and the music for *Do I Hear a Waltz?* (1965) and *Rex* (1976).   Ken Bloom

Rodin, *roh DAN,* **Auguste,** *oh GOOST* (1840-1917), a French sculptor, is often considered the greatest sculptor of the 1800's. Rodin created an enormous number of sculptures of the human figure. Many have a great deal of emotional intensity, and explore a wide range of human passions. The inner feelings of his figures are expressed through a vigorous sense of movement and by gestures that emphasize different parts of the body. Many of his figures are incomplete or fragmentary. These works consist of just a torso, a head, or hands.

Rodin was primarily a modeler, preferring to work with clay and wax rather than to carve in stone. After he

Bronze statue (1902-1904); the Rodin Museum, Philadelphia, gift of Jules E. Mastbaum

Auguste Rodin's *The Thinker,* *above,* is one of the French sculptor's most famous works. Several versions of this statue exist. Like many of Rodin's sculptures, *The Thinker* portrays the human figure in an attitude of great emotional intensity.

created the original model, his assistants would translate it into marble or bronze. Inspired by the Renaissance sculptor Michelangelo, Rodin's marble figures are often beautifully smooth and finished, emerging from parts of the marble that are often very rough. The surfaces of his bronze works combine a thorough understanding of anatomy with a rough texture that allows light and shadow to enliven the work.

Rodin was born in Paris. He did not win public recognition for many years, and had to earn his living designing popular sculpture and ornament for commercial firms. Indifference and misunderstanding greeted his first exhibits, but appreciation for his work gradually spread. By 1880, his genius began to be more widely appreciated and by the 1900's he was world famous.

In 1880, Rodin was commissioned by the French government to create a large sculptural door for the Museum of Decorative Art in Paris. The subject was the "Inferno" from Dante's *Divine Comedy.* The door was never finished, but Rodin did many figures for it. Later he developed many of them as independent sculptures. The best known include *The Thinker* and *The Kiss.* Rodin's most important later works include the monumental group *The Burghers of Calais* and the monument to Balzac. The Balzac statue appears in the **France** (Arts) article. *Orpheus* appears in the **Sculpture** article.

Joseph F. Lamb

Additional resources

Butler, Ruth. *Rodin.* Yale, 1993.
Lampert, Catherine. *Rodin: Sculpture & Drawings.* Yale, 1987.
Levkoff, Mary L. *Rodin in His Time.* Thames & Hudson, 1994.

Rodney, Caesar, *SEE zuhr* (1728-1784), an American statesman, was a Delaware signer of the Declaration of Independence. Rodney was one of the political leaders most responsible for Delaware's participation in the Revolutionary War in America (1775-1783). He served in the Delaware legislature almost continuously from 1761 to 1776. As a delegate to the Continental Congress in 1776, he voted for independence after riding 80 miles (130 kilometers) on horseback to cast his vote in time. Rodney was born in Dover, Delaware. He led opposition to British taxes before the Revolution and was elected to the Continental Congress of 1774 and 1775. In 1777, he commanded the Delaware militia. The next year, he was elected president (governor) of the state. A statue of Rodney represents Delaware in the United States Capitol.   Robert A. Becker

Rodó, *roh DOH,* **José Enrique,** *ayn REE kay* (1872?-1917), was a Uruguayan thinker and essayist. He believed in the human spirit's infinite capacity to renew itself, but he feared that humanity was pursuing material goals at the expense of the spirit. Rodó was a leader of the Modernist movement in Spanish literature (see **Latin-American literature** [Modernism]). In his landmark essay *Ariel* (1900), Rodó urged young Latin Americans to maintain their ideals in their intellectual and spiritual development, avoiding the materialism he claimed was damaging the potential of United States culture. In his philosophical work *Motives of Proteus* (1909), Rodó continued his recommendations for the direction of the mind and spirit. He discouraged the pursuit of technical knowledge in favor of the total cultivation of wisdom. Rodó was born in Montevideo.   Naomi Lindstrom

Roe v. Wade was a 1973 landmark case in which the Supreme Court of the United States ruled that state laws could not forbid a woman to have an abortion during the first three months of pregnancy. The court also ruled that during the second three months, a state could regulate abortions only to protect women's health. Before *Roe v. Wade,* many U.S. states prohibited abortions in almost all circumstances.

The court based its decision in part on the principle that the Bill of Rights of the U.S. Constitution created a "zone of privacy" into which a state could not intrude. Seven of the court's nine justices supported the decision, which was written by Justice Harry A. Blackmun.

Roe v. Wade arose after Norma McCorvey, an unmarried carnival worker, was denied an abortion in Texas in 1969. Texas law permitted abortions only when the woman's life was in danger. McCorvey sued Henry Wade, the Dallas County district attorney, in an attempt to prove that the law was unconstitutional. McCorvey was called Jane Roe in the case to conceal her identity.

In *Roe v. Wade,* the Supreme Court divided the nine months of pregnancy into three stages called *trimesters.* It ruled that a state cannot regulate abortions in the first trimester, except for requiring that the doctor be licensed by the state. The court ruled that during the second trimester, the state may prevent a woman from having an abortion, but only to protect the woman's health. It ruled that in the third trimester, the state may prohibit abortions entirely, except when an abortion is needed to save the woman's life. The court based this last decision on two considerations: (1) during the third trimester, the fetus is more likely to survive outside the mother; and (2) abortion is a serious medical procedure during the third trimester.

Roe v. Wade soon became the subject of a great national controversy. Some people considered it an important advance toward equality for women because it gave women the right to choose when and whether to have a child. However, people who opposed abortion—particularly those who feel that life begins at conception—strongly disagreed with the court's decision.

After *Roe v. Wade,* the number of legal abortions performed in the United States rose. Many states enacted new laws designed to restrict abortions, and the Supreme Court had to decide whether some of these new laws conflicted with the principles of *Roe v. Wade.* In some cases, the court allowed restrictions to stand. But it also upheld the basic principles of *Roe v. Wade.* For more information about Supreme Court decisions after *Roe v. Wade,* see **Abortion** (Abortion in the United States). Susan Gluck Mezey

Roentgen. See **Ion** (Producing ions).

Roentgen, *REHNT guhn,* **Wilhelm Conrad** (1845-1923), a German physicist, in 1901 won the first Nobel Prize in physics for his discovery of X rays. During an experiment in 1895, Roentgen covered a *Crookes tube* (an evacuated glass tube through which an electric current was passed) with black paper. He noticed that a dark image appeared on a photographic plate substance near the tube when he turned on the electric current.

Roentgen assumed that unknown, invisible rays, which he called *X rays,* were coming from the tube. These rays passed easily through some substances, such as flesh, but were largely stopped by others, such as metal or bone. Because of this, Roentgen found he could photograph the bone structure of his wife's hand with the rays. The use of X rays revolutionized medical and surgical techniques, and eventually provided scientists with new insights into the nature of radiation and the structure of the atom. In Germany, X rays were called *Roentgen rays* in his honor.

Roentgen was born in Lennep (now Remscheid), Germany. He was a professor at the University of Würzburg when he made his famous discovery. Roger H. Stuewer

See also **Physics** (picture: Wilhelm Roentgen); **X rays.**

Roethke, *REHT kee,* **Theodore** (1908-1963), an American poet, received the Pulitzer Prize for poetry in 1954 for *The Waking: Poems 1933-1953. Words for the Wind* (1958) won seven awards, including the Bollingen Prize in 1958 and the National Book Award in 1959. Roethke shifted his style often between his first published work, *Open House* (1941), and his last collection, *The Far Field* (1964). His early poems had the concentrated quality of the poetry of Emily Dickinson. His next works showed the meditative mysticism of T. S. Eliot's poems. His later poems showed the influence of William Butler Yeats.

Roethke's concerns, however, remained constant. His field was the inner life rather than the political or social life. He looked for a sense of self in memories of childhood and for a sense of life in growing things. His father's greenhouse revealed nature (rooting, blossoming, dying) and art (grafting stems, forcing bloom). Roethke also wrote poems for children. He was born in Saginaw, Michigan. Bonnie Costello

See also **Poetry** (Forms).

Rogers, Carl Ransom (1902-1987), was an American psychologist. He is known for developing a form of psychotherapy called *client-centered therapy.*

Client-centered therapy is based on the belief that individuals are controlled by their own values and choices rather than by such other factors as the environment or unconscious drives. Its goal is to help people fulfill their unique potential, which is called *self-actualization.* In developing client-centered therapy, Rogers emphasized the need for a close relationship between the patient (client) and the therapist (counselor). He stressed the importance of the client's personal understanding of his or her experiences instead of the counselor's interpretation of them. In client-centered therapy, clients gain insights into their problems through the examination of their experiences. The counselor does not explain the meaning of experiences or tell the clients what to do.

Rogers was born in Oak Park, Illinois. He wrote a number of books. *On Becoming a Person* (1961) is probably his best-known work. Robert G. Weyant

Rogers, Ginger (1911-1995), was an American actress perhaps best known as Fred Astaire's dancing partner in musical comedies of the 1930's. Rogers was also a skilled dramatic performer, winning the 1940 Academy Award as best actress for her performance in *Kitty Foyle.*

Rogers was born in Independence, Missouri. Her real name was Virginia Katherine McMath. She got her first big break in show business in a leading role in the Broadway musical *Top Speed* (1929). She also appeared in the musical *Girl Crazy* (1930) before moving to Hollywood in 1931 to start her movie career.

Rogers played wisecracking young women in such movies as *42nd Street* (1933) and *Gold Diggers of 1933* (1933) before making *Flying Down to Rio* (1933), her first film with Astaire. Their graceful dancing and the chemistry between them led to nine more musicals. They were *The Gay Divorcee* (1934), *Roberta* and *Top Hat* (both 1935), *Follow the Fleet* and *Swing Time* (both 1936), *Shall We Dance?* (1937), *Carefree* (1938), *The Story of Vernon and Irene Castle* (1939), and *The Barkleys of Broadway* (1949). Rogers retired from movies in 1965 after making about 70 pictures. She wrote an autobiography, *Ginger: My Story* (1991). Dan Zeff

Rogers, Robert. See **Rogers's Rangers.**

Rogers, Roy (1911-1998), was a popular star of Western motion pictures known as the "King of the Cowboys." His greatest fame extended from the late 1930's to the mid-1950's. Rogers sang in most of his films. Comedy was provided by his sidekick, George "Gabby" Hayes. The movies also featured Rogers's palomino horse, Trigger, and heroine Dale Evans, who married Rogers in 1947. Rogers and Evans starred in "The Roy Rogers Show" on television from 1951 to 1956.

Rogers was born in Cincinnati, Ohio. His real name was Leonard Franklin Slye. He began his career as a Western singer on radio and helped found the Sons of the Pioneers vocal group in the early 1930's. Rogers's first starring film role was in the Western *Under Western Skies* (1938). Soon, he was making several low-budget Westerns a year for Republic Pictures. He appeared in about 90 films before retiring from movies in the early 1950's. Rogers also became a successful businessman, establishing a chain of restaurants. Louis Giannetti

Rogers, Will (1879-1935), was an American humorist and social critic. He began his career as a cowboy and rose to international fame as an author; lecturer; and star of vaudeville, motion pictures, and radio. Rogers was known for his homespun humor, his down-to-earth philosophy, and his generosity.

Bettmann Archive
Will Rogers

Rogers gained much of his popularity as an easy-going lecturer on current events. During his lectures, he chewed gum and performed rope tricks while kidding about business, government, people, and politics. Rogers also wrote a column that appeared in more than 350 daily newspapers. He began most of his lectures and columns by saying, "All I know is what I read in the papers." This expression became a byword during the 1920's. Rogers appeared in 50 silent movies and 21 talking films and was popular on radio. He also wrote six books.

William Penn Adair Rogers was born on a ranch near Oologah in the Indian Territory (now Oklahoma). He was partly of Cherokee Indian ancestry, of which he often expressed pride. "My ancestors may not have come over on the *Mayflower,* but they met 'em at the boat," he drawled. As a young man, Rogers worked on cattle drives and in ranching.

In 1902, Rogers left home to seek adventure in Argentina. That same year, he went to South Africa and joined Texas Jack's Wild West Show as a trick roper. He later toured Australia and New Zealand with the Wirth Brothers' Circus. Rogers returned to the United States in 1904 and began his vaudeville career in 1905 as a trick roper and humorist. He gained fame while appearing on Broadway in the *Ziegfeld Follies of 1916.*

Rogers died in a plane crash near Point Barrow, Alaska. He was killed while flying with Wiley Post, a pioneer American aviator. A statue of Rogers stands in the United States Capitol in Washington, D.C. Another statue, at the Will Rogers Memorial in Claremore, Oklahoma, bears the statement for which he was best known: "I never met a man I didn't like."

Critically reviewed by the Will Rogers Memorial

See also **Oklahoma** (Places to visit [with picture]).

Additional resources

Bennett, Cathereen L. *Will Rogers.* Lerner, 1995. Younger readers.
Carter, Joseph H. *Never Met a Man I Didn't Like: The Life and Writings of Will Rogers.* Avon, 1991.

Rogers's Rangers were frontier scouts who served with the British Army during the French and Indian War (1754-1763). Led by Captain Robert Rogers, they scouted and conducted raids on enemy positions.

The Rangers were formally commissioned by Major General William Shirley in 1756 to help the British Army fight in the American wilderness. At first, they consisted of a group of about 60 men under Rogers's command. By mid-1758, Rogers had been promoted to major and given command of nine companies. His command included about 600 men. Most of the Rangers were farmers from New England frontier towns. Rogers taught them to move quietly through the woods and to fight under a variety of conditions.

The Rangers made many long-distance patrols and raids. The most notorious was a surprise attack on a Canadian Indian village in October 1759. Rogers and his Rangers burned the village and killed many villagers, including women and children.   Fred W. Anderson

Roget, *roh ZHAY* or *RAHZH ay,* **Peter Mark** (1779-1869), was a British physician and scholar. He is known as the compiler of *Roget's Thesaurus of English Words and Phrases* (1852). This book lists synonyms under many headings. It has been revised several times. Roget was born near London. He received a medical degree from the University of Edinburgh and lectured on anatomy and physiology throughout Europe.   Patricia A. Moody

Roland was the greatest of the legendary knights who served the medieval king Charlemagne. Stories of Roland circulated during the 1000's, but the oldest surviving version is *The Song of Roland,* an epic poem written about 1100 by an unknown French author. The work may have been based on an actual event in A.D. 778, but it describes the hero as though he lived in the author's time. In the epic, Roland shows his courage and devotion by accepting the dangerous assignment of protecting Charlemagne's army from the Muslims as it crossed the Pyrenees, a mountain chain between France and Spain. A traitor betrays Roland and his men. They die in battle against the Muslims, but Roland's bravery reflects the knightly ideal of service to one's lord. Later German and Italian authors also wrote about Roland. Most of their works are longer than *The Song of Roland* and tell a more complicated story.   Carl Lindahl

See also **French literature** (Early French literature).

Roland de la Platière, *RAW LAHN duh lah* PLAH *TYAIR,* **Marie Jeanne** (1754-1793), known as Madame Roland, was a political adviser and hostess to the Girondist group during the French Revolution (1789-1799). She was intelligent, ambitious, and attractive. She dominated her husband, Jean-Marie Roland de la Platière, a minor government official. Madame Roland took an active interest in the revolutionary movement. Her husband became minister of the interior under the Girondists in 1792, and Madame Roland helped him administer this office. She also served as hostess to many of the leaders of the Girondists.

Madame Roland felt a strong dislike for Maximilien Robespierre and, particularly, Georges-Jacques Danton, who were leaders of another political group known as the Jacobins. Her feelings contributed to a struggle for power between the Girondists and the Jacobins. When the Girondist leaders were arrested in June 1793, Madame Roland also went to prison. After a political trial, she was executed by the guillotine in November 1793. Her husband, who had escaped arrest, committed suicide when he learned of her death. The *Memoirs* she wrote in prison explained her beliefs and became very popular. Madame Roland was born in Paris.

Eric A. Arnold, Jr.

See also **Girondists.**

Role playing is a method of teaching and learning. A real-life problem, such as a disagreement between people, is described. Members of a group then act out roles. Each member tries a different way of behaving in the situation. Other members of the group observe the effects of the behavior. Then the group discusses what happened and often suggests other ways of handling the problem.

Role playing, sometimes called *sociodrama,* was perfected in the 1930's and has been used in schools, industry, social work, and adult education. Doctors use a form of role playing, called *psychodrama,* to treat mentally ill patients. Role playing helps people understand the feelings of others. It also allows people to test new solutions to problems.   C. M. Charles

Rolfe, *rahlf,* **John** (1585-1622), was an early English settler in Jamestown, Virginia. In 1614, he married Pocahontas, daughter of the Indian chief Powhatan. This marriage marked the beginning of a period of peace between Indians and the Jamestown colonists.

Rolfe arrived in Jamestown in 1610. In 1612, he succeeded in cultivating a type of tobacco from the West Indies. This tobacco became the foundation of Virginia's economy. Rolfe served as the colony's secretary from 1614 to 1619. Rolfe, Pocahontas, and their infant son, Thomas, traveled to England in 1616. Pocahontas died there in 1617. Rolfe then returned to America and later remarried. He became a member of the governor's council in 1619 and joined the Council of State in 1621. Rolfe was probably born in Heacham, England, in the county of Norfolk.   Karen Ordahl Kupperman

See also **Pocahontas; Powhatan.**

Rolland, *raw LAHN,* **Romain,** *raw MAN* (1866-1944), a French author, won the 1915 Nobel Prize for literature. His reputation is based on his 10-volume novel *Jean-Christophe* (1904-1912), the story of a young German-born musician somewhat resembling Ludwig van Beethoven. Rolland called the work a *roman-fleuve,* by which he meant that its form corresponded to the unpredictable whims of life, rather than to any preconceived design or plot. In *Jean-Christophe,* Rolland criticized modern civilization and commented on the artist's place in society. The novel expresses Rolland's idealism, his opposition to egotism and hypocrisy, and his love of courage, sincerity, and enthusiasm. Rolland was born in Clamecy in Burgundy.   Elaine D. Cancalon

Roller is the name of 12 species of brightly colored birds that live in Africa, Europe, and Asia. Most rollers are striking shades of blue, pink, and cinnamon. The roller gets its name from the acrobatic flight the male performs when trying to attract a female. The male flies sharply upward over the treetops, then dives downward, calling loudly, twisting and rolling as it tumbles toward the ground.

The *European roller* has a blue head and breast, a chestnut back, and a greenish-blue and brown tail. It measures about 12 inches (30 centimeters) long. It nests in holes in trees or among rocks, where the female lays four to five white eggs. This bird breeds in Europe and winters in Africa.

Scientific classification. Rollers belong to the roller family, Coraciidae. The scientific name for the European roller is *Coracias garrulus.*   Peter G. Connors

See also **Bird** (picture: Birds of Europe and Asia).

Roller coaster is a thrill ride found in amusement and theme parks. It consists of small open cars that run on inclined railway tracks, driven by gravity and momentum. Their path often includes twists, loops, and drops. Roller coasters are designed to appear danger-

ous, but they are safe as long as riders follow prescribed precautions.

The earliest known devices resembling roller coasters were ice-covered wooden slides constructed in Russia in the 1400's. The first American roller coaster was built at Coney Island in New York City in 1884. By the 1920's, there were about 2,000 roller coasters in North America. Today, there are about 175 large, permanent roller coasters in the United States, some with reported speeds of about 70 miles (110 kilometers) per hour.
        Don B. Wilmeth

Roller skating is a form of recreation and a sport in which people glide on wheeled boots called *roller skates.* Some people skate for recreation on sidewalks and in parks, and others skate to music at indoor skating centers. Many take part in competitive roller skating. Joseph Merlin of Belgium invented the roller skate about 1760.

Roller skates. Most roller skates have two major parts, the *boot* and the *skate assembly.* The boots are usually made of leather. Boots worn for recreational and artistic skating have high tops and are laced up the front to a point above the ankle. Speed skaters wear boots with low-cut tops.

The skate assembly is a metal or plastic structure attached to the sole of the boot. There are two main assembly styles, the *quad* and the *in-line.* The main parts of a quad assembly are the *plate,* two *truck assemblies,* four *wheels,* and the *toe stop.* The plate is a piece of metal or plastic fastened to the boot. The truck assemblies are attached to the front and back of the plate. They have movable parts that enable skaters to control the direction in which they want to move. A pair of wheels are attached to an axle on each truck assembly. The toe stop, found on most skates, allows skaters to stop quickly and to perform maneuvers. Some people wear *clamp-on skates,* which are skate assemblies that attach to their shoes. Beginning in the mid-1980's, skates with in-line wheels have become popular. In-line wheels are arranged one behind the other, resembling an ice-skating blade.

Early roller skate wheels were made of metal or wood. In the mid-1970's, wheels made of a hard plastic called *polyurethane* became popular. Such wheels are quieter than those made of wood or metal, and skaters

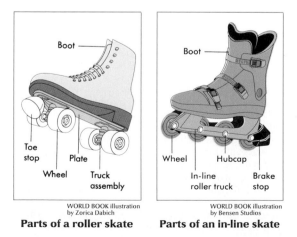

WORLD BOOK illustration
by Zorica Dabich

WORLD BOOK illustration
by Bensen Studios

Parts of a roller skate   **Parts of an in-line skate**

can move faster and more smoothly on them.

Competitive roller skating includes three types of events. *Artistic skating* and *speed skating* are similar to competitive ice skating (see **Ice skating**). *Roller hockey* combines elements of hockey and basketball. Artistic skaters use quad skates. Speed skating and roller hockey use both quad and in-line skates.

Artistic skating competitors perform graceful movements, often to music. Artistic skating consists of *figure skating, free skating,* and *dance skating.* In figure skating, athletes retrace circular patterns marked on the floor. They are judged on accuracy and control.

Free skating can be performed by an individual or a team. There are separate events for men and women. Individual free skaters, called *singles,* combine jumps, spins, and dance footwork with music. They are judged on the speed, accuracy, and difficulty of their jumps, the speed and form of their spins, the originality of their footwork, and their musical expression. Free skating teams, called *pairs,* consist of one man and one woman. They combine the moves of singles free skaters with lifts and other movements. They are judged by the same standards as singles skaters. But the judges also consider the pair's ability to precisely mirror each other's movements.

Dance skating is performed by two skaters, known as a team, or by a solo skater. Both team and solo skaters perform compulsory dances to music.

Speed skating has separate events for indoor and outdoor competition. Athletes are divided into nine age groups, with separate races for men and women. Indoor events take place on a flat, 100-meter oval track. Distances for indoor races range from 100 meters to 5,000 meters. Outdoor competitions take place on either a road course or on a banked, oval track. Outdoor events vary in distance from 300 meters to 20,000 meters. There are also indoor and outdoor relay events for teams of two, three, or four skaters.

Roller hockey is a noncontact team sport. Teams consist of four "floor" players and a goalkeeper. Players score points by passing a hard plastic ball into the opponent's goal. They move the ball along the ground with short, curved sticks like those used in hockey.

Critically reviewed by the Roller Skating Associations and the United States Amateur Confederation of Roller Skating

Rolling Stones are a popular English rock band. The band's music has often been aggressive, rebellious, and sexual. The group is known for the excitement of its live performances.

The Rolling Stones were formed in 1962 and took their name from a song by the American blues singer Muddy Waters. The original members of the group were lead singer Mick Jagger (1943-), guitarists Keith Richards (1943-) and Brian Jones (1942-1969), bassist Bill Wyman (1936-), and drummer Charlie Watts (1941-). Jones left the band in 1969, shortly before his death. He was replaced by guitarist Mick Taylor, who quit the group in 1974. Ron Wood has been the Stones's second guitarist since then.

The Rolling Stones were formed to play the music of earlier blues and rock artists. But Jagger and Richards soon began writing most of the band's material. Their hit songs include "(I Can't Get No) Satisfaction" (1965), "Get Off of My Cloud" (1965), "Honky Tonk Women" (1969),

"Brown Sugar" (1971), and "Start Me Up" (1981).

In the 1980's, the individual members of the Rolling Stones began involving themselves in solo projects, but continued to enjoy success with the band. Wyman retired after the band's 1989 tour and no permanent replacement was named. The Rolling Stones appeared in several filmed versions of their concerts. Jagger also appeared in the movies *Ned Kelly* (1969), *Performance* (1970), and *Freejack* (1992).   Don McLeese

See also **Rock music** (picture).

Roman alphabet. See **Alphabet** (The Roman alphabet).

Roman Catholic Church is the largest body of Christians in the world. It has about 1 billion members—nearly a fifth of the world's population. Roman Catholics are most heavily concentrated in Europe, North America, and South America. But the percentage of the Catholic population in both Africa and Asia is growing.

The Roman Catholic Church traces its beginnings to about A.D. 30, when Jesus Christ instructed the apostles, His followers, to spread His teaching about the Kingdom of God. Roman Catholics believe that Christ rose from the dead after being crucified and sent the Holy Spirit to guide the apostles.

Roman Catholics believe that Jesus Christ founded the church to carry to all people the salvation He brought to the world. They also believe that, with God's assistance, the church has faithfully preserved the teachings of Christ. According to Catholic teaching, the Holy Spirit continues to guide the church.

The pope, who is the bishop of Rome, serves as the head of the Roman Catholic Church. He governs the church from Vatican City, a tiny independent country within the city of Rome. Throughout the world, other bishops lead local churches.

The Roman Catholic Church has been an important force in world history. During much of the Middle Ages, for example, the church had great political power in Western Europe. Its universities and monasteries were centers of learning, and they preserved much of the heritage of the Greek and Roman cultures. During the 1500's and 1600's, Catholic missionaries traveled to Africa, Asia, and the Americas, preaching the gospel and spreading European culture.

Throughout its history, the Catholic faith has inspired many great works of art. These works include the Gothic cathedrals built in France in the Middle Ages and the frescoes painted in the Vatican in the early 1500's by the Italian artist Michelangelo.

This article describes the beliefs and worship of Roman Catholics. It also discusses the organization and history of the Roman Catholic Church.

Roman Catholic beliefs

For Catholics, religious faith means, above all, a wholehearted acceptance of God's *revelation,* which is the knowledge of Himself and His will that God has revealed to humanity through Christ. A Catholic's faith in God is expressed in certain teachings. These teachings, based on the Bible, are found in declarations of church councils and popes and in short statements of faith called *creeds.* The oldest and most authoritative of these creeds are the Apostles' Creed and the Nicene Creed. Catholics recite the Nicene Creed at their central act of worship, called the *Eucharist* or *Mass.*

The creeds summarize Catholic beliefs concerning (1) the Trinity and creation; (2) sin, the Incarnation, and salvation; (3) the nature of the church; and (4) life after death. These core doctrines, in turn, form the basis of Catholic *morality*—that is, guidelines for how Catholics should live their lives.

The Trinity and creation. Catholics believe there is only one God. But this one God exists as a union of three Persons—the Father; the Son, who is Christ; and the Holy Spirit. These three Persons form the *Trinity.* Each Person is distinct and is truly God. Yet there is only one God, who has no beginning or end, is beyond time and space, and is perfect and unchanging. Catholics believe that the universe owes its beginning to God, who created everything freely, from love. They believe that the world and humanity could not survive without God's continuing care.

Sin, the Incarnation, and salvation. The Catholic Church teaches that humanity was created not only *by* God but also *for* God. Its destiny is to share God's life forever, in union with God and one another. God intended humanity to achieve this destiny by lovingly obeying His will. But *original sin* interfered with God's plan for humanity. The Bible describes Adam, the first man, as sinning by an act of disobedience to God. Adam's sin affects every person born in the world.

Catholics believe that God sent His Son, the second Person of the Trinity, to save humanity from all sin—the original sin people inherit as well as the sins they themselves commit during their lifetime by deliberately turning from God. Without ceasing to be God, the Son of God became man. He was born to the Virgin Mary. Catholics especially commemorate this *Incarnation* of God in Jesus Christ at Christmas.

Catholics believe that Christ saved humanity through His life and death and by rising from the dead and entering heaven. While on earth, Jesus taught that salvation would be given to all who truly turn to God and live justly in God's sight.

The nature of the church. Salvation was not complete when Christ left the earth. Salvation must be brought to each new generation. Jesus therefore commissioned His apostles to gather all human beings into a church. Catholics describe this church as the people of God, united with God and one another through Christ. They believe that the Holy Spirit guides and strengthens the church on the way to salvation. They also consider the church to be a missionary people with the function of drawing everyone into a communion of love.

Life after death. According to Catholic doctrine, life does not end with the death of the body. Instead, the soul leaves the body and enters heaven, purgatory, or hell. On the final Judgment Day, when this world has ended, all souls will be reunited with their bodies.

Heaven is the eternal communion of those who have reached their destiny. They see God as He is and love Him and one another with complete joy. Purgatory is a temporary state for souls who die in God's love but must be purified of all unholiness. The Roman Catholic Church defines hell as the absence of God, which results in complete despair. It is the punishment people bring on themselves who have abandoned God and refused communion with Him.

Catholic morality—how Catholics should behave—can be largely summarized as follows: The church teaches Catholics to love God with their whole heart and to love their fellow human beings as they love themselves. The church asks Catholics to do this in imitation of Jesus, who offered Himself for the world's salvation. The Roman Catholic Church believes that all people must follow their conscience. But a Catholic's conscience is formed not only by personal opinion of what is right and wrong. It is especially formed by the Bible, church teaching, and the faith and worship of the Christian community.

Worship

The acts of worship that Catholics perform together are called the *liturgy.* The central act of liturgy is the Eucharist or Mass. The Eucharist and certain other important liturgical acts make up the seven *sacraments* of the Roman Catholic Church. The sacraments are (1) baptism, (2) confirmation, (3) Eucharist, (4) penance, (5) holy orders, (6) marriage, and (7) anointing of the sick.

Baptism is the liturgical celebration in which a child or adult is cleansed of sin and begins a new life with God. Water poured in the name of the Trinity over the head of the person being baptized is a sign of the person's cleansing from sin. Because water is necessary to life, the baptismal water also is a sign of new spiritual life. Thus, baptism marks the beginning of a Catholic's oneness with Christ and entry into the church.

Confirmation enables baptized people to grow to spiritual adulthood. A bishop, and sometimes also a priest, puts holy oil, called *chrism,* on the forehead of the people being confirmed. The chrism signifies that these people have been strengthened by the Holy Spirit so that they may live up to their faith.

The Eucharist or Mass is the celebration of the Lord's Supper. Catholics believe the Mass makes present Christ's sacrifice of Himself. The Mass has two main parts. The first part, the *liturgy of the word,* consists of prayers, hymns, readings from the Bible, a sermon, and the recitation of the Nicene Creed. The second part is the *liturgy of the Eucharist.* During this part, according to Catholic teaching, the priest, acting in Jesus's name and by the power of the Holy Spirit, transforms bread and wine into Christ's body and blood. The congregation is then invited to receive Christ Himself in Holy Communion.

Catholics believe that during the Mass, Christ is truly present, sins are forgiven, and God's Spirit is given. The members of the congregation are closely united with one another, the whole church, and their fellow human beings. Catholics must participate in the Mass on Saturday evenings or Sundays and on *holy days of obligation,* such as Christmas. They must receive Holy Communion at least once a year, at Easter time.

Penance, also called *confession,* is the sacrament in which Catholics confess their sins to a priest, express their sincere sorrow for having sinned, and promise to avoid sin in the future. The priest forgives the sinner in God's name. The effect of penance is to bring the Roman Catholic back to God and the Christian community. Catholics must confess their sins at least once a year if the sins are serious. However, the church urges believers to receive penance as well as the Eucharist more often.

Holy orders is the sacrament in which men are made deacons, priest, or bishops. These men become ministers of God's word and sacraments, and spiritual leaders of the community.

Marriage is the sacrament in which a man and woman promise themselves to each other for life. This sacrament helps them be faithful to the duties of marriage and family life. In general, Catholics may marry only once, unless their partner dies.

Anointing of the sick is the sacrament given to people who are dangerously ill or very old. The priest anoints these people with oil, a sign of healing. The priest prays that they will receive the grace of the Holy Spirit, so they may be freed from sin, comforted and strengthened in soul and body, and restored to health.

Church organization

Roman Catholics are members of a local *parish,* led by a priest called a *pastor.* The parishes in an area form a *diocese,* a territorial district headed by a bishop. The pope appoints bishops, and they are responsible to him. Bishops in turn appoint and oversee pastors.

The pope is the head of the Roman Catholic Church. He is the highest member of its *clergy* (ordained ministers). There are three *orders* (ranks) within the clergy—deacons, priests, and bishops. The organization of the clergy by rank is the church's *hierarchy.* Each order—from deacons up through the pope, who is the bishop of Rome—has more responsibilities and wider powers of ministry and government than the one below it.

Catholics believe the pope is Christ's representative on earth and a successor of Saint Peter, who is regarded as the first pope. They believe that the pope is *infallible* (free from error) when he formally defines matters of faith and morals. The pope is aided in governing the church by *cardinals* and the *Roman Curia.*

Cardinals are bishops chosen by the pope to be his main advisers. As a group, they form the College of Cardinals. They hold the highest rank below the pope, and they have the responsibility of electing a new pope after a reigning pope dies or resigns.

The Roman Curia is the pope's administrative arm. It consists of the Secretariat of State and a number of other departments called congregations, tribunals, councils, and offices. Cardinals and *archbishops* (highest-ranking bishops) head the various departments of the Curia.

The Secretariat of State assists the pope most directly in governing the church and in communicating with the rest of the Curia. The congregations do most of the Curia's administrative work. Tribunals have judicial powers. For example, the tribunal called the Roman Rota serves as a court to settle disputes about the validity of marriages. The councils deal with matters of Christian unity and handle relations with non-Christians. The offices are responsible for such functions as drafting papal documents and gathering church statistics.

Bishop and diocese. Bishops are considered successors to Christ's apostles. A bishop appoints the pastors of the parishes in his diocese, and the pastors are responsible to him. He also supervises the many church-supported agencies that serve local needs in the diocese, including schools, hospitals, and newspapers.

The bishops of the church, together with the pope as

Robert Fried

The Eucharist or Mass is the central act of Roman Catholic worship. According to Catholic teaching, the priest transforms bread and wine into the body and blood of Jesus Christ.

their head, form the *college of bishops* and share authority over the church. They are responsible for teaching and guiding the church as a whole. For example, when the bishops met at Vatican Council II (1962-1965), they issued statements that had great impact on Catholic life and practice.

Pastor and parish. A *territorial parish* includes all Catholic residents in a given area. A *national parish* primarily serves an ethnic group whose members may live in several territorial parishes. The pastor of a parish is its spiritual leader. Pastors of large parishes are assisted by other priests, by deacons, and, increasingly, by the *laity* or *lay people*—people who are not ordained.

The role of lay people is to live according to the principles of their faith. They are united with the clergy in worship and prayer, and they are called to exemplify the vision and values of the gospel at all times. Lay people participate in such church governing bodies as parish councils and parish school boards. At Mass, they act as readers, reading aloud passages from the Bible, and they help distribute Holy Communion.

Religious institutes are societies of Catholic men or women who live according to a set of regulations called a *rule.* Members of the institute are called *religious.* They take vows of poverty, chastity, and obedience. Some of the men are also ordained. Well-known Catholic institutes for men include the Jesuits, the Franciscans, and the Dominicans. Institutes for women include the Sisters of Charity, the Ursulines, and the Benedictines.

These institutes are governed directly by their own appointed or elected leaders.

The early church

The first 300 years. Catholics trace the beginnings of their church to Palestine, where Jesus preached, healed others, and was crucified. There, according to the Bible, after Christ rose from the dead, He told the apostles to preach the gospel to all peoples. In Jerusalem, the Holy Spirit came upon the apostles on what Catholics call the feast of Pentecost.

The first Christians were Jews who believed Jesus was the *Messiah,* the savior expected by the Jews. The early church gradually separated itself from Judaism, the religion of the Jews, and achieved its own identity. But the church accepted the Jewish Scriptures as the record of God's dealings with His chosen people and as a guide leading to salvation in Jesus Christ.

Saint Paul became the most important person to carry the gospel to the *gentiles* (non-Jews). He regarded himself as a divinely appointed apostle to the gentiles. Paul founded many churches and exercised authority over them through visits and letters. He also represented their interests with the mother church in Jerusalem. After Paul's death, about A.D. 67, the number of gentile churches continued to expand rapidly. By the 100's, the center of Christianity had passed from Jerusalem to Christian communities in the cities of Antioch in Syria, Alexandria in Egypt, and especially Rome.

In its early years, the church grew steadily in spite of persecution by the Romans, whose empire covered most of Europe, the Middle East, and northern Africa. The Romans believed loyalty to the emperor involved honoring the gods of the state and often the emperor. They regarded Christians who refused to give such honor as traitors and atheists. The Christian ideal became the *martyr*—a person who suffered persecution and even death rather than abandon Christianity. Although the church suffered widespread persecution, many of these attacks were local and brief. The church thus had time to grow and develop a distinct structure.

While the church faced persecution from outside, many movements threatened to divide it from within. Some of these movements taught what the church declared to be *heresies*—that is, teachings opposed to basic Christian beliefs. The most serious heresy during the church's first 200 years was *Gnosticism.* It was a religious philosophy that had many followers throughout the Roman Empire. It held that Christ was a spiritual being who only appeared to be human; and thus He did not actually suffer and die. The struggle against Gnosticism was a difficult and important battle in church history.

The earliest Christians relied on the apostles, led by Saint Peter, as their authority in settling questions of doctrine and government. After the death of the apostles, the church faced the problem of where to turn for authority in such matters. In the 100's, two developments helped solve the problem. First, the church gradually recognized the books of the New Testament as sources of authority in doctrine. Second, the basic orders of Christian ministry—bishops, *presbyters* (later called priests), and deacons—became more clearly defined.

The recognition of Christianity. Constantine the Great was the first Roman emperor to become a Christian. In 313, Constantine and Licinius, the emperor of Rome's eastern provinces, granted freedom of worship and equal rights to all religious groups in the empire. By the late 300's, Christianity had become the favored religion of the empire.

The recognition of Christianity had some unfortunate effects on the church. For the first time, the church attracted many people who lacked the dedication of the early Christians. Emperors intruded into the internal affairs of the church. In the mid-300's, for example, the Roman Emperor Constantius II tried to force the Eastern heresy known as *Arianism* on the West. Arianism is named for Arius, a priest in Egypt who claimed that Christ was not truly God.

But on the whole, the empire's recognition of Christianity benefited the church. The church was able to influence civil laws. It also expanded its work among the poor and began missionary work outside the empire.

Bishops from throughout the Christian world met several times to resolve major theological disputes in the early church. These meetings are called *general* or *ecumenical councils.* The first council, Nicaea I, met in 325 and condemned the teachings of Arius. The creed of the council, which Catholics pray at Mass, affirms that Jesus Christ is truly God, "one in being with the Father." In 451, the Council of Chalcedon denounced *Monophysitism,* which denied Christ's human nature. The council completed the teaching of Nicaea by declaring that Christ is truly man.

Some of the most distinguished literature in church history was produced between 325 and 451. The most notable writers of this period included the historian Eusebius; the bishops and theologians Saint Ambrose, Saint Athanasius, and Saint Augustine; the preacher Saint John Chrysostom; the poet Prudentius; and the Biblical scholar Saint Jerome. Their writings had a great influence on church thought in later centuries.

Monasticism began to develop in the 300's. This way of life, in which a person withdraws from worldly affairs and is completely devoted to prayer and the service of God, was to play an important part in church history. As persecution ceased and Christianity prospered, the monk replaced the martyr as the Christian ideal. The two basic models for monastic life were the Egyptians Saint Anthony and Saint Pachomius. Anthony lived the solitary life of a hermit. Pachomius organized monastic communities governed by a rule.

Pope Saint Leo I, who reigned from 440 to 461, was perhaps the greatest early pope. Leo persuaded the Huns and the Vandals, two barbarian tribes, to halt their attacks on Italy. By the time Leo began his reign, the huge Roman Empire had been split into Eastern and Western empires. Leo emphasized that popes were successors to Saint Peter and so had *primacy* (supreme authority) as head of the universal church.

Conflict with the East. Before the 400's, a single Christian church existed. But it consisted of several nationalities. Each nationality expressed the Christian faith in its own language and liturgy and, at times, its own theology. Gradually, cultural, geographic, political, and religious differences led to the development of several separate churches in the East Roman Empire. Beginning in the 400's, the Eastern churches began to drift away from the authority of Rome and the church in the West.

Several events helped widen the gulf between Western and Eastern Christianity. One event was the condemnation by the Council of Ephesus in 431 of the teachings of Nestorius, the *patriarch* (bishop) of Constantinople. Nestorius asserted that Mary was the mother of Christ but not the mother of God. In reaction to the council's condemnation, the East Syrian Church separated itself from the Western Church. The gulf widened after the Council of Chalcedon condemned Monophysitism. After this condemnation, the Armenian Church, the Coptic Church of Egypt, the Ethiopian Church, and the Syrian Jacobite Church all broke away from those churches that accepted the teaching of the Council of Chalcedon.

Growth of the church in Europe

The Early Middle Ages. In A.D. 476, barbarian forces led by the Germanic general Odoacer deposed the last emperor of the West Roman Empire. Many historians use this date to mark the end of the Roman Empire in the West and the start of the Middle Ages. During the Middle Ages, the influence and power of the church reached its peak.

The collapse of the West Roman Empire meant that no one power had political control in the West. Instead, all of Western Europe except Ireland came to be ruled by barbarian kings, who were either Arians or non-Christians. Beginning with the reign of Pope Gregory the Great in 590, the church set out to create a Christian world in the West. Its chief instruments were the papacy and monasticism.

The papacy gradually replaced the empire as the center of authority in Western Europe. Ireland had been converted to Christianity in the 400's, mainly through the efforts of Saint Patrick. In 496, the king of the Franks, Clovis I, was converted. His conversion brought Gaul into the church and checked the spread of the Arian heresy there. Gaul was a huge region now occupied by Belgium, France, and part of western Germany. From the 500's to the 700's, the papacy directed the conversion of other peoples of the West. These peoples included the Visigoths in Spain, the Anglo-Saxons in England, and the Croats in central Europe.

Meanwhile, the growth of monasticism played a large part in the increasing influence of the church. Monasticism created centers of Christian society, renewed the spiritual life of religious communities, and helped transform a dying Western culture into a Christian civilization. In the early 500's, Saint Benedict of Nursia founded Benedictine monasticism. The Benedictine rule was both moderate and humane in setting forth how its followers should live. These qualities influenced the rule of many later orders.

In the early 700's, Muslims, who followed the religion of Islam, conquered Spain. Also in the 700's, Viking raiders from northern Europe began to attack England and other Christian countries. The conquest of Spain and the Viking attacks greatly disrupted Western European economic, political, and social life. In the midst of these disruptions, the church stood out as the major force for unifying and civilizing the West.

Charlemagne, the greatest king of the Franks, became one of the most important people in European as well as church history. During his reign, he laid a foundation for the organized, civilized society that was later built in Western Europe. This foundation resulted from the ideals that Charlemagne pursued—orderly government, religious reform, and the expansion of the Christian world through conquest and missionary activity.

Charlemagne involved himself deeply in church affairs and became protector of the popes. In 800, Pope Leo III crowned him emperor of the Romans, restoring the idea of empire in the West. Charlemagne's empire formed the basis of what became the Holy Roman Empire in 962. The Holy Roman Empire lasted until 1806. It consisted largely of German and Italian states ruled by German emperors.

Cluniac reform was the name given to a vast reform movement within the church. It began in the 900's and lasted about 200 years. It was centered in the Benedictine abbey of Cluny, France. The movement introduced significant changes in the way monasteries were governed and monks lived. It also helped correct abuses within the church, such as *simony* (buying or selling sacred things or church offices). The Cistercian order—founded in 1098 in Cîteaux, France—also became a leading force for church renewal, particularly under the leadership of Saint Bernard of Clairvaux.

Split with the East. Since the 400's, the Eastern churches had continued to drift away from the church in the West. Then, in the 800's, Photius, patriarch of Constantinople, had a serious dispute with the papacy. A major issue in the dispute was the pope's claim to authority over Eastern Christians. In the 1000's, a conflict also developed between Rome and the patriarch of Constantinople, Michael Cerularius. Part of this conflict arose from claims by each church that the other was interfering in its affairs. Serious *schisms* (splits) emerged from these disagreements. The disagreements led to a formal division between the Eastern churches that employed the Byzantine rite and the Western church that followed the Latin rite and acknowledged the primacy of the bishop of Rome. However, some Eastern churches eventually reunited with the Roman Catholic Church, forming what are now called the Eastern Catholic Churches.

Innocent III became pope in 1198. He was one of the most powerful popes of the Middle Ages. He influenced the political affairs of much of Europe. Innocent called one of the most important church councils of the period, the Fourth Lateran Council, which met in 1215. The council enacted 70 *decrees* (official decisions) regulating church affairs. Innocent also encouraged the founding of the Dominican and Franciscan religious orders. Saint Dominic and Saint Francis of Assisi established these *mendicant* (begging) orders. The members sought to live a life of poverty in community as they preached the gospel.

Innocent's reign led to the establishment of the religious court known as the Inquisition. The Inquisition was set up in 1231 to investigate and combat heresy. But the inquisitors often misused their power, and they had some suspects tortured or even put to death.

Scholasticism. In the 1100's, the system of thought called *medieval scholasticism* began to develop. It reached its peak in the 1200's. Its scholars, called *scholastics,* tried to better understand Christian doctrine by the use of reason. The writings on logic by the ancient

Greek philosopher Aristotle had an early influence on scholasticism. The scholastics put various doctrines and their explanations into systematic order. They also tried to resolve conflicting views in Christian theology.

The leading scholastics included Saint Albertus Magnus of Germany, Roger Bacon of England, Saint Bonaventure of Italy, and especially Saint Thomas Aquinas of Italy. The center of scholasticism was the University of Paris, where Bonaventure and Thomas Aquinas taught.

Boniface VIII became pope in 1294. He tried to unify the Christian world more closely under the papacy. Boniface insisted that kings of individual nations were subject to the Holy Roman emperor and that the emperor's power, in turn, came from the pope. In 1302, Boniface issued a *bull* (papal decree) called *Unam sanctam.* The bull declared that, for salvation, every human being must be subject to the pope. The bull angered the French king, Philip IV, who said Boniface was trying to claim authority over the French king and the French people.

The Avignon papacy. In 1309, Pope Clement V moved from Rome to Avignon, in what is now France. The popes did not return to Rome until 1377. One reason that the popes lived in Avignon was that they wished to avoid the civil wars that were disrupting Italy in the 1300's. Also, the popes came to be increasingly influenced by the powerful French kings. During the Avignon period, papal reform efforts continued, and the church sent missionaries to Asia and encouraged the expansion of universities. But hostility against a French-dominated papacy began to grow outside of France.

The Great Schism. From 1378 to 1417, a controversy called the *Great Schism* deeply divided the church. During this time, candidates from Avignon and Rome both claimed to be the rightful pope. In 1409, the Council of Pisa tried to untangle the dispute but instead created a third claim to the office. Each of the three men demanded obedience from the Christian faithful, which caused much confusion and doubt.

In 1417, bishops and other high-ranking clergymen meeting at the Council of Constance finally ended the Great Schism by electing a fourth man, Martin V, as the single rightful pope. But the controversy had caused damage within the church. For example, reform efforts had been slowed. A conflict also had developed over the idea that a general council of bishops had greater authority than the pope.

The close of the Middle Ages. From the 1300's through the 1500's, medieval Europe gradually gave way to modern Europe. During these 300 years, the Middle Ages overlapped a period called the *Renaissance.* This was a time of great cultural and intellectual activity, when ideas and customs that had been accepted for hundreds of years were questioned or swept away. The Renaissance began in Italy in the 1300's and spread throughout Western Europe in the 1400's and 1500's.

The Renaissance emphasized the great dignity of humanity and the beauty of life on earth and had both good and bad effects on Catholicism. Popes supported Renaissance artists and scholars, but the papacy also suffered a moral decline. The church sponsored important historical scholarship, but the popes often became involved in Italian politics. Reform efforts within the church slackened.

Meanwhile, during the 1400's, a revival of deep religious feeling occurred among clergy and the laity. Many Catholics expressed this feeling in emotional *devotions* (pious practices) to the sufferings and death of Jesus. During this time, however, piety was being divorced from its roots in theology, and theology was hardening into conflicting schools of thought and losing much of its vitality.

The Council of Florence, which began in 1438, reunited the Western church with some Eastern churches. However, the reunification lasted only a few years. In 1453, Muslims captured Constantinople and ruled over most Eastern Christians until the 1800's.

The Reformation. Medieval Christian civilization ended with the *Reformation,* a religious revolution that gave birth to Protestantism in the 1500's. As a result of the Reformation, Europe became divided between Roman Catholic and Protestant countries.

By the early 1500's, the conditions in the church that led to the Reformation were apparent. The papacy was dominated by temporal concerns. The Roman Curia often was corrupt. Many bishops lived like princes and neglected the faithful. A great number of clergymen were uneducated and ignored their pastoral duties. Members of religious orders had become worldly. Fear and superstition were common among the laity. The liturgy no longer held much meaning or inspiration for the people, and theology had generally become dry and unrelated to real life.

Some councils, popes, saints, scholars, and movements among the people had indeed attempted to reform the church during the late Middle Ages. However, the church remained largely unreformed.

In 1517, Martin Luther, a member of the Augustinian order, issued his famous Ninety-Five Theses in Wittenberg, Germany. The theses were statements attacking the church's doctrine of indulgences and the abuses that arose in granting indulgences. An indulgence is a release from part or all of temporal punishment due for sin, provided that the sin has already been forgiven. The church's doctrine on indulgences was basically sound. But it was not always understood properly. Also, many preachers sold indulgences. Many people bought them from the church, hoping the indulgences would hasten the release of a dead person's soul from purgatory. Luther's attack on indulgences began the Reformation.

By the late 1500's, the Reformation had divided Western Europe into Protestant and Roman Catholic lands. Catholicism was reduced primarily to the Mediterranean countries, as well as to Hungary, Poland, and small areas within the Holy Roman Empire. But while the church lost much ground in Europe to Protestantism, it achieved enormous success in other parts of the world. Beginning in the 1500's, Catholic missionaries converted many people in Africa, Asia, and the Americas.

The Counter Reformation, also known as the Catholic Reformation, was a reform movement within Catholicism that increased in intensity as the church reacted to the Protestant Reformation. It took place during the 1500's and 1600's.

Beginning in the 1520's, such reform popes as Adrian VI, Paul III, and especially Paul IV concentrated on correcting abuses in the Roman Curia and hierarchy. By the end of the reign of Saint Pius V in 1572, the papacy had clearly committed itself to church reform.

A leading force in the Counter Reformation was the Society of Jesus, commonly called the Jesuits. Saint Ignatius Loyola founded the Jesuits in 1534, and Paul III confirmed the order in 1540. Loyola did not found the Jesuits specifically to counteract Protestantism. But the order proved well equipped for the task. The Jesuits were flexible, practical, and completely at the pope's service. They were intelligent, deeply religious men who revived Catholicism both intellectually and spiritually. To a large extent, the Jesuits helped halt the advance of Protestantism, even regaining vast areas that had come under Protestant influence in Belgium, Luxembourg, the Netherlands, France, and eastern and central Europe.

Perhaps the greatest single force in renewing Catholic life and worship was the Council of Trent (1545-1563). The council issued decrees on the Mass and other areas of doctrine and discipline that eliminated much confusion within the church. Its decrees on such topics as the training of priests and the granting of indulgences reformed church life wherever they were put into effect.

The Counter Reformation drew strength from the spiritual renewal led by Saint Teresa of Avila and Saint John of the Cross. It found artistic expression in the *baroque* churches and monasteries built during this period and in the *polyphonic* music composed for religious services by the Italian composer Giovanni Palestrina and the English composer William Byrd.

A number of religious and political wars broke out during the Counter Reformation. Between 1562 and 1598, the Catholic majority in France and French Protestants called Huguenots fought eight civil wars called the Wars of Religion. The Thirty Years' War destroyed much of Germany. It began as a civil war between Protestants and Catholics in the German states but eventually involved most European countries. The Peace of Westphalia, which ended the war in 1648, declared that the people of each state must follow the religion of their ruler. This principle greatly weakened the Holy Roman Empire. It also ended the medieval idea of a Christian commonwealth of nations harmoniously directed by the supreme authority of pope and emperor.

Catholic revival in France. Perhaps the most outstanding example of church renewal in the 1600's occurred in France. Several people especially helped to create this renewal. Saint Francis de Sales, bishop of Geneva, inspired many Christians by his uniting of humanism and piety. Saint Vincent de Paul devoted his life to serving the poor. He founded the Vincentians, an order of missionary priests to country districts in France. Saint Louise de Marillac worked with Vincent de Paul in assisting the needy. She was one of many women who helped restore a sense of charity and deep religious feeling to both convent and Catholic family life.

During the 1600's, several French clergymen founded religious institutes that helped inspire a new emphasis on spirituality in the priesthood. Pierre Cardinal de Bérulle established the French Oratory in 1611. Jean Jacques Olier founded the Company of Saint Sulpice in 1642, and Saint John Eudes established the Congregation of Jesus and Mary in 1643.

Gallicanism. The period from the end of the Thirty Years' War in 1648 to the outbreak of the French Revolution (1789-1799) has been called the Revolt of the Catholic Kings. The period was marked by quarrels between church and state, especially over *Gallicanism*—the view that the authority of national churches should be increased at the expense of papal authority.

Gallicanism developed in France, and the dispute over it became most critical there. King Louis XIV and Pope Innocent XI quarreled over Louis's attempts to increase his influence in French religious affairs. The quarrel led many French clergymen to adopt doctrines that the papacy could not in conscience accept. For example, some French clergymen believed that a general church council was superior to the pope. Although the controversy died down in the 1690's, the French clergy remained anti-Roman for many years.

Gallicanism, with its emphasis on nationalism, became popular in every European country ruled by a Catholic monarch. During the late 1700's, the Holy Roman emperor, Joseph II, tried to separate the Catholic Church in Austria from Rome. Joseph considered the church a department of state whose task was to promote morality. He controlled all levels of the clergy and even interfered with the liturgy. Rulers in Naples, Sardinia, Spain, and Venice followed Joseph's example.

Jansenism. While the church faced challenges from Catholic rulers, it also was disrupted from within by theological disputes. The most serious dispute was over a religious movement known as *Jansenism.* Jansenism arose in France in the mid-1600's. It was based on the writings of Cornelius Jansen, bishop of Ypres, Belgium. Jansen developed doctrines on divine grace that played down human freedom and denied that Christ died for all humanity. The church attacked some Jansenist doctrines as heresy.

The movement tore Catholic France apart. It divided many French bishops from Rome and even attracted the attention of Kings Louis XIV and Louis XV. The Catholic philosopher and mathematician Blaise Pascal became a leading spokesman for Jansenism and a fierce critic of the Jesuits, who spoke against it. Three popes condemned Jansenism—Innocent X in 1653, Alexander VII in 1656, and Clement XI in 1713. But their condemnation only fueled the controversy.

Jansenism finally began to lose influence in the 1730's. But its harsh idea of God and emphasis on divine punishment still influence some Catholics today.

The Age of Reason was a period during which philosophers emphasized the use of reason as the one sure method of learning truth. The Age of Reason lasted from the late 1600's to the late 1700's. During this time, many people attacked organized religion in general and the Catholic Church in particular. They claimed that the church favored obedience to authority over individual freedom and that it sacrificed reason to tradition. They also believed that the Catholic clergy's obedience to Rome violated national sovereignty. The leaders of the period included such French intellectuals as Denis Diderot, Jean-Jacques Rousseau, and Voltaire.

Suppression of the Jesuits. During the middle and late 1700's, several nations banned the Jesuit Order from their country and colonies. Portugal banned the Jesuits in 1759, France in 1764, and Spain in 1767. In 1773, pressure from Catholic rulers helped force Pope Clement XIV to suppress the Jesuits in all countries.

The Jesuits were banned for several reasons. Some

Catholic rulers and churchmen were jealous of the order's influence. Some accused the Jesuits of accumulating too much power and wealth. Gallicans opposed the order's total obedience to the pope, and Jansenists objected to the order's emphasis on human freedom.

The suppression of the Jesuits was never completely effective. For example, the order survived in Russia through the friendship of Empress Catherine the Great. Pope Pius VII lifted the ban in 1814. But the suppression caused a severe setback in Catholic education and missionary activity.

The decline of church influence. The forces of democracy and nationalism swept across Europe from the start of the French Revolution through the 1800's. These forces often were accompanied by fierce opposition to the Roman Catholic Church because the church was viewed as a supporter of the traditional order.

The church suffered enormous losses as a result of the French Revolution. For example, many of the great abbeys of Europe disappeared, and with them the influence of the monastic orders as centers of scholarship and spiritual renewal. Catholic influence over public life was severely lessened, often by civil laws. Catholic universities yielded to state-sponsored education. Theology came to be studied mostly in seminaries rather than in universities, and it became increasingly separated from modern thought and problems.

In many countries, the church suffered from a shortage of priests. This was especially true in France. During the French Revolution, the church lost half its clergy. Many priests were executed or died in prison. Others left the church.

The papacy had governed certain territories called the Papal States, which were gradually absorbed by Italy. By 1870, the papacy had lost the last of the land that once made up the Papal States. The pope's territory was reduced to Vatican City. Although that seemed at the time to be a loss, it freed the papacy from political pressures and concerns.

Although the church suffered setbacks and hostility during the 1800's, Catholic life itself experienced renewal. The restoration of the Jesuit Order in 1814 enabled it to play a large role in that renewal. New religious orders of women became active in education in Belgium, France, and Germany. In Germany, the Congress of Mainz founded the Catholic Union in 1848. The union was an association of Catholics dedicated to promoting the ideals of their religion in social life.

Vatican Council I. In 1846, Pius IX became pope. He ruled until 1878—the longest reign in papal history. Pius's reign reached a high point when he summoned Vatican Council I (1869-1870). The council defined as Catholic doctrine the pope's primacy over the whole church. It also declared him to be *infallible*—that is, incapable of error when, as supreme pastor of the church, he formally defines matters of faith and morals.

Leo XIII. A new age of church history began after Leo XIII became pope in 1878. Leo tried to convince the governments of his time that they and the church could live in harmony. He faced especially strong antichurch feeling in Germany, France, and Italy. He succeeded in easing the German government's restrictions against the church, but he failed in France and Italy. In fact, the French government passed new antichurch laws in 1880, including laws that expelled religious orders from France and banned religious education in the schools.

Leo sought to make the church more active in confronting issues and problems of the modern world. He began a new policy of maintaining contact between the papacy and everyday Catholic life. He established this contact through letters to the Catholic world, called *encyclicals.* The encyclicals dealt with such subjects as philosophy and Bible studies, theology and church law, and the relations between the state and the working class. Leo's most important statement on social questions was called *Rerum Novarum* (1891).

Pius X. The papacy of Saint Pius X, which lasted from 1903 to 1914, featured the most impressive reform activity since the Council of Trent in the 1500's. Reforms were made in such areas as liturgy, the reception of Holy Communion, seminary education, and church law.

However, Pius vigorously opposed *Modernism,* a movement that began in the late 1800's among Catholic intellectuals in several European countries. Modernists desired to bring Catholic thought into what they felt was a closer relation to the knowledge and outlook of the time. A number of church leaders believed that Modernism challenged important Catholic teachings. Some other Catholics believed that the Modernists raised valid issues. Pius formally condemned Modernism, but such Modernist issues as Biblical scholarship were discussed in the 1960's at Vatican Council II.

During the 1920's and 1930's, the church made *concordats* (agreements) with many nations to guarantee its freedom and its spiritual authority over Catholics in the countries involved. During this period, the church also updated its worldwide missionary activities. Meanwhile, many clergy and laity made significant contributions to learning and scholarship, especially in the areas of Bible and church history.

Facing opposition. Throughout most of the 1900's, the church faced hostility from European dictatorships. During the 1920's and 1930's, dictatorships in Germany, Italy, and the Soviet Union often opposed the church. After World War II (1939-1945), the church faced persecution in the Communist countries of Eastern Europe. In the 1940's and 1950's, Pope Pius XII worked constantly to preserve the religious freedom of Catholics living under dictatorships. Pius's encyclicals on the liturgy and other topics prepared the way for the great reforms of Vatican Council II.

Vatican Council II. Pope John XXIII succeeded Pius in 1958. John called Vatican Council II, which met from 1962 to 1965. The council marked a turning point in the history of the Roman Catholic Church. The council issued 16 documents that tried to give a deeper understanding of the church and its doctrines and help the church serve the needs of the modern world. These documents led to a number of reforms. These major reforms included celebration of the liturgy in the language of the people rather than in Latin, a renewed emphasis on the importance of Bible reading and study, and an encouragement of active participation of the laity in the life of the church. The council also involved the church more fully in the *ecumenical movement* to unite all Christians.

Paul VI, who succeeded John XXIII in 1963, guided the council to its completion. He led the church through

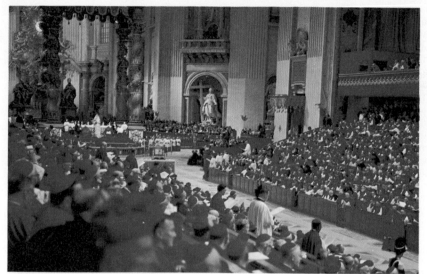

Vatican Council II marked a turning point in the history of the Roman Catholic Church. Church leaders met in Rome from 1962 to 1965. The meeting led to a number of reforms, including worship services in the language of the people instead of in Latin.

the turmoil of the late 1960's, when much in society as well as the church was undergoing radical change.

Paul disheartened liberals by reaffirming the church's traditional teaching on sexual morality in his 1968 encyclical *Humanae Vitae.* But he also promoted the council's liturgical reforms and spoke out strongly on behalf of social justice, especially for developing nations. He directed a reform of the Roman Curia, made the College of Cardinals a more international body, and increased the number of bishops from developing countries. Paul also traveled widely. He visited the United States as well as countries in Latin America, Africa, and Asia. He showed, both in word and deed, that the Roman Catholic Church was no longer a Europe-centered church.

Growth of the church outside Europe

Before the 1500's, the Roman Catholic Church had spread to only a few areas outside Europe. But during the 1500's, due to the activities of Catholic missionaries, the church began to take root throughout the world.

In Africa in the 1500's, the most successful Catholic missions were those in the Portuguese colonies of Angola, the Congo, and Mozambique. Missionaries had begun accompanying Portuguese explorers to Africa by the late 1400's. The missions in Africa eventually declined, however, particularly because of a lack of priests. By the beginning of the 1800's, Christianity had almost completely died out on the continent. In the mid-1800's, many European countries started colonizing Africa, and missionary activity began again. The church eventually spread throughout the continent. Today, Africa has the fastest growing Catholic population in the world.

In Asia, Catholic missionaries were sent to every country that European colonial interests discovered in the 1500's. They were most successful where Spanish control was strong. In the Philippines, missionaries first arrived in 1564. By the 1800's, the majority of the Philippine population had become Catholic.

Missionaries who reached Japan in 1549 established a Roman Catholic community in Kyushu. Japanese rulers later turned away from Western influence, and in 1614

Japanese Catholics were persecuted and killed for their faith. It was not until 1873 that religious freedom was granted once more. A small group of secret Christians survived in spite of the persecution, and the church has many members in southern Japan.

In India, Catholic missionaries, especially the Jesuit Saint Francis Xavier, established churches in Goa and surrounding areas during the early 1500's. Goa was then a Portuguese colony. Today, the largest Indian Roman Catholic communities are in the southwestern states of Goa and Kerala.

In Latin America. Soon after Christopher Columbus arrived in the Western Hemisphere in 1492, Spain and Portugal claimed nearly all of Latin America. Catholic missionaries accompanied Spanish and Portuguese explorers and colonists and converted most Latin American Indians.

Many natives of Latin America accepted Christianity only under pressure from colonial rulers and, in fact, still retained their old religious beliefs. As a result, the church tried to strengthen the faith of the converts. For example, it helped establish universities in Lima, Peru; Mexico City; and elsewhere. The church also recruited clergy from among Latin Americans. But the number of native-born priests proved inadequate for church needs. Catholicism in Latin America thus remained almost totally dependent on the church in Europe.

In the 1800's, the church in Latin America declined after many colonies gained their independence from Spain and Portugal. The church had had close ties with the colonial powers, and many clergymen had opposed the independence movements. As a result, many Latin Americans became hostile toward the church, and it lost much influence in Latin American life.

In Latin America today, there is a renewal of Catholicism, mainly because bishops and priests have become involved in social problems. Following a movement called *liberation theology,* they have established local Christian groups, called *base communities,* for prayer, reflection, and social action. However, Protestantism has won many people away from Catholicism, and anticlerical feeling remains strong in many countries.

In Canada. Canada became a flourishing territory for Catholic missionaries beginning with French colonial rule in 1534. In 1763, Canada became a British colony. Until 1774, Britain restricted the religious freedom of French Canadians, who were Catholics. In 1774, the British Parliament passed the Quebec Act, which restored religious liberties to French Canadians.

Today, the Roman Catholic Church is the country's largest single body of Christians. The church plays a particularly influential role in the province of Quebec, where most of the people are Catholics.

In the United States. Spanish missions covered an immense territory from Florida to northern California. The missions of New France extended from the Great Lakes in the north, through the Mississippi Valley, and south to Louisiana. In the 13 English colonies, along the Atlantic coast, Maryland had the largest concentration of Catholics.

The mainstream of Catholic life emerged from the minority Catholics of the English colonies rather than from the state-favored Catholics of the French and Spanish colonies. Occasionally, the governments of the English colonies passed anti-Catholic legislation. But generally they followed a policy of religious freedom. This freedom and the growing separation of church and state helped make the Catholic Church acceptable to non-Catholics. In 1789, Catholic priests in the United States elected John Carroll as the country's first bishop.

During the 1800's, waves of immigration shaped the nature of the church in the United States. From 1790 to the mid-1860's, more than 2 million Catholics arrived, mainly from Germany and Ireland. From 1870 to 1900, over 3 million more Catholics came, most of them from Italy, Austria-Hungary, and Poland. By 1900, Irish Americans had become the most powerful force in the church in the United States.

Some native-born Americans subjected many Catholic immigrants to a form of prejudice called *nativism.* They questioned the patriotism, morals, and religion of the immigrants. Nativism sometimes led to violence, such as the burning of the Ursuline convent in Charlestown, Massachusetts, in 1834. During the Civil War (1861-1865), Catholics on both sides showed such loyalty and courage that they won increased acceptance in the North and the South.

From 1865 to 1900, several conflicts developed within the church in the United States. Many Catholics believed that Catholic children should be educated in state-supported public schools. Others believed Catholic children should attend schools operated by the church. Some Catholics supported the Knights of Labor, an early labor organization. Others attacked the organization, partly because they claimed its social programs were too extreme. Conflicts sometimes broke out among the various nationalities of Catholic immigrants, especially between German Catholics and Irish Catholics.

In 1887, bishops of the United States established the Catholic University of America in Washington, D.C. They founded the school as the official national Roman Catholic university in the United States.

During the late 1800's, some European Catholic leaders accused American Catholics of a tendency toward nationalism. The Europeans labeled this tendency *Amer-*

icanism and saw in it an attempt to dilute the church's doctrines to make them fit modern culture. American Catholics denied the charges. In 1899, Pope Leo XIII condemned the views of Americanism without naming anyone as holding its principles.

During the 1900's, the church in the United States grew strong. American bishops coordinated their various activities through national meetings and, after Vatican II, established the National Conference of Catholic Bishops. An increasing number of American missionaries went to other lands. Catholic education, from the elementary to the university level, spread throughout the country. The study of liturgy and theology made great strides. Catholics became a powerful political factor, especially in such large cities as Boston, Chicago, and New York. The election in 1960 of John F. Kennedy, a Catholic, as President symbolized the final assimilation of the church into American society.

Today, major concerns of the church in the United States include financial problems and a growing shortage of priests. Because of the shortage, some Catholics argue that priests should be allowed to marry and that women should be eligible to become priests. Others insist such changes would be contrary to the church's tradition.

The church today

John Paul II was elected pope in 1978. A native of Poland, he became the first non-Italian pope since the Renaissance. Many people believe he played an important part in bringing about the collapse of Communism in Eastern Europe and the Soviet Union in the late 1980's and early 1990's.

In 1983, John Paul issued a new code of church law that incorporated the reforms of Vatican Council II into the institutional life of the church. For example, the code called for an active role for lay people in parish and diocesan advisory bodies. In 1992, John Paul announced the publication of a new *Cathechism of the Catholic Church,* a comprehensive statement of Catholic doctrine, liturgical practice, and morality. It is intended primarily for bishops for use in religious education.

John Paul has traveled throughout the world, and he has written extensively. He addressed issues of social justice in his encyclical *Centesiumus Annus* (1991), written on the hundredth anniversary of Leo XIII's *Rerum Novarum* (1891). He discussed principles of Catholic morality in *Veritatis Splendor* (1993) and *Evangelium Vitae* (1995). John Paul wishes to prepare the church for the task of a *new evangelization*—preaching the gospel to a world he considers to be often aimless and adrift. He has encouraged ecumenical dialogue with the Eastern Orthodox Church and has furthered understanding and respect between Catholics and Jews.

Challenges. The Roman Catholic Church as a whole faces a number of challenges. A major challenge is to preserve its strong unity in faith, even as it encourages different cultural expressions of that faith throughout the world. This issue of *inculturation* has received much discussion and debate among Catholics. Another pressing task is to further the full participation of the laity, both men and women, in all areas of the church's life and mission. Finally, the church is aware of a need to find a balance between Roman Catholicism's distinctive

UPI/Bettmann

Pope Paul VI addressed the United Nations General Assembly in New York City in 1965 to plead for world peace. Paul was the first pope to travel widely outside of Europe. In addition to the United States, he visited countries in Latin America, Africa, and Asia.

insistence on the primacy of the pope and the renewed realization that the bishops share leadership responsibilities.   Robert P. Imbelli

Related articles in *World Book* include:

Biographies

See the separate articles **Pope**, with its table: The popes; **Cardinal**, with its tables: Canadian cardinals and American cardinals; and **Saint**, and its list of *Related articles.* See also:

Abelard, Peter
Damien de Veuster, Joseph
Day, Dorothy
De Smet, Pierre Jean
Duns Scotus, John
Eck, Johann
Eckhart, Johannes
Erasmus, Desiderius
Fénelon, François de Salignac
  de la Mothe-
Flanagan, Edward J.
Jansen, Cornelius
Lanfranc
Las Casas, Bartolomé de

Lombard, Peter
Maritain, Jacques
Merton, Thomas
Nicholas of Cusa
Peter the Hermit
Savonarola, Girolamo
Serra, Junípero
Sheen, Fulton J.
Teilhard de Chardin, Pierre
Teresa, Mother
Tetzel, Johann
Thomas à Kempis
Torquemada, Tomás de

Doctrines, beliefs, and ceremonies

Advent
Annunciation
Anointing of the
  sick
Apostles' Creed
Baptism
Bible
Canonization
Communion
Confirmation

Excommunication
Feasts and
  festivals
Immaculate
  Conception
Indulgence
Lent
Liberation
  theology

Liturgy
Mass
Pentecost
Purgatory
Rosary
Sacrament
Transubstantiation
Trinity

Hierarchy

Abbot
Archbishop
Bishop

Cardinal
Friar
Metropolitan

Monk
Nun
Patriarch

Pope
Priest

History

Arianism
Canada, History of
  (The Quebec
  Act)
Counter Reformation
Crusades
Freedom of religion

Gnosticism
Holy Roman Empire
Inquisition
Middle Ages
Mission life in
  America
Missionary
Nicene Councils

Papal States
Reformation
Renaissance
Scholasticism
Trent, Council of
Vatican City
Vatican Council I
Vatican Council II

Organizations

Catholic Conference, United States
Catholic Library Association
Catholic Youth Organization
Knights of Columbus

Religious institutes

For a list of articles on religious institutes, see the *Related articles* at the end of the **Religious life** article.

Other related articles

Abortion
Birth control
Bull
Christianity
Divorce
Eastern Catholic Churches
Eastern Orthodox Churches
Encyclical

Fátima, Our Lady of
Index of Forbidden Books
Jesus Christ
Lourdes
Old Catholic churches
Regina Medal
Sainte-Anne-de-Beaupré
World Council of Churches

Outline

I. Roman Catholic beliefs
II. Worship
III. Church organization
IV. The early church
V. Growth of the church in Europe
VI. Growth of the church outside Europe
VII. The church today

Questions

What event marked the beginning of the Reformation?
What is a *creed?*
Who wrote the first *encyclicals?*
What are some responsibilities of the Roman Curia?
Why did the church in Latin America decline in the 1800's?
Where did *Gallicanism* develop?
What are the two main parts of the *Eucharist?*
How was the *Great Schism* brought to an end?
What reforms resulted from Vatican Council II?
Why did the Eastern and Western churches split?

Additional resources

Collinge, William J. *Historical Dictionary of Catholicism.* Scarecrow, 1997.
McBrien, Richard P. *Catholicism.* Rev. ed. HarperSanFrancisco, 1994.
McBrien, Richard P., and others, eds. *The HarperCollins Encyclopedia of Catholicism.* HarperCollins, 1995.
New Catholic Encyclopedia. McGraw, 1967-. Multivolume work.

Roman Empire. See Rome, Ancient.
Roman Forum. See Forum, Roman.
Roman gods. See Mythology.
Roman law. See Law (Ancient Roman law); **Justinian I; Rome, Ancient** (The law).
Roman mythology. See Mythology.
Roman numerals are symbols that stand for numbers. All Roman numerals are written using seven basic symbols, either alone or in combination. These seven symbols are I (1), V (5), X (10), L (50), C (100), D (500), and M (1,000).

Roman numerals from 1 to 1,000,000

1	I		50		L
2	II		60		LX
3	III		70		LXX
4	IIII or IV		80		LXXX
5	V		90		LXXXX or XC
6	VI		100		C
7	VII		200		CC
8	VIII		300		CCC
9	VIIII or IX		400		CCCC or CD
10	X		500		D
11	XI		600		DC
12	XII		700		DCC
13	XIII		800		DCCC
14	XIIII or XIV		900		DCCCC or CM
15	XV		1,000		M
16	XVI		2,000		MM
17	XVII		3,000		MMM
18	XVIII		4,000		MMMM or M$\overline{\text{V}}$
19	XVIIII or XIX or IXX		5,000		$\overline{\text{V}}$
			10,000		$\overline{\text{X}}$
20	XX		25,000		$\overline{\text{XXV}}$
30	XXX		50,000		$\overline{\text{L}}$
40	XXXX or XL		100,000		$\overline{\text{C}}$
			500,000		$\overline{\text{D}}$
			1,000,000		$\overline{\text{M}}$

S. H. and D. H. Cavanaugh, Robert Harding Picture Library Ltd.

Emperor Hadrian's wall, built across northern England in the A.D. 120's, consisted of fortified sites joined together by a great wall. The ruins in some places are still 5 to 6 feet (1.5 to 1.8 meters) high and wide enough to walk on.

Roman numerals are written from left to right, using the principle of addition in most cases. A person first writes the thousands, then the hundreds, then the tens, and finally the units. To write 2,763, first write MM (2,000), then DCC (500+200=700), next LX (50+10=60), then III (3). The number 2,763 appears as MMDCCLXIII. A bar is sometimes placed over a Roman numeral to multiply it by 1,000. For example, 5,000 appears as $\overline{\text{V}}$.

In Roman numerals, a smaller numeral appearing before a larger numeral indicates that the smaller numeral is subtracted from the larger one. This principle is generally used for 4's and 9's. Thus, 4 usually appears as IV (5 minus 1), and 9 usually appears as IX (10 minus 1). The principle is usually applied to any number beginning with 4 or 9, such as 40 (XL) and 90 (XC). However, the principle of addition can also be used in writing such numbers. For example, 400 can be written as CCCC instead of CD.

The ancient Romans invented Roman numerals. But the early Roman system of about 500 B.C. differed from the system people commonly use today. For example, the Romans always wrote 4 as IIII and 9 as VIIII. In addition, they had different symbols for numbers that can be divided by 1,000.

People throughout Europe used Roman numerals until the A.D. 1500's. They found it easy to add and subtract using Roman numerals but difficult to perform other calculations. In the late 1500's, people began using Arabic numerals instead. Today, the Roman system is used to number the faces of clocks, to list topics in outlines, and to record dates on monuments and public buildings.   Karen Connors Fuson

See also **Arabic numerals; Numeration systems** (History).

Roman Republic. See Rome, Ancient (Government; History).

Roman walls were barriers that the Romans built where no natural territorial boundaries existed. By A.D. 100, they had built a line of walls in what is now Romania and Germany. They later built Hadrian's Wall and the Antonine Wall along the northern edge of the province

of Britain. These walls were named for two Roman emperors, Hadrian and Antoninus Pius, and are the most famous Roman walls. The walls discouraged raids and revolts. But their main purpose was to remind the tribes on both sides that the Romans were masters. The walls also made it easier for the Romans to control trade and to collect taxes.

Hadrian's Wall was built in the A.D. 120's. It extended 73 miles (117 kilometers), from the mouth of the Tyne River to the Solway Firth. Parts still stand. The wall was about 10 feet (3 meters) wide at its base and 20 feet (6 meters) high. For half its length, it was all stone. The rest was stone and turf. Forts stood about 1 mile (1.6 kilometers) apart along the wall, with watch towers every $\frac{1}{3}$ mile (0.5 kilometer). A ditch lay in front of it, with a wider ditch 10 feet (3 meters) deep behind it.

The Antonine Wall was built in the A.D. 140's, north of Hadrian's Wall. It was a simpler wall, made of turf, and it stretched for 37 miles (60 kilometers).

The Romans allowed Hadrian's Wall to decay until 211, when they could no longer defend the Antonine Wall. Then they rebuilt Hadrian's Wall carefully. They rebuilt it twice more in the 300's, and defended it until nearly 400.   Arthur M. Eckstein

Romance is a long work of fiction that is less realistic than a novel. Most novelists try to present life realistically. Writers of romance concentrate on telling an entertaining story. Many use fantastic and supernatural plots and characters.

The meaning of the term *romance* has changed many times since the first romances appeared in Greece almost 2,000 years ago. In ancient Greek literature, most fiction dealt with either love or war. War stories were called epics, and love stories were called romances. The word *romance* is still used for a love story.

By about the 1200's, most Western Europeans spoke a *Romance language* (language based on Latin), such as French, Italian, or Spanish. All fiction written in Romance languages was called romance. In most Romance languages today, the word for *romance* refers to long prose fiction. The word for *novel* means short prose fiction. English is the only language in which the words *novel* and *romance* distinguish between realistic and unrealistic fiction.

The first important romance was *Daphnis and Chloë,* (A.D. 100's or 200's) by a Greek named Longus. The greatest romances were written by medieval authors from the 1100's to the 1400's. Often written in verse, these romances mingle knightly combat, adventure, and courtship. Many describe the adventures of King Arthur and his knights of the Round Table. Others tell about the ancient conqueror Alexander the Great; the Spanish hero The Cid; and the emperor Charlemagne and his devoted knight, Roland.

The romance flourished again during the late 1700's and 1800's. In England, Horace Walpole's *The Castle of Otranto* (1764) began a trend for romances that emphasized mystery, terror, and the supernatural. These romances became known as *Gothic novels.* In the United States, the famous author Nathaniel Hawthorne insisted that he wrote romances, not novels. Elements of romance continue to appear in popular novels about courtship as well as in novels about the American frontier, in Western films, and in science fiction.

Paul Strohm

Related articles in *World Book* include:

Amadís of Gaul	Hawthorne, Nathaniel
French literature (Romances)	Novel (Ancient Greek and Roman narratives)
Gawain, Sir	Round Table
Gothic novel	

Romance languages are a group of languages that developed from Latin and are spoken in places that were once part of the Roman Empire. They include French, Italian, Portuguese, Romanian, and Spanish. Other Romance languages are Catalan of northeastern Spain and Provençal of southeastern France. The group also includes the Sardinian dialect and Rhaeto-Romanic dialects from certain parts of Switzerland and the Tyrol region of western Austria and northern Italy.

Latin was the official language of the Roman Empire. The word *romance* comes from a Latin adverb that referred to speakers of Latin who were said to "fabulare romanice," which means "to speak in the Roman way." These people spoke one of two forms—*classical* Latin or *vernacular* Latin. The educated classes spoke classical Latin. The common people spoke vernacular Latin. Romance languages developed from vernacular Latin spoken in certain conquered European countries that became Roman provinces. This vernacular Latin adopted words and features of pronunciation from the languages of the conquered countries. For example, the vernacular Latin word *caballus* (horse) became *cheval* in French, *cavallo* in Italian, and *caballo* in Spanish.

The Romance languages developed from the many dialects of vernacular Latin over several centuries. The earliest evidence of Romance languages appeared in the 800's. By the late 1200's, much literature was written in the Romance languages. So many literary works centered on the topic of love that they became known as *romances.* The word *romance* meaning *an affair of the heart* comes from this usage. Richard P. Kinkade

Related articles in *World Book* include:

French language	Portuguese language
Italian language	Romance
Latin language	Spanish language

Giraudon/Art Resource

A typical Romanesque church had thick walls and heavy curved arches. Notre-Dame-la-Grande (1130-1145) in Poitiers, France, is noted for its richly decorated west front.

Romanesque architecture was the prevailing architectural movement in western Europe from about A.D. 800 to the 1100's. Romanesque architecture developed into a number of regional styles, including Aquitaine, Brittany, Burgundy, Île-de-France, Norman, and Provence. Romanesque buildings were frequently isolated from the few developed cities of the period. The massive character of these buildings was a response to the demands for security and defense that such locations required.

The Romanesque style was especially well developed in churches and monastic structures. The plan of a typical Romanesque church was in the shape of a *Latin cross*—that is, a cross with a vertical arm and a shorter horizontal crosspiece above the center. The roof over the *nave* (main gathering area) consisted of vaults of stone constructed on the principle of the arch. Side aisles flanked the nave. Large columns called *piers* supported the roof vaults. Round arches were built in openings in the walls and between the piers. The openings and piers were decorated with stone sculpture and carvings depicting Biblical scenes and people. Walls of the church were painted in fresco and also portrayed religious subjects.

By the mid-1100's, the Romanesque style had evolved into Gothic architecture. The chief reasons for the evolution included less need for defensive buildings and a desire to celebrate Christianity in lighter and higher churches. J. William Rudd

See also **Architecture** (Romanesque architecture; pictures); **Norman architecture; Leaning Tower of Pisa.**

Additional resources

Conant, Kenneth J. *Carolingian and Romanesque Architecture: 800-1200.* 4th ed. 1959. Reprint. Yale, 1992.

Erlande-Brandenburg, Alain. *The Cathedral.* Cambridge, 1994.

Kubach, Hans E. *Romanesque Architecture.* 1975. Reprint. Rizzoli, 1988.

Yarwood, Doreen. *The Architecture of Europe, Vol. II: The Middle Ages 650-1550.* Batsford, 1992.

William Gelman, FPG

Farm villages are scattered throughout the Romanian countryside. Rich farmland covers about 60 percent of Romania, and agriculture employs many of the nation's people.

Romania

Romania, also spelled *Rumania,* is a country in eastern Europe. The country was part of the Roman Empire during ancient times, and its name means *land of the Romans.* The Romanian people are the only Eastern Europeans who trace their ancestry and language back to the ancient Romans. Bucharest is Romania's capital and largest city.

Romania is located west of the Black Sea and north of the Balkan Peninsula, Europe's southeastern tip. A long string of mountains curves through the northern and central parts of Romania. Breathtaking scenery, hiking trails, and ski and vacation resorts make the mountains a favorite recreation area. Picturesque farm villages dot fertile flatlands around the mountains. In addition, Romania's warm, sunny east coast—which borders the Black Sea—has dozens of sandy beaches and a huge wildlife preserve.

The colorful folk culture of Romania's rural people adds to the beauty and charm of the country. Each year, these people hold festivals at which they dance to the lively sounds of Romanian folk music. This music was influenced by the melodies of music played by Gypsies, nomads who once wandered through Romania by the thousands.

Romania has a wealth of natural resources, including fertile soil, mineral deposits, and vast forests. Even so, it has always been one of Europe's least developed nations. Foreign nations controlled the country through much of its history and did little to develop its economy. Romania also suffered from an overdependence on one economic activity, agriculture.

Communists took over Romania's government in the 1940's. At first, they ran the country according to the wishes of the Soviet Union, which was Europe's strongest Communist nation. However, beginning in the 1960's,

Romania's Communists succeeded in reducing Soviet control of the country. In addition, they adopted their own domestic policies. Chief among these policies was a program to expand industry. As industry grew, many people left rural areas to find jobs in cities. The industrial program changed Romania from an agricultural country to an industrial country. However, Romania still remains poor by European standards.

In the late 1980's, the Soviet Union made reforms toward giving its people more freedom. As a result, reform movements increased in Romania and other European Communist countries. In late 1989, Romanians revolted against the dictatorship of Nicolae Ceauşescu, Romania's president and Communist Party leader.

Facts in brief

Capital: Bucharest.
Official language: Romanian.
Official name: Republica România (Republic of Romania).
Area: 92,043 sq. mi. (238,391 km²). *Greatest distances*—east-west, about 450 mi. (724 km); north-south, about 320 mi. (515 km). *Coastline*—130 mi. (209 km).
Elevation: *Highest*—Mount Moldoveanu, 8,343 ft. (2,543 m) above sea level. *Lowest*—sea level.
Population: *Estimated 2000 population*—22,607,000; density, 246 persons per sq. mi. (95 per km²); distribution, 55 percent urban, 45 percent rural. *1992 census*—22,810,035.
Chief products: *Agriculture*—corn, potatoes, wheat, milk, sugar beets, grapes, wool. *Manufacturing*—machinery, cement, iron and steel, petroleum products, processed foods, clothing and shoes, wood products. *Mining*—petroleum, natural gas, coal.
National anthem: "Deşteapta-te, Române" ("Romanian, Arise").
Money: *Basic unit*—leu. One hundred bani equal one leu.

William Gelman, Artstreet

The Palace of the Republic in Bucharest, the capital of Romania, is part of a complex of government buildings. It houses government offices and an art museum.

Symbols of Romania. Romania's flag has stripes of blue, yellow, and red. The three stripes represent Romania's national colors. The eagle on Romania's coat of arms, *right*, is a symbol of the region of Walachia. The other symbols on the coat of arms represent each of Romania's five other regions.

Ceaușescu was executed, and a temporary government was set up. Free multiparty elections have been held since 1990.

Government

The Communist Party became Romania's ruling political party in the 1940's. It exerted its power over the country's entire governmental structure. Only a small percentage of Romania's people belonged to the Communist Party. However, Communist leaders held important positions at all levels of government and in major nongovernmental organizations. The general secretary, who headed the Communist Party, had the authority of a dictator.

The Communist Party leaders made the country's laws and planned every detail of its economy. They also controlled Romania's police and armed forces, and therefore had power over the lives of the people.

Romania's Constitution guaranteed such rights as freedom of speech, freedom of the press, and freedom of religion. However, the Communists interpreted the Constitution to mean that they could limit these rights in order to maintain power.

In December 1989, Romanians revolted and overthrew the Communist government. Free multiparty elections to select a president and members of a national legislature were held in mid-1990. Romania adopted a new Constitution in late 1991.

National government. Romania's top government official is the president, who is elected by the people. The president appoints a prime minister, who selects a Cabinet to help carry out the operations of government. The people elect a 486-member two-house legislature. It consists of the 143-member Senate and the 343-member Chamber of Deputies.

Political parties. Romania has about 50 political parties. The largest of these parties is the Democratic Convention of Romania. The country's other political parties include the Social Democratic Party of Romania, the Social Democratic Union, the Hungarian Democratic Union of Romania, the Greater Romania Party, and the Party of Romanian National Unity.

Local government. Romania is divided into 40 counties and 1 special district, the city of Bucharest. Each unit has its own local government, as do cities, towns, and *communes* (rural areas) within the counties.

Courts. The Supreme Court is Romania's highest court. It hears appeals from the country's lower courts. The city of Bucharest and each of Romania's 40 counties have a county court and a variety of lower courts.

Armed forces. Romania's regular army, navy, and air force have a total of about 200,000 men. Men 18 years old may be drafted, usually for 16 months.

People

Ancestry. More than 85 percent of Romania's people are Romanians by ancestry. The Romanians are descended from the Dacians, Romans, and such tribes as the Goths, Huns, and Slavs. The Dacians lived in what is now Romania as early as the 300's B.C. The Romans occupied the country in the A.D. 100's and 200's, and the tribes began living there after the Romans left.

Hungarians form the largest minority group in Romania, making up about 8 percent of the population. Germans make up about 2 percent. Smaller groups include Gypsies, Jews, Turks, and Ukrainians.

Language. Romanian is the nation's official language and is spoken by almost all the people. Many of Romania's Germans and Hungarians prefer to speak their own ethnic languages among themselves.

Romanian developed from Latin, the language of the

WORLD BOOK map

Romania lies in eastern Europe. It is bordered by Ukraine, Moldova, the Black Sea, Bulgaria, Yugoslavia, and Hungary.

Romans who ruled the country in ancient times. Romanian is the only Eastern European language that comes from Latin. As a result, it is much different from all the other languages that are spoken in the region. Romanian most closely resembles French, Italian, Portuguese, and Spanish. These Western European languages also developed from Latin.

Way of life. The Romanian people have one of the lowest living standards in Europe. Almost all of the workers in Romania earn enough to pay for their families' food, clothing, and shelter, and have a little left over for recreation. But few Romanians can afford many luxury items. For example, only about 15 per cent of the people own a television set, and fewer than 2 per cent own an automobile.

Most rural Romanians live in two- or three-room wooden cottages. The houses are plain and simple, but many people beautify them with a variety of art objects that they make themselves. These objects include wall rugs with skillfully woven patterns, colorfully decorated plates, and woodcarvings on furniture, building frames, and fences.

Festivals held to celebrate such things as weddings, christenings, and holidays are the most important part of social life in rural Romania. At the festivals, the people wear colorful costumes, and they play and dance to Romanian folk music.

Romania's cities present a striking contrast between the old and the new. Many city buildings are hundreds of years old. Others are modern structures built since industrialization began in the 1960's. Population growth has caused a housing shortage in the cities. Most city people live in crowded apartments.

Both old Romanian traditions and modern, Western

Kurt Scholz, © ZEFA from Publix

Crowds of vacationers enjoy the sandy beaches and sunny weather along Romania's Black Sea coast. Fashionable resort hotels line the streets in this popular recreation area.

culture are part of city life. Many people enjoy going to restaurants and to concert halls where orchestras play Romanian folk music. They also visit exhibits of rural Romanian folk art that the government sets up in cities. But many people—especially the young—like rock music and Western movies, plays, and books.

Before the 1989 revolt, the lives of the Romanian people were affected by the Communist government in many ways. The government decided what kind of jobs students should prepare for in school. It owned or managed most of the country's businesses and farms, and so almost all the people worked for the government. Romanians could not change their jobs or leave the country without the government's permission. After the revolution, the non-Communist government lifted most of these restrictions.

Recreation. Romanians have two favorite vacation spots—the mountains and the Black Sea coast. The mountains offer skiing, hiking, mountain climbing, and beautiful scenery. Romanians go to the Black Sea coast to swim and to relax in the sun. Soccer is the most popular spectator sport in Romania.

Food and drink. Romanians enjoy grilled meats, including *mititei* (meat balls shaped like cylinders) and *patricieni* (sausages). Another favorite food in Romania is *mamaliga,* a bread or mush made from corn meal, which can be cooked and served in many ways. Wine and a plum brandy called *tzuica* are popular drinks in Romania.

Education. Romanian law requires children from 6 to 16 to attend school. Elementary school lasts eight years. Students then take tests that are prepared by the government to determine what kind of course they will study in secondary school. About half the students are assigned to vocational courses. These students learn the basic skills that are needed for work on farms or in factories. Most of the other students take courses that train them in advanced technical skills, in the arts, or in teach-

Kurt Scholz, © ZEFA from Publix

Bucharest is Romania's capital and largest city. Many parts of the city have wide boulevards and modern buildings constructed since the 1960's. Other sections are centuries old.

James Theologos, Keystone

Colorful festivals are held by rural Romanians to celebrate holidays, weddings, and other occasions. Bright costumes and lively folk dances are traditional features of such celebrations.

ing. The top elementary school graduates—about 5 percent of the total—are assigned to courses that prepare them for college.

Romania has seven universities. The largest Romanian university is in Bucharest.

Religion. About three-fourths of all Romanians belong to the Romanian Orthodox Church, an Eastern Orthodox Church. About 7 percent of the people—chiefly Hungarians—are Roman Catholics. Other faiths that are practiced in Romania include Islam, Judaism, and various forms of Protestantism.

In order to avoid popular protests, the prerevolution Communists allowed churches to operate as long as the churches avoided political activities. After the revolution, the churches were granted complete religious freedom.

The arts. Romania's rural culture has had a strong influence on the country's professional art. The lives and customs of rural Romanians have long been favorite topics of Romanian writers. The works of many composers show the influence of Romanian folk music. The best-known Romanian paintings are medieval works that appear on the outside walls of churches. These works were done outside, rather than inside, to remind peasants passing by of their faith.

In the 1950's, the government forced Romanian artists to use their works to promote Communism. Romanian art grew dull from a lack of self-expression. However, since the 1960's, the government has allowed artists more freedom, and art has flourished in Romania. Old Romanian themes and styles are still popular. But many artists have turned to modern styles, and deal with such themes as humanity's relation to the universe.

The composer Georges Enesco, the sculptor Constantin Brancusi, and the playwright Eugène Ionesco probably rank as the best-known Romanian-born artists. But each man did most of his work in France. Enesco's masterpieces, called *Romanian Rhapsodies,* are based on

Romanian folk music. Some of Brancusi's sculptures contain elements of Romanian folk art. Ionesco's plays show some influence of his youth in Romania before the outbreak of World War II in 1939.

Land and climate

Romania is bordered on the north and northeast by Moldova, on the east by Ukraine, on the west by Hungary and Yugoslavia, and on the south by Bulgaria. The country has only 130 miles (209 kilometers) of coastline, where it borders the Black Sea in the southeast.

Surface features. A series of mountain ranges curves through northern and central Romania, forming a circular pattern. The mountains surround a vast flatland known as the Transylvanian Plateau. The mountains are, in turn, surrounded by plains on the east, south, and west.

Romania's mountains are all part of the Carpathian Mountain System. The eastern part of the Carpathian range stretches from the northern border to the center of the country. The Southern Carpathians, or Transylvanian Alps, extend westward from the Moldavian range. The Bihor Mountains and other ranges make up the Western Carpathians, which run through western Romania.

Romania's mountains are neither extremely high nor steep, and several passes cut through them. As a result, they are not major barriers to transportation. Most of them are from 3,000 to 6,000 feet (910 to 1,800 meters) high. Mount Moldoveanu, in the Southern Carpathians, is Romania's highest mountain. It rises 8,343 feet (2,543 meters).

The Transylvanian Plateau lies about 1,200 feet (366 meters) above sea level, and Romania's plains lie at or

James Theologos, Keystone

Religious paintings decorate the outside walls of many Romanian churches. This form of art developed in Romania during the 1500's to remind passers-by of their religious faith.

near sea level. These flatlands have the country's best farmland and most of its cities and towns. Vast forests cover parts of the Transylvanian Plateau and the mountains.

Romania has many rivers. The longest and most important one by far is the Danube River. It flows about 900 miles (1,400 kilometers) through Romania. Most of the way, it flows west to east along the southern border. The Danube turns northward near the Black Sea, then eastward again, and empties into the sea. Most of Romania's other major rivers flow into the Danube from the north. They include, from west to east, the Jiu, Oltul, Argeş, Ialomiţa, Siretul, and Prut.

Romania has about 2,500 lakes. Most of them are small. The biggest lakes lie near the Danube. Numerous tiny lakes add beauty to Romania's mountains.

Land regions. Romania can be divided into six land regions. They are Transylvania, Bukovina, Moldavia, Walachia, Banat, and Dobruja.

Transylvania is the country's largest and most varied region. It extends throughout central and northwestern Romania, and includes most of the country's mountains, the Transylvanian Plateau, and the northwestern plain. The plateau and plain have good soil for farming. The plateau and the mountains yield valuable forest products and minerals. The beauty of the mountains and their ski slopes and other recreation facilities make them a favorite vacation area. Several cities have grown up in Transylvania because of its rich resources.

Bukovina, northeast of Transylvania, is a thickly forested region in the Moldavian Carpathian Mountains. It

has ski slopes and lovely scenery. The people of Bukovina live in small villages in the valleys.

Moldavia, Walachia, and Banat. Moldavia, in northeastern Romania, extends from Transylvania to the Prut River along the border with Moldova. Walachia, in the south, stretches from the southernmost mountains to the Danube. Banat, in western Romania, extends from the western mountains to Yugoslavia and Hungary. All of these regions have a similar physical makeup. The land in each descends from mountains near Transylvania, to hills, and then to plains. These plains are Romania's best farmland. Walachia has more people than any other Romanian region, chiefly because Bucharest is there. Banat has several cities, but Moldavia has few.

Dobruja is a small plain between the northern course of the Danube River and the Black Sea. The Danube Delta covers northeastern Dobruja. This marshy area has an amazing variety of wildlife. Sturgeon, the source of caviar, and numerous other kinds of fish live in its waters. About 300 species of birds, including the pelican, also live in the delta. Farmland covers most of southern Dobruja. The Danube-Black Sea Canal flows through this area. Completed in 1984, it provides a shortcut from the Danube to the Black Sea. Sandy beaches and beautiful seaside resorts line Dobruja's Black Sea coast. Constanţa, Romania's major port city, is on the coast.

Climate. Romania has hot, sunny summers and cold, cloudy winters. The average July temperature is 70 °F (21 °C), and the average January temperature is 30 °F (−1 °C). Romania's plains are warmer than its mountain areas. *Precipitation* (rain, melted snow, and other forms

Scholz, Bavaria

The land region of Walachia in southern Romania includes mountains, rolling hills, and some of the country's best farmland. The village of Bran, *left,* is located near Brasov, in the Transylvanian Alps.

Romania

WORLD BOOK map

▬ International boundary	▬ Railroad	• Other city or town
▬ Expressway	▬ Canal	+ Elevation above sea level
▬ Road	⊛ National capital	− Dam

Romania map index

Cities and towns

Aiud ....31,894 ..C 3
Alba Iulia ......71,168 ..C 3
Alexandria .....58,478 ..F 4
Arad ....190,114 ..C 1
Bacău ....205,029 ..C 5
Baia Mare ....149,205 ..B 3
Băilești ....22,344 ..F 3
Balș ....24,640 ..E 3
Bîrlad ....77,518 ..C 6
Bistrița ....87,710 ..B 4
Blaj ....22,425 ..C 3
Bocșa ....19,152 ..D 1
Botoșani .....126,145 ..A 5
Brad ....18,861 ..C 2
Brăila ....234,110 ..D 6
Brașov ....323,736 ..D 4
Breaza ....19,329 ..D 5
Bucharest ..2,067,545 ..E 5
          *2,350,984 ..E 5
Buftea ....19,399 ..E 5
Buhuși ....21,621 ..C 5
Buzău ....148,087 ..D 5
Calafat ....20,445 ..F 2
Călărași ....76,952 ..E 6
Caracal ....39,130 ..F 3
Caransebeș ....31,985 ..D 2
Carei ....26,372 ..A 2
Cîmpia
  Turzii ......29,307 ..C 3

Cîmpina ......41,554 ..D 5
Cîmpulung ....44,125 ..D 4
Cîmpulung
  Moldo-
  venesc .....22,143 ..B 4
Cisnădie ....17,807 ..D 3
Cluj-Napoca ..328,602 ..B 3
Comănești .....25,020 ..C 5
Constanța ....350,581 ..E 7
Corabia ....22,386 ..F 4
Craiova ....303,959 ..E 3
Curtea
  de Argeș ....35,824 ..D 4
Dej ....41,216 ..B 3
Deva ....78,438 ..D 2
Dorohoi ....33,739 ..A 5
Drăgășani .....22,126 ..E 4
Drobeta-
  Turnu
  Severin ....115,259 ..E 2
Făgăraș ....44,931 ..D 4
Fălticeni ......32,807 ..B 5
Fetești ....35,374 ..E 6
Focșani ......101,335 ..D 6
Galați ....326,141 ..D 6
Gheorgheni ....21,433 ..C 4
Gherla ....26,277 ..B 3
Giurgiu ....74,191 ..F 5
Hunedoara .....81,337 ..D 2
Huși ....32,673 ..C 6
Iași ....344,425 ..B 6

Lipova ....12,059 ..C 2
Luduș ....18,789 ..C 3
Lugoj ....50,939 ..D 2
Lupeni ....32,853 ..D 3
Mangalia ......43,960 ..F 7
Marghita ......19,071 ..B 2
Medgidia ......46,657 ..E 7
Mediaș ....64,484 ..C 4
Miercurea-
  Ciuc ....46,228 ..C 5
Moldova Nouă ..16,874 ..E 2
Odorheiu
  Secuiesc ....39,959 ..C 4
Oltenița ....31,821 ..F 5
Onești ....58,810 ..C 5
Oradea ....222,741 ..B 2
Orăștie ....24,174 ..D 3
Petrila ....29,302 ..D 3
Petroșani ......52,390 ..D 3
Piatra Neamț ..123,360 ..B 5
Pitești ....179,337 ..E 4
Ploiești ......252,715 ..E 5
Rădăuți ....31,074 ..A 5
Reghin ....39,240 ..B 4
Reșița ....96,918 ..D 2
Rîmnicu Sărat ..41,405 ..D 5
Rîmnicu
  Vîlcea ......113,624 ..D 3
Roman ....80,328 ..B 5
Roșiori de
  Vede ....37,640 ..F 4

Săcele ....30,226 ..D 5
Salonta ....20,660 ..B 2
Satu Mare ....131,987 ..A 3
Sebeș ....29,754 ..C 3
Sibiu ....169,656 ..D 3
Sighetul
  Marmației ...44,185 ..A 3
Sighișoara .....36,170 ..C 4
Slatina ....85,168 ..E 3
Slobozia ....56,048 ..E 6
Suceava ....114,462 ..B 5
Tecuci ....46,825 ..D 6
Timișoara .....334,115 ..D 1
Tîrgoviște .....98,117 ..E 4
Tîrgu Jiu ......98,238 ..D 3
Tîrgu Mureș ...164,445 ..C 4
Tîrgu Neamț ...22,282 ..B 5
Tîrnăveni ......30,520 ..C 4
Toplița ....17,212 ..B 4
Tulcea ....97,904 ..D 7
Turda ....61,200 ..C 3
Turnu
  Măgurele ....36,966 ..F 4
Urziceni ....19,303 ..E 5
Vaslui ....80,614 ..C 6
Vatra Dornei ...18,488 ..B 4
Vișeu de Sus ...19,167 ..A 4
Vulcan ....34,524 ..D 3
Zalău ....68,404 ..B 3
Zărnești ....26,319 ..D 4
Zimnicea ....17,128 ..F 4

Physical features

Argeș River ....E 4
Bega Canal ....D 1
Bihor Mountains ....C 2
Bîrlad River ....C 6
Bistrița River ....B 5
Black Sea ....E 7
Buzău River ....D 6
Calimani Mountains .....B 4
Carpathian Mountains ...B 4
Codru Mountains ....C 2
Crișul Alb River ....C 2
Crișul Repede River .....B 2
Danube River ....E 6
Dîmbovița River ....E 4
Harghita Mountains .....C 4
Ialomița River ....E 5
Jiu River ....E 3
Lake Razelm ....E 7
Lake Sinoe ....E 7
Moldova River ....B 5
Moldoveanu (mtn.) ......D 4
Mureș River ....C 4
Olt River ....F 4
Prut River ....B 6
Rodnei Mountains ....B 4
Siret River ....A 5
Someș River ....B 3
Southern Carpathian
  Mountains ....D 3

*Population of metropolitan area, including suburbs.
Source: 1992 census.

Land regions of Romania

The map below shows the six land regions of Romania: Transylvania, Bukovina, Moldavia, Dobruja, Walachia, and Banat.

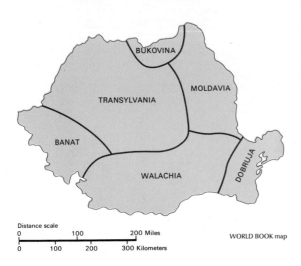

Distance scale

WORLD BOOK map

of moisture) ranges from about 40 inches (100 centimeters) yearly in some mountain areas to less than 20 inches (50 centimeters) on the plains.

Economy

Before the 1960's, Romania's economy was based on agriculture. But since then, the government has built many new factories and power plants and taken other steps to increase industry in the country. Under the Communist government, industry—including manufacturing, mining, and construction—passed agriculture as the leading producer of income in Romania. Industry also passed agriculture as the leading employer.

Under the Communists, the national government controlled Romania's economy. It owned the country's factories, mines, and banks, and owned or controlled most of its farms. It decided how much of each product should be produced, and it set the price of most goods. After the 1989 revolution, the non-Communist government loosened government control of the economy and allowed some private enterprise. In mid-1992, the government took a large step toward creating a free enterprise economy. It began selling shares in state-owned companies and distributing vouchers that could be exchanged for shares in other state-owned businesses. During the mid-1990's, the government also began to sell some state-owned companies. In addition, many new private businesses were set up.

Natural resources. About 60 percent of Romania's land is fertile cropland and rich pastureland. Another 25 percent has forests that provide timber. The mountains and plateau have valuable mineral deposits. Natural gas and petroleum rank as Romania's most important mineral products. Other important minerals include bauxite, coal, copper, gold, iron ore, lead, silver, and zinc.

Industry. Romania had very little industry when the Communists took over. To get industry started, the Communists stressed the production of *capital goods.* Capital goods include raw materials needed for industry,

buildings in which industrial work is done, machines and tools needed to do the work, and power plants that supply energy for the work. Production of *consumer goods* (those manufactured for use by people) lags far behind production of capital goods.

The manufacture of machinery for farms, factories, and mines is the leading industrial activity. Romania also produces cement and other construction materials, iron and steel, petroleum products, and wood products. Food processing and the manufacture of clothing and shoes are the only consumer goods activities among the top industries in Romania. Bucharest is the chief industrial center. Other industrial centers include Brașov, Cluj-Napoca, Ploiești, and Timișoara.

Services. Trade and transportation are the leading employers among service industries in Romania. These industries are responsible for getting the country's agricultural and industrial products from producers to buyers. Other service activities include education, health care, housing, and national defense.

Agriculture. Crops account for about three-fifths of the value of Romania's agricultural products, and livestock for about two-fifths. Grains, especially corn and wheat, are the leading crops. Other crops include grapes and other fruits, potatoes, and sugar beets. Farmers raise more sheep than any other kind of livestock. They also raise cattle, horses, pigs, and poultry.

In pre-Communist days, almost all of Romania's farmland was privately owned. But the Communist government gradually took control of 90 percent of the land. It created collective farms and state farms. Hundreds of families worked together on each collective farm. The crops and livestock they produced belonged to the whole group. Workers received wages and farm products, and part of the income earned from the sale of the products. Officially, the people owned the collectives. But the government told them what to produce and how to manage the farms. State farms were owned and operated by the government. The farmers received wages. The government provided much modern farm equipment for the state farms. But collective farmers still relied heavily on old-fashioned equipment.

William Gelman, Artstreet

Heavy machinery is Romania's leading manufactured product. Each year, the country's latest agricultural and industrial products are displayed at an exhibition held in Bucharest, *above.*

William Gelman, Black Star

Agriculture employs many Romanians. Although large farms have modern equipment, many smaller farms use old-fashioned methods, as shown here.

After the 1989 revolution, the government passed land-reform laws that allowed some collective farms to be broken up and their land redistributed to farmworkers. Some farmers whose lands had been taken away by the Communists were again able to own their own farms. At first, the land-reform laws did not break up state farms. Many farmers whose land had been incorporated into the state farms were issued shares of stock in new agricultural companies. These companies took the place of state farms. But in the late 1990's, the government began to break up some state farms. Today, about 80 percent of agricultural land is privately owned.

Trade. Industrial machinery, fuels, and chemicals are important exports and imports. Other exports include cement, clothing and shoes, processed foods, and lumber. Iron ore, coal, and cotton are other major imports.

Until the 1960's, Romania carried on about 80 percent of its trade with the Soviet Union and other Communist nations. But in the 1960's—as part of its policy to free itself from Soviet control—the country began expanding its trade with Western European nations and the United States. The Soviet Union broke up in 1991. Today, however, Romania's major trading partners still include countries that made up the former Soviet Union, especially Russia and Ukraine.

Transportation and communication. Trains are Romania's chief means of long-distance travel. Buses provide most of the transportation within cities. Fewer than 2 percent of Romanians own a car. Bucharest has the nation's main airport. The government owns Romania's railroads, bus lines, and major airlines.

About 40 daily newspapers are published in Romania. The government owned most radio and television stations under Communism, but many independent stations were set up in the early 1990's.

History

Romanians trace their history back to the 300's B.C. But Romania did not become an independent, unified country until the mid-1800's. During most of the time in between, various foreign peoples ruled all or part of it.

Early days. Historians do not know when Romania was first settled. But a people called the Dacians were known to be living there by the 300's B.C. The Dacians farmed, mined gold and iron ore, and traded with neighboring peoples. Romania was called *Dacia* during this period.

The Romans, under Emperor Trajan, conquered Dacia in A.D. 106 and made it a province of the Roman Empire. Roman soldiers occupied Dacia, and Roman colonists settled there. The Romans intermarried with the Dacians, who adopted Roman customs and the Latin language. Dacia became known as *Romania* because of the Roman occupation and influence.

Barbarians from the east and north began invading Romania during the A.D. 200's. They forced the Romans to abandon the province in the late 200's. The invasions were to continue off and on until the 1100's. The invaders included Bulgars, Goths, Huns, Magyars, Slavs, and Tatars. These groups, especially the Slavs, intermarried with the Romanians.

Unification movement. The period of invasions slowed the development of Romania into a unified nation. For hundreds of years, various groups fought for control of the region, and no one group gained full control. The first steps toward unification took place between 1250 and 1350. The people of Walachia, a region in southern Romania, gradually united and formed an independent state under a single ruler. The people of Moldavia, in eastern Romania, did the same. A prince ruled each state, and so they were called *principalities*.

Earlier, during the 1000's, Hungary had taken over most of what is now northern Romania. This area, called *Transylvania,* had many Romanian people. But it did not become part of Romania until the 1900's.

Ottoman rule. The independence of the principalities was short-lived. The Ottomans of Asia Minor (now Turkey) swept into Europe in the mid-1400's. They conquered Walachia in 1476 and Moldavia in 1504. The Ottoman Empire ruled these lands almost continuously for over 300 years. The peasants in the principalities—who made up most of the population—led hard lives even before the Ottomans took over. They were poor farmers, but they had to pay high taxes to the ruling nobles. Conditions grew worse under the Ottomans, who let Romanian nobles rule in their name, but demanded increased taxes from the peasants for themselves.

The Romanian nobles made several attempts to gain freedom from the Ottoman Empire. As a result, in the early 1700's, the empire sent wealthy Greeks to govern the principalities. These Greeks were called *Phanariots* because they came from the Phanar district of Constantinople (now Istanbul, Turkey). They taxed the peasants far more than ever before and treated them harshly. Phanariot rule lasted until 1821, when a revolt by Romanians forced the Ottomans to remove the Greeks from power. Many scholars believe Romania's peasants never suffered more than they did during the Phanariot period.

Russian control. During the late 1700's, the Ottoman Empire suffered a series of military defeats at the hands of Russia. Little by little, the Ottomans lost parts of their empire. Officially, Ottoman rule of the principalities lasted until 1878. But, in effect, it ended in 1829, when Russian troops occupied the principalities.

Russia drew up a constitution for the principalities in

the early 1830's. The constitution, called *Organic Statutes,* gave governing power in each principality to an assembly of nobles. This marked the beginning of representative government in Romania. Russia's troops withdrew from the principalities in 1834.

The origins of modern Romania. The idea of uniting Moldavia and Walachia existed almost from the time the principalities were founded. The unification movement grew rapidly during the mid-1800's. In 1859, the assemblies of the two principalities elected Prince Alexander John Cuza as their common ruler. In 1861, Moldavia and Walachia, unified under the name *Romania,* received international recognition.

Many leaders of the unification movement were young Romanians who had studied in Paris. There, they learned about a revolutionary spirit that was sweeping through Europe. Many Europeans were demanding an end to undemocratic government and calling for improvements in living conditions for the lower classes. The young Romanians demanded reforms after they returned home. Prince Cuza responded. His government bought much land from wealthy Romanians and gave it to peasants. It also increased the number of free schools for the poor. Many of the wealthy Romanians opposed Cuza. They forced the prince to resign in 1866.

The wealthy Romanians selected Karl of Hohenzollern to replace Cuza. Karl was a German prince who knew little about Romania. According to one story, he even had to consult a map to learn where the country was. But he was to rule Romania for nearly 50 years.

Karl took the name Prince Carol. In 1878, the major nations of Europe officially recognized Romania's full independence from the Ottoman Empire. In 1881, Romania became a kingdom, and Carol became King Carol I.

At the start of Carol's reign, Romania's first political parties were established, and the people were given the right to elect their government representatives. But a complex election system kept the peasants from having many representatives. Romania's economy improved under Carol. Wealthy Romanians benefited from the economic growth, but the peasants gained little from it. In 1907, Romania's peasants revolted. They burned the houses and destroyed the crops of many wealthy landowners. The Romanian Army put down the revolt,

killing at least 10,000 peasants. Carol died in 1914, and his nephew Ferdinand became king.

World War I was fought from 1914 to 1918. Romania remained neutral at first. But in 1916, it joined France, the United Kingdom, and the other Allies in their fight against the Central Powers (chiefly Austria-Hungary and Germany). Romania wanted to gain Banat, Bukovina, and Transylvania—three provinces of Austria-Hungary that had large Romanian populations. The Allies won the war, and Romania received the territories it wanted as part of the peace settlement. As a result, Romania about doubled in size and population. For the first time, Romania's territory included almost all the land where large numbers of Romanians lived.

Depression and fascism. Liberal political parties headed Romania's government after World War I. They divided the estates of many of the wealthy landowners into small farms and sold the farms to peasants. The liberals wanted to continue helping the peasants, but a worldwide depression that began in 1929 destroyed Romania's economy. Millions of Romanians lost their jobs, and poverty became severe throughout the country.

Romania's economic problems caused many people to seek new leadership in the early 1930's. The Iron Guard soon became a strong authoritarian movement. Its followers were fascists who sought to destroy Romania's government and establish a dictatorship. This group used terror against its political opponents and blamed Communists, Jews, and liberals for Romania's problems.

King Ferdinand died in 1927, and his son Carol became King Carol II three years later. The popularity and power of the Iron Guard grew during the early years of Carol's reign. Fearing a loss of his own authority, Carol made himself dictator of Romania. He outlawed the Iron Guard and all political parties.

World War II began in Europe in September 1939, as a struggle between Germany and the Allies—a group of nations led by France and the United Kingdom. Romania remained neutral at first. By June of 1940, Germany had gained a great military advantage over the Allies. Germany allowed Hungary to take northern Transylvania from Romania. The Soviet Union took part of northeastern Romania. Bulgaria took territory in the southeast.

Romania—History   The map at the left shows the principalities of Moldavia and Walachia before they fell under Ottoman control. The center map shows Romania in 1861, when the union of the principalities was internationally recognized. The map at the right shows Romania before the outbreak of World War II, in 1939. The boundaries of present-day Romania are shown in red.

1350

1861

1939

WORLD BOOK maps

The territorial losses turned the people against King Carol, and he gave up his throne on Sept. 6, 1940. Carol's son Michael became king, but Premier Ion Antonescu ruled. Antonescu cooperated with Germany, and German troops occupied Romania in October. Romania then joined the war on the side of Germany.

By August 1944, the tide of the war had turned against Germany. King Michael then overthrew Antonescu, and Romania joined the Allies. The war ended in 1945, and the Allies took northern Transylvania from Hungary and returned it to Romania. The Soviet Union and Bulgaria kept the Romanian territory they had taken.

Communist control. The Soviet Union had been formed as a Communist nation under Russia's leadership in 1922, and it existed until 1991. During World War II, the Soviet Union fought on the side of the Allies. Soviet troops occupied Romania in 1944 and stayed there until the late 1950's.

Romania's Communist Party had never been strong before World War II. But under the protection of the Soviet troops, Romanian Communists took over the government after the war. They killed or imprisoned their political opponents and forced King Michael to give up his throne on Dec. 30, 1947.

The Communists declared Romania an "independent people's democracy." But Romania was a *Soviet satellite* (country controlled by the Soviet Union). In 1948 and 1952, Romania adopted constitutions that praised the Soviet Union. Romania's government, educational system, and other institutions were modeled on those of the Soviet Union. Soviet leaders directed Romania's economy and forced the country to emphasize agriculture and neglect industry. They also set foreign policy.

Opposition to the Soviet Union. Resentment of Soviet interference in Romania's affairs grew during the 1950's. In the early 1960's, Romania's Communists—led by Communist Party head Gheorghe Gheorghiu-Dej—

began to oppose this interference openly. Gheorghiu-Dej died in 1965. Nicolae Ceaușescu, who succeeded him as party head, continued the opposition.

In 1962, Romania insisted that each Communist country should be free to develop its own economic system, trade freely with all nations, and make its own foreign policy. Romania's leaders then began expanding industry and increasing trade with Western nations. In 1964, Romania exchanged ambassadors with the United States. Romania's leaders hosted a visit by U.S. President Richard M. Nixon in 1969. They also declared Romania neutral in a dispute between the Soviet Union and China. In 1965, Romania adopted a Constitution that called for the nation's complete independence. In 1977, Romania began strengthening its ties with the nations of the *nonaligned movement.* These nations, primarily in Asia and Africa, had refused to support either the Communist or non-Communist bloc.

Also in 1977, an earthquake struck Bucharest and other parts of Romania. It caused about 1,500 deaths and over $1 billion in damage.

The government's industrialization policy increased the size of Romania's urban communities. Each year, thousands of young people moved from rural areas to cities to work in industry and government.

In the 1980's, new jobs were created, but Romania's living standard remained low and consumer goods were scarce. Reasons for the struggling economy included corruption in the Communist Party and overreliance on central government economic planning. In addition, Romania had to borrow heavily from Western European banks to finance its industrial build-up. Paying off this debt took funds away from further development and slowed economic growth.

Protests and political change. Ceaușescu's government maintained an extensive system of restrictions on the lives of the people. In mid-December 1989, thousands of people in the city of Timișoara staged demonstrations, calling for greater freedom from the Communist government and for an improved standard of living. Government security forces responded to the protests by firing on the people and killing hundreds. Antigovernment protests then spread across Romania. In Bucharest, tens of thousands gathered in the streets and called for increased freedoms and for Ceaușescu's resignation. Security forces fired on the crowds, bringing the death toll of demonstrators into the thousands. Army units joined the revolt, and fierce fighting between the army and Ceaușescu's security forces followed.

On December 22, Ceaușescu and his wife, Elena, fled Bucharest during a massive antigovernment demonstration. However, they were soon captured by the army. A secret trial took place and Ceaușescu and his wife were charged with murder and embezzlement of government funds. They were found guilty and were executed on December 25. The National Salvation Front, a group made up chiefly of former Communists, took control of the government. Ion Iliescu, leader of the Front, became the acting president. The Front canceled a number of Ceaușescu's restrictions on freedom. Free multiparty elections took place in May 1990. Iliescu won the presidency. The Front also won a wide majority in the legislature. Iliescu then stepped down as the Front's leader in accordance with a law established in early 1990. The law

Important dates in Romania

300's B.C.	Dacians lived in what is now Romania.
A.D. 100's	Romania became a province of the Roman Empire.
200's to 1100's	Barbarian tribes invaded Romania.
1250 to 1350	Moldavia and Walachia gradually became independent principalities.
c. 1500	The principalities fell under Ottoman rule.
1861	The union of Moldavia and Walachia as Romania received international recognition.
1919	Romania about doubled in size when Transylvania and other surrounding lands became part of it.
1940-1945	Romania fought in World War II—first on the German side and then on the side of the Allies.
1947	Romania officially became a Communist country.
1950's	The Soviet Union had nearly complete control over Romania.
1965	A new Romanian Constitution stressed the nation's control over its own affairs.
1977	An earthquake caused about 1,500 deaths and about $1 billion in property damage in Romania.
1989	Communist Party leader Nicolae Ceaușescu was overthrown and executed following widespread protest over his policies and corruption in his government.
1990	Romania held its first free multiparty elections since the end of World War II.

states that the head of state cannot be a party leader.

Opposition parties complained of abuse and intimidation by members of the ruling party during the election. In mid-1990, progovernment and antigovernment demonstrators clashed on the streets of Bucharest. Hundreds were injured. Large antigovernment demonstrations continued in the early 1990's, often in protest of economic conditions. In late 1991, following strikes and riots staged by miners, the government of the National Salvation Front resigned. It was replaced by a coalition government dominated by the Front. Iliescu remained president. New national elections were held in late 1992. Iliescu was reelected president. But in this election, he represented a political party called the Democratic National Salvation Front. This party broke away from the National Salvation Front in 1992. In 1993, it changed its name to the Social Democratic Party of Romania.

Recent developments. Ion Iliescu's government was dominated by former Communists who favored only limited political and economic reform. In 1996, Emil Constantinescu, who supported more rapid reform, was elected president. His party, the Democratic Convention of Romania, also won the most seats in the legislature. However, the progress of economic reform in Romania during the late 1990's remained slow.

Vladimir Tismaneanu

Related articles in *World Book* include:

Biographies

Outline

Questions

Who were the first known people to live in Romania?
What are some of Romania's natural resources?
How did the Communists influence life in Romania?
How did Romania get its name?
Who was Nicolae Ceauşescu? Ion Iliescu?
What are some favorite recreational activities in Romania?
Why is the Romanian language unusual?
What was the Iron Guard?
What are some features of Romania's folk culture?

Romanov, *ROH muh NAWF,* was the name of the family that ruled Russia from 1613 to 1917. The first Romanov ruler was Czar Michael, the son of Czar Ivan IV and Anastasia Romanov. Michael was elected czar in 1613. His son, Czar Alexis, acquired Ukraine and sponsored the introduction of Western education, technology, and military methods in Russia.

Sixteen more Romanov rulers followed. One of the most famous was Alexis's son Peter the Great. Rulers after 1762 either were foreigners or had little Russian ancestry, but they kept the Romanov name. The last Romanov ruler, Czar Nicholas II, gave up his throne in March 1917. He and his immediate family were killed by Bolshevik revolutionaries in July 1918. Other family members survived and escaped from Russia.

Joseph T. Fuhrmann

Related articles in *World Book* include:

Romanov, *ROH muh NAWF,* **Grigoriy Vasilyevich,** *gryih GAW RYUH ih vuh SYEEL yuh vyihch* (1923-   ), was a leading official of the Communist Party of the Soviet Union. Romanov served as a full member of the party's Politburo from 1976 to 1985, and as a member of the Secretariat of the party's Central Committee from 1983 to 1985. He also belonged to the Presidium from 1970 to 1985. The Politburo made the party's policies. The Secretariat managed its daily affairs. The Presidium was an important body of the Soviet government. In 1985, Romanov asked to be removed from his posts for health reasons. Many analysts believe he was removed because he had lost influence in the Communist Party.

Romanov was born in Zikhnovo, near Novgorod. He joined the Communist Party in 1944. Romanov became known as a strict follower of traditional Communist beliefs and policies.   Melvin Croan

Romans, Epistle to the, the sixth book of the New Testament, is a letter from the apostle Paul to the Christians in Rome. Paul wrote the Epistle, probably from Corinth, Greece, about A.D. 56. The Epistle was a letter of introduction, preparing for a visit Paul intended to make on his way to do missionary work in Spain.

The Epistle to the Romans is Paul's longest and most systematic letter. The main theme of the first 11 chapters is that Jews and Gentiles are equally in need of salvation, and that both have access to salvation through faith in Jesus Christ. In the five remaining chapters, Paul discusses problems in Christian living. Some scholars doubt that Chapter 16 was originally part of the letter, mainly because Paul, who had never been to Rome, greets many people by name in this chapter. These scholars believe that the chapter is a letter Paul wrote to another place, which a later editor attached to the letter to the Romans.   Terrance D. Callan

See also **Paul, Saint** (Paul's letters and ideas); **Bible** (Books of the New Testament).

Romanticism is a style in the fine arts and literature. It emphasizes passion rather than reason, and imagination and intuition rather than logic. Romanticism favors full expression of the emotions, and free, spontaneous action rather than restraint and order. In all these ways, romanticism contrasts with another style called *classi-*

cism (see **Classicism**). Periods of romanticism often develop as a revolt against classicism. Artists and writers throughout history have shown romantic tendencies. But the term *romantic movement* usually refers to the period from the late 1700's to the mid-1800's.

The qualities of romanticism

Romantics yearn for the infinite. The English romantic poet William Blake thought he could "see a World in a Grain of Sand/And a Heaven in a Wild Flower." Romantics view nature as a living spirit, attuned to human feelings of love and compassion.

Romanticism stresses freedom for the individual. It rejects restricting social conventions and unjust political rule. In literature, the romantic hero, such as Lord Byron's "Manfred," is often a rebel or outlaw.

Just as the romantic hero is in revolt against social conventions, the romantic artist is in revolt against artificial ideas of good form. In drama, for example, romantic writers reject the classical unities of time, place, and action. They allow the events in their plays to range widely in time and space. Jean Racine's play *Phèdre* is rigidly classical in form. Johann Wolfgang von Goethe's play *Faust* is romantic.

Romanticism in the arts

Romanticism in literature. During the romantic movement, most writers were discontented with their world. It seemed commercial, inhuman, and standardized. To escape from modern life, the romantics turned their interest to remote and faraway places, the medieval past, folklore and legends, and nature and the common people. The romantics were also drawn to the supernatural.

Many romantic characteristics were united in the *Gothic novel.* This was a type of horror story, filled with violence and supernatural effects, and set against a background of gloomy medieval Gothic castles. The Gothic novel influenced the American writers Nathaniel Hawthorne and Edgar Allan Poe. The novels of Sir Walter Scott of Scotland and James Fenimore Cooper of the United States reveal the typically romantic interest in the past. *Grimm's Fairy Tales,* collected by Jakob and Wilhelm Grimm, are famous examples of the romantic interest in legends and folklore.

Many typically romantic characteristics appear in the poetry of William Wordsworth of England. Wordsworth preferred a reflective "vacant and pensive mood" to a restless search for scientific knowledge. He believed we learn more by communing with nature or talking to country people than by reading books. He also believed that harmony with nature is the source of all goodness and truth.

Romanticism in painting. Romantic painters often used bold lighting effects and deep shadow to cast a visionary gleam over their subjects. Classical forms and themes were abandoned for faraway exotic subjects such as the Asian scenes painted by Frenchman Eugène Delacroix.

Romanticism in music. Romantic composers modified the formalism of classical music, and aimed at lyric expression and organic unity. Many romantic composers gave their works a nationalistic character by using folk songs as themes. Romantic composers include Franz Schubert of Austria; Felix Mendelssohn, Robert Schumann, and Carl Maria von Weber of Germany; and Frédéric Chopin of Poland.

Romanticism and society. The French philosopher Jean-Jacques Rousseau taught that people are naturally good but have been corrupted by the institutions of civilization. He idealized the *noble savage,* an individual unspoiled by luxury and sophistication, and he argued that in a virtuous society children would grow up honest and free. Influenced by these ideas, many romantics opposed political tyranny and took part in liberal and revolutionary activities. The revolutions in America and France during the late 1700's were influenced by romantic ideals.

Many of Rousseau's theories influenced educational theory and practice. Romanticism also became associated with economic and social reform, especially in the United States.   Lawrence Lipking

Related articles. There is a separate biography in *World Book* for each person discussed in this article. For the historical development of romanticism, see:

Ballet (Romantic ballet)	Latin-American literature (Romanticism)
Classical music (The romantic era)	Painting (The 1800's)
Drama (Romanticism)	Poetry (Romantic poetry)
English literature (Romantic literature)	Russian literature (The Age of romanticism)
French literature (Romanticism)	Sculpture (Sculpture from 1600 to 1900)
German literature (1750-1830)	Spanish literature (Neoclassicism, romanticism, and realism)
Gothic novel	

Additional resources

Curran, Stuart M., ed. *The Cambridge Companion to British Romanticism.* Cambridge, 1993.
Peckham, Morse. *The Romantic Virtuoso.* Univ. Pr. of New England, 1995.
Ratner, Leonard G. *Romantic Music.* Schirmer Bks., 1992.

Romberg, Sigmund (1887-1951), was a famous composer of operettas. He wrote the music for such famous operettas as *Maytime* (1917), *The Student Prince* (1924), *The Desert Song* (1926), *My Maryland* (1927), *The New Moon* (1928), and *Up in Central Park* (1945). He adapted the music of the Austrian composer Franz Schubert for another popular operetta, *Blossom Time* (1921). Romberg's many popular songs include "Deep in My Heart, Dear," "The Desert Song," "Stouthearted Men," and "When I Grow Too Old to Dream." He also wrote music for motion pictures and gained praise as a conductor of light classical music.

Romberg was born in Nagykanizsa, Hungary. Although he studied the violin as a child, Romberg planned to become an engineer. To help finance his engineering studies in a Vienna technical school, he worked as assistant manager at the Theater-an-der-Wien, Vienna's leading theater for operettas. The productions Romberg saw there persuaded him to pursue a career in music.

Romberg moved to New York City in 1909. He eventually formed a small orchestra. Romberg was soon hired to write songs for musicals presented by J. J. and Lee Shubert, two brothers who operated theaters throughout the United States. Romberg composed music in the American ragtime fashion for several years before he began writing the European-style operettas for which he became famous.   Gerald Bordman

Central Rome, seen here looking northeast from Trastevere, displays its long history in the varied styles of its buildings. The white Victor Emmanuel Monument rises dramatically in the upper right part of the picture. The Tiber River, marked by the trees, winds through Rome.

Rome

Rome is the capital of Italy and one of the world's great historic cities. It has been an important center of civilization for over 2,000 years. Because of its long history, Rome is called the *Eternal City.* It is also one of the world's most beautiful cities. Its ancient monuments and magnificent churches and palaces stand as reminders of Rome's past glory. Gleaming new buildings are a sign of its modern-day importance.

Rome ruled the ancient Western world as the capital of the mighty Roman Empire. For hundreds of years, Rome was the supreme power of Europe, northern Africa, and western Asia. Ancient Rome's influence can still be seen today in such fields as architecture, government, language, and law.

As the home of the popes, Rome also became the center of the Roman Catholic Church. During the 1500's and 1600's, the popes brought a new splendor to Rome. They hired great artists who gave the city beautiful buildings and priceless works of art. Today, thousands of visitors come every year from all parts of the world to enjoy these masterpieces, and to see the ruins of ancient Rome.

Visitors also enjoy the colorful life of sunny Rome. They stroll through the city's fashionable shops and open-air markets and ride in horse-drawn carriages. Like the Romans, visitors enjoy relaxing at sidewalk cafes or in the many beautiful squares. The people of Rome are friendly and proud of their city. They are happy to help strangers find their way, select the most delicious foods in restaurants, or just to chat.

Facts in brief

Population: 2,775,250.
Area: 582 sq. mi. (1,508 km²).
Climate: *Average temperature*—January 45°F (7°C); July, 78°F (26°C). *Average annual precipitation* (rainfall, melted snow, and other forms of moisture)—38 in. (97 cm). For the monthly weather in Rome, see Italy (Climate).
Government: *Chief executive*—mayor (4-year term). *Legislature*—80-member City Council (4-year terms).
Founded: 753 B.C. (according to legend).

Anthony James Joes, the contributor of this article, is Director of the International Relations Program at St. Joseph's University.

Rome lies on both banks of the Tiber River in central Italy, 10 miles (16 kilometers) east of the Tyrrhenian Sea. The city stretches over about 20 hills, but its outskirts have some wide expanses of flat ground. These hills include the famous seven hills on which ancient Rome was built—the Aventine, Caelian, Capitoline, Esquiline, Palatine, Quirinal, and Viminal hills.

Today, the ruins of ancient buildings cover most of the Aventine, Caelian, and Palatine hills. The Palatine also has a modern public park. Crowded commercial districts spread over the Esquiline and Viminal hills. The Italian presidential palace and some of Rome's government buildings stand on the Quirinal, the tallest of the seven hills. The streets of ancient Rome extended from the Capitoline, a center of Roman life. Today, this hill has famous art museums, the City Council building, and a square designed by Michelangelo, the great Renaissance artist.

Throughout the city are many beautiful squares connected by busy streets. In the heart of Rome is the *Piazza Colonna* (Colonna Square). Banks, hotels, luxury shops, office buildings, restaurants, and theaters make it the busiest place in the city. Rome's main street, the *Via del Corso* (Way of the Course), runs 1 mile (1.6 kilometers) through the Piazza Colonna and links two other squares to the north and south. The street received its name because it was used as a horse-racing course in the Middle Ages.

Vatican City, the administrative and spiritual center of the Roman Catholic Church, lies in northwestern Rome. The Vatican, as it is sometimes called, is the smallest independent country in the world. It covers only 109 acres (44 hectares), or about $\frac{1}{6}$ square mile (0.4 square kilometer). See **Vatican City.**

Rome is also one of the world's most important art centers. Actors, musicians, painters, sculptors, and writers take part in the city's busy cultural life.

Parks and gardens. Romans enjoy the city's many public parks and gardens on the grounds of magnificent old *villas* (large estates). The villas were once owned by wealthy families. The great Villa Borghese, which was opened to the public in 1902, is the finest of these parks. Its hills, meadows, and woods seem like natural countryside. It also has a large zoo.

Many campers visit the Villa Ada, the former residence of the kings of Italy. The Villa Glori, a park honoring Italy's war dead, is covered with pine trees. The Villa Sciarra has famous fountains and rare plants. Gardens on top of the Janiculum Hill are especially popular with children.

Music and theater. The National Academy of St. Cecilia has one of Rome's leading symphony orchestras. Rome's orchestras also include the Rome Philharmonic and the Radiotelevisione Italiana. The world's oldest academies of music are in Rome.

Romans, like most Italians, enjoy opera. The Opera House offers performances from December to June. In July and August, operas are presented in an outdoor setting. Rome's many theaters offer plays and musical comedies, including productions from other countries.

Museums and art galleries. Countless visitors come to see Rome's priceless art collections. Many of the finest paintings and statues are displayed in the Vatican Palace. They include masterpieces by such famous artists as Leonardo da Vinci, Michelangelo, and Raphael. Some of Michelangelo's greatest paintings decorate the ceiling and front wall of the Vatican's Sistine Chapel.

The oldest art collection in Rome, begun in 1471, is in the Capitoline Museum. It includes many fine sculptures of ancient Rome. The National Museum of the Villa Giulia has a collection of art from central Italy dating from pre-Roman times. Greek and Roman sculptures and other articles from ancient civilizations are exhibited in the National Roman Museum. The Borghese Collection in the Villa Borghese includes works of art by almost every master of the Renaissance. The national Gallery of Modern Art contains masterpieces that are chiefly of the 1800's and 1900's.

Churches, palaces, and fountains. Saint Peter's Basilica in Vatican City is Europe's largest Christian church. It is an outstanding example of Renaissance architecture. Michelangelo helped design the church during the 1500's. Many famous art masterpieces can be seen inside it (see **Saint Peter's Basilica**). Other well-known churches of Rome also date from the Renaissance, as well as from earlier and later periods.

The most famous of Rome's many palaces is the Venezia Palace, built during the mid-1400's. The Italian dictator Benito Mussolini established his office there in the Fascist period of the 1920's and 1930's. The palace now houses an art museum. The Madama Palace, once owned by the powerful Medici family, has been the seat of the Italian Senate since 1871. The Quirinal Palace is

Rome

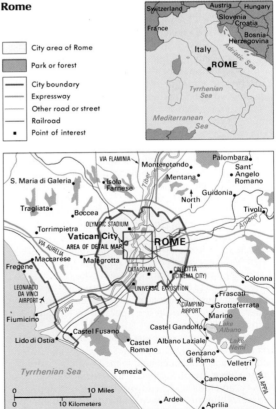

☐	City area of Rome
▨	Park or forest
──	City boundary
──	Expressway
──	Other road or street
──	Railroad
▪	Point of interest

WORLD BOOK maps

The Fountain of Neptune is in Rome's Piazza Navona, a historic square surrounded by beautiful churches and palaces.

The Baths of Caracalla were public baths dating from the A.D. 200's. Visitors to the site enjoy its splendid architecture.

the Italian president's official residence. It was the home of popes until 1870 and of kings of Italy from 1871 until 1946.

Rome has many magnificent fountains that are considered great works of art. The Trevi Fountain, which was completed in 1762, is the most popular with visitors from other countries. A legend says that visitors who throw coins into this fountain will someday return to the city.

Schools. The University of Rome, founded in 1303, is Italy's largest university. Various religious societies of the Roman Catholic Church operate a number of schools in Vatican City. There, students from many countries attend seminaries to become priests, or take university graduate studies. Some seminaries have been established for students from one country only. For example, the North American College has graduated thousands of priests from the United States since it was founded in 1859.

Roman children must attend school between the ages of 6 and 14, which takes them through junior high school. They may also attend public schools at the next level of education. These schools include senior high schools and schools of fine arts, teacher training, and technical job training. Students pay small fees to attend all these higher-level schools. A number of private schools are operated by religious groups.

The Vatican Library, established in the 1400's, is one of the most important libraries in the world. The library owns many old Latin manuscripts. Rome also has nine public libraries with a total of about three million books. Other libraries in the city are operated by Roman Catholic orders.

Sports. Soccer is the most popular sport in Rome, as it is throughout Italy. Huge crowds attend club and international soccer matches held in the Olympic Stadium. Horse shows are performed in the *Piazza di Siena* (Siena Square) and the Capannelle and Tor di Valle Hippodromes. Other popular sports include basketball, boxing, and tennis.

Economy. Rome is not a heavily industrialized city. Most Romans earn their living through jobs related to commerce and government. Many Romans work in restaurants and in the building trades. Tourism also provides a large part of the city's income. Only about a fifth of the workers in Rome are employed in industry. The city's factories produce clothing and textiles, processed foods, and other products. Most of the factories in Rome are in the northwestern part of the city.

Motion-picture production is an important part of Rome's economy. The city is one of the film capitals of the world. Motion-picture companies of Italy and other countries have produced many famous films in Rome's studios and streets.

Rome is a major transportation center of Italy. Railways and roads connect Rome with cities in most parts of the country. Airlines link the city with the rest of Italy and other parts of the world. Rome's central railroad station is one of the largest and most beautiful stations in the world. The Metropolitana, Rome's subway system, runs southwest from the railroad station to the port of Ostia. Buses, streetcars, taxis, and trolleys also serve Rome. Beginning in 1973, all private vehicles were banned from part of the ancient section of the city to reduce traffic jams and air and noise pollution.

Rome has many daily newspapers, of which the most important are *Il Messaggero* (The Messenger), *Il Tempo* (The Time), and *La Repubblica* (The Republic). The Vatican publishes the semiofficial newspaper of the Roman Catholic Church, *L'Osservatore Romano* (The Roman Observer). Many other specialized newspapers are published in Rome, including *Corriere dello Sport* (Sport Courier). Some papers are official dailies of political parties. These include *Avanti!* (Forward!) of the Socialist Party, *Il Popolo* (The People) of the Christian Democratic Party, and *L'Unità* (Unity) of the Democratic Party of the Left. Italy's radio and television system, Radiotelevisione Italiana, has its headquarters in Rome.

Government. Rome is governed by a City Council consisting of 80 members, who are elected every four

© Francesco Garufi, Contrasto from Grazia Neri

SCALA/Art Resource

The University of Rome, founded in 1303, is the largest university in Italy. About 200,000 men and women study there.

The Sports Palace was built for the 1960 Summer Olympic Games. It lies on the southwestern outskirts of the city.

years. The City Council elects one member of its group as mayor. The council also elects 18 of its members to the City Executive Committee. The mayor and the members of this committee all serve four-year terms. The mayor heads the committee as well as the general city administration. Fifteen departments direct the city's affairs, including health, markets, public works, and transportation.

Central Rome

This map shows the central area of Rome and locates many of its famous landmarks. The Tiber River flows through the area. Vatican City, the world's smallest independent country and the headquarters of the Roman Catholic Church, is surrounded by Rome.

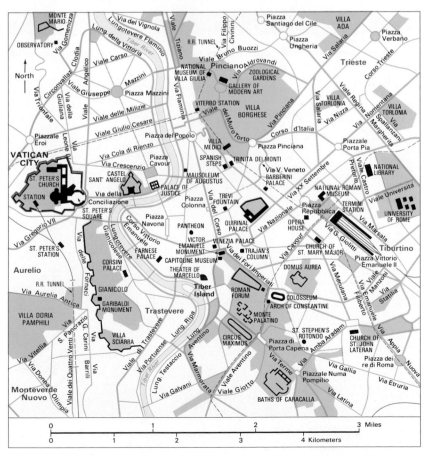

Park

Vatican City boundary

Major street

Other street

Railroad

Subway (Metropolitana)

Point of interest

WORLD BOOK map

FPG

The Roman Forum was the center of Roman government.

SCALA/Art Resource

The Pantheon was a temple dedicated to Roman gods.

Mario Gerardi Photography

The Arch of Constantine celebrated a military victory.

The Photo Source from Shostal

Trajan's Column stands 100 feet (30 meters) high.

Ancient Rome

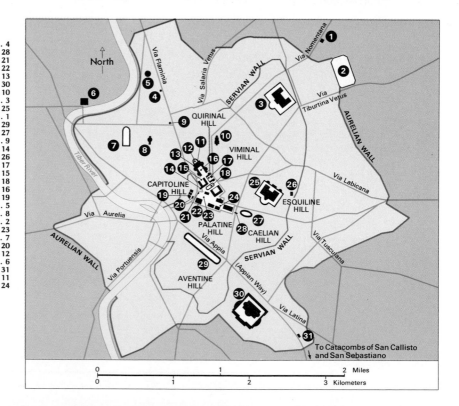

WORLD BOOK map

Remains of the splendors of ancient Rome may be seen throughout the city, especially in an area east of the Tiber River. Since the 1800's, the Italian government has cleared the main sites of the ruins and surrounded them with trees and gardens. Thousands of tourists visit these attractions yearly.

Forums. The centers of ancient Roman life were open marketplaces called *forums,* where public meetings were held. The Roman Forum, the most important one, was the center of Roman government. Many important buildings and monuments stood there. Ruins in the Roman Forum include the *Curia* (Senate House), the triumphal Arch of Septimius Severus, the Temple of Saturn, and the Basilica Julia, an assembly hall.

Most streets of ancient Rome were narrow and crooked, but a few were wide and beautiful, with high arches and white marble buildings. The chief street, the *Via Sacra* (Sacred Way), crossed the Roman Forum. Victorious emperors and generals returning from war paraded over its lava pavement. See **Forum, Roman; Rome, Ancient** (picture: A triumphal procession).

Many Roman rulers built forums of their own. The ruins of five of these forums still stand—those of Augustus, Julius Caesar, Nerva, Trajan, and Vespasian. Trajan's Forum is the finest. Most of its buildings, including the Basilica Ulpia and the Temple of Trajan, are in ruins. But Trajan's Column, 100 feet (30 meters) tall, is almost whole. It has carvings of scenes from Trajan's wars. Nearby stand the Markets of Trajan, a large semicircle of three-storied shops. One of the shops has been rebuilt to show how it looked in ancient times. See **Trajan.**

The Colosseum, dedicated in A.D. 80, is one of the chief landmarks of Rome. In this huge amphitheater, now half-ruined, Romans watched trained fighters called *gladiators* battle each other or fight wild animals. The audiences also saw persecuted Christians killed by lions. See **Colosseum.**

Baths. Only wealthy Romans could afford to own private baths, but the city had many public ones. During the time of the emperors, the public baths became luxurious meeting places. They looked like great square-shaped swimming pools and were surrounded by gardens, columned marble porches, and libraries. The bath buildings had facilities for warm and cold baths, steam baths, and massages.

The most splendid remains of baths are those of Caracalla and of Diocletian. The Baths of Caracalla, which date from the early A.D. 200's, are especially impressive. They were decorated with precious marble, statues, and *mosaics* (pictures formed of bits of colored glass, stone, or wood). Few of these decorations remain. But many tourists continue to visit the ruins each year for their history and architecture. The Baths of Diocletian, completed in the early A.D. 300's, were the largest of all Roman baths. They could serve 3,000 people at a time. Most of the site has been built over, but some rooms can still be seen.

The catacombs were systems of underground passages and rooms used as Christian burial places and chapels. The early Christians dug them from the A.D. 100's to the early 400's and hid there during periods of persecution. The catacombs are decorated with paintings on walls and ceilings and with Christian symbols. The most famous catacombs include those of San Callisto, San Sebastiano, and Sant' Agnese. See **Catacombs.**

Other remains. The Pantheon is the best preserved of all the remains of ancient Rome. The Romans built it as a temple in honor of all their gods (see **Pantheon**). The triple Arch of Constantine, built about A.D. 315, also is well preserved. It includes three connected arches, side by side, richly decorated with sculpture.

The ruins of the *Domus Aurea* (Golden House) are in a popular public park. This building was the palace of Emperor Nero. The ruins, which lie mainly underground, occupy a large area. Paintings cover some of the walls. The well-preserved Column of Marcus Aurelius, built during the A.D. 100's, honors Roman victories in battle. It has carvings of war scenes. Stairs inside the hollow marble column lead to the top, where a statue of Saint Paul has stood since 1589.

The Mausoleum of Augustus, begun about 28 B.C., is the tomb of Augustus and the principal members of his family. Augustus, the first Roman emperor, built the nearby *Ara Pacis* (Altar of Peace) after establishing the *Pax Romana* (Roman Peace), which lasted 200 years. These buildings stood on the *Campus Martius* (Field of Mars), which had been used for military training. During the A.D. 200's, barbarian tribes attacked the empire, and Rome built the Aurelian Wall and other walls for defense. Many parts of these walls are still standing.

Gerald Clyde, FPG

The Colosseum was a huge amphitheater.

SCALA/Art Resource

The catacombs were used for Christian burial places.

Early days. A legend says that Rome was founded by twin brothers in 753 B.C. For an account of this story, see **Romulus and Remus.** Rome expanded and became the supreme power of the Western world. For the history of Rome through the fall of the West Roman Empire in A.D. 476, see **Rome, Ancient** (History).

After Rome fell to Germanic tribes, most of the once-splendid city became an unhealthful area of marshes. In the mid-500's, Emperor Justinian I of the Byzantine Empire drove the Ostrogoths from Rome. He reestablished Roman rule of the city as a Byzantine territory, but the decay of Rome continued. See **Byzantine Empire.**

Rome had far-reaching importance as the official center of the Christian Church. During the 700's, the popes greatly increased their political power. When invading Lombards threatened Rome, Pope Stephen II asked for help from Pepin the Short, king of the Franks. Pepin saved Rome twice and gave the city and nearby lands to the pope in 756. Pepin's son Charlemagne later expanded these *Papal States,* as they were called. See **Papal States; Pepin the Short.**

Feudal times and the Renaissance. For hundreds of years after the 800's, Rome was torn by struggles among kings and princes. Various European rulers tried to control the powerful popes, especially by influencing papal elections. In 1305, through the efforts of King Philip IV of France, a French archbishop was elected pope. The new pope, Clement V, moved his court to Avignon, France. It was returned to Rome in 1377. See **Pope** (The troubles of the papacy).

During this period, Cola di Rienzo, an Italian patriot, rebelled against the nobles. He established a popular republic in 1347. But Cola soon became cruel and greedy for power and was later killed in a riot.

Rome became one of the most splendid cities of the Renaissance. In 1527, raiding German and Spanish troops destroyed or stole many of the city's treasures and killed thousands of Romans. Soon afterward, the job of rebuilding Rome began. During the rest of the 1500's and the 1600's, the popes built hundreds of magnificent structures. They appointed the finest painters and sculptors, including Michelangelo, to design and decorate the buildings.

Under Napoleon. In 1798, after Napoleon conquered the Italian Peninsula, the victorious French troops entered Rome. Napoleon ended the pope's political power in 1809. He made the Papal States a part of his empire. He also declared Rome to be the second city of his em-

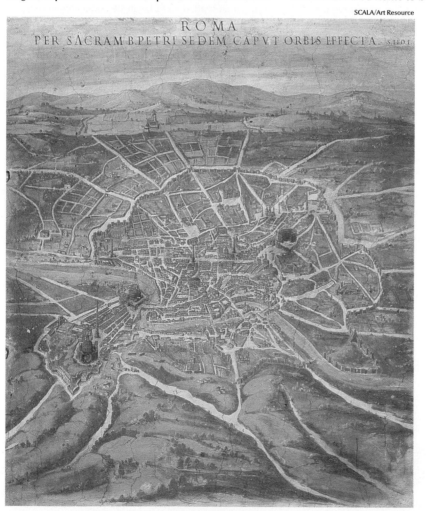

ROMA
PER SACRAM B.PETRI SEDEM CAPVT ORBIS EFFECTA. S.LEO.I

A map of Rome shows the city's layout during the 1500's. Some of the 20 hills of Rome rise in the background. The Tiber River flows through the city. St. Peter's Basilica stands on what was then the city's southwestern edge.

pire, after Paris. Pope Pius VII fought these changes, and Napoleon jailed him. After Napoleon's defeat, most of the Papal States were returned to the pope in 1815.

Republic of Rome. During the early 1800's, movements for unity and freedom from foreign rule swept the Italian peninsula. But the popes opposed these movements. In 1848, revolutionists made Rome a republic, and Pope Pius IX fled. French troops captured Rome in 1849 and restored the pope to power the next year.

Italy's capital. In 1861, when Victor Emmanuel II became king of a united Italy, Rome was not yet a part of the new kingdom. Italian volunteers tried to take Rome in 1867, but French defenders stopped them. In 1870, after the French had left, Victor Emmanuel entered Rome almost without bloodshed. He ended the pope's political power and made Rome his capital in 1871. In protest, Pius IX shut himself up in the Vatican and refused to deal with the government. Succeeding popes followed the same policy until 1929. That year, by treaty, Vatican City became an independent state, and Roman Catholic Church officials recognized Rome as Italy's capital.

Period of construction. The 1900's were a period of widespread construction in Rome. New buildings and roads were built, and the city restored many ancient buildings and monuments. During the 1920's and 1930's, the Fascist dictator Benito Mussolini promoted much poorly planned construction. It later led to severe traffic jams and other city problems. Mussolini completed a new University of Rome campus in 1935 and began work on a huge central railroad station in 1938. But construction was halted by World War II (1939-1945). Rome suffered little damage during the war. Neither side wanted to endanger the life of Pope Pius XII, who was in Vatican City. The central railroad station was completed in 1950 according to improved new plans.

In 1938, Mussolini began building the *Esposizione Universale di Roma* (Universal Exhibition of Rome, or E.U.R.). This world's fair was to have opened in 1942, and plans called for its buildings to form a government center later. The construction was interrupted by the war and was resumed in 1951. In 1955, Rome's subway linked the 1,075-acre (435-hectare) E.U.R. with the new railroad station. Some of the 1960 Summer Olympic Games were held near the E.U.R. in the city's new Sports

Palace. The E.U.R. was completed in 1976. Many large companies and government agencies operate there.

During the early 1980's, Rome's city government adopted a plan to restore many of Rome's ruins. Several monuments, including Trajan's Column, the Arch of Constantine, and the Trevi Fountain, were restored.

Recent developments. In the mid-1990's, Rome began another ambitious program of restoration and construction. New projects included the Rome Auditorium, designed by Italian architect Renzo Piano. Some projects undertaken in the late 1990's to accommodate millennial celebrations stirred controversy because they threatened historic sites.   Anthony James Joes

Related articles in *World Book* include:

Catacombs	Mazzini, Giuseppe	Romulus and
City (picture)	Michelangelo	Remus
Cola di Rienzo	Pantheon	Saint Peter's
Colosseum	Papal States	Basilica
Forum, Roman	Pope	Sistine Chapel
Garibaldi,	Quirinal Hill	Tiber River
Giuseppe	Rome, Ancient	Vatican City

Outline

I. **The city today**
  A. Parks and gardens   E. Schools
  B. Music and theater   F. Sports
  C. Museums and art   G. Economy
     galleries   H. Government
  D. Churches, palaces, and
     fountains
II. **The ancient city**
  A. Forums   D. The catacombs
  B. The Colosseum   E. Other remains
  C. Baths
III. **History**

Questions

Why is Rome called the *Eternal City?*
Where were public meetings held in ancient Rome?
What is the largest church in Europe?
What is Rome's most popular sport?
What great painter decorated the Sistine Chapel?
How did the Via del Corso get its name?
Between which two points does Rome's subway run?
What were the catacombs? What were they used for?
What is the legend of the Fountain of Trevi?

Additional resources

Belford, Ros, and others. *Rome.* Dorling Kindersley, 1993.
Hibbert, Christopher. *Rome.* 1985. Reprint. Penguin, 1987.
Insight Guide to Rome. Houghton, published annually.

Rome, New York (pop. 44,350), is a historic city in the central part of the state. For location, see **New York** (political map). With Utica, Rome forms part of a metropolitan area of 316,633 people. Rome's chief products are copper wire and other copper products. The Rome Laboratory, a United States Air Force research facility, is in the city. Rome stands on the site of Fort Stanwix and is the home of the Fort Stanwix National Monument. The city was originally named Lynchville. But it was renamed Rome in 1819. Some people believe that the Stars and Stripes flew there for the first time in battle in 1777, during the Battle of Oriskany in the Revolutionary War in America. Groundbreaking for the construction of the Erie Canal took place in Rome on July 4, 1817. Today, the Erie Canal Village stands on the site of the groundbreaking. The village is a reconstruction of the area in the 1800's. Rome was incorporated in 1870. It has a mayor-council form of government.   John Kenneth White

Shostal

A huge complex called the *Esposizione Universale di Roma* (Universal Exhibition of Rome, or E.U.R.) includes numerous modern buildings. Many large companies and government agencies have their offices in the E.U.R.

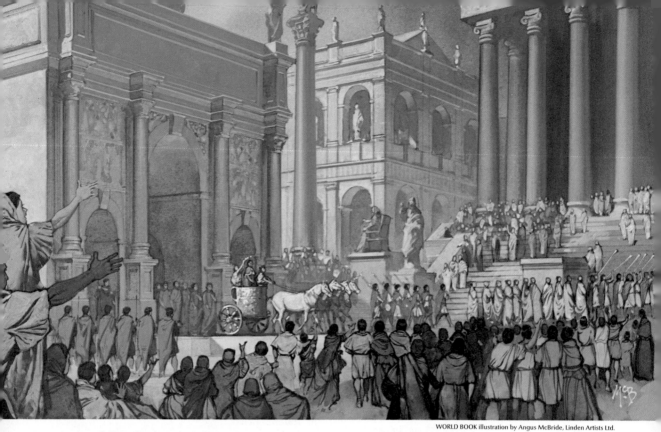

A triumphal procession paraded through the Roman Forum, the chief public square of ancient Rome, when a victorious general returned from war. The general rode in a chariot followed by his army. Before him marched trumpeters and Roman senators and other high government officials.

Ancient Rome

Rome, Ancient. The story of ancient Rome is a tale of how a small community of shepherds in central Italy grew to become one of the greatest empires in history—and then collapsed. According to Roman legend, the city of Rome was founded in 753 B.C. By 275 B.C., it controlled most of the Italian Peninsula. At its peak, in the A.D. 100's, the Roman Empire covered about half of Europe, much of the Middle East, and the north coast of Africa. The empire then began to crumble, partly because it was too big for Rome to govern. In A.D. 476, Germanic tribes overthrew the last Roman emperor.

The millions of people who lived in the Roman Empire spoke many languages and followed many different customs and religions. But the Roman Empire bound them together under a common system of law and government. This remarkable achievement has aroused interest and admiration from ancient times until today.

Ancient Rome had enormous influence on the development of Western civilization because the empire was so vast and lasted so long. The language of the ancient Romans, Latin, became the basis of French, Italian, Spanish, and the other Romance languages. Roman law provided the foundation for the legal systems of most of the countries in Western Europe and Latin America. Roman

Erich S. Gruen, the contributor of this article, is Professor of History at the University of California in Berkeley.

principles of justice and the Roman political system contributed to the building of governments in the United States and other countries. Roman roads, bridges, and aqueducts—some of which are still used—served as models for engineers in later ages.

This article provides a broad overview of the people, achievements, government, and history of ancient Rome. Many separate *World Book* articles have detailed information. For a list of these articles, see the *Related articles* at the end of the article.

The Roman world

The land. Ancient Rome arose on seven wooded hills along the Tiber River in central Italy. The Tiber provided a convenient route to the sea, which lay about 15 miles (24 kilometers) to the west. But Rome was far enough from the sea to escape raids by pirates. Rome's hills were very steep, and so the city could be easily defended against enemy attacks. Fertile soil and excellent building materials lay nearby.

The Italian Peninsula gradually came under Roman rule. The peninsula jutted far out into the Mediterranean Sea. Italy thus occupied a central position among the lands bordering the Mediterranean. To the north, the Alps helped protect Italy against invaders from central Europe. But mountain passes let through a slow stream of settlers, who were attracted by Italy's mild climate and fertile soil. In time, the steadily growing population provided the soldiers Rome needed for expansion.

Roman rule slowly spread over all the lands bordering the Mediterranean Sea. The Romans called the Mediterranean *Mare Nostrum* (Our Sea) or *Mare Internum* (Inland Sea). At its greatest size, in the A.D. 100's, the Roman Empire also extended as far north as the British Isles and as far east as the Persian Gulf.

The Roman Empire had many natural resources. They included fertile grainfields in Sicily and northern Africa, rich mineral deposits in Spain and Britain, and marble quarries in Greece. There were also thick forests in Asia Minor and thriving vineyards and olive orchards in Gaul (now France, Belgium, and part of Germany).

The people. The Roman Empire probably had from 50 to 70 million people at its height. Of that number, nearly I million people lived in Rome, and from 5 to 6 million lived in the rest of Italy.

The peoples of the Roman Empire differed greatly in their customs and spoke many languages. Peoples in Mesopotamia, Palestine, Egypt, and Greece had cultures far older than that of Rome. But many peoples in Britain, Germany, and Gaul were introduced to more advanced civilization by the Romans. Throughout the empire, government officials and members of the upper class spoke Latin and Greek. But most conquered peoples continued to use their native languages. For example, people spoke Celtic in Gaul and Britain, Berber in northern Africa, and Aramaic in Syria and Palestine.

The people of ancient Rome were divided into various social classes. Very few Romans belonged to the upper classes. Members of the Senate and their families made up the most powerful upper-class group. Most people belonged to the lower classes and had little social standing. Within this group, Romans distinguished between citizens and slaves. Citizens included small farmers, city workers, and soldiers. Most slaves were people captured in warfare. In time, slaves could buy or be given their freedom and become citizens.

As the Roman world expanded, a new social class became important. This class consisted of prosperous landowners and business people, who were called *equites* (pronounced *EHK wuh teez*). Under the Roman emperors, equites held important government positions and helped run the empire's civil service.

Roman citizenship was eventually granted to most peoples of the empire. Citizenship meant protection under Roman law. The privilege of citizenship promoted loyalty to the empire and gave peoples of all classes and all regions a greater stake in its success.

Life of the people

City life. Rome was the capital and the largest city of the Roman Empire. It had almost a million inhabitants at its height. No earlier city had achieved such size and splendor. Alexandria, in Egypt, was the empire's second largest city. It had about 750,000 people. Other important cities included Antioch in Syria and Constantinople (now Istanbul, Turkey).

Cities in the Roman Empire served as centers of trade and culture. Roman engineers planned cities carefully. They located public buildings conveniently and provided for sewerage and water supply systems. Emperors or wealthy individuals paid for the construction of such large public buildings as baths, sports arenas, and theaters. At the heart of a Roman city lay the *forum*—a large open space surrounded by markets, government buildings, and temples. Rich and poor mingled in the bus-

tling forum and at the baths, theaters, and arenas.

Rural life. The first Romans were shepherds and farmers. In early Rome, farmers who worked their own land formed the backbone of the Roman army. They planted their crops in spring and harvested them in fall. During the summer, they fought in the army.

Rural life changed after Rome began to expand its territory. Many farmers were sent to fight wars abroad for long periods, and so they had to sell their land. Wealthy Romans then built up large estates on which they raised crops and livestock to sell for a profit. They bought slaves to work for them and also rented land to tenant farmers. For most farmers, life was hard. But they could look forward to regular festivals, such as those at planting and at harvesttime, which provided athletic games and other entertainment.

Family life. The head of a Roman household was the *paterfamilias* (father of the family). He had total power over all members of his household. The paterfamilias even had the power to sell his children into slavery or have them killed. As long as his father lived, a son could not own property or have legal authority over his own children. Many households were therefore large and included married sons and their families.

Children in ancient Rome enjoyed many of the same kinds of toys and games that delight children today. For example, they had dolls, carts, hobbyhorses, and board games. They also had dogs, cats, and other pets. But Roman children took on adult responsibilities sooner than most children do today. In poor rural families, children had to work in the fields. In wealthier families, children married early. Most boys married when they were 15 to 18 years old, and most girls when they were 13 or 14. Parents selected marriage partners for their children, who had little say in the matter. Many marriages were arranged for the economic or political benefits they would bring to the families.

Education. Ancient Rome had no public schools. Children received their earliest education at home under their parents' supervision. From the age of 6 or 7 until about 10 or 11, most boys and some girls attended a private school or studied at home. They learned reading, writing, and arithmetic. Slaves taught the children in many homes. Some slaves, especially those from Greece, had more education than their masters.

Most Roman children who received further education came from wealthy families. Until age 14, they studied mainly Latin and Greek grammar and literature. They also studied mathematics, music, and astronomy.

Higher education in ancient Rome meant the study of *rhetoric*—that is, the art of public speaking and persuasion. Only upper-class Romans who planned a career in law or politics studied rhetoric. Training in rhetoric provided the skills needed to argue cases before law courts or to debate issues in the Roman Senate. To improve their abilities as public speakers, students might also read philosophy and history. Few women studied rhetoric because women were forbidden to enter politics.

Religion. The earliest Romans believed that gods and goddesses had power over agriculture and all aspects of daily life. For example, Ceres was the goddess of the harvest, the goddess Vesta guarded the hearth fire, and the god Janus stood watch at the door. Even Jupiter, who later became the supreme Roman god, was first worshiped as a sky god with power over the weather.

During the 300's B.C., the Romans came into increasing contact with Greek ideas. They then began to worship Greek gods and goddesses. They gave them Roman names and built temples and shrines in their honor.

The government controlled the religion of ancient Rome. Priests were government officials, who were either elected or appointed to office. They performed public ceremonies to win the favor of the gods and goddesses for the state.

By A.D. 100, many Romans had lost interest in their religion. They became attracted to the religions of the Middle East, which appealed strongly to the emotions. Some of these religions promised salvation and happiness after death. Christianity, one of the Middle Eastern religions, gained many followers.

Food, clothing, and shelter. The Romans began their day at sunrise. Daylight was precious because the oil lamps the people used after dark gave off little light. Breakfast was usually a light meal of bread and cheese.

A Roman house

The illustration at the right shows a typical large house of a wealthy Roman. A courtyard called an *atrium* served as a reception room. An opening in the atrium roof let in air and light. Other rooms opened onto the atrium. Brightly colored wallpaintings and marble floor tiles decorated some atriums, such as the one below. A second courtyard, called a *peristyle,* was planted with trees, flowers, and shrubs. It might also have had a fishpond and a fountain. Fruits and vegetables were grown in a walled garden at the rear of the house. In some houses, small shops faced the street.

WORLD BOOK illustrations by Richard Hook, Linden Artists Ltd.

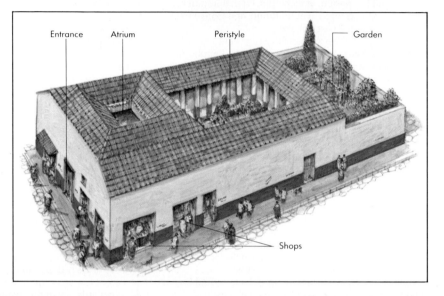

Entrance   Atrium   Peristyle   Garden

Shops

Trained warriors called *gladiators* battled to the death before huge crowds in ancient Rome. Some gladiators wore armor and carried a sword and a shield. Others used only a net and a spear. They tried to entangle their opponent in the net before driving in the spear.

Most Romans ate lunch just before midday. For wealthy Romans, it consisted of meat or fish and olives or fruit. Dinner, the main meal, began in the late afternoon so that it could end before sunset.

Wealthy Romans feasted on several courses at dinner. Their first course might include eggs, vegetables, and shellfish. The main course featured meat, fish, or fowl. For dessert, they usually ate honey-sweetened cakes and fruit. Poorer Romans ate much simpler meals. For example, their dinners consisted mainly of porridge and bread plus some olives, fruit, or cheese.

The Romans wore simple clothes made of wool or linen. The main garment for both men and women was a gown called a *tunic.* It hung to the knees or below. The tunic also served as sleepwear. Over the tunic, men wore a *toga* and women wore a *palla.* Both garments resembled a large sheet, which was draped around the body. Men almost always wore white clothing, though the toga of upper-class Romans had a purple border. Women's clothing might be dyed various colors.

In the cities, most Romans lived in crowded apartment buildings from three to five stories high. Only rich Romans could afford houses. Their houses were built around a courtyard called an *atrium.* Most rooms surrounding the atrium were small and windowless. But the atrium was spacious and had a roof opening that let in light and air. Large houses had a second courtyard, called a *peristyle,* which served as a garden. Poor people in farm areas lived in huts made of sun-dried bricks.

Recreation. The Romans observed many holidays. Most holidays were religious festivals in honor of gods and goddesses. Holidays had become so numerous by the A.D. 100's that Emperor Marcus Aurelius limited them to 135 days a year. On many holidays, the emperor or wealthy government officials sponsored free, public entertainments in outdoor arenas called *amphitheaters.*

The most famous amphitheater in the city of Rome, the Colosseum, seated about 50,000 spectators. Many of the entertainments held there were violent and bloody. For example, trained warriors called *gladiators* fought one another to the death. Most gladiators were slaves, prisoners of war, or condemned criminals. In other events, armed men fought wild animals, or starving beasts attacked condemned criminals or Christians.

Chariot races drew huge crowds in ancient Rome. The races took place in a long, oval arena called a *circus.* The Circus Maximus, the largest arena in Rome, held about 250,000 people. Skilled charioteers became popular heroes. Many Romans bet on their favorites.

Three theaters in Rome staged comedies and serious dramas by Greek and Roman authors. But most Romans preferred *mimes* (short plays about everyday life) or *pantomimes* (stories told through music and dancing).

Roman emperors built lavish public baths decorated in marble and gold to encourage daily exercise and bathing. Bathers moved through steam rooms and indoor pools of warm, hot, and cold water. Romans also visited the baths for recreation and to meet with friends. Gymnasiums, exercise grounds, gardens, sitting rooms, and libraries surrounded the bathing areas.

Work of the people

Agriculture. About 90 per cent of the people of the Roman world lived by farming. The Romans understood the need to rotate crops. They also knew that by leaving half of every field unplanted each year the soil would be enriched for a crop the next year. However, few small landowners could afford that practice.

In fertile valleys north and south of Rome, farmers grew such grains as wheat, rye, and barley. On hillsides and in less fertile soil, they planted olive groves and vineyards and grazed sheep and goats. Roman farmers also raised pigs, cattle, and poultry. As the empire expanded, farms in Gaul, Spain, and northern Africa supplied Rome with many agricultural products.

Manufacturing. The city of Rome never became a manufacturing center in ancient times. It imported most of its manufactured goods. Other Italian communities supplied the capital with such products as pottery, glassware, weapons, tools, and textiles. They also made the bricks and lead pipes needed by Rome's booming construction industry. As the empire expanded, important manufacturing centers developed outside Italy. They produced goods for local use and for export to Rome.

Mining was one of ancient Rome's most important activities. The empire's great building projects required large supplies of marble and other materials. Marble came from Greece and northern Italy. Italy also had copper and rich deposits of iron ore. Most of the empire's gold and silver came from Spain. Mines in Britain produced lead and tin. Work in the mines was hard and unhealthful. The Romans forced slaves, condemned criminals, and prisoners of war to work in the mines.

Trade thrived as the Roman Empire expanded. Huge sailing ships carried cargo from one end of the Mediterranean Sea to the other. Carts and wagons hauled goods over the empire's vast network of roads.

The city of Rome's chief imports included foods, raw materials, and manufactured goods. The Italian Peninsula exported wine and olive oil. The Romans also traded with lands outside the empire. For example, they imported silk from China, spices and precious gems from India, and ivory from Africa. The Roman government issued coins of gold, silver, copper, and bronze and controlled the supply of money, which made trade easier.

Transportation and communication. An excellent system of roads crisscrossed the Roman Empire. The roads covered about 50,000 miles (80,000 kilometers) and helped hold the empire together. The Roman army built the roads to speed the movement of troops. But the roads also promoted trade and communication. The highly organized Roman postal system depended on the road system. The straight, smooth roads designed by Roman engineers were superior to all other roads of the time.

The Romans built up the largest fleet of cargo ships of ancient times. Their ships traveled to all ports on the Mediterranean Sea and on such large rivers as the Rhine, Danube, and Nile.

In Rome, a government newssheet called *Acta Diurna* (*Daily Events*) was posted throughout the city. The paper reported on new laws and other important events.

Arts and sciences

Architecture and engineering. The ancient Romans adopted the basic forms of Greek architecture. These forms included the temple surrounded by columns and the covered walkway known as a *portico*. The Romans also created new kinds of structures, such as public baths and amphitheaters, that held many people. In gen-

WORLD BOOK illustration by Richard Hook, Linden Artists Ltd.

Crowded shops occupied the ground story of many buildings in ancient Rome. In the various shops, women marketed, men drank wine with friends, and workers sold goods they had crafted. Public fountains in the narrow streets provided water for Roman homes.

Aqueduct construction, *above,* was one of the peacetime activities of the Roman army. Roman aqueducts carried water long distances from rivers and mountain springs. The water ran in a channel along the top of an aqueduct. Roman soldiers also built roads, bridges, tunnels, and walls.

eral, the Romans designed larger and grander buildings than did the Greeks.

Two achievements of Roman engineering made the large Roman buildings possible. They were the arch and concrete. Arches supported such structures as bridges and the aqueducts that carried water to Roman cities. Arched roofs called *vaults* spanned vast interior spaces of buildings. Vaults eliminated the need for columns to hold up roofs. Although the Romans did not invent the arch, they were the first people to realize its possibilities. Concrete, which the Romans did invent, provided a strong building material for walls and vaults.

Sculpture and painting. Roman sculptors and painters borrowed from Greek art and native Italian traditions. Their works thus reflected both the lifelike but idealized human figures of Greek art and the specific details of Italian traditions.

Roman sculptors created realistic portraits that revealed individual personalities. They also illustrated historical events by means of carvings on large public monuments. For example, the richly decorated Ara Pacis (Altar of Peace) celebrated the peace brought to the empire by Emperor Augustus. Carvings on tall columns and triumphal arches told of military campaigns.

Large wallpaintings decorated the houses of well-to-do Romans. Such paintings showed garden landscapes, events from Roman mythology, and scenes of everyday life. The richly colored, carefully created paintings made rooms in Roman houses seem larger and brighter.

Literature of ancient Rome was greatly influenced by Greek poetry and drama. The Roman poets and dramatists Naevius and Ennius and the playwrights Terence and Plautus adapted Greek forms to Roman audiences. Cato and Sallust based their historical writings on Greek models. Powerful and original works were produced by

Rome's greatest poets—Catullus, Lucretius, Ovid, and Virgil—and by its most brilliant historian, Tacitus. Other important works of Latin literature include the speeches of Cicero, the satires of Horace and Juvenal, and the letters of Cicero and Pliny the Younger.

Science. The ancient Romans made few scientific discoveries. But the work of Greek scientists flourished under Roman rule. The Greek geographer Strabo traveled widely in the Roman Empire and wrote careful descriptions of what he saw. Ptolemy, a Greek astronomer living in Egypt, developed a system of astronomy that was accepted for nearly 1,500 years. Galen, a Greek physician, proposed important medical theories based on scientific experiments. The Romans themselves assembled important collections of scientific information. For example, Pliny the Elder gathered the scientific knowledge of his day in a 37-volume encyclopedia.

Government

A series of kings ruled ancient Rome at the beginning of its history. Each king was advised by a Senate made up of the heads of Rome's leading families. Citizens met in assemblies to vote on decisions made by the king and the Senate.

The Roman Republic was established in 509 B.C., after Roman nobles overthrew the king. The new government kept many features of the earlier system, including the Senate and citizen assemblies. Two elected officials called *consuls* headed the government. The consuls shared power, but either consul could veto the actions of the other. A consul served for only a year.

The Senate was the most powerful government body of the Roman Republic. The Senate conducted foreign policy, passed *decrees* (official orders), and handled the government's finances. Senators, unlike consuls, served

Hadrian's Wall was built for defense across northern Britain by Emperor Hadrian.

Britain

London •

Atlantic Ocean

The Roman Army conquered vast territories for the empire and defended its frontiers.

Germanic Lands

Rhine River

Danube River

Roman Law was based on common-sense notions of fairness. It spread throughout the empire.

Farms in Gaul supplied Rome with wine and food. Gaul also produced pottery and glassware.

Gaul

Agriculture provided a living for about 90 per cent of the people in the Roman Empire.

Illyria

Spain

Corsica

Italy

Rome ★

Huge Aqueducts supplied about 200 cities in the Roman Empire with water.

Sardinia

Chariot Racing was a popular entertainment in ancient Rome. People bet on their favorite drivers.

Sicily

Mediterranean Sea

Carthage •

Mauretania

Roman Warships, which were propelled by oars and sails, ruled the Mediterranean Sea.

Timgad, like many other Roman cities, had an orderly plan and was originally built as an army camp.

Wild Animals caught in Africa were shipped to Rome to fight people in bloody public games.

WORLD BOOK illustrations by Angus McBride, Linden Artists Ltd.

The Roman world

Roman rule gradually spread over all the lands bordering the Mediterranean Sea. At the time of its greatest size, the Roman Empire also stretched from Britain in the north to Mesopotamia in the east. The peoples who lived in the Roman Empire spoke many languages and followed different customs. Yet the Roman Empire united them under a common system of law and government.

Military Engineers built a vast system of roads throughout the Roman Empire.

Dacia

Black Sea

Greek Culture greatly influenced the Romans. They copied Greek art and worshiped Greek gods.

Emperor Constantine made Byzantium (now Istanbul, Turkey) his capital in A.D. 330. He renamed it Constantinople.

Armenia

Constantinople

Saint Paul preached the teachings of Jesus Christ in Asia Minor and Greece during the A.D. 50's.

Parthia

Macedonia

• Pergamum

Ephesus •

Mesopotamia

• Athens

Antioch • **Syria**

Tigris River

Euphrates River

Greece

Cyprus

Crete

Cargo Ships brought goods to Rome. The Romans had the largest merchant fleet of ancient times.

Judea

Jerusalem •

Alexandria •

Grain from Egypt helped feed the Roman people. The Romans made bread and porridge from wheat.

The Destruction of Jerusalem occurred in A.D. 70. After the Jews revolted against Roman rule, Roman soldiers burned the city.

Caspian Sea

Egypt

Arabia

Nile River

Red Sea

for life. At first, all senators were *patricians*—that is, members of Rome's oldest and richest families. Patricians controlled not only the Senate but also the assembly that elected the consuls and other important officials. All the rest of Rome's citizens, who were called *plebeians,* had little political influence.

To obtain political rights, plebeians formed their own assembly, the *Concilium Plebis,* and elected leaders called *tribunes.* Largely through the work of the tribunes, plebeians gradually gained the same political rights as the patricians. In time, a new and larger assembly, the *Comitia Tributa,* developed. It represented both patricians and plebeians, but plebeians largely controlled the assembly.

The Roman Republic lasted nearly 500 years, until 27 B.C. It combined strong heads of state, a respected Senate of senior statesmen, and assemblies where the people could be heard. For centuries afterward, historians and political scientists viewed the Roman Republic as a model of balanced government.

The Roman Empire was established in 27 B.C., after the republic was destroyed by 20 years of civil war. The empire lasted until Rome fell in A.D. 476. During that time, emperors held supreme authority. The republican institutions of government were kept. But emperors nominated the consuls and appointed new senators. The citizen assemblies had little power. Emperors headed the army and directed the making of laws. They relied more on their own advisers than on the Senate. A vast civil service handled the empire's day-to-day business.

The law. The Romans published their first known code of law about 450 B.C. This code, called the Laws of the Twelve Tables, set down accepted practices in written form. Roman law remained flexible. It depended on the interpretations of skilled lawyers and judges.

Through the years, a general set of legal principles developed that governed all the various peoples living under Roman rule. Roman lawyers called this set of principles the *jus gentium* (law of nations). The jus gentium was based on common-sense notions of fairness. It took into account local customs and practices.

The army. Under the Roman Republic, the army was made up only of citizens who owned land. The Romans felt that property owners had a greater stake in the republic than did landless people and would therefore defend it better.

As Rome began to fight wars overseas, it required more soldiers, and they had to serve for longer periods. The government abolished the property requirement in 107 B.C. and opened the army to volunteers. The army then offered a long-term career for many Romans. In time, more and more soldiers were recruited from the provinces. By about 20 B.C., some 300,000 men served in the Roman army. The number of soldiers changed little thereafter. Most soldiers were professionals, whose training and discipline made the Roman army one of the greatest fighting forces in history.

Roman soldiers did not only fight. They also built roads, aqueducts, walls, and tunnels. After Rome reached its greatest size, the army's main task was to defend the empire's frontiers. Many troops were thus stationed along the Rhine and Danube rivers. Other important army posts stood in Egypt, Syria, and Britain.

History

Beginnings. Historians know little about the early days of ancient Rome. According to Roman legend, twin brothers, Romulus and Remus, established a settlement

Highlights in the history of ancient Rome

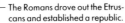

According to legend, Romulus and Remus founded Rome.

Rome began its expansion overseas by defeating Carthage in three Punic Wars.

753 B.C. 509 B.C. 264-146 B.C. 27 B.C.

The Romans drove out the Etruscans and established a republic.

Augustus became the first Roman emperor.

Bronze sculpture; Museo del Palazzo dei Conservatori, Rome (SCALA/Art Resource)

The legendary founders of Rome were twin brothers named Romulus and Remus. According to Roman mythology, a wolf nursed them as babies.

Tomb painting (500's B.C.) in Tarquinia, Italy (SCALA/Art Resource)

The Etruscan culture of central Italy influenced Rome during the 500's B.C. Under Etruscan rule, Rome grew from a village into a prosperous city.

Marble sculpture by an unknown artist; Uffizi Gallery, Florence, Italy (SCALA/Art Resource)

Cicero, the great Roman statesman and orator, supported Rome's republican government. But the Roman Republic ended soon after he died in 43 B.C.

in 753 B.C. on the Palatine Hill, one of Rome's hills over-looking the Tiber River. Greek legend told of the Trojan hero Aeneas, who founded a settlement in central Italy after the destruction of Troy by the Greeks in the Trojan War. Some versions combined the two myths and made Romulus and Remus descendants of Aeneas.

The first known settlers of ancient Rome lived on the Palatine Hill about 1000 B.C. Most historians believe that these settlers were a people called Latins. Latins also inhabited many neighboring towns in Latium, the region surrounding Rome.

About 600 B.C., Rome and other towns in Latium came under the control of the Etruscans, a people who lived north of Latium. The Etruscans had the most advanced civilization in Italy. They built roads, temples, and public buildings in Rome. They also promoted trade and introduced the idea of the citizen assembly. Under Etruscan rule, Rome grew from a village of farmers and shepherds into a prosperous city. The city became so powerful that the people were able to drive out the Etruscans in 509 B.C.

The early republic. The Roman Republic was established in 509 B.C., after the overthrow of the monarchy. However, the institutions of republican government developed gradually through a long struggle between the landowning upper class—that is, the patricians—and all the other citizens, the plebeians. At first, only patricians held political office, served as priests, and interpreted Roman law. Plebeians had few political rights and often received unfair treatment from judges.

Plebeians fought for political rights during the 400's and 300's B.C. By 287 B.C., they had won the right to hold any public or religious office and had gained equality under the law. But vast differences in wealth and social position still separated most plebeians from patricians.

Meanwhile, Rome was slowly gaining military control over the rest of the Italian Peninsula. In 493 B.C., Rome entered an alliance with the Latin League, a federation of cities of Latium. Rome had become the largest city in Latium by 396 B.C. and thereafter used the league's resources to fight wars with its neighbors. Rome offered protection and certain privileges of Roman citizenship to the cities it conquered. In return, the conquered cities supplied the Roman army with soldiers.

During the 300's B.C., Rome won victories over the Etruscans. Rome also defeated the Gauls, who had invaded Italy from the north and burned Rome in 390 B.C. In 338 B.C., Rome overpowered and disbanded the Latin League. In 290 B.C., the Romans conquered the Samnites, a mountain people who lived south of Rome. Rome ruled most of the Italian Peninsula by 275 B.C., after a victory over the Greek colony of Tarentum in southern Italy.

Expansion overseas made Rome a mighty empire during the 200's and 100's B.C. Rome came into conflict first with Carthage, a sea power and trading center on the coast of northern Africa. Rome and Carthage fought for mastery of the Mediterranean Sea in three struggles called the Punic Wars. In the First Punic War (264-241 B.C.), Rome conquered Sicily, an island off the tip of Italy, and made it the first Roman province. Rome also seized two other Mediterranean islands—Sardinia and Corsica. In the Second Punic War (218-201 B.C.), the brilliant Carthaginian general Hannibal led his army over the Alps into Italy. He won several key battles, but Roman manpower and endurance eventually wore him down. Under Publius Cornelius Scipio's leadership, the Roman forces defeated Hannibal in 202 B.C. In the

The Roman Empire reached its height of power and prosperity.

A.D. 96-180

The Roman Empire split into two parts—the West Roman Empire and the East Roman Empire.

A.D. 395

The last emperor of the West Roman Empire, Romulus Augustulus, was overthrown by a Germanic tribe.

A.D. 476

Mosaic (A.D. 200's); Bardo Museum, Tunis, Tunisia (Giraudon/Art Resource)

Latin literature flourished in the Age of Augustus, from 27 B.C. to A.D. 14. The poet Virgil, *seated*, wrote of Rome's creation in his great epic, the *Aeneid*.

Relief sculpture (A.D. 100's); The Louvre, Paris (André Martin, Arthaud)

The praetorians were soldiers who guarded the emperor. In time, the emperors grew removed from the people and were worshiped as gods after death.

Wall painting (A.D. 200's) in Rome; (SCALA/Art Resource)

Christianity spread rapidly in the Roman Empire, though Christians were often persecuted. Christians were granted freedom of worship in A.D. 313.

Third Punic War (149-146 B.C.), Rome destroyed Carthage. These victories brought the Mediterranean coasts of Spain and Africa under Roman control.

After the Second Punic War, Rome began to expand in the east. At first, Rome acted to protect its allies along Italy's east coast from pirate raids. But it soon became involved in conflicts between Greece and Macedonia. Macedonia, which lay north of Greece, had conquered the Greeks in 338 B.C. Rome posed as the liberator of the Greeks. But by the 140's B.C., it had taken control of Greece and Macedonia. In 133 B.C., King Attalus III of Pergamum, a Roman ally, died and left his kingdom (now part of Turkey) to Rome.

Two reasons help explain Rome's remarkable expansion overseas. First, Rome built an alliance of cities in Italy that supplied the army with enormous manpower. Second, pride in their military power and government institutions gave the Romans great confidence in their superiority and in the justness of their cause.

Breakdown of the republic. Although the Romans had triumphed overseas, they faced growing discontent at home. Wealthy Romans profited from the tax revenues, slaves, and looted property that poured into Rome from defeated lands. But unemployment rose as plantations worked by slaves drove out the small farmers, and the gap between rich and poor widened. In 133 and 123 B.C., two Roman tribunes tried to help the poor. Tiberius Gracchus and his brother, Gaius Gracchus, promoted a program to distribute state-owned land to the poor. But the majority of the Senate opposed them, and both brothers were assassinated.

Conflicts among leaders caused upheaval in the Roman Republic during its last 100 years. Revolts by Rome's Italian allies, a war in Asia, and unrest at home weakened the republic. In 82 B.C., the Roman general Lucius Sulla became dictator. Sulla restored stability to the government and strengthened the Senate by bringing in new leaders. Sulla retired in 79 B.C., but he had given Rome a taste of one-man rule.

In the 60's B.C., Rome again began to expand overseas. The Roman general Pompey conquered eastern Asia Minor, Syria, and Judea. He returned to Rome a popular hero, but the Senate refused to recognize his victories. As a result, Pompey and two other Roman leaders—Julius Caesar and Marcus Crassus—formed a three-man political alliance called the First Triumvirate in 60 B.C. Crassus died in warfare in 53 B.C. Other Roman leaders then tried to split the two surviving members of the Triumvirate.

From 58 to 51 B.C., Caesar conquered Gaul, thereby adding the huge territory west of the Rhine River to the Roman world. Pompey and the Senate feared Caesar's power and ambition, and they ordered him to give up his command. But Caesar marched his troops across the Rubicon, a stream that separated Italy from Gaul, and invaded Italy in 49 B.C. In the civil war that followed, Caesar defeated Pompey and his followers. By 45 B.C., Caesar had become sole ruler of the Roman world. A group of aristocrats who hoped to revive the Roman Republic assassinated him in 44 B.C.

Civil war again broke out after Caesar's death. In 43 B.C., Caesar's adopted son and heir, Octavian, formed the Second Triumvirate with two army officers, Mark Antony and Marcus Lepidus. Octavian and Antony defeated Caesar's enemies and soon pushed Lepidus aside. Octavian and Antony then fought each other for control of Rome. Antony sought the support of Cleopatra, queen of Egypt, and they fell in love. In 31 B.C., Octavian defeated the forces of Antony and Cleopatra in the Battle of Actium off the west coast of Greece. The next year, the Romans conquered Egypt and made it a Roman province.

After the defeat of Antony, Octavian was the unchallenged leader of the Roman world. In 27 B.C., he became the first Roman emperor and took the name Augustus, meaning *exalted.* In spite of his power, Augustus avoided the title of emperor. He preferred to be called *princeps,* meaning *first citizen.* Nearly 20 years of civil war had destroyed the republic. Only a strong central authority seemed able to govern the empire.

The height of the empire. The reign of Augustus marked the beginning of a long period of stability, which became known as the *Pax Romana* (Roman Peace). The Pax Romana lasted about 200 years. Augustus reestablished orderly government and the rule of law. The Senate, consuls, and tribunes still functioned, but Augustus had supreme power. He commanded the army, controlled the provinces, and filled the Senate with his supporters.

Augustus established strong defenses along the fron-

Growth of the Roman Empire

Ancient Rome began to expand during the 300's B.C. and by 275 B.C. ruled much of Italy. Expansion overseas made Rome the dominant Mediterranean power by 133 B.C. The Roman Empire grew relatively little after the death of Augustus in A.D. 14. It reached its greatest size under Trajan, who ruled until A.D. 117.

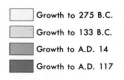

Growth to 275 B.C.
Growth to 133 B.C.
Growth to A.D. 14
Growth to A.D. 117

World Book map

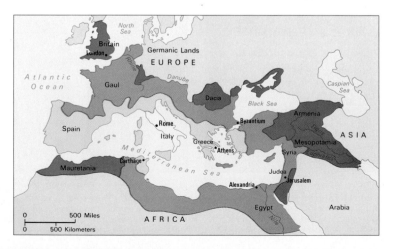

Division of the Roman Empire

The Roman Empire grew weaker during the A.D. 300's. In 395, it was split into the West Roman Empire and the East Roman Empire. Each empire was subdivided into two parts called *prefectures*. The West Roman Empire soon fell to Germanic tribes. But the East Roman Empire survived as the Byzantine Empire until 1453.

West Roman Empire
- Prefecture of Gaul
- Prefecture of Italy and Africa

East Roman Empire
- Prefecture of Illyricum
- Prefecture of the East

WORLD BOOK map

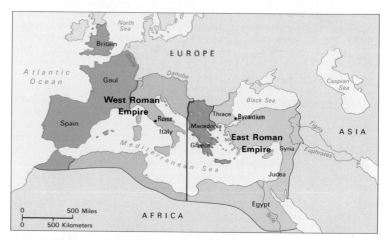

tiers of the Roman Empire and kept the provinces under control. He began to develop a civil service staffed by skilled administrators to help govern the empire. Trade flourished, and art and literature reached a high point during what has been called the *Augustan Age.*

Augustus died in A.D. 14. He had groomed his stepson Tiberius to succeed him, thereby preparing the way for a succession of emperors. Members of Augustus's family, known as the Julio-Claudians, ruled until A.D. 68. They were followed by the Flavian family, which reigned until A.D. 96. The Roman Empire reached its height of power and prosperity during the reign of the Antonines, from A.D. 96 to 180. The Antonine rulers—Nerva, Trajan, Hadrian, Antoninus Pius, and Marcus Aurelius—were noted for their wisdom and ability.

The Roman Empire grew relatively little after the reign of Augustus. In A.D. 43, Emperor Claudius invaded Britain. Trajan seized Dacia (now part of Hungary and Romania) in A.D. 106. The stable political and military situation encouraged Romans to invest in land. Small farms and large estates thrived. Roman roads made excellent communications possible. Roman emperors encouraged the founding of new towns and cities, even in remote areas. The civil service grew increasingly skilled at running the day-to-day business of the empire. Provincial governors usually served long terms and so gained familiarity with the territories they controlled.

The authority of the Roman emperors gradually grew stronger. An emperor's order overruled any act of the Senate. The Romans worshiped an emperor as a god after his death. Emperor worship provided a common base of loyalty among the empire's peoples, who otherwise observed many different religions and traditions.

In the eastern part of the Roman Empire, a new religion developed based on the teachings of Jesus Christ. Although the Romans crucified Jesus for treason about A.D. 30, His followers spread Christianity throughout the empire. The Roman government took little notice of Christianity at first. Persecutions of Christians stemmed from local hostility rather than orders from Rome.

Growing disorder. Marcus Aurelius became emperor in A.D. 161. He defended the Roman Empire against attacks by Germanic tribes from the north and Parthians from the east. But growing disorder plagued the empire after his son, Emperor Commodus, died in 192. Many

emperors seized power by force, and rival leaders fought for the throne. From 235 to 284, 60 men were proclaimed emperor. Most of the men were army commanders whose troops named them emperor.

The enormous size of the Roman Empire hastened its

Emperors of Rome

Name	Reign†	Name	Reign†
*Augustus	27 B.C.-A.D. 14	*Aurelian	270-275
*Tiberius	14-37	Tacitus	275-276
*Caligula	37-41	Florian	276
*Claudius	41-54	Probus	276-282
*Nero	54-68	Carus	282-283
Galba	68-69	Carinus	283-285
Otho	69	Numerianus	283-284
Vitellius	69	*Diocletian (E)	284-305
*Vespasian	69-79	Maximian (W)	286-305
*Titus	79-81	Constantius I (W)	305-306
Domitian	81-96	Galerius	305-311
Nerva	96-98	Severus	306-307
*Trajan	98-117	*Constantine I	306-337
*Hadrian	117-138	Licinius	308-324
*Antoninus Pius	138-161	Maximinus	310-313
*Marcus Aurelius	161-180	Constantius II	337-361
Lucius Verus	161-169	Constantine II	337-340
Commodus	180-192	Constans	337-350
Pertinax	193	*Julian	361-363
Didius Julianus	193	Jovian	363-364
Septimius Severus	193-211	*Valentinian I (W)	364-375
Caracalla	211-217	Valens (E)	364-378
Macrinus	217-218	Gratian (W)	367-383
Elagabalus	218-222	Valentinian II (W)	375-392
Severus		Eugenius	392-394
Alexander	222-235	*Theodosius I	379-395
Maximinus			
Thrax	235-238	**Emperors of the west**	
Gordian I and		Honorius	395-423
Gordian II	238	*Valentinian III	425-455
Pupienus	238	Petronius	
Balbinus	238	Maximus	455-457
Gordian III	238-244	Majorian	457-461
Philippus	244-249	Libius Severus	461-467
Decius	249-251	Anthemius	467-472
Gallus	251-253	Olybrius	472-473
Aemilianus	253	Glycerius	473-474
Valerian	253-260	Julius Nepos	474-475
*Gallienus	253-268	Romulus	
Claudius II	268-270	Augustulus	475-476

*Has a separate article in *World Book.*
†Rome was ruled by two emperors from 161 to 169 and by two or more emperors much of the time from 283 to 395. Sometimes, the empire's eastern (E) and western (W) parts were ruled by separate emperors. At other times, as many as four emperors ruled.

breakdown. A central authority in Rome could no longer hold the empire together. In addition, the struggles for power among Roman generals seriously weakened the empire's defenses. The Goths, a Germanic people, invaded Roman territory many times during the 200's, and the Persians overran Mesopotamia and Syria.

Temporary recovery. Diocletian, a Roman general, was proclaimed emperor by his troops in 284. Diocletian realized that one man could no longer govern the empire. To restore order, he divided the provinces into smaller units. Each unit had its own government and army. He appointed a soldier named Maximian to be co-emperor and two deputies to succeed them. Maximian ruled the western part of the empire, and Diocletian ruled the eastern part. Diocletian's reforms temporarily halted the empire's collapse. But heavy taxes were needed to pay for the larger army and government.

Christians suffered severe persecution during the 200's. Many Romans blamed them for causing the evils of the time by having offended the traditional Roman gods. In 303, Diocletian forbade Christian worship.

Constantine I was named emperor of Rome's western provinces in 306. Diocletian's system of shared rule and succession quickly broke down as several men struggled for the throne. In 312, Constantine defeated his major rival after having had a vision promising victory if he fought under the sign of the cross. In 313, Constantine and Licinius, emperor of the eastern provinces, granted Christians freedom of worship. Constantine and Licinius ruled jointly until 324, when Constantine defeated the co-emperor in war. Constantine, who later became known as "the Great," moved his capital to Byzantium in 330 and renamed the city Constantinople.

Decline and fall. After Constantine died in 337, his three sons and two of his nephews fought for control of the Roman Empire. One of the nephews, Julian, became emperor in 361. Julian tried to check the spread of Christianity and restore the traditional Roman religion. But by the late 300's, Christianity had become the official religion of the empire. The empire was permanently split into the West Roman Empire and the East Roman Empire after Emperor Theodosius I died in 395.

The West Roman Empire grew steadily weaker. The Vandals, Visigoths, and other Germanic peoples invaded Spain, Gaul, and northern Africa. In 410, the Visigoths looted Rome. The fall of the empire is often dated 476. That year, the Germanic chieftain Odoacer forced Romulus Augustulus, the last ruler of the empire, from the throne. Germanic chiefs had already begun to carve up the empire into several kingdoms. The East Roman Empire survived as the Byzantine Empire until 1453, when the Turks captured Constantinople.

The Roman heritage. The Roman Empire fell from political power. But its culture and institutions survived and shaped Western civilization and the Byzantine world. Roman law became the base of many legal systems in western Europe and Latin America. Latin remained the language of learned Europeans for over 1,000 years. French, Italian, Spanish, and other Romance languages developed from Latin. Roman architecture inspired building design in Europe and North America.

The Roman Empire transmitted its social and economic system to the Middle Ages, the period of European history that followed ancient times. During the Middle Ages, the Roman Catholic Church replaced the Roman Empire as the unifying force in Europe. The church modeled its administrative structure on the organization of the Roman Empire. It used the Latin language and preserved the classics of Latin literature.

Learning about ancient Rome

Most of our knowledge about ancient Rome comes from written records of the Romans. These records include such documents as law codes, treaties, and decrees of the emperors and the Roman Senate. Other written records are masterpieces of Latin literature. In many works, the authors wrote about events they lived through. Such works include the letters and speeches of Cicero and the letters of Pliny the Younger. Julius Caesar wrote about his conquest of Gaul in *Commentaries on the Gallic War.* Roman historians supplied the narrations that connected many of the events that other writers described. Livy told of Rome's development from its legendary origins to his own time, the Augustan Age. Tacitus described the period of Roman history from Emperors Tiberius to Domitian. Suetonius wrote biographies of the rulers from Julius Caesar to Domitian.

Not all the records left by the Romans are written. Scenes carved on monuments also portray events in Roman history. For example, Trajan's Column and the Column of Marcus Aurelius, both in Rome, tell about Trajan's and Marcus Aurelius' military campaigns.

The remains of Roman towns and cities also provide valuable information. Pompeii and Herculaneum, which lay south of Rome, were buried when Mount Vesuvius erupted in A.D. 79. Excavations of the sites have told us much about everyday life in Roman times.

Interest in the study of ancient Rome reawakened during the Renaissance, the great cultural movement that swept across Europe from the early 1300's to about 1600. The Renaissance started in Italy as scholars rediscovered the works of ancient Greek and Roman authors. In modern times, the first major history of Rome was *The History of the Decline and Fall of the Roman Empire* (1776-1788), a six-volume work by the British historian Edward Gibbon. During the 1800's, German scholars made important studies of ancient Roman texts. The German historian Theodor Mommsen produced some of the most important studies on Roman law and history. His *History of Rome* (1854-1856) has influenced all later scholarship on ancient Rome.   Erich S. Gruen

Related articles in *World Book* include:

Biographies

See the table *Emperors of Rome* with this article. For biographies of Roman authors, see the *Related articles* at the end of **Latin literature.** See also:

Agrippina the Younger	Galen
Antony, Mark	Gracchus family
Brutus, Marcus Junius	Marius, Gaius
Caesar, Julius	Octavia
Cassius Longinus, Gaius	Pilate, Pontius
Catiline	Plotinus
Cato, Marcus Porcius, the Elder	Pompey the Great
	Porphyry
Cato, Marcus Porcius, the Younger	Regulus, Marcus Atilius
	Scipio Africanus, Publius Cornelius
Cincinnatus, Lucius Q.	
Coriolanus, Gaius Marcius	Spartacus
Crassus, Marcus Licinius	Sulla, Lucius Cornelius

Buildings and works

Appian Way
Aqueduct
Archaeology (pictures)
Atrium
Basilica
Catacombs

Colosseum
Column
Forum, Roman
Pantheon
Road
Roman walls

Cities and regions

Galatia
Gaul
Herculaneum
Latium
Numidia
Pompeii
Rome (Ancient city; pictures)

Contributions to civilization

Architecture
Drama (Roman drama)
Exploration (The Romans)
Geology (The Romans)
Julian calendar
Justinian Code
Latin language
Latin literature
Law (Ancient Roman law)

Library (History)
Mythology
Oratory (Classical orators)
Painting
Roman numerals
Romance languages
Sculpture
Twelve Tables, Laws of the

Daily life

Augur
Bath (History)
Clothing (Clothing through the ages)
Education (History)
Food (Ancient times)
Furniture (Ancient Rome)
Gladiator
Lares and Penates
Saturnalia
Sibyl
Toga

Government

Consul
Dictatorship
Equestrian order
Fasces
Legion
Patricians

Plebeians
Praetor
Praetorian guard
Tribune
Triumvirate

History

See the *History* section of articles on countries that Rome ruled, such as **England** (History). See also:
Actium, Battle of
Barbarian
Byzantine Empire
Etruscans
Flag (pictures: Historical flags of the world)
Punic Wars
Romulus and Remus
Rubicon
Sabines
Ship (Roman ships; pictures)
World, History of the (The Romans)

Outline

I. **The Roman world**
  A. The land B. The people
II. **Life of the people**
  A. City life
  B. Rural life
  C. Family life
  D. Education
  E. Religion
  F. Food, clothing, and shelter
  G. Recreation

III. **Work of the people**
  A. Agriculture
  B. Manufacturing
  C. Mining
  D. Trade
  E. Transportation and communication
IV. **Arts and sciences**
  A. Architecture and engineering
  B. Sculpture and painting
  C. Literature
  D. Science
V. **Government**
  A. The Roman Republic
  B. The Roman Empire
  C. The law
  D. The army
VI. **History**
VII. **Learning about ancient Rome**

Questions

Why did rhetoric play an important role in higher education in ancient Rome?

From where does most of our knowledge of ancient Rome come?

What steps did Diocletian take to restore order in the Roman Empire?

What was an *atrium* and what purpose did it serve?

Why was the army of the Roman Republic made up only of property owners?

Why was building a network of roads so important to the Romans?

What two reasons help explain Rome's remarkable expansion overseas?

Where do Roman legal principles survive today?

What two engineering achievements made it possible for the Romans to construct large buildings?

How did Roman emperors limit the role of the members of the Roman Senate?

Additional resources

Adkins, Lesley and R. A. *Handbook to Life in Ancient Rome.* Facts on File, 1994.

Boardman, John, and others, eds. *The Oxford History of the Roman World.* Oxford, 1991.

Bunson, Matthew. *Encyclopedia of the Roman Empire.* Facts on File, 1992.

Cornell, Tim, and Matthews, John. *Atlas of the Roman World.* Facts on File, 1982.

Nardo, Don. *The Roman Empire.* Lucent Bks., 1994. *The Roman Republic.* 1994.

Rome, University of, is the largest university in Italy. It has divisions of architecture; economics and commerce; education; engineering; law; letters and philosophy; mathematics, physics, and chemistry; medicine; pharmacy; political science; and statistical sciences. The university is coeducational and has about 180,000 students. Its library owns about 1 million books and pamphlets.

The University of Rome was founded in 1303 by Pope Boniface VIII. During the 1500's, it became famous as a center for the study of medicine and other sciences. The Italian government has controlled the university since 1870.   P. A. McGinley

See also **Rome** (picture: The University of Rome).

Romero, Oscar Arnulfo (1917-1980), served as archbishop of El Salvador from 1977 until his death. As archbishop, he was the highest official of the Roman Catholic Church in the country. Romero at first avoided becoming involved in political affairs. However, in time he came to believe the church should take an active role in bringing social justice to the people. Romero became an outspoken critic of the violence and human rights abuses that El Salvador's military government committed against its citizens and opponents. In 1980, he was assassinated by an unknown gunman while celebrating Mass. Romero's death became a symbol for those who sought peace and change in the country.

Oscar Arnulfo Romero y Galdamez was born in Ciudad Barrios, El Salvador, near the city of San Miguel. He was ordained as a priest in 1942. From 1968 to 1972, Romero served as executive secretary to the Central American Bishop's Secretariat. In 1974, he became bishop in Santiago de Maria.   Morris J. Blachman

Rommel, *RAW muhl,* **Erwin** (1891-1944), a German field marshal, was one of the most brilliant generals of World War II. He led the Afrika Korps, and his clever tactics earned him the nickname of The Desert Fox. But in 1942, he was stopped by British forces in Egypt.

In 1944, Rommel led some of the troops that opposed the Allied invasion of Normandy. After he recognized the significance of the superiority of the Allied air forces, he reported to Adolf Hitler that it was futile for Germany to continue the war. He was implicated in the plot to kill Hitler in July 1944. Rommel was given his choice of trial or poison. He chose death by poison. Rommel was born in Heidenheim.   Donald M. McKale

Romulo, *RAHM yu loh* or *roh MOO loh,* **Carlos Pena,** *PAY nah* (1899-1985), a Filipino diplomat and author, served as Philippine secretary (later minister) of foreign affairs from 1965 to 1984. He had previously held several important government posts. Romulo served as Philippine ambassador to the United States in 1952 and 1953, and from 1955 to 1962. He was his country's representative at the United Nations (UN) from 1946 to 1954. In 1949, he became the first Asian president of the UN General Assembly. Romulo represented the Philippines on the UN Security Council in 1957. He served as the president of the University of the Philippines from 1962 to 1969 and was also secretary of education from 1966 to 1969.

Romulo was born in Manila and educated at the University of the Philippines and Columbia University. For 20 years, he edited a chain of Philippine newspapers. He won a Pulitzer Prize in 1942 for a series of articles he wrote on political and military affairs in Southeast Asia.

Socorro L. Reyes

Romulus and Remus, *RAHM yuh luhs, REE muhs,* in Roman mythology, were twin brothers who founded the city of Rome. The Romans considered Romulus their first king.

According to tradition, Romulus and Remus were born in the ancient Italian city of Alba Longa. King Numitor ruled Alba Longa until Amulius, his younger brother, deposed him. Amulius killed Numitor's sons and forced Rhea Silvia, Numitor's daughter, to become a Vestal Virgin. Vestal Virgins were priestesses who were required by law to remain virgins. Amulius hoped that Rhea Silvia's being a Vestal Virgin would prevent her from bearing children who might threaten his rule. But the god Mars seduced Rhea Silvia, and she gave birth to Romulus and Remus. Amulius had Rhea Silvia executed and ordered the babies placed in a basket and thrown into the Tiber River.

After floating downstream, the twins were washed ashore. A female wolf found the infants and nursed

them. Romulus, Remus, and the wolf became popular subjects for Roman artists. Several ancient statues show the babies with their animal protector.

A shepherd named Faustulus discovered Romulus and Remus. Faustulus and his wife raised the boys as their own children. After the twins became young men, they learned their true identity. They overthrew Amulius, killed him, and restored Numitor to the throne.

Soon, Romulus and Remus set out to found their own city. However, the brothers quarreled over the site where the city should be built. To settle the argument, they agreed that the one who saw the largest number of vultures in flight should choose the site. Romulus claimed he saw 12 vultures, which he declared was a sign from the gods that his location was the proper one. Remus, who saw only 6 vultures, thought his brother had cheated. After Romulus began to build a wall around his chosen site, Remus leaped over the ditch that was to hold the foundation of the wall. As he did so, he mocked Romulus. For this act of disloyalty, Remus was killed, either by Romulus himself or by one of Romulus's followers. Romulus then became the sole ruler of the city, which he named Rome for himself.

Rome prospered, but only men lived there. To provide wives for his subjects, Romulus had women kidnapped from the neighboring Sabine people (see **Sabines**). Romulus was a wise and popular ruler and a fine military leader. He expanded Rome until it became the most powerful city in its region.

After a long reign, Romulus disappeared mysteriously during a storm. According to a later myth, he became the god Quirinus.   Daniel P. Harmon

See also **Mythology** (Roman mythology); **Rome, Ancient** (picture: The legendary founders of Rome).

Roncalli, Angelo Giuseppe. See **John XXIII** (pope).

Rondo, *RAHN doh,* is a form of musical composition in which the principal section or theme is repeated at least three times in the same key. Contrasting sections appear between the principal themes. Because it constantly returns to the main idea, this form is cyclic, and so is called a *rondo.* If *A* represents the principal section or theme, and *B* and *C* the contrasting sections, the sequence of sections might be ABACA, or ABACABA, and so on.   Thomas W. Tunks

Ronsard, *rawn SAR,* **Pierre de,** *pyair duh* (1524-1585), often called the Prince of Poets, led an influential group of French poets called the *Pléiade.* The *Sonnets for Hélène* (1578), perhaps his best-known work, explored the joys and sorrows of love in masterful and descriptive verse. Ronsard's *Odes* (1550-1556) were inspired by Greek and Latin poetry. Ronsard also wrote many volumes of love poetry in addition to the *Sonnets for Hélène,* and the moral and philosophical *Hymnes* (1555-1556). In *Discours* (1560-1563), he wrote stirring attacks against the Protestant movement during the religious wars that shook France in the 1560's.

Ronsard was born near Vendôme and trained to be a diplomat. He turned to literature after he became partially deaf.   Robert B. Griffin

See also **French literature** (The Pléiade).

Roof is the cover of any building. The term also includes the materials that support the roof. Climate often determines the design of roofs. Ancient Syrians and Egyptians used flat roofs because of the hot sun and the

Types of roofs

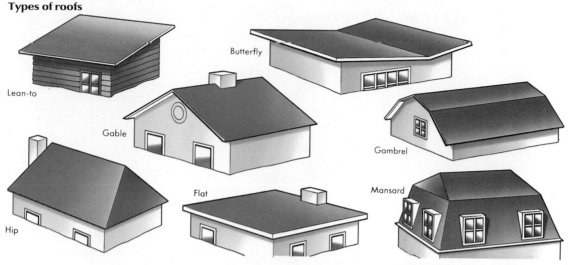

Lean-to

Butterfly

Gable

Gambrel

Hip

Flat

Mansard

WORLD BOOK illustrations by Oxford Illustrators Limited

lack of rain. Steep, sloping roofs covered the homes of central Europe, to help drain off heavy rains.

There are many variations of flat and sloping roofs. A *gable* roof has two sides sloping up to a center ridge. The *hip* roof has four sides sloping up from all four walls. The *lean-to* is a single slope over a small building, usually set against a larger building. A *gambrel* roof has two added ridges parallel to the center gable ridge, making steep slopes below each side of the upper, flatter slopes. *Mansard* roofs also have ridges below the center one, but on four sides, like the hip roof. Water is drained beyond the walls of a building by the *eaves* (overhang) of the roof.   Jack M. Landers

See also **Architecture** (pictures); **House; Shelter.**

Rook, also called *Eurasian rook,* is a bird found in Europe and Asia. The rook belongs to the crow family. Unlike other members of the crow family, however, the rook has a purple gloss on its black plumage. It feeds primarily on insects and grain. When rooks reach adulthood, about 1 year of age, they shed the feathers of their face, which then becomes a grayish-white color. Rooks measure about 18 inches (46 centimeters) long.

Rooks nest in communities of many hundreds, known as *rookeries.* Rooks that nest in central Europe remain in the same region the year around. Those that nest farther north migrate southward for the winter. Tame rooks sometimes learn to imitate human speech.

Martha Hatch Balph

Scientific classification. The rook belongs to the crow family, Corvidae. Its scientific name is *Corvus frugilegus.*

See also **Crow.**

Roosevelt, *ROH zuh vehlt,* **Eleanor** (1884-1962), the wife of President Franklin D. Roosevelt, became a distinguished public figure in her own right. She was one of the most active first ladies in American history. Roosevelt, a niece of President Theodore Roosevelt, won fame for her humanitarian work and became a role model for women in politics and public affairs.

Eleanor Roosevelt was christened Anna Eleanor Roosevelt. But her family called her Eleanor, and she rarely used her real first name. In 1905, she married Franklin D.

Roosevelt, a distant cousin. She began to work politically in his behalf after polio crippled him in 1921. During Franklin Roosevelt's terms as governor of New York and, later, as president, she frequently made fact-finding trips for him. While first lady, she traveled nationwide on lecture tours, held 350 press conferences for women reporters only, and wrote a daily newspaper column and many articles for magazines. She also worked with young people and the underprivileged, and fought for equal rights for minority groups.

Karsh, Ottawa

Eleanor Roosevelt

From 1945 to 1951, Roosevelt was a delegate to the United Nations General Assembly. In 1946, she was elected chairman of the UN's Human Rights Commission, part of the Economic and Social Council. She helped draft the Universal Declaration of Human Rights (see **Human Rights, Universal Declaration of**). In 1961, she returned to the General Assembly. Later that year, President John F. Kennedy appointed her head of the Commission on the Status of Women.

Eleanor Roosevelt wrote several books. They include *This Is My Story* (1937), *This I Remember* (1950), *On My Own* (1958), and *Tomorrow Is Now* (published in 1963, after her death).   Maurine H. Beasley

See also **First ladies** (picture); **Roosevelt, Franklin Delano.**

Additional resources

Beasley, Maurine H. *Eleanor Roosevelt and the Media.* Univ. of Ill. Pr., 1987.

Black, Allida M. *What I Hope to Leave Behind: The Essential Essays of Eleanor Roosevelt.* Carlson Pub., 1995.

Cook, Blanche W. *Eleanor Roosevelt, Vol. I: 1884-1933.* Viking, 1992.

Freedman, Russell. *Eleanor Roosevelt.* Clarion, 1993. Younger readers.

32nd President of the United States 1933-1945

John N. Garner
Vice President
1933-1941

Henry A. Wallace
Vice President
1941-1945

Harry S. Truman
Vice President
1945

Hoover
31st President
1929-1933
Republican

F. D. Roosevelt
32nd President
1933-1945
Democrat

Truman
33rd president
1945-1953
Democrat

United Press Int.

Roosevelt, *ROH zuh vehlt,* **Franklin Delano,** *DEHL uh noh* (1882-1945), served as President for more than 12 years, longer than any other person. He was the only President elected four times. Roosevelt led the United States through its worst depression and through its worst war. He died just 83 days after becoming President for the fourth time.

Roosevelt took office as President at the depth of the Great Depression. About 25 per cent of the workers in the United States had lost their jobs. Many families had no money to buy food. Others had lost their homes because they could not pay their mortgages. Millions of Americans feared what would happen next. In Roosevelt's inaugural address, he called for faith in America's future. "The only thing we have to fear is fear itself," he declared boldly.

A new era in American history began under Roosevelt. He called his program the *New Deal.* For the first time, the federal government took strong action to help make the United States prosperous. Roosevelt said he wanted to help the average American, whom he called the "forgotten man." He promised relief for unemployed workers. He said he would aid farmers. Under his leadership, the government put stronger controls on business companies than ever before. It spent billions of dollars on relief and public works to "prime the pump" of business activity. Dozens of new government agencies were set up. Many were known by their initials, such as CCC, TVA, and NRA. Roosevelt himself became widely known by his initials, F.D.R.

Probably no other President since Abraham Lincoln has been so bitterly hated or so deeply loved. Critics charged that Roosevelt's policies gave the federal government too much power. They accused him of taking over many rights that belonged to the states under the Constitution. Many Americans thought that government controls over business might destroy the free enterprise system and lead to socialism. But millions believed that Roosevelt was the friend and protector of the "common man." Their faith was the key to Roosevelt's success in politics.

The start of World War II in 1939 tended to divide Roosevelt's presidency into two parts. Until the German invasion of Poland that year, the government worked hard to end the depression. The war then became the chief concern of Roosevelt and the United States.

Born into a wealthy family, Roosevelt entered politics because he believed it offered great opportunity for public service. Before he was elected President, he served in the New York state senate, as assistant secretary of the Navy, and as governor of New York.

Roosevelt had a colorful personality. He was known for his friendly smile, flashing eyes, and genial manner. He had two famous "trademarks." These were the glasses that he wore clipped to the bridge of his nose, and the cigaret holder that jutted upward at a jaunty angle from his mouth. He was a fine speaker, with a warm, pleasing voice.

People in all parts of the world admired Roosevelt for his personal courage. Although he was crippled by

The Great Depression created widespread unemployment throughout the United States.

The attack on Pearl Harbor led the U.S. into World War II.

The world of President Franklin D. Roosevelt

Nazi leader Adolf Hitler ruled Germany from 1933 until his death in 1945. His expansionist policies led to World War II, and his anti-Semitism resulted in the killing of about 6 million Jews in Germany and German-controlled countries.

Dust storms in the Great Plains in the 1930's blew away precious topsoil and led to the ruin of many farm families. Some migrated to California. Their plight was told in John Steinbeck's novel, *The Grapes of Wrath,* published in 1939.

Labor leader John L. Lewis formed the Committee for Industrial Organization (CIO) in 1935 to organize workers in the steel, rubber, automobile, and other industries.

Italian dictator Benito Mussolini conquered Ethiopia in 1936 and joined with Germany and Japan in World War II.

Edward VIII gave up the throne of Great Britain in 1936 to marry Wallis Warfield Simpson, an American divorcee.

American track star Jesse Owens became a hero when he won four gold medals at the 1936 Olympics in Berlin.

The Spanish Civil War raged from 1936 to 1939 and ended in a victory for the rebel forces of Francisco Franco.

American aviator Amelia Earhart disappeared over the Pacific in 1937 during an attempted around-the-world flight.

The "big band" era of popular music featured groups led by Glenn Miller, Count Basie, Tommy and Jimmy Dorsey, and Duke Ellington. Clarinetist Benny Goodman became known as the "King of Swing," and Americans enjoyed such dance crazes as the big apple and the jitterbug.

Research on the atomic bomb advanced after Dec. 2, 1942, when workers at the University of Chicago produced the first artificially created nuclear chain reaction.

Women joined the American work force in unprecedented numbers during World War II. "Rosie the Riveter" was a nickname that symbolized the millions of women working in wartime industries.

Library of Congress; Wide World

polio at the age of 39, he refused to give up his career of public service. As he struggled to regain the use of his legs, his physical appearance changed. As a young man, Roosevelt had been slender and tall. After his illness, he became stocky and heavy-set. Roosevelt could never again stand without help. But a little more than 11 years after being stricken, he was elected President.

Early life

Boyhood. The Roosevelt family traced its beginnings to Klaes Martensen Van Roosevelt. Van Roosevelt was a Dutch landowner who in the 1640's had settled in New York City (then New Amsterdam). Van Roosevelt was also an ancestor of Theodore Roosevelt, the 26th President of the United States. Franklin and Theodore were fifth cousins.

Franklin Delano Roosevelt was born on Jan. 30, 1882,

Important dates in Roosevelt's life

1882	(Jan. 30) Born in Hyde Park, N.Y.
1905	(March 17) Married Eleanor Roosevelt.
1913	Appointed assistant secretary of the Navy.
1920	Ran unsuccessfully for Vice President of the United States.
1921	Stricken with polio.
1928	Elected governor of New York.
1932	Elected President of the United States.
1936	Reelected President.
1940	Reelected President.
1944	Reelected President.
1945	(April 12) Died in Warm Springs, Ga.

on his father's estate, Springwood, in Hyde Park, N.Y. He was the only child of James and Sara Roosevelt. James Roosevelt was a wealthy vice president of the Delaware and Hudson Railway. His wife was a member of the wealthy Delano family. The estates of both the Delanos and the Roosevelts overlooked the Hudson River. When Franklin was born, his mother was 26 years old and his father was 53.

Franklin's parents brought him up with loving firmness. His mother made him live by a rigid schedule. She set definite times for such daily activities as eating,

Springwood, oil painting on canvas by I. V. Lounsbery;
Franklin D. Roosevelt Library, Hyde Park, N.Y.

Franklin D. Roosevelt's birthplace was this house at Springwood, the family estate on the Hudson River in Hyde Park, N.Y. This painting shows the house as it looked before 1900.

Bachrach

The Roosevelt family posed for this photograph in 1919. Franklin and Eleanor Roosevelt are surrounded by, *left to right,* Anna, Franklin Delano, Jr., Elliott, John, and James.

studying, and playing. Sara Roosevelt was a domineering woman. Even after her son was grown and had children of his own, she would tell him to put on his rubbers before going outdoors in rainy weather. James Roosevelt made sure his son had all the advantages that wealth could buy. But he taught Franklin that being wealthy also brought with it the responsibility of helping persons who were not so lucky.

Education. From the time he was 3 years old, Franklin's parents usually took him on their yearly trips to Europe. He studied under governesses and private tutors until he was 14. He learned to speak and write both German and French. Roosevelt attended a public school only once—for six weeks, during a family trip in Germany. His mother thought the experience might improve his German. He was 9 years old at the time.

At the age of 14, Roosevelt entered the Groton School, a preparatory school in Groton, Mass. He made good grades, but was shy and had few close friends. He was graduated from Groton in 1900.

Roosevelt enrolled that same year at Harvard University. He majored in history and earned fair grades. He joined intramural rowing and football teams. He also was elected secretary of the Freshman Glee Club. Roosevelt was proud of his appointment in 1903 as an editor of the *Harvard Crimson,* the school newspaper. His college activities helped him make friends more easily.

Roosevelt graduated from Harvard in 1903. But he continued his studies for another year. In 1904, he entered the Columbia University Law School. He passed the bar examination in 1907. But he had little interest in the study of law and left school that year before receiving a degree. Roosevelt worked as a clerk for a law firm in New York City for the next three years. However, he showed no enthusiasm for legal work.

Roosevelt's family. Roosevelt and his distant cousin, Eleanor Roosevelt (1884-1962), had known each other

slightly since childhood. He began to court her seriously while at Harvard. In 1903, after they became engaged, Roosevelt told his mother of his plans to marry. Sara Roosevelt did not want another woman in her son's life. She tried to change his mind, and even took him on a Caribbean cruise in hope that he would forget Eleanor. But Roosevelt went ahead with his plans. He and Eleanor were married on March 17, 1905. President Theodore Roosevelt, Eleanor's uncle, gave the bride away. See **Roosevelt, Eleanor.**

While the Roosevelts were on their honeymoon, his mother rented a house for them and furnished it completely. Eleanor was disappointed to learn that she could not furnish her own home. But, rather than anger her mother-in-law, she accepted the arrangement. She learned to take the older woman's interference silently, and to go her own way quietly. Roosevelt never seemed to mind his mother's attempts to dominate him.

The Roosevelts had six children. They were Anna Eleanor (1906-1975); James (1907-1991); Franklin Delano, Jr. (died in infancy, 1909); Elliott (1910-1990); Franklin Delano, Jr. (1914-1988); and John (1916-1981). James and Franklin, Jr., both served in the United States House of Representatives.

Roosevelt was a great companion to his children. He enjoyed swimming, sailing, and sledding with them. He often competed with them in races and contests. The Roosevelts called their children "the chicks."

Entry into politics

State senator. In 1910, Roosevelt accepted an invitation from state Democratic leaders to run for the New York senate. He joined the Democratic Party chiefly because his father had been a Democrat. Roosevelt's task seemed impossible. The Republicans had controlled his district for more than 50 years. Roosevelt called for clean government and declared his opposition to "big-city bosses." He surprised veteran politicians by winning the election.

Roosevelt entered the state senate at the age of 29. He soon became known as a bold and skillful political fighter. At that time, U.S. senators were elected by the state legislatures. Roosevelt led a group of Democratic legislators in a successful revolt against a candidate chosen by the party bosses. His action angered Tammany Hall, the Democratic organization in New York City (see **Tammany, Society of**).

Assistant secretary of the Navy. In 1912, Roosevelt supported Woodrow Wilson against his cousin Theodore Roosevelt in the presidential election. Wilson became President and in 1913 appointed Franklin Roosevelt as assistant secretary of the Navy. Roosevelt was delighted with his new post. "I now find my vocation combined with my avocation in a delightful way," he said. Politics was his "vocation," or work. His "avocation," or hobby, was ships and naval history.

Josephus Daniels was secretary of the Navy and Roosevelt's immediate superior. He taught Roosevelt much about national politics, and especially about ways to get along with Congress.

In 1914, Roosevelt sought the Democratic nomination as a candidate for the U.S. Senate. He lost by a wide margin, chiefly because Tammany Hall opposed him.

After the United States entered World War I in April

As assistant secretary of the Navy, Roosevelt reviewed the troops at a U.S. naval air station in France in 1918. President Woodrow Wilson had appointed Roosevelt in 1913.

1917, Roosevelt wanted to enter military service. But Daniels persuaded him to stay at his desk. Roosevelt worked on many wartime projects, including a plan to lay antisubmarine mines in the North Sea. He became known as a man who "got things done." In 1918, he toured European battlefields and met with military leaders overseas. Roosevelt had become a national figure.

Candidate for Vice President. In 1920, the Democratic National Convention nominated Governor James M. Cox of Ohio for President. In order to "balance the ticket," the delegates wanted a vice presidential candidate from an eastern state. Partly for this reason, the convention nominated Roosevelt.

Cox and Roosevelt campaigned on a platform calling for U.S. membership in the League of Nations. But the Senate had blocked American membership in the League. In addition, most voters were indifferent to the League. The Republican candidates, Senator Warren G. Harding of Ohio and Governor Calvin Coolidge of Massachusetts, defeated Cox and Roosevelt easily.

The defeat did Roosevelt little harm. He was only 38, and had established himself as a leader among progressive Democrats. In 1920, he became a vice president of the Fidelity and Deposit Company of Maryland, a surety-bonding firm. He took charge of the company's New York City office.

Crippled by polio

Tragedy strikes. The Roosevelt family had a summer home on Campobello Island, off New Brunswick, Canada. On Aug. 8, 1921, Roosevelt fell from a friend's boat into frigid water. The next day, he felt tired but remained active. On August 10, Roosevelt felt even worse, but he sailed, jogged, and swam. He commented later that he had expected the swim to refresh him, but it had not. Later, at home, he sat in his wet bathing suit reading his mail. He suddenly felt chilled and went up to bed.

The next morning, Roosevelt could hardly get out of bed. His left leg dragged, he ached all over, and he had a slight fever. Eleanor sent for a doctor. At first, the doc-

tor thought Roosevelt had an unusually heavy cold. But by the next day, Roosevelt could not stand or even move his legs. He suffered severe pain. His back, arms, and hands became partially paralyzed. He could no longer hold a pen to write.

Roosevelt did not know for certain that he had a severe case of polio, but he suspected the truth. "While the doctors were unanimous in telling me that the attack was very mild . . . ," he recalled, "I had, of course, the usual dark suspicion that they were just saying nice things to make me feel good." Later, lying in bed in New York City, he showed his withered legs to his children. He explained how polio had damaged his muscles. He wanted them to understand his illness.

In January 1922, Roosevelt's condition suddenly became worse. He remained cheerful despite more weeks of severe pain. One day, Josephus Daniels visited Roosevelt in the hospital. Roosevelt beckoned him close to the bed, then struck Daniels on the chest so hard it made him stagger. "You thought you were coming to see an invalid," Roosevelt said with a laugh, "but I can knock you out in any bout."

Many persons thought Roosevelt's political career had ended. His mother urged him to retire. But he continued his political activity—writing letters, issuing statements, and holding conferences in his home. He received encouragement and help from his wife and from his aide, Louis Howe.

He began to fight back against the disease that had crippled him. He regained the use of his hands, and the paralysis left his back. By exercising regularly, Roosevelt developed great strength in his arms and shoulders. After many months, using gymnasium equipment, he began trying to learn to walk again. He had several bad falls but did not give up. His legs improved a little, but he never again could walk unaided, or without braces.

The Warm Springs Foundation. In addition to his other exercises, Roosevelt went swimming as often as he could. "The water put me where I am, and the water has to bring me back," he said. Roosevelt was referring to the swim he had taken just before he had the first polio attack. Now, swimming gave him a chance to exercise his legs.

In 1924, Roosevelt began to spend several months of each year at Warm Springs, Georgia. Many polio victims had been helped by swimming in the pool of warm mineral water there. At the springs, Roosevelt met patients who could barely afford the cost of polio treatment. In 1926, he bought the springs and surrounding land. The next year, with a group of friends, he established the Georgia Warm Springs Foundation. For many years, the foundation provided low-cost treatment for "polios," as Roosevelt affectionately called his fellow victims.

Return to politics

While learning to walk again, Roosevelt devoted more and more time to politics. Aided by Louis Howe, he corresponded with Democratic leaders throughout the country.

Roosevelt made a spectacular return to national politics in 1924. He nominated Governor Alfred E. Smith of New York for President at the Democratic National Convention. He ignored the advice of friends who said he should not support a Roman Catholic for the presi-

Franklin D. Roosevelt Library

Swimming was one of Roosevelt's favorite forms of exercise after he contracted polio in 1921. He is shown here at Warm Springs, Ga., where he set up a foundation to treat polio victims.

International Newsreel photo from Franklin D. Roosevelt Library

Roosevelt helped Alfred E. Smith, *left,* win the 1928 Democratic presidential nomination. Smith lost the 1928 election, but Roosevelt ran for governor of New York and won.

dency. The nominating speech was Roosevelt's first major public appearance since his polio attack. Thundering cheers greeted him as he moved slowly to the podium, aided by his son James. Smith did not get the nomination. But Roosevelt gained importance as a Democratic leader and as a man who had conquered personal tragedy.

In 1928, again with Roosevelt's support, Smith won the Democratic nomination for President. Smith asked Roosevelt to run for governor of New York. At first, Roosevelt refused to run. He wanted to continue his polio treatments at Warm Springs. But Smith insisted, feeling that Roosevelt's candidacy would strengthen his own chances. Roosevelt finally consented. He barely defeated his Republican opponent, Albert Ottinger, the attorney general of New York. Smith lost the presidential election to Herbert Hoover, and did not even carry New York.

Governor of New York. As governor, Roosevelt supported a variety of progressive legislation. He obtained tax relief for farmers. After the Great Depression began in October 1929, he established the first system of relief for the unemployed in New York. He brought about tighter control of public utilities. He also created a power authority to develop the water power of the St. Lawrence River. Other laws modernized the state prison system and established old-age pensions. A broad conservation and reforestation program also went into effect.

In 1930, Roosevelt won reelection by about 725,000 votes, a record for the state at that time. The victory proved that he was popular with voters.

Election of 1932. Roosevelt had gained wide public respect for his work as governor by 1932. By then, he was seeking the Democratic presidential nomination. James A. Farley, Democratic Party chairman in New York state, directed his campaign. In a nationwide radio address, Roosevelt outlined a program to meet the economic problems of the nation. Such a program, he said, had to be built for the average American, whom he called the "forgotten man." The Democratic National Convention nominated Roosevelt on the fourth ballot. John Nance Garner of Texas, the Speaker of the House

of Representatives, was chosen for Vice President. The Republicans renominated President Herbert Hoover and Vice President Charles Curtis.

Roosevelt flew to the convention in Chicago to accept the nomination. It was the first time a presidential nominee had made an acceptance speech at a national convention. Roosevelt promised a "new deal" to lead the nation out of the depression. He said he would set up economic safeguards to prevent future depressions.

During the election campaign, Roosevelt visited 38 states. He wanted to show the voters that he was physically able to be President. He promised to provide relief for the unemployed, to help the farmers, and to balance the budget. He also said he would end Prohibition (see **Prohibition**). In the election, Roosevelt received 472 electoral votes to only 59 for Hoover. Many persons sang a popular song, "Happy Days Are Here Again," to celebrate Roosevelt's victory. This tune had been the Democratic campaign song.

On Feb. 15, 1933, Giuseppe Zangara, a mentally ill bricklayer, tried to assassinate Roosevelt in Miami, Fla. Roosevelt escaped injury, but the shots fired by Zangara killed Mayor Anton J. Cermak of Chicago. Zangara, who said he had visions of killing a "great ruler," was executed on March 20, 1933.

Roosevelt's first Administration (1933-1937)

Roosevelt became President on March 4, 1933, at the age of 51. The inauguration was the last held in March. Under Amendment 20 to the Constitution, all later inaugurations have been held in January.

The depression had grown steadily worse. Thousands of unemployed workers were standing in bread lines to get food for their families. Many farmers and city workers had lost their homes. Even more were about to lose them because they could not pay their mortgages.

The banking crisis. About three weeks before Roosevelt took office, a banking panic began. It spread throughout the country as anxious depositors hurried to their banks to get cash and gold. The panic created "runs" that ruined many banks.

Roosevelt declared a "bank holiday" that began on

Roosevelt's first election

Place of nominating convention	...Chicago
Ballot on which nominated	........4th
Republican opponent	.............Herbert Hoover
Electoral vote*	.....................472 (Roosevelt) to 59 (Hoover)
Popular vote	.......................22,825,016 (Roosevelt) to 15,758,397 (Hoover)
Age at inauguration	51

*For votes by states, see **Electoral College** (table).

United Press Int.

"Fireside chats" became a regular feature of Roosevelt's presidency. These informal radio reports to the American people enabled Roosevelt to gain widespread support for his programs.

March 6, 1933. He closed all banks in the United States until the Department of the Treasury could examine every bank's books. Banks in good financial condition were to be supplied with money by the Treasury and allowed to reopen. Those in doubtful condition were kept closed until they could be put on a sound basis. Many banks that had been badly operated never reopened.

The President's action restored confidence and ended the bank crisis. People knew that if a bank opened its doors, it was safe. Few people wished to withdraw their money from a bank that was sound. See **Bank holiday.**

The "Hundred Days." On March 9, 1933, Congress began a special session called by Roosevelt. The President at once began to submit recovery and reform laws for congressional approval. Congress passed nearly all the important bills that he requested, most of them by large majorities. This special session of Congress came to be known as the "Hundred Days." It actually lasted 99 days, from March 9 to June 16. Important laws passed included the Agricultural Adjustment Act (AAA), the Tennessee Valley Authority (TVA) Act, and the National Industrial Recovery Act (NIRA). See **New Deal** (table: Leading New Deal agencies).

On March 12, Roosevelt gave the first of his famous "fireside chats," speaking to the nation by radio. He explained what action had been taken and what he planned for the immediate future. See **Radio** (The Golden Age of Broadcasting; picture).

Many of the advisers who helped Roosevelt during his presidential campaign continued to aid him after he entered the White House. From time to time they included Adolf A. Berle, Harry L. Hopkins, Raymond Moley, Samuel I. Rosenman, and Rexford G. Tugwell. A newspaperman once described the group as "Roosevelt's Brain Trust." The name stuck.

Roosevelt's Cabinet included Frances Perkins as secretary of labor. She was the first woman ever named to a

Franklin D. Roosevelt Library

Roosevelt ran for President in 1932 with John Nance Garner of Texas as his running mate. He promised to end Prohibition, as well as enact programs to lead the nation out of the depression.

Cabinet post. Harold L. Ickes, a Chicago lawyer who had been chairman of the National Progressive League for Roosevelt and Garner, was named secretary of the interior. Henry Morgenthau, Jr., became secretary of the treasury in 1934.

The New Deal, as Roosevelt called his reform program, included a wide range of activities. The President described it as a "use of the authority of government as an organized form of self-help for all classes and groups and sections of our country."

Unemployment legislation. At first, Roosevelt favored only emergency measures. At his request, Congress appropriated $500 million for relief to states and cities through the Federal Emergency Relief Administration. In the winter of 1933-1934, the government started a relief program called the Civil Works Administration (CWA). The CWA supplied funds to local authorities such as mayors of cities and governors of states. These funds made possible such public projects as building streets, roads, bridges, and schoolhouses; cleaning up parks; or doing other useful tasks. A number of persons criticized the CWA. They said many CWA employees merely raked leaves or held other useless jobs.

Roosevelt ended the CWA after a few months. But other employment relief programs were more permanent. The Civilian Conservation Corps (CCC) operated from 1933 until 1942. The CCC gave work and training to $2\frac{1}{2}$ million young people. It achieved great success with its programs of flood control, forestry, and soil conservation. The Works Progress Administration (WPA) was established in 1935 to provide work for people without jobs. In 1939, it was renamed the Work Projects Administration. It employed an average of 2 million workers annually between 1935 and 1943.

All these government projects cost a great deal of money—much more than the government was collecting through taxes. The deficit was made up partly by raising taxes and partly by borrowing. The government borrowed money by selling government bonds. The national debt rose higher than ever before.

Keystone

The Works Progress Administration (WPA) provided jobs for workers in construction and other fields. It was one of the relief programs that Roosevelt began during the Great Depression.

Vice presidents and Cabinet

Vice president . . . .*	John N. Garner
	* Henry A. Wallace (1941)
	* Harry S. Truman (1945)
Secretary of state . . . .*	Cordell Hull
	* Edward R. Stettinius, Jr. (1944)
Secretary of the treasury	William H. Woodin
	* Henry Morgenthau, Jr. (1934)
Secretary of war	George H. Dern
	Harry H. Woodring (1937)
	Henry L. Stimson (1940)
Attorney general	Homer S. Cummings
	Frank Murphy (1939)
	* Robert H. Jackson (1940)
	Francis Biddle (1941)
Postmaster general . . . .*	James A. Farley
	Frank C. Walker (1940)
Secretary of the Navy	Claude A. Swanson
	Charles Edison (1940)
	* Frank Knox (1940)
	* James Forrestal (1944)
Secretary of the interior . . . .*	Harold L. Ickes
Secretary of agriculture . . . .*	Henry A. Wallace
	Claude R. Wickard (1940)
Secretary of commerce	Daniel C. Roper
	* Harry L. Hopkins (1938)
	Jesse H. Jones (1940)
	* Henry A. Wallace (1945)
Secretary of labor . . . .*	Frances Perkins

*Has a separate biography in WORLD BOOK

Other reforms. During Roosevelt's first year in the White House, Congress passed laws to protect the investments of persons who buy stocks and bonds. Other legislation helped the oil and railroad industries, small businesses, and homeowners. In December 1933, Amendment 21 to the Constitution ended prohibition. The Social Security Act of 1935 authorized unemployment relief and old-age pensions. The National Labor Relations Act of 1935 greatly strengthened the right of workers to bargain collectively (see **Labor movement** [The New Deal]).

Opposition to the New Deal. By 1935, some New Deal measures were meeting strong opposition, chiefly from the nation's business leaders. The WPA and the National Labor Relations Act received heavy criticism. Critics charged that these measures wasted money and favored unions.

Good Neighbor Policy. Roosevelt described his foreign policy as that of a "good neighbor." This phrase came to be used to describe the U.S. attitude toward the countries of Latin America. Under Roosevelt's Good Neighbor Policy, the United States took a stronger lead in promoting good will among these nations.

The Platt Amendment of 1901 had given the United States the right to intervene in the affairs of Cuba (see **Cuba** [The Platt Amendment]). On May 31, 1934, the government repealed this amendment. It also withdrew American occupation forces from some Caribbean republics, and settled long-standing oil disputes with Mexico. Reciprocal trade treaties were signed with some Latin American countries between 1934 and 1937. These countries included Brazil, Colombia, Costa Rica, Cuba, El Salvador, Guatemala, Haiti, Honduras, and Nicaragua (see **Reciprocal trade agreement**). In 1935, the United States signed treaties of nonaggression and conciliation with six Latin American countries. The desire for hemispheric ties soon spread to include Canada. The United States and Canada signed several reciprocal trade agreements.

Roosevelt also used personal diplomacy. In July 1934,

he took a trip to Cartagena, Colombia, and became the first president to visit South America. In 1936, he attended the Inter-American Conference for the Maintenance of Peace, in Buenos Aires, Argentina. On the way home, he visited Montevideo, Uruguay.

Relations with the Soviet Union. Roosevelt hoped that trade could be resumed between the United States and the Soviet Union. Partly for this reason, his Administration recognized the Soviet government in November 1933. Relations between the United States and the Soviet Union had been broken off after the Russian Revolution of 1917. In 1933, for the first time in 16 years, the two countries exchanged diplomatic representatives.

Election of 1936. The Democratic National Convention renominated Roosevelt by acclamation in 1936. The delegates also renominated Vice President Garner. The Republicans picked Governor Alfred M. Landon of Kansas for president and Frank Knox, publisher of the *Chicago Daily News,* for vice president.

In the campaign, the Republicans charged that Roosevelt had not kept his promise to balance the budget. Roosevelt replied by pointing to the action taken by his Administration to fight the depression and return the nation to prosperity.

Roosevelt won reelection in a landslide. He received 523 electoral votes to 8 for Landon, and carried every state except Maine and Vermont.

Roosevelt's second Administration (1937-1941)

The Supreme Court. According to the United States Constitution, only Congress has the power to make laws binding upon every American. The Constitution also states that Congress may "regulate" various activities, such as interstate commerce. However, Congress is too large and has too many other duties to do an effective job of regulating. So the courts have held that Con-

Roosevelt's second election

Place of nominating convention	. . . Philadelphia
Ballot on which nominated	. . . . 1st
Republican opponent	. . . . Alfred M. Landon
Electoral vote*	. . . . 523 (Roosevelt) to
	8 (Landon)
Popular vote	. . . . 27,747,636 (Roosevelt) to
	16,679,543 (Landon)
Age at inauguration	 54

*For votes by states, see **Electoral College** (table).

gress may delegate its regulatory power to various government agencies.

But when is a rule a mere regulation, and when is it a law? This difficult question arose over the regulations of some New Deal agencies. In 1935, a chicken dealer sued the government to nullify the National Industrial Recovery Act. The case eventually went to the Supreme Court. The Court ruled the act unconstitutional because it delegated lawmaking powers to the National Recovery Administration (NRA). This decision ended the NRA, one of the chief New Deal projects. See **National Recovery Administration.**

The Agricultural Adjustment Act, the Railroad Retirement Act, and a number of other New Deal measures were also declared unconstitutional. The President feared his whole program might be defeated by the nine Supreme Court justices.

In 1937, shortly after his second inauguration, Roosevelt proposed a reorganization of the Supreme Court. Congress approved six of the seven changes recommended by the President. In the seventh, Roosevelt proposed that when a Supreme Court justice reached the age of 70, a younger person should be appointed to sit with the justice on the court. The total number of justices was not to exceed 15.

The seventh proposal provoked many people, who charged that Roosevelt was trying to "pack" the Supreme Court with judges who would always favor the New Deal. While Congress was debating the President's proposal, the Supreme Court approved some legislation considered essential to the New Deal program. For these reasons, the proposal did not pass. By 1944, so many justices had retired or died that all but two Court members were Roosevelt appointees.

Attitude toward Japan. In the mid-1930's, President Roosevelt realized that Japanese attacks on China were a threat to world peace. He tried to arouse the nation to the danger. In October 1937, he called on peaceful countries to unite and "quarantine" war in the same way that doctors quarantine, or isolate, a contagious disease. But he did not follow up on this speech, and no such action occurred.

Roosevelt and Secretary of State Cordell Hull believed that the United States needed a policy that would help the country arm for defense. The President tried to strengthen the Army and the Navy, although Congress often opposed him. He refused to recognize the Japanese puppet state of Manchukuo in northern China. He believed Japan should respect American rights in the Pacific and Far East. The President demanded that Japan apologize and pay for the sinking of the American gunboat *Panay* in 1937. The Japanese met his demands at once.

Neutrality acts of the 1930's reflected the desire of many Americans to isolate the United States from other nations (see **Isolationism**). Congress passed the first Neutrality Act in 1935. It prohibited the United States from furnishing weapons or supplies to any nation at war. President Roosevelt said he hoped that any future neutrality laws "might provide for greater flexibility." But in 1936 and 1937, Congress and Roosevelt approved other legislation to keep America free of "foreign entanglements."

Roosevelt did not like the neutrality laws because they treated all nations the same—whether a country had attacked another country, or had been attacked itself. These laws made it all but impossible for the United States to aid any friendly nation. Roosevelt wanted to give "all aid short of war" to nations opposing the Axis powers—Germany, Italy, and Japan. He believed that an Axis victory would endanger democracy everywhere in the world.

World War II began on Sept. 1, 1939, when Germany invaded Poland. Still, many Americans did not agree that the situation was as dangerous as Roosevelt believed. These "isolationists" thought the United States could stay out of the war.

As tension increased, Americans became more concerned about the war in Europe. Some isolationists accused Roosevelt of *warmongering,* or trying to get America into the war.

Shortly after German troops attacked Poland, Congress passed the Neutrality Act of 1939. This law made it possible for a nation fighting the Axis to buy war supplies from the United States. But it had to pay for the weapons in cash and furnish its own ships to carry them. In November 1941, Congress repealed two sections of the act. These sections had kept American vessels out of war zones and had forbidden them to carry guns.

Election of 1940. The Democratic Party broke precedent in 1940 by nominating Roosevelt for a third consecutive term. Secretary of Agriculture Henry A. Wallace was chosen as his vice presidential running mate. The Republicans nominated Wendell L. Willkie of Indiana, a corporation president, to oppose Roosevelt. They picked Senator Charles L. McNary of Oregon for their vice presidential candidate. Willkie supported Roosevelt's foreign policy and favored many of the New Deal programs for social reform. However, Willkie opposed the controls that the Democratic Administration had put on business.

To obtain the support of both Republicans and Democrats for his military program, Roosevelt appointed two Republicans to his Cabinet in 1940. Henry L. Stimson became secretary of war. He had held this office under President William Howard Taft, and had been secretary of state under President Hoover. Stimson replaced Harry H. Woodring, who was regarded as an isolationist. Newspaper publisher Frank Knox became secretary of the Navy.

The Republicans based their campaign on the tradition that no President had ever sought three terms in succession. Roosevelt defended his Administration's programs. He promised to try to keep the nation out of war. In June, France had surrendered to Germany. The defeat of the French army, believed by many to be the strongest in the world, shocked the United States.

The voters decided Roosevelt's leadership and experience were needed for another term. He carried 38 of the 48 states, and won 449 electoral votes to 82 for Willkie.

Roosevelt's third Administration (1941-1945)

The eve of war. By the time Roosevelt took his third presidential oath of office, the United States was preparing to give the United Kingdom all aid short of war. In the summer of 1940, Britain gave the United States 99-year leases on several naval bases in the Atlantic. The British navy received 50 old American destroyers in return. The United States adopted its first peacetime selective service, or draft, law in September.

In August 1941, Roosevelt met British Prime Minister Winston Churchill on a cruiser anchored off Newfoundland. The two men adopted a declaration that became known as the *Atlantic Charter.* They pledged not to seek gains, "territorial or otherwise"; to respect the right of every nation to choose its own form of government; to guarantee freedom of the seas; and to conduct peaceful world trade. See **Atlantic Charter.**

In a speech on Jan. 6, 1941, Roosevelt declared that all people are entitled to freedom of speech, freedom of worship, freedom from want, and freedom from fear. These basic rights came to be called the *four freedoms.* On March 11, Congress passed the Lend-Lease Act. This law authorized the government to provide war supplies to any nation that the President deemed vital to U.S. security. See **Lend-Lease.**

Relations with Japan became increasingly tense. Germany, Italy, and Japan had signed a defense pact in 1940. Beginning in 1940, the United States tried to stop Japanese aggression in Southeast Asia. The government reduced trade with Japan and issued occasional warnings. Roosevelt described this policy as "babying the Japanese along." After Japan invaded southern Indochina in July 1941, the U.S. government cut off exports to Japan.

America goes to war. On Sunday, Dec. 7, 1941, Secretary of State Hull conferred with two Japanese diplomats. While they talked, Japanese planes attacked the U.S. Pacific Fleet, which lay at anchor in Pearl Harbor, Hawaii (see **Pearl Harbor**).

President Roosevelt addressed Congress the next day. He said December 7 was "a date which will live in infamy." The United States declared war against Japan. Three days later, on December 11, Germany and Italy declared war on the United States. America then declared war on those countries.

Most Americans realized that the nation faced a serious situation. The war extended across the Atlantic and Pacific oceans. The Navy had been crippled by the attack on Pearl Harbor. But the draft had given the Army more than a million men with at least a year's training.

A great decision confronted the President after Pearl Harbor. He had to decide where to strike first. On the

Roosevelt's third election

Place of nominating convention	Chicago
Ballot on which nominated	1st
Republican opponent	Wendell L. Willkie
Electoral vote*	449 (Roosevelt) to 82 (Willkie)
Popular vote	27,263,448 (Roosevelt) to 22,336,260 (Willkie)
Age at inauguration	58

*For votes by states, see **Electoral College** (table).

Library of Congress

Roosevelt signed a declaration of war against Japan on Dec. 8, 1941, the day after Japan attacked Pearl Harbor. He said December 7 was "a date which will live in infamy."

Franklin D. Roosevelt Library

During the war, Roosevelt traveled overseas several times to confer with Allied leaders. Here he is shown riding in a jeep in Sicily with Allied Commander Dwight D. Eisenhower.

Quotations from Franklin Roosevelt
Some of Franklin Roosevelt's most famous speeches are quoted or paraphrased in the text of this article. The following are additional quotations from some of his speeches and writings.

It is common sense to take a method and try it. If it fails, admit it frankly and try another. But above all, try something.
Speech in Atlanta, Ga., May 22, 1932

The fate of America cannot depend on any one man. The greatness of America is grounded in principles and not on any single personality.
Speech in New York City, Nov. 5,1932

Democracy is not a static thing. It is an everlasting march.
Speech in Los Angeles, Oct. 1, 1935

Nationwide thinking, nationwide planning, and nationwide action are the three great essentials to prevent nationwide crises for future generations to struggle through.
Speech in New York City, April 25, 1936

I should like to have it said of my first Administration that in it the forces of selfishness and lust for power met their

match. I should like to have it said of my second Administration that in it these forces met their master.
Speech in New York City, Oct. 31, 1936

The test of our progress is not whether we add more to the abundance of those who have much; it is whether we provide enough for those who have too little.
Second Inaugural Address, Jan. 20, 1937

Our Security is not a matter of weapons alone. The arm that wields them must be strong, the eye that guides them clear, the will that directs them indomitable.
Message to Congress, May 16, 1940

True individual freedom cannot exist without economic security and independence. People who are hungry and out of a job are the stuff of which dictatorships are made.
Message to Congress, Jan. 11, 1944

West Coast, many people felt that Japan was the most important foe. In the East, many wanted Germany defeated first.

Roosevelt conferred with Churchill in the White House in December 1941, and January 1942. The two leaders realized that the United States could not strike an effective blow against Japan until the Navy had recovered from its losses at Pearl Harbor. In addition, German scientists were developing new weapons that could mean defeat for the Allies. Both British and Soviet citizens wanted to see Germany defeated as soon as possible. For these reasons, Roosevelt and Churchill decided that Germany, the most powerful enemy nation, must be defeated first.

Roosevelt suggested the name *United Nations* for the alliance that fought Germany, Italy, and Japan. This alliance formed the basis for the peacetime United Nations organization that later was established in 1945. See **United Nations.**

For a description of life in the United States and Canada during World War II, see **World War II** (On the home front).

North African invasion. On Nov. 8, 1942, the Allies invaded North Africa. It was the greatest landing operation in history up to that time. After the landings began, Roosevelt spoke by radio to the French people in their own language. He explained that the Allies had to drive the Germans out of French territory in North Africa. See **World War II** (In northern Africa).

The Big Three. President Roosevelt left the United States many times during the war for conferences with Allied leaders. He was the first President to leave the country in wartime. Early in 1943, he met with Churchill in Casablanca, Morocco. The two leaders announced that they would accept only unconditional surrender by the Axis nations. In other conferences, Roosevelt discussed problems of war and peace with both Churchill and Premier Joseph Stalin of the Soviet Union. They came to be known as the "Big Three." Roosevelt also conferred with Generalissimo Chiang Kai-shek of China in 1943.

Early in the war, the Soviet Union asked for a "second front" against the Germans in Western Europe. Churchill believed the Allies should first attack the Germans in Africa or in other places where they were relatively weak.

He also feared that the Soviet Union would take control of Eastern Europe after the war. In November 1943, the Big Three met at Teheran, Iran. During and after this conference, Roosevelt worked to get Churchill and Stalin to agree on major war aims. At Teheran, he refused to have lunch with Churchill before meeting with Stalin. The President did not want Stalin to think he and Churchill had made a separate agreement. See **Teheran Conference.**

Life in the White House was relaxed and informal during Roosevelt's presidency. His many grandchildren stayed in the Executive Mansion from time to time. An indoor swimming pool was installed so the President could continue to exercise his crippled legs. In the summer of 1934, the executive offices in the West Wing of the White House were enlarged, and a new Cabinet Room was added. The East Wing was also enlarged and remodeled.

The Roosevelts entertained a great deal until the Japanese attack on Pearl Harbor. In 1939, King George VI and Queen Elizabeth became the first British monarchs to visit the United States. They stayed at the White House as guests of the Roosevelts.

Many changes in White House routine were made after the United States entered World War II. The Roosevelts reduced their entertaining. Wartime security regulations went into effect in the White House. Machine guns were set up on the White House roof, and Secret Service agents took over a special office in the building's East Wing. Engineers built a bomb shelter in the White House basement.

Election of 1944. In June 1944, the Republicans nominated Governor Thomas E. Dewey of New York for President and Governor John W. Bricker of Ohio for Vice President. Roosevelt had not said whether he would run for a fourth term. He finally declared that he wanted to retire, but felt it was his duty to run again. Roosevelt said he wanted to avoid a wartime change in leadership. Many Democratic leaders felt that he might not live through a fourth term. But the President easily won renomination. Senator Harry S. Truman of Missouri was nominated for Vice President. See **Truman, Harry S.** (Vice President).

In the campaign, the Republicans argued that no person should be President for 16 years. The Democrats answered by saying that America should not "change horses in mid-stream." Republicans charged that Roosevelt was in poor health. The President replied by driving around New York City in an open car for four hours during a rainstorm—and then making a major speech. Roosevelt won an easy election victory. He carried 36 of the 48 states, and received 432 electoral votes to 99 votes for Dewey.

Roosevelt's fourth Administration (1945)

Roosevelt's inaugural address of January 1945, was one of the shortest in American history. It lasted only six minutes. The President declared that Americans had learned "we cannot live alone at peace, that our own well-being is dependent on the well-being of nations far away . . ."

Roosevelt was in poor health when he started his fourth term. A series of colds had bothered him for more than a year. He had lost about 15 pounds (7 kilograms). In the fall and winter of 1944, Roosevelt had been busy directing his legislative program and dealing with increasingly difficult international problems. The presidential election campaign of 1944 had weakened him even further.

Yalta Conference. Two days after his fourth inauguration, Roosevelt left to meet Churchill and Stalin at Yalta, a famous resort in the Crimea in the southern Soviet Union. On Feb. 11, 1945, the three leaders issued the Crimea Declaration. It repeated the principles of the Atlantic Charter and the Casablanca conferences. The leaders mapped the final assault on Germany and the postwar occupation of that country. They also planned a meeting in San Francisco to lay the foundations for the peacetime United Nations organization. In a secret agreement, the Soviet Union promised to enter the war

Roosevelt's fourth election

Place of nominating convention	. . . Chicago
Ballot on which nominated	. . . . 1st
Republican opponent	. . . . Thomas E. Dewey
Electoral vote*	. . . . 432 (Roosevelt) to 99 (Dewey)
Popular vote	. . . . 25,611,936 (Roosevelt) to 22,013,372 (Dewey)
Age at inauguration	 62

*For votes by states, see **Electoral College** (table)

Highlights of Roosevelt's Administrations

1933	Congress enacted New Deal recovery measures during the "Hundred Days." Prohibition was repealed.
1935	The Social Security Act and the first Neutrality Act were passed.
1937	Roosevelt's "court-packing" recommendations started the Supreme Court controversy.
1939	The United States began selling arms to friendly countries on a "cash-and-carry" basis.
1940	Congress passed the Selective Service Act.
1941	The Atlantic Charter was issued. (Dec. 7) Japan attacked Pearl Harbor.
1942	Twenty-six nations signed the Declaration of the United Nations.
1943	Roosevelt and Churchill announced the goal of unconditional surrender by the Axis powers. Roosevelt, Churchill, and Stalin conferred in Teheran, Iran.
1944	(June 6) The Allies invaded Normandy, France.
1945	Roosevelt, Churchill, and Stalin met at Yalta, in the Crimea.

against Japan within three months after the surrender of Germany. In return, the Soviet Union was to receive the Kuril Islands and other concessions. Critics later charged that Roosevelt had been cheated by Stalin. See **Yalta Conference.**

While reporting to Congress on the Yalta meeting on March 1, Roosevelt made one of his rare public references to his physical handicap. "I hope that you will pardon me for this unusual posture of sitting down . . . ," he said, "but . . . it makes it a lot easier for me not to have to carry about 10 pounds of steel around at the bottom of my legs."

During the next few weeks, Roosevelt began to have doubts about the good will of the Soviets. He was anxious, he told Churchill, about "the development of the Soviet attitude."

Death. On March 29, 1945, the President left for a rest at Warm Springs. He had prepared a speech for broadcast on April 13. Roosevelt had written: "The only limit to our realization of tomorrow will be our doubts of today. Let us move forward with strong and active faith."

April 12 began as usual. The President read newspapers and mail that had been flown from Washington. Roosevelt planned to attend a barbecue in the afternoon.

The **"Big Three"**—British Prime Minister Winston Churchill, President Roosevelt, and Soviet Premier Joseph Stalin—met at the Yalta Conference in February 1945.

Mourners lined the streets of Washington as Franklin Roosevelt's funeral procession headed toward the White House. Millions of people around the world mourned his death.

U.S. Army

Before the barbecue, Roosevelt was working at his desk while an artist, Elizabeth Schoumatoff, painted his portrait. Suddenly he fell over in his chair. "I have a terrific headache," he whispered. These were Roosevelt's last words. He died a few hours later of a cerebral hemorrhage. As news of Roosevelt's death spread, a crowd gathered in front of the White House, silent with grief. Millions of people in all parts of the world mourned the dead President.

Roosevelt was buried at Hyde Park. His home was set aside as the Home of Franklin D. Roosevelt National Historic Site in 1944. In 1997, the Franklin Delano Roosevelt Memorial was dedicated on the National Mall in Washington, D. C.   James T. Patterson

Related articles in *World Book* include:

Atlantic Charter
Bank holiday
Churchill, Sir Winston
Dewey, Thomas E.
Garner, John N.
Georgia (picture: The Little White House)
Great Depression
Hull, Cordell
Landon, Alfred M.
National Recovery Administration

New Deal
New York (Places to visit)
President of the U.S.
Roosevelt, Eleanor
Roosevelt Campobello International Park
Teheran Conference
Truman, Harry S.
Wallace, Henry A.
Willkie, Wendell L.
World War II
Yalta Conference

Outline

I. Early life
  A. Boyhood
  B. Education
  C. Roosevelt's family
II. Entry into politics
  A. State senator
  B. Assistant secretary of the Navy
  C. Candidate for Vice President
III. Crippled by polio
  A. Tragedy strikes
  B. The Warm Springs Foundation

IV. Return to politics
  A. Governor of New York
  B. Election of 1932
V. Roosevelt's first Administration (1933-1937)
  A. The banking crisis
  B. The "Hundred Days"
  C. The New Deal
  D. Good Neighbor Policy
  E. Relations with the Soviet Union
  F. Election of 1936
VI. Roosevelt's second Administration (1937-1941)
  A. The Supreme Court
  B. Attitude toward Japan
  C. Neutrality acts
  D. Election of 1940
VII. Roosevelt's third Administration (1941-1945)
  A. The eve of war
  B. America goes to war
  C. North African invasion
  D. The Big Three
  E. Life in the White House
  F. Election of 1944
VIII. Roosevelt's fourth Administration (1945)
  A. Yalta Conference
  B. Death

Questions

What illness almost ended Roosevelt's career?
What were the two critical periods during which Roosevelt served as President?
What was Roosevelt's first federal office?
What was the *New Deal*?
How did the "bank holiday" help end the financial crisis that occurred in 1933?
Why was Roosevelt criticized for his proposal to reorganize the Supreme Court?
How did Roosevelt first use the phrase "good neighbor"? What did the phrase come to mean?
What were the "Hundred Days"?
How did Roosevelt try to end unemployment?
Why was Roosevelt's election in 1940 unique?

Additional resources

Davis, Kenneth S. *FDR*. Random Hse. 1972-   . Multivolume work.
Freedman, Russell. *Franklin Delano Roosevelt*. Clarion, 1990. Younger readers.
Freidel, Frank B. *Franklin D. Roosevelt*. 4 vols. Little, Brown, 1952-1973. *Franklin D. Roosevelt: A Rendezvous with Destiny*. 1990.
Goodwin, Doris K. *No Ordinary Time: Franklin and Eleanor Roosevelt: The Home Front in World War II*. Simon & Schuster, 1994.
Graham, Otis L., Jr., and Wander, M. R., eds. *Franklin D. Roosevelt: His Life and Times*. 1985. Reprint. Da Capo, 1990.
Larsen, Rebecca. *Franklin D. Roosevelt*. Watts, 1991. Younger readers.
Morris, Jeffrey. *The FDR Way*. Lerner, 1996.
Ward, Geoffrey C. *Before the Trumpet: Young Franklin Roosevelt, 1882-1905*. 1985. Reprint. Smithmark, 1994. *A First-Class Temperament: The Emergence of Franklin Roosevelt*. Harper, 1989.

Roosevelt, *ROH zuh VEHLT,* **Nicholas J.** (1767-1854), was an American inventor and engineer. He helped pioneer the development of steamboats.

Roosevelt was born in New York City. He became interested in mechanics as a youth and, at about the age of 15, he designed a paddle wheel to drive a model boat. Roosevelt later opened a metal shop in New Jersey.

In 1809, Roosevelt and the inventor Robert Fulton joined in a venture to introduce steamboats on Western rivers. In 1812, Roosevelt completed a voyage from Pittsburgh to New Orleans in their boat, the *New Orleans*. The trip was the first steamboat voyage on the Ohio and Mississippi rivers. The *New Orleans* was a success and continued to travel for about two years. Roosevelt patented the use of vertical paddle wheels in 1814. They became the chief method of propelling steamboats.

David F. Channell

Theodore Roosevelt

**26th President of
the United States 1901-1909**

McKinley
25th President
1897-1901
Republican

T. Roosevelt
26th President
1901-1909
Republican

Taft
27th President
1909-1913
Republican

**Charles W.
Fairbanks**
Vice President
1905-1909

Oil painting on canvas (1903) by John Singer Sargent; © White House Historical Association (National Geographic Society)

Roosevelt, *ROH zuh VEHLT,* **Theodore** (1858-1919), was the youngest man ever to become President of the United States. He took office at the age of 42. Roosevelt had been Vice President for only six months when President William McKinley was assassinated in September 1901. Roosevelt won wide popularity, and millions of Americans affectionately called him "Teddy" or "T.R." In 1904, the voters elected him to a full term as President. He ran for President again in 1912, as the "Bull Moose" party candidate, but lost to Woodrow Wilson.

Roosevelt was a man of great energy and practiced what he called the "strenuous life." He enjoyed horseback riding, swimming, hunting, hiking, and boxing. He often expressed enthusiasm for something by describing it as "bully." Cartoonists liked to draw Roosevelt with his rimless glasses, bushy mustache, prominent teeth, and jutting jaw. One cartoon showed him with a bear cub. Soon, toymakers were producing stuffed animals that are still known as "teddy bears."

As commander of the fearless Rough Riders, Roosevelt became a national hero during the Spanish-American War in 1898. He led this famous cavalry regiment against the Spaniards in Cuba. Roosevelt came home and won election as governor of New York. Two years later, he was elected Vice President.

As President, Roosevelt used his power of leadership to help the United States meet challenges at home and abroad. "I did not usurp power," Roosevelt said, "but I did greatly broaden the use of executive power."

Roosevelt fought for reforms that would benefit the American people. He became known as a "trust buster" because he tried to limit the power of great business corporations. During his Administration, Congress passed laws to regulate the railroads, to protect the public from harmful foods and drugs, and to conserve the nation's forests and other natural resources.

In foreign relations, Roosevelt worked to make the United States a world leader. He felt that this leadership must be supported by strong armed forces. He expressed his foreign policy as: "Speak softly and carry a big stick." Roosevelt strengthened the U.S. Navy, began the construction of the Panama Canal, and kept European nations from interfering in Latin America. He helped end the Russo-Japanese War, and became the first American to receive the Nobel Peace Prize.

While Roosevelt was President, millions of Americans traveled by bicycle—even women in their sweeping, ankle-length skirts. But automobiles, along with electric lights and telephones, started to come into widespread use. Guglielmo Marconi sent the first radio message across the Atlantic Ocean, and a telegraph cable was laid across the Pacific to the Philippines. The air age was born when the Wright brothers flew the first successful airplane. Roosevelt enjoyed taking a ride in one of the early models.

Roosevelt regarded public life as a great stage. As President, he joyfully held the center of that stage. When Roosevelt left office, he wrote: "I do not believe that anyone else has ever enjoyed the White House as much as I have." He was probably right.

Early life

Boyhood and education. Theodore Roosevelt was born in New York City on Oct. 27, 1858. He was the second of the four children of Theodore and Martha Bulloch Roosevelt. "Teedie," as the family called him, was younger than his sister Anna, and older than his brother Elliott and his sister Corinne.

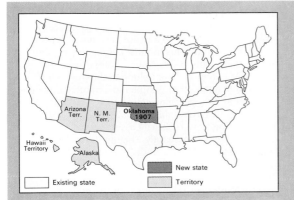

Oklahoma became a state in 1907, bringing the number of states in the Union to 46. The United States had four territories during President Roosevelt's Administration.

There were 46 stars on the United States flag when Roosevelt left office. A star was added for Oklahoma on July 4, 1908.

The world of President Theodore Roosevelt

Architect Frank Lloyd Wright began designing homes in his famous "prairie style" In 1902. He eventually became one of the nation's most influential architects.

The world's first successful airplane flights were made by Orville and Wilbur Wright at Kitty Hawk, N.C., on Dec. 17, 1903.

The first movie to tell a story, *The Great Train Robbery,* was produced in 1903. Its tremendous popularity led to the development of nickelodeons, the first movie theaters.

Russia's Revolution of 1905 began when soldiers fired on unarmed workers who came to the czar's palace in St. Petersburg to ask for reforms.

Albert Einstein revolutionized scientific thought with his theory of relativity, which he proposed in 1905.

The San Francisco earthquake and fire of 1906 left most of the city in ruins and killed at least 3,000 people.

"Muckrakers" was a term first used by President Roosevelt in 1906 to describe writers who used a realistic style to portray social evils. The works of such writers as Upton Sinclair, Ida Tarbell, and Lincoln Steffens helped bring about much-needed reforms.

Musical theater delighted audiences of the early 1900's. George M. Cohan wrote musicals that featured such patriotic tunes as "I'm a Yankee Doodle Dandy." Victor Herbert became popular for his operettas, and Florenz Ziegfeld began to produce the *Ziegfeld Follies.*

The Model T Ford was introduced in 1908. It became the most popular car in the United States.

WORLD BOOK map

Roosevelt's ancestors, the Van Roosevelts, had come to America from Holland in the 1640's. One of these ancestors, Klaes Martensen Van Roosevelt, settled in New York, which was then called New Amsterdam. Klaes was also an ancestor of Franklin D. Roosevelt, the 32nd President of the United States. Most of the Van Roosevelts were wealthy landowners and business leaders.

Theodore Roosevelt's mother came from a prominent Georgia family. One of her brothers was an admiral in the Confederate Navy. She sympathized with the South during the Civil War. Her husband, an importer of plate glass, supported the North. But the Roosevelts did not let their differences keep them from providing a happy home life for their family.

Like his father, Teedie had great energy, curiosity, and determination. He enjoyed an active childhood although he was puny and frequently ill. He suffered greatly from asthma. While playing with friends one day, he discovered that he also was nearsighted. The other

Important dates in Roosevelt's life

1858	(Oct. 27) Born in New York City.
1880	(Oct. 27) Married Alice Hathaway Lee.
1882-1884	Served in the New York state assembly.
1884	(Feb. 14) Mrs. Alice Roosevelt died.
1886	(Dec. 2) Married Edith Kermit Carow.
1889	Appointed to the U.S. Civil Service Commission.
1897	Named assistant secretary of the Navy.
1898	Led the Rough Riders in the Spanish-American War.
1898	Elected governor of New York.
1900	Elected Vice President of the United States.
1901	(Sept. 14) Became President of the United States.
1904	Elected to full term as President.
1912	Defeated for President on the "Bull Moose" ticket.
1919	(Jan. 6) Died at his home in Oyster Bay, N.Y.

children easily read an advertisement on a billboard some distance away. "Not only was I unable to read the sign, but I could not even see the letters," Roosevelt

Woman's Roosevelt Memorial Association

Roosevelt's birthplace in New York City is now a National Historic Site. His father built a gymnasium in the house, where "Teedie," a weak and sickly child, exercised regularly.

Theodore Roosevelt Collection, Harvard College Library

Alice Hathaway Lee married Theodore Roosevelt in 1880, on his 22nd birthday. She died in 1884, two days after giving birth to a daughter, also named Alice.

wrote later. From then on Theodore wore glasses.

Theodore loved both books and the outdoors. He combined these interests in nature study. His bureau drawers smelled of dead mice and birds, and so, often, did Theodore. When he was 10, and again when he was 14, Theodore went with his family on year-long trips abroad. He visited Europe and the Middle East.

When Theodore was about 12, his father told him that he would need a strong body to give his mind a chance to develop fully. The next year, while alone on a trip to Maine, Theodore was tormented by two mischievous boys. He felt ashamed because he was not strong enough to fight back. Roosevelt's father built a gymnasium in the family home, and Theodore exercised there regularly. He overcame his asthma and built up unusual physical strength.

Roosevelt studied under tutors until he entered Harvard University in 1876 at the age of 18. He earned good grades in college. Once he asked so many questions during a lecture that the professor exclaimed: "Now look here, Roosevelt, let me talk. I'm running this course!" Roosevelt graduated from Harvard in 1880.

First marriage. In October 1879, Roosevelt met Alice Hathaway Lee (1861-1884). She was the daughter of a wealthy official of a Boston investment firm. Roosevelt courted Alice during his senior year at Harvard. They were married on his 22nd birthday.

A double tragedy struck on Feb. 14, 1884. Alice Roosevelt died two days after the birth of a daughter, also named Alice (1884-1980). On the same day, Roosevelt's mother died of typhoid fever.

Political and public activities

State legislator. After graduation from Harvard in 1880, Roosevelt did not know what to do for a living. His father, who had died in 1878, had left him some money. But Theodore needed to earn more in order to live comfortably. He enrolled in the Columbia University Law School, but the courses did not interest him. While

studying law, he wrote *The Naval War of 1812,* a technically excellent but dull book.

Roosevelt decided to enter politics as a means of public service. He joined a Republican club in New York City. He recalled that his friends "laughed at me, and told me that politics were 'low . . .' I answered that . . . the people I knew did not belong to the governing class, and that the other people did—and that I intended to be one of the governing class."

In the fall of 1881, at the age of 23, Roosevelt won election to the New York state assembly. He wore sideburns and dressed elegantly. The other legislators thought he looked like a "dude." But his intelligence, courage, and energy won their respect. He was reelected twice, in 1882 and 1883.

Party leader. In 1882, Roosevelt served briefly as leader of the Republican minority in the assembly. State party bosses expected him to follow orders, but he refused to obey blindly. The bosses removed him as minority leader. However, Roosevelt remained the most influential man in the assembly. He worked closely with Governor Grover Cleveland, a Democrat, and became interested in civil service reform.

Rancher and writer. After the death of his wife and mother in 1884, Roosevelt left politics. He ran two cattle ranches on the Little Missouri River in the Dakota Territory. The hard life and endless activity of a rancher helped him recover from his sorrow. Wearing cowboy clothes, Roosevelt often spent 14 to 16 hours a day in the saddle. He hunted buffalo and other wild animals, tended cattle, and even helped law officers capture a band of outlaws.

Roosevelt wrote steadily. In one period of less than three months, he completed a biography of Senator Thomas Hart Benton of Missouri. Roosevelt also wrote a four-volume series called *The Winning of the West.*

Severe snowstorms in the winter of 1885-1886 de-

White House Historical Association

Edith Kermit Carow had known Roosevelt since childhood. They were married in 1886 and had five children. She was a devoted mother, as well as a gracious White House hostess.

stroyed most of Roosevelt's cattle. He returned to New York City in 1886 and at the request of Republican leaders, ran for mayor. He was badly defeated.

Second marriage. During several trips home from his ranches, Roosevelt had visited a childhood friend, Edith Kermit Carow (1861-1948). They were married on Dec. 2, 1886, and lived in Sagamore Hill, Roosevelt's home in Oyster Bay, Long Island, N.Y. Edith Roosevelt had a strong influence on her husband. He came to depend on her advice. "Whenever I go against her judgment, I regret it," he said.

The Roosevelts had five children: Theodore, Jr. (1887-1944); Kermit (1889-1943); Ethel Carow (1891-1977); Archibald Bulloch (1894-1979); and Quentin (1897-1918). Mrs. Roosevelt reared Alice Roosevelt, Theodore's daughter by his first wife, as her own child. Roosevelt loved to play with his children.

Civil Service commissioner. Benjamin Harrison won the Republican nomination for President in 1888. Roosevelt went on a speaking tour for Harrison, who was elected in November. Partly as a reward for Roosevelt's service, Harrison appointed him to the Civil Service Commission. Roosevelt brought publicity to the commission, which previously had attracted little attention. He improved the merit system by establishing examinations for some Civil Service jobs. He opposed the awarding of government jobs to political friends. Many Republicans resented his attitude. But President Grover Cleveland reappointed him in 1893.

Police commissioner. In 1895, Roosevelt gladly accepted the post of president of the Board of Police Commissioners in New York City. For the next two years, he fought to stamp out dishonesty on the police force. Sometimes he patrolled the streets at night to check on police officers suspected of illegal activities.

A national figure

Assistant secretary of the Navy. In 1895, some friends asked Roosevelt if he might be a candidate for President. "Don't you dare ask me that!" Roosevelt exclaimed. "Don't you put such ideas into my head . . . . I must be wanting to be President. Every young man does. But I won't let myself think of it . . . because if I do, I will begin to work for it, I'll be careful, calculating, cautious. . . and so—I'll beat myself. See?"

Roosevelt campaigned vigorously for William McKinley, the Republican candidate for President in 1896. McKinley won, and Roosevelt asked him for a government appointment. McKinley did not want this brash young man in Washington, but Roosevelt had powerful support. The President finally made him an assistant secretary of the Navy.

Roosevelt believed that sea power was the decisive factor in world history. He worked to strengthen the Navy. He also believed that war for a righteous cause brought out the finest virtues in people and nations. "No triumph of peace is quite so great as the supreme triumphs of war," he said soon after taking office. "The diplomat is the servant, not the master, of the soldier."

The Rough Riders. Since 1895, Cuban rebels had been revolting against their Spanish rulers. Many Americans demanded that the United States help the Cubans. On Feb. 15, 1898, the U.S. battleship *Maine* blew up in Havana harbor. Roosevelt tried to rush preparations for

Library of Congress

As assistant secretary of the Navy, which he became in 1897, Roosevelt worked to strengthen U.S. naval forces. He resigned in 1898 to fight in the Spanish-American War.

war against Spain. He became impatient with McKinley's attempts to avoid war. In private, Roosevelt complained that the President had "no more backbone than a chocolate éclair."

On April 25, 1898, the United States declared war on Spain. Roosevelt immediately resigned as assistant secretary of the Navy so he could fight. Even before resigning, he had started to recruit men for a cavalry regiment. This unit became the First Volunteer Cavalry Regiment. Under Roosevelt's command, it won fame as the Rough Riders. Most of the men were former college athletes and Western cowboys.

On July 1, 1898, American troops attacked a ring of fortified hills surrounding Santiago, Cuba. Colonel Roosevelt led his men in a charge up Kettle Hill, which flanked the Spanish blockhouse on San Juan Hill. He and the Rough Riders became nationally famous. Twenty years later he declared: "San Juan was the great day of my life." See **Spanish-American War.**

Governor of New York. The Republicans faced defeat in New York in 1898 because of a scandal over state canal contracts. The state party leader, Senator Thomas C. Platt, did not like Roosevelt. But Platt knew that Roosevelt's reputation might save the Republicans. Roosevelt agreed to run for governor. He won, largely because of his war record.

As governor, Roosevelt did not break with Platt. Neither did he follow Platt's wishes. He described this policy to a friend: "I have always been fond of the West African proverb: 'Speak softly and carry a big stick, you will go far.'" Roosevelt became an efficient, independent administrator. He supported mild reform legislation, including a law affecting civil service in the state. He angered large business interests by approving a bill for the taxation of corporation franchises.

Vice President. McKinley's renomination in 1900 seemed certain. Roosevelt had no wish to oppose the President, who he knew had nationwide support. But Roosevelt wondered whether he himself might get the

The Rough Riders, a regiment led by Roosevelt, became nationally famous for their role in helping to win the Battle of San Juan Hill in the Spanish-American War.

Library of Congress

nomination in 1904. As the Republican National Convention drew near, a movement began to nominate him for Vice President.

Roosevelt felt that being Vice President would take him out of active politics. In this way, his chances for the presidential nomination in 1904 would be weakened. Roosevelt also knew that Senator Platt wanted to get rid of him as governor of New York. Roosevelt felt he might not win a second term as governor in opposition to Platt. He finally consented to be McKinley's running mate. The Republicans nominated both men by acclamation. In the election, McKinley and Roosevelt defeated their Democratic opponents, William Jennings Bryan and former Vice President Adlai E. Stevenson.

On Sept. 6, 1901, only six months after his second inauguration, President McKinley was shot by an assassin. The tragedy occurred while McKinley was at the Pan American Exposition in Buffalo, N.Y. Doctors told Roosevelt that McKinley would probably recover. But, while vacationing in the Adirondack Mountains, Roosevelt learned McKinley was near death. He hurried to Buffalo, but McKinley died before Roosevelt arrived. That same day, Sept. 14, 1901, Roosevelt took the oath of office as President. See **McKinley, William** (Assassination).

Roosevelt's first Administration (1901-1905)

Roosevelt became President just six weeks before his 43rd birthday. He kept all the members of McKinley's Cabinet. He said he would continue McKinley's policies "absolutely unbroken." But Roosevelt had too much originality to follow another person's plans.

Most business leaders feared Roosevelt because of some reforms he had introduced as governor of New York. Several of these reforms had brought about stricter government control over industry. Early in his Administration, Roosevelt tried to convince business people that he would not interfere with them. He also tried to persuade conservative Republican leaders that he was not dangerous. But he never won them over completely. They considered much of his legislation dangerously progressive, even socialistic. The Republicans controlled Congress throughout Roosevelt's presidency. But because of conservative opposition, Roosevelt had increasing difficulty getting Congress to act on his recommendations.

"Trust buster." Many Americans had become worried about the *trusts,* or large business monopolies. These trusts were increasing rapidly in both number and power. The trusts had increased productivity and had raised the standard of living. But prices had also risen, and the people blamed the trusts. In his first message to Congress, in December 1901, Roosevelt expressed this feeling. "Captains of industry . . . have on the whole done great good to our people," he said. But he also pointed to "real and grave evils." Roosevelt recommended that "combination and concentration should be, not prohibited, but supervised and, within reasonable limits, controlled."

In 1902, the government sued the Northern Securities Company on charges of trying to reduce competition. This firm had been formed by J. P. Morgan and other financiers to control key railroads in the West. Roosevelt said he did not want to use the power of the government to ruin Morgan. Rather, he wanted to keep order among all the great economic forces in the nation. The Supreme Court upheld the government's view in 1904. It dissolved the Northern Securities Company.

During Roosevelt's presidency, the government filed suits against 43 other corporations. In major cases, the government ended John D. Rockefeller's oil trust and James B. Duke's tobacco trust. Many people called Roosevelt a "trust buster." But the President declared that he wanted the government to regulate, not "bust," trusts.

Friend of labor. Roosevelt wanted the government to act justly toward labor unions as well as toward business. Government intervention in labor disputes was not new. But it had usually favored management.

In May 1902, about 140,000 members of the United Mine Workers went on strike in the hard-coal fields of Pennsylvania. Public opinion favored the strikers, who demanded more pay and better working conditions. As the strike continued, coal supplies began to run low in

Eastern cities. Many hospitals and schools had no fuel. Winter was approaching.

Roosevelt had no legal authority to intervene in the strike. But he called a conference of leaders of both sides. He proposed that the strike be settled by arbitration. The miners agreed, but the mine owners refused. Roosevelt threatened to have the army seize and operate the mines. At Roosevelt's request, J. P. Morgan helped reach a compromise with the mine owners. The miners got a pay raise the next March. Roosevelt said later that he had tried to give the miners a "square deal." He often used this phrase to refer to his policy of social reform. In 1903, Congress established the Department of Commerce and Labor (see **Labor, Department of**).

Foreign policy. Roosevelt believed that the government needed a "big stick," or threat of force, to carry out its foreign policies. He used this policy in relations with Europe and Latin America.

The Venezuela Affair. The Monroe Doctrine held that the United States should keep European powers out of the Western Hemisphere. Roosevelt upheld this doctrine in what was known as the Venezuela Affair.

Venezuela had borrowed large sums of money in Europe. In December 1902, German and British ships blockaded Venezuelan ports to force payment of the debts. Roosevelt feared that Germany planned to seize Venezuelan territory. He warned the Germans that he might have to use force if they took any part of Venezuela. The Germans withdrew their warships. Later, Roosevelt helped settle the dispute peacefully.

The "Roosevelt Corollary." In 1904, Santo Domingo (now the Dominican Republic) found it could not pay its debts to several European countries. Again, Roosevelt feared European intervention. He announced that the United States might be forced "in flagrant cases of . . . wrongdoing or impotence, to the exercise of an international police power." This policy was called the "Roosevelt Corollary" of the Monroe Doctrine.

Theodore Roosevelt Collection, Harvard College Library

Roosevelt spoke out against trusts on various occasions. Although he denied being a "trust buster," Roosevelt believed government should regulate large business monopolies.

Roosevelt ordered American officials to take over the customs system of Santo Domingo in 1904. American control, which began the next year, brought order to Santo Domingo's finances.

The Panama Canal. Between 1902 and 1905, Roosevelt persuaded Congress to approve building 10 battleships and 4 armored cruisers for the U.S. Navy. He believed the larger fleet would give the nation greater influence in international affairs. But the fleet would need to shift rapidly between the Atlantic and Pacific oceans. A canal across Central America seemed necessary.

In 1902, Roosevelt began negotiating with Colombia for the right to build a canal across Panama, a province of Colombia. The negotiators signed a treaty, but the Colombian Senate rejected it. Roosevelt then supported a revolutionary government that took control of Panama, and the United States recognized the Republic of Panama. Less than two weeks later, the United States and Panama signed a treaty granting to the United States the use and control of a strip of land on which to dig a canal. Roosevelt said he was prouder of the canal than of any other accomplishment of his Administration. He visited Panama in 1906—the first President to travel in a foreign country while in office. See **Panama Canal** (picture: President Theodore Roosevelt).

The Alaskan boundary dispute. No one cared about the exact boundary between Canada and Alaska until gold was discovered in the Klondike in 1896. Then Canada claimed a line that gave it control of important routes to the gold fields. The United States disputed the claim. Early in 1902, Great Britain asked that the matter be settled by arbitration. At first, Roosevelt refused. But then he agreed that the dispute should be settled by a tribunal of six "impartial jurists" appointed by both countries. In 1903, the tribunal ruled in favor of the United States.

Conservation. Roosevelt made notable achievements in conservation. He added about 150 million acres (61 million hectares) to the national forests and in 1905 established the United States Forest Service. He also set up five new national parks. Congress passed the Reclamation Act of 1902, which provided for the reclamation and irrigation of dry Western lands. Roosevelt then started 25 irrigation or reclamation projects (see **Roosevelt Dam**). He also set aside 18 sites as national monuments and worked to preserve wildlife. By executive order, he created the first 51 federal bird reservations and established the first four national game preserves.

Life in the White House was never dull during Roosevelt's presidency. The Roosevelt children and their friends became known as the "White House Gang." The President sometimes joined in the children's games. One day, he heard that the gang was preparing an "attack" on the White House. He sent a message to the children through the War Department, ordering them to call off the "attack." Once Roosevelt scolded his sons for decorating a portrait of President Andrew Jackson with spitballs. But he allowed the boys to bring their pets, including a pony and snakes, into the White House.

The President often played tennis on the White House lawn with friends. These friends came to be known as the "tennis cabinet." The group also went horseback riding and hiking. More than once, on winter hikes, Roose-

Roosevelt went to Panama in 1906 to inspect progress on the construction of the Panama Canal. He considered the canal the greatest achievement of his presidency.

Culver

velt and his friends swam across the Potomac River through chunks of floating ice.

In 1902, the White House was remodeled and enlarged. The east and west wings were built. Workers installed new plumbing, heating, and electrical systems.

Edith Roosevelt was an efficient and gracious White House hostess. She carefully kept out of politics. The President's daughter by his first marriage was called "Princess Alice" by newspaper reporters. In 1906, Alice married Representative Nicholas Longworth of Ohio, who later served as Speaker of the House of Representatives. Their wedding took place in the White House.

Election of 1904. The Republicans unanimously nominated Roosevelt for President at their 1904 national convention. They chose Senator Charles W. Fairbanks of Indiana for Vice President. The Democrats nominated Judge Alton B. Parker of the New York Supreme Court for President, and Henry G. Davis of West Virginia for Vice President.

During the election campaign, Roosevelt called on the voters to support his "square deal" policies. Parker appealed for an end to what he called "rule of individual caprice" and "usurpation of authority" by the President. Roosevelt won the election by more than $2\frac{1}{2}$ million popular votes. No earlier President had won by so large a margin.

Roosevelt's second Administration (1905-1909)

Domestic problems. Roosevelt believed that laws were badly needed to control the nation's railroads. The Elkins Act of 1903 had prohibited railroads from making *rebates,* or returning sums of money, to favored shippers. But the act had not stopped such practices, which often put rival shippers out of business. Roosevelt demanded legislation to curb the abuses. In 1906, Congress passed the Hepburn Railway Rate Act despite conservative opposition. The act did not end the rebates, but it was a step in that direction.

The food and drug industries were also affected by reforms. In 1906, Roosevelt read Upton Sinclair's new novel *The Jungle.* It described unsanitary conditions in the meat-packing industry. Roosevelt ordered an investigation and received what he called a "sickening report." He threatened to publish the report if Congress did not correct the situation. That same year, Congress passed the Meat Inspection Act and the Food and Drugs Act. See **Pure food and drug laws.**

In 1907, the stock market slumped. A financial panic spread throughout the country. The business community blamed Roosevelt and his progressive legislation.

Vice President and Cabinet

Vice President	* Charles W. Fairbanks
Secretary of state	* John Hay
	* Elihu Root (1905)
	Robert Bacon (1909)
Secretary of the treasury	Lyman J. Gage
	Leslie M. Shaw (1902)
	George B. Cortelyou (1907)
Secretary of war	* Elihu Root
	* William Howard Taft (1904)
	Luke E. Wright (1908)
Attorney general	Philander C. Knox
	William H. Moody (1904)
	Charles J. Bonaparte (1906)
Postmaster general	Charles E. Smith
	Henry C. Payne (1902)
	Robert J. Wynne (1904)
	George B. Cortelyou (1905)
	George von L. Meyer (1907)
Secretary of the Navy	John D. Long
	William H. Moody (1902)
	Paul Morton (1904)
	Charles J. Bonaparte (1905)
	Victor H. Metcalf (1906)
	Truman H. Newberry (1908)
Secretary of the interior	Ethan A. Hitchcock
	James R. Garfield (1907)
Secretary of agriculture	James Wilson
Secretary of commerce and labor	George B. Cortelyou
	Victor H. Metcalf (1904)
	Oscar S. Straus (1906)

*Has a separate biography in *World Book*

Sagamore Hill, Roosevelt's home on Long Island, New York, provided a spacious setting for his large, active family. It served as a summer White House during his presidency.

John Todaro

Roosevelt's election

Place of nominating convention	. .Chicago
Ballot on which nominated	. . . . . . .1st
Democratic opponent	. . . . .Alton B. Parker
Electoral vote*	. . . . .336 (Roosevelt) to 140 (Parker)
Popular vote	. . . . .7,626,593 (Roosevelt) to 5,082,898 (Parker)
Age at inauguration	46

* For votes by states, see **Electoral College** (table).

But most historians believe that speculation and inefficient business management actually caused the panic. Prosperity returned by 1909.

Friction with Japan. In 1905, Roosevelt helped end the Russo-Japanese War. He brought representatives of Russia and Japan together in Portsmouth, New Hampshire. Then the president served as mediator in the peace talks that led to the Treaty of Portsmouth. In 1906, Roosevelt received the Nobel Peace Prize. He was the first American to win a Nobel Prize.

As the victors in the war, the Japanese demanded compensation payments from Russia. During the peace talks, Roosevelt had opposed this demand. His attitude angered the Japanese and also Japanese Americans in the United States. Their anger grew in 1906, when the San Francisco school board decided to segregate children of Japanese descent.

Relations between the United States and Japan became more strained. Roosevelt feared a Japanese attack on the Philippines. Many Americans thought war with Japan was near. But the president persuaded the San Francisco school board to end its segregation policy. He also negotiated a *gentlemen's agreement* with Japan to keep Japanese laborers out of the United States (see **Gentlemen's agreement**). In 1908, Japan and the United States signed the Root-Takahira Agreement. In this pact, the two nations promised not to seek territorial gains in the Pacific, and to honor the Open-Door Policy in China (see **Open-Door Policy**).

In 1907, Roosevelt decided to display American naval power. He sent 16 new battleships on a good-will tour of the world. These ships became known as the *Great White Fleet* because they were painted white. The fleet

received enthusiastic welcomes in Japan and other countries. Roosevelt viewed the tour as a part of "big stick" diplomacy.

European power balance was maintained with Roosevelt's help. In 1905, Germany demanded a share in the control of Morocco, which was dominated by France. Two alliances of nations—one headed by Germany, the other by Britain and France—came close to war. Roosevelt persuaded Germany to attend an international conference in Spain in 1906. At the conference, the United States sided with France and Britain. Germany backed down on its demand.

A party split developed among the Republicans as Roosevelt neared the end of his presidency. Conservative Republicans put up increased resistance to Roosevelt's progressive policies. Roosevelt fought harder for "political, social, and industrial reform." But during his last year in office, he got little congressional action. His Republican opponents dared to resist him because they believed he would leave office in 1909.

Roosevelt had declared after his election in 1904 that he would "under no circumstances" run for president again. He decided to keep this pledge. He selected William Howard Taft, his secretary of war, to succeed him. At the Republican National Convention of 1908, he persuaded most of the delegates to support Taft for president. In this way, he assured Taft's nomination. Taft won an easy election victory over the Democratic candidate, William Jennings Bryan.

Later years

After leaving the presidency in March 1909, Roosevelt sailed for Africa to hunt big game. Some conservative congressmen wished "health to the lions." But Roosevelt and his party brought down 296 big-game animals, including 9 lions. When Roosevelt arrived home in June 1910, he found himself the center of national attention. Progressive Republicans felt that Taft had betrayed them. They turned to Roosevelt.

"Bull Moose" candidate. Roosevelt tried to bring together the progressive and conservative wings of the Republican Party. But he failed. He had become identified too closely with the progressives.

In 1910, on a speaking tour of the West, Roosevelt

proclaimed a policy of "New Nationalism." It became the policy of the progressive Republicans. Roosevelt declared that the president must be the "steward of public welfare." He frightened conservatives with his views on private property. Roosevelt said that property was "subject to the general right of the community to regulate its use to whatever degree the public welfare may require it."

In 1912, Roosevelt gave in to pleas that he run for a third term as president. He said that his statement in 1904 had meant not running for a third *consecutive* term. He won many victories in primary elections. These victories indicated he was the popular choice of the party. But President Taft controlled the party machinery and was renominated by the Republican National Convention. Roosevelt and his followers formed the Progressive Party, or *Bull Moose* party. The name came from Roosevelt's reply when a reporter asked how he felt. "I feel as strong as a bull moose," he said.

On Oct. 14, 1912, a saloonkeeper named John N. Schrank tried to assassinate Roosevelt. Schrank shot Roosevelt just before he made a speech in Milwaukee. A glasses case in Roosevelt's pocket deflected the bullet and probably saved his life. Even with the bullet in his chest, Roosevelt insisted on making the speech. He recovered from the wound in about two weeks. Schrank was committed to a mental hospital.

Roosevelt's candidacy split the Republican vote. The Democratic candidate, Governor Woodrow Wilson of New Jersey, easily won the election. See **Wilson, Woodrow** (Presidential candidate).

World War I began in 1914. Roosevelt called for American preparedness against a "strong, ruthless, ambitious, militaristic … Germany." He developed an intense dislike of Wilson, mostly because the president did not lead the nation into war immediately. After the United States entered the war in 1917, Roosevelt asked Wilson for permission to raise a division of troops to fight in France. Wilson refused the request.

Roosevelt's sons served in France. Quentin, an aviator, was killed in an air battle with a German pilot.

Death. In 1914, Roosevelt had explored the River of Doubt in the Brazilian jungle. He contracted a form of jungle fever and returned weak and prematurely aged. Early in 1918, Roosevelt underwent operations to remove abscesses on his thigh and in his ears. The abscesses resulted from the jungle fever. He lost the hearing in his left ear. At about this time, Roosevelt revealed that he had been blind in his left eye since 1908. He lost the sight in the eye as a result of an injury he received boxing with a military aide in the White House.

Roosevelt opposed American membership in the League of Nations, which he felt would limit the United States in foreign relations. He might have won the Republican presidential nomination in 1920. But Roosevelt died unexpectedly of a blood clot in the heart on Jan. 6, 1919. He was buried in Youngs Memorial Cemetery, near Sagamore Hill in Oyster Bay, New York. His second wife died in 1948 and was buried beside him.

Roosevelt's birthplace in New York City and Sagamore Hill are national historic sites, as is the Wilcox Mansion in Buffalo, New York, where Roosevelt took the oath of office in 1901. Theodore Roosevelt National Park, in western North Dakota, includes one of the ranches

Roosevelt operated in the 1880's. Roosevelt's other ranch is nearby. Theodore Roosevelt Island, in the Potomac River in Washington, D.C., has a large statue of the former president. Roosevelt is also one of the four presidents whose faces are carved on Mount Rushmore in South Dakota.　　John A. Gable

Related articles in *World Book* include:

Antitrust laws	President of the United States
Conservation (The rise of the conservation movement)	Progressive Party
	Pure food and drug laws
Fairbanks, Charles Warren	Roosevelt, Theodore, Jr.
McKinley, William	Roosevelt Dam
Mount Rushmore National Memorial	Rough Riders
	Spanish-American War
Panama Canal (picture)	Taft, William Howard
Parker, Alton Brooks	White House (History)

Outline

I. Early life
　A. Boyhood and education
　B. First marriage
II. Political and public activities
　A. State legislator
　B. Party leader
　C. Rancher and writer
　D. Second marriage
　E. Civil Service commissioner
　F. Police commissioner
III. A national figure
　A. Assistant secretary of
　　the Navy
　B. The Rough Riders
　C. Governor of New York
　D. Vice President
IV. Roosevelt's first Administration (1901-1905)
　A. "Trust buster"
　B. Friend of labor
　C. Foreign policy
　D. Conservation
　E. Life in the White House
　F. Election of 1904
V. Roosevelt's second Administration (1905-1909)
　A. Domestic problems
　B. Friction with Japan
　C. European power balance
　D. A party split
VI. Later years
　A. "Bull Moose" candidate
　B. World War I
　C. Death

Questions

As a boy, how did Roosevelt build up his strength?
What was the "White House gang"?
What phrase did Roosevelt use to describe his foreign policy?
Why did Roosevelt become known as a "trust buster"?
How did the "Bull Moose" party get its name?
What were some of Roosevelt's achievements in conservation?
How did Roosevelt first win national fame?
What did the "Roosevelt Corollary" proclaim?
What was the *Great White Fleet*?
What did Roosevelt call "the great day of my life"?

Additional resources

DeStefano, Susan. *Theodore Roosevelt.* 21st Century Books, 1993. Younger readers.
Fritz, Jean. *Bully for You, Teddy Roosevelt!* Putnam, 1991. Younger readers.
Gould, Lewis L. *The Presidency of Theodore Roosevelt.* Univ. Pr. of Kans., 1991.
McCullough, David G. *Mornings on Horseback.* Simon & Schuster, 1981.
Meltzer, Milton. *Theodore Roosevelt and His America.* Watts, 1994.

Miller, Nathan. *Theodore Roosevelt.* 1992. Reprint. Quill Paperbacks, 1994.

Whitelaw, Nancy. *Theodore Roosevelt Takes Charge.* Whitman, 1992.

Roosevelt, *ROH zuh vehlt,* **Theodore, Jr.** (1887-1944), was the oldest son of President Theodore Roosevelt. Like his father, he was a soldier, statesman, and author.

Roosevelt was born in Oyster Bay, New York. He commanded an infantry battalion in 1917 and 1918 and an infantry regiment in late 1918 during World War I. He won the Silver Star and the Distinguished Service Cross. In 1919, he helped organize the American Legion. A Republican, he served in the New York State Assembly in 1920 and 1921 and as assistant secretary of the Navy from 1921 to 1924. Roosevelt served as governor of Puerto Rico from 1929 to 1932 and governor general of the Philippines in 1932 and 1933, both appointed posts. A brigadier general during World War II, he won the Medal of Honor for his actions on D-Day (June 6, 1944), when he led troops ashore at Utah Beach, in France. He died of a heart attack in France on July 12. Roosevelt wrote many books and articles on hunting, adventure, and public policy.   John A. Gable

Roosevelt Campobello International Park, *ROH zuh vehlt KAM puh BEHL OH,* covers about 2,800 acres (1,100 hectares) on Campobello Island in New Brunswick, Canada. For the location of the park, see **New Brunswick** (physical map). The summer home of United States President Franklin D. Roosevelt is in the park. Roosevelt's family often spent vacations there. He was stricken with poliomyelitis on the island in 1921. The United States and Canada dedicated the park in 1964. A joint U.S.-Canadian commission administers it. The Franklin D. Roosevelt International Bridge connects the island and Lubec, Maine.

Critically reviewed by Roosevelt Campobello International Park

Roosevelt Dam, *ROH zuh vehlt,* is part of the Salt River irrigation project in south-central Arizona. It was originally constructed by the U.S. Bureau of Reclamation as a rubble-masonry arch-gravity dam in 1911. It was officially named the Theodore Roosevelt Dam in 1959. An extensive renovation project was completed on the dam in 1996. The dam is 357 feet (109 meters) high and has a crest length of 1,210 feet (369 meters). Its reservoir covers about 21,500 acres (8,700 hectares) and can store about 1.6 million acre-feet (2 billion cubic meters) of water. The dam is used for flood control, water storage, and power production.

Critically reviewed by the Bureau of Reclamation

Roosevelt Memorial. See Franklin Delano Roosevelt Memorial.

Rooster. See Chicken.

Root, in arithmetic, is a quantity that yields a given quantity when it is taken as a factor a specified number of times (see **Factor**). The number of times the root is taken as a factor is called its *index.* Roots are named from their indexes. Thus, 3 is a *fourth* root of 81, because $3 \times 3 \times 3 \times 3 = 81$. Roots with indexes of 2 and 3 are also called *square roots* and *cube roots,* respectively. The positive n th root of a positive number p is indicated by $\sqrt[n]{p}$. Thus, $\sqrt{81} = 3$. The symbol $\sqrt{\ }$ is called a *radical sign.* When no index is shown, the index 2 is understood.

A root in algebra is a solution of an equation—that is, it is a quantity which, when substituted for the variable in an equation, satisfies the equation. For example, 3 is a root of $x + 2 = 5$, because if 3 is substituted for the variable x, the equation correctly reads $3 + 2 = 5$. See also **Algebra; Cube root; Square root.**   Robert M. Vancko

Root is one of the three main organs of a plant. The others are the stem and the leaf. Most roots are long and round and grow underground. They anchor the plant in the soil. They also absorb water and minerals that the plant needs to grow. In addition, many roots store food for later use by the plant.

Plants with roots include all seed-producing plants and most spore-producing plants, such as ferns and horsetails. Liverworts, hornworts, and mosses do not have true roots.

Kinds of roots

The first root to develop from a seed is the *primary* root. It produces many branches called *secondary* roots. The secondary roots produce branches of their own.

There are two main kinds of root systems, *taproot* or *fibrous.* In a taproot system, the primary root grows straight down and is called the *taproot.* The taproot remains larger than any of the secondary roots throughout the life of the plant. In some plants, including beets and carrots, the taproot becomes *fleshy* (swollen).

Grass is an example of a plant with a fibrous root system. In such a system, the primary root does not remain larger than the others. Many slender secondary roots grow out in all directions. A fibrous root system may become very extensive. For example, the roots of a rye plant may have a combined length of about 380 miles (612 kilometers).

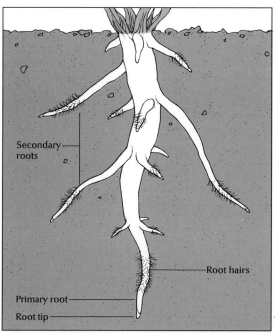

WORLD BOOK diagram by Robert Keys

The main parts of a root system appear in this illustration. The *primary root* develops first and produces branches called *secondary roots. Root hairs* grow just above the tip of each root.

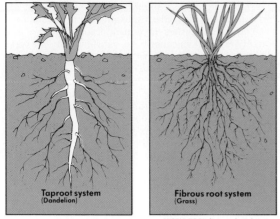

Taproot system
(Dandelion)

Fibrous root system
(Grass)

WORLD BOOK diagrams by Robert Keys

The two chief kinds of root systems. In a *taproot system,* the primary root grows straight down and remains larger than secondary roots. In a *fibrous root system,* secondary roots grow in all directions and may be as long as the primary root.

Some plants have modified roots that perform special functions. Roots that grow from the primary root or its branches are called *adventitious roots.* They include the *prop roots* of corn and certain other plants. Prop roots grow down into the soil from the lower part of the stem and help brace the plant against the wind. Some species of orchids and other plants that live on tree branches send out *aerial roots,* which cling to the branches. Aerial roots absorb water and minerals from the surface of the tree and from the air. Mistletoe is one of the few plants with roots that penetrate the limbs of a tree. These roots, called *sinkers,* absorb food, water, and minerals directly from the tree.

Parts of a root

The root tip. A root grows in length from an area at its *apex* (tip). This growth area is called the *apical meristem.* A meristem is any part of a plant where the cells divide rapidly, forming new cells continually. The apical

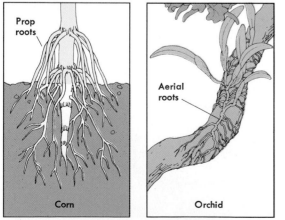

Prop roots

Aerial roots

Corn

Orchid

WORLD BOOK diagrams by Robert Keys

Specialized roots. *Prop roots* grow from a stem and help brace a plant against the wind. *Aerial roots* cling to tree branches and absorb water and minerals from the tree and the air.

meristem produces the *root cap,* a thimble-shaped group of cells. The root cap protects the delicate root tip from damage as the root grows in length and the tip pushes through the soil.

The cells produced by the apical meristem are all small and nearly identical. In the *region of elongation,* just behind the apical meristem, the cells rapidly grow longer. Farther back lies the *region of maturation.* There, the cells *differentiate*—that is, they take on a different structure and appearance according to their functions in the mature root. The distance from the root cap to the region of maturation is only a few tenths of an inch or a few millimeters.

The outer tissues. The outer layer of cells of a root is called the *epidermis.* It serves as a sort of skin and protects the tissues beneath. Tiny, hairlike extensions called *root hairs* grow from the epidermis. The root hairs absorb most of the water and minerals that a plant takes in from the soil. In most kinds of plants, the root hairs live only a few days. They occupy the *root hair zone,* an area just above the root tip. This area is only a few tenths of an inch or a few millimeters long.

A thick layer of rounded cells called the *cortex* lies just inside the epidermis. These cells contain stored food and water. The inner layer of cells of the cortex makes up the *endodermis.*

The core, or *stele,* is the central portion of the root. Its outer layer of cells is called the *pericycle.* Branch roots grow from the pericycle. Inside the pericycle are two kinds of tissues, *xylem* and *phloem.* Xylem includes rows of dead, tubular cells called *vessels,* which conduct water and minerals up to the stem and leaves. Phloem consists largely of rows of long, living cells called *sieve tubes.* These cells transport food down from the leaves for use or storage by the root. In most roots, the xylem forms a pattern shaped like a star or the spokes of a wheel. The phloem lies between the points of the star or between the spokes.

Secondary tissues. All the tissues described so far have been *primary tissues.* Such tissues differentiate from cells created in the apical meristem. Many plants that live just one year have only primary tissues in their roots. But other plants, especially those that live more than one year, have *secondary tissues* in their roots in addition to primary tissues. The growth of primary tissue adds to the length of a root. Secondary tissues add to the root's thickness. Secondary-tissue growth produces the large, brown, woody roots in trees, shrubs, and other plants that live for many years.

Secondary tissues develop from two meristems. One, called the *cork cambium,* originates beneath the epidermis, generally in the pericycle. It produces cork cells and pushes them toward the outside of the root. As the cork expands outward, the endodermis, cortex, and epidermis die and peel off. The cork replaces them and becomes the outer covering of the root. The other secondary meristem, the *cambium,* lies between the primary xylem and the primary phloem. It produces secondary xylem cells toward the center of the root, and secondary phloem cells toward the outside.

The importance of roots

Fleshy taproots rank among the most important vegetables. Fleshy taproots include beets, carrots, radishes,

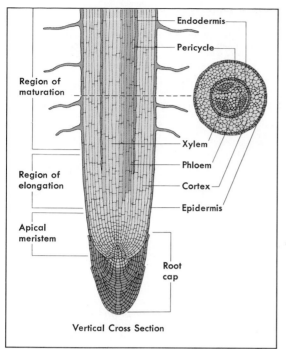

The root tip comprises the regions in which cells divide *(apical meristem)*, grow longer *(region of elongation)*, and become specialized *(region of maturation)*. The *root cap* protects the tip.

rutabagas, and turnips. Sweet potatoes are a root used not only as food, but also in making alcohol, starch, and syrup. Roots of the cassava plant are a popular food in the tropics. The roots of tropical yams are used in producing cortisone and related drugs.

Roots help prevent erosion of soil by wind and water. Soil is held in place by the dense network of roots of grasses, trees, and other plants. Plants called *legumes,* which include clover, peas, and soybeans, help enrich the soil. Swellings on their roots contain bacteria that

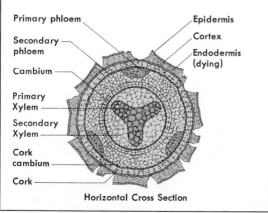

Secondary tissues develop in some kinds of roots. The *cambium* produces secondary xylem and phloem. The *cork cambium* produces cork. As the cork expands, the outer tissues die.

convert nitrogen from the air into compounds. These compounds are useful to the plant. After the plant dies, the compounds become part of the soil.

Richard C. Keating

See also **Alfalfa** (picture); **Carrot; Mangrove; Plant** (Factors affecting plant growth; pictures).

Root, Elihu (1845-1937), an American statesman, is best remembered for his efforts to assure international peace. From 1905 to 1909, he served as secretary of state under President Theodore Roosevelt. As secretary of state, Root worked to improve United States relations with Latin American countries and Japan. He also negotiated many treaties in order to end disputes between the United States and other countries. In 1912, he received the Nobel Peace Prize for his contributions to world peace.

Root served as president of the Carnegie Endowment for International Peace from 1910 to 1925. In 1920 and 1921, he helped organize the Permanent Court of International Justice. For the next 10 years, he battled unsuccessfully to get the United States to join the court.

Root was born in Clinton, New York. He graduated from the New York University Law School in 1867. He soon became a highly successful corporate lawyer in New York City.

Root served as United States secretary of war from 1899 to 1904, under Presidents William McKinley and Theodore Roosevelt. In 1901, he founded the Army War College. Root also drafted the Platt Amendment to the Constitution of Cuba. This amendment, adopted in 1901, gave the United States the right to intervene in Cuban affairs. Root represented New York in the United States Senate from 1909 to 1915. In 1916, he unsuccessfully sought the Republican presidential nomination.

Robert W. Cherny

See also **Nobel Prizes** (picture).

Root, John Wellborn (1850-1891), was one of the most important architects of the Chicago School. The school was an influential group of architects trained in Chicago during the late 1800's. Root became a leader in the aesthetic and technical development of modern office skyscrapers.

Root gained acclaim for the skyscrapers he designed in Chicago with Daniel Hudson Burnham. The two formed a famous partnership in 1873. Their first important project was the 10-story Montauk Block office building (1881-1882). One of their most influential designs was the Rookery office building (1885-1888). Root designed the structure to resemble a hollow square. Masonry walls supported the exterior while the walls around an interior court were supported by a light iron frame. Root's Rand McNally building (1889-1890) was the first to have an all-steel frame, a structural element that became basic to modern design. Root also designed the 22-story Masonic Temple (1890-1892), which was the world's tallest building for a time. Before his death, Root helped design the Reliance Building in Chicago, one of the great skyscrapers of the period. Root was born in Lumpkin, Georgia. Leland M. Roth

See also **Architecture** (Early modern architecture in America); **Burnham, Daniel Hudson.**

Rope consists of strands of yarn or wire that have been twisted together. It ranges in size from $\frac{1}{16}$ inch (4.8 millimeters) to more than 6 inches (152 millimeters) in diameter. Rope that is less than $\frac{3}{16}$ inch thick is called *twine* or *cord. Cordage* is the general term for rope, twine, or cord made from yarn.

People have made and used ropes since prehistoric times. Today, ropes are used for lifting loads, for towing, and for many other purposes. There are three kinds of rope, depending on the material from which they are made: (1) natural-fiber rope, (2) synthetic-fiber rope, and (3) wire rope.

Natural-fiber rope is made from fibers that come from plants. The natural fiber most widely used in rope is *manila,* a hard fiber taken from the leaf stems of the abacá plant. Abacá grows mainly in the Philippines, and most manila rope is manufactured there. Manila rope has great strength and good resistance to wind, rain, and sun. See **Abacá.**

Other natural fibers used in rope include *sisal* and *henequen.* Sisal comes from the leaves of the sisal plant, which grows mainly in Brazil and eastern Africa. It is a hard fiber that has about 80 per cent of the strength of manila. Henequen is taken from the henequen plant, which grows chiefly in Mexico. Henequen is not as strong as sisal and is used primarily in twine and lower grades of rope. See **Henequen; Sisal.**

In the past, much rope was also made from soft natural fibers, such as *hemp* and *jute.* Today, soft fibers are used mostly in twine and in the art of *macramé.* See **Hemp; Jute; Macramé.**

Synthetic-fiber rope is stronger, lighter, and, in most cases, more flexible than natural-fiber rope. Synthetic fibers have greater resistance to chemical damage and do not rot, as do natural fibers.

The first synthetic-fiber rope was made from *nylon* during World War II (1939-1945) and used for parachute cords and glider towropes. Nylon rope is almost three times as strong as manila rope. The great elasticity of nylon rope makes it the best rope for towing and anchor lines. Rope made from *polyester* fibers is expensive, but it is the best rope for general use. It has almost the same strength as nylon rope but does not have as much

Parts of a three-strand rope

Rope consists of many fibers that have been spun into yarns. The yarns are then twisted into thick strands. The most common type of rope has three strands *laid* (twisted) together.

WORLD BOOK diagram by Richard Fickle

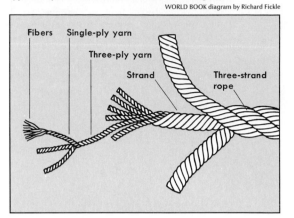

stretch. Polyester rope resists damage from *abrasion* (scraping) and the sun's ultraviolet rays better than any other synthetic-fiber rope. *Polypropylene* rope is about 50 per cent stronger than manila rope but has poor abrasion resistance. Also, special chemical compounds must be added to polypropylene rope to give it ultraviolet resistance.

Manufacturers make extremely strong rope from synthetic fibers called *aramids.* Rope made from aramid fibers can be used under hotter conditions than other synthetic fibers because it has a high melting point. It also resists stretching.

Manufacturers also produce ropes that combine the desirable features of two or more synthetic fibers. A common combination—polyester and polypropylene—provides a cheaper substitute for polyester.

Wire rope consists of steel wires twisted together. It is stronger and wears better than most fiber rope,

Some uses of rope   Rope has a wide variety of uses. Window washers hang their scaffold with manila rope, which comes from the fibers of the abacá plant. Nylon rope is widely used as *mooring line* to tie ships and boats to docks. Wire ropes secure the cables of huge suspension bridges.

Artstreet

Manila rope

George Hall

Nylon rope

George Hall

Wire rope

but it is much heavier and not as flexible as rope made from fibers. Wire rope, often called *cable,* is used in operating such equipment as elevators, oil well derricks, and shovels used in construction work.

How rope is made. Ropes must be carefully designed to meet such usage requirements as abrasion resistance, chemical and ultraviolet resistance, strength, stretch, and weight. Rope manufacturers buy bales of natural fibers from fiber brokers. A machine called a *card* combs the fibers and lays them parallel, forming a continuous ribbon. The ribbon is drawn out until it is thin enough for spinning. A machine spins the ribbon into yarn, and strands are made by twisting together two or more yarns. Three or more strands are *laid* (twisted) together to form rope.

Manufacturers buy most synthetic fibers in *filament* form. A machine called a *twister* twists the long filament yarns into *plied yarns,* which are then made into rope in the same way as natural fiber yarn.

Most rope has three strands, but four- and eight-strand ropes are also popular. Another common type, called *cable-laid rope,* consists of three three-strand ropes *closed* (wrapped) together.

Manufacturers make wire rope by twisting a number of wires together to form strands and then closing the strands around a core. The strongest wire ropes have wire cores.   Christine W. Jarvis

See also **Century plant; Cowboy** (His rope); **Fiber; Knots, hitches, and splices.**

Rorqual. See Whale (Rorquals).

Rosario, *roh ZAH ree OH* (pop. 1,079,359), is the third largest city in Argentina. Only Buenos Aires and Córdoba have more people. Rosario is located on the Paraná River, in the east-central part of the country. For the location of Rosario, see **Argentina** (political map). The city is a major inland seaport and an important industrial center.

Rosario was founded in 1730 on the eastern edge of the *Pampa,* a huge fertile plain. The city first became important in the late 1800's, when farmers on the Pampa began producing large quantities of agricultural products. Rosario's location on the Paraná River made it an ideal point from which to ship the products to places outside the region. Today, five railway systems and five major highways link various parts of northern and central Argentina to Rosario's excellent port facilities. Many factories in Rosario produce processed foods from farm products. The city's other industries include petroleum refining and the manufacture of chemicals, metal products, and textiles. Rosario is modern in appearance and has many boulevards and attractive parks.

Richard W. Wilkie

Rosary, *ROH zuhr ee,* is a string of beads used as an aid to memory and concentration while praying. The beads may be made of wood, metal, or stone. The rosary commonly used by Roman Catholics consists of 50 small beads divided into equal sections by four large beads. A pendant, composed of two large beads, three small ones, and a crucifix, hangs from the rosary. Worshipers recite the Lord's Prayer on the large beads. They use the small beads for prayers to the Virgin Mary that are commonly called "Hail Marys." At the end of each group of Hail Marys, a short verse in praise of God is recited. The Apostles' Creed is recited on the crucifix.

While worshipers recite the prayers, they are expected to reflect on the mysteries of the faith.

Prayer beads are of ancient origin and were probably first used by Buddhists in an attempt to combine vocal prayer with mental prayer. Buddhists, Hindus, and Muslims use them in certain forms of their prayer. Early forms of praying with a rosary began in Christianity during the Middle Ages, but became widespread only in the 1400's and 1500's.   Richard L. Schebera

Rosas, Juan Manuel de. See Argentina (Forming a national government).

Roscius, *RAHSH ee uhs,* **Quintus,** *KWIHN tuhs* (126? B.C.-62? B.C.), a Roman actor, was so famous in his day that his name came to stand for "great actor." He excelled in both tragic and comic parts. He founded a school for actors and wrote a book on acting and speaking. One of his admirers was the orator Cicero, who defended him in a famous speech. Quintus Roscius Gallus was born near Rome and became rich through his acting.   Don B. Wilmeth

Rose is one of the most beautiful of all flowers. It is a symbol of fragrance and loveliness. Its name calls to mind pictures of the sweetbrier, or wild rose, the loveliest wild flower of the country roadsides.

Flower experts recognize three main classes of cultivated roses. Members of the first class, sometimes called *old roses,* bloom once a year, usually in early summer. They include the yellow briers, damask roses, moss roses, and many climbers. The second kind of roses bloom in early summer and again in fall. The best-known members of this class—called *perpetual roses* or *summer-and-autumn roses*—are the hybrid perpetuals. Members of the third main class, the *everblooming hybrids,* flower almost constantly during the growing season. These roses include floribundas, grandifloras, hybrid teas, and polyanthas.

Roses come in many colors, including various shades of pink, red, yellow, and white. Rose growers have not developed a blue rose, but they do grow lavender varieties. Some roses, such as the teas and hybrid teas, smell like tea or fruit. Others have a fragrant "rose" scent, and still others have little odor.

The most popular garden roses are *hybrids*—that is, they were bred from two different varieties. For example, hybrid teas were developed from the everblooming hybrid teas and the hardier hybrid perpetuals. Floribundas were bred from the hybrid teas and polyanthas. Grandifloras, one of the newer kinds of roses, resulted from crossing hybrid teas with floribundas.

The climbing and rambler roses can be trained on trellises and fences. Others creep over the ground and may cover steep banks. Some climbers have large flowers, but true ramblers have clusters of small flowers. Climbers have to be hardy. Those with the small flowers are usually the hardiest.

Another important group is the shrub roses. The rugosas grow large bushes, 6 to 15 feet (1.8 to 4.6 meters) tall, with thorny stems. They usually have fragrant flowers. The sweetbrier and its cultivated forms are tall, graceful bushes, with fragrant leaves.

Miniature roses, another popular group, range in height from 4 to 18 inches (10 to 46 centimeters). Some have flowers no larger than a nickel.

Cabbage roses have flowers with many petals. These

Hybrid tea roses have only a few flowers on each plant. This popular type of rose includes the peace rose, *above.*

Floribunda roses bear flowers in clusters and thrive with little care. The vogue variety of floribunda is pictured above.

petals overlap in a way similar to the leaves of a head of cabbage. Moss roses, a type of cabbage rose, have rough sepals and stems that resemble moss.

Wild roses are erect or climbing shrubs. They bear thorns, and their flowers have one layer of five petals. Such one-layered blossoms are called *singles.* Most cultivated roses have *double blossoms.* This means that the flower has many petals arranged in several layers. Some cultivated roses lack thorns.

Roses grow in many parts of the world, in various soils and climates. They do especially well in temperate and mild climates. Roses thrive under cultivation, and thousands of varieties have been developed.

Popular roses. Of the thousands of different varieties of roses, some are popular year after year. Others disappear because plant breeders produce better ones. For example, the American beauty rose was once popular but is no longer grown commercially. It is a hybrid perpetual, famous for its fragrant crimson flowers.

The following list gives some popular varieties of roses and the colors of their flowers:

Hybrid teas.   Charlotte Armstong, light red
             Chrysler imperial, fragrant red
             Crimson glory, dark red
             Pascali, pure white
             Peace, yellow with pink shadings at the edges of
               the petals
             Rubaiyat, light rose-red
             Summer sunshine, deep yellow
             Tiffany, pink and gold blend
             Tropicana, coral-orange
Climbers. Dr. J. H. Nicholas, long-stem, rose-pink
             Golden showers, yellow
             New dawn, soft pink
             Paul's scarlet, vivid scarlet
Hybrid perpetuals. Frau Karl Druschki, taffy-white
Floribundas. Circus, red and yellow blend
             Fashion, coral-pink

             Floradora, cinnabar-red
             Iceberg, pure white
             Red pinocchio, dark red
             Vogue, coral-red
Grandifloras. Granada, red and yellow blend
             Montezuma, deep coral
             Mount Shasta, pure white
             Queen Elizabeth, medium pink

How to grow roses. Most roses are grown from *slips*—that is, cuttings. But almost all new varieties start as seedlings. Most cultivated varieties seldom bear seeds, and, if there are seeds, only a few are good. In double roses, the parts of the flower that produce seeds have changed to extra petals and, as a result, few seeds are possible.

The plot for a rose garden should be protected from cold winds and open to sunlight several hours a day. A deep, rich loam is usually the best soil for roses. But hybrid roses will grow in sandy and gravelly soil. Any soil must be well drained. Roses do not grow well in wet ground. Sometimes they need artificial drainage.

A few weeks before planting, the soil should be mixed with about one-third its bulk of well-rotted manure to a depth of 2 feet (61 centimeters). Fresh manure should not be used as it may injure rose roots.

The time for planting depends on the kind of rose and on the location. Some hardy roses can be planted in autumn, but the general rule is to plant in the spring. After the plants are received from the nursery, do not let the wind dry out the roots before they are planted. If necessary, cover them with burlap or similar material, and keep them damp. The holes should be deep enough to let the roots point downward and slant outward. The roots must not lie flat. Arrange the plants so that the beds are easy to water and weed. A good rule is to have the beds not over 5 feet (1.5 meters) wide. The

Jim Collins

Climbing roses develop long stems. Such climbers as the blaze rose, *above,* may fasten to fences or other supports.

plants should be from $1\frac{1}{2}$ to $2\frac{1}{2}$ feet (46 to 76 centimeters) apart. The exact distance depends on their spreading habits. A garden tine and a sharp steel rake should be used to keep the soil loose and the weeds out. However, plants should not be cultivated deeply.

The rose is the national flower of the United States and Iran. Several states and a Canadian province have also chosen the rose as their official flower. The District of Columbia has taken the American beauty rose. Georgia has chosen the Cherokee rose. This variety is a white Chinese rose. The wild rose is the official flower of Iowa, North Dakota, and Alberta. A series of battles in English history are called the Wars of the Roses (see **Wars of the Roses**). In addition, the rose is the flower for the month of June.

The rose family is one of the largest and most important families of flowering plants. There are about 3,400 species of trees, shrubs, and herbs in the rose family. Members of the family include plants that produce such fruits as apples, pears, berries, peaches, apricots, plums, and cherries. The rose family's many ornamental plants include the meadowsweet, mountain ash, rowan tree, and hawthorn. Plants of this family also give us many useful products. Several fine woods are used in cabinetmaking. Attar, an oil from rose petals, is used to make toilet water and perfumes (see **Attar; Rose water**). The fruits of some rose plants, called *hips,* are sometimes used in jellies and other foods.

Plants of the rose family have regular flowers. Each flower has five petals, a calyx with five lobes, many stamens, and one or more carpels. These plants bear seeds, and so they are classed as *angiosperms.* When the seeds *germinate* (begin to develop), they have two seed leaves, called *cotyledons.* Rose plants and other angiosperms that bear two cotyledons are classified as *dicotyledons,* or *dicots.*

Scientific classification. Roses belong to the rose family, Rosaceae. They make up the genus *Rosa.* Botanists disagree on how to divide them into species. Estimates of the number of species range from 30 to 250.   Peter H. Raven

Related articles in *World Book* include:

Angiosperm	Crab apple	Mountain ash
Apple	Eglantine	Peach
Apricot	Flower (picture: Gar-	Pear
Attar	den perennials	Plum
Bramble	[Flowering	Quince
Bridal wreath	shrubs])	Raspberry
Cherry	Hawthorn	Spiraea
Cinquefoil	Loquat	Strawberry

Rose, Ernestine Potowski (1810-1892), was a leading reformer in the United States during the mid-1800's. She became especially known as an early supporter of efforts to obtain equal rights for women.

In the 1840's, Rose led a campaign in New York for legislation permitting women to keep control of property they had owned before marriage. Laws of the day gave their husbands control of such possessions. The state legislature passed the bill in 1848. Rose then became active in the new women's rights movement, which started at Seneca Falls, N.Y., in 1848 (see **Woman suffrage**).

Rose was an excellent orator. She addressed women's rights conventions and state legislatures. She also worked to abolish slavery and to end the manufacture of alcoholic beverages. In 1869, she joined Susan B. Anthony and Elizabeth Cady Stanton in founding the National Woman Suffrage Association, which campaigned for women's right to vote.

Ernestine Potowski was born in Piotrków (now Piotrków Trybunalski), Poland. She and her husband, William E. Rose, a British silversmith, settled in the United States in 1836. The Roses moved to England about 1870.   Nancy Woloch

Rose, Sir John (1820-1888), was Canadian minister of finance from 1867 to 1869, during the first term of Prime Minister John A. Macdonald. As minister of finance, Rose proposed procedures that helped establish the national banking system of Canada.

In 1869, Rose moved to London, where he became a partner and British representative in the banking firm of Morton, Rose and Company. At various times, Macdonald asked Rose to serve as an agent of the Canadian government in Britain. Rose achieved great success in handling a number of diplomatic and financial matters for Canada. In 1869 and 1870, he helped the Canadian government acquire land in western Canada previously held by the Hudson's Bay Company, a British fur-trading firm. Rose was knighted in 1870. During the 1880's, he sold bonds and other securities in Britain to help provide financial aid for construction of the Canadian Pacific Railway (now CP Rail) across Canada. Rose was born in Turriff, Scotland, near Fraserburgh.   D. M. L. Farr

Rose, Pete (1941-   ), was one of baseball's all-time leading hitters and most exciting players. He made 4,256 hits in his career—the highest total in major-league history. Rose broke the record of 4,191 hits set by Ty Cobb, whose career ended in 1928. Rose hit safely in 44 straight games in 1978, tying an all-time National League record set in 1897 by Wee Willie Keeler. Rose was the National League's Most Valuable Player in 1973 and the league batting champion in 1968, 1969, and 1973.

Peter Edward Rose was born in Cincinnati. He played for the Cincinnati Reds from 1963 to 1978 and for the Philadelphia Phillies from 1979 to 1983. Rose played for the Montreal Expos for part of the 1984 season before returning to Cincinnati as player-manager. He ended his playing career after the 1986 season. Rose began his career as a second baseman, but later played the outfield, third base, and first base. In addition to his batting skills, Rose was noted for his aggressive style of play.

In 1989, Baseball Commissioner A. Bartlett Giamatti banned Rose from baseball for life. Giamatti based his action on evidence from an investigation conducted by his office into charges that Rose violated baseball rules by betting on baseball games. Rose denied betting on games but did not challenge Giamatti's ruling. In 1990, Rose pleaded guilty to two counts of filing false federal income tax returns. His penalty included a prison sentence of five months and a fine.   Donald Honig

Rose Bowl. See Football (College competition); Pasadena.

Rose chafer, often called the *rose bug,* is a beetle about $\frac{1}{3}$ inch (8 millimeters) long. It is light brown, and has long, spiny legs. It feeds on many plants and is often found on roses, ornamental plants, grapes, and various fruit trees. The beetles eat the blossoms of grapes and roses, and often apples. They also attack many fruits. The rose chafer is particularly destructive in localities where there are large areas of grassland. It lives throughout the eastern and central regions of the United States.

After feeding for three or four weeks, the beetles disappear. The females deposit their eggs in the soil. These eggs hatch, and the larvae feed upon the roots of grass. Nearly full grown by fall, they go below the frost line for the winter. The larva, which looks like a white grub, comes near the surface in the spring and becomes a pupa. There is only one generation each year.

When the beetles are very numerous, the best means of preventing injury is to cover small plants with cloth, or to pick the beetles off by hand. Large numbers can be collected in a pan containing water and kerosene. Commercial plantings of grapes, apples, and other fruit may be protected by cultivating all nearby areas during May and June to destroy any eggs that may have been laid. Insecticides may also be used on the plants.

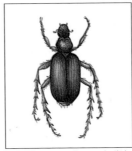

WORLD BOOK illustration by Shirley Hooper, Oxford Illustrators Limited

Rose chafer

Ellis W. Huddleston

Scientific classification. The rose chafer belongs to the family Scarabaeidae. Its scientific name is *Macrodactylus subspinosus.*

Rose of Jericho. See Resurrection plant.
Rose of Lima, Saint (1586-1617), was the first person born in the Western Hemisphere to be *canonized* (declared a saint) by the Roman Catholic Church. She was canonized in 1671. She was born in Lima, Peru, and her life was modeled upon that of Saint Catherine of Siena. In 1606, Rose joined the Dominican religious order. She ran an infirmary for poor children and old people in the garden of her home. She was loved by people from all of Lima's social classes. Rose practiced extreme mortification and penance and had remarkable mystical experiences and visions. She is the Patroness of South America. August 30 is her feast day.   Anne E. Carr

Rose of Sharon, also called *Althaea,* is a large hibiscus shrub with lovely rose, purple, white, or blue flowers about 3 inches (8 centimeters) wide. The flowers bloom from midsummer to early fall. The rose of Sharon grows about 12 feet (3.7 meters) high and has large, three-lobed leaves. It is hardy and does well under unfavorable conditions, either in the city or in the country. It is native to Eastern Asia and grows in many North American gardens. Gardeners have developed several forms of the shrub. The rose of Sharon may be grown in pots and later transplanted outdoors.   Walter S. Judd

Scientific classification. The rose of Sharon is in the mallow family, Malvaceae. Its scientific name is *Hibiscus syriacus.*

See also Hibiscus; Flower (Garden perennials; picture).

Rose water is a clear, colorless solution made from fresh rose flowers and used in making perfumes and certain medicines. Rose water has a fragrant odor much like that of fresh rose blossoms. It is made by distilling with water the fragrant parts of the flowers, such as the petals and the *sepals* (leaflike divisions of the outer covering of the flowers). This is done by placing the flowers in water, boiling the water, and separating the vapor into a vessel. The vapor is then condensed back into a liquid, which is rose water.   Patricia Ann Mullen

Roseau, *roh ZOH* (pop. 11,000), is the capital and largest city of Dominica, an island country in the Caribbean Sea. The city lies on the southwestern coast of the island, at the mouth of the Roseau River. For location, see Dominica (map).

Roseau has a busy port whose import and export activities are the basis of the city's economy. The city includes modern commercial buildings as well as stone structures dating from the 1700's. Many of Roseau's people live in small wooden or cement-block houses.

Roseau was founded in the mid-1700's by French settlers. They named the site *Roseau,* which means *reed* in French, because reeds grew there. From the 1600's to 1759, France and Britain struggled for control of Dominica. Britain ruled the country from 1759 to 1978, when Dominica gained independence. Hurricanes have sometimes struck Roseau, causing deaths and damage to the city.   Gustavo A. Antonini

Rosecrans, William Starke (1819-1898), was a Union general in the American Civil War (1861-1865). He commanded forces in western Virginia in 1861, and at Corinth and Iuka, Mississippi, in 1862. He became commander of the Army of the Cumberland in 1862. He fought in the Battle of Stones River (Murfreesboro), and later forced the Confederates out of Chattanooga. But he was defeated at Chickamauga in 1863. He was then assigned command of the Department of the Missouri.

Rosecrans was born in Delaware County, Ohio. He graduated from the U.S. Military Academy in 1842. He was minister to Mexico in 1868 and represented California in Congress from 1881 to 1885.   John F. Marszalek

Rosemary is an evergreen shrub of the mint family noted for the fragrance of its leaves. Rosemary grows wild in the Mediterranean region and measures from 2 to 6 feet (60 to 180 centimeters) high. It bears shiny, dark-green leaves and small, pale-blue flowers. In masses, blossoming rosemary looks like blue-gray mist blown inland from the sea. Its name comes from the Latin word *rosmarinus,* meaning *sea dew.*

Rosemary is used fresh or dried as an herb for seasoning. The plant yields an oil used in perfumes. The dried leaves have been used in *sachets* (small bags of perfumed powder), as a moth repellant, and to brew tea for stomachaches and headaches. Rosemary has long been a symbol of remembrance. Europeans carried rosemary at weddings and funerals because they believed it would aid their memories.

Donna M. Eggers Ware

Scientific classification. Rosemary belongs to the mint family, Lamiaceae or Labiatae. Its scientific name is *Rosmarinus officinalis.*

Rosenberg, *ROH zuhn behrk,* **Alfred** (1893-1946), was the philosopher of the German Nazi movement. His *Myth of the Twentieth Century* (1930) stressed "Aryan" racial superiority and depicted Judaism and Christianity as deadly enemies of the Germanic spirit. He wanted to replace Christianity with a Germanic pagan religion. During World War II (1939-1945), Rosenberg looted the art treasures of France and other Nazi-occupied countries and shipped them to Germany. He was born of German parents in Estonia. He became minister for Germany's eastern occupied territories during the war. Rosenberg pressed for extermination of the Jews. In 1946, he was executed for war crimes.   Donald M. McKale

Rosenberg, *ROH zuhn burg,* **Julius and Ethel,** were American citizens, husband and wife, who were executed for spying for the Soviet Union during World War II (1939-1945). They became the first United States civilians ever put to death for wartime spying.

Julius Rosenberg (1918-1953) and Ethel Greenglass Rosenberg (1915-1953) were born and raised on the Lower East Side of New York City. They were married in 1939. By then, both had been involved in radical political activities. In 1940, Julius began working for the United States Army Signal Corps as a civilian junior engineer. Early in 1945, the Army fired him for being a Communist. Between 1946 and late 1949, Julius worked with Ethel's brother David Greenglass in a small machine shop they owned in New York City. In 1944 and 1945, Greenglass had worked as a machinist at Los Alamos, New Mexico, on the U.S. project to make an atomic bomb.

In 1950, Greenglass was arrested for spying for the Soviet Union while working at Los Alamos. The U.S. government charged that the information he supplied was used to build the first Soviet atomic bomb. Greenglass claimed Julius had recruited him to collect the information. As a result, the Rosenbergs were arrested and accused of passing secret atomic-bomb information to the Soviet Union. The Rosenbergs pleaded innocent.

In 1951, a jury found the Rosenbergs guilty of conspiracy to commit espionage. Judge Irving Kaufman sentenced the Rosenbergs to die in the electric chair. Protests against the conviction and sentence were organized in the United States and Europe. Numerous people felt that the Rosenbergs did not get a fair trial or that their sentence was too harsh. Many respected people, including the great scientist Albert Einstein and

AP/Wide World

Julius and Ethel Rosenberg, husband and wife, were U.S. citizens executed as spies in 1953. They were convicted of giving atomic bomb secrets to the Soviet Union during World War II.

Pope Pius XII, urged clemency. The case was appealed to the Supreme Court of the United States, but the court denied all appeals. President Dwight D. Eisenhower twice rejected pleas for clemency. The Rosenbergs were executed in 1953 at Sing Sing prison in Ossining, New York. Greenglass was sentenced to 15 years in prison. He was released in 1960.   Thomas C. Reeves

Additional resources

Meeropol, Michael, ed. *The Rosenberg Letters: A Complete Edition of the Prison Correspondence of Julius and Ethel Rosenberg.* Garland, 1994.
Radosh, Ronald, and Milton, Joyce. *The Rosenberg File.* 2nd ed. Yale, 1997.

Rosenquist, James Albert (1933-   ), is an American painter who came to prominence as a member of the pop art movement in the 1960's. Rosenquist's works combine realistically painted, magnified fragments of everyday objects and images. He uses extremely large canvases, bright colors, and a painting style that resembles billboard and outdoor sign art. He often attaches actual objects to his canvases. Rosenquist's placement and recombination of seemingly unrelated items make his works seem somewhat surrealistic, but the title of each painting helps to bring the message into focus.

Rosenquist's most famous painting, *The F-111* (1965), is 86 feet (26.2 meters) long. It includes images of a fighter plane, a little girl under a hairdryer, a light bulb, a mass of spaghetti, an umbrella, and an atomic explosion. The title refers to an American fighter-bomber used in the Vietnam War (1957-1975). It is an indictment of American society of the time, particularly attacking consumerism and war.

Rosenquist was born in Grand Forks, North Dakota. He supported himself painting billboards before and after moving to New York City in 1955.   Deborah Leveton

Roses, Wars of the. See Wars of the Roses.

Rosetta stone, *roh ZEHT uh,* gave the world the key to the long-forgotten language of ancient Egypt. A French officer of Napoleon's engineering corps discovered it in 1799. He found the stone half buried in the mud near Rosetta, a city near Alexandria, Egypt. The Rosetta stone was later taken to England, where it is still preserved in the British Museum.

On the stone is carved a decree by Egyptian priests to commemorate the crowning of Ptolemy V Epiphanes, king of Egypt from 203 to 181 B.C. The first inscription is in ancient Egyptian hieroglyphics. The second is in demotic, the popular language of Egypt at that time. At the bottom of the stone the same message is written again in Greek. See **Hieroglyphics**.

The stone is made of black basalt, 11 inches (28 centimeters) thick. It is about 3 feet 9 inches (114 centimeters) high and 2 feet 4 $\frac{1}{2}$ inches (72 centimeters) across. Part of the top and a section of the right side are missing.

The language of ancient Egypt had been a riddle to scholars for hundreds of years. A French scholar named Jean François Champollion used the Rosetta stone to solve the riddle. Using the Greek text as a guide, he studied the position and repetition of proper names in the Greek text and was able to pick out the same names in the Egyptian text. This enabled him to learn the sounds of many of the Egyptian hieroglyphic characters.

Champollion had a thorough knowledge of Coptic, the last stage of the Egyptian language that was written mainly with Greek letters. This knowledge enabled him to recognize the meanings of many Egyptian words in the upper part of the inscription. After much work, Champollion could read the entire text. In 1822, he published a pamphlet, *Lettre à M. Dacier,* containing the re-

British Museum, London (Bridgeman Art Library/Art Resource)

The Rosetta stone is a fragment of a black basalt tablet covered with ancient Egyptian hieroglyphics. The stone provided the key to translating the language of the ancient Egyptians.

sults of his work. This pamphlet enabled scholars to read the literature of ancient Egypt.   Leonard H. Lesko

Additional resources

Andrews, Carol. *The British Museum Book of the Rosetta Stone.* Bedrick, 1985.
Giblin, James C. *The Riddle of the Rosetta Stone.* T. Y. Crowell, 1990. Younger readers.

Rosewood is the name of several kinds of wood used to make knife handles, brush handles, and ornamental furniture. Rosewood is valued for its ability to take a high polish and for its rich color, which ranges from dark reddish-brown to purplish-brown. Its name comes from the roselike odor of the wood when it is sawed. The wood is sometimes called *blackwood.*

Rosewood comes from trees in the genus *Dalbergia.* These trees grow in Brazil, Central America, Southern Asia, and Madagascar.   Jim L Bowyer

Rosh Ha-Shanah, *rohsh hah SHAH nah* or *rohsh hah shah NAH,* is the Jewish New Year celebration. The Hebrew words *Rosh Ha-Shanah* (which are also written *Rosh Hashanah*) mean *Beginning of the Year.* During this solemn religious festival, Jews pray for God's forgiveness, for a good year, and for long life. Rosh Ha-Shanah usually begins in September, on the first day of the Hebrew month of Tishri, and lasts two days. Some Reform Jews celebrate it for one day.

Rosh Ha-Shanah begins the Ten Days of Penitence, which end on Yom Kippur, the Day of Atonement (see **Yom Kippur**). Jews believe Rosh Ha-Shanah is the beginning of God's annual judgment of humanity. At that time, God decides who will continue to live and who will die during the coming year.

Jews attend synagogue services on Rosh Ha-Shanah. These services emphasize the themes of judgment, penitence, and forgiveness. A ram's horn, called a *shofar,* is blown to call the people to repentance and to awaken the Jews to the service of God. Three special groups of prayers are recited during the holiday. The first group reminds the people that God rules the world. The second group tells them that God responds to the sound of the shofar, and the third group that He remembers people's deeds.   Lawrence H. Schiffman

See also **Judaism** (The High Holidays).

Rosicrucian Order, *ROH zuh KROO shuhn,* is an international nonsectarian fraternity that studies the higher principles of life as expressed in humanity and nature. Members of the Rosicrucian Order learn about philosophy and the arts and sciences. The organization originated in ancient Egypt, where schools were formed to study humanity and nature.

The Rosicrucian Order first came to America in 1694. Many of its members made important studies in music, art, and painting. Today, Rosicrucians study the trends of history and attempt to apply their philosophy to meeting life's problems. Members believe that people must understand and live in harmony with nature. The Rosicrucian Order is not a religion.

The full name of the Rosicrucian Order is the *Ancient Mystical Order Rosae Crucis.* Its emblem is a gold cross with a red rose in the center. Headquarters are in San Jose, California.   Critically reviewed by the Rosicrucian Order

Rosin, *RAHZ uhn,* is resin derived from several varieties of North American and European pine trees. It ranges in color from pale yellow to dark brown and dark red. There are three main types of rosin. *Gum rosin* is produced by distilling resin collected from living trees. The crude resin is obtained from the trees by making lengthwise cuts in them. The resin then flows from the cuts. *Wood rosin* is extracted from tree stumps with the use of solvents. *Sulfate rosin,* also called *tall oil rosin,* is a by-product of the manufacture of wood pulp.

Rosin has many industrial uses. For example, it is used with other substances to *size* (coat) paper. The sizing helps keep the paper from absorbing moisture. Rosin is also used in the preparation of paints, varnishes, adhesives, sealants, and printing inks.   Lewis T. Hendricks

See also **Resin.**

Ross, Alexander (1783-1856), was a Scottish-born explorer, fur trader, and author. He explored much of the Oregon region, which then extended from present-day Alaska to California.

Ross was born in Morayshire, Scotland. He moved to Canada in 1804 and became a schoolteacher. In 1810, he went to work for John Jacob Astor's Pacific Fur Company. The next year, he aided in the building of Fort Astoria, which was the first white settlement in the Oregon region. From 1811 to 1813, Ross was at Fort Okanagan. There, he took an Okanagan Indian woman as his wife. Ross was a member of the group that founded Fort Nez Perce, also called Fort Walla Walla. He was in charge of that fort for five years. Beginning in 1824, Ross did extensive exploration of what is now Idaho.

In 1825, Ross moved to the Red River area, near the present site of Winnipeg. He received a grant of land there. He served as sheriff of Assiniboia (now southern Manitoba) in 1835 and as justice of the peace from 1839 to 1851. He died at the Red River colony in 1856.

Ross wrote extensively. He was one of western Canada's early historians. His works include *Adventures of the First Settlers on the Oregon or Columbia River* (1849), *The Fur Hunters of the Far West* (1855), and *The Red River Settlement* (1856).   Barry M. Gough

Ross, Barnaby. See Queen, Ellery.

Ross, Betsy (1752-1836), was a seamstress who made flags in Philadelphia at the time of the Revolutionary War in America (1775-1783). Some people believe she made the first American flag that had stars and stripes.

Betsy Ross was born in Philadelphia, the daughter of Samuel Griscom, a Quaker carpenter. She is believed to have attended the Friends School. In 1773, she eloped with John Ross, an upholsterer. Soon afterward, Ross was killed. Mrs. Ross took over his shop and became known as an expert seamstress. She remarried twice and had seven daughters.

William J. Canby, a grandson of Betsy Ross, wrote a paper about her in 1870. Canby said that when he was 11, his 84-year-old grandmother told him the story of how she made the first official United States flag. As the story goes, a committee headed by General George Washington visited Mrs. Ross in June 1776. George Ross, a signer of the Declaration of Independence and an uncle of Betsy Ross's first husband, was a member of the committee. These men asked Mrs. Ross to make a flag according to the rough design they gave her. Washington wanted six-pointed stars in the flag, but the seamstress persuaded him to make the stars five-pointed. No proof has been found that this incident actually happened. But it is known that Betsy Ross was an official

flagmaker for the Pennsylvania Navy. The stars-and-stripes design she may have sewed was adopted by Congress on June 14, 1777.   Whitney Smith

See also **Flag** (First United States flags); **Philadelphia** (Downtown Philadelphia).

Ross, Edmund Gibson (1826-1907), was an American statesman. Though he opposed President Andrew Johnson, he voted in the United States Senate against convicting Johnson during the impeachment trial in 1868. This vote earned him the hatred of his fellow Republicans, but won him a reputation for political courage. Ross was born in Ashland, Ohio. In 1856, he led settlers to Kansas to oppose slavery in the territory. He served in the U.S. Senate from 1866 to 1871 and then became a newspaper editor. He was governor of the New Mexico Territory from 1885 to 1889.   James E. Sefton

Ross, George (1730-1779), a Pennsylvania lawyer, signed the Declaration of Independence. From 1768 to 1776, he served in the Pennsylvania assembly, where he opposed the governor. He helped draft Pennsylvania's first constitution in 1776. Ross also served as a delegate to the Continental Congress from 1774 to 1777. In 1779, he was commissioned an admiralty judge of the state of Pennsylvania. He served in the position until his death. Ross was born in New Castle, Delaware.   Jack N. Rakove

Ross, Harold Wallace (1892-1951), founded *The New Yorker* magazine and edited it for 26 years, until his death. Ross began *The New Yorker* in 1925 as a publication for and about New York City. It became a national magazine famous for excellent writing, clever cartoons, and penetrating observations.

Ross was born in Aspen, Colo. He left school at 14 to work for newspapers. In World War I, which the United States entered in 1917, he was editor of *The Stars and Stripes,* a newspaper for U.S. soldiers.   Daniel W. Pfaff

Ross, Sir James Clark (1800-1862), was a British polar explorer. He led an expedition to the Antarctic aboard the ships *Erebus* and *Terror* from 1839 to 1843 and discovered the Ross Ice Shelf, Victoria Land, and Mount Erebus, an active volcano. He reached 78° 10′ south latitude, the southernmost point reached by any person until 1900. His uncle, Sir John Ross, and Sir William Edward Parry trained him during six Arctic voyages in search of the Northwest Passage between 1818 and 1834. Ross discovered the north magnetic pole in 1831 while serving under his uncle. Ross was born in London.

William Barr

Ross, John (1790-1866), was the principal chief of the Cherokee Indians from 1828 to 1866. His father was Scottish, and his mother was Scottish and Cherokee. But he won the support of the tribe and led it through one of its most difficult periods.

As chief, Ross resisted pressure from federal and state governments to move the Cherokee from their homelands in the Southeastern United States to Indian Territory, in what is now Oklahoma. In the 1830's, non-Indians began taking Cherokee lands, particularly in Georgia. Ross appealed to the courts, Congress, and President Andrew Jackson, but he could not stop the flow of illegal settlers. In the winter of 1838-1839, Ross unwillingly led his people to the Indian Territory. Thousands of Cherokee died on the way. Ross was born near Lookout Mountain, Tennessee.   Gary E. Moulton

See also **Cherokee Indians.**

Ross, Nellie Tayloe (1876-1977), an American politician and public official, was the first woman governor in the United States. She was elected to succeed her husband, William B. Ross, as governor of Wyoming after his death in 1924. She served as governor from 1925 to 1927. In 1933, President Franklin D. Roosevelt named her director of the United States Mint, a position she held until 1953. She was the first woman to hold that post. For several years she served as a vice chairman of the Democratic National Committee in charge of the activities for women of the Democratic Party. Ross was born in St. Joseph, Mo.   James S. Olson

Ross Dam was built in a narrow gorge of the Skagit River north of Seattle, Wash. The arch-type dam was one of the world's highest when it was constructed in 1949. It is a unit of the Seattle power system and produces 360,000 kilowatts of power. Ross Dam is 540 feet (165 meters) high and 1,300 feet (396 meters) long. It forms a lake 24 miles (39 kilometers) long, which can store about $1\frac{1}{2}$ million acre-feet (1.9 billion cubic meters) of water.
        Edward C. Pritchett

Ross Dependency is a wedge-shaped section of Antarctica that includes Ross Sea, Ross Ice Shelf, and Mc-Murdo Sound. It covers about 160,000 square miles (414,400 square kilometers) of land area, and about 130,000 square miles (337,000 square kilometers) of permanent ice shelf. The Ross Dependency is uninhabited except for scientific personnel located at Scott Base. New Zealand has been responsible for the administration of the area since 1923. *Little America,* the base set up by Richard E. Byrd in 1928, is located on the Ross Dependency.   W. B. Johnston

Rossetti, *roh SEHT ee,* **Christina Georgina** (1830-1894), was a gifted English poet. Many of her poems are melancholy and deal with symbolic religious themes. One of her best works is "Goblin Market" (1862), a fantasy about a girl's love for her sister. She wrote "Goblin Market" in an exciting, fast-paced style that makes the poem particularly effective when read aloud. Rossetti's other works include *Sing-Song* (1872), a nursery rhyme collection; and two volumes of religious prose—*Annus Domini* (1874) and *Seek and Find* (1879).

Rossetti was born in London. She lived a quiet, religious life. Her brother Dante Rossetti was a famous English poet and painter.   K. K. Collins

Rossetti, *roh SEHT ee,* **Dante Gabriel,** *DAN tee* (1828-1882), was one of the most famous English poets and painters of the 1800's. Rossetti was a central figure in the Pre-Raphaelite Brotherhood, an art movement he helped found in 1848 (see **Pre-Raphaelite Brotherhood**).

Rossetti's poetry is noted for its unconventional and sensuous language, vivid descriptions, and fantastic and symbolic themes. In spite of his brief training as a painter, Rossetti produced many works that are noted for their rich colors and attention to detail.

Many of Rossetti's poems and paintings were inspired by Elizabeth Siddal, whom he married in 1860. She died less than two years later, and the grief-stricken Rossetti buried the only copy of his poems with her.

Rossetti agreed in 1869 to get the manuscript from his wife's grave. The collection was published in 1870 as *Poems* and made Rossetti known as a major poet. In 1881, he published *Ballads and Sonnets.* Rossetti's best-known poems include "The Blessed Damozel," "Sister

The Wedding of St. George and Princess Sabra (about 1857), a water color; Tate Gallery, London

A Rossetti painting is typical of the artist's style in its bright colors and many details. The subject reflects Rossetti's interest in religious and historical themes.

Helen," and a series of love sonnets, *The House of Life.* He also translated many European works into English.

Rossetti was born in London. His sister Christina also was a famous poet.   K. K. Collins

Rossini, *roh SEE nee,* **Gioacchino Antonio,** *JOH ahk KEE noh* (1792-1868), was perhaps the most popular and important Italian opera composer during the first half of the 1800's. *The Barber of Seville* (1816) is probably the greatest comic opera ever written.

Rossini was born in Pesaro and received advanced musical training in Bologna. His second opera, *La Cambiale di matrimonio* (1810), made him an important force in Italian music, and was the first of his operas to be performed. For the next 13 years, Rossini wrote *opera buffa* (comic opera) and *opera seria* (serious opera), sometimes as many as three or four a year. The most popular ones include *The Italian in Algiers* (1813), *The Turk in Italy* (1814), *Otello* (1816), *Cinderella* (1817), *Moses in Egypt* (1818), *The Lady of the Lake* (1819), and *Semiramide* (1823). They are noted for their rich and catchy melodies, surging vitality, and expert vocal writing.

In 1824, Rossini moved to Paris, then the opera capital of the world. In 1826 and 1827, he revised two of his Italian operas for French words. He then composed—to French texts—the masterly comic *Le Comte Ory* (1828) and his serious masterpiece *William Tell* (1829), which represented a high point in Rossini's operatic style.

Rossini composed no operas after 1829, partly because he was often in poor health, and partly because he did not like the new operatic styles. His compositions after that year include the religious work *Stabat Mater* (1842) and many small instrumental and vocal pieces that he called *Péchés de vieillesse* (*Sins of Old Age*). Rossini had intelligence, wit, and humor, and became a famous host while living in Paris.   Charles H. Webb

See also **Opera** (*Barber of Seville, The*).

Rostand, *raw STAHN,* **Edmond,** *ehd MAWN* (1868-1918), was a French playwright best known for his fourth play, *Cyrano de Bergerac* (1897). It is set in the 1600's and tells the touching story of Cyrano, a swashbuckling poet who has a long, ugly nose. Because of his appearance, he is ashamed to woo the beautiful woman he loves. Instead, he writes letters to her signed by a handsome young friend who also loves her. The woman falls in love with the young man through the letters, not knowing that Cyrano is the true author.

Rostand wrote romantic plays in verse during a period when most dramatists preferred a style known as *naturalism*. A typical naturalistic play is extremely realistic, pessimistic, and written in prose. Rostand's first play, *Les Romanesques* (1894), is a charming story of young love. It became the basis for the American musical *The Fantasticks* (1960). Edmond Eugene Alexis Rostand was born in Marseille.   Malcolm Goldstein

See also **Cyrano de Bergerac, Savinien de.**

Rostock, *RAHS tahk* (pop. 242,729), is a German seaport and industrial center on the Baltic Sea. For location, see **Germany** (political map). The city lies at the mouth of the Warnow River and has been an important shipping point for hundreds of years. It is an important port of entry for much of Germany's petroleum supplies. Rostock's industries produce machinery, motors, container ships, and cargo ships. A railroad ferry runs from suburban Warnemünde to Denmark.

Rostock was chartered in 1218. The city was a member of the Hanseatic League in the Middle Ages (see **Hanseatic League**). The University of Rostock was founded in 1419.   John W. Boyer

Rostov-on-Don, also called Rostov, *ruh STAWF* (pop. 983,000), is one of Russia's most important cities. Rostov (Rostov-na-Donu in Russian) lies on the Don River, 25 miles (40 kilometers) from where it empties into the Sea of Azov (see **Russia** [political map]). The city is the gateway to the Caucasus (see **Caucasus Mountains**). Rostov is a railroad and industrial center and a river port. It has one of the largest farm-machinery plants in Europe.

Rostov was founded in 1780. It began a long period of development as a trading center in the 1800's. During World War II, German forces took control of Rostov in 1942 after a long, bitter battle. They occupied the city until 1943.   Roman Szporluk

Rostropovich, *rahs truh POH vihch,* **Mstislav,** *MIHS tuh slahv* (1927-   ), is one of the world's great cello players. He is also a distinguished conductor. As a cellist, Rostropovich expresses emotion and imagination through a range of tone variety. Many composers have written works for him, notably Sergei Prokofiev, Dimitri Shostakovich, and Aram Khachaturian of the Soviet Union and Benjamin Britten of the United Kingdom. In 1977, Rostropovich became music director of the National Symphony Orchestra in Washington, D.C.

Rostropovich was born in Baku, Azerbaijan, then part of the Soviet Union. In 1953, he was appointed to the cello faculty at the Moscow Conservatory. That same year, he played cello recitals in London and New York City that established his international reputation. In the 1970's, he protested Soviet oppression, especially of Russian writer Alexander Solzhenitsyn. Rostropovich left the Soviet Union in 1974. After the collapse of the Soviet Union during the early 1990's, he resigned from the National Symphony and announced his intention to return to Russian musical life.   Stephen Clapp

Roszak, *RAW shahk,* **Theodore** (1907-1981), was an American sculptor. Roszak became best known for welded metal forms that are violent and expressionistic in appearance. His works in this style frequently deal with menacing, fossilized savage birds and animals. He described these works as "blunt reminders of primordial strife and struggle."

Roszak was born in Poznań, Poland, and moved to Chicago with his family in 1909. He studied at the Art Institute of Chicago, the National Academy of Design, and Columbia University. His earliest works were paintings. From 1935 to 1945, he produced sculptured abstract works, severely geometrical and impersonal in style.

George Gurney

Steel brazed with copper sculpture (1951); Cleveland Museum of Art, Gift of the Cleveland Society for Contemporary Art

Theodore Roszak's *Mandrake* is typical of the fierce, menacing, birdlike forms that appear in many of the sculptor's works.

Rot is a symptom of many plant diseases in which the plant decays. The decaying part of the plant may be soft and watery or it may be firm and dry. Rot diseases are caused by bacteria or fungi that infect the plant and kill the plant's cells. Rot destroys fruits and vegetables. Plant growers help prevent rot by spraying plants with pesticides.

Common rot diseases include *bitter rot, black rot, brown rot, dry rot, heart rot, potato late blight,* and *soft rot.* Bitter rot occurs chiefly in apples but also attacks quinces, pears, and other plants. It is caused by a fungus that destroys the fruit, twigs, and limbs of the trees. The fungus produces a brown spot in the fruit that grows and may give the fruit a bitter taste.

Black rot attacks cultivated plants, including apples, grapes, pears, quinces, and sweet potatoes. The disease causes dark brown spots in the infected parts. Brown rot destroys peaches and other stone fruits, such as cherries and plums. Small brown spots appear on the fruit and grow until the entire fruit rots. Dry rot and heart rot affect chiefly timber. Potato late blight produces rot in potatoes. It caused the potato crop of Ireland to fail from 1845 to 1847. Soft rot is a common disease of vegetables that occurs during storage and transit. It may result in serious crop losses.   Joseph G. Hancock

Rotary engine is a type of internal-combustion engine that uses a *rotor* (rotating part) instead of a piston. A West German engineer, Felix Wankel, developed the first practical rotary engine, called the *Wankel engine,*

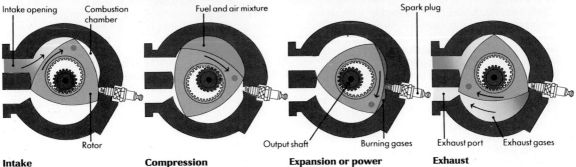

How a rotary engine works A rotary engine uses triangular rotors instead of pistons in its specially shaped combustion chambers. As a rotor turns, each of its three sides goes through a four-step cycle that produces power. These steps are (1) intake, (2) compression, (3) expansion or power, and (4) exhaust.

WORLD BOOK diagram

Intake

Fresh air mixed with fuel is drawn into the engine as a tip of the rotor, shown by a dot, passes the intake opening.

Compression

The rotor begins to compress the fuel and air mixture when the following tip of the rotor passes the intake opening.

Expansion or power

The spark plug ignites the mixture. The burning gases expand and move the rotor around the output shaft.

Exhaust

The burned gases leave through the exhaust port after the rotor tip uncovers it. The cycle then begins again.

during the 1950's. It has a triangular rotor design.

A rotary engine differs from a piston engine in several ways. For example, a rotary engine has fewer parts than a piston engine of the same power. A rotary engine also uses lower-octane gasoline. However, it burns fuel less efficiently and thus uses more fuel and emits more exhaust pollutants. The noise and vibration produced by a rotary engine tend to be opposite to those of a piston engine. At high speed, a rotary engine operates more quietly and smoothly than a piston engine. But at low speed, a rotary engine makes more noise and vibrates more. When it was introduced, the rotary engine was smaller and weighed less than a piston engine of equal power. But by the early 1980's, manufacturers produced comparably small and lightweight piston engines that were more efficient than rotary engines.

How a rotary engine works. The most important parts of a rotary engine are its triangular rotor and specially shaped chamber. The rotor moves so that its tips always touch the walls of the chamber and divide the chamber into three areas. A different part of the combustion process takes place in each of the three areas of the chamber. A rotary engine may have several rotors, each with its own chamber.

A rotary engine, like a piston engine that operates on a four-stroke cycle, goes through four steps to complete one combustion cycle: (1) *intake,* (2) *compression,* (3) *expansion* or *power,* and (4) *exhaust.* During the intake step, a combustible mixture of air and gasoline enters the chamber. Then the mixture is compressed. One or two spark plugs then ignite the mixture. The burning produces expanding gases that move the rotor. The exhaust step pushes the burned gases from the engine.

In a piston engine, each piston must move back and forth twice and stop four times to complete the cycle (see **Gasoline engine** [diagram: How a four-stroke cycle gasoline engine works]). A rotary engine operates continuously. It completes three combustion cycles with each full rotation of its rotor. Each revolution of the rotor produces three power strokes. The output shaft connected to the rotor makes three revolutions each time the rotor turns once. As a result, a single-rotor engine produces one power stroke per turn of its output shaft. A piston engine produces one power stroke every other time a piston moves down its cylinder. A dual-rotor engine therefore generates the same number of power strokes as a four-cylinder piston engine.

History. Felix Wankel developed the basic principles of the rotary engine during the early 1950's. By 1958, Wankel and researchers at a West German engine plant had worked out the engine's design. Automobile manufacturers rejected the engine at first because of its poor fuel economy, short operating life, and dirty exhaust. But after engineers began to solve some of these problems, the rotary engine's simplicity and low cost attracted interest. Several automakers in Japan, West Germany, and the United States sought to develop efficient rotary engines. But by the 1980's, the engine's original problems caused many manufacturers to reduce their development efforts.   William H. Haverdink

Rotary International is the worldwide association of all Rotary clubs. A Rotary club is a group of community leaders, each in a different profession or business. The association supervises member clubs and works for the advancement of Rotary. Members provide humanitarian services, encourage high ethical standards, and help build good will and peace in the world.

The Rotary Foundation of Rotary International sponsors scholarships for study abroad and the exchange of young business and professional people between countries. The foundation also sponsors projects to improve worldwide health. For example, it funds immunization projects in developing countries to protect children against infectious diseases, especially polio.

Paul P. Harris, a lawyer in Chicago, founded Rotary in 1905. It got its name from an early practice of members meeting in rotation at their places of business. There are about 24,500

Rotary International has a cogwheel for an emblem.

Rotary clubs in 167 countries, with about 1,100,000 members. The official Rotary magazine is called *The Rotarian.* Rotary headquarters are in Evanston, Illinois.

Critically reviewed by Rotary International

ROTC. See **Reserve Officers Training Corps.**

Rotenone, *ROH tuh nohn,* is a poisonous substance taken from the root of the derris and cube plants. It is frequently used in garden sprays because it is poisonous to cold-blooded creatures, but is fairly harmless to warm-blooded animals. Vegetable farmers often use rotenone because this poison kills insects but will not harm the people who may later eat the vegetables.

Rotenone is commonly used in home gardens. It is also used to control animal parasites, including cattle grubs in dairy cattle, and fleas, lice, and ticks. It is used in fruit sprays to control certain pests.

Indians in South America use crushed cube roots to catch fish. Although the rotenone in the roots kills the fish, the Indians can safely eat them.   Harold D. Coble

See also **Insecticide** (Botanical insecticides).

Roth, Henry (1906-1995), was an American author known for his novel *Call It Sleep* (1934). The book is considered perhaps the greatest working-class novel about Jewish immigrants in New York City in the early 1900's.

The novel covers two years in the life of young David Schearl. Early reviewers praised Roth for his realistic treatment of Jewish slum life and his intense, poetic style. But some critics disapproved of the book's frank language, violence, preoccupation with sex, and unsparing look at a troubled Jewish family. Both the book and Roth dropped from public view for almost 25 years. The novel was reissued to unexpected acclaim in 1960. Critics in the 1960's, especially Jewish critics, recognized the artistic merit of Roth's account of an important time in America's multiethnic urban experience.

Roth was born in Ukraine. His family immigrated to New York City when he was 18 months old. The first volume of a projected six-novel series, *Mercy of a Rude Stream,* was published in 1994.   James M. Mellard

Roth, Mark (1951-   ), is one of the greatest professional bowlers in the history of the sport. Roth had the highest average among professionals five times—in 1976, 1977, 1978, 1979, and 1981. His average of 221.662 in 1979 also set a record. In 1978, he won a record eight Professional Bowlers Association (PBA) titles. Roth has been named PBA Player of the Year four times—in 1977, 1978, 1979, and 1984. He won the U.S. Open and the Touring Players Championship in 1984. He was elected to the PBA Hall of Fame in 1987. Roth was born in Brooklyn, New York. He became a member of the PBA in 1970.

Nelson Burton, Jr.

Roth, Philip (1933–   ), is an American novelist and short-story writer. He became known for his frank, comic, and often satirical portraits of modern Jewish society and family life in the United States.

Roth first gained fame for *Goodbye, Columbus* (1959), a collection of five short stories and a novelette. In the title novelette, Roth explored the material attractions and spiritual costs he saw in suburban upper-class Jewish life. Roth's most famous novel is *Portnoy's Complaint* (1969). Some critics have praised it as a funny, intimate, and accurate study of the guilt feelings of a typical American Jewish son. The book generated controversy because of its explicit sexual descriptions.

Roth's related novels *The Ghost Writer* (1979), *Zuckerman Unbound* (1981), and *The Anatomy Lesson* (1983) describe the artistic struggles and psychological problems of a Jewish-American author. The three novels were reissued in a single volume called *Zuckerman Bound.* The book also included an additional short story called "The Prague Orgy." A fourth Zuckerman novel, *The Counterlife,* was published in 1986. Zuckerman also narrates *The Human Stain* (2000), the final novel in a trilogy about American society after the end of World War II in 1945. The first two novels are *American Pastoral* (1997), which won the 1998 Pulitzer Prize for fiction, and *I Married a Communist* (1998).

Roth's other novels include *Letting Go* (1962), *When She Was Good* (1967), *Our Gang* (1971), *The Great American Novel* (1973), *My Life as a Man* (1974), *The Professor of Desire* (1977), *Deception* (1990), *Operation Shylock* (1993), and *Sabbath's Theater* (1995). He also wrote an autobiography, *The Facts* (1988), and *Patrimony* (1991), an account of his father's battle against a fatal illness. Roth was born in Newark, New Jersey.   Arthur M. Saltzman

Rothko, *RAHTH koh,* **Mark** (1903-1970), an American painter, was a leader of the abstract expressionist movement. His best-known paintings are large, boldly simplified abstract compositions. In these works, he relied chiefly on color and ambiguous boundaries on rectangular forms to create a range of moods. See **Abstract expressionism.**

Rothko was born in Russia. His family settled in Portland, Oregon, in 1913. His real name was Marcus Rothkovitz. Until the early 1940's, Rothko mainly painted recognizable subjects, including city scenes, plants, and

Oil painting on canvas (1952); collection of Mr. and Mrs. Burton Tremaine, Meriden, Conn. (WORLD BOOK photo by Lee Boltin)

A typical painting by Mark Rothko emphasizes rectangles of color. Rothko used this type of composition in this painting, called *Number 8,* and in hundreds of other large works. Different combinations color vary the mood of his paintings.

animals. Gradually, he began to adapt themes from ancient myths to a poetic semiabstract style. From there he moved into a highly personal reduction of forms to the moody, veillike surfaces of glimmering color of his mature style. Shortly before his death, Rothko completed a group of murals for the interdenominational Rothko Chapel In Houston. He worked with dark, low-keyed colors to induce a meditative atmosphere.   Dore Ashton

Rothschild, *RAHTH chyld,* is the name of a German family that founded a famous banking firm in the late 1700's. The family opened banks in several European countries in the 1800's, and the company became known as the House of Rothschild. Today, the family operates a bank in England and an investment firm in the United States. The family has also been prominent in industry, philanthropy, politics, and science.

Mayer Amschel Rothschild (1743-1812), who founded the banking dynasty, was the son of a merchant of Frankfurt, Germany. Mayer Rothschild opened a bank in Frankfurt, where he made profitable investments for the royal families of several European nations. He trained his five sons in conservative money management. Rothschild made investments that produced reasonable profits rather than excessive earnings. These methods helped him make a spectacular fortune.

After Rothschild's death, his sons expanded the family business. The oldest son, Amschel Mayer Rothschild (1773-1855), took control of the Frankfurt bank. Branches of the House of Rothschild were opened in Vienna, Austria, by Salomon Mayer Rothschild (1774-1855); in Naples, Italy, by Karl Mayer Rothschild (1788-1855); and in Paris, France, by James Mayer Rothschild (1792-1868).

Nathan Mayer Rothschild (1777-1836), the third son of Mayer Rothschild, founded the London branch of the House of Rothschild. He later became a financial agent of the English government. Rothschild helped Britain defeat France in the Napoleonic Wars (1796-1815) by providing funds for the British Army.

Lionel Rothschild (1808-1879), Nathan Rothschild's oldest son, won election to Parliament six times between 1847 and 1857. But each time he was denied admission because, as a Jew, he refused to take an oath supporting Christianity. Rothschild worked to change the law that required the oath and, in 1858, he became the first Jewish member of the House of Commons. In 1885, his son Nathan Mayer Rothschild (1840-1915) became the first Jew admitted to the House of Lords.

Guy de Rothschild (1909-   ), the great-greatgrandson of Mayer Rothschild, was president of the family's bank in Paris from 1949 to 1981. The French government took control of all privately owned banks in France in 1981. The Rothschild bank in Paris had controlled many of the family's industrial holdings, which the government also nationalized. The Paris branch had been the family's main bank since its bank in Austria closed in 1938, just before World War II. In 1981, Rothschild and his cousin Evelyn de Rothschild, chairman of the London bank, became co-chairmen of the family's American investment company.   Brison D. Gooch

Rotifer, *ROH tuh fuhr,* is a type of tiny multicellular animal that lives in water. The largest rotifers are about $\frac{1}{26}$ inch (1 millimeter) long. Rotifers have cylinder- or vase-shaped bodies. Most species live in lakes, rivers, or streams. Some live in the ocean.

The name *rotifer* means *wheel bearer* and refers to the circles of hairlike projections called *cilia* on the animal's head (see **Cilia**). The cilia create a circular water current that draws food to the rotifer. This water current also enables most species of rotifers to "swim." Other species spend their entire lives attached to such objects as stones and leaves.

In many rotifer populations, the male has no role in reproduction. The female produces young by herself. This kind of reproduction, called *parthenogenesis,* produces only female offspring.   P. A. McLaughlin

Scientific classification. Rotifers make up the phylum Rotifera.

Rotterdam, *RAHT uhr DAM* (pop. 558,832; met. area pop. 1,025,580), is the second largest city in the Netherlands. Only Amsterdam is larger. Rotterdam has the world's busiest seaport. The city lies on both banks of the Nieuwe Maas River about 19 miles (31 kilometers) east of the North Sea (see **Netherlands** [map]). In 1872, engineers completed a channel called the Nieuwe Waterweg, which links Rotterdam with the sea. The Nieuwe Maas, a branch of the Rhine River, links Rotterdam with many other cities.

Almost all the buildings in the heart of Rotterdam have been constructed since World War II ended in 1945. German bombs had destroyed most of the city's central area (see **Netherlands** [picture]). One of the few surviving buildings there, the medieval St. Laurens (or St. Lawrence) Church, is a major landmark of the city. It was badly damaged by the bombing but was repaired after the war. Rotterdam's old harbor district, Delfshaven, escaped destruction. It has many buildings that date from the 1600's. Some of the Pilgrims who sailed to America in 1620 began their journey from Delfshaven.

Most Rotterdammers live in single-family houses or apartment buildings constructed since World War II. Rotterdam has many shopping districts, including the Lijnbaan, a pedestrian shopping mall.

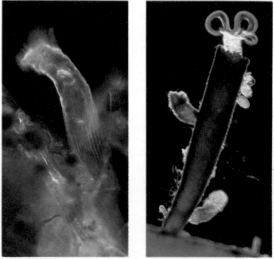

John Walsh, Science Photo Library

Rotifers are microscopic animals that live in fresh water. The common rotifer, *left,* uses its hairlike cilia to swim. The tube-building rotifer, *right,* can be seen atop a brown tube that it has formed from its own body secretions.

The Boymans-Van Beuningen Museum houses a large collection of Dutch art. A music center, the Doelen, includes several concert halls. Erasmus University of Rotterdam was founded in 1973.

Rotterdam's economy depends largely on its huge shipping industry. Europoort, the city's vast harbor, serves the Netherlands, major industrial regions of Germany, and parts of France, Switzerland, and the United Kingdom. Other important industries include oil refining, shipbuilding and repair, insurance, and banking.

Rotterdam became a city in 1328, when it received a municipal charter. Rotterdam was a small fishing community until the 1600's, when merchants increased their trade with England and France. Rotterdam became a thriving port in the late 1800's after the Nieuwe Waterweg enabled large ships to travel between the city and the North Sea.

The German destruction of the city and its port during World War II (1939-1945) almost ruined Rotterdam's economy, but the port was quickly rebuilt. Since then, Rotterdam has become the world's busiest shipping center.   Jan de Vries

See also **Europe** (picture).

Rottweiler, *RAHT wy luhr,* is a muscular dog with short, coarse black hair. This breed of dog has tan or mahogany markings on the head, chest, and legs. When full-grown, rottweilers stand from 22 to 27 inches (56 to 69 centimeters) high. Most males are larger than the fe-

WORLD BOOK photo by E. F. Hoppe
Powerful rottweilers once guarded Roman herds.

males. Rottweilers were developed in southern Germany, near the village of Rottweil. They are descended from the camp dogs that followed Roman armies in their conquest of southern Europe about 1,900 years ago. The Romans used these dogs to herd the cattle and sheep that provided meat for the armies.

Critically reviewed by the American Rottweiler Club

Rouault, *roo OH,* **Georges,** *zhawrzh* (1871-1958), was a French artist. He was a deeply religious man with strong moral convictions, and his works show his hatred of hypocrisy, poverty, sin, and war.

Rouault was born in Paris. From 1885 to 1890, he worked for a maker of stained-glass windows. Rouault's paintings, with their thick black outlines and intense,

Oil painting on canvas (1938); Museum of Art, Carnegie Institute, Pittsburgh, Pa. (WORLD BOOK photo by Elton Schnellbacher)

Rouault's *The Old King* resembles a stained-glass window with its thick black lines enclosing areas of bright color.

glowing color, show the influence of stained-glass design. About 1905, Rouault was briefly associated with a group of painters called the Fauves (see **Fauves**). The Fauves' bold brushstrokes and dramatic color contrasts became important parts of his style. From about 1903 to 1916, he painted religious subjects and sad clowns, and satirical pictures of prostitutes and corrupt judges. These works reflect misery and pain as expressed by the crude, rugged forms with their hacked-out edges.

From 1916 to 1927, Rouault worked on a series of 58 aquatints and etchings. This series, called *Miserere,* was published in 1948 and ranks among the great achievements in modern printmaking. From 1927 until his death, Rouault painted clowns and religious pictures, but chose fewer satirical subjects.   Alison McNeil Kettering

Rouen, *roo AHN* (pop. 105,470; met. area pop. 380,161), is a city in France that is both a major industrial center and a treasure house of artistic masterpieces. It lies in northern France, on the banks of the Seine River. For location, see **France** (political map).

Rouen's many industries include food processing, petroleum refining, shipping, and the production of chemicals, medicines, metals, paper, and textiles. A magnificent Gothic cathedral built between the 1200's and 1500's stands near the center of Rouen. The city has several other beautiful old churches, art museums that house outstanding collections, and a university. The *Grosse Horloge,* a huge clock dating from the 1300's, is

The Cathedral of Rouen stands near the center of the city. It was built from the 1200's to the 1500's and ranks as a masterpiece of French Gothic architecture.

© Jean Guamy, Magnum

another landmark. Rouen serves as the capital of the Seine-Maritime *department* (administrative district) and the Haute-Normandie (Upper Normandy) region.

A settlement existed at what is now Rouen in ancient times. In 1431, the English—who controlled Rouen at the time—burned Joan of Arc at the stake in the city (see **Joan of Arc, Saint**). Rouen suffered heavy damage in World War II (1939-1945), but was rebuilt after the war.

Mark Kesselman

Rough Riders is the nickname for a famous American regiment that fought in Cuba under Theodore Roosevelt's leadership during the Spanish-American War of 1898. The official name of the regiment was the First United States Volunteer Cavalry. About 1,000 men enlisted in the unit—all, Roosevelt said, "born adventurers." The press named them the "Rough Riders" during their training in San Antonio. Leonard Wood commanded the Rough Riders when the regiment was first formed. Later, Roosevelt became colonel in command.

The Rough Riders fought at the Battle of Las Guasimas on June 24, 1898. In the Battle of San Juan Hill on July 1, Roosevelt led a victorious charge up Kettle Hill, near San Juan Hill. In the charge, 15 of the regiment's men were killed and 76 were wounded. The daring of the Rough Riders helped make Roosevelt a national hero and, later, President of the United States.   Lewis L. Gould

See also **Spanish-American War** (picture).

Roughy, *RUHF ee,* is the name of a group of fish that live in temperate oceans throughout the world. Roughies range from 3 to 20 inches (8 to 51 centimeters) long. The *orange roughy* is the most common and one of the largest species. It is important commercially, especially

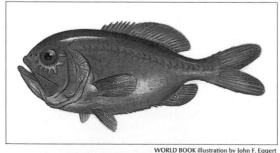

WORLD BOOK illustration by John F. Eggert

Orange roughy is a popular food fish.

around New Zealand. It is sold fresh or frozen. A freshly caught adult orange roughy is actually red. It turns orangish after several hours out of the water.

Unlike most fish, orange roughies have a *swim bladder* (baglike organ) that is filled with oil and wax. Most fish have a gas-filled swim bladder. Oil from the swim bladder of orange roughies is similar to the oil in sperm whales and in jojoba, a desert shrub. It is used in such products as lubricants and cosmetics.

Studies indicate that the orange roughy takes 18 to 20 years to mature. Some research indicates that the orange roughy may live 100 years or more.

Scientific classification. Roughies belong to the family Trachichthyidae. The scientific name for the orange roughy is *Hoplostethus atlanticus.*   Don Robertson

Roulette, *roo LEHT,* is a popular game in gambling casinos. A roulette table consists of a wheel located at one end and a betting layout extending across the rest of the table surface. There are 38 symbols around the circumference of the wheel, numbered 1 through 36 plus a 0 and 00. Many wheels in Europe do not have 00. Each symbol has an identical small slot on the wheel. The numbers are marked on a background alternately of red and black, with the 0 and 00 on a green background.

Players bet by placing chips on the betting layout. Then the dealer, often called the *croupier,* rotates the wheel while spinning a small white ball on the rim of the wheel in the direction opposite that of the turning wheel. The ball finally drops into a slot, whose symbol and color become the winner for that spin. Players can bet on the red or black colors, a single symbol, or combinations of symbols.   Dwight Chuman

Roumania, a variant of Romania. See **Romania**.

Round. See Canon.

Round Table was the table at which King Arthur, the legendary British ruler, sat with his knights. The term *Round Table* also refers to Arthur's entire royal court. The Round Table inspired some of the greatest literature of the Middle Ages. The fullest English account of Arthur and his knights appears in *Le Morte Darthur* (about 1470), a group of *romances* collected and rewritten by Sir Thomas Malory. A romance, in medieval literature, was a long work of fiction that described the remarkable adventures of a hero. See also **Merlin**.

Origin. The first mention of the Round Table occurs in *Le Roman de Brut* (1155), a verse history by the Norman poet Wace. This book tells how Arthur decided to seat his knights around a circular table to avoid quarrels over who should occupy the seats of honor. Since the knights were all "noble and equal," no knight could boast of sitting higher than his peer.

About 1205, the English priest Layamon adapted Wace's book into an English version called *The Brut.* In *The Brut,* bloody fighting broke out among Arthur's knights over the choicest seats at a Christmas feast. To avoid such conflicts, Arthur had a Welsh carpenter build a wondrous round table. The table would seat 1,600 men and yet fold up so it could be carried on horseback. According to still another source, Merlin the magician had the table built for Uther, Arthur's father. Uther apparently gave the table to King Leodegan. Later, Leodegan gave the table to Arthur after Arthur married Guenevere, Leodegan's daughter.

Another tradition describes the Round Table as seating 12 and resembling the table at the Last Supper, with an empty place representing Judas' seat. This seat was called the *Siege Perilous,* and was reserved for the knight so pure that he would someday find the Holy Grail, the cup or dish used by Jesus at the Last Supper. Any other knight who sat in the seat would die. One day, Sir Galahad's name appeared on the seat. From then on, he occupied the Siege Perilous. He later was one of three knights who found the Holy Grail.

The knights of the Round Table. In medieval literature, knights considered membership at the Round Table a great honor. Brave men came to Arthur's court from many countries hoping to be chosen a member.

Many romances describe the career of various knights of the Round Table. Several tell of the adventures of Sir Tristram. These stories describe his skill as a hunter and harp player and his bravery in killing a dragon and a giant. The best-known tale concerns his love affair with Isolt, the wife of his uncle, King Mark.

Sir Gawain was another famous knight of the Round Table. The great English romance *Sir Gawain and the Green Knight* describes Gawain's bravery and sense of honor as he faces possible death from the gigantic Green Knight. Gawain also shows his moral purity by refusing to be seduced by the Green Knight's beautiful but deceitful wife. Other Round Table heroes included Ban, Bedevere, Ector, Gareth, Kay, Lancelot, Launfal, Palomides, Sagramore, and Ywain.

The decline of the Round Table. For several reasons, the fellowship of the Round Table declined and in time was destroyed. The greatest adventure of the Round Table was the search for the Holy Grail. However, only three knights—Bors, Galahad, and Perceval—were morally perfect and thus able to find the Grail. The fact that so many of Arthur's knights proved themselves morally imperfect damaged the reputation of the Round Table. A scandal also developed over the love affair between Queen Guenevere and Sir Lancelot, perhaps the greatest of the Round Table knights. The scandal destroyed the bonds of respect and friendship that had united all the knights.

The villainous actions of Sir Modred, a knight who was either Arthur's nephew or his son, led to the final destruction of the fellowship of the Round Table. Modred seized Arthur's throne while the king was in France. Arthur quickly returned to Britain after learning of Modred's treachery, and war broke out between the forces of the two men. Arthur killed Modred in battle but received wounds that led to his death. The brotherhood of the Round Table dissolved following the death of Arthur.   Edmund Reise

Related articles in *World Book* include:

Arthur, King	Holy Grail
Chrétien de Troyes	Lancelot, Sir
Galahad, Sir	Launfal, Sir
Geoffrey of Monmouth	Malory, Sir Thomas

Roundheads. See England (The Civil War).

Roundworm, also called *nematode,* is any of more than 10,000 species of worms. Many species of roundworms live freely in soil, water, dead plants, or dead animals. All other roundworms are *parasites.* They live and feed on living plants and animals, which serve as *hosts.* Some parasitic species cause serious diseases in human beings and other hosts.

Roundworms range in size from microscopic to about 3 feet (0.9 meter) long. They have slender, round bodies with tapered ends. Roundworms have remarkable powers of reproduction and are extremely numerous. Researchers have found more than 90,000 roundworms in a single rotting apple.

Nearly all species of roundworms reproduce by laying eggs. Some species produce great quantities of eggs. For example, females of the species *Ascaris lumbricoides* each lay about 200,000 eggs per day for at least 10 months. Among some species of roundworms, the eggs hatch into tiny young that look like the adults. Eggs of other species hatch into young called *larvae,* which gradually transform into adults. Species of roundworms that do not lay eggs give birth to larvae.

Parasitic roundworms may infect a host in a number of ways. Some species enter the host when the host swallows food that contains the roundworm, its eggs, or its larvae. Among other species, the larva burrows into the skin of the host. In other species of roundworms, the larva is taken up by an insect, such as a fly or a mosquito, and transmitted through the bite of that insect to the host.

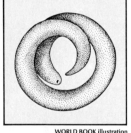

WORLD BOOK illustration by Patricia Wynne

A roundworm has a slender body with tapered ends.

At least 14 species of roundworms cause infection in human beings. *A. lumbricoides,* which inhabits the small intestine, infects about 65 million people throughout the world. It causes a disease called *ascariasis.* Symptoms of this disease include pneumonia and intestinal pain. The roundworm *Trichuris trichiura* infects the large intestine and occurs in about 350 million people worldwide. It causes *trichuriasis,* a disease characterized by diarrhea. Other common roundworms that cause disease in humans include *filariae, hookworms, pinworms,* and *trichinae* (see **Filaria; Hookworm; Pinworm; Trichina**).

Scientific classification. Roundworms make up the roundworm phylum, Nematoda.   David F. Oetinger

See also **Worm** (picture); **Vinegar eel.**

Rous, *rows,* **Francis Peyton,** *PAY tuhn* (1879-1970), an American medical researcher, proved that viruses cause some types of cancer. In 1910, Rous ground up a cancerous tumor from a chicken and filtered out everything larger than a virus. The resulting liquid produced cancer when injected into other chickens. For many years, scientists scoffed at Rous's discovery. These scientists believed cancer could not be caused by a virus because the disease is not contagious. In 1966, Rous shared the Nobel Prize for physiology or medicine for his work.

Rous was born in Baltimore and earned an M.D. from Johns Hopkins University in 1905. He joined the Rockefeller Institute for Medical Research (now Rockefeller University) in 1909 and worked there for more than 60 years. In 1915 and 1916, during World War I, Rous helped develop a method of storing blood for transfusions. This technique made possible the establishment of blood banks.   Eric Howard Christianson

Rousseau, *roo SOH,* **Henri,** *ahn REE* (1844-1910), was a French artist who painted some of the most unusual pictures in early modern art. He is called a *primitive* painter because he had no professional training.

The bold colors and decorative patterns of Rousseau's paintings indicate his debt to works by artists called *impressionists* and *nabis.* But unlike such artists, Rousseau portrayed each detail precisely and polished the surfaces of his canvases to a high gloss. He took many of his subjects—such as a wedding party or a patriotic celebration—from French middle-class life. But he also painted realistic figures and objects in fantastic or mysterious relationships and exotic environments. Such pictures strongly influenced the surrealism movement of the 1920's (see **Surrealism**).

Rousseau was born in Laval. He worked as a minor customs official in Paris until about 1885, when he retired to devote his life to painting.   Nancy J. Troy

Rousseau, *roo SOH,* **Jean-Jacques,** *jhahn zhahk* (1712-1778), was a French philosopher. He was the most important writer of the Age of Reason, a period of European history that extended from the late 1600's to the late 1700's. Rousseau's philosophy helped shape the political events that led to the French Revolution. His works have influenced education, literature, and politics.

Early life. Rousseau was born in Geneva, in what is now Switzerland. The Rousseau family was of French Protestant origin and had been living in Geneva for nearly 200 years. Rousseau's mother died as a result of giving birth to him, leaving the infant to be raised by his quarrelsome father. As the result of a fight in 1722, Rousseau's father was forced to flee Geneva. The boy's uncle then took responsibility for his upbringing.

In 1728, Rousseau ran away from Geneva and began a life of wandering, trying and failing at many jobs. He was continually attracted to music. For years, Rousseau was undecided between careers in literature or music.

Shortly after leaving Geneva, at the age of 15, Rousseau met Louise de Warens, a well-to-do widow. Under her influence, Rousseau joined the Roman Catholic Church. Although he was 12 or 13 years younger than Madame de Warens, Rousseau settled down with her near Chambéry in the Duchy of Savoy. He described the happiness of their relationship in his famous autobiography, *Confessions* (written 1765 or 1766-1770, published in 1782, 1788). However, the relationship did not last and Rousseau eventually left in 1740.

In 1741 or 1742, Rousseau was in Paris seeking fame and fortune and hoping to establish himself in a musical career. His hope lay in a new system of musical notation that he had invented. He presented the project to the Academy of Sciences, but it aroused little interest.

In Paris, Rousseau became friends with the *philosophes,* a group of famous writers and philosophers of the time. He gained the patronage of well-known financiers. Through their sponsorship, he served in Venice as secretary to the French ambassador in 1743 and 1744.

The turning point in Rousseau's life came in 1749, when he read about a contest sponsored by the Academy of Dijon. The

Pastel portrait on paper (1753) by Maurice Quentin de La Tour; Musée Antoine Lécuyer, Saint-Quentin, France

Jean-Jacques Rousseau

academy was offering a prize for the best essay on the question: Whether the revival of activity in the sciences and arts was contributing to moral purification. As he read about the contest, Rousseau realized the course his life would take. He would oppose the existing social structure, spending the rest of his life indicating new directions for social development. Rousseau submitted an essay to the academy. His "Discourse on the Sciences and the Arts" (1750 or 1751) attacked the arts and sciences for corrupting humanity. He won the prize and the fame he had so long desired.

Later life. When Rousseau converted to Catholicism, he lost his citizenship in Geneva. To regain his citizenship, he reconverted to Protestantism in 1754. In 1757, he quarreled with the philosophes, feeling they were persecuting him. Rousseau's last works are marked by emotional distress and guilt. They reflect his attempt to overcome a deep sense of inadequacy and to find an identity in a world that seemed to have rejected him.

In three *Dialogues,* also called *Rousseau, Judge of Jean-Jacques* (written 1772-1776, published 1782), Rousseau tried to answer charges by his critics and those he believed were persecuting him. His final work was the beautiful and serene *Reveries of the Solitary Stroller* (written 1776-1778, published 1782). Rousseau also wrote poetry and plays in both verse and prose. His musical works include many essays on music, an influential opera called *The Village Soothsayer* (1752), a highly respected *Dictionary of Music* (1767), and a collection of folk songs entitled *The Consolation of My Life's Miseries* (1781). In addition, he wrote on botany, an interest he cherished, especially during the last years of his life.

His ideas. Rousseau criticized society in several essays. For example, in "Discourse on the Origin and Foundations of Inequality" (1755), he attacked society and private property as causes of inequality and oppression. *The New Heloise* (1761) is both a romantic novel and a work that strongly criticizes the false codes of morality Rousseau saw in society. In *The Social Contract* (1762), a landmark in the history of political science, Rousseau gave his views concerning government and the rights of citizens. In the novel *Émile* (1762), Rousseau stated that children should be taught with patience and understanding. Rousseau recommended that the teacher appeal to the child's interests, and discouraged strict discipline and tiresome lessons. However, he also felt that children's thoughts and behavior should be controlled.

Rousseau believed that people are not social beings by nature. He stated that people, living in a natural condition, isolated and without language, are kind and without motive or impulse to hurt one another. However, once they live together in society, people become evil. Society corrupts individuals by bringing out their inclination toward aggression and selfishness.

Rousseau did not advise people to return to a natural condition. He thought that people could come closest to the advantages of that condition in a simple agricultural society in which desires could be limited, sexual and egotistical drives controlled, and energies directed toward community life. In his writings, he outlined institutions he believed were necessary to establish a democracy in which all citizens would participate.

Rousseau believed that laws should express the general will of the people. Any kind of government could be considered legitimate, provided that social organization was by common consent. According to Rousseau, all forms of government would eventually tend to decline. The degeneration could be restrained only through the control of moral standards and the elimination of special interest groups. Robespierre and other leaders of the French Revolution were influenced by Rousseau's ideas on the state. Also, many Socialists and some Communists have found inspiration in Rousseau's ideas.

His literary influence. Rousseau foreshadowed *Romanticism,* a movement that dominated the arts from the late 1700's to the mid-1800's. In both his writings and his personal life, Rousseau exemplified the spirit of Romanticism by valuing feeling more than reason, impulse and spontaneity more than self-discipline. Rousseau introduced true and passionate love to the French novel, popularized descriptions of nature, and created a lyrical and eloquent prose style. His *Confessions* created a fashion for intimate autobiographies.   Jean Terrasse

See also **Age of Reason; Romanticism; Philosophes.**

Additional resources

Cranston, Maurice W. *Jean-Jacques.* 1983. Reprint. Univ. of Chicago Pr., 1991. *The Noble Savage.* 1991. *The Solitary Self.* 1997. A three-volume biography.
Hulliung, Mark. *The Autocritique of Enlightenment: Rousseau and the Philosophes.* Harvard Univ. Pr., 1994.

Route 66 is perhaps the most famous highway in the United States. Officially named U.S. Highway 66 in 1926, this nearly 2,500-mile (4,000-kilometer) road between Chicago and Los Angeles was one of the first paved highways. It crossed parts of Illinois, Missouri, Kansas, Oklahoma, Texas, New Mexico, Arizona, and California.

Route 66 linked small towns to larger cities and gave rise to a network of roadside motels, diners, and gas stations. The popularity of these enterprises helped cement the relationship between Americans and their cars.

In the 1930's, hundreds of thousands of farmers traveled west on Route 66 to California to escape the "Dust Bowl," a region of the southern Great Plains devastated by severe dust storms. John Steinbeck nicknamed Route 66 the "Mother Road" in his 1939 novel, *The Grapes of Wrath.* The novel vividly portrayed a Dust Bowl family's

hardships. After World War II (1939-1945), Route 66 came to symbolize postwar optimism and freedom, as thousands of returning soldiers and their families traveled west to forge new lives.

In the late 1950's, Route 66 began to be replaced by interstate highways, which enabled motorists to travel faster. The last section of the original road was replaced by an interstate highway in 1984. Although no longer on current maps, parts of the road are still maintained and designated "Historic Route 66."   Bruce E. Seely

Rowan, *ROH uhn,* **Carl Thomas** (1925-2000), an American journalist, was director of the United States Information Agency (USIA) in 1964 and 1965. He was the first African American to serve on the National Security Council. He also served as deputy assistant secretary of state for public affairs from 1961 to 1963 and as ambassador to Finland in 1963 and 1964. He was a columnist for the *Chicago Daily News* from 1965 to 1978, when he became a columnist for the *Chicago Sun-Times.*

Rowan was an outstanding reporter for the *Minneapolis Tribune* from 1948 to 1961. His books include *South of Freedom* (1952), *Go South in Sorrow* (1957), and *Dream Makers, Dream Breakers* (1993). In 1997, Rowan won the Spingarn Medal for his achievements.

Rowan was born in Ravenscroft, Tennessee. He attended Oberlin College and received a master's degree from the University of Minnesota.   Michael Emery

Rowan tree. See Mountain ash.

Rowing is the act of propelling a boat with oars. Many people find rowing on lakes, rivers, and lagoons to be a pleasant form of exercise. Rowing races have also developed into well-organized amateur sporting events.

Types of rowing. In racing, there are two main kinds of rowing: (1) sculling and (2) sweep oar rowing.

In *sculling,* each rower, or *sculler,* uses two oars. Both the boat and the oars are called *sculls.* Sculling crafts include *single* sculls, for one person; *double* sculls, for two people; and *quadruple* sculls, for four. A few eight-place sculls, known as *octuples,* have also been built.

In *sweep oar rowing,* each person uses one oar. Sweep oars are larger and longer than sculling oars. The boats used hold two, four, or eight people, and are called *pairs, fours,* and *eights.* Eights, some fours, and pairs are designed to hold an additional crew member called the *coxswain.* The coxswain steers the boat. The

M. L. Thomas

Rowing in a race, the rowers respond to the commands of the coxswain, who faces them. The coxswain also steers the shell.

coxswain may also direct the timing of the oar strokes for the *stroke,* the rower who sits closest to the coxswain and sets the pace for the other rowers.

Racing boats are lighter and more fragile than ordinary rowboats. For this reason, they are called *shells.* There are no rules limiting the length, width, or shape of a shell. A single scull may weigh a minimum of 30 pounds (14 kilograms). An eight shell may be 60 feet (18 meters) long, 2 feet (60 centimeters) wide, and weigh a minimum of 205 pounds (93 kilograms).

Competition. The Olympic Games offer 14 rowing events in open weight classes for both men and women. World championships are held each year for junior and lightweight classes. World championships for open weight classes are held each non-Olympic year. The events are held by the Fédération Internationale des Sociétés d'Aviron (FISA), the ruling body for rowing.

Racing meets called *regattas* are held annually throughout the world. A number are open to contestants from all nations. The Henley Royal Regatta, an English event that began in 1840, is held each year at Henley-on-Thames. Other important regattas include the American Rowing Championships at Camden, New Jersey, and the Royal Canadian Henley at St. Catharines, Ontario.

History. Thomas Doggett, an English comedian, helped originate boat racing in the 1700's. He offered a trophy known as the "Doggett Coat and Badge" to the winner of a race on the River Thames. Later, regattas became important sporting events at many universities. The first race, between Oxford University and Cambridge University, took place in 1829. In the United States, the oldest collegiate regatta is held annually by Harvard University and Yale University. It started in 1852.

Critically reviewed by the United States Rowing Association

See also **Olympic Games** (table: Rowing).

Rowland, *ROH luhnd,* **Henry Augustus** (1848-1901), was an American physicist. He invented the concave grating for spectrum analysis and built an improved ruling and dividing engine for making precise rulings on glass or metal surfaces. In his Berlin experiment in 1876, he proved that electrostatic charges of electricity in motion produce a magnetic field similar to the field produced by an electric current in a wire. Rowland also determined the mechanical equivalent of heat, and the value of the *ohm,* the unit used for measuring resistance to the flow of an electric current (see **Ohm**). Rowland was born in Honesdale, Pennsylvania. He was a professor of physics at Johns Hopkins University from 1875 to 1901. Richard G. Olson

Rowling, *ROH lihng,* **J. K.** (1965-   ), a British children's author, became an international sensation with her fantasy novels about Harry Potter. The series begins when Harry, an 11-year-old schoolboy, discovers he is the orphaned son of wizards. The stories center on his adventures at the Hogwarts School of Witchcraft and Wizardry.

Rowling said that the series would cover seven novels, following Harry through seven years at Hogwarts. The character ages one year in each book. The first novel in the series was published in the United Kingdom in 1997 as *Harry Potter and the Philosopher's Stone.* It appeared in a slightly revised version in the United States in 1998 as *Harry Potter and the Sorcerer's Stone.* The next three novels are *Harry Potter and the Chamber of Secrets* (1998), *Harry Potter and the Prisoner of Azkaban* (1999), and *Harry Potter and the Goblet of Fire* (2000).

Joanne Kathleen Rowling was born in Chipping Sodbury, northeast of Bristol, England. She spent several years in Portugal teaching English and then returned to the United Kingdom, settling in Edinburgh, Scotland. Rowling said she conceived the idea for the characters while sitting in a train in London in 1990 and completed the first novel while she was an unemployed teacher in Edinburgh. Zena Sutherland

See also **Potter, Harry.**

Roxas y Acuña, *RAW hahs ee ah KOO nyah,* **Manuel,** *mah NWEHL* (1892-1948), served as the first president of the Philippine Republic, after it received its independence from the United States on July 4, 1946. He fought the Japanese in World War II (1939-1945), first as a colonel and then as a guerrilla on the island of Mindanao. The Japanese captured him and forced him to serve as a minor official under the puppet government of José P. Laurel. Roxas used his position to shield a spy ring he formed to aid the United States.

Roxas was born in Capiz (now Roxas), on Panay Island. He studied law at the University of the Philippines and became governor of his home province. As speaker of the House of Representatives, he became well known as a supporter of independence. Socorro L. Reyes

See also **Philippines** (History).

Roy, Gabrielle (1909-1983), was a French-Canadian novelist. Roy wrote with sympathy and understanding about the sufferings of ordinary, often underprivileged people. Her writing has been praised for its psychological subtlety and vivid descriptions. Roy gained fame for her first novel, *Bonheur d'occasion* (1945), translated into English as *The Tin Flute* (1947). The novel describes the poverty-stricken lives of a working-class family in the slums of Montreal during the 1930's and early 1940's. Other novels include *Street of Riches* (1955), *The Road Past Altamont* (1966), and *Garden in the Wind* (1975).

Roy was born in St.-Boniface (now part of Winnipeg), Manitoba. She taught school in rural Manitoba from 1928 to 1937, and the province served as the setting for much of her writing. Rosemary Sullivan

Roy, Ram Mohan (1772-1833), was a social and religious reformer in India. He helped change Hinduism in a time when it had come under criticism from India's British colonial rulers, Christian missionaries, and others. Roy is sometimes called the father of modern India.

Roy sought to change religion and society within Indian traditions by claiming that ancient Hindu writings supported his ideas for reform. For example, he rejected the *polytheism* (belief in many gods) that Hindus practiced at that time. He argued instead that certain Hindu texts supported the belief in one supreme being. He held that Hinduism was an ethical religion and one that was based on reason. Roy objected to such traditional Hindu practices as idolatry and *suttee,* in which a widow was burned along with her dead husband. He also opposed the caste system's rigid structure and strict rules.

Roy was born in West Bengal. In 1828, he founded the Brahmo Samaj (Society of God). This organization played an important role in reforming Indian society and religion in the 1800's. Ian J. Kerr

Roy, Rob. See Rob Roy.

Royal Air Force. See Air force (The British Air Force; World War II); **World War II** (The Battle of Britain).

Royal Canadian Legion is Canada's largest organization of veterans. Its membership consists of former and active members of the Canadian Armed Forces and the Royal Canadian Mounted Police, their children, and others who support the legion's aims. Wives of members may join the Ladies Auxiliary, which has about 100,000 members and supports legion programs and activities.

The legion encourages patriotism and national unity, assists needy veterans and former service members and their families, and promotes government programs for veterans. It sponsors memorial services on Remembrance Day, November 11, a national holiday that honors Canadians who died in war. The legion also performs community service. It supports housing projects for veterans and senior citizens and awards grants and scholarships to students. Each November, legion members distribute poppies. The donations received are used to fund legion activities.

The legion was formed in 1925 when a number of veterans' groups merged. It has about 600,000 members in 1,750 Canadian, United States, and German branches. Headquarters are in Ottawa.

Critically reviewed by the Royal Canadian Legion

Royal Canadian Mounted Police (RCMP) is the national law enforcement department of Canada. The fame of the Mounted Police has spread throughout the world since the force began in 1873. Today, the Mounted Police travel in motor vehicles instead of on horses. But the heroic officers on horseback still live in the many books and motion pictures about them. The badge of the Royal Canadian Mounted Police bears the force's motto, *Maintiens le droit* (Maintain the right).

Organization and duties. The Royal Canadian

Royal Canadian Mounted Police

The RCMP badge has a motto in French that means *Maintain the right.*

Mounted Police enforces federal law throughout Canada. It is the only police force in the Northwest Territories, the Yukon Territory, and Nunavut. RCMP members serve as provincial police in all provinces except Ontario and Quebec, which have their own police forces. They also provide police protection in some municipalities.

More than 19,000 people serve in the RCMP. Applicants must be Canadian citizens, at least 19 years of age, and have at least an 11th-grade education. Recruits receive six months training at Regina, Saskatchewan. They graduate as *constables.*

The force also maintains the Canadian Police Col-

Royal Canadian Mounted Police

Royal Canadian Mounted Police perform the *Musical Ride,* a series of complex movements including the "Dome," *shown here.*

Royal Canadian Mounted Police badges of rank

Officers

Enlisted personnel

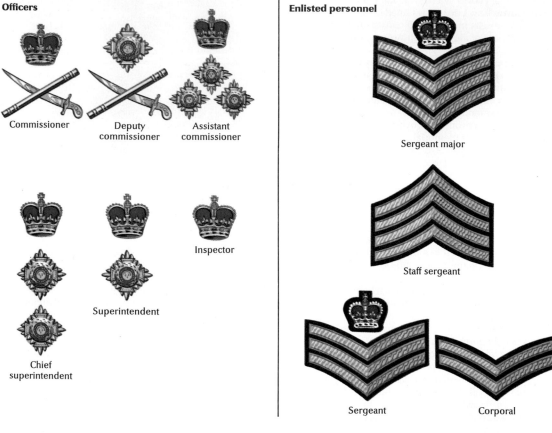

Commissioner

Deputy commissioner

Assistant commissioner

Inspector

Superintendent

Chief superintendent

Sergeant major

Staff sergeant

Sergeant

Corporal

WORLD BOOK illustration by Tom Morgan

Royal Canadian Mounted Police

Mounted Police use snowmobiles as well as airplanes to patrol the vast, thinly populated areas of the Northwest Territories and the Yukon Territory in northern Canada.

Royal Canadian Mounted Police

A Mounted Police officer uses the two-way radio in her patrol car to speak to police headquarters. The Royal Canadian Mounted Police began to admit women to the force in 1974.

lege. Senior members of the force and police officers invited from other countries study the latest methods of crime prevention and detection there.

The Royal Canadian Mounted Police maintains over 4,500 land motor vehicles, including cars, trucks, and snowmobiles. It has police dogs and horses, but the horses are used only for ceremonies. The force also has air and marine services. The air services maintain aircraft at strategic points throughout Canada. The marine services operate about 15 patrol vessels and over 300 small boats on Canada's two coasts, the St. Lawrence River, and the Great Lakes.

The solicitor general of Canada oversees the force. A commissioner directs its activities from headquarters in Ottawa. The RCMP has 13 police divisions with headquarters in the provincial capitals. Three other divisions deal with administration and training.

Uniform. The working uniform of male members of the Mounted Police includes a cloth cap, brown *tunic* (jacket), brown leather gloves, dark blue trousers with broad yellow stripes, oxford shoes, and side-arm equipment. The women's uniform is similar, but female members may wear dark blue skirts when side arms are not required. At ceremonies, the Mounted Police still wear their famed uniforms with wide-brimmed hats and scarlet dress tunics. The dress uniform for women includes a cloth cap, scarlet tunic, and dark blue skirt.

The color of the dress tunic is the only part of the uniform that has never changed. Scarlet was chosen because Indians considered it a symbol of justice and fair dealing. The Indians respected the British soldiers who came to Canada's western plains before the Mounted Police. The soldiers wore scarlet coats.

Mounted Police of 1873 wore gray riding breeches, loose-fitting tunics, black riding boots, and spurs. Their hats were either white cork helmets or caps shaped like pillboxes. By 1878, the loose-fitting jacket was replaced by a short, tight-fitting tunic. Blue breeches with a yellow stripe replaced gray breeches.

About 1900, broad-brimmed hats became part of the uniform. Mounted Police had complained that the helmets were hot and that the pillbox caps did not protect them from the blazing prairie sun. Brown boots replaced the black ones. Since that time, other changes have been made in the uniform.

History. In 1870, Canada's Dominion government acquired the vast, thinly populated territory of the Canadian Northwest. Disputes broke out there between Indians and whiskey traders, and criminal bands began to cause trouble. Government officials feared that war would develop between the Indians and white settlers after settlers began to arrive in the Northwest. The government decided that the area must be controlled. On May 23, 1873, the Canadian Parliament created a mounted police force to prevent bloodshed and to preserve order in the region. This force soon became known as the North-West Mounted Police.

The first members of the force were trained during the winter of 1873-1874. The following summer, about 300 riders headed west across the plains between Manitoba and the Rocky Mountains. They established posts there and quickly halted the smuggling of whiskey across the border. In cooperation with the Blackfoot chief Crowfoot and other Indian leaders, the N.W.M.P. soon brought law and order to the plains.

In 1885, the North West Rebellion broke out in what is now central Saskatchewan. The North-West Mounted Police helped the militia stop the uprising, and later aided many settlers who wanted to establish homes on the prairies. During the gold rush to the Klondike in the late 1890's, the N.W.M.P. helped maintain order in the Yukon gold camps.

King Edward VII officially recognized the North-West Mounted Police in 1904 when he granted it the prefix *Royal.* The force became the Royal Canadian Mounted Police in 1920 when it merged with the Dominion Police and took over federal law enforcement.

Part of the Northwest Territories became the provinces of Alberta and Saskatchewan in 1905, and the Mounted Police continued to enforce the law in the new provinces. This arrangement ended in 1917 but was revived in Saskatchewan in 1928. In 1932, the RCMP also began serving in Manitoba, Alberta, New Brunswick, Nova Scotia, and Prince Edward Island.

During World War II (1939-1945), the Royal Canadian Mounted Police maintained Canada's internal security. Men from its ranks also served with the Canadian army overseas. In 1950, the RCMP took over provincial law enforcement in British Columbia and Newfoundland. In 1974, the RCMP began to admit women to the force.

Canadian Pacific

The Royal Canadian Mounted Police were first called the North-West Mounted Police. The force was established in 1873 to eliminate illegal trade in whiskey, collect customs duties, calm unrest among Canadian Indians, and fight lawlessness in western Canada.

In 1977, the solicitor general of Canada, who supervises the RCMP, revealed to Parliament that RCMP members had illegally broken into a Montreal computer firm and seized records of the Parti Québécois (PQ) in 1973. The PQ, a political party, was then working to make the province of Quebec an independent nation. The solicitor general also reported that the force had used other unlawful methods, such as wiretapping and opening of mail, in national security investigations. Two government commissions were appointed to investigate RCMP activities, one on the federal level and the other a provincial commission in Quebec. In 1981, as a result of the federal investigation, the RCMP was stripped of its role in domestic intelligence.   Roderick C. Macleod

See also **Police** (In Canada; picture).

Additional resources

Cruise, David, and Griffiths, Alison. *The Great Adventure: How the Mounties Conquered the West.* St. Martin's, 1997.
Horrall, Stanley W. *The Pictoral History of the Royal Canadian Mounted Police.* McGraw. 1973.
McKenzie, James. *Troop 17: The Making of Mounties.* Temeron, 1992. Follows RCMP recruits through their training.

Royal Dutch/Shell Group is one of the world's major industrial enterprises. It has interests in more than 2,000 firms, which operate in over 100 countries. The group's parent companies are the Royal Dutch Petroleum Company of the Netherlands and The "Shell" Transport and Trading Company, P.L.C., of the United Kingdom.

The Royal Dutch/Shell Group's major activities involve all operations of the petroleum industry—exploration, production, transportation, refining, marketing, sales, and research. The companies also have interests in the chemical, coal, metal, and natural gas industries. The group grew out of an alliance made in 1907 by the parent companies. For information about the group's sales, assets, and number of employees, see **Manufacturing** (table: 25 leading manufacturers outside the U.S.).

Critically reviewed by the Royal Dutch/Shell Group

Royal Geographical Society is a British organization composed of people interested in geographical education and discoveries. It has the world's largest private map collection, which is open to the public, and a large library. The society organizes geographical research projects and sponsors scientific expeditions. It publishes two magazines: *The Geographic Journal* and *Geographical Magazine.* The society was founded in 1830. It now has about 10,500 members in many countries. Headquarters are in London.

Critically reviewed by the Royal Geographical Society

Royal Gorge is a canyon of the Arkansas River, extending about 10 miles (16 kilometers) from Canon City, Colorado. The gorge is more than 1,000 feet (300 meters) deep. A railroad passes through this remarkable chasm. The canyon is only 30 feet (9 meters) wide at some points. Many bridgelike structures had to be built along the walls of the gorge for the railroad tracks. This roadway provides a water-level route through a mountainous section of the Rockies. The highest suspension bridge in the world, 1,053 feet (321 meters) above the water, spans the gorge at the top.   John L. Dietz

See also **Arkansas River.**

Royal Greenwich Observatory. See Greenwich Observatory, Royal.

Royal Household of the United Kingdom includes officials who conduct the private business of the monarch and supervise court life. They have few powers of government. The *lord chamberlain* supervises the household. The *lord steward* controls household finances and supervises the treasurer and the comptroller of the household. The *master of the horse* cares for the royal stables. The queen's chief attendant is the *mistress of the robes.* She attends the queen on state occasions. The *ladies of the bedchamber* are the queen's personal attendants. The original household offices, such as marshal, steward, and chamberlain, are hereditary in some families. These officials act only on ceremonial occasions.   Richard W. Davis

Royal Institution is a scientific society founded in England in 1799. King George III granted the society a charter in 1800. Its purpose is to encourage scientific study and to spread technical knowledge. The society has about 1,500 members.

Headquarters of the Royal Institution are in London. Many scientists have made important discoveries there. They include Sir Humphry Davy, who invented the safety lamp for use in mines, and Michael Faraday, who did important work in the field of electrical research. A museum in the building houses Faraday's research equipment and manuscripts. Scientific research continues today in the building's Davy Faraday Research Laboratory.

Critically reviewed by the Royal Institution

Royal Military College of Canada is a university in Kingston, Ontario, that trains young men and women to become officers in the Canadian Armed Forces. It provides a broad program of academic, military, and physical training. Graduates receive a bachelor's degree in arts, engineering, or science, and a commission as an officer in the Canadian Armed Forces. The college also has a program of graduate studies for officers.

The school is one of three Canadian Military Colleges. The others are the Royal Roads Military College, near Victoria, British Columbia, and the Collège militaire royal de Saint-Jean, in Saint-Jean, Quebec. Students may begin their studies at any of the three colleges. But all engineering students and most science students will spend their last two years at the Royal Military College. The college was founded in 1874 and opened in 1876.

Critically reviewed by the Royal Military College of Canada

Royal palm is a tall, graceful tree common in tropical America. The tree's trunk resembles a pillar, and a cluster of featherlike leaves crowns its top. The royal palm grows in southern Florida, the West Indies, and Central America. See also **Palm** (picture).

Scientific classification. The royal palm is in the palm family, Arecaceae or Palmae. It makes up the genus *Roystonea.*

Royal Society is the world's oldest continuously existing scientific organization. Its full title is the Royal Society of London for Improving Natural Knowledge. The organization was founded in 1660 to promote the natural sciences. Its fellowship consists largely of leading British and Commonwealth scientists in such fields as chemistry, engineering, mathematics, and physics. The society has more than 1,000 members.

The society encourages scientific advancement by supporting scientific research and its applications throughout the world. It maintains extensive international contacts with scientists and scientific academies;

provides advice on scientific matters to many groups, including the British government; and promotes science education.

The Royal Society has a library of about 120,000 books and 200,000 manuscripts. It publishes several journals, including *Philosophical Transactions* and *Proceedings*. Its offices are in London.

Critically reviewed by the Royal Society

Royal Society of Canada is a national organization that promotes learning and research in the arts and sciences. The organization elects as its members people who have made important contributions in the humanities, sciences, or literature. They must be Canadian or have worked in Canada for at least five years. The society, which has about 1,300 members, awards medals for achievement and administers scholarships to aid research. It publishes papers annually in volumes called *Transactions.* The organization also publishes the proceedings of its conferences and studies on matters of public interest.

The Royal Society of Canada was founded in 1882. Its headquarters are in Ottawa.

Critically reviewed by the Royal Society of Canada

Royall, Anne Newport (1769-1854), was an early American newspaperwoman. She wrote for two Washington, D.C., newspapers that she founded when in her 60's. She published a weekly newspaper, *Paul Pry,* from 1831 to 1836. In 1836, she founded another newspaper, *The Huntress,* which appeared until shortly before her death.

Royall was born near Baltimore. Before she became a newspaperwoman, she traveled through the United States and wrote a number of books about her experiences. Royall became an author in her 50's in order to earn a living. Her husband's family had cheated her out of the money he left her upon his death. Social historians still value Royall's descriptions of the 1800's.

Miriam Schneir

Royalty, a commission. See **Writing.**

Royalty. See **King** and its *Related articles.*

Royce, Josiah, *joh SY uh* (1855-1916), an American philosopher, was the leading representative of a movement that was called *Idealism.* Royce emphasized the religious aspect of philosophy and the need for a philosophical interpretation of religion. In addition, he developed a philosophy of loyalty that included a system of ethics, a theory of self-knowledge, and a theory of human society.

According to Royce, a person gains self-knowledge through interaction with other people, not in isolated contemplation. Royce urged people to be "loyal to loyalty." He believed that humanity's deepest problems can be solved by harmonizing conflicting interests through a commitment to a higher loyalty. For example, Royce regarded Christianity as the religion of loyalty that binds its followers together in a "beloved community."

Royce was born in Grass Valley, California. His best-known works include *The Spirit of Modern Philosophy* (1892), *The World and the Individual* (two volumes, 1900-1901), *The Philosophy of Loyalty* (1908), and *The Problem of Christianity* (1913). John E. Smith

Ruanda-Urundi, *roo AHN dah oo ROON dee,* was a European-controlled territory in east-central Africa from 1896 to 1962. It consisted of two kingdoms, Rwanda and Burundi. Both of these kingdoms became independent nations in 1962. The Europeans used the spellings *Ruanda* and *Urundi.* The Germans set up a military post in the region in 1896. In 1899, the Germans established the boundaries of Ruanda-Urundi and made it part of German East Africa. Belgium gained control of the territory in 1916, during World War I. In 1923, Ruanda-Urundi became a mandated territory, administered by Belgium under the League of Nations (see **Mandated territory**). In 1946, it became a United Nations trust territory under Belgian control.

The peoples of Ruanda-Urundi spoke nearly identical Bantu languages. One group, the Tutsi (sometimes called the Batusi, or Watusi), formed a small minority that dominated a larger group, the Hutu, politically and economically. The Europeans strengthened Tutsi dominance by giving them privileged access to education at missions and to administrative training.

During the 1950's, tension created by Tutsi domination led to social unrest. In 1962, after much fighting, the Hutu gained control of the newly independent Rwanda government. In Burundi, the Tutsi continued to dominate a large Hutu majority, even after the kingdom gained its independence in 1962. David Lee Schoenbrun

See also **Burundi; Hutu; Rwanda; Tutsi.**

Rubaiyat, *ROO by yaht* or *ROO bee yaht,* is the shortened form of *The Rubaiyat of Omar Khayyam.* This title was given by English writer Edward FitzGerald to his translation of a group of short poems attributed to the Persian poet, astronomer, and mathematician Omar Khayyam. FitzGerald published four editions of the *Rubaiyat*—in 1859, 1868, 1872, and 1879. He changed the work considerably each time.

The title of the collection comes from the plural of the Arabic word *rubai,* which the Persians used to refer to a form of poetry. A rubai is a *quatrain* (four-line stanza) in which usually the first, second, and fourth lines rhyme with each other. Occasionally all four lines rhyme. In theory, the name *rubaiyat* can be used to refer to any group of such quatrains by any poet. In English, however, it is almost always used to refer to FitzGerald's version of Khayyam.

In the original Persian, each quatrain is a separate poem. FitzGerald made a selection from the many hundreds of these poems attributed to Khayyam and arranged them into one long poem forming a continuous narrative. The narrative describes a day in the life of a disillusioned would-be philosopher. Finding no meaning in the world and its hardships, he looks for comfort in friendship, wine, and love. Many of FitzGerald's quatrains are frequently quoted in English. They include:

> The Moving Finger writes; and, having writ,
> Moves on: nor all thy Piety nor Wit
> Shall lure it back to cancel half a Line,
> Nor all thy Tears wash out a Word of it.

> A book of Verses underneath the Bough,
> A Jug of wine, a Loaf of Bread—and Thou
> Beside me singing in the Wilderness—
> Oh Wilderness were Paradise enow!

A few of FitzGerald's quatrains are translated from passages written by other Persian poets. One or two quatrains are entirely his own creation. Dick Davis

See also **FitzGerald, Edward; Omar Khayyam.**

Photo Researchers

Natural rubber comes chiefly from rubber trees grown on plantations in hot, moist regions. Workers remove a white juice called *latex* by cutting grooves in the bark, *above*. Latex, which is about one-third rubber, is refined to produce crude rubber.

Goodyear Tire & Rubber Co.

Synthetic rubber is made by mixing chemicals to produce latex that looks like natural latex from rubber trees. Manufacturers make some synthetic rubber in crumb form, *above*. Synthetic rubber performs better than natural rubber in many ways.

Rubber is one of our most interesting and most important raw materials. *Natural rubber* comes from the juice of a tree. *Synthetic rubber* is manufactured from chemicals.

Rubber is especially useful for several reasons. It holds air, keeps out moisture, and does not readily conduct electricity. But its chief importance to us is that it is *elastic*. When you stretch a rubber band and let it go, its elasticity makes it quickly spring back to its original shape. A rubber ball bounces because of this same springiness. Your rubber heels absorb shock when you walk because they have elasticity.

We depend so much on rubber that it would be almost impossible to get along without it. This is not the case with most other materials. If we lack one material, we can usually substitute another. A house can be built using such materials as wood, brick, stone, concrete, glass, or metal. Clothes can be made of cotton, silk, wool, or other fibers.

But what about the tires of an automobile, truck, or bus? It is hard to imagine making them of anything but rubber. Only rubber is elastic, airtight, water-resistant, shock-absorbing, and long-wearing.

Manufacturers make between 40,000 and 50,000 rubber products. A typical automobile has about 600 rubber parts. Some cars, of course, use less rubber than this, and some use more. Many trucks and buses even have springs made of rubber instead of steel.

Uses of rubber

About three-fifths of the rubber used in the United States goes into tires and tubes. These are used on automobiles, airplanes, buses, trucks, tractors, and construction machinery. About one-tenth is used for mechanical products such as gaskets, sealing devices, belting, and printing rollers.

Manufacturers use rubber to make waterproof aprons, boots, raincoats, gloves, and hats, and to give elasticity to other types of clothing and household fabrics. Hard-rubber goods include hair combs and automobile storage-battery cases. Doctors use rubber hot-water bottles, ice bags, syringes, elastic tapes, and surgeon's gloves. Hearing aids, oxygen tents, and many other pieces of equipment have rubber parts.

Swimmers wear rubber bathing suits and caps, goggles, and ear stoppers, and sunbathe on rubber rafts. Many sports are played with rubber balls that range in size from small golfballs to large beach balls. Other rubber products include thread, bottle stoppers, toys, jar rings, elastic bands, and rubber-based paints.

Air pockets in sponge and foam rubbers make them springy. Manufacturers use such kinds of rubber for cushions, mattresses, pillows, and upholstery padding. They are also used as an insulating material. For example, some shoes have a layer of foam rubber next to the leather to keep out the cold.

Rubber cement can be used to hold pieces of paper together, but the pieces can be pulled apart easily. This cement is made of a solution of raw natural rubber in a chemical solvent. The solvent evaporates, and the sticky rubber holds the pieces of paper together.

The development of rubber

First uses. When the early European explorers came to Central and South America, they saw the Indians playing with bouncing balls made of rubber. The explorers learned that the Indians made "waterproof" shoes from *latex,* the milky white juice of the rubber tree. They spread the latex on their feet and let it dry. The Indians also made waterproof bottles by smoothing latex on a bottle-shaped clay mold. They dried the latex over a fire and then washed out the clay.

The South American Indians called the rubber tree *cahuchu,* which means *weeping wood.* The drops of latex oozing from the bark made them think of big white tears. A French explorer, Charles Marie de La Condamine, gathered samples of hardened latex in Peru in 1735, and took them back to France. The French called this new material *caoutchouc,* the French pronunciation of the Indian name *cahuchu.* Variations of the French spelling are used as the word for rubber in most European countries. In 1770, the English chemist Joseph Priestley discovered that the material could be used as an eraser to *rub* out pencil marks. From this use, we get the name *rubber.*

The rubber industry begins. By the late 1700's, scientists had found that hardened latex dissolved in turpentine made a waterproofing liquid for cloth. In the early 1820's, the English inventor Thomas Hancock built a machine to knead scraps of rubber into a solid mass. His inventions and experiments led to the development of present-day rubber processing.

In 1823, Charles Macintosh, a Scottish chemist, began manufacturing the "mackintosh" raincoats that became world famous. He made them with a layer of rubber between two layers of cloth. Manufacturers in Europe and the United States began to make rubber products, including elastic bands, raincoats, hoses, tubes, and shoes.

Discovery of vulcanization. Early rubber products became sticky in hot weather, and stiff and brittle in cold weather. In 1839, Charles Goodyear, a Connecticut inventor, discovered a way to make rubber stronger and give it resistance to heat and cold. Goodyear accidentally spilled a sulfur-rubber mixture containing other ingredients on a hot stove while conducting an experiment. The rubber compound was "cured" by the heat, and stayed tough and firm in heat and cold. The process of heating sulfur-rubber mixtures became known as *vulcanization,* after Vulcan, the Roman god of fire. With vulcanized rubber, manufacturers could make dependable products, and the rubber industry grew rapidly. Vulcanized rubber was elastic, airtight, and watertight. It could be used to make tight seals between the moving parts of machinery.

The first plantations. At first, manufacturers used only wild rubber. Most of it came from the Amazon Valley of Brazil, although some was from latex-bearing vines in Africa. In 1876, a botanist brought rubber tree seeds to England. Some of the seeds sprouted and were taken to Ceylon (now Sri Lanka) and Malaya for replanting on plantations. Almost all the plantation trees in the Far East come from these seedlings. The British, Dutch, and French developed plantations in Indonesia, Thailand, Indochina, and other countries of the Far East.

The invention of the automobile in the late 1800's created a tremendous demand for rubber. By 1914, the yearly production of plantation rubber exceeded that of wild rubber. Later, plantations were established in Africa, South and Central America, and the Philippines.

Development of synthetic rubbers. The importance of rubber in wartime became obvious during World War I. Armies needed rubber-tired vehicles to carry troops and supplies. The Germans were cut off from their natural-rubber supplies by the Allied blockade. They began to make synthetic rubber, but it did not work well. Experiments in producing synthetic rubber continued in the 1920's, chiefly by scientists in Germany and the United States.

When World War II began in 1939, Germany was manufacturing two chief types of synthetic rubber: (1) *Buna S,* made from *butadiene* (a gas) and *styrene* (a liquid made from coal tar and petroleum); and (2) *Buna N,* made from butadiene and acrylonitrile (a liquid obtained from acetylene and hydrocyanic acid). Before 1939, experimenters in the United States made small amounts of several types of synthetic rubber. However, the estimated cost of making these synthetic rubbers was much higher than that of natural rubber.

In 1942, the Japanese captured the rubber-growing lands of the Far East. This cut off nine-tenths of the natural-rubber supply to the United States. Almost overnight, the United States developed a synthetic-rubber industry.

The world now uses more synthetic rubber than natural rubber. This is because synthetic rubber has a greater variety of uses and can be produced cheaply enough to compete with the cost of natural rubber. But the rising cost of petroleum, used in making synthetic rubber, has slowed the growth of synthetic rubber production. Synthetic rubber production has also been affected by the increasing popularity of long-lasting radial tires. These tires require more natural rubber than does another kind of tire called a *bias tire* (see **Tire**).

The chemistry of rubber

In 1826, the English chemist and physicist Michael Faraday discovered that rubber is a hydrocarbon—that is, it consists of the chemical elements hydrogen and carbon. In 1860, another English scientist, Greville Williams, heated some rubber and obtained a liquid he called *isoprene.* Each isoprene molecule contains five carbon atoms and eight hydrogen atoms. In natural rubber, thousands of tiny isoprene molecules link up into a chain to form large molecules of rubber. Chemists call these molecular chains *polymers.* They call the single molecules, such as isoprene, *monomers.*

The particular chainlike structure of the rubber polymer explains why rubber is elastic. Polymer molecules of unstretched rubber fold back on themselves somewhat like irregular coils. Vulcanization attaches the polymer coils to each other. Stretching the rubber straightens the chain of folded molecules. Releasing the rubber lets the chain return to its coiled position.

For years, scientists tried to duplicate the true rubber polymer with isoprene monomers. They finally built the first successful synthetic rubbers from the monomers of other hydrocarbons, including butadiene, styrene, and isobutylene.

The rubber industry

Production and uses. More than 80 percent of the world's natural rubber grows on plantations in the Far East, chiefly in Thailand, Indonesia, and Malaysia. Other Far Eastern countries that produce natural rubber include Cambodia, China, Myanmar, the Philippines, and Vietnam. India and Sri Lanka grow about 10 percent of the world's supply of natural rubber, and Africa grows about 5 percent. The rest comes from South America. The world's annual production of natural rubber is about $7\frac{1}{3}$ million short tons (6.7 million metric tons). The United States uses about a sixth of the world's total natural rubber production.

The world's synthetic rubber production is about 10 million short tons (9 million metric tons) a year. The United States accounts for more than a fourth of the world's total production. The country exports only a small amount of its synthetic rubber. Other important synthetic rubber producers include, in order of production, Japan, France, Russia, China, and Germany.

Leading rubber manufacturers usually grow part of their natural rubber on their own plantations, and produce synthetic rubber in their own plants. These rubber companies make varied products such as tires, mechanical goods, industrial products, shoe materials and footwear, aircraft parts, and rubberized textiles. Some companies also produce, for their own use and for sale to other firms, raw materials used to make synthetic rubber. More rubber is used in the manufacture of tires than for any other purpose. The number of tire manufacturers decreased during the 1980's as large companies bought smaller companies. Today, the two largest tire manufacturers in the world in sales are Michelin, a French company, and the Goodyear Tire & Rubber Company of the United States.

Research in rubber is directed mainly toward making better synthetic rubbers to provide improved rubber products for home, automotive, and industrial use. In addition, many unusual types of rubber are required in the age of nuclear energy and space travel. As new planes and missiles fly higher and faster, they require rubber parts that can withstand temperatures from −120 to 700 °F (−84 to 370 °C). Chemists hope to develop rubbers that will increase protection against harmful radiation in nuclear power plants.

U.S. scientists are studying the possible use of the guayule plant as an inexpensive source of natural rubber. This plant could reduce the nation's dependence on foreign sources of natural rubber and on synthetic rubbers made from petroleum.

Natural rubber

Latex is found in a wide variety of trees and other types of plants. You can see latex oozing from the broken stem of a dandelion or from a cut branch of goldenrod. Scientists are not sure of its use to the plant. Some scientists believe that latex acts as a kind of protective substance when a plant has been wounded.

Chemical analysis shows that about 30 to 35 percent of latex consists of pure rubber. Water makes up another 60 to 65 percent. Latex holds little *globules* (particles) of rubber in the same way that milk holds butterfat. Latex spoils easily, and must be processed into *crude rubber* as soon as possible after tapping. This is done by separating the natural rubber in the latex from water and other materials. About 99 percent of all natural rubber comes from the latex of the *Hevea brasiliensis*. This is the tree that we call the *rubber tree*.

The rubber tree. The hevea tree grows best in hot, moist climates in acid, well-drained soils. The finest rubber-growing regions lie within a *rubber belt* that extends about 700 miles (1,100 kilometers) on each side of the equator. Almost all natural rubber comes from huge plantations of rubber trees in the Far East.

The rubber tree cultivated on plantations grows straight and slender, about 60 to 70 feet (18 to 21 meters) tall. It has smooth, light-colored bark and shiny, dark leaves. When its pale yellow blossoms fade, seed pods grow in their place. Each pod contains three brownish, speckled seeds about 1 inch (2.5 centimeters) long. The latex containing the rubber flows through a series of tubes in the tree's *cambium layer,* the outer wood layer directly under the bark. When this layer is pierced, the milky white latex oozes out. By grafting and breeding, botanists have developed trees that produce over 10 times as much natural rubber as the wild hevea.

Rubber has also been collected from *landolphia* vines that grow in Africa. In Mexico, *guayule* bushes have been cultivated for their rubber, but they produce only a small amount. In Brazil, a small amount of rubber comes from wild hevea trees. Other rubber-bearing trees include the *manihot* tree, also found in Brazil, and the trees of the genus *Castilloa* found in Central America, Colombia, and Ecuador.

Tapping the tree. Rubber plantations employ workers called *tappers* who collect latex from the trees. A tapper cuts a narrow groove in the bark of a tree about 4 feet (1.2 meters) above the ground. The groove slants diagonally downward about halfway around the trunk. At the bottom of the cut, the tapper attaches a U-shaped metal spout, and below the spout, a small cup. Latex

Leading natural rubber producing countries

Tons of rubber produced in a year

Thailand	●●●●●●●●●●●●● 2,431,000 tons (2,206,000 metric tons)
Indonesia	●●●●●●●●● 1,918,000 tons (1,740,000 metric tons)
Malaysia	●●●●●◖ 976,000 tons (886,000 metric tons)
India	●●●◖ 652,000 tons (591,000 metric tons)
China	●●◖ 496,000 tons (450,000 metric tons)

Figures are for 1998.
Source: International Rubber Study Group, London.

Leading synthetic rubber producing countries

Tons of rubber produced in a year

United States	●●●●●●●●●●●●●● 2,877,000 tons (2,610,000 metric tons)
Japan	●●●●●●●●◖ 1,676,000 tons (1,520,000 metric tons)
France	●●●◖ 667,000 tons (606,000 metric tons)
Russia	●●●◖ 660,000 tons (599,000 metric tons)
China	●●●◖ 649,000 tons (589,000 metric tons)

Figures are for 1998.
Source: International Rubber Study Group, London.

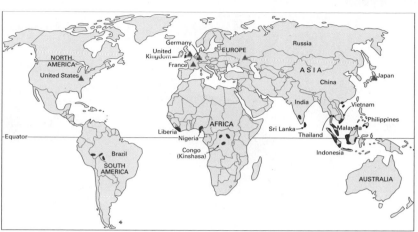

Rubber comes from two main sources. Natural rubber is provided chiefly by rubber trees grown on plantations in hot, humid areas. Synthetic rubber is manufactured in many industrialized nations. The map shows the leading countries for each type of rubber production.

 Natural rubber harvesting areas

▲ Synthetic rubber producing countries

WORLD BOOK map

oozes from the cut and flows down the groove through the spout into the cup. Tappers collect about a teacupful of latex at each tree. The latex is then transported to the factory for processing into liquid latex or dry rubber.

Some plantations tap the trees every other day. Other plantations tap every day for 15 days, and then allow the trees to "rest" for 15 days. On each tapping, the worker slices off a thin shaving of bark from the bottom edge of the groove near the cambium layer. The tapper does not cut into the cambium layer of the tree, because deep cuts that penetrate the wood harm the tree. After three or four years, the groove reaches the ground, and the tapper cuts the bark on the opposite side of the trunk. By the time the second groove reaches the ground, the bark has grown back on the first groove, and it can be tapped again.

Workers begin to tap rubber trees about five to seven years after planting. But younger trees do not give as much rubber as they do about the 10th year, when they are fully grown. Rubber trees yield their full capacity of latex for about 25 to 30 years. About 100 trees grow on 1 acre (0.4 hectare), and each full-grown tree produces from 1 to 4 gallons (4 to 15 liters) of latex a year. One acre of trees on a large, well-developed plantation may yield about 1,800 pounds (816 kilograms) of dry crude rubber a year.

Separating the latex. Most plantations make crude rubber from latex by *coagulation.* Tappers pour latex from their collecting pails into tanks and add an equal amount of water. They strain the diluted latex through sieves to remove dirt, bark, and twigs. Formic acid is then added to the strained latex to make it *coagulate,* or form solid particles. The rubber particles rise to the surface and form a curdlike mass of crude rubber.

Processing crude rubber. Workers feed the crude rubber through rollers that squeeze out the water and form it into a sheet. *Crumb rubber* is produced by special machines that chop or shred the sheets into fine, wet crumbs. The crumb rubber is dried in hot air tunnels and then compressed into 75-pound (34-kilogram) bales for shipment to market.

Ribbed smoke sheet is made by putting crude rubber through rollers that give the sheets a ribbed appearance. The sheets are hung to dry for several days in a

hot smokehouse. The smoke turns the rubber sheets brown and kills mold and bacteria that would damage them. The dried sheets are pressed into bales for shipment.

Crepe rubber is formed by passing the curdlike mass through rollers that roughen and crinkle the sheets so that they look like thick crepe paper. The rubber is constantly washed while being rolled. The sheets hang in heating rooms to dry. Workers bale the pale, crinkled sheets for shipment.

Processing latex. Sometimes, all the latex collected on plantations is not coagulated. Workers place part of the fresh latex in machines called *separators* that remove part of the water from the latex. Ammonia or another preservative keeps the latex from coagulating and prevents spoiling. The preserved liquid latex is sent to market in drums or tanks. Rubber manufacturers use

How a rubber tree is tapped

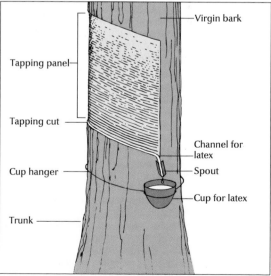

WORLD BOOK illustration by David Cunningham

This diagram shows how latex is obtained from a rubber tree. The liquid oozes down to the spout through the channel produced by the tapping cut. It flows down the spout into the cup.

Freshly tapped latex flows from a tank truck into vats at a processing plant, *above*. The plant uses a process called *coagulation* to remove impurities from latex and form crude rubber.

Sheets of crepe rubber, *above,* are formed by rollers that roughen and crinkle doughy masses of crude rubber passing through them. The rubber is constantly washed as it is rolled.

latex to make articles such as surgeon's gloves, foam-backed carpeting, tubing, and elastic thread.

Synthetic rubber

Rubberlike materials made from chemicals were called synthetic rubbers because they were intended as substitutes for natural rubber. Chemists use the word *elastomer* for any substance, including rubber, that stretches easily to several times its length, and returns to its original shape.

Manufacturers group synthetic rubbers into two classes: general-purpose and special-purpose. General-purpose rubbers have many uses. Special-purpose rubbers have special properties such as resistance to oils and fuels, air, and extreme temperatures, that make them better than natural rubber for certain uses.

General-purpose synthetic rubbers. The most important general-purpose rubber is styrene-butadiene rubber (SBR). It usually consists of about three parts butadiene and one part styrene. Butadiene, a gas, is made from petroleum. It must be compressed or condensed into liquid form for use in making rubber. Styrene is a liquid made from coal tar or petroleum.

Styrene and butadiene usually come to the synthetic-rubber plant in tank cars or tank trucks. Sometimes they are piped in directly from the plants that produce them. Correct amounts of styrene and butadiene are pumped into a big tank containing a mixture of soap and water. The mixture is heated or cooled depending on the type of SBR being made. A catalyst causes the styrene and butadiene to combine with each other (see **Catalysis**). Gradually, with stirring, the ingredients change to a milky white fluid, also called *latex.*

Workers pump the latex into another tank where *antioxidants* are added to prevent the rubber from decaying. The latex is sent to a third tank containing acids and

salts. The salts and acids coagulate the latex. The rubber forms into lumps that float on top of the liquid. Washing the rubber lumps removes extra chemicals. After drying, the lumps may be packed as loose crumbs or pressed into big bales of dry rubber.

SBR can also be prepared in a hydrocarbon solution. An *organometallic* catalyst, which contains metal atoms bonded to carbon atoms, causes butadiene to react with styrene to form SBR. The rubber is then recovered by adding the solution to hot water and removing the solvent with steam. The crumbs of rubber are then filtered from the water, dried, and baled.

Special-purpose rubbers. Contact with gasoline, oils, sunlight, and air harms natural rubber. Special-purpose synthetic rubbers resist these "enemies" better than natural rubber or SBR do. Also, some of these special-purpose rubbers have greater resistance to heat and cold. They cost more than natural rubber or SBR, but their special properties make them worth the difference. Special-purpose rubbers include butyl rubber, neoprene rubber, and polyurethane rubbers.

Manufacturing rubber products

Manufacturers obtain bales of dry rubber from plantations and from synthetic-rubber manufacturing plants. Latex comes to them in big tanks on ships and in tank cars. Manufacturers usually process natural and synthetic rubber in much the same way, although latex requires different steps.

Plasticization involves only dry rubber. It is a series of processes that makes dry rubber softer and easier to mold.

Workers first slice the big bales into small pieces of rubber that they can handle easily. The lower grades of natural rubber receive a thorough washing in a wringer-like machine called a *wash mill.* Then the rubber slices

Firestone Tire & Rubber Company

Washed and shredded rubber is dried by an *extrusion-dryer,* such as the one shown here. The dried rubber is baked and pressed into bales for shipment to rubber manufacturers.

are fed into mixing mills and other machines that *plasticize,* or soften, them into a doughlike mass. Manufacturers plasticize the rubber faster by heating it and adding materials called *plasticizers* and *softeners.*

Compounding and mixing. Compounding means adding carefully measured amounts of various ingredients to plasticized rubber and to latex. The compounding "recipe" helps control the elasticity, strength, and other properties of the final product. Sulfur is commonly added to bring about vulcanization, a process that takes place later in rubber manufacturing. Other ingredients used include accelerators, which speed vulcanization; fillers, which increase the volume and strength of the rubber; and antioxidants, which slow down the rate at which the rubber wears out.

Shaping. Manufacturers use several methods to shape rubber into final products. These include (1) calendering, (2) extrusion, (3) molding, and (4) dipping.

Calendering means rolling rubber into sheets. It is done on a machine that has two to five rolls. The rubber passes between the rolls to form sheets. Workers cut the sheets into various sizes and patterns, or stack the sheets in layers to make many products. These products include rubber flooring, toys, bed sheets, baby pants, and mechanical goods, such as wrapping tapes, washers, rings, and disks.

Extrusion is the final step in the processing of some rubber products. The word *extrude* means to push out. *Tube machines* push soft rubber through a hole, much as toothpaste is squeezed from a tube. Extruded products include hoses, inner tubes, and rubber strips used on refrigerators and automobile windshields.

Molding produces shoe soles and heels, rubber tires, hot-water bottles, mattresses, hard-rubber articles, and industrial products, such as gaskets and fittings. Workers prepare pieces of rubber in the approximate size and shape of the finished product. They put the pieces in molds shaped to form the product. Many products are molded and vulcanized at the same time.

Dipping is used only to make products from liquid latex. Products made by dipping include rubber gloves and toy balloons. Workers dip molds, usually made of metal, glass, or ceramic materials, into tanks of latex. They drain the excess latex and dry the mold at low temperatures. By repeating this process, they build up several layers on the mold.

Vulcanization is usually the last step in preparing a final product. It gives strength, hardness, and elasticity to rubber by treating it with heat and vulcanizing agents, such as sulfur. During vulcanization, the heat causes the sulfur to combine with the rubber and cure it. This makes the rubber stronger and more durable. Generally, the more sulfur that is added, the firmer the vulcanized compound will be. Vulcanization may take from a few minutes to several hours.

Manufacturers vulcanize and shape molded products at the same time by heating the molds under pressure. They vulcanize extruded and sheet products on pans in hot-air or steam chambers. Dipped products are vulcanized in hot water, hot air, or open steam while still on the molds. Foam products in their molds are vulcanized in steam chambers or in boiling water.

Sponge rubber may be made either from dry rubber or from latex. *Blowing* produces one type of sponge rubber from dry rubber. During vulcanization, the chemicals that have been added turn to gas and "blow" tiny bubbles of air in the rubber compound. When the rubber *gels,* or sets, in the mold, the bubbles are trapped in it. Blown sponge rubber may be either hard or soft.

Foam rubber is a type of sponge rubber made by whipping air into latex, much as a cook whips air into egg whites. Vulcanization takes place after the foam gels in a mold. Foam rubber has millions of tiny cells filled with air. Some types may be nine-tenths air and only one-tenth rubber. Foam rubber is used for upholstery and foam strips for surgical use.   Howard A. Colvin

Questions

Who first used the name "rubber"? Why?
What accident led to the discovery of vulcanization?
What country first developed synthetic rubber?
What event brought about the first successful mass production of synthetic rubber?
What countries grow the most natural rubber?
What is latex? Why is it said to be something of a mystery?
How does the chemical structure of rubber explain its elasticity?
How are rubber trees tapped?
What is crude rubber?
Which two countries produce about half the world's synthetic rubber?

Additional resources

Cannon, William A. *How to Cast Small Metal and Rubber Parts.* 2nd ed. TAB, 1986.
Love, Steve, and Giffels, David. *Wheel of Fortune: The Story of Rubber in Akron.* Univ. of Akron Pr., 1998.
Mark, James E., and others. *Science and Technology of Rubber.* 2nd ed. Academic Pr., 1994.

Rubber plant is the common name for a house plant that is really a kind of fig. The rubber plant can grow well in the heat and low humidity of houses. It grows tall rapidly and lives a long time. The leaves of the rubber plant are large and broad and may grow from 2 to 12 inches (5 to 30 centimeters) long. The upper surface of the leaf is a shiny, dark green, and the underside is dull and lighter green.

The rubber plant requires little care. It will grow well if the soil in the pot is rich in minerals and the plant is given enough sunlight, water, and room. The plant should be placed outdoors during the summer so that it will get enough sunlight to last the winter. A rubber plant may grow so tall that it may be necessary to cut it back to make it branch. Sometimes a new plant can be grown from the tip of the stem that is cut off.

Rubber plants are often attacked by scale insects.

Paul Robert Perry

The attractive rubber plant is frequently grown in pots in the home. It has thick, rubberlike leaves.

These pests can be destroyed by spraying the plants with nicotine. Commercial rubber does not come from these rubber plants, but from a tropical tree that belongs to the castor-bean family.   Alwyn H. Gentry

Scientific classification. Rubber plants are in the mulberry family, Moraceae. The scientific name for the common rubber plant is *Ficus elastica.* The more decorative rubber plant is the fiddle fig, *F. lyrata.*

Rubella is a common contagious disease that most often affects children. It is also called *German measles.* Most cases of rubella are not serious. But if a woman develops the disease during early pregnancy, it may result in her baby having one or more birth defects. Such birth defects may include mental retardation, impaired vision and hearing, and malformations of the heart.

Rubella is caused by a virus, which is spread chiefly in droplets expelled when an infected person coughs or sneezes. Two to three weeks after contact with the disease, a person may develop a runny nose or mild fever. Pink, slightly raised spots appear on the face and spread to the trunk and limbs. Lymph nodes on the back of the scalp, behind the ears, and on the side of the neck may become tender. These symptoms usually disappear in a few days. In adolescents and adults, the symptoms often are more severe than in children and may include painful, swollen joints. In some cases of rubella, no symptoms appear. Infected people can spread the virus to others from about seven days before the rash develops until about five days after its appearance.

There is no specific treatment for rubella. A case of rubella results in *immunity* (resistance) to the disease for the rest of a person's life. In 1969, a vaccine became available that also provides immunity to rubella. Doctors recommend that children 15 months of age or older be given this vaccine and that a second dose be given from 4 to 12 years of age. It is generally combined with vaccines for measles and mumps.   Neil R. Blacklow

See also **Measles.**

Rubens, Peter Paul (1577-1640), was the greatest Flemish painter of the 1600's. In addition to his paintings, Rubens made designs for book illustrations and tapestries, and occasionally for architecture and sculpture. He was also a scholar and a respected diplomat.

His life. Rubens was born in Siegen, Germany, of Flemish parents. After his father died in 1587, his mother returned with her children to her native city of Antwerp, in what is now Belgium. There, Rubens studied under local painters. He went to Italy in 1600 to study art. In Italy, he was employed as a painter by Vincenzo Gonzaga, duke of Mantua. In 1603, the duke sent Rubens to Spain as a member of a diplomatic mission. Rubens also spent time in Genoa and Rome.

Rubens went back to Antwerp in 1608, to visit his sick mother, but she died before he arrived. In Antwerp, Rubens was offered several important commissions for paintings, and he decided to remain in the city. In 1609, he married Isabella Brant, a member of a prominent Antwerp family. They had four children.

Also in 1609, Rubens became court painter to the Governors of the Netherlands, Archduke Albert and the Infanta Isabella, at Brussels. Rubens' fame as a painter spread, and nobility and royalty throughout Europe sought his services. He also received many commissions from the Roman Catholic Church.

To carry out commissions for large-scale works, Rubens formed a large workshop with assistants. Rubens never claimed any of his assistants' pictures as his own unless he had retouched them thoroughly. His most famous assistant was the Flemish artist Sir Anthony Van Dyck.

After his wife died in 1626, Rubens accepted several diplomatic assignments involving peace negotiations between England and Spain. His assignments took him to Madrid in 1628 and to London in 1629. King Charles I of England knighted Rubens for his skill in diplomacy.

Rubens married again in 1630 and gradually withdrew from political life. His second wife was a beautiful 16-year-old girl, Hélène Fourment. Hélène, like Rubens' first wife, was a member of a prominent Antwerp family. Rubens painted her many times. They had five children. After 1635, Rubens spent much time at his country estate near Brussels. The beautiful landscape there became the setting for many of his late works. Rubens died in Antwerp.

His art. The most important influence on Rubens' style was the ancient Roman sculpture he studied in Italy. He was also influenced by the paintings and sculptures of such Italian Renaissance artists as Michelangelo, Raphael, Tintoretto, Titian, and Veronese. Among the artists of his own time, Rubens especially admired Caravaggio and Carracci.

Rubens was the most important baroque artist of northern Europe. His paintings are known for their vast scale, brilliant colors, and emotional intensity. Rubens completed an enormous number of works. In one commission during the 1620's, he painted 21 large pictures on the life of Marie de Médicis, the widow of King Henry IV of France. From 1630 to 1635, he painted nine huge canvases for the Banqueting House at Whitehall in London. In the mid-1630's, he organized the artists of Antwerp to decorate structures in the city according to his designs to celebrate the visit of a new Spanish governor of the Netherlands. His last major commission was for a series of paintings to decorate the hunting lodge of King Philip IV of Spain.

Rubens' subjects include hunting scenes, Biblical episodes, stories from classical mythology, portraits and self-portraits, and landscapes. *Battle of the Amazons* is an example of his baroque style. It is reproduced in the **Painting** article. Eric M. Zafran

See also **Baroque; Daniel, Book of** (picture); **Drawing** (picture: A chalk drawing); **Jesus Christ** (picture: *Le Coup de Lance*).

Additional resources

McLanathan, Richard. *Peter Paul Rubens*. Abrams, 1995. Younger readers.
Scribner, Charles, III. *Rubens*. Abrams, 1989.
Sutton, Peter C., and others. *The Age of Rubens*. Abrams, 1993.
White, Christopher. *Peter Paul Rubens*. Yale, 1987.

Rubeola. See Measles.

Rubicon, *ROO buh kahn,* is a stream near Rimini, Italy, that Julius Caesar made famous when he was governor of Gaul. The Rubicon was part of the boundary between Roman Italy and the Roman province of Cisalpine Gaul (the Po Valley). Caesar and other Roman governors were forbidden to cross the boundary with troops. Caesar was commanding troops in Gaul when the Roman Senate, fearing his power, ordered him to give up his command. Caesar refused and led his men across the Rubicon on Jan. 10, 49 B.C. This action symbolized the start of Caesar's successful drive for the leadership of Rome. The expression *to cross the Rubicon* means to make a decision that cannot be changed.

The name Rubicon comes from the Latin word *rubeus* meaning *red.* The stream got its name because its waters are colored red by mud deposits. It may be the same as the present-day Fiumicino River. Arther Ferrill

See also **Caesar, Julius.**

Rubidium, *roo BIHD ee uhm,* is a soft, silvery-white metallic element. The German scientists Gustav Kirchhoff and Robert Bunsen discovered it in 1861. Rubidium occurs abundantly in the earth's crust. But, it is so widely distributed that its production is limited. It is usually obtained from minerals used for lithium production. Industry uses rubidium as a catalyst, and in making photocells and vacuum tubes.

Rubidium has the chemical symbol Rb. Its atomic number is 37, and its atomic weight is 85.4678. Rubidium oxidizes readily in air and is a fire hazard. It reacts violently with water and acids and melts at 38.84 °C.

Duward F. Shriver

Rubin, Robert Edward (1938-   ), was United States secretary of the treasury under President Bill Clinton from 1995 to 1999. Before Rubin became secretary, he had been director of the National Economic Council since 1993. As the council's director, Rubin helped shape the Clinton Administration's economic policies.

Hélène Fourment and Her Children (1637), an oil painting on canvas; The Louvre, Paris (SCALA/Art Resource)

An affectionate Rubens portrait of his second wife and two of their children reflects the intimacy and serenity of the works the artist painted during the final 10 years of his life.

He also helped win congressional approval of the North American Free Trade Agreement (NAFTA) between the United States, Canada, and Mexico. Before he became director of the National Economic Council, Rubin had been a major political fund-raiser for Clinton and other Democratic presidential nominees.

Rubin was born in New York City. He earned a bachelor's degree from Harvard University in 1960 and studied at the London School of Economics in 1960 and 1961. He graduated from Yale Law School in 1964. That same year, Rubin began working as a corporate lawyer in New York City. In 1966, he joined Goldman, Sachs & Co., a New York investment-banking firm. He was cochairman of the firm from 1990 to 1992. After stepping down as secretary of the treasury in 1999, Rubin joined Citigroup, a large U.S. financial services company, becoming a cochairman.   Alan Greenblatt

Rubinstein, *ROO bihn STYN,* **Anton Gregor,** *ahn TAWN* (1829-1894), was a Russian pianist and composer. He was one of the greatest pianists of the 1800's, and his tours through Europe and America also made him the most famous pianist of his time. Rubinstein composed many works, but few of them are performed today. Rubinstein was born near Balta, Ukraine. At 10, he made his first public appearance in Moscow.

When Rubinstein was 16, he began to teach in Vienna, Austria. Two years later, he went to St. Petersburg, Russia. There, the Grand Duchess Helen became his patroness and gave him many opportunities to be heard in public. In 1858, he became court pianist and concert conductor. The following year, he became director of the Royal Russian Musical Society, and four years later he founded the St. Petersburg Conservatory. He served as its director until 1867, and again from 1887 to 1890. Rubinstein came to the United States in 1872 and toured the country.   Lydia Hailparn Ledeen

Rubinstein, *ROO bihn styn,* **Arthur** (1887-1982), was a Polish-born concert pianist. He became famous throughout the world for his warmly expressive interpretations of music by Romantic composers of the 1800's, especially Frédéric Chopin.

Rubinstein also gained praise for his performances of works by the composers Franz Liszt, Robert Schumann, Peter Ilich Tchaikovsky, Manuel de Falla, and Heitor Villa-Lobos. Besides his solo concerts, Rubinstein performed chamber music with other prominent musicians.

Rubinstein was born in Łódź, Poland. He studied in Berlin and Warsaw with the composer Max Bruch and the pianist Ignace Paderewski, among others. Rubinstein made his concert debut at the age of 11. He moved to the United States in 1939 and became a U.S. citizen in 1946. Rubinstein wrote two autobiographies, *My Young Years* (1973) and *My Many Years* (1980).   F. E. Kirby

Ruble, *ROO buhl,* also spelled *rouble,* is the monetary unit of Russia, Belarus, and Tajikistan. The value of the ruble in each of these three countries is determined independently. The Russian ruble and the Belarusian ruble are each divided into 100 *kopecks.* The Tajik ruble is divided into 100 *tanga.* Currency in circulation in Russia includes treasury notes (paper money) and coins. Treasury notes are available in various ruble denominations. Coins are issued in several small denominations of rubles and in various denominations of kopecks.

Burton H. Hobson

Ruby is the red gem variety of the mineral corundum. Varieties of corundum are called *sapphires* if they are blue and *fancy sapphires* if they are any color other than red or blue. Chemically, corundum is an aluminum oxide.

Rubies get their color from traces of chromium in the aluminum oxide. The red of most rubies

Art Resource

Red ruby

has a brownish or yellowish tint. But the most highly valued rubies have a bluish tint called *pigeon's blood red.*

Rubies and sapphires are second only to diamonds in hardness, and fine-quality rubies are among the costliest of all gems. The finest rubies come from Myanmar. Today, commercially important deposits are mined in Thailand. India produces many rubies of lesser quality, but its *star rubies* are excellent. A star ruby appears to have a six-rayed star within it when seen in a bright light.

Millions of carats of inexpensive synthetic rubies are produced each year. But a demand for real gems has allowed the natural stones to maintain their high value. It can be difficult to distinguish between natural and synthetic rubies, even for experts. Red garnets are sometimes substituted for rubies. These garnets may appear under misleading names, such as *Arizona ruby* or *Cape ruby.* The ruby is the birthstone for July.   Robert I. Gait

See also **Corundum; Gem** (Imitation and synthetic gems); **Sapphire.**

Rudolf, Lake. See Lake Turkana.

Rudolph, Paul (1918-1997), was an American architect. He became best known for his dramatic and complex designs, especially buildings for urban and academic environments. His imaginative use of concrete and the

© ESTO

A building by Paul Rudolph serves as the home of the schools of art and architecture at Yale University. The building features an exterior of glass and roughly textured concrete. The absence of ornamentation is typical of the architect's designs.

absence of ornamentation in his exteriors show the influence of the French architect Le Corbusier (see **Le Corbusier**).

Rudolph served as chairman of the architecture department at Yale University in New Haven, Connecticut, from 1958 to 1965. Several of his important buildings are located in New Haven. Rudolph's most controversial work is the Art and Architecture Building (1963) at Yale, a complicated, 9-story building with 36 interior levels. The Temple Street parking garage (1963) is an example of his skill in integrating structures into urban settings. The garage is also an attempt to turn a simple, functional building into an object of beauty. During the 1960's, Rudolph began to design low-cost, prefabricated residential buildings, such as Crawford Manor (1966) in New Haven.

Rudolph was born in Elkton, Kentucky. He studied with architect Walter Gropius at Harvard University from 1941 to 1943 and in 1947.   Nicholas Adams

Rudolph, Wilma (1940-1994), was an American athlete. In the 1960 Olympic Games in Rome, she became the first American woman to win three gold medals in track and field competition. She won the 100-meter and 200-meter individual races, and she was a member of the winning American 400-meter relay team. During her career, Rudolph set world records in the 100-meter and 200-meter races.

Wilma Glodean Rudolph was born in St. Bethlehem, Tennessee. At the age of 4, she suffered an attack of double pneumonia and scarlet fever, followed by polio, which left her unable to walk properly until she was 11 years old. Rudolph competed in her first Olympics at the age of 16 in the 1956 games. She won a bronze medal as a member of the American Olympic 400-meter relay

UPI/Bettmann Newsphotos
Wilma Rudolph

team. After retiring from competition, Rudolph worked with young people, in both sports and educational pro grams.   Michael Takaha

Ruff is a sandpiper native to the Eastern Hemisphere. Ruffs range in color from black and chestnut to buff and whitish. During the mating season, the male develops a tuft of feathers on its neck that it can erect into a ruff. The female, called a *reeve,* has more modest plumage than the male. Ruffs are occasionally seen on the East Coast of North America.   Fritz L. Knopf

Scientific classification. The ruff belongs to the family Scolopacidae. The scientific name for the ruff is *Philomachus pugnax.*

Ruffe, *ruhf,* is a small freshwater fish that is a major pest in North America. Ruffe are native to Europe and Asia. But they appeared in the Great Lakes of North America in the 1980's and quickly became plentiful. Their explosive growth threatened the food supply of many fish native to the Great Lakes. Ruffe further endangered these native fish by eating the fishes' eggs and *larvae* (young). Ruffe grow up to 10 inches (25 centimeters) in length

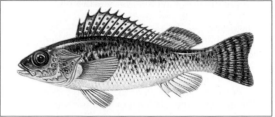

WORLD BOOK illustration by Colin Newman, Bernard Thornton Artists
The ruffe has a greenish back and a yellowish belly. Sharp spikes stick out of both the *dorsal* (back) fin and the bones that cover the gills. Ruffe are major pests in North America.

and have a drooping, scaleless head. Their bodies are brownish-green in color on the back and yellowish on the belly. Sharp spikes stick out of both the *dorsal* (back) fin and the bones that cover the gills. Ruffe live in lakes and slow-moving rivers. In addition to eggs and larvae of other fish, the ruffe's diet includes a variety of insects and shellfish.

Ruffe were first discovered in Lake Superior in 1987. Ships probably transported ruffe larvae from Europe to North America. The larvae may have been trapped in the ships' *ballast* (water kept in the hold of a ship to stabilize the vessel). Once the ships reached Lake Superior, they unintentionally released the young fish with the ballast.
          John E. McCosker

Scientific classification. The ruffe belongs to the freshwater perch family, Percidae. Its scientific name is *Gymnocephalus cernuus.*

Ruffed grouse is a thickly feathered grouse of North America. It is famous for the drumming sounds that the male bird makes with his wings during the spring. He chooses a log for his drumming and perches on it daily early in the morning. For many years, naturalists thought that the bird drummed by beating his wings against the log, against his breast, or against each other. High-speed photographs have shown that the bird actually beats the air with his wings, creating a sonic boom. At first the sounds are dull and well spaced, but as the

© Harry Engels, Animals Animals
A male ruffed grouse beats the air with its wings, *above,* making a drumming sound that can be heard far away.

speed of the flapping increases, the drumming becomes a long roll. The sound of the ruffed grouse can be heard for a great distance.

A thick collar of feathers around the ruffed grouse's neck gives the bird its name. During courtship, the male lifts these gleaming black feathers outward until they look like a ruff. Adult males are about 17 inches (43 centimeters) long. The ruffed grouse usually makes its nest at the foot of a tree. The nest may be formed from leaves and may contain from 9 to 14 eggs. The birds do not fly south in the autumn. In winter, the leg feathers of the ruffed grouse grow longer for warmth, and a weblike structure grows between its toes, enabling the bird to walk on top of snow. The ruffed grouse is the state bird of Pennsylvania.   Bertin W. Anderson

Scientific classification. The ruffed grouse belongs to the grouse subfamily, Tetraoninae, in the family Phasianidae. It is *Bonasa umbellus.*

See also Grouse; Partridge.

Ruffin, Edmund (1794-1865), was a noted Virginia agriculturist and a strong supporter of slavery. Ruffin favored *secession* (withdrawal) from the Union, and he was given the honor of firing the first shot on Fort Sumter, South Carolina, where the American Civil War was started in 1861.

Ruffin was born in Prince George County, Virginia. He experimented in crop rotation and with improved plowing, drainage, and fertilizing methods. He wrote about his theories and experiments, and helped bring about important changes in farming methods in the South. Ruffin founded the *Farmer's Register,* an agricultural journal, in 1833, and headed the Virginia State Agricultural Society from 1852 to 1854. Ruffin was so disturbed when the South lost the Civil War that he committed suicide.   James M. McPherson

Rugby football is a fast contact sport played by two teams. Players on each team try to score by kicking, passing, or carrying the ball until they can kick it over the opponent's goal or touch it down behind the opponent's goal line. The team that scores the most points wins the match.

There are two versions of Rugby football—*Rugby Union* and *Rugby League.* Rugby Union, the older of the two, is played by both amateurs and professionals. Professionals play Rugby League. Both types of Rugby football originated in Britain in the 1800's and both are now played worldwide.

Both forms of Rugby football feature almost continuous play. Stoppages occur only when a player is injured, when points are scored, if the ball crosses the boundaries of the field, or when there is a restart of play resulting from a rules violation. A match is divided into two 40-minute halves separated by a half-time rest period of no more than 5 minutes.

Both Rugby Union and Rugby League matches involve tackling and other physical play, but the players are allowed little protective equipment. A typical uniform consists of a shirt, shorts, knee-length stockings, and cleated boots. Some of the players wear shin guards and mouth guards.

Rugby Union

The field and equipment. The field is a maximum of 69 meters (75 yards) wide and 144 meters (157 yards)

long. The goal lines are 100 meters (109 yards) apart. An area called the *in-goal* extends up to 22 meters (24 yards) beyond each goal line. A halfway line and other lines parallel to the goal lines divide the field.

There are two goal posts that stand on each goal line. The posts are 5.6 meters ($6\frac{1}{8}$ yards) apart and are connected by a crossbar that is 3 meters ($3\frac{1}{3}$ yards) above the ground.

For more information about the Rugby Union field, see the diagram in this article.

The Rugby Union ball is an inflated oval rubber bladder encased in leather. It measures from 28 to 29 centimeters (11 to $11\frac{1}{2}$ inches) in length and weighs between 400 and 450 grams (14 to 16 ounces).

The officials. A *referee* and two *touch judges* officiate a match. The referee controls the game, and his judgment is final. The touch judges signal when and where the ball goes *into touch* (out of bounds), and they indicate whether a kick at goal is successful. They also inform the referees of any foul play.

The team consists of 15 players—8 forwards and 7 backs. The forwards attempt to win possession of the ball. The backs then advance the ball toward the goal by running, passing, or kicking. Forwards may also participate in the running, passing, and kicking activity.

Scoring. A team can score a *try,* a *conversion,* and a *goal.* A try is scored when any player touches the ball down on the ground in the opponent's in-goal area. A try counts 4 points. After a try is scored, a player on the scoring team attempts to *convert* the try. To convert a try, the player *place-kicks* the ball over the crossbar from a point opposite the spot where the player's team scored the try. Place-kicking involves kicking the ball from a prepared piece of turf called a "place." Defensive players stand behind their own goal line during the attempted conversion. A successful conversion scores 2 points.

There are two kinds of goals, a *penalty goal* and a *dropped goal.* Each counts 3 points. A player scores a goal by *drop-kicking*—dropping the ball and kicking it on the first bounce—or place-kicking the ball over the crossbar on a *penalty kick.* A penalty kick is awarded when the opposing team infringes certain rules. A player scores a dropped goal by drop-kicking the ball over the crossbar while the ball is in play.

How to play Rugby Union. The kickoff starts a Rugby Union match and also starts play in the second half. A player restarts play after either team has scored by place-kicking or drop-kicking from the center spot. The receiving team is positioned behind its 10-meter line.

Advancing the ball. The team that secures possession of the ball tries to gain territory toward the opponent's goal line by running, passing, or kicking the ball. Players are not allowed to pass the ball *forward* (toward the opponent's goal). The ball can only be passed laterally or backward. In addition, players cannot *knock on* (hit the ball toward the opponent's goal line with their hand or arm).

Players can tackle any opponent who is carrying the ball. The ball carrier avoids a tackle by dodging opponents or by passing the ball to a teammate. The ball carrier also may avoid a tackle by *handing off* the opponent, called a *fend.* That is, the player may push the opponent away by using the palm of the hand. However, no player can strike or punch any opponent. When a player is tackled, the player must release the ball to allow play to continue. Any player may pick up the ball and run with it or kick it.

A player may kick the ball directly over the touch line or side line only from behind his own team's 22-meter line. He can kick the ball over the touch line or side line from in front of the 22-meter line only if the ball bounces before going over the touch line or side line.

Substitutions. In international rugby matches, up to three players may leave a game only after a doctor determines that the player is not fit to continue playing. Substituted players may not reenter the match. In noninternational matches, six players who leave a game may be replaced.

The scrum. A scrum restarts play after one of the teams has committed a minor violation, such as a forward pass. In a scrum, the two opposing sets of forwards link themselves together tightly, bending forward from the waist to form a tunnellike formation. The halfback from the team not responsible for the violation "feeds" the ball into the tunnel. The two sets of forwards push from opposite sides as soon as the ball enters the scrum. Each side attempts to move the scrum into a po-

sition that allows its *hooker* to heel the ball back through his own team scrum to gain possession. The hooker is positioned in the front and center of the front row of the forwards in the scrum.

The line out. A line out restarts play after the ball has gone over the side line or into touch. A player from the team not responsible for putting the ball in touch throws the ball in bounds between two opposing lines of forwards. Each set of forwards tries to outjump the other and secure possession of the ball for its backs.

The forwards also form a *ruck* or a *maul*. Both formations continue play without interruption after a tackle. In a ruck, the forwards close in around the ball after the ball carrier has been tackled and the ball has gone to ground. The forwards attempt to heel, or "ruck," the ball back for their backs to continue play. A maul occurs when several forwards surround the ball carrier during a tackle and the tackled player is able to remain on his feet. The opposition players in the maul attempt to wrestle the ball from the ball carrier.

Rugby League

The field. The field is a maximum of 68 meters (74 yards) wide. The goal lines are 100 meters apart. An in-

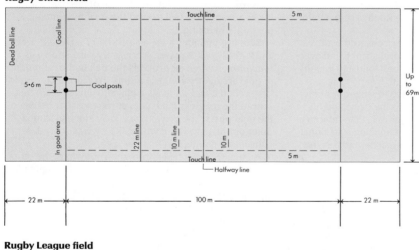

Rugby Union field

Rugby League field

A **Rugby football field** consists of the field of play and the in-goal areas. The field of play is a rectangle bordered by the touch lines and the goal lines. The in-goal areas are behind each goal line and are enclosed by the goal lines and dead-ball lines. Rugby League and Rugby Union fields are about the same size, but they have some different markings. The diagram at the upper left shows a Rugby Union field. The diagram at the lower left shows a Rugby League field.

WORLD BOOK diagrams

Mickey Pfleger

A line out restarts play in Rugby Union after the ball has gone out-of-bounds. A player tosses the ball in between two lines of forwards, and each group tries to pass the ball to its backs.

Focus on Sports

A scrum puts the ball in play in Rugby League. The ball is tossed into a tunnellike formation made by the forwards from each team. Players in the center try to kick it to a teammate.

goal area from 6 to 11 meters ($6\frac{1}{2}$ to 12 yards) extends beyond each goal line. The field is divided into quarters with a halfway line in the middle. Two goal posts stand on each goal line. The posts are 5.5 meters (6 yards) apart.

For more information about the Rugby League field, see the diagram in this article.

The ball is an inflated rubber sack covered with leather or synthetic material. It is oval-shaped and averages about 28 centimeters (11 inches) long and weighs about 410 grams ($14\frac{1}{2}$ ounces).

The officials. A referee and two touch judges officiate the match. The referee controls the game and his judgment is final. The touch judges assist the referee in all phases of the game. Their chief function is to signal with a flag whether the ball or ball carrier crosses the

WORLD BOOK illustrations by David Cunningham

Plays in Rugby. A player can pass the ball laterally, *upper left.* A player with the ball can *hand off* an opponent, *upper right,* by pushing the opponent with the palm of the hand. Teams score a try, *lower left,* by touching the ball down in the opponent's in-goal area. They score a goal, *lower right,* by kicking.

sideline. They also can inform the referee of player misconduct and indicate whether points have been correctly scored.

A team has 13 players—6 forwards and 7 backs. The forwards attempt to win possession of the ball. The backs advance the ball toward the goal by running, passing, or kicking.

Scoring includes a *try,* a *conversion,* a *penalty kick,* and a *field goal.* A player scores a try (also known as a *touchdown*) when he grounds the ball in the opponent's in-goal area. A try counts 4 points. To score a conversion (also called a *kick at goal*), a player from the team that scored the try kicks the ball over the crossbar between the goal posts. The player place-kicks the ball from a point opposite the spot where the try was scored. A conversion counts 2 points.

A penalty kick is taken from the spot where the other team's violation occurred. The kick is worth 2 points. The team awarded the penalty kick may choose to gain yardage instead of taking the kick by kicking the ball into the field from outside the touch lines.

A player scores a field goal by drop-kicking the ball through the goal posts and over the crossbar at any time during the game. A field goal counts 1 point.

How to play Rugby League. The kickoff starts a Rugby League match and also starts play in the second half. A player place-kicks the ball from the center spot on the halfway line. The receiving team stands behind the 10-meter line.

Advancing the ball. The team in possession of the ball tries to move it over the opponent's goal line. Any player can run with the ball and kick it in any direction. He may pass, throw, or knock the ball to any teammate not in front of him. Only the player carrying the ball is allowed to be tackled.

Substitutions. Up to four players may be substituted in a match for any reason. A replaced player cannot re-enter the game.

Playing the ball. During a game, a team in possession is allowed 6 tackles, or *downs,* to score points. If the team does not score, a *hand-over* occurs to allow the opposing team 6 tackles. After each tackle is completed, the ball carrier places the ball on the ground and *plays the ball* back with the foot to one of his teammates. That player can then pick up the ball to continue play. All players from both teams must be 5 meters (5½ yards) away and cannot move up until the ball is played.

The scrum. A scrum, or *scrummage,* restarts play after one of the teams has committed a minor violation or a ball carrier goes over the sideline. In a scrum, the two opposing sets of forwards link themselves together tightly and lower their heads to make a tunnellike formation. A player from the team not responsible for the violation tosses the ball into the scrum. The two sets of forwards push from opposite sides as soon as the ball enters the scrum. Each side attempts to move the scrum into a position that allows its hooker to kick the ball out of the scrum to a teammate.

History

According to tradition, Rugby football originated from a soccer game played at Rugby School in Rugby, England, in 1823. During the game, a student named William Webb Ellis broke the rules of soccer by picking up the ball and running with it. Players of the new game adopted use of an oval-shaped ball to make passing and carrying easier.

Rugby football quickly became popular throughout Britain. Teams could play with an unlimited number of players at one time, and there were few rules. In 1871, a conference of Rugby clubs formed the English Rugby Union, made up of 17 amateur clubs. The conference set the number of players on a team at 15 and established other general rules. Scotland formed its Rugby Union in 1873, and Ireland organized a Rugby Union in 1874. The Welsh Rugby Union formed in 1881.

In 1895, 21 teams from the northern counties of England broke from the Rugby Union to form the Northern Rugby Union. The players on these teams wanted to play Rugby professionally, which the Rugby Union did not allow. The Northern Rugby Union changed its name to the Rugby Football League in 1922. The International Rugby Board, formed in 1948, was established to govern both Rugby Union and Rugby League.

Andy Haden and Neville N. Kesha

Rugby School is a famous English public school founded in 1567 at Rugby, England. England's "public" schools are not free schools. They are privately supported institutions for secondary education. Rugby's playground was one of the founding places of Rugby football. The school became one of the leading public schools in England under Thomas Arnold, who served as headmaster from 1828 to 1842. Arnold is the popular headmaster who appears in the novel *Tom Brown's School Days,* by Thomas Hughes. Rugby's average enrollment is more than 750.   P. A. McGinley

Rugs and carpets are fabrics used as floor coverings. They add beauty, comfort, and warmth to a room, and they help absorb sound. Rugs and carpets also protect floors and provide a less slippery surface than a waxed or tiled floor. Most rugs and carpets are used in homes and other buildings, but some cover outdoor surfaces. Some rugs are used as decorative wallhangings.

The words *rug* and *carpet* are sometimes used interchangeably, but they refer to different types of floor cov-

erings. A rug covers only part of the floor of a room and is not fastened down. A carpet covers an entire floor and is nailed, tacked, or glued down.

Most rugs and carpets are mass-produced and are made in a variety of textures and an almost unlimited number of colors and patterns. Some rugs are manufactured in standard sizes, such as 4 feet by 6 feet (1.2 meters by 1.8 meters) or 9 feet by 15 feet (2.7 meters by 5 meters). Other rugs are cut from large rolls of carpeting. Most carpeting is produced in 12-foot (3.7-meter) widths, but some is 15 feet (5 meters) wide. Other carpeting is cut into 9-, 12-, or 18-inch (23-, 30-, or 46-centimeter) squares called *carpet tiles.* Carpeting made on a loom or other machine more than 6 feet (1.8 meters) wide is called *broadloom carpeting.*

Rugs may also be made by hand. Handmade Oriental rugs are valued for their rareness and beauty.

The United States produces about 1⅓ billion square yards (1 billion square meters) of rugs and carpets annually. Georgia is the leading state in the production of rugs and carpets, making more than 70 percent of these floor coverings. California ranks second in the production of rugs and carpets.

Materials used in rugs and carpets

. Rugs and carpets have two main parts, the *pile,* or *face,* and the *backing.* The pile is the top surface, and

© Mason Morfit, FPG

Modern carpeting is mass-produced by machines in a variety of textures, colors, and patterns. Rugs and carpets help protect floors and provide beauty and warmth to a room.

the backing is the undersurface. Various manufactured or natural fibers are used in making both the pile and the backing. A few manufacturers produce pile with a blend of both manufactured and natural fibers.

The chief manufactured materials in pile fibers are nylon, olefin, and polyester. All these materials resist soiling and staining well. About 75 per cent of the rugs and carpets manufactured in the United States have nylon pile. Nylon fibers are durable and easy to dye. Olefin fibers make up the pile in about 14 per cent of the rugs and carpets produced in the United States. People use olefin floor coverings widely both indoors and outdoors because olefin resists moisture and fading. About 10 per cent of the rugs and carpets have polyester pile. Polyester fibers can absorb and hold brighter colors of dye than other manufactured fibers can. A small number of rugs and carpets have acrylic pile. Acrylic floor coverings are bulky but light in weight, and they resist fading. Tough nylon fibers make up the pile in *artificial turf,* a type of carpet used both indoors and outdoors for landscaping and playing surfaces.

Wool is the main natural fiber used in making pile. Until the 1940's, nearly all rugs and carpets manufactured in the United States were made of wool. Today, wool is used for only about 1 per cent of the rugs and carpets made in the United States. Wool floor coverings are attractive, soft, and durable. Many people consider them the finest made. But most wool floor coverings cost more than those made from manufactured fibers.

The backing of most rugs and carpets is made of olefin or of jute, a natural fiber. Linen, polyester, and cotton are also used.

Kinds of rugs and carpets

Rugs and carpets are classified according to their pile textures. There are six main kinds of rugs and carpets: (1) level loop, (2) multilevel loop, (3) plush, (4) saxony, (5) frieze, and (6) cut and loop.

Level loop and multilevel loop floor coverings have a *loop pile,* which consists of loops of yarn. Plush, saxony,

Kinds of rugs and carpets   Rugs and carpets are classified according to the texture of their top surface, called the *pile.* Examples of the six main types of rugs and carpets are shown below.

Bigelow-Sanford, Inc. (WORLD BOOK photos); WORLD BOOK illustrations by Koralik Associates

Level loop

 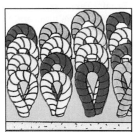

Multilevel loop

Plush

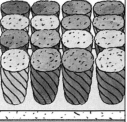

Saxony

 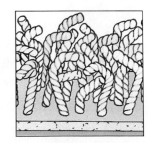

Frieze

 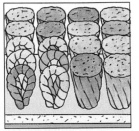

Cut and loop

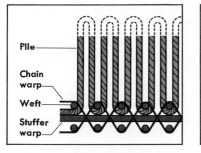

A **velvet weave** is the simplest type. Almost all the pile yarn appears on the surface of the floor covering.

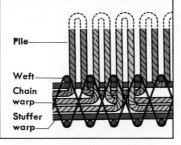

A **Wilton weave** has all its yarns running in rows along the backing, but only one color is raised to the surface at a time.

An **Axminster weave** has each pile yarn inserted independently. Most of the pile yarn appears on the surface.

WORLD BOOK diagrams by Zorica Dabich

and frieze rugs and carpets have a *cut pile.* They are made with loops of yarn, but each loop is then cut in two, producing a surface of cut ends. The cut and loop type has a combination pile.

Level loop rugs and carpets have a smooth, tight texture. All the loops of yarn that make up the pile have the same height.

Multilevel loop rugs and carpets have an uneven texture. The loops of their pile vary in height, giving the surface a patterned effect.

Plush rugs and carpets are soft and have a luxurious appearance. The yarns of plush pile are short and loosely twisted. Plush pile provides a thick, level floor covering that is often desired in formal settings.

Saxony rugs and carpets resemble the plush type. However, each yarn of a saxony floor covering stands erect and is clearly distinguishable. The ends of the yarn in plush pile tend to blend together.

Frieze rugs and carpets have a rougher texture than the other members of the cut pile group. The yarns of a frieze pile are tightly twisted, and they curl when inserted into the surface.

Cut and loop rugs and carpets have yarns that vary in height. The longer yarns provide a cut pile. The shorter yarns are looped and may be hidden by the longer ones.

How rugs and carpets are made

More than 95 per cent of the rugs and carpets produced in the United States are made by a process called *tufting.* The rest are made by weaving or by other methods.

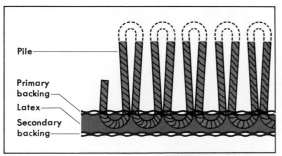

WORLD BOOK diagram by Steven Liska

A **tufted floor covering** consists of pile yarns called *tufts,* which are forced through a backing by needles.

Tufting is the fastest and cheapest method of making rugs and carpets. Tufted floor coverings consist of clusters of pile yarns called *tufts.* Eyed needles insert the tufts into the backing.

A tufting machine has hundreds of needles set in a row on a device called a *needle bar.* When the needle bar is lowered, each needle forces a loop of yarn through a layer of backing called *primary backing.* The loops form a row of tufts. As the needle bar is lifted, devices called *loopers* hold the tufts in place to form a looped pile. A cut pile can be made by attaching a knife blade to each looper.

A synthetic latex compound is applied to the primary backing to secure the tufts. A layer of backing called *secondary backing* may be added over the latex to provide extra durability. The secondary backing is made of jute or synthetic materials. Some tufted floor coverings have a layer of plastic foam instead of a secondary backing.

Weaving was the chief method of manufacturing rugs and carpets in the United States until the development of tufting in the 1950's. Woven floor coverings are made on looms by interlacing the pile yarns with backing yarns. Weaving the two kinds of yarns together holds the pile yarns securely in the backing.

The pile of a woven rug or carpet is formed from one set of yarns. The backing is made from two sets. The pile yarns are woven into the backing in rows. During the weaving process, these yarns form loops over long, flat pieces of metal called *wires* that lie across the loom. This action creates a looped pile. A cut pile is produced by wires that have a knife blade at one end. In the backing, one set of yarns, called the *weft,* runs crosswise on the loom. Another set, called the *warp,* runs lengthwise. There are two kinds of warp yarns, *chains* and *stuffers.* Chain warps cross over and under the weft yarns to form the weave. Stuffer warps are extra yarns that run through the backing in order to give it greater bulk and strength.

There are three chief types of woven rugs and carpets: (1) velvet, (2) Wilton, and (3) Axminster. They differ in the way their pile yarns are woven into the backing, and each type is made on a different kind of loom. The backing for all three is made in basically the same way.

Velvet rugs and carpets are made with the simplest type of weave. They are woven on looms similar to those used in making regular cloth. The majority of velvet floor coverings have a pile of one color, and a design cannot be woven into the surface. Most of the pile yarn is on the surface of the rug or carpet.

Wilton rugs and carpets are woven on a loom that has a special device called a *Jacquard mechanism.* With this device, as many as six different colored yarns may be used in each row of the pile. A design, if desired, may be created on the surface. All the yarns run in rows along the backing, but only one yarn is raised to the surface at a time. Thus, a yarn of the desired color appears in the proper place in the design. The other yarns run under the surface, where they give strength and springiness to the backing.

Axminster rugs and carpets may be produced in an unlimited number of colors and patterns. Most of the pile yarns of an Axminster floor covering appear on the surface. Each pile yarn is inserted into the carpet independently. As each yarn is inserted, it is interwoven with the backing yarns.

Other methods include *knitting, needle-punching, braiding, embroidering,* and *hooking.*

Knitted rugs and carpets are produced on knitting machines by a process that is similar to hand knitting. The pile yarns and the backing yarns are knitted together. Needle-punched floor coverings are made from fibers that have been tangled together by means of barbed needles. This tangled mass is then compressed into thick, feltlike material that can be used both indoors and outdoors.

Braided floor coverings are manufactured from individual braids of yarn or fabric. The braids are sewn together and coiled into a circle, an oval, or some other shape. Embroidered floor coverings are created by stitching designs onto the backing. The designs form

the pile. Hooked rugs are produced by punching yarns through the backing with a metal hook.

Oriental rugs

People who live in Asia have traditionally created beautiful handmade rugs. Authentic Oriental rugs have pile yarns that are hand-knotted onto a woven backing. These rugs are made in such countries as China, India, Iran, and Turkey.

Oriental rugs are valuable because they have intricate designs and take a long time to weave. The value of an Oriental rug depends in part on the type of material used to create the rug and on the size and closeness of the rug's weave. Tightly woven Oriental rugs are more expensive because they require the most time to make and are the most durable. Age, condition, and color also contribute to a rug's value.

An Oriental rug is not as perfect as a mass-produced rug. The size and shape of an Oriental rug may not be exact, and the color in various areas of the rug may differ slightly.

Oriental rugs are woven on simple looms. A small rug may be woven by one person, but most large Oriental rugs are made by several weavers. First, the rug makers knot a row of pile yarns to the warp yarns. Next, they weave one or more weft yarns through the warp. The knots and weft yarns are then packed down tightly on the previously woven rows with a comblike device. The knotting process is then repeated. Trimming the ends of the knotted pile yarns creates the rug's even surface.

Almost every Oriental rug is made with one of two types of knots. A *Persian,* or *Sehna, knot* twists the pile and warp yarns together. A *Turkish,* or *Ghiordes, knot*

Detail of a silk rug (1500's) of the Safavid period; the
Metropolitan Museum of Art, Bequest of Benjamin Altman, 1913

Persian rugs are prized for their soft colors and graceful patterns. They are made by hand in Iran (formerly Persia). At left, a weaver ties a colorful yarn to two vertical strands of a Persian rug. Patterns woven into such rugs include pictures of leaves, flowers, and animals, *right.*

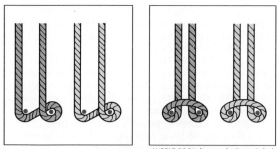

WORLD BOOK diagrams by Zorica Dabich

Knots for most Oriental rugs are made in one of two ways. A *Persian,* or *Sehna, knot, left,* twists the pile and warp yarns together. A *Turkish,* or *Ghiordes, knot, right,* ties them together.

ties the yarns. Most Oriental rugs have from 50 to 500 knots per square inch (8 to 78 knots per square centimeter).

Most Oriental rugs have wool pile yarns, but some have pile yarns of silk. The warp and weft yarns of most Oriental rugs are made of cotton or wool. Hemp, jute, and silk are less commonly used.

The chief colors in most Oriental rugs are blue, brown, red, and white. Most of the yarns are treated with chemical dyes to obtain various shades of these colors. Before these chemical dyes were developed, the yarns were colored with natural dyes made from plants and minerals. Today, a few rug makers still use natural dyes.

Oriental rugs called *prayer rugs* are made in Islamic regions of Asia. The design of a prayer rug includes a pointed or arch-shaped pattern representing the prayer niche of the mosque. Muslims face Mecca, their holy city, as they kneel in prayer, and the rug is placed with the design pointed toward it.

There are six chief types of Oriental rugs. They are (1) Caucasian rugs, (2) Chinese rugs, (3) Indian rugs, (4) Persian rugs, (5) Turkish rugs, and (6) Turkoman rugs. Oriental rugs are named for regions where they are made.

Caucasian rugs come from the Caucasus Mountains between Europe and Asia. These rugs have geometric designs woven in bold reds, blues, yellows, and other colors.

Chinese rugs have designs that feature philosophical and religious symbols of China. The designs are woven into backgrounds originally of blue, red, and yellow. Time may have changed the reds in some older rugs to lighter colors.

Indian rugs resemble Persian rugs in color and pattern. Many of the designs feature plants and animals.

Persian rugs are made in Iran (formerly Persia). Their graceful patterns feature flowers, leaves, and birds. Some Persian rugs feature animal combat scenes. Persian rugs have soft, blended colors.

Turkish rugs are known for their rectangular patterns and their floral designs arranged in rows. Most of these rugs have large areas of solid colors.

Turkoman rugs come from Turkestan, a region of central Asia. They are woven primarily in reddish tones and have simple geometric designs.

History

Some prehistoric people may have used animal skins as floor coverings in their caves or huts. After people learned to weave, they made floor mats from grasses and other plant material.

No one knows when rug making began. The earliest known fabric made with pile is called the *Pazyryk rug.* It was made around the 400's B.C. and was discovered in a tomb in southern Siberia.

Crusaders who traveled to the Middle East during the A.D. 1100's and 1200's probably brought rugs back to Europe. In the 1200's, Spain became the first European country to produce rugs. England started making pile rugs in the 1500's.

During the 1600's, France began to make a style of rug called the *Savonnerie,* which had a deep pile. In the 1700's, England was the center of the European rug and carpet industry. An English inventor named Edmund Cartwright developed the power loom in the 1780's.

In North America, the most common rugs during colonial times were braided rugs, hooked rugs, and *rag rugs,* which were made from scraps of cloth. The first U.S. carpet mill was set up in 1791 in Philadelphia.

Joseph M. Jacquard, a French weaver, invented the Jacquard mechanism about 1800. Erastus B. Bigelow, a Massachusetts inventor, perfected a power loom for making carpets in the early 1840's. A power loom for producing Axminster carpets was patented in 1856.

The tufting machine for carpeting was introduced in the early 1950's. By the mid-1950's, more tufted rugs and carpets than woven ones were being produced in the United States.   R. Carroll Turner

Related articles in *World Book* include:

Artificial turf	Industry (pictures)
Asia (picture: Skilled craft workers)	Interior design (Floor coverings)
Carpet beetle	Islamic art (picture)
Cartwright, Edmund	Jacquard, Joseph M.
Indian, American (picture: The Navajo)	Tapestry Weaving

Genesis by Helen Webber; Edward Fields, Inc. (WORLD BOOK photo)

A handmade rug used as a wallhanging adds a modern decorative touch to a home or office.

Ruhr, *roor,* is an industrial region in western Germany. Several branches of the Rhine River run through the region, including the Ruhr River, from which it takes its name. The area most commonly known as the Ruhr is rectangular, with corners roughly at Hamm, Lüden-scheid, Mönchengladbach, and Wesel. The Ruhr covers about 2,830 square miles (7,330 square kilometers). People sometimes refer to a greater Ruhr area, which includes the Cologne and Bonn regions.

The people and their work. The Ruhr is one of the most crowded sections of Europe. It has a population of about 8,500,000, excluding the Cologne and Bonn areas. Dortmund, Duisburg, Düsseldorf, Essen, and Wuppertal

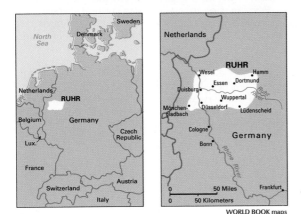

The Ruhr is a region in western Germany.

are large industrial cities in this region. The entire area along the Ruhr River from Duisburg to Dortmund forms practically one continuous city.

The Ruhr includes one of the largest concentrations of industry in the world. It has a great transportation network that includes railroads and river and canal developments. The region's industries produce chemicals, iron and steel, and textiles.

History. The Ruhr became important to German industry in the mid-1800's. Its huge coal fields and fine transportation facilities made it important as a coal-mining area. In 1871, Germany won control of almost all of Alsace and part of Lorraine after the Franco-Prussian War. This made iron ore from Lorraine available to German industries without customs duties. Industrialists in the Ruhr area began to bring in ore from Lorraine, and the region developed into an industrial center.

Germany lost Lorraine after World War I (1914-1918). For a time it seemed the Ruhr would again become only a mining district. But the German government paid huge sums to iron manufacturers for the loss of Lorraine. With this money, the industrialists built smelting works that could process iron ore from Sweden.

By 1922, Germany had fallen behind in paying France and Belgium for damages caused during World War I. French and Belgian troops occupied the Ruhr in January 1923 to force Germany to make its payments. But the German government encouraged Ruhr workers to follow a policy of passive resistance and to produce as little as possible during the occupation.

The French took harsh steps to increase German production. But all their measures failed. The decrease in production of the Ruhr soon affected the economic life

of France and Germany disastrously. Both countries headed toward national bankruptcy. The occupation cost Germany about $833 million, and France lost about $200 million worth of coal.

On Sept. 27, 1923, Germany finally ended its passive resistance in the Ruhr. At the same time, France saw that it was useless to occupy the Ruhr any longer. Under the terms of the Dawes Plan, French and Belgian troops left the region by Aug. 1, 1925.

Adolf Hitler came to power in Germany in 1933. He used Ruhr industries to supply the Nazi war machine. During World War II (1939-1945), Allied bombers made many devastating raids on the Ruhr. American armies finally captured the Ruhr, and British troops occupied the area. After the war, Germany was divided into two states—West Germany and East Germany. The Ruhr became part of West Germany. In 1990, Germany was reunified.　　John W. Boyer

Ruhr River, *roor,* rises in Westphalia, Germany, and flows 144 miles (232 kilometers) through the famous industrial region of the Ruhr Valley. It joins the Rhine River near Duisburg. See **Ruhr.**

Another Ruhr (Roer) River rises on the Belgian frontier and flows north through Germany for 67 miles (108 kilometers). It enters the Maas (Meuse) River at Roermond, the Netherlands.　　Hugh D. Clout

Ruisdael, *ROYS dahl,* **Jacob van,** *YAH kawp vahn* (1628?-1682), was the greatest Dutch landscape painter

Ewing Galloway

Ruisdael's *The Mill at Wijk,* completed about 1665, shows the painter's dramatic interpretation of the Dutch countryside.

of his time. His name is also spelled *Ruysdael.* Other artists of Ruisdael's time stressed the placid character of the Dutch countryside, but Ruisdael depicted nature as filled with drama and mood. He painted stormy seas, rushing waterfalls, melancholy ruins, dark forests, and clouded skies that were pierced by rays of light. Romantic painters of the 1800's admired Ruisdael's poetic approach to nature and often imitated his style and subject matter.

Ruisdael was born in Haarlem and in 1648 became a member of the painters' guild there. In 1656, Ruisdael moved to Amsterdam, where he produced his finest paintings. In Amsterdam, he expanded his range of subjects to include urban scenes.   Linda Stone-Ferrier

Ruiz, *roo EES,* **Juan** (1283?-1350?), ranks among Spain's important poets on the strength of a single known work. His *Book of Good Love* (*Libro de buen amor,* 1330, revised and enlarged 1343), a collection of stories in verse and song, is the most entertaining and human book in medieval Spanish literature. "Good love" in the title stands for love of God and the Virgin Mary, a popular topic in medieval Spain. However, the work is more a praise of human love than spiritual love. See **Spanish literature** (Early medieval literature).

Ruiz was born in Alcalá de Henares and was archpriest of Hita, a small town in Castile. He probably suffered a long prison term by order of the Archbishop of Toledo. Ruiz' *Book of Good Love* mingles mock allegories, tales from medieval French literature, and references to classical authors with realistic episodes.

Harry Sieber

Ruiz Cortines, *roo EES kawr TEE nays,* **Adolfo** (1891-1973), served as president of Mexico from 1952 to 1958. A civil servant for 30 years, he was governor of Veracruz from 1944 to 1948 and secretary of the interior under President Miguel Alemán.

As president, Ruiz Cortines fought dishonesty and corruption in reforming the civil service. He also consolidated gains made by Alemán's administration in developing agriculture and industry. In addition, Ruiz Cortines took measures that led to a decrease in Mexico's high inflation rate. He directed reform of Mexico City's government, and effectively met the crisis caused by an earthquake in 1957. Ruiz Cortines was born in Veracruz.

W. Dirk Raat

Rules of order. See **Parliamentary procedure.**
Rum. See **Alcoholic beverage** (Rum).
Rumania. See **Romania.**
Rumba, also spelled *rhumba,* is a Latin ballroom dance that originated in Africa and achieved its modern form in Cuba. Couples perform the rumba in $\frac{4}{4}$ time with a quick-quick-slow rhythm. The rumba emphasizes a swaying hip motion that is achieved by taking small steps with the knees relaxed. Steps are typically performed in a square pattern. The rumba is most often accompanied by music with a repeated beat played on percussion instruments.

A version of the rumba was first introduced into the United States from Cuba about 1914. However, the dance's exaggerated hip movements were considered too sexually suggestive and the dance did not gain acceptance. A more refined version was introduced about 1930. The dance maintained its popularity in the 1930's and 1940's, especially in England, where ballroom dance teachers standardized the figures and step rhythms. Rumbas also appear in music not intended for ballroom dancing, as in Darius Milhaud's ballet *La creation du monde* (1923).   Patricia W. Rader

Ruminant is the name given to a grazing animal that has a highly specialized digestive system and split hoofs. Such mammals as sheep, cows, oxen, deer, antelope, camels, llamas, and giraffes are ruminants. Most kinds of ruminants have a stomach with four *cavities* (compartments). Each cavity helps digest food with the aid of numerous microorganisms, such as bacteria and yeasts, that live in the stomach. The microorganisms break

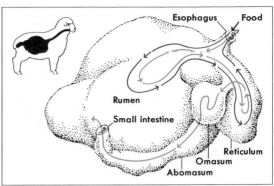

WORLD BOOK illustration by Marion Pahl

Most ruminants have a stomach with four compartments: the *rumen, reticulum, omasum,* and *abomasum.* These drawings show a sheep's stomach. Food enters the rumen and reticulum, *red arrows,* and is then rechewed as cud. Cud eventually passes into the omasum and abomasum, *blue arrows.*

down *cellulose,* a substance found in the cell walls of plants, into important nutrients. These nutrients provide the main source of energy for many ruminants.

A ruminant chews its food with its molars. It does not have any *incisors* (biting teeth) in the upper jaw. When a ruminant eats, it swallows its food, which is usually grass, after chewing it only slightly. The food goes down the *esophagus* (food pipe) into the first cavity of the stomach. This cavity is called the *rumen* or *paunch.* Most of the food collects in the rumen, but some passes directly into the second cavity, called the *reticulum.* The reticulum has tiny pockets in its walls, which look like a honeycomb.

Food stored in the rumen eventually passes into the reticulum, where it is softened and formed into soft masses called *cuds.* As the animal rests, the muscles of the reticulum send the food back to the mouth to be chewed and mixed with saliva. The animal chews with a roundish motion of the jaw and swallows again. The cud then passes through the rumen and reticulum to the third cavity, called the *omasum.* The rumen, reticulum, and omasum all serve as "vats" for storing the stomach's microorganisms.

Finally, the food enters the fourth cavity, the *abomasum.* This cavity is the "true stomach." It functions the same way as the stomach in human beings and other mammals that are not ruminants. There, the food mixes with stomach juice and passes into the intestine, where digestion is completed. The digested food is absorbed through the lining of the intestine and passes to all parts of the body through the bloodstream.

Scientific classification. Ruminants are in the class Mammalia. They are in the order Artiodactyla, and make up the suborder Ruminantia.   C. Richard Taylor

Rump Parliament was a name given the English Parliament during the civil war in the mid-1600's. That Parliament had less than a fourth of the usual number of members. The other members had been excluded by troops of the Puritan leader Oliver Cromwell.

Civil war broke out in 1642 between the forces of King Charles I and those of the *Long Parliament* (see **Long Parliament**). Later, members of Parliament disagreed on the conduct of the war. On Dec. 6, 1648, soldiers led by Colonel Thomas Pride surrounded the House of Commons. They arrested 47 members of Parliament who opposed the trial of the king, and excluded many others. This action was called *Pride's Purge.* The remaining members were known as the *Rump Parliament,* because they were the *rump* (end) of the larger body. They supported the execution of Charles I in 1649.

The Rump Parliament fought later against many demands made by Cromwell's army. Cromwell entered Parliament in 1653 at the head of a troop of soldiers and ordered it disbanded. The Rump Parliament met twice after Cromwell's death. In 1660, after the members expelled by Colonel Pride had been recalled, the Long Parliament disbanded itself and ordered the election of a new Parliament. Later that year, the monarchy was restored under Charles II.   Charles Carlton

See also **Charles I** (of England); **Cromwell, Oliver.**

Rune, *roon,* is any one of the characters of the earliest written alphabet used by the Germanic peoples of Europe. The oldest runic writings date back to the A.D. 200's. Most runic inscriptions known today were written before the 1000's. Many runes were carved in wood, but most surviving runes were written in stone.

The word *rune* comes from a Gothic word meaning *secret.* Members of early Germanic tribes associated runes with secrecy or mystery because few people understood the inscriptions. Runic characters were probably first used by pagan priests in making charms and magic spells. The characters were also scratched on coins, jewelry, monuments, and slabs of stone or wood. The earliest runes consisted almost entirely of straight lines, arranged singly or in combinations of two or more. Later runes had more complex forms.

Archaeologists have discovered more than 4,000 runic inscriptions. Over 3,000 of these writings were found in Sweden, and many dated from the 800's to the 1000's, the period of the Vikings. Other runic writings were discovered in Denmark, England, Germany, and Norway. By the 1000's, missionaries had converted the Germanic peoples to Christianity. Their conversion led to the introduction of the Roman alphabet, which eventually replaced runic characters.   James E. Cathey

See also **Kensington rune stone.**

Running is a vigorous form of exercise and a popular sport. Millions of people run because they enjoy the activity or want to be physically fit. Some runners compete in long-distance races that do not form part of organized track meets. Most of these races are run on city streets

Focus on Sports

Running is an effective form of exercise and a popular sport. These runners are competing in the New York City Marathon.

and roads. This article includes information on such long-distance races. For information about other kinds of running events, see **Track and field.**

Some people use the terms *running* and *jogging* interchangeably. However, running is usually considered faster than jogging. In addition, people jog only to exercise, not to compete against others.

Running requires no special skills or facilities. The only equipment needed is well-cushioned, flexible shoes and comfortable clothing. People considering a running program should have a complete medical examination before starting.

A daily running program improves a person's physical condition. Running is an *aerobic exercise*—that is, it promotes the circulation of oxygen through the bloodstream to the organs and tissues. It also builds up the heart and increases endurance. Running strengthens the leg muscles and makes the body more limber. It helps control weight because runners burn up more than 100 calories per mile (62 calories per kilometer). Running also helps relieve emotional stress.

Running competitions have been held since ancient times. The Olympic Games feature several running events, including the *marathon.* Officially, a marathon is a race that covers 26 miles 385 yards (42.2 kilometers).

Letters of the runic alphabet were used for writing ancient Anglo-Saxon inscriptions.

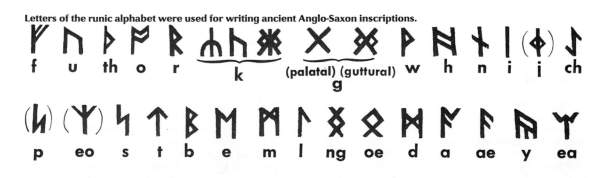

Many cities in the United States hold annual marathons. About 24,000 runners compete in the New York City Marathon, more than in any other marathon in the world. However, races covering 10 kilometers (6.2 miles) are more popular than official marathons.

Running became extremely popular throughout the United States during the 1960's and 1970's. In the book *Aerobics* (1968), Kenneth Cooper, an American physician, brought attention to the advantages of running. A large number of newspaper and magazine articles described the benefits of running, and many more books about running were published.   Michael Takaha

See also **Cross-country; Jogging; Marathon; Physical fitness**.

Runnymede, *RUHN ih MEED,* is a meadow in England on the south bank of the River Thames, about 36 miles (58 kilometers) southwest of London. At this site in June 1215, the barons of England forced King John to approve Magna Carta, a document that limited the powers of the king.

A monument to Magna Carta was built at Runnymede in 1957. In 1965, a memorial to United States President John F. Kennedy was dedicated there.

Emily Zack Tabuteau

See also **Magna Carta**.

Runyon, Damon (1884-1946), was an American short-story writer and journalist. His best-known stories deal with colorful gamblers, chorus girls, and various characters who live on the fringes of the criminal world in the Broadway district of New York City. Runyon wrote these stories in a distinctive style that was noted for its use of wisecracks and slang. The popular musical comedy *Guys and Dolls* (1950) is based on the Runyon tale "The Idylls of Sarah Brown" and on characters from other Runyon stories.

Runyon's full name was Alfred Damon Runyon. He was born in Manhattan, Kansas. In 1911, he began working as a sports reporter for the *New York American*. Runyon soon became the highest paid sportswriter of his time. He based many stories on his experiences in the sports world. Throughout his newspaper career, Runyon wrote short stories for magazines. These stories were published in a number of collections, beginning with *Guys and Dolls* (1931).   Arthur M. Saltzman

Rupee, *roo PEE,* is the chief monetary unit of India and the basic unit in India's decimal currency system. It is divided into 100 smaller units called *paise*. Paise circulate

WORLD BOOK photo by James Simek

A rupee coin of India pictures Jawaharlal Nehru, India's first prime minister, *left.* The image of three lions on the other side, *right,* is India's national emblem.

as nickel, copper-nickel, or bronze coins. Ten million rupees, or 100 *lacs,* are called a *crore.* The monetary systems of Mauritius, Nepal, Pakistan, and Sri Lanka are also based on rupees. But all of these rupees have different monetary values.   Burton H. Hobson

Rupert's Land. See Canada, History of (Growth of the Dominion [1863-1913]).

Rupp, Adolph (1901-1977), was one of the top college basketball coaches in the United States. Rupp coached the University of Kentucky basketball team to 876 victories, a college record until it was broken by Dean Smith in 1997. Under Rupp, Kentucky won the National Collegiate Athletic Association (NCAA) championship in 1948, 1949, 1951, and 1958. His Kentucky teams also won 27 Southeastern Conference championships. Rupp became coach at Kentucky in 1930 and retired in 1972. That same year, he became president of the Memphis Tams of the American Basketball Association.

Adolph Frederick Rupp was born in Halstead, Kansas. He played guard on the University of Kansas basketball team from 1921 to 1923. Rupp's coach at Kansas was Forrest C. (Phog) Allen. Allen ranked as the college coach with the most victories until 1967, when Kentucky won its 772nd game under Rupp.   Bob Logan

Rupture. See Hernia.

Rural delivery is a service that provides mail delivery to rural and suburban communities throughout the United States. Rural carriers place letters and packages into boxes, most of which stand along curbs. Each carrier has an assigned delivery route. The carriers use their own automobiles or U.S. Postal Service vehicles to deliver mail, and they travel about $2\frac{1}{2}$ million miles (4 million kilometers) daily.

Before 1896, there was no rural delivery system in the country. Farmers' organizations, especially the National Grange, were active in getting the United States Congress to provide money for free delivery of mail to rural areas. In 1896, the first rural deliveries were made in West Virginia. The system was called Rural Free Delivery (R.F.D.). The number of delivery routes increased during the early 1900's. In 1917, the service was extended to most rural areas.

The development of the rural delivery system was important to the development of farm areas. For the first time, the farmer could receive the newspaper daily by mail. The system led to parcel-post service and the development of great mail-order firms.

Critically reviewed by the United States Postal Service

See also **Post office** (picture: Rural free delivery).

Rural Electrification Administration (REA) was an agency of the United States Department of Agriculture from 1935 to 1994. It made insured loans and loan guarantees to rural electric and telephone cooperatives and companies in 47 states and many U.S. territories. The loans financed the construction, operation, and improvement of electric and telephone service. The agency also provided its borrowers with engineering and management assistance. In addition, the REA lent money to its borrowers for them to invest in economic development projects in their communities. An administrator appointed by the president with the approval of the U.S. Senate headed the REA.

Electric program. When the REA was established in 1935, about 10 percent of the farms in the United States had electricity. By the early 1990's, 99 percent of all U.S. farms had electric service, and REA-financed systems served about half of them. About 95 percent of the REA's electric loans were made to *cooperatives* (independent, private, nonprofit organizations). Other borrowers included public power districts and other public bodies.

Telephone program. When the telephone program began in 1949, about 35 percent of all farms in the United States had telephone service. By the early 1990's, more than 95 percent of the nation's farms had telephones. About 75 percent of the borrowers in the telephone program were commercial telephone companies. Almost all the rest were cooperatives. Borrowers received insured loans and loan guarantees as well as supplemental loans from the Rural Telephone Bank, which was established in 1971.

Rural development program. Beginning in 1989, the REA was authorized by Congress to make rural development loans. In most cases, the rural electric and telephone utilities receiving the loans made these funds available to businesses or other organizations to promote economic development and create jobs. The loans were interest-free, and most of them ran for 10 years.

History. President Franklin D. Roosevelt established the REA in 1935 as an emergency relief program. The Rural Electrification Act of 1936 made the REA a provider of loans for rural electrification. In 1949, the organization was authorized to make loans to improve and extend telephone service in rural areas. It was authorized to guarantee the loans of other organizations in 1973. In 1994, the agency was replaced by the Rural Utilities Service. The new service became responsible for providing funds for the development of water and waste-disposal systems in rural areas.

Critically reviewed by the Department of Agriculture

Rural life. See Farm and farming.

Rush is the common name for a group of grasslike plants that generally grow in marshes and meadows, and sometimes in standing water. The true rushes belong to one family. They have round stems with three rows of leaves, and their tiny flowers are greenish or brown. The small seed pod contains many dustlike brown seeds. The *slender rush* is a wiry, dark-green plant that often grows on damp paths and lawns. Most other species grow in marshes or damp meadows. Rushes are used to weave baskets, mats, and chair seats. At one time, the pith of the stems was used for wicks in candles called *rushlights.* Various plants called rushes are not true rushes. *Scouring rushes,* also called *horsetails,* are related to the ferns (see **Horsetail**). *Bulrushes* are actually sedges (see **Bulrush**). David A. Francko

Scientific classification. Rushes belong to the rush family, Juncaceae. The slender rush is *Juncus tenuis.*

Rush, Benjamin (1745-1813), was an American physician and a prominent figure in the public life of his time. He was the most influential physician in the United States, but his ideas were controversial. His beliefs in bloodletting and in purging with calomel were extreme even for his day. But his efforts to improve the treatment of the mentally ill were advanced and humane.

Rush was born in Byberry, Pennsylvania, near Philadelphia. He graduated from the College of New Jersey (now Princeton University) at the age of 15. In 1768, he received his degree in medicine from the University

of Edinburgh. Later, he practiced in Philadelphia and served as professor of chemistry and medicine at the medical college there. In 1783, Rush joined the Pennsylvania Hospital, and became interested in social reform. In 1786, he opened the first free clinic in the U.S.

Rush believed strongly in the republican form of government. He helped found the first American antislavery society, served as a member of the Continental Congress, and signed the Declaration of Independence.

During the Revolutionary War in America, Rush served as surgeon general in the Continental Army. With James Wilson, he led Pennsylvania to *ratify* (approve) the federal Constitution. He also helped frame the Pennsylvania state constitution. He served as treasurer of the U.S. Mint from 1797 to 1813. Matthew Ramsey

Rush-Bagot Agreement. See Monroe, James (Diplomacy).

Rushdie, *RUHSH dee* or *ROOSH dee,* **Salman,** *SAHL man* (1947-), is a noted Indian-born novelist. Rushdie has gained praise for his skill as a storyteller and for his imaginative style, which often features fantasy and high-spirited humor. His major themes include homelessness, exile, and the redefinition of identity.

Rushdie became the center of an international controversy with the publication in 1988 of *The Satanic Verses.* The novel plays upon the legend that Satan inserted certain verses into the revelation of the Quran, the sacred book of Islam. The prophet Muhammad later rejected the verses after an angel revealed they were fake. Many Islamic leaders denounced the novel as blasphemy. In 1989, Iran's spiritual leader, Ayatollah Ruhollah Khomeini, pronounced a *fatwah* (death sentence) on Rushdie. Fearing assassination, the writer went into hiding.

Rushdie first won literary recognition with *Midnight's Children* (1981), his second novel. It is a panoramic account of the history of India since the country's independence from Britain in 1947. In the novel, actual historical figures mingle with deities and bizarre fictional human characters. The novel is an example of *magic realism,* a narrative style that combines detailed realism with grotesque and fantastic elements to achieve a dreamlike quality. *Shame* (1983), Rushdie's next novel, is set in an imaginary country that resembles Pakistan. It shuttles between memory and prophecy and between the past and the future to demonstrate how the forces of history and culture can distort human relationships.

Rushdie wrote most of his books in hiding during the 1990's. They included the short story collection *East, West* (1994) and the novels *Haroun and the Sea of Stories* (1990) and *The Moor's Last Sigh* (1995). In 1998, the Iranian government announced it would no longer support the death sentence. Rushdie then came out of hiding. His long novel *The Ground Beneath Her Feet* was published in 1999.

Ahmed Salman Rushdie was born in Bombay (now Mumbai). Since 1961, he has lived mainly in England. Ranjit Hoskote

Rushmore, Mount. See Mount Rushmore National Memorial.

Rusk, Dean (1909-1994), served as United States secretary of state from 1961 to 1969 under Presidents John F. Kennedy and Lyndon B. Johnson. As secretary of state, he became a leading spokesman for the Johnson Administration's Vietnam War policy.

Rusk was born David Dean Rusk in Cherokee County, Georgia. He graduated from Davidson College in North Carolina in 1931 and studied at Oxford University as a Rhodes scholar in 1933 and 1934. In 1934, he became a political science professor at Mills College in California. He was made dean of the faculty at Mills in 1938.

Rusk joined the Department of State in 1946 and served as director of its office of United Nations affairs from 1947 to 1949. During these years, he helped bring the Marshall Plan and the North Atlantic Treaty Organization (NATO) into being. From 1950 to 1952, during the Korean War, Rusk served as assistant secretary of state for far eastern affairs. From 1952 to 1960, he was president of the Rockefeller Foundation. Rusk was made a "distinguished fellow" by the foundation in 1969. In 1970, he became a law professor at the University of Georgia.

James I. Lengle

Ruskin, John (1819-1900), was probably the most influential English critic of the 1800's. His many writings on art, literature, and social issues helped form the tastes of Victorian England.

Ruskin was born in London. While a student at Oxford University, he became a strong supporter of the British artist J. M. W. Turner, whose paintings had aroused much controversy. Ruskin's first book, *Modern Painters I* (1843), defended Turner's style (see **Turner, J. M. W.**). Ruskin's other works on art and architecture include four more volumes of *Modern Painters* (1846-1860), *The Seven Lamps of Architecture* (1849), and *The Stones of Venice* (three volumes, 1851-1853).

Ruskin believed that education, morality, and healthy social conditions were needed to produce good art. As a result, he concerned himself with social and economic issues. In lectures, essays, and books, Ruskin questioned the operations and motives of the free enterprise system. He attacked the quality of mass-produced products and encouraged workers to express their individuality. Ruskin had little political effect on his own time, but his ideas later influenced many British socialists, such writers as D. H. Lawrence and Leo Tolstoy, and the Hindu spiritual leader Mohandas Gandhi.

Ruskin's writings on social issues include four essays, published as *Unto This Last* (1862), and *Fors Clavigera,* a series of letters to British workers published from 1871 to 1884. In his last years, Ruskin's last important work was an unfinished autobiography, *Praeterita,* written from 1885 to 1889. K. K. Collins

See also **Whistler, James Abbott McNeill.**

Russell, Bertrand (1872-1970), was a British philosopher and mathematician. Russell ranks among the greatest philosophers of the 1900's. He has also been called the most important *logician* (expert in logic) since the ancient Greek philosopher Aristotle.

Russell made his most important contributions in formal logic and the theory of knowledge. However, his influence extends far beyond these fields. Russell developed a prose style of extraordinary clarity, wit, and passion. He received the 1950 Nobel Prize for literature.

Russell became an influential and controversial figure on social, political, and educational issues. He was an outspoken pacifist and advocated extremely liberal attitudes toward sex, marriage, and methods of education. Russell was a critic of World War I (1914-1918). He was imprisoned in 1918 for statements considered harmful

to British-American relations, and again in 1961 for "incitement to civil disobedience" in a campaign for nuclear disarmament.

Russell made his major contributions to philosophy and mathematics in the early 1900's. He wanted to derive all of mathematics from logic, thus putting it on a sure foundation. Russell collaborated with the English mathematician and philosopher Alfred North Whitehead on the monumental three-volume *Principia Mathematica* (1910-1913). This work attempts to show that all pure mathematics follows from premises that are strictly logical and uses only those concepts that can be defined in purely logical terms. Although Russell's ideas have been refined and corrected by later mathematicians, all modern work in logic and the foundations of mathematics begins with his ideas.

Russell made important contributions to the history of philosophy in such books as *A Critical Exposition of the Philosophy of Leibniz* (1900) and *A History of Western Philosophy* (1945). He expressed his social and political ideas in a number of works, including *German Social Democracy* (1896), *Roads to Freedom* (1918), *Power* (1938), and *Authority and the Individual* (1949). Russell also influenced morality and education in essays and such books as *Why I Am Not a Christian* (1927), *Marriage and Morals* (1929), and *The Conquest of Happiness* (1930). Russell wrote many accounts of his life, including a three-volume autobiography (1967 to 1969).

Russell was born near Trellek, Wales, north of Chepstow. His full name was Bertrand Arthur William Russell. He was a member of an old and noble family. In 1931, he inherited the family title and became Earl Russell. See also **Russell family.** W. W. Bartley III

Additional resources

Clark, Ronald W. *The Life of Bertrand Russell.* 1976. Reprint. Da Capo, 1990.
Moorehead, Caroline. *Bertrand Russell.* Viking, 1992.

Russell, Bill (1934-   ), became one of the finest defensive players in basketball history. A 6-foot 10-inch (208-centimeter) center for the Boston Celtics, Russell became a master at blocking shots and rebounding. He ranks second only to Wilt Chamberlain among the leading rebounders in the history of the National Basketball Association (NBA).

William Felton Russell was born in Monroe, Louisiana. He helped lead the University of San Francisco to win 57 of 58 games during the 1954-1955 and 1955-1956 seasons. Russell joined the Celtics in the 1956-1957 season and helped lead the team to 11 NBA championships in the 13 years he played.

Russell served as player-coach of the Celtics from 1966 to 1969. He was the first African American head coach in major league professional sports. Russell retired as a player in 1969. He served as general manager and coach of the Seattle SuperSonics of the NBA from 1973 to 1977. He coached the Sacramento Kings of the NBA from 1987 to 1988, and served as a vice president for the team in 1988 and 1989. Russell was a TV sports commentator between coaching assignments. He discussed his life and his views on basketball in *Go Up for Glory* (1970) and *Second Wind* (1979). Bob Logan

Russell, Charles Marion (1864-1926), was an American painter and sculptor famous for his scenes of cowboys and life in the West. Russell's work shows action and great detail, with authentic backgrounds and settings. Russell taught himself art. He worked almost equally well with pen-and-ink, oil paint or water color, and clay. He also wrote stories about the West, which were published with his illustrations.

Russell was born in St. Louis, Missouri. As a child, he loved to sketch and model animals, cowboys, and Indians. Because of his interest in the West, his parents let him visit the Montana Territory when he was 16 years old. He quickly made Montana his permanent home. Russell earned his living as a hunter for 2 years and then worked as a cowboy for about 10 years. He lived with the Blood Indians in Canada one winter. His experiences provided dramatic, often humorous material for his paintings and sculptures.

In 1893, Russell gave up cowboy living so that he could paint and sculpt full-time. Three years later, he married Nancy Cooper, who encouraged his artistic career. Russell's statue represents Montana in Statuary Hall in the U.S. Capitol.   Sarah E. Boehme

See also **Cowboy** (picture); **Dodge City** (picture).

Russell, George William (1867-1935), was an Irish poet, painter, and journalist. He was a leader of the Irish Literary Revival, a movement that began in the late 1800's. This movement encouraged the creation of works based exclusively on Irish culture.

Russell's mystical poetry and paintings reflect his deep love of nature. He developed a personal religion that sought spiritual truths in nature. Russell was born in Lurgan, in what is now Northern Ireland. He spent most of his adult life as a journalist in Dublin. He wrote under the pen name "AE," which he took from a printer's error on one of his essays. Russell was an authority on farming and devoted much time to improving Irish agriculture.   James MacKillop

Russell, Henry Norris (1877-1957), an American astronomer, influenced the growth of theoretical astrophysics in the United States. Around 1910, he and the Danish astronomer Ejnar Hertzsprung independently developed a diagram that relates the brightness of a star to its surface temperature. Research based on this diagram has helped scientists interpret the physical nature and evolution of stars. In 1929, Russell presented strong evidence that hydrogen is by far the most abundant chemical element in the atmosphere of stars.

Russell was born in Oyster Bay, New York. From 1912 to 1947, he was director of the observatory at Princeton University.   Karl Hufbauer

See also **Star** (The Hertzsprung-Russell diagram [diagram]).

Russell, Lord John (1792-1878), served as prime minister of Britain from 1846 to 1852 and in 1865 and 1866. But he is probably more famous for his earlier leadership of the British reform movement.

Russell was born in London, a son of the sixth Duke of Bedford. His family had been active in the Whig Party and was known for its support of civil rights. Russell was elected to the British House of Commons in 1813. In 1828, he made a motion that led to the repeal of the Test acts and the Corporation Act. As a result, Protestants who did not belong to the Church of England were allowed to participate fully in English politics. Russell also helped write and pass the Reform Act of 1832, which

gave more middle-class men the right to vote. He became Earl Russell in 1861.   Richard W. Davis

See also **United Kingdom** (The era of reform).

Russell, Lillian (1861-1922), an American actress and singer, was the ideal of feminine beauty in the late 1800's. She made her debut in 1879 in the chorus in *H.M.S. Pinafore*. She became famous in the 1880's when she was billed at Tony Pastor's Theatre in New York City as "the beautiful English ballad singer." Her costumes, especially her hats, became the talk of the town. Beginning in 1899, she performed for five seasons with the musical comedy troupe of Weber and Fields. Russell was born in Clinton, Iowa. Her real name was Helen Louise Leonard.   Don B. Wilmeth

Brown Bros.

Lillian Russell

Russell, Richard Brevard (1897-1971), a Georgia Democrat, became one of the most influential people in the United States Senate. Russell served as chairman of the Senate Armed Services Committee in 1951 and 1952 and again from 1955 until 1969, when he became chairman of the Senate Appropriations Committee. In 1969, he also was elected president *pro tempore* of the Senate. As chairman of the appropriations group, Russell had great influence on the nation's spending, especially in gaining Senate approval of military budgets. He also opposed civil rights legislation.

Russell was born in Winder, Georgia, and graduated from the University of Georgia School of Law. He was elected to the Georgia House of Representatives in 1920 and became Speaker of the House in 1927. In 1930, he was elected governor of Georgia. In 1932, he was elected to complete the term of U.S. Senator William J. Harris, who had died. Russell served in the Senate from 1933 until his death. He was an unsuccessful candidate for the Democratic presidential nomination in 1948 and 1952.   Kenneth Coleman

Russell family became one of England's most famous families. Its best-known members included Bertrand Russell, a mathematician and philosopher, and Lord John Russell, a prime minister (see **Russell, Bertrand; Russell, Lord John**). Several other members became prominent in politics.

John Russell (1486?-1555) distinguished himself as a soldier and diplomat during the reign of King Henry VIII. In 1549, he was made the first Earl of Bedford. Francis Russell (1593-1641) played an important part in Parliament's struggle to limit the power of King Charles I. William Russell (1613-1700) switched his support from Parliament to Charles I and then back to Parliament during the English Civil War in the 1640's.

Hastings William Sackville Russell (1888-1953) was a pacifist. He defended some of Adolf Hitler's policies during World War II (1939-1945). John Robert Russell (1917-   ) was a journalist and farmer in South Africa. He made his land at Woburn a public park in 1955.   Richard W. Davis

Red Square in Moscow, Russia's capital and largest city, is the site of such famous landmarks as St. Basil's Cathedral, *left,* V. I. Lenin's tomb, *center,* and the Kremlin, *right.* The large plaza took its name in Russian from an old word meaning both *beautiful* and *red.*

Russia

Russia is the world's largest country in area. It is almost twice as big as Canada, the second largest country. From 1922 until 1991, Russia was the most important republic in the Soviet Union, which was the most powerful Communist country in the world. The Soviet Union broke apart in 1991. After the breakup, Russia set up new political, legal, and economic systems.

Russia extends from the Arctic Ocean south to the Black Sea and from the Baltic Sea east to the Pacific Ocean. It covers much of the continents of Europe and Asia. Moscow is the capital and largest city of Russia. St. Petersburg, on the coast of the Baltic Sea, is Russia's chief seaport.

Most of Russia's people are ethnic Russians—that is, descendants of an early Slavic people called the Russians. More than 100 minority nationalities also live in

Russia. Approximately three-fourths of the people make their homes in urban areas. Russian cities have better schools and health-care facilities than the rural areas do. However, the cities suffer from such urban problems as overcrowding, crime, and environmental pollution.

Russia has abundant natural resources, including vast deposits of petroleum, natural gas, coal, and iron ore. Many of these reserves, however, lie far from settled areas. Russia's harsh, cold climate makes it difficult to take advantage of many of the country's valuable resources.

Russia traces its history back to a state that emerged in Europe among the East Slavs during the 800's. Over time, large amounts of territory and many different peoples came under Russian rule. For hundreds of years, *czars* (emperors) and empresses ruled Russia. They had almost complete control over most aspects of Russian life. Under these rulers, the country's economic development lagged behind the rapid industrial progress that began in Western Europe in the 1700's. Most of the people were poor, uneducated peasants.

Russia made many great contributions to the arts dur-

Donald J. Raleigh, the contributor of this article, is Pardue Professor of History at the University of North Carolina at Chapel Hill.

Fields of wheat spread over vast areas of Russian farmland. Russia ranks as one of the world's major producers of wheat and other grains.

Scene from a Kirov Ballet production of *Don Quixote* (ITAR-Tass from Sovfoto)

Russian ballet troupes perform throughout the world. They are famous for their skill and beauty.

Snow covers more than half of Russia for six months of the year. This village is near the city of Irkutsk in Siberia.

ing the 1800's. Such authors as Anton Chekhov, Fyodor Dostoevsky, and Leo Tolstoy wrote masterpieces of literature. Russian composers, including Modest Mussorgsky, Nikolai Rimsky-Korsakov, and Peter Ilich Tchaikovsky, created music of lasting greatness. Russians also made valuable artistic contributions in the fields of architecture, ballet, and painting.

Opposition to the czars' absolute power increased during the late 1800's and the early 1900's. Revolutionaries overthrew the Russian government in 1917. The next year, Russia became the Russian Soviet Federative Socialist Republic (R.S.F.S.R.).

In 1922, the R.S.F.S.R. and three other republics established a new nation called the Union of Soviet Socialist Republics (U.S.S.R.), also known as the Soviet Union. The R.S.F.S.R. became the largest and most influential republic of the Soviet Union, which included 15 republics by

1956. In 1991, Communist rule in the Soviet Union collapsed, and the country broke apart. Russia and most of the other republics formed a new, loose federation called the Commonwealth of Independent States.

After the breakup of the Soviet Union, Russia entered a transitional period. The Communist leaders of the Soviet Union had controlled all aspects of the country's economy and government. Russia's new national government worked to move the country from a state-controlled economy to one based on private enterprise. The government also began to establish new political and legal systems in Russia.

This article deals with Russia from its early history to the present. For more detailed information about the history of Russia between 1922 and 1991—when it was part of the Soviet Union—see **Union of Soviet Socialist Republics.**

Russia in brief

General information

Capital: Moscow.
Official language: Russian.
Official names: *Rossiya* (Russia) or *Rossiyskaya Federatsiya* (Russian Federation).
Largest cities (1990 official estimates)
Moscow   8,801,000
St. Petersburg 4,468,000

The Russian flag has stripes of white, blue, and red. It was adopted in 1991. The Russian Empire used the flag from 1699 to 1918.

The state seal was adopted in 1993. It includes symbols of the Russian Empire.

Land and climate

Land: Russia is the world's largest country in area. It covers a large part of both Europe and Asia. It has coastlines on the Arctic Ocean, Baltic Sea, Black Sea, Caspian Sea, and Pacific Ocean. Russia borders eight European countries, three Asian countries, and three countries with lands in both Europe and Asia. Much of the west is a large plain. The Ural Mountains separate Europe and Asia. Siberia, east of the Urals, has low western plains, a central plateau, and a mountainous wilderness in the east. Major Russian rivers include the Lena in Asia and the Volga in Europe. Lake Baikal in Siberia is the world's deepest lake.
Area: 6,592,850 sq. mi. (17,075,400 km²). *Greatest distances*—east-west, 6,000 mi. (9,650 km); north-south, 2,800 mi. (4,500 km).
Elevation: *Highest*—Mount Elbrus, 18,510 ft. (5,642 m). *Lowest*—coast of Caspian Sea, 92 ft. (28 m) below sea level.
Climate: Most of Russia has long, bitterly cold winters and mild to warm—but short—summers. In northeastern Siberia, the country's coldest area, January temperatures average below –50 °F (–46 °C). Rainfall is moderate in most of Russia. Snow covers more than half of the country during six months of the year.

WORLD BOOK map

Government

Form of government: Republic.
Head of state: President.
Head of government: Prime minister.
Legislature: Russia's parliament is called the Federal Assembly. It consists of two houses—the 450-member State Duma and the 178-member Federation Council.
Executive: The president is the chief executive and most powerful official.
Judiciary: Highest court is the Constitutional Court.
Political subdivisions: 49 *oblasts* (regions), 6 *krais* (territories), 21 republics, 10 autonomous areas, 1 autonomous region. Moscow and St. Petersburg each have special region status. Many of the political subdivisions are divided into *raions* (districts).

People

Population: *2000 estimate*—145,552,000. *1989 census*—147,021,869.
Population density: 22 persons per sq. mi. (9 per km²).
Distribution: 73 percent urban, 27 percent rural.
Major ethnic/national groups: About 83 percent Russian. Smaller groups include Tatars (or Tartars), Ukrainians, Chuvash, Bashkirs, Belarusians, Mordvins, Chechen, Germans, Udmurts, Mari, Kazakhs, Avars, Jews, and Armenians.
Major religions: The Russian Orthodox Church is the largest religious group. Other religious groups include Muslims, Protestants, Roman Catholics, and Jews.

Population trend

Year	Population
1926	93,459,000
1939	109,277,000
1959	117,534,000
1970	130,090,000
1979	137,552,000
1989	147,022,000

Economy

Chief products: *Agriculture*—barley, cattle, flax, fruits, hogs, oats, potatoes, rye, sheep, sugar beets, sunflowers, wheat. *Fishing*—cod, haddock, herring, salmon. *Manufacturing*—chemicals, construction materials, electrical equipment, iron and steel, lumber, machinery, paper. *Mining*—coal, iron ore, manganese, natural gas, nickel, petroleum, platinum-group metals.
Money: *Basic unit*—ruble.
International trade: *Major exports*—chemicals, machinery, mined products, natural gas, paper products, petroleum, wood products. *Major imports*—consumer goods, food and beverages, industrial equipment, machinery. *Major trading partners*—Ukraine, Belarus, Kazakhstan, Germany, Uzbekistan, Lithuania, Georgia, Italy.

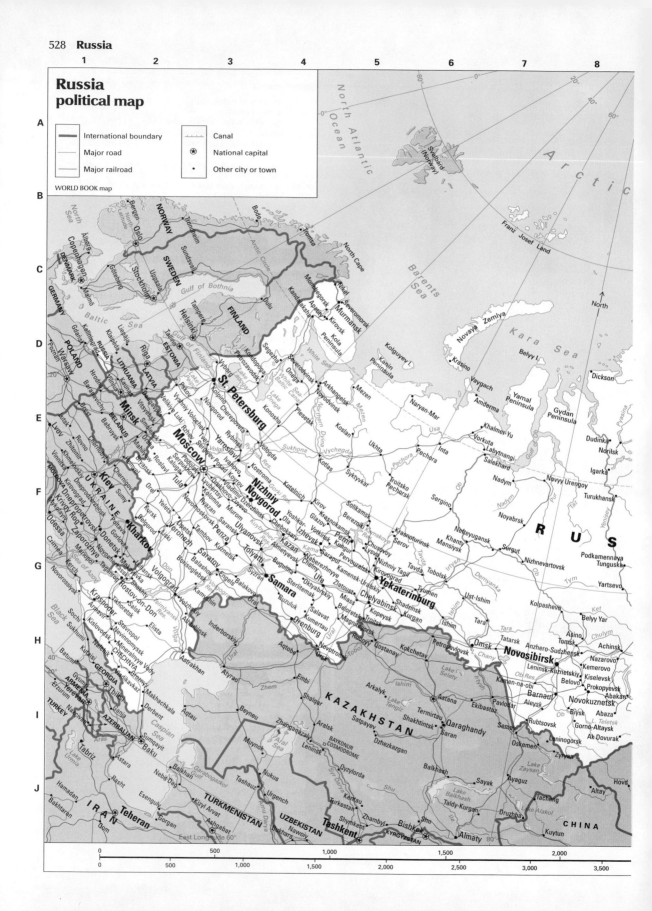

Russia
political map

International boundary
Major road
Major railroad
Canal
National capital
Other city or town

WORLD BOOK map

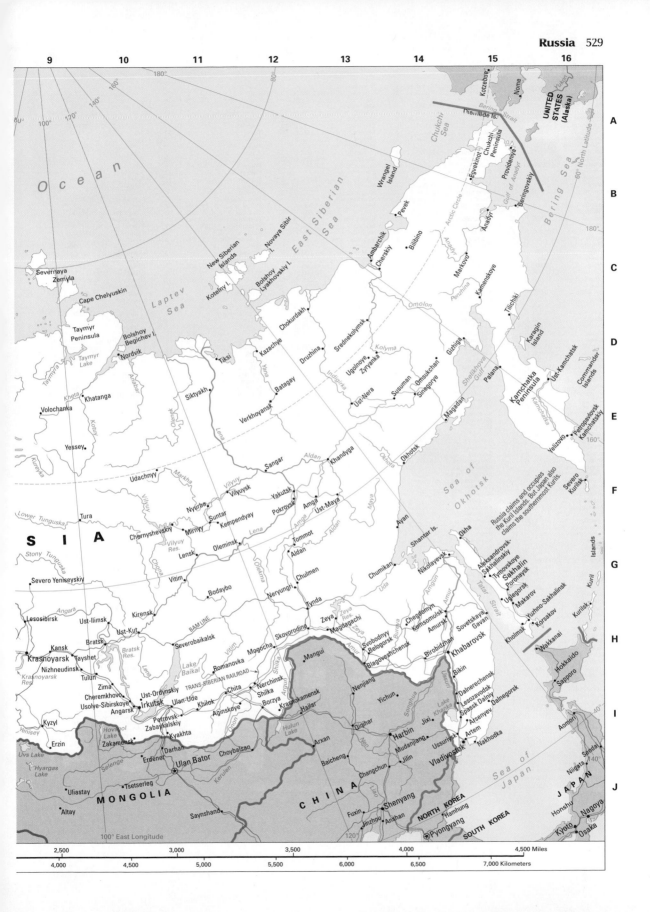

9   10   11   12   13   14   15   16

A B C D E F G H I J

Ocean

Laptev Sea

East Siberian Sea

Chukchi Sea

Bering Sea

UNITED STATES (Alaska)

Severnaya Zemlya

Cape Chelyuskin

Taymyr Peninsula

Taymyr Lake

Nordvik

Bolshoy Begichev I.

Khatanga

Volochanka

Yessey

New Siberian Islands

Novaya Sibir I.

Koteľny I.

Bolshoy Lyakhovskiy I.

Tiksi

Kazachye

Chokurdakh

Srednekolymsk

Druzhina

Chersky

Ambarchik

Bilibino

Pevek

Wrangel Island

Kotzebue

Nome

Diomede Is.

Egvekinot

Chukchi Peninsula

Providen
ya

Beringovskiy

Anadyr

Markovo

Kamenskoye

Tilichiki

Kanchin Island

Ust-Kamchatsk

Commander Islands

Petropavlovsk-Kamchatsky

Yelizovo

Kamchatka Peninsula

Severo-Kuriľsk

Palana

Gizhiga

Magadan

Okhotsk

Ayan

Shantar Is.

Sea of Okhotsk

Russia claims and occupies the Kuril Islands. But Japan also claims the southernmost Kurils.

Nikolayevsk

Okha

Aleksandrovsk-Sakhalinsk

Tymovskoye

Poronaysk

Uglegorsk

Makarov

Yuzhno-Sakhalinsk

Korsakov

Kholmsk

Kuril Islands

Sakhalin

Tatar Strait

Sovetskaya Gavan

Wakkanai

HOKKAIDO

Sapporo

JAPAN

Aomori

Sea of Japan

Volochanka

Udachnyy

Tura

Severo Yeniseyskiy

Lesosibirsk

Ust-Ilimsk

Bratsk

Tayshet

Kansk

Krasnoyarsk

Nizhneudinsk

Tulun

Zima

Cheremkhovo

Usolye-Sibirskoye

Angarsk

Irkutsk

Ust-Ordynskiy

Ulan-Ude

Petrovsk-Zabaykalskiy

Kyakhta

Zakamensk

Kyzyl

Erzin

Uliastay

Altay

Saynshand

Tsetserleg

Ulan Bator

Erdenet

Darhan

Choybalsan

MONGOLIA

CHINA

Fuxin

Jinzhou

Anshan

Shenyang

Pyongyang

NORTH KOREA

Hamhung

SOUTH KOREA

Changchun

Jilin

Baicheng

Harbin

Mudanjiang

Arxan

Nenjiang

Yichun

Qiqihar

Jixi

Ussuriysk

Vladivostok

Nakhodka

Dalnegorsk

Arsenyev

Artem

Spassk Dalniy

Lesozavodsk

Dalnerechensk

Bikin

Khabarovsk

Birobidzhan

Blagoveshchensk

Belogorsk

Svobodnyy

Komsomolsk

Amursk

Chegdomyn

Magdagachi

Zeya

Tynda

Neryungri

Chumikan

Chulmen

Tommot

Aldan

Olekminsk

Vitim

Bodaybo

Kirensk

Ust-Kut

Severobaikalsk

Bratsk Res.

Lake Baikal

Romanovka

Mogocha

Chita

Nerchinsk

Shilka

Borzya

Aginskoye

Khilok

Krasnokamensk

Hailar

Mangui

Skovorodino

TRANS-SIBERIAN RAILROAD

BAM LINE

Vilyuy Res.

Chernyshevskiy

Mirnyy

Nyurba

Vilyuysk

Suntar

Kempendyay

Lensk

Pokrovsk

Yakutsk

Amga

Ust-Maya

Khandyga

Ust-Nera

Susuman

Omsukchan

Sinegorye

Zyryanka

Ugolnoye

Verkhoyansk

Batagay

Sangar

S I A

Yuryung

2,500   3,000   3,500   4,000   4,500 Miles

4,000   4,500   5,000   5,500   6,000   6,500   7,000 Kilometers

Russia map index

Cities and towns

Abakan ...157,000..I 8
Abaza ...I 8
Achinsk ...122,000..H 8
Aginskoye ...I 11
Ak Dovurak ...I 8
Aldan ...G 12
Aleksandrovsk
  Sakhalinskiy ...G 15
Aleksin* ...70,000..F 2
Aleysk ...I 7
Almetyevsk ...130,000..G 4
Ambarchik ...C 13
Amderma ...E 6
Amga ...F 13
Amursk ...H 15
Anadyr ...B 15
Andropov, see
  Rybinsk
Angarsk ...267,000..I 10
Anzhero-
  Sudzhensk ...108,000..H 8
Apatity ...74,000..I 4
Arkhangelsk ...419,000..D 4
Armavir ...162,000..H 1
Arsenyev ...I 15
Artem ...71,000..I 15
Arzamas* ...111,000..F 3
Asbest* ...81,000..G 5
Asino ...H 8
Astrakhan ...510,000..H 2
Ayan ...F 14
Azov* ...79,000..I 1
Balakovo ...200,000..G 3
Balashikha* ...137,000..F 3
Balashov ...97,000..G 3
Barnaul ...603,000..I 7
Batagay ...E 12
Bataysk* ...95,000..G 1
Belgorod ...306,000..F 2
Beloretsk ...74,000..G 5
Belovo ...116,000..I 8
Belyy Yar ...H 8
Berdsk* ...74,000..H 7
Berezniki ...201,000..F 5
Beringovskiy ...B 15
Bikin ...I 15
Bilibino ...C 14
Birobidzhan ...77,000..H 14
Biysk ...234,000..I 8
Blagove-
  shchensk ...208,000..H 13
Bodaybo ...G 11
Borisoglebsk ...G 2
Borzya ...I 12
Bratsk ...258,000..H 10
Brezhnev, see
  Naberezhnyye
  Chelny
Bryansk ...456,000..F 2
Bugulma ...85,000..G 4
Buzuluk ...79,000..G 4
Chapayevsk* ...86,000..G 4
Chay-
  kovskiy* ...76,000..G 4
Cheboksary ...429,000..F 4
Chegdomyn ...H 14
Chelya-
  binsk ...1,148,000..G 5
Cherem-
  khovo ...73,000..I 10
Chere-
  povets ...313,000..E 3
Cherkessk* ...115,000..H 1
Chernogorsk* ...77,000..I 9
Cherskiy ...C 13
Chita ...372,000..I 11
Chokurdakh ...D 12
Chulmen ...G 12
Chumikan ...G 14
Chusovoy ...G 5
Dalnegorsk ...I 15
Dalnerechensk ...I 15
Derbent ...78,000..I 2
Dickson ...D 8
Dimitrov-
  grad* ...133,000..G 4
Druzhina ...D 13
Dudinka ...E 8
Dzerzhinsk ...286,000..F 3
Egvekinot ...B 15
Elektrostal* ...153,000..F 3
Elista ...80,000..H 2
Engels ...183,000..G 3
Erzin ...I 9
Gatchina* ...78,000..D 3
Gizhiga ...D 15
Glazov ...105,000..F 4
Gorki, see
  Nizhniy Novgorod
Gorno-Altaysk ...I 8

Groznyy ...401,000..H 2
Gubkin* ...70,000..F 2
Gus-Khrust-
  alnyy* ...74,000..F 3
Igarka ...F 8
Inta ...E 6
Irkutsk ...635,000..I 10
Ishim ...H 6
Ivanovo ...482,000..F 3
Izhevsk
  (Ustinov) ...642,000..F 4
Kalinin, see
  Tver
Kaliningrad
  (Konigs-
  berg) ...406,000..D 1
Kaliningrad* ...161,000..F 3
Kaluga ...314,000..F 2
Kamen-na-
  Obi ...I 7
Kamenskoye ...C 15
Kamensk
  Shakh-
  tinskiy* ...75,000..G 2
Kamensk-
  Uralskiy ...208,000..G 5
Kamyshin ...123,000..G 3
Kandalaksha ...D 4
Kansk ...110,000..H 9
Kazachye ...D 12
Kazan ...1,103,000..G 4
Kemerovo ...521,000..H 8
Kempendyay ...F 11
Khabarovsk ...608,000..H 14
Khalmer-Yu ...E 6
Khandyga ...F 13
Khanty ...G 6
Khasavyurt* ...72,000..I 2
Khatanga ...E 9
Khilok ...I 11
Khimki* ...135,000..F 3
Kholmsk ...H 15
Kineshma* ...105,000..F 3
Kirensk ...H 10
Kirov ...487,000..F 4
Kirovo-
  Chepetsk* ...83,000..F /
Kirovograd ...G 5
Kirovsk ...D 4
Kiselevsk ...128,000..H 8
Kislovodsk ...116,000..H 1
Klin* ...94,000..E 3
Klintsy* ...71,000..F 2
Kolomna ...163,000..F 3
Kolpashevo ...H 8
Kolpino ...143,000..E 3
Komsomolsk ...318,000..H 14
Kondopoga ...D 3
Konigsberg, see
  Kaliningrad
Konosha ...E 4
Kopeysk ...134,000..G 5
Korsakov ...H 15
Koslan ...E 5
Kostroma ...280,000..F 3
Kotelnich ...F 4
Kotlas ...F 4
Kovrov ...161,000..F 3
Krasino ...D 6
Krasnodar ...627,000..G 1
Krasno-
  gorsk* ...86,000..F 15
Krasno-
  kamensk ...I 12
Krasnokamsk ...F 5
Krasnoturinsk ...F 5
Krasnoyarsk ...922,000..H 9
Kropotkin* ...73,000..G 2
Kumertau ...82,000..G 4
Kungur ...82,000..F 5
Kur ...430,000..F 2
Kurgan ...360,000..H 5
Kuybyshev,
  see Samara
Kuznetsk ...97,000..G 3
Kyakhta ...I 10
Kyzyl ...73,000..I 9
Labytnangi ...E 6
Leningrad, see
  St. Petersburg
Leninsk-
  Kuznetskiy ...134,000..H 8
Lensk ...G 11
Lesosibirsk ...H 9
Lesoza-
  vodsk ...I 15
Lipetsk ...455,000..F 2
Liski ...G 2
Lysva ...76,000..G 5
Lyubertsy ...165,000..F 3
Magadan ...154,000..E 14
Magdagachi ...H 13

Magnito-
  gorsk ...443,000..H 5
Makarov ...H 15
Makhach-
  kala ...327,000..I 2
Mansiysk ...G 5
Markovo ...C 15
Maykop* ...151,000..G 1
Mezen ...E 5
Mezhdure-
  chensk* ...107,000..F 5
Miass ...169,000..G 5
Michurinsk* ...109,000..F 3
Mineralnyye
  Vody ...72,000..H 2
Mirnyy ...F 11
Mogocha ...H 12
Monchegorsk ...C 4
Moscow ...8,801,000
  †8,967,000..F 3
Murmansk ...472,000..D 4
Murom ...125,000..F 3
Mytishchi* ...153,000..F 3
Naberezhnyye
  Chelny
  (Brezhnev) ...507,000..G 4
Nadym ...F 7
Nakhodka ...163,000..I 15
Nalchik ...237,000..H 1
Naryan-Mar ...E 5
Neftekamsk* ...109,000..G 4
Nefteyugansk ...72,000..G 7
Nerchinsk ...I 12
Neryungri ...G 12
Nevinno-
  myssk ...122,000..H 1
Nikel ...C 4
Nikolayevsk ...G 14
Nizhne-
  kamsk* ...193,000..G 4
Nizhneudinsk ...H 9
Nizhnevar-
  tovsk ...246,000..G 7
Nizhniy
  Novgorod
  (Gorki) ...1,443,000..F 3
Nizhniy
  Tagil ...440,000..G 5
Noginsk* ...123,000..F 3
Nordvik ...D 10
Norilsk ...173,000..E 8
Novgorod ...232,000..E 3
Novochebok-
  sarsk* ...117,000..G 3
Novocher-
  kassk ...188,000..G 2
Novokuyby-
  shevsk* ...114,000..G 3
Novokuz-
  netsk ...601,000..I 8
Novo-
  moskovsk ...F
Novo-
  rossiysk ...188,000..G 1
Novoshakh-
  tinsk* ...108,000..G 1
Novosi-
  birsk ...1,443,000..H 7
Novo-
  troitsk ...107,000..H 5
Novyy
  Urengoy ...F 7
Nyurba ...F 11
Obinsk* ...137,000..F 2
Odintsovo* ...127,000..F 2
Okha ...G 15
Okhotsk ...F 14
Oktya-
  brskiy* ...106,000..G 4
Oleminsk ...F 12
Omsk ...1,159,000..H 6
Omsukchan ...D 14
Onega ...D 4
Ordzhonikidze,
  see Vladikavkaz
Orekhovo-
  Zuyevo ...137,000..F 3
Orel ...342,000..F 2
Orenburg ...552,000..H 4
Orsk ...271,000..G 4
Palana ...D 15
Pavlovo* ...70,000..F 3
Pavlovskiy
  Posad* ...71,000..F 3
Pechora ...E 6
Penza ...548,000..G 3
Perm ...1,094,000..G 5
Pervo-
  maysk* ...76,000..F 3
Pervouralsk ...143,000..G 5
Petro-
  dvorets* ...77,000..D 3

Petropavlovsk-
  Kam-
  chatskiy ...271,000..E 16
Petrovsk
  Zabaykalskiy ...I 11
Petroza-
  vodsk ...274,000..D 3
Pevek ...B 14
Plesetsk ...E 4
Podka-
  mennaya
  Tunguska ...G 8
Podolsk ...209,000..F 3
Pokrovsk ...F 12
Poronaysk ...G 15
Prokop-
  yevsk ...274,000..I 8
Provideniya ...A 15
Pskov ...206,000..E 2
Pushkin* ...91,000..D 3
Pushkino* ...74,000..F 3
Pyatigorsk* ...130,000..H 1
Ramen-
  skoye* ...84,000..F 3
Romanovka ...H 11
Roslavl ...E 2
Rostov-on-
  Don ...1,025,000..G 1
Rubtsovsk ...172,000..I 7
Ryazan ...522,000..F 3
Rybinsk
  (Andro-
  pov) ...252,000..E 3
Rzhev ...70,000..E 2
St. Petersburg
  (Lenin-
  grad) ...4,468,000
  †5,020,000..D 3
Salavat ...151,000..H 4
Salekhard ...E 6
Salsk ...G 2
Samara
  (Kuyby-
  shev) ...1,258,000..G 4
Sangar ...F 12
Saransk ...316,000..F 3
Sarapul ...111,000..G 4
Saratov ...909,000..G 3
Segezha ...D 4
Sergino ...F 6
Sergiyev
  Posad
  (Zagorsk) ...115,000..E 3
Serov ...104,000..F 5
Serpukhov ...144,000..F 3
Severo-
  baikalsk ...H 11
Severo-
  dvinsk ...250,000..D 4
Severo
  Kurilsk ...F 16
Severomorsk ...D 4
Severo
  Yeniseyskiy ...G 9
Shadrinsk ...86,000..G 5
Shakh-
  tersk* ...71,000..H 15
Shakhty ...227,000..G 2
Shchekino* ...70,000..F 2
Shchelkovo* ...109,000..F 3
Shilka ...I 12
Shostka* ...84,000..E 2
Shuya* ...72,000..F 3
Siktyakh ...E 11
Sinegorye ...D 14
Skovarodino ...H 11
Smolensk ...346,000..F 2
Sochi ...339,000..H 1
Solikamsk ...110,000..F 5
Sovetskaya
  Gavan ...H 15
Spassk
  Dalniy ...I 15
Srednekolymsk ...D 13
Stalingrad,
  see Volgograd
Staryy
  Oskol* ...178,000..F 2
Stavropol ...324,000..H 1
Sterlitamak ...250,000..G 4
Stupino* ...72,000..F 3
Suntar ...F 11
Surgut ...256,000..G 7
Susuman ...E 14
Sverdlovsk, see
  Yekaterinburg
Svobodnyy ...H 13
Syktyvkar ...235,000..F 5
Syzran ...174,000..G 3
Taganrog ...293,000..G 1
Tambov ...307,000..F 3
Tara ...H 7

Tatarsk ...H 7
Tavda ...G 6
Tayshet ...H 9
Tikhoretsk ...G 1
Tiksi ...D 11
Tilichiki ...D 15
Tobolsk ...72,000..G 6
Tolyatti ...642,000..G 3
Tommot ...G 12
Tomsk ...506,000..H 8
Torey ...87,000..I 10
Troitsk ...90,000..H 5
Troitsko
  Pechorsk ...F 5
Tula ...543,000..F 2
Tulun ...H 10
Tura ...F 9
Turukhansk ...F 8
Tver
  (Kalinin) ...454,000..E 2
Tymoskoye ...G 15
Tynda ...H 12
Tyumen ...487,000..G 6
Udachnyy ...F 10
Ufa ...1,094,000..G 4
Uglegorsk ...G 15
Ugolnoye ...D 13
Ukhta ...111,000..E 5
Ulan-Ude ...359,000..I 11
Ulyanovsk ...638,000..G 3
Usolye-Sibir-
  skoye ...107,000..I 10
Ussuriysk ...159,000..I 14
Ust-
  Ilimsk ...93,000..H 10
Ustinov, see
  Izhevsk
Ust-Ishim ...G 6
Ust-Kamchatsk ...E 16
Ust-Kut ...H 10
Ust-Maya ...E 13
Ust-Nera ...E 13
Ust-
  Ordynskiy ...I 10
Velikiye
  Luki ...115,000..E 2
Verkhoyansk ...E 12
Vilyuysk ...F 11
Vitim ...G 11
Vladikavkaz
  (Ordzho-
  nikidze) ...303,000..H 2
Vladimir ...353,000..F 3
Vladivostok ...643,000..J 15
Volgodonsk* ...178,000..G 2
Volgograd
  (Stalin-
  grad) ...1,005,000..G 2
Volochanka ...E 9
Vologda ...286,000..E 3
Volzhskiy ...275,000..G 2
Vorkuta ...117,000..E 7
Voronezh ...895,000..F 2
Voskre-
  sensk* ...79,000..F 3
Votkinsk ...104,000..G 4
Vyborg ...79,000..D 3
Vyshniy
  Volochek ...71,000..E 3
Yakutsk ...191,000..F 12
Yaroslavl ...636,000..E 3
Yartsevo ...G 8
Yegoryevsk* ...73,000..F 3
Yekaterinburg
  (Sverd-
  lovsk) ...1,372,000..G 5
Yelets ...115,000..F 2
Yelizovo ...E 16
Yessentuki* ...82,000..H 1
Yeysk* ...75,000..G 1
Yoshkar-
  Ola ...246,000..F 4
Yurga* ...87,000..H 7
Yuzhno-Sakh-
  alinsk ...162,000..H 15
Zagorsk, see
  Sergiyev
  Posad
Zakamansk ...I 10
Zeleno-
  dolsk* ...88,000..G 4
Zelenograd* ...160,000..F 3
Zeya ...H 13
Zheleznodo-
  rozhnyy* ...84,000..F 3
Zhelezno-
  gorsk* ...74,000..F 2
Zhukovskiy* ...101,000..F 3
Zima ...I 10
Zlatoust ...208,000..G 5
Zyryanka ...D 13

*Does not appear on map; key shows general location.
†Population of metropolitan area, including suburbs.
Sources: 1990 official estimates for places over 100,000; 1989 census for metropolitan areas; 1984 official estimates for other places.

Government

National government. In 1992—shortly after the Soviet Union broke up—Russia established a *transitional* (temporary) government headed by Boris N. Yeltsin. Yeltsin had been elected president of the R.S.F.S.R. in 1991. After the breakup of the Soviet Union, Yeltsin continued to serve as president of Russia until he resigned in 1999. In December 1993, Russia adopted a new constitution that established a permanent government.

The president of Russia is the government's chief executive, head of state, and most powerful official. The president is elected by the people to a four-year term.

The president, with the approval of the lower house of parliament, appoints a prime minister to serve as head of government. The prime minister is the top-ranking official of a Council of Ministers (cabinet). The council carries out the operations of the government.

Russia's parliament, called the Federal Assembly, consists of a 450-member lower house known as the State Duma and a 178-member upper house called the Federation Council. The State Duma makes the country's laws. Legislation proposed by the Duma must be approved by the Federation Council and by the president before becoming law. However, the State Duma can override a veto by the Federation Council and send legislation directly to the president. The Federation Council approves government appointments and such presidential actions as the declaration of martial law and the use of armed forces outside of Russia.

Members of the State Duma are elected by the people to four-year terms. Members of the Federation Council are local government officials. These members include regional governors and leaders of local legislatures. They are not elected directly to the council but gain membership when they attain the local office. All Russian citizens 18 years of age and older may vote in the country's elections.

Local government. Russia consists of 89 federal administrative units. These include 49 *oblasts* (regions), 21 republics, 10 *okrugs* (areas), 6 *krais* (territories), 1 autonomous oblast, and 2 federal cities, Moscow and St. Petersburg. Some of these divisions may contain smaller units called *raions* (districts). Councils called *soviets* manage local affairs in both urban and rural areas.

Many of the administrative units have taken more control over their own affairs since the breakup of the Soviet Union. Some have pressed for independence from Russia. In 2000, however, the president and the State Duma began passing measures designed to reassert federal control over local governments.

Politics. The Communist Party was the only legal political party in the Soviet Union until March 1990. At that time, the Soviet Constitution—which gave the Communist Party its broad powers—was amended. A loose coalition of political parties with a democratic platform, known as the Democratic Russia Movement, began to play a key role in the reform movement. The Democratic Russia Movement secured Yeltsin's victory in a free presidential election held in June 1991.

The collapse of the Soviet Union led to the end of the Democratic Russia Movement. Its component groups broke apart and developed into separate political parties. Since then, Russia's political landscape has constantly shifted. There are numerous political parties and coalitions, and power changes hands with each election.

After the 1993 parliamentary elections, Russia's Choice, now called Russia's Democratic Choice, held the most seats in the State Duma. This party favors reducing government control of the economy and other reforms. The Liberal Democratic Party, an extreme nationalist group, gained the second highest number of seats.

In the 1995 parliamentary elections, the Communist Party won the largest number of seats in the State Duma. As it did in the Soviet era, the Communist Party supports more government control of land and industries. Our Home Is Russia, a moderate reform party, gained the second highest number of seats in the State Duma.

In the 1999 parliamentary elections, the Communist Party again won the largest number of seats in the State

ITAR-Tass from Sovfoto

The State Duma makes Russia's laws. Russia's parliament consists of the State Duma and the Federation Council. This photo shows Duma members in session in their Moscow meeting chambers.

Duma. A new political group called Unity won the second highest number of seats. Unity favors continuing the reforms begun by Yeltsin's administration. Surprisingly, Unity formed a coalition government with the Communists, who had opposed Yeltsin's reforms. The coalition was put together by Vladimir V. Putin, who had been named acting president of Russia in 1999 and was elected president in 2000.

Other political parties represented in the Duma include Fatherland-All Russia, the Union of Right Wing Forces, and *Yabloko,* which means *apple* in Russian. All of these parties favor continued economic and political reform, but they all have different plans and priorities.

Courts. The former Soviet government had a political police system called the Committee on State Security, known as the KGB. The KGB could interfere with and influence the legal system, and major violations of human rights took place. The KGB no longer exists in Russia.

Today, Russia has two security agencies. The Federal Security Service handles internal security, and the Foreign Intelligence Service collects information from other countries. In addition, Russia's 1993 Constitution protects the civil rights of all Russian citizens. The *prosecutor-general,* who serves as the chief legal officer of Russia, is nominated by the president and is approved by the Federation Council.

Russia's highest court is called the Constitutional Court. This court, which was established in 1992, rules on the constitutionality of the country's laws. Russia's local courts are called *people's courts.*

Armed forces. The Soviet Union had the largest armed forces in the world. About 4 million people served in its army, navy, and air force. When the Soviet Union collapsed, command of its armed forces passed to the Commonwealth of Independent States. Several former republics—including Russia—said they would also create their own armed forces. In 1992, Russia began to form its own armed forces and absorbed some of the former Soviet forces. About 1 million people serve in Russia's armed forces. Russian men must serve two years in the military. Women may volunteer to serve.

People

The people of Russia are distributed unevenly throughout the country. The vast majority live in the western—or European—part of Russia. The more rugged and remote areas to the east are sparsely inhabited.

Ancestry. More than 80 percent of Russia's people are of Russian ancestry. These ethnic Russians make up the largest group of Slavic peoples. Members of more than 100 other nationality groups also live in Russia. The largest groups include Tatars (or Tartars), Ukrainians, Chuvash, Bashkirs, Belarusians, Mordvins, Chechen, Germans, Udmurts, Mari, Kazakhs, Avars, Armenians, and Jews, who are considered a nationality group in Russia. Many of them live in Russia's autonomous territories. Remote parts of the Far North are sparsely inhabited by small Siberian groups, including Aleuts, Chukchi, Inuit (also called Eskimos), and Koryaks. These northern peoples differ from one another in ancestry and language, but they share a common way of life shaped by the harsh, cold climate.

The government of the Soviet Union had granted special political and economic privileges to Russians who were loyal to the Communist Party. It repressed the distinctive cultures of other nationalities and did not always uphold their rights. This policy sharpened resentment among some peoples. Today, pride in their culture and the desire for greater independence are growing among the members of many nationalities, including Russians.

Ethnic Russians are descended from Slavs who lived in eastern Europe several thousand years ago. Over time, migration split the Slavs into three subgroups—the East Slavs, the West Slavs, and the South Slavs. The Russians trace their heritage to the first East Slav state, Kievan Rus, which emerged in the 800's.

Kievan Rus suffered repeated invasions by Asian tribes, including the Pechenegs, Polovtsians, and Mongols. The Mongol invasions forced some people to migrate to safer, forested regions near present-day Moscow. Moscow became an important Russian state in

Population density

The map at the right shows the population density throughout Russia. Most of Russia's people live in the western part of the country. Central and eastern Russia are sparsely inhabited.

Major cities

● More than 2 million inhabitants

• Less than 2 million inhabitants

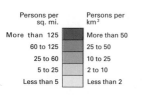

Persons per sq. mi.	Persons per km²
More than 125	More than 50
60 to 125	25 to 50
25 to 60	10 to 25
5 to 25	2 to 10
Less than 5	Less than 2

WORLD BOOK map

the 1300's. This area has remained at the heart of Russia ever since. But people of many ethnic groups have lived in Russia, especially since the 1500's, when extensive expansion and colonization began.

Language. Russian is the official language of Russia. Spoken Russian sounds fairly uniform from one end of the country to the other. Nevertheless, the language has three major regional accents—northern, southern, and central. The small differences rarely interfere with communication among Russian speakers. Russian is written in the Cyrillic alphabet (see **Alphabet** [The Cyrillic alphabet]). Many minority nationality groups in Russia have their own language and speak Russian as a second language.

Way of life

The government of the Soviet Union controlled many aspects of life in the country. It exerted great influence over religion, education, and the arts. The independence of Russia following the breakup of the Soviet Union brought greater freedom and triggered many other changes in the lives of the people.

City life. About three-fourths of Russia's people live in urban areas. Approximately 35 cities in Russia have populations over 500,000. Two of Russia's cities—Moscow and St. Petersburg—each have more than 4 million inhabitants.

Some Russian cities remain crowded. Beginning in the 1930's, large numbers of people migrated from the countryside to urban areas. During World War II (1939-1945), bombs destroyed many houses and other buildings. These circumstances combined to create a severe housing shortage in Russian cities. Many families had to share kitchen and bathroom facilities. Although the situation has greatly improved, millions of city dwellers live in small apartments in high-rise buildings. Single-family houses are more common in small towns and in the older neighborhoods of many cities. Some of these dwellings lack indoor plumbing and other modern conveniences. At the same time, Russia's newly wealthy inhabit luxury apartments and large homes.

Shortages of food, services, and manufactured goods have been common features of city life in Russia. The shift toward capitalism that began in the 1990's has not yet cured the shortages. Even when goods become available, they are often too expensive for many people to afford. Russian cities also face such urban problems as crime and environmental pollution.

Rural life. About one-fourth of the Russian population lives in rural areas. Single-family housing is common in these areas, but the Soviet government built many city-style apartment buildings. In the most remote areas of Russia, some homes lack gas, plumbing, running water, and electric power. In addition, the quality of education, health care, and cultural life is lower than in the cities. Rural life is changing, however. Rural stores, for example, have a wider selection of goods available than they once offered.

When Russia was part of the Soviet Union, most rural people worked on huge farms run by the government. After the Soviet Union collapsed, Russia began to break up these farms. New laws allow people to withdraw from the government farms and set up private farms.

Clothing. Most people in the Soviet Union wore plain clothing. Stores offered little variety in styles, and most people had a limited number of outfits. In the 1970's, consumers began to demand greater variety. They preferred to buy imported clothing whenever it was available. As a result, Soviet clothing manufacturers began to pay more attention to style and quality.

Now that Russia has opened its markets, stylish clothing made in Russia and in other parts of the world has become more widely available. Many young people dress fashionably. Russia's harsh winters affect styles.

Andy Hernandez, Gamma/Liaison

Western products are available in Russia, though they are often expensive. Here, vendors offer an American soft drink at a concert in Moscow's Red Square.

High-rise apartment buildings, such as those shown in this photograph, house millions of people in Russia's cities. Nevertheless, a housing shortage persists in some urban areas.

Traditional Russian clothing consists of colorfully embroidered shirts and blouses, embroidered headwear, and shoes woven from *bast,* a tough fiber from the bark of certain trees. Rural dwellers wore these costumes on special occasions, such as weddings and holidays. The traditional costume is rarely worn today, however.

Food and drink. The traditional Russian diet is hearty. Eating habits are changing, however, as more people turn to convenience and fast foods. Beef, chicken, pork, and fish are popular main dishes. The most commonly eaten vegetables include beets, cabbage, carrots, cucumbers, onions, potatoes, radishes, and tomatoes. Russians are fond of soups, breads, and dairy products, and they consume large quantities of sugar. Frying remains a widespread method of preparing food.

Many Russian dishes are popular around the world. They include *blinis* (thin pancakes served with smoked salmon or other fillings and sour cream) and *beef Stroganoff* (beef strips cooked with onions and mushrooms in a sour cream sauce). Other favorite dishes include *borscht* (beet soup) and *piroshki* (baked or fried dumplings filled with meat and cabbage).

Typical breakfast foods in Russia include eggs, porridge, sausages, cheese, bread, butter, and jam. Most of the people eat their main meal at midday. It consists of a salad or appetizer; soup; meat or fish with potatoes or *kasha* (cooked buckwheat); and dessert, such as stewed fruit or pastries. In the evening, most Russians eat a light supper.

Russians drink large quantities of tea, but coffee has become popular, especially among urban Russians. *Kvass,* a beerlike beverage made from fermented black bread, is especially popular in summer. Russians also enjoy soft drinks, juices, and mineral water.

Vodka is Russia's trademark alcoholic beverage. Russians also drink wine, champagne, cognac, beer, and other alcoholic beverages. Alcohol abuse has been and remains a major social problem in Russia.

Health care in the Soviet Union was free. The Russian government remains committed to meeting the basic health-care needs of its people. An insurance program to finance health care was introduced in 1993. A private health-care sector has begun to grow. Russia has many doctors, nurses, and health-care facilities. However,

At outdoor markets, farmers sell fresh produce to city dwellers. The produce is often fresher than that found in urban stores but also often more expensive. This market is in Krasnodar, a city in southwestern Russia.

Soccer is the most popular sport in Russia, among both participants and spectators. Russia has many sports camps and clubs, recreational centers, and other athletic facilities for children and adults.

tight government budgets for health care, shortages of medicines and equipment, low wages for health-care providers, and bureaucracy continue to create problems. Conditions in rural areas are worse than in the cities.

Recreation. Russians enjoy watching television, reading, playing chess, seeing motion pictures and plays, visiting museums, walking, and taking part in sports. The government actively promotes athletic activities, especially team sports. Soccer is the most popular participant and spectator sport in Russia. Other popular sports include gymnastics, basketball, and such winter sports as hockey, ice skating, and skiing. Tennis is growing in popularity.

Russia has many athletic clubs, stadiums, recreational centers, and other sporting facilities. Schools provide physical education at all levels. There are also special sports camps and clubs for children and adults.

The people of Russia are avid nature lovers, and they enjoy spending time in the countryside. Many Russians have country cottages called *dachas*. There, they garden, hike, bicycle, swim, fish, gather mushrooms, and take part in other outdoor activities.

The majority of Russia's people vacation in the summer. Price increases, an end to government support, and ethnic unrest have made vacationing away from home more difficult for many Russians. However, resort areas along the Black Sea, the Baltic Sea, and the Volga River—and in Siberia—remain popular destinations.

Religion. The Russian Orthodox Church is the largest religious denomination in the country. January 7, the Russian Orthodox Christmas, is a national holiday. In addition to Russian Orthodoxy, religions that have full freedom in Russia include Buddhism, Islam, Judaism, and certain Christian denominations. These religions enjoy full freedom because they were recognized by the state prior to the fall of the Soviet Union.

Religions that were not registered in Russia prior to

the fall of the Soviet Union face certain restrictions. Many of these religions conduct intense recruiting efforts in Russia. Restricted religions include Baptists, Mormons, Pentecostalists, Roman Catholics, and Seventh-day Adventists. These groups must register annually for 15 years before they are allowed to participate in such activities as publishing religious literature and operating religious schools. However, the Russian government has not strictly enforced the law.

Education. The Soviet government controlled education and considered it a major vehicle of social advancement. As a result, almost all Russians can read and write. Today, public education in Russia remains free for all citizens. New private schools are also opening. The Soviet government had banned such schools. Russian educators are changing the school curriculum to better prepare students for the new economy. They are also trying to satisfy the needs of Russia's many nationality groups.

All children attend school for 11 years, from age 6 to 17. Elementary education includes nine primary and intermediate grades. When pupils finish ninth grade, they may choose to complete their schooling by enrolling in a secondary school or vocational school. The secondary schools emphasize science and mathematics. They also teach language, literature, history, social sciences, and physical education. English is the most widely taught foreign language. The vocational schools prepare young people for careers as technicians or in various branches of industry and agriculture.

Starting with the intermediate grades, pupils must pass annual exams to advance to the next grade. Students who pass a national examination upon the completion of secondary school receive a certificate, and those who score well also get a gold or silver medal. Schools use a number grading scale of 1 to 5, with 5 being the highest.

Many gifted children attend special schools. These schools stress individual subjects, such as mathematics or physics, languages, or the arts. Russia also has schools for children with physical or learning disabilities.

Students must pass an entrance exam to be admitted to a university or institute of higher education. Russia has about 550 institutions of higher education equivalent to colleges and universities, with about $2\frac{1}{2}$ million students. Moscow State University, the largest university in Russia, has 28,000 students.

Museums and libraries. The people of Russia spend more time in museums than do the people of the United States or most European countries. Russia has more than 660 museums. The State Historical Museum in Moscow is the country's chief historical museum. Several museums deal with the Russian Revolution. They include the Central Museum of the Revolution, which is located in Moscow. The Hermitage Museum in St. Petersburg has one of the largest art collections in the world.

Russia has about 62,000 libraries. Most towns and large villages have a public library. There are also libraries that specialize in particular subjects and libraries run by factories, schools, labor unions, and professional and civic organizations. The Russian State Library in Moscow is the largest library in Russia. Other major libraries in Moscow include the All-Russian State Library of Foreign Literature, INION (Institute of Scholarly Information for the Social Sciences of the Academy of Sciences), the State Historical Library, and the Gorki Library at Moscow State University. St. Petersburg is home to the Saltykov-Shchedrin State Library and the Library of the Russian Academy of Sciences.

The arts

The arts in Russia date back to the earliest days of the country. But Russian artists did not produce internationally recognized works in many fields until the early 1800's. Throughout much of the 1800's and the early 1900's, Russia became an international leader in classical music, ballet, drama, and literature. Several Russian painters and sculptors also gained worldwide fame.

This section discusses Russian architecture, music, ballet, painting, and sculpture. For information on Russian drama and literature, see **Russian literature** with its list of *Related articles.*

Architecture in Russia has been shaped by religious and Western influences combined with local traditions. About 988, Grand Prince Vladimir I, ruler of the state of Kievan Rus, was converted to the Byzantine (Eastern Orthodox Christian) faith. For hundreds of years, Russian architecture reflected the influence of the Byzantine style. The most important structures were churches, which had distinctive onion-shaped domes. The best-known Byzantine church is St. Basil's Cathedral in Moscow, built by Czar Ivan IV (also called Ivan the Terrible), from 1555 to 1560. See **Byzantine art.**

In 1682, Peter I, also known as Peter the Great, became czar. Peter introduced Western European artistic styles into Russia. He founded the city of St. Petersburg in 1703 and brought Western European architects and artists to help design it. Many of the buildings dating from his reign and through the mid-1700's were designed in the Western European baroque style by Italian and French architects. A famous example is the Great Palace, which was begun in the early 1700's at Peterhof (now Petrodvorets), near St. Petersburg.

Among the most widely recognized architectural works in Russia are the buildings within the enclosed fortress in Moscow called the Kremlin. The Kremlin includes churches, palaces, and other buildings erected from the late 1400's to the mid-1900's. Some Kremlin buildings house Russia's government, and others serve as museums.

Music. Until the mid-1700's, Russian music consisted almost entirely of vocal music sung in church worship services and of folk music, which was also mainly vocal. Nonreligious music began to flower during the reign of Elizabeth, the empress of Russia from 1741 to 1762. She established the Academy of Arts in 1757, which taught music. Italian opera became popular during her reign. The popularity of music in Russia expanded further during the reign of Catherine II, known as Catherine the Great, who ruled from 1762 to 1796. The earliest written collection of Russian folk songs appeared in four vol-

The Hermitage Museum in St. Petersburg is Russia's largest art museum. Its outstanding collection includes masterpieces of ancient Greek and Roman art; Islamic art; baroque and Renaissance paintings and sculpture; and French Impressionist paintings.

St. Basil's Cathedral in Moscow has colorful onion-shaped
domes that have made it one of the most widely recognized
buildings in Russia. The Byzantine-style cathedral was built from
1555 to 1560 by Czar Ivan IV (also called Ivan the Terrible).

The Trinity by Andrei Rublev; Tretyakov Gallery, Moscow

Religious paintings called *icons* dominated Russian art from
the late 900's to the late 1600's. Icons were created for Russian
Orthodox worship services and were considered sacred.

umes published between 1776 and 1795.

Mikhail Glinka is credited with founding a distinc-
tively Russian school of classical music in the early and
middle 1800's. He blended folk songs and religious
music into his works and also introduced subjects from
Russian history. His most influential work is probably his
second opera, *Ruslan and Lyudmila* (1842), based on a
fairy tale written by the Russian poet Alexander Pushkin.

By the late 1800's, Russian music flourished. Such
composers as Modest Mussorgsky, Nikolai Rimsky-
Korsakov, Peter Ilich Tchaikovsky, and Alexander Borodin wrote operas and instrumental music. Much of their
work was based on Russian history and folklore. In the
early 1900's, Sergei Rachmaninoff and Igor Stravinsky
gained international fame for their musical compositions. Stravinsky wrote several influential ballet scores,
including *The Firebird* (1910), *Petrouchka* (1911), and *The
Rite of Spring* (1913). See the list of Russian composers
in the *Related articles* section of **Classical music.**

Ballet. Russian ballet became internationally famous
starting in the mid-1800's. The leading ballet companies,

which continue to perform today, are the Kirov Ballet
(formerly the Russian Imperial Ballet) of St. Petersburg
and the Bolshoi Ballet of Moscow. See **Ballet** (History);
Bolshoi Ballet.

Painting and sculpture. Until the early 1900's, the
most important Russian paintings were created for religious purposes. Russian artists decorated the interiors
of churches with wallpaintings and mosaics. Stylized
paintings called *icons* were produced for many centuries. An icon is a religious painting considered sacred in
Eastern Orthodox Christianity. Icons were produced according to strict rules established by the church, and
their style changed little over the years. See **Icon.**

By the mid-1800's, Moscow and St. Petersburg had
busy art schools. Russian artists also began to create
paintings and sculptures on more varied subjects.

A burst of creativity in Russian art exploded during
the years before the start of World War I in 1914. Russian artists were strongly influenced by the modern art
movements emerging in Western Europe. The painters
Marc Chagall, Alexei von Jawlensky, and Wassily
Kandinsky eventually settled in Western Europe.

Artists who remained in Russia developed two major
art movements, *suprematism* and *constructivism.* Both
movements produced paintings that were *abstract*—that
is, they had no recognizable subject matter. The leading
suprematist was Kasimir Malevich. The major construc-
tivists included Naum Gabo, Antoine Pevsner, and Vladimir Tatlin. See **Malevich, Kasimir; Chagall, Marc; Gabo,
Naum; Kandinsky, Wassily; Pevsner, Antoine.**

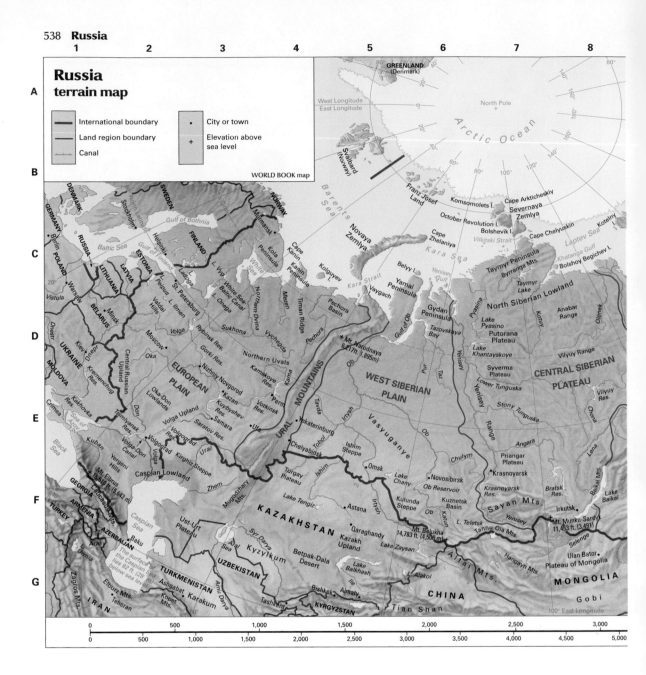

Russia
terrain map

- International boundary
- Land region boundary
- Canal
- • City or town
- + Elevation above sea level

WORLD BOOK map

Physical features

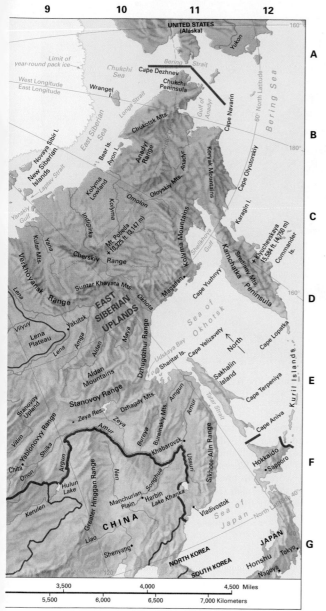

Map grid references (top): 9 10 11 12

Limit of year-round pack ice

West Longitude / East Longitude

UNITED STATES (Alaska)

Yukon

Chukchi Sea

Cape Dezhnev

Bering Strait

Chukchi Peninsula

Wrangel I.

Gulf of Anadyr

Cape Navarin

60° North Latitude

Bering Sea

180°

Nordvik Sibir I.

New Siberian Islands

Bear Is.

Ayon I.

Chukotsk Mts.

Anadyr Range

Anadyr

Koryak Mountains

Cape Olyutorskiy

East Siberian Sea

Laptev Strait

Yanskiy Gulf

Kolyma Lowland

Omolon

Oloysky Mts.

Kolyma Mountains

Karagin I.

Commander Is.

Kolyma

Indigirka

Mt. Pobeda +10,325 ft. (3,147 m)

Shelikhova Gulf

Klyuchevskaya +15,584 ft. (4,750 m)

Sredinnyy Mts.

Kular Mts.

Yana

Cherskiy Range

Kamchatka Peninsula

Verkhoyansk Range

Suntar Khayata Mts.

Okhota

Magadan

Cape Yuzhnyy

160°

Lena

Vilyuy

Lena Plateau

Yakutsk

EAST SIBERIAN UPLANDS

Maya

Dzhugdzhur Range

Sea of Okhotsk

Cape Lopatka

Amga

Aldan

Udskaya Bay

Shantar Is.

Cape Yelizavety

North

Kuril Islands

Aldan Mountains

Cape Terpeniya

Stanovoy Upland

Stanovoy Range

Zeya Res.

Dzhagdy Mts.

Zeya

Sakhalin Island

Vitim

Yablonovyy Range

Shilka

Bureinsky Mts.

Amgun

Amur

Tatar Strait

Cape Aniva

Chita

Onon

Argun

Bureya

Khabarovsk

Sikhote-Alin Range

Ussuri

Nen

Hulun Lake

Greater Hinggan Range

Manchurian Plain

Songhua

Harbin

Lake Khanka

Vladivostok

Sea of Japan

North Latitude 40°

Hokkaido

Sapporo

Kerulen

CHINA

Liao

Shenyang

NORTH KOREA

SOUTH KOREA

JAPAN

Honshu

Tokyo

Nagoya

120°

Scale:
3,500 4,000 4,500 Miles
5,500 6,000 6,500 7,000 Kilometers

Grid letters (right side): A B C D E F G

Land and climate

Russia is the largest country in the world. It has an area of 6,592,850 square miles (17,075,400 square kilometers), almost twice that of Canada, the second largest country. A train trip between Moscow in the west and Vladivostok in the east takes seven days and passes through eight time zones, including that of Moscow.

Land regions. Many scientists divide Russia into four zones according to soil conditions and plant life, which are based mainly on climate. The zones form broad belts across Russia, and no sharp transitions separate them. From north to south, the zones are (1) the tundra, (2) the forest zone, (3) the steppes, and (4) the semidesert and mountainous zone.

The tundra lies in the northernmost part of Russia. It is largely a treeless plain. The tundra has short summers and long, severe winters. About half the region has permanently frozen soil called *permafrost.* Few people live in this bleak area. Plant life consists chiefly of low shrubs, dwarf trees, and moss. Animals of the tundra include reindeer, Arctic foxes, ermines, hares, and lemmings. Waterfowl live near the Arctic Sea in summer.

The forest belt lies south of the tundra. The northern part of this belt is called the *taiga.* It consists of *coniferous* (cone-bearing) trees, such as cedar, fir, pine, and spruce. This area has poor, ashy soil, known as *podzol,* that makes it largely unfit for agriculture. Farther south, the coniferous forests give way to mixed forests of conifers, aspen, birch, elm, maple, oak, and other species. The soils in this zone support agriculture in some areas, and the area has a mild, moist climate. Brown bears, deer, elk, lynx, reindeer, and smaller animals, such as beavers, rabbits, and squirrels, roam the forests.

Grassy plains called *steppes* stretch across Russia south of the forests. The northern part of the steppe zone consists of wooded plains and meadows. The massive southern part is largely a treeless prairie. The best soils in Russia—brown soil and black, rich soil called *chernozem*—are found there. Most of the steppe zone is farmland. Birds, squirrels, and mouselike mammals called *jerboas* live in the steppes. Antelope inhabit the eastern steppes.

The semidesert and mountainous zone, the southernmost zone in Russia, has diverse soils and climate due to variations in elevation. It includes the dry, semidesert lowlands near the Caspian Sea, as well as the lush vegetation and mild climate of the Caucasus Mountains.

Geologists also divide Russia into five land regions that differ from the soil and vegetation zones. From west to east, the regions are (1) the European Plain, (2) the Ural Mountains, (3) the West Siberian Plain, (4) the Central Siberian Plateau, and (5) the East Siberian Uplands.

The European Plain makes up most of the European part of Russia. It is the most densely populated region in the country. The European Plain is predominantly flat, averaging about 600 feet (180 meters) above sea level. Most of the nation's industries are there, but the region is poor in natural resources. Forests cover much of the northern European Plain. The southern part is largely cropland. The plain is home to a variety of animal life. The Caucasus Mountains rise at the southern edge of the plain, between the Black and the Caspian seas. The mountains include 18,510-foot (5,642-meter) Mount El-

© Patrick David, Sipa Press

The East Siberian Uplands are mainly a wilderness of mountains and plateaus. The region has valuable mineral resources, but its harsh climate makes it difficult to use them. Small towns, such as the one shown here, are sparsely scattered throughout the East Siberian Uplands.

brus, the highest point in Europe.

The Ural Mountains form the traditional boundary between the European and Asian parts of Russia. These mountains, worn down by streams, reach an average height of only about 2,000 feet (610 meters). The middle and southern Ural Mountains are rich in deposits of iron, copper, and other metals. The middle section is the region's most heavily populated and highly industrialized area. Major cities in the region include Yekaterinburg and Chelyabinsk.

The West Siberian Plain is the largest level region in the world. This enormous plain covers more than 1 million square miles (2.6 million square kilometers) and rises no more than 500 feet (150 meters) above sea level.

© Bill Swersey, Liaison Agency

A belt of rich farmland stretches across Russia from east to west. In this photograph, farmworkers harvest potatoes on the European Plain. This mainly flat landform makes up most of the European part of Russia.

It is drained by the Ob River system, which flows northward into the Arctic Ocean. But drainage is poor, and the plain is marshy. The West Siberian Plain is rich in oil and natural gas deposits, and it is being developed rapidly. Cropland covers the southern-most part of the plain. The cities of Novosibirsk and Omsk are in this region.

The Central Siberian Plateau slopes upward toward the south from coastal plains along the Arctic Ocean. It has an average height of about 2,000 feet (610 meters). Streams cut deeply through the region. The Sayan and Baikal mountains rise more than 11,000 feet (3,350 meters) along the plateau's southern edge. Thick pine forests cover much of the Central Siberian Plateau, and its climate reaches extremes of heat and cold. The region has a wide variety of rich mineral deposits. Krasnoyarsk and Irkutsk are its largest cities.

The East Siberian Uplands are mainly a wilderness of mountains and plateaus. The mountains rise to 10,000 feet (3,000 meters) and form part of a series of ranges along the eastern coast of Asia and some offshore islands. About 25 active volcanoes are found on the Kamchatka Peninsula. The tallest volcano, snow-capped Klyuchevskaya, rises 15,584 feet (4,750 meters). The region has valuable mineral resources, but its harsh climate makes it difficult to tap them. Vladivostok on the Pacific Ocean and Khabarovsk on the Amur River are the region's most important cities.

Rivers and lakes. Russia's many large rivers have served as important means of communication and commerce. The construction of canals further improved these activities.

The Lena River in Siberia, 2,734 miles (4,400 kilometers) long, is Russia's longest river. It empties into the Arctic Ocean. Other major rivers in Siberia include the Amur, Ob, and Yenisey rivers, all frozen seven to nine months a year. The Volga River is the longest river in European Russia. It originates in the Valdai Hills northwest of Moscow and flows 2,300 miles (3,700 kilometers) to the Caspian Sea. The Volga freezes for about three months each year. Other important rivers in European Russia include the Don and the Northern Dvina.

Russia has about 200,000 lakes. The Caspian Sea, a saltwater lake 92 feet (28 meters) below sea level, is the world's largest inland body of water. It touches the southern part of European Russia. Lake Ladoga, near St. Petersburg, covers 6,835 square miles (17,703 square kilometers). It is the largest lake entirely in Europe. Lake Baikal, near the Baikal Mountains, is the deepest lake in the world. It plunges 5,315 feet (1,620 meters) deep.

A thick forest blankets the northern part of Russia from Europe to the Pacific Ocean. It covers much of Siberia. Few people live in this vast area.

ITAR-Tass from Sovfoto

© Paolo Koch, Photo Researchers

Lake Baikal, the deepest lake in the world, lies in Siberia. It has a depth of 5,315 feet (1,620 meters). A small community, *right,* is nestled between Lake Baikal and the surrounding mountains.

Climate. Russia is known for its long and bitter winters. The country's harsh climate helped stop various invaders during its history, including the large armies of Napoleon in 1812 and of Adolf Hitler in 1941 and 1942. In the Moscow region, snow covers the ground for about five months each year. In the northernmost part of Russia, snow abounds for eight to nine months a year. Half the land has permafrost beneath the surface. Russia's main cropland, in the southwest part of the country, has a short growing season and insufficient rainfall. Most of the coastal waters, lakes, and rivers freeze for much of the year.

Russia's weather varies from extremely cold to extremely hot. Northeastern Siberia is one of the coldest regions in the world. January temperatures there average below −50 °F (−46 °C). Temperatures as low as −90 °F (−68 °C) have been recorded. The average July temperature in this region is 60 °F (16 °C), but it can climb to nearly 100 °F (38 °C). No other part of the world registers such a wide range of temperatures.

Precipitation (rain, melted snow, and other forms of moisture) is light to moderate. The European Plain and parts of the East Siberian Uplands receive the most rain. Vast inland areas get little rain. The heaviest snowfalls—up to 4 feet (120 centimeters) of snow a year—occur in western and central Siberia.

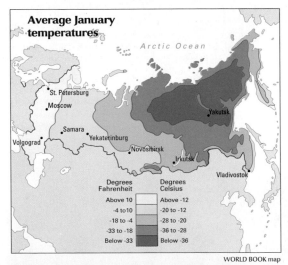

ITAR-Tass from Sovfoto

Winters are long and cold in most parts of Russia. Snow covers the ground in the Moscow region for about five months each year. This photograph shows a Moscow street in winter.

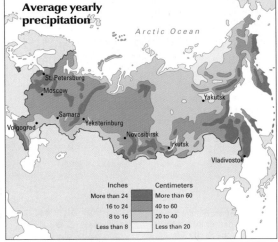

WORLD BOOK map

Rainfall in Russia is heaviest on the European Plain, in parts of the East Siberian Uplands, and in mountainous regions along the southern border. Vast areas of the interior get little rain.

WORLD BOOK map

January temperatures in eastern Siberia are among the coldest in the world, dropping as low as −90 °F (−68 °C). January temperatures in Russia average above 10 °F (−12 °C) only in the westernmost part of the country.

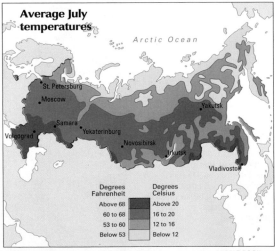

WORLD BOOK map

July temperatures in Russia vary widely. Most of the country has an average July temperature above 60 °F (16 °C), but temperatures can hit almost 100 °F (38 °C) in northeastern Siberia and drop below 32 °F (0 °C) on islands in the Arctic Ocean.

Economy

Since the fall of the Soviet Union in 1991, Russia has struggled to reform its economic system. The country has attempted to shift from a state-controlled economy to a market-driven economy.

In the Soviet Union, central government agencies planned almost all aspects of economic life. The government owned and controlled all factories and farms, and private businesses were illegal. Soviet leaders transformed Russia from a farming country into an industrial giant. Heavy industry—such as chemicals, construction, machine tools, and steel—developed rapidly. Government ministries supplied factories with materials, set production quotas, and told managers what to produce and to whom to sell their goods. This planning led to rapid industrial development and impressive economic gains. But central control also tended to suppress new ideas and to discourage quality.

Russia inherited both the successes and the problems of the Soviet Union's industrial policy. The Russian government has been converting state-owned property, including large factories and farms, to private ownership. Many small businesses and joint ventures with foreign partners have started. Russia turned to Western countries and Japan for assistance in modernizing and restructuring its manufacturing sector.

When the Soviet Union collapsed, the economy was in a state of disorder. To stabilize the Russian economy, reduce inflation, and attract foreign investment, the government allowed the ruble to be exchanged for other currencies at international rates. The government also promoted the development of a modern banking system. When the government lifted price controls on most items in 1992, prices soared. Although the ruble stabilized, average wages fell, making many consumer items too expensive for most people. Retirees and other Russians living on fixed incomes had a particularly hard time making ends meet.

The Russian government's bold effort to quickly introduce a Western-style economy caused great instability in the country throughout the 1990's. Industrial output fell, and inflation rose dramatically. In August 1998, the Russian government was unable to make payments on its loans. The value of the ruble fell. An economic crisis followed, and the political debate over how to restore

Russia's gross domestic product

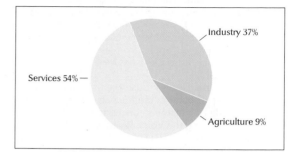

- Industry 37%
- Services 54%
- Agriculture 9%

Russia's gross domestic product (GDP) was $354,407,000,000 in 1995. The GDP is the total value of goods and services produced within a country in a year. The GDP measures a nation's total economic performance and can be used to compare the economic output and growth of countries.

Production and workers by economic activities

Economic activities	Percent of GDP produced	Employed workers	
		Number of people	Percent of total
Manufacturing, mining, & utilities	29	16,631,700	25
Trade, hotels, & restaurants	16	6,071,400	9
Community, government, & personal services	13	21,451,800	32
Transportation & communication	13	5,252,900	8
Finance, insurance, & real estate	12	820,300	1
Agriculture & forestry	9	10,442,800	16
Construction	8	5,770,000	9
Total	100	66,440,900	100

Figures are for 1995.
Sources: International Labour Office; International Monetary Fund.

the Russian economy intensified.

On the positive side, Russia has a skilled labor force and an abundance of natural resources. Many new businesses have been started, and young Russians are committed to a market economy. However, corrupt and illegal business practices are common, and Russian gangsters control many businesses.

Sovfoto/Eastfoto

Mining is an important industry in Russia. The country is rich in minerals and has abundant deposits of coal, natural gas, and petroleum. A coal miner, *shown here,* operates equipment that twists coal out of the side of a coal pit in the northern Ural Mountains.

Natural resources. Russia is one of the richest countries in terms of natural resources. It has the world's largest forest reserves, enormous energy supplies, vast stretches of farmland, extensive mineral deposits, and many potential sources of hydroelectric power. Many of its resources, however, are far from the factories where they are put to use. Russia also has a wide variety of plant and animal life.

Manufacturing. Heavy industry remains the most highly developed sector of the Russian economy. The machine-building industry is concentrated in Moscow, St. Petersburg, along the Volga River, and in the Ural Mountains. It makes a variety of tractors and other heavy machinery and electrical equipment. The chemical industry produces chemical fibers, mineral fertilizers, petrochemicals, plastics, soda ash, and synthetic resins. The construction materials industry is also important.

The Moscow area is Russia's leading manufacturing center. Its factories produce chemicals, electrical equipment, electronics, motor vehicles, processed foods, steel, and textiles. Ships and industrial equipment are manufactured in St. Petersburg. Metal processing and machinery production are important in the Urals. Most oil refining takes place in the Volga-Urals region. New industries are being developed in Siberia to make use of the region's mineral and hydroelectric resources. Light industry, particularly textile production, is centered in the region around Moscow and along the Volga River. The paper industry operates along the southern edge of the forest belt.

Agriculture. Russia has a large amount of farmland. But a short growing season, insufficient rainfall, and a lack of fertile soil make farming difficult. The Soviet Union's wasteful and inefficient system of state-run farms added to Russia's agricultural problems.

When the Soviet Union collapsed, there were about 15,000 large state-controlled farms in Russia. About half were state farms operated like government factories, called *sovkhozy.* Workers on sovkhozy received wages. The rest were collective farms called *kolkhozy,* which were government-controlled but managed in part by farmers.

The Russian government introduced a program to break up the state-controlled farms. The farms set up committees whose job it was to decide how to divide the farms into producer cooperatives or joint-stock companies. Many farms have been reorganized. But many farmers, afraid of the changes, have resisted the move to free-market agriculture. Private farms control only a small percentage of the farmland.

Economy of Russia

This map shows the major uses of land in Russia. The map also shows where the leading farm, fishing, mineral, and forest products are produced, and it locates the chief manufacturing centers.

- Wheat-growing land
- Other cropland
- Mostly grazing land
- Forestland
- Tundra or mountainous area
- Fishing
- Manufacturing center
- Mineral deposit

WORLD BOOK map

Long pipelines, such as the one shown here, transport natural gas from fields in Siberia to European Russia. The gas is burned to provide energy for industry and heat for homes. It is also a natural resource for the production of certain chemicals.

Approximately 13 percent of Russia's land is cropland. One of the main agricultural regions is the Black Earth Belt, a portion of the steppes stretching from the Ukrainian border to southwestern Siberia that is famous for its dark chernozem soil. Other important farming regions are the Volga area, the northern Caucasus Mountains, and western Siberia.

Russia is one of the world's major grain producers. The country still must import grain for food, however. Major crops grown in Russia include barley, flax, fruits, oats, potatoes, rye, sugar beets, sunflowers, vegetables, and wheat. Russian farmers also grow many *fodder crops* (food crops for animals). Grasses and corn are the most important fodder crops.

Livestock breeding is another main component of Russian agriculture. Cattle, hogs, and sheep are the livestock most commonly raised in the country.

Mining. Russia has vast amounts of most of the minerals used in modern industrial production. The country has abundant coal deposits and huge reserves of petroleum and natural gas. Other resources include calcium phosphate minerals and phosphorites, used in fertilizers, and diamonds.

Russia is a major producer of iron ore. Iron ore is mined primarily in the western and southern parts of the country. Nickel is mined in the Kola Peninsula, eastern Siberia, and the southern Urals. The country ranks as a leading producer of gold, lead, platinum, salt, tin, and tungsten. It is also an important source of copper, silver, and zinc. Bauxite, a material used in making aluminum, is mined in western Siberia.

A fishing crew brings in sturgeon from the mouth of the Volga River. Sturgeon eggs are used to make a salty delicacy called *caviar.* Russia is famous for its flavorful caviar.

Railroads transport freight and passengers between Russia's major cities, many of which are separated by vast distances. This photograph shows a train on the Trans-Siberian Railroad, which runs between Vladivostok in the southeast and Moscow in the west.

ITAR-Tass from Sovfoto

Fishing industry. In the northern Barents Sea and the White Sea, Russian fishing crews catch cod, haddock, herring, salmon, and other fishes. Sturgeon are caught in the Caspian Sea. *Caviar,* the salted eggs of sturgeon, is a famous Russian delicacy. Crews also fish in inland waterways, the Atlantic and Pacific oceans, and the Baltic and Black seas.

Service industries are industries that produce services, not goods. In the former Soviet Union, these industries were underdeveloped. Most service-industry workers were poorly trained and underpaid. They had little incentive to satisfy their customers, who competed for services that were in short supply. Today, private economic activity in the service sector is flourishing. Many individuals and families operate small businesses, such as restaurants, dry cleaners, and taxi services.

Energy sources. Russia has enormous natural energy reserves, especially petroleum and natural gas. The country is the world's largest producer of crude oil. Oil fields in western Siberia supply more than half of Russia's petroleum. The Volga-Ural Oil-Gas Region, the Northern Caucasus, and the Timan-Pechora Oil-Gas Basin are also important. Russia also produces large amounts of coal and natural gas. Pipelines carry oil and natural gas from western Siberia to European Russia. The largest coal mines are in the Kuznetsk and Pechora basins. Peat bogs also furnish some of Russia's fuel.

Most of Russia's electric power plants are steam-turbine plants. Hydroelectric plants also generate electric power. In addition, Russia is a major producer of nuclear power.

Trade. The Soviet Union traded mainly with Eastern European Communist countries, such as Bulgaria, Hungary, and Poland. Since the overthrow of the Communist regimes of Eastern Europe and the breakup of the Soviet Union, Russia's trading activity with those countries

has declined. Russia's main trading partners are the other former Soviet republics, China, Germany, Italy, Japan, the United Kingdom, and the United States.

Russia exports mostly petroleum, natural gas, minerals, machinery, chemicals, and wood and paper products. Major imports include consumer goods, foods and beverages, industrial equipment, and machinery.

Transportation and communication. Because of Russia's vast size and harsh climate, transportation facilities and communications systems are unevenly distributed throughout the country. They are less efficient than the transportation and communications networks of Western Europe, the United States, and Japan.

Railroads handle most freight transportation in Russia. But the system is heavily loaded and in urgent need of modernization. Russia's poorly developed highway network, combined with the country's vast size, make truck transport ineffective and costly. Trucks account for only about 5 percent of total freight movement. River transportation carries only a small percentage of Russia's freight traffic, because most rivers are frozen for much of the year. Canals, including the Volga-Don Canal and the Moscow Canal, which connects Moscow with the Volga River, make an important contribution to the country's river traffic.

Russia inherited its national airline, Aeroflot, from the Soviet Union. Aeroflot must now compete with new, privately owned companies. Russia's airlines carry freight and passengers between Russian cities and between Russia and other countries. Rising ticket costs have reduced air traffic.

Russia's most important seaports—Arkhangelsk, Kaliningrad, Murmansk, Nakhodka, St. Petersburg, and Vladivostok—handle a large portion of the country's foreign trade. The water at many Russian ports is frozen for many months of the year, however.

Automobile production is increasing, but it remains small in comparison with other developed nations. Only about 60 of every 1,000 Russians own cars.

Public transportation is modern and inexpensive, but crowded. Several large cities, including Moscow, have clean, efficient subway systems. Buses, trams, and trolleys also operate in the cities. Bicycles are seen in large cities, but they are more common in rural and vacation areas. Horses and buggies can also be found in rural parts of Russia.

Russia has an underdeveloped telecommunications system, but it is being modernized. There is only about one telephone for every six Russians, compared to about one telephone per person in the United States.

During the Soviet era, the government required all broadcasts and publications to follow Communist Party policies. Such censorship began to ease in the 1980's, and the number of independent newspapers and publishing houses increased dramatically. The government still exerts some control over the media, however. Most families own radios and televisions. Although costly for many families, videocassette players are popular, as are personal computers and the Internet.

History

Russia's unique geographic location astride both Europe and Asia has influenced its history and shaped its destiny. Russia never has been entirely an Eastern or a Western country. As a result, Russian intellectuals have long debated the country's development and contribution to world history.

This section traces the major developments of Russian history. In 1917, revolutionaries overthrew the Russian czarist government. They changed Russia's name to the Russian Soviet Federative Socialist Republic (R.S.F.S.R.). In 1922, the R.S.F.S.R. and three other republics formed a new nation called the Union of Soviet Socialist Republics (U.S.S.R.), also known as the Soviet Union. The U.S.S.R. broke apart in 1991, and Belarus, Russia, and Ukraine invited the other republics to join a federation called the Commonwealth of Independent States. For more detailed information about this period, see **Union of Soviet Socialist Republics** (History).

Early days. Beginning about 1200 B.C., the Cimmerians, a Balkan people, lived north of the Black Sea in what is now southern Ukraine. They were defeated about 700 B.C. by the Scythians, an Iranian people from central Asia. The Scythians controlled the region until about 200 B.C. They fell to the Sarmatians, another Iranian group. The Scythians and Sarmatians lived in close contact with Greek colonies—later controlled by the Romans—along the northern coast of the Black Sea. They absorbed many Greek and Roman ways of life through trade, marriage, and other contacts. See **Cimmerians.**

Germanic tribes from the West, called the Goths, conquered the region about A.D. 200. The Goths ruled until about 370, when they were defeated by the Huns, a warlike Asian people. The Huns' empire broke up after their leader, Attila, died in 453. The Avars, a tribe related to the Huns, began to rule the region in the mid-500's. The Khazars, another Asian people, won the southern Volga and northern Caucasus regions in the mid-600's. They became Jews and established a busy trade with other peoples. See **Goths; Hun.**

By the 800's, Slavic groups had built many towns in eastern Europe, including what became the European part of Russia. They had also developed an active trade. No one knows where the Slavs came from. Some historians believe they came in the 400's from what is now Poland. Others think the Slavs were farmers in the Black Sea region under Scythian rule or earlier. Slavs of what are now Belarus, Russia, and Ukraine became known as East Slavs. See **Slavs**.

The earliest written Russian history of the 800's is the *Primary Chronicle,* written in Kiev, probably in 1111. It says that quarreling Slavic groups in the town of Novgorod asked a Viking tribe to rule them and bring order to the land. The Vikings were called the *Varangian Russes.* Historians who accept the *Primary Chronicle* as true believe that Russia took its name from this tribe. According to the *Primary Chronicle,* a group of related Varangian families headed by a prince named Rurik arrived in 862. Rurik settled in Novgorod, and the area became known as the "land of the Rus."

Many historians doubt that the Slavs of Novgorod invited the Vikings to rule them. They believe the Vikings invaded the region. Some historians claim the word *Rus,* from which Russia took its name, was the name of an early Slavic tribe in the Black Sea region. It is known, however, that the first state founded by East Slavs—called Kievan Rus—was established at present-day Kiev in the 800's. Kiev, now the capital of Ukraine, was an important trading center on the Dnepr River. Whether it had been developed by the Vikings is unclear.

The state of Kievan Rus. The *Primary Chronicle* states that Oleg, a Varangian, captured Kiev in 882 and

Important dates in Russia

A.D. 800's East Slavs established the state of Kievan Rus.
1237-1240 The Mongols conquered Russia.
c. 1318 The Mongols appointed Prince Yuri of Moscow as the Russian grand prince.
1480 Ivan III broke Mongol control over Russia.
1547 Ivan IV became the first Russian ruler to be crowned czar.
1604-1613 Russia was torn by civil war, invasion, and political confusion during the Time of Troubles.
1613 Michael Romanov became czar. He started the Romanov line of czars, which ruled until 1917.
1703 Peter I founded St. Petersburg and began building his capital there.
1812 Napoleon invaded Russia but was forced to retreat.
1861 Alexander II freed the serfs.
1905 Japan defeated Russia in the Russo-Japanese War. A revolution forced Czar Nicholas II to form a parliament.
1914-1917 Russia fought Germany and Austria-Hungary in World War I.
1917 The February Revolution overthrew Czar Nicholas II. The Bolsheviks (who were later called Communists) seized power in the October Revolution. V. I. Lenin became head of the government. Russia withdrew from World War I.
1918-1920 The Communists defeated their anti-Communist opponents in a civil war.
1922 The U.S.S.R. was established.
1941-1945 The U.S.S.R. fought Germany in World War II.
1957 The U.S.S.R. launches Sputnik 1, the earth's first artificial satellite.
1991 Communist rule ended, and the Soviet Union was dissolved. Russia and the other Soviet republics became independent nations.

ruled as its prince. During the 900's, the other *principalities* (regions ruled by a prince) of Kievan Rus recognized Kiev's major importance. Kiev lay on the main trade route connecting the Baltic Sea with the Black Sea and the Byzantine Empire. In addition, Kiev's forces defended Kievan Rus against invading tribes from the south and east. The ruler of Kiev came to be called *grand prince* and ranked above the other princes of Kievan Rus.

About 988, Grand Prince Vladimir I *(Volodymyr* in Ukrainian) became a Christian. At that time, the East Slavs worshiped the forces of nature. Vladimir made Christianity the state religion, and most people under his rule turned Christian. Vladimir later became a saint of the Russian Orthodox Church.

Several grand princes were strong rulers, but Kiev's power began to decrease after the mid-1000's. The rulers of other Kievan Rus principalities grew in power, and they fought many destructive wars. In Novgorod and a few other towns with strong local governments, the princes were driven out. Badly weakened by civil wars and without strong central control, Kievan Rus fell to huge armies of Mongols called Tatars, or Tartars, who swept across Russia from the east during the 1200's (see **Tatars**).

Mongol rule. In 1237, Batu, a grandson of the conqueror Genghis Khan, led between 150,000 and 200,000 Mongol troops into Russia. The Mongols destroyed one Russian town after another. In 1240, they destroyed Kiev, and Russia became part of the Mongol Empire. It was included in a section called the Golden Horde. The capital of the Golden Horde was at Sarai, near what is now Volgograd.

Batu forced the surviving Russian princes to pledge allegiance to the Golden Horde and to pay heavy taxes. From time to time, the Mongols left their capital and wiped out the people of various areas because of their disloyalty. The Mongols also appointed the Russian grand prince and forced many Russians to serve in their armies. But they interfered little with Russian life in general. The Mongols were chiefly interested in maintaining their power and collecting taxes.

During the period of Mongol rule, which ended in the late 1400's, the new ideas and reforming spirit of the Renaissance were dramatically changing many aspects of life in Western Europe. But under Mongol control, Russia was to a great extent cut off from these important Western influences.

The rise of Moscow. In the early 1300's, Prince Yuri of Moscow married the sister of the Golden Horde's *khan* (ruler). Yuri was appointed the Russian grand prince about 1318. Mongol troops helped him put down threats to his leadership from other principalities. The Mongols also began letting the grand prince of Moscow collect taxes for them. This practice started with Ivan I (called the Moneybag) about 1330. Ivan kept some of the tax money. He bought much land and expanded his territory greatly. Other princes and *boyars* (high-ranking landowners) began to serve in Moscow's army and government. In addition, Ivan persuaded the chief bishop of the Russian Orthodox Church to remain in Moscow. Until then, Kiev had been the spiritual center of Russia.

Moscow grew stronger and richer as the Golden Horde grew weaker, chiefly because of struggles for leadership. In 1380, Grand Prince Dmitriy defeated a Mongol force in the Battle of Kulikovo, near the Don River. The victory briefly freed Moscow of Mongol control. The Mongols recaptured Moscow in 1382, but they no longer believed they could not be beaten.

During the late 1400's, Moscow became the most powerful Russian city. Ivan III (called Ivan the Great) won control of Moscow's main rival cities, Novgorod and Tver, and great numbers of boyars entered his service. In 1480, Ivan made the final break from Mongol control by refusing to pay taxes to the Golden Horde. Mongol troops moved toward Moscow but turned back to defend their capital from Russian attack.

Ivan the Terrible. After the rise of Moscow, its grand prince came to be called *czar.* In 1547, Ivan IV, also known as Ivan the Terrible, became the first ruler to be crowned czar. Ivan made the power of the czar over all Russia complete.

Ivan was brutal, extremely suspicious, and perhaps, at times, insane. He formed a special police force and began a reign of terror in which he ordered the arrest and murder of hundreds of aristocrats. Ivan gave his victims' estates as payment to the *service gentry* (landowners serving in the army and government). He also established strict rules concerning the number of warriors and horses each landowner had to supply to the army. Ivan burned many towns and villages, and he killed church leaders who opposed him. In a fit of rage, Ivan even struck and killed his oldest son.

The number of service gentry increased rapidly. But their estates had no value unless the peasants remained on the land and farmed it. Ivan and later czars passed a series of laws that bound the peasants to the land as *serfs.* Serfdom became the economic basis of Russian power. The development of Russian serfdom differed sharply from changes occurring in Western Europe at the time. There, during the Renaissance, the growth of

Illustration from a Russian manuscript of the 1500's;
Russian State Library, Moscow (Historical Pictures Service)

The Battle of Kulikovo in 1380 was the first Russian victory over the Mongol forces. It took place near the Don River.

trade led to the use of money as royal payment. It also led to the disappearance of serfdom in Western Europe. See **Serf**.

Ivan fought Tatars at Astrakhan and Kazan to the southeast, and he won their lands. Russian forces then crossed the Ural Mountains and conquered western Siberia. Ivan also tried to win lands northwest to the Baltic Sea, but he was defeated by Lithuanian, Polish, and Swedish armies.

The Time of Troubles developed because of a breakdown of the czar's power after Ivan's death. Fedor I, Ivan's second son, was a weak czar. His wife's brother, Boris Godunov, became the real ruler of Russia. Fedor's younger brother, Dmitriy, was found dead in 1591, and Fedor died in 1598 without leaving a male heir.

The *zemskii sobor* (land council), a kind of parliament with little power, elected Boris czar. But a man believed to be Gregory Otrepiev, a former monk, posed as Dmitriy. This *False Dmitriy* claimed Dmitriy had not died, and he fled to Lithuania to avoid arrest. In 1604, False Dmitriy invaded Russia with Polish troops. The invaders were joined by many discontented Russians. This invasion marked the beginning of the Time of Troubles. Russia was torn by civil war, invasion, and political confu-sion until 1613.

False Dmitriy became czar in 1605, but a group of boyars killed him the next year. Prince Basil Shuisky then became czar. In 1610, Polish invaders occupied Moscow. They ruled through a powerless council of boyars until 1612. Meanwhile, a new False Dmitriy and a number of other pretenders to the throne won many followers. Peasant revolts swept through Russia. Landowners and frontier people called Cossacks fought each other, and sometimes joined together to fight powerful aristocrats (see **Cossacks**). The Polish control of Moscow led the Russians to unite their forces and drive out the

Czars and empresses of Russia

Ruler	Reign	Ruler	Reign
* Ivan IV	1547-1584	Peter II	1727-1730
Fedor I	1584-1598	Anne	1730-1740
Boris Godunov	1598-1605	Ivan VI	1740-1741
Fedor II	1605	Elizabeth	1741-1762
False Dmitriy	1605-1606	Peter III	1762
Basil Shuisky	1606-1610	* Catherine II	1762-1796
Michael		Paul	1796-1801
Romanov	1613-1645	* Alexander I	1801-1825
Alexis	1645-1676	* Nicholas I	1825-1855
Fedor III	1676-1682	* Alexander II	1855-1881
Ivan V	1682-1696	* Alexander III	1881-1894
* Peter I	1682-1725	* Nicholas II	1894-1917
Catherine I	1725-1727		

*Has a separate article in *World Book*.

invaders. They recaptured the capital in 1612.

The early Romanovs. After the Poles were defeated, there was no one of royal birth to take the throne. In 1613, the zemskii sobor elected Michael Romanov czar. The Romanov czars ruled Russia for the next 300 years, until the February Revolution of 1917 ended czarist rule.

During the 1600's, Russia annexed much of Ukraine and extended its control of Siberia eastward to the Pacific Ocean. During this same period, the Russian Orthodox Church made changes in religious texts and ceremonies. People called *Old Believers* objected to these changes and broke away from the church. This group still follows the old practices today.

Peter the Great. In 1682, a struggle for power resulted in the crowning of two half brothers—Peter I (later known as Peter the Great) and Ivan V—as co-czars. Both were children, and Ivan's sister Sophia ruled as *regent* (temporary ruler) until Peter's followers forced her to retire in 1689. Peter made close contact with the many Western Europeans living in Moscow and absorbed

Oil painting (1885) by I. Repin; Tretyakov Gallery, Moscow (ITAR-Tass from Sovfoto)

Ivan the Terrible became the first Russian ruler to be crowned czar, in 1547. He expanded Russia's territory and made Moscow his capital. This painting shows Ivan holding his son after he killed him in a fit of rage.

RIA-Novosti from Sovfoto

Peter the Great ruled Russia from 1682 until his death in 1725. Peter was a powerful ruler whose many conquests expanded Russia's empire. He also reorganized the government.

much new information from them. He came into full power in 1696, when Ivan died.

Peter was greatly influenced by ideas of commerce and government then popular in Western Europe. A powerful ruler, he improved Russia's military and made many important conquests. During Peter's reign, Russia expanded its territory to the Baltic Sea in the Great Northern War with Sweden. In 1703, Peter founded St. Petersburg on the Baltic, and he moved the capital there in 1712. After traveling throughout Europe, he introduced Western-type clothing, factories, and schools in Russia, and reorganized Russia's government to make it run more efficiently.

Peter forced Russia's nobility to adopt many Western customs. He also increased the czar's power over the aristocrats, church officials, and serfs. He dealt harshly with those who opposed these changes. Under Peter, the legal status of serfs further deteriorated.

Catherine the Great. After Peter's death in 1725, a series of struggles for the throne took place. The service gentry and the leading nobles were on opposite sides. Candidates for the throne who were supported by the service gentry won most of these struggles and rewarded their followers. The rulers increased the gentry's power over the serfs and local affairs. The gentry's enforced service to the state was gradually reduced. It was ended altogether in 1762. Later that year, Empress Catherine II, known as Catherine the Great, came to power.

Magnificent royal parties and other festivities, all in the latest Western fashion, took place during the 1700's. The arts were promoted, and many new schools were started, mainly for the upper classes. The Russian Imperial School of Ballet was founded, and Italian opera and

chamber music were brought to Russia. It also became fashionable in Russia to repeat the newest Western ideas on freedom and social reform, especially during the rule of Catherine the Great. In 1767, Catherine called a large legislative assembly to reform Russian laws. However, the assembly achieved nothing.

The great majority of Russians remained in extreme poverty and ignorance during this period. In 1773 and 1774, the peasants' discontent boiled over in a revolt led by Emelian Pugachev, a Cossack. The revolt swept through Russia from the Ural Mountains to the Volga River. It spread almost to Moscow before being crushed by government troops. In 1775, Catherine further tightened the landowners' control over the serfs.

Under Catherine the Great, Russia rose to new importance as a major world power. In the late 1700's, Austria, Prussia, and Russia gradually divided Poland among themselves. Russia gained nearly all of Belarus, Lithuania, and Ukraine from Poland. In wars against the Ottoman Empire (based in present-day Turkey), Russia gained the Crimea and other Ottoman lands. Catherine died in 1796. She was succeeded by her son, Paul.

Alexander I. Paul's five-year rule ended with his murder in 1801. Alexander I, Paul's son, became czar and talked about freeing the serfs, building schools for all young Russians, and even giving up the throne and making Russia a republic. He introduced several reforms, such as freeing many political prisoners and spreading Western ways and ideas. But he did nothing to lessen the czar's total power or to end serfdom. Alexander knew that Russia's military strength and its position as a major world power depended on income that was provided by serfdom. Under Alexander's rule, Russia continued to win territory from Persia, Sweden, and the Ottoman Empire.

In June 1812, Napoleon led the Grand Army of France into Russia. He wanted to stop Russian trade with the United Kingdom, France's chief enemy, and to halt Russian expansion in the Balkan region. The French swept forward and reached Moscow in September 1812. Most people had left the city, and Napoleon and his army entered easily.

Soon afterward, fire destroyed most of Moscow. Historians believe the Russians themselves set the fire. After 35 days, the French left the city because they feared they might not survive the approaching bitter Russian winter. They began a disastrous retreat with little food and under continual attack by the Russians. Of the estimated 600,000 French troops in Russia, about 500,000 died, deserted, or were captured. Russia then became a major force in the campaign by several European countries that defeated Napoleon. See **Napoleon I** (Disaster in Russia).

Although Alexander had begun some reforms, harsh rule continued in Russia. Beginning in 1816, many young aristocrats became revolutionaries. They formed secret groups, wrote constitutions for Russia, and prepared to revolt. Alexander died in 1825, and Nicholas I became czar. In December of 1825, a group of revolutionaries, later called the *Decembrists,* took action. At the urging of the Decembrists, about 3,000 soldiers and officers gathered in Senate Square in St. Petersburg, and government troops arrived to face them. After several hours, the Decembrists fired a few shots. Government

RIA-Novosti from Sovfoto

Catherine the Great became empress of Russia in 1762. She expanded the country's territory and encouraged the development of the arts. But she preserved and extended serfdom.

cannons ended the revolt by the Decembrists.

Nicholas I. The Decembrist revolt deeply impressed and frightened Nicholas. He removed aristocrats, whom he now distrusted, from government office and replaced them with professional military officers. He tightened his control over the press and education, reduced travel outside Russia, and prohibited organizations that might have political influence. He established six special government departments. These departments, which included a secret police system, handled important economic and political matters. Through the special departments, Nicholas avoided the regular processes of Russian government and increased his control over Russian life.

In spite of Nicholas's harsh rule, the period was one of outstanding achievement in Russian literature. Nikolai Gogol, Mikhail Lermontov, Alexander Pushkin, and others wrote their finest works. Fyodor Dostoevsky, Leo Tolstoy, and Ivan Turgenev launched their careers. Many educated Russians began to debate the values of Westernized Russian life against those of old Russian life. The pro-Western group argued that Russia must learn from the West and catch up with it economically and politically. The other group argued for the old Russian ways, including the czarist system, a strong church, and the quiet life of the Russian countryside.

Nicholas became known as the "policeman of Europe" because he sent troops to put down revolutions in Poland and Hungary. Nicholas also declared himself the defender of the Eastern Orthodox Churches and fought two wars with the Muslim Ottoman Empire. In the war of 1828 and 1829, Russia gained much territory around the Black Sea. Russia also won the right to move merchant ships through the straits connecting the Black Sea

with the Mediterranean Sea. The Ottoman Empire controlled these straits.

In 1853, the Crimean War broke out between Russia and the Ottoman Empire. The United Kingdom and France, which objected to Russian expansion in the Black Sea region, aided the Ottomans. Russia was defeated and signed the Treaty of Paris in 1856. This treaty forced Russia to give up some of the territory it had taken earlier from the Ottomans, and the pact forbade warships on and fortifications around the Black Sea.

Expansion in Asia. After its defeat in the Crimean War, Russia began to expand in Asia. In the Far East, Russia won disputed territories from China. In 1858 and 1860, the Chinese signed treaties giving Russia lands north of the Amur River and east of the Ussuri River. By 1864, Russian forces defeated Muslim rebels in the Caucasus. Central Asia was won during a series of military campaigns from 1865 to 1876. In 1867, Russia sold its Alaskan territory to the United States for $7,200,000.

Alexander II. Nicholas I died in 1855, during the Crimean War. His son, Alexander II, became czar. Russia's defeat in the Crimean War taught Alexander a lesson. He realized that Russia had to catch up with the West to remain a major power. Alexander began a series of reforms to strengthen the economy and Russian life in general. In 1861, he freed the serfs and distributed land among them. He began developing railroads and organizing a banking system. Alexander promoted reforms in education, reduced controls on the press, and introduced a jury system and other reforms in the courts. He also established forms of self-government in towns and villages and modernized the armed forces.

But many young Russians believed that Alexander's reforms did not go far enough. Some revolutionary groups wanted to establish socialism in Russia. Others wanted a constitution and a republic. These groups formed a number of public and secret organizations. After a revolutionary tried to kill Alexander in 1866, the czar began to weaken many of his reforms. The revolutionaries then argued that Alexander had never been a sincere reformer at all. During the mid-1870's, a group of revolutionaries tried to get the peasants to revolt. They wanted to achieve either socialism or *anarchism* (absence of government) for Russia (see Anarchism). After this effort failed, a terrorist group called the People's Will tried several times to kill the czar. Alexander then decided to set up a new reform program. But in 1881, he was killed by a terrorist's bomb in St. Petersburg.

Alexander III, Alexander's son, became czar and soon began a program of harsh rule. Alexander III limited the freedom of the press and of the universities, and he sharply reduced the powers of Russia's local self-governments. He set up a special bank to help the aristocrats increase their property. He also appointed officials called *land captains* from among the aristocrats and gave them much political power over the peasants. Alexander started some programs to help the peasants and industrial workers. But their living and working conditions improved little during his reign.

Nicholas II became Russia's next, and last, czar in 1894. The revolutionary movement had been kept in check until the 1890's, when a series of bad harvests caused starvation among the peasants. In addition, as industrialization increased, discontent grew among the rising middle class and workers in the cities. Discontented Russians were attracted to three political movements. (1) The *liberal constitutionalists* wanted to replace czarist rule with a Western type of parliamentary government. (2) The *populists*, who later formed the Socialist Revolutionary Party, sought to promote a revolution among rural peasants and workers in the cities. (3) The *Marxists* wanted to promote revolution among the city workers. The Marxists followed the socialist teachings of Karl Marx, a German social philosopher (see **Marx, Karl**). In 1898, the Marxists established the Russian Social Democratic Labor Party.

Between 1899 and 1904, the discontent of the Russian people increased. Worker strikes and other forms of protest took place. In 1903, the Russian Social Democratic Labor Party split into two groups—the *Bolsheviks* (members of the majority) and the *Mensheviks* (members of the minority). V. I. Lenin was the leader of the Bolsheviks, later called Communists.

The Revolution of 1905. On Jan. 22, 1905, thousands of unarmed workers marched to the czar's Winter Palace in St. Petersburg. The workers were on strike, and they planned to ask Nicholas II for reforms. Government troops fired on the crowd and killed or wounded hundreds of marchers. After this *Bloody Sunday* slaughter, the revolutionary movement, led mainly by the liberal constitutionalists, gained much strength. In February, Nicholas agreed to establish an elected lawmaking body, called the Duma, to advise him. More strikes broke out during the summer, however, and peasant and military groups revolted. In part, the growing unrest was linked to the increasingly unpopular Russo-Japanese War. This war had broken out in February 1904 after a Japanese attack on Russian ships. The war ended with Russia's defeat in September 1905.

In October 1905, a general strike paralyzed the country. Revolutionaries in St. Petersburg formed a *soviet* (council) called the Soviet of Workers' Deputies. Nicholas then granted the Duma the power to pass or

reject all proposed laws. Many Russians were satisfied with this action, but others were not. The revolution continued, especially in Moscow, where the army crushed a serious uprising in December.

Each of the first two Dumas, which met in 1906 and 1907, was dissolved after a few months. The Dumas could not work with Nicholas and his high-ranking officials, who refused to give up much power. Nicholas illegally changed the election law and made the selection of Duma candidates less democratic. The peasants and workers were allowed far fewer representatives in the Duma than the upper classes. The third Duma served from 1907 to 1912, and the fourth Duma met from 1912 to 1917. During this period, Russia made important advances in the arts, education, farming, and industry.

World War I. By the time World War I began in 1914, Europe was divided into two tense armed camps. On one side was the Triple Entente (Triple Agreement), consisting of Russia, France, and the United Kingdom. Russia and France had agreed in 1894 to defend each other against attack. France and the United Kingdom had signed the Entente Cordiale (Friendly Understanding) in 1904, and Russia had signed a similar agreement with the United Kingdom in 1907. The Triple Entente developed from these treaties. Fighting against the Triple Entente was the Triple Alliance, which was an alliance formed in 1882 by Austria-Hungary, Germany, and Italy.

On Aug. 1, 1914, Germany declared war on Russia. Soon afterward, Russia changed the German-sounding name of St. Petersburg to Petrograd. German troops crushed the Russian army at Tannenberg, in East Prussia. However, the Russians defeated an Austrian army in the Battles of Lemberg in the Galicia region of Austria-Hungary, near present-day Lvov, Ukraine.

In 1915, Austrian and German forces drove back the Russians. The next year, the Russians attacked along a 70-mile (113-kilometer) front in Galicia. They advanced about 50 miles (80 kilometers). Russian troops moved into the Carpathian Mountains in 1917, but the Germans

Expansion of Russia

This map shows the increase in territory that took place in Russia between 1462 and 1914. Russia gained these lands through wars, conquests, and annexations. The boundary of present-day Russia appears as a solid red line on the map.

- - - - - - - Boundary of Moscow 1462

▢ Expansion 1462-1533

▢ Expansion 1533-1584

▢ Expansion 1584-1689

▢ Expansion 1689-1914

───── Boundary of present-day Russia

WORLD BOOK map

Sovfoto

V. I. Lenin, *with raised arm,* led the Bolshevik take-over of the Russian government in the October Revolution of 1917. He became the first leader of the Soviet Union.

pushed them back. For more information on Russia's role in the war, see **World War I.**

The February Revolution. During World War I, the Russian economy could not meet the needs of both the soldiers and the people at home. The railroads carried military supplies and could not serve the cities. The people suffered severe shortages of food, fuel, and housing. Russian troops at the front were loyal, but the untrained soldiers behind the fighting lines began to question the war. They knew they would probably be sent to the front and be killed. The soldiers and civilians behind the lines grew increasingly dissatisfied.

By the end of 1916, almost all educated Russians opposed the czar. Nicholas had removed many capable executives from high government offices and replaced them with weak, unpopular officials. He was accused of crippling the war effort by such acts. Many Russians blamed his action on the influence of Grigori Rasputin, adviser to the czar and the czarina. The royal couple believed that Rasputin was a holy man who was saving their sick son's life. In December 1916, a group of nobles murdered Rasputin. But the officials who supposedly had been appointed through his influence remained.

In March 1917, the people of Russia revolted. (The month was February in the old Russian calendar, which was replaced in 1918.) Violent riots and strikes over shortages of bread and coal accompanied the uprising in Petrograd, the capital of Russia. (Petrograd was known as St. Petersburg until 1914, was renamed Leningrad in 1924, and again became St. Petersburg in 1991.) Nicholas ordered the Duma to dissolve itself, but it ignored his command and set up a *provisional* (temporary) government. Nicholas had lost all political support, and he gave up the throne on March 15. Nicholas and his family were then imprisoned. Bolshevik revolutionaries shot the czar and his family to death in July 1918.

Many soviets were established in Russia at the same time as the provisional government was formed. The soviets rivaled the provisional government. Workers and soldiers tried to seize power in Petrograd in July, but the attempt failed.

The October Revolution. In August 1917, General Lavr Kornilov tried to curb the growing power of the soviets. But the attempt failed, and the Russian masses became increasingly radical. On November 7 (October 25 in the old Russian calendar), workers, soldiers, and sailors led by the Bolsheviks took over the Winter Palace, a former royal residence that had become the headquarters of the provisional government. They overthrew the provisional government and formed a new government headed by Lenin. Lenin immediately withdrew Russia from World War I. The new government soon took over Russia's industries and also seized most of the peasants' farm products.

In 1918, the Bolsheviks made Moscow the capital of Russia. They also changed the name of the Russian Social Democratic Labor Party to the Russian Communist Party. This name was later changed to the Communist Party of the Soviet Union. See **Communism.**

Civil war and the formation of the U.S.S.R. From 1918 to 1920, civil war raged between the Communists and the anti-Communists over control of Russia. The anti-Communists received support from several other countries, including France, Japan, the United Kingdom, and the United States. Nevertheless, the Communists defeated their opponents. They also established Communist rule in Georgia, Ukraine, eastern Armenia, Belarus, and Central Asia. The civil war contributed to the increasing discontent among the Russian people.

In 1921, peasant uprisings and workers' strikes broke out in opposition to Bolshevik policies. That same year, Lenin established a New Economic Policy to strengthen Russia. Under this policy, the government controlled the most important aspects of the economy, including banking, foreign trade, heavy industry, and transportation. But small businesses could control their own operations, and peasants could keep their farm products.

In December 1922, the Communist government created a new nation called the Union of Soviet Socialist Republics (U.S.S.R.). It consisted of four republics—the Russian Soviet Federative Socialist Republic, Byelorussia (formerly Belarus and now again known by that name), Transcaucasia, and Ukraine. By late 1940, Transcaucasia had been divided into Azerbaijan, Armenia, and Georgia, and 10 other republics had been established. The new republics included what are now Estonia, Kazakhstan, Kyrgyzstan, Latvia, Lithuania, Moldova (then Moldavia), Tajikistan, Turkmenistan, and Uzbekistan.

Stalin. Lenin died in 1924. Joseph Stalin, who had been general secretary of the Communist Party since 1922, rapidly gained power. He defeated his rivals one by one. By 1929, Stalin had become dictator of the Soviet Union.

In the late 1920's, Stalin began a socialist economic program. It emphasized the development of heavy industry and the combining of privately owned farms into large, government-run farms. Many citizens of the Soviet Union opposed Stalin's policies.

In the mid-1930's, Stalin started a program of terror called the Great Purge. His secret police arrested millions of people. Most of the prisoners were shot or sent to prison labor camps. Many of those arrested had helped Stalin rise to power. Stalin thus eliminated all possible threats to his power and tightened his hold over the Soviet Union.

World War II. By the late 1930's, German dictator Adolf Hitler was ready to conquer Europe. In August 1939, the U.S.S.R. and Germany signed a *nonaggression pact,* a treaty agreeing that neither nation would attack the other. In September, German forces invaded Poland from the west. The Soviet Union's forces quickly occupied the eastern part of Poland.

In June 1941, Germany invaded the Soviet Union and began a rapid advance into the country. The turning point of the war in the Soviet Union was the Soviet defeat of the Germans in the Battle of Stalingrad (now Volgograd) in 1943. Soviet troops then drove the Germans back out of the country and across eastern Europe. They attacked Berlin in April 1945. Berlin fell to the Soviets on May 2, and German troops surrendered to the Allies five days later.

In August 1945, the U.S.S.R. declared war on Japan. Japan surrendered to the Allies on Sept. 2, 1945, ending World War II. For more information on Russia's role in the war, see **World War II.**

The Cold War. After World War II ended, the Soviet Union extended the influence of Communism into Eastern Europe. By early 1948, several Eastern European countries had become *Soviet satellites* (countries controlled by the Soviet Union). The satellites were Bulgaria, Czechoslovakia, Hungary, Poland, Romania, and—later—East Germany. The U.S.S.R. also influenced Communist regimes in Albania and Yugoslavia. It cut off nearly all contact between its satellites and the West. Mutual distrust and suspicion between East and West developed into a rivalry that became known as the Cold War. The Cold War shaped the foreign policy of the Soviet Union and of many Western countries until the late 1980's.

Stalin died on March 5, 1953. In September of that year, Nikita S. Khrushchev became the head of the Communist Party. In 1958, he also became premier of the Soviet Union.

Khrushchev eased the terror that had characterized Stalin's dictatorship and relaxed some of the restrictions on communication, trade, and travel between East and

West. He also improved the Soviet people's standard of living. However, the U.S.S.R. continued working to expand its influence in non-Communist countries. Khrushchev improved Soviet relations with the West, but many of his other policies failed.

In 1964, the highest-ranking Communists overthrew Khrushchev. Leonid I. Brezhnev became Communist Party head, and Aleksei N. Kosygin became premier. Brezhnev and Kosygin increased the production of consumer goods and the construction of housing, and they expanded Soviet influence in Africa.

By the mid-1970's, Brezhnev was the most powerful Soviet leader. He sought to ease tensions between East and West, a policy that became known as *détente.* However, détente began to collapse in the late 1970's. Relations between the Soviet Union and the United States worsened over such issues as Soviet violations of human rights, the Soviet invasion of Afghanistan, and an increase in the number of nuclear weapons held by both the Soviet Union and the United States.

The rise of Gorbachev. In 1985, Mikhail S. Gorbachev became head of the Communist Party. Gorbachev instituted many changes in the U.S.S.R., including increased freedom of expression in politics, literature, and the arts. He worked to improve relations between the Soviet Union and the West and to reduce government control over the Soviet economy.

In 1989, the U.S.S.R. held its first contested elections for the newly created Congress of People's Deputies. The following year, the government voted to allow non-Communist political parties. Many Communist Party members and other Soviet officials opposed Gorbachev's reforms. But in March 1990, Gorbachev was elected by the Congress of People's Deputies to the newly created office of president of the Soviet Union.

The breakup of the U.S.S.R. During the late 1980's, people in many parts of the Soviet Union increased their demands for greater freedom from the central government. In June 1990, the Russian republic declared that laws passed by its legislature took precedence over laws passed by the central government. By the end of the year, each of the other 14 Soviet republics had made similar declarations.

In July 1991, Gorbachev and the leaders of 10 republics agreed to sign a treaty giving the republics a large amount of self-government. Five of the republics were scheduled to sign the treaty on August 20. But on August 19, conservative Communist Party leaders staged a coup against Gorbachev's government. They imprisoned Gorbachev and his family in their vacation home. The president of the Russian republic, Boris N. Yeltsin, led popular opposition to the coup. The coup collapsed on August 21. Gorbachev then regained his office as president but resigned as head of the Communist Party.

With the coup's collapse, the republics renewed their demands for more self-government. In September 1991, an interim government was established to rule until a new union treaty and constitution could be written and approved. This government included a State Council, made up of Gorbachev and the leaders of the republics.

On Dec. 8, 1991, Yeltsin and the presidents of Belarus and Ukraine announced the formation of the Commonwealth of Independent States (C.I.S.). They declared that the Soviet Union had ceased to exist and invited the re-

ITAR-Tass from Sovfoto

Leonid I. Brezhnev pursued a policy of friendly relations with the West called *détente.* In the 1970's, Brezhnev, *left,* and U.S. President Richard M. Nixon signed an agreement limiting production of nuclear weapons as a result of a series of meetings called the Strategic Arms Limitation Talks (SALT).

AP/WideWorld

Boris N. Yeltsin, *center, holding papers,* led opposition to the coup against Soviet leader Mikhail S. Gorbachev in 1991. The coup failed, and the Soviet Union rapidly dissolved. Yeltsin continued leading Russia through a difficult transition period.

maining republics to join the commonwealth. The members would be independent countries tied by economic and defense links. Most of the republics joined the C.I.S.

Yeltsin took control of what remained of the central government of the Soviet Union, including the Kremlin. On Dec. 25, 1991, Gorbachev resigned as Soviet president, and the Soviet Union ceased to exist.

The new nation. With the end of the Soviet Union, the Russian republic resumed its course as an independent nation. The breakup of the Soviet Union helped to ease remaining tensions between East and West.

In 1992, the Russian government slashed military spending and reduced the number of people employed in the armed forces. These cutbacks forced large numbers of former military personnel to find homes and jobs as civilians. That same year, the other former Soviet republics with nuclear weapons on their lands—Ukraine, Belarus, and Kazakhstan—agreed to eliminate all nuclear weapons on their territories within seven years. By the end of 1996, the three countries had turned over their nuclear weapons to Russia.

Russia had to establish new relationships with the C.I.S. members. Some Russian leaders wanted the country to take a leading role. But the smaller states feared domination by Russia because of its size and power.

Russia also faced the challenges of setting up new economic and governmental systems. The government ended price controls. The lifting of controls caused prices to soar and resulted in a lower standard of living for the Russian people. President Yeltsin and his government took steps to increase private ownership of businesses. For example, the government issued vouchers

that citizens used to buy shares in state-owned firms.

Opposition to Yeltsin's economic policies grew in parliament, which included many Communist Party members and former Soviet Union leaders. In a referendum held in April 1993, a majority of the voters supported Yeltsin and his economic policies. Opposition to Yeltsin in parliament continued, however. In September, Yeltsin suspended Vice President Alexander V. Rutskoi, who had become a leader of the anti-Yeltsin group. Later that month, Yeltsin dissolved parliament and called for new parliamentary elections in December. Parliament, in turn, voted to remove Yeltsin from office and to make Rutskoi acting president.

Rutskoi and many other foes of Yeltsin barricaded themselves in the parliament building in Moscow. At Yeltsin's order, police and forces of the internal affairs ministry blockaded the building, known as the White House. In October 1993, anti-Yeltsin crowds rioted and tried to break up the blockade. The next day, Yeltsin ordered the military to take control of the White House. Rutskoi and other leaders of the movement against Yeltsin were arrested.

The elections Yeltsin had called for took place in December 1993. Russia's voters elected a new parliament and approved a new constitution. The new document formally defined the powers of the president and of the parliament. In February 1994, the new State Duma granted amnesty both to those who revolted against Yeltsin in 1993 and to those who led the failed coup in 1991.

In parliamentary elections in 1995, the Communist Party won the largest number of seats in the State Duma. Many voters had initially shunned the Communists after the fall of the Soviet Union. However, the turmoil of transforming Russia into a democratic, capitalist nation brought voters back to the party. In 1996, Yeltsin won a second term as Russia's president.

In 1991, the government of Chechnya, a republic in southwestern Russia, demanded independence. In 1992, violence broke out between the Chechen government and citizens who wanted the region to remain part of Russia. In December 1994, Russia sent troops against the separatist forces, and serious fighting resulted. A cease-fire ended the fighting in August 1996. In May 1997, Yeltsin and the Chechen leader signed a peace treaty.

In 1998, Russia faced severe economic problems. In March, Yeltsin abruptly dismissed his cabinet, including Prime Minister Viktor S. Chernomyrdin. He forced parliament to accept young, reform-minded Sergei Kiriyenko as prime minister. In August, Yeltsin dismissed Kiriyenko and tried to bring back Chernomyrdin. But parliament forced Yeltsin to nominate another candidate. In September 1998, parliament approved Yevgeny M. Primakov, the minister of foreign affairs, as the new prime minister. In October, Yeltsin, who had been in poor health for some time, turned over most of his duties to Primakov. Russia's economic crisis continued.

Recent developments. In May 1999, Yeltsin abruptly dismissed Primakov and the rest of the cabinet members. Yeltsin appointed the minister of internal affairs, Sergei V. Stepashin, as prime minister. In August, Yeltsin replaced Stepashin with Vladimir V. Putin, former head of Russia's domestic intelligence service.

Shortly after Yeltsin's dismissal of Primakov, the State Duma took a vote on whether to impeach Yeltsin for a number of his past actions. But the Duma voted against impeachment.

In August 1999, Islamic militants who wanted to unite Chechnya and the neighboring republic of Dagestan seized several towns in Dagestan. Russia invaded Chechnya to oppose the rebellion. Russian attacks heavily damaged Chechnya's cities and killed many civilians. Many nations protested Russia's handling of the conflict.

In parliamentary elections in December 1999, the Communist Party again won the largest number of seats in the State Duma. Unity, a political group supported by Prime Minister Putin, won the second highest number of seats. Unity favors continuing the economic reforms begun during Yeltsin's tenure.

On Dec. 31, 1999, Yeltsin resigned and appointed Putin as acting president. In presidential elections in March 2000, Russians formally elected Putin. The war in Chechnya dragged on.   Donald J. Raleigh

Related articles in *World Book.* For more information about Russia between 1917 and 1991, see **Union of Soviet Socialist Republics** and its list of *Related articles.* See also:

Biographies

See the *Related articles* of **Classical music; Drama;** and **Russian literature.** See also:

Alexander I (czar)	Nicholas II (czar)
Alexander II (czar)	Peter I, the Great
Alexander III (czar)	Primakov, Yevgeny M.
Catherine the Great	Putin, Vladimir V.
Chernomyrdin, Viktor S.	Rasputin, Grigori E.
Fabergé, Peter Carl	Romanov
Ivan III, the Great	Rutskoi, Alexander
Ivan IV, the Terrible	Stalin, Joseph
Kerensky, Alexander F.	Stepashin, Sergei V.
Krupskaya, Nadezhda K.	Trotsky, Leon
Lenin, V. I.	Vladimir I
Nicholas I (czar)	Yeltsin, Boris N.

Cities

Arkhangelsk	Nizhniy	Samara
Irkutsk	Novgorod	Vladivostok
Kaliningrad	Novgorod	Volgograd
Kazan	Novosibirsk	Yekaterinburg
Magnitogorsk	Omsk	
Moscow	Rostov-on-Don	
Murmansk	Saint Petersburg	

History

Berlin, Congress of	Hungary (History)	Russo-Turkish wars
Bolsheviks	Mensheviks	Scythians
Crimean War	Mongol Empire	World War I
Czar	Poland (History)	World War II
Duma	Russo-Japanese War	

Physical features

Amur River	Kamchatka Peninsula	Novaya Zemlya
Azov, Sea of	Kara Sea	Ob River
Black Sea	Kuril Islands	Okhotsk, Sea of
Caspian Sea	Lake Baikal	Sakhalin
Caucasus Mountains	Lake Ilmen	Ural Mountains
Commander Islands	Lake Ladoga	Ural River
Don River	Lake Onega	Volga River
Dvina River	Lake Peipus	White Sea
Franz Josef Land	Lena River	Yablonovyy Mountains
	Mount Elbrus	Yenisey River

Other related articles

Air force (The Russian Air Force)	Army (The world's major armies)

Balalaika	Doll (Traditional dolls; picture)	Ruble
Ballet (Ballet in Russia)	Drama (Russian drama and Chekhov)	Russian language
Chechnya		Russian literature
Clothing (picture: Traditional costumes)	Karelia	Siberia
	Kremlin	Tatars
Commonwealth of Independent States	Mir	Theater (Russia)
	Nihilism	Tuva
	Novel (Russia)	Strategic Arms Reduction Treaty

Outline

I. Government
   A. National government   D. Courts
   B. Local government   E. Armed forces
   C. Politics

II. People
   A. Ancestry   B. Language

III. Way of life
   A. City life   D. Food and drink   H. Education
   B. Rural life   E. Health care   I. Museums and libraries
   C. Clothing   F. Recreation
               G. Religion

IV. The arts
   A. Architecture   C. Ballet
   B. Music   D. Painting and sculpture

V. Land and climate
   A. Land regions   C. Climate
   B. Rivers and lakes

VI. Economy
   A. Natural resources   F. Service industries
   B. Manufacturing   G. Energy sources
   C. Agriculture   H. Trade
   D. Mining   I. Transportation and
   E. Fishing industry   communication

VII. History

Questions

What is Russia's longest river?
Who led the October Revolution?
What is Russia's most popular sport?
How did composer Mikhail Glinka influence Russian music?
When did the Soviet Union cease to exist?
What is the most important type of building in Russian Byzantine architecture?
What part of Russia receives the heaviest snowfall?
Where in Russia does the vast majority of the population live?
What is the largest religious denomination in Russia?
Why did Czar Alexander II enact reforms?

Additional resources

Level I
Murrell, Kathleen B. *Russia.* Knopf, 1998.
Rice, Terence M. G. *Russia.* Gareth Stevens, 1999.
Russia. Lerner, 1992.
Schomp, Virginia. *Russia: New Freedoms, New Challenges.* Benchmark Bks., 1995.
Vail, John J. *Peace, Land, Bread! A History of the Russian Revolution.* Facts on File, 1996.

Level II
Brown, Archie, and others, eds. *The Cambridge Encyclopedia of Russia and the Former Soviet Union.* 2nd ed. Cambridge, 1994.
Curtis, Glenn E., ed. *Russia: A Country Study.* U.S. Government Printing Office, 1998.
Duffy, James P., and Ricci, V. L. *Czars: Russia's Rulers for over One Thousand Years.* Facts on File, 1995.
Figes, Orlando. *A People's Tragedy: A History of the Russian Revolution.* Viking, 1997.
Kort, Michael. *Russia.* Rev ed. Facts on File, 1998.
Milner-Gulland, Robin R. *The Russians.* Blackwell, 1997.
Raymond, Boris, and Duffy, Paul. *Historical Dictionary of Russia.* Scarecrow, 1998.
Service, Robert W. *A History of Twentieth-Century Russia.* Harvard Univ. Pr., 1998.

Russian language is one of the world's most important languages. About 153 million people speak Russian as their native tongue. Russian is the third most widely spoken European language, after English and Spanish, and is one of the six official languages of the United Nations. More science material is printed in Russian than in any other language except English.

Russian is the official language of Russia. It was the dominant language of the Soviet Union before that country was dissolved in 1991. It served as the common means of communication among most of the Soviet Union's many ethnic groups.

Russian, or Great Russian, belongs to the eastern branch of the Slavic linguistic family. Ukrainian (or Little Russian) and Belarusian (or White Russian) also belong to this branch. Russian is closely related to other Slavic tongues, such as Polish, Czech, Slovak, Slovenian, Serbo-Croatian, Macedonian, and Bulgarian. Russian has three main dialects: northern, central, and southern. Modern literary Russian is based on the central dialect, the speech of Moscow and the surrounding areas. The present literary Russian dialect became fairly stabilized by the end of the 1700's. It has changed little since that time.

Alphabet. The Russian alphabet has 33 letters. It uses the Cyrillic alphabet, which is based on the Greek alphabet. The letters and their approximate sounds in English are as follows:

The letters ъ, ы, and ь never occur at the beginning of a word or syllable. Most Russian consonants have two distinct pronunciations—an ordinary *hard* sound and a *soft* sound. Soft consonants are pronounced with the tongue raised and touching the hard *palate* (roof of the mouth). This position adds a short *y* sound to the consonant before the following vowel. The soft vowels— е, ё, и, ю, and я (as well as ь)—are pronounced *eh, oh, ee, oo,* and *ah,* and normally indicate that the preceding consonant is soft. Thus, ву is pronounced *voo,* and вю is pronounced *vyoo,* or somewhat like the French *vu.* At the beginning of a word or syllable, the soft vowels е, ё, ю, and я indicate a distinct *y* sound preceding the vowel: *ye, yoh, yu, ya.*

Russian spelling, like English, tries to combine a historical principle with a phonetic one. That is, some words retain their traditional spelling even though they are no longer pronounced as they used to be.

Grammar. Russian belongs to the Indo-European family of languages. Like Latin, Greek, and German, its words can have many different endings. Nouns have six cases and three genders. Adjectives change their forms to agree with the words they represent or modify. In addition, Russian has special forms for predicate adjectives and for the comparative and superlative forms. Russian verbs have only three tense forms—present, past, and future. Completed, continued, and repetitive actions are expressed by *aspect,* an essential feature of all Russian verb forms. The Russian language has a marked stress. The accent of a given word may change, depending on the grammatical form. The word order in a Russian sentence is not rigid. However, important new information tends to be placed at the end of the sentence.

Vocabulary. Comparatively few basic words in everyday Russian are easily recognizable as related to English. But many Russian and English words have a common ancestor. A few Russian words have been adopted into English. They include *czar, sputnik,* and *vodka.*

History. All the Slavic languages probably developed from a primitive Common-Slavic tongue. Old Church Slavonic, the language of the Russian Orthodox Church, resembles Common-Slavic more closely than does any other existing language. This tongue played a role in the history of Russian similar to that played by Latin in the history of the Romance languages. A great many modern Russian words, most of them compound forms with prefixes and suffixes, are actually Old Church Slavonic in origin. Russian has many word pairs. The native Russian form is used for a word with a concrete, everyday meaning, and the Old Church Slavonic is used to express a more technical or abstract concept. This characteristic resembles word pairs in English, which often consist of a common word derived from Anglo-Saxon (*house*) and a more formal word derived from Latin through French (*residence*).

The earliest formal literature in Russia was written chiefly in Old Church Slavonic, with some native Russian words and forms. The oldest manuscripts indicate that a distinct Russian language existed as early as the 1000's. Old Russian legal and business documents were written in the native dialect. By the 1700's, works of literature were written in Russian, which gradually replaced Old Church Slavonic entirely except for religious use.

Donald K. Jarvis

Russian		Roman equivalent	Approximate sound in English
А	а	a	*far*
Б	б	b	*b*og
В	в	v	*v*ault
Г	г	g	*g*o
Д	д	d	*d*og
Е	е	ye	*ye*t
Ё	ё	yo	*yo*lk
Ж	ж	zh	a*z*ure
З	з	z	*z*one
И	и	i	*fee*t
Й	й	y	bo*y*
К	к	k	*c*alm
Л	л	l	*l*aw
М	м	m	*m*oose
Н	н	n	*n*ot
О	о	o	*aw*e
П	п	p	*p*ot
Р	р	r	th*r*ice (rolled)
С	с	s	*s*oot
Т	т	t	*t*oe
У	у	u	f*oo*l
Ф	ф	f	*f*or
Х	х	kh	lo*ch*
Ц	ц	ts	i*ts*
Ч	ч	ch	*ch*eeks
Ш	ш	sh	*sh*ucks
Щ	щ	shch	fre*sh ch*erry
Ъ	ъ	—	indicates a break for syllable and *ye*-sound before next vowel
Ы	ы	y	rh*y*thm
Ь	ь	—	usually softens preceding consonant, adding a *ye*-sound, as *n* in canyon
Э	э	e	*e*ffort
Ю	ю	yu	*u*se
Я	я	ya	*ya*rd

Novosti Press Agency, Moscow

Russian literature includes many famous works, such as *The Three Sisters,* a drama by Anton Chekhov. A scene from a production of the play by the Moscow Art Theater is shown above.

Russian literature

Russian literature includes some of the greatest masterpieces ever written. Russian authors have used all literary forms, but are best known for their novels and poetry. Style, content, and keen character analysis contribute to the excellence of Russian writing. The most famous Russian works show a deep concern for moral, religious, and philosophical problems.

History has had an important influence on Russian literature. The widespread acceptance of Christianity in Russia during the late 900's resulted in literature that consisted mostly of religious works. Themes of the *Tatar* (Mongol) invasion and conquest dominated Russian literature from the 1200's to the late 1400's. The Tatar occupation isolated Russia from Western Europe for more than 200 years. But by the end of the 1600's, translations and imitations of Western European works were appearing in many Russian writings. By the late 1700's, literature included expressions of social protest against the czars, serfdom, and moral and political corruption.

The greatest Russian poetry, prose, and drama were written during the 1800's. The mid-1800's was the age of realism in Russian literature. Beginning in the 1890's, an artistic and cultural revival known as the Silver Age emerged. It developed from a combination of Russian religious philosophy, the ideas of the German philosopher Friedrich Nietzsche, and artistic doctrines and poetry from France. Most of the great Russian poets of the 1900's appeared during this period, which ended shortly after the Communist Revolution of 1917.

After 1917, literary activity was controlled by the Communist government. In 1922, the Communist government formed the Soviet Union, which existed until 1991. Government censors required that literature portray Soviet society as being full of optimism and joy of life.

Writers who ignored such regulations faced the threat of severe punishment. However, the constant struggle of Soviet writers against censorship led to periods of creative freedom and experimentation.

Early literature

Religious literature. The first Russian literature appeared at about the time of the nation's conversion to Christianity in A.D. 988. The literature, like the new religion, came from the Byzantine Empire and the Slavic kingdoms of Bulgaria and Serbia. The writings were largely religious in the form of sermons, hymns, and biographies of saints. Many of these works, despite their religious themes, were characterized by imagination and vivid details of Russian life. Some works were original, but many were based on Greek writings.

Early Russian literature was written in a mixture of Russian and *Old Church Slavonic,* a related language. Old Church Slavonic came from the Slavic peoples of central and Balkan Europe. The Russians also were Slavs, and could understand the new language without much difficulty. Old Church Slavonic became the official language of the Russian Orthodox Church. Elements of this language's style were used even in nonreligious literature to give it a more dignified tone.

Most of Russia's first literary works were both written and read by clergymen. Until 1564, when the first books were printed in Russia, the clergymen copied all manuscripts by hand.

Anna Lisa Crone, the contributor of this article, is Associate Professor of Slavic Languages and Literatures at the University of Chicago.

Nonreligious literature. The *chronicles,* which were records of outstanding events, were probably the most important early nonreligious Russian writings. The capital of each *principality* (region ruled by a prince) had its own chronicle. During the 1100's, some of these chronicles carried frequent warnings against the danger of a divided Russia. Later chronicles, particularly those of Moscow, claimed that their principalities had the right to reunite and rule all Russia. Much of a chronicle was dry narrative, but some accounts were vivid descriptions of military or political battles. Others were fantastic stories based on legend rather than fact.

The greatest work of early Russian literature was "The Lay of Igor's Campaign," written by an anonymous author of the late 1100's. This epic prose poem, famous for its vivid imagery and nature symbolism, describes the defeat of a Russian prince by the Polovtsians, an Asian tribe, in 1185. This work pleads for cooperation among the princes to prevent a foreign invasion. It warns that squabbles among Russian princes would lead to national destruction. The poem was a prophecy. The Tatars invaded Russia in 1223 and 1237. By 1240, they controlled most of Russia.

The literature of Tatar captivity reflected less original thought than did the literature of any other period in Russian history. Tatar rule, which lasted until 1480, provided the dominant theme of the small amount of literature that did appear. The "Zadonshchina" ("The Battle Beyond the Don"), an important work of the 1400's, describes the first major Russian victory over the Tatars. It describes this great victory with solemnity rather than jubilation. Christian imagery appears throughout "Zadonshchina." This work imitates the literary language and imagery of "The Lay of Igor's Campaign."

Muscovite literature developed as Moscow rose to power following the final defeat of the Tatars in 1480. All Russian-speaking territories were united into a single state under the grand prince of Moscow. Russia eventually became an empire, and the grand prince became known as czar. Main themes of Muscovite literature included the right of Moscow to rule the Russian land, and the czar's right to absolute authority. One work, the *Domostroy* (*Household Management*), advises a man to rule his family with complete authority, while obeying God, the czar, and the state. Other works praise the grandeur of the new Russian Empire. The most remarkable stylistic development of the Muscovite period is the elaborate *word-weaving.* It emphasizes style rather than content, including the formation of words and complex devices used in speaking and writing.

Beginnings of modern literature

Western influences. The 1600's saw an almost complete reshaping of Russian literature. Western Europe, from which Russia had been isolated since the 1100's, began to have a strong influence on Russian writing. Western works, such as anecdotes, fables, moral tales, poetry, and stories of knighthood, were translated and imitated. For the first time, rhymed verse appeared in Russian literature. Russian folklore provided a source for many fairy tales, *satires* (writings that ridiculed persons or their actions), and other works. Some authors discarded Old Church Slavonic, the old literary language, and wrote in Russian.

The greatest writer of the new literature was Avvakum, a conservative clergyman who belonged to a group called the *Old Believers.* This group opposed changes made in the ritual of the Russian Orthodox Church in the 1650's, which led to a split in the church. Avvakum's autobiography illustrates his colorful personality and religious convictions. His expressive language and vivid descriptions of daily life make his writings some of the most revealing works of this period.

Simeon Polotsky, a monk who received a Western education in Kiev, was an outstanding author of the period. His most important contribution to literature was the introduction of a rigid syllabic system into Russian verse. Each line of poetry has a fixed number of syllables with regularly placed pauses. Polotsky wrote quaint but serious verse. Many of his works praise the czar and the ruling family. He also wrote several plays on Biblical subjects.

Another playwright influenced by Western literature was Johann Gregori, a German Lutheran pastor in Moscow. Gregori's crude comedies, based on Biblical stories, were specially performed for the czar.

Czar Peter I (the Great), whose rule officially began in 1682, Westernized Russia. This adoption of Western culture and institutions led to great changes in Russian literature. Peter encouraged the translation of many European works and sent people abroad to study Western ways of life. He also invited large numbers of Europeans to Russia. European historians, architects, musicians, dancers, and writers came to Russia during and following Peter's rule.

The complete Westernization of Russian literature took place during the 1700's. Despite the many political changes that occurred in Russia, European culture continued to flourish there. Many French, German, and English works influenced Russian authors.

Antioch Kantemir, a leading poet and diplomat, wrote nine satires in syllabic verse supporting Peter the Great's reforms and the spread of Western culture. Kantemir used everyday speech in his works, and the informal language helped his characters appear lively and typically Russian.

Mikhail Lomonosov has been called the founder of modern Russian literature and the forerunner of classicism. His dignified *odes* (lyric poems) praise the czar and the greatness of God. Lomonosov introduced the modern Russian type of verse, featuring a regular pattern of stressed and unstressed syllables. He also established a system of three literary styles. These styles varied among (1) the highest, or most dignified, language; (2) the middle language based on spoken Russian, but without the vulgarisms; and (3) the lowest, or most popular, speech.

The classical movement, introduced by Lomonosov's literary reforms, emerged fully in Russia in the 1740's. The classical movement stressed the importance of reason and analysis in the interpretation of life. Classicism came to Russia as part of the continual cultural flow from Western Europe. It followed strict rules for composition, style, and subject matter. These guidelines were inspired by models of ancient Greek and Roman literature and were influenced by the literary criticism in *The Art of Poetry* (1674) by Nicolas Boileau-Despréaux of France.

The most typical Russian classicist was Alexander Sumarokov. His works included fables, plays, satires, and songs. Many of his comedies were amusing, but his tragedies were crude and monotonous.

Vasili Ivanovich Maykov, one of Sumarokov's followers, wrote a mock epic poem called *Elisey, or Bacchus Infuriated* (1771). This realistic work describes the hilarious adventures of a drunken coachman. Another important classicist, Denis Fonvizin, became famous for his satirical comedies. *The Adolescent* (1782), though it has obvious flaws, is considered his finest work. This play attacks the ignorance and cruelty of country landowners. Fonvizin was forced out of literature in the 1780's after Empress Catherine II (the Great) prohibited him from publishing his writings.

The outstanding poet of the 1700's was Gavriil Derzhavin who, like Lomonosov, wrote mostly odes. In "Ode to Felitsa" (1783) and other poems, Derzhavin praises Catherine and ridicules the vices of her courtiers. He did much to make the ode a fresh poetry of life and feeling. His work marked the turning point in Russian literature from classical to romantic writing.

During the late 1700's and early 1800's, fables were the most popular form of literature. Russia's greatest writer of fables was Ivan Krylov. His works, typically Russian in their everyday language and humorous characterizations, ridiculed ignorance and vanity.

The age of romanticism

Romanticism, which originated in Germany and England, stressed the full expression of emotions in literature. The movement developed as a revolt against the logic and formality used by classical writers. Romantic characteristics began to appear in Russian literature during the late 1700's. But romanticism did not become a significant influence until the early 1800's.

Sentimentalism, one of the strongest early romantic trends, came to Russia from Europe in the 1790's. The followers of this movement emphasized the importance of feelings and imagination. However, the sentimentalists continued to use classical forms in poetry.

The leading Russian sentimentalist was Nikolai Karamzin. His *Letters of a Russian Traveler* (written in 1789 and 1790) is filled with the excitement of his trip to the West and his meetings with famous writers. "Poor Liza" (1792) is a popular tale about a peasant girl who was abandoned by her lover, a nobleman. Karamzin's *History of the Russian State* (1816-1829) is still an important work of Russian history.

Preromanticism. Another group of writers of the early 1800's are known as preromantics. They showed a greater interest in nature and more love of moods than did the sentimentalists. Preromantics continued to use forms of classicism in their works. Leading preromantic writers included Vasili Zhukovsky and Konstantin Batyushkov. Zhukovsky, a gifted poet, translated works of several German and English romantics. Batyushkov was famous primarily for his *elegies* (sad poems on love and death). He also wrote sad, passionate lyrics.

Early romanticism. A new generation of poets appeared during the 1820's, marking the beginning of the *Golden Age* of Russian poetry. These poets, like the pre-

Important periods in the development of Russian literature

Early Russian literature (Late 900's to 1600's)	The age of romanticism (Late 1700's to the early 1840's)	The age of realism (Early 1840's to the early 1900's)
Early Russian literature consisted primarily of religious works written by clergymen. Some important nonreligious writings, mostly historical works, also appeared during this period.	The romantic movement in literature developed as a revolt against classicism. Romantic writing featured a new freedom of form and admiration for human emotion.	Realism in literature was a reaction against romantic writing. The realists felt that literature should portray life honestly. Russian realists wrote about social and political problems.
The chronicles "The Lay of Igor's Campaign" The "Zadonshchina"	**Sentimentalism** (Late 1700's and early 1800's)	**Early realism** (Early 1840's to the early 1860's)
Beginnings of modern Russian literature (1600 to the late 1700's)	Nikolai Karamzin *Letters of a Russian Traveler* (1789-1790)	Ivan Turgenev *Rudin* (1856) *Fathers and Sons* (1862)
Western Europe began to have a strong influence on Russian literature during the 1600's. Russian authors translated English, French, and German writings and imitated Western literary forms.	**Preromanticism** (Early 1800's) Vasili Zhukovsky Konstantin Batyushkov	Alexander Ostrovsky *Poverty Is No Crime* (1854) *The Storm* (1860)
Archpriest Avvakum Antioch Kantemir Mikhail Lomonosov	**Early romanticism** (1820 to the early 1830's)	**The period of great Russian novels** (Early 1860's to the early 1880's)
The classical movement, which began in Western Europe, appeared in Russia in the 1740's. Classical writers followed the formal rules of composition developed by the Greeks and Romans.	Alexander Pushkin *Eugene Onegin* (1825-1832) *Boris Godunov* (1825) Alexander Griboyedov *Woe from Wit* (1825)	Leo Tolstoy *War and Peace* (1869) *Anna Karenina* (1875-1877) Fyodor Dostoevsky *Crime and Punishment* (1866) *The Brothers Karamazov* (1879-1880)
Alexander Sumarokov Gavriil Derzhavin	**Late romanticism** (Early 1830's to the early 1840's)	**Late realism** (Early 1880's to the early 1900's)
	Mikhail Lermontov *A Hero of Our Times* (1840) Nikolai Gogol *Taras Bulba* (1835) *Dead Souls* (1842)	Anton Chekhov *Uncle Vanya* (1899) *The Three Sisters* (1901) Maxim Gorki *The Lower Depths* (1902)

romantics, combined classical forms with romantic sentiments. However, the early romantics showed a greater concern for individual freedom and an interest in a broader range of subjects. The poets of the Golden Age were strongly influenced by two English authors, William Shakespeare and Lord Byron.

Russia's greatest lyric poet, and the leading writer of early romanticism, was Alexander S. Pushkin. His poems are distinguished by their economical but very expressive language. Pushkin's concise style makes his works difficult to translate, or to be appreciated in any language except Russian. Pushkin's narrative poems deal with the place of human beings in society. Many of his main characters, such as the title hero of *Eugene Onegin* (1825-1832), are unable to find a purpose in life. They end up bored and insensitive to love.

In 1825, Pushkin wrote *Boris Godunov,* a historical drama in blank verse. It was an attempt to introduce Shakespeare's type of chronicle play into Russian drama. "The Bronze Horseman" (written in 1833), one of Pushkin's greatest narrative poems, centers on Peter the Great's Westernization of Russia and its effect on ordinary Russians. The work tells of both the glorious and tragic consequences of his grand design for Russia.

Pushkin also wrote a novel and several stories. His novel, *The Captain's Daughter* (1836), resembled the historical novels of Sir Walter Scott, a Scottish romantic. One of Pushkin's best stories, "The Queen of Spades" (1834), is about a gambler who goes mad after failing to win a fortune at cards.

Other poets of the Golden Age included Yevgeny Baratynsky, Baron Anton Delvig, and Wilhelm Kuchelbecker. Baratynsky became famous for his precise, original style. His narrative poems include *Eda* (1825), *The Ball* (1828), and *The Gypsy Girl* (1842).

Another important writer of the 1820's was Alexander Griboyedov. His most famous work, *Woe from Wit* (1825), is a satirical comedy written in rhymed verses. The hero, Chatsky, like Pushkin's Eugene Onegin, is unable to fit into the society of his time. Onegin and Chatsky became known as "superfluous" or useless men whose weak natures prevent them from pursuing constructive goals. Later writers used this character type to describe Russian nobles who could not provide strong liberal leadership in support of political and social reforms. The superfluous man appeared in Russian literature several times during the 1800's and early 1900's.

Late romanticism featured a new freedom of form and style, and an admiration for human feelings and passions. This movement, which began in the 1830's, also stressed the deep significance of dreams, visions, and fantasies. Political and moral corruption were the themes of some late romantic Russian literature. However, censorship had become severe under Czar Nicholas I, whose rule began in 1825. There was strict censorship of all literary works critical of Russian society, especially serfdom. The leading writers of this period included Mikhail Lermontov, Fyodor Tyutchev, and Nikolai V. Gogol.

Lermontov was an outstanding poet and novelist. His lyrics expressed intense frustration and boredom with life in Russia. In several of his poems, Lermontov

Literary revival (1890's to 1920's)	Soviet literature (1917 to 1991)	
The spirit of revolution, which swept through the country from the 1890's until the 1920's, was a period of social change with a renewed interest in the arts. This period was known as the Silver Age.	For many years after the Bolshevik Revolution of 1917, the government attempted to use literature as a propaganda tool. Soviet writers were told to present only favorable descriptions of life in the Soviet Union, and government censorship limited the free expression of ideas. The works of many Soviet writers were published only outside the Soviet Union. During the late 1900's, the government greatly relaxed its censorship policy.	
Symbolism, a literary trend that began in Russia during the mid-1890's, opposed a realistic portrayal of life in writing.	During the 1920's, several important works were written about the revolution and the civil war that followed from 1918 to 1920.	The 1950's and 1960's were marked by the appearance of several liberal writers who attacked social and political conditions in the Soviet Union.

Alexander Blok
  The Twelve (1918)
Andrey Bely
  St. Petersburg (1913-1914)
	Isaak Babel
	  Red Cavalry (1926)
	Alexei N. Tolstoy
	  Road to Calvary (1921-1941)
		Poets
		Yevgeny Yevtushenko
		Andrey Voznesensky
		Novelists

Post-symbolism, which began about 1910, was a revolt against the vague works of the symbolists. It stressed simplicity and clarity in literature.	From 1928 to 1932, Soviet writers helped promote Soviet industry by producing works that dealt with such subjects as agriculture and manufacturing.	Boris Pasternak
		  Doctor Zhivago (1957)
		Alexander Solzhenitsyn
		  The First Circle (1968)
		  The Gulag Archipelago, 1918-1956 (1973-1976)

Anna Akhmatova Osip Mandelshtam Vladimir Mayakovsky	Valentin Kataev *Time, Forward!* (1932)	In the 1970's and 1980's a number of writers continued to criticize the selfishness and hypocrisy of Soviet society.
	Many works written during the 1930's and 1940's were based on historical events, such as the revolution or the war against Germany from 1941 to 1945.	Yuri Trifonov *Another Life* (1975)

	Mikhail Sholokhov
	  The Quiet Don (1928-1940)
	Konstantin Simonov
	  Days and Nights (1943-1944)
		Vladimir Voinovich
		  The Life and Extraordinary Adventures of Private Ivan Chonkin (1975)

dreamed of an unattainable paradise. Pride and unrestrained desire cause the hero of *The Demon* (about 1839) to lose this ideal state. Lermontov's *A Hero of Our Times* (1840) was the first psychological novel in Russian literature. The hero, Pechorin, is another superfluous man. He wastes his life in senseless adventures because the strictness of Russian social and political life keeps him from any useful activities except his military duties.

Tyutchev, another brilliant romantic poet, wrote on such themes as the place of human beings in the universe, the limits of their understanding of nature, and their ability to communicate through language. His poems include "Silentium" (1830), "A Dream at Sea" (1833), and "Nature Is Not What You Think" (1836).

Gogol was one of Russia's greatest writers. His early works give colorful descriptions of life in Ukraine, where he was born. *Taras Bulba* (1835), a historical novel, praises the past glory of Ukrainian Cossacks. Literary critics regarded many of Gogol's later works as political satires. But Gogol's main objective was to make fun of humanity's spiritual weaknesses. The characters in *The Inspector-General* (1836) represent common human vices. "The Overcoat" (1842), the story of a pathetic copy clerk, protests the spiritual poverty of human beings. *Dead Souls* (1842), though never completed, is one of Gogol's most brilliant satires. The hero of the story travels around Russia buying up titles to dead serfs whose names are still in the census. He plans to use the titles in a swindle. This tale, an attack on moral corruption, was misinterpreted by readers of Gogol's day as a criticism of political corruption.

The age of realism

In the 1840's, realism emerged as an important literary trend in Russia. Its followers were influenced partly by the teachings of Vissarion Belinsky, a leading literary critic. Belinsky believed realistic literature should give an honest picture of life and, at the same time, preach social reform. His view that literature should serve the needs of society became an established principle in Russian criticism during much of the 1800's. This view continued to influence the choice of themes and their treatment in Russian prose in the 1900's.

Early realism. The literature of the 1840's and the 1850's had both romantic and realistic traits. Early realists combined romantic sentiments and feelings with realistic portrayals of social and political problems.

Ivan Turgenev, an outstanding novelist and playwright, displayed a deep understanding of Russian society and people. *A Sportsman's Sketches* (1852) helped stir up public sympathy for Russia's serfs. Turgenev described the serfs as kind and dignified, and portrayed landowners as crude and insensitive. In *Rudin* (1856), Turgenev shows the traditional superfluous man as a frustrated liberal. *Fathers and Sons* (1862) was superior to Turgenev's other works in dramatic content and in character analysis. It shows the *nihilists* (radical Russian youths of the early 1860's) as strong-willed, and disrespectful of authority and tradition. They want to change Russian society, but the country is not yet ready for a revolution. The hero, Bazarov, dies inactive and frustrated. One of Turgenev's favorite themes was young love, the subject of *Asya* (1858) and *First Love* (1860). In *First Love,* a boy experiences his first crush, only to learn

that the girl is his father's mistress. Turgenev's most successful play, *A Month in the Country* (completed in 1850), tells a similar story. A girl and her guardian compete for the love of a young tutor.

The novelist Ivan Goncharov tried to convince Russian liberals that only practical action, not sentiment, leads to social reform. In *Oblomov* (1859), the superfluous man is portrayed as a well-bred landowner, Oblomov, a charming and intelligent man whose almost total failure to act keeps him from achieving his youthful dreams. After this novel, Russians began to refer to inactivity within the privileged class as "Oblomovism."

Alexander N. Ostrovsky, one of the most popular and most productive Russian dramatists, wrote plays criticizing the middle classes. His use of everyday Russian speech gives his work strong national appeal. Ostrovsky's villains, products of the merchant world, are greedy, dishonest, and dominating. In *Poverty Is No Crime* (1854), a selfish businessman decides that his daughter must marry a wealthy swindler. Ostrovsky's greatest work, *The Storm* (1860), tells the tragic story of a merchant's wife who is driven to suicide by her domineering mother-in-law.

Sergey Aksakov, another leading writer of the 1850's, based his vivid descriptions of nature and people on childhood experiences. Unlike other Russian realists, Aksakov neither attacked nor defended Russian society in his writings. His works include *Family Chronicle* (1856) and *The Childhood of Bagrov the Grandson* (1858).

The 1860's and 1870's brought an end to romanticism in Russian literature. Russian realists began to write about social conditions in their works. A simplified prose replaced the elegant style of romanticism. The novel became the principal literary form. Many novels had vivid characters but little plot structure.

Count Leo N. Tolstoy, perhaps Russia's greatest writer of realistic fiction, produced his major novels during the 1860's and 1870's. Tolstoy discarded romantic values of heroism and spiritual love. Instead, he showed a deep concern for the natural stages of human development, such as birth, marriage, and death. Tolstoy's magnificent novel *War and Peace* (1869) captures the color and fire of the French invasion of Russia in 1812. But the novel also opposes war and reveals Tolstoy's desire for a quiet life in close harmony with nature. In *Anna Karenina* (1875-1877), Tolstoy attacked romantic love as self-indulgence, and encouraged a sense of moral duty and love of family instead.

Fyodor Dostoevsky was another great Russian novelist. His works are famous for their dramatic portrayals of inner conflicts. His characters experience a violent spiritual struggle between their belief in God and their strong sense of pride and self-centeredness. *Crime and Punishment* (1866), Dostoevsky's most exciting novel, describes the drama of a murderer who is tortured by his conscience. The hero is spiritually redeemed when he finally confesses his crime and accepts the punishment. *The Brothers Karamazov* (1879-1880), Dostoevsky's last and greatest novel, tells about the murder of an evil man by one of his four sons. The symbolic redemption of the other sons represents the author's faith in the saving power of God.

Late realism. Alexander III, who became czar in 1881, opposed many of the reforms made by his father,

Scene from *The Lower Depths* (1902); Theatre Collection, New York Public Library at Lincoln Center

Maxim Gorki's *The Lower Depths* is an example of the realism that dominated Russian drama during the late 1800's and early 1900's. The play describes the miserable lives and secret hopes of the inhabitants of a cheap boarding house.

Alexander II. Themes of despair and bitterness, resulting from the czar's harsh rule, appeared in Russian writings of the 1880's and 1890's. Stories and plays became the major literary forms of late realism.

Anton Chekhov was a leading writer of short stories and plays. Many of his works deal with the boredom and frustration of life. "Ionych" (1898) tells the story of a sensitive, idealistic doctor who becomes lazy and conceited as he grows older. *The Three Sisters* (1901) describes a family whose members are too weak-willed to change their dull lives.

Maxim Gorki, the last of the great Russian realists, wrote novels, plays, and stories. His early works, reflecting his Communist philosophy, describe the terrible poverty of the lower classes. Gorki's most famous play, *The Lower Depths* (1902), dramatizes the miserable lives of the inhabitants of a flophouse. A frequent theme of Gorki's later works was the decline of the upper middle class, shown in the novel *The Artamanovs' Business* (1925). Gorki also wrote a multivolume autobiography and published reminiscences of his meetings and friendships with leading Russian authors.

Literary revival

A spirit of revolution spread throughout Russia from the 1890's until the 1920's. This period was known as the Silver Age. This period of social upheaval and transition in Russia was also a time of tremendous vitality and renewal in the arts, especially literature.

Symbolism in Russian poetry and fiction began in the mid-1890's. The symbolists opposed the realistic portrayal of everyday life and its problems. Russian writers, particularly Tyutchev, Lermontov, and Dostoevsky, and several authors of Western Europe inspired the symbolists. Followers of the movement returned to the dreams and fantasies of the romantics. Some concentrated on religious and philosophical theories. Leading symbolists included Alexander Blok and Andrey Bely.

Blok, a poet, expressed his religious ideals in his early works. His later poetry describes the ugliness of the world. Blok's most famous work, *The Twelve* (1918), interprets the *Bolshevik* (Communist) revolution of 1917 as a spiritual purification of Russia.

Bely was an outstanding novelist and also a poet. His *St. Petersburg* (1913-1914) pictures the Russian capital as a place where Eastern and Western philosophies meet and conflict with almost explosive violence.

Leonid Andreyev combined elements of realism and symbolism in his works. He wrote sensational stories with themes of sex, madness, and terror. Examples of this style include the short story "The Red Laugh" (1904) and the play *He Who Gets Slapped* (1915).

Another leading writer of the early 1900's was Ivan Bunin. Although he was not a symbolist, his work, dominated by themes of love and death, resembles the literature of the symbolists. Bunin's masterpiece, "The Gentleman from San Francisco" (1915), is a story about an American millionaire who works too hard and is later unable to enjoy life.

Post-symbolism grew out of symbolism and represented a revolt against the vague, philosophical works of the symbolists. It began in Russia around 1910. The *acmeists,* one of the most important post-symbolist groups, began to write poetry that focused on the present world. They used clear-cut images and more concrete language. Leading acmeists included Nikolai Gumilev, Osip Mandelshtam, and Anna Akhmatova. A radical post-symbolist group called the *futurists* departed from traditional poetic themes and diction. Vladimir Mayakovsky, the most famous futurist and later an outspoken Communist, shocked readers with his strong language and unusual imagery.

Boris Pasternak, one of the greatest poets of the 1900's, created highly original poetry about nature and life. He achieved world fame with his epic novel *Doctor Zhivago* (1957). Marina Tsvetaeva, another great poet, experimented with Russian sounds and words. She strongly influenced the younger generation of Russian poets.

Soviet literature

The Communist Revolution of 1917 marked the dawn of a new era in Russian literature. The government greatly tightened censorship, which had existed under the czars. Many writers who opposed the Soviet government left the country or were imprisoned or executed. Those who stayed had to serve the interests of the state and could not criticize the government. Writers were told to describe Soviet life as happy and prosperous.

From 1917 to 1920. Following the revolution, literary activity decreased considerably. Publishing houses closed, and book production and sales dropped. Newspapers and magazines became political tools of the Communist Party. Printing presses were taken over by the state. The government encouraged the development of a *proletarian* literature to express the interests of Russian workers and peasants. However, few works of value were written during this period.

The period of rebirth in Russian literature occurred during the 1920's. The poor writing of the first few years of Communist rule resulted in a more lenient government policy. The government restored a certain amount of literary freedom, and reopened publishing houses. It also permitted literary criticism to resume. A new group of poets and novelists called *fellow travelers* appeared in the Soviet Union. Isaak Babel wrote a series of stories called *Red Cavalry* (1926) about the horrible conditions resulting from war. Leonid Leonov, inspired by Dostoevsky, told about the psychological effects of the revolution on the Russian people. His greatest novels are *The Badgers* (1924) and *The Thief* (1927). Alexei N. Tolstoy wrote *Road to Calvary,* a three-novel work consisting of *The Sisters* (1921), *1918* (1927), and *Bleak Morning* (1941). The novels deal with Russian intellectuals and members of the Russian middle class from 1914 to 1920.

The period of industrial literature began in 1928 with the Soviet Union's First Five-Year Plan. This plan aimed, in part, to build up Soviet industry. Writers were expected to produce works concerning economic problems. During this period, *factory* and *production novels* appeared in the Soviet Union. They dealt with such subjects as the building of a factory or the organization of collective farming. Most of this literature is inferior, but a few works, such as *Time, Forward!* (1932) by Valentin Kataev, are interesting and skillfully written.

The period of socialist realism started in the early 1930's. The government, headed by Joseph Stalin, banned all private literary organizations and established the Union of Soviet Writers. The union, which all professional writers were required to join, endorsed the newly developed theory of *socialist realism.* According to this doctrine, the main purpose of literature is to portray the building of a socialist society. The government-controlled union ordered Soviet authors to produce optimistic works that were easy to understand and similar to the style of such writers as Tolstoy and Gorki. Censorship eliminated undesirable material from manuscripts.

By forcing writers to meet the requirements of socialist realism, the government gained more control over literature. Writers who ignored the doctrine were expelled from the union. This meant the end of their careers. Some writers were imprisoned.

Historical literature became common during the 1930's and early 1940's. One of the finest works about the revolution and the civil war was *The Quiet Don* (1928-1940) by Mikhail A. Sholokhov. This long epic novel tells the story of a young Cossack whose happiness is destroyed by the tragedy of war. Sholokhov received the Nobel Prize for literature in 1965.

World War II. During the war against Germany from 1941 to 1945, the Soviet government gave writers somewhat greater freedom. Soviet leaders were more interested in fighting the Germans than in building socialism. Themes of individual suffering and death dominated this period. *Days and Nights* (1943-1944) by Konstantin Simonov was one of many patriotic war novels that appeared. The government reestablished strict controls over literature after the war. It also forced several leading authors out of the Union of Soviet Writers. These writers included Anna Akhmatova and Mikhail Zoshchenko, a noted humorist and satirist.

Modern Soviet literature. The death of Stalin in 1953 was followed by another period of relaxed restrictions in Soviet life and literature. This change became known as *The Thaw,* the name of a short novel written by Ilya Ehrenburg in 1954. In contrast to the policy of describing Soviet life as happy and optimistic, Ehrenburg wrote about frustrated, lonely people. Strict censorship returned after the publication in 1962 of *One Day in the Life of Ivan Denisovich* by Alexander Solzhenitsyn. This short novel describes Soviet labor camps under Stalin.

A number of young liberal writers appeared in the Soviet Union during the 1960's. Two popular young poets were Yevgeny Yevtushenko and Andrey Voznesensky. Both supported freedom and creativity in Soviet life. In "Babi Yar" (1961), Yevtushenko attacks the prejudice against Jews in the Soviet Union. The main theme of Voznesensky's work is self-analysis through personal experience. Several talented young prose writers, including Vasily Aksyonov, wrote about the shortcomings of Soviet life. Vasily Shukshin and other writers describe the hardships suffered by collective farmers.

Censorship in the Soviet Union prevented many works from being published, though typewritten or mimeographed copies of some of the manuscripts were circulated secretly. Some Soviet writers had works published abroad that had not been officially published in their own country. In 1957, Boris Pasternak's novel *Doctor Zhivago* appeared in Italy. Pasternak was awarded the 1958 Nobel Prize for his works, including this novel. He refused the prize because of pressure from the Soviet government.

Andrey Sinyavsky, writing under the name of Abram Tertz, wrote several short stories that were published abroad beginning in 1959. Sinyavsky's works, including *The Trial Begins,* describe the terrors of life in a police state. *The First Circle* by Alexander Solzhenitsyn was published in the West in 1968. This novel tells about the life of political prisoners in a research institute during the Stalin era. Solzhenitsyn won the Nobel Prize for literature in 1970.

From 1970 to 1980, political restrictions increased the difficulty of publishing in the Soviet Union. But a number of writers continued to criticize Soviet society. Valentin Rasputin wrote about the decay of morals and standards in rural areas. Vladimir Voinovich wrote a humorous satire of Soviet life in *The Life and Extraordinary Adventures of Private Ivan Chonkin* (1975). Yuri Trifonov dealt with moral dilemmas faced by Soviet intellectuals.

In the mid-1980's, Soviet leader Mikhail Gorbachev introduced a policy of *glasnost* (openness) that greatly relaxed censorship and led to freer public expression of information and opinion. The Soviet Union began publishing works of important Soviet writers, such as Akhmatova and Pasternak.

The post-Gorbachev period of political transition in Russia saw the massive publication of formerly undesirable writers. They include Tsvetaeva, Mandelshtam, and Solzhenitsyn, and once-suppressed religious thinkers, such as Nicolas Berdyaev and Vasily Rozanov. A talented group of women writers gained popularity, including Liudmila Petrushevskaia and Aleksandra Tolstaya. In 1969, Venedikt Erofeev wrote a short novel, translated as *Moscow to the End of the Line,* that became a cult favorite in the new Russia. The book contains the reflections of an imaginative alcoholic on a short train ride and seems to symbolize the odyssey of a lost Russia in search of herself. The era of Soviet literature ended in 1991 when the Soviet Union broke up into many independent countries.

Modern Russian literature

Russian literature today is marked by dynamism and diversity, though no clear trends have emerged since the breakup of the Soviet Union. Several newer writers have gained prominence. Vladimir Makanin has written novels that treat the guilt of Russian intellectuals during the Soviet period. Viktor Erofeev has produced fiction dealing with sex, violence, horror, absurdity, and power used for evil. Notably newer poets include Olga Sedakova, David Samoilov, and Viktor Krivulin.   Anna Lisa Crone

Related articles in *World Book* include:

Andreyev, Leonid	Pushkin, Alexander
Brodsky, Joseph	Sholokhov, Mikhail
Bunin, Ivan	Solzhenitsyn, Alexander
Chekhov, Anton	Tolstoy, Alexei
Dostoevsky, Fyodor	Tolstoy, Leo
Gogol, Nikolai	Turgenev, Ivan
Gorki, Maxim	Yevtushenko, Yevgeny
Pasternak, Boris	

Outline

I. Early literature
 A. Religious literature
 B. Nonreligious literature
 C. The literature of Tatar captivity
 D. Muscovite literature
II. Beginnings of modern literature
 A. Western influences
 B. The classical movement
III. The age of romanticism
 A. Sentimentalism
 B. Preromanticism
 C. Early romanticism
 D. Late romanticism
IV. The age of realism
 A. Early realism
 B. The 1860's and 1870's
 C. Late realism

V. Literary revival
 A. Symbolism   B. Post-symbolism
VI. Soviet literature
 A. From 1917 to 1920
 B. The period of rebirth
 C. The period of industrial literature
 D. The period of socialist realism
 E. World War II
 F. Postwar Soviet literature
VII. Modern Russian literature

Questions

What was the literary language used in early Russia?
What were the *chronicles*?
How did Western culture affect Russian literature?
Who was the founder of modern Russian literature?
What were the characteristics of Russian romanticism?
How did *glasnost* affect Soviet literature?
What was the "superfluous" man?
Who were Russia's greatest novelists?
Who were the *acmeists*? The *futurists*?
What is the theory of *socialist realism*?

Additional resources

Brown, Clarence, ed. *The Portable Twentieth-Century Russian Reader.* Rev. ed. Viking Penguin, 1993.
Brown, William E. *A History of Russian Literature of the Romantic Period.* 4 vols. Ardis, 1986.
Kasack, Wolfgang. *Dictionary of Russian Literature Since 1917.* Columbia Univ. Pr., 1988.
Moser, Charles A., ed. *The Cambridge History of Russian Literature.* Rev. ed. Cambridge, 1992.
Terras, Victor. *A History of Russian Literature.* Yale, 1992.
Terras, Victor, ed. *Handbook of Russian Literature.* 1985. Reprint. Yale, 1990.
Woodward, James B. *Form and Meaning: Essays on Russian Literature.* Slavica, 1993.

Russian Revolution. See Russia (History); Union of Soviet Socialist Republics (History).

Russo-Finnish wars. During World War II, the Soviet Union and Finland fought each other in two wars. They battled in the brief "Winter War" of 1939-1940. The second war, called the "Continuation War," took place from 1941 to 1944. Finland lost both wars.

"The Winter War." Germany conquered Poland in 1939. The Soviet Union feared a German invasion by way of Finnish territory. It maintained that it needed Finland's Karelian Isthmus, only 25 miles (40 kilometers) from the Soviet city of Leningrad (now St. Petersburg), to protect its borders. The Soviet Union demanded that Finland cede this territory and allow it to set up defenses along the Finnish coast. The Finns refused. After failed talks, the Soviet Union broke diplomatic ties with them.

On Nov. 30, 1939, the Soviet Union attacked Finland without formally declaring war. In the early stages of a harsh winter campaign, the Finns demonstrated that a small army using advantages of terrain and climate could outfight a larger and better-equipped force. But by February, the tide turned. The Finns suffered heavy losses, and received little help from other countries. On March 12, 1940, Finland had to accept harsh Soviet terms and sign the Peace of Moscow.

The Soviet Union took even more than it had first demanded. Finland lost one-tenth of its total area, including most of Karelia, the industrialized areas of Lake Ladoga, strategic islands in the Gulf of Finland, and the Petsamo region on Finland's Arctic coast near the Soviet port of Murmansk. The Soviet Union also received a 30-year lease on the Hangö Peninsula.

"The Continuation War." Between the first and second Russo-Finnish wars, Finland entered into a closer relationship with Nazi Germany. In September 1940, Finnish military leaders secretly agreed to allow German troops and war supplies to enter Finland. On June 22, 1941, Germany invaded the Soviet Union. Finland sought to regain territory it lost in the "Winter War." It joined in the war against the Soviet Union. The Soviet Union immediately bombed Finland.

Britain had already declared war on Germany. It now declared war on Finland, in December 1941. As the war turned against the Germans, Finnish enthusiasm for the war cooled. In September 1944, Finland accepted severe Soviet peace terms. The treaty restored the 1940 Finnish-Soviet border. The Finns lost the Arctic port of Petsamo and nearby nickel mines. They regained the Hangö Peninsula, but had to grant the Soviet Union a 50-year lease on the Porkkala Peninsula, near Helsinki. Finland agreed to pay the Soviet Union $300 million for war damages, and to disarm the German troops in Finland. The Soviet Union returned the Porkkala Peninsula to Finland early in 1956. In 1962, the Soviet Union agreed to lease to Finland part of the Saimaa Canal lost to the Soviet Union in 1940. Stefan T. Possony

See also Finland (History).

Russo-Japanese War brought recognition to Japan as a major world power. Russia's poor showing in the war sharpened the dissatisfaction of its people with the Russian government. This discontent helped shape the course of the Russian Revolution of 1905. The Russo-Japanese War began on Feb. 8, 1904, when Japan attacked Lüshun (also called Port Arthur) in Manchuria. It ended on Sept. 5, 1905, with the signing of the Treaty of Portsmouth.

Underlying causes of the war were the conflicting ambitions of Russia and Japan. Russia had been expanding its holdings and its interests in the Far East throughout the late 1800's. In 1891, Russia began to build the Trans-Siberian Railroad connecting Moscow and Vladivostok. In 1896, a treaty between Russia and China allowed Russia to build the Chinese Eastern Railway across Manchuria. In 1898, Russia leased the Liaodong Peninsula from China and built there the naval base of Lüshun and the commercial port of Dalian. As a result of the Boxer Rebellion in China (1900-1901), Russia increased its influence in Manchuria (see **Boxer Rebellion**). Russia also expanded its influence in Korea during these years.

These actions disturbed Japan, which also wanted to extend its power at the expense of China. After Japan defeated China in a war (1894-1895), it tried to seize the Liaodong Peninsula. But Russia, Germany, and France prevented that move. Japan became angry when Russia leased Liaodong. The two nations were also rivals in Korea, whose location was important to them both. Japan wanted to control Korean trade and industry. It already owned the Korean railroads and had sent thousands of Japanese settlers to Korea.

Japan sought a settlement with Russia over their rival interests in Manchuria and Korea. But Russia rejected Japan's offers. The Japanese therefore made an alliance with Britain in 1902 and began to prepare for war.

Attack on Lüshun. Japan broke off diplomatic relations with Russia on Feb. 6, 1904. On February 8, Vice Admiral Heihachiro Togo's fleet attacked Russian ships at Lüshun without warning. Japan declared war against Russia on February 10. Russia seemed so much more powerful than Japan that most people expected Russia to win the war easily. But Russia had only 80,000 troops in the Far East when the war began. More soldiers and all supplies for the army had to be shipped over 5,000 miles (8,000 kilometers) from western Russia on the uncompleted Trans-Siberian Railroad. Also, Russia was weakened by social and political problems that would lead to a revolution in 1905.

Final battles. Japan had 200,000 troops in North China, and another large army nearby. Japan lay closer to the scene of the fighting, and its people supported the government. Japanese warships and mines soon bottled up in Lüshun most of Russia's Pacific squadron. The Japanese destroyed most of the Russian ships that tried to escape. They also defeated the Russians at Vladivostok in the Battle of the Sea of Japan. Russia then ordered its Baltic Fleet to the Far East. This fleet steamed from the Baltic Sea around Africa, across the Indian Ocean, and into the Korean Strait. But the Japanese nearly annihilated it in the Battle of Tsushima Straits.

The land war went just as badly for the Russians. The Russians were handicapped by poor leadership and a lack of troops and supplies. The Japanese were trained and well-organized and had modern equipment. Japanese forces gradually drove the Russian forces back into Manchuria and defeated them at the Battle of Mukden in 1905. After a two-month siege, Lüshun surrendered to Japan. By then, both countries were ready to stop the war. The Japanese were running out of war funds. The Russian government wanted to end an unpopular war because revolution had broken out at home.

Treaty at Portsmouth. In 1905, at the secret suggestion of Japan, President Theodore Roosevelt of the United States arranged a peace conference at Portsmouth, New Hampshire. The Treaty of Portsmouth gave southern Sakhalin Island to Japan and forced Russia to remove its troops from Manchuria. Russia had to give Lüshun and Dalian to Japan and also leave Korea for the Japanese. But Russia kept control of the Chinese Eastern Railway. Donald J. Raleigh

Russo-Turkish wars were a series of conflicts between the Russian Empire and the Ottoman Empire, which was based in what is now Turkey. From the 1400's to the 1900's, these two empires engaged in nearly constant warfare with each other. At first, they clashed over lands that were claimed by both the Russians and the Crimean Tatars, who were allies of the Ottomans. Most of these lands lie in what is now Ukraine. Beginning in the late 1600's, Russian advances into Ottoman territory on the Black Sea and in southeastern Europe caused further fighting between the empires.

Peter the Great and then Catherine the Great of Russia each fought successful wars against the Ottomans. During the late 1600's, Peter forced them out of most of present-day Ukraine. During the 1700's, Catherine's armies conquered the Crimea, a peninsula in southern Ukraine, and completed the opening of the southern lands to Russian settlement. Catherine also forced the Ottomans to allow Russian merchant vessels to sail the Black Sea.

Russia and Austria allied themselves against the

Ottoman Empire during a war fought from 1736 to 1739. They also formed an alliance against the Ottomans in the two Russo-Turkish wars (1768-1774 and 1787-1792) fought in the reign of Catherine the Great. Russia and the Ottomans were allies briefly in the early 1800's, but this unusual arrangement did not last.

During the 1800's, Russia and the Ottomans fought four wars against each other: 1806-1812, 1828-1829, 1853-1856, and 1877-1878. At the end of the first war, Russia acquired Bessarabia (now parts of Moldova and Ukraine). It also gained a special position in the Balkans, a region that included present-day Albania and Bulgaria and much of what became Yugoslavia. The second war gave Russia control of the eastern coast of the Black Sea. The Ottomans won the third war, known as the Crimean War. As a result, Russia lost its dominant position in the Balkans and Black Sea area. However, it regained these losses after the 1877-1878 war.

During World War I (1914-1918), the Ottomans fought on the side of Germany against Russia and the other Allies. Both the Russian and Ottoman empires were destroyed in the war. The nations that succeeded the Ottoman and Russian empires—Turkey and the Soviet Union, respectively—continued to oppose each other. The Soviet Union attempted to seize portions of the Turkish Republic after World War II ended in 1945. But firm Turkish refusal and an alliance between Turkey and the United States blocked the attempt.   Justin McCarthy

See also **Berlin, Congress of; Crimea; Crimean War.**

Russwurm, John Brown (1799-1851), was an early spokesman against slavery and an important figure in a black American "back-to-Africa" movement. Russwurm expressed his antislavery views chiefly through *Freedom's Journal,* a newspaper he and Samuel Cornish started in New York City in 1827. The newspaper was the first in the United States to be owned and operated by blacks. Russwurm soon came to believe that blacks could never gain full citizenship in the United States. In 1829, he moved to Liberia, in Africa. Liberia had been founded in 1822 as a place where free blacks from the United States could settle. Russwurm served as governor of a colony at Cape Palmas, Liberia.

Russwurm was born in Jamaica and raised in Maine. He graduated from Bowdoin College.   Richard Bardolph

Rust is the common name of a group of diseases caused by fungi that are parasites on plants. Rusts are especially harmful to cereal crops. The rust diseases are named for the spores produced by the fungi. These spores are brownish and resemble iron rust. Rusts have special organs resembling threads that grow among the cells of the host plant and absorb the food of the plant cells. This action robs the plant of nutrients and may cause the leaves and stems to wither. Badly rusted crops produce shriveled and worthless grain. Rust-causing fungi also attack other types of plants. For example, *asparagus rust* damages asparagus, *blister rust* attacks white pine trees, and *cedar rust* harms apples.

Every species of rust-causing fungi goes through a certain life cycle. Each period or stage in this life cycle is marked by a different type of spore formation. Some rust-causing fungi have as many as five different types of spores, while others have only two or three. Some species of rust-causing fungi spend their entire life cycle on one host. These species are called *autoecious.* Other

species must spend their life cycle on two different hosts. This type is called *heteroecious.* The second host is known as the *alternate host.*

A common heteroecious type of rust-causing fungus causes *black stem rust* of wheat plants. This species has five different kinds of spores and must live its life cycle on two hosts, the wheat plant and the American barberry plant (see **Barberry**). In the spring, small cups filled with spores appear on the lower side of the leaves of the barberry plant. These spores are carried by the wind and spread to wheat plants. The spores germinate and send out threads. These enter the tissues of the wheat plant and there produce reddish spores that are carried to other healthy wheat plants. This is the first stage. The second stage occurs in the fall, when there is a growth of tiny black spores on the stalks and stubble. These black spores sprout in the spring and produce small colorless spores called *sporidia,* which mark the third stage of life. The sporidia cannot grow on the wheat plant and will grow only on the barberry plant. These sporidia are carried by the wind to the barberry. The fourth stage is the development of tiny yellow spores on the upper surface of the barberry leaves. Later, yellow-orange cups containing spores appear on the undersurface of the barberry leaves. This marks the fifth stage. These spores are not able to infect the barberry plants. They must be carried on the wind to wheat plants. There the life cycle begins again.

One method of controlling a rust that grows on two hosts is to destroy the alternate host. In the case of black stem rust, wheat crops have been saved by destroying barberry plants. Another method is to breed rust-resistant plants. Rust is sometimes controlled by destroying or uprooting crops affected by the disease. Crop rotation also helps prevent rust.   Joseph G. Hancock

Rust is a brownish-red substance that forms on the surface of iron or steel when it is exposed to damp air. The term used alone means *iron rust,* which consists mainly of hydrated iron oxide ($3Fe_2O_3 \cdot H_2O$). Rust is formed by the union of the oxygen of the air with the iron by a process called *oxidation* (see **Oxidation**).

Rust not only corrodes the surface but also weakens the metal. Long exposure to air and moisture will cause nails to rust off, and rust holes to form in sheet iron. Iron can be *alloyed* (mixed) with other chemical elements to create rust-resistant metals called *stainless steels.* Iron and steel that are not rust resistant should be kept dry or coated with some substance, such as chrome or paint, that will resist the action of oxygen. Polished tools may be easily protected if wiped with a cloth soaked in oil. Coating metal objects with heavy greases or spray-on plastics, or wrapping them in special chemically treated paper, also prevents rust.

A coat of rust may be removed by scrubbing in water or using a polishing powder. Removal of a thick coat requires use of an emery wheel, a grindstone, or a file. Acids also dissolve rust.   Raymond E. Davis

See also **Corrosion; Stainless steel.**

Rustin, Bayard, *BY* urd (1910-1987), was an American civil rights leader. A Quaker and a pacifist, he believed in achieving civil rights by nonviolent means. Rustin was the chief organizer of the 1963 March on Washington. Over 200,000 people took part in the march to protest racial injustice in the United States. He also planned the organization of the Southern Christian Leadership Conference, led by Martin Luther King, Jr. In 1947, Rustin helped organize the first "freedom ride" into the South to protest racial discrimination. In 1964, he became executive director of the A. Philip Randolph Institute in New York City. This group works toward economic and social reforms to benefit Americans of all races. Rustin was born in West Chester, Pennsylvania.   C. Eric Lincoln

Rutabaga, *ROO tuh BAY guh,* is a plant with an edible root that tastes like a turnip. It is also called *Swedish turnip* and *Russian turnip.* Rutabagas are hardier than turnips, and so are usually harvested later in the year. The yellow roots are rich in vitamins and minerals. The blue-green leaves also may be eaten. The leaves usually are harvested in early summer because they become spongy and bitter in hot weather.

Scientific classification. Rutabaga is in the mustard family, Brassicaceae or Cruciferae. Its scientific name is *Brassica napus,* variety *napobrassica.*   Albert Liptay

Rutgers The State University of New Jersey has its main campus in New Brunswick, New Jersey. It also has coeducational undergraduate colleges and graduate and professional schools in Newark and Camden, and offers extension courses throughout the state.

The New Brunswick campus has one undergraduate college for women only—Douglass College—and three coeducational undergraduate colleges—Livingston College, Rutgers College, and Cook College. University College, which has divisions in Newark and Camden, offers evening courses. The New Brunswick campus includes the Institute of Microbiology and graduate and professional schools of applied and professional psychology; arts and sciences; communication and information and library studies; creative and performing arts; education; engineering; environmental sciences, agriculture, and life sciences; pharmacy; and social work. The Newark campus has the Newark College of Arts and Sciences; a college of nursing; and graduate schools of arts and sciences, business, criminal justice, and law. The Camden campus includes the Camden College of Arts and Sciences, a graduate school, and a law school.

Rutgers was founded in 1766 as Queen's College and took its present name in 1825.

Critically reviewed by Rutgers The State University of New Jersey

Ruth, Babe (1895-1948), was the first great home run hitter in baseball history. His batting ability and colorful personality attracted huge crowds wherever he played. He made baseball more exciting by establishing homers as a common part of the game. Ruth set many major league records, including 2,056 career bases on balls and 72 games in which he hit two or more home runs. He had a .342 lifetime batting average.

George Herman Ruth was born in Baltimore. He began his baseball career in 1914 with the Baltimore Orioles, a minor league team at the time. Later that same year, he joined the Boston Red Sox as a pitcher. In the 1916 and

New York Yankees
Babe Ruth

1918 World Series, Ruth pitched $29\frac{2}{3}$ consecutive scoreless innings. He won 94 games and lost 46 during his major league career. But Ruth had even greater talent as a hitter and began to play regularly in the outfield in 1918. That year also marked his first big home run season, when he hit 11. In 1920, the Red Sox sold Ruth to the New York Yankees. He attracted so many fans that Yankee Stadium, which opened in 1923, was nicknamed "the House That Ruth Built."

In 1927, Babe Ruth set a record of 60 home runs during a 154-game season. In 1961, Roger Maris hit 61 home runs during a 162-game season. Both feats were considered major league records until 1991, when Maris's 61 home runs were recognized as the sole record. Ruth hit 714 homers during his career, a record until Henry Aaron hit his 715th home run in 1974.

The Yankees released Ruth after the 1934 season, and he ended his playing career in 1935 with the Boston Braves. In the final game he started in the outfield for Boston, Ruth hit three home runs. In 1936, Ruth became one of the first five players elected to the National Baseball Hall of Fame.   Jack Lang

See also **Baseball** (The Babe Ruth Era; picture).

Additional resources

Creamer, Robert W. *Babe.* 1974. Reprint. Simon & Schuster, 1992.
Sanford, William R., and Green, C. R. *Babe Ruth.* Crestwood, 1992. Younger readers.

Ruth, Book of, is a book of the Hebrew Bible, or Old Testament. The story centers on the loving and loyal behavior of Ruth, a Moabite woman married to an Israelite. Left widowed and childless in Moab, Ruth resolves to leave her homeland and follow her mother-in-law, Naomi, to Bethlehem. When Naomi urges her to stay among her people, Ruth responds with the famous words "Whither thou goest, I will go. . . . Thy people shall be my people, and thy God my God. Where thou diest I will die, and there will I be buried" (Ruth 1: 16-17). Continuing her bold actions, Ruth manages to obtain food for herself and Naomi and to marry Boaz, a kinsman, and thus secure the family heritage.

The story of Ruth is a beautifully crafted piece of literature. It conveys the resources of individuals in dealing with life's problems. It shows Israelite openness to all peoples and offers a glimpse of the independent and courageous actions of women in ancient Israel. Since Ruth is portrayed as the great-grandmother of King David, the book links her to the genealogy of Israel's royal family.   Carol L. Meyers

Ruthenia is a historic region in Ukraine. Ruthenia lies on the southern slopes of the Carpathian Mountains and on the nearby southwest highland. It covers approximately 4,940 square miles (12,800 square kilometers) and has about 1,196,000 people. Uzhgorod is the region's principal city.

Most Ruthenians are farmers. The principal industries of the region include wood processing, winemaking, and such handicrafts as basket weaving, embroidery, and leathercraft. Ruthenia's chief natural resources are timber and rock salt.

In the 900's and 1000's, Ruthenia was part of Kievan Rus, the first state founded by the East Slavs. It later came under the control of *Magyar* (Hungarian) landlords. In 1919, Ruthenia became a province of Czechoslovakia.

Ruthenia once had great strategic value because of its location near several countries. Germany, Hungary, Poland, and the Soviet Union all tried to gain control of the area in the 1930's. In 1939, Hungary took control of the entire region. The Soviet Union occupied Ruthenia in 1944, during World War II. It officially annexed the region in 1945. Ruthenia was made part of the Ukrainian Soviet Socialist Republic. In 1991, the republic became the independent country of Ukraine.   Vojtech Mastny

Ruthenium, *roo THEE nee uhm,* is a rare, silver-white metallic element. It is used mainly in jewelry as a hardener of the metals platinum and palladium. Alloys of ruthenium with those metals are highly resistant to wear and are used for electrical contacts in the ignition systems of some aircraft engines. Karl Klaus, a Russian chemist, discovered ruthenium in 1844. Ruthenium has an atomic number of 44 and an atomic weight of 101.07. It melts at about 2300 °C and boils at about 4000 °C. Its chemical symbol is Ru.   R. Craig Taylor

Rutherford, Ernest (1871-1937), a British physicist, established the nuclear model of the atom in 1911. Later, he became the first person to break up the nucleus of an atom. Because of his many contributions to science, he is often regarded as the father of nuclear science.

In the nuclear model of the atom, Rutherford theorized that atoms are constructed much like the solar system. That is, a heavy part, called the *nucleus,* forms the center of each atom. Particles with a negative electric charge, called *electrons,* form the outer part, most of which consists of empty space. In 1913, Niels Bohr combined this nuclear model of the atom with the quantum theory in the Bohr theory of atomic structure (see **Bohr, Niels**).

In 1902, Rutherford and the British chemist Frederick Soddy published their discovery of *atomic transmutation.* Their observations proved that radioactive elements give off electrically charged particles known as alpha and beta particles. This process changes the *parent* (original) atom into a *daughter* atom. The daughter atom is a different chemical element. This achievement won Rutherford the 1908 Nobel Prize in chemistry.

Rutherford produced the first artificial atomic transmutations in a series of experiments from 1917 to 1919. He bombarded nitrogen atoms with alpha particles. In rare collisions, an alpha particle pushed a *proton,* a positively charged particle, out of a nitrogen nucleus. At the same time, the nucleus absorbed the alpha particle, becoming an oxygen nucleus.

Rutherford was born in Nelson, New Zealand. He taught at McGill University in Montreal, the University of Manchester, and Cambridge University. In 1903, he was elected a Fellow of the Royal Society. He wrote several books, including *Radioactive Substances and Their Radiations* (1913). In 1931, he received the title of Baron Rutherford of Nelson.   Roger H. Stuewer

Rutherfordium is an artificially produced radioactive element with 104 protons—that is, with an *atomic number* of 104. Scientists have discovered 10 *isotopes* of rutherfordium, forms of the element with the same number of protons but different numbers of neutrons. The *atomic mass numbers* (total numbers of protons and neutrons) of these isotopes range from 253 to 262. The

most stable isotope has a mass number of 261 and a *half-life* of 65 seconds—that is, due to radioactive decay, only half the atoms in a sample of isotope 261 would still be atoms of that isotope after 65 seconds.

In 1964, scientists at the Joint Institute for Nuclear Research in Dubna, near Moscow, claimed they had produced the element. Dubna was then part of the Soviet Union and is now in Russia. The Soviet scientists had bombarded plutonium, whose atomic number is 94, with neon, whose atomic number is 10. From 1966 to 1970, Dubna presented additional claims for the element. In 1969, scientists at the Lawrence Radiation Laboratory (now Lawrence Berkeley National Laboratory) in Berkeley, California, made a rival claim. The Americans had bombarded californium, whose atomic number is 98, with carbon, which has an atomic number of 6.

In 1986, the International Union of Pure and Applied Chemistry (IUPAC) and the International Union of Pure and Applied Physics formed a working group to review the histories of the elements with atomic numbers from 101 to 109. IUPAC is the recognized authority in crediting the discovery of elements and assigning names to them. The group concluded that the Berkeley claim and a 1969-1970 Dubna claim—but not the 1964 claim—were strong. In 1993, IUPAC accepted the group's recommendation that credit for the discovery be shared by the two institutions. Disagreements about what to name the element delayed an official naming until 1997, however.

Rutherfordium is named after British physicist Ernest Rutherford. The symbol for rutherfordium is Rf. Before being named, rutherfordium was commonly referred to as *element 104.*   Richard L. Hahn

Rutland (pop. 18,230) is the second largest city in Vermont. Only Burlington has more people. Rutland lies 65 miles (105 kilometers) southwest of Montpelier (see **Vermont** [political map]). It is the trading center for a region of about 150,000 people. Marble finishing and the manufacture of weighing scales, fire clay, and stoneworking machinery are important industries. Ski resorts are an important source of income in the Rutland area. Rutland is the home of the College of St. Joseph. The *Rutland Herald,* established in 1794, is the oldest continuously published newspaper in Vermont. Rutland has a mayor-council government.   John McCardell

Rutledge, Ann (1813-1835), became famous as Abraham Lincoln's first sweetheart. Romantic stories of their tragic love affair are based more on legend than on fact.

Ann Rutledge was the daughter of the innkeeper in New Salem, Illinois, where Lincoln lived for a time. She was engaged to John McNamar, a wealthy settler. He left for the East, and there was doubt that he would return to marry Ann. Meanwhile, she may have accepted a proposal of marriage from Lincoln. However, she soon became ill and died.   Mark E. Neely, Jr.

Rutledge, Edward (1749-1800), a lawyer and statesman, was a South Carolina signer of the Declaration of Independence. He represented South Carolina in the First and Second Continental Congresses from 1774 to 1776. He defended American rights within the British Empire but accepted independence only reluctantly.

Rutledge was born in or near Charleston, South Carolina. He studied law in Britain. During the Revolutionary War in America (1775-1783), he was a captain of artillery. The British captured him when Charleston fell in 1780 and held him prisoner for about a year. His brother John Rutledge was a signer of the Constitution of the United States.

From 1782 to 1795, Edward Rutledge was a state representative. He served in the South Carolina Senate from 1796 to 1798 and was governor of South Carolina from 1798 to 1800.   Robert M. Weir

Rutledge, John (1739-1800), was a South Carolina signer of the Constitution of the United States. At the Constitutional Convention of 1787, he favored efforts to develop a strong national government. Rutledge also helped convince Northern delegates that the Southern States would withdraw from the United States if the Constitution prohibited slavery.

Rutledge was born in or near Charleston, South Carolina, and was educated in Charleston and London. He represented South Carolina in the First Continental Congress in 1774 and the Second Continental Congress in 1775. From 1776 to 1778, Rutledge was South Carolina's first executive, with the title of president. He was governor of South Carolina from 1779 to 1782. He served in the Congress of the Confederation from May 1782 to September 1783 and in the South Carolina House of Representatives from 1784 to 1790.

President George Washington appointed Rutledge an associate justice of the Supreme Court of the United States in 1789. But Rutledge served only a short time, and in 1791 became chief justice of South Carolina. In 1795, Washington nominated Rutledge as chief justice of the United States. Rutledge presided during the August term. But the U.S. Senate rejected his nomination, largely because of his opposition to the Jay Treaty of 1794.   Robert M. Weir

Rutskoi, *root SKOY,* **Alexander Vladimirovich,** *vluh DYEE myih raw vyihch* (1947-   ), was vice president of Russia from 1991 to 1993. He was elected with President Boris Yeltsin in Russia's first presidential election. Yeltsin forced Rutskoi from office because Rutskoi opposed Yeltsin's policies. In 1996, Rutskoi became governor of the Kursk region, in southwestern Russia.

Rutskoi was born in Kursk. He became a military pilot. He was elected to Russia's parliament in 1990. In 1991, after becoming vice president, he began to disagree openly with Yeltsin's policies. He charged that Yeltsin and his advisers had no clear idea of how to improve the economy. He argued that their economic experiments were proving too costly for the people. In 1992, Yeltsin stripped Rutskoi of nearly all responsibilities.

In September 1993, a commission headed by Yeltsin accused Rutskoi of corruption. Yeltsin suspended Rutskoi from office, but parliament declared the suspension unconstitutional. Yeltsin dissolved parliament. Parliament, in turn, voted to remove Yeltsin from office and to make Rutskoi acting president. A struggle for power followed. Rutskoi and his allies barricaded themselves in the parliament building in Moscow. In October, the military, on Yeltsin's orders, forced Rutskoi and his allies out of the building. Rutskoi and others were arrested and jailed. Rutskoi was released in 1994.   Nicolai N. Petro

Ruysdael, Jacob van. See Ruisdael, Jacob van.

Rwanda, *roo WAHN duh,* is a small country in east-central Africa, just south of the equator. It is one of the poorest and most crowded countries on the continent. It has little industry and more people than the land can

Rwanda

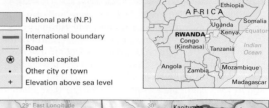

National park (N.P.)
International boundary
Road
⊛ National capital
•   Other city or town
+   Elevation above sea level

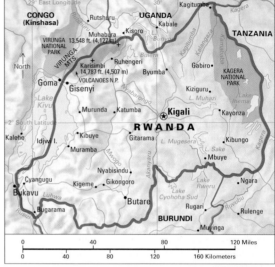

WORLD BOOK maps

support. Kigali is Rwanda's capital and largest city.

Although Rwanda is near the equator, it has a cool, pleasant climate. This is because it lies on a series of high plateaus. Rwanda's landscape ranges from volcanic mountains to winding river valleys, and from beautiful lakes to grassy plains. Volcanoes National Park in the Virunga Mountains of northwestern Rwanda is a refuge for mountain gorillas, an endangered species.

From 1946 to 1962, Rwanda formed the northern half of Ruanda-Urundi, a United Nations (UN) trust territory administered by Belgium. What is now Burundi formed the southern half. In 1962, the two parts became the independent nations of Rwanda and Burundi.

Facts in brief

Capital: Kigali.
Official languages: English, French, and Kinyarwanda.
Official name: Rwandese Republic.
Area: 10,169 sq. mi. (26,338 km²). *Greatest distances*—east-west, 145 mi. (233 km); north-south, 110 mi. (177 km).
Population: *Estimated 2000 population*—7,640,000; density, 751 persons per sq. mi. (290 persons per km²); distribution, 95 percent rural, 5 percent urban. *1991 census*—7,142,755.
Chief products: *Agriculture*—bananas, beans, cassava, cattle, coffee, pyrethrum, sorghum, sweet potatoes, tea. *Mining*—tin, wolframite.
Flag: The flag has three vertical stripes of red, yellow, and green, with a large black *R* in the center. See Flag (picture: Flags of Africa).
Money: *Basic unit*—franc. One hundred centimes equal one franc.

A large majority of Rwanda's people belong to the Hutu (also called Bahutu) ethnic group. The Tutsi (also called the Batutsi or Watusi) form a minority of the population. The Tutsi monarchy dominated the Hutu politically and economically for hundreds of years. In 1959, the Hutu rebelled against the Tutsi. After a period of bloody fighting, the Hutu gained control of the government and the economy. In 1994, after another major bloody conflict between the two groups, the Tutsi took control. See the *History* section of this article for details.

Government. A president is the head of Rwanda's government. A prime minister heads a cabinet, which helps carry out the operations of the government. Under Rwanda's constitution, the people elect the president and the president appoints the prime minister and members of the cabinet. But after Tutsi rebels overthrew the government in 1994, they appointed these officials.

From 1974 to 1991, Rwanda had only one party, the National Revolutionary Movement for Development, now called the National Republican Movement for Democracy and Development. In 1991, the Constitution was changed to a multiparty system. Important opposition parties include the Christian Democratic Party, Liberal Party, Republican Democratic Movement, and Social Democratic Party.

People. About 90 percent of the people of Rwanda are Hutu. Most of the rest are Tutsi. These two groups share a common language and culture. Most Hutu are farmers who raise crops to feed their families. Some of them also raise cattle or grow coffee, Rwanda's chief export. Other Hutu work in Rwanda's towns. About 5 percent of the Rwandese people belong to the Tutsi ethnic group. Most Tutsi keep cattle or work in businesses or government agencies.

The Twa, a Pygmy group, make up less than 1 percent of Rwanda's population. They once made their living by hunting, but some now live and work in the towns. Only a few Europeans live in Rwanda. Some are farmers who raise tea and pyrethrum, which is used in making insecticides. A few are executives in the mining industry. Others are Christian missionaries.

English, French, and Kinyarwanda are the official languages. Most of the people speak Kinyarwanda, a Bantu language. Most of the people are Roman Catholics. A small percentage practices traditional African religions. The Roman Catholic and other Christian churches operate most of the elementary and high schools. The National University of Rwanda operates in Butare. Public education is free and compulsory for children from 7 through 15 years of age, but there are not enough classrooms to accommodate all the children. Many adult Rwandese cannot read and write. For the country's literacy rate, see **Literacy** (table: Literacy rates).

Land. Much of Rwanda's land is rugged and mountainous. The highest mountains, in the west and northwest, were formed by volcanoes. Lake Kivu and the Rusizi River form Rwanda's western border and are part of Africa's Great Rift Valley. The Kagera River forms the eastern border, and the Akanyaru River forms part of the southern border. The land rises sharply from Lake Kivu to about 9,000 feet (2,700 meters) above sea level. The Virunga Mountains rise to about 14,800 feet (4,510 meters) in the northwest. Heavy rainfall in western Rwanda has *leached* (washed away) chemicals that enrich soil.

A series of plateaus in eastern Rwanda range from 5,000 to 7,000 feet (1,500 to 2,100 meters) above sea level and slope down toward the east. Each one is bounded on the east by an *escarpment* (steep edge) with a marsh at its foot. Forests once covered the plateaus, but most of this land has been cleared for farming.

The Great Rift Valley areas in the west have an average annual temperature of 73 °F (23 °C) and an average annual rainfall of 30 inches (76 centimeters). The mountainous areas in the west have an average annual temperature of 63 °F (17 °C) and an average annual rainfall of 58 inches (147 centimeters). On the plateaus, the temperature averages 68 °F (20 °C) annually. Annual rainfall is about 47 inches (119 centimeters).

Economy. Most Rwandese are farmers. But many farmers can grow only enough food to feed their own families. Food crops include bananas, beans, cassava, sorghum, and sweet potatoes. Some rural people also raise cattle. Coffee is the country's chief export. Tea and pyrethrum are also important exports. The farming varies according to the altitude. For example, farmers raise *robusta* coffee on land up to about 4,500 feet (1,370 meters) above sea level. This coffee is used to make instant coffee. From about 4,500 to 6,000 feet (1,370 to 1,800 meters), farmers grow *arabica* coffee, the kind used for regular brewing.

Tin and wolframite are the chief minerals in Rwanda. They account for about one-fourth of the country's exports. Rwanda has few manufacturing industries. It has no railroads. Its main highways are surfaced, but most of the roads are dirt. Kigali has an international airport.

In the past, Rwanda's exports were shipped through Burundi mainly to the ocean ports of Dar es Salaam in Tanzania; Lobito in Angola; and Beira in Mozambique. But fighting between Hutu and Tutsi strained relations between Rwanda and Burundi. When possible, Rwandan exports are now hauled to Kampala, Uganda, and then shipped by train to Mombasa, Kenya. This process makes it difficult and expensive for Rwanda to export and import goods and products.

History. What is now Rwanda was first inhabited by Hutu farmers and Twa hunters. During the 1300's or 1400's, the Tutsi, a warrior people with large herds of big-horned cattle, migrated to the area. Eventually, a

Bernard Gerard, Explorer

Rwanda is a country in east-central Africa. Small towns, villages, and farms dot the country's landscape. This photograph shows a street scene in the town of Gitarama.

kingdom was established in which the Hutu farmers paid tribute to the cattle-keeping Tutsi aristocrats. However, much intermarriage and change of economic status occurred between the groups. Over time, the Hutu and Tutsi developed a common language and culture.

Germany conquered the area that is now Rwanda and Burundi in 1897. It ruled this area as part of German East Africa. Belgian troops occupied the area, then called Ruanda-Urundi, in 1916, during World War I. Germany lost its African colonies after the war. Ruanda-Urundi became a mandated territory under Belgian administration in 1923 (see **Mandated territory**). Under Belgian colonial rule, the inequalities between the Hutu and Tutsi intensified. The Belgians favored the Tutsi, who received greater employment and educational opportunities under them than the Hutu or Twa did. The Belgians also formalized the ethnic divisions in the territory by requiring the people to carry passes identifying themselves as Hutu, Tutsi, or Twa. In 1946, Ruanda-Urundi became a UN trust territory administered by Belgium.

Political unrest followed the death of *Mwami* (King) Mutara III in 1959. The Hutu rebelled against the Tutsi. Fighting between the Hutu and Tutsi resulted in about 150,000 deaths. The Tutsi suffered the heaviest casualties. During and after the rebellion, about 150,000 Tutsi fled to Burundi and other neighboring countries.

Elections held in 1960 gave the Hutu control of the government. In 1961, the people of Ruanda voted to make their country a republic. Ruanda-Urundi became independent as two countries, Rwanda and Burundi, on July 1, 1962. The people of Rwanda then elected Hutu leader Gregoire Kayibanda as the first president. They reelected him in 1965 and 1969. In 1973, military leaders led by Major General Juvenal Habyarimana, a Hutu, overthrew Kayibanda and took control of the government. Habyarimana declared himself president.

In 1990, Rwandese rebels, called the Rwandan Patriotic Front (RPF), began launching attacks against Rwanda's government. Most of the rebels were Tutsi, who had been living in exile in Uganda.

In August 1993, the government and the RPF signed a peace treaty. In April 1994, Habyarimana was killed in an airplane crash. Extremist Hutu militias broke the peace. They killed up to 800,000 people, mostly Tutsi. A Hutu-dominated government was formed, but the Tutsi-dominated RPF refused to recognize it. By mid-July, the RPF had defeated the Hutu forces. The RPF took control of the government. But it appointed a multiparty government, including some moderate Hutu officials. About 2 million refugees, mostly Hutu, left Rwanda to escape RPF forces during the fighting. The majority of them went to the area near the town of Goma, Zaire. Tens of thousands of the refugees died from cholera and other diseases, or from starvation.

In 1996 and 1997, Zairian rebels overturned the government of Zaire and renamed the country the Democratic Republic of Congo. The fighting forced the Rwandan refugees from the camps. Many returned to Rwanda, but some fled deeper into Congo or to neighboring countries. Michael Chege

Related articles in *World Book* include:

Bantu	Hutu	Pygmies
Burundi	Kigali	Tutsi

Rx. See ℞ (symbol) alphabetized between **R** and **Ra.**

Ryan, Nolan (1947-   ), ranks among the greatest pitchers in baseball history. During his major league career, Ryan struck out 5,714 batters, a record. In 1973, Ryan set a major league record of 383 strikeouts for a single season. He pitched 7 no-hit games and 12 one-hit games in the major leagues. No other pitcher has more than four major league no-hitters. In 1990, Ryan became the 20th major league pitcher to win 300 games. During his career, he won 324 games. Ryan became especially famous for his blazing fast ball and his durability.

Lynn Nolan Ryan was born in Refugio, Texas. He began his major league career with the New York Mets in 1966 and pitched again for the Mets from 1968 to 1971. He played for the California (now Anaheim) Angels from 1972 to 1979 and the Houston Astros from 1980 to 1988. He pitched for the Texas Rangers from 1989 until his retirement after the 1993 season. Ryan was elected to the National Baseball Hall of Fame in 1999. Donald Honig

See also **Baseball** (picture).

Ryder, Albert Pinkham (1847-1917), is considered one of the most original of American painters. He is best known for his brooding night scenes of the sea and dreamlike landscapes. His paintings are based on stories from the Bible, William Shakespeare, and other literary sources. Ryder conceived simple, bold designs. He often used dark and pale tones in dramatic contrast. He laid paint on thickly, worked on a painting for a long time, and repainted until layers of color were built up. Romantic and independent by nature, he worked in seclusion and was largely self-taught. His imaginative style, often resembling abstract design, influenced many painters Ryder was born in New Bedford, Massachusetts. He later settled in New York City. Sarah Burns

Rye is a cereal grain similar to wheat and barley. The plant has slender seed spikes with long, stiff *awns* (beards). The dark-colored grains grow in pairs. Rye flowers, unlike those of wheat, oats, and barley, open for pollination. The flowers shed their pollen into the air, and the pollen is spread by the wind. Rye is used to make bread and certain types of liquors. Rye probably originated from wild species in eastern Europe or Asia. Wild rye still grows in these regions and in northern Africa.

Production. Rye is an important crop in the cool climates of northern Europe, Asia, and North America.

WORLD BOOK illustration by John D. Dawson

A rye seed spike, *left,* has long, stiff beards. Rye grains, *right,* grow in pairs. Rye is a major crop in many countries.

Albert Ryder's painting *The Race Track or Death on a Pale Horse* illustrates the moody, mystical quality of his work. This dreamlike vision illustrates the artist's ability to create a feeling of mystery and power in his imaginative paintings.

Oil painting on canvas (about 1910); Cleveland Museum of Art

Poland and Russia rank among the world's leading rye-growing countries. In North America, most rye is grown in central Canada, the Dakotas, and Georgia. The world produces about 900 million bushels of rye annually. A bushel of rye weighs 56 pounds (25 kilograms).

Uses. In most countries, rye is used chiefly for human food. The food value of rye is nearly as great as that of wheat. But American farmers feed much of the grain to livestock. Rye hay and *middlings* (medium-sized particles which are a by-product of bran flour milling) are frequently used as livestock feed. Young rye plants make good pasture in spring and autumn. But sometimes, cows that graze on rye give milk that has an unusually strong flavor.

Farmers frequently grow rye to improve or to protect the soil. For example, a crop of rye may be raised alternately with other crops to protect the soil. Then, it is called a *cover crop*. If it is plowed under before it ma-

tures, it is called a *green manure crop*.

The heavy, black bread of Europe is made from rye. Rye does not contain as much gluten as wheat. Because of this, yeast cannot raise rye dough as easily as wheat dough, and rye bread is heavier and more compact. In the United States, bakers usually add much wheat flour to the rye so that the bread is not so dark as the bread made in Europe. During the past few hundred years, wheat bread has become more popular than rye bread.

Distillers use malt made from rye for rye whiskey and Holland gin. Rye straw is long, smooth, and easy to bend. Packers use the straw as a packing material. Manufacturers use it to make hats, paper, mats, and mattress stuffing. Rye straw is also used in European countries for thatched roofs because it decays less rapidly than most other kinds of straw.

Construction workers use rye to conserve soil. They plant rye in the raw soil along new roadbeds. The plants

Leading rye-growing countries

Bushels of rye grown in a year

Country	Bushels
Poland	217,349,000 bushels
Russia	190,260,000 bushels
Germany	179,440,000 bushels
Belarus	53,841,000 bushels
Ukraine	48,397,000 bushels

One bushel equals 56 pounds (25 kilograms).
Figures are for a three-year average, 1997-1999.
Source: Food and Agriculture Organization of the United Nations.

Leading rye-growing states and provinces

Bushels of rye grown in a year

State/Province	Bushels
Saskatchewan	5,584,000 bushels
Manitoba	3,082,000 bushels
Alberta	2,725,000 bushels
Ontario	1,883,000 bushels
Georgia	1,433,000 bushels

One bushel equals 56 pounds (25 kilograms).
Figures are for a three-year average, 1996-1998.
Sources: U.S. Department of Agriculture; Statistics Canada.

grow in the infertile subsoil and keep it from eroding.

Cultivation. Rye grows well in much poorer soils than those necessary for most cereal grains. Thus, it is an especially valuable crop in regions where the soil has sand or peat. Rye plants withstand cold better than other small grains do. Most farmers grow winter ryes, which are planted and begin to grow in autumn. In spring, the plants develop and produce their crop.

Like all cereal grains, rye plants are annuals and new seeds must be planted each year. Most American farmers use grain drills to plant rye. These machines plant the seeds in rows 6 to 7 inches (15 to 18 centimeters) apart. About 84 to 112 pounds of seed are sown per acre (93 to 124 kilograms per hectare). In the United States, rye yields an average of about 30 bushels of grain per acre (75 bushels per hectare). In some European countries, the crop may yield two to three times this amount. Because of the low rye yields and a greater demand for wheat, U.S. farmers usually grow wheat instead of rye whenever possible.

Ergot is a poisonous fungus that often destroys rye grain. Ergot replaces the grain with a hornlike blackish body several times longer than the normal grain. These ergot bodies poison livestock and human beings who eat the grain or products made from it. This disease is called *ergotism.* Doctors use small doses of drugs made from ergot to ease migraine headaches, to control bleeding, and as an aid to childbirth.   Robert D. Wych

Scientific classification. Rye belongs to the grass family, Poaceae or Gramineae. Its scientific name is *Secale cereale.*

See also **Ergot; Triticale.**

Rye House Plot was a scheme concocted by radical members of the English Whig Party in 1682 and 1683. The conspirators planned to kill Charles II, king of England, and his brother James, Duke of York, who was a Roman Catholic and heir to the throne. Some of the plotters favored a republic, and others wanted to place Charles's illegitimate son, the Protestant Duke of Monmouth, on the throne. The assassination was to have occurred near a country home called the Rye House as the king and his brother returned to London from Newmarket in Cambridgeshire. The scheme failed after the royal party left Newmarket earlier than expected.

The Rye House Plot is often confused with another plot of 1682 and 1683, which involved a more prominent group of conspirators. In the second plot, Monmouth, Lord Russell, and political theorist Algernon Sidney planned a rebellion to force Charles to support Monmouth as his successor rather than James. Russell, Sidney, and some of their accomplices were tried and executed. Monmouth was forced into exile.

Richard L. Greaves

See also **Glorious Revolution.**

Ryukyu Islands, *ree OO KYOO,* are a group of more than 100 islands in the North Pacific Ocean that belong to Japan. They stretch from the main islands of Japan to Taiwan. They have a land area of 1,205 square miles (3,120 square kilometers) and a population of about 1,222,000. Some of the islands have no people. The Ryukyus can be divided into five groups from north to south—(1) the Osumi Islands, (2) the Tokara Islands, (3) the central Ryukyus including the Amami Islands and Okinawa, (4) the Miyako Islands, and (5) the Yaeyama Islands.

Ryukyu Islands

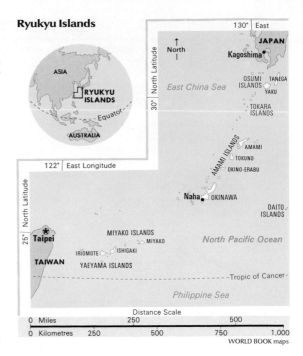

WORLD BOOK maps

People. Farming is the most important occupation of the islanders, though the soil is rocky and hilly. The people grow rice, but their main food crop is sweet potatoes. They export sugar cane and pineapple. Fishing is another important activity for income and food.

The Ryukyuans speak a language similar to Japanese. Their religion has been influenced by both China and Japan. Burial of the dead in large family tombs and ceremonies honoring ancestors are important parts of the Ryukyuan religion. Ryukyuans also worship things connected with nature, such as trees and fire.

Land and climate. Most of the Ryukyu Islands are mountainous. The highest elevation above sea level, more than 6,000 feet (1,800 meters), is on Yaku Island. Some of the islands have active volcanoes. The Ryukyus have a warm, wet climate. The average temperature is about 70 °F (21 °C), and the annual rainfall ranges from 53 to 120 inches (135 to 305 centimeters). Typhoons bring damaging winds and rains in summer and fall. Winters are usually cloudy and chilly, with less rain.

History. Ancestors of the Ryukyuans probably came from Japan and Taiwan, and possibly from the Philippines. Some scientists believe that prehistoric people may have lived on the islands during the most recent ice age, which ended about 11,500 years ago. Chinese and Japanese expeditions stopped in the Ryukyu Islands as early as the A.D. 600's. During the 1400's and 1500's, Okinawa was part of a trade network that linked China, Japan, Korea, and Southeast Asia.

China and Japan both claimed the Ryukyus until 1874, when China recognized Japanese rule. In 1879, the islands became part of two *prefectures* (provinces) of Japan. After World War II, the United States took over the Ryukyus. In 1953, the islands north of Okinawa were returned to Japan. Okinawa and the southern Ryukyus were returned in 1972.   Kenneth B. Pyle

See also **Okinawa.**